Biographical Dictionary
of
American Music

Biographical Dictionary of American Music

Charles Eugene Claghorn

PARKER PUBLISHING COMPANY, INC.
West Nyack, New York

PARKER PUBLISHING COMPANY, INC.

West Nyack, New York

Library of Congress Cataloging in Publication Data

Claghorn, Charles Eugene
Biographical dictionary of American music.

1. Music--United States--Bio-bibliography.
I. Title.
ML106.U3C6 780'.92'2 [B] 73-5534
ISBN 0-13-076331-4

Printed in the United States of America

To

my wife

Eileen

A Word from the Author

There has been a great need for a dictionary or encyclopedia of *only American* composers, lyricists, musicians, singers, and teachers. Such a compilation does not exist now. Dictionaries presently on the market are worldwide in scope, primarily containing the names of Europeans, with very few Americans included. There are specialized books on the opera, symphonies, concert music, jazz, rhythm and the blues, folk and country music, sacred and gospel music, popular songs, and so on. The purpose of this book is to be inclusive of all forms of music, and to include lyricists, librettists, and hymnists as well as composers, musicians, and singers.

All individuals included are listed alphabetically. There are numerous song books on the market which give the name of the composer and the lyricist, but usually no further information. Record covers give the names of the vocalist and the band. This book lists various bands alphabetically, giving the names of the musicians and vocalists in each band. The information included in this book is not available in any other *one* volume published.

Since the purpose of this book is to be all-inclusive, and to include over 5,200 individuals, biographical sketches of noted composers and musicians are not extensive in scope, since information on these individuals is available in other sources. However, biographical information on thousands of other musicians and singers that is not available in the other worldwide dictionaries is included here.

The text is limited to those persons who were born in the United States, or came to America and lived and worked here for an extended period of time. During the rise of Nazism, hundreds of noted composers and musicians fled Germany and made America their new home. As a result, thousands of Europeans are included here.

The book covers the entire span of musical America, from the seventeenth century to the present day. You will find biographical information on persons active in American musical life during the Colonial period, the Revolution, and during the 1790s in Boston, New York City, Philadelphia, and Charleston, South Carolina. Many popular songs were written during the Civil War period, and again during World Wars I and II. The composers and lyricists of songs during these periods are all included.

Black people in the United States have a long and worthy musical heritage, and are so designated as blacks in this volume in tribute to their accomplishments. This provides an easy reference for the student of black studies.

Considerable research was undertaken to compile the information in this dictionary. For instance, most books on music state that James Hewitt was the first American to write an opera, *Tammany*, which was presented in New York City in 1794, but no mention is made as to the librettist. Diligent research revealed that the story was written by Ann Julia Hatton. But who was she? Further research revealed that her maiden name was Ann Julia Kemble, and that she was the younger sister of Mrs. Sarah Kemble Siddons, the great English actress.

Research also revealed many stories. Will Hays, who wrote "The Drummer Boy of Shiloh" in 1862, was a war correspondent for the old *Louisville Democrat* and was traveling through the Confederate lines when he was captured in New Orleans in 1862. He was charged with writing seditious songs and thrown into prison on orders of General Ben Butler, the Union Commander there. General Butler also punished A.E. Blackmar, a music publisher in New Orleans. He ordered Blackmar's entire stock of published music destroyed and fined him $500 for publishing Confederate songs.

When Teresa Carreno, the child piano prodigy from Caracas, Venezuela, played in the White House for President Lincoln in 1863 when she was nine years old, he told her he knew only two tunes. Since his favorite was "Listen to the Mocking Bird," she played that song for the President. It was written by Septimus Winner in 1855, based on a melody he heard from Richard Milburn, a black singer and whistler in Philadelphia.

Often performing artists falsify their ages, to appear three or four years younger than their actual age. As a result, birthdates of musicians and singers sometimes vary in different reference books. Usually the older date is the correct one. For example, in his earlier years Leopold Stokowski gave his year of birth as 1887 instead of 1882, but was happy and proud to celebrate his ninetieth birthday in 1972. Also, in some cases, dates of birth or death were unavailable. A question mark has been used to designate this lack of information.

Gene Claghorn

ACKNOWLEDGMENTS

The compiler wishes to thank One Spot Publishers, Mt. Prospect, Illinois, for copies of their *Popular Guide* covering titles and artists listing records and albums; the American Society of Composers, Authors and Publishers for information on lyricists, which otherwise would be difficult to obtain; The Hymn Society of America for information on hymnists; James J. Fuld, author of *The Book of World-Famous Music*, for information supplied.

Notes for the Reader

Abbreviations

The following are symbols employed in this book:

arr.	*arranged*
b.	*born*
ca.	*circa (about)*
d.	*died*
m.	*music*
op.	*opus*
prob.	*probably*
pseud.	*pseudonym*
w.	*words (lyrics)*

Typography

In accordance with *A Manual of Style*, 12th edition, The University of Chicago Press, © 1969, the following serves as a guideline for the typographical treatment of the various works listed:

Italics: Titles of long musical works, e.g., motets, oratorios, operas, symphonies, tone poems.
Also italicized: books, collections of poetry and long poems, magazines, movies, names of ships, newspapers, plays, record album titles, and paintings, drawings, statues, other works of art.

Quotation marks: Titles of songs and short musical works, e.g., anthems, hymns (both tune and words), marches, parts of larger musical works, rags.
Also in quotation marks: poems, radio shows, television shows.

AARONSON, IRVING

b. 1895 New York City, d. 1963 Hollywood, California. Pianist and bandleader. Studied at David Mannes Music School, New York City; with Albert Sendry; pianist in theaters at age eleven; formed the Versatile Sextet, later The Commanders in the 1930s; Artie Shaw was in his band; wrote "Boo-Hoo-Hoo," "The Song Angels Sing."

ABBEY, ALONZO JUDSON

b. 1825 Olive, Ulster County, New York, d. 1887 Chester, New Jersey. Composer. His birthplace was wiped out when the Ashokin Reservoir was built; composed the tune "Cooling" for "I Worship Thee, O Holy Ghost" (w. W.F. Warren, 1877), also for "I Know Not What the Future Hath" (w. John Greenleaf Whittier).

ABBEY, HENRY EUGENE

b. 1846 Akron, Ohio, d. 1896 New York. Opera house manager. First manager of the Metropolitan Opera House, New York City (1880-84) which incurred heavy losses. It was managed again by Abbey, Schoeffel, and Grau (1890-97).

ABBOTT, EMMA

b. 1850 Chicago, Illinois, d. 1891 Salt Lake City, Utah. Soprano. Debut in 1876 in Covent Garden, London, and in New York City (1877); organized the English Grand Opera Company in 1878 which toured the United States (her husband, Eugene Wetherell, was the manager).

ABBOTT, GEORGE

b. 1887 Forestville, New York.
Lyricist and librettist. Librettist for *On Your Toes* (1936, m. Richard Rodgers); *Damn Yankees* (1955) with Douglass Wallop (m. Richard Adler, lyrics Jerry Ross); *Fiorello!* (1959) with Jerome Weidman (m. Jerry Bock and Sheldon Harnick); *Tenderloin* (1960) with Weidman (m. Bock).

ABDUL-MALIK, AHMED

b. 1927 Brooklyn, New York.
Bass, tuba player, violinist, cellist and pianist. Studied violin at age seven at Vardi's Conservatory; with Art Blakey (1945); Don Byas (1946); also with Sam Taylor, Thelonious Monk and others; studied at New York College of Music (1965).

à BECKET, THOMAS, *see* BECKET, THOMAS, à

ABEL, FREDERICK L.

b. 1794 Ludwigslust, Mecklenburg, Germany, d. 1820 Savannah, Georgia. Pianist, violinist, composer, and teacher. Settled in Savannah before 1815 and instructed Lowell Mason in harmony and composition (1815); died in the yellow fever epidemic of 1820; composed for the pianoforte *American Rondo, The Copenhagen Waltz* (arrangement), *General Jackson's Triumph,* also the song "Whip-poorwill" (w. Dr. I.M. Harney).

ABNEY, JOHN DONALD (DON)

b. 1923 Baltimore, Maryland.
Pianist. Accompanist for Ella Fitzgerald in mid-1950s, again in 1961; in Los Angeles, California, after 1962 in TV orchestras.

ABORN, MILTON

b. 1864 Marysville, California, d. 1933 New York City. Impresario. Founded and managed the Aborn Opera Company (1902) in New York City (the operas were in English); later staged Gilbert and Sullivan productions.

ABORN, SARGENT

b. 1866 Boston, Massachusetts, d. 1956.
Manager. Brother of Milton Aborn; with Aborn Opera School, New York City.

ABOTT, BESSIE PICKENS

b. 1878 Riverdale, New York, d. 1919 New York City. Soprano. Sang in light opera from 1894-1900 in New York City; after 1900 in grand opera in Paris and in the United States; supported Geraldine Farrar in *Mignon* at the Metropolitan Opera, N.Y. City (1908); married T.W. Story (1912).

ABRAHAMS (ABRAMS), MAURICE

b. 1883 Russia, d. 1931 New York City. Composer, lyricist, and publisher. Publisher in New York City after 1923; married singer Belle Baker; with Lewis F. Muir, wrote "Cowboy Joe" and "Hitchy-Koo" (1912).

ACE, JOHNNY

b. 1932 Memphis, Tennessee, d. 1954 Houston, Texas. Black singer and pianist. Born John Marshall Alexander, Jr.; played piano in Adolph Duncan's band in Memphis (1949); his hit record, "Pledging My Love" (by Don Robey and Ferdinand Washington), won Billboard's Triple Crown; while thousands awaited his appearance at the Houston Civic Auditorium, he shot himself playing Russian Roulette.

ACHILLES, ROBERT WILLIAM (BOB)

b. 1937 Evansville, Indiana.
Clarinetist and saxophonist. Graduated University of Illinois in 1960 in music; studied with Lyle "Spud" Murphy in Los Angeles; with Harry James' band after 1963.

ACHRON, ISIDOR

b. 1892 Warsaw, Poland, d. 1948 New York City. Pianist and composer. Came to America ca. 1920; studied with Nicolai Doubassoff and Anatol Liadoff; piano soloist with London Symphony; New York Philharmonic; conducted his own works with Miami (Florida) Symphony, 1939; music teacher in New York City; wrote *Hebrew Melody, Gavotte Grotesque, Minuet Grotesque, Valse Dramatique, Valse Intime, March of Toys.*

ACHRON, JOSEPH

b. 1886 Losdzeye, Lithuania. d. 1943 Los Angeles, California. Pianist and composer. Studied in St. Petersburg, Russia, under Leopold Auer; when he came to America he first settled in Chicago, then moved to New York, then Los Angeles; composed *The Fiddler's Soul,* stage music; *Golem,* a suite; the *Hebrew Dance;* his *Children's Suite* was a collection of twenty piano pieces.

ACKROYD, JAMES E.

b. 1854 England, d. 1897 Philadelphia, Pennsylvania. Organist and choirmaster. Came to Philadelphia (1870); studied with David Wood; organist at Church of the Epiphany, Philadelphia (1880-97), directed a fine boys' choir there; his daughter, Helen Ackroyd Clare, contralto, sang in Philadelphia after 1909.

ACUFF, ROY

b. 1903 Haynardville, Tennessee.
Singer. Joined Grand Ole Opry, Nashville, Tenn. (1940); had records on the best-selling lists during the 1940s; was the Republican candidate for governor (1948), but lost the election; with Fred Rose formed the Acuff-Rose Company, music publishing firm; when nominated to the Country Music Hall of Fame (1963), his record sales had exceeded thirty million; at Grand Ole Opry, Nashville, Tenn. (1972).

ADAMOWSKI, JOSEPH (JOZEF)

b. 1862 Warsaw, Poland, d. 1930 Cambridge, Massachusetts. Noted cellist. Studied at Warsaw Conservatory; then with Fitzenhagen, Tchaikovsky, and Pabst in Moscow; graduated University of Moscow; played in Poland and Germany (1883-89); with Boston Symphony Orchestra (1889-1907); with his wife, pianist Antoinette Szumowska, and brother, violinist Timothee Adamowski, formed the Adamowski Trio in Boston in the 1890s; studied at New England Conservatory; one of the founders of Boston Symphony Pension Fund.

ADAMOWSKI, TIMOTHEE

b. 1858 Warsaw, Poland, d. 1943 Boston, Massachusetts. Violinist. Brother of Joseph Adamowski; came to the United States (1879) and was with the Boston Symphony Orchestra (1884-1908) (conducted their popular summer concerts 1890-94); was first violinist in the Adamowski Quartet (1888), (A.E. Fielder, second violinist, D. Kunst, viola, and Giuseppe Campanari, cello; in 1890 it consisted of A. Moldauer, second violin, and Max Zach, viola).

ADAMS, ALTON AUGUSTUS

b. 1889.
Black bandmaster and composer. First black bandmaster in the United States Navy; studied in St. Thomas, Virgin Islands; organized band in the Virgin Islands for the U.S. Navy (1917); composed "Virgin Islands March" and "Spirit of the United States Navy."

ADAMS, B. M.

b. (?), d. 1903.
Composer of hymns. Was a Methodist minister in Brooklyn, New York; participated in the camp meetings at Vineland, New Jersey (1867), and Hamilton, New York (1870); wrote

the hymn with chorus "All I Have I Leave with Jesus," which was included in *The Revivalist* (1868).

ADAMS, CHARLES R.

b. 1843 Charlestown, Massachusetts, d. 1900 West Harwich, Massachusetts. Noted tenor. At Covent Garden, London (1865); in Vienna (1867-76); in German opera in U.S. (1877-78); sang the part of Rienzi in Wagner's opera at the Academy of Music, New York City (1878); later taught in Boston.

ADAMS, DERROLL

b. 1925 Portland, Oregon.
Singer, banjoist, composer. Born Derroll Lewis Thompson; at age sixteen enlisted in the army; studied art at Reed College, Portland; composed "Portland Town," which became a favorite country song; was married and divorced three times; appeared at the 1958 Brussels World's Fair with Jack Elliott.

ADAMS, ERNEST HARRY

b. 1886 Waltham, Massachusetts, d. 1959. Composer, pianist and teacher. Studied with Benjamin Cutter and Henry Dunham; piano works—*At Parting, Concerto Impromptu, Espringdale, Dance of the Gnomes, Ice Carnival, In the Flower Garden, Parade of the Clowns, Spooks and Shadows, The Wind in the Willows, The King's Jester.*

ADAMS, FRANK R.

b. 1883 Morrison, Illinois, d. 1963 White Lake, Michigan. Lyricist. Educated at University of Chicago, Ph.B.; reporter on *Chicago Tribune, Daily News & Examiner;* with Will M. Hough wrote "I Wonder Who's Kissing Her Now" (1909, m. Joe E. Howard and Harold Orlob).

ADAMS, FRANKLIN PIERCE

b. 1881 Chicago, Illinois, d. 1960 New York City. Journalist and lyricist. Wrote "Don't Tell Me What You Dreamed Last Night" (m. Brian Hooker).

ADAMS, JOHN GREENLEAF

b. 1810 Portsmouth, New Hampshire, d. 1887 Melrose, Massachusetts. Hymnist and compiler. Was a Universalist minister; with Dr. E.H. Chapin, edited *Hymns for Christian Devotion* (1846) and he compiled *Gospel Psalmist* (1861); wrote the hymn "Heaven Is Here, Where Hymns of Gladness" (tune "Austrian Hymn"—F. J. Haydn).

ADAMS, J.T.

b. 1926 Sulphur Springs, Texas.
Gospel singer, Graduated East Texas State Teachers College, Commerce, Texas; his albums are *Voices Skyward, Word, J.T. Adams and the Men of Texas.*

ADAMS, LEE

b. 1924 Mansfield, Ohio.
Lyricist and librettist. Graduated Ohio State, Columbus, Ohio, and Columbia Graduate School of Journalism; with composer Charles Strouse wrote the words for the Broadway musicals *Golden Boy, Bye Bye Birdie* (book—Michael Stewart), *Applause,* and *Six.*

ADAMS, NEHEMIAH

b. 1806 Salem, Massachusetts, d. 1878.
Hymnist. Graduated from Harvard (1826) and Andover Seminary (1829); was a Congregational minister in Boston (1834-70); wrote "Come, Take His Offers Now," which appeared in *Church Pastorals* (1864), and "Saints in Glory, We Together," in *Hymns and Songs of Praise* (1874).

ADAMS, PARK ("PEPPER")

b. 1930 Highland Park, Illinois.
Baritone saxophonist. Played in Detroit, Michigan, after 1946; served in army in Korean War; in New York after 1956 with Maynard Ferguson and Benny Goodman; later with Thad Jones-Mel Lewis band.

ADAMS, STANLEY

b. 1907 New York City.
Lyricist. Graduated New York University Law School; elected a director of the American Society of Composers, Authors and Publishers (1934); President of ASCAP 1953-56 and after 1959; wrote songs for Broadway musicals and films; wrote "Little Old Lady" (m. Hoagy Carmichael), "There Are Such Things" (1943, m. Abel Baer and George Meyer).

ADAMS, SUZANNE

b. 1872 Cambridge, Massachusetts, d. 1953 London, England. Soprano. Debut at the Paris Opera in 1894 as Juliette, and again as Juliette at the Metropolitan Opera, New York City, in 1899; married cellist Leo Stern; at Covent Garden (1898-1906); lived in England after 1903.

ADAMSON, HAROLD

b. 1906 Greenville, New Jersey.
Lyricist. Educated at the University of Kansas, and Harvard University; wrote lyrics

for Broadway shows and Hollywood films; wrote "It's a Most Unusual Day" (m. Jimmy McHugh); "A Love Affair to Remember" and "The Legend of Wyatt Earp" (both m. Harry Warren); with John Latouche wrote lyrics for Eddie Cantor's show *Banjo Eyes* (1941, m. Vernon Duke); with Mack Gordon, "Time on My Hands" (1930, m. Vincent Youmans).

ADCOCK, EDWARD

b. 1938 Scottsville, Virginia.
Singer and mandolin player. Started as a gospel singer on radio station WCHV, Charlottesville, Virginia; joined the group known as the "Country Gentlemen." (*See* Charlie Waller)

ADDERLEY, JULIAN EDWIN ("CANNONBALL")

b. 1928 Tampa, Florida.
Black alto saxophonist and bandleader. Band director of Dillard High School, Ft. Lauderdale, Florida (1948-56); leader of 36th Army Dance Band while in the army (1950-52); studied at U.S. Naval School of Music, Washington, D.C. (1952), where he led his own combo; toured with his brother Nat in 1956-57; later with Miles Davis and then with George Shearing; formed own group with his brother (1959); married actress Olga James (1962); toured Japan (1963), and Europe (1964); Cannonball Adderley Quintet at the Apollo Theatre, Harlem, New York City (1972).

ADDERLEY, NATHANIEL (NAT)

b. 1931 Tampa, Florida.
Black cornetist. Brother of Cannonball Adderley; played in Woody Herman's band; with his brother's combo after 1959; wrote "Work Song" (w. Oscar Brown, Jr.) (*Note:* original tune for "Work Song" by Lowell Mason, 1864).

ADDISON, BERNARD

b. 1905 Annapolis, Maryland.
Black guitarist. Played with Art Tatum and others in 1920s; with Fats Waller, Fletcher Henderson, the Mills Brothers and others in 1930s; served in army in World War II; later in Canada; then on tours with the Ink Spots.

ADE, GEORGE

b. 1866 Kentland, Indiana, d. 1944.
Librettist and humorist. Graduated Purdue University, Lafayette, Indiana, and became a newspaper columnist; wrote the operetta *The Sultan of Sulu* (1902), and with Gustav Luders *The Sho Gun* (1904), and *The Fair Co-ed* (1909).

ADGATE, ANDREW

b. (?), d. 1793 Philadelphia, Pennsylvania.
Compiler and teacher. Founded the Institute for Vocal Music in Philadelphia, which gave its first concert in 1785; published *Select Psalms and Hymns* (1787); *Rudiments of Music* (1788); *The Philadelphia Songster* (1789); *The Philadelphia Harmony* (1790); died in the yellow fever epidemic of 1793.

ADINY, ADA

b. ca. 1855 Boston, Massachusetts, d. 1924 Dieppe, France. Soprano. Sang in opera at the Academy of Music in New York City and in London under her real name, Ada Chapman, then sang leads in the Paris Opera starting in 1898 as Ada Adiny; at La Scala and in Brussels; married Paul Milliet, librettist.

ADLER, CLARENCE

b. 1886.
Singer, concert pianist, and teacher. Father of Richard Adler, composer.

ADLER, HENRY

b. 1915 New York, New York.
Drummer, publisher and teacher. Played in Wingy Manone's band; later with Red Norvo and Charlie Barnet; played at Randall's Island Jazz Concert (1938).

ADLER, HUGO

b. 1895, d. 1955.
Cantor and composer. Cantor of Temple Emanuel, Worcester, Massachusetts; composed *Nachlat Israel* for Friday evening, *Shirah Chadashah, Balak und Bilam,* "Behold the Jew," and "Bearers of Light."

ADLER, LARRY

b. 1914 Baltimore, Maryland.
Musician. Album—*Larry Adler Again.*

ADLER, PETER HERMAN

b. 1899 Jablonec, Czechoslovakia.
Conductor. Conducted opera performances on radio and television over the NBC network, New York City.

ADLER, RICHARD

b. 1921 New York.
Composer of popular songs and musical shows. Educated at the University of North Carolina, Chapel Hill (1943); served as an officer on a YP-PC boat in the Pacific in World War II; with Jerold Ross, wrote "Rags to Riches," "Teasin'," "Now Hear This," and "You're So Much a Part of Me," also the score for *The Pajama Game* (1954, book—

Richard Bissell's *7-1/2 Cents*) and *Damn Yankees* (1945, book—Douglas Wallop).

ADLER, SAMUEL

b. 1928 Mannheim, Germany.
Composer. Came to the U.S. (1939); educated at Boston University and Harvard University, M.A.; studied with Walter Piston, Randall Thompson, et al.; conducted 7th Army Symphony, U.S. Army (1950-52); also conductor in Europe; musical director Temple Emanu-El, Dallas, Texas (1952); taught at North Texas State after 1958; composed the overture "Summer Stock"; three symphonies (no. 1 with a colorful Jewish background); *Toccata for Orchestra.*

AFONSKY, NICHOLAS

b. 1894 Kiev, Russia, d. 1971 New York City.
Conductor. Studied at the Kiev Conservatory and directed the Kiev Military Chorus (1915-18); director of the choir of the Russian Cathedral in Paris, France, (1922), then came to America; director of the choir of the American Russian Orthodox Cathedral, New York City (1950-71).

AGER, MILTON

b. 1893 Chicago, Illinois.
Pianist and composer of popular songs. With George W. Meyer wrote "Everything Is Peaches Down in Georgia" (1918, w. Grant Clarke); served in the army in World War I; composed "A Young Man's Fancy" (1920, w. Jack Yellen and J.M. Anderson), "Ain't She Sweet" (Yellen), and "Happy Days Are Here Again" (Yellen), which became Franklin D. Roosevelt's theme song in the 1932 presidential campaign.

AGRAMONTE, EMILIO

b. 1844 Puerto Principe, Cuba, d. 1918.
Conductor and teacher. Studied law in Madrid; then piano under Marmontel and composition with Malden in Paris; singing with Delle Sedie in Paris and Selva in Madrid; came to New York (1869); musical director of Eight O'Clock Musical Club and Amateur Operatic Club; conductor of Gounod Choral Society at New Haven, Conn.; also taught singing.

AHBEZ, EDEN

b. 1908 Brooklyn, New York.
Composer. Studied piano; wrote "Nature Boy," recorded by Nat King Cole, which became a hit.

AHLERT, FRED E.

b. 1892 New York, d. there 1953.
Composer of popular songs. Educated at City College of New York and Fordham Law School; wrote "Beets and Turnips" (1914, w. Cliff Hess), "My Mammy's Arms" (1920, w. Sam Lewis and Joe Young); with lyrics by Roy Turk—"I'll Get By" (1928), "Mean to Me," "Where the Blue of the Night Meets the Gold of the Day" (with Bing Crosby), "I'm Gonna Sit Right Down and Write Myself a Letter" (w. Joe Young).

AIKEN, CHARLES

b. 1818 Goffstown, New Hampshire, d. 1882.
Teacher. Educated at Dartmouth; teacher of music in Cincinnati, Ohio, after 1839; compiled school singing books.

AINSLIE, HEW

b. 1792 Ayrshire, Scotland, d. 1878 Louisville, Kentucky. Compiler. Came to America (1822); published *Scottish Songs, Ballads and Poems* (1855).

AITKEN, JOHN

b. 1745 Dalkeith, Scotland, d. 1831 Philadelphia, Pennsylvania. Compiler and music publisher in Philadelphia. Came to America about 1785; published *A Compilation of the Litanies and Vespers, Hymns and Anthems as They Are Sung in the Catholic Church* (1787), *The Scots Musical Museum* (1797), *The Goldsmith's Rant* (1802), *Aitken's Collection of Divine Music* (1806), *A Collection of Sacred Music* (1807), *Aitken's New Musical Museum* (1807), and *Aitken's Fountain of Music* (1811).

AKEMAN, DAVID ("STRINGBEAN")

b. 1915 Annville, Kentucky, d. 1973.
Singer, banjoist, and comedian. Radio debut on WLAP, Lexington, Kentucky (1935); joined Uncle Dave Macon on Grand Ole Opry, Nashville, Tenn. (1942); single records were "Barnyard Banjo Picking," "Big Ball in Nashville," "Run Little Rabbit Run," "Crazy Viet Nam War."

AKERMAN, LUCY EVELINA METCALF

b. 1816 Wrentham, Massachusetts, d. 1874, Providence, Rhode Island. Hymnist. Married Charles Akerman of Portsmouth, N.H.; wrote "Nothing But Leaves, the Spirit Grieves," which appeared in *Scottish Family Treasury* (1859, m. S. J. Vail).

AKERS, HOWARD E.

b. 1913 Laddonia, Missouri.
Trombonist, conductor, and composer. Studied at Curtis Institute of Music, Philadelphia, and at colleges; trombonist in theater, symphony, and studio orchestras; served in United States Marine Corps in World War II; professor of music at Millikin University, Decatur, Illinois; wrote "Michigan State," "Purdue," "Indiana," "The Showman," "Show Business," "Little Classical Suite."

AKIRA, ENDO

b. 1938 Japan.
Conductor. Came to U.S. (1954); studied violin in Long Beach, California; conductor of Long Beach Symphony Orchestra (1966); conductor of American Ballet Theater (1971).

AKST, HARRY

b. 1894 New York City, d. 1963 Hollywood, California. Composer. Served in the army in World War I; met Irving Berlin and went to work for him; wrote "Laddie Boy" (1918), "Dinah" (1925, w. Sam Lewis and Joe Young), "Baby Face" (1926, w. Benny Davis), "All My Love" (1947, w. Al Jolson and Saul Chaplin), also for musicals—*Stand Up and Cheer* (1934, w. Lew Brown).

ALABAMA STATE COLLEGIANS, *see* ERSKINE HAWKINS

ALABAMIANS, THE [band] *see* CAB CALLOWAY

ALBAM, EMMANUEL (MANNY)

b. 1922 Samana, Dominican Republic.
Composer and teacher. Brought to New York City at age of six weeks; debut with Don Joseph Quintet on alto sax (1940); later on baritone sax; wrote for Muggsy Spanier, Boyd Raeburn and others; in army (1945-46); later teacher at Eastman School of Music, Rochester, New York; composed jazz ballet, music for TV shows and films.

ALBANI, EMMA

b. 1847 Chambly, Quebec, Canada, d. 1930 London, England. Noted soprano. Born Marie Louise Cecile Emylie de Lajeunesse; studied music at age five; placed in the Convent of the Sacred Heart, near Montreal (1857); church organist and soloist in Albany, N.Y. (1866); studied under Gilbert Duprez in Paris (1868) and Lamperti in Milan; debut in *La Sonnambula* in Messina (1870), debut at Covent Garden, London (1872); toured Europe; American debut as Amina at New York Academy of Music under Max Strakosch (1874); married Ernest Gye (1877); with Metropolitan Opera in New York after 1890; retired from opera (1896); later sang in concert and in vaudeville theaters.

ALBANY, JOSEPH (JOE)

b. 1924 Atlantic City, New Jersey.
Pianist. With Leo Watson in Los Angeles (1941); with Benny Carter's band; in New York at the Pied Piper (1944); recorded with George Auld (1945); with Charlie Parker and Howard McGhee (1946); in San Francisco after 1959; wrote songs for Anita O'Day; came to New York City (1963), and played in small groups; lived in California after 1964; one of the first important bop pianists.

ALBEE, AMOS

b. 1772 Medfield, Massachusetts, d. (?).
Singer, composer, and teacher. Compiled *The Norfolk Collection of Sacred Music* (1805) and assisted Oliver Shaw and Herman Mann in *The Columbian Sacred Psalmonist* (1808); composed the tunes "Tennessee" and "Medfield," and also wrote "General Crane's March"; in 1820 he and his wife Judith were dismissed from the church in Medfield, Massachusetts, and they moved to Watertown, Connecticut.

ALBEE, EDWARD F.

b. 1928.
Lyricist and playwright. Wrote the words for "Song for a Winter Child" (1950, m. William Flanagan) and "Lady of Tearful Regret" (1958, m. Flanagan).

ALDEN, JOHN CARVER

b. 1852 Boston, Massachusetts, d. 1935 Cambridge, Massachusetts. Pianist and teacher. Student of Faelten in Boston and with Paperitz, Paul, and Plaidy in Leipzig; taught at New England Conservatory, Boston, after 1880; later at Converse College, Spartanburg, S.C.; headed piano department at Quincy Mansion School, Wollaston, Massachusetts; wrote Piano Concerto in G Minor.

ALDEN, JOSEPH REED

b. 1886 Grand Rapids, Michigan, d. there 1951. Songwriter. Graduated University of Michigan, Ann Arbor; studied with Francis Mills; wrote songs for vaudeville and later for Broadway shows; with Richard A. Whiting and Ange Lorenzo wrote "Sleepy Time Gal."

ALDRICH, MARISKA

b. 1881 Boston, Massachusetts.
Soprano. Studied with Giraudet and Hen-

schel; debut in New York (1908); sang with the Metropolitan Opera Company, New York (1909-13); sang the part of Brunnhilde at Bayreuth (1914).

ALDRICH, PERLEY DUNN

b. 1863 Blackstone, Massachusetts, d. 1933 New York City. Singer, composer, and teacher. Pupil of Shakespeare, Trabadello, and Sbriglia; professor of music at the University of Kansas, Lawrence (1885-87), at Utica Conservatory (1889-91), at Rochester, New York (1891-93), after 1903 in Philadelphia and New York; composed the cantatas *La Belle Dame Sans Merci* (1895) and *The Sleeping Wood Nymph* (1896), also anthems and songs; wrote *Vocal Economy.*

ALDRICH, RICHARD

b. 1863 Providence, Rhode Island, d. 1937 Rome, Italy. Critic. Music critic of the *Providence Journal* (1885-89), the *Washington Evening Star* (1889-91) while secretary to Senator N.F. Dixon, with the *Herald Tribune* until 1902 and thereafter with the *New York Times*; with H.E. Krehbiel, wrote the *History of the Philharmonic Society*; went to Rome to meet his brother, head of the Roman American Academy, and died there.

ALDRICH, THOMAS BAILEY

b. 1836 Portsmouth, New Hampshire, d. 1907 Boston, Massachusetts. Lyricist and editor. Editor of *Every Saturday,* Boston (1865-72) and editor of the *Atlantic Monthly* (1881-90); wrote the lyrics for "Little Maud" (1870, m. J. P. Webster).

ALDRIDGE, IRA

b. 1807, d. 1867.
Black singer and actor. Known as a singer of Negro songs; also Shakespearean actor; appeared at the African Grove, New York City (1822) and sang "'Possum Up a Gum Stump."

ALEXANDER, CHARLIE

b. 1900.
Black jazz pianist. Known as a barrelhouse player.

ALEXANDER, JAMES WADDELL

b. 1804 Hopewell, New Jersey, d. 1859 Sweet Springs, Virginia. Hymnist. Educated at Princeton Seminary and became a Presbyterian minister in New Jersey, New York, and Virginia; translated the hymn "O Sacred Head, Now Wounded" from the German (tune, "Passion Chorale"—Hans Leo Hassler, harmonized by Bach).

ALEXANDER, JOSEPH ADDISON

b. 1809 Philadelphia, Pennsylvania, d. 1860 Princeton, New Jersey. Hymnist. Brother of James W. Alexander; graduated from Princeton (1826), then taught there; was a Presbyterian minister; wrote *The Doomed Man* (1837, book of poems), part of which, the hymn, "There Is a Time, We Know Not When," appeared in the *New York Church Praise Book* (1881).

ALEXANDER, ROLAND E.

b. 1935 Boston, Massachusetts.
Saxophonist and pianist. Graduated Boston Conservatory; went to New York City (1959) and played in small groups.

ALEXANDER, VAN

b. 1915 New York City.
Conductor, composer, and arranger. Educated at Columbia University, New York City; led own orchestra; conductor and arranger for Gordon and Sheila MacRae; with Al Feldman arranged "A-Tisket, A-Tasket" (w. F. Shaw, 1879) for Ella Fitzgerald; also "Where, O Where, Has My Little Dog Gone?" (Septimus Winner, 1864).

ALEXANDRIA, LOREZ

b. 1929 Chicago, Illinois.
Singer. Conducted *a capella* choral group consisting of her mother, sister, and other relatives; sang in King Fleming's band; also with Jimmy Hill; composed, "My Very First Love"; moved to Los Angeles, Calif. (1961); married agent Dave Nelson; sang on Steve Allen's TV show.

ALI, RASHEID

b. 1935 Philadelphia, Pennsylvania.
Drummer. Studied at Granoff School; came to New York (1963); gave concerts at Judson Hall with Bill Dixon and others; with John Coltrane combo after 1965.

ALLEN, BENJAMIN DWIGHT

b. 1831 Sturbridge, Massachusetts, d. 1914 Wellesley, Massachusetts. Organist and teacher. Organist in Worcester, Massachusetts for many years; taught at the New England Conservatory, Boston (1871-76), and was head of the music department at Beloit College, Beloit, Wisconsin (1894-1901), and later organist for the Manhattan Congregational Church, New York City, and Teachers College (1902-05); a founder of the American Guild of Organists and of the Worcester Festivals; wrote songs and anthems.

ALLEN, BETTY

b. 1930 Campbell, Ohio.
Black mezzo-soprano. Educated at Wilberforce University in Ohio; toured with fellow student Leontyne Price as the Wilberforce Singers; studied at Hartford School of Music in Connecticut (1950) and Berkshire Music Center (1951); soloist in Bernstein's *Jeremiah* Symphony; New York debut in Virgil Thomson's *Four Saints in Three Acts* (based on play by Gertrude Stein).

ALLEN, BYRON

b. 1940 Omaha, Nebraska.
Alto saxophonist and composer. Played sax at age eight; played in small groups in New York City.

ALLEN, EDWARD (ED)

b. 1897 Nashville, Tennessee, d. 1974.
Black jazz trumpeter. Raised in St. Louis, Missouri; played for Clarence Williams and others in 1920s; later played in various night spots in New York City; recorded with Clarence Williams in 1920s.

ALLEN, GEORGE NELSON

b. 1812 Mansfield, Massachusetts, d. 1877 Cincinnati, Ohio. Composer and teacher. Graduated Oberlin College, Ohio; professor of sacred music there after 1841; paved the way for establishment of Conservatory (1865); published *The Oberlin Social and Sabbath School Hymn Book* (1844), and *The Social and Sabbath Hymn Book* (1849); composed tunes "Maitland" (1844), "Must Jesus Bear the Cross Alone" (w. Thomas Shepherd), and "The Ocean Burial" (1849, w. E. H. Chapin), "Bury Me Not in the Deep, Deep Sea," the tune of which was later used by William Jossey for "Bury Me Not on the Lone Prairie" (1907).

ALLEN, HEMAN

b. 1836 St. Albans, Vermont, d. 1876.
Violinist, pianist, organist, and teacher. Active in faculty chamber music concerts in Philadelphia between 1862-67.

ALLEN, HENRY JAMES, JR., ("RED")

b. 1900 Algiers, Louisiana, d. 1969.
Black jazz trumpeter. Son of Henry James Allen, bandleader; studied violin with Peter Bocage; called "Red" because his light face lit up when he blew his horn; joined King Oliver in St. Louis (1917), became homesick and returned to New Orleans where he played with Walter "Fats" Pichon, pianist; played on Mississippi river boats (1928-29); with Luis Russell (1929); then with Fletcher Henderson; joined Blue Rhythm Band under Lucky Millinder (1934); with Louis Armstrong (1935-40); formed his own orchestra (1941); toured Europe with Kid Ory (1959); toured again (1964).

ALLEN, LORENZO B.

b. 1812 Jefferson, Maine, d. 1872.
Hymnist. Entered the Baptist ministry (1840); wrote "How Sweet Is the Sabbath, How Hallowed Its Hours."

ALLEN, MARSHALL

b. 1924 Louisville, Kentucky.
Alto saxophonist, clarinetist, flutist, and oboe player. Played clarinet at age ten; played in an army band; with Art Simmons in Paris (1949-50); studied at Paris Conservatory; then with Sun Ra's Solar Arkestra in Chicago and New York.

ALLEN, NATHAN HALE

b. 1848 Marion, Massachusetts, d. 1925 Hartford, Connecticut. Organist, compiler, and teacher. Pupil of Haupt in Berlin, Germany; taught in Hartford, Connecticut; composed cantatas, etc.; a founder of AGO; with Leonard W. Bacon edited *The Hymns of Martin Luther*, New York City (1883); original member of New York Manuscript Society.

ALLEN, PAUL HASTINGS

b. 1883 Boston, Massachusetts, d. 1952.
Composer. Studied in Italy for twenty years; awarded first prize in 1910 Paderewski competition for his Symphony in D Major; wrote the operas *Il Filtro*, and *Milda*, both produced in Italy.

ALLEN, REX

b. 1924 Willcox, Arizona.
Singer, guitarist, and songwriter. Joined the "National Barn Dance," Chicago (1945-50), then went with CBS in Hollywood, California where the "Rex Allen Show" became very popular; his recording of "Crying in the Chapel" was one of the top ten of 1953; appeared in a number of western films; wrote over 300 songs, many of which appeared in *Faith of a Man* and *Rex Allen Sings and Tells Tales* (1963).

ALLEN, RICHARD

b. 1760 Philadelphia, Pennsylvania, d. 1831.
Black compiler. Born a slave in the family of Benjamin Chew, Philadelphia lawyer; became an African Methodist Episcopal minister; published *A Collection of Spiritual Songs and Hymns* (1801).

ALLEN, ROSALIE

b. 1924 Old Forge, Pennsylvania.
Singer, guitarist, and "Queen of the Yodelers." Own radio show in New York for several years; produced a number of records with Eldon Britt, another yodeler, their best seller being *Quicksilver* (1950); most popular record was *He Taught Me How to Yodel*; during the 1960s she was a disc jockey for WOV radio, New York City.

ALLEN, STEPHEN VALENTINE PATRICK WILLIAM (STEVE)

b. 1921 New York City.
Pianist, comedian, and songwriter. Attended high school in Chicago; educated at Drake University, Des Moines, Iowa, and Arizona State (1942); radio announcer on station KOY, Phoenix; in army five months and discharged for asthma; disc jockey on various stations; wrote "Let's Go to Church Next Sunday" (recorded by Perry Como and Margaret Whiting), "Cotton Candy," "An Old Piano Plays the Blues," "Little Man," "Gravy Waltz" (1962, with Ray Brown), which recorded Steve's piano playing.

ALLEN, WILLIAM

b. 1784 Pittsfield, Massachusetts, d. 1868 Northampton, Massachusetts. Hymnist. Graduated from Harvard (1802) and was President of Dartmouth University (1817-20), and President of Bowdoin (1820-39); wrote 200 hymns which appeared in *Psalms and Hymns* (1835).

ALLEN, WILLIAM FRANCIS

b. 1830 Northborough, Massachusetts,d.there 1889. Compiler. With Charles P. Ware and Lucy McK. Garrison, compiled *Slave Songs of the United States* (1867), the first book of Negro spirituals.

ALLEN'S BRASS BAND OF ALGIERS, LOUISIANA (black jazz band)

Organized by Henry James Allen, Sr. ca. 1912; Jack Carey, trombone; Oscar "Papa" Celestine, trumpet; William Young; later Red Allen, trumpet; King Oliver, trumpet.

ALLERS, FRITZ

b. 1905 Karlsbad, Czechoslovakia.
Conductor. Conducted a number of ballets and musical shows in New York City.

ALLINE, HENRY

b. 1748 Newport, Rhode Island, d. 1784 North Hill, Nova Scotia. Hymnist. Minister in Falmouth, Nova Scotia; published *Hymns and Spiritual Songs* in five editions (1795-1802).

ALLISON, MOSE JOHN, JR.

b. 1927 Tippo, Mississippi.
Black pianist, singer, and composer. Studied piano at age six, later trumpet; educated at Louisiana State University; in army (1946-47); after 1956 with Stan Getz, then Gerry Mulligan; own trio in New York City (1958); toured Europe (1959); influenced by early jazz roots; leader of his own trio during the 1960s in New York and California.

ALLMAN, DUANE

b. 1947, d. 1971 Macon, Georgia.
Rock musician. Leader of Allman Brothers rock band; killed in motorcycle accident; album—*Allman Brothers Band.*

ALLYSON, JUNE

b. 1923 Lucerne, New York.
Singer and actress. Started by replacing Betty Hutton in *Panama Hattie*; started in films (1943) in *Best foot Forward;* appeared in many nonsinging rolls in films; married Dick Powell (1945); replaced Ruby Keeler in the road company of *No, No Nanette* (1971).

ALMANAC SINGERS

Pete Seeger, Woody Guthrie, Lee Hays, Millard Lampell, et al.

ALMAND, CLAUDE

b. 1915 Winnsboro, Louisiana.
Composer. Composed *The Waste Land,* a symphony (Civic Orchesta of Rochester, New York, 1940); a steamboat overture, "John Gilbert" (Louisville, Kentucky, Philharmonic Orchestra under Robert Whitney, 1949); *Piano Concerto* (1949).

ALMEIDA, LAURINDO

b. 1917 Sao Paolo, Brazil.
Guitarist and composer. Recorded with Bud Shank (1953-54), and later reissued when the bossa nova movement became popular; joined the Modern Jazz Quartet (1963); toured Europe with Quartet (1964); wrote "Discantus for Three Guitars," "Choro for People in Love," "Sahra's Samba," "Twilight in Rio."

ALPERT, HERB

b. 1935 Los Angeles, California.
Trumpeter and bandleader. Studied classical music with first trumpet of San Francisco Symphony; with Jerry Moss, began recording Mexican music (1962); his record, *The Lonely Bull,* sold over one million copies; leader of

The Tijuana Brass; albums—*Herb Alpert's Ninth, Beat of the Brass, Brass are Comin', Going Places, Greatest Hits, S.R.O., South of the Border, Tijuana Brass, Warm, Whipped Cream.*

ALPERT, HERMAN ("TRIGGER")

b. 1916 Indianapolis, Indiana.
Bass player and arranger. Educated at Indiana University; with Glenn Miller after 1940; served in army in World War II in Miller's band; later with Tex Beneke, Woody Herman; also Benny Goodman; arranger for "Gary Moore Show"; with CBS (1950-65); recorded with Louis Armstrong, Ella Fitzgerald, Ray McKinley and others; considered as one of the greatest bassists.

ALSOP, FRANCES (JORDAN)

b. (?) England, d. 1821 New York City.
Singer and popular composer. Daughter of Mrs. Jordan, the actress; American debut in *The Country Girl* at the Park Theatre, New York City (1820); composed "Last New Year's Day" (arr. A. Clifton), "The Poor Hindoo" (w. Mrs. Opie, arr. A. Clifton), "William and Mary" (arr. A. Clifton).

ALTER, LOUIS

b. 1902 Haverhill, Massachusetts.
Popular composer. Studied at the New England Conservatory, then toured Europe and America with Nora Bayes as her accompanist (1925-29); served with the Special Forces in World War II providing musical entertainment; composed "Blue Shadows" (1927, w. Ray Klages), "Manhattan Serenade" (1928), "Manhattan Moonlight" (1930), "Metropolitan Nocturne" (1935), "Twilight on the Trail" (a favorite of President Franklin D. Roosevelt).

ALTHOUSE, PAUL SHEARER

b. 1889 Reading, Pennsylvania, d. 1954 New York City. Tenor. Graduated from Bucknell University, Lewisburg, Pennsylvania, and made his debut as Dmitri in *Boris Godunov* at the Metropolitan Opera (1913); sang in Berlin, Stockholm, Stuttgart, Philadelphia, Chicago, then after 1934 with the Metropolitan Opera, New York City, in Wagnerian roles.

ALVIS, HAYES

b. 1907 Chicago, Illinois.
Black double bass player. With Lionel Hampton, Sid Catlett, Jelly Roll Morton (1927) on drums; on bass with Blue Rhythm Band (1931), Duke Ellington (1935-38), and others; in army (1943-45); later with Dave Martin, Sy Oliver and others.

AMATO, PASQUALE

b. 1878 Naples, Italy, d. 1942 New York City. Baritone. Debut in Naples (1900); sang in Milan, Trieste, then with the Manhattan Opera Company, New York City (1909-11) and after 1911 with the Metropolitan Opera; later taught at Louisiana State University, Baton Rouge, Louisiana.

AMBOY DUKES, THE

Ted Nugent, lead guitar; Steve Farmer, rhythm guitar; Dave Palmer, drums; Greg Arama, bass; Andy Solomon, piano and organ; Rusty Day, lead vocals; albums—*Amboy Dukes, Journey to the Center of Your Mind* (1968).

AMBROSE, ROBERT STEELE

b. 1824 Chelmsford, Essex, England, d. 1908 Hamilton, Ontario, Canada. Organist and composer. Emigrated to Canada with his parents in 1825; became organist at St. George's, Guelph, St. George's Cathedral, Kingston, and the Church of the Ascension, Hamilton, Ontario; composed the tune "Dolce Domum" ("One Sweetly Solemn Thought" w. Phoebe Cary).

AMERICA (vocal group)

Dan Peek (b. 1951 Florida); Gerry Beckley (b. 1953 Texas); Dewey Bunnell (b. 1952 Yorkshire, England, raised in Texas); album—*America* (1972), which included the no. 1 hit, "A Horse with No Name."

"AMERICAN BANDSTAND" (TV show)

Teen variety show with Dick Clark, host; many popular performers appeared, including Sam Cooke.

AMERICAN BREED

Chuck Colbert, Gary Loizzo, Lee Graziano, Al Ciner; albums—*American Breed* (1967), *Bend Me, Shape Me* (1968), *Pumpkin, Powder, Scarlet and Green* (1968), *Lonely Side of the City* (1968).

AMERICAN RAGTIME OCTETTE *see* NAT D. AYER

"AMERICAN SWINGAROUND"

Chicago radio show featuring country-western talent, including Lynn Anderson.

AMES BROTHERS

Ed and Leon Ames (b. 1903 Portland, Indiana); albums—*Ames Brothers, Featuring Ed Ames, Best of the Ames.*

AMFITHEATROF, DANIELE

b. 1901 St. Petersburg, Russia.
Conductor and composer. Studied music privately and at Conservatory and Pontifical Academy of Sacred Music, Vatican, Rome; came to U.S. (1937); associate conductor of Minneapolis (Minnesota) Symphony (1937); American delegate to Florence Music Film Congress (1950); wrote *The Miracle of the Roses, Poem of the Sea, Prelude to a Requiem Mass, Piano Concerto, American Panorama* (Grand Prix du Disque); became U.S. citizen (1944); wrote background music for films; member of Screen Composers Assn. and Motion Picutre Academy of Arts and Sciences.

AMMONS, ALBERT

b. 1907 Chicago, Illinois, d. 1949.
Black pianist. Played in Chicago; had own band (1934-38); boogie-woogie pianist in New York after 1938 with Pete Johnson; played in New York City nightspots; noted boogie-woogie pianist.

AMMONS, EUGENE (GENE, "JUG")

b. 1925 Chicago, Illinois, d. 1974.
Black tenor saxophonist. Son of Albert Ammons, boogie-woogie pianist; played in Billy Eckstine and Woody Herman's band in 1940s; with Sonny Stitt in 1950s; the Chess Brothers cut his record "My Foolish Heart," used the first echo chamber effect to enhance his tenor sax by dangling a mike in the studio toilet.

AMRAM, DAVID WERNER, III

b. 1930 Philadelphia, Pennsylvania.
Composer and French horn player. Cousin of conductor Otto Klemperer; studied piano and trumpet, also at Curtis Institute, Philadelphia; with National Symphony in Washington, D.C. (1951-52); in army (1952-54) with 7th Army Symphony in Germany; recorded with Lionel Hampton; after 1955 played with Sonny Rollins, Charlie Mingus and others; wrote scores for *Echo of an Era* (Brussels World Fair prize, 1958), *Turn of the Screw* (1959); wrote opera, *The Final Ingredient* presented on ABC-TV (1965); *Dirge and Variations*; also played in the Amram-Barrow Quartet; conductor of the National Symphony Orchestra, Washington, D.C. (1972).

AMSTERDAM, MOREY

b. 1912 Chicago, Illinois.
Singer, comedian, and lyricist. Educated at University of California; Master of Ceremonies, comedian on radio, Los Angeles, Calif.; also in night clubs; wrote lyrics for "Rum and Coca-Cola."

AMY, CURTIS EDWARD

b. 1929 Houston, Texas.
Saxophonist, clarinetist, and flutist. Studied under high school band director; in service (1946-47); graduated Kentucky State College, Frankfort, Kentucky (1952) in music; settled in Los Angeles (1955); recorded as leader of Pacific Jazz band (1960); plays tenor sax, also alto sax and soprano sax.

ANDERSEN, ARTHUR OLAF

b. 1880 Newport, Rhode Island, d. 1958 Tucson, Arizona. Teacher and composer. Studied at American Conservatory in Chicago; studied with d'Indy, et al.; taught at American Conservatory (1908-33); Chicago Musical College (1933-35); wrote *Arizona Sketches Numbers 1 and 2, Suite for Strings, Piano and String Trio, Quartet for Flute and Strings, A Chinese Ballet, Arizona Hi-Ho* (operetta), Symphony in F.

ANDERSEN, MICHAEL

b. 1938 Los Angeles, California.
Composer. Educated at University of Southern California at Los Angeles; won Alchin Fellowship; wrote scores for films; composed *Trumpet Concerto, Concert Overture, Seven Songs for Voice and Orchestra, Variations on a Georgian Theme for Violin and Piano, Music for Brass, Serenade for Two Flutes and String Quartet, Suite for Solo Viola.*

ANDERSON, ED

b. 1906, Jacksonville, Florida
Black jazz trumpeter.

ANDERSON, ELIZABETH JANE (LIZ)

b. 1930 Roseau, Minnesota.
Singer. Attended high school in Grand Forks, North Dakota, and business college in Redwood City, California; albums—*Strangers* (1966); *Liz Anderson Sings*, and *Cookin' Up Hits* (1967); *Liz Anderson Sings Her Favorites*, and *Like a Merry-Go-Round* (1968).

ANDERSON, ERNESTINE IRENE

b. 1928 Houston, Texas.
Singer. With Lionel Hampton's band (1952-53); toured Sweden, recorded "Hot Cargo" in Stockholm which became popular in Sweden and the U.S.; sang in night clubs in London after 1965.

ANDERSON, IAN

b. 1947.
Singer and flutist. Leader of Jethro Tull, rock group, organized 1967; played at Madison Square Garden, New York City (1971) with "bounce"; albums—*Benefit, This Was Jethro Tull, Stand Up.*

ANDERSON, IVY (IVIE)

b. 1904 Gilroy, California, d. 1949 Los Angeles, California. Black singer. Singer for Duke Ellington (1931-42); recorded with Ellington.

ANDERSON, JAMES WILLIAM, III (BILL)

b. 1937 Columbia, South Carolina.
Singer, guitarist, and songwriter. Graduated from the University of Georgia, Athens, in journalism; wrote "City Lights" (1959), "That's What It's Like to be Lonesome" (1960), "Tips of My Fingers" (1960), "I Missed Me" (1960), "Happy Birthday to Me" (1961), "We Missed You" (1962), "My Name Is Mud" (1962), "Still" (1963), "Peel Me a 'Nanner" (1964), "Strangers" (1965), "Three AM" (1965), "I Love You Drops" (1966), "Nobody But a Fool" (1966).

ANDERSON, JOHN MURRAY

b. 1886 St. John's, Newfoundland, d. 1954 New York City. Lyricist and producer. Studied at Edinburgh Academy, Scotland, and Lausanne University, Switzerland; with American Bureau of Information in World War I; director of Greenwich Village Follies, and Music Box Revue of 1924; with Jack Yellen wrote lyrics for *A Young Man's Fancy* (1920, m. Milton Ager); *John Murray Anderson's Almanac* (1929), also 1953 included Sheldon Harnick's "Merry Minuet"; also many other shows; wrote lyrics for A. Baldwin Sloane and Carey Morgan.

ANDERSON, LEROY

b. 1908 Cambridge, Massachusetts, d. 1975. Popular composer and teacher. Studied at the New England Conservatory, Boston, and at Harvard (1929); organist at the East Congregational Church, Milton, Massachusetts (1929-32) and taught at Radcliffe College; served in the army in World War II in Iceland and Washington, D.C. as a captain; composed "Blue Tango," "Bugler's Holiday," "A Christmas Festival," "The Irish Suite," "The Typewriter."

ANDERSON, LYNN RENE

b. 1947 Grand Forks, North Dakota.
Singer. Attended high school in Fair Oaks, California; American River College, Sacramento, California (1966); on "American Swingaround," Chicago (1967-68); "Lawrence Welk's Champagne Music Makers" after 1967; albums—*Ride, Ride, Ride* (1967); *Promises, Promises,* and *Big Girls Don't Cry* (1968); at the 1971 Country Music Association awards, Nashville, Tennessee, she was named Female Vocalist of the Year.

ANDERSON, MARIAN

b. 1902 Philadelphia, Pennsylvania.
Black contralto. Studied with Giuseppe Boghetti and made her debut with the Philadelphia Philharmonic Orchestra (1925); sang in Berlin, Paris, and Vienna (1930-35); conductor Arturo Toscanini said, "A voice like hers comes once in a century"; first black person to sing with the Metropolitan Opera, New York City (1955); President Eisenhower appointed her a United States delegate to the United Nations (1958); she was refused by the Daughters of the American Revolution to sing in Constitution Hall, Washington D.C. in 1939 because she was black; she sang instead at the Lincoln Memorial before a crowd of 75,000 people; later she was permitted by the DAR to sing in Constitution Hall after a surge of public outrage.

ANDERSON, MAXWELL

b. 1888 Atlantic, Pennsylvania, d. 1959 Stamford, Connecticut. Librettist and dramatist. Graduated from the University of North Dakota, Grand Forks, and Stanford University, Stanford, California; wrote the librettos *Knickerbocker Holiday* (m. Kurt Weill), *Lost in the Stars* (Weill); also wrote many successful plays.

ANDERSON, THOMAS JEFFERSON

b. 1928 Coatesville, Pennsylvania.
Black composer. Graduated West Virginia State, Institute, West Virginia (1950); master's degree at Penn State (1951); studied at Cincinnati Conservatory; doctorate from State University of Iowa, Ames, Iowa (1958); also at Aspen School of Music; taught at West Virginia State, Langston University, Oklahoma, and Tennessee A & I College, Nashville, after 1963; then composer-in-residence to Atlanta Symphony (1969) on a Rockefeller Foundation grant; wrote *New Dances for Orchestra* (1960); *Symphony in Three Movements* (1965); *Personals* (1966); *for Orchestra* (1965); *Personals* (1966); *Rotations, for Band* (1967); *Chamber* Symphony (1968).

ANDERSON, WALTER

b. 1915 Zanesville, Ohio.
Black organist and teacher. Head of music department of Antioch College, Yellow Springs, Ohio.

ANDERSON, WILLIAM ALONZO ("CAT")

b. 1916 Greenville, South Carolina.
Black trumpeter. With Duke Ellington's band (1944-47 and again 1950-59); led own band (1947-50); also with Lionel Hampton, Lucky Millinder, and Erskine Hawkins; toured with Ellington's band during 1960s in U.S. and overseas; with Lionel Hampton's band at Newport Jazz Festival, New York City (1972).

ANDERSON, WILLIAM KETCHAM

b. 1888 Bronx, New York, d. 1947.
Composer. Educated at Wesleyan University, Middletown, Connecticut, Union Theological Seminary, and Columbia University, N.Y. City; was a Methodist minister in the Northeast Ohio (1912), Ohio (1915), and Pittsburgh Conferences (1920), then in Johnstown, Pennsylvania; composed the tune "Journey's End" (1930) for "When on My Day of Life the Night Is Falling" (w. John G. Whittier).

ANDRADE, DANIEL RAY ("HANK THE DRIFTER")

b. 1929 Taunton, Massachusetts.
Singer. Leader of the Drifters (1944-48) and the Hayshakers (1949-51); albums—*Pictures, Life's Other Side, Driftin' with Hank* (1966), *Hank Is Singing Again* (1968).

ANDRES, HENRY GEORGE

b. 1838 Nancy, France, d. 1921.
Pianist. Studied under his father; at age fourteen went to Paris where he studied for seven years; came to the United States (1860); gave concerts in Cincinnati, Ohio; taught at the Cincinnati Conservatory of Music upon its founding by Clara Bauer in 1867; toured the States with Armin W. Doerner in 1889.

ANDREWS, GEORGE WHITFIELD

b. 1861 Wayne, Ohio, d. 1932 Honolulu, Hawaii. Organist and teacher. Organist in churches in Meadville, Pennsylvania and Toledo, Ohio (1879-86); began teaching at Oberlin Conservatory, Oberlin, Ohio, in 1886 and became professor of organ, composition and orchestration in 1892.

ANDREWS, J. WARREN

b. 1860 Lynn, Massachusetts, d. 1932 Grantwood, New Jersey. Pianist, organist and teacher. Organist in Swampscott, Lynn, and Cambridge, Massachusetts; Newport, Rhode Island; Minneapolis, Minnesota (1895), and New York City (1898), and also taught piano in Minneapolis and New York.

ANDREWS, JULIE

b. 1935 Walton, England.
Singer and actress. American debut in an off-Broadway musical, *The Boy Friend*; played the lead in *My Fair Lady* (1956, m. Frederick Loewe); later appeared in pictures (scores by Lennie Hayton); also had the lead in *Camelot* (1960, m. Loewe).

ANDREWS, LA VERNE

b. 1915 Minneapolis, Minnesota, d. 1967.
Singer. Formed the Andrews Sisters with Maxene and Patty; toured with bandleader Larry Rich (1932); appeared in many films after 1937; also appeared with Bing Crosby on radio shows; popular during World War II.

ANDREWS, MAXENE

b. 1918 Minneapolis, Minnesota.
Singer. With sisters La Verne and Patty, famous as the Andrews Sisters.

ANDREWS, PATTY

b. 1920 Minneapolis, Minnesota.
Singer. With sisters La Verne and Maxene, famous as the Andrews Sisters.

ANDRUS, CHARLES E., JR. (CHUCK)

b. 1928 Holyoke, Massachusetts.
Bass player. Studied at Manhattan School of Music; led own jazz group in Springfield, Massachusetts; during 1950s with Charlie Barnet, Claude Thornhill, and others; with Woody Herman (1961-65); toured Europe with Herman (1964); played with small groups in New York City.

ANGLIN, JACK

b. 1916 Columbia, Tennessee, d. 1963 Madison, Tennessee. Singer, guitarist, and songwriter. Teamed with Johnny Wright to form The Tennessee Mountain Boys which toured the Southern states and appeared on various radio stations during the 1940s and 1950s; their best sellers were "Crying Heart Blues" and "Poison Love" (1951); "Beware of It" and "I Get So Lonely" (1954), "South of New Orleans" (1953), and "The Moon Is High and So Am I"; killed in an auto accident on the way to funeral services for Patsy Cline and group who were killed in a plane crash.

ANKA, PAUL

b. 1941 Ottawa, Ontario, Canada.
Singer and composer. At age fifteen he composed ten songs including "Diana,"

which he sang and recorded, and was number one for thirteen weeks in 1957; toured the world (1957-59); sang at the Copacabana, N. Y. City (1960); wrote "You Are My Destiny," "Put Your Head on My Shoulder," "Lonely Boy," "Crazy Love," "Puppy Love," "My Home Town," "Don't Gamble on Love," "Train of Love" (recorded by Annette); toured Japan (1972).

ANSCHUTZ, KARL

b. 1815 Coblenz, Germany, d. 1870 New York City. Conductor. Came to New York City in 1857 as conductor of the Strakosch-Ullmann Opera troupe; conducted the Arion Society of New York (1860-62).

ANTES, JOHN

b. 1740 Frederickstown, Pennsylvania, d. 1811 Bristol, England. Musical inventor and composer. Left America in 1764 as a Moravian missionary to Egypt, was tortured and crippled there; invented a machine to turn pages, an instrument for better violin tuning, improvements for the piano keyboard hammer, and the violin bow; also made instruments.

ANTHEIL, GEORGE

b. 1900 Trenton, New Jersey, d. 1959 New York City. Noted pianist and composer. Studied under Constanin Sternberg and Ernest Bloch; toured Europe as a concert pianist (1922); best known for *Ballet Mecanique*, introduced in Paris (1926), Symphony no. 4 introduced by Leopold Stokowski and the NBC Symphony Orchestra (1944), Sonata no. 4 for Piano (1948), and Symphony no. 6 introduced by the San Francisco Orchestra under Frederick Marvin (1948).

ANTHONY AND THE IMPERIALS (formerly Little Anthony and the Imperials)

Anthony Gourdine, vocals; Ernest Wright, vocals; Clarence Collins, vocals; Sam Strain, vocals; Kenny Seymour, guitar; albums—*Best of Little Anthony and the Imperials* (Volumes 1 and 2) (1968), *Goin' Out of My Head, Greatest Hits of Little Anthony and the Imperials, I'm on the Outside, Movie Grabbers, Payin' Our Dues, Reflections* (1967).

ANTHONY, RAY

b. 1922 Cleveland, Ohio.
Trumpeter and bandleader. Played with Al Donahue (1938); later with Jimmy Dorsey and Glenn Miller; served in the navy in World War II; organized his own band after the war; his band played in a number of films.

ANTOINE, JOSEPHINE L.

b. 1908 Boulder, Colorado, d. 1971 Jamestown, New York. Soprano. Studied at the Juilliard School, New York City; debut with the Metropolitan Opera Company, New York (1935); later sang with opera companies in Chicago, San Francisco, and Cincinnati; professor of voice at University of Rochester Eastman School, Rochester, New York.

APPLETON, THOMAS

b. 1785, d. 1872.
Organ maker. Employee of William M. Goodrich of Templeton, Massachusetts; left him about 1807 to join Alpheus Babcock to form the firm of Hayts, Babcock, and Appleton; firm dissolved (1840), went in business with Ebenezer Goodrich; later with Samuel R. Warren.

APTHORP, WILLIAM FOSTER

b. 1848 Boston, Massachusetts, d. 1913 Vevey, Switzerland. Critic and writer. Program annotator for the Boston Symphony Orchestra (1892-1901) and music critic for the *Boston Transcript*; wrote *Musicians and Music Lovers* (1894), *By the Way About Music and Musicians* (1898), and with John D. Champlin edited the *Cyclopaedia of Music and Musicians* (1888-1890).

ARBUCKLE, MATTHEW

b. 1828, Glasgow, Scotland, d. 1883 New York. Cornetist and writer. Wrote *The Complete Cornet Method*, published in Boston; played the cornet and was a bandmaster.

ARCHER, FREDERICK

b. 1838 Oxford, England, d. 1901 Pittsburgh, Pennsylvania. Conductor and composer. Studied in London and in Leipzig; came to New York in the early 1880s and was an organist at the Plymouth Church, Brooklyn; became conductor of the Boston Oratorio Society in 1887 and conductor of the Pittsburgh (Pa.) Orchestra (1895-98); composed organ pieces and a cantata; published *The Keynote*, a monthly music magazine, after 1880.

ARCHER (AURACHER), HARRY

b. 1888 Creston, Iowa, d. 1960 New York City. Composer of musical shows. Educated at Knox College, Galesburg, Illinois, and Princeton University; wrote the score for *Little Jesse James* (1923), *Paradise Alley* (1924), *Merry Merry* (1925), and *Twinkle Twinkle* (1926).

ARCHER, JOHN BENJAMIN

b. 1872 Blackinton, Massachusetts, d. 1954. Composer. Studied at Williams College, Williamstown, Massachusetts (1889-93), then the University of Michigan, Ann Arbor (LL.B. 1896).

ARCHEY, JAMES H. (JIMMY)

b. 1902 Norfolk, Virginia, d. 1967.
Black jazz trombonist. With Edgar Hayes in New York debut (1926); after 1928 with King Oliver and Luis Russell until 1937; with Benny Carter, Noble Sissle, and others; toured Europe with own sextet (1952); later with Mez Mezzrow; with Earl Hines' combo (1955-62).

ARDELLI, NORBERT

b. 1902 Trieste, Austria-Hungary, d. 1972 New York City. Tenor and teacher. Born Norbert Adler; brought to U.S. as a boy; studied voice with Pasquale Amato; appeared in opera in Europe and South America; New York Stadium debut (1939) as Rhadames in a concert version of *Aïda*; taught voice after 1950; married dramatic soprano Selma Siegel who sang professionally as Selma Segalli.

ARENS, FRANZ XAVIER

b. 1856 Rheniser, Prussia, Germany, d. 1932 Los Angeles, California. Conductor. Conducted the May Music Festivals in Indianapolis, Indiana (1892-96) and was president of the Metropolitan School of Music; moved to New York City in 1897 where he established and conducted the People's Symphony Society; composed a symphonic fantasia and other works.

ARIZONA, JOHNNIE

b. 1921 Tucson, Arizona.
Songwriter. With Grand Ole Opry (1942-45); wrote "Jealous Blues," "Just Back from Texas," "Forgive Me," "Boomrang Baby," "Time Will Tell the Tale," "I Love Every Worldly Thing."

ARIZONA TRAILBLAZERS *see* SMOKEY WARREN

ARKANSAS COTTON PICKERS (band) *see* PAUL HOWARD

ARKIN, ALAN

b. 1934 Brooklyn, New York.
Singer, guitarist, composer and actor. Attended Bennington College, Bennington, Vermont, Los Angeles City College and Los Angeles State in California; joined The Tarriers folk quartet (1956); became an actor on Broadway and in the movies; composed the background music for two plays, and the songs "Cuddle Bug," "That's Me" and "Best Time of the Year."

ARLEN, HAROLD

b. 1905 Buffalo, New York.
Pianist and popular composer. Born Hyman Arluck, and was pianist for the Cotton Club in New York City; with lyrics by Ted Koehler, he wrote "I Love a Parade," "Happy as the Day Is Long," and "Stormy Weather"; with Johnny Mercer, "Blues in the Night," "That Old Black Magic," "Accentuate the Positive," and "Come Rain or Come Shine"; also, "It's Only a Paper Moon" (w. Billy Rose and E. Y. Harburg) and "Over the Rainbow" (w. E. Y. Harburg for *The Wizard of Oz*, 1939).

ARMSTRONG, DANIEL LOUIS ("SATCHMO")

b. 1900 New Orleans, Louisiana, d. 1971 Queens, New York City. Black trumpeter and bandleader. At age twelve and a half he shot off his father's .38 revolver on New Year's Eve, and was sent to the Colored Waif's Home for Boys, where his teacher taught him to read music and play the drums, bugle and cornet; got his start with King Oliver (1922); then with Fletcher Henderson in New York at the Roseland Ballroom (1924), where he switched from the cornet to the trumpet; played before King George V at the London Palladium; his record *Hello Dolly!* sold over a million discs; at his funeral Peggy Lee sang "The Lord's Prayer," old-time jazz vocalist Al Hibbler sang "Nobody Knows the Trouble I've Seen," Professor Hugh Porter, musical director at Canaan Baptist Church, New York City, sang "Just a Closer Walk with Thee," and Hibbler sang "When the Saints Go Marching In."

ARMSTRONG, HENRY W. (HARRY)

b. 1879 Somerville, Massachusetts, d. 1951 New York City. Singer, pianist, and composer. Was a prize fighter, pianist, booking agent, producer; entertained in hospitals during World War I; entertainer in night clubs, on radio, and TV; wrote "Sweet Adeline" (1903, w. Richard H. Gerard).

ARMSTRONG, WILLIAM DAWSON

b. 1868 Alton, Illinois, d. there 1936.
Composer, organist and teacher. Instructor at Forest Park University, St. Louis, Missouri (1888-90); organist in Alton, Illinois (1890-96); taught at Western Military Academy (1898-1908); composed the opera *The Spectre Bridegroom*, produced in St. Louis in 1899.

ARNDT, FELIX

b. 1889 New York City, d. 1918 Harmon, New York. Pianist and popular composer. Educated at the New York Conservatory and worked as staff pianist for various New York publishing houses; wrote the piano pieces "Nola" (1915), "Desecration," "Clover Club," "Love in June," "Marionette," "Soup to Nuts," and "Toots."

ARNHEIM, GUS

b. 1897 Philadelphia, Pennsylvania, d. 1955 Los Angeles, California. Bandleader and composer. Had his own band; Russ Columbo played violin in his orchestra; with Harry Tobias and Jules Lemare, wrote "Sweet and Lovely" (1931).

ARNOLD, EDDIE

b. 1918 near Henderson, Tennessee.
Singer, guitarist, songwriter, known as the "Tennessee Plowboy." Top feature on WTJS radio station, Jackson, Tennessee (1942-48); wrote "Easy on the Eyes" (1952); during the 1940s, '50s, and '60s his records were top hits of country music; toured all fifty states, and large crowds attended all his engagements. (*See also* Jimmy Driftwood).

ARNOLD, HORACE

b. 1937 Louisville, Kentucky.
Drummer. Studied piano at Los Angeles City College (1957) while in the Coast Guard; played drums with Roland Kirk in Indianapolis, Indiana (1959); played in trio in Louisville with Cecil McBee and Kirk Lightsey; after 1960 in New York City; played with Mingus, Kirk, and others; studied composition with Heine Stadler (1966).

ARNOLD, MAURICE

b. 1865 St. Louis, Missouri, d. 1937.
Composer and teacher. Born Maurice Strothotte; studied at the Cincinnati College (1883), in Berlin, at the Cologne Conservatory, and with Max Bruch, Breslau; after publication of his *American Plantation Dances* in 1894, he became an instructor at the National Conservatory at the invitation of Antonin Dvořák; his comic opera *The Merry Benedicts* was produced in 1896 in Brooklyn, New York.

ARNOLD, RICHARD

b. 1845 Eilenburg, (East) Germany, d. 1918 New York City. Violinist. His parents brought him to America (1853); pupil of Ferdinand David; first violinist of Theodore Thomas' orchestra (1878); leader of the New York Philharmonic Club (1891); organized a sextet (1897).

ARONSON, RUDOLPH

b. 1856 New York City, d. there 1919.
Conductor. Promoted popular concerts at the Metropolitan Concert Hall and at the Casino after 1890.

ARRAU, CLAUDIO

b. 1903 Chillan, Chile.
Concert pianist and teacher. When he was eight years old the Chilean government sent him to Berlin, Germany, where he studied under Martin Krause, a pupil of Franz Liszt; toured Europe and America as a concert pianist.

ARROYO, MARTINA

b. 1936 New York City.
Black soprano. Graduated Hunter College, New York City, in three years; won Metropolitan Opera auditions (1958); sang in Europe; debut at Met (1965) replacing the ailing Birgit Nilsson in *Aïda*; married Emilio Poggioni, Italian violist.

ARS NOVA (rock group)

Wyatt Day, rhythm guitar; John Pierson, lead singer and bass trombone; Sam Brown, lead guitar; Jimmy Owens, trumpet and cornet; Art Koenig, bass; Joe Hunt, drums; albums—*Ars Nova* (1968); *Sunshine and Shadows* (1969).

ARTHUR, ALFRED

b. 1844 Pittsburgh, Pennsylvania, d. 1918 Lakewood, Ohio. Tenor, composer, conductor, and teacher. Graduated the Boston School of Music (1869) and sang in the Church of the Advent, Boston (1869-71); founded the Cleveland School of Music in 1885; composed the operas *Adeline, The Water Carrier* and *The Roundheads and Cavaliers.*

ASCHER, LEO

b. 1880 Vienna, Austria, d. 1942 New York City. Composer. Composed *Soldat der Marie* and *Hoheit tanzt Walzer.*

ASHBY, DOROTHY JEANNE

b. 1932 Detroit, Michigan.
Singer, harpist, and pianist. Daughter of Wiley Thompson, jazz guitarist; educated at Wayne State University, Detroit, Mich.; played in many concerts during 1950s in Detroit; also on radio; known as a jazz harpist.

ASHBY, HAROLD KENNETH

b. 1925 Kansas City, Missouri.
Tenor saxist. Served in U.S. Navy; played with Tommy Douglas (1946); later in Chicago, then New York with Mercer Ellington.

ASHTON, JOSEPH NICKERSON

b. 1868 Salem, Massachusetts, d. 1946.
Organist and teacher. Graduated Brown University, Providence, Rhode Island (1891), and Harvard (M.A., 1893); taught musical history and theory at Brown University (1898-1904).

ASHWORTH, CHARLES STEWART

b. 1777, d. (?).
Conductor and writer. Director of the United States Marine Band (1804-16); wrote *Rules to be Observed by Young Drummers* (1812).

ASHWORTH, ERNIE

b. 1928 Huntsville, Alabama.
Singer, guitarist, and songwriter. Worked for radio station WSIX, Nashville, Tennessee in the 1950s; some of his songs were recorded by MGM under the name Billy Worth; hit the number one spot in 1963 with "Talk Back Tremblin' Lips"; joined the Grand Ole Opry cast (1964).

ASPLUND, JOHN

b. (?), d. 1807.
Compiler of hymns. Compiled *J. Asplund's New Collection*, Baltimore, Maryland (1793). (*See* Thomas Baldwin)

ASSOCIATION, THE (rock group)

Russ Giguere, vocals and guitar; Ted Bluechet, Jr., drums; Brian Cole, bass vocals, bass guitar, and clarinet; Terry Kirkman, vocals and twenty-three instruments; Larry Ramos, lead guitar and vocals; Jim Yester, tenor vocals, and rhythm guitar; albums—*And Then . . . Along Comes the Association* (1966), *Renaissance* (1967), *Insight Out* (1967), *Birthday* (1968), *Association's Greatest Hits* (1968).

ASSUNTO, FRANK JOSEPH

b. 1932 New Orleans, Louisiana, d. 1974.
Trumpeter and bandleader. Leader of the Dukes of Dixieland in Las Vegas, Nevada (1949); toured other cities; toured Japan (1964).

ASSUNTO, FRED J.

b. 1929 New Orleans, Louisiana, d. 1966 Las Vegas, Nevada. Trombonist. Toured with his brother's Dukes of Dixieland. (*See* Frank J. Assunto)

ASSUNTO, JACOB ("PAPA JAC")

b. 1905 Lake Charles, Louisiana.
Trombonist and banjoist. Father of Frank and Fred Assunto; toured with the Dukes of Dixieland.

ATCHER, JAMES ROBERT OWEN (BOB)

b. 1914 Hardin County, Kentucky.
Singer, guitarist, and songwriter. Attended Kentucky State University, Frankfort; sang on radio station WHAS, Louisville, Kentucky, then on WBBM Chicago (1938-43); served in the army in the Pacific Theatre during World War II, performing at army bases and in hospitals; Columbia recorded his top hits in an LP record, *Bob Atcher* (1965).

ATCHER, RANDALL I. (RANDY)

b. 1918 Tip Top, Kentucky.
Singer and songwriter. Attended high school in West Point, Kentucky; Western Kentucky College, Bowling Green, Kentucky (1936-37); served as a major in the air force during World War II; wrote "Flying High," "Them Soft Shoulders," "Give Back My Heart," "Indian Rock," "I Need You Baby," "You're a Living Doll," "Heart Break Avenue."

ATCHISON, JOHN BUSH

b. 1840 Wilson, New York, d. 1882.
Hymnist. Was a Methodist clergyman; wrote the hymn "Not Half Has Ever Been Told" (1875, m. O.F. Presbry, "I Have Read of a Beautiful City").

ATCHISON, SHELBY DAVID ("TEX")

b. 1912 Rosine, Kentucky.
Singer, fiddler, bandleader, and songwriter. With "National Barn Dance," WLS Chicago (1931-40); WHO Des Moines, Iowa (1940-41); KXLA Los Angeles (1942-60); leader of his own band (1945-60); wrote "Old Kentucky Fox Chase," "Sick, Sober and Sorry," "Sleepy Eyed John," "Honky Tonkitis."

ATHERTON, PERCY LEE

b. 1871 Roxbury, Massachusetts, d. 1944 Atlantic City, New Jersey. Composer. Graduated Harvard (1893); composed the comic operas *The Heir Apparent* (1890), *The Maharajah* (1900), and the symphonic poem, *Noon in the Forest.*

ATKINS, BOYD

b. 1900 Paducah, Kentucky.
Black saxophonist, violinist, and composer. Played with Fate Marable, Carroll Dickerson, and Louis Armstrong; later had his own band; wrote "Heebie Jeebies" (1925).

ATKINS, CHESTER BURTON (CHET)

b. 1924 Luttrell, Tennessee.
Singer, guitarist, and songwriter. Started with radio station WNOX, Knoxville, Tennessee, then went with several other stations; joined Grand Ole Opry, Nashville, Tennessee (1946), then went to work for RCA Victor in Nashville (1957); guest soloist at the 1960 Newport (R.I.) Jazz Festival and at the Press Photographers' Ball at the White House for President Kennedy (1961).

ATKINSON, JOHN

b. 1835 Deerfield, New Jersey, d. 1897.
Hymnist. Was a Methodist minister; wrote the hymn "We Shall Meet Beyond the River" (1867), soon after the death of his mother (m. H. P. Main, second tune by S. J. Vail); the song appeared in *Bright Jewels* (1869).

ATKINSON, ROBERT WHITMAN

b. 1868, d. 1933.
Composer. Wrote "Floating 'Mid the Lilies," "I Am Thinking Love of Thee."

ATTERIDGE, (RICHARD) HAROLD

b. 1886 Lake Forest, Illinois, d. 1938 Lynnbrook, New York. Lyricist. Educated at University of Chicago, Ph.B.; staff writer for Shuberts; librettist for numerous Broadway shows; wrote lyrics for "Come Dance with Me" (1911, m. Louis A. Hirsch), "By the Beautiful Sea" (m. Harry Carroll), songs for the *Passing Show* (1913, (m. Jean Schwartz), also eleven other editions of the *Passing Show*.

AUBERT, HENRI

b. 1926 Paris, France, d. 1971 Cragsmoor, New York. Concert violinist. Studied in Warsaw, then at the Paris Conservatory; sent to Auschwitz concentration camp at age fifteen, later to Buchenwald; toured Israel (1948); came to America (1950); resided in New York City.

AUDEN, WYSTAN HUGH

b. 1907 York, England.
Poet and lyricist. Wrote *The Age of Anxiety* which was set to music by Leonard Bernstein in his second symphony (1949); taught at the University of Michigan, Ann Arbor, and at Smith College, Northampton, Massachusetts; became an American citizen in 1946; wrote *Hymn to Peace* (m. Pablo Casals) conducted by Casals at the United Nations General Assembly (1971).

AUER, LEOPOLD

b. 1845 Veszprem, Hungary, d. 1930 near Dresden, (East) Germany. Concert violinist. Soloist for the Czar; taught at the St. Petersburg Conservatory (1868); director of the Imperial Musical Society (1887-92); came to New York City to live in 1918.

AULD, ALEXANDER

b. 1836, d. 1889.
Composer, compiler, and teacher. Resided in Deersville, Ohio; organized and conducted singing schools in Ohio; published *The Key of the West* (1836), *The Ohio Harmonist* (1847), *The Farmers' and Mechanics' Minstrel* (1867), and *The Golden Trumpet*.

AULD, GEORGIE

b. 1919 Toronto, Canada.
Saxophonist and bandleader. Born John Altwerger; played with Bunny Berigan, Artie Shaw, Jan Savitt, and Benny Goodman; served in World War II; led own orchestra (1944-46); later led small groups.

AUSTIN, GENE

b. 1900 Gainesville, Texas, d. 1972 Palm Springs, California. Tenor and songwriter. Born Eugene Lucas, took the surname of his stepfather, Jim Austin; lived in Louisiana, then Baltimore, Maryland; served in France in the army in World War I; became a crooner, his theme song, "My Blue Heaven" sold over twelve million records; wrote "When My Sugar Walks Down the Street," "Those Wedding Bells Are Breaking Up That Old Gang of Mine"; he had no musical training and composed by ear.

AUSTIN, LARRY

b. 1930 Duncan, Oklahoma.
Composer and teacher. Graduated North Texas State, Denton (1951, M.S. 1952); studied composition with Darius Milhaud and others; taught at the University of California after 1958; wrote *Piano Variations; A Broken Consort; The Maze; Changes* for trombone and tape; *Current*, for clarinet and piano; *Piano Set; Bass; Improvisations* for orchestra and jazz soloists (performed by Leonard Bernstein and the New York Philharmonic, 1964); *Duet Amphitryon*, taped electronic music (1967).

AUSTIN, LOVIE

b. 1887 Chattanooga, Tennessee.
Black pianist and orchestra leader. Born Cora

Calhoun; studied at Roger Williams University in Nashville, and Knoxville College; led the Serenaders in 1923; accompanied Ma Rainey, blues singer; pianist in pit bands in theaters; later pianist at Jimmy Payne's dancing school; recorded with Ida Cox, Ma Rainey, and Johnny Dodds.

AUTREY, HERMAN

b. 1904 Evergreen, Alabama.
Black jazz trumpeter. Played with Thomas "Fats" Waller; recorded on Swingville with Zutty Singleton; also played with Fletcher Henderson and Claude Hopkins; later led own group.

AUTRY, ORVON ("GENE")

b. 1907 Tioga, Texas.
Singer, guitarist and actor. Known on radio station KVOO as "Oklahoma's Singing Cowboy"; joined station WLS, Chicago (1930) with his own program; wrote "That Silver Haired Daddy of Mine" (1931), which sold over five million records, "You're the Only Star in My Blue Heaven" and "Dust" (1938), "Tears on My Pillow" and "Be Honest with Me" (1941), "Tweedle O Twill" (1942) and "Here Comes Santa Claus" (1948); appeared in his first film in 1934; was a pilot in the Army Air Corps in the Pacific area during World War II; later formed his own record company, Challenge Records, put together a chain of radio stations, formed a TV production company, and became part owner of the Los Angeles Angels (baseball team) (1962), and took part in the ceremonies opening the new stadium at Anaheim, California (1966).

AVALON, FRANKIE

b. 1940 Philadelphia, Pennsylvania.
Singer and trumpeter. Played the trumpet on "Horn & Hardart's Children's Hour" (1955); his song "Venus" (1959) hit the number one spot; albums—*Frankie Avalon; Fifteen Greatest Hits.*

AVERILL, PERRY

b. 1862 New Haven, Connecticut, d. 1935.
Opera singer. Operatic debut as Count di Luna in *Il Trovatore* in Boston in 1895.

AVERY, STANLEY R.

b. 1879 Yonkers, New York, d. after 1910.
Organist. Organist in Yonkers, New York (1895-1910).

AVOLA, ALEXANDER ALBERT (AL)

b. 1914 Boston, Massachusetts.
Guitarist, composer and arranger. Educated at Suffolk University, Boston, Massachusetts, LL.B.; guitarist and arranger for Frankie Carle, Tony Pastor and Artie Shaw; with Raymond Scott orchestra; wrote film scores; instrumentals "Blossoms" (Tony Pastor theme); "Carle Boogie" (for Frankie Carle).

AVSHALOMOFF, AARON

b. 1894 Nicolaevsk, Siberia, d. 1965.
Composer. Studied in Zurich, Switzerland, then went to China (1914); came to America, returned to China (1928), but returned to America and settled in Hollywood, California; composed *Kuan Yin*, an opera; *The Soul of China*, a ballet; *The Peiping Hutungs*, a symphonic fantasy; *The Great Wall*, an opera.

AVSHALOMOFF, JACOB

b. 1919 Tsingtao, China.
Composer, conductor and teacher. Son of Aaron Avshalomoff, and came to America with his father; instructor at Columbia University, New York City, then conductor of the Junior Symphony Orchestra, Portland, Oregon; composed the choral work, *Tom O'Bedlam* (a cantata), a sinfonietta, and chamber music.

AYER, NAT D.

b. 1887 Boston, Massachusetts, d. 1952 Bath, England. Popular composer. Went to England with the American Ragtime Octette; wrote the music for a number of musical shows and reviews produced in England—*The Bing Boys Are Here* (1916, w. Clifford Grey), *The Bing Girls Are There* (1917, w. Grey), *The Bing Boys on Broadway* (1918, w. Grey); these shows were produced at the Alhambra Theatre, London, England; also wrote "Oh, You Beautiful Doll" (1911, w. Seymour Brown).

AYERS, ROY E., JR.

b. 1940 Los Angeles, California.
Vibraharpist. Studied music at Los Angeles City College; in Las Vegas Jazz Festival (1962); co-leader with Hamp Haws in quartet; led own quartet (1965-66).

AYLER, ALBERT

b. 1936 Cleveland, Ohio.
Black saxophonist. Brother of Don Ayler, trumpeter; organized Albert Ayler Trio in Greenwich Village, New York City; toured Europe with his brother, recorded in Denmark.

AYLER, DONALD (DON)

b. 1942 Cleveland, Ohio.
Black trumpeter. Brother of Albert Ayler; studied at Miller Academy of Music in Cleveland, then at Cleveland Institute of

Music; toured Sweden (1963); with Albert Ayler Quintet after 1964.

AYLER TRIO, ALBERT (black jazz rock group)

Albert Ayler, saxophone; Gary Peacock, electric bass; Sonny Murray, drums; albums—*My Name Is Albert Ayler, Albert Ayler in Greenwich Village* (1967), *Love Cry* (1968), *New Grass* (1969), *Music Is the Healing Force of the Universe.*

AZNAVOUR, CHARLES

b. 1924 France.

Singer. Albums—*Aznavour Canta en Espanol; Aznavour Italiano; Aznavour Sings His Love Songs in English; Aznavour Way* (in French); *Grande Charles; Live at the Olympia* (in concert); *World of Charles Aznavour.*

B

BABASIN, HARRY

b. 1921 Dallas, Texas.
Cellist and bass player. Educated at North Texas State College; played with Gene Krupa, Boyd Raeburn, and Charlie Barnet; later with Benny Goodman (1945); toured with Woody Herman (1948); formed own group, The Jazzpickers (1956); studied composition at San Fernando Valley State College, California (M.A., 1961); with Phil Moody after 1963.

BABBITT, MILTON BYRON

b. 1916 Philadelphia, Pennsylvania.
Noted composer. Attended public schools in Jackson, Mississippi, graduated from New York University (1935), then studied privately in New York with Roger Sessions; taught music at Princeton University; composed *Music for the Masses* (1941), *Three Compositions for Piano* and *Composition for Four Instruments* (1947), *The Widow's Lament in Springtime* (1950, w. William Carlos Williams for Bethany Beardslee), *Composition for Synthesizer* (1961, composed electronically), *Vision for Prayer* (1961, electronically synthesized, w. Dylan Thomas), *Relata I* for symphony orchestra (1966), performed by the Cleveland Orchestra with Gunther Schuller conducting.

BABCOCK, JOSEPH T. (JOE)

b. 1932 North Loup, Nebraska.
Singer and songwriter. Graduated University of Nebraska, Lincoln (1957), and UCLA, Los Angeles (1958); with Glaser Brothers Band (1959-61), Marty Robbins Band (1961-65), and Town and Country Singers (1966-68); wrote "Prairie Fire," "Won't You Forgive," "Ghost Train," "Dusty Winds," "Georgia Moon," "I Washed My Hands in Muddy Water."

BABCOCK, MALTBIE DAVENPORT

b. 1858 Syracuse, New York, d. 1901 Naples, Italy. Poet and hymnist. Educated at Syracuse University and Auburn Theological Seminary; became a Presbyterian minister in Lockport, New York, and Baltimore, Maryland, then at the Brick Presbyterian Church, New York City; wrote "This is My Father's World" (1901, tune "Terra Beata"—F.L. Shepard) and "Be Strong! We Are Not Here to Play" (tune "Fortitude"—David S. Smith).

BABIN, VICTOR

b. 1908 Moscow, Russia, d. 1972 Cleveland, Ohio. Pianist and composer. Studied at Riga (Latvia) Conservatory and Berlin Hochschule; pianist after 1933; U.S. debut (1937), then settled here; married Vitya Vronsky, and they played as a two-piano team; composed *Variations on Theme by Purcell* for cello and piano, *Six Etudes* for two pianos, *Strains from Far-off Lands* for two pianos, string quartets, concerto for two pianos and orchestra, *Sonata-Fantaisie* for cello and piano, and a song cycle, *Beloved Stranger*, to words by Witter Bynner.

BACCUS, EDDIE

b. 1936 Lawndale, North Carolina.
Organist. Studied piano at age ten at School for Blind Children in Raleigh, North Carolina, and later at School for the Blind in Columbus, Ohio; joined Roland Kirk's group as a pianist, then organist; formed his own trio and recorded in 1962.

BACHARACH, BURT F.

b. 1928 Kansas City, Missouri.
Singer, composer, and conductor. Educated at McGraw University, Mannes School of Music, New York City, and Music Academy of the West, Santa Barbara, California; studied with Darius Milhaud, et al.; served in army (1950-52); arranger for Vic Damone, Ames Brothers, and Marlene Dietrich; albums—*Burt Bacharach, The Man and His Songs; Butch Cassidy and The Sundance Kid; Casino Royale* (soundtrack); *Make It Easy on Yourself; Reach Out;* wrote "What's New Pussycat" (1965, w. Hal David).

BACON, ERNST

b. 1898 Chicago, Illinois.
Composer. Studied in Chicago and Vienna; pupil of Ernest Bloch and others; composed *Ford Theatre*, suite for orchestra; operas—*A*

Tree on the Plains and *A Drumlin Legend* (Columbia University production under Alice M. Ditson Fund); also symphonies, chamber works, songs.

BACON, KATHERINE

b. 1896 Chesterfield, England.
Concert pianist. Pupil of Arthur Newstead, whom she married (1916); toured the United States and Canada, then taught at the Juilliard School of Music, New York City.

BACON, LEONARD W.

b. 1802 Detroit, Michigan, d. 1881 New Haven, Connecticut. Hymnist and compiler. Graduated Yale and Andover Theological Seminary and in 1824 became pastor of the First Congregational Church, New Haven, Connecticut, until 1865; wrote the lyrics for "O God, Beneath Thy Guiding Hand" (1833, tune "Duke Street"—Hatton, 1793); with Nathan H. Allen, edited *The Hymns of Martin Luther*, New York City (1883), and with Dr. E. T. Fitch, *Psalms and Hymns for Christian Worship* (1845) which included five of his hymns.

BACON, LOUIS

b. 1904 Louisville, Kentucky, d. 1967.
Black jazz trumpeter.

BAER, ABEL

b. 1893 Baltimore, Maryland.
Popular composer. Orchestral conductor in Boston (1918-20); wrote "Lucky Lindy" (1927, w. L. Wolfe Gilbert) to celebrate Charles A. Lindbergh's flight, "All That I Need Is You" (1921, w. Lester Santly), "Mama Loves Papa" (1924, with Cliff Friend), "There Are Such Things" (1943, with George Meyer, w. Stanley Adams), "Don't Wake Me Up, Let Me Dream" (1925, with Mabel Wayne, w. L. Wolfe Gilbert).

BAERMANN, CARL

b. 1839 Munich, Germany, d. 1913 Newton, Massachusetts. Pianist and teacher. Studied under Liszt; came to Boston (1881); noted teacher there.

BAEZ, JOAN

b. 1941 Staten Island, New York.
Singer and guitarist, known as the "Queen of the Folksingers." Graduated from high school in Los Angeles and attended Boston University, but dropped out; sang in coffee houses in Boston, then at the Newport Jazz Festivals of 1959 and 1960; her Vanguard record entitled *Joan Baez* was a sensation; lived in Carmel,California, and was a crusader against the Vietnam war.

BAEZ, MIMI

b. 1945.
Singer. Younger sister of Joan Baez; married Richard Farina, who was killed in a motorcycle accident (1966); albums—*Celebrations for a Grey Day* (1965), *Reflections in a Crystal Wind* (1966), *Memories* (1968).

BAGLEY, EDWIN E.

b. 1857, d. 1922.
Bandmaster and composer. Wrote the "National Emblem March" (1906), this tune used for "And the monkey wrapped its tail around the flagpole."

BAGWELL, WENDELL LEE (WENDY)

b. 1930.
Gospel singer and songwriter. Attended high school in Atlanta, Georgia; albums—*Old Time Religion, Family Bible, Keep Walking, Hand in Hand, Reunion in Heaven, Just Over the Rainbow, Heavenly Flight;* he wrote "Pearl Buttons," "Unbelievable," "Good Bye Devil," "Little Country Preacher."

BAILES, WALTER BUTLER

b. 1920 North Charleston, West Virginia.
Gospel singer and songwriter. Wrote "Pretty Flowers," "Dust on the Bible," "Will the Angels Have a Sweetheart," "I Want to be Loved," "Whiskey Is the Devil," "Drunkard's Grave."

BAILEY, DANIEL (compiler) *see* DANIEL BAYLEY

BAILEY, DONALD ORLANDO ("DONALD DUCK")

b. 1934 Philadelphia, Pennsylvania.
Drummer. Toured with organist Jimmy Smith for eight years; then played in Los Angeles night clubs.

BAILEY, ERNEST HAROLD (BENNY)

b. 1925 Cleveland, Ohio.
Black trumpeter. Went to Europe (1948) with Dizzy Gillespie, Lionel Hampton, and Quincy Jones; with Swedish radio band (1957-59); first recorded in U.S. in 1960.

BAILEY, MARIE LOUIS (MRS. APFELBECK)

b. 1876 Nashville, Tennessee.
Pianist and composer. Studied in Leipzig, and was a pupil of C. Reinecke and later with Leschetizky; debut in Leipzig (1893); became chamber-virtuoso to King Albert of Saxony; after 1900 toured Europe and the United States.

BAILEY, MILDRED RINKER

b. 1907 Tekoa, Washington, d. 1951 Poughkeepsie, N.Y. Singer. Joined Benny

Goodman's band (1927); married Red Norvo; they had their own band (1937-39); on the "Camel Caravan" radio series in 1940's; she was a large woman of part Indian blood; considered by some jazz writers as the greatest singer of all time.

BAILEY, PEARL

b. 1918 Newport News, Virginia.
Black singer. Toured with Cootie Williams' band; later singer in night clubs, Broadway shows; TV appearances; also appeared in films; sang at a church service in the White House for President and Mrs. Nixon (October 1971); married drummer Louis Bellson (1952); resided in Northridge, California.

BAILEY, SAMUEL DAVID (DAVE)

b. 1926 Portsmouth, Virginia.
Black drummer. Served in Army Air Force (1942-46); studied at Music Center Conservatory, New York City (1947); with Herbie Jones (1951-53); with Hodges, Mingus, and others in 1950s; with Gerry Mulligan (1955-59), toured Europe; later with Clark Terry-Bob Brookmeyer Quintet; toured Brazil; early promoter of the bossa nova.

BAILEY, WILLIAM C. ("BUSTER")

b. 1902 Memphis, Tennessee, d. 1967.
Black clarinetist. Played in Lucky Millinder's band; also with John Kirby and Fletcher Henderson (1924-25); previously with King Oliver; member of Saints and Sinners Orchestra (1961-65); with Jackie Gleason (1962-63); at Newport Jazz Festival (1960-61) with Red Allen.

BAKER, BENJAMIN FRANKLIN

b. 1811 Wenham, Massachusetts, d. 1889 Boston, Massachusetts. Singer, composer, compiler, and teacher. Choirmaster in churches in Salem and Boston (1831-41); taught music in Boston public schools (1841-47); founded and was principal of the Boston Music School (1851-68); assisted Isaac B. Woodbury in compiling *The Boston Musical Educational Society's Collection* (1842) and *The Choral* (1845), and published *Through Brass and Harmony* (1870); wrote the cantatas *The Storm King, The Burning Ship, Camillus,* and *The Roman Conqueror.*

BAKER, CHESNEY H. (CHET)

b. 1929 Yale, Oklahoma.
Jazz trumpeter and singer. Served in 298th Army Band in Germany (1946-48); studied at El Camino College, Los Angeles; in Presidio Army Band in San Francisco (1950-52); with Gerry Mulligan (1953); formed own group (1953); toured Europe (1955-57); arrested in Italy on a narcotics charge and in jail there (1960-61); spent some time in a sanatorium in Germany; returned to New York (1963) and played in night clubs.

BAKER, DAVID NATHANIEL, JR. (DAVE)

b. 1931 Indianapolis, Indiana.
Black composer. Graduated Indiana University (B.A. and M.A. in music); taught at Indiana Central College, Indianapolis, Lincoln University, Jefferson City, Missouri, and Indiana University; toured Europe in 1961 with Quincy Jones; wrote *A Summer's Day* (1945) for jazz ensemble and tape recorders, *Reflections* for symphony orchestra and jazz ensemble, *But I Am a Worm* for chorus, jazz ensemble, and string orchestra, and *Psalm 22, A Modern Jazz Oratorio.*

BAKER, HAROLD ("SHORTY")

b. 1914 St. Louis, Missouri, d. 1966.
Black trumpeter. Organized his own band with his brother; played in Don Redman's band; also with Teddy Wilson, Andy Kirk, Mary Lou Williams and Duke Ellington; toured Europe with Ellington.

BAKER, JOSEPHINE

b. 1906 St. Louis, Missouri, d. 1975.
Black singer. Sang in New York City night clubs; went to Paris (1925) with the show *Revue Négre,* where she was the star and where she remained; sang in the *Folies Bergère* (some of her material was composed by Spencer Williams); became the "Toast of Paris"; married a Frenchman.

BAKER, KENNY

b. 1912 Monrovia, California.
Trumpeter. Album—*Spectacular Trumpet of Kenny Baker.*

BAKER, PHIL

b. 1896 Philadelphia, Pennsylvania, d. 1963 Copenhagen, Denmark. Accordionist and comedian. In vaudeville; with Ed Janis in violin-accordian act; later with Ben Bernie; served in navy in World War I; appeared in films.

BAKER, THEODORE

b. 1851 New York City, d. 1934 Dresden, Germany. Compiler and writer. In 1900 he published *Baker's Biographical Dictionary of Musicians.*

BALATKA, HANS

b. 1827 Hoffnungsthal, Moravia (Czechoslovakia), d. 1899 Chicago, Illinois. Conductor. Studied in Vienna, Austria, and came to America (1849); founded Musikverein in Milwaukee, Wisconsin, (1851), and later founded the northwest Sangerbund; became conductor of the Chicago Philharmonic Society (1860); conductor of Chicago Musical Union (1863-65).

BALDWIN, D.H.

b. ?, d. 1889.
Piano maker. Founded the D. H. Baldwin Company, Cincinnati, Ohio (1862).

BALDWIN, RALPH LYMAN

b. 1872 Easthampton, Massachusetts, d. 1943 Canaan, New Hampshire. Teacher and composer. Joined the faculty of the Institute of Music Pedagogy, Northampton, Massachusetts in 1900.

BALDWIN, SAMUEL ATKINSON

b. 1862 Lake City, Minnesota, d. 1949 New York City. Organist and composer of hymns. Organist of the Plymouth Church, Chicago (1885-89), People's Church, St. Paul, Minnesota (1889-95), and the Chapel of the Intercession, New York City (1895-1902); composed the anthem "Tarry with Me"; became a teacher at City College, New York City (1895).

BALDWIN, THOMAS

b. 1753 Norwich, Connecticut, d. 1825.
Hymnist. Pastor of the Second Baptist Church, Boston (1790-1825); wrote "From Whence Does This Union Rise?" which appeared in *J. Asplund's New Collection,* Baltimore (1793), and "Almighty Saviour, Here We Stand" which appeared in *Collection of Sacred and Devotional Hymns,* Boston (1808).

BALES, RICHARD

b. 1915 Alexandria, Virginia.
Composer. Studied at Eastman School of Music, Rochester, New York, and at Juilliard, New York City; conductor of National Gallery of Art after 1943; works—*The American Revolution, The Confederacy, The Union, Theme and Variations* (strings), *National Gallery Suite No. 3, Gate of the Year* (choral), *Holiday at the White House* (piano), *The Lincoln Room* (violin, piano), *Mary's Gift* (voice, piano).

BALL, ERNEST R.

b. 1878 Cleveland, Ohio, d. 1927 Santa Ana, California. Popular composer. Studied at the Cleveland Conservatory, then worked as a pianist and staff composer for Witmark, New York City; wrote "Will You Love Me in December as You Do in May" (1905, w. J. J. Walker), "Love Me and the World Is Mine" (1906, w. Dave Reed), "Mother Machree" (1910, with C. Olcott, w. Rida J. Young), "When Irish Eyes Are Smiling" (1912, w. C. Olcott and George Graff, Jr.), "A Little Bit of Heaven, Sure They Call It Ireland," "Rose of Killarney" (1927, w. William Davidson).

BALLANTINE, EDWARD

b. 1886 Oberlin, Ohio, d. 1971 Vineyard Haven, Martha's Vineyard, Massachusetts. Pianist and composer. Studied piano with Schnabel and Ganz, and composition with Spalding and Converse; joined the faculty of Harvard University (1912); wrote *The Eve of Saint Agnes,* introduced by the Boston Symphony (1917), and other chorus, piano and violin pieces; other orchestra pieces included—*From the Garden of Hella, Prelude to the Delectable Forest,* and *By a Lake in Russia,* played by the Boston Pops.

BALLOU, HOSEA

b. 1771 Richmond, New Hampshire, d. 1852. Hymnist. Was a Universalist preacher in Portsmouth, New Hampshire (1807), Salem Massachusetts (1815), and Boston (1817); wrote "When God Descends with Men to Dwell," which appeared in *Hymns Compiled by Different Authors* (1808).

BALOGH, ERNO

b. 1897 Budapest, Hungary.
Pianist and composer. Studied at Budapest Conservatory with Bartok and Kodaly; came to U.S. (1924); composed *Portrait of a City,* suite for strings and piano (WQXR); *Pastorale and Capriccio,* for piano, flute, clarinet and strings (WQXR, 1943); piano pieces.

BALSLEY, PHILIP E.

b. 1939 Augusta County, Virginia.
Baritone. Member of the Statler Brothers vocal quartet.

BALTAZAR, GABRIEL RUIZ, JR. (GABE)

b. 1929 Hilo, Hawaii.
Alto saxist, clarinetist, flutist, and pianist. Studied at Peabody Conservatory in Baltimore; in Stan Kenton's band (1960-64), toured Mexico and Great Britain; at 1963 Newport Jazz Festival; appeared with small groups after 1964.

BALTZELL, WINTON JAMES

b. 1864 Shiremanstown, Pennsylvania, d. 1928 New York City. Editor and teacher. Son of the Rev. Isaiah Baltzell (1832-93); educated at Lebanon Valley College, Annville, Pennsylvania (1884), and New England Conservatory (1889); taught singing in Lebanon,

Pennsylvania; assistant editor of *The Etude* (1897-99); professor at Ohio Wesleyan University, Delaware, Ohio (1899-1900); editor of *The Etude* (1900-07).

BAMBERGER, CARL

b. 1902 Vienna, Austria.
Teacher. Came to America and taught opera at the Mannes College of Music, New York City.

BAMPTON, ROSE

b. 1909 Cleveland, Ohio.
Soprano. Studied at the Curtis Institute of Music, Philadelphia, with Horatio Connell and Queena Mario; sang with the Chautauqua, New York Opera Association (1929), the Philadelphia Grand Opera Company, the Philadelphia Orchestra, and after 1933 with the Metropolitan Opera Company, New York City.

BANCROFT, JAMES HENRY

b. 1819 Boston, Massachusetts, d. there 1844.
Hymnist. Graduated Amherst (1839) and Andover (1842); wrote "Brother, Though from Yonder Sky," which appeared in *The Psalmist, A New Collection of Hymns for the Use of Baptist Churches*, Boston (1843).

BANCROFT, SILAS ATKINS

b. 1823 Boston, Massachusetts, d. 1886.
Organist, composer, and compiler. Organist of the Mount Vernon Congregational Church, Boston (1848-60), then the Emmanuel Church (1860-80); assisted William Mason in compiling *The Social Glee Book* (1848), and Samuel P. Tuckerman in compiling *The National Lyre* (1848).

BAND OF PIRATES *see* FREDDY MARTIN

BAND, THE (rock group)

Rick Danko, bass and vocals; Levon Helm, vocals and drums; Garth Hudson, vocals and organ; Richard Manuel, vocals and piano; Robbie Robertson, vocals and lead guitar; albums—*Band; Music from Big Pink; Stage Fright* (1970).

BANG, MAIA

b. 1877 Norway, d. 1940 New York City.
Violinist and teacher. Studied at the Leipzig Conservatory, and with Marteau and Auer; she made her debut in Oslo, Norway (1900); came to New York City (1919) to teach in Auer's Academy.

BAQUET, GEORGE F.

b. 1883 New Orleans, Louisiana, d. 1949 Philadelphia, Pennsylvania. Black clarinetist. Resided in New Orleans; played in Bill Johnson's Original Creole Ragtime Band (1914); settled in Philadelphia (1918); taught Sidney Bechet to play the clarinet.

BAQUET, THEOGÈNE

b. 1860 New Orleans, Louisiana, d. 1920. Black cornetist. Played in New Orleans.

BARBARIN, PAUL

b. 1901 New Orleans, Louisiana, d. 1969.
Jazz drummer. Played in King Oliver's band; with Oliver, he wrote "Tack Annie" (1927) and "Every Tub" (1927); played with Freddie Keppard (1918); also with Bill Johnson (1918); with the Luis Russell Band (1928); recorded with King Oliver and his Dixie Syncopators.

BARBER, SAMUEL

b. 1910 West Chester, Pennsylvania.
Noted composer. Educated at the Curtis Institute, Philadelphia; composed Symphony no. 1 (Rome, 1936), *Adagio for Strings* (introduced by the NBC Symphony under Arturo Toscanini, 1938), Essay no. 1 (by the NBC Symphony under Toscanini, 1938), Essay no. 2 (by the New York Philharmonic under Bruno Walter, 1942), Symphony no. 2 (by the Boston Symphony under Serge Koussevitsky, 1944), *Concerto for Cello and Orchestra* (1946), *Medea* ("Cave of the Heart," ballet in New York City, 1946), *Vanessa* (1958); opera, *Antony and Cleopatra*, Metropolitan Opera (1966).

BARBIERI, LEANDRO ("GATO")

b. 1933 Rosario, Argentina.
Tenor saxist. Played in Europe with Lalo Schifrin, Ted Curson, and Jim Hall; with Don Cherry Quintet after 1966.

BARBOUR, DAVID MICHAEL (DAVE)

b. 1912 Flushing, New York, d. 1965 Malibu, California. Guitarist and songwriter. Played with Wingy Manone, Red Norvo, Artie Shaw and Benny Goodman; married singer Peggy Lee (1943); they wrote "Mañana," "It's a Good Day," "I Don't Know Enough about You."

BARCELONA, DANIEL (DANNY)

b. 1929 Honolulu, Oahu, Hawaii.
Drummer. Joined Trummy Young (1948); formed own sextet (1951), the Hawaiian Dixieland All-Stars and toured the Far East;

joined Louis Armstrong's band (1958); toured with Armstrong during the 1960s.

BARE, ROBERT JOSEPH (BOBBY)

b. 1935 Ironton, Ohio.
Singer, guitarist, and songwriter. Went to California in the 1950s, then into the army; wrote "All-American Boy" at that time, then "Detroit City" (1963) which won him a Grammy Award, "500 Miles Away from Home" (1963), "Four Strong Winds" (1964), "Miller's Cave" (1964), "It's All Right" (1965), "The Streets of Baltimore" (1966).

BAREFIELD, EDWARD EMANUEL (EDDIE)

b. 1909 Scandia, Iowa.
Black clarinetist. Debut with Edgar Pillows in Des Moines, Iowa (1926); studied at Chicago Conservatory (1930); later with Teddy Wilson, Art Tatum, and others; with Cab Calloway (1934-37); then with Les Hite, Fletcher Henderson, and others; with ABC (1942-46); later with Sy Oliver; with Cab Calloway off and on (1957-60), toured U.S. and South America; conducted and arranged Jazz Train revue in Europe (1960); with Paul Lavalle at 1965 World's Fair.

BARENBOIM, DANIEL

b. 1942 Buenos Aires, Argentina.
Pianist. Family took him as a child to Tel Aviv, Israel, in order to be raised properly in the Jewish faith; at age ten toured the capitals of the world as a concert artist; married cellist Jacqueline Du Pre (b. 1945 Oxford, England); gave joint concert with his wife at Manhattan's Philharmonic Hall (1971); guest conductor of Cleveland Orchestra at Carnegie Hall concert, New York City (1972).

BARÉS, BASILE

b. 1845 New Orleans, Louisiana, d. there 1902. Black musician and composer after the Civil War.

BARKER, DANIEL (DANNY)

b. 1909 New Orleans, Louisiana.
Black guitarist and banjoist. In New York after 1930, played with James P. Johnson, Cab Calloway, Benny Carter and other leading bands; assistant to curator of New Orleans Jazz Museum after 1965.

BARKER, HORTON

b. 1889 Laurel Bloomer, Tennessee.
Folk singer. Raised in Staunton, Virginia; first appeared at the White Top Mountain Folk Festival, near Marion, Virginia (1933), then sang there and other places for years afterwards; sang at the first annual University of Chicago Folk Festival (1961); recorded a number of his folk songs for the Archives of American Folk Song of the Library of Congress, Washington, D.C.

BARKSDALE, EVERETT

b. 1910 Detroit, Michigan.
Black guitarist. Played with Art Tatum; afterwards a staff musician at ABC network in New York City.

BARLOW, HOWARD

b. 1892 Plain City, Ohio, d. 1972 Bethel, Connecticut. Conductor. Graduated Reed College, Portland, Oregon; studied music with Lucien Becker, and at Columbia University, New York City, with Frank E. Ward and Cornelius Rybner; conductor of the Reed College choral society, the Riverdale Choral Society, New York (1915), and later became a conductor on radio programs; on "Voice of Firestone" programs after 1943.

BARLOW, JOEL

b. 1755 Redding, Connecticut, d. 1812 Krakow, Poland. Lyricist. Served in the Continental Army in the American Revolution; graduated from Yale (1778) and became a lawyer; let Robert Fulton test Fulton's steam torpedo boat on Rock Creek on his estate in Washington, D.C.; wrote "Hasty Pudding," "Columbia," and "Along the Banks" (1799, tune "Melton"—Lowell Mason); went to Poland for a meeting with Emperor Napoleon, and died there.

BARLOW, SAMUEL LATHAM MITCHELL

b. 1892 New York City.
Composer and teacher. Studied at Harvard and later in Rome with Respighi, et al; wrote the operas *Mon Ami Pierrot* (w. Sacha Guitry) produced in Paris (1934), and *Amanda* (1936); also orchestral works, and chamber music.

BARLOW, WAYNE

b. 1912 Elyria, Ohio.
Composer. Graduated Eastman School of Music, Rochester, New York; taught at the Eastman School; won Lillian Fairchild Award (1935); composed *Sarabande* (for orchestra), *The Winter's Passed* (for oboe and strings), *Lyrical Piece* (for clarinet and piano, or strings), *Madrigal for a May Morning, Twenty-third Psalm* (for tenor, mixed choir, and organ, or orchestra).

BARNABEE, HENRY CLAY

b. 1833 Portsmouth, New Hampshire, d. 1917 Boston, Massachusetts. Opera singer. Sang with the Boston Ideal Opera Company; with

Tom Karl, organized "The Bostonians" in 1887.

BARNARD, REV. JOHN

b. 1681 Bristol, Massachusetts, d. 1770. Hymnist. Pastor in Marblehead, Massachusetts; wrote versifications of the Psalms (1752).

BARNES, EDWARD SHIPPEN

b. 1887 Sea Bright, New Jersey, d. 1958. Idyllwild, California. Organist and composer. Studied at Yale and in Paris; organist at churches in New York City, Rutgers, New Jersey, Philadelphia, and Santa Monica, California, at the First Presbyterian Church there since 1938; arranged the tune "Gloria" for "Angels We Have Heard on High" (w. French); also composed two symphonies.

BARNES, GEORGE

b. 1921 Chicago Heights, Illinois.
Guitarist. Studied with his father; toured with own quartet (1935-39) through the Middle West; with Bud Freeman; in army during World War II; with ABC radio (1946-51); later in New York City; formed duo with guitarist Carl Kress (1963); toured U.S. and Japan (1965); later taught at Famous Guitarists School; played at Upstairs at the Downstairs, New York City (1972) with Bucky Pizzarelli, later with Art Ryerson on the seven string guitar, and with singer Peter Dean.

BARNES, PAUL D. ("POLO")

b. 1901 New Orleans, Louisiana.
Black clarinetist and soprano saxist. Studied at St. Paul Lutheran College; formed own group, Diamond Jazz Band (1919), later known as Young Tuxedo Band; with Papa Celestin, composed and recorded "My Josephine" (1926); with King Oliver and Jelly Roll Morton; in U.S. Navy (1942-45); with Celestin's Tuxedo Band (1946-51); played in New Orleans after 1964.

BARNES, WILL C.

b. 1858 Minneapolis, Minnesota, d. 1936 Phoenix, Arizona. Lyricist and writer. In the Signal Corps from 1879-82 and was awarded the Congressional Medal of Honor "for bravery in action with hostile Apache Indians" at Fort Apache, Arizona, in September, 1881; was a writer in Holbrook, Arizona, and also Phoenix; wrote the words for "A Cowboy's Dream" (1893) to the tune "In the Sweet Bye and Bye" (m. J. P. Webster); the lyrics are also attributed to others, but Barnes had a strong claim.

BARNET, CHARLES DALY (CHARLIE)

b. 1913 New York City.
Bandleader and tenor saxist. Educated at Rumsey Hall and Blair Academy; formed his first band in 1933; at the Palomar in Los Angeles (1939), then the ballroom burned to the ground; recorded Ray Noble's tune "Cherokee" (1939) which became his theme song; featured singers Harry Von Zell, then Lena Horne and baritone Bob Carroll (1941), later Kay Starr; at various times his band included trumpeters Eddie Sauter, Tutti Camarata, Chris Griffin, Neal Hefti, Al Killian, and Peanuts Holland; bassist Oscar Pettiford, clarinetist Buddy De Franco, guitarist Barney Kessel, also trumpeters Doc Severinsen, Jimmy Nottingham, and Clark Terry; his guitarist Bus Etri and trumpeter Lloyd Hundling were killed in an auto accident (1941).

BARNETT, ALICE

b. 1886 Lewiston, Illinois.
Composer. Studied at Chicago Musical College, and American Conservatory, Chicago; taught in San Diego High School (California) 1917-26; also music chairman of San Diego Symphony; wrote musical settings for poems—"In a Gondola," "In May," "Harbour Lights."

BARNETT, BOBBY GLEN

b. 1936 Cushing, Oklahoma.
Singer and songwriter. Album—*Bobby Barnett at the Crystal Palace, Tombstone, Arizona* (1964); wrote "Just Gotta Be Love," "Cheatin' Kathleen," "Worst Thing That Could Happen," "Break Your Habit of Breaking My Heart."

BARNUM, H.B.

b. 1936 Houston, Texas.
Singer and arranger. Known as the "Barnum Wonder Boy"; debut as singer and pianist at age four; appeared in films; arranger for rhythm and blues artists in Hollywood, California, during the 1960s.

BAROMEO, CHASE (CESARE)

b. 1893 Augusta, Georgia.
Bass. Graduated from the school of music at the University of Michigan, Ann Arbor, and studied music in Italy; sang at La Scala (in Buenos Aires, Argentina), with the Chicago Opera, and after 1935 with the Metropolitan Opera Company, New York City.

BARRERE, GEORGES

b. 1876 Bordeau, France, d. 1944 Kingston, New York. Flutist and conductor. Studied at the Paris Conservatory (1895) and joined the Paris Opera Company; member of the New York Symphony Orchestra (1905-28); taught at the Institute of Musical Art, New York City after 1910; member of the trio with Carlos Salzedo and Horace Britt; composed chamber works.

BARRETT, EMMA ("SWEET EMMA")

b. ca. 1905 New Orleans, Louisiana.
Black singer and pianist. With Papa Celestin (1923); played with Armand J. Piron; leader of her own band after 1961; known as "Sweet Emma the Bell Gal."

BARRIS, HARRY

b. 1905 New York City, d. 1962 Burbank, California. Singer, pianist, and songwriter. Member of the Rhythm Boys, Paul Whiteman, Bing Crosby, and Al Rinker (1928-29); entertainer in China-Burma-India Theatre of War (1943-44).

BARRON, KENNETH (KENNY)

b. 1943 Philadelphia, Pennsylvania.
Pianist. Brother of Bill Barron; played in Mel Melvin's band (1957); with Yusef Lateef in Detroit (1960); with Dizzy Gillespie Quintet after 1962.

BARRON, WILLIAM, JR. (BILL)

b. 1927 Philadelphia, Pennsylvania.
Tenor saxist and songwriter. Toured with Carolina Cottonpickers; in army band (1944-46); studied at Ornstein School of Music in Philadelphia; played in Philadelphia night clubs (1948-58); in New York City after 1958; co-leader with Ted Curson; toured Europe.

BARROWS, DONALD S.

b. 1887 New Haven, Connecticut.
Choirmaster and composer of hymns. Graduated from the New York School of Law (1898); was vice-president of the Symington-Gould Corp., Rochester, New York (1924-47); choirmaster in churches in Rutherford, N.J., Boonton, N.J., and New York City; composed the tunes "*Cura Dei*" (1941, for "God Who Made the Earth," w. Sarah Betts Rhodes), and "O North with All Thy Vales of Green" (w. William C. Bryant).

BARROWS, JOHN R., JR.

b. 1913 Glendale, California.
Composer. Studied horn at Eastman School in Rochester, New York, and later at Yale School of Music;. pupil of Baumgartner, Donovan and Smith; played first horn with San Diego Symphony and with New Haven, Connecticut Symphony; wrote *Nocturne* (for English horn, played by San Diego Symphony), *Quintet* (for woodwinds, American Musical Festival at Yaddo), *Divertimento* (for string trio broadcast over WICC Mutual Network).

BARRYMORE, LIONEL

b. 1878 Philadelphia, Pennsylvania, d. 1954 Van Nuys, California. Composer and actor. Son of Maurice Barrymore, brother of Ethel and John Barrymore; stage debut in *The Rivals* (1893); appeared in numerous plays and films; works—*Farewell* Symphony (one-act opera), *Elegie* (piano pieces), *Fugue Fantasia, Preludium and Fugue, Rondo for Piano, Russian Dances, The Woodman and the Elves.*

BART, JAN

b. 1919 Sambor, Poland, d. 1971 Brooklyn, New York. Cantor, tenor and lyricist. Born Jan Strauser; attended Warsaw Academy of Music and Berlin Academy; came to U.S. (1930) and attended Columbia University, New York City; most popular singer of Yiddish songs; had his own program on station WEVD for thirty years; wrote *Book of Yinglish Songs* (Yiddish songs with his English lyrics); sang in Yiddish and English at night clubs and on the radio; broadcast with the American Jewish Caravan of Stars.

BARTH, HANS

b. 1896 Leipzig, Germany, d. 1956.
Composer. Brought to America at age six; studied at Leipzig Conservatory under Rechendorf; piano debut at age twelve in New York City; invented a portable, sectional, quarter-tone piano; his *Concerto for Quarter-Tone Strings and Quarter-Tone Piano* was played by Philadelphia, Cincinnati, and Havana orchestras; also wrote *Sonata,* for piano (op.14).

BARTHOLOMEW, MARSHALL MOORE

b. 1885 Belleville, Illinois.
Composer, conductor, teacher, and writer. Graduate of Yale University, University of Pennsylvania (B.M), and Berliner Hochschule fur Musik; director of National War Work Council in World War I; Yale Glee Club (1921-53); director, then president of Intercollegiate Music Council (1927-39); professor at Yale (1939-53); wrote *Music for Everybody, Mountain Songs of North Carolina, Seventy Songs for School and High School Singers,* and *Yale Song Book.*

BARTLETT, HOMER NEWTON

b. 1846 Olive, New York, d. 1920 Hoboken, New Jersey. Organist and composer. Studied with S. B. Mills, Max Braun and Jacobson; organist in New York City churches, including the Madison Avenue Baptist Church; wrote the cantata *The Last Chieftan*, the oratorio *Samuel*, and an opera, *La Valliere*.

BARTLETT, JAMES CARROLL

b. 1845 Harmony, Maine, d. after 1920. Singer, organist, composer, and teacher. Wrote "The Day Is Ended" and "An Evening Hymn."

BARTLETT, MARO LOOMIS

b. 1847 Brownhelm, Ohio, d. 1919.
Singer, conductor, and teacher. Studied at Oberlin Conservatory, Oberlin, Ohio; conductor of Philharmonic Society in Meadville, Pennsylvania; taught in Orange, New Jersey; bass soloist in New York City; conductor of Mozart Club, Chicago after 1880; director of Chicago Musical College; director of music at First Congregational Church there; then director of Musical College in Des Moines, Iowa; senior editor of *Sacred Gems;* author of *Class and Chorus.*

BARTOK, BELA

b. 1881 Nagyszentmiklos, Hungary, d. 1945 New York City. Noted pianist and composer. Studied piano at age five with mother; concert debut at Nagyszollos; studied with Erkel in Pozsony, Koessler, and Thoman in Budapest (1899); researched Hungarian folk songs; his opera *Prince Bluebeard's Castle* performed in Budapest (1918); came to America (1940), toured U.S.; folk song research at Columbia University (1940-42); wrote choral and orchestral works, piano pieces, and chamber music; his *Concerto for Orchestra* (1943) was introduced by Serge Koussevitzky and the Boston Symphony; Concerto no. 3 in Philadelphia (1945).

BARTON, WILLIAM ELEAZER

b. 1861 Sublette, Illinois, d. 1930 Brooklyn, New York. Compiler. Was a Congregational Minister in Oak Park, Illinois, for twenty-five years; compiled *Old Plantation Hymns* (1899) which included, for the first time, "Were You There When They Crucified My Lord?" and "She'll Be Comin' Round the Mountain" (based on the old Negro spiritual "When the Chariot Comes"); on March 21, 1971, while deliberating the fate of Lt. William L. Calley, Jr., the jury took a Sunday recess to sing "Were You There When They Crucified My Lord?"

BASCOMB, WILBUR ODELL ("DUD")

b. 1916 Birmingham, Alabama.
Black trumpeter. With Erskine Hawkins' band in 1930s; recorded new version of "Tuxedo Junction" (1960); own combo (1961-63); with Sam "The Man" Taylor after 1963; toured Japan.

BASIE, WILLIAM ("COUNT")

b. 1904 Red Bank, New Jersey.
Black pianist and bandleader. His jazz band became famous in the 1930s; with Otho Lee Gaines, wrote "One O'clock Jump" (1937); recorded with tenor sax greats Don Byas and Buddy Tate on RCA's *Big Bands' Greatest Hits* (1971); played at a command performance at Buckingham Palace (1957) for Queen Elizabeth II; continued popularity in 1960s; appeared at Roseland Dance City, New York (1972), broadcast on WHN radio; at 1972 Newport Jazz Festival, New York.

BASSETT, FRANKLIN

b. 1852 Wheeling, W. Virginia, d. 1915.
Organist and teacher. Taught at Cleveland Conservatory of Music, which became a department of the Western Reserve University, Cleveland, Ohio.

BASSETT, KAROLYN WELLS

b. 1892 Derby, Connecticut, d. 1931.
Composer and pianist. Studied with Van York, Carl and Reinhold Faelton; first piano recital at age six; wrote *Yellow Butterfly, Little Brown Baby, The Moon of Roses, A Child's Night Song.*

BASSETT, LESLIE

b. 1923 Hanford, California.
Composer. Attended Fresno State College; played the trombone in the 13th Armored Division Band in Germany in World War II; then studied composition at the University of Michigan, Ann Arbor, and in Paris, then taught at the University; composed several pieces which won him the Prix de Rome (1961); known for his *Five Movements for Orchestra*, performed by the RAI Orchestra of Rome with Massimo Freccia conducting, and for his *Variations for Orchestra* performed in Rome (1963) with Ferruccio Scaglia conducting, and by the Philadelphia Orchestra (1965) with Eugene Ormandy; wrote *Collect for Peace*, performed (1972) by St. Olaf Choir at Philharmonic Hall, New York City, conducted by Kenneth L. Jennings.

BASSFORD, WILLIAM KIPP

b. 1839 New York City, d. there 1902. Organist and composer. Pupil of Samuel Jackson; toured the United States as a concert pianist, then later became an organist in East Orange, New Jersey.

BASSMAN, GEORGE

b. 1914 New York City.
Pianist, composer, and arranger. Arranger for Andre Kostelanetz; wrote "I'm Getting Sentimental Over You" (Tommy Dorsey's signature tune); wrote music for numerous MGM films.

BATE, STANLEY

b. 1912 Plymouth, England.
Composer. Studied with Nadia Boulanger in Paris; awarded Guggenheim Fellowship; came to U.S. to live; composed music for ballets, chamber music, a sinfonietta for orchestra.

BATES, KATHERINE LEE

b. 1859 Falmouth, Massachusetts, d. 1929 Wellesley, Massachusetts. Lyricist and hymnist. Professor of music at Wellesley College; in 1893 she visited the Columbian Exposition in Chicago and decided to travel west and visit Pike's Peak, Colorado, where she was so impressed with the beauty of the view that she wrote "America, the Beautiful" which appeared in *The Congregationalist* (1895, later it was set to the tune "Materna" by Samuel A. Ward); also wrote the hymns "The Kings of the East Are Riding" (1914, tune "Wallace"—C.G. Hamilton), and "Dear God, Our Father, at Thy Knee Confessing" (1928, m. L.B. Longacre).

BATSON, FLORA (BERGEN)

b. 1870 Providence, Rhode Island, d. 1906. Black singer. She made concert tours in the United States, Europe, Australia, New Zealand, and Africa.

BATTISTA, JOSEPH

b. 1918 Philadelphia, Pennsylvania.
Pianist. Studied at Settlement Music School, Philadelphia Conservatory, and Juilliard School, New York City; appeared in concerts and recitals in Philadelphia and New York, including Youth Concert with the Philadelphia Orchestra (1939).

BAUDUC, RAY

b. 1909 New Orleans, Louisiana.
Jazz drummer. With Bob Crosby's band; at the P & M New Orleans Barbecue in Chicago operated by Paul Mares during the late 1930s; later very successful in New York City.

BAUER, CLARA

b. (?) Wurtemberg, Germany, d. 1912 Cincinnati, Ohio. Educator. Founder and director of the Cincinnati Conservatory (1867-1912); succeeded by her niece, Bertha Bauer; the Conservatory was taken over by the Institute of Fine Arts (1930).

BAUER, HAROLD

b. 1873 New Malden, England, d. 1951 Miami, Florida. Concert pianist. Debut as a violinist at the age of nine; studied with Gorski, in Paris, then piano with Paderewski, and made his debut as a pianist in Paris (1893); toured America after 1900 and resided in New York City for many years; founded the Beethoven Association (1919), and became its president.

BAUER, MARION EUGENIE

b. 1887 Walla Walla, Washington, d. 1955 South Hadley, Massachusetts. Composer and musicologist. Taught history of music at New York University; composed the ballet *Pan and Syrinx*, choral works for Jewish services, and piano pieces; wrote *Twentieth Century Music*, and with Ethel Peyser, *Music Through the Ages* and *How Music Grew*.

BAUER, WILLIAM HENRY (BILLY)

b. 1915 New York City.
Guitarist. With Herman and Goodman bands in 1940s; with Lennie Tristano and Lee Konitz in 1950s; staff guitarist for Ice Capades after 1963.

BAUMBACH, ADOLPH

b. ca. 1830 Germany, d. 1880 Chicago, Illinois. Pianist, organist, composer, and teacher. Came to America in 1855 and settled in Boston, where he taught piano and organ; later he moved to Chicago; composed "Let the Words of My Mouth" (from Psalm 19) which appeared in Baumbach's *Sacred Quartets, A Collection of Pieces for the Opening and Close of Service*, Boston (1862).

BAXTER, LES

b. 1922 Mexia, Texas.
Pianist, singer, conductor, and composer. Studied at the Detroit Conservatory, and Pepperdine College, Los Angeles; began as a concert pianist; sang for Mel Torme's Mel Tones (1945); conducted a number of radio shows including the "Bob Hope Show"; wrote *Le Sacre du Sauvage*.

BAXTER, LYDIA

b. 1809 Petersburg , New York, d. 1874 New York City. Hymnist. She and her sister helped form a Baptist Church in Petersburgh; wrote the hymn "Take the Name of Jesus with You" (tune "Precious Name" by William H. Doane) which appeared in *Pure Gold* (1871); published her poems in *Gems by the Wayside* (1855).

BAYES, NORA

b. ca. 1880 probably Joliet, Illinois, d. 1928 Brooklyn, New York. Singer. Born Dora Goldberg; debut as vaudeville singer; sang Harry von Tilzer's "Down Where the Wurzburger Flows" in Brooklyn (1902); at Palace Theatre, London (1905); in *Ziegfeld Follies* of 1907; wrote lyrics "Shine On, Harvest Moon" with second husband actor-composer Jack Norworth for Follies of 1908; they introduced "When It's Apple Blossom Time in Normandy" (1912); popularized Cohan's "Over There" (1917); she was married five times.

BAYLEY, DANIEL

b. 1725 West Newbury, Massachusetts, d. 1799. Organist, compiler, and writer. Organist at St. Paul's Episcopal Church, Newburyport, Massachusetts; published *A New and Complete Introduction to the Grounds and Rules of Music* (1764), *American Harmony* (1769), *Essex Harmony* (1770), *New Universal Harmony* (1775), *A Collection of Anthems and Hymn Tunes* (1784), *The Psalm Singer's Assistant* (1785), *The New Harmony of Zion, or Complete Melody* (1788).

BAZLEY, ANTHONY (TONY)

b. 1936 New Orleans, Louisiana.
Drummer. With Air Force show (1956-57) in Iceland, Newfoundland, Greenland, and Japan; studied at Los Angeles Conservatory; with Eric Dolphy (1958); played in small combos.

BEACH, AMY MARCY CHENEY (MRS. H.H.A. BEACH)

b. 1867 Henniker, New Hampshire, d. 1944 New York City. Composer. Pupil of E. Perabo, K. Baerman (piano), and Junius W. Hill (harmony); President of the Board of Councillors at the New England Conservatory, Boston; composed *Gaelic* Symphony, *Mass with Orchestra*, choral works.

BEACH BOYS (vocal group)

Organized in Los Angeles in 1966 by three brothers: Brian Wilson (b. 1942), Dennis Wilson (b. 1944), Carl Wilson (b. 1946); their cousin Mike Love (b. 1941); friends Al Jardine (b. 1944) and Bruce Johnston (b. 1944); later Brian Wilson dropped out of the group.

BEACH, DR. HENRY HARRIS AUBREY

b. 1844, d. 1910.
Singer. Husband of Amy Marcy Cheney Beach, the composer.

BEACH, JOHN PARSONS

b. 1877 Gloversville, New York, d. 1953.
Composer. Graduated New England Conservatory, Boston, and also studied in Europe; composed *Mardi Gras* (for baritone and orchestra, New Orleans, under Henri Wehrman with William Broussard, soloist, 1926), *New Orleans Street Cries at Dawn* (Philadelphia Orchestra under Stokowski, 1927), *The Phantom Satyr* (ballet, Asolo, Italy, under de Guarnieri, 1925, and as concert by Little Symphony, Rochester, New York, under Hanson, 1926), operas.

BEACON STREET UNION (rock group)

Dropouts from Boston University (1967), they wrote "Speed Kills" (antidrug) and "Incident" (*re* a knifing); Paul Tartachny, vocals and lead guitar; Wayne Ulaky, vocals and bass guitar; John Wright, lead singer and percussion; Richard Weisburg, drums; Robert Rhodes, piano and brass; albums—*Clown Died in Marvin Gardens*, and *Eyes of the Beacon Street Union*.

BEARDSLEY, CAROLINE (LATTIN)

b. 1860 Huntington, Connecticut, d. 1944.
Organist. Organist of the Second Congregational Church of Bridgeport, Connecticut (1883-1938) and also of B'nai Israel Temple (1909-38).

BEAU BRUMMELS (rock group)

Sal Valentino, vocals; Ron Meagher, bass; Ron Elliott, guitar; albums—*Beau Brummels* (1966), *Best of Beau Brummels* (1967), *Triangle* (1967), *Bradley's Barn* (1968).

BEAVERS, CLYDE WINFREY

b. 1932 Tennga, Georgia.
Singer, guitarist, and songwriter. After high school enlisted in the Air Force for two years; joined the Grand Ole Opry (1961); wrote "My Mom and Santa Claus," "Crazy Little Things," "I'd Rather Fight Than Switch," "That's You, Still Loving You."

BECHET, SIDNEY

b. 1891 New Orleans, Louisiana, d. 1959 Paris, France. Famous black clarinetist, soprano saxophonist, and composer. Played with Bunk Johnson in the Eagle Band (ca. 1912); then in New Orleans; on tour with Louis Wade, pianist (1917); then with King Oliver, Freddie Keppard, and Tony Jackson (1919); toured Europe (1919) with Will Marion Cook, violinist; gave concerts at the Royal Philharmonic Hall, London, and Paris, Berlin, Moscow, and Frankfort (1925); jailed in Paris (1928) for eleven months for being involved in a shooting scrape in a Montmartre night club, then deported; with Noble Sissle after 1929; wrote "Petite Fleur," "The Fishseller," "As-tu la Cafard," "Viper Mad," "Southern Sunset," "Delta Mood," "The Broken Windmill."

BECK, JOHANN HEINRICH

b. 1856 Cleveland, Ohio, d. there 1924. Violinist. Studied at the Leipzig Conservatory; founded the Cleveland Schubert Quartet (1889); composed overtures to Lord Byron's *Lara,* Shakespeare's *Romeo and Juliet,* the cantata *Deukalion* (Bayard Taylor).

BECKEL, JAMES COX

b. 1811 Philadelphia, Pennsylvania, d. there 1880. Organist and composer. Father was also an organist; organist in Philadelphia (1830-80); wrote "Old Easy Chair by the Fire."

BECKER, JOHN J.

b. 1886 Henderson, Kentucky, d. 1961. Composer, teacher and writer. Graduated Wisconsin Conservatory; was Director of Music at Notre Dame University, Indiana; after 1950 Director of Music at Barat College of the Sacred Heart, Lake Forest, Illinois; his Symphony no. 2 was played at the ISCM Festival at Frankfort-au-Main, Germany (1937) and Symphony no. 3 by the New York Philharmonic Orchestra.

BECKET, THOMAS à

b. ca. 1817, d. ca. 1871.
Popular composer and actor. Composed "He Was Such a Nice Young Man" (1840, w. R.W. Allridge), "Columbia, Gem of the Ocean" (1843), and "Adieu, Sweet Maid" (1845). In 1843 David T. Shaw, a singer, asked Becket to write a patriotic song for a benefit at the Chinese Theatre in Philadelphia. Shaw gave Becket several lines which he had written. Becket found them to be deficient in measure and ungrammatical, so he rewrote the entire song, "Columbia, Gem of the Ocean," which he gave to Shaw. Several weeks later, while acting in a show in New Orleans, Becket came across a printed copy of the song giving credit to Shaw as the lyricist and composer, and Becket as the arranger. But to the end, Becket insisted that he alone was the lyricist and composer, and finally had the song published under his own name as written and composed by Becket.

BECKET, THOMAS à, JR.

b. 1843 Philadelphia, Pennsylvania, d. there 1918. Pianist and teacher. Son of Thomas à Becket, and taught piano at Girard College (a school for orphans) in Philadelphia (1873-1918); composed *Rural Pictures,* twelve piano pieces published by Hatch in 1900; edited *Vocal and Instrumental Classics* (ca. 1893), and *Our Favorite Songs* (1913).

BEE, MOLLY

b. 1939 Oklahoma City, Oklahoma.
Singer and actress. Born Molly Beachboard; at the age of eleven, she sang on the "Hometown Jamboree" TV show in Los Angeles, at thirteen with "Pinky Lee Show," and at sixteen with Tennessee Ernie Ford; successful records include "Single Girl," "Losing You," "Hate to See Me Go," and "Miserable Me," also the LP *Swingin' Country.*

BEECHER, CHARLES

b. 1815 Litchfield, Connecticut, d. 1900 Georgetown, Massachusetts. Hymnist. Congregational minister in Georgetown, Massachusetts; son of Lyman Beecher and brother of Henry Ward Beecher and Harriet Beecher Stowe; wrote "We Are on Our Journey Home," which appeared in the *Plymouth Collection* (1855), which he edited with Henry W. Beecher and John Zundel.

BEECHER, HENRY WARD

b. 1813 Litchfield, Connecticut, d. 1887 Brooklyn, New York. Compiler. Brother of Harriet Beecher Stowe; graduated from Amherst and Lane Seminary; minister of Presbyterian churches in Lawrenceburg, Indiana, and Indianapolis (1837-47), then pastor of the Congregational Plymouth Church in Brooklyn (1847-87); edited *The Plymouth Collection of Hymns and Tunes* (1855, the music was edited by John Zundel and the Rev. Charles Beecher, his brother).

BEERS, ETHELINDA ELIOT

b. 1827 Goshen, New York, d. 1879 New York City. Lyricist. She wrote the lyrics "All Quiet Along the Potomac Tonight" (1861, m. J. H. Hewitt, 1863) originally called "The Picket Guard."

BEERS, EVELYNE CHRISTINE SAUER (ANDRESSEN)

b. 1925 Chicago, Illinois.
Singer. Met Robert Beers in St. Louis, and after they were married, they moved to Chicago; with her husband, Robert, and later their daughter Martha Christine, they were known as the "Singing Beers Family"; she was featured on a Prestige LP, *The Gentle Art;* they both appeared on *Walkie in the Parlor* (1961), and *Fiddler Beers and Evelyne Songs;* later they moved to Fox Hollow, New York.

BEERS, ROBERT HARLAN

b. 1920 Clearfield, Pennsylvania, d. 1972 Williamstown, Massachusetts. Singer and fiddler. Went to grade school in Joliet, Illinois, then the family moved to St. Louis; studied music at Northwestern University, Evanston, Illinois; served in World War II, and returned to college; concertmaster of the Symphony Orchestra, Billings, Montana (1951-55); with his wife Evelyne, sang in the Ozark Festivals (1957-58), the National Folk Festival at Oklahoma City (1957), and the Newport Festivals in the 1960s, with their daughter Martha; sponsored the annual Beers Family Festival of Traditional Music and Arts, also known as the "Fox Hollow Music Festival" in Petersburg, New York; with his wife performed in the White House on Christmas Day 1969; he was killed in a three-car collision.

BEESON, JACK

b. 1921 Muncie, Indiana.
Composer and teacher. Studied at Eastman School, Rochester, New York (1939-44); Mac Dowell Professor of Music at Columbia University, New York City after 1967; wrote the operas *Hello Out There* (1954 w. William Saroyan), *The Sweet Bye and Bye* (libretto—Kenward Elmslie, Juilliard Opera Theatre, 1957), *Lizzie Borden* (Richard Plant and Kenward Emslie, New York City Opera, 1965), *My Heart's in the Highlands* (Saroyan, NET Opera Theatre TV, 1970).

BEIDERBECKE, LEON ("BIX")

b. 1903 Davenport, Iowa, d. 1931 Queens, New York. Cornetist, pianist, bandleader and composer. Became a legendary figure in jazz; wrote "Davenport Blues" (1925), "In a Mist" (1927); recorded with Gennett Records (1922); played with Frankie Trumbauer's band in the Arcadia Ballroom in St. Louis (1924).

BEISSEL, JOHANN CONRAD

b. 1690 Eberbach, Germany, d. 1768.
Composer and compiler. Came to Boston in 1720, then founded and was choirmaster of the Kloster of Seventh Day Baptists (Dunkards) at Ephrata, Lancaster County, Pennsylvania (1735); with Ludwig Blum and Peter Miller developed seven-part singing and published the hymn collections *Turtle Taube* (1747), and *Paradisches Wunderspiel* (1754).

BEKKER, PAUL

b. 1882 Berlin, Germany, d. 1937 New York City. Critic and writer. Violinist in the Berlin Philharmonic, became a conductor, then music critic for the *Frankfurt Zeitung* (1911-25); became general manager of the Kassel Opera House (1925), and the Wiesbaden State Theatre (1927), but the rise of Nazism forced him to come to New York where he became music critic of *Staats-Zeitung und Herold;* wrote biographies of Beethoven, Jacques Offenbach, Franz Schreker, and *Die Sinfonien Gustav Mahlers.*

BELAFONTE, HAROLD GEORGE, JR. (HARRY)

b. 1927 New York City.
Black singer and actor. Lived in Jamaica (1935-40); served in the U.S. Navy during World War II; sang in night clubs in New York City, being successful at the Village Vanguard and the Blue Angel; sang in musical shows on Broadway and produced specials on Negro music on NBC-TV; his RCA Victor LP *Calypso* was a top seller; toured all fifty states and sang in other parts of the world, always drawing a large crowd.

BELASCO, DAVID

b. 1853 San Francisco, California, d. 1931. Producer. Raised in Victoria, British Columbia, Canada; worked as an actor, playwright, and stage manager in San Francisco; at Madison Square Theatre, New York City (1879); built Belasco Theatre in Washington, D.C. (1904), designed to fit all his requirements.

BELASCO, F. pseudonym of MONROE H. ROSENFELD

BELCHER, JOSEPH

b. 1794 Birmingham, England, d. 1859 Philadelphia, Pennsylvania. Writer. Came to America in 1844; wrote *Historical Sketches of Hymns, Their Writers and Their Influence* (1859).

BELCHER, SUPPLY

b. 1751 Stoughton, Massachusetts, d. 1836 Farmington, Maine. Violinist and composer. In 1785 he moved to Hallowell, Maine, then in 1791 to Farmington; original collection of tunes, *The Harmony of Maine,* was published 1794; his tune "Canton" was included in *The Hallowell Collection of Sacred Music,* published by Ezekiel Goodale at Hallowell, Maine (1817).

BELEW, CARL ROBERT

b. 1931 Salina, Oklahoma.
Singer, guitarist, and composer. Played in small clubs, then on radio station KWKH, Shreveport Louisiana; composed "Lonely Street," "Stop the World" (1958, with W.S. Stevenson), "Am I That Easy to Forget" (1959), "Hello Out There" (1962), "Boston Jail, I Spent a Week There One Day."

BELKNAP, DANIEL

b. 1771 Framingham, Massachusetts, d. 1815 Pawtucket, Rhode Island. Composer. Published his music in *The Harmonist's Companion* (1797), *The Evangelical Harmony* (1800), and *The Village Compilation of Sacred Music* (1806); composed "Belknap's March" (1809).

BELLSON, LOUIS

b. 1924 Rock Falls, Illinois.
Jazz drummer. Born Louis Balassoni; with Benny Goodman and Tommy Dorsey in 1940s; with Harry James (1950-51) and Duke Ellington (1951-53); organized own combo; married singer Pearl Bailey; toured Sweden (1962) with Count Basie's band; composed and produced jazz ballet at Las Vegas, Nevada Jazz Festival (1962); at 1964 World Jazz Festival in Japan.

BEMAN, NATHAN SIDNEY SMITH

b. 1785 Canaan, New York d. 1871 Carbondale, Illinois. Hymnist. Graduated Middlebury College, Vermont (1807); Congregational minister, Portland, Maine (1810-12), minister in Georgia (1812-22), then at the First Presbyterian Church, Troy, New York (1823-63); wrote "Jesus, We Bow Before Thy Throne" (*Spiritual Songs,* 1831), "Hark, the Judgment Trumpet Sounding" and "Jesus I Come to Thee" (both published in his *Sacred Lyrics,* 1832).

BENATZKY, RALPH

b. 1887 Moravske Budejovice, Austria, d. 1957 Zurich, Switzerland. Composer. Studied with Veit, Klinger, and Mottl; came to U.S. (1938); composed the operettas *White Horse Inn, Meet My Sister, The Apaches, Cocktail, Casanova,* staged in London and New York City.

BENDIX, MAX

b. 1866 Detroit, Michigan, d. 1945 Chicago, Illinois. Violinist, conductor, and teacher. Studied with Jacobsohn; became concertmaster of the Metropolitan Opera, New York City (1886), also was assistant conductor of Thomas' Orchestra; founded the Bendix quartet; conductor at the Manhattan Opera (1906), and the Metropolitan Opera (1909-10); at the San Francisco Exposition (1915), then became a teacher in New York City.

BENEDICT, ERASTUS CORNELIUS

b. 1800 Branford, Connecticut, d. 1880 New York City. Writer. Graduated Williams College (1821); an attorney and President of the New York Board of Education (1850-54) and Regent of New York University; published "Hymn of St. Hildebert," New York (1867).

BENHAM, ASAHEL

b. 1757 Hartford, Connecticut, d. 1815.
Composer, compiler, and teacher. Published *Federal Harmony,* New Haven, Connecticut (1790, same title used later by Timothy Swan), *Social Harmony,* Wallingford, Connecticut (1798); composed "Hymn for Wallingford" (1812).

BENNETT, LOU (LOUIS BENOIT)

b. 1926 Philadelphia, Pennsylvania.
Organist and composer. Studied piano with mother; served in U.S. Army; had own trio in Baltimore; played organ and formed trio (1957); toured eastern and midwestern U.S.; played in Paris after 1960; played at 1964 Newport Jazz Festival and 1966 Prague Jass Festival.

BENNETT, MAX

b. 1928 Des Moines, Iowa.
Bass player. Studied at University of Iowa; with Herbie Fields, Georgie Auld, and others; in army (1951-53); with Stan Kenton (1954); accompanist for Peggy Lee, also for Ella Fitzgerald on European tour (1958) and for Peggy Lee on European tour (1961); with Jimmy Rowles Trio in Burbank, California, after 1963.

BENNETT, ROBERT RUSSELL

b. 1894 Kansas City, Missouri.
Noted composer. Studied harmony with Carl Busch; went to work for G. Schirmer, music publishers, New York City (1916); spent a year in the army in World War I; then studied with Nadia Boulanger in Paris; his *Abraham*

Lincoln Symphony was introduced by Leopold Stokowski and the Philadelphia Orchestra (1931); wrote the operas *Maria Malibran* (1935, libretto—Robert A. Simon), and *The Enchanted Kiss* (1945, libretto—Simon, story by O. Henry), *A Commemoration* Symphony (1959); his score for *Oklahoma!* (film adaptation) won the Motion Picture Academy Award for 1955.

BENNETT, SANFORD FILLMORE

b. 1836, d. 1898 Elkhorn, Wisconsin.
Lyricist. Medical doctor in Elkhorn and collaborated with Joseph P. Webster in writing a number of popular songs and hymns. One day Webster wasn't feeling too well and he visited Dr. Bennett's office. The doctor asked, "What's the matter?" and Webster replied, "Oh, everything will be all right, bye and bye." That gave the doctor the inspiration to write "In the Sweet Bye and Bye" (1867), which Webster set to music; they also wrote "The Irish Volunteer" (1861), "The Soldier to His Mother" (1862), "Old Abe Has Gone and Did It Boys" (1862), and "The Negro Emancipation Song" (1863).

BENNETT, TONY

b. 1926 Queens, New York.
Singer. Born Anthony Dominick Benedetto; served in the army in World War II; sang on Bob Hope tours and for Mitch Miller; his recording of "Cold, Cold Heart" (1951) raised him to stardom; made several solo appearances in Carnegie Hall, New York City; also with 103-piece London Philharmonic Orchestra (1971); completed thirteen TV shows in London for his "This Is Music" program (1972); then at Vegas International, Las Vegas.

BENOIT, LOUIS

b. ca. 1780 France, d. ca. 1835 New York City.
Composer, conductor, and teacher. Also known as Lewis Bennett; came to New York City (1800) and became leader of the City Assembly's Orchestra; composed *La Cesarine*, a set of cotillions for the Grand Ball for General Lafayette at Castle Garden (1824), and *A New Set of Cotillions* for the Grand Military Greek Ball (1824).

BENSON, GEORGE

b. 1943 Pittsburgh, Pennsylvania.
Singer and guitarist. Played ukulele on streets for money at age eight; played in clubs with stepfather; first recorded as singer in 1954; with Jack McDuff (1962-65); formed own group in 1965; at the CTI Summer Jazz Festival, New York City (1972).

BENSON, LOUIS FITZGERALD

b. 1855 Philadelphia, Pennsylvania, d. there 1930. Hymnist and compiler. Graduated from the University of Pennsylvania, became an attorney for seven years, then entered Princeton Theological Seminary; pastor of the Church of the Redeemer in Germantown, Philadelphia; wrote the hymn "O Thou Whose Feet Have Climbed Life's Hill" (1894, tune "St. Magnus," 1709); with William W. Gilchrist, edited the *Presbyterian Hymnal* of 1895.

BENTEEN, FREDERICK D.

b. (?), d. 1864.
Publisher. Published music in Baltimore; published numerous songs of Stephen Foster, including "Oh Susanna" (1848), "Old Uncle Ned" (1848), "Camptown Races" (1850), "Laura Lee" (1851), (Foster's other publishers were Firth, Pond & Company in New York City (1848-63), later William A. Pond & Company).

BENZELL, MIMI

b. 1923 Bridgeport, Connecticut, d. 1970 Manhasset, New York. Singer. Operatic debut in Mexico City, Mexico (1944) as a soprano; sang in *Don Giovanni* and *The Magic Flute* at a Mozart festival there, which led to her first appearance at the Metropolitan Opera in New York City; later she switched from opera to become a popular singer.

BERAULT, CHARLES

b. ca. 1798, d. ca. 1836.
Violinist and dancing master. Violinist at concerts in New York City (1798); dancing master there until 1836.

BERCKMAN, EVELYN

b. 1900 Philadelphia, Pennsylvania.
Pianist, composer, and writer. Composed music for orchestra and chamber ensembles; a temporary attack of paralysis resulting from intensive piano practice delayed her career for seven years; wrote the soprano solos, *Die Nebelstadt* and *Sturm* (1924) published by M. Senart, Paris.

BEREZOWSKY, NICOLAI T.

b. 1900 St. Petersburg, Russia, d. 1953 New York City. Composer. Studied at the Imperial Capella and came to America in 1922; studied at the Juilliard School, New York City with R.

Goldmark and Kochanski, then played in the New York Philharmonic; wrote *Hebrew Suite* introduced by the New York Philharmonic, the opera *Prince Batrak*, two symphonies (first played by the Boston Symphony Orchestra).

BERGER, ARTHUR VICTOR

b. 1912 New York City.
Composer, critic, and writer. Music critic of the *New York Herald-Tribune*, and also wrote a monograph on Aaron Copland; known for his ballet, *Entertainment Piece*, the *92nd Psalm for Choir*, *Serenade Concertante for Violin and Orchestra*, and *Ideas of Order*, which was introduced by the New York Philharmonic Symphony with Mitropoulos conducting.

BERGER, WILLIAM (WILHELM)

b. 1861 Boston, Massachusetts, d. 1911 Jena, Germany. Composer. His parents took him to Bremen as a child; studied under Kiel; wrote *Meine Gottin* (w. Goethe) which won a prize in 1898, also composed *Gesang der Geister uber den Wassern* for mixed choir and orchestra.

BERGH, ARTHUR

b. 1882 St. Paul, Minnesota, d. 1962 Los Angeles, California. Violinist, conductor, and composer. With Metropolitan Opera, New York City (1903-08); conductor of Municipal concerts, New York (1911-14); music director, phonograph companies (1915-30), and advertising agencies (1931-38); music librarian after 1941; works—*The Raven*, *The Pied Piper of Hamelin* (melodramas with orchestra), *Festival March*, *In Arcady* (operetta), *Honor and Glory;* song—"The Red, White and Blue."

BERGHOFER, CHARLES CURTIS (CHUCK)

b. 1937 Denver, Colorado.
Bass player. Lived in Los Angeles after 1945; studied with Bob Stone and Ralph Pena; played with Shelly Manne in 1960s.

BERGMANN, KARL

b. 1821 Ebersbach, Saxony, Germany, d. 1876 New York City. Conductor. Came to America in 1850; with the Germania Orchestra (1850) and later its conductor until 1854; conductor of the Handel and Haydn Society, Boston (1852-54); alternate conductor of the New York Philharmonic (1855), sole conductor (1862-76).

BERGSMA, WILLIAM LAURENCE

b. 1921 Oakland, California.
Composer. Studied at the University of Southern California, Los Angeles, under Howard Hanson, at Stanford University, Palo Alto, California, and at the Eastman School of Music, Rochester, New York under Bernard Rogers; wrote a string quartet which won the Bearns Prize of Columbia University (1943), a ballet, *Gold and the Señor Commandante* (1942), second string quartet (1944), third string quartet (1956), the opera *The Wife of Martin Guene* (1956), and *Serenade, To Await the Moon* for chamber orchestra (1965).

BERIGAN, ROLAND BERNARD ("BUNNY")

b. 1908 Fox Lake, Wisconsin, d. 1942 New York City. Jazz trumpeter. Played trumpet on "Saturday Night Swing" with Jerry Colona and Raymond Scott (1936); debut with his own band (1937) at the Pennsylvania Roof, New York City; died of cirrhosis of the liver.

BERLE, MILTON

b. 1908 New York City.
Comedian and songwriter. With the Tobias brothers, Henry, Charles, and Harry, wrote "Here Comes the Girl" (1937).

BERLIN, IRVING

b. 1888 Temun, Russia.
Popular composer. Born Israel Baline; became a singing waiter at Pelham's Cafe in Chinatown, New York City (1906) and at Jimmy Kelly's on Union Square; he could neither read nor write music, and could play the piano in a single key only (F-sharp); composed the words and music for "Alexander's Ragtime Band" (1911), and "When I Lost You" (1912); sergeant at Camp Upton during World War I; wrote "Oh How I Hate to Get Up in the Morning," and "Mandy" (1918), "Say It Isn't So," "Let's Have Another Cup of Coffee" (1932), "Easter Parade" (1933), "Cheek to Cheek," "I've Got My Love to Keep Me Warm," "God Bless America" (1938); during World War II he wrote "White Christmas" (1942), and the musical *This Is the Army* (1942); also wrote "The Girl That I Marry" and "Doin' What Comes Naturally" (1946), "Count Your Blessings" (1954); his musical shows include *Face the Music* (1932, book—Moss Hart), *Louisiana Purchase* (1940), *Annie Get Your Gun* (1946) starring Ethel Merman, *Call Me Madam* also starring Ethel Merman.

BERMAN, SAUL ("SONNY")

b. 1924 New Haven, Connecticut, d. 1947 New York City. Trumpeter. With Woody Herman (1945-47); died of a heart attack.

BERNARD, CAROLINE RICHINGS

b. 1827 England, d. 1882 Richmond, Virginia. Singer, teacher, and composer. Came to

America as a child; debut as a pianist in Philadelphia (1847); sang in *La Fille du Regiment* (1852); married P. Bernard, tenor (1867); organized Old Folks Concert Company, which was unsuccessful; taught in Baltimore; sang in her operetta, *The Duchess*, in Baltimore (1881); taught in Richmond; died there of smallpox.

BERNARDI, MARIO

b. 1930 Kirkland Lake, Ontario, Canada.
Conductor. Graduated Venice Conservatory, Italy, at age seventeen; studied at Royal Conservatory, Toronto; conducted opera in Canada (1957); later music director of Sadler's Wells Opera in London; conducted Mostly Mozart Festival and New York City Opera; conductor of Ottawa Orchestra (formed 1968); at Tully Hall, New York City (1972).

BERNHARDT, LEWIS F.

b. ca. 1780 Germany, d. after 1820.
Pianist, composer and teacher. Taught in Philadelphia, Pennsylvania (1804-20); wrote "The Beggar Boy" (published by G. Willig), "The Month of May," and "O'er the Deep Waters" (w. Henry John Sharpe).

BERNIE, BEN (ANSELWITZ)

b. 1891 New York City, d. 1943 Beverly Hills, California. Bandleader. Known as "The Ol' Maestro"; top band in the 1920s and '30s; played at the Pabst Blue Ribbon Casino during the 1933 Chicago World's Fair; with Frank Prince, crooner, and Dick Stabile, saxophonist; later featured a newcomer, Dinah Shore.

BERNSTEIN, ARTHUR (ARTIE)

b. 1909 Brooklyn, New York, d. 1964 Los Angeles, California. Bass player. During 1930s played with Red Nichols, the Dorsey Brothers and Benny Goodman; later staff musician in Los Angeles; died of cancer.

BERNSTEIN, ELMER

b. 1922 New York City.
Conductor and composer. Studied at Juilliard School, New York City, with Aaron Copland, et al.; wrote scores of Army Air Force radio shows, and United Nations show (1940); also scores for motion pictures—*Sudden Fear* (1952), *Man with the Golden Arm* (1955), *Sweet Smell of Success* (1957), *The Ten Commandments* (1956).

BERNSTEIN, LEONARD

b. 1918 Lawrence, Massachusetts.
Famous conductor and composer. Studied at Harvard (1939), Curtis Institute of Music, Philadelphia, and the Berkshire Music Center at Tanglewood, Lenox, Massachusetts; became assistant conductor of the New York Philharmonic Orchestra (1943) and music director (1958); his *Jeremiah* Symphony was introduced in Pittsburgh (1944), and his ballet *Fancy Free* in New York City (1944); wrote musicals *Wonderful Town* (1953, book—Ruth McKenny), and *West Side Story* (1957, book—Arthur Laurents); wrote second symphony *The Age of Anxiety* (1949, w. W. H. Auden), third symphony *Kaddish* (1963); his *Mass* (w. Stephen Schwartz), commissioned by Mrs. Jacqueline Onassis, was performed September, 1971, at the John F. Kennedy Center for the Performing Arts, Washington, D.C.

BERRY, CHARLES EDWARD (CHUCK)

b. 1926 St. Louis, Missouri.
Black singer and composer. Wrote "Mabelline" (1955), "Roll Over Beethoven" (hit by the Beatles in 1964), "Rock & Roll Music," "School Days" ("Ring! Ring! Goes the Bell"), "Johnny B. Goode," "Sweet Little Sixteen," "Almost Grown" (1959), "Surfin' U.S.A." (made famous by the Beach Boys); his albums—*After School Sessions, One Dozen Berrys, Chuck Berry—Golden Decade, Golden Hits, Greatest Hits;* at the Festival of Hope rock concert, Westbury, L.I., New York (1972).

BERRY, EMMETT

b. 1916 Macon, Georgia.
Black trumpeter. With Fletcher and Horace Henderson's bands in 1930s; later with Teddy Wilson and Count Basie, in 1940s; with Johnny Hodges, and Cootie Williams in 1950s; toured France and North Africa (1956) with Sammy Price, Europe with Buck Clayton (1959); later played in small groups.

BERRY, LEON ("CHEW," "CHU")

b. 1910 Wheeling, West Virgina, d. 1941 Conneaut, Ohio. Black tenor-saxophonist. Played in Cab Calloway's band (1937-41); killed in an automobile crash.

BERRY, WILLIAM R. (BILL)

b. 1930 Benton Harbor, Michigan.
Trumpeter and flügelhorn player. Raised in South Bend, Indiana; studied piano there; with Herb Pomeroy (1955-57); Woody Herman (1957-60); also with Duke Ellington; with Thad Jones-Mel Lewis band after 1966.

BERT, EDDIE

b. 1922 Yonkers, New York.
Trombonist. Played with Stan Kenton and

Benny Goodman's bands in 1940s and '50s; with Elliot Lawrence (1955-65); at 8th International Jazz Festival, Caracas, Venezuela (1964).

BERTON, VIC

b. 1896 Chicago, Illinois, d. 1951 Hollywood, California. Jazz drummer. Played with Paul Whiteman, Vincent Lopez, Red Nichols, and others.

BESEKIRSKY, VASILLY

b. 1879 Moscow, Russia.
Concert violinist. Son of Vasilly V. Besekirsky, concert violinist and composer; came to America in 1914 and taught here; also toured.

BEST, DENZIL DE COSTA

b. 1917 New York City, d. there 1965.
Black jazz drummer. With Coleman Hawkins, Ben Webster, and Chubby Jackson in 1940s; with George Shearing Quintet (1949-52); with Artie Shaw (1954); Erroll Garner (1956-57); fell down the subway steps in New York City, fractured his skull and died the next day.

BETHUNE, GEORGE WASHINGTON

b. 1905 New York City, d. 1862 Florence, Italy. Hymnist. Graduated Dickinson College, Carlisle, Pennsylvania (1822) and Princeton University; became pastor of the Reformed Dutch Church,Rhinebeck, New York (1827), then to Utica (1830), Philadelphia (1834), and Brooklyn (1850); wrote "Tossed Upon Life's Raging Billow" (*Christian Lyre,* 1830), and other hymns.

BETHUNE, THOMAS GREENE ("BLIND TOM")

b. 1849 Columbus, Georgia, d. 1908.
Black pianist and composer. Blind from birth; sold as a slave to Colonel Bethune; debut at recital in Savannah, Georgia (1858) at age nine; toured U.S. and Europe; the Bethune family made a fortune on Tom's ability; he could play over 700 pieces from memory on demand.

BIBB, LEON

b. 1926 Louisville, Kentucky.
Black singer and guitarist. Served in the army, then went to New York City where he sang in the revival of Kurt Weill's *Lost in the Stars* (1958), *Annie Get Your Gun, Finian's Rainbow;* played in night club spots in New York and San Francisco; toured Russia in 1964; records include *Leon Bibb Sings Folk Songs,* (1959), and *Leon Bibb Sings Love Songs* (1960); on "Someone New," NBC-TV program (1972).

BIEDERMANN, EDWARD JULIUS

b. 1849 Milwaukee, Wisconsin, d. 1933. Organist, composer, and teacher. Wrote *A Vassar Chant.*

BIGARD, LEON ALBANY ("BARNEY")

b. 1906 New Orleans, Louisiana.
Black clarinetist. With King Oliver's band; with King he wrote "Showboat Shuffle" (1927); with Duke Ellington (1928-42); also with Luis Russell and Kid Ory; with Louis Armstrong's All-Stars (1947-55); toured Europe and Africa for U.S. State Department (1961-62); played in Eddie Condon's band at the 1972 Newport Jazz Festival, New York City.

BIG BAND 72 (sounds of the '40s and '50s)

Teddy Sommers, leader, and vocalist Marian Herrman; at the Riverboat, Empire State Building, New York City (1972).

BIG BOPPER *see* J.P. RICHARDSON

BIG BROTHER AND THE HOLDING COMPANY (rock group)

Janis Joplin, lead vocals (died 1970); Peter Albin, bass and vocals; Sam Andrew, lead and rhythm guitar; James Gurley, lead, rhythm guitar, and vocals; David Getz, drums and vocals; albums—*Big Brother and the Holding Company; Cheap Thrills.*

BIGGS, ARTHUR H.

b. 1906 Trenton, New Jersey.
Organist and composer. Educated at Eastern Washington College, Cheney, Washington (1928); organist at the Westminster Congregational Church, Spokane, Washington (1929-38), then at the Cathedral of St. John the Evangelist; taught in the Spokane public schools (1930-42); composed the tunes "Charlotte" (1941, "Lord, Who at Cana's Wedding Feast," w. Adelaide Thrupp), and "Summer" (1941, "Day by Day," w. Old English).

BIGGS, RICHARD KEYS

b. 1886 Glendale, Ohio, d. 1962 Hollywood, California. Organist and composer. Educated at Cincinnati College of Music, and University of Michigan; solo organist at San Diego Exposition (1915); served in U.S. Naval Hospital unit in World War I; taught at Mount St. Mary's Immaculate Heart College; works—*Queen of All Saints, Saint Ambrose, Our Lady of Lourdes, Sunset Meditation, St. Joseph the Worker.*

KEL, THEODORE

b. 1924 Vienna, Austria.
Singer and guitarist. Learned Yiddish and Hebrew, but with the rise of Nazism, the family fled to Palestine (1938); actor in Tel Aviv (1943-47); went to London where he appeared in plays and movies; came to New York (1955) and acted in several plays; his LP records include—*Bravo Bikel* (1958), *Folk Songs of Israel, Songs of a Russian Gypsy, An Actor's Holiday.* (*See* Cynthia Gooding).

BILLINGS, WILLIAM

b. 1746 Boston, Massachusetts, d. there 1800. Composer. Apprenticed as a tanner, but later taught singing in Stoughton, Massachusetts; born with vision in only one eye, a withered arm and legs of uneven length; published *The New England Psalm Singer* (1770, the frontispiece was engraved by Paul Revere), *Billings' Best* (1776), *Music in Miniature* (1779), *The Psalm Singer's Amusement*(1781), *The Suffolk Harmony* (1786), *The Continental Harmony* (1794); tunes were "Chester" (1775), "Retrospect," Independence," "Columbia"; wrote "Lamentation Over Boston" to his tune "By the Waters of Babylon" and also "An Anthem for Easter" (1785).

BINDER, ABRAHAM WOLFE

b. 1895 New York City, d. 1966.
Composer and conductor. Choirmaster of the Free Synagogue in New York when the rabbi was Stephen Wise; wrote *Hibbath Sabbath* (1928), *Sabbath in Israel,* a collection of fifteen songs for the Yom Kippur afternoon service (1956), *Ha-Chalutzim, Holy Land Impressions, Palestinian Song Suite, In Memory of the Defenders of the Warsaw Ghetto,* and *Israel Reborn,* an oratorio.

BING, RUDOLF

b. 1903 Vienna, Austria.
Manager. Born Rudolf Landau; studied at the University of Vienna; manager of a concert there; later administrative director of the theatre in Darmstadt, Germany, then at the *Staedtische Oper,* Berlin; with the rise of Nazism, he emigrated to England and finally to America, when he was asked to take over the administration of the Metropolitan Opera, New York City, in 1950; retired in 1971.

BINGHAM, SETH

b. 1882 Bloomfield, New Jersey, d. 1972 New York City. Organist. Studied at Yale and in Paris; organist in churches in New Haven, Connecticut, Rye, New York, and at the Madison Avenue Presbyterian Church, New York City (1912); professor of music at Columbia University, New York City; composed *Pioneer America* for orchestra, and choral music; his *Wall Street Fantasy* for orchestra was presented by the New York Philharmonic (1916).

BIRCHFIELD, BENNY

b. 1937 Isaban, West Virginia.
Singer and guitarist. In 1959 he joined the "Osborne Brothers," Bob and Sonny Osborne.

BIRD, ARTHUR

b. 1956 Cambridge, Massachusetts, d. 1923 Berlin, Germany. Composer. Pupil of Haupt, Loschhorn, and Rohde in Berlin (1875-77); organist and teacher in Halifax, Nova Scotia, and founded the first male chorus there; studied with Liszt at Weimar; wrote the comic opera *Daphne* (New York, 1897), the ballet *Rubezahl,* a symphony, three suites for orchestra.

BISCHOFF, JOHN W.

b. 1850 Chicago, Illinois, d. 1909 Washington, D.C. Organist, compiler and composer. Became blind at the age of two years; served as organist of the First Congregational Church, Washington, D.C. (1874-1909); with O.F. Presbrey, compiled *Crystal Songs* (1877) which included thirty-two of his tunes, and with Presbrey and J.E. Rankin compiled *Gospel Bells* (1883); arranged "God Be with You" (1880, J.E. Rankin and W.G. Tomer), and "Not Half Has Been Told" (1877, J.B. Atchinson and Presbrey).

BISHOP, ANNA RIVIERE

b. 1810 London, England, d. 1884 New York City. Soprano. Daughter of Jules Riviere, married Sir Henry Bishop (1831), and deserted him for the harpist Bochsa; toured with Bochsa giving concerts in various parts of the world.

BISHOP, STEPHEN

b. 1940 Los Angeles, California.
Pianist. Studied with Dame Myra Hess in England (1959); recorded Beethoven's Sonata no. 5 in C Minor, and Piano Concerto no. 1 in C (Philips, 1972); piano soloist with Boston Symphony, Colin Davis conducting at Carnegie Hall, New York City (1972)

BISHOP, THOMAS BRIGHAM

b. 1835 Wayne, Maine, d. 1905.
Popular composer. With lyricist George Cooper wrote "Pretty as a Picture," and "God Bless My Boy at Sea."

BISHOP, WALTER

b. 1905 Kingston, Jamaica.
Black pianist and songwriter. Studied music under the Federal Music Project, and at New York University, the Schillinger System; served in World War II; works—*Skyline*, tone poem; wrote *Happy and Satisfied* (m. Edgar Melvin Sampson).

BISHOP, WALTER, JR.

b. 1927 New York City.
Black pianist. With Art Blakey in 1940s; with Charles Parker and Kai Winding in 1950s; with Curtis Fuller (1960); formed own trio with G.T. Hogan and Jimmy Garrison (1961); toured with Terry Gibbs' Quartet (1964); later in Europe.

BISPHAM, DAVID SCULL

b. 1857 Philadelphia, Pennsylvania, d. 1921 New York City. Baritone. Pupil of Vannuccini and William Shakespeare (1885-87); in opera at Covent Garden and later in America; his repertoire included 50 operatic roles, over 100 oratorio parts, and some 1,500 recital numbers; popular at Carnegie Hall, New York City in early 1900s.

BIVONA, GUS

b. 1917 New London, Connecticut.
Clarinetist. On Steve Allen's TV shows after 1958; led own combo in Los Angeles night clubs during 1960s.

BLACK, JAMES M.

b. 1856 New York State, d. 1938 Williamsport, Pennsylvania, Compiler and composer of hymns. Edited several gospel song books and was one of the editors of the *Methodist Hymnal* of 1905; Sunday School teacher in the Mulberry Methodist Church in Williamsport (As he called the roll one Sunday in 1893, one of the little girls failed to answer. Later he heard she was ill, and expected to die. Then he remembered the roll call, and wondered if he would be there to answer when his time came, so he wrote "When the Roll Is Called Up Yonder"); also wrote "I Remember Calvary," "Where Jesus Is 'tis Heaven," "We Shall Reign with Him in Glory," "When the Saints Are Marching In" (1896, w. Katherine E. Purvis, tune for "When the Saints Go Marching In"), "Where He May Lead Us" (1900).

BLACK KANGAROO

Led by guitarist Peter Kaukonen, brother of Jorma Kaukonen, guitarist with the Jefferson Airplane; played at the Family Dog (Friends and Relations Hall), San Francisco, California (1971).

BLACK MUSLIMS

Band in New York City led by Elijah Muhammad, born Elijah Poole.

BLACK, WILLIAM PATTON (BILL)

b. 1926 Memphis, Tennessee, d. 1965.
Singer and songwriter. Attended schools in Oakville, Tennessee, and Whitehaven, Tennessee; wrote *Smokie* (album, 1959); "Crank Case," "Cyclone Bop," "Special Duty," Before Dawn," "The Wheel"; died of a brain tumor.

BLACKBURN, LOU

b. 1922 Rankin, Pennsylvania.
Trombonist. Educated at Roosevelt University, Chicago; in U.S. Army (1948-56); with 7th Army Symphony in Europe (1955-56); played in Club Harlem, Atlantic City, New Jersey (1956-57); with Lionel Hampton's band (1958-60); toured Europe and North Africa; with Duke Ellington (1961); later settled in Los Angeles.

BLACKMAR, ARMAND EDWARD ("A.E.")

b. 1826 Vermont, d. 1888.
Composer and publisher. Went to Cleveland, Ohio (1834); graduated Western Reserve College (1845); music teacher in Huntsville, Alabama; taught at Centenary College, Jackson, Lousiana (1852-55); opened music store in Jackson, Mississippi (1856); with brother, Henry Clay Blackmar, opened store in New Orleans (1860); known as the "Voice of the South"; when Union forces under General Ben Butler occupied New Orleans in March 1862, Butler ordered Blackmar's entire stock of published music destroyed and fined him $500 for publishing Confederate songs; Henry fled to Augusta, Georgia, where he resumed publishing; wrote "The Southern Marseillaise" (1861), which became the rallying song of the Confederacy, "God and Our Rights" (1861, w. Catherine A. Warfield-Wm. M. Johnston), "That Bugler, or the Upidee Song" (w. D.G. Knight), "Goober Peas," "For Bales" (m. P.S. Gilmore), "Our Brutus" (1865), "The Sword of Robert E. Lee" (w. Father A.J. Ryan), "Wearin' of the Gray" (tune—"Wearin' of the Green"—Irish), "The Southern's Chant of Defiance" (w. Warfield). (*See also* Will Hays; Septimus Winner)

BLACKWOOD, CECIL STAMPS

b. 1934 Ackerman, Mississippi.
Singer and publisher. Attended high school in Memphis, Tennessee; joined Blackwood Brothers Quartet (1954, *see* James W. Black-

wood); with Stamps Music Company and Blackwood House of Music, Memphis, Tennessee.

BLACKWOOD, DOYLE J.

b. 1911 Ackerman, Mississippi.
Singer. Attended high school in Chester, Mississippi; with Blackwood Brothers Quartet since 1934; record distributor in Memphis.

BLACKWOOD, EASLEY

b. 1933 Indianapolis, Indiana.
Composer. Studied at Indiana University, Bloomington, with Bernard Heiden, and at Yale with Paul Hindemith (1954), and in Paris with Nadia Boulanger, then taught at the University of Chicago; first symphony was introduced by Charles Munch and the Boston Symphony (1958), second symphony by George Szell and the Cleveland Orchestra (1961); wrote a *Symphonic Fantasy* (1967) and a fourth symphony produced in 1968 at the Ravinia Festival, near Chicago.

BLACKWOOD, JAMES WEBRE

b. 1919 Ackerman, Mississippi.
Gospel singer. Attended school in Chester, Mississippi; leader of Blackwood Brothers Quartet since 1934; owner of Stamps Quartet; over forty albums include *All Day Singing; Blackwood Brothers; Fill My Cup, Lord; Give Us This Day; Gospel Classics; Just a Closer Walk with Thee; On the Jericho Road; Sound of Gospel Music.*

BLACKWOOD, JAMES WEBRE, JR.

b. 1943 San Diego, California.
Singer. Attended school in Memphis, Tennessee and Stamps Quartet School of Music, Dallas, Texas (1962); with Junior Blackwood Brothers Quartet (1962-65); with Stamps Quartet after 1965.

BLAIR, JANET

b. 1921 Altoona, Pennsylvania.
Singer and actress. Born Janet Lafferty; started as singer with Hal Kemp's band; later actress in many films.

BLAKE, CHARLES D.

b. 1847 Walpole, Massachusetts, d. 1903.
Composer and publisher. Studied under Dr. Paine of Harvard and J.C.D. Parker; composed over 1,200 piano pieces.

BLAKE, GEORGE E.

b. 1775 Yorkshire, England, d. 1871 Philadelphia, Pennsylvania. Clarinetist and publisher. Came to Philadelphia in 1793 during the yellow fever epidemic there, and assisted in caring for the sick and dying; taught the clarinet and started publishing music in 1802; published *The Vocal Harmony,* (ca. 1808); *Blake's Young Flutist Magazine* (1833).

BLAKE, JAMES HUBERT ("EUBIE")

b. 1883 Baltimore, Maryland.
Famous black pianist and composer. Took piano lessons at age six; pianist in bawdy houses in the Baltimore tenderloin at age sixteen; later played in Atlantic City, N.J., and New York City; studied with Llewellyn Wilson, conductor of the Baltimore Negro Symphony; in 1915 joined with Noble Sissle, singer and lyricist, who later became a bandleader; wrote "Charleston Rag" (1899), "Chevy Chase" (1914), "Fizz Water" (1914), "I'm Wild About Harry" and "Love Will Find a Way (both w. Sissle) in *Shuffle Along* (1921-24), "Dixie Moon" (w. Sissle) in *Chocolate Dandies* (1924), "Bugle Call Rag" (1926) in *Blackbirds* of 1930 (w. Andy Razaf) with Ethel Waters and the Berry Brothers; "Eubie's Boogie," "Brittwood Rag," "Blue Rags in 12 Keys" (1969); gave concert with Willie "The Lion" Smith at Whitney Museum, New York City (1972) at age 89.

BLAKE, JAMES W.

b. 1862 New York City, d. there 1935.
Lyricist and vaudeville actor. Salesman in a hat shop when he met Charlie Lawlor, who helped him write "The Sidewalks. of New York" (1894); together they wrote "Pretty Jenny Slattery" (1896), "Best in the House" (1896), "Every Boy Has Quarrelled with His First Sweetheart" (1896), and "Daisy McIntyre" (1897); Blake joined Lawlor in vaudeville; "The Sidewalks of New York" become the theme song of Alfred E. Smith when he was a candidate for the Presidential nominations in 1920 and 1924, and the Democratic nominee in 1928; even though he became blind, Blake continued in vaudeville until the end.

BLAKE, RAN

b. 1935 Springfield, Massachusetts.
Pianist and organist. Accompanist for Jeanne Lee after 1957; toured Europe (1963); appeared at Town Hall, New York City (1964).

BLAKEY, ART

b. 1919 Pittsburgh, Pennsylvania.
Black jazz drummer. With Fletcher Henderson (1939); then Billy Eckstine (1944-47); Buddy De Franco Quartet (1951-53); leader of Jazz Messengers after 1954; toured Europe; at the 1972 Newport Jazz Festival, New York City.

BLANCHARD, DONALD F. ("RED")

b. 1914 Pittsville, Wisconsin.
Singer and songwriter. On WLS "National Barn Dance," Chicago, Illinois (1931-59); wrote "Too Many People," "She Went and Gone Away," "I'm Lonesome in the Saddle (Since My Old Horse Died)."

BLANCHARD, RICHARD LOWELL

b. 1910 Palmer, Illinois.
Producer and songwriter. Attended high school in Morrisonville, Illinois; graduated University of Illinois, Urbana (1933); writer, producer and M.C. on "Midday Merry-Go-Round" and "Tennessee Barn Dance," WNOX, Knoxville, Tennessee (1936-64); wrote "Woman Driver," "God Had a Son in Service," "I Heard My Mother Weeping."

BLANCHARD, WILLIAM GODWIN

b. 1905 Greencastle, Indiana.
Teacher and composer. Educated at the School of Music of DePauw University, Greencastle, and at the University of Michigan, Ann Arbor; music teacher at Pomona College, Claremont, California; composed the tune "Godwin" ("God of the Strong, God of the Weak," w. R.W. Gilder).

BLAND, JAMES A.

b. 1854 Queens, New York City, d. 1911 Philadelphia, Pennsylvania. Famous black composer. Member of the all-Negro minstrel troupe headed by Billy Kersands; wrote the words and music for "Carry Me Back to Old Virginny" (1878, adopted as the official state song of Virginia in 1940), "Oh Dem Golden Slippers" (1879), "In the Evening by the Moonlight" (1879), "Christmas Dinner" (1879), "Hand Me Down My Walking Cane" (1880), and "De Golden Wedding" (1880); buried in Merion, Pennsylvania.

BLAND, ROBERT CALVIN (BOBBY)

b. 1930.
Black singer. Raised in Rosemark, Tennessee; sang in Adolph Duncan's band in Memphis (1949); was a chauffeur for Roscoe Gordon, blues singer; signed with Duke Records (1954); had hits "I Pity the Fool" (1961), and "That's the Way Love Is" (1963); albums—*Ain't Nothing You Can Do; Best of Bobby Bland; Bobby Bland; Here's the Man; Like'er Hot; Soul of the Man; Touch of the Blues; Two Steps from the Blues.*

BLANE, RALPH

b. 1914 Broken Arrow, Oklahoma.
Singer, lyricist, and composer. Educated at Northwestern University, Evanston, Illinois; studied with Estelle Liebling; joined the quartet, the Martins; with Hugh Martin wrote "Buckle Down, Winsocki" (*Best Foot Forward*, 1941) and "The Trolley Song" (*Meet Me in St. Louis*, 1944 film); wrote "The Stanley Steamer" (m. Harry Warren); works—*Duty, Honor and Country* (musical setting for General MacArthur's speech).

BLANTON, JIMMY

b. 1921 Chattanooga, Tennessee, d. 1942 Los Angeles, California. Black jazz bass player. With Duke Ellington's band; previously in Fate Marable's band in the 1930s on the Mississippi river boats between St. Louis and New Orleans.

BLAUFUSS, WALTER

b. 1883 Milwaukee, Wisconsin, d. 1945 Chicago, Illinois. Pianist, conductor, and composer. Educated at Chicago Musical College, and Sherwood Music School; accompanist to Mary Garden, Emma Calve, and Fritzi Scheff; conductor in theatres and on radio; with Egbert van Alstyne wrote "Your Eyes Have Told Me So" (w. Gus Kahn).

BLAUVERT, LILLIAN EVANS

b. 1873 Brooklyn, New York, d. 1947 Chicago, Illinois. Soprano. Studied at National Conservatory, New York, and in Paris; debut in opera in *Faust* at Covent Garden, London (1903); successful singer in America and Europe until 1914.

BLEDSOE, JULES

b. 1899 Waco, Texas, d. 1943.
Black baritone. Graduated Bishop College, Marshall, Texas; debut in Aeolian Hall, New York City (1924); concert singer on tours of the United States; appeared in the lyric drama, *Deep River* (1926, m. Frank Harling); Verdi's *Aïda;* opera, *The Emperor Jones* (1933, m. Louis Gruenberg, play—Eugene O'Neill); *Show Boat* (m. Jerome Kern); appeared with symphony orchestras in *The Creation*, poem (w. James Weldon Johnson, m. Louis Gruenberg).

BLESSING, LYNN

b. 1938 Cicero, Indiana.
Vibraharpist and drummer. At 1960 Los Angeles Jazz Festival; with Paul Horn (1965-66) as member of the Horn Quintet.

BLEY, CARLA BORG

b. 1938 Oakland, California.
Pianist and composer. Father a piano teacher and church organist; married Paul Bley, pianist; with Charles Moffet and Pharaoh

Saunders at the Porpoise Club, New York City (1964); with Mike Mantler as co-leader of Jazz Composer's Orchestra after 1964; toured Europe (1965).

BLEY, PAUL

b. 1932 Montreal, Quebec, Canada.
Pianist and composer. Played with Charles Mingus, Ornette Coleman, and Don Cherry during 1950s; organized his own group (1964); at Judson Hall concerts, New York City; toured Europe (1960) and Japan (1963) with Sonny Rollins.

BLISS, PHILIP P. (PHILIPP)

b. 1838 Rome, Pennsylvania, d. 1876 Ashtabula, Ohio. Composer. After attending a revival meeting near Elk Run, Pennsylvania, at the age of twelve, he joined the Baptist church; worked for Root and Cady, music publishers in Chicago, then toured the states with Major D.W. Whittle, the evangelist; wrote "Goodby Jeff" (1863), "Hold the Fort" (1864), "I Gave My Life for Thee," "Pull for the Shore," "I Am So Glad" (1870, w. Emily S. Oakey), "Sowing by the Daylight Fair" (w. Oakey), "What Shall the Harvest Be?," "Eternity" (w. Ellen Gates), "When Jesus Comes" (1872) while in Peoria, Illinois. While in church one Sunday, Bliss heard the preacher read from Acts 26:28 "Then (King) Agrippa said unto Paul, Almost thou persuadest me to be a Christian." This verse so impressed Bliss that he wrote his hymn "Almost Persuaded" (ca. 1870). Once Dwight L. Moody, the famous evangelist, preached a sermon about a ship on the Great Lakes coming into Cleveland in a bad storm. "Are you sure this is Cleveland?" asked the captain, seeing only one light from the lighthouse. "Where are the lower lights?" "Gone out, sir," was the reply. Because the people turned out their lights before going to bed, the ship crashed and the crew perished. Bliss, thus inspired, wrote his hymn "Let the Lower Lights Be Burning" (1871). Although Bliss was a Baptist, the hymn was included in the Methodist hymnal, due to so many urgent requests from devout Christians living on the coastline of the Great Lakes. Bliss was in the great railway wreck of 1876 in Ashtabula, Ohio; he actually survived the accident, but died trying to save his wife.

BLITZSTEIN, MARC

b. 1905 Philadelphia, Pennsylvania, d. 1964 Fort-de-France, Martinique. Noted composer. Studied at the University of Pennsylvania and the Curtis Institute, Philadelphia; served in the Eighth Air Force during World War II; composed *The Cradle Will Rock* (opera, New York City, 1937), The Airborne (a symphony, introduced by Leonard Bernstein and the New York Symphony, 1946), *Regina* (musical play, book–Lillian Hellman, Boston, 1949), *No for an Answer* (one-act play), *The Condemned* (the trial of Sacco and Vanzetti), *Juno* (1959, play–Sean O'Casey), adapted Kurt Weill's *Three Penny Opera.*

BLOCH, ERNEST

b. 1880 Geneva, Switzerland, d. 1959 Portland, Oregon. Noted composer. Educated in Geneva and Germany; wrote the opera *Macbeth,* performed by the Paris Opera Comique (1910); came to America (1916), was director of the Cleveland Institute of Music (1920-25), then lived in San Francisco, in Switzerland, then Agate Beach, Oregon; composed the *Israel* Symphony (1916), *Schelomo* (1916), *Baal Shem* (1923), *Sacred Service* (1924), *A Voice in the Wilderness* (1936), *Concerto for Violin and Orchestra* (1938), and *Concerto Symphonique* (1948).

BLOCH, RAYMOND A. (RAY)

b. 1902 Alsace-Lorraine, Germany.
Orchestra leader, pianist, and composer. Came to U.S. during World War I; organized own orchestra, toured U.S. in vaudeville; music director on radio and television, including the "Ed Sullivan Show."

BLOCH, SIDNEY S.

b. 1895 New York City.
Violinist and conductor. Studied in Berlin, then became a violinist at the Royal Opera in Berlin.

BLOCK, FREDERICK

b. 1899 Vienna, Austria, d. 1945 New York City. Composer. His opera *Samum* was introduced in Bratislava (1936); he came to New York City (1936); composed the operas *Play of Shadows, Tinsel, America, Pan, Ester,* several symphonies and chamber music.

BLODGETT, BENJAMIN COLMAN

b. 1838 Boston, Massachusetts, d. 1925 Seattle, Washington. Organist, composer, and teacher. Wrote *Fair Smith;* director of the Smith College School of Music (1880-1903).

BLONDELL, WILLIAM

b. ca. 1800, d. after 1834.
Organist, teacher, and compiler. Came to New York City (1823); taught there; organist at St. Paul's Chapel (1826-34); with Abner Jones compiled *Melodies of the Church* (1832).

BLOOD, SWEAT AND TEARS (rock group)

David Clayton-Thomas, blues singer; Bobby Colomby, drums; Jim Fielder, bass; Dick Halligan, keyboard; Jerry Hyman, trombone; Steve Katz, vocals, guitar, and harmonica; Fred Lipsius, alto sax and piano; Chuck Winfield, trumpet and flügelhorn; Louis Soloff, trumpet and flügelhorn; albums—*Blood, Sweat & Tears*, and *Child Is Father to the Man.*

BLOOM, MILTON ("MICKEY")

b. 1906 Brooklyn, New York.
Trumpeter and songwriter. Studied with Max Schlossberg; played in Hal Kemp's band; also with Vincent Lopez, Dorsey Brothers, Benny Goodman, Artie Shaw, Russ Morgan, Matty Malneck; toured Europe with Irving Aaronson; served in AAF Radio Orchestra in World War II.

BLOOMFIELD-ZEISLER, FANNY

b. 1863 Bielitz, Poland, d. 1955 Chicago, Illinois. Concert pianist. Student of Theodor Leschetizky, in Vienna, Austria, then became a concert pianist; popular at Carnegie Hall, New York City, in early 1900s.

BLOSSOM, HENRY

b. 1866 St. Louis, Missouri, d. 1919 New York City. Librettist and lyricist. Insurance broker; wrote libretto *Mlle. Modiste* (1905, m. Victor Herbert) which included his song "Kiss Me Again"; also *The Red Mill* (1906, m. Victor Herbert) which featured Fred Stone and David Montgomery and included his song, "The Streets of New York," (or "In Old New York").

BLUE CHEER (rock group)

Paul Whaley, drums; Dick Peterson, bass; Randy Holden, guitar; albums—*Blue Cheer; New Improved Blue Cheer, Outsideinside; Vicebus Eruptum.*

BLUEGRASS BOYS *see* BILL and CHARLIE MONROE

BLUE RHYTHM BAND (black band)

Organized by Irving Mills, manager; Lucky Millinder, singer and leader; Henry Allen, trumpeter; J.C. Higgenbotham, trombonist; Buster Bailey, clarinetist; Joe Garland, tenor sax; John Kirby, double bass player; recorded in 1934 a Tiger Rag variant entitled "Ride, Red, Ride" which became a hit.

BLUE RIDGE BOYS *see* JIM EANES

BLUE RIDGE QUARTET (vocal)

Elmo Fagg, second tenor and manager; Henry Gates, baritone and pianist; Edward Sprouse, first tenor; George Younce, bass.

BLUE SKY BOYS *see* BILL and EARL BOLICK

BLUES MAGOOS (rock group)

Ralph Scala, vocals and organ; Ron Gilbert, bass; Geoff Daking, drums; Mike Esposito, lead guitar; Emil "Peppy" Thielhelm, vocals and guitar; albums—*Psychedelic Lollipop; Electric Comic Book; Basic Blues Magoos; Never Goin' Back to Georgia.*

BLUES PROJECT (rock group)

Andy Kulberg, flute, bass, and piano; Roy Blumenfeld, drums; John Gregory, guitar and vocals; Donald Gretmar, bass sax; Richard Greene, violin; albums—*Best of the Blues Project; Blues Project; Live at the Cafe à Go Go; Live at Town Hall; Planned Obsolescence; Projections.*

BLUES SERENADERS (black group) *see* IDA COX

BLUMENSCHEIN, WILLIAM LEONARD

b. 1849 Brensbach, Germany, d. 1916 Dayton, Ohio. Conductor and teacher. Brought to America as a child; raised in Pittsburgh; graduated Leipzig Conservatory (1872); director of Portsmouth, Ohio Harmonic Society (1876-78); leader of Philharmonic Society of Dayton, Ohio after 1878; principal of the Conservatory of Music at Dayton, Ohio.

BLYTH, SAM

b. 1744, d. 1795.
Spinet maker, violin maker, and teacher.

BLYTHE, JIMMY

b. 1899 Louisville, Kentucky, d. 1931.
Black jazz pianist. Known as a barrelhouse player; recorded with Johnny Dodds after 1924.

BOATNER, EDWARD H.

b. 1898 New Orleans, Louisiana.
Black singer, choirmaster and composer. Studied at Boston Conservatory of Music; graduated Chicago College of Music (1932); father of Sonny Stitt, jazz saxophonist; taught music for fifty years; produced "The Life of Christ" from his arrangements of Negro spirituals at the Cathedral Church of St. John the Divine, New York City (1971); composed

or arranged "I Want Jesus to Walk with Me," "On Ma Journey," "Tramping," "Oh, What a Beautiful City"; honored by National Federation of Music Associations (1919) and National Association of Negro Musicians (1964).

BOB CATS *see* BOB CROSBY'S BAND

BOBO, WILLIE

b. 1934 New York City.
Bongo and conga drummer. Born William Correa; played with Tito Puente (1954-58); Cal Tjader (1958-61), and Herbie Mann (1961-63); at 1959 Monterey Jazz Festival with Tjader, and at Newport (1963) with Mann.

BOCK, JERRY

b. 1928 New Haven, Connecticut.
Popular composer. Educated at the University of Wisconsin, Madison; came to New York City to work and resided in New Rochelle, New York; joined with Larry Holofcener, the lyricist, writing songs for TV and stage shows; they wrote "Mr Wonderful" and "Too Close for Comfort" (1956), *Fiorello!* (1959, book—Jerome Weidman and George Abbott), and he composed *Tenderloin* (1960, book—Weidman and Abbott with Sheldon Harnick, lyricist), *Fiddler on the Roof* (1964, book—Joseph Stein, based on the tales of Sholom Aleichem, choreography by Jerome Robbins, and starring Zero Mostel), *The Apple Tree* (1966, w. Harnick, starring Barbara Harris).

BODANZKY, ARTUR

b. 1877 Vienna, Austria, d. 1939 New York City. Conductor. Opera conductor in Berlin, Prague, and Mannheim, then came to New York as conductor of the Metropolitan Opera (1915-39); also musical director of the Friends of Music (1921-31).

BOEHM (BÖHM), KARL

b. 1894 Graz, Austria.
Conductor. Conducted Munich Opera (1921), Darmstadt (1927), Dresden Opera (1933), and at Metropolitan Opera, New York City after 1957; Verdi's *Otello* (1972).

BOEKELMAN, BERNARDUS

b. 1838 Utrecht, Netherlands, d. 1930 New York City. Pianist, conductor, and teacher. Pupil of his father, A.J. Boekelman; studied at the Leipzig Conservatory and in Berlin; came to New York (1866); conductor of the New York Trio Club (1883-88); musical director of Miss Porter's School, Farmington, Connecticut; composed a number of pieces for orchestra.

BOEPPLE, PAUL

b. 1896 Basel, Switzerland, d. 1970 Brattleboro, Vermont. Choral director. Studied at Basel University and the Dalcroze Institute in Geneva; came to New York in 1926 as director of the Dalcroze School there, until 1944; taught at Bennington College, Vermont (1944-64); conducted the Dessoff Choirs in Arthur Honegger's *Judith* and *King David*, and Handel's *Israel in Egypt*.

BOGGS, MORAN L.

b. 1898 Norton, Virginia.
Singer and banjoist. Played the banjo at the age of twelve; was a coal miner for forty-one years, but couldn't sing or play in public since his wife thought country music was sinful; after retirement in the 1960s he appeared publicly at colleges and concert halls across the nation, including the Jazz Festival at Newport; his record *Dock Boggs* appeared 1964 and a second record in 1965.

BOGGS, NOEL EDWIN

b. 1917 Oklahoma City, Oklahoma.
Singer and songwriter. Leader of Noel Boggs Four since 1956; wrote "Boggs Boogie," "Texas Blues," "Stealin' Home," "You Put Me on My Feet," "Magic Isle," "Day Sleeper."

BOHANON, GEORGE ROLAND, JR.

b. 1937 Detroit, Michigan.
Trombonist. Member of Chico Hamilton Quintet; led own group; played for Detroit Jazz Society.

BOHLMANN, T.H.F.

b. 1865 Osterwieck am Harz, Germany, d. 1926 Memphis, Tennessee. Pianist and teacher. Debut in Berlin (1890); toured Germany, then became a professor at the Cincinnati Conservatory; later founded his own school in Memphis.

BOISE, OTIS BARDWELL

b. 1844 Oberlin, Ohio, d. 1912 Baltimore, Maryland. Organist and teacher. Studied in Leipzig and in Berlin; organist and teacher in Cleveland, Ohio (1864-70), New York (1870-76), then taught in Berlin; settled in Baltimore (1901); composed symphonies, overtures, pianoforte concertos; wrote *Music and Its Master* (1902).

BOLDEN'S BAND, BUDDY (black band)

At various times—Buddy Bolden, cornetist and trumpeter; Buddy Botley, singer, dancer, and M.C.; Frankie Dusen, trombonist; Lorenzo Stall, banjoist; Bunk Johnson, cornetist and trumpeter (replaced Bolden); Jimmy Johnson, bass; Willy Cornish, trombonist; Willy Warner, clarinetist; Brock Mumford, guitarist; Frank Lewis, clarinetist; organized by Bolden in New Orleans in the 1890s.

BOLDEN, CHARLES ("BUDDY THE KING")

b. 1868 New Orleans, Louisiana, d. Jackson, Louisiana 1931. Black cornetist, trumpeter, and bandleader. Pioneer of New Orleans jazz; formed his band before 1895; had been a barber; after taking a kidding about his love life, slashed a friend's face with a razor; Frankie Dusen, trombonist, took over the band; Bolden went berserk on the street while playing in a parade with Henry Allen, Sr.'s Brass Band (1907); committed to the East Louisiana State Hospital, diagnosed as a paranoid; spent the rest of his life there (1907-31).

BOLICK, EARL A.

b. 1919 Hickory, North Carolina.
Earl and Bill Bolick, brothers, were a vocal and instrumental duo. Started with radio station WWNC, Ashville, North Carolina (1935), then with WNAO, Raleigh, North Carolina, in the 1940s; retired from public appearances (1951), but came back in 1964 for the University of Illinois Folksong Concert and the UCLA and New York Folk Festivals (1965); Capitol issued the LP record *The Blue Sky Boys* (1965).

BOLICK, WILLIAM A.

b. 1917 Hickory, North Carolina.
Bill and his brother Earl were folk singers and an instrumental duo known as the "Blue Sky Boys." (*See* Earl Bolick)

BOLTON, GUY REGINALD

b. 1884 Broxbourne, Hertfordshire, England. Lyricist and librettist. Born in England of American parents; studied architecture at Pratt Institute, Brooklyn, New York and Ecole des Beaux Arts, Paris; wrote libretto *Oh, Lady! Lady!* (1918, with P.G. Wodehouse, m. Jerome Kern), *Sally* (1920, also with Wodehouse and Kern) which included "Look for a Silver Lining" (sung by Marilyn Miller); also numerous other shows.

BONANO, JOSEPH G. ("SHARKEY")

b. 1900 Milneburg, Louisiana, d. 1972 New Orleans, Louisiana. Jazz trumpeter. Started playing a second-hand cornet at age twelve, later the trumpet; played in the Original Dixieland Jazz Band; also led his own group in New Orleans; rarely left the city, but in 1959 he and his Kings of Dixieland played at the Roundtable in New York City.

BOND, CARRIE (JACOBS)

b. 1862 Janesville, Wisconsin, d. 1946 Hollywood, California. Popular composer. Disaster struck her in 1895; her husband lost all his money in wild mining speculations and died, and she fell on an icy sidewalk and became an invalid, so she took to writing songs; popular songs were—"I Love You Truly," "Just A-Wearyin' for You," and "When It Comes to the End of a Perfect Day"; wrote *The Road of Melody, My Story* (1927), her autobiography.

BOND, CYRUS WHITFIELD ("JOHNNY")

b. 1915 Enville, Oklahoma.
Singer, guitarist, and songwriter. Attended the University of Oklahoma, Norman, Oklahoma; joined the Jimmy Wakely Trio on CBS radio (1937-40), then with Gene Autry (1940-54); wrote "Cimarron," "Glad Rags," "Tomorrow Never Comes," "Gone and Left Me Blues," "I'll Step Aside"; LP albums—*Live It Up and Laugh It Up, Johnny Bond* (1962), *Songs That Made Him Famous* (1963), *Johnny Bond's Best* (1964).

BOND, EDDIE J.

b. 1933.
Singer. Attended school in Memphis, Tennessee; albums—*Country Gospel Hits; Country Hits from Down Home.*

BOND, JAMES E., JR. (JIMMY)

b. 1933 Philadelphia, Pennsylvania.
Bass and tuba player. Traveled with George Shearing; with Paul Horn Quintet (1959-61); also toured with Lena Horne; later played in Hollywood film studios.

BONDS, MARGARET

b. 1913 Chicago, Illinois, d. 1972.
Black pianist and composer. Studied at Northwestern University, Evanston, Illinois (master's degree), also at Juilliard; won Julius Rosenwald fellowship, Roy Harris scholarship, and Wanamaker Award (1932); wrote *Migration* (a ballet), *Spiritual Suite for Piano,* Mass in D Minor, *Three Dream Portraits.*

BONFA, LUIZ FLORIANO

b. 1922 Rio de Janeiro, Brazil.
Singer, guitarist, and composer. Studied guitar at age twelve under his father, a

guitarist; debut in 1946; wrote music for Brazilian film, *Black Orpheus*, including "Manha de Carnival" and "Samba de Orfeu"; came to New York City (1958) and played with Stan Getz; toured Germany and Italy (1962); album—*The Brazilian Scene*.

BONN, SKEETER

b. 1923 Canton, Illinois.
Yodeler. Born Junior Lewis Bougham; with WWVA radio, Wheeling, West Virginia.

BONNER, EUGENE MAC DONALD

b. 1889 Washington, North Carolina.
Composer. Studied at Peabody Conservatory, Baltimore; in army in France in World War I; musical editor of *The Outlook* (1927-29); critic on *Brooklyn Daily Eagle* after 1929; wrote the operas—*Barbara Frietchie* (1921), *The Venetian Glass Nephew* (1927), *The Gods of the Mountain* (1936); also orchestral works and chamber music.

BONNER, ROBERT

b. 1854 Brighton, England, d. 1899.
Organist and composer. Graduated Leipzig Conservatory (1868); came to Providence, Rhode Island (1869); organist of St. John's Church there; secretary of American College of Musicians; taught piano, organ, violin, and theory in Providence; composed church music and piano pieces.

BONNHORST, CARL FRANZ WILHELM VON *see* VON BONNHORST, CARL

BONO, CHERYL LA PIERE

b. 1946 El Centro, California.
Singer. With her husband, they formed the team of Sonny and Cher; both in concert at the Nassau Coliseum, Uniondale, New York (1972).

BONO, SALVATORE (SONNY)

b. 1935 Detroit, Michigan.
Singer. With his wife, Cheryl La Piere, they formed the very successful team of Sonny and Cher; his original "I Got You, Babe" sold over four million discs; their albums include *Best of Sonny and Cher, Good Times, In Case You're in Love, It's Gonna Rain, Look at Us* and *Wondrous World of Sonny and Cher;* starred on their own TV show (1972).

BONVIN, LUDWIG

b. 1850 Siders, Switzerland, d. 1939 Buffalo, New York. Organist and teacher. Studied medicine in Vienna; entered Jesuit novitiate in the Netherlands (1874); became organist-choirmaster; music director of Canisius College, Buffalo, New York (1887); composed masses.

BONYUN, WILLIAM

b. 1911 Brooklyn, New York.
Singer and guitarist. Attended Wesleyan University, Middletown, Connecticut, University of Connecticut at Storrs, and Columbia University, New York City; lived in Brookhaven, Long Island, N.Y.; sang each summer at Old Sturbridge Village in Sturbridge, Massachusetts in the 1950s; with Gene Bonyun, recorded old New England tunes on *Yankee Legend*, LP record (1957).

BOOKER T & THE M.G.'S (rock group)

Steve Cropper, lead guitar; Al Jackson, drums; Donald "Duck" Dunn, bass; Booker T. Jones, organ; albums—*And Now, Back to Work, Best of Booker T. & the M.G.'s, Booker T. Set, Doin' Our Thing, Green Onions, Hip Hug-Her, McLemore Avenue, Soul Dressing, Soul Limbo, Up Tight.*

BOOKER, WALTER M., JR.

b. 1933 Prairie View, Texas.
Bass player. Raised in Washington, D.C.; studied clarinet with father, clarinetist; graduated Morehouse College, Atlanta, Georgia; in U.S. Army (1956-58); studied bass with Joseph Willens in Washington; with JFK Quintet (1960-63); went to N.Y. City (1964); played with Don Byrd, Sonny Rollins, Ray Bryant, and Art Farmer.

BOONE, BLIND

b. 1864 Miami, Missouri, d. after 1900.
Black concert pianist. Successful career as a concert pianist, but was also interested in ragtime; retired in Columbia, Missouri; arranged *Boone's Rag Medleys, No. 1 Strains from the Alley* which included the folk tune "Make Me a Ballet on the Floor"; *No. 2 Strains from Flat Branch* had the strains of "Carrie's Gone to Kansas City," "I'm Alabama Bound," "So They Say" and "Oh, Honey, Ain't You Sorry?" published in the 1890s.

BOONE, CHARLES EUGENE ("PAT")

b. 1934 Jacksonville, Florida.
Singer and actor. Raised in Nashville, Tennessee; attended North Texas State College, Denton; married Shirley Foley, daughter of Red Foley; graduated Columbia University, N.Y. City (1958); on the "Arthur Godfrey Show," New York (1955); appeared in several films; had his own TV show.

BOOTT, FRANCIS

b. 1813 Boston, Massachusetts, d. 1904 Cambridge, Massachusetts. Composer. Pupil of L. Picchianti in Florence, Italy; composed under the pseudonym "Telford."

BORETZ, BENJAMIN

b. 1934.
Composer. Studied with Milton Babbitt at Princeton; also with Roger Sessions.

BORGE, VICTOR

b. 1909 Copenhagen, Denmark.
Pianist and entertainer. Attended Conservatory of Copenhagen; studied with Egon Petri and Frederic Lammond; debut as concert pianist (1922); came to the United States (1940); gave concerts throughout the United States and Europe; made records and TV appearances; resided in Greenwich, Connecticut: album—*Great Moments of Comedy;* on "Vibrations," TV Channel 13 program (1972).

BORI, LUCREZIA

b. 1888 Valencia, Spain, d. 1960.
Noted soprano. Born Lucrezia Borgia; pupil of Vidal; made her debut in *Carmen* in Rome (1908); joined the Metropolitan Opera Company, New York (1912-36); elected a member of the board of directors of the opera company.

BORNSCHEIN, FRANZ CARL

b. 1879 Baltimore, Maryland, d. there 1948. Conductor, composer, and teacher. Studied at Peabody Conservatory, Baltimore, and with Van Husteyn, et al.; conductor of Baltimore Music School Orchestra and Music Club Chorus; taught at Peabody Conservatory; wrote *The Sea God's Daughter, Onawa* (cantata), *Sea Cycle, The Willow Plate* (operetta), *String Quartet, Leif Ericson, Southern Night, Phantom Canoe Suite, Joy* (NFMC Award).

BOROWSKI, FELIX

b. 1872 Burton, Westmorland, England, d. 1956 Chicago, Illinois. Composer. Graduated Conservatory of Music in Cologne, Germany; director at Chicago Musical College after 1897; president of college (1916-25); music editor for *Chicago Evening Post* and *Chicago Herald;* wrote *Concerto for Piano and Orchestra* (1913, played by Chicago and Minneapolis Symphony Orchestras), *Two Pieces for String Orchestra, Elegie Symphonique; Allegro de Concert for Organ and Orchestra* (1915), all performed by Chicago and other symphony orchestras.

BOSTIC, EARL

b. 1913 Tulsa, Oklahoma, d. 1965 Rochester, New York. Alto saxophonist and composer. Suffered a heart attack (1956); played in small groups in Los Angeles after 1959; moved to Detroit (1965) and went on the road again with his own combo, but was stricken in Rochester.

BOSWELL, CONNEE

b. 1912 New Orleans, Louisiana.
Singer. She made several records with the Casa Loma orchestra during the 1930s; studied with Otto Finck; with sisters, Martha and Vet, appeared in theatres and films; later appeared alone; entertained U.S. Armed Forces during World War II; appeared in Broadway shows, and in films.

BOTSFORD, GEORGE

b. 1874 Sioux Falls, South Dakota, d. 1949 New York City. Ragtime composer. Wrote "The Katy Flyer"(1899), "Black and White Rag" (1908), "Klondike Rag" (1908), "Texas Steer Rag" (1909), "Old Cow Rag" (1909), "Chatterbox Rag" (1910), "Grizzly Bear Rag" (w. Irving Berlin), "Royal Flush Rag" (1911), "Eskimo Rag" (w. Jean C. Havez), "Buckeye Rag" (1913), "Rag, Baby Mine" (1913), "Sailing Down Chesapeake Bay" (1913, w. Jean C. Havez), "Boomerang Rag" (1916).

BOTT, JEAN JOSEPH

b. 1826 Kassel, Germany, d. 1895 New York City. Violinist and composer. Became court-conductor (1852); was pensioned (1878); came to New York (1885); composed two operas.

BOTTA, LUCA

b. 1882 Italy, d. 1917 New York City.
Tenor. Sang with the Pacific Coast Opera Company (1912), and with Metropolitan Opera, New York City (1914) until his death.

BOTTOME, FRANCIS

b. 1823 Belper, Derbyshire, England, d. 1894 England. Hymnist. Came to America in 1850 and entered the Methodist ministry; received the degree of Doctor of Divinity at Dickinson College, Carlisle, Pa.; wrote the hymn "O Bliss of the Purified, Bliss of the Free" (1869, m. W.B. Bradbury, "Songs of the Beautiful" in *Fresh Laurels*).

BOWERS, FREDERICK V.

b. 1874 Boston, Massachusetts, d. 1961 Los Angeles, California. Singer and popular composer. Also a vaudeville actor, teamed with Charles Horwitz, the lyricist; with Horwitz, Bowers composed "Because" (1898),

"Always" (1899), "Sweet, Sweet Love" (1899), "Wait" (1900), "When I Think of You," "In Naples Fair" (1900).

BOWERS, THOMAS J.

b. 1836 Philadelphia, Pennsylvania, d. 1885. Black organist and tenor. Organist at Thomas' African Episcopal Church, Philadelphia; debut there (1854); toured northern states and Canada; known as the "Colored Mario"; sang ballads, oratorios, and standard arias from operas.

BOWES, EDWARD

b. 1874, d. 1946.
Producer. His famous "Major Bowes' Amateur Hour" on radio and on tour started many young singers and musicians on the road to stardom, including Theresa Brewer; the Eva Jessye Choir (black group) appeared on his show.

BOWES, MARGIE

b. 1941 Roxboro, North Carolina.
Singer and guitarist. Won first prize on the Pet Milk Talent Show, Nashville, and appeared in many TV shows; later appeared on Red Foley's "Jubilee USA" for several years; her record "Poor Old Heartsick Me" was a top hit of 1959, and her records in the 1960s "Big City," "Overnight," "Our Thing," "Lost," and "Look Who's Lonely," were also hits.

BOWIE, WALTER RUSSELL

b. 1882 Richmond, Virginia, d. 1969.
Hymnist. Educated at Harvard (M.A. 1905); became an Episcopal rector in churches in Greenwood and Richmond, Virginia, then came to Grace Church, New York City (1923); chaplain of a base hospital during World War I; wrote the hymns "O Holy City, Seen of John" (tune, "Ford Cottage"—F.C. Baker), and "Lord Christ, When First Thou Cam'st to Men" (tune, "Wachterlied"—German).

BOWLES, PAUL FREDERIC

b. 1910 New York City.
Composer. Studied with Aaron Copland and Virgil Thomson; composed the ballets *Pastorela* and *Yankee Clipper* (Ballet Caravan and Philadelphia Orchestra under Smallens, 1937), a cantata, a suite for small orchestra, songs, "Scenes d'Anabase" (a song circle, w. J. Perse).

BOWMAN, DAVID W. (DAVE)

b. 1914 Buffalo, New York, d. 1964 Miami, Florida. Pianist. Worked with Bobby Hackett, Jack Teagarden, Muggsy Spanier, and Bud Freeman; worked with hotel bands in Florida during 1950s; with Phil Napoleon's Dixieland Band (1964); killed in an automobile accident.

BOWMAN, DONALD

b. 1937 Lubbock, Texas.
Singer and guitarist. Disk jockey, then signed with RCA Victor in Nashville; best-known records were "Chet Atkins," "Make Me a Star," and "Wrong House"; as a singing comedian, he was known as the "world's worst guitarist"; guest player in Grand Ole Opry.

BOWMAN, EDGAR MORRIS

b. 1848 Barnard, Vermont, d. 1913 Brooklyn, New York. Organist and teacher. Pupil of William Mason and J.P. Morgan, New York, also studied in Berlin and Paris; founded and was first president of the American College of Musicians (1884-93, discontinued, 1895), and became professor at Vassar College, Poughkeepsie, New York (1895).

BOWMAN, EUDAY L.

b. 1887 Fort Worth, Texas, d. 1949 New York City. Composer and lyricist. Wrote "12th Street Rag" (1914), recorded by Earl Fuller's Rector Novelty Orchestra (ca. 1917).

BOXTOPS (rock group)

Alex Chilton, lead singer; Billy Cunningham, bass guitar; Gary Talley, lead guitar; Danny Smythe, drums; John Evans, organ and guitar; albums—*Boxtops, Boxtops' Super Hits, Cry Like a Baby, Dimensions, Non-Stop.*

BOYD, CHARLES N.

b. 1875 Pleasant Unity, Pennsylvania, d. 1937 Pittsburgh, Pennsylvania. Organist and teacher. Graduated University of Pittsburgh; organist and conductor there (1894-1903); taught at Western Theological Seminary (1903); appointed director of the Pittsburgh Musical Institute and treasurer of the National Association of Schools of Music (1924).

BOYD, WILLIAM (BILL)

b. 1911 Fannin County, Texas.
Singer, guitarist, and songwriter. Started with station WRR, Dallas, Texas (1932) and lasted over thirty years; wrote "Boyd's Blues," "David's Blues," and "New Fort Worth Rag"; appeared in many Hollywood westerns; bandleader for The Cowboy Ramblers.

BOYLE, GEORGE FREDERICK

b. 1886 Sydney, Australia, d. 1948 Philadelphia, Pennsylvania. Pianist, teacher, and composer. Taught at the Peabody Conservatory, Baltimore (1910), then at the Curtis Institute of Music, Philadelphia, and later at the Institute of Musical Art and the Juilliard School, New York City; composed a piano concerto which he conducted at a New York Philharmonic concert (1912); also cantatas and chamber works.

BRADBURY, WILLIAM B.

b. 1816 York, Maine, d. 1868 Montclair, New Jersey. Noted composer. Student of Lowell Mason in Boston; taught music in Machias, Maine (1836); became organist at the Baptist Temple in New York City (1840); held a music convention in Somerville, New Jersey (1851); lived for a time in Bloomfield, New Jersey; with his brother, he formed a company to manufacture pianos; composed the music for "Just as I Am" (1849, w. Charlotte Elliott), "Saviour, Like a Shepherd Lead Us" (1856, Dorothy Thrupp), "Jesus Loves Me" (1859, w. Anna B. Warner), "Sweet Hour of Prayer" (1860, w. Walter W. Walford), "Marching Along" (1861, Civil War song), "He Leadeth Me" (1864, w. J.H. Gilmore, "Victory at Last" (1865, w. Mrs. M.A. Kidder), "O Blessed Thought" and "Jesus the Water of Life Will Give" (1867, w. Fanny Crosby), "I Love to Steal Awhile Away" (w. Phebe H. Brown).

BRADFORD, ANDREW

b. 1686 Pennsylvania, d. 1742 Philadelphia, Pennsylvania. Hymnist and publisher. Published sacred music in Philadelphia (1739).

BRADFORD, CLEA ANNAH ETHELL

b. 1936 Charleston, Missouri.
Black singer. Studied with grandfather, a voice teacher; debut at Faust Club in East St. Louis, Illinois; sang in Playboy Clubs (1955-56); toured Soviet Union with Earl Hines (1966).

BRADFORD, PERRY

b. 1893 Montgomery, Alabama, d. 1970.
Black singer and pianist. Arranged a session for black singer Mamie Smith (1920); later a publisher; wrote his autobiography, *Born with the Blues* (1965).

BRADLEY, HAROLD RAY

b. 1926 Nashville, Tennessee.
Guitarist. With Owen Bradley's orchestra (1950-62); albums—*Misty Guitar* (1964), *Guitar for Lovers Only* (1965).

BRADY, PAT

b. 1914 Toledo, Ohio, d. 1972 Green Mountain Falls, Colorado. Singer, guitarist, and actor. Both parents were in show business; played bass guitar with his father in a nightclub in Sunset Beach, California; joined Leonard Sly (Roy Rogers) and Sons of the Pioneers singing group; served in France in General Patton's Third Army in World War II; appeared in eighty films as Roy Roger's side-kick.

BRAFF, REUBEN ("RUBY")

b. 1927 Boston, Massachusetts.
Trumpeter. Played at 1954 Newport Jazz Festival, and also at subsequent festivals; toured United States during 1960s; also played with George Wein, pianist-producer; toured Europe with a jazz group (1965); also soloist in England.

BRAHAM, DAVID

b. 1838 London, England, d. 1905 New York City. Popular composer. Started as a violinist in Tony Moore's Minstrels, then became music director of Tony Pastor's, New York City (1865); Ed Harrigan wrote the lyrics and Braham the music for "The Mulligan Guard" (1873), "The Skidmore Guard" (1874), "Patrick's Day Parade" (1874), "Sweet Mary Ann" (1879), and *The Skidmore Fancy Ball* (1879) which included the song "The Babies on Our Block"—these songs and shows were produced by Harrigan and Hart; Braham also wrote "Eily Machree" (w. C.L. Stout), "To Rest, Let Him Gently Be Laid" (w. George Cooper), "Sway the Cot Gently for Baby's Asleep" (w. Hartley Neville), "The Eagle" (Stout), "Emancipation Day" (Stout).

BRAINARD, JOHN GARDINER CALKINS

b. 1796 New London, Connecticut, d. 1828 Hartford, Connecticut. Hymnist. Graduated Yale; attorney in Middletown, Connecticut, and edited a paper in Hartford; wrote"To Thee, O God, the Shepherd King," which appeared in *Congregational Psalms and Hymns* (1845).

BRAINARD, SILAS

b. 1814 Lempster, New Hampshire, d. 1871. Publisher. Music publisher in Cleveland, Ohio, during the 1860s; moved the business to Chicago, Illinois (1869).

BRAINE, ROBERT

b. 1896 Springfield, Ohio, d. 1940.
Conductor, composer, and editor. Wrote *Brown Men* (w. M.S. Burt), *S.O.S.* (1927), *The Raven* (for baritone, 1928), *The Song of Hiawatha* (suite, 1930), *Concerto in Jazz* (for violin, 1931), *Quartet in Jazz* (for two violins, viola, and cello, 1935).

BRAITH, GEORGE (GEORGE BRAITHWAITE)

b. 1939 Bronx, New York.
Black saxophonist. At age ten led his own group; studied with Garvin Bushell; toured with his own combo (1957); toured Netherlands; played soprano sax and tenor sax.

BRAND, MAX

b. 1896 Vienna, Austria.
Composer. Wrote the opera *Maschinist Hopkins*, which was successful in Germany, and then *Requiem*, accepted by the Berlin State Opera (1932), but it was cancelled by the Nazis when they seized power, so he came to New York City; while living there, he wrote the choral, *The Gate*, and the symphonic poem *The Wonderful One-Horse Shay* (w. Oliver W. Holmes), first performed by the Philadelphia Orchestra. (*See* Harold Rome).

BRAND, OSCAR

b. 1920 Winnipeg, Canada.
Singer, banjoist, guitarist, and songwriter. While still young, his family moved to Minneapolis, Chicago, then New York City; attended Brooklyn College, then served in the army in World War II; started his "Folksong Festival" on station WNYC in 1945, and it ran for more than twenty years; wrote the music for *A Joyful Noise* (1966), and *In White America* (off-Broadway production); also wrote the song "A Guy Is a Guy," and recorded over fifty LP folk song records; in concert at Folk Concert, Battery Park, New York City (1972).

BRANDEIS, FREDERICK (FRANCIS)

b. 1835 Vienna, Austria, d. 1899 New York City. Pianist and composer. Studied under Czerny; but one day in 1848 Brandeis appeared in a revolutionary uniform, and Czerny, a staunch imperialist, chased him out of the house; Brandeis' father's fortune was confiscated; the family came to New York (1848); appeared as solo pianist and with William Vincent Wallace's concert company, toured the country; later organist of St. Peter and St. Paul's Roman Catholic church, Brooklyn, N.Y., and of Forty-fourth Street Synagogue, New York; composed *Waltz, Poem* (dedicated to and played by S.B. Mills), Polonaise in C, Tocca in C, Gavotte in A Minor, (played by Mme. Rive-King, also played by Thomas' orchestra under the name *Danse Heroique*), *Andante Elegiaco, Tarantelle Caprice, Tantum Ergo,* festival for solo, chorus and organ.

BRANSCOMBE, GENA

b. 1881 Picton, Ontario, Canada.
Composer. Studied at the Chicago Conservatory; later pupil of Humperdinck in Germany; married John F. Tenny and lived in New York City; she wrote *Pilgrims of Destiny* (a cantata, 1928), *Quebec Suite* (1930).

BRANT, HENRY DREFUSS

b. 1913 Montreal, P.Q., Canada
Composer. Studied at the Juilliard School of Music, New York City, under James Friskin and Rubin Goldmark, then studied privately; taught at Juilliard (1947-55) and since 1957 at Bennington College, Vermont; wrote *The Marx Brothers* (Chico, Groucho, and Harpo, 1938, for piccolo and chamber orchestra), *The Great American Goof* (William Saroyan and Eugene Loring, choreography, debut at the Ballet Theatre, New York, 1940); wrote the scores for films produced by the office of War Information during World War II; known for his First Symphony in B-flat (1945), *December* (1954), *Millennium* (1954), *Grand Universal Circus* (1956), *Atlantis* (1960); wrote the music for the Jewish film *My Father's House,* also composed *Fire in Cities* (1961), and *Voyage Four* (1964).

BRASLAU, SOPHIE

b. 1892 New York City, d. there 1935. Soprano. Debut at Metropolitan Opera, New York City (1913) as Feodor in *Boris Godunov;* with Metropolitan Opera (1913-20); toured Scandinavia, the Netherlands, and England.

BRATTLE, THOMAS

b. 1658 Boston, Massachusetts, d. there 1713. Organist. Owned the first organ in New England (1711) in Boston, which he presented to Queen's Chapel, Boston, in August 1713, but prejudice against it was so great it remained unpacked for seven months, erected in 1714 and remained there until 1756, when it was sold to St. Paul's Church, Newburyport, Mass., and in use there until 1836 when sold to St. John's Church, Portsmouth, N.H.

BRATTON, JOHN W.

b. 1867 Wilmington, Delaware, d. 1947 Brooklyn, New York. Popular composer. Walter H. Ford wrote the lyrics and Bratton the music for "I Love You in the Same Old Way, Darling Sue" (1896), "I'm Nothing to You Now" (1898), "Beneath the Evening Star" (1900); also wrote "Best in the House" (1898, w. C.B. Lawler).

BRAUD, WELLMAN

b. 1891 St. James, Louisiana, d. 1966. Black double bass player. Played with Jelly Roll Morton (1917), Lawrence Duhe (1919), with Duke Ellington (1926-35), Bunk Johnson (1947); used the slap technique to great effect.

BRAUN, JOHN F.

b. (?), d. 1939 Philadelphia, Pennsylvania. Tenor, pianist, violinist, and cellist. Made several appearances as a soloist with the Philadelphia Orchestra, in concert form under Stokowski, and with the Cincinnati and St. Louis Orchestras.

BRAUN, MATITIAHU

b. 1940. Violinist. With New York Philharmonic; also own group, Voces Intimae Trio, at Tully Hall, Lincoln Center, New York City (1972).

BRAY, JOHN

b. 1782 England, d. 1822. Composer and actor. With the Royal York Theatre in London; came to America; with Chestnut Street Theatre (1805-14); in Boston (1814-20); wrote "General Harrison's Grand March" (1812), "Hull's Victory" (1812), "Madison's March" (1814), "Columbia, Land of Liberty" (1814, w. General J.N. Barker), "Arise, Columbia" (1820), "Our Rights on the Ocean," "Soft as Yon Silver Ray That Sleeps," an operetta, *The Indian Princess,* performed in Philadelphia (1808).

BRAZOS VALLEY BOYS *see* HANK THOMPSON

BREAU, HAROLD

b. 1916 Pea Cove, Maine. Singer. Leader of the Lone Pine Mountaineers and Lone Pine Stage Show; on radio, Bangor, Maine, and radio-TV Canadian Maritime Provinces; father of Lenny Breau, guitarist.

BRECK, CARRIE ELLIS

b. 1855 Walden, Vermont, d. 1934 Portland, Oregon. Hymnist. Married Frank A. Breck; wrote "Face to Face" (1899, m. G.C. Tullar), "Go to the Deeps of God's Promise," "There Was One Who Was Willing," "They Are Nailed to the Cross."

BREEDEN, HAROLD LEON

b. 1921 Guthrie, Oklahoma. Bandleader, saxophonist, and educator. Raised in Wichita Falls, Texas; with Ray McKinley (1952); conducted jazz bands at North Texas State College, Denton, Texas, winners at college festivals at Notre Dame and University of Kansas.

BREIL, JOSEPH CARL

b. 1870 Pittsburgh, Pennsylvania, d. 1926 Los Angeles, California. Tenor and composer. Studied in Leipzig and Milan; sang in Juch Opera Company and later in Pittsburgh; theater conductor after 1897; composed comic operas and a grand opera, *The Legend,* performed by the Metropolitan Opera Company, New York City (1919).

BREMNER (BENNER), JAMES

b. (?) England, d. 1780 Philadelphia, Pennsylvania. Organist and teacher. Came to Philadelphia (1763); organist at St. Peter's Church and then at Christ Church; music teacher, one of the students was Francis Hopkinson; with Hopkinson presented the first subscription concerts in Philadelphia in 1764.

BRENDEL, ALFRED

b. 1931. Pianist. Began playing at age six; debut at age seventeen; won Italy's Concorso Busoni prize (1949); recorded thirty-six long-playing sides of Beethoven's piano works for Vox Records; played at the Mostly Mozart Festival in New York's Philharmonic Hall (1971); in concert at Carnegie Hall, New York City (1972).

BRENNAN, J. KEIRN

b. 1873 San Francisco, California, d. 1948 Hollywood, California. Singer and lyricist. Sang in vaudeville; wrote "A Little Bit of Heaven, Sure They Call It Ireland" (m. Ernest Ball) which appeared in the show *The Heart of Paddy Wack,* New York City (1914).

BRETT, ARABELLA

b. (?) England, d. 1803. Singer and actress. Sister of Mrs. King and Mrs. Hodgkinson; played Maiden of Uri in *The Archers* (opera, w. W. Dunlap, m. B. Carr, produced in New York City, 1796); leading operatic singer and actress with Mrs. Oldmixon and Miss Broadhurst in Philadelphia (1793-1800).

BREWER, JOHN HYATT

b. 1856 Brooklyn, New York, d. there 1931. Organist. Organist at churches in New York City, the last being the Lafayette Avenue Presbyterian Church (1881).

BREWER, LEIGH RICHMOND

b. 1839 Berkshire, Vermont, d. 1916 Helena, Montana. Hymnist. Educated at Hobart College, Geneva, New York, and General Theological Seminary; served in churches in New York until he became Missionary Bishop of Montana; wrote the hymn "Long Years Ago O'er Bethlehem's Hills" (tune "Weinhnacht" by K.P. Harrington).

BREWER, TERESA

b. 1937 Toledo, Ohio.
Singer. Toured on the "Major Bowes' Amateur Hour" from ages five to twelve; then on the "Pick & Pat Show"; appeared on "Eddie Dowling's Big Break"; married Bill Monahan; later appeared on the "Perry Como Show" and "Ed Sullivan Show."

BRICE, FANNY

b. 1891, d. 1951.
Singer and entertainer. Star of the Ziegfeld Follies (1910) and sang "Lovey Joe" (w. Joe Jordan, m. Will M. Cook); sang "The Vamp from East Broadway" (by Harry Ruby and Irving Berlin) in the Follies of 1920.

BRICKEN, CARL ERNST

b. 1898 Shelbyville, Kentucky.
Conductor and composer. Conductor of the University of Chicago Symphony (1931), and of the Seattle Symphony, Seattle, Washington (1944).

BRIDGETOWER, GEORGE POLGREEN

b. 1779, d. 1860.
Black violinist and composer. Studied with Haydn; gave first performance of Beethoven's Violin Sonata op. 47, the Kreutzer Sonata, in Vienna, Austria (1803); known as the "Abyssinian Prince."

BRIEL, MARIE

b. 1896 Peru, Illinois.
Organist and teacher. Educated at Northwestern University, Evanston, Illinois (Mus. M., 1925); then taught at Marionville College, Missouri, Iowa Wesleyan, Mt. Pleasant, Iowa, the Columbia School of Music, Chicago, and the American Conservatory of Music, Chicago; organist in the Methodist church, Wilmette, Illinois; composed music for the Holy Communion services.

BRIGGS, GEORGE WALLACE

b. 1875, d. 1959.
Hymnist. Wrote "Come, Risen Lord, and Deign to Be Our Guest" (1931, m. Frank K. Owen, also tune by George Henry Day); "Christ Is the World's True Light"(1941, m. Percy E. B. Coller).

BRIGGS, G. WRIGHT

b. 1916 Taunton, Massachusetts.
Composer and teacher. Graduated Harvard University, Harvard Business School, and Harvard Graduate School (M.A.); studied at New England Conservatory with Walter Piston, et al.; taught at New England Conservatory (1942-55); with advertising firm after 1955; works—"Commemoration March," "Concord and Lexington March," "Boston's on the Move Again," *Andante* for violin, cello and piano, and *Twentieth Century Gavotte.*

BRIGHT, HOUSTON

b. 1916 Midland, Texas.
Composer. Graduated West Texas State College, Canyon, Texas, and University of Southern California, Los Angeles (Ph.D.); studied with Halsey Stevens, et al.; served in World War II; taught at West Texas State College; works—Prelude and Fugue in F (for band), *Three Short Dances* (for woodwind quintet), *Two Short Pieces* (for brass quartet), *Marche de Concert, Four Pieces for Piano.*

BRIGHT, RONNELL

b. 1930 Chicago, Illinois.
Pianist and composer. Accompanist for Sarah Vaughn during 1950s and Lena Horne (1961); with Nancy Wilson after 1964.

BRIGNOLA, NICHOLAS THOMAS (NICK)

b. 1936 Troy, New York.
Baritone saxist. Played in Troy area during 1950s, also on West Coast; with Woody Herman (1963) and Sal Salvador (1963-64); had his own group in Troy area after 1964.

BRISTOW, GEORGE FREDERICK

b. 1825 Brooklyn, New York, d. 1898 New York City. Noted violinist and composer. Violinist with the New York Philharmonic Orchestra (1842); his compositions were a cantata, *Eleutheria* (1849); an opera, *Rip Van Winkle* (second opera to have been written by a native American—its debut was at Niblo's Theatre, New York City in 1855); also wrote the oratorios *Praise to God* (1861) and *Daniel* (1867), and the symphony, *Niagara.*

BRISTOW, WILLIAM RICHARD

b. 1803 England, d. 1867 New York City.
Conductor in New York City. Father of George F. Bristow.

BRITAIN, RADIE

b. 1903 Silverton, Texas.
Composer. Educated at Clarendon Junior College, Texas, and American Conservatory (B.M.); studied with Leopold Godowsky, et al.; teacher at Clarendon College; works—*Southern* Symphony, *Bondage, Light, Heroic Poem* (Hollywood International prize and Juilliard publ. award), *Epic Poem* (first prize, National Contest of American Pen Women),

Suite for Strings (first prize, American Women Composers), *Nirvana* (first prize, Texas Federation of Music Clubs).

BRITT, ELTON

b. 1913 Marshall, Arkansas.
Singer and guitarist. Born James Britt Baker; sang on radio in Los Angeles at age fourteen; later signed with RCA Victor and recorded over 700 discs between 1937-59, then recorded for Decca and other labels; his hit recordings were "There's a Star Spangled Banner Waving Somewhere" (World War II), "Chime Bells" (1948), "Candy Kisses" (1949), and "Quicksilver" (1950, with Rosalie Allen).

BRITT, HORACE

b. 1881 Antwerp, Belgium, d. 1971 Austin, Texas. Concert cellist. Studied at the Paris Conservatory and was soloist with the Lamoureux Orchestra (1897); American debut with the Chicago Symphony (1907); toured the United States with Georges Barrere, flutist, and Carlos Salzedo, harpist, and founded the Barrere-Britt Concertino, (1937); taught at the University of Texas, Austin (1948-65).

BROCKMAN, HARRY

b. 1904 Kishinov, Russia, d. 1972 Brooklyn, New York. Cantor. Debut as a singer at age eight; graduated Kishinov Music Conservatory; came to America at age sixteen; studied here under Cantor David Roitman; cantor at Congregation Shaare Torah of Flatbush, Brooklyn (1943-72); awarded fellowship in music by the Jewish Theological Seminary (1960).

BROCKMAN, JAMES

b. 1886, d. 1967.
Composer and lyricist. Studied at Cleveland Conservatory; was a comedian in musicals; later a songwriter for films; wrote "I'm Forever Blowing Bubbles" (with James Kendis and Nat Vincent, m. John William Killette), introduced by June Caprice in *The Passing Show* of 1918.

BROCKWAY, HOWARD A.

b. 1870 Brooklyn, New York, d. 1951.
Composer. Studied in Berlin (1890-95), then toured the United States as a concert pianist, then taught; his Symphony in D was produced in Berlin; also composed a cantata, *Ballade and Scherzo,* for orchestra.

BROMFIELD, EDWARD, JR.

b. 1723 Boston, Massachusetts, d. 1806.
Organ maker. Graduated Harvard University (1742); constructed first organ built in America in Boston (1745), for Rev. Thomas Prince.

BROOKMEYER, ROBERT (BOB)

b. 1929 Kansas City, Kansas.
Jazz trombonist. Played with Claude Thornhill; formed his own combo with Clark Terry (1961); toured Europe with Mulligan (1963-64), and Japan (1964); staff musician on Merv Griffin's TV show after 1965; married composer-lyricist Margo Guryan (1964).

BROOKS, CHARLES TIMOTHY

b. 1813 Salem, Massachusetts, d. 1883 Newport, Rhode Island. Hymnist. Educated at Harvard University and Divinity School (1829-35); became a Unitarian minister in Newport, R.I.; Brooks and John S. Dwight translated from the German, "God Bless Our Native Land" (1834, tune "Dort" by Lowell Mason), it was originally sung to "God Save the King (Queen)."

BROOKS, HARRY

b. 1895 Homestead, Pennsylvania, d. 1970 Teaneck, New Jersey. Pianist and composer. Studied with Walter Spriggs; played in dance orchestras; composer and arranger for publishing companies; with Fats Waller and Andy Razaf, wrote the score for *Hot Chocolates* (1929) which included the song "Ain't Misbehavin'."

BROOKS, JACK

b. 1912 Liverpool, England.
Composer and lyricist. Came to U.S. with family at age four; wrote material for Bing Crosby, Phil Harris, and Fred Allen; wrote film background scores; wrote the libretto for *The Dybbuk* and *You Wonderful You* (with Harry Warren and Saul Chapin).

BROOKS, PHILLIPS

b. 1835 Boston, Massachusetts, d. there 1893. Hymnist. Graduated from Harvard (1855) and the Episcopal Divinity School, Alexandria, Virginia (1859); pastor of the Church of the Advent, and then of Holy Trinity, Philadelphia, when he wrote the words of the Christmas carol, "O Little Town of Bethlehem" (1868, m. L.H. Redner); elected Bishop of the diocese of Massachusetts in 1891.

BROOKS, SHELTON

b. 1886 Amesbury, Ontario, Canada.
Black popular composer, pianist, and vaudeville entertainer. His family moved to Detroit when he was young; wrote "Some of

These Days" (1910, sung by Sophie Tucker in Chicago), "The Darktown Strutter's Ball" (1917), "There'll Come a Time" (1911), "Jean," "All Night Long," "You Ain't Talkin' to Me," and "Honey Gal" (sung by Al Jolson in the Winter Garden).

BROONZY, "BIG BILL" (WILLIAM LEE CONLEY)

b. 1893 Scott, Mississippi, d. 1958 Chicago, Illinois. Black singer, fiddler, guitarist, and songwriter. Served in France in the army in World War I; wrote "Saturday Night Rub," "Big Bill Blues," "House Rent Stomp," "Date with an Angel Blues," "The Walking Blues," "Bull Cow Blues," "Milk Cow Blues," "Serve It to Me Right Blues," and "Mama Let's Cuddle Some More"; toured Europe in 1951, which was very successful; recorded several Big Bill Broonzy LP records.

BROTHERHOOD, THE (rock group)

Drake Levin, guitar; Phil Volk, bass; Michael "Smitty" Smith, drums; Ron Collins, organ and piano; group originally with Paul Revere and the Raiders; album—*Brotherhood.*

BROTHERS FOUR, THE

Bob Flick, Michael Kirkland, John Paine, and Richard Foley.

BROUNOFF, PLATON

b. 1869 Elizabethgrad, Russia, d. 1924 New York City. Conductor and composer. Pupil of Rubinstein and Rimsky-Korsakov at the St. Petersburg Conservatory; his cantata *The Angel* was produced at court in Russia; conductor of the Russian choral society in New York City; composed operas, piano suites, and songs.

BROWN, ARTHUR LAWRENCE

b. 1877, d. 1954.
Composer. Wrote *Glad Light.*

BROWN, BARTHOLOMEW

b. 1772 Sterling, Massachusetts, d. 1854 Boston, Massachusetts. Compiler and composer. Graduated from Harvard (1799), became an attorney, but changed to music; taught music in Abington, Mass. and in Boston; composed the tune "Tilden" (ca. 1800); with Nahum Mitchell and Benjamin Holt, he compiled *The Columbian and European Harmony* (*Bridgewater Collection of Sacred Music,* 1802.)

BROWN, BONNIE GEAN

b. 1938 Sparkman, Arkansas.
Singer. Attended schools in Pine Bluff, Arkansas; Arkansas A&M College, Monticello (1955); member of The Browns, with brother Jim Edward and sister Maxine; married Dr. Gene Dale Ring.

BROWN, CLIFFORD

b. 1930 Wilmington, Delaware, d. 1956 on Pennsylvania Turnpike. Black jazz trumpeter. Played with Miles Davis, Fats Navarro, and others; killed in an automobile crash.

BROWN, EARLE A., JR.

b. 1926 Lunenburg, Massachusetts.
Composer. Attended Northwestern University, Evanston, Illinois; studied Schillinger system of composition and orchestration with Kenneth McKillop; taught in Denver; devised a system of notation using symbolic ideograms; director of the Contemporary Sound Series (Time Records); wrote *Folio Pieces* (1952), *Pentahis* (for nine instruments, 1958), *Available Forms I* (for eighteen players,) *Darmstadt* (1961).

BROWN, EDDY

b. 1895 Chicago, Illinois, d. 1974.
Violinist. Studied with Hubay and Auer; debut with London Philharmonic Orchestra (1909); toured Europe and America.

BROWN, GARNETT, JR.

b. 1936 Memphis, Tennessee.
Trombonist. Played wtih Chico Hamilton (1962); toured Europe with George Russell (1964).

BROWN, FLEMING

b. 1926 Marshall, Missouri.
Singer and banjoist. Taught at the Old Town School of Folk Music, Chicago, Illinois; his LP record *Fleming Brown Sings Folk Songs* was issued in 1962.

BROWN, HYLO

b. 1920.
Singer. Regular on WWVA "Jamboree," Wheeling, West Virginia; member of the Timberliners; albums—*Hylo Brown, Bluegrass Oldies but Goodies, Bluegrass Balladeer, Starday.*

BROWN, JAMES ("MR. DYNAMITE")

b. 1928 near Augusta, Georgia.
Black singer and songwriter. Top rock singer; sang in Harlem's Apollo Theatre; later at Madison Square Garden (1966); sings, shouts, raves, and screams; started as a prize fighter; his first hits were "Please, Please, Please" (1956), "Try Me" (1958), "If I Ruled the World" (1964), "I Got You" (1965), "Pap's

Got a Brand New Bag" (1965), "It's a Man's Man's World" (1966); entertained troops in Vietnam (1968); called to Washington, D.C. by President Lyndon Johnson to help quell the riots there; lives in a castle with a drawbridge and moat in St. Albans, New York; wrote "Don't Be a Drop Out,""Prisoner of Love" (with Russ Columbo), "Say It Loud, I'm Black and I'm Proud" (1968); at the Festival of Hope rock concert, Westbury, L.I., New York (1972); albums—*Ain't It Funny, Amazing James Brown-Flames, James Brown and Famous Flames Tour the U.S.A., Live at the Apollo, Live at the Garden, Plays New Breed, Plays the Real Thing, Presents His Show of Tomorrow, Sings and Plays 22 Giant Hits, Cold Sweat, Grits and Soul, Handful of Soul, I Got the Feelin'.*

BROWN, J. HAROLD

b. 1909 Shellman, Georgia.
Black organist and composer. Graduated Fisk University, Nashville, master's at Indiana University; director of music at Florida A&M, Tallahassee; at Southern University, Baton Rouge; later director at Karamu House and Huntington Playhouse, Cleveland, in 1950s; wrote *Job* (oratorio), *The Saga of Rip Van Winkle* (for chorus), *The African Chief* (cantata).

BROWN, JAMES OSTEND ("PETE")

b. 1906 Baltimore, Maryland, d. 1963.
Black alto and tenor saxist. Joined John Kirby Sextet (1938); considered one of the great alto players in jazz history; died of a kidney ailment.

BROWN, JEWEL HAZEL

b. 1937 Houston, Texas.
Singer. Studied under her brother, a pianist; vocalist with Earl Grant (1957-58); with Louis Armstrong after 1961; toured all over the world with Armstrong's band.

BROWN, JIM EDWARD

b. 1934 Sparkman, Arkansas.
The Browns—vocal trio, consisting of Maxine, Jim Edward and Bonnie; Jim studied at Arkansas State Teacher's College; the Browns were regulars on the "Ozark Jamboree," Springfield, Missouri (1955), then Jim went into the army; they made a hit with "Jimmy Brown" (1959, based on "Three Bells"), "Scarlet Ribbons" and "The Old Lamplighter"; they were regulars on Grand Ole Opry (1963-67), while Jim lived in Brentwood, Tennessee.

BROWN, JOHN NEWTON

b. 1803 New London, Connecticut, d. 1868. Hymnist. Graduated Madison University (1823); professor at New Hampton, N.H. (1838-45) and pastor in Lexington, Virginia (1845-49); wrote "Go, Spirit of the Sainted Dead" which appeared in *The Psalmist* (1843) compiled by the Rev. B. Stow and S.F. Smith.

BROWN, LAWRENCE

b. 1905 Lawrence, Kansas.
Jazz trombonist. With Duke Ellington (1932-51), also after 1960; recorded with Johnny Hodges.

BROWN, LESTER RAYMOND (LES)

b. 1912 Reinerton, Pennsylvania.
Bandleader. Educated at Ithaca College and Duke University, Durham, N.C.; formed own band (1938), Band of Renown; toured until 1947; Doris Day sang in his band; conductor for Bob Hope radio and TV shows (1947-62); albums—*Les Brown Concert at the Palladium, Les Brown's in Town, Hits from Sound of Music, My Fair Lady, and Others, Impact (Band Meets Band), Les Dance with Les Brown, Sign of the Times, World of the Young;* on NBC TV for Chrysler Corp. (1972).

BROWN, LEW

b. 1893 Odessa, Russia, d. 1958 New York City. Lyricist. His family came to America (1898) and settled in New Haven, Connecticut, then moved to New York City; he wrote lyrics for Albert von Tilzer, and with Buddy de Sylva for Ray Henderson's music for *George White's Scandals* (1925); also wrote lyrics for Harry Akst, Sammy Fain, and Sammy Stept; hit songs include "Beer Barrel Polka," "Don't Sit Under the Apple Tree with Anyone Else but Me."

BROWN, LUCY

b. 1913 Crestwood, New York, d. 1971 New York City. Concert pianist and teacher. Taught at the Peabody Conservatory of Music, Baltimore; studied under Manfred Malkin; debut in Town Hall (1931), and later was accompanist for Paul Robeson.

BROWN, MARION, JR.

b. 1935 Atlanta, Georgia.
Black alto saxophonist. Played in an army band; with Johnny Hodges in Atlanta (1957); went to New York City and played with Archie Shepp; with Jazz Composers Guild Orchestra; organized own group (1965).

BROWN, MARSHALL RICHARD

b. 1920 Framingham, Massachusetts. Bandleader and songwriter. Organized and led the Newport Youth Band (1959); publisher; as trombonist toured during 1960s with Pee Wee Russell, Bobby Hackett, Ruby Braff, and Wild Bill Davidson.

BROWN, MAXINE

b. 1932 Sparkman, Arkansas.
Singer. Member of the Browns, with brother Jim Ed and Bonnie Brown; married Tom Russell.

BROWN, NACIO HERB

b. 1896 Deming, New Mexico, d. 1964 San Francisco, California. Popular composer. Attended the University of California, Los Angeles, for a year; became a tailor and made a fortune in Beverly Hills real estate; with Arthur Freed, lyricist, he wrote "Broadway Melody" and "The Wedding of the Painted Doll" (1929); also wrote "You Were Meant for Me" (1929), "The Pagan Love Song" (1929), "You Are My Lucky Star" (1935), "Broadway Rhythm" (1935), and "Love Is Where You Find It" (w. Gus Kahn).

BROWN, NATHAN

b. 1807 New Ipswich, New Hampshire, d. 1886 Yokohama, Japan. Hymnist. Baptist missionary in Burma (1833); translated hymns into Burmese and Japanese.

BROWN, NORMAN

b. (?), d. 1969.
Black guitarist. Played with the Miles Brothers for over thirty years (1936-1969); he joined the group as a guitarist after John Miles, Jr. died.

BROWN, OSCAR, JR.

b. 1926 Chicago, Illinois.
Black singer and songwriter. Served in army (1954-56); wrote "Brown Baby," recorded by Mahalia Jackson; with Max Roach wrote "Freedom Now Suite"; wrote lyrics for "Work Song" (m. Nat Adderley), "Dat Dere" (m. Bobby Timmons), "All Blues" (m. Miles Davis), "So Help Me" (m. Les McCann), "One Foot in the Gutter" (m. Clark Terry); master of ceremonies on "Jazz Scene USA" (1962 TV show).

BROWN, PHOEBE (HINSDALE)

b. 1783 Canaan, New York, d. 1861 Marshall, Illinois. Poetess and hymnist. Hew husband was a journeyman house painter, and they were the parents of the Rev. Samuel R. Brown, D.D., pioneer missionary to Japan; she wrote a nine-stanza poem, "An Apology for My Twilight Rambles," addressed to a lady whose garden she often visited; a hymn was made from the poem "I Love to Steal Awhile Away" (m. D. Dutton—tune "Woodstock," second tune—"Brown"—W.B. Bradbury), which appeared in Asahel Nettleton's *Village Hymns* (1824).

BROWN, RAY FRANCIS

b. 1897 Roxbury, Vermont.
Organist. Studied at Oberlin College, Oberlin, Ohio, and taught there (1925-27) while playing the organ in Elyria, Ohio, then at Fisk University, Nashville, and the General Theological Seminary in New York City (1933-34); organist in churches in New York City and Bronxville, New York, then after 1943 at the Church of the Resurrection, New York City; arranged the tune "Chelsea Square" (1941, "Put Forth O God, Thy Spirit's Might," w. H.C. Robbins).

BROWN, RAYMOND MATTHEWS (RAY)

b. 1926 Pittsburgh, Pennsylvania.
Black jazz bass player. Known for his humming technique similar to Slam Stewart; with Oscar Peterson after 1951; toured Europe and Japan (1964); in Hollywood after 1966; wrote "Gravy Waltz" (w. Steve Allen), popularized on the "Steve Allen Show."

BROWN, SEYMOUR

b. 1885 Philadelphia, Pennsylvania, d. there 1947. Actor and lyricist. Wrote lyrics "Oh, You Beautiful Doll" (1911, m. Nat D. Ayer).

BROWN, TONI

b. 1938.
Singer, pianist, organist, and songwriter. With Terry Garthwaite, organized the Joys of Cooking, at Los Angeles (1967); she wrote and recorded "Only Time Will Tell Me" (gospel song).

BROWN, WILLIAM ("SONNY")

b. 1928 Cincinnati, Ohio.
Black composer, pianist, flutist, guitarist, and saxophonist. Served in the navy (1945-48); settled in Los Angeles, played in night clubs; developed the heroin habit; went to jail for stealing a record player; organized the "Fallen Sparrows" at California Correctional Institute at Tehachapi (1967); toured other prisons, taped TV show at Bakersfield, played at high schools and colleges in California;

recorded for RCA (1970); on National Educational TV (1972).

BROWNING, MORTIMER

b. 1891 Baltimore, Maryland, d. 1953 Milford, Delaware. Composer, organist and pianist. Studied at Peabody Conservatory, Baltimore, Chicago Musical College, and David Mannes School, New York City; with Percy Grainger, et al.; taught at Greensboro College, N.C., School of Musicanship, New York City, and Westchester Conservatory; organist in churches in Baltimore and New York City; works—*Trio for Violin, Cello and Piano,* Piano Suite in D, *Concerto for Theramin, Scherzo Rondo* (for violin and orchestra), *Caprice Burlesque* (for violin).

BROWNLEE, JOHN

b. 1901 Geelong, Australia, d. 1969.
Baritone. Studied with Gilly; discovered by Dame Nellie Melba; sang at Melba's Covent Garden Farewell (1926); debut at Metropolitan Opera, New York City (1937) as the lead in *Rigoletto;* with Metropolitan Opera (1937-54); later director of the Manhattan School of Music, New York City.

BROWNS, THE (vocal group)

James Edward, Maxine, and Bonnie Gean Brown.

BROWN'S FERRY FOUR

Alton and Rabon Delmore, Grandpa Jones, Red Foley, and Merle Travis.

BRUBECK, CHRIS

b. 1952.
Guitarist and leader. Son of Dave Brubeck; leader of the New Heavenly Blue rock group (family group of Dave Brubeck and sons—pianist Darius, guitarist Chris, and drummer Danny); at the Westbury Music Fair, L.I., New York (1972).

BRUBECK, DARIUS
Leader. Son of Dave Brubeck; leader of his own group; in concert with his brother, Chris, his father, Gerry Mulligan, and Paul Desmond at Carnegie Hall, New York City (1972).

BRUBECK, DAVID W. (DAVE)

b. 1920 Concord, California.
Composer and pianist. Studied with Milhaud; also with Schoenberg; formed a quartet which recorded a version of *Perdido* at Oberlin College (1953); later issued an album in 5/4 and 7/4 jazz meter entitled *Time Out;* albums—*Angel Eyes, Anything Goes, Bernstein Plays Brubeck-Brubeck Plays Bernstein, Blue Roots, Bossa Nova USA, Brandenburg Gate Revisited, Dave Brubeck at Carnegie Hall, Dave Brubeck in Amsterdam, Dave Brubeck Quartet in Europe;* at the Newport Jazz Festival, New York City (1972).

BRUNIES BROTHERS OF NEW ORLEANS

Creole players with different groups—George (known as Brunis), trombone and drums; Albert ("Abbie") cornet, trumpet, bass and drums; Henry, trombone; Richard, trumpet; Merritt, horn and trumpet.

BRUNIS, GEORG

b. 1902 New Orleans, Louisiana, d. 1974.
Creole trombonist. Born George Brunies; played in Friar's Society Orchestra, later known as the New Orleans Rhythm Kings; then with Ted Lewis (1918-35); did female impersonations; at a Town Hall concert manipulated the trombone slide with his foot; played in Chicago (1951-59); with Ted Lewis again (1962-65); in Eddie Condon's band at Newport Jazz Festival, New York City (1972).

BRUNSWICK, MARK

b. 1902 New York City, d. 1971 London, England. Composer. Studied under Rubin Goldmark, Nadia Boulanger, and Ernest Bloch; taught at Kenyon College, Gambier, Ohio, Brooklyn College, and the Greenwich House Music School Settlement, New York City (1938-45); wrote Symphony in B-flat (1945), *Lysistrata-Suite for Orchestra and Chorus, Eros and Death* (choral symphony), and *Fragment of Sappho* (motet); he was touring Europe when he died of a heart attack in London.

BRYAN, ALFRED

b. 1871 Brantford, Ontario, Canada, d. 1958 Gladstone, New Jersey. Lyricist. Wrote the lyrics for "Rainbow" (1908, m. Percy Wenrich), "Peg O' My Heart" (1913, m. Fred Fisher), "It's a Cute Little Way of My Own" (m. Harry Tierney) sung by Anna Held in *Follow Me* (1917).

BRYAN, CHARLES FAULKNER

b. 1911 McMinnville, Tennessee, d. 1955 Pinson, Alabama. Singer, teacher, and composer. Studied at the Nashville Conservatory of Music (1930-34); taught at Tennessee Polytech and received his M.A. at George Peabody College, Nashville, where he taught (1947-52), then at the Indian Springs School, Helena, Alabama; composed *The Bell Witch* (1946, folk cantata), *Cumberland Interlude 1790, White Spiritual* Symphony,

Birmingham Suite (1953), *Singin' Billy* (opera), and *Strangers in This World* (a musical folk play).

BRYAN, VINCENT

b. 1883, d. 1937 Hollywood, California. Lyricist. Wrote "In My Merry Oldsmobile" (1905, m. Gus Edwards).

BRYANT, ANITA

b. 1941 Barnsdall, Oklahoma. Singer. Noted gospel singer; albums—*ABC Stories of Jesus, Abiding Love, As Long as He Needs Me, Anita Bryant, Anita Bryant's Greatest Hits, How Great Thou Are, I Believe, Kisses Sweeter than Wine, Mine Eyes Have Seen the Glory, Whispering Hope.*

BRYANT, BOUDLEAUX

b. 1920 Shellman, Georgia. Fiddler and songwriter. Raised in Moultrie, Georgia; joined a jazz band, and while in Milwaukee, met and married Felice (1945); they wrote "Country Boy" (1949), "It's a Lovely, Lovely World," "Our Honeymoon" (1952), "Hey Joe" (1953), "Just Wait 'Till I Get You Alone," "Back Up, Buddy" (1954), "I've Been Thinking" and "Richest Man" (1955), "Bye Bye Love" (1957), "Bird Dog" (1958), "Blue Boy" (1958), "Mexico" (1961), "Baltimore" and "I Love to Dance with Annie" (1964).

BRYANT, DAN

b. 1833 Troy, New York, d. 1875 New York City. Actor and popular lyricist. Born Daniel W. O'Brien; was an early minstrel showman; in 1849 he joined the minstrel troup the Sable Harmonists; in 1857 Dan and his brothers Jerry and Neil formed Bryant's Minstrels; he wrote the lyrics "Turkey in the Straw" (1861) based on the tune "Zip Coon"; died of pneumonia.

BRYANT, GILMORE WARD

b. 1859 Bethel, Vermont, d. 1946. Organist, pianist, and teacher. His wife was also a singer and teacher; he studied with Petersilea in Boston; taught at Wesleyan Female Institute, Staunton, Virginia; wrote piano pieces.

BRYANT, IVY ("JIMMY")

b. 1925 Pavo, Georgia. Singer and guitarist. On radio in Panama City, Florida (1936-38); WRC, Washington, D.C. (1946-47); with "Russell Hayden Show" (1947-48); Roy Rogers (1949-53); Cliffie Stone's "Hometown Jamboree," Hollywood (1950-58).

BRYANT, PAUL C.

b. 1933 Long Branch, New Jersey. Organist. Studied at Gray's Conservatory of Music at Los Angeles; appeared on CBS radio at age nine; appeared in films (1938-48); played in Los Angeles night clubs in 1950s; also on "Steve Allen's Jazz Scene USA" TV series.

BRYANT, RAPHAEL ("RAY")

b. 1931 Philadelphia, Pennsylvania. Black pianist and composer. Formed his own trio (1960); wrote "Little Susie" and "Cubano Chant."

BRYANT, THOMAS HOYT ("SLIM")

b. 1908 Atlanta, Georgia. Sing r and songwriter. Member of the Georgia Wildcats (1931-34); organized his own group (1935), later known as Slim Bryant and His Wildcats; wrote—"Eeny Meeny Dixie Deeny" (1947), "The Golden Train," "Gal with This Coal Black Hair," "Rose of Shenandoah Valley."

BRYANT, WILLIAM CULLEN

b. 1794 Cummington, Massachusetts, d. 1878 New York City. Poet and hymnist. Educated at Williams College, Williamstown, Mass. and admitted to the bar in 1815; practiced law for ten years, and later was editor of the *New York Evening Post* for almost fifty years; wrote "Thou, Whose Unmeasured Temple Stands" (1835, tune—"Dundee," included in *Congregational Hymns*, London, 1864) and "O North, with All Thy Vales of Green" (1869, m. Donald S. Barrows), and "The Hunter's Serenade" (old German air).

BRYANT, WILLIAM STEVEN (WILLIE)

b. 1908 New Orleans, Louisiana, d. 1964 Los Angeles, California. Black bandleader. Led his own big band (1933-39); later in films and on TV; died of a heart attack.

BRYMM, JAMES TIM

b. 1881 Kinston, North Carolina, d. 1946 New York City. Black composer and bandleader. With Chris Smith, wrote "Good Morning Carrie" (w. Cecil Mack); bandmaster of the "Seventy Black Devils" of the 350th Infantry (formerly 8th Illinois) during World War I.

BUCHANAN, ANNABEL (MORRIS)

b. 1889 Groesbeck, Texas. Teacher and compiler. She studied at Landon Conservatory, Dallas, Texas, and taught in schools in Texas and Oklahoma, then at Stonewall Jackson College, Abington,

Virginia; organized the annual White-Top Folk Festivals in Virginia (1931); compiled *Folk-Hymns of America* (1938); with Hilton Rufty and John Powell, compiled *Twelve Folk Hymns* (1934).

BUCHANAN, JAMES GILBERT ("GOOBER")

b. 1917 Hillsdale, Kentucky.
Vocal leader. Leader of the Kentuckians (1938 and 1943-55).

BUCK, DUDLEY

b. 1839 Hartford, Connecticut, d. 1909 Orange, New Jersey. Noted organist and composer. Studied in Leipzig (1856-61) and then in Paris; organist in Hartford, Chicago, Boston, and at Holy Trinity, Brooklyn, New York (1877-1901); wrote *The Centennial Meditation of Columbia* (w. Sidney Lanier) which was conducted by Theodore Thomas at the Centennial in Philadelphia (1876), *The Light of Asia, The Golden Legend* (1880, w. H.W. Longfellow), Te Deum in B Minor and the Easter anthem "As It Began to Dawn."

BUCK, EDWARD EUGENE (GENE)

b. 1885 Detroit, Michigan, d. 1957 Great Neck, New York. Lyricist. Educated at University of Detroit, and Detroit Art School; early designer of sheet music covers; with David Stamper, composer, wrote lyrics for *Ziegfeld Follies:* "Daddy Has a Sweetheart and Mother Is Her Name" (1912), "Just You and I and the Moon," "Without You," "Everybody Sometime Must Love Somebody" (1913).

BUCK, RICHARD HENRY

b. 1870 Philadelphia, Pennsylvania, d. 1956 Manhasset, New York. Lyricist. Wrote the lyrics "Kentucky Babe" (1896, m. Adam Geibel, the song was popularized by Bessie Davis); also wrote "Dear Old Girl" (1903, m. T.F. Morse), and "Where the Southern Roses Grow" (m. Morse).

BUCKAROOS, THE

Buck Owens, Don Rich, Tom Brumley, Doyle Holley, Willie Cantu, et al.

BUCKINGHAMS, THE (rock group)

Denny Tufano, lead vocals; Carl Giammarese, lead guitar; Jon-Jon Poulos, drums; Nick Fortune, bass; Marty Grebb, organ; originated in Chicago; albums—*Buckinghams' Greatest Hits, In One Ear and Gone Tomorrow* (1968), *Portraits, Time and Charges* (1967).

BUCKLEY, HELEN DALLAM

b. 1899 Chicago, Illinois.
Singer, composer, teacher, and writer. Educated at American Conservatory, Chicago (later taught there), also at Academy of Allied Arts, New York City; works—*Quartet for Strings, Piano* (Chicago News prize), *An Indian Legend* (Chicago News prize), *The Slave, Temple Song, Earth in Cycle* (soprano, harp, strings and quartet).

BUCKLEY, R. BISHOP

b. ca. 1810 England, d. 1867 Quincy, Massachusetts. Minstrel showman. Organized Buckley's Minstrels (1843); credited by some persons as having written "Wait for the Wagon" (1851, w. George P. Knauff).

BUCKNER, JOHN EDWARD ("TEDDY")

b. 1909 Sherman, Texas.
Black trumpeter. Played in name bands during 1950s; later led his own band; played at the Huddle in West Covina, California (1962-66); also on "Steve Allen's Jazz Scene USA."

BUDIMER, DENNIS MATTHEW

b. 1938 Los Angeles, California.
Guitarist. Played with Harry James and Chico Hamilton in 1950s; in armed forces (1961-63); accompanied Julie London and Bobby Troup on tour of Japan (1963); recorded with Bud Shank, Dizzy Gillespie and others.

BUDWIG, MONTY

b. 1929 Pender, Nebraska.
Bass player. Played in various combos in Los Angeles during 1950s; later with Benny Goodman Quartet in New York City; toured Japan (1964); recorded with S. Manne, Bill Evans, and Victor Feldman.

BUELL, MRS. HARRIETT EUGENIA (PECK)

b. 1834 Cazenovia, New York, d. 1910 Washington, D.C. Hymnist. One summer in 1878, while at Thousand Island Park, New York, she wrote the hymn "Child of a King"; she sent it to the *Northern Christian Advocate,* Syracuse, New York, which published the poem; it was first sung in the Manlius Methodist Church, Manlius, New York.

BUFFALO SPRINGFIELD (rock group)

Richie Furay, vocals and rhythm guitar; Neil Young, vocals and lead guitar; Jim Messina, bass guitar; Dewey Martin, vocals and drums; Stephen Stills, vocals, guitar, and songwriter;

started in Los Angeles; albums—*Buffalo Springfield, Buffalo Springfield Again, Last Time Around, Retrospective.*

BUHLIG, RICHARD

b. 1880 Chicago, Illinois, d. 1952 Los Angeles, California. Pianist. Studied with Leschetizky in Vienna; toured Europe; made his American debut with the Philadelphia Orchestra (1907); taught at the Institute of Musical Art, New York City (1918-20), then lived in Los Angeles.

BUKOFZER, MANFRED

b. 1910 Oldenburg, Germany, d. 1955 Berkeley, California. Teacher and writer. Studied musicology in Heidelberg, Berlin, and Basel; taught in Basel, Cambridge, and Oxford, then came to America where he became an instructor at the University of California, Berkeley (1941); wrote *Music in the Baroque Era, Music in the Classic Period 1750-1827* and compiled the *Complete Works of John Dunstable.*

BULFINCH, STEPHEN GREENLEAF

b. 1809 Boston, Massachusetts, d. 1870 Washington, D.C. Hymnist and compiler. Educated at Columbian College (now George Washington University), and Harvard Divinity School (1830); as a Unitarian minister in Charleston, South Carolina (1831), he assisted the Rev. Dr. Samuel Gilman; then he was pastor of churches in Pittsburgh and Washington, D.C.; published *Contemplations of the Saviour* (1832) which included twenty-eight of his hymns, and *The Harp and the Cross* (1857).

BULL, AMOS

b. 1744, d. ca. 1805 Hartford, Connecticut. Teacher and composer. In 1766 he was living in New Haven, Connecticut, and in 1795 in Hartford; published *The Responsary* (1795), which included some of his music.

BULLARD, FREDERICK F.

b. 1864 Boston, Massachusetts, d. there 1904. Popular composer. Wrote the music for "A Stein Song" (1898, w. Richard Hovey), "A June Lullaby," "From Dreams of Thee," "The Pigtail," "Beam from Yonder Star," "Sweet and Clear the Birds Are Singing," "The Indifferent Mariner" (w. A. Macy).

BUNCH, JOHN L., JR.

b. 1921 Tipton, Indiana.
Pianist. With Woody Herman and Benny Goodman; formed own quartet (ca. 1955); toured with Goodman to Soviet (1962) and Mexico (1963); with Gene Krupa Quartet (1961-64); appeared on many TV shows.

BUNKER, LAWRENCE BENJAMIN (LARRY)

b. 1928 Long Beach, California.
Drummer and vibraharpist. Studio musician in Hollywood; led own quartet (1963); with Bill Evans on drums (1964-65) and toured Europe; with Judy Garland in Australia (1964); with Stan Getz in Japan (1965).

BUNN, TEDDY

b. 1909 Freeport, L.I., New York.
Black guitarist and songwriter. Wrote "If You See Me Comin'" (with Mezz Mezzrow).

BURDETT, GEORGE ALBERT

b. 1856 Boston, Massachusetts, d. 1943.
Organist, composer, and writer. Wrote "O Little Town of Bethlehem" (not to be confused with carol of same title by Phillips Brooks and L.H. Redner).

BURGESS, GEORGE

b. 1809 Providence, Rhode Island, d. 1866 Haiti. Hymnist. Graduated Brown University (1826); rector of Christ Church, Hartford, Connecticut (1834); became bishop of Maine (1847) and rector of Christ Church, Gardiner, Maine; wrote "Lord, in Thy Name We Spread the Sail" (*Connecticut Psalms and Hymns,* 1845), and "The Harvest Dawn Is Near" (in his *Book of Psalms,* 1839).

BURGESS, WILMA

b. 1939 Orlando, Florida.
Singer. Graduated Stetson University, De Land, Florida; moved to Nashville; hit records were *Baby* (1966), *Fifteen Days* (1967), *Wilma Burgess Sings Misty Blue* (1967), *Parting* (1969).

BURGSTALLER, ALOIS

b. 1871 Holzkirchen, Germany, d. 1945 Gmund, Austria. Tenor. Pupil of Bellurth and Kniese, sang at Bayreuth after 1894; with Metropolitan Opera, New York City from 1903.

BURKE, BILLIE

b. 1885 Washington, D.C.
Singer and actress. She sang "My Little Canoe" (m. Jerome Kern) in *The School Girl* at the Pavilion Music Hall, London, England (1903); later she became a stage and screen star; married Florenz Ziegfeld.

BURKE, JOE

b. 1884 Philadelphia, Pennsylvania, d. 1950 Upper Darby, Pennsylvania. Pianist and popular composer. Wrote "Down Honolulu Way" (1916, with Earl Burnett, w. James E. Dempsey), "Tip Toe Through the Tulips with Me" (1929, w. Al Dubin, in *Gold Diggers of Broadway*), "Carolina Moon" (1928, w. Benny Davis), "Moon Over Miami" (1936, w. Edgar Leslie), "It Looks Like Rain in Cherry Blossom Lane" (1937, w. Leslie), "By the River of Roses" (1944, Marty Symes), "Ramblin' Rose" (1948, Joseph McCarthy, Jr.).

BURKE, JOHNNY

b. 1908 Antioch, California, d. 1964 New York City. Lyricist and publisher. Attended Crane College, Chicago, Illinois, and University of Wisconsin, Madison; staff songwriter for music firms in Chicago and New York; wrote the lyrics for a number of songs for James V. Monaco, James van Heusen, and Victor Schertzinger; his hit lyrics include "Pennies from Heaven," "Swinging on a Star" (which won an Academy Award for the best song of 1944).

BURKETT, HAROLD BRENT

b. 1939 Steubenville, Ohio.
Singer. Member of the Four Guys, vocal group.

BURLEIGH, CECIL

b. 1885 Wyoming, New York.
Violinist and composer. Studied in Berlin, then in Chicago with Sauret, Hugo Heerman, and Felix Borowski, concert violinist; taught after 1909 in Denver, Colorado, Sioux City, Iowa, and Missoula, Montana; later taught at the University of Wisconsin, Madison; composed violin works and songs.

BURLEIGH, HENRY THACKER

b. 1866 Erie, Pennsylvania, d. 1949 Stamford, Connecticut. Noted black singer and composer. Student of Antonin Dvořák in New York City; baritone soloist at St. George's Episcopal Church, New York City (1894) and sang *The Palms* in that church every Sunday for the next fifty years; made a number of arrangements of Negro spirituals and folk songs; best known for his arrangement of "Deep River."

BURLEIGH, WILLIAM HENRY

b. 1812 Woodstock, Connecticut, d. 1871 Brooklyn, New York. Hymnist. Raised in Plainfield, Connecticut; became editor of *The Christian Freeman*, Hartford, Connecticut (1843); later he was an editor in Syracuse, New York, then Harbour Master at New York City for fifteen years; wrote the hymn "Lead Us, O Father, in the Paths of Peace" (tune—"Petrie" from an old Irish air adapted by Martin Shaw, and second tune "Burleigh" by Joseph Barnby).

BURLIN, NATALIE CURTIS

b. 1875 New York City, d. 1921 Paris, France. Composer, writer, and pianist. She wrote about Indian and Negro music; married Paul Burlin, the painter.

BURMEISTER, RICHARD

b. 1860 Hamburg, Germany, d. 1944.
Teacher. Studied with Liszt at Weimar for three years; came to America; taught at Peabody Institute, Baltimore; composed Concerto in D Minor, for piano and orchestra; also other piano pieces.

BURNAP, UZZIAH C.

b. 1834, d. 1900.
Compiler of hymns. With John K. Paine, he was musical editor of *Hymns and Songs of Praise* (1874).

BURNETT, CAROL

b. 1935 San Antonio, Texas.
Singer and M.C. (Mistress of Ceremonies) on her own TV show on CBS; guest stars included Cass Elliott and Bernadette Peters 1971; albums—*Here's Carol, Julie and Carol at Carnegie Hall, Once Upon a Mattress, Together Again for the First Time* (with Martha Raye).

BURNETT, CHESTER ARTHUR ("HOWLIN' WOLF")

b. 1910 Aberdeen, Mississippi.
Black singer. Formed a band in West Memphis, Arkansas, in the 1940s; recorded "Moanin' at Midnight" (1951), "Sitting on Top of the World" (1957), wrote "Killing Floor," later called "Killing Ground"· was a sensation at the 1966 Folk Festival at Newport, R.I.; albums—*Howlin' Wolf, Tune Box, Evil, Real Folk Blues—Howlin' Wolf, More Real Folk Blues, Moanin' in the Moonlight.*

BURNETT, ERNIE

b. 1884 Cincinnati, Ohio, d. 1959 Saranac Lake, New York. Composer and vaudeville entertainer. Studied in Italy and Austria, and at Charlottenburg Conservatory; returned to U.S. (1901); vaudeville pianist; served in 89th Division, AEF in World War I; led own dance orchestra; founded own publishing company;

wrote "My Melancholy Baby" (1911, w. George A. Norton).

BURNETT, JOE

b. 1927 Dallas, Texas.
Trumpeter and flügelhorn player. With Woody Herman (1953-54), M. Ferguson (1956-58), also with Stan Kenton and Charlie Barnet; toured Japan with Julie London (1964); married singer Irene Kral.

BURNETTE, LESTER ALVIN

b. 1911 Summun, Illinois, d. 1967.
Songwriter. Writer in films after 1934, spent ten years at Republic Studios and ten years with Columbia Pictures writing westerns; songs included "Hominy Grits," "Ridin' Down the Canyon," "Mamma Don't Allow No Music," "It's My Lazy Day," "My Home Town," "Cat Fish Take a Look at That Worm," "Jackass Mail."

BURNS, KENNETH C. ("JETHRO")

b. 1920 Knoxville, Tennessee.
Singer and mandolin player. Partner with Henry D. Haynes in the team "Homer & Jethro"; their hit records were "Battle of Kukamonga," "Daddy Sang Bass," "Hound Dog in the Window" and "Let Me Go Lover"; they made fifty albums; their LP-Victor records included *Barefoot Ballads, Worst of Homer & Jethro* (1958), *Life Can Be Miserable* (1959), *Songs My Mother Never Sang* (1961).

BURNS, RALPH

b. 1922 Newton, Massachusetts.
Pianist and composer. With Woody Herman's band (1944); later with small combos; wrote *Summer Sequence, Bijou, Early Autumn.*

BURR, WILLARD, JR.

b. 1852 Ravenna, Ohio, d. 1915 Boston, Massachusetts. Composer and writer. Studied with Haupt in Berlin; later resided in Boston; composed chamber music, piano pieces.

BURRELL, KENNETH EARL (KENNY)

b. 1931 Detroit, Michigan.
Guitarist. Graduated Wayne State University, Detroit (1955); played with Dizzy Gillespie and Benny Goodman; later led his own group; played at the Newport Jazz Festival, New York City (1972).

BURRITT, WILLIAM NELSON

b. 1852 Albion, Michigan, d. 1929.
Teacher. Studied under Vannuccini, Vannini, and George Henschel; teacher of voice in St. Paul, Minnesota.

BURROWS, ABRAM S. (ABE)

b. 1910 Brooklyn, New York.
Librettist. Librettist for *Guys & Dolls* (1950) with Jo Swerling (m. Frank Loesser), and *How to Succeed in Business Without Really Trying* (1961) with Jack Weinstock and Willie Gilbert (m. Frank Loesser).

BURT, BATES GILBERT

b. 1878 Wheeling, West Virginia, d. 1948 Edgewood, Maryland. Composer. Educated at Kenyon College, Gambier, Ohio, and Seabury Divinity School and ordained (1904); served as a chaplain in France in World War I; rector of All Saint's Church, Pontiac, Michigan (1922-47); wrote the tunes "Shaddick" (1941) for "City of God, How Broad and Far" (w. Samuel Johnson), "Prayer Is the Soul's Sincere Desire" (w. James Montgomery), and "Lynne" (1935) for "O God of Youth, Whose Spirit."

BURT, NATHANIEL CLARK

b. 1825 Fairton, New Jersey, d. 1874 Rome, Italy. Compiler. Graduated Princeton (1846); Presbyterian minister in Springfield, Ohio, Baltimore, Maryland, and Cincinnati, Ohio; in 1844 with John Cole, he compiled and issued *Music for the Church*, for his church in Baltimore; the volume included sixty-two Psalm and hymn tunes by Christopher Meinecke among others.

BURTON, FREDERICK RUSSELL

b. 1861 Jonesville, Michigan, d. 1909 Lake Hopatcong, New Jersey. Composer. Graduated Harvard; founded a choral society in Yonkers, New York (1896); composed a cantata *Hiawatha.*

BURTON, GARY

b. 1943 Anderson, Indiana.
Vibraharpist. Debut in Nashville (1960); toured South America (1962) with the Gary Burton Quartet; toured Japan (1963) with George Shearing; with Stan Getz (1964-66); appeared in films; albums—*Gary Burton Quartet in Concert, Country Roads & Other Places, Duster, Genuine Tong Funeral, Lofty Fake Anagram, Tennessee Firebird, Throb, Time Machine.*

BUSCH, ADOLF G. W.

b. 1891 Siegen, Germany, d. 1952 Guilford, Vermont. Violinist and composer. Studied at the Cologne Conservatory; first violinist with the Vienna Orchestra (1912-18); toured Europe (1918-22); came to America where he toured the states as a soloist with leading orchestras; composed orchestral and chamber works, and songs.

BUSCH, CARL

b. 1862 Bjerre, Denmark, d. 1943 Kansas City, Missouri. Conductor and composer. Studied at the Brussels Conservatory; came to Kansas City (1887), organized and became conductor of the Kansas City Symphony (1912); composed cantatas, orchestral and chamber works, anthems and songs.

BUSHKIN, JOE

b. 1916 New York City.
Pianist and songwriter. Played with Tommy Dorsey and Benny Goodman in 1940s; with Louis Armstrong in 1950s; led his own quartet in 1960s; retired in Kamuela, Hawaii.

BUTCHER, DWIGHT

b. 1911 Oakdale, Tennessee.
Singer and songwriter. Sang under the names of Slim Oakdale and Hank Hall, in addition to his own name; wrote "When Jimmie Rodgers Said Goodbye" (1933), "Love Letters Bring Memories of You" (1933), "Best Time of All."

BUTLER, CARL ROBERTS

b. 1927 Knoxville, Tennessee.
Singer, guitarist, and songwriter. Joined Grand Ole Opry, Nashville (1948); wrote "If Teardrops Were Pennies," "Crying Alone," "Grief in My Heart," "Loving Arms," "So Close," "Country Mile," "Too Late to Try Again" (1964); his wife Pearl joined him as a team and they made a hit with "Don't Let Me Cross Over" (1962); LP successes were *Carl Butler* (1963) and *Loving Arms* (1964).

BUTLER, FRANK

b. 1928 Kansas City, Missouri.
Drummer. With Dave Brubeck (1950); with Duke Ellington (1954); played in Los Angeles night clubs with small groups in 1960s.

BUTLER, JERRY

b. 1940 Philadelphia, Pennsylvania.
Black singer and songwriter. Joined the Impressions at the age of eighteen; recorded "For Your Precious Love" then went out on his own; organized Butler Music Workshop (1969) with black songwriters—Billy Butler (his brother), Terrace Callier, Larry Wade, Sam Brown, Charles Jackson, and James Blumenberg; albums—*Jerry Butler's Golden Hits, Live, Gift of Love, Ice Man Cometh, Ice on Ice, Just Beautiful, Mr. Dream Merchant, Soul Artistry, Soul Goes On;* at Alice Tully Hall, New York City (1972); conducted Jerry Butler Workshop (soul music) in Chicago (1972).

BUTTERFIELD, BILLY

b. 1917 Middletown, Ohio.
Jazz trumpeter. Played in Bob Crosby's band; also in Benny Goodman's band.

BUTTERFIELD, DON

b. 1923 Centralia, Washington.
Tuba player. Played with Teddy Charles and Charles Mingus in 1950s; at the Antibes Festival on the French Riviera (1962) with Dizzy Gillespie's band; at 1963 Newport Jazz Festival with Dakota Staton with Oliver Nelson at first jazz concert at Philharmonic Hall, New York City.

BUTTERFIELD, JAMES A.

b. 1837 Hertfordshire, England, d. 1891 Chicago, Illinois. Teacher and popular composer. Came to America in 1856 and resided in Chicago, Illinois; wrote "The South, Our Country" (1861, w. E.M. Thompson), "The Volunteer's Farewell, The Soldier's Request" (w. Mrs. Clara Eastland), "Lincoln's Requiem" (1865, w. Irene Boynton), "When the Boys Come Home" (1865, w. Robert Morris); when Butterfield came across a book of poems entitled *Maple Leaves* by George W. Johnson, he was attracted to the poem "When You and I Were Young Maggie," and set it to music (1866).

BUTTERFIELD, PAUL

b. 1941 Chicago, Illinois.
Singer and harmonica player. Leader of Paul Butterfield Blues Band since 1965; started in Chicago; albums—*Butterfield Blues Band, Keep on Moving, East-West, In My Own Dream, Resurrection of Pigboy Crabshaw, You Are What You Eat* (soundtrack).

BUTTERWORTH, HEZEKIAH

b. 1839 Warren, Rhode Island, d. there 1905. Hymnist. On the editorial staff of the *Youth's Companion* for twenty-five years; wrote the hymns "O Church! Arise and Sing" (m. C.C. Case), the cantata *Under the Palms—Captive Judah in Babylon* (m. George F. Root), and the lyrics "The Bird with the Broken Pinion" (m. F.M. Lamb and second tune by George C. Stebbins); published *Story of the Hymns* (1875) and *Story of the Tunes* (1890); also wrote "The Schoolhouse and the Flag" (m. Southwick).

BUZZI-PECCIA, ARTURO

b. 1854 Milan, Italy, d. 1943 New York City. Composer. Studied with his father, Antonio

Buzzi, also with Saint-Saëns; educated at Royal Conservatory of Milan; came to the U.S. (1898); wrote *Mariolina: A Love Call, Forza d'Amore* (opera), and *Voyage des Noces* (piano suite).

BYARD, JOHN A., JR. ("JAKI")

b. 1922 Worcester, Massachusetts.
Black pianist and songwriter. With Maynard Ferguson (1959-62); then with Charles Mingus; also led his own bands; wrote "Here to Here," "Twelve."

BYAS, CARLOS WESLEY ("DON")

b. 1912 Muskogee, Oklahoma, d. 1972 Amsterdam, Netherlands. Black tenor saxist. Played with Don Redman, Lucky Millinder, Eddie Mallory, and Andy Kirk during 1930s; later with Count Basie and Dizzy Gillespie; toured Europe after 1946 and remained there; at Berlin Jazz Festival (1965); toured Japan with Art Blakey (1971); died of cancer.

BYERS, WILLIAM MITCHELL (BILLY)

b. 1927 Los Angeles, California.
Trombonist. Performer, conductor, and arranger during the 1950s in Los Angeles and New York; arranger for Quincy Jones after 1959; later with Count Basie.

BYLES, NATHAN

b. 1706, d. 1788.
Hymnist. Educated at Harvard (1725); Congregational minister in Boston; wrote "When Wild Confusion Wrecks the Air" which appeared in the *Appendix to Tate & Brady*, published by S. Kneeland (1760) and also included in *Belknap's Selection* (1795).

BYRD, CHARLES L. (CHARLIE)

b. 1925 Suffolk, Virginia.
Guitarist. Played in his own Showboat Club in Washington, D.C. in 1960s; toured South America (1961); recorded "Jazz Samba" with Stan Getz (1962) in Washington, D.C.; influential in starting the bossa nova craze in the United States; gave a recital in the White House (1965) for Mrs. Lyndon Johnson; Charlie Byrd Trio played at Newport Jazz Festival, New York City (1972).

BYRD, DONALD

b. 1932 Detroit, Michigan.
Black jazz trumpeter and composer. Studied with Nadia Boulanger in Paris (1963); taught at Music and Art High School in New York City; played at jazz festivals in Europe; wrote "Cecile," "Pure D. Funk," "The Cat Walk," "Shangri-La," "Elijah," "Noah," "Bossa."

BYRD, GENE ("JOE")

b. 1933 Chuckatuck, Virginia.
Bass player. Brother of Charlie Byrd; studied at Peabody Conservatory in Baltimore; joined his brother's group (1964).

BYRD, JERRY LESTER

b. 1920 Lima, Ohio.
Singer, guitarist, and songwriter. Member of Ernie Lee's Pleasant Valley Boys (1944-46); leader of the Pleasant Valley Boys (1948-51); wrote "Steelin' the Chimes," "Steelin' the Blues," "Stars and Steel Guitars," "Blues Guaranteed," "Rominiscing," "Waltz Tropicalo."

BYRDS (rock group)

Started by Roger McGuinn, lead vocals and guitar; Gene Clark, David Crosby, Mike Clarke and Chris Hillman; played at Ciros on Hollywood's Sunset Strip; later all dropped out except McGuinn; joined by Jay Yorke, bass; Clarence White, guitar; Gene Parsons, drums; albums—*Ballad of Easy Rider, Byrd's Greatest Hits, Dr. Byrds and Mr. Hyde, Fifth Dimension, Mr. Tambourine Man, Notorious Byrd Brothers, Sweetheart of the Rodeo, Turn, Turn, Turn.*

CACERES, ERNIE

b. 1911 Rockport, Texas, d. 1971 San Antonio, Texas. Jazz clarinetist and baritone saxophonist. Played in bands led by Bobby Hackett, Jack Teagarden, Benny Goodman, Tommy Dorsey and played the clarinet and alto sax on Glenn Miller recordings (1939-42); served in the army in World War II; formed the Caceres Trio with his brother, Emilio Caceres, jazz violinist and guitarist, in the 1930s.

CADMAN, CHARLES WAKEFIELD

b. 1881 Johnstown, Pennsylvania, d. 1946 Los Angeles, California. Noted composer—operas, for orchestra and popular songs. Composed *Shanewis* (opera), *Thunderbird* (orchestral suite), and the songs "At Dawning" and "The Land of the Sky-blue Water"; he was interested in Indian music.

CADY, CALVIN BRAINERD

b. 1851 Barry, Illinois, d. 1928.
Writer, publisher, and teacher. Nephew of C.M. Cady; studied at Oberlin College, Ohio; then at Leipzig Conservatory; taught at Oberlin (1874-79), at University of Michigan at Ann Arbor (1880-88), and at Chicago Conservatory after 1888.

CAESAR, IRVING

b. 1895 New York City.
Lyricist. Studied to be a concert pianist at the Third Street Music School Settlement, New York City, at the age of six; the school was founded by Emily Wagner (1894); wrote the lyrics for "Crazy Rhythm" (m. Joseph Meyer and Roger Wolf), and with Otto Harbach the lyrics "Tea for Two" (m. Vincent M. Youmans), which appeared in *No, No Nanette,* also "Swanee" (m. George Gershwin), introduced by Arthur Pryor's band at the Capital Theatre, New York City (1919).

CAGE, JOHN MILTON, JR.

b. 1912 Los Angeles, California.
Noted composer. Attended Pomona College, Claremont, California, and studied with Fannie Charles Dillon and later with Lazare Levy in Paris, then taught at the Cornish School, Seattle; later he taught at Mills College, Oakland, California, and the New School for Social Research, New York City; known for his *Sonatas and Interludes* (1946-48), *Water Music* and *Williams Mix* (1952, composed while throwing Chinese dice for the mix); in his *Variations* (1958-65) the performer improvises sounds heard in everyday movement—scraping, scratching, etc.

CAGLE, BUDDY

b. 1936 Concord, North Carolina.
Singer and guitarist. Raised in the Children's Home, Winston-Salem, N.C.; after four years in the air force, he started singing professionally; hit recordings were "The Gold Cup," "Sing a Sad Song," "Your Mother's Prayer," "Tonight I'm Coming Home," and "Apologize."

CAHIER, MME. CHARLES

b. 1875 Nashville, Tennessee, d. 1951 Manhattan Beach, California. Contralto. Born Sara Jane Layton-Walker; studied with Jean de Reszke; debut in opera as "Orfeo" (Nice, 1904); joined Vienna Royal Opera (1909), and Metropolitan Opera, New York City (1912).

CAHILL, MARIE

b. 1870 Brooklyn, New York, d. 1933 New York City. Singer and actress. Debut in road company of *Kathleen Mavourneen* in 1880s; in *C.O.D.* at Poole's Eighth St. Theatre, New York City (1888); in Charles Hoyt's *The Tin Soldier* (1888); made a hit singing "Nancy Brown" in *The Wild Rose* (1902) and "Under the Bamboo Tree" in *Sally in Our Alley* (1902); appeared in various musicals (1903-30); died of chronic Bright's disease.

CAHN, SAMMY

b. 1913 New York City.
Lyricist. With Saul Chaplin, he wrote "Bei Mir Bist du Schoen" (based on a Yiddish song), made famous by the Andrews Sisters (1938); wrote lyrics for Alfred Newman, Jule Styne, and James van Heusen; won Academy Awards for "Three Coins in a Fountain" (1954, m. Jule Styne), "All the Way" (1957, m.

van Heusen), "High Hopes" (1959, m. van Heusen), "Call Me Irresponsible" (1963, m. van Heusen).

CAIN, JACQUELINE RUTH (JACKIE)

b. 1928 Milwaukee, Wisconsin.
Singer. Vocalist for Charlie Ventura; married Roy Kral (1948); worked with her husband in Las Vegas night clubs during 1950s; in New York after 1962; appeared on TV shows.

CAIOLA, ALEXANDER EMIL (AL)

b. 1920 Jersey City, New Jersey.
Guitarist. With Hugo Winterhalter (1955), Percy Faith (1956), and Andre Kostelanetz (1957); led own group after 1958; accompanist for Caterina Valente in Rome (1962).

CALDWELL, ALBERT ("HAPPY")

b. 1903 Chicago, Illinois.
Black tenor saxist. Played with Armstrong, Condon, Waller, and Henderson; with Louis Metcalf, Jimmy Rushing and others during 1960s; led his own quintet.

CALHOUN, EDDIE

b. 1921 Clarksdale, Mississippi.
Bass player. Served in army during World War II; with Prince Cooper in Chicago after 1946; with Dick Davis (1947), Ahmad Jamal (1949), Horace Henderson (1952), and Johnny Griffin (1954); with Erroll Garner after 1955.

CALLAHAN, J. WILL

b. 1874 Columbus, Indiana, d. 1946 New Smyrna Beach, Florida. Singer and lyricist. Wrote "Smiles" (1917—"There are smiles that make us happy" m. Lee S. Roberts).

CALLAS, MARIA

b. 1923 New York City.
Soprano. Born Maria Cecilia Sophia Kalogeropoulos; studied with Elvira de Hidalgo in Athens; debut in opera there; at the Arena in Verona, Italy as La Gioconda (1947); sang *Norma* in Chicago, Dallas, and at the Metropolitan Opera, New York City (1956); due to her stirring singing, acting, and fiery temperament, became a widely known singer; married Giovanni Battista Meneghini, later divorced; sang in *Tosca* (1965); taught at Juilliard (1972).

CALLAWAY, PAUL SMITH

b. 1909 Atlanta, Illinois.
Organist and bandmaster. Studied at Westminster College, Fulton, Missouri, and William Jewell College, Liberty, Missouri; organist in Rock Falls, Illinois, New York City, Grand Rapids, Michigan, and the Washington Cathedral, Washington, D.C. (1939); army bandmaster in World War II.

CALLENDER, GEORGE ("RED")

b. 1918 Richmond, Virginia.
Tuba and bass player. With Armstrong, L. Young, and E. Garner in 1940s; on NBC-TV staff after 1964; at 1962 Monterey Jazz Festival; with C. Mingus (1964); wrote "Primrose Lane."

CALLOWAY, CABELL (CAB)

b. 1907 Rochester, New York.
Black bandleader and singer. Raised in Baltimore; studied law in Chicago; led a band called "The Alabamians" then "The Missourians" which took his name in 1930; appeared in films; broke up his band (1948); appeared with small groups; appeared in night clubs and on television.

CALVÉ, EMMA

b. 1858 Decazeville, France, d. 1942 Millau, France. Noted dramatic soprano. Born Rosa Calvert; at the Convent of the Sacred Heart, Montpellier (1868-73); studied in Paris with Puget (1880); debut as Marguerite in Brussels (1882); studied with Mme. Marchesi; debut in Paris (1884) as Bianca; with Opera Comique (1885-87); as Ophelia in Milan (1887) and hissed there; at Covent Garden, London (1892); with Metropolitan Opera in New York (1893); toured Europe (1894) and America (1895); was a sensation as Carmen; at Manhattan Opera House New York (1908).

CAMERATA SINGERS AND SYMPHONY ORCHESTRA

Conducted by Abraham Kaplan at Carnegie Hall, New York City (March 1972).

CAMERO, CANDIDO

b. 1921 Havana, Cuba.
Conga drummer, bongos. Came to New York (1952); with Kenton, Gillespie, and his own group; appeared on TV shows (1962); toured U.S. (1964) with all-Mexican revue; played in Virgin Islands and Puerto Rico (1965); with Edgar Sampson, wrote "I'll Be Back for More" (w. Sammy Gallop).

CAMERON, JAY

b. 1928 New York City.
Baritone saxist. Played with R. Stewart, Woody Herman, and M. Ferguson; with Slide Hampton (1960-62); toured France (1962) with Hampton; had his own quartet.

CAMMERHOF, JOHANN FRIEDRICH

b. 1721 Magdeburg, East Germany, d. 1751 Bethlehem, Pennsylvania. Hymnist. Was a

Moravian minister, then became bishop of the Unity (United Brethren) (1747); his hymns appeared in Moravian hymnals.

CAMPANARI, LEANDRO

b. 1857 Rovigo, Italy, d. 1939 San Francisco, California. Conductor, violinist, and teacher. Studied at the Milan Conservatory; came to America (1879), organized Campanari String Quartet in Boston; taught at New England Conservatory (1883), and Cincinnati Conservatory (1890); conductor at Milan (1897-1905), and at Manhattan Opera House, New York City (1906); after 1907 taught in San Francisco.

CAMPANINI, CLEOFONTE

b. 1860 Parma, Italy, d. 1919 Chicago, Illinois. Conductor. Studied at the Milan Conservatory, later taught there; conductor at La Scala, Covent Garden, and at the Metropolitan Opera House, New York City (1906-09); married Eva Tetrazzini, operatic soprano (sister of Luisa); conductor of the Chicago Opera (1910) and after 1913 artistic director.

CAMPBELL, ARCHIE

b. 1914 Bulls Gap, Tennessee.
Singer. Started with radio station WNOX, Knoxville, Tennessee on the "Mid-Day Merry-Go-Round" show; served in the navy in World War II; had his own show on WROL-TV, Knoxville; his specialty was rocking gospels and comic songs such as "Beeping Sleauty," "Trouble in the Amen Corner," "Pee Little Thrigs," "Rindercella," and "Bedtime Stories for Adults."

CAMPBELL, FRANCIS JOSEPH

b. 1832 Franklin County, Tennessee, d. 1914. Pianist, manager, and teacher. Lost sight in both eyes at age three; attended a school for the blind in Nashville; taught at Perkins Institute for the Blind in Boston; pupil of Theodore Kullak and Carl Tausig in Berlin; went to England (1871) and started a school in Norwood, London, which became the Royal Normal College and Academy of Music for the Blind, of which he became principal.

CAMPBELL, GLEN

b. 1937 Delight, Arkansas.
Singer and guitarist. Started with his uncle's band in Albuquerque, New Mexico, then formed his own band; hits were "Turn Around, Look at Me" (1961), "Too Late to Worry—Too Blue to Cry," "Gentle on My Mind" (1967, m. John Hartford), "By the Time I Get to Phoenix" (1967, Jim Webb), "Hey Little One" (1968), "Wichita Lineman" (1968), "Galveston" (1969); appeared in films.

CAMPBELL, JIMMY

b. 1903 Scotland, d. 1967.
Trumpeter and songwriter. With Ray Noble and Reg Connelly, wrote "Good Night Sweetheart, Till We Meet Tomorrow" (1931, w. Rudy Vallee); with Harry Woods and Reg Connelly wrote "Try a Little Tenderness."

CAMPBELL, JOHN B.

b. 1856 Bloomington, Indiana, d. 1938.
Composer. Studied at New England Conservatory in Boston; composed many songs.

CAMPBELL, S. BRUNSON ("THE RAGTIME KID")

b. 1884 Washington, Kansas.
Black pianist. Ran away from home to Oklahoma City, then to Sedalia, Missouri, where he studied under Scott Joplin; lived in Arkansas City, Kansas, and El Reno, Oklahoma; played in various bars and night spots in the southwest.

CAMPBELL-TIPTON, LOUIS

b. 1877 Chicago, Illinois, d. 1921 Paris, France. Composer. Studied in Chicago, Boston and Leipzig; composed *Heroic,* sonata for piano; the piano suites, *The Four Seasons* and *Suite Pastorale* for piano and violin, also songs.

CANDIDO *see* CANDIDO CAMERO

CANDLYN, T. FREDERICK H.

b. 1892 England, d. 1964 Point Lookout, New York. Organist. Organist in New York City (1914), then at St. Paul's (Episcopal) Church, Albany, New York; served in the U.S. Army (1917-19), then returned to St. Paul's; afterwards he became organist at St. Thomas' Church, New York City (1943).

CANDOLI, SECONDO ("CONTE")

b. 1927 Mishawaka, Indiana.
Jazz trumpeter. Brother of Pete Candoli; with Howard Rumsey combo (1954-60) at Hermosa Beach, Calif.; later with Woody Herman, Terry Gibbs, and Gerry Mulligan; with Shelly Manne quintet (1961-66); also on TV staff orchestras.

CANDOLI, WALTER JOSEPH ("PETE")

b. 1923 Mishawaka, Indiana.
Trumpeter. Played in Will Bradley's band; left him (1942) to go with Ray McKinley; later with Woody Herman and Teddy Powell; with Hollywood studios after 1955; married singer Betty Hutton.

CANNED HEAT (blues group)

Adolfo De La Parra, drums; Bob "The Bear" Hite, lead vocals; Larry Taylor, bass guitar; Henry Vestine, lead guitar; Alan Wilson, guitar; white blues band from Los Angeles; albums—*Canned Heat, Canned Heat Cookbook, Hallelujah, Livin' the Blues, Vintage.*

CANNON, GUS ("BANJO JOE")

b. 1883 Red Banks, Mississippi.
Black singer, banjoist, and bandleader. Recorded with Victor (1901), blues record; leader of the Jug Stompers; recorded again with Victor (1927).

CANNON, HUGHIE

b. 1877 Detroit, Michigan, d. 1912 Toledo, Ohio. Composer, lyricist, and pianist. Pianist in vaudeville shows; wrote "Bill Bailey, Won't You Come Home?" (1902), "He Done Me Wrong, or Death of Bill Bailey" (1904, tune for *Frankie & Johnny*).

CANOVA, JUDY

b. 1916 Starke, Florida.
Singer and comedienne. Comedienne on Paul Whiteman's radio show; later had the "Judy Canova Show" on NBC for twelve years.

CANSLER, LOMAN

b. 1924 Long Lane, near Springfield, Missouri. Singer and guitarist. Served in the navy in World War II, then attended the University of Missouri, Columbia; taught in North Kansas City, Missouri; recorded *Missouri Folk Songs* (1959) which included "The Blue and the Gray," "When I Leave for to Take My Leave," "Judgment Day," "Far Away," "Kickin' Mule," "Arthur Clyde."

CANTOR, EDDIE

b. 1892 New York City, d. 1964 Beverly Hills, California. Singer and comedian. Born Edward Iskowitz; became famous by singing "Oh! How She Could Yacki, Hacki, Wicki, Woo" (by Albert Von Tilzer) in the *Ziegfeld Follies* of 1916; starred in *Kid Boots* (1923, w. Joseph McCarthy, m. Harry Tierney); also starred in *Banjo Eyes* (1941, m. Vernon Duke).

CAPTAIN BEEFHEART AND HIS MAGIC BAND (blues group)

Don Van Vliet, Alex Snoffer, Doug Moon, Gerald Handley, and John French; albums—*Safe as Milk, Strictly Personal, Trout Mask Replica.*

CAPTAIN STUBBY AND THE BUCCANEERS *see* TOM C. FOUTS

CARAWAN, GUY

b. 1927 Los Angeles, California.
Singer and guitarist. Graduated from the University of California, Los Angeles; attended the World Youth Festival in Moscow (1957) as a folk singer, then toured Red China and Europe; helped form the Sea Island Singers on Johns Island, South Carolina, a group of black folk singers which later appeared at the Newport Folk Festivals.

CAREY, BRUCE ANDERSON

b. 1877 Hamilton, Ontario, Canada.
Conductor. Studied at the Royal College of Music, London, also in Florence and Munich; founder and conductor of the Hamilton Elgar Choir for seventeen years, later Philadelphia Mendelssohn Club and musical director at Girard College (school for orphan boys in Philadelphia); conductor of the Bethlehem (Pa.) Bach Choir (1933-38).

CAREY, MATTHEW

b.1760 Dublin, Ireland, d. 1839 Philadelphia, Pennsylvania. Publisher. Came to Philadelphia before 1790 and published music; published *Philadelphia Harmony or Adgate's Music Improved* (1801); in 1808 he published *A Valuable Selection of Psalm and Hymn Tunes* compiled by Stephen Addington and first published in London (1792); published music for The Independent Tabernacle, which became the Seventh Presbyterian Church in 1819.

CAREY, MUTT ("PAPA")

b. 1891 Hahnville, Louisiana, d. 1948 Los Angeles, California. Black jazz trumpeter and cornetist. Played in Kid's Ory's Band in New Orleans after 1911; later played in Kid Ory's new band in Los Angeles (1944) on the Orson Wells radio show.

CARISI, JOHN E. (JOHNNY)

b. 1922 Hasbrouck Heights, New Jersey. Trumpeter and composer. Played with Glenn Miller's U.S. Air Force Band; later with Claude Thornhill and Charlie Barnet; wrote *Israel*, which was played by Miles Davis' group; toured Southeast Asia and the Middle East as accompanist for a dance company sponsored by the State Department; wrote a chamber piece for New York Saxophone Quartet's concert at Town Hall, New York City (1965).

CARL, WILLIAM CRANE

b. 1865 Bloomfield, New Jersey, d. 1936 New York City. Organist and compiler. Organist of the First Presbyterian Church, Newark, New

Jersey (1882-90) and then at the First Presbyterian Church, New York City (1890-1936); compiled *Masterpieces for the Organ* (1898).

CARLE, FRANKIE

b. 1903 Providence, Rhode Island.
Bandleader and pianist. Started as pianist with Horace Heidt's band; had own band (1944) at Cafe Rouge of Hotel Pennsylvania, New York City, with arrangements by Al Avola; Betty Bonney, soloist (formerly with Les Brown), also Judy Johnson, later Phyllis Lynne, then Marjorie Hughes (later revealed as Carle's daughter); his rendition of "Sunrise Serenade" was included in RCA's *Big Bands' Greatest Hits* (1971).

CARLISLE, CLIFFORD RAYMOND (CLIFF)

b. 1904 Taylorsville, Kentucky.
Singer and guitarist. Cliff and his brother Bill were a team and first appeared on a radio station in Lexington, Kentucky (1931), then Louisville, (1937) and later in Charlotte, N.C.; their LP record was *Fresh from the Country* (1959); their other hits were "Rainbow at Midnight" (comic rendition), "No Help Wanted" and "Too Old to Cut the Mustard"; they joined Grand Ole Opry, Nashville (1954).

CARLISLE, GEORGE F.

b. 1911 Brandon, Manitoba, Canada.
Singer. Raised in Vancouver, British Columbia; leader of the Sierra Range Riders (Georgie Sue Carlisle, Clyde Gummow, Jr., and Howard Lilly, 1950-66).

CARLISLE, WILLIAM (BILL)

b. 1908 Wakefield, Kentucky.
Singer, guitarist, and songwriter. Bill and his brother Cliff were a team; Bill was featured on radio station WSB, Atlanta, Georgia (1949); he wrote "No Help Wanted," "Too Old to Cut the Mustard," "Is Zat You Myrtle" (with the Louvin brothers), "Knothole," "What Kinda Deal Is This" (1966); his LP record is *Best of Bill Carlisle.*

CARLLILE, KENNETH RAY ("THUMBS")

b. 1931 St. Louis, Missouri.
Singer and guitarist. With Jimmy Dickens' band (1949-52), Bill Wimberly's Country Rhythm Boys (1954-57), and Roger Miller's band after 1963; albums—*All Thumbs*, (1966), *Walking in Guitar Land* (1968).

CARLSON, FRANK L.

b. 1914 New York City.
Drummer. Played in Woody Herman's band; recorded with Glenn Miller and Benny Goodman; member of Neophonic Orchestra (1965); worked on TV shows.

CARMICHAEL, HOAGLAND ("HOAGY")

b. 1899 Bloomington, Indiana.
Pianist and popular composer. Studied law at Indiana University, Bloomington, but became a musician instead; composed "Stardust" (1927, w. Mitchell Parish), "Little Old Lady" (w. Stanley Adams), "Small Fry" (w. Frank Loesser), "The Lamplighter's Serenade" (w. P.F. Webster), and with lyrics by Johnny Mercer: "Lazybones" (1932), "The Old Music Master," and "In the Cool, Cool of the Evening."

CARNEY, HARRY HOWELL

b. 1905 Boston, Massachusetts, d. 1974.
Black baritone saxist and composer. Joined Duke Ellington's band (1926) and remained with Ellington for over forty years; with Ellington, wrote "Rockin' in Rhythm" (1930).

CARNEY, JULIA ABIGAIL (FLETCHER)

b. 1823 Boston, Massachusetts, d. 1908.
Hymnist. School teacher in Boston; wrote "Little Drops of Water" which was published in the *Boston Primary School Reader* in 1845 (tune "Camber"—Martin Shaw).

CAROLINA MOUNTAINEERS (vocal group) *see* CHARLES B. MOORE, JR.

CARPENTER, JOHN ALDEN

b. 1876 Park Ridge, Illinois, d. 1951 Chicago, Illinois. Noter composer. Educated at Harvard and studied privately with Sir Edward Elgar in London; resided in Chicago; composed *Adventures in a Perambulator* (for orchestra, 1915), *Krazy Kat* (1921), *Skyscrapers* (a ballet, 1925), and *Sea-Drift* (symphonic poem for orchestra introduced by the Chicago Symphony Orchestra under Frederick Stock, 1933); awarded the National Institute of Arts and Letters gold medal (1947), presented only once in music every nine years.

CARPENTERS, THE (pop singing pair)

From Downey, California. Richard (b. 1947) and his sister Karen (b. 1950), album—*The Carpenters: A Song for You* (1972).

CARR, BENJAMIN

b. 1768 London, England, d. 1831 Philadelphia, Pennsylvania. Noted organist, composer, and publisher. Came to Philadelphia (1793) with his father, Joseph, and brother, Thomas; he opened their third music shop in New York City; organist at St.

Joseph's Roman Catholic Church, Philadelphia, and in charge of music at St. Augustine's Roman Catholic Church there (1801-31); composed *The Archers, or the Mountaineers of Switzerland* (w. William Dunlap) which was produced in the John Street Theatre, New York City, April 18, 1796; compiled *Masses, Vespers, Litanies* (1805, approved by the Rt. Rev. John Carroll, Bishop of Baltimore), *Collection of Chants* (1816), and the *Chorister* (1820); the first to publish "Hail Columbia" (w. Joseph Hopkinson, m. Philip Phile) in Philadelphia in 1798.

CARR, BRUNO

b. 1928 Bronx, New York.
Black drummer. Cousin of Connie Kay, drummer; in U.S. Army (1951-53); bouncer in New York City night clubs (1953-55); played with Ray Charles on European tour (1960-62); with Sarah Vaughan and Shirley Scott (1964); also with Betty Carter, Abbey Lincoln and others.

CARR, JOSEPH

b. 1739 England, d. 1819 Baltimore, Maryland. Publisher. Came to America (1793) with his sons, Benjamin and Thomas, where they opened a music shop and publishing house in Philadelphia; later Joseph and Thomas opened a shop and publishing house in Baltimore (1803); he operated the shop (1803-19); they were the first to publish the "Star Spangled Banner" (Francis Scott Key) in 1814.

CARR, LEROY

b. 1899 Nashville, Tennessee, d. 1935 Indianapolis, Indiana. Black singer, guitarist and pianist. Traveled with Josh White, guitarist and singer, during the 1930s; mellow blues balladeer; wrote "How Long, How Long Blues," "In the Evening When the Sun Goes Down"; also accompanied by Scrapper Blackwell; credited with making the "blues" popular with the whites; died of nephritis brought on by excessive drinking to alleviate the pain of arthritis.

CARR, THOMAS

b. 1780 London, England, d. 1849 Baltimore, Maryland. Organist and publisher. Came to Philadelphia (1793) with his father, Joseph, and his brother, Benjamin; with his father, opened a music store and publishing house in Baltimore, (1803); Thomas operated the shop (1820-23); organized the St. Cecilia Society in Philadelphia (1824) and was its first director.

CARREÑO, TERESA

b. 1853 Caracas, Venezuela, d. 1917 New York City. World-famous pianist. Pupil of L.M. Gottschalk and G. Mathias; in 1863 she toured the United States and played "Listen to the Mocking Bird" (Septimus Winner) in the White House for President Lincoln; composed a string-quartet and piano pieces; her four husbands were E. Sauret, Giovanni Tagliapietra, Eugen d'Albert, and Arturo Tagliapietra (brother of Giovanni); her daughter, Teresa Tagliapietra, was also a pianist.

CARROLL, DIAHANN

b. 1935 Bronx, New York.
Black singer. Albums—*Diahann Carroll, Fun Life, No Strings, Nobody Sees Me Cry.*

CARROLL, GEORGIA LILLIAN

b. 1914 Weed, California.
Singer and songwriter. Sang with Fanchon and Marco; sang in musical comedy; wrote, directed, and appeared in radio show, "Phyllis & Don"; married Kay Kyser, bandleader.

CARROLL, HARRY

b. 1892 Atlantic City, New Jersey, d. 1962 Mt. Carmel, Pennsylvania. Popular composer. Arranger and pianist in Tin Pan Alley, New York City, then a vaudeville actor; wrote "The Trail of the Lonesome Pine" (1913, w. Ballard MacDonald), "By the Beautiful Sea" (w. Harold Atteridge), "I'm Always Chasing Rainbows" (1918, w. Joseph McCarthy, based on a tune by Chopin).

CARROLL (CARRELL), JAMES P.

b. 1787, d. 1854.
Compiler. Resided in Harrisonburg, Virginia; published *Songs of Zion* (1820) and *The Virginia Harmony* (1831).

CARROLL, JIMMY

b. 1913 New York City, d. 1972 Los Angeles, California. Composer and arranger. Graduated Eastman School of Music; attended Juilliard School and Yale Music School; studied with Vittorio Giannini, Nathan Van Cleave, and Joseph Schillinger; arranger for many Mitch Miller recordings; his original music using advanced synthesizer and computer sounds appeared on LP *The Jimmy Carroll Computer Music Maker* (1972).

CARROLL, JOE ("BEBOP")

b. 1919 Philadelphia, Pennsylvania.
Singer. Vocalist for Dizzy Gillespie (1949-53); later soloist; with Woody Herman (1964-65).

CARSON, JAMES

b. 1918 Richmond, Kentucky.
Gospel singer. Son of "Fiddlin' Doc" Roberts; born James William Roberts; attended high school in Union City, Kentucky; first recorded with his father (1929) for Gennett Records in Richmond, Indiana; with Cas Walker's radio and TV shows, Knoxville, Tennessee since 1953; records include "Jesus Spoke to Me" (1947), "The Man of Galilee" (1948), "He Set Me Free" (1948), "Comin' to Carry Me Home" (1955), "When He Heard My Plea" (1956).

CARSON, MARTHA

b. 1921 Neon, Kentucky.
Singer, guitarist, and songwriter. First appearance was on radio station WHIS, Bluefield, West Virginia (1939), then in Atlanta, Georgia, and Knoxville, Tennessee; joined Grand Ole Opry, Nashville (1952); wrote "Satisfied, I'm Gonna Walk and Talk with My Lord" and "I Can't Stand Up Alone."

CARSON, SALLY (BONNIE LOU)

b. 1926 Bloomington, Illinois.
Singer, yodeler, and guitarist. Bonnie Lou was a teenage singer on radio station KMBC, Kansas City, Kansas (1944) when discovered by Bill McCluskey, who hired her for the "Midwestern Hayride," WLW, Cincinnati, Ohio, where she was a favorite for over twenty years; LP album was *Bonnie Lou Sings.*

CARTER, ALVIN PLEASANT

b. ca. 1897 Maces Spring, Virginia, d. there 1960. Singer, guitarist, and songwriter. The vocal group originally consisted of A.P. Carter, his wife Sara, and sister-in-law Maybelle Carter; they cut their first record in Bristol, Tennessee (1927) and became famous as folk singers; he wrote "I'm Thinking Tonight of My Blue Eyes," "Lonesome Valley" and "Jimmy Brown the Newsboy"; they were on radio station XERA, Mexico, near Del Rio, Texas (1938-41), then WBT Charlotte, North Carolina (1941-43).

CARTER, ANITA INA

b. 1934 Maces Spring, Virginia.
Singer. Member of the Carter Sisters—Mother Maybelle, Helen, June, and Anita; albums—*Anita Carter, Folk Songs.*

CARTER, BENNETT LESTER (BENNY)

b. 1907 New York City.
Black jazz bandleader and alto-saxophonist. Considered by some as one of the greatest of all jazz musicians; his first band opened in Harlem's Savoy Ballroom, New York City (1939); organized other bands which fizzled; then on the West Coast; with Savannah Churchill who sang the blues, "Hurry, Hurry"; played at the Swing Club, Hollywood (1944); at the Newport Jazz Festival, New York City (1972).

CARTER, BETTY

b. 1930 Flint, Michigan.
Singer. Born Lillie Mae Jones; sang in night clubs; toured Japan with Sonny Rollins (1963); at Annie Ross' club in London, England (1964).

CARTER, ELLIOTT COOK, JR.

b. 1908 New York City.
Composer. Graduated from Harvard (1930) and studied with Walter Piston and Gustav Holst, later with Nadia Boulanger in Paris; taught at St. John's College, Annapolis, Maryland (1939-41); with the Office of War Information during World War II; first symphony was introduced by the Eastman-Rochester Symphony under Howard Hanson (1944), his *Holiday Overture* by the Baltimore Symphony (1946), *The Minotaur* by the Ballet Society of New York (1947), *String Quartet* in New York (1952), his second string quartet won the Pulitzer Prize (1960), two-movement *Concerto for Piano and Orchestra* appeared (1965).

CARTER, ERNEST TROW

b. 1866 Orange, New Jersey, d. 1953 Wallack's Point, Connecticut. Composer. Studied in New York and Berlin; organist in Berlin, then at Princeton University (1899-1901); composed the comic opera *The Blonde Donna,* opera *The White Bird* (Chicago, 1924), pantomine *Namba.*

CARTER, JUNE

b. 1929 Maces Spring, Virginia.
Singer, autoharpist, and songwriter. Daughter of Mother Maybelle Carter, and with her sisters, Helen and Anita, they became known as the Carter Sisters (1943); they were featured on radio stations in Charlotte, N.C., Richmond, Va., and Knoxville, Tenn.; with Johnny Cash she wrote "The Matador" (1963), with Merle Kilgore "Ring of Fire" (1963), and with Cash and Kilgore "Happy to Be with You" (1966); teamed with Johnny Cash (1967), and shortly thereafter married him.

CARTER, MOTHER MAYBELLE

b. 1909 Nickelsville, Virginia.
Singer, autoharpist, and songwriter. Sister-in-law of A.P. Carter; their records made them

the royalty of American folk music; her daughters Helen, June, and Anita also became famous folk singers; after she broke up with A.P. Carter, Maybelle and the Carter Sisters joined station WRVA Richmond, Virginia (1943); she wrote "A Jilted Love" and "Walk a Little Closer"; her LP records included *Songs of the Famous Carter Family, Mother Maybelle* and *Mother Maybelle Carter.*

CARTER, RONALD LEVIN (RON)

b. 1937 Ferndale, Michigan.
Black cellist and bass player. Graduated Eastman School of Music, Rochester, New York (1959), and Manhattan School of Music, New York City, (M.M. 1961); with Eastman Philharmonic Orchestra; with Miles Davis after 1963; toured Europe (1963-64) and Japan (1964); with Friedrich Gulda in Europe (1965); at the CTI Summer Jazz Festival, New York City (1972).

CARTER, SARAH

b. 1898 Flatwoods, near Coeburn, Virginia. Singer. Married A.P. Carter (1915); original member of the Carter Family singers; divorced (1932); married Coy Bayes (1939); albums—*Great Original Carter Family, 'Mid the Green Fields of Virginia, The Famous Carter Family, Great Sacred Songs.*

CARTER, WILF

b. 1904 Guysboro, Nova Scotia, Canada.
Singer, guitarist, and songwriter. Started with radio station CFCN, Calgary, Ontario (1933), then to Radio Vancouver, British Columbia, then to New York City, where he became known as "Montana Slim"; wrote "I'm Hittin' the Trail" and "Swiss Moonlight Lullaby"; also a yodeler; his LP record was *Montana Slim-Wilf Carter.*

CARTWRIGHT, PETER

b. 1785 Amherst County, Virginia, d. 1872 Pleasant Plains, Illinois. Gospel singer. Started as a blacksmith and became a singing circuit preacher and evangelist; probably the first traveling gospel singer in America.

CARUSI, GAETANO

b. ca. 1773 Catania, Italy, d. after 1846. Clarinetist and composer. Hired as director of the United States Marine Band in Italy (1805); came to Washington, D.C. (1805) but denied the position; taught in Philadelphia (1813); U.S. citizen (1820); composed *Circus Tunes* (1811).

CARUSO, ENRICO

b. 1873 Naples, Italy, d. there 1921.
Famous tenor. Pupil of Vergine; debut (1895), La Scala (1899), St. Petersburg, Russia (1899-1903), also in Buenos Aires, Argentina; appeared with Melba at Monte Carlo (1902) and also at Covent Garden; with Metropolitan Opera House, New York City (1903-20); last role was Eleazar in *La Juive* (Christmas Eve, 1920), at the Metropolitan, when stricken with a hemorrhage of the throat; after an operation he sailed for Naples.

CARY, ALICE

b. 1820 near Cincinnati, Ohio, d. 1871 New York City. Hymnist. She and her sister Phoebe published their first volume, *Poems* (1850).

CARY, ANNIE LOUISE

b. 1842 Wayne, Maine, d. 1921 Norwalk, Connecticut. Operatic and concert contralto. Studied in Boston and Milan, with Viardot-Garcia, et.al.; debut Hamburg, Germany (1868); toured Europe and came to New York (1870); married C.M. Raymond of Cincinnati, Ohio.

CARY, PHOEBE

b. 1824 near Cincinnati, Ohio, d. 1871 Newport, Rhode Island. Hymnist. Sister of Alice Cary; Phoebe wrote the hymn "Nearer Home" ("One Sweetly Solemn Thought"), which appeared in her book *Religious Poems and Hymns* (1852, tune "Nearer Home" or "Woodbury"—I.B. Woodbury, second tune "Dunbar"—Robert S. Ambrose); with Dr. Charles F. Deems, she compiled *Hymns for All Christians* (1869).

CARY, RICHARD DURANT (DICK)

b. 1916 Hartford, Connecticut.
Pianist, trumpeter, and composer. With Armstrong, Goodman, and others during 1940s and '50s; after 1959 in Los Angeles; toured Australia, New Zealand and Japan with Condon (1964); at Monterey Jazz Festival (1964) with Pee Wee Russell.

CARYLL, IVAN

b. 1861 Liege, Belgium, d. 1921 New York City. Noted composer of operettas. Born Felix Tilken; studied at Liege Conservatory and later with Camille Saint-Saëns; came to America (1911); wrote the operettas *The Pink Lady* (1911), *Oh, Oh, Delphine* (1914), *Chin-Chin* (1914), *Jack O'Lantern* (1917), *The Girl Behind the Gun* (1918), *The Canary* (1918), and *Tip Top* (1920).

CASA LOMA (band)

Originally led by Henry Biagini, with Glen Gray (Knoblaugh) on sax; trombonists Walter (Peewee) Hunt and Billy Rausch; pianist

Howard (Joe the Horse) Hall joined (1927); and in 1929, guitarist-arranger Gene Gifford and tenor-saxophonist Pat Davis; later Biagini was dismissed; joined were drummer Tony Briglia, bassist Stan Dennis, trumpeter Bobby Jones; played at Roseland Ballroom (1929); appeared on the "Camel Caravan" (1933-34); played in the R 'nbow Room atop the R.C.A. building, New York (1935).

CASADESUS, JEAN

b. 1927 Paris, France, d. 1972 near Renfrew, Ontario, Canada. Pianist. Studied under his parents, Robert and Gaby Casadesus, and also with his aunt, Rose Casadesus; entered Paris Conservatory at age eleven; came to America (1940) with his parents; studied at Princeton University; debut (1946) under Eugene Ormandy; won first prize (1947) at Geneva International Competition; appeared on "Bell Telephone Hour"; taught at American Conservatory at Fontainebleau after 1954, and after 1965 half the year at the State University at Binghamton; killed in an auto crash.

CASADESUS, ROBERT MARCEL

b. 1899 Paris, France, d. 1972.
Pianist. Entered Paris Conservatory at age thirteen; won first prize in piano; appeared at concerts in France, Belgium, Holland, etc.; came to America (1935); debut as soloist with New York Philharmonic; taught at American Conservatory at Fontainebleau; at Musica Aeterna Orchestra's concert in Tully Hall, New York City (1971) as soloist, and in duo with his wife, Gaby, for a spirited performance of Mozart's Two Piano Concerto in E-flat.

CASALS, PABLO

b. 1876 Vendrell, Tarragona, Spain, d. 1973. World-famed cellist and composer. Pupil of Jose Garcia, Rodereda, and Breton; composed *La Vision de Fray Martin* for chorus and orchestra, many cello pieces, etc.; resided in San Juan, Puerto Rico, for many years; came to Washington, D.C. to play in the White House for President and Mrs. Kennedy; conducted his *Hymn to Peace* (w. W.H. Auden—commissioned by Secretary General Thant) at the United Nations General Assembly (1971) at age 94; at Marlboro Music Festival in Marlboro, Vermont (1972); held master classes for cellists in residence.

CASE, ANNA

b. 1889 Clinton, New Jersey.
Soprano. Studied with Augusta Ohrstrom-Renard, sang with the Metropolitan Opera, New York City (1909-16); married Clarence H. Mackay.

CASEY, ALBERT ALOYSIUS

b. 1915 Louisville, Kentucky.
Black guitarist. Played with Fats Waller during 1930s and '40s; later with King Curtis' All-Stars.

CASH, JOHN R. (JOHNNY)

b. 1932 Kingsland, Arkansas.
Singer, guitarist, and songwriter. Born and raised in a sharecropper's shack where his two brothers died; served in the air force; wrote "So Doggone Lonesome," "There You Go" and "I Walk the Line" (all 1956 hits), "Train of Love" and "Next in Line" (1957), "Don't Take Your Guns to Town" (1958), "Frankie's Man Johnny" and "I Got Stripes" (1959); his records continued to be top hits in the 1960s and 1970s; his LP record *Johnny Cash at Folsom Prison* (1968) was his greatest success.

CASH, THOMAS R. (TOMMY)

b. 1940 Dyess, Arkansas.
Singer. Brother of Johnny Cash; attended schools in Dyess and in Memphis, Tennessee (1958), and the University of Frankfurt, Germany (1960); albums—*Tommy Cash, Your Lovin' Takes the Leavin' Out of Me, Here Comes Tommy Cash, Six White Horses.*

CASSEL, IRWIN M.

b. 1886 New York City, d. 1971 Miami Beach, Florida. Lyricist. Wrote the lyrics for ninety songs, mostly to music composed by his wife, Mana-Zucca; among the songs were "I Love Life," "There's Joy in My Heart" and "Romany Gypsy"; also wrote *In Bibleland*, a group of twelve songs; founded the Cromer Cassels department store, which became the Richards store chain in Florida.

CASTELMARY (COMTE ARMAND DE CASTAN)

b. 1834 Toulouse, France, d. 1897 New York City. Baritone. Sang in the Metropolitan Opera Company, New York City; died on the stage just after the first act of *Martha.*

CASTELNUOVO-TEDESCO, MARIO

b. 1895 Florence, Italy, d. 1968.
Noted composer. Studied at the Cherubini Royal Institute; came to America (1939) and settled in Los Angeles; composed the opera *La Mandragola* (1926), *Overture to Twelfth Night* (1933), Concerto no. 2 for Piano and Orchestra (1937), *Cipressi* for orchestra and piano (1940), the opera *Merchant of Venice* (1958), *Indian Songs and Dances, Five*

Humoresques on Foster's Themes and *An American Rhapsody.*

CASTLE, IRENE

b. 1894 New Rochelle, New York, d. 1969. Dancer. Married Vernon Castle (1887-1918), English actor in 1911; they pooled their $400 savings in 1912 and went to Paris where they became overnight sensations dancing the Texas Tommy and the Grizzly Bear; in 1918 Vernon was killed in a training plane accident in Fort Worth, Texas, and Irene rarely danced after that; she became patron of Orphans of the Storm, a dog haven in Deerfield, Illinois.

CASTRO, JOSEPH (JOE)

b. 1927 Miami, Arizona.
Pianist. Played in clubs in Hollywood; with Tony Martin (1961-63); accompanied June Christy to Australia (1963); also Anita Day; formed own record company, Clover (1965); resides in Honolulu, Hawaii.

CAT MOTHER AND THE ALL NIGHT NEWSBOYS (jug-rock band)

Charley Chin, guitar, banjo, and bass; Roy "Bones" Michaels, banjo, guitar, and bass; Bob Smith, piano and drums; Michael Equine, drums, guitar, etc; Larry Israel Packer, violin, mandolin, etc.; started in 1969; toured with Jimi Hendrix; album—*Street Giveth and Street Taketh Away.*

CATLETT, GEORGE JAMES ("BUDDY")

b. 1933 Long Beach, California.
Black bass player. Played with Cal Tjader and Quincy Jones in late 1950s; with Chico Hamilton, Count Basie, Maynard Ferguson and Louis Armstrong in 1960s; toured Europe and Japan with Basie (1963), and Europe with Armstrong (1965).

CATLETT, SIDNEY ("BIG SID")

b. 1910 Evansville, Indiana, d. 1951 Chicago, Illinois. Black jazz drummer. Played with Benny Carter, Fletcher Henderson, Don Redman, and Louis Armstrong; recorded on Victor with Sidney Bechet's group (1940-41); recorded "Shake It and Break It"; played in Jimmy Ryan's Club on 52nd Street, New York City.

CAVALLARO, CARMEN

b. 1913 New York City.
Pianist. Played with Al Kavelin's band (1935); had his own band, with Larry Douglas, singer; later a semipop concert pianist; wrote *While the Nightwind Sings, Masquerade Waltz.*

CAVANAUGH, WALTER PAGE

b. 1922 Cherokee, Kansas.
Pianist and singer. With small groups in 1940s and '50s; formed The Page 7 in 1962 which appeared on TV; at clubs in New York City and Studio City, California.

CAVE, JAY

b. 1932 Altoona, Pennsylvania.
Bass player. Toured with Ralph Sharon, Chris Connor, Billie Holiday, Red Rodney, and Nina Simone in 1950s; joined Al Hirt (1965).

CAZDEN, NORMAN

b. 1914 New York City.
Composer. Studied at Juilliard Graduate School, New York City; composed *Concerto for Ten Instruments* (Juilliard Graduate School under Bernard Wagenaar, 1937), *Preamble and Three Dances* (for orchestra), *Elegy Before Dawn—On the Death of a Spanish Child* (for symphonic band or chamber orchestra), songs.

CELESTIN, OSCAR ("PAPA")

b. 1884 Lafourche, Louisiana, d. 1954 New Orleans, Louisiana. Black cornetist. Member of Allen's Brass Band of Algiers, Louisiana after 1912.

CELLA, THEODORE

b. 1897 Philadelphia, Pennsylvania, d. 1960. Harpist and composer. Played with the Boston Symphony Orchestra; his composition *Through the Pyrenees* (1932) was presented the first time by the New York Philharmonic; *The Lido* by the Boston Symphony, Philharmonic Society of New York, and the Philadelphia orchestras.

CEROLI, NICK

b. 1939 Warren, Ohio.
Drummer. With Ralph Marterie after 1958; then Ray Anthony, Lionel Hampton, Les Brown and others; with Tijuana Brass after 1965; at Monterey Jazz Festival with Gerlad Wilson (1963).

CHAD AND JEREMY

Chad Stuart and Jeremy Clyde; albums—*The Ark, Before and After, Best of Chad and Jeremy, Distant Shores, I Don't Wanna Lose You Baby, Of Cabbage and Kings.*

CHADWICK, GEORGE WHITFIELD

b. 1854 Lowell, Massachusetts, d. 1931 Boston, Massachusetts. Noted composer. Studied at the New England Conservatory of

Music (1872); taught at Olivet College, Olivet, Michigan, then studied at the Leipzig Conservatory and in Munich, Germany; in 1882 started teaching at the New England Conservatory, Boston, and became its director (1897); known for his Third Symphony in F Major (1886), debut Boston Symphony (1894), overture *Melpomene* (1887), *Symphonic Sketches* (1908), *Suite Symphonic* (1911), *Aphrodite* (a symphonic fantasy, 1912) and *Tam o'Shanter* (1915), both introduced at the Norfolk Festivals.

CHADWICK, JOHN WHITE

b. 1840 Marblehead, Massachusetts, d. 1904 Brooklyn, New York. Hymnist. Graduated Harvard Divinity School, Cambridge (1864) and became minister of the Second Unitarian Church in Brooklyn; wrote the hymns "Eternal Ruler of the Ceaseless Round" (1864, tune "Song I," Orlando Gibbons), "It Singeth Low in Every Heart" (1876, tune "Auld Lang Syne"—Scotch).

CHAJES, JULIUS

b. 1910 Lvov, Russia.
Composer. Studied in Vienna, then went to Tel Aviv, Israel; settled in Detroit (1938), was conductor at Temple Beth-El, then musical director at the Jewish Community Center in Detroit; composed *Psalm 142* for choir, the cantata *The Promised Land* and the *Palestinian Suite* for orchestra, and also chamber music.

CHAMBERS BROTHERS (black soul-rock group with a white drummer)

George Ernest Chambers, bass; Willie Mack Chambers, vocals and guitar; Joe Chambers, vocals and guitar; Lester Chambers, vocals, tambourine, and cow bells; Brian Keenan, drums; Mississippi-born gospel group (1961-65); albums—*Chambers Brothers Live at B. Graham's Fillmore East; Chambers Brothers Now; Chambers Brothers Shout; Feelin' the Blues; Groovin' Time; Love, Peace and Happiness; New Time—A New Day; People Get Ready;* George and Willie Chambers and Jerome Brailey, all of Stamford, Connecticut, arrested in Winter Park, Florida, in March, 1972 for possession of marijuana.

CHAMBERS, HENDERSON CHARLES

b. 1908 Alexandria, Louisiana, d. 1967.
Trombonist. Played in large bands during 1930s and '40s; later with small combos; with Ray Charles (1961-63); then with Count Basie after 1964.

CHAMBERS, JOSEPH ARTHUR (JOE)

b. 1942 Stoneacre, Virginia.
Drummer. Raised in Chester, Pennsylvania; played with Eric Dolphy, Freddie Hubbard, Jimmy Giuffre, and Andrew Hill during 1960s; with Hill at Toronto University Concert (1965).

CHAMBERS, PAUL LAURENCE DUNBAR, JR.

b. 1935 Pittsburgh, Pennsylvania.
Black drummer. Played in small combos in Detroit (1949-54); in New York with Miles Davis (1955-63); formed a trio with Wynton Kelly and Jimmy Cobb (1963-66); then with Tony Scott.

CHAMBERS, STEPHEN

b. 1940.
Black composer. Studied at Manhattan School of Music and the New School for Social Research, New York City; works played by Young Men's Hebrew Association under Max Pollikoff; wrote *Elements* (1967, for strings, flutes, clarinets, piano, glass and bamboo chimes), *Sound Images* (1969, for percussion, brass, bass, and six female voices).

CHAMLEE, MARIO

b. 1892 Los Angeles, California, d. 1967.
Tenor. Born Archer Chalmondeley; pupil of Achille Alberti and Riccardo Dellera; debut at Metropolitan Opera, New York City (1920) in *Tosca;* with the Metropolitan Opera (1920-26); later with the Scotti and Ravinia Opera companies; again with the Metropolitan Opera (1935-39); married soprano Ruth Miller; conducted a vocal studio in Hollywood.

CHAMPAGNE MUSIC MAKERS *see* LAWRENCE WELK

CHAMPLIN, JOHN DENISON

b. 1834 Stonington, Connecticut, d. 1915.
Editor and compiler. With William Foster Apthorp, edited the *Cyclopaedia of Music and Musicians* (1888-90).

CHANDLER, LEN

b. 1935 Akron, Ohio.
Black singer, guitarist, and songwriter. Studied at the University of Akron and at Columbia University, New York City; wrote over fifty folk songs, including *The Wicked Weirs* (songs commemorating civil rights martyr Medgar Evers of Mississippi); best-known LP record was *To Be a Man* (1966).

CHANDLER, S.

b. 1760 d. after 1812.
Composer. Lived in Troy, New York around 1800; composed the tune "Ganges" (also called "Hull") for "Awaked by Sinai's Awful Sound" (ca. 1790, w. Samson Occum), which appeared in John Wyeth's *Repository of Sacred Music* (1812).

CHANLER, THEODORE WARD

b. 1902 Newport, Rhode Island, d. 1961 Boston, Massachusetts. Composer. Pupil of Arthur Shepherd, Percy Goetschius, and Ernest Bloch; also at Oxford University and with Nadia Boulanger in Paris; composed *Eight Epitaphs* (song cycle), *Five Short Colloquies* (for piano), *Sonatina* (for chamber ensemble), sonata for violin and piano, and *Mass* (for two women's voices).

CHANNING, CAROL

b. 1923 Seattle, Washington.
Singer and actress. Sang in *Gentlemen Prefer Blondes* (1949, m. Jule Styne, book by Joseph Fields and Anita Loos); was a hit in *Hello Dolly!* (1964, m. Jerry Herman, book—Michael Stewart).

CHAPIN, AMZI

b. 1768, d. 1835.
Composer. Younger brother of Lucius Chapin; joined his brother in the Shenandoah Valley, Virginia (1791); was a singing master there; composed the music for "Christians, If Your Hearts Are Warm" (1805, w. John Leland).

CHAPIN, EDWIN HUBBELL

b. 1814 Union Village, Washington County, New York, d. 1880. Lyricist. Educated at Bennington College, Vermont; Universalist minister in Richmond, Virginia (1837), Boston (1846), and New York City (1848); wrote the lyrics "O Bury Me Not in the Deep, Deep Sea," which appeared in the *Southern Literary Messenger* (1839, m. George N. Allen, 1849); with Dr. John Greenleaf Adams, he edited *Universalist Hymns for Christian Devotion* (1846).

CHAPIN, LUCIUS

b. 1760, d. 1842.
Composer and teacher. Resided in Massachusetts and enlisted as a fifer in the Revolutionary War; singing master in the Shenandoah Valley, Virginia, after 1787; credited with seven tunes in John Wyeth's *Repository of Sacred Music, Part Second* (1813); also tunes in Ananias Davisson's *Kentucky Harmony* (1815-16).

CHAPLIN, SAUL

b. 1912 Brooklyn, New York.
Conductor, pianist, and songwriter. Educated at New York University; pianist in same band with Sammy Cahn, violinist; with Harry Warren and Jack Brooks wrote "Wonderful You"; with Harry Akst and Al Jolson wrote "All My Love" (1947).

CHAPMAN, WILLIAM ROGERS

b. 1855 Hanover, Massachusetts, d. 1935 Palm Beach, Florida. Conductor and composer. Founded and led the Apollo Club, New York City, then conductor of the Maine Festivals in Portland and Bangor after 1897, the Rubinstein Club (1887).

CHARIG, PHIL

b. 1902 New York City, d. there 1960.
Popular composer. Wrote the music for the following Broadway shows: *Yes, Yes Yvette* (1927), *Polly* (1929), *Artists and Models* (1943), *Follow the Girls* (1944).

CHARLES, ERNEST

b. 1895 Minneapolis, Minnesota.
Singer and composer. Educated at University of Southern California; singer in vaudeville; Broadway shows: *Earl Carroll's Vanities* (1928) and *George White's Scandals* (1929); wrote "And So, Goodbye," "The Sussex Sailor," "The House on the Hill," "Oh Lovely World."

CHARLES, RAY

b. 1918 Chicago, Illinois.
Conductor and composer. Director of the Ray Charles Singers; appeared on "Hit Parade"; on the "Perry Como Show" after 1954.

CHARLES, RAY

b. 1930 Albany, Georgia.
Black singer and pianist. Born Ray Charles Robinson; became blind at age six; studied at state school for the blind in Orlando, Florida; orphaned at age fifteen; played in Henry Washington's orchestra in Jacksonville, Florida; in Joe Anderson's band in Orlando; with Manzie Harris combo in Tampa; played piano with Florida Playboys; first recorded in 1951; first hit "I Got a Woman" (1955); traveled with Lowell Fulson; main attraction at 1958 Newport Jazz Festival; arrested in Indianapolis (1961) for possession of narcotics, entered a clinic in California for treatment (1965); albums—*Best of Ray Charles, Ray Charles and Betty Carter, Ray Charles at Newport, Dedicated to You, Doing His Thing, Ray Charles in Person, Ray Charles Live in Concert, Crying Time, Genius*

After Hours, Genius Hits the Road, Genius of Ray Charles, Genius Plus Soul Equals Jazz, Genius Sings the Blues, The Great Ray Charles, Greatest Ray Charles; at the Newport Jazz Festival, New York City (1972).

CHARLES, ROOSEVELT

b. 1919 Louisiana.
Black singer and songwriter. In 1937 he killed a man in a drunken brawl and was sentenced to Angola prison in Louisiana; when out of prison he did odd jobs for Harry Oster of Baton Rouge, Louisiana who taped Charles' songs; wrote "The Boll Weevil" and "The Bale Weevil"; his long-playing record was *Blues, Prayer, Work and Trouble Songs;* went back to prison in 1961 as a four-time loser.

CHARLES, TEDDY

b. 1928 Chicopee Falls, Massachusetts.
Vibraharpist. Born Theodore Charles Cohen; played in various combos during 1940s and '50s; organized own record company, Polaris, in 1965.

CHARLTON, MELVILLE

b. 1880 New York City.
Black organist and composer. Graduated City College of New York; studied at National Conservatory of Music, New York; organist at St. Philips Church; later at Temple Emanu-El and at Union Theological Seminary; composed piano and organ pieces.

CHASINS, ABRAM

b. 1903 New York City.
Pianist and composer. Musical director for station WQXR in New York City; known for two piano concertos, *Twenty-four Preludes for Piano,* and other pieces.

CHATMAN, PETER *see* MEMPHIS SLIM

CHAUVIN, LOUIS

b. 1883 St. Louis, Missouri, d. 1908 Chicago, Illinois. Black pianist, composer, and entertainer. Formed a singing and tap dancing duo with Sam Patterson in St. Louis and toured America; wrote "Heliotrope Bouquet" (1907, with Scott Joplin), "The Moon Is Shining in the Skies" (1903, w. Sam Patterson), "Babe, It's Too Long Off" (1906, w. Elmer Bowman), the musical revue *Dandy Coon* (1903, w. Sam Patterson).

CHEATHAM, CATHARINE SMILEY ("KITTY")

b. 1864 Nashville, Tennessee, d. 1946 Greenwich, Connecticut. Mezzo-soprano. She gave numerous concerts of folk music and children's songs.

CHECKER, CHUBBY

b. 1941 Philadelphia, Pennsylvania.
Black singer and dancer. Born Ernest Evans; cut up chickens for a market in South Philadelphia; recorded "The Class" (by Kal Mann), sang "The Twist" (1960, by Hank Ballard, 1958), and recorded the album *Twist with Chubby Checker* (1961) which became a nationwide hit; appeared in the film *Twist Around the Clock;* started another dance craze (1962) with "Limbo Rock"; at "The Legend of Rock 'n Roll" show at Hollywood Bowl, California (1972).

CHEEVER, GEORGE BARRELL

b. 1807 Hallowell, Maine, d. 1890 Englewood, New Jersey. Hymnist. Graduated Bowdoin College, Brunswick, Maine (1825); Congregational minister in Salem, Massachusetts (1833-39), and New York City (1839-67); imprisoned for a month in 1835 in Salem for writing *Deacon Giles' Distillery;* many of his hymns are in *Christian Melodies* (1851), which he compiled; also published the *Common Place Book* (1831).

CHERICO, EUGENE V. (GENE)

b. 1935 Buffalo, New York.
Bass player. Drummer in U.S. Army band, but injured his right arm in a train accident in Germany (1955); took up bass as physical therapy; studied at Berklee School; worked with Toshiko Akiyoshi, Herb Pomeroy, and Maynard Ferguson during 1950s; with Red Norvo, Benny Goodman, Stan Getz, and Peggy Lee in 1960s.

CHEROKEE COUNTY BOYS *see* LITTLE JIMMY DEMPSEY

CHERRY, DONALD E. (DON)

b. 1936 Oklahoma City, Oklahoma.
Black trumpeter. Played in Ornette Coleman's Quintet after 1959; played with Sonny Rollins (1963); in Europe after 1964; led his own band in Europe.

CHESLOCK, LOUIS

b. 1899 London, England.
Composer. Came to U.S. (1901); studied at Peabody Conservatory, Baltimore; U.S. citizen (1913); studied violin under Van Hulsteyn and Gittelson, and composition with Strobe; violinist with Baltimore Symphony Orchestra (1916), later guest conductor and assistant concertmaster; composed *Symphonic Prelude* (1927, performed in Baltimore

and Rochester), *Three Tone Poems* (1922, in Baltimore, Chicago, and San Diego).

CHESTER, ROBERT T. (BOB)

b. 1908 Detroit, Michigan.
Conductor and composer. Orchestra leader (1939-52); Stan Getz, saxophonist, played in his band; wrote "Sunburst" (theme), "Octave Jump," "You're the One."

CHESTER, WILLIAM SIDELL

b. 1865 Englewood, New Jersey, d. 1900.
Composer. Graduated from Stevens Institute of Technology, Hoboken, New Jersey (1886); organist and choirmaster of St. George's Church, New York City (1888); composed the tune "Chester" (1897, "Jesus Calls Us," w. C. Frances Alexander).

CHEVALIER, ANTOINE LOUIS

b. 1770 France, d. 1823 New York City.
Pianist, composer, dancing master, and publisher. Music publisher in New York City (1820-23); published *Collection of Quadrilles for Pianoforte or Harp.*

CHICAGO (rock group)

Jim Guercio, producer; Lee Loughnane, trumpeter; and others; Robert Lamm's "A Hit by Varese" included in their album *Chicago V.*

CHICAGO BLUES BAND *see* JUNIOR WELLS

CHICKERING, JONAS

b. 1798 New Ipswich, New Hampshire, d. 1853 Boston, Massachusetts. Piano maker. Established the firm of Chickering & Sons, piano makers (1823); in 1908 the firm was merged with the American Piano Company; his sons in the business were Thomas E. (1824-71), Charles Frank (1827-91), and George H. (1830-96).

CHILD, FRANCIS JAMES

b. 1825 Boston, Massachusetts, d. there 1896. Compiler. Graduated Harvard University (1846) and was appointed Boylston professor there (1851); compiled *English and Scottish Ballads* published in eight volumes (1857-58), and *The English and Scottish Popular Ballads* published in five volumes (1896-98, after his death).

CHILDERS, MARION ("BUDDY")

b. 1926 St. Louis, Missouri.
Jazz trumpeter. Played in Stan Kenton's band off and on between 1943-54.

CHILDREN OF GOD, THE (rock and soul group)

Gerry Moore, lead vocals, trumpet, sax, etc.; Eddie Vernon, lead vocals, organ, tambourine, etc.; Tom Everett, lead vocals, bass guitar and piano; Gil Silva, lead vocals, lead guitar, and banjo; Chris Sigwald, drums, conga, etc.; album—*This Is Our Time.*

CHITTISON, HERMAN

b. 1909 Flemingsburg, Kentucky, d. 1967.
Black jazz pianist. Accompanist for Stepin Fetchit, Ethel Waters and others; later formed his own trio.

CHIVERS, THOMAS HOLLEY

b. 1807 Washington County, Georgia, d. there 1858. Lyricist and poet. Graduated Transylvania College, Lexington, Kentucky (M.D., 1830); met Edgar Allan Poe in New York (1845) and was Poe's friend until his death in 1849; wrote "Corn Song" (1828, based on folk music) to be sung by the slaves at corn shucking on his father's plantation.

CHOTZINOFF, SAMUEL

b. 1889 New York City, d. 1964.
Musical director. Brother-in-law of Jascha Heifetz and also his accompanist; music critic, then joined the staff of NBC (1936), where he became musical director.

CHOU WEN-CHUNG

b. 1923.
Composer. Studied with Edgard Varèse; orchestral works: *All in the Spring Wind* (1953), *And the Fallen Petal* (1954).

CHRISTENSEN, AXEL W.

b. 1881 Chicago, Illinois.
Pianist and teacher. Opened a ragtime class in Chicago (1903); by 1915 he directed a nationwide network of thirty-five schools; known as the "Czar of Ragtime"; published *Christensen's Instruction Book No. 1 for Ragtime Piano Playing* (1904, yearly editions thereafter), the *Christensen Instruction Book for Ragtime* (1927, later changed to jazz piano), *Modern Swing Music.*

CHRISTIAN, CHARLIE

b. 1917 Dallas, Texas, d. 1942 New York City. Black guitarist. Played in Benny Goodman's band (1939-41); played in Minton's Playhouse, Harlem, New York City during the 1940s with Thelonious Monk (pianist), Kenny Clarke (drummer), and Dizzy Gillespie (trumpeter); developed what was called "bebop," later simply "bop."

CHRISTIAN TROUBADOURS *see* WAYNE D. WALTERS

CHRISTIANI, STEFANO

b. 1768 Bologna, Italy, d. ca. 1835 Philadelphia Pennsylvania. Composer. Came to Philadelphia in 1818; wrote "*Chactas au tombeau d' Atala,*" a march for President James Monroe (1819), "Blue Eye'd Mary" (1819), "*Una brunetta,*" "All of Life Is Love" (1820), "Commodore Decatur's Funeral March" (1820).

CHRISTIANSEN, F. MELIUS

b. 1871 Eidsvald, Norway, d. 1955.
Organist, conductor, and teacher. Came to America (1888) and led the Scandinavian Band, Marinette, Wisconsin; educated at Augsburg College, Minneapolis, and the Northwest Conservatory of Music (1894); organist at Lutheran churches in Minneapolis and head of the music department at St. Olaf's College, Northfield, Minnesota (1903) and choirmaster of St. Olaf's Lutheran Choir.

CHRISTY (CHRISTIE), EDWIN P.

b. 1815 Philadelphia, Pennsylvania, d. 1862 New York City. Minstrel showman and popular composer. First organized his minstrels in 1842 in Buffalo, New York, as the Virginia Serenaders; Christy's Ethiopian Minstrels opened at Palmo's Opera House in New York City (1846); wrote the words and music "Farewell Ladies," or "Goodnight Ladies," in 1847 and composed the music for "My Heart's O'er the Deep Blue Sea" (w. George Cooper); became depressed and committed suicide by jumping out of his hotel room window in New York City.

CHRISTY, JUNE

b. 1925 Springfield, Illinois.
Singer. Vocalist for Stan Kenton (1945-49); married saxophonist Bob Cooper (1946); toured Europe with Cooper in late 1950s; toured Australia and Japan (1964), and England (1965); at Newport Jazz Festival, New York City with Stan Kenton (1972).

CHRYSALIS (rock group)

Paul Album, bass; J. Spider Barbour, vocals and rhythm cicada; Ralph Kotkov, vocals and piano; Nancy Nain, vocals; John Sabin, guitar; Dahaud Shaar, percussion; started in Ithaca, New York (1966); album—*Definition.*

CHUCK WAGON GANG (gospel singers)

D.P. Carter (deceased), tenor; Eddie Carter; Rose Karnes, soprano; Anna Gordon, alto; Jim Carter, bass and guitarist; Howard Gordon (deceased); Louise Clark; Ronnie Page, tenor; Howard Wellborn; Ronald Crittenden.

CHURCH, JOHN

b. 1834, d. 1890.
Publisher. Music publisher in Cincinnati, Ohio. (*See also* J.R. Murray).

CHURCHILL, FRANK E.

b. 1901 Rumford, Maine, d. 1942 Castaic, California. Popular composer. After 1930 he composed music for Walt Disney; with words by various lyricists, he composed the music for "Some Day My Prince Will Come," "Who's Afraid of the Big Bad Wolf," "Heigh-ho," "Whistle While You Work," "One Song," "With a Smile and a Song," "Casey Junior," "Look Out for Mr. Stork."

CHURCHILL, SAVANNAH

b. 1919 New Orleans, Louisiana.
Black singer. Raised in Brooklyn, New York; sang with Benny Carter in 1940s.

CIMARRON BOYS *see* LEON MC AULIFFE

CIRCUS MAXIMUS (rock group)

Jerry Jeff "Mr. Bojangles" Walker, vocals and guitar; Bob Bruno, vocals, lead guitar, etc.; David Scherstrom, drums; Gary White, vocals and bass; Peter Troutner, vocals, guitar, and tambourine; played a baroque-rock mix with the New York Pro Musica at Carnegie Hall (1967); album—*Circus Maximus and Neverland Revisited* (1968); group disbanded.

CIRILLO, WALLACE JOSEPH (WALLY)

b. 1927 Huntington, New York.
Pianist. Played with John La Porta and Charles Mingus in 1950s; taught at Palm Beach, Florida school after 1961; led own group in Fort Lauderdale-Miami area (1962-65).

CITKOWITZ, ISRAEL

b. 1909 Russia, d. 1974.
Teacher and composer. His parents brought him to New York as a child; studied with Copland and Sessions, and also with Nadia Boulanger in Paris; taught at the Dalcroze School, New York City; composed orchestral and choral works, chamber music.

CLAASSEN, ARTHUR

b. 1859 Stargard, Prussia, Germany, d. 1920 San Francisco, California. Conductor. Pupil of Muller-Hartung, Gottschalk, Sulze, and Weimar Music School; conductor in Gottingen and Magdeburg (1880-84); came to Brooklyn (1884), conductor at Arion Society there; established the Claassen Musical Institute; after 1910 was orchestra and choral conductor in San Antonio, Texas; composed choral pieces and a symphonic poem.

CLAFLIN, AVERY

b. 1898 Keene, New Hampshire.
Composer. Attended Harvard; studied composition with Archibald T. Davison; became president of the French-American Banking Corporation, New York City; wrote four operas: *The Fall of Usher* (1921), *Hester Prynne* (1932), *La Grande Breteche* (1947), *Uncle Tom's Cabin* (1966); also for chorus, *Mary of Nazareth, Lament for April 15;* for orchestra, *Moby Dick Suite* (1929); also symphonies, a ballet, chamber music.

CLANCY, THOMAS

b. (?) Carrick-on-Suir, Ireland.
Singer, actor, and director. The Clancy Brothers (Patrick, Liam and Tom) joined with Tommy Makem as a vocal and instrumental group) their LP records included *Clancy Brothers with Tommy Makem* (1961), *Hearty and Hellish* and *The Boys Won't Leave the Girls Alone* (1962), *In Person* (1963), *First Hurrah* (1964), *The Irish Uprising* (1966); Tom staged the Newport Folk Festival (1966) and the International Dublin Folk Festival (1967).

CLAPP, PHILIP GREELEY

b. 1888 Boston, Massachusetts, d. 1954.
Composer and teacher. Graduated Harvard University; studied in Europe as Sheldon Fellow of Harvard; director of music at Dartmouth (1915-19), then professor of music at the University of Iowa, Iowa City; composed choral works.

CLARE, SIDNEY

b. 1892 New York City.
Comedian, dancer, and lyricist. Wrote "Ma—He's Making Eyes at Me" (1921, m. Con Conrad); went to Hollywood (1933); wrote film scores and songs for films.

CLARK, ALEXANDER

b. 1834 Jefferson County, Ohio, d. 1879 Atlanta, Georgia. Hymnist. Journalist and editor of the *Methodist Recorder,* Pittsburgh; wrote the hymn "Heavenly Father, Bless Me Now" (1872, tune, "Seymour"—Carl Maria von Weber); was on a lecture tour in Atlanta when taken ill; Governor Colquitt took Clark to the Executive Mansion, where he died three weeks later.

CLARK, ALGERIA JUNIUS ("JUNE")

b. 1901 Long Branch, New Jersey, d. 1963. Black trumpeter. Played with Willie "The Lion" Smith, Charlie Smith, Sugar Ray Robinson's touring group, and others.

CLARK, CONRAD YEATIS ("SONNY")

b. 1931 Herminie, Pennsylvania, d. 1963 New York City. Pianist. Played in Buddy De Franco Quartet, also with Wardell Gray, Oscar Pettiford, and H. Rumsey's Lighthouse All-Stars during 1950s; hospitalized with a leg infection and died of a heart attack a few days after he was released.

CLARK, FREDERICK HORACE

b. 1861 Independence, Texas, d. 1917.
Pianist and teacher. Studied at New England Conservatory, Boston; piano soloist and teacher of piano in Corpus Christi, Texas.

CLARK, PETULA

b. 1934 Ewell, Surrey, England.
Singer. Appeared in English films; became a singing star in France; married a Frenchman; came to America (1967) to appear in Hollywood films; albums—*Downtown* (1964), *Petula Clark* (1965), *I Couldn't Live Without Your Love, I Know a Place* (1965), *My Love* (1966), *This Is Petula Clark* (1966), *Color My World/Who Am I* (1967), *These Are My Songs* (1967), *Other Man's Grass Is Always Greener* (1968), *Petula* (1968), *Finian's Rainbow* (1968), *Just Pet.*

CLARK, RAYMOND LE ROY ("YODELING SLIM")

b. 1917 Springfield, Massachusetts.
Singer and yodeler. Attended school in Petersham, Mass.; World's Champion Yodeler (1947); albums—*Yodel Songs, Cowboy Songs, Cowboy and Folk Songs.*

CLARK, RICHARD (DICK)

b. 1929 Mt. Vernon, New York.
Producer and entertainer. Many singers appeared on the popular "Dick Clark Show."

CLARK, ROY LINWOOD

b. 1933 Meaherrin, Virginia.
Singer, banjoist, and guitarist. Joined Jimmy Dean on ABC-TV, New York City; then with Wanda Jackson at the Golden Nugget, Las Vegas (1960); also with Hank Thompson at

Harrah's Club, Reno, Nevada; his LP records include *Lightning* (1962), *Tips of My Fingers* (1963), *Happy to Be Unhappy* and *The Lightning Fingers of Roy Clark* (1967).

CLARK, WILLIS GAYLORD

b. 1810 Otisco, New York, d. 1841.
Hymnist. Editor of the *Philadelphia Gazette;* wrote "We Have Met in Peace Together," for the Eighth Anniversary of the American Sunday School Union (1832).

CLARKE, BUCK

b. 1932 Washington, D.C.
Conga drummer and bongos. Served two years in the army; played with Arnett Cobb combo; formed his own quintet (1959) in Washington, D.C.

CLARKE, GRANT

b. 1891 Akron, Ohio, d. 1931 California.
Lyricist and publisher. Wrote material for Bert Williams, Fanny Brice and others; staff writer for New York music publishing firms; later publisher; wrote the lyrics "Everything Is Peaches Down in Georgia" (1918, m. Milton Ager), "You Love and I Love Angels" (m. Jean Schwartz), "Back to Carolina" (m. Jean Schwartz).

CLARKE, HERBERT LINCOLN

b. 1867 Woburn, Massachusetts, d. 1945 Los Angeles, California. Cornetist and teacher. Son of William Horatio Clarke, organist; cornet soloist and teacher in Toronto, Ontario, Canada; member of Patrick Gilmore's Band; 7th Regiment Band under Victor Herbert; made four European tours with John Philip Sousa; wrote *Flirtations* (cornet trio), *Sounds from the Deep, Birth of Dawn.*

CLARKE, HUGH ARCHIBALD

b. 1839 Toronto, Ontario, Canada, d. 1927 Philadelphia, Pennsylvania. Organist and teacher. Son of James Peyton Clarke; came to America and became professor of music at the University of Pennsylvania (1875); composed an oratorio *Jerusalem* (1891), *Acharnians.*

CLARKE, JAMES FREEMAN

b. 1810 Hanover, New Hampshire, d. 1888.
Compiler and hymnist. Grandson of James Freeman; graduated Harvard (1829), and Divinity School (1833); Unitarian pastor in Louisville, Kentucky (1833-40) and in Boston after 1841; compiled *Chapel Hymn Book* (1838); contributed five hymns to *Hymn Book for the Church of the Disciples* (1844) which he edited, and the enlarged edition (1852). (*See* Julia Ward Howe)

CLARKE, KENNETH SPEARMAN (KENNY)

b. 1914 Pittsburgh, Pennsylvania.
Black jazz drummer. Played in Dizzy Gillespie's band; later with Edgar Hayes, toured Scandinavia; recorded with Sidney Bechet's group (1940-41); played with Red Allen in Chicago (1942-46); played in Minton's Playhouse, Harlem, New York City during 1940s with Charlie Christian (guitarist), Dizzy Gillespie (trumpeter), Thelonious Monk (pianist); developed "bebop," later called simply "bop."

CLARKE, TERENCE MICHAEL (TERRY)

b. 1944 Vancouver, B.C., Canada.
Drummer. Played with local groups (1959); then with B. Kessel and V. Guaraldi; came to U.S. (1965); played with John Handy Quintet in San Francisco; at 1965 Monterey Jazz Festival with Handy.

CLARKE, WILLIAM HORATIO

b. 1840 Newton, Massachusetts, d. 1913 Reading, Massachusetts. Organist and writer. Organist at Tremont Temple (1878-87) in Boston; had a chapel of music, Clarigold Hall, on his estate in Reading, Mass. with a huge four-manual organ with 100 stops; wrote *Outline of the Structure of the Pipe-Organ* (1877), and fourteen other instructive books.

CLAY, SHIRLEY

b. 1902 Charleston, Missouri, d. 1951.
Black trumpeter. Played in Earl Hines and Don Redman's orchestras.

CLAYTON, EDITH

b. 1897 Orange, New Jersey.
Hymnist. Educated at Columbia University School of Journalism, New York City; wrote the hymns "Father, We Come, with Youth and Vigor Pressing" (1922, tune, "St. Osyth"—Thomas Wood) and "Fisherman's Night Hymn" (1941, m. Channing Lefebvre); wrote *Litany of Youth* and *Post-War Litany* (1942).

CLAYTON, PAUL

b. 1933 New Bedford, Massachusetts.
Singer, guitarist, and dulcimer player. Attended the University of Virginia, Charlottesville; his LP records include *Bay State Ballads, Foc'sle Songs and Shanties, Whaling and Sailing Songs from the Days of Moby Dick, Bloody Ballads, Waters of Tyne, Whaling Songs and Ballads, British Broadside Ballads in Popular Tradition, Concert of British and American Folksongs,*

Folk Songs and Ballads of Virginia, Dulcimer Songs and Solos.

CLAYTON, WILBUR ("BUCK")

b. 1912 Parsons, Kansas.
Trumpeter. Played in Count Basie's band (1936-43); served in army in World War II; with Jazz at the Philharmonic for two years; played with Joe Bushkin's Quartet in New York City (1951-53); toured Europe (1949, '53, '59, '62, '63); to Australia and Japan (1964); instrumentals—"Red Band Boogie," "7th Avenue Express," "Swingin' at the Copper Rail," "Stan's Dance," "Blues Blase."

CLEF CLUB ORCHESTRA (black band) *see* JAMES R. EUROPE

CLEMENS, BENJAMIN S.

b. ca. 1790 England, d. 1854.
Composer and piano maker. Came to Philadelphia (1818); composed "Jackson's Grand March" (1818), and "The Columbia March" (1818).

CLEMENS, CLARA

b. 1874 Elmira, New York, d. 1921.
Mezzo-soprano. Daughter of Mark Twain; married Ossip Gabrilowitsch, the conductor; in 1938 she published a biography of Gabrilowitsch entitled *My Husband.*

CLEMENTS, CHARLES EDWIN

b. 1858 Plymouth, England, d. 1933 Cleveland, Ohio. Organist, teacher, and writer. Studied at the Royal College of Music; organist at St. Paul's Church, Cleveland (1896), then at the Euclid Avenue Presbyterian Church (1911); taught at Western Reserve University (1898, now Case Western Reserve); wrote *Modern Progressive Pedal Technique* (1894) and *Modern School for the Organ* (1903).

CLEMM, JOHN *see* JOHANN GOTTLOB KLEMM

CLEVA, FAUSTO

b. 1902 Trieste, Austria- Italy, d. 1971 Athens, Greece. Conductor. Came to New York City at age eighteen as assistant chorus master at the Metropolitan Opera; later chorus master until 1942; became U.S. citizen; conducted San Francisco Opera (1942-44, 1949-55); rejoined Metropolitan Opera (1950).

CLEVELAND, CHARLES DEXTER

b. 1802 Salem, Massachusetts, d. 1869.
Compiler of hymns. Graduated Dartmouth College, Hanover, N.H. (1827); professor at Dickinson College, Carlisle, Pa. (1830) and the University of New York (1832); opened a school for young ladies in Philadelphia (1824); compiled *Lyra Sacra Americana* (1868).

CLEVELAND, JAMES MILTON (JIMMY)

b. 1926 Wartrace, Tennessee.
Black trombonist. Played in various bands in 1950s; later played in TV orchestras; also in orchestras for Broadway shows.

CLEVELAND SINGERS (gospel singers)

James Cleveland, leader; albums—*James Cleveland and the Angelic Choir, James Cleveland and Gospel Girls, James Cleveland and Voices of the Tabernacle.*

CLIBURN, HARVEY LAVAN ("VAN")

b. 1934 Shreveport, Louisiana.
Pianist. Raised in Kilgore, Texas; studied piano from age three with his mother, former concert pianist; at Juilliard School in New York City; won International Tchaikovsky Competition in Moscow against pianists from nineteen other countries, thus gaining world-wide attention; upon return to New York City, he received the first ticker-tape parade ever given a musician.

CLIFTON, ARTHUR

b. 1784 Edinburgh, Scotland, d. 1832 Baltimore, Maryland. Composer and music publisher. Born Philip Anthony Corri; brother of M.P. Corri and brother-in-law of Jan Ladislav Dussek; since his wife was Catholic, and he could not get a divorce, he left his wife, came to Baltimore (ca. 1814) and changed his name; composed "The Carrollton March" for the laying of the first stone of the Baltimore & Ohio Railroad (1828), a march for the visit of General Lafayette to Baltimore (1824), "Annual Coronation Ode" (1831), the operetta *The Enterprise,* arranged music for Frances Jordan Alsop, the singer, also composed pianoforte sonata on the death of Jan L. Dussek, *Oh Tell Me How from Love to Fly.*

CLIFTON, BILL

b. 1931 Riverwood, Maryland.
Singer and songwriter. Attended St. Paul's School, Concord, N.H. (1944-47), and Adirondack School, Coconut Grove, Florida (1947-49); graduated University of Virginia, Charlottesville (1954); M.A. (1959); wrote "Take Back Your Heart," "Lonely Heart Blues," "When Autumn Leaves Begin to Fall."

CLIFTON, CHALMERS

b. 1889 Jackson, Mississippi, d. 1966. Conductor and composer. Pupil of d'Indy and Gedalge; conducted Cecilia Society, Boston (1915-17), and American Orchestra Society, New York (1922-30); composed orchestral and piano works, and songs.

CLIFTON, WILLIAM

b. ca. 1800, d. ca. 1870. Popular composer. Wrote "Oh I Was Born in Ole Virginny" (1836), "Shinbone Alley" (arr. of "Long Time Ago"), "The Orphan's Fear" (1839), "Ding Along Josey" (1840), "The Last Link Is Broken" (1840, w. J.C. Barker), "We Won't Go Home 'Till Morning" (1842, arr. of an old French tune), "Don't Be Foolish Joe" (1848), "Huzza! Here's Columbia Forever" (1859), and "Richmond Is Ours!" (1865).

CLINE, PATSY

b. 1932 Winchester, Virginia, d. 1963 Camden, Tennessee. Singer and pianist. Real name was Virginia Patterson Hensley; hit records were "Walkin' After Midnight" (1957), "I Fall to Pieces" (1961), "Crazy" (1961), "When I Get Through with You, You'll Love Me Too" and "She's Got You" (1962), "Faded Love," "Leavin' on Your Mind" and "Sweet Dreams" (1963); died in an airplane crash March 5th, eighty-five miles west of Nashville while returning from a benefit performance in Kansas City for the family of DJ Cactus Call who was killed in a traffic accident.

CLOKEY, JOSEPH WADDELL

b. 1890 New Albany, Indiana, d. 1961 San Dimas, California. Composer and teacher. Educated at Miami University, Oxford, Ohio, and the Cincinnati Conservatory (1915); taught organ and theory at Miami University (1915-26) and at Pomona College, Claremont, California (1926-39); composed a drama with music, *A Rose from Syria.*

CLOONEY, ROSEMARY

b. 1928 Maysville, Kentucky. Singer. As a child, she sang with her sister Betty to help her grandfather win a mayoral election; later moved to Cincinnati, Ohio; appeared on station WLW there; joined Tony Pastor's orchestra (1946); became solo vocalist (1949) and made many successful records.

CLOUGH-LEITER, HENRY

b. 1874 Washington, D.C., d. 1956 Wollaston, Massachusetts. Organist and composer. Pupil of Edward Kimball, H. Xande and J.H. Anger; organist in Washington, D.C. and Providence, R.I.; composed *Lasca* (for tenor and orchestra), *A Day of Beauty* (for string quartet), four cantatas, and many songs.

CLOUSE, ROSE

b. 1865 Mound City, Illinois, d. after 1900. Pianist and teacher. Studied in Leipzig, Germany; taught in Toledo, Ohio.

COASTERS (black rock group)

Carl Gardner, lead singer; albums—*Coast Along, Coasters, Coasters' Greatest Hits, One by One;* at the "Legend of Rock 'n Roll" show at Hollywood Bowl, California (1972).

COBB, WILBUR JAMES (JIMMY)

b. 1929 Washington, D.C. Black drummer. Worked with Dinah Washington in 1950s; then with C. Adderley, Stan Getz, and Dizzy Gillespie; between 1958-63 with Miles Davis; played in Wynton Kelly Trio with bassist Paul Chambers; toured Japan (1964) in group led by J.J. Johnson.

COBB, WILL D.

b. 1876 Philadelphia, Pennsylvania, d. 1930 New York City. Lyricist. Educated at Girard College, Philadelphia; department store salesman; later lyricist with composer Gus Edwards; wrote "I Couldn't Stand to See My Baby Lose" (1899), "I Can't Tell Why I Love You But I Do" (1900), "School Days" (1906), "Goodby, Dolly Gray" (1897, m. Paul Barnes).

COBURN, RICHARD

b. 1886 Ipswich, Massachusetts, d. 1952 Los Angeles, California. Singer and lyricist. Born Frank D. de Long; wrote lyrics for "Whispering" (1920, m. John Schonberger and Vincent Rose).

COCHRAN, EDDIE

b. 1938 Oklahoma City, Oklahoma, d. 1960 England. Rock singer and songwriter. Wrote "Summertime Blues," recorded by The Who and also by Blue Cheer; killed in a car accident while touring England with Gene Vincent; albums—*Summertime Blues* (1958), *Eddie Cochran* (1960), *Never to Be Forgotten.*

COCHRAN, HENRY

b. 1935 Greenville, Mississippi. Singer and songwriter. With Harlan Howard, he wrote "I Fall to Pieces" (1961), also wrote in 1962: "She's Got You," "A Little Teddy Bear," "Funny Way of Laughing," "Tears Broke Out on Me" and "Willingly," "Make the World Go Away" and "You Comb Her Hair" (1963), "I Want to Go With You" and

"Don't Touch Me" (1966); his LP records were *Hank Cochran* (1965) and *Hits from the Heart* (1966).

COERNE, LOUIS ADOLPHE

b. 1870 Newark, New Jersey, d. 1922 New London, Connecticut. Organist, teacher, and composer. Studied at Stuttgart and Paris (1876-80), then Harvard University, then in Munich; organist in Boston, at the Columbian Exposition, Chicago (1893); director of Liedertafel, Buffalo (1893-96); then taught at Harvard, and later Smith College, Northampton, Mass., Olivet College, and Connecticut College; composed opera *Zenobia* (performed at Bremen, 1905), also *The Maid of Marblehead* (opera), vocal music.

COFFIN, HENRY SLOANE

b. 1877 New York City, d. 1954.
Hymnist and compiler. Educated at Yale University, the New College, Edinburgh, and the University of Marburg; served the Bedford Park and Madison Avenue (Presbyterian) Churches, New York City and became president of the Union Theological Seminary in 1926; translated stanzas 2 and 3 of "O Come, O Come, Immanuel" from the Latin, and headed the committee that compiled *Hymns of the Kingdom of God* (1910).

COHAN, GEORGE MICHAEL

b. 1878 Providence, Rhode Island, d. 1942 New York City. Popular composer. As a youth he toured the vaudeville circuit with his parents and sister as "The Four Cohans"; wrote the musical shows *Little Johnny Jones* (1904, including his songs "The Yankee Doodle Boy" and "Give My Regards to Broadway") *Forty-five Minutes from Broadway* (1906, including "Mary's a Grand Old Name"), and the songs "You're a Grand Old Flag" (1906), "There's Something About a Uniform" (1909), and "Over There" (1917); his career was filmed in *Yankee Doodle Dandy* (1942) with James Cagney.

COHEN, JOHN

b. 1932 New York City.
Singer and guitarist. Graduated Yale (1956); formed the New Lost City Ramblers, which was featured in folk concerts across the country and at the Newport Folk Festival, Newport, R.I.; filmed the story of Roscoe Holcomb, folk singer, entitled *The High Lonesome Sound* (1964); compiled *New Lost City Ramblers Song Book* (1964).

COHEN, LEONARD

b. 1933 Canada.
Singer and songwriter. Came to New York (1966); wrote "Suzanne" recorded by Judy Collins (1966), "So Long, Marianne" recorded by Noel Harrison, "Sisters of Mercy"; appeared on stage with Judy Collins at a concert in New York's Central Park (1967); albums—*Songs of Leonard Cohen, Songs from a Room.*

COHN, ALVIN GILBERT (AL)

b. 1925 Brooklyn, New York.
Jazz saxophonist. Played with Elliot Lawrence; also with Henry Jerome; wrote arrangements for Georgie Auld and Elliot Lawrence; married Mary Ann McCall, singer in Woody Herman's band; at the Newport Jazz Festival, New York City (1972).

COHN, ARTHUR

b. 1910 Philadelphia, Pennsylvania.
Composer. Studied at Juilliard School, New York City; director of music division, New York Public Library; director of Edwin A. Fleisher Music Collection; composed *Retrospections*, for string orchestra (Philadelphia Chamber Orchestra under Isadore Freed, 1935), *Histrionics*, for string quartet or string orchestra (New York String Quartet, 1935), *Four Symphonic Documents* (National Symphony Orchestra under Kindler, 1941), *Four Preludes* (Greenwich Orchestra, 1937).

COHN, GEORGE THOMAS ("SONNY")

b. 1925 Chicago, Illinois.
Trumpeter. With Walter Dyett and Red Saunders in 1940s and '50s; with Count Basie after 1960.

COKER, CHARLES MITCHELL ("DOLO")

b. 1927 Hartford, Connecticut.
Pianist. Raised in Florence, S.C.; studied music at Mather Academy, Camden, S.C.; with Ben Webster in Philadelphia (1946); with Kenny Dorham, S. Stitt, G. Ammons, Clyde McPhatter and others in 1950s; went to Los Angeles and formed own trio there (1961).

COKER, HENRY L.

b. 1919 Dallas, Texas.
Jazz trombonist. Played with Benny Carter and Eddie Heywood in 1940s; with Count Basie (1952-63); toured with Ray Charles (1966).

COKER, JERRY

b. 1932 South Bend, Indiana.
Tenor sax and bandleader. With Woody Herman (1953-54); also Stan Kenton; studied composition at Yale (1958); led jazz bands at Sam Houston College, Huntsville, Texas (1960-62), Monterey Peninsula College (1963-64), Indiana University (1965), and Miami

University (1966); toured the Near East (1966) under State Department program.

COLCORD, LINCOLN

b. 1883 at sea off Cape Horn, South America, d. 1947 Belfast, Maine. Lyricist. Graduated University of Maine (1906); wrote the "Maine Stein Song" (1901, m. E.A. Fensted) popularized by Rudy Vallee.

COLE, EDWIN LE MAR ("BUDDY")

b. 1916 Irvington, Illinois, d. 1964 North Hollywood, California. Pianist and organist. Accompanist to Bing Crosby, Judy Garland, Nat King Cole and others; died of a heart attack.

COLE, JOHN

b. 1774 Tewksbury, England, d. 1855 Baltimore, Maryland. Composer and publisher. His family came to Baltimore (1785), where he was with the firm of Neal, Wills & Cole, music publishers (1812-15); composed the tune "Geneva" ("When All Thy Mercies, O My God," ca. 1830, w. Joseph Addison); leader of The Independent Blues Regimental Band which was present at the North Point battle during the War of 1812; issued *Episcopal Harmony* (1800), *Divine Harmonist* (1808), *Ecclesiastical Harmony* (1810), *The Minstrel* (1812, a book of songs), *Devotional Harmony* (1814), *Songs of Zion* (1818, psalm tunes), *The Seraph* (1821), *Beauties of Psalmody* (1827), *Sacred Melodies* (1828), *Laudate Dominum* (1842), *Collection of Anthems* (fifty-six pages, no date), *Music for the Church* (1844, jointly with N.C. Burt).

COLE, NAT ("KING")

b. 1917 Montgomery, Alabama, d. 1969 Santa Monica, California. Black singer, pianist, and bandleader. Born Nathaniel Coles; learned to play the piano at age four; played the church organ at age twelve; had his own band in high school; pianist at the Swanee Club, Hollywood; played at the 331 Club, Los Angeles; recorded "Nature Boy" (by Eden Ahbez) which became a hit; toured South America (1959); toured Europe (1960) where he gave a command performance for Queen Elizabeth; died of lung cancer.

COLE, ROBERT A. (BOB)

b. 1863 Athens, Georgia, d. 1911.
Black composer, singer, and vaudeville actor. Graduated Atlanta University; wrote "Louisiana Lize" (1899); the vaudeville team of Bob Cole and Billy Johnson wrote "The Wedding of the Chinese and the Coon" (1897) and "Chicken" (1899); their greatest success was "La Hoola Boola" (1897) which later became "Boola Boola" of Yale University; with Cole and the Johnson Brothers (James Weldon Johnson and J. Rosamond Johnson, 1901-06); with J. Rosamond Johnson wrote "Under the Bamboo Tree," "The Maiden with the Dreamy Eyes," and "Lazy Moon."

COLE, ROSSETTER GLEASON

b. 1866 near Clyde, Michigan, d. 1952 Chicago, Illinois. Teacher and composer. Graduated University of Michigan; studied in Berlin with Max Bruch (1890-92); taught at Ripon College, Wisconsin (1892-94), at Iowa College (1894-1901), then after 1902 taught in Chicago; composed a sonata for violin, ballade for cello and orchestra, songs.

COLE, SAMUEL WINKLEY

b. 1848, d. after 1900.
Conductor, teacher, and writer. Taught sight singing and vocal music at New England Conservatory, Boston.

COLE, ULRIC

b. 1905 New York City.
Composer. Studied with Homer Grunn in Los Angeles, Goetschius in New York, at Juilliard School, New York City, and with Nadia Boulanger in Paris; composed *Two Sketches* for string orchestra (Mutual Broadcasting String Symphony under Wallenstein, 1938), *Concerto for Piano and Orchestra, Two Sonatas* for violin and piano, *Divertimento* for string orchestra and two pianos.

COLE, WILLIAM R. ("COZY")

b. 1909 East Orange, New Jersey
Black jazz drummer. Recorded with Jelly Roll Morton (1930); then with Cab Calloway, the Armstrong All-Stars, Hines, Teagarden; led own combo after 1958; toured West Africa (1962-63) on State Department program.

COLEMAN, EARL

b. 1925 Port Huron, Michigan.
Baritone. Sang with Ernie Fields, Earl Hines, Jay McShann, and King Kolax in 1940s; with Gene Ammons in 1950s; with Gerald Wilson's band in Los Angeles (1960); in London and Paris (1962); in New York City after 1962.

COLEMAN, GEORGE

b. 1935 Memphis, Tennessee.
Tenor saxist and alto saxist. With B.B. King, John Gilmore, and Max Roach during 1950s; with Slide Hampton, Wild Bill Davis, and Miles Davis in early 1960s; with Lionel Hampton after 1964; wife, Gloria, is an organist.

COLEMAN, ORNETTE

b. 1930 Fort Worth, Texas.
Black alto saxophonist. Studied on a Guggenheim Fellowship; played in bands with John Coltrane, saxophonist, and Eric Dolphy, clarinetist; instrumentals—"Lonely Woman," "Sadness," "Ramblin'," "Turnaround."

COLEMAN, WILLIAM JOHNSON (BILL)

b. 1904 Centerville, near Paris, Kentucky.
Black jazz trumpeter. Played in Teddy Hill's band in Harlem's Savoy Ballroon, New York City; played with Sidney Bechet; went to Paris (1935); played with Teddy Wilson, Andy Kirk, and John Kirby in New York City in 1940s; returned to Paris (1948) to live there; toured England (1966).

COLES, GEORGE

b. 1792 Stewkley, England, d. 1858 New York City. Composer. Came to America as a young man and joined the New York (Methodist) Conference; was a flutist; assistant editor of *The Christian Advocate* and editor of the *Sunday School Advocate;* composed the tune "Duane Street" (1835, used for "Jesus My All to Heaven Is Gone," w. John Cennick) and "A Poor Wayfaring Man of Grief" (w. James Montgomery).

COLES, JOHNNY

b. 1926 Trenton, New Jersey.
Trumpeter. Played with military band (1941); with Slappy and His Swingsters, and Eddie Vinson in 1940s; with Philly Joe Jones, Bull Moose Jackson, and James Moody in 1950s; recorded with Gil Evan's band (1959); with George Coleman at Newport Jazz Festivals in 1960s; also with Hunter College jazz concerts.

COLESWORTHY, DANIEL C.

b. 1810 Portland, Maine, d. 1893.
Compiler. Published *Sabbath School Hymns* (1833) and *Opening Buds* (1838).

COLLER, PERCY E.B.

b. 1895 Liverpool, England.
Composer. Educated at Liverpool University; served in the British army in World War I; emigrated to Canada, where he became organist-choirmaster at St. Peter's Church, Mount Royal, Montreal, Quebec; composed the tune "St. Joan" ("Christ Is the World's True Light" 1941, w. G.W. Briggs).

COLLETTE, WILLIAM MARCELL ("BUDDY")

b. 1921 Los Angeles, California.
Black saxist, flutist, clarinetist, and composer. Played with Benny Carter, Gerald Wilson, and Chico Hamilton Quintet in 1940s and '50s; with T. Monk and Charles Mingus in 1960s; wrote five fugues, three arrangements for T. Monk (1964), "Jazz As I Feel It," with Earl Bostic; with Los Angeles Neophonic Orchestra (1965).

COLLIE, HIRAM ABIFF

b. 1926 Little Rock, Arkansas.
Singer, trumpeter, and disk jockey. Started with radio station KMAC, San Antonio, Texas (1943), then with stations in Browning, Alice, and Houston, Texas; master of ceremonies for the "Philip Morris Country Music Show" (1957-58), which toured thirty-seven states; later went with station KFOX, Long Beach, California; produced the "Academy of Country and Western Music Show" in Beverly Hills, California (1967).

COLLIER, MARY ANN

b. 1810 Charlestown (Boston), Massachusetts, d. 1866 Alexandria, Virginia. Hymnist. Wrote "The Sun That Lights Yon Broad Blue Sky."

COLLINS, DOROTHY

b. 1926 Windsor, Ontario, Canada.
Singer. Album—*Dorothy Collins.*

COLLINS, JOHN ELBERT

b. 1913 Montgomery, Alabama.
Guitarist. With Art Tatum, Roy Eldridge, Dizzy Gillespie, and Slam Stewart; with Nat King Cole (1951-65); joined Bobby Troup Trio (1965).

COLLINS, JOYCE

b. 1930 Battle Mountain, Nevada.
Pianist and singer. Studied at College of the Pacific, Stockton, California; with Oscar Pettiford in San Francisco (1955); with Bob Cooper in Los Angeles (1960); led own duo and trio after 1960; played in Paris (1960) and Mexico City (1965).

COLLINS, JUDY

b. 1939 Seattle, Washington.
Singer and guitarist. When she was young, the family moved to Boulder, Colorado; made her folk concert debut at New York's Town Hall (1964), which was greeted with wild applause; her LP record *The Judy Collins Concert* (1969) was a hit of the year.

COLLINS, LAWRENCE ALBERT

b. 1944 Tulsa, Oklahoma.
Singer, guitarist, and songwriter. Larry and his sister Lorrie were a team; the family moved to Sapulpa, Oklahoma when they were young; they made their debut on the "Town

Hall Party Show," Compton California (1953); they wrote "In My Teens," "My First Love," "Go 'Way Don't Bother Me," "Hop, Skip and Jump," "Young Heart," "Heart Beat," "Whistle Bait," "Mercy" and "Sweet Talk"; their albums included *Country Spectacular* (1957) and *Town Hall Party* (1958).

COLLINS, LAWRENCINE MAY (LORRIE)

b. 1942 Tahlequah, Oklahoma.
Singer. (*See* Lawrence Albert Collins)

COLLINS, LEE

b. 1901 New Orleans, Louisiana, d. 1960 Chicago, Illinois. Black jazz trumpeter. With King Oliver's Band (1924) as replacement for Louis Armstrong; played in Paris (1951) at the Salle Pleyel with the Mezz Mezzrow Dixieland group.

COLLINS, RUDOLPH ALEXANDER (RUDY)

b. 1934 New York City.
Drummer. Appeared with Cootie Williams, Roy Eldridge, Austin Powell and others in 1950s; with Herbie Mann (1959-60), toured Africa; with Dizzy Gillespie (1962-66).

COLLINS, TOMMY

b. 1930 Oklahoma City, Oklahoma.
Singer, guitarist, and songwriter. Born Leonard Raymond Sipes; attended Oklahoma Central State College, Edmond, Oklahoma; settled in Bakersfield, California; wrote "Whatcha Gonna Do Now," "You Gotta Have a License" and "You Better Not Do That" (1954), "It Tickles" (1955), "If You Can't Bite, Don't Growl" (1966); his LP records include *Light of the Lord* (religious), *This Is Tommy Collins* (1959).

COLONNA, JERRY

b. 1904 Boston, Massachusetts.
Trombonist, comedian, and songwriter. Played with Columbia Symphony (1931-36); later on Bob Hope TV show; appeared in films; played on "Saturday Night Swing" with Raymond Scott, pianist, and Bunny Berigan, trumpet player.

COLTRANE, JOHN

b. 1926 Hamlet, North Carolina, d. 1967.
Black saxophonist. Played in bands with Eric Allan Dolphy, clarinetist, and Ornette Coleman, saxophonist; with Miles Davis (1955-60); formed own combo (1960); considered one of the great saxophonists.

COLUMBO, RUSS

b. 1908, d. 1934.
Singer, violinist, and bandleader. Played violin in Gus Arnheim's band; organized own band; while cleaning his loaded hunting rifle, accidentally shot himself to death.

COLVER, NATHANIEL

b. 1794 Orwell, Vermont, d. 1870.
Hymnist. Became a Baptist minister (1836) in Boston, then Detroit, Cincinnati, and Chicago; founded Colver Institute, Richmond, Virginia (1865); contributed seventeen hymns to Banvard's *Christian Methodist*, Boston (1848).

COLWELL-WINFIELD BLUES BAND
(blues band)

"Moose" Sorrento, vocals; Chuck Purro, drums; Jack Shroer, sax; Bill Colwell, guitar; Mike Winfield, bass; Collin Tilton, tenor sax and flute; album—*Cold Wing Blues* (1968).

COMBS, GILBERT RAYNOLDS

b. 1863 Philadelphia, Pennsylvania, d. 1934 Mt. Airy, Pennsylvania. Organist and teacher. Organist and teacher in Philadelphia; founded the Broad Street Conservatory of Music (1885), of which he was director.

COMDEN, BETTY

b. 1915 New York City.
Lyricist and librettist. Attended New York University; with Adolph Green, wrote the book and lyrics for Leonard Bernstein's first Broadway show, *On the Town* (1944), with Green, *High Button Shoes* (1947, m. Jule Styne), with Green, *Two on the Aisle* (1951, m. Styne), *Wonderful Town* (1953, m. Bernstein), *Peter Pan* (1954, Styne, starring Mary Martin).

COMER, THOMAS

b. 1790, d. 1862.
Composer. Edited *Music of King's Chapel*, Boston (1835), which included many of his tunes and was written for Unitarian churches; also a singer, conductor, and teacher; wrote "The Captain with His Whiskers," which was very popular with the Confederate Army.

COMO, PERRY

b. 1912 Canonsburg, Pennsylvania.
Singer. Seventh son of Italian immigrants; was a singer-barber at age fifteen in his own barber shop; sang for Ted Weems' band (1936-42); own show on CBS radio, New York City after 1943; first real hit record was " 'Till the End of Time" (1945); with NBC-TV after

1955; at the Hilton International, Las Vegas (1972).

COMSTOCK, OSCAR FRANKLIN

b. 1865 Brooklyn, New York, d. 1944. Teacher. Studied with George F. Bristow; later in Leipzig and with the St. Caecilia Society in Rome; taught in Cleveland, Ohio.

CONDON, ALBERT EDWIN (EDDIE)

b. 1904 Goodland, Indiana, d. 1973. Guitarist and bandleader. Played with Red McKenzie in the Mound City Blue Blowers, New York (1928); his group made the first jazz performance on TV (1942); opened own night club in New York (1946); had own TV series (1948); played at 1954 Newport Jazz Festival; his combo toured Australia, New Zealand, and Japan (1964); taken ill (1964), but made a comeback (1965); played at Newport Jazz Festival, New York City (1972).

CONFREY, EDWARD ("ZEZ")

b. 1895 Peru, Illinois, d. 1971 Lakewood, New Jersey. Composer and jazz pianist. Zez and his older brother, Jim, pianist, formed their own band (1915); served in navy in World War I; in the navy touring show, "Leave to the Sailors"; played with Benny Kabelski, violinst (Jack Benny); later played in Paul Whiteman's band; wrote "Stumbling" (1922), "Dizzy Fingers" (1923), "Nickel in the Slot" (1926), "Kitten on the Keys" (1924, introduced in Aeolian Concert Hall the same day George Gershwin introduced *Rhapsody in Blue*).

CONKEY, ITHAMAR

b. 1815 Shutesbury, Massachusetts, d. 1867 Elizabeth, New Jersey. Composer. Organist at the Central Baptist Church, Norwich, Conn.; later was a bass singer in the choir of Calvary Church, New York City; composed the tune "Rathburn" ("In the Cross of Christ I Glory" 1847, w. John Bowring, also used for "Tell Me Not in Mournful Numbers," w. Henry W. Longfellow).

CONLEY, ARTHUR

b. 1947. Black singer and songwriter. Discovered by Otis Redding (1965); albums—*Shake, Rattle and Roll, Soul Directions, Sweet Soul Music, More Sweet Soul.*

CONN, CHARLES GERARD

b. 1844 Manchester, New York, d. 1931. Instrument maker. Brought to Elkhart, Indiana (1850); served in the Civil War (1861-65) as a captain; started making brass instruments (1872); invented many improvements for the cornet; lost his factory in a fire (1883), but rebuilt the factory; opened a branch in Worcester, Mass. (1887); also made brass clarinets; was mayor of Elkhart for four years.

CONN, IRVING

b. 1898 London, England, d. 1961 Fort Lee, New Jersey. Conductor and composer. Born Irving Cohn; educated at Juilliard, New York City; served in U.S. Army in World War I; conducted his own orchestra in hotels in New York City; wrote "Yes, We Have No Bananas" (1923, w. Frank Silver).

CONNECTICUT YANKEES (band) *see* RUDY VALLEE

CONNELLY, MARC

b. 1890 McKeesport, Pennsylvania. Playwright and librettist. Librettist for *Helen of Troy* (1926) with George S. Kaufman (m. Harry Ruby).

CONNIFF, RAY

b. 1916 Attleboro, Massachusetts. Trombonist, conductor, and arranger. Studied at the Juilliard School, New York City; played with Bunny Berigan, Bob Crosby, and Artie Shaw; served in the army in World War II; also arranger for Harry James; his album *'S Wonderful* (1956) sold in the millions.

CONNOR, CHRIS

b. 1927 Kansas City, Missouri. Singer. With Stan Kenton (1953); she sang in various clubs during the 1960s; Austin Jazz Festival (1966).

CONNORS, CHARLES (CHUCK)

b. 1930 Maysville, Kentucky. Bass trombonist. With Dizzy Gillespie (1957); joined Duke Ellington (1961).

CONRAD, CON

b. 1891 New York City, d. 1938 Van Nuys, California. Popular composer. Born Conrad K. Dober; vaudeville actor on the Keith circuit; composed "Margie" (1920, w. Benny Davis), "Ma—He's Making Eyes at Me" (1921, w. Sidney Clare), "Barney Google" (w. Billy Rose), "The Continental" (1934, w. Herb Magidson), "Prisoner of Love" (w. Leo Robin).

CONVERSE, CHARLES CROZAT

b. 1832 Warren, Massachusetts, d. 1918 Highwood, New Jersey. Noted composer. Received his musical training in Berlin and

Leipzig, Germany, but returned to America to study law; for many years he practiced law in Erie, Pa., and retired in Highwood, N.J.; composed the music for "What a Friend We Have in Jesus" (w. Joseph Scriven, ca. 1855, tune "Converse"), "The Ninety and Nine" (w. Elizabeth Clephane), and "The Death of Minnehaha" (1856, w. Henry W. Longfellow, "The Rock Beside the Sea").

CONVERSE, FREDERICK SHEPHERD

b. 1871 Newton, Massachusetts, d. 1940 Boston, Massachusetts. Noted composer. Studied at Harvard University with J.K. Paine (1889-93), then in Munich; taught at the New England Conservatory, then at Harvard (1901-07), and at the N.E. Conservatory (1921-38); known for *The Mystic Trumpeter* (1905, based on poem by Walt Whitman), the opera *The Pipe of Desire* (1906, libretto G.E. Burton); in World War I he enlisted as a private and attained the rank of captain in the 13th Regiment Massachusetts State Guard; wrote *American Sketches* (1935, based on Carl Sandburg's *The American Songbag*).

COOK, HERMAN ("JUNIOR")

b. 1934 Pensacola, Florida.
Tenor saxist. With Horace Silver Quintet (1958-64); then with Blue Mitchell after 1964.

COOK, JOHN ("WILLIE")

b. 1923 East Chicago, Indiana.
Black trumpeter. Played with Earl Hines, Dizzy Gillespie, Duke Ellington and others.

COOK, MARTHA ANN (WOODBRIDGE)

b. 1807, d. 1874.
Hymnist. Resided in Bridgeport, Conn. and Lynn, Mass.; her husband was the Rev. Parsons Cook (1800-65), editor of the *Puritan Recorder*, Boston; she wrote the hymn "In Some Way or Other the Lord Will Provide" (m. Calvin S. Harrington, second tune by Philip Phillips).

COOK, MAY A.

b. 1870 Michigan.
Pianist and teacher. Established Cook's Musical Institute, Portland, Oregon; also concert pianist.

COOK, RUSSELL STURGIS

b. 1811 New Marlborough, Massachusetts, d. 1864 Pleasant Valley, New York. Hymnist. Congregational minister and Secretary of the American Tract Society (1839-56); wrote "Just as Thou Art," "Burdened with Guilt, Wouldn't Thou Be Blessed" (*Sabbath Hymn Book*, 1858).

COOK, WILL MARION

b. 1869 Washington, D.C., d. 1944 New York City. Noted black composer. Son of a professor of law at Howard University; studied the violin at Oberlin Conservatory, Oberlin, Ohio, when he was only thirteen, and at fifteen he won a scholarship to study with Joseph Joachim in Berlin; when he returned to the states he studied with Antonin Dvořák at the National Conservatory of Music in New York City; composed the ragtime operetta *Clorinda* which was produced on Broadway in 1898; the hit tunes "That's How the Cake Walk Is Done" and "Emancipation Day," were a success; also wrote "I May Be Crazy but I Ain't No Fool," "I'm Comin' Virginia," "Rain Song," "Darktown Out Tonight" (1898) and "Who Dat Say Chicken in Dis Crowd?" (w. P.L. Dunbar); married Abbie Mitchell, soprano.

COOKE, CHARLES L. ("DOC")

b. 1891 Louisville, Kentucky, d. 1958 Wurtsboro, New York. Black composer. Graduated Chicago Musical College, also received doctorate there; led own orchestra; staff arranger for Detroit publishing firms and for RKO pictures, later for Radio City Music Hall, New York City; wrote scores for *Cabin in the Sky* (1940), *Banjo Eyes, The Hot Mikado, Follow the Girls;* his *Sketches of the Deep South* were performed at an ASCAP Silver Jubilee concert (1939).

COOKE, JAMES FRANCIS

b. 1875 Bay City, Michigan, d. 1960 Philadelphia, Pennsylvania. Pianist, teacher, and writer. Studied at the Wurzburg R. Conservatory and in New York; became editor of *The Etude* (1907), then president of the Presser Foundation (1917); wrote *Standard History of Music, Musical Playlets, Music Masters Old and New, Great Pianists upon Piano Playing, Mastering Scales and Arpeggios.*

COOKE, SAM

b. 1935 Chicago, Illinois, d. 1964 Los Angeles, California. Black singer. Sang for the Soul Stirrers, gospel group at the Shrine Auditorium, Los Angeles; his first record, "You Send Me," sold over two million copies; appeared on "American Bandstand" TV show during the 1960s; shot to death in a Los Angeles motel in a gun fight.

COOLIDGE, RITA

b. 1945.
Singer. Raised in Nashville; daughter of a Baptist preacher, sang in her daddy's choir;

back-up singer for Delaney & Bonnie; album—*Rita Coolidge;* with Kris Kristofferson in concert at Philharmonic Hall, New York City (1972).

COOMBS, CHARLES WHITNEY

b. 1859 Bucksport, Maine, d. 1940 Montclair, New Jersey. Organist and composer. Organist in an American church in Dresden, Germany (1887-91), Church of the Holy Communion, New York (1892), St. Luke's (1908); composed *The Vision of St. John* (cantata with orchestra and organ) and songs.

COOPER, BOB

b. 1925 Pittsburgh, Pennsylvania.
Tenor saxist, oboe player, and composer. With Stan Kenton (1945-51); with Howard Rumsey's Lighthouse All-Stars and other groups in 1950s; married singer June Christy; composed *Music for Jazz Saxophones and Symphony Orchestra* (1963) for Ford TV shows (1964-65); toured Japan with June Christy (1961).

COOPER, EMIL

b. 1879 Odessa, Russia, d. 1960 New York. Conductor. Conductor in Kiev, Moscow, and St. Petersburg, then toured Europe and South America; became conductor of the Metropolitan Opera in New York City.

COOPER, GEORGE

b. 1838 New York City, d. there 1927.
Lyricist. Closest friend Stephen Foster had in New York City, found Foster bleeding from an accident in Foster's hotel room in the Bowery, and took him to Bellevue Hospital, where Foster died there three days later in January 1864; Cooper wrote the lyrics, and Foster the music, for "Mr. and Mrs. Brown" and "Bring Back My Brother to Me" (1862); Cooper wrote the lyrics for many other composers—with J.R. Thomas, "Linger Not, Darling" (1863), "Our Noble Chief Has Passed Away" (1865, on the death of President Lincoln), "Must We Then Meet as Strangers" (1875), "Golden Hours" (1875), "Rose of Killarney" (1876); with J.P. Skelly, "Twinkle, Twinkle Little Star" and "Strolling on the Brooklyn Bridge" (1883); with David Braham, "To Rest Let Him Gently Be Laid"; with Adam Geibel, "Joys of Spring" (1879); with F.W. Meacham, "There Is No Place Like New York After All" (1895); with Ira D. Sankey, "There Are Lonely Hearts to Cherish," "While the Days Are Going By"; with Henry Tucker, "Sweet Genevieve"; with Thomas B. Bishop, "Pretty as a Picture" and "God Bless My Boy at Sea"; with E.P. Christy, "My Heart's O'er the Deep Blue Sea"; with Harrison Millard, "The Pilot Brave" and "Ship Ahoy!"; with M.R. Osgood, "Come Little Leaves."

COOPER, GEORGE ("BUSTER")

b. 1929 St. Petersburg, Florida.
Trombonist. Played with Lionel Hampton during 1950s; later lived in Paris; joined Duke Ellington (1962).

COOPER, JACKIE

b. 1922 Los Angeles, California.
Drummer and actor. Drummer in Claude Thornhill's orchestra while serving in the navy in the Pacific theatre in World War II; famous as an actor.

COOPER, STONEY

b. 1918 Harman, West Virginia.
Singer and fiddler. Married Wilma Lee Leary and they became a team; they sang on radio stations in Fairmont and Wheeling, West Virginia, and Harrisonburg, Virginia; they joined Grand Ole Opry, Nashville (1957); their top records were "Come Walk with Me," "There's a Big Wheel" and "Big Midnight Special" (1959), "Wreck on the Highway" (1961).

COOPER, WILMA LEE (LEARY)

b. 1921 Valley Head, West Virginia.
Singer, guitarist, banjoist, organist, and songwriter; graduated from Davis and Elkins College, Elkins, West Va.; sang with the "Leary Family"; married Stoney Cooper, and they became a team; she wrote (some jointly with Stoney), "Cheated Too" (1956), "I Tell My Heart," "Loving You" and "My Heart Keeps Crying" (1957), "He Taught Them How" (1958), "Heartbreak Street," "Tomorrow I'll Be Gone" and "Big Midnight Special" (1959).

COOTS, J. FRED

b. 1897 Brooklyn, New York.
Popular composer. Composed song material for Sophie Tucker and the team of Van & Schenk, vaudeville entertainers; wrote the songs for the musicals *Sally, Irene and Mary* (1922), *Artists and Models, June Days* and *Gay Paree* (1925), *The Merry World* (1926), *A Night in Paris* (1926), *White Lights* (1927), *Sons o' Guns* (1928); wrote "Love Letters in the Sand" (w. Nick Kenny), "Santa Claus Is Coming to Town" (w. Haven Gillespie), "Precious Little Thing Called Love" (w. Lou Davis).

COPAS, LLOYD ESTEL ("COWBOY")

b. 1913 Muskogee, Oklahoma, d. 1963.
Singer and guitarist. Regular performer on radio stations in Knoxville, Tennessee, and Cincinnati, Ohio; hit records were "Filipino Baby," "Tragic Romance," "Signed, Sealed and Delivered," "Tennessee Waltz" and "Kentucky Waltz" (1946), "Tennessee Moon" (1948), "Candy Kisses" (1949), "Strange Little Girl" (1951), "Alabam' " (1960), "Flat Top" (1961); star on Grand Ole Opry, Nashville, when he was killed in an airplane accident with Patsy Cline and Hawkshaw Hawkins.

COPELAND, BENJAMIN

b. 1855 Claredon, New York, d. 1940.
Hymnist. Educated at Genesee Wesleyan Seminary, then served in the Methodist circuit around Bradford, Pa.; later entered the Genesee Conference and served western New York for forty-two years, settling in Buffalo, N.Y.; wrote the hymn "Christ's Life Our Code, His Cross Our Creed" (1900), while serving the Frank Street Methodist Church, Rochester, N.Y. (tune "Copeland"—K.P. Harrington).

COPELAND, GEORGE

b. 1882 Boston, Massachusetts, d. 1971 Princeton, New Jersey. Concert pianist. Studied with Carlo Buonamici in Italy; met Debussy in 1911 and visited him almost daily for four months; became a Debussy expert, playing only his works most of the time; celebrated the fiftieth anniversary of his New York debut at Carnegie Hall in 1957.

COPELAND, RAY M.

b. 1926 Norfolk, Virginia.
Trumpeter and flügelhorn player. Played with big bands during 1940s; in Roxy Theater Orchestra, New York City (1959-61); later on various TV shows; with Pearl Bailey and Louis Bellson (1962-64); with Ella Fitzgerald (1965); Ray Copeland Jazz Band at Bryant Park, New York City (1972).

COPENHAVER, LAURA (SCHERER)

b. 1868 Marion, Virginia, d. 1940.
Hymnist. Wrote the hymn "Heralds of Christ, Who Bear the King's Commands" (tune "National Hymn"—G.W. Warren).

COPLAND, AARON

b. 1900 Brooklyn, New York.
Famous composer. Born Aaron Kaplan; studied at the Fontainebleau School of Music and with Nadia Boulanger in Paris; composed *Symphony for Organ and Orchestra* (1924), *Music for the Theatre* (1925), *El salon Mexico* for orchestra (1936), *Billy the Kid* (ballet 1938), *A Lincoln Portrait* for narrator and orchestra (1942), *Appalachian Spring* (ballet, 1945), Symphony no. 3 (1946), *Concerto for Clarinet and String Orchestra* (1948), which was adapted into the ballet, *The Pied Piper,* introduced by the New York City Ballet.

CORB, MORTIMER G. (MORTY)

b. 1917 San Antonio, Texas.
Bass player and composer. With Louis Armstrong, Benny Goodman, Jack Teagarden, and Bob Crosby during 1940s and '50s; then in Hollywood studio orchestras; wrote "Oasis," "Goodbye My Love," "Bayou Blues."

CORCORAN, GENE PATRICK ("CORKY")

b. 1924 Tacoma, Washington.
Tenor saxist. With Harry James at various times between 1941-57; led own combo in Seattle; back with Harry James after 1962.

COREA, ARMANDO ANTHONY ("CHICK")

b. 1941 Chelsea, Massachusetts.
Pianist. With Mongo Santamaria, Willie Bobo, Blue Mitchell, and Herbie Mann during 1960s; played in New York City.

CORIGLIANO, JOHN, JR.

b. 1938 New York City.
Composer. Son of John Corigliano, concertmaster of New York Philharmonic for twenty-two years; with David Hess wrote *The Naked Carmen,* rock extravaganza (Mercury Records, 1970) which included Mary Bruce and Her Starbuds, actor-singer George Turner, pianist John Atkins, tenor Robert White, rock singer Melba Moore, soprano Anita Darian, Metropolitan Opera singer William Walker, and the Detroit Symphony under Paul Paray.

CORN HUSKERS *see* NAT STUCKEY

CORNELL, DON

b. 1921 New York City.
Singer. Sang in Sammy Kaye's band; albums—*I'll Walk Alone, It Isn't Fair.*

CORNELL, JOHN HENRY

b. 1838 New York City, d. 1894.
Composer. Organist at St. Paul's Chapel, Trinity Church, New York City; composed the tunes "St. Kevin" (ca. 1865, "I Think When I Read That Sweet Story," w. Jemima T. Luke), and "Neale" ("Fierce Was the Wild Billow," translated from the Greek by J.M. Neale).

CORWIN, ROBERT (BOB)

b. 1933 Hollis, New York.
Pianist. With Don Elliott, Flip Phillips, and Anita O'Day during 1950s; with Peggy Lee, Anita O'Day, Louis Ney, Ruth Price, and Paul Horn during 1960s; toured Japan with Anita (1963); married Amanda Mercer, daughter of Johnny Mercer.

CORY, GEORGE

b. 1920 Syracuse, New York.
Pianist, conductor, and composer. Educated at University of California; served in U.S. Army in World War II; assistant to Gian-Carlo Menotti (1946-50); pianist in night clubs; wrote "I Left My Heart in San Francisco" (Grammy Award, 1963), same was sung by Claramae Turner, accompanied by the composer, at the fiftieth anniversary of the San Francisco Opera (1972).

COSTA, EDWIN JAMES (EDDIE)

b. 1930 Atlas, Pennsylvania, d. 1962 New York City. Vibraharpist and pianist. Noted soloist; albums—*In Their Own Sweet Way, Pair of Pianos;* killed in an auto crash.

COTNER, CARL B.

b. 1916 Lake Cicott, Indiana.
Bandleader and actor. Attended schools in Idaville, Indiana; Cincinnati College of Music (1937); leader of the Melody Ranch Band since 1939.

COTTEN, ELIZABETH ("LIBBA")

b. 1893 Chapel Hill, North Carolina.
Black singer and guitarist. Worked as a maid for Charles Seeger in Washington, D.C.; folk singer; recorded "Freight Train," which she wrote at age thirteen, it became a success in 1962.

COTTLOW, AUGUSTA

b. 1878 Shelbyville, Illinois, d. 1954 White Plains, New York. Pianist. Studied in Chicago and made her debut there (1889); then was a pupil of Seidl in New York (1891); studied in Berlin with Busoni and Boise; toured Europe, then America (1900).

COTTON, JAMES

b. 1925 Tunica, Mississippi.
Black singer and bandleader. Played the harmonica; at the age of nine, after hearing Sonny Boy Williamson play the harmonica on the radio, ran away from home to find his hero, was adopted by Williamson; with Muddy Waters' band (1954-66); formed his own band (1966); played at the Fillmore West Auditorium, San Francisco.

COTTON BLUES BAND, JAMES (blues band)

James Cotton, vocals and harmonica; Luther Tucker, lead guitar; Bob Anderson, bass; Albert Gianquinto, piano; Francis Clay, drums; albums—*James Cotton Blues Band, Pure Cotton, Cotton in Your Ears, Cut You Loose.*

COTTON PICKERS (jazz band) *see* JOHN NESBIT

COUNCE, CURTIS LEE

b. 1926 Kansas City, Missouri, d. 1963 Los Angeles, California. Black bass player. Active in Los Angeles after 1950; led his own trios and quintets; died of a heart attack.

COUNTRY BOYS *see* HOWARD VOKES

COUNTRY DRIFTERS *see* EDDIE NESBITT

COUNTRY GENTLEMEN

Charlie Waller, John Duffy, Eddie Adcock, and Jim Cox.

COUNTRY JOE AND THE FISH (folk-rock band)

Joe McDonald, lead vocals and rhythm guitar; Barry Melton, vocals and lead guitar; Bruce Barthol, bass and harmonica; Chicken Hirsch, drums; David Cohen, organ and guitar; started in 1965, debut at Fillmore West, San Francisco; albums—*Electric Music for the Mind and Body, I Feel Like I'm Fixin' to Die, Together, C.J. Fish, Greatest Hits, Here We Are Again.*

COUNTRY LADS *see* DICK FLOOD

COUNTRY RHYTHM BOYS (Bill Wimberly's band) *see* THUMBS CARLLILE

COVINGTON, WARREN

b. 1921 Philadelphia, Pennsylvania.
Trombonist and bandleader. After Tommy Dorsey died in 1956, Covington led Dorsey's band; led same band under his own name after 1961; featured his wife, singer Kathee Covington.

COWBOY RAMBLERS, THE *see* BILL BOYD

COWELL, HENRY DIXON

b. 1897 Menlo Park, California, d. 1965 Shady (Catskill Mts.), New York. Pianist and composer. Studied at the University of California; bandmaster in the army during World War I; studied at the Institute of Applied Music in New York; during World War II served with the Office of War Information in charge of music short-wave broadcasts; composed *Tales of Our Coun-*

tryside for piano and orchestra (1940), Hymn and Fuguing Tune no. 2 for string orchestra (1944, based on *Southern Harmony*, Billy Walker, 1835), Short Symphony no. 4 (1946, introduced by the Boston Symphony Orchestra, 1947).

COWLES, CECIL M.

b. 1898 San Francisco, California.
Pianist and composer. Studied with Hugo Mansfeldt, Otto Bendix, Reigger, Engle, et.al.; debut at age nine; gave recitals in United States, Europe and Near East; works—*Jesu Bambino* (mass), *Oriental Sketches, Shanghai Bund, Cubanita, Nocturne in A-flat.*

COWLES, EUGENE

b. 1860, d. 1948.
Singer. Introduced "Gypsy Love Song" from the *Fortune Teller* (w. Harry B. Smith and m. Victor Herbert) at the Grand Opera House in Toronto, Ontario, Canada (1898).

COWSILLS (rock group)

John, vocals and drums; Bob, vocals and guitar; Barry, vocals and bass; Bill, vocals and guitar; Susan, vocals; and Mini-Mom Barbara Cowsills, vocals; albums—*Best of the Cowsills, Captain Sad and His Ship of Fools, The Cowsills, In Concert, Plus the Lincoln Park Zoo, Two by Two, We Can Fly.*

COX, CHRISTOPHER CHRISTIAN

b. 1816 Baltimore, Maryland, d. 1882 Washington, D.C. Hymnist. Graduated Yale (1835); physician in Baltimore (1838) and Talbot County, Maryland (1843); brigade surgeon (1861); wrote the hymn "Silently the Shades of Evening" (Woodworth's *Cabinet*, 1847) and set to music, later the tune "Stockwell" was used, composed by D.E. Jones (1850).

COX, IDA

b. 1889 Cedartown, Georgia, d. 1967.
Black singer. Joined the Rabbit Foot Minstrels at age fourteen; also with Silas Green's Minstrels from New Orleans; led the Blues Serenaders; known as the "Uncrowned Queen of the Blues"; married her accompanist, Jesse Crump, pianist, of Paris, Texas, who was seventeen years younger than she; recorded on Black Swan disks with Lovie Austin and also with the Pruett Twins.

COX, JAMES

b. 1930 Vansant, Virginia.
Bassist and banjoist. Joined the group known as the "Country Gentlemen" (*See* Charles Waller)

COX, W. RALPH

b. 1884 Galion, Ohio, d. 1941 New York City. Composer and organist. Studied at Oberlin Conservatory, Guilmant Organ School, and Wooster University; studied under d' Aubigne, Braggiotti, et.al.; organist and choirmaster of Greenwich Presbyterian Church, New York City; later First Presbyterian Church, Orange, New Jersey; wrote "Pansies," "In a Southern Garden," "To a Hilltop," "The Road to Spring."

COXE, ARTHUR CLEVELAND

b. 1818 Mendham, New Jersey, d. 1896 Clifton Springs, New York. Hymnist. Graduated University of the City of New York (1838) and the General Theological Seminary (1841); Episcopal rector in Hartford, Conn., Baltimore, Md. then of Calvary Church, New York City; Bishop of Western New York (1865); wrote "O Where Are Kings and Empires Now" (1840, tune "St. Anne") and "How Beauteous Were the Marks Divine" (1840, tune "Canonbury"—Robert Schuman).

CRABBÉ, ARMAND

b. 1884 Brussels, Belgium, d. 1948 Buenos Aires, Argentina. Baritone. Studied at the Brussels Conservatory; sang with the Manhattan Opera House, New York City (1908-10), then with the Chicago Opera Company after 1910.

CRAFT, MARCELLA

b. 1880 Indianapolis, Indiana, d. 1959.
Soprano. Pupil of Charles Adams, also studied in Milan, Italy; opera debut (Morbegno, 1902); sang with the Munich Opera (1900-14); in America (1917-18); later returned to Germany.

CRAMER, FLOYD

b. 1933 Shreveport, Louisiana.
Singer and pianist. His family moved to Huttig, Arkansas, when he was young; started with radio station KWKH, Shreveport (1951) on "Louisiana Hayride," and was very popular; around 1955 he went to Nashville and joined Grand Ole Opry; first major hit was "Last Date" (1961); LP records are *Floyd Cramer* (1964) and *Class of 65, Class of 66, Class of 67, Class of 68, Class of 69, America's Biggest Selling Pianist.*

CRANSHAW, MELBOURNE R. ("BOB")

b. 1932 Evanston, Illinois.
Bass and tuba player. Studied drums from age ten; father was a drummer in Kansas City; played tuba while in army in Korea; with Eddie Harris and Walter Perkins in Chicago

during 1950s; with Sonny Rollins and Junior Mance in New York during 1960s; also toured England and Scotland with George Shearing and Joe Williams.

CRAWFORD, BENNY ROSS, JR. ("HANK")

b. 1934 Memphis, Tennessee.
Black saxist, pianist, and composer. Studied at Tennessee State University; played baritone sax with Ray Charles (1958); then switched to alto sax; with the band on European tours (1961-63); formed his own seven-piece band (1963); at the Monterey Jazz Festival (1964); wrote "The Peeper," "Dig These Blues," "Stony Lonesome"; at the CTI Summer Jazz Festival, New York City (1972).

CRAWFORD, HOLLAND R. ("RAY")

b. 1924 Pittsburgh, Pennsylvania.
Guitarist. With Fletcher Henderson as sax soloist and with Ahmad Jamal as guitarist during 1940s; later in New York with Gil Evans and others; moved to Los Angeles.

CRAWFORD, JIMMY

b. 1910 Memphis, Tennessee.
Black jazz drummer. Played in Jimmie Lunceford's band; in U.S. Army band during World War II; later played in orchestras for Broadway shows.

CRAWFORD, RUTH PORTER (Mrs. Charles Seeger)

b. 1901 East Liverpool, Ohio, d. 1953 Chevy Chase, Maryland. Composer. Studied in Chicago; won Guggenheim Fellowship for study in Paris and Berlin; composed *Three Songs* (Amsterdam Festival, 1933).

CREAMER, DAVID

b. 1812 Baltimore, Maryland, d. there 1887. Writer. Wrote the *Methodist Hymnology* (1848), being annotations of *The Methodist Hymn Book* of 1836; when the Sixth Massachusetts Infantry passed through the streets of Baltimore on April 19, 1861, many Union soldiers were killed, and it was through the efforts of Creamer that their families in Massachusetts learned of the care given to the dead and wounded in Baltimore; in 1863 he became assessor of internal revenue.

CREAMER, HENRY S.

b. 1879 Richmond Virginia, d. 1930 New York City. Black singer and songwriter. Co-founder of Clef Club; with Gotham-Attucks Music Co., New York City; teamed with Turner Layton in the vaudeville act of Layton and Johnson; were popular entertainers in England; with Layton, composer, wrote "After You've Gone" (1918), "Way Down Yonder in New Orleans" (1922), "Dear Old Southland" (1921).

CREEDENCE CLEARWATER REVIVAL (rock group)

Doug Clifford, drums; Stuart Cook, piano and electric bass; John Fogerty, guitar, harp, piano, and organ; Tom Fogerty, guitar; albums—*Bayou Country, Creedence Clearwater Revival, Green River, Willy and the Poor Boys.*

CREHORE, BENJAMIN

b. (?), d. 1819.
Instrument maker and publisher. Carpenter for Federal Street Theatre in Boston; was making violins, cellos, guitars, drums, and flutes in 1791; published music with Peter Albrecht Van Hagen, Sr. in Boston (1798-1803); constructed first piano in America in 1803 in Milton, Massachusetts.

CREOLE JAZZ BAND *see* KING OLIVER

CRESTON, PAUL

b. 1906 New York City.
Noted composer. Took private lessons; composed *Threnody* for orchestra (op. 16 introduced by the Pittsburgh Symphony under Fritz Reiner, 1938), *Two Choric Dances* for orchestra (op. 17 introduced at the Yaddo Music Festival, Saratoga Springs, New York by Arthur Shepherd, 1938), Symphony no. 1 (Brooklyn, New York, 1940), Symphony no. 2 (by the New York Philharmonic under Artur Rodzinski, 1944), Symphony no. 3 (by the Philadelphia Orchestra under Eugene Ormandy at the Worcester Music Festival, 1950).

CRISS, WILLIAM ("SONNY")

b. 1927 Memphis, Tennessee.
Alto saxist. With H. McGee and G. Wilson in Los Angeles during 1940s; led own combos during 1950s; went to Paris (1962) and played in night clubs there; also in Germany and Belgium; returned to Los Angeles (1965).

CRIST, BAINBRIDGE

b. 1883 Lawrenceburg, Indiana.
Composer. Studied with Juon, Emerich, and Shakespeare; taught in Boston after 1914; composed the dance-drama *Le Pied de la Momie,* songs, and orchestra and chamber music.

CRITTERS (rock group)

Chris Daraway, autoharp; Kenny Gorke, bass; Jeff Pelosi, drums; Jim Ryan, guitar; Bob Spinella, organ; albums—*Younger Girl, Touch 'n Go with the Critters.*

CROOKER, EARLE T.

b. 1899 Boston, Massachusetts.
Lyricist. Educated at University of Pennsylvania (Ph.D.); wrote special material for Beatrice Lillie (1926-41); with Frederick Loewe wrote scores for *Salute to Spring* (1937) and *Great Lady* (1938).

CROOKS, RICHARD

b. 1900 Trenton, New Jersey, d. 1972.
Noted tenor. Studied with Sydney H. Bourne and made concert appearances at age twelve; served in World War I; later was a soloist with the New York Symphony, Hamburg Opera (1927), Berlin Opera, then with the Metropolitan Opera Company, New York City (1933-43).

CROSBY, DAVID

b. 1941.
Rhythm guitarist, singer, and songwriter. His parents were both in the New York Social Register; with Crosby, Stills, Nash and Young; albums—*Crosby, Stills and Nash, Déjà Vu.*

CROSBY, FRANCES J. (FANNY)

b. 1820 South East, Putnam County, New York, d. 1915 Bridgeport, Connecticut.
Lyricist and hymnist. Lost her eyesight at age six weeks and was blind for ninety-five years; at the New York Institute for the Blind she was a pupil of George F. Root and wrote the lyrics for a number of his popular songs including "The Hazel Dell" (1853), "Rosalie, the Prairie Flower" (1855), "There's Music in the Air" (1854); married a blind musician, Alexander van Alstyne; wrote the hymns "Jesus the Water of Life Will Give" (tune "Fresh Laurels"—W.B. Bradbury, 1867), "Jesus Keep Me Near the Cross" (1869, m. W.H. Doane), "Praise Him, Praise Him" (1869, English tune), "Blessed Assurance" (1873, m. Phoebe P. Knapp), "All the Way My Savior Leads Me" (1875, m. Robert Lowry), "Tell Me the Old, Old Story" (1878, m. W.H. Doane), "Speed Away, Speed Away!" (1890, m. I.B. Woodbury, 1848).

CROSBY, GEORGE ROBERT (BOB)

b. 1913 Spokane, Washington.
Singer and bandleader. Younger brother of Bing Crosby; attended Gonzaga University, Spokane; sang for Anson Weeks' band (1933); worked for a New York band (1935) which became Bob Crosby's Bob Cats; served as a lieutenant in the marines in the Pacific in World War II; reorganized his band after the war; then appeared again as a singer; with his band at Roseland Dance City, New York (1972).

CROSBY, HARRY LILLIS ("BING")

b. 1904 Tacoma, Washington.
Singer and actor. Studied law for a time, then joined a dance band in Los Angeles (1924); member of the "Rhythm Boys" singing trio with Paul Whiteman's orchestra (1931); became famous as an actor, winning the Academy award for his part as a singing priest in *Going My Way* (1944); with Fred Ahlert, he wrote "Where the Blue of the Night Meets the Gold of the Day."

CROSBY, ISRAEL

b. 1919 Chicago, Illinois, d. there 1962.
Double bass player. Played in Raymond Scott's band; with the Ahmad Jamal Trio and Benny Goodman during 1950s; joined George Shearing (1962).

CROSS, ALLEN EASTMAN

b. 1864 Manchester, New Hampshire, d. 1943.
Hymnist. Educated at Amherst College, Amherst, Mass. and Andover Seminary; Congregational minister in Cliftondale, Mass. Springfield, Mass., then the Old South Church, Boston (1901-11); wrote the hymn "Jesus, Kneel Beside Me" (1907, tune "Eudoxia"—Sabine Baring-Gould).

CROSS, BENJAMIN

b. 1786 Philadelphia, Pennsylvania, d. 1857.
Noted organist, pianist, singer, conductor, composer, and teacher. Succeeded Benjamin Carr as organist at St. Augustine's Roman Catholic Church, Philadelphia (1831); wrote "The News and the Old Song" (pub. Willig, 1839), "I Saw Thee but an Hour" (pub. Nunns, ca. 1837), "Still Floats the Spangled Banner" (S. T. Gordon, N.Y., 1861).

CROSS, MICHAEL HURLEY

b. 1833 Philadelphia, Pennsylvania, d. there 1897. Organist and conductor. Studied piano with his father, Benjamin Cross, and theory with Dr. Meignen; also violin and cello; conducted the Orpheus Club, Arion men's singing society in Germantown, Euridice chorus of women, Cecelian mixed chorus; organist at the Cathedral of St. Peter and St. Paul, Philadelphia (1862-80); at Holy Trinity (1880-97).

CROSS, MOSES SMITH

b. 1854, d. 1911 Esparto, California.
Composer. Methodist Episcopal minister of the Rock River Conference, the California Conference (1890), then became a professor at

the University of the Pacific, Stockton, Calif. (1891); composed the tune "Resignation"—"We Hope in Thee, O God" (w. Marianne Hearn).

CROSSWELL, WILLIAM

b. 1804 Hudson, New York, d. 1851 Boston, Massachusetts. Hymnist. Graduated Yale (1822) and Hartford College; rector of Christ Church, Boston (1829), Auburn, N.Y. (1840), then Boston (1844); wrote several hymns.

CROUCH, FREDERICK W. NICHOLS

b. 1808 London, England, d. 1896 Portland, Maine. Basso, cellist, and singing teacher. Composed two operas and a number of songs, including "Kathleen Mavourneen" (1840); came to America (1849); resided in Baltimore; enlisted in the Richmond (Va.) Greys in the Civil War; when he returned to his old home in Baltimore, found it reduced to ashes.

CROUSE, RUSSELL

b. 1893 Findlay, Ohio, d. 1966.
Playwright and librettist. With Howard Lindsay, he wrote the libretto for *Anything Goes* (1934, m. Cole Porter), *Call Me Madam* (1950, m. Irving Berlin), *Sound of Music* (1959, m. Richard Rodgers).

CROW, WILLIAM ORVAL (BILL)

b. 1927 Othello, Washington.
Bass player. With Stan Getz, T. Gibbs, M. McPartland, and G. Mulligan during 1950s; with A. Cohn, Z. Sims, Mulligan Concert Jazz Band, Quincy Jones and others in 1960s; toured Soviet Russia (1962) with Benny Goodman band; also Europe (1963) and Japan (1964) with Mulligan.

CROWN JEWELS, THE (rock group)

At Barney Google's, New York City (1972).

CROZIER, DAVID E.

b. 1863 Illinois, d. 1935 Philadelphia, Pennsylvania. Organist and composer. Organist at the Hollond Presbyterian Church, Philadelphia (1898-1901); at Calvary Presbyterian Church (1907-25); composed church music.

CRUMIT, FRANK

b. 1889 Jackson, Ohio, d. 1943 Longmeadow, Massachusetts. Singer and popular composer. Raised in Jackson, Ohio; attended Culver Military Academy in Indiana; graduated University of Ohio, Athens; sang with Paul Biese's orchestra; president of the Lambs' Club (1935); wrote or arranged—"A Gay Caballero," "Donald the Dub," "Down in de Cane Break," "The Song of the Prune," "Down by the Railroad Track."

CUGAT, XAVIER

b. 1900 Gerona, Spain.
Violinist, bandleader, and arranger. Family moved to Havana, Cuba (1904); studied at the conservatory there; played violin in a theatre there at age nine; first violinist in Havana's National Theatre Symphonic Orchestra at age twelve; gave concert in Carnegie Hall, New York City (1925); played with Vincent Lopez's band; organized his own band in Hollywood; then at the Waldorf-Astoria, New York City in the 1930s when he became known as the "Rumba King."

CULLY, WENDELL PHILIPS

b. 1906 Worcester, Massachusetts.
Black trumpeter. Played in Count Basie's orchestra; recorded with Basie and also with Lionel Hampton.

CULVER, ROLLAND PIERCE (ROLLIE)

b. 1908 Fond du Lac, Wisconsin.
Drummer. With Red Nichols after 1945; on tour of Europe and Asia (1960); at World Jazz Festival in Japan (1964).

CUMMINS, BETTY (FOLEY)

b. 1933 Chicago, Illinois.
Singer and guitarist. Raised in Berea, Kentucky, the daughter of "Red" Foley; top records were "Tennessee Whistling Man" (1955), "Satisfied Mind" (1955, with Red), "Sweet Kentucky Rose" (1956), "Old Man" (1959); appeared with her father on his "Ozark Jubilee," ABC-TV, Springfield, Missouri.

CUMMINS, EVELYN (ATWATER)

b. 1891 Poughkeepsie, New York.
Hymnist. Associate editor of *The Chronicle* and became police commissioner of Poughkeepsie (1947); wrote the hymn "I Know Not Where the Road Will Lead" (1922, tune "Laramie"—A.G.H. Bodie).

CUNINGGIM, MAUD (MERRIMON)

b. 1874 Raleigh, North Carolina.
Hymnist. Taught school in Nashville for eleven years; wrote the hymn "Living Christ, Chief Corner Stone" (1926, tune "Arlington"—Thomas A. Arne) for ceremonies at Scarritt College, Nashville.

CUNNINGHAM, ARTHUR

b. 1928 Piermont, New York.
Black pianist and composer. Graduated Fisk University, Nashville (1951), Columbia University Teachers College (M.A.); studied at Juilliard and at Metropolitan School with Wallingford Riegger; his compositions performed in concert by the National Association of Negro Musicians (1951); wrote *Adazio for String Orchestra and Oboe* (1954) "Patsy Patch" and "Susan's Dream," for stage show, *Ostrich Feathers* (1963), *Concentrics for Orchestra* (1968), music for show, *Shango* (1969).

CURLESS, RICHARD

b. 1932 Fort Fairfield, Maine.
Singer and guitarist. Started with a radio station in Ware, Mass. (1948); served in the Special Forces in Korea during the Korean War; hit records were "A Tombstone Every Mile" (1965, m. Dan Fulkerson), "Six Times a Day" (1965), "Tater Raising Man" (1966), "Travelin' Man" (1967).

CURRIER, EVERETT RAYMOND

b. 1877 Yarmouth, Nova Scotia, d. 1954.
Composer. Came to New York City (1900); president of the Currier Press, N.Y.; composed a festival Te Deum for the seventy-fifth anniversary of the Church of the Holy Trinity, Westport, Conn., composed the tune "Bourne" (1941, "In Christ There Is No East or West," w. John Oxenham).

CURRY, ARTHUR MANSFIELD

b. 1866 Chelsea, Massachusetts, d. after 1911.
Violinist and composer. Studied with Franz Kneisel and Edward A. MacDowell; conductor and teacher in Boston; composed the overture "Blomidon" (Worcester, Mass. Festival, 1902), symphonic poem *Atala* (Boston Symphony, 1911), *The Winning of Amarac.*

CURSON, THEODORE (TED)

b. 1935 Philadelphia, Pennsylvania.
Black trumpeter and composer. Studied with Jimmy Heath; with Mal Waldron, Red Garland, Philly Joe Jones, and Cecil Taylor during 1950s; with Charlie Mingus (1959-61); later led his own groups; wrote "Nosruc Waltz," "Straight Ice," "Flip Top," "Flatted Fifth."

CURTIS, GEORGE WILLIAM

b. 1824 Providence, Rhode Island, d. 1892 Staten Island, New York. Critic. Wrote articles on music for the *Harbinger,* New York City (1844-47); editor of *Harper's Weekly* (1863-92).

CURTIS, H. HOLBROOK

b. 1856 New York City, d. there 1920.
Writer. Graduated Yale (1887, M.D. 1880); prominent throat specialist; wrote *Voice Building and Tone Placing.*

CURTIS, KING

b. 1935 Fort Worth, Texas, d. 1971 New York City. Black saxophonist, bandleader, and composer. Born Curtis Ousley; his staccato style on the tenor sax was known as "a yackity sax"; become a member of Lionel Hampton's band; later had his own band; composed "Soul Serenade," "Memphis Soul Stew," "Instant Groove," "Teasin'," "Soulful 13"; records include *Best of King Curtis; King Curtis Plays the Great Memphis Hits; Eternally, Soul; Have Tenor Sax, Will Blow; Soul Battle; Soul Meeting; Soul Twist;* stabbed to death on the front steps of his home in New York City.

CURWEN, JOHN

b. 1817, d. 1880.
Hymnist and compiler. Wrote "God Is Near Thee" which appeared in *Standard Course* (1860), and "I'm a Little Pilgrim"; compiled *John Curwen's Tune Book* (1842).

CUSHING, CATHERINE CHISHOLM

b. 1874 Mt. Perry, Ohio, d. there 1952.
Composer, lyricist, playwright, and librettist. Wrote the lyrics "L'Amour, Toujours L'Amour" (m. Rudolf Friml).

CUSHING, WILLIAM ORCUTT

b. 1823 Hingham, Massachusetts, d. 1902.
Hymnist. Wrote the hymn "When He Cometh, When He Cometh" (1856, tune "Jewel Hymn"—George F. Root); eight of his hymns appeared in Ira D. Sankey's *Sacred Songs and Solos.*

CUTLER, HENRY STEPHEN

b. 1824 Boston, Massachusetts, d. there 1902.
Composer. Organist of Grace Church, Boston (1864), then organist and choirmaster at the Church of the Advent, Boston, and Trinity Church, New York City (1858-65), then positions in Brooklyn, Providence, R.I., Philadelphia, and Troy, N.Y.; wrote the music for "The Son of God Goes Forth to War"

(1828, R. Heber, tune "All Saints New," 1872); published the *Trinity Psalter* (1864) and *Trinity Anthems* (1865).

CUTSHALL, ROBERT DEWEES ("CUTTY")

b. 1911 Huntington, Pennsylvania, d. 1968. Trombonist. With Benny Goodman in 1940s; with Eddie Condon after 1949; toured England and Scotland with Condon (1957); at Aspen Jazz Festival in Colorado (1963-66).

CUTTER, BENJAMIN

b. 1857 Woburn, Massachusetts, d. 1910. Violist, violinist, composer, teacher, and writer. Taught violin and viola at New England Conservatory of Music, Boston.

CUTTER, WILLIAM

b. 1801 North Yarmouth, Maine, d. 1867. Hymnist. Graduated Bowdoin College, Brunswick, Maine (1821); lived in Portland, Maine, and Brooklyn, N.Y.; wrote several hymns.

CUTTING, SEWELL SYLVESTER

b. 1813 Windsor, Vermont, d. 1882 Brooklyn, New York. Hymnist. Graduated University of Vermont, Burlington (1835); Baptist pastor in Southbridge, Mass. (1837-45); editor of the *New York Recorder* (1845-50 and 1853-55), the *Christian Review* (1850-53 and 1855-68); professor at the University of Rochester, New York (1868); wrote several hymns.

CYRKLE, THE (rock group)

Don Dannemann, lead guitar; Tom Dawes, bass, twelve-string guitar, etc.; Marty Fried, drums; Mike Losekamp, piano and organ; started as the Rhondells (1962); as the Cyrkle (1966); disbanded (1968); albums—*Red Rubber Ball, Neon.*

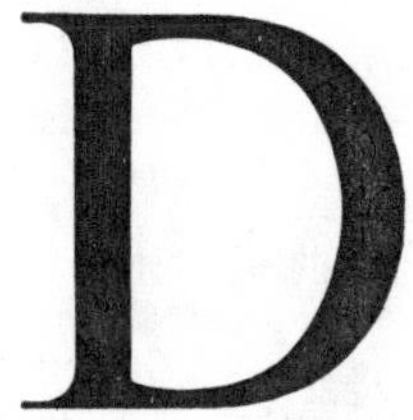

DABNEY, FORD T.

b. 1883 Washington, D.C., d. 1958 New York City. Black bandleader and composer. Official court musician to the President of Haiti (1904-07); joined Tempo Club in New York City (1913); conducted the Ziegfeld Follies orchestra; wrote music for Vernon and Irene Castle's dance numbers.

DABNEY, WENDELL PHILLIPS

b. 1865 Richmond, Virgina, d. 1952.
Black guitarist and writer. Graduated Oberlin Conservatory, Oberlin, Ohio; resided in Cincinnati, Ohio; wrote *Dabney's Complete Method of Guitar and Dabney's Complete Method of Mandolin and Guitar.*

DA COSTA, NOEL

b. 1930 Lagos, Nigeria.
Black composer. Came to New York City with parents (1941); educated at Queens College and Columbia University, New York City; studied with Luigi Dallapiccola in Florence, Italy on Fulbright grant; wrote *In the Circle* (for four electric guitars, bass and percussion, 1969), *The Confessional Stone* (for soprano and ten instruments, w. Owen Dodson), *The Last Judgment* (for women's chorus, narrator, piano and percussion, 1970, w. James Weldon Johnson).

DADMUN, JOHN W.

b. 1819 Hubbardstown, Massachusetts, d. 1890 Boston, Massachusetts. Composer. Studied at the Methodist Academy at Wilbraham, Mass. and became a minister in Ludlow, Mass.; member of the Christian Commission of the Army of the Potomac (1864-65); in 1868 he became chaplain in the prison on Deer Island in Boston Harbor; composed the music for "Land of Beulah" ("I Am Dwelling on the Mountain," w. Wm. Hunter), "Rest for the Weary" ("In the Christian's Home in Glory," w. William Hunter), "Come All Ye Saints to Pisgah's Mount"; popular songs were "Homeward Bound" (w. W.F. Warren, another tune by C.E. Harrington), "The Empty Sleeve" (1862, w. Mrs. P.A. Hanaford, a Civil War amputee case), and "Songs of the Negro Boatman" (1862, w. John Greenleaf Whittier); compiled *Revival Melodies* (1858, *The Melodeon* (1860), *Army Melodies* (1861), *Musical String of Pearls* (1862), *The Sacred Harmonium* (1864 with Lewis Hartsough), and *The New Melodeon* (1866).

DAFFAN, THERON EUGENE (TED)

b. 1912 Beauregarde Parish, Louisiana.
Singer, guitarist, and songwriter. Started with radio station KTRH, Houston, Texas (1932); wrote "Truck Driver Blues" (1939), "Worried Mind" (1940), "No Letter Today" and "Born to Lose" (1943), "I'm a Fool to Care" (1954), "I've Got Five Dollars and It's Saturday Night," "Tangled Mind" (1954), "Last Ride" and "Rocking Rolling Ocean" (1958); his band was known as "Ted Daffan and the Texans."

DAILEY, ALBERT PRESTON (AL)

b. 1938 Baltimore, Maryland.
Pianist. Studied piano at age six; at Peabody Conservatory, Baltimore (1956-59); with Damita Jo, had own trio; with Bill English, Sarah Vaughan, Art Farmer and others during 1960s.

DALEY, JOSEPH ALBERT (JOE)

b. 1918 Salem, Ohio.
Tenor saxist, clarinetist, and flutist. Studied at Chicago Musical College (1953); with Woody Herman, Judy Garland, Tony Bennett and others during 1950s; formed own trio (1963).

DALHART, VERNON

b. 1883 Jefferson, Texas, d. 1948.
Singer. Born Marion T. Slaughter; his records include "Barbara Allen," "Mollie Darling," "The Prisoner's Song," "The Wreck of the Old 97," "Sourwood Mountain," "In the Baggage Coach Ahead," "The Letter Edged in Black," "Oh! Bury Me Not on the Lone Prairie," "My Little Home in Tennessee," "Carolina Sunshine," "Tumbled Down Shack."

DALLAPICCOLA, LUIGI

b. 1904 Pisino, Istria, Yugoslavia, d. 1975. Noted composer. Studied at the Cherubini Conservatory in Florence, Italy; professor at Queens College, New York City (1956); composed *Three Studies for Soprano and Chamber Orchestra* (introduced in Venice, 1932), *Marsia* (ballet, 1943), *Il Prigioniero* (opera, 1947, introduced on the stage at the Florentine May Music Festival, 1950).

DALMORES, CHARLES

b. 1871 Nancy, France, d. 1939.
Tenor. Studied at the Paris and Lyons Conservatories; sang in the Metropolitan Opera, New York City (1896), and Chicago Opera (1910); later settled in Los Angeles as a vocal teacher.

DAMBOIS, MAURICE

b. 1889 Liege, Belgium.
Cellist. Studied at the Liege Conservatory; toured Europe, then came to America to live (1917); composed chamber pieces, orchestral works, and songs.

DAMERON, TADLEY EWING (TADD)

b. 1917 Cleveland, Ohio, d. 1965 New York City. Black pianist. Arranger for Dizzy Gillespie's band during the 1940s; led a quintet (1948); with Miles Davis at the Paris Jazz Festival (1949); arrested and jailed (1958) on a narcotics charge; with Blue Mitchell, Milt Jackson, and Sonny Stitt after 1961; suffered a series of heart attacks, but died of cancer.

D'AMICO, HENRY (HANK)

b. 1915 Rochester, New York, d. 1965 Queens, New York. Clarinetist. Played with Red Norvo (1936-39); with Bob Crosby; then with ABC orchestra (1944-45); at World's Fair, New York City (1964) with Morey Feld Trio.

DAMONE, VIC

b. 1928 Brooklyn, New York.
Singer. Born Vito Farinola; won audition on "Arthur Godfrey's Talent Scouts" (1945); appeared in films and on his own radio show (1947-49); served in the army (1951-53); sang in Hollywood night clubs.

DAMROSCH, FRANK HEINO

b. 1859 Breslau, Poland, d. 1937 New York City. Conductor and teacher. Son of Leopold Damrosch; choral director in Denver, Colorado, then became chorus master at the Metropolitan Opera, New York; founded the Institute of Musical Art, which later became the Juilliard School of Music.

DAMROSCH, FRANK, JR.

b. 1888 New York City.
Hymnist. Educated at Yale, General Theological Seminary, and Berkeley Divinity School (1913); rector in churches in Mechanicsville, N.Y. (1914-15), Bristol, R.I. (1918-22), Brockport, N.Y. (1922-24), Brooklyn, N.Y. (1924-27), Newark, N.J. (1927-35), then St. Paul's, Doylestown, Pa. after 1935; wrote the hymn "God, Deigning Man to Be" (1939, tune "Little Cornard"—Martin Shaw).

DAMROSCH, LEOPOLD

b. 1832 Posen, Germany, d. 1885 New York City. Composer. Composed songs, duets, violin pieces, and the cantatas *Ruth and Naomi*, and *Sulamith;* instrumental in founding the Oratorio Society and the New York Symphony Society.

DAMROSCH, WALTER JOHANNES

b. 1862 Breslau, Poland, d. 1950 New York City. Noted composer. Son of Leopold Damrosch; wrote the operas *The Scarlet Letter, Cyrano de Bergerac* (after Rostand's play, which was produced by the Met in New York, 1913), *The Man Without a Country* (book—Edward W. Hale), *The Opera Cloak*, and the comic opera *The Dove of Peace;* also composed a violin sonata and vocal works; became head of the New York Symphony Orchestra (1903).

DANA, CHARLES ANDERSON

b. 1819 Hinsdale, New Hampshire, d. 1897 Glen Cove, New York. Writer. Editor and part owner of the *New York Sun;* wrote seven articles in *The Harbinger*, New York City, on the 1847-48 Italian opera season.

DANA, CHARLES HENSHAW

b. 1846 West Newton, Massachusetts, d. 1883 Worcester, Massachusetts. Pianist and composer.

DANA, MARY STANLEY BUNCE PALMER

b. 1810 Beaufort, South Carolina, d. 1883 Texas. Hymnist. Married Charles E. Dana, New York City, 1835; lived in Muscatine, Iowa; Dana died (1839); married Robert D. Shindler, professor at Shelby College, Kentucky (1851); published *Southern Harp* (1840) and *Northern Harp* (1841); later eight of her hymns were published in T.O. Summers' *Songs of Zion* (1852); wrote "I'm a Pilgrim, and I'm a Stranger" (tune "Buono Notte"—anonymous) and "O Sing to Me of Heaven" (1840, m. E.W. Dunbar, second tune by William Miller).

DANA, WILLIAM HENRY

b. 1846 Warren, Ohio, d. 1916.
Conductor, teacher, and writer. Founded the Dana Musical Institute, Warren, Ohio in 1869.

DANE, BARBARA

b. 1927 Detroit, Michigan.
Singer and guitarist. Real name is Barbara Spillman; started on radio stations in Berkeley, Calif.; LP records are *Trouble in Mind, Living with the Blues, Night at the Ash Grove, When I Was a Young Girl.*

DANIEL, ROBERT T.

b. 1773 Middlesex County, Virginia, d. 1840 Paris, Tennessee. Hymnist. Was a blacksmith, became a Baptist minister (1803), and served in North and South Carolina, Virginia, Mississippi, and Tennessee; wrote "Lord, in Humble, Sweet Submission" (in Broaddus' *Dover Selection,* 1828-31).

DANIELS, CHARLES N.

b. 1878, d. 1943 San Francisco, California. Composer and lyricist. While residing in Kansas City, Missouri, wrote "Hiawatha—A Summer Idyl" (w. Jim O'Dea, 1901) under the pseudonym Neil Moret; became an arranger for Whitney-Warren (later Remick) in Detroit; wrote "You Tell Me Your Dream, I'll Tell You Mine," Porries," "Chloe"; later established Villa Moret publishing house in San Francisco; wrote the lyrics "She's Funny That Way" (m. Richard A. Whiting), and "The Call of the Rockies" (1934, m. Harry Tobias).

DANIELS, EDWARD KENNETH (EDDIE)

b. 1941 Brooklyn, New York.
Tenor saxist and clarinetist. Graduated Brooklyn College (1963); M.A. from Juilliard (1966); with Tony Scott (1965); then with Thad Jones-Mel Lewis band after 1966; at Vienna International Jazz Competition (1966) won first prize on tenor sax.

DANIELS, MABEL WHEELER

b. 1878 Swampscott, Massachusetts.
Composer. Graduated Radcliffe College, Cambridge, Mass.; studied under George Chadwick and Ludwig Thuille; taught at Simmons College, Boston (1913-18); works—*The Story of Jael* (cantata), *Deep Forest, Exultate Deo* (for Radcliffe's fiftieth anniversary), *Three Observations for Three Woodwinds, The Wild Ride* (National League of American Pen Women Prize), *A Psalm of Praise, Canticle of Wisdom.*

DANISE, GIUSEPPE

b. 1883 Naples, Italy, d. 1963.
Opera baritone. Debut in Naples (1906), then toured widely; sang with the Metropolitan Opera, New York City after 1920, and later with the Ravina Opera Company.

DANKS, HART PEASE

b. 1834 New Haven, Connecticut, d. 1903 Philadelphia, Pennsylvania. Composer and bass singer. Family moved to Saratoga Springs, N.Y., when he was a boy; became a carpenter and was self-taught in music; later moved to Chicago; wrote "Anna Lee" (1856), "The Old Lane" (1856), "Don't Be Angry with Me, Darling" (1870), "Silver Threads Among the Gold" (1873, w. Eben E. Rexford), "Little Darling" (1873, w. S.M. Mitchell), "Amber Tresses Tied in Blue" (1874, Mitchell), "The Sparrows Are Calling" (1878, w. A.A. Dayton), the tunes "Spitta" and "Delphine" (1901); died in poverty, and on his desk were scribbled the words on a scrap of paper: "It's hard to die alone."

DANN, HOLLIS ELLSWORTH

b. 1861 Canton, Pennsylvania, d. 1939 New York City. Teacher and author. Taught music in the public schools in Ithaca, N.Y. (1887-1903), then Cornell University (1906-21), Pennsylvania State College (1921-25), New York University (1925-35); wrote books on school music and compiled school songs.

DANNREUTHER, GUSTAV

b. 1853 Cincinnati, Ohio, d. 1923 New York City. Violinist and teacher. Studied in Berlin, lived in London, then returned to America (1877) and joined the Mendelssohn Quintet Club of Boston; became a member of the Boston Symphony (1880); director of the Philharmonic Society, Buffalo, N.Y. (1882-84); later founded the Dannreuther Quartet, New York City; after 1907 taught at Vassar College, Poughkeepsie, N.Y.

DA PONTE, LORENZO

b. 1749 Ceneda, Italy, d. 1838 New York City. Librettist. Born Emmanuele Conegliano, a Jew, but when the bishop persuaded his father to turn Roman Catholic, the boy was named after the bishop (1763); decided to write for opera, went to Vienna, was hired by the opera manager, met Mozart, and wrote the libretto *Le Mariage de Figaro,* also *Don Giovanni* (1787), and *Cosi fan tutte;* as the result of a letter he wrote to the Emperor, he was banished from the country (1792); fled to Paris, London, and then came to America where he lived in New York City,

Elizabethtown, and Sunbury, Pennsylvania; returned to New York City where he opened an Italian bookstore at 342 Broadway and an Italian opera house at the corner of Church and Leonard Streets, which closed after only twenty-eight performances; wrote his memoirs which portrayed European musical life in an interesting fashion, but were unreliable concerning himself; died a disappointed and broken man, but his name remains alive due to his association with Mozart.

D'ARCY, HUGH A.

b. 1843 Paris, France, d. 1925 New York City. Lyricist. Came to New York City (1872); managed several productions including *The Prince and the Pauper, The Wishing Ring* and *The Bachelor;* in 1893, while in Joe Schmidt's barroom at Fourth Avenue and 14th Street, New York City, a drunkard was thrown out of the bar, and when D'Arcy went to help him, the man said: "I am an artist," which was the inspiration for D'Arcy's poem, "The Face on the Floor," set to music as "The Face on the Barroom Floor" (1893, by William B. Gray).

DARE, ELKANAH KELSAY

b. 1782, d. 1826.
Composer. Methodist pastor, dean of boys at Wilmington College, Wilmington, Delaware; published *The Periodical Harmony* (1810); composed the tune "Fairton," "God of Mercy, Hear My Call," w. Isaac Watts), which appeared in the *Repository of Sacred Music, Part Second* (1813), published by John Wyeth of Harrisburg, Pa., which also included twelve other tunes by Dare.

DARENSBOURG, JOSEPH

b. 1906 Baton Rouge, Louisiana.
Black clarinetist. Studied with Alphonse Picou; played with Fate Marable on Mississippi River boats; later with Kid Ory; formed his own group.

DARIN, BOBBY

b. 1936 Bronx, New York City, d. 1973.
Singer. Born Walden Robert Cassotto; stricken with rheumatic fever at age eight; learned to play the piano, guitar, and drums; wrote radio commercials with Donnie Kirschner; composed and recorded "Splish, Splash" which became a hit; recorded "Mack the Knife" from *The Threepenny Opera,* another hit; at Copacabana, New York City (1969); married actress Sandra Dee, later separated; suffered from fibrulations (irregular heart beats) for twenty-six years, finally underwent a successful operation (1971); back at the Copacabana (1972); NBC-TV show (1972).

DARLEY, FRANCIS THOMAS SULLY

b. ca. 1835 Philadelphia, Pennsylvania, d. after 1900. Composer. Son of William H.W. Darley and grandson of Thomas Sully, artist; wrote *The Cities of the Plain* (oratorio, produced by Harmonic Society of Philadelphia, 1855, and by Musical Fund Society, 1857), *Fortunio* (comic opera, produced by Academy of Music, Philadelphia, 1883); active in founding of Philadelphia Orchestra (1900) and was vice-president of the orchestra.

DARLEY, WILLIAM HENRY WESTRAY

b. 1813 England, d. 1858.
Organist, composer, and teacher. Married Jane Cooper Sully (1833), daughter of Thomas Sully, noted artist; organist at St. Stephens, Philadelphia, after 1839; member of the Anacreontic Society in Philadelphia; wrote "On a Bright Sunny Morn" (1822), "They're a Noddin' "; with J.C.B. Standbridge, compiled *Music of Christ Church and St. Stephen's* (1839), *Four Voice Harmony and Piano or Organ Accompaniment, Chants of the Episcopal Church* (1840), *The Sacred Chorister* (1844).

DARLING, ERIK

b. 1933 Baltimore, Maryland.
Singer, guitarist, and banjoist. Attended New York University; was accompanist for Ed McCurdy, then formed a group "The Tarriers" whose hit was "The Banana Boat Song" (1956), then "The Folk Singers" with the hit "Run Come Hear" (1958); his solo LP records are *Folksongs* (1958), *True Religion* and *Train Time!;* joined "The Weavers" (1958), then formed the "Rooftop Singers" (1962), whose LPs were *Walk Right In* (1963) and *Good Time!* (1964).

DARRELL, JOHNNY

b. 1940 Cleburne County, Alabama.
Singer and songwriter. Wrote "At the Sight of You," "Passing Through."

DAVENPORT, CHARLES ("COW COW")

b. 1894 Anniston, Alabama, d. 1955 Cleveland, Ohio. Pianist and singer. Known as a boogie-woogie pianist; educated at Selma University, Alabama; singer and pianist in vaudeville, teamed with Dora Carr, singer; wrote "Cow Cow Blues," "State Street Jive," "Hobson City Stomp."

DAVID, HAL

b. 1921 New York City.
Lyricist. Brother of composer Mack David; educated at New York University; wrote "What's New Pussycat" (1965, m. Burt Bacharach), and other songs.

DAVID, HANS T.

b. 1902 Frankfurt, Germany.
Compiler and teacher. Wrote an analytical edition of Bach's *Das Musikalische Opfer* (1927), and a practical edition of *Das Musikalische Opfer;* forced to leave Germany after Hitler came to power; after he came to America, he became professor at the University of Michigan at Ann Arbor; with Arthur Mendel, he compiled and edited *The Bach Reader.*

DAVID, MACK

b. 1912 New York City.
Songwriter. Brother of Hal David, lyricist; educated at Cornell University, Ithaca, N.Y., and St. John's Law School; with Jerry Livingston, wrote "Haven't We Met Before?" (1934), "Just a Kid Named Joe," "My Destiny" (1950), also with Clyde Hager and Jerry Livingston, "That's All Brother."

DAVIDOVSKY, MARIO

b. 1934 Medanos, Buenos Aires, Argentina.
Composer and teacher. Studied in Buenos Aires; came to New York (1960); professor at Manhattan School of Music, New York City; wrote *Electronic Study* No. 1 and No. 2; *Synchronisms* No. 1, No. 2 and No. 3.

DAVIES, DAVID

b. 1855 Talsarn, South Wales, d. 1921.
Singer and teacher. Came to America at age thirteen; studied with Dr. John Parry at Aberystwith; oratorio singer in London; returned to America (1880) and toured the country; taught singing in Cincinnati.

DAVIES, DENNIS RUSSELL

b. 1944.
Pianist. Studied at Juilliard, New York City; also under Jean Morel; with composer Luciano Berio, formed Juilliard Ensemble (1968), later called the Ensemble; gave concerts at Tully Hall, New York City during 1972; also conducted Norwalk (Conn.) Symphony in six concerts.

DAVIES, SAMUEL

b. 1723 Summit Bridge, Delaware, d. 1761 Princeton, New Jersey. Hymnist. Presbyterian minister in Virginia, then became president of New Jersey College (now Princeton University), 1759; wrote the hymn "Lord, I Am Thine, Entirely Thine" (tune "Sessions"—Luther O. Emerson); sixteen of his hymns appeared in Dr. Gibbons' *Hymns Adapted to Divine Worship* (1769).

DAVIS, ARTHUR (ART)

b. 1934 Harrisburg, Pennsylvania.
Bass player. Studied at Juilliard and Manhattan School of Music, New York City; with Max Roach (1958); with Dizzy Gillespie, NBC orchestra, Radio City Symphony Orchestra and Symphony of the New World during 1960s; at Newport Jazz Festivals (1958-61); toured Europe and Africa.

DAVIS, AUGUSTE

b. (?), d. after 1895.
Composer. Resided in New Orleans; wrote "La Mazurka" (1861), "Nelly Was Bright and Happy" (1864), "Le Rondeau des Zou! Zou!," "Peoples' Rights Quick Step" (ca. 1895).

DAVIS, BENNY

b. 1895 New York City.
Bandleader and songwriter. Appeared in vaudeville at age fourteen; toured country with Benny Fields as accompanists to Blossom Seeley; with Con Conrad and J.R. Robinson, wrote "Margie" (1920), "Baby Face" (1926, m. Harry Akst), "Carolina Moon" (1928, m. Joe Burke), "Falling in Love with You" (1928, m. Joseph Meyer).

DAVIS, BETTY JACK

b. 1932 Corbin, Kentucky, d. 1953 near Cincinnati, Ohio. Singer. Joined with Mary F. Penick, who called herself Skeeter Davis, as the "Davis Singers"; they were featured on radio stations in Lexington, Ky., Detroit, Mich., Cincinnati, Ohio, and Wheeling, West Virginia; their hit song was "I Forgot More Than You'll Ever Know"; while returning to Cincinnati with Skeeter Davis, Betty Jack was killed in an accident by a car which crossed over the dividing line and crashed into their car.

DAVIS, BILLY

b. 1940 St. Louis, Missouri.
Black singer. Sheet metal worker; went to Hollywood; met Ron Townson and Lamonte McLemore, singers; with Marilyn McCoo, Miss Bronze California 1962 and Florence LaRuse, Miss Bronze California 1963, formed a group which later became the Fifth Dimension.

DAVIS, CHARLES

b. 1933 Goodman, Mississippi.
Black baritone, tenor saxist, and composer. With Jack McDuff, Al Smith Orchestra, Sun Ra, Dinah Washington, and Jenny Dorham during 1950s; led own quintet (1965-66); wrote "Half and Half," "Turbo," "Azan," "Some Other Time," "Linda."

DAVIS, DANNY

b. 1930 Philadelphia, Pennsylvania.
Comedian and writer. Educated at American Theatre Wing, and Columbia University; partner of Eddie Davis for three years; writer for TV; featured on the Nashville Brass.

DAVIS, DON S.

b. 1928 Calvert, Alabama.
Singer and bandleader. Attended schools in Satsuma, and Mobile, Alabama; leader of the Dixie All-Stars (1957-63).

DAVIS, EDDIE

b. 1921 New York City.
Tenor saxist. With various bands during 1940s; led own group in New York City in 1950s; with Count Basie after 1964.

DAVIS, GUSSIE L.

b. 1863 Dayton, Ohio, d. 1899.
Black composer. Started his musical career by sweeping floors at the Conservatory of Music, Cincinnati, Ohio; he composed "On the Sandy Shore" (1891), "Irene, Goodnight" (1892), "The Fatal Wedding" (1893, w. W.H. Windom), "Picture 84" (1894, m. C.B. Ward), "My Creole Sue" (1898), "Get on Your Sneak Shoes Children" (1898), "In the Baggage Coach Ahead" (1896).

DAVIS, JAMES HOUSTON (JIMMIE)

b. 1902 Quitman, Louisiana.
Singer, guitarist, songwriter, and governor. Raised in Beech Springs, La., graduated from Louisiana College, Pineville, and Louisiana State, Baton Rouge (M.A.), later taught at Dodd College; co-authored "You Are My Sunshine" and "It Makes No Difference Now"; served as governor of Louisiana (1944-48 and again 1960-64); LP records are *Jimmie Davis Sings* (1964), *Near the Cross, Highway to Heaven, Hymn Time, Songs of Faith, Suppertime, Sweet Hour of Prayer, The Door Is Always Open, Hail Him with a Song, No One Stands Alone, Watching Over You, How Great Thou Art, Beyond the Shadow.*

DAVIS, JESSIE BARTLETT

b. 1860 near Morris, Illinois, d. 1905 Crown Point, Indiana. Contralto. Studied under Frederic W. Root in Chicago; also De Rialp and Albites in New York and Sara Robinson Duff of Chicago; debut as Buttercup in *Pinafore* (1879); sang with Patti (1883) in *Faust* and *Dinorah;* with Carleton Opera Company; later with American Opera Company (1886-88); introduced "Oh Promise Me" in *Robin Hood* (1889, m. Reginald de Koven), also "I Love Thee, I Adore Thee" with W.H. MacDonald in *The Serenade* (m. Victor Herbert) which opened in Cleveland, Ohio (1897).

DAVIS, JOHN

b. 1773 Paris, France, d. 1839 Mandeville, Louisiana. Impresario. Emigrated to Saint-Dominque, West Indies; then to Cuba; to New Orleans (1809); opened his theatre in New Orleans (1819); his New Orleans opera company presented eighty-five different operas by thirty-two composers between 1827-33; toured New York City and Philadelphia (1827-33), Boston (1828 and 1833), and Baltimore (1829-30 and 1833).

DAVIS, KARL VICTOR

b. 1905 Mt. Vernon, Kentucky.
Singer and songwriter. Wrote "Kentucky," "House Where We Were Wed," "I'm Here to Get My Baby Out of Jail," "Everlasting Love," "Country Hall of Fame," "The Good Book Song," "Mighty Everglades," "I Would Send You Roses," "The B-I-B-L-E."

DAVIS, LOU

b. 1881 New York City, d. there 1961.
Lyricist. Wrote "Precious Little Thing Called Love" (m. J. Fred Coots).

DAVIS, MILES DEWEY, JR.

b. 1926 Alton, Illinois.
Black trumpeter and bandleader. With Charles Parker, Billy Eckstine and others in 1940s; led own combo after 1950 with Gil Evans, his arranger; at World Jazz Festival in Japan (1964); made a successful tour of Europe (1971); played at Gaslight au Go Go in New York City; concert at Manhattan's Philharmonic Hall (1971); considered a top trumpeter; in concert at Philharmonic Hall (1972).

DAVIS, NATHAN TATE

b. 1937 Kansas City, Kansas.
Tenor and soprano saxist, flutist, and clarinetist. Studied at Kansas City Conservatory and the University of Kansas; served in U.S. Army; went to Paris, with Kenny Clarke, Donald Byrd, and Eric Dolphy; on

Paris TV with own quintet; also with Kenny Clarke in Rome.

DAVIS, OZORA STEARNS

b. 1866 Wheelock, Vermont, d. 1931.
Hymnist. Educated at Dartmouth College, Hanover, N.H., Hartford Theological Seminary, and the University of Leipzig, Germany; Congregational minister in Springfield, Vermont, Newtonville, Mass., and New Britain, Conn.; President of the Chicago Theological Seminary (1909-20); wrote the hymns "At Length There Dawns the Glorious Day" (tune "St. Michel's") and "We Bear the Strain of Earthly Care" (1909, tune "Azmon"—C.G. Glazer).

DAVIS, RICHARD

b. 1930 Chicago, Illinois.
Black bass player. With Benny Goodman and others during 1940s to '50s; with Orchestra U.S.A. (1961-64); also with Igor Stravinsky and Leonard Bernstein (1964); visited Europe with Gunther Schuller Orchestra; considered by many as the greatest bass player in the world; played at the Newport Jazz Festival, New York City (1972).

DAVIS, SAMMY

b. 1885 New Orleans, Louisiana.
Black pianist. One of the greatest manipulators in the world on piano, according to Jelly Roll Morton.

DAVIS, SAMMY, JR.

b. 1925 New York City.
Black singer, dancer, and actor. Appeared in vaudeville at age four with his parents in the Will Mastin troupe; served in the army in World War II; the Mastin Trio (Will, Sammy, and his father) were a hit at Slapsie Maxie Rosenbloom's night club in Hollywood (1945); toured with leading performers; Sammy at the Copacabana, New York City (1954); later appeared in a number of films; hospitalized (1971) with cirrhosis of the liver, Sammy said the doctors told him to "stay away from the bottle."

DAVIS, SKEETER

b. 1931 Dry Ridge, Kentucky.
Singer and songwriter. Real name is Mary Frances Penick; joined with Betty Jack Davis (1949-53) as the Davis Sisters; co-wrote "Homebreaker"; top records were "Set Him Free" (1959), "I'm Falling Too" (1960), "Optimistic" (1961), "Where I Ought to Be" (1962), "The End of the World" (1963), "Gonna Get Along Without You Now" (1964), "Singin' in the Summer Sun" (1966), "My Heart's in the Country" (1967).

DAVIS, WILLIAM STRETHEN ("WILD BILL")

b. 1918 Glasgow, Missouri.
Black organist and pianist. Led own trio after 1951; recorded with Johnny Hodges during 1960s.

DAVISON, ARCHIBALD T.

b. 1883, d. 1961 Brant Rock, Massachusetts.
Organist, conductor, editor, composer, and teacher. Conducted the Harvard University Glee Club (1919-34).

DAVISON, WILLIAM ("WILD BILL")

b. 1906 Defiance, Ohio.
Cornetist and bandleader. Record debut (1924) with Chubb Steinberg; went to Chicago (1927); later in Milwaukee; in New York after 1940; served in the army (1943-45); with Art Hodes and others during late '40s and '50s; during 1960s played in New York City, toured England and the continent; played at the Newport Jazz Festival, New York City (1972).

DAWSON, ALAN

b. 1929 Marietta, Pennsylvania.
Drummer. Played with various groups in Boston; toured with Lionel Hampton's band; taught at the Berklee School of Music in Boston; member of the Boston Percussion Trio; at the Berlin Jazz Festival (1965) with Sonny Rollins and Bill Evans; wrote *A Manual for the Modern Drummer.*

DAWSON, WILLIAM LEVI

b. 1897 Anniston, Alabama.
Black trombonist and composer. Attended Tuskegee Institute, Alabama and Horner Institute for Fine Arts, Kansas City, Chicago Musical College, and American Conservatory of Music (master's, 1927); played in Chicago Civic Orchestra; directed Tuskegee Institute Choir until 1955; won three Wanamaker awards; wrote *Negro Folk Symphony,* with Philadelphia Orchestra under Leopold Stokowski (1934); rewritten (1952) after visit to West Africa, Movement I—*The Bond of Africa,* II—*Hope in the Night,* III—*O Let Me Shine!*

DAY, DENNIS

b. 1917 New York City.
Singer. Sang in Claude Thornhill's orchestra while in the Pacific in the navy during World War II; albums—*Johnny Appleseed, My Wild Irish Rose, Shillelaghs and Shamrocks.*

DAY, DORIS

b. 1924 Cincinnati, Ohio.
Singer and actress. Born Doris Kapplehoff;

danced with the Fanchon and Marco stage show at age twelve; broke her leg in a car-train accident and took singing lessons; sang in Barney Rapp's band at age seventeen; then with Les Brown; appeared in several films for Warner Brothers (1948-54); then with Metro-Goldwyn-Mayer; her singing of "Sentimental Journey" with Les Brown's band was included in RCA's *Big Bands' Greatest Hits* (1972)

DAY, EDITH

b. 1896 Minneapolis, Minnesota, d. 1971 London, England. Singer. Became the toast of London in the 1920s; starred in the London productions of *Irene, Rose Marie* and *The Desert Song;* introduced "Alice Blue Gown" (m. Harry Tierney) in *Irene* on Broadway, New York City (1919).

DAY, GEORGE HENRY

b. 1883 New York City, d. (?).
Composer, graduated New York University and New York College of Music (1913) and Lincoln and Jefferson University (D. Mus., 1923); organist-choirmaster in churches in New York City, Wilmington, Del. and Rochester, N.Y., then Trinity Church, Geneva, N.Y. after 1935; composed the tunes "Geneva" (1940, "Not Alone for Mighty Empire, w. W.P. Merrill) and "Edsall" ("Come, Risen Lord, and Deign to Be Our Guest," w. G.W. Briggs).

DAYE, IRENE

b. 1918, d. 1971 Greenville, South Carolina. Singer. Began her singing career with the Jan Murphy band while a teenager; later sang in the bands of Mal Hallett and Gene Krupa; married Charlie Spivak, bandleader (1950).

DE ABRAVANEL, MAURICE

b. 1903 Salonika, Greece.
Conductor. Studied in Switzerland; became a conductor in Berlin, but due to his Spanish-Portuguese-Jewish ancestry he was forced to leave (1933); came to America, was with the Metropolitan Opera, Broadway shows, then with the Utah Symphony Orchestra, Salt Lake City.

DEAN, DONALD WESLEY

b. 1937 Kansas City, Missouri.
Drummer. Played in Los Angeles after 1961 with Art Blakey and others.

DEAN, EDDIE

b. 1907 Posey, Texas.
Singer and songwriter. Wrote "One Has My Name, the Other Has My Heart"; with H. Sothern and Tex Ritter wrote "I Dreamed of a Hillbilly Heaven" (1961).

DEAN, JIMMY RAY

b. 1928 Plainview, Texas.
Singer, guitarist, pianist, and songwriter. Real name is Seth Ward; served in the Merchant Marine (1944-46), then the Army Air Force; his Texas Wildcats joined station WARL, Arlington, Va. (1953); wrote "Big Bad John" (1961), "Dear Ivan" (1961); started with ABC-TV (1963); LP records include *Jimmy Dean Is Here, Most Richly Blessed* (1967).

DE BLANC, DAMITA JO

b. 1933 Austin, Texas.
Singer. Studied music at University of California and at Sam Houston State, Huntsville, Texas; vocalist for Steve Gibson and the Red Caps; later soloist on TV and in night clubs.

DE CISNEROS, ELEANORA BROADFOOT

b. 1878 New York City, d. there 1934.
Soprano. Pupil of Mme. Murio-Celli; debut as Rossweise in *Die Walküre* at the Metropolitan Opera House, New York City (1900); after 1902 traveled and sang widely in Europe, Central and South America, and Australia; after 1910 with the Chicago Opera Company.

DE COPPET, EDWARD J.

b. 1855 New York City, d. there 1916.
Music patron. Established chamber music concerts in his home in 1886; the Flonzaley Quartet, consisting of Adolfo Betti, Alfred Pochon, Ugo Ara, and Iwan d'Archambeau, was organized for these events (1902); later they toured America and Europe; in 1917 Ugo Ara was succeeded as violist by Louis Bailly; the Flonzaley Quartet was named after de Coppet's summer home in Switzerland.

DÉDÉ, EDMUND

b. 1829 New Orleans, Louisiana, d. 1903 Paris, France. Black violinist, conductor, and composer. Studied clarinet with Debarque and violin with Gabici; played in Mexico and England; toured the United States after the Civil War; later became director of the Bordeaux Orchestra; wrote *Le Sement de l'Arabe, Vaillant Belle Rose Quadrille, Le Palmier Overture.*

DEE, JOEY

b. 1940 Passaic, New Jersey.
Bandleader. Leader of Joey Dee and The Starliters; played the twist at the Peppermint Lounge (1961); singles—"Hot Pastrami with Mashed Potatoes," "Peppermint Twist" (two parts), "Shout" (two parts), "What Kind of Love Is This."

DEEMS, JAMES MONROE

b. 1818 Baltimore, Maryland, d. 1901. Violo-cellist, composer, and teacher. Studied under Captain William Rountree, bandleader of 53rd Regiment of Maryland Infantry; studied in Dresden under J.J.F. Dotzauer; professor of music at University of Virginia, Charlottesville (1849-58); Major of 21st Maryland Cavalry after 1861; later Brigadier-General; cornetist at Franklin Square Baptist church in Baltimore; composed a grand opera, comic opera, oratorio, *Nebuchadnezzar.*

DEEP PURPLE (rock group)

Rod Evans, vocals; Jon Lord, vocals and organ; Nicky Simper, vocals; Ritchie Blackmore, lead guitar; Ian Paice, drums; albums—*Shades of Deep Purple* (1968), *Book of Taliesyn, Deep Purple, Deep Purple and the Royal Philharmonic Orchestra.*

DEFAUW, DÉSIRÉ

b. 1885 Ghent, Belgium, d. 1960. Conductor. Conductor of Chicago Symphony Orchestra (1943-47).

DE FRANCO, BONIFACE FERDINAND LEONARDO ("BUDDY")

b. 1923 Camden, New Jersey. Clarinetist and bandleader. Played with Gene Krupa, Charlie Barnet, Tommy Dorsey, and Count Basie during the 1940s; led various groups during 1950s; at the Kansas City Jazz Festival (1965); also played the bass clarinet; led the Glenn Miller band after 1966; at Roseland Dance City, New York City (1972).

DE GANTE, PEDRO

b. ca. 1500, d. ca. 1572. Teacher. Father de Gante established a musical school at Texoco, Mexico (1524); built an organ there (1527); later established a school in Mexico City, where he taught until he died.

DE GOGORZA, EMILIO

b. 1874 Brooklyn, New York, d. 1949 New York City. Baritone. Resided as a youth in Spain and France; debut with Sembrich (1897); toured widely; with Emma Eames, whom he married (1911), later taught at the Curtis Institute, Philadelphia.

DE HAVEN, GLORIA

b. 1926 Los Angeles, California. Singer and actress. Started with Jan Savitt's band; later appeared in many films.

DEIS, CARL

b. 1883, d.1960 New York City. Organist, composer, and teacher. Wrote *A Lovers Lament* (w. W.M. Johnson), *Waiting* (w. C.H. Towne).

DE KOVEN, HENRY LOUIS REGINALD

b. 1859 Middletown, Connecticut, d. 1920 New York, N.Y. Popular composer. With Harry B. Smith, librettist, he wrote the operettas *Don Quixote* (1889), *Robin Hood* (1890), *The Knickerbockers* (1892), *The Algerian* (1893), *Rob Roy* (1894), *The Begum* (1897), *The Highwayman* (1897); among his songs were "Brown October Ale" (1889), "Oh Promise Me" (1889, w. Clement Scott, introduced by Jessie B. Davis in *Robin Hood*), "The Armorer's Song" (1891), "Do You Remember Love" and "Moonlight Song" (1897); conducted the Philharmonic Orchestra in Washington, D.C. from 1902-05.

DE LAMARTER, ERIC

b. 1880 Lansing, Michigan, d. 1953 Orlando, Florida. Organist and composer. Studied with G.H. Fairclough, Guilmant and Widor; music critic (1908-14); organist at Fourth Presbyterian Church, Chicago (1914-36); assistant conductor of Chicago Symphony (1918-36); works—*The Black Orchid* (ballet), four symphonies, *The Giddy Puritan* (overture), *The 144th Psalm* (choral, Eastman School public award).

DELANEY, ROBERT MILLS

b. 1903 Baltimore, Maryland, d. 1956 Santa Barbara, California. Composer. Studied with Honegger, also with Nadia Boulanger in Paris; composed suite of music for *The Constant Couple* (play by Farquhar, Rochester Philharmonic under Hanson, 1928), *Going to Town* (orchestral suite), Symphonic Piece no. 1 (1936), Work no. 22 (scherzo for orchestra, Harvard University Orchestra under Malcolm Holmes, 1939), *John Brown's Body* (choral symphony).

DE LANGE, DANIEL

b. 1841 Rotterdam, Netherlands, d. 1918 Point Loma, California. Composer. Brother of Samuel de Lang, composer; studied at Lemberg Conservatory (1860-63), with Mme. Dubois in Paris, and with others; directed the Amsterdam Conservatory (1895-1913); composed two symphonies, the opera *De Val Van Kuilenburg*, the overture *Willem van Holland.*

DE LANGE, EDGAR (EDDIE)

b. 1904 Long Island City, New York, d. 1949. Lyricist and composer. Organized a band with

Will Hudson (1934) and wrote many songs with him—"Moonglow" (1934), "Organ Grinder's Swing," "With All My Heart and Soul," "The Least Little Thing You Do"; also wrote "String of Pearls" (with W.B. Gray), "Solitude" (with Duke Ellington, w. Irving Mills), "Along the Navajo Trail" (with Charles Marks), and with Jimmy van Heusen "Deep in a Dream" and "Heaven Can Wait."

DE LANGE, HANS

b. 1884 Istanbul, Turkey.
Conductor. Studied at the Prague Conservatory; concertmaster of Frankfort Opera (1910); concertmaster and assistant conductor of the New York Philharmonic (1924-36); then assistant conductor of the Chicago Symphony; Albuquerque Symphony Orchestra (1950).

DELLO JOIO, NORMAN

b. 1913 New York City.
Noted composer. Studied at the Musical Institute, Juilliard, and the Berkshire Music Center; taught at Sarah Lawrence College, Bronxville, N.Y. (1944-50); composed *Concerto for Harp and Orchestra* (1944), *Ricercari* (for piano and orchestra, 1946), *Variations Chaconne, and Finale* (for orchestra, 1947), *New York Profiles* (suite for orchestra, produced in La Jolla, California, under the direction of Nikolai Sokoloff, 1949), and *Meditation on Ecclesiastes* (won the Pulitzer Prize in Music, 1957).

DELMORE, ALTON

b. 1908 Elkmont, Alabama, d. 1964 Nashville, Tennessee. Singer, guitarist, and songwriter. With his brother, Rabon, they were known as the Delmore Brothers; they joined Grand Ole Opry, Nashville (1932); they wrote "Blues Stay Away from Me" (1949), and with Arthur Smith, Alton wrote "Beautiful Brown Eyes."

DELMORE, RABON

b. 1910 Elkmont, Alabama, d. 1952 Athens, Alabama. Singer, guitarist, and songwriter. With his brother, Alton, they were known as the Delmore Brothers; they wrote "Blues Stay Away from Me" (1949); they appeared on radio stations in Nashville, Raleigh, N.C., Greenville, S.C. Birmingham, Ala., Cincinnati, Ohio, Indianapolis, Memphis, and Ft. Smith, Arkansas; he died of lung cancer.

DELTA RHYTHM BOYS (jazz group) *see* BILLY MOORE

DE LUCA, GIUSEPPE

b. 1876 Rome, Italy, d. 1950 New York City. Baritone. Studied at the St. Cecilia Academy; debut in *Valentin*, Piacenza, Italy (1897); sang at La Scala in Milan for eight years, then with Metropolitan Opera, New York City (1915-35).

DE LUCE, NATHANIEL

b. ca. 1795, d. 1842 New York City.
Composer and teacher. Teacher in Philadelphia (1817-24); in New York City (1825-41); his wife was a prominent singer; wrote *Love and Music* (1819).

DE LUSSAN, ZELIE

b. 1863 New York City, d. 1949 London, England. Singer. Pupil of her mother; debut on stage (1886) and in concerts; with Carl Rosa Company, London (1889); with Metropolitan Opera, New York (1894-95); at Covent Garden, London (1895-1902).

DEMAREST, MARY AUGUSTA (LEE)

b. 1838 Croton Falls, New York, d. 1888 Los Angeles, California. Lyricist. Wrote "My Ain Countree" (1864, m. Mrs. Ione T. Hanna of Denver, Colorado, harmonized by Hubert P. Main, 1873), "I Am Far from My Hame an' I'm Weary Aften Whiles"; resided in Passaic, New Jersey, and later moved to Pasadena, California.

DE MENASCE, JACQUES

b. 1905 Bad Ischl, Austria, d. 1960.
Composer. Composed *Lecho dodi* for cantor, choir, and organ for the synagogue Menasce.

DEMPSEY, JAMES CLIFFORD ("LITTLE JIMMY")

b. 1937 Atlanta, Georgia.
Singer, bandleader, and songwriter. Leader of the Cherokee County Boys (1958-62); the Little Dempsey Trio after 1962; wrote "Turn Around," "Bessie Was a Good Old Cow," "Loneliness," "Betcha Can't Eat Just One," "Answer from Your Heart," "But First, a Word from Our Sponsor."

DEMPSTER, WILLIAM R.

b. 1809 Scotland, d. 1871 London, England. Popular composer. Lived in America for a number of years, but was constantly traveling back and forth to England, where he died; wrote the music for "Rainy Day" (1847, w. Henry W. Longfellow), "The Blind Boy" (w. Longfellow), "The Death of Warren" (w. Epes Sargent) and "Thou'st Ever at My Side" (w. C.H. Waterman).

DENCKE, JEREMIAS

b. 1735 Germany, d. 1795.
Composer. Came to America (1760) as a Moravian pastor in Bethlehem, Pa.; first to

compose sacred music (in America) with instruments; wrote three sets of sacred songs for soprano, strings and organ, including *Ich will singen von einem Könige.*

DENNÉE, CHARLES FREDERICK

b. 1863 Oswego, New York, d. 1946.
Teacher and composer. Studied with Emery in Boston; taught piano at New England Conservatory of Music, Boston.

DENNI, LUCIEN

b. 1886 Nancy, France, d. 1947 Hermosa Beach, California. Composer. Came to America and resided in St. Louis; wrote *Oceana Roll* (1911).

DENNIS, KENNETH CARL (KENNY)

b. 1930 Philadelphia, Pennsylvania.
Drummer. Played with Earl Bostic, Erroll Garner, Sonny Stitt, and Billy Taylor during 1950s; with Lena Horne in Los Angeles (1960); at Rubaiyat Room in Los Angeles (1960-63); married singer Nancy Wilson.

DENNIS, MATT

b. 1914 Seattle, Washington.
Pianist and composer. His mother was a vaudeville actress with the Five Musical Lovelands; attended high school in San Rafael, Calif.; arranger for Jo Stafford, Connie Haines, Martha Tilton, and Margaret Whiting; served in the Army Air Force in World War II as an entertainer; had his own show on NBC-TV; appeared in films; wrote "Let's Get Away from It All," "Relax," "Everything Happens to Me," "The Night We Called It Day," "Violets for Your Furs," "Angel Eyes."

DENNIS, WILLIE

b. 1926 Philadelphia, Pennsylvania, d. 1965.
Trombonist. Born William De Berardinis; played with Benny Goodman, Charles Mingus and others during 1950s; toured Soviet Russia with Goodman (1962); later TV studio musician; killed in an auto accident.

DENNY, MARTIN

b. 1911 New York City.
Pianist and bandleader. Studied piano at age ten; attended high school in Los Angeles; then University of Southern California; formed a jazz band (1931) which toured South America; formed a new band after the war which played in Honolulu, Hawaii; recorded many albums based on Hawaiian tunes, his first album, *Exotica I,* was a great success.

DENSMORE, JOHN HOPKINS

b. 1880 Sommerville, Massachusetts, d. 1943 Boston, Massachusetts. Composer. Educated at Harvard University; wrote "Veritas" (Harvard football song), "April," "If God Left Only You."

DE PARIS, SIDNEY

b. 1903 Crawfordsville, Indiana, d. 1967.
Black trumpeter. With McKinney's Cotton Pickers and Don Redman in 1930s; with Benny Carter (1940-41); recorded with Sandy Williams on trombone and Sidney Catlett on drums; with his brother Wilbur De Paris' combo after 1943.

DE PARIS, WILBUR

b. 1900 Crawfordsville, Indiana, d. 1973.
Black trombonist. With Original Blue Rhythm Band in 1920s; with Noble Sissle, Benny Carter, Teddy Hill, and Louis Armstrong in 1930s; with Ella Fitzgerald and Duke Ellington in 1940s; formed own band (1947) with his brother Sidney De Paris; at Jimmy Ryan's in New York City until 1962; at Cannes Festival (1960).

DE PAUR, LEONARD

b. 1915 Summit, New Jersey.
Black choirmaster and bandleader. Graduated University of Colorado, Boulder; studied at Juilliard School of Music, New York City; associate director of Hall Johnson Choir; served as choral director of Air Force's Winged Victory show in World War II; organized glee club of 372nd Infantry Regiment; organized De Paur's Infantry Chorus.

DEPPENSCHMIDT, BUDDY

b. 1936 Philadelphia, Pennsylvania.
Drummer. With Billy Butterfield (1958-59); Charlie Byrd (1960-62); toured South America.

DE PRIEST, JAMES ANDERSON

b. 1936 Philadelphia, Pennsylvania.
Black conductor and drummer. Nephew of Marion Anderson; studied under Jules Benner; conducted first Modern Music Festival at University of Pennsylvania (1956); directed concerts for Contemporary Music Guild.

DE QUINONES, FRAY CRISTOBAL

b. (?), d. 1609 New Mexico.
Teacher. First music teacher in New Mexico, and brought the first organ to America (ca. 1598) which he installed in the chapel of the monastery at San Felipe Pueblo.

DE ROSE, PETER

b. 1900 New York City, d. there 1953. Popular composer. With Billy Hill, lyricist, he wrote "Wagon Wheels" (1934), "In a Mission by the Sea," Down the Old Oregon Trail"; he also wrote "Deep Purple" (for piano, 1933, later words were written by Mitchell Parish), "Autumn Serenade" (w. Sammy Gallop), "As Years Go By" (w. Charles Tobias).

DESABAYE, MARK

b. (?), d. 1837 New York City. Teacher, composer, and publisher. Taught in New York City (1814-37).

DESMOND, JOHNNY

b. 1925 Detroit, Michigan. Composer, singer, and lyricist. Educated at Detroit Conservatory; vocalist with Gene Krupa, Glenn Miller, and Bob Crosby; wrote "Please Don't Forget Me Dear," "When," "Dancing Man"; album—*Johnny Desmond.*

DESMOND, PAUL (BREITENFELD)

b. 1924 San Francisco, California. Alto saxist. With Dave Brubeck after 1951; also recorded with guitarist Jim Hall and others; albums—*Blues in Time, Bossa Antigua, Desmond Blue, Paul Desmond, Easy Living, From the Hot Afternoon, Glad to Be Unhappy, Gerry Mulligan Quartet-Paul Desmond Quintet, Summertime, Take Ten, Two of a Mind* (with Gerry Mulligan); in concert with Dave Brubeck and Gerry Mulligan at Carnegie Hall, New York City (1972), and at Newport Jazz Festival.

DE SYLVA, GEORGE GARD ("BUDDY")

b. 1895 New York City, d. 1950 Hollywood, California. Lyricist. With Lew Brown he wrote lyrics for Ray Henderson; they wrote "The Best Things in Life Are Free" (1927), "Button Up Your Overcoat," "You Are My Lucky Star," "Sonny Boy" (1928, for Al Jolson), "Keep Your Sunny Side Up" (1929), for Joseph Meyer he wrote the lyrics "California Here I Come" (1922), "If You Knew Susie Like I Know Susie" (1925), for Richard A. Whiting "You're an Old Smoothie" (1932), also "Rise 'n Shine" (Vincent M. Youmans), "April Showers" (m. Louis Silvers).

DE TAR, VERNON

b. 1905 Detroit, Michigan. Organist. Graduated Syracuse University, New York (1927); organist in Episcopal churches in New York City (1929-39), then at the Church of the Ascension after 1939.

DETHIER, EDOUARD

b. 1885 Liege, Belgium, d. 1962. Violinist. Studied at the Liege and Brussels Conservatories; taught at the Institute of Musical Art, New York City after 1906; toured as a soloist and also gave recitals with his brother Gaston.

DETHIER, GASTON MARIE

b. 1875 Liege, Belgium, d. 1958 New York City. Organist and teacher. Graduated Liege Conservatory (1892); became organist at St. Xavier's Church, New York City (1894); taught at the Institute of Musical Art, New York City after 1907; gave concert recitals with his brother Edouard.

DETT, ROBERT NATHANIEL

b. 1882 Drummondsville, Quebec, Canada, d. 1943 Battle Creek, Michigan. Black composer. Studied at Oberlin College, Ohio, and Columbia University, New York City; taught at Lane College, Jackson, Tenn., Lincoln Institute, and Hampton (Va.) Institute after 1913; composed choral works, piano music, and spiritual settings.

DEUTSCH, LEONHARD

b. 1887 Vienna, Austria, d. 1951 New York City. Compiler. Edited *A Treasury of the World's Finest Folksongs, A Treasury of Slovak Folksongs, Folksongs of Florida* (with Alton C. Morris), and wrote *Individualpsychologie im Musikunterricht* and *Die Schule des Primavista-Spielens.*

DE WITT, LEW C.

b. 1938 Roanoke County, Virginia. Tenor and songwriter. Member of the Statler Brothers vocal quartet; wrote "Flowers on the Wall" which was number one on the popular charts in 1965.

DE WOLFE, JOHN

b. 1786 Bristol, Rhode Island, d. there 1862. Hymnist. Educated at Brown University, Providence, R.I.; professor there (1817-38); wrote "Angel Bands in Strains Sweet Sounding" (1815, in *Protestant Episcopal Hymnal,* 1871).

DEXTER, AL

b. 1902 Jacksonville, Texas. Singer, guitarist, and songwriter. Real name is Albert Poindexter; formed the Texas Troopers (1934); wrote the hymn "Going Home to Glory"; also wrote "Pistol Packin'

Mama," "Honky Tonk Blues" and "Rosalita" (1942); LP record is *Pistol Packin' Mama.*

DEXTER, HENRY MARTYN

b. 1821 Plymouth, Massachusetts, d. 1890 New Bedford, Massachusetts. Hymnist. Graduated Yale (1840) and Andover Divinity School (1844); for twenty-three years he was editor of the *Congregationalist;* wrote the lyrics "Shepherd of Tender Youth" based on "Clement's Hymn" (ca. 200 A.D., m. W.H. Monk, tune "St. Ambrose").

DIAMOND, DAVID LEO

b. 1915 Rochester, New York.
Composer. Studied at the Cleveland Institute of Music; Eastman School of Music, Rochester, Dalcroze School, New York City, and under Nadia Boulanger in Paris; composed *Rounds* (for string orchestra, 1944), Symphony no. 3 (introduced by the Boston Symphony under Charles Munch, 1950), Symphony no. 4 (introduced by the Boston Symphony under Leonard Bernstein, 1948), *Romeo and Juliet* (symphonic suite introduced by the Little Orchestra Society, New York City, 1947), Symphony no. 6 (1954).

DIAMOND, NEIL

b. 1942 Brooklyn, New York.
Singer and composer. Wrote "I'm a Believer" (1967), and "A Little Bit Me, A Little Bit You," both recorded by the Monkees; albums—*Brother Love's Travelling Salvation Show, Neil Diamond's Greatest Hits, Feel of Neil Diamond, Just for You, Touching You, Touching Me, Velvet Gloves and Spit.*

DICKENS, JIMMY

b. 1925 Bolt, West Virginia.
Singer, guitarist, and songwriter. Attended the University of West Virginia, Morgantown; started with station WJLS, Beckley, West Virginia, later in Fairmont, West Va.; joined Grand Ole Opry, Nashville (1948); wrote "Sea of Broken Dreams" and "I Sure Would Like to Sit a Spell with You"; hit records were "Take an Old Cold Tater" (1949), "Country Boy" (1949), "Hillbilly Fever" and "A-Sleeping at the Foot of the Bed" (1950), "May the Bird of Happiness Fly Up Your Nose" (1965).

DICKENSON, VICTOR (VIC)

b. 1906 Xenia, Ohio.
Black jazz trombonist. Played in Count Basie's band; also with Benny Carter; recorded with Sidney Bechet's group in the early 1940s; played at the Brussels World's Fair (1958) with the Bechet group; with Wild Bill Davison (1961-63); toured South Pacific (1964) with Eddie Condon; Europe (1965); at Columbus Jazz Festival (1965); with Yank Lawson at Newport Jazz Festival, New York City (1972).

DICKERSON, WALT

b. 1931 Philadelphia, Pennsylvania.
Vibraphonist and composer. Graduated Morgan State College, Baltimore (1953); served in U.S. Army; played in New York City night spots after 1960; later at Montmarte Club in Copenhagen, Denmark.

DICKEY, MARK

b. 1885 Ludlow, Massachusetts, d. (?).
Composer. Organist at Congregational churches in Rochester, N.H., Somersworth, N.H., Dover, N.H., Kennebunk, Maine, and the First Baptist Church, Arlington, Mass.; composed the anthem "Let Not Your Heart Be Troubled" (1932), and the tune "Pater Omnipotens" (1941, "Almighty Father, Who Dost Give" w. J.H.B. Masterman).

DICKINSON, CHARLES ALBERT

b. 1849 Westminster, Vermont, d. 1906 California. Hymnist. Educated at Harvard University; became a Congregational minister; moved to California (1899); wrote the hymn "Blessed Master, I Have Promised" (tune "Bullinger"—Ethelbert W. Bullinger).

DICKINSON, CLARENCE

b. 1873 Lafayette, Indiana, d. 1969.
Noted composer. Educated at Miami University, Oxford, Ohio, and Northwestern University, Evanston, Illinois (1894, Mus. D. 1917); organist in churches in Evanston, Chicago, then after 1909 at the Brick Presbyterian Church and Temple Beth-El, New York City; professor at the Union Theological Seminary (1912-45); composed the *Storm King* symphony; compiled *Choruses Ancient and Modern, Forty Antiphons* and published *The Technique and Art of Organ Playing.*

DICKINSON, JOHN

b. 1732 Talbot County, Maryland, d. 1808 Wilmington, Delaware. Lyricist. Served in the Continental Congress (1765); favored reconciliation with England; later resided near Dover, Delaware; as a delegate from

Delaware, helped draft the U.S. Constitution; Dickinson College in Carlisle, Pa., named after him; wrote the lyrics "The Liberty Song, or Song for American Freedom" (1768, based on the tune "Hearts of Oak" by Dr. William Boyce, 1759).

DIDDLEY, BO

b. 1928 McComb, Mississippi.
Black singer and guitarist. Born Ellas McDaniel; sang and played at the Apollo in Harlem, New York City; albums—*Bossman; Bo Diddley; Bo Diddley and Company; Beach Party; Is a Gunslinger; Is a Lover; 500 Per Cent More Man; Go Bo Diddley; Have Guitar, Will Travel; Hey Good Lookin'; In the Spotlight; Road Runner; 16 All-Time Hits; Surfin' with Bo Diddley; Two Great Guitars* (with Chuck Berry).

DIETRICH, MARLENE

b. 1901 Berlin, Germany.
Singer, entertainer, and actress. Born Maria Magdalene von Losch; appeared in the musical *Broadway* (1928, George Abbott production); appeared in many films; sang in night clubs; entertained soldiers in World War II; albums—*Marlene Dietrich, Dietrich in London, Marlene Dietrich's Berlin, Marlene, Magic of Marlene, Wiedersehen Mit Marlene.*

DIETZ, HOWARD

b. 1896 New York City.
Lyricist and librettist. Attended Columbia University, New York City; served in the navy in World War I; joined Metro-Goldwyn-Mayer (1924); wrote "Moanin' Low" (1929, m. Ralph Rainger), "Something to Remember You By" (1930, m. Arthur Schwartz), "Dancing in the Dark" (1931, m. Schwartz), also lyrics for many musical shows. (*See* Arthur Schwartz).

DI FILIPPI, ARTURO

b. 1894 Italy, d. 1972 Miami, Florida.
Tenor and impresario. Came to United States (1912); concert singer on stage and network radio opera in New York City; founded the Opera Guild of Greater Miami (1941) and was its impresario for thirty-one years.

DIGGLE, ROLAND

b. 1887 London, England, d. 1954 Los Angeles, California. Composer. Educated at the Royal Academy of Music and came to America (1904); organist-choirmaster in Wichita, Kansas (1908-11), Quincy, Illinois (1911-14), and St. John's (Episcopal) Church, Los Angeles after 1914; composed the tune "Racine" (1941, "Lord God of Hosts, Whose Almighty Hand," w. John Oxenham).

DILLARD & CLARK (duo)

Started (1968) with Doug Dillard of the Dillards and Gene Clark of the Byrds; albums—*Fantastic Expedition of Dillard and Clark* (1968), *Through the Morning, Through the Night.*

DILLARD, DOUGLAS F.

b. 1937 Salem, Missouri.
Singer and banjoist. With Rod, his brother, Dean Webb, and Mitch Jayne, he formed a group known as "The Dillards"; their LP records include *Bluegrass* (1963) and *The Dillards Live* (1964), *Back Porch Bluegrass, Dillards-Copperfields, Pickin' and Fiddlin', Wheatstraw Suite.*

DILLARD, RODNEY

b. 1942 Salem, Missouri.
Singer and guitarist. Doug, his brother, Dean Webb, and Mitch Jayne were a group known as "The Dillards"; one of their early engagements was with the Buddha Club, Oklahoma City, Oklahoma.

DILLARDS, THE (bluegrass group)

Rodney Dillard, lead guitar, etc.; Herb Pedersen, guitar and banjo; Mitch Jayne, bass; Joe Osborn, bass; Toxey French, drums; Jimmy Gordon, drums; started in Los Angeles (1962); previous member Douglas Dillard left to join Gene Clark; albums—*Back Porch Bluegrass, Dillards-Copperfields, Dillards Live, Pickin' and Fiddlin', Wheatstraw Suite.*

DILLON, FANNIE CHARLES

b. 1881 Denver, Colorado, d. 1947 Los Angeles, California. Pianist, composer, teacher, and writer. Educated at Pomona College, Calif.; debut as pianist (1908); taught at Pomona College (1910-13), and Los Angeles HS (1918-47); works—*Celebration of Victory, The Cloud, A Letter from the Southland, Birds at Dawn* (for piano).

DILLON, WILLIAM A. (WILL)

b. 1877 Cortland, New York, d. 1966 Ithaca, New York. Composer, lyricist, and actor. Vaudeville actor; with Harry von Tilzer, wrote "I Want a Girl Just Like the Girl That Married Dear Old Dad" (1911), also "Take Me to My Alabam' " and "That Girl of Mine" (both with Harry Tobias, 1916).

DINO, DESI AND BILLY (trio)

Dino Martin, Jr., guitar; Desi Arnaz, Jr., drums (Dean Martin's son and the son of Desi

Arnez); Billy Hinsche, guitar; albums—*Follow Me* (soundtrack), *I'm a Fool, Memories Are Made of This.*

DI NOVI, EUGENE (GENE)

b. 1928 Brooklyn, New York.
Pianist. With Buddy Rich, Lena Horne, Chubby Jackson and others during 1940s and '50s; with Lena Horne in London (1961); then wrote for Dick Van Dyke TV shows from Los Angeles; played in TV orchestras.

DION AND THE BELMONTS (folk rock group)

Dion DiMucci, lead singer and guitar; Angelo D'Aleo; Fred Milano, piano; Carlo Mastrangelo, drums; albums—*Dion, Dion Sings 15 Million Sellers, Dion's Greatest Hits, More of Dion's Greatest Hits, Sit Down Old Friend, Wonder Where I'm Bound.*

DIPPEL, ANDREAS

b. 1866 Kassel, Germany, d. 1932 Hollywood, California. Tenor. Pupil of Hey, Leoni, and Rau; with Bremen opera (1887-92), then in New York City; later in Breslau, Vienna, Bayreuth, Covent Garden, London; in management with the Metropolitan Opera, New York City (1908); directed opera in Chicago and Philadelphia (1910-13), then taught singing in Los Angeles.

DITON, CARL ROSSINI

b. 1886 Philadelphia, Pennsylvania, d. 1969.
Black pianist and composer. Graduated University of Pennsylvania, Philadelphia (1909); studied in Germany; toured as a concert pianist; taught at Paine College, Augusta, Georgia after 1911; at Talladega College, Talladega, Alabama until 1918; returned to Philadelphia; first black pianist to make a transcontinental tour; wrote *Four Spirituals* (1914), *The Hymn of Nebraska* (oratorio, 1921).

DITSON, OLIVER

b. 1811 Boston, Massachusetts, d. there 1888.
Publisher. Started as a partner with Col. S.H. Parker (1832); Col. Parker retired (1840); John C. Haynes joined the firm (1845); his son, Charles Healy Ditson (1845-1929) took charge of the New York branch (1867); and James Edward (d. 1881) the Philadelphia branch (1875); the firm was sold to Theodore Presser Company (1932).

DIXIE ALL-STARS *see* DON S. DAVIS

DIXIE BLUE BOYS *see* BILL NETTLES

DIXIE JASS BAND (jazz band) *see* NICK LA ROCCA

DIXIE PARTNERS (vocal group) *see* CHARLES B. MOORE, JR.

DIXIELAND BAND, THE SAL PACE (jazz band)

At the Grand Concourse Branch of the Public Library, New York City (1972).

DIXON, DEAN (CHARLES)

b. 1915 New York City.
Black conductor. Conducted Gateborg Symphony Orchestra in Sweden, and Frankfort Opera in Germany.

DIXON, DORSEY MURDOCK

b. 1897 Darlington, South Carolina.
Singer, guitarist, and songwriter. Started working for the Darlington Cotton Mills at the age of twelve; later worked for the mills in Lancaster and Greenville, S.C. and East Rockingham, N.C.; with his brother, Howard, the "Dixon Brothers" first appeared on WBT, Charlotte, N.C. (1934); wrote "The Cleveland Schoolhouse Fire" (1929) and "Crash on the Highway"; his records include *Old Time Music at Newport* (1963) and *Babies in the Mill* (1966).

DIXON, ERIC

b. 1930 Staten Island, New York.
Flutist, tenor saxist, and clarinetist. With Johnny Hodges, Cootie Williams and others during 1950s; with Count Basie after 1962.

DIXON, GEORGE WASHINGTON

b. 1808, d. 1861 New Orleans, Louisiana.
Singer. Early ministrel showman of importance and performed as early as 1827; known as the "celebrated buffo singer"; early tunes were "Coal Black Rose" and "Long Tailed Blue"; introduced "Coal Black Rose" (by John Clemens) in Philadelphia (1829), and "Zip Coon" at the Arch Street Theatre, Philadelphia (1834, song later known as "Turkey in the Straw").

DIXON, HOWARD

b. 1903 Darlington, South Carolina, d. 1961.
Singer and guitarist. Joined with his brother, Dorsey, as the "Dixon Brothers," but both of them continued working for the Darlington Cotton Mills.

DIXON, MORT

b. 1892 New York City, d. 1956 Bronxville, New York. Lyricist and vaudeville actor. Served in World War I; with Billy Rose wrote "That Old Gang of Mine" (1923, m. Ray Henderson); "Bye, Bye Blackbird" (m. Henderson), "River, Stay Away from My

Door" (1931, m. Harry Woods); with composer Allie Wrubel wrote "Flirtation Walk" (1934), "Fare Thee Well" (1935), "The Lady in Red" (1935), "Mine Alone" (1935); with composer Harry Warren wrote "Nagasaki," "I Found a Million Dollar Baby in a Five & Ten Cent Store"; also "I'm Looking Over a Four Leaf Clover" (1927, m. Harry Woods).

DIXON, WILLIAM ROBERT

b. 1925 Nantucket, Massachusetts.
Trumpeter and composer. Raised in New York City; educated at Boston University; served in U.S. army; studied at Hartnett School of Music (1946-51); leader of his own group during 1950s; also worked with Cecil Taylor; played his own compositions after 1962.

DIXON, WILLIE

b. 1915 Vicksburg, Mississippi.
Black bassist, singer, and songwriter. Played bass on Muddy Waters' records; wrote "Little Red Rooster" (recorded by the Rolling Stones), "Seventh Son" (recorded by the Challengers and others), "I Just Want to Make Love to You" (by Bo Diddley and others), "Bring It on Home" (by The Animals, et al.), "Hootchie Cootchie Man" (by Muddy Waters et al.); his own albums—*I Am the Blues, Memphis Slim and Willie Dixon, At the Village Gate.*

DIXON'S BRASS BAND (black band)

Originated in 1827 by Samuel Dixon in Newburgh, New York.

DLUGOSZEWSKI, LUCIA

b. 1931 Detroit, Michigan.
Composer and writer. She attended Detroit Conservatory of Music and Wayne State University, Detroit, Mich.; taught at New York University; composed over thirty works commissioned by dancing schools; wrote *Space Is a Diamond,* trumpet solo (1970); also other instrumental and vocal numbers; has invented numerous percussion instruments including the "timbre piano."

DOANE, GEORGE WASHINGTON

b. 1799 Trenton, New Jersey, d. 1859.
Hymnist. Graduated Union College, Schenectady, New York (1818) and General Theological Seminary; served as assistant minister at Trinity Church, New York; professor of belles-lettres at Washington (Trinity) College, Hartford; rector of Trinity Church, Boston; became the second Episcopal Bishop of New Jersey in 1832; wrote the lyrics "Softly Now the Light of Day" (1824, m. Geo. Hewes, tune "Holley"), "Fling Out the Banner" (1848, m. J.F. Wolle, tune "Palmarum," other tunes by J.B. Calkin), "Thou Art the Way, to Thee Alone" (1824, tune "St. James," 1697); published *Songs by the Way* (1824). (*See* H.W. Greatorex).

DOANE, WILLIAM CROSWELL

b. 1832 Boston, Massachusetts, d. 1913 Albany, New York. Hymnist. Son of G.W. Doane; graduated Burlington College (1850); became his father's assistant at St. Mary's Church, Burlington, N.J. then rector of St. John's Church, Hartford, and St. Peter's Church, Albany; first Episcopal bishop of the diocese of Albany; wrote the lyrics "Ancient of Days" (1886, m. J.A. Jeffrey, tune "Albany," 1892).

DOANE, WILLIAM H.

b. 1832 Preston, Connecticut, d. 1915 South Orange, New Jersey. Composer. President of a woodworking factory in Cincinnati, Ohio; received the degree of Doctor of Music from Denison University, Granville, Ohio in 1875; composed the music for "Safe in the Arms of Jesus" (1868), "The Prodigal Child" (w. Mrs. Ellen H. Gates), "Near the Cross" (1869, w. Fanny Crosby), "Pass Me Not" (w. Crosby), "To the Work" (1871, w. Crosby), "Tell Me the Old, Old Story" (1878, w. Katherine Hankey), "My Faith Still Clings to Thee," "This I Know," and "Sound the Alarm."

DR. JOHN, THE NIGHT TRIPPER (voodoo rock)

Mack Rebenneck, leader; albums—*Gris-Gris, Babylon, Remedies.*

DODDS, JOHNNY ("JOLIET")

b. 1892 New Orleans, Louisiana, d. 1940 Chicago, Illinois. Black clarinetist. Brother of Warren "Baby" Dodds; played in Kid Ory's band (1911-18); joined Mack's Merrymakers (1917) with Mutt Carey; joined King Oliver's band (1920-24); played at Burt Kelly's Stable (1924-30); died of a stroke.

DODDS, WARREN ("BABY")

b. 1894 New Orleans, Louisiana, d. 1959.
Black jazz drummer. Brother of Johnny Dodds; played in Fate Marable's Band on the Mississippi River boats between St. Louis and New Orleans after 1917; played with King Oliver until 1924; in Johnny Dodds' group (1924-30); recorded with Louis Armstrong (1923) at Gennett Record Co., Richmond, Indiana; recorded with Bunk Johnson (1944). Johnson (1944).

DODGION, JERRY

b. 1932 Richmond, California.
Alto saxist and flutist. With Gerald Wilson, Benny Carter, and Red Norvo during 1950s; later led own quartet with his wife, Dottie Dodgion, on drums; toured South America (1961); with Benny Goodman in Soviet Russia (1962); with the Mel Lewis-Thad Jones band after 1966.

DODSON, HOWARD J.

b. 1910, d. 1971 New York City.
Black organist. Studied at the Juilliard School, New York City; organist-choirmaster of the Abyssinian Baptist Church, New York City (1946-71).

DOERNER (DÖRNER), ARMIN W.

b. 1852 Marietta, Ohio, d. 1924 Denver, Colorado. Pianist and teacher. Family moved to Cincinnati (1859); studied in Berlin (1871) at New Academy under Kullak, also pupil of Franz Bendel and Carl Weitzmann; studied at Stuttgart Academy; in Paris with Edward Wolff; taught at Cincinnati College of Music after 1879 (when established); wrote *Technical Exercises.*

DOGGETT, WILLIAM BALLARD (BILL)

b. 1916 Philadelphia, Pennsylvania.
Organist and pianist. Active with various bands during 1950s; led own combo; at Juan-les-Pins Jazz Festival (1962); with Ella Fitzgerald (1963).

DOLAN, JIMMIE

b. 1924 Missouri.
Singer, guitarist, and bandleader. Started with radio station KWK, St. Louis, then joined the navy and spent five years in the Pacific during World War II; formed his own band in Los Angeles (1946) and became known as America's Cowboy Troubadour; top hit was "Hot Rod Race" (1951).

DOLE, NATHAN HASKELL

b. 1852 Chelsea, Massachusetts, d. 1935 Yonkers, New York. Writer. Wrote the lyrics for numerous songs based on French and German folk music, such as "Butterflies," "The Holiday," "My Pony," "Santa Claus," "The Tall Clock," "Winter," "Summer," "May Song," "Goodnight," "The Fountain of Knowledge."

DOLL, ANDY JOSEPH

b. 1921 Wauzeka, Wisconsin.
Singer and songwriter. Attended La Crosse Teachers College, La Crosse, Wisconsin (1941); taught in elementary schools; wrote "Sandy Haired Stranger," "Goodby Mary Ann," "Have I Lived," "Honey Dew."

DOLLAR, JIMMY

b. 1936 Kilgore, Texas.
Singer, guitarist, and songwriter. Served in the marines during World War II; for a time he was leader of the Texas Sons and appeared on radio in Dallas, Texas, and Shreveport, Louisiana; wrote "Lumberjack" and other songs; top hits were "Tear Talk," and "Stop the Start" (1966), "Your Hands," "Watching Me Losing You," and "The Wheels Fell Off the Wagon" (1967).

DOLLAR, JOHN WASHINGTON, JR. (JOHNNY)

b. 1933 Kilgore, Texas.
Singer and songwriter. Attended high school in Sheridan, Texas, and junior college in Kerrville, Texas; leader of the Texas Sons (1953-54); wrote "Stop the Start," "Big Red," "Crazy Eyes," "Your Hands," "Windburn," "Watching Me Losing You," "Did You Talk to Him Today," "Don't Take the Future from Me."

DOLLY, ROSIKA (singer) *see* JEAN SCHWARTZ

DOLLY SISTERS (singers) *see* JEAN SCHWARTZ

DOLPHY, ERIC ALLAN

b. 1928 Los Angeles, California, d. 1964 Berlin, Germany. Black bass clarinetist. Played in bands with Charlie Mingus (bass player), John Coltrane (saxophonist), and Ornette Coleman (saxophonist); toured Europe with Mingus (1964); suffered with diabetes; apparently died of a heart attack.

DOMINGO, PLACIDO

b. 1941 Madrid, Spain.
Tenor. Debut in *La Traviata* with Mexico's National Opera (1961); also in 1961 with Dallas Civic Opera and Israel National Opera in Tel Aviv; debut with New York City Opera in Ginastera's *Don Rodrigo* (1966) at Lincoln Center.

DOMINIQUE, ANATIE ("NATTY")

b. 1896 New Orleans, Louisiana.
Black trumpeter. With Jimmie Noone, Carroll Dickerson and others; later with King Oliver and Zutty Singleton.

DOMINO, ANTOINE, JR. ("FATS")

b. 1928 New Orleans, Louisiana.
Black pianist, bandleader, and composer.

While working in a bedspring factory in his teens, his hand was gashed, almost destroying his career as a pianist; obtained his first band job at age nineteen; later appeared in many night clubs and in films; wrote "Poor Me," "I'm Walkin'," "Ain't That a Shame."

DOMINOES (band) *see* JACKIE WILSON

DONAHUE, SAM KOONTZ

b. 1918 Detroit, Michigan.
Tenor saxist, trumpeter, and bandleader. Led his own band (1957-59); then with Stan Kenton; led the old Tommy Dorsey band after 1961, featuring Frank Sinatra as vocalist; visited World Jazz Festival in Japan (1964); toured South America (1965).

DONALDA, PAULINE

b. 1884 Montreal, Quebec, Canada, d. 1970.
Soprano. Born Pauline Lightstone; studied at the Victoria and Paris Conservatory; debut as Manon in Nice, France (1904); sang at the Manhattan Opera House, New York City (1905); at the Paris Opera (1907).

DONALDSON, LOU

b. 1926 Badin, North Carolina.
Alto saxist. Played in New York City night clubs during the 1950s and '60s; in Stockholm, Sweden (1965).

DONALDSON, WALTER

b. 1893 Brooklyn, New York, d. 1947 Santa Monica, California. Popular composer. Entertained at Camp Upton, New York in World War I; composed "Back Home in Tennessee" (1915, w. William Jerome), with lyrics by Sam Lewis and Joe Young: "How Ya Gonna Keep 'Em Down on the Farm?" (1919) and "My Mammy" (1920, made famous by Al Jolson), with lyrics by Gus Kahn: "Carolina in the Morning" (1922), "Yes Sir, That's My Baby" (1925), and "Love Me or Leave Me" (1928), also "My Buddy" (1922, w. Kahn), "Let It Rain, Let It Pour" (1925, w. Cliff Friend), and "My Blue Heaven" (1927, w. George Whiting).

DONATO DE OLIVEIRA, JOAO

b. 1934 Rio Branco Acre, Brazil.
Pianist and composer. Played in Rio de Janeiro and Sao Paolo during 1950s; came to U.S. (1959); with Mongo Santamaria, Tito Puente, and Herbie Mann; later formed his own trio; wrote "Aquarius," "Caminho de Casa," "Jodel," "Sambou, Sambou," "Sugar Cane Breeze," "Bossa Nova Carnival" (recorded by Dave Pike).

DONEGAN, DOROTHY

b. 1924 Chicago, Illinois.
Black pianist. Studied at Chicago Conservatory and Chicago College of Music; played in New York City night clubs.

DONNELLY, DOROTHY

b. 1880 New York City, d. there 1928.
Lyricist and actress. Wrote lyrics for composer Sigmund Romberg—"Song of Love" (1921). "Drinking Song" in *The Student Prince* (1924).

DONOVAN, RICHARD FRANK

b. 1891 New Haven, Connecticut.
Composer. Studied at Yale University Music School, at Institute of Musical Art, New York City, and with Widor in Paris; taught at Yale School of Music; composed *Smoke and Steel* (symphonic poem, Carl Sandburg), *Symphony* (for chamber orchestra, Yaddo Festival, 1937), *Ricercare*, (for oboe and strings, Eastman School Little Symphony, Rochester, N.Y., 1939).

DOOLITTLE, AMOS

b. 1754 Cheshire, Connecticut, d. 1832 New Haven, Connecticut. Editor and publisher. Doolittle and Simeon Jocelyn opened a music shop and publishing house in New Haven, Conn. in 1782; they published *The Chorister's Companion.*

DOOLITTLE, ELIAKIM

b. 1772, d. 1850 Argyle, New York.
Teacher and composer. Attended Yale for a time; published forty-one tunes and one anthem in *The Psalm Singers Companion* (1806); moved to Hampton, N.Y. in 1802, and in later years lived in Pawlet, Vermont; after the *Hornet* sank the British man-of-war *Peacock* in 1813, he composed a popular war song, "The Hornet Stung the Peacock."

DOORS, THE (rock group)

Jim Morrison, vocals; Ray Manzarek, organ; Robbie Krieger, guitar; John Densmore, drums; organized in Los Angeles; began playing at the now defunct club the London Fog on Sunset Strip; Morrison died (1971); albums—*The Doors* (1967), *Morrison Hotel-Hard Rock Cafe, Soft Parade, Strange Days, Waiting for the Sun.*

DORATI, ANTAL

b. 1906 Budapest, Hungary.
Conductor. Came to America and was musical director of the Ballet Russe, conductor of the Dallas Symphony Orchestra, then of the

Minneapolis Symphony (1949); musical director of the National Symphony Orchestra, opened its forty-first season in the concert hall of the John F. Kennedy Center for the Performing Arts on September 9, 1971 with President and Mrs. Nixon in the presidential box; conducted National Symphony Orchestra in Oliver Messiaen's *La Transfiguration de Notre Signeur Jesus Christ* at Carnegie Hall, New York City, Easter Sunday 1972, with Yvonne Loriod (Mrs. Messiaen) as piano soloist.

DOREE, DORIS

b. 1909 Newark, New Jersey, d. 1971 New York City. Dramatic soprano and teacher. Studied at the Settlement School of Music in Philadelphia, an adjunct of the Curtis Institute; operatic debut at Metropolitan Opera, New York City in Wagner's *Gotterdammerung* (1942); later leading soprano for two seasons at Covent Garden Opera, London.

DORHAM, MC KINLEY HOWARD ("KENNY")

b. 1924 Fairfield, Texas, d. 1972.
Black trumpeter. Played with Dizzy Gillespie, Billy Eckstine, and Lionel Hampton during 1940s; later with Charlie Parker Quintet; with Art Blakey, Max Roach, and his own groups in 50s; at Longhorn Jazz Festival in Austin, Texas (1966).

DORR, JULIA CAROLINE (RIPLEY)

b. 1825 Charleston, South Carolina, d. 1913 Vermont. Hymnist. Wrote the lyrics "How Can I Cease to Pray for Thee?" (1879, m. H. Lawes, 1638, tune "Battle").

DORSEY, JAMES (JIMMY)

b. 1904 Shenandoah, Pennsylvania, d. 1957 New York City. Clarinetist and bandleader. Played in his father's band as a teenager; formed the Dorsey Novelty Band with his brother Tommy (1920-22); later played with Paul Whiteman, Jean Goldkette, Rudy Vallee, and Victor Young; formed his own band (1934); joined Tommy again (1953) as the Fabulous Dorseys.

DORSEY, THOMAS, JR. (TOMMY)

b. 1905 Mahanoy Plane, Pennsylvania, d. 1956, Greenwich, Connecticut. Trombonist and bandleader. Played in his father's band as a teenager; formed a band with his brother (1920-22); again (1933-35); formed his own band in New York City (1935); disc jockey in the 1950s; with his brother again (1953-56).

DOUGLAS, CHARLES WINFRED

b. 1867 Oswego, New York, d. 1944.
Composer. Received his B.Mus. from Syracuse University, Syracuse, N.Y. (1891); organist and choirmaster of the Church of Zion and St. Timothy, New York City (1892-93), then went west to the Cathedral of St. John in the Wilderness, Denver (1894), and settled in Evergreen, Colorado; after further study at St. Matthew's Hall, Denver, he became canon at St. Paul's Cathedral, Fond du Lac, Wisconsin (1897-1907); assisted in compiling *The Choral Service* (1927), *The American Psalter* (1929), and *The Plainsong Psalter* (1932); composed the tunes "Dexter Street" (1940, "The Sabbath Day Was By," w. H.C. Robbins), and "St. Dunstan's" (1917, "He Who Would Valiant Be," w. John Bunyan).

DOUGLAS, LARRY

b. 1917 Detroit, Michigan.
Singer and composer. Sang in Carmen Cavallaro's band; wrote "Black Pearl," "Dancing Under Latin Skies," "A New Tomorrow," "Copenhagen, Denmark."

DOUGLASS, JOSEPH

b. 1869 Washington, D.C. d. 1935.
Black violinist. Grandson of Frederick Douglass, writer and orator; studied in Washington, D.C. and at New England Conservatory in Boston; also studied in Europe; married Fannie Howard, pianist; played at Columbian Exposition, Chicago (1893); played for Presidents William McKinley and William Howard Taft; taught at Howard University, Washington, D.C., and the Music Settlement School in New York City; first black violinist to record for the Victor Talking Machine Company of Camden, New Jersey (now RCA-Victor).

DOUTY, NICHOLAS

b. 1870 Philadelphia, Pennsylvania, d. 1955.
Organist, singer, composer, and writer. Organist in 1887; concert tenor (1895-1930); for twenty-five years sang solo parts at the Bach Festival in Bethlehem, Pennsylvania.

DOWDY, BILL

b. 1933 Benton Harbor, Michigan.
Drummer. Played in Chicago; with quintet (1956), later a trio with Gene Harris, pianist; played in night clubs in New York City; known as The Three Sounds.

DOWNBEATS (rock group) *see* PAUL REVERE AND THE RAIDERS

DOWNES, EDWIN OLIN

b. 1886 Evanston, Illinois, d. 1955 New York City. Music critic and pianist. Music critic with the *Boston Post* (1906-24), *New York Times* after 1924; with Elie Siegmeister, he edited *A Treasury of American Song;* appeared as a pianist in chamber music recitals.

DOWNES, LEWIS THOMAS

b. 1824, d. 1910.
Composer. Organist in Providence, Rhode Island; composed the tune "Solitude" (1850, "Now May He Who from the Dead," w. John Newton).

DOWNEY, MORTON

b. 1901 Wallingford, Connecticut.
Singer, pianist, and songwriter. Sang in Greenwich Village theatres; toured Europe (1927); opened own night club, The Delmonico, New York City (1930); sang over radio.

DOWN TOWNERS *see* KENNY ROBERTS

DRAKE, ERVIN M.

b. 1919 New York City.
Producer and songwriter. Educated at City College of New York; studied at Juilliard; writer and producer for TV shows; with Harry Lend wrote words for "Perdido" (1942, m. Juan Tizol and Duke Ellington).

DRAKE, JAMES G.

b. 1802 England, d. 1852 Louisville, Kentucky. Composer. Came to America (1810); lived in Cincinnati (1825), Pensacola, Florida (1830), then Louisville, Kentucky; wrote "Beautiful Isle Where the Sun Goes Down," "Shall We Meet Again, Mary," "Tam Breeze," "Parlez bas," "Gie Each a Cup and Fill It Fu'."

DRAKE, PETER

b. 1933 Augusta, Georgia.
Guitarist. Played the steel guitar and formed his own band, The Sons of the South (1951); they broadcast on WLMA, Atlanta, Georgia and WTJH, East Point, Georgia, then he moved to Nashville (1959); his hits were "Talking Steel Guitar," "Forever," "I'm a Fool to Care," and "Mystic Dream."

DRAPER, RAYMOND ALLEN (RAY)

b. 1940 New York City.
Black tuba player and composer. With John Coltrane, Jackie McLean, and Max Roach during 1950s; formed own group in Los Angeles with Philly Joe Jones (1964); wrote *Crisis in Algiers, Tone Poem on the Watts Riots.*

DRESSER, PAUL

b. 1857 Terre Haute, Indiana, d. 1906 Brooklyn, New York. Popular composer. Born Paul Dreiser; the brother of Theodore Dreiser, the novelist; wrote "The Letter That Never Came" (1886), "The Outcast Unknown" (1887), "The Blue and the Gray" (1890), "Just Tell Them That You Saw Me" (1895), "Show Me the Way" (1896, popular on records but absent from hymnals), "On the Banks of the Wabash" (1897, state song of Indiana), "Sweet Savannah" (1898), "In Good Old New York Town" (1899), "I'll Still Believe You True" (1900, introduced by Charles Kent), and "My Gal Sal" (1905, but died too soon to enjoy the royalties).

DREW, KENNETH SIDNEY (KENNY)

b. 1928 New York City.
Pianist. With Lester Young and Charlie Parker in New York City in 1950s; later with Buddy De Franco and his own trio in Los Angeles; went to Paris (1961); at Bologna Jazz Festival (1962); played in Copenhagen, Denmark night spots after 1964.

DRIFTERS, THE (blues group)

Clyde McPhatter, lead singer; albums—*Drifters' Golden Hits, Good Life with the Drifters, I'll Take You Where the Music's Playing, Save the Last Dance for Me, Under the Boardwalk, Up on the Roof.*

DRIFTWOOD, JIMMY

b. 1917 Mountain View, Arkansas.
Guitarist and songwriter. Real name is Jimmy Morris; graduated from Arkansas State Teachers College, Conway, Arkansas; wrote "The Battle of New Orleans," based on old folk music (recorded by Johnny Horton, 1958), and "Tennessee Stud" (recorded by Eddy Arnold, 1959); recorded *Newly Discovered Early American Folk Songs* (1958), and *Best of Jimmy Driftwood;* founded (with federal funds) five million dollar folk center in Mountain View, Arkansas (1972).

DRUSKY, ROY FRANK

b. 1930 Atlanta, Georgia.
Singer, guitarist, and songwriter. Served in the navy, then attended Emory University, Atlanta, Georgia; formed the Southern Ranch Boys who played on radio in Decatur, Georgia, and Atlanta; wrote "Alone with You" (1958), "Another and Anymore" (1960), "Yes, Mr. Peters" (1965), and "White

Lightning Express" (1966); his hits by other writers were "Three Hearts in a Tangle" (1961), "Second Hand Rose" (1963), "Strangers" (1965).

DUBENSKY, ARCADY

b. 1890 Viatka, Russia, d. 1966.
Composer. Studied at the Moscow Conservatory, then came to America (ca. 1917) and was a violinist with the Philadelphia Orchestra; composed the opera *Romance with Double Bass* (Moscow Imperial Opera, 1916), *The Raven* (w. Edgar Allan Poe), a symphony *Russian Bells* (New York Symphony Orchestra, 1927), *Fugue* for eighteen violins.

DUBIN, AL

b. 1891 Zurich, Switzerland, d. 1945 New York City. Lyricist. Family came to Perkiomen, Pennsylvania (1893); staff writer for New York music publishers; served in 77th Division in France in World War I; returned to songwriting after the war; with composer Joe Burke wrote "Tip Toe Through the Tulips," "The Kiss Waltz"; with composer Harry Warren "Shuffle Off to Buffalo," "Lullaby of Broadway" (1935 Oscar winner); "South American Way" (m. Jimmy McHugh), "Feudin' and Fightin' " (1944, m. Burton Lane).

DUBOIS, WILLIAM

b. ca. 1774, d. ca. 1854 New York City.
Clarinetist, composer, and music publisher. Came to Philadelphia (ca. 1795), gave a benefit concert there (1799); composed the "Freemasons March"; moved to New York City, publisher there (1817-21) and with Dubois and Stodart (1821-26); published "By the Side of a Willow Weeping" (J. Whitaker), "Thine Am I My Faithful Fair" (1818, J. Whitaker).

DUCHIN, EDDY

b. 1909, d. 1951.
Pianist and bandleader. Played with Leo Reisman's band at the Central Park Casino, New York City; led the band in 1931; Lew Sherwood was his trumpeter, vocalist, and confidant; played on radio for Ed Wynn and Texaco; toured South America in the 1940s; served as a lieutenant in the navy in World War II; died of leukemia.

DUDLEY, DAVID (DAVE)

b. 1928 Spencer, Wisconsin.
Singer and guitarist. Raised in Stevens Point, Wisconsin, where he started on radio station WTWT as a singer and guitarist; moved to stations in Waterloo, Iowa, then to Charles City, Idaho, then Minneapolis; hit records were "Six Days on the Road" (1962), "Cowboy Boots" (1963), "Mad" and "Last Day in the Mines" (1964), "Truck Drivin' Son-of-a Gun," and "What We're Fighting For" (1965).

DUFF, ARLEIGH ELTON (ARLIE)

b. 1924 Warren, Texas.
Singer and songwriter. Graduated Stephen F. Austin State College, Nacogdoches, Texas (1951 B.S. and M.A.); wrote "Y'All Come" (1932), "She's Just a Housewife, That's All," "I'll Always Wonder."

DUFFIELD, GEORGE, JR.

b. 1818 Carlisle, Pennsylvania, d. 1888 Detroit, Michigan. Hymnist. Educated at Yale and Union Theological Seminary; Presbyterian minister in Brooklyn, N.Y., Bloomfield, N.J., Philadelphia, Pa., Galesburg, Ill., then Adrian, Saginaw, Ann Arbor, and Lansing, Michigan; wrote the hymn "Stand Up, Stand Up for Jesus" (tune "Geibel"—Adam Geibel and also G.J. Webb). During the great revival of 1858 in Philadelphia, the Rev. Dudley Tyng caught his arm in a corn-shelling machine, and it was torn off. As Tyng lay dying, several ministers came to his bedside, including Duffield. When someone asked if Tyng had a message for his congregation, Tyng said: "Let us all stand up for Jesus," which inspired Duffield to write his hymn.

DUFFIELD, SAMUEL AUGUSTUS WILLOUGHBY

b. 1843 Brooklyn, New York, d. 1887.
Hymnologist. Son of Dr. George Duffield, Jr.; minister in Detroit, Michigan; wrote *English Hymns, Their Authors and History.*

DUFFY, JOHN

b. 1934 Washington, D.C.
Singer and guitarist. Raised in Washington, D.C., and Bethesda, Maryland; he was working for radio station WFMD, Frederick, Maryland, when he met Charlie Waller; they formed a team, and later Eddie Adcock and Jim Cox joined the group, which became known as the "Country Gentlemen." (*See* Charlie Waller).

DUKE, JOHN WOODS

b. 1899 Cumberland, Maryland.
Composer. Studied at Peabody Conservatory, Baltimore, later with Nadia Boulanger in Paris; taught at Smith College, Northampton,

Mass.; composed Overture in D Minor for string orchestra (Smith College Symphony Orchestra under composer, 1928); Concerto in A Major for piano and string orchestra (Springfield, Massachusetts Federation Symphony, composer soloist, Milton Aronson, conductor, 1939); chamber music, songs.

DUKE, VERNON (VLADIMER DUKELSY)

b. 1903 Pskov, (North) Russia, d. 1969 Santa Monica, California. Composer. Studied at the Conservatory at Kiev; fled Russia to Turkey (1920) then to the U.S. (1921); went to Paris (1924) and London, then returned to the United States (1929), eventually settling in Pacific Palisades, California; composed the music for the ballet *Zephyr et Flore* (1925), the musicals *Walk a Little Faster* (1932, which included "April in Paris"), the *Ziegfeld Follies* (1934-35), *The Show Is On* (1934-35-36), *Cabin in the Sky* (1940, book by Lynn Root), *Banjo Eyes* (1941, starring Eddie Cantor) *Sadie Thompson* (1944), *Two's Company* (1952, w. Ogden Nash), and the ballets *Public Gardens* (1935), *Washerwoman's Ball* (1946), *Emperor Norton* (1957), *Lady Blue* (1961).

DUKES OF DIXIELAND *see* FRANK J. ASSUNTO AND EDMOND HALL

DULCKEN, FERDINAND QUENTIN

b. 1837 London, England, d. 1902 Astoria, New York. Pianist and composer. Pupil of Mendelssohn; became a professor at the Warsaw Conservatory, toured Europe, then came to New York; composed the opera *Wieslav*, and a mass.

DUMAS, JAMES MADISON ("DUKE")

b. 1941 Hamburg, Arkansas.
Singer and bandleader. Co-leader of Roller Coasters (1961-64); leader of The Rhoderunners (1964-67); member of Stamps Quartet after 1967; albums—*The Best of the Stamps Quartet* (1967), *Gospel Music's No. 1 Band* (1968), *In the Sweet Bye and Bye* (1968).

DUNBAR, PAUL LAURENCE

b. 1872 Dayton, Ohio, d. there 1906.
Black lyricist. Son of former slaves; started writing poetry as a youth; wrote "Oak and Ivy" (1893), "Majors and Minors" (1895), "Lyrics of Lowly Life" (1896), the last two praised by William Dean Howells; wrote the song "Li'l Gal" (m. J. Rosamond Johnson).

DUNCAN, R. TODD

b. 1903 Danville, Kentucky.
Black baritone. Graduated Butler University, Indianapolis, Indiana (1925), master's degree from Columbia University, New York City (1930); appeared in Masacagni's *Cavalleria Rusticana* (in New York City, 1934), *Porgy and Bess* (1935, m. George Gershwin), *The Sun Never Sets* (at Drury Lane Theatre, London, 1938), *Cabin in the Sky* (1940, London; with New York City Opera in Leoncavallo's *Pagliacci* and Bizet's *Carmen*); toured as a concert singer; taught at Howard University, Washington, D.C. after 1931.

DUNCAN, TOMMY

b. 1911 Hillsboro, Texas, d. 1967.
Singer. Joined Bob Wills' Texas Playboys (1932); died of a heart attack.

DUNHAM, HENRY MORTON

b. 1853 Brockton, Massachusetts, d. there 1929. Organist and composer. Studied at the New England Conservatory, Boston; later became professor of organ at the New England Conservatory; composed a symphony, tone poem *Easter Morning*, three organ sonatas, *Meditation* for organ, harp and violin.

DUNLAP, WILLIAM

b. 1766 Perth Amboy, New Jersey, d. 1839 New York City. Librettist and playwright. Blinded in one eye from a boyhood accident; moved to New York City (1777); studied arts of design with Benjamin West in London (1784-89); wrote libretto for the opera, *The Archers or the Mountaineers of Switzerland* (m. Benjamin Carr, performed in New York City, 1796); also lyrics "Come My Love to the Window Come" (a duet, sung by Mrs. Johann C.G. Graupner and Mrs. Villers in the play *Count Benjowsky* at the Boston Theater, 1799).

DUNLOP, FRANCIS (FRANKIE)

b. 1928 Buffalo, New York.
Drummer. Played with Thelonious Monk, Sonny Rollins, Charlie Mingus, and Maynard Ferguson in 1950s; toured Europe with Monk (1961) and Japan (1963).

DUNN, JAMES PHILIP

b. 1884 New York City, d. 1936 Jersey City, New Jersey. Organist, composer, and writer. Educated at City College of New York and Columbia University; studied with MacDowell and Rybner; church organist in New York City, Bayonne, and Jersey City; works—Piano Quintet, Violin Sonata, two string quartets, *We* (tone poem), *The Phantom Drum* (cantata), *Overture on Negro Themes*, *The Galleon* (opera), Mass in C, songs.

DUNN, JOHNNY

b. 1897 Memphis, Tennessee, d. 1937. Black trumpeter. Known as a "plunger trumpeter"; recorded with Jelly Roll Morton (1928); recorded "Buffalo Blues" (later called "Mister Joe"), "Dunn's Bugle Call Blues" (adapted from "Milenberg Blues").

DUNN, ROBINSON PORTER

b. 1825, d. 1867.
Hymnist. Professor at Brown University, Providence, R.I.; translated a number of hymns from the Latin.

DUPORT, PIERRE LANDRIN

b. 1762 Paris, France, d. 1841 Washington, D.C. Dancing master, composer, and teacher. Came to America (1790); taught music and dancing in Philadelphia, New York City, Boston, Baltimore, Norfolk, then Washington, D.C.; wrote "Commodore Perry's March" (1813), "Decatur's March" (1813); his *Fancy Menuit* was danced before General Washington (1792), and his *Fancy Menuit with Figure Dance* performed by two young ladies for Mrs. Washington in Philadelphia (1792).

DUQUES, AUGUSTIN

b. 1899 Toulouse, France, d. 1972 New York City. Clarinetist. Studied at the National Conservatory in Paris; teacher at Institute of Musical Art (later Juilliard), New York City after 1923; joined Goldman Band in Brooklyn, New York in 1920s; first clarinet with NBC Symphony (1931-49); with Goldman Band in concert (1972).

DURAN, FATHER NARCISO

b. 1776, d. 1846.
Composer and choir leader in the Franciscan mission in San Diego, California. Composed *Misa de Catalein* and compiled a book of mission music in 1813.

DURANG, JOHN

b. 1768 York, Pennsylvania, d. 1822.
Singer and dancer. Debut in Philadelphia (1784); married dancer Mary McEwen (1787); with Old American Company (1789-96); sang in *The Archers* (w. William Dunlap, m. Benjamin Carr) produced in New York City (1796).

DURANTE, JIMMY

b. 1893 New York City.
Pianist, singer, and actor. Pianist at Coney Island, New York; organized his own band (1916); vaudeville actor with Eddie Jackson and Lou Clayton; appeared in *Show Girl* and other Broadway musicals; at Palladium, London (1936); appeared in many films; wrote "Inka Dinka Doo"; at "A Salute to Television's 25th Anniversary," ABC-TV (1972).

DURBIN, DEANNA

b. 1922 Winnipeg, Manitoba, Canada.
Singer and actress. Appeared in numerous films; album—*Deanna Durbin.*

DUSEN, FRANK (FRANKIE)

b. ca. 1880, d. 1940.
Black trombonist and bandleader. Played in Buddy Bolden's band before 1900; took over the band after Buddy was confined to a mental institution and renamed it the Eagle Band; played with Jelly Roll Morton (1917-22).

DU SHON, JEAN ATWELL

b. 1936 Detroit, Michigan.
Singer. Studied at Detroit Conservatory of Music; debut at age fifteen; worked with Cootie Williams; sang with Ramsey Lewis Trio; later at Las Vegas night clubs.

DUTREY, HONORÉ

b. 1892 New Orleans, Louisiana, d. 1937 Chicago, Illinois. Black trombonist. Played in King Oliver's orchestras; previously played in Bolden's Eagle Band; left King Oliver (1924); played with Johnny Dodds' group (1924-30).

DUTTON, DEODATUS, JR.

b. 1808 Monson, Massachusetts, d. 1832 New York City. Composer. Educated at Brown University, Providence, R.I., and Trinity College, Hartford, Conn. (1828), where he played the first organ in the Center Church; composed the tune "Woodstock"—"I Love to Steal Awhile Away" (w. Phebe H. Brown); with Elam Ives, Jr. he issued the *American Psalmody* (1830), called *The Hartford Collection.*

DUX, CLAIRE

b. 1885 Witkowicz, Poland.
Soprano. Studied in Milan, Italy; debut in Cologne, Germany (1906); sang with Berlin Opera (1911-18), and Chicago Opera (1921-23); concert performer in Europe and America; she married Charles H. Swift and established residence in Chicago (1926).

DVOŘÁK, ANTONIN

b. 1841 Muhlhausen, Bohemia (now Czechoslovakia), d. 1904 Prague, Bohemia.

Noted composer and teacher. From 1892-95 he headed the National Conservatory of Music, New York City; among his students were the black composers Will Martin Cook and Henry T. Burleigh, who introduced the American Negro spirituals to Dvořák, and which made a profound impression on him; composed his 5th symphony, op. 95 *From the New World* (1893), *Humoresque* (1894, piano solo), and *The American Flag* (1895, while residing in New York City).

DWIGHT, JOHN SULLIVAN

b. 1813 Boston, Massachusetts, d. there 1893. Critic. Graduated from Harvard; published the *Journal of Music* from 1852 to 1881; leading music critic; when Patrick S. Gilmore held his Peace Jubilee in Boston in 1869 a coliseum seating 30,000 people was erected, with four organs that required relays of twelve men to pump. 10,000 choral singers, an orchestra of 84 trombones, 83 tubas, 83 cornets, 75 drums, 330 strings and 110 woodwinds, plus 100 members of the fire department beating on 100 anvils produced the loudest performance of the anvil chorus from *Il Trovatore* ever given. President U.S. Grant attended, unsmiling, but Dwight fled the scene to escape the thunderous din!; Dwight and C.T. Brooks translated "God Bless Our Native Land" from the German (m. Lowell Mason, tune "Dort").

DWIGHT, TIMOTHY

b. 1752 Northampton, Massachusetts, d. 1817 Philadelphia, Pennsylvania. Hymnist. Graduated Yale University at age thirteen, and became President of Yale in 1795; before becoming President of Yale, he was a school teacher in New Haven, a chaplain in the American army, and pastor of the Congregational Church in Greenfield, Conn.; wrote the lyrics "I Love Thy Kingdom, Lord" (m. Aaron Williams, 1734-1776, English, adapted from Handel); in 1800 he revised and published *Isaac Watt's Psalms.*

DYER, SAMUEL

b. 1785 Wellshire, England, d. 1835 Hoboken, New Jersey. Composer and compiler. Came to New York City (1811), went to Philadelphia (1812) where he conducted a series of sacred concerts, then to Baltimore (1815) where he published *Dyer's New Selection of Sacred Music* (1817); to introduce his book he traveled south to Savannah, Georgia, north to Norfolk, Va. and to Salem, Mass., visiting other cities along the way; the sixth edition was called the *Philadelphia Collection of Sacred Music* (1828), and *Anthems* separately in 1822; composed the tune "Mendon" often attributed to Lowell Mason.

DYER-BENNET, RICHARD

b. 1913 Leicester, England.
Singer, lutist, guitarist, and songwriter. Spent his early years in Canada, then the family came to America (1925); graduated from the University of California, Berkeley, then studied under Sven Scholander in Sweden, where he learned European folk songs on the lute; later he changed to the Spanish guitar; LP records are *Gems of Minstrelsy* (1960), *Dyer-Bennett* (1962), *Songs of the Spirit of 1601* (1963), and *Of Ships and Seafaring Men* (1965).

DYKEMA, PETER WILLIAM

b. 1873 Grand Rapids, Michigan, d. 1951 Hastings, New York. Teacher. Studied in Berlin and at the Institute of Musical Art, New York City; director of music at the Ethical Culture School (1901-13); professor of music at the University of Wisconsin, Madison (1913-24); professor at Teachers College, Columbia University after 1924.

DYLAN, BOB

b. 1941 Duluth, Minnesota.
Singer, guitarist, pianist, and songwriter. Real name is Robert Zimmerman; raised in Hibbing, Minnesota and as a youth ran away from home many times; attended the University of Minnesota only six months, then went to New York City; wrote "Blowin' in the Wind," "The Times They Are A-Changin'," "Masters of War," "Don't Think Twice, It's All Right," "Spanish Harlem Incident," "Chimes of Freedom"; LP records were *Bob Dylan* (1961), *John Wesley Harding* (1968), and *Nashville Skyline* (1969).

EAGLE BAND (black jazz band)

Led by Frankie Dusen, successor to Buddy Bolden's Band in New Orleans; included Honoré Dutrey, trombonist.

EAMES, EMMA HAYDEN

b. 1865 Shanghai, China, d. 1952 New York City. Noted soprano. Family moved to Bath, Maine (1870); studied in Boston and Paris; debut as Juliette at the Paris Grand Opera (1889), and sang there (1889-91); then in *Faust* at Covent Garden, London, in Madrid (1892-93 and 1895-96), then at the Metropolitan Opera in New York until 1909; married Julian Story, the painter (1891), and later Emilio de Gogorza, baritone (1911) and toured with him; later separated.

EAMES, HENRY PURMONT

b. 1872 Chicago, Illinois, d. 1950.
Pianist, composer, and teacher. Wrote *Onward.*

EANES, HOMER ROBERT, JR. ("JIM")

b. 1923 Mountain Valley, Virginia.
Singer and bandleader. Sang in various groups; leader of the Blue Ridge Boys (1950-51) and Shenandoah Boys (1951).

EARDLEY, JON

b. 1928 Altoona, Pennsylvania.
Jazz trumpeter. Player with Buddy Rich, Gene Williams, Gerry Mulligan and others.

EARHART, WILL

b. 1871 Franklin, Ohio, d. 1960 Portland, Oregon. Teacher and writer. Became musical director of the School of Education, University of Pittsburgh in 1913.

EARTH OPERA (contemporary group)

Peter Rowan, vocals, guitar and tenor sax; David Grisman, vocals, mandolin, etc; Paul Dillon, vocals, drums, etc.; John Nagy, electric bass, etc.; started in Boston; albums—*Earth Opera* (1968), *The Great American Eagle Tragedy.*

EASTBURN, JAMES WALLACE

b. 1797 London, England, d. 1819 Santa Cruz. Hymnist. Family came to New York (1803); graduated Columbia University (1816); rector in Accomac, Virginia (1818); wrote "O Holy, Holy, Holy Lord, Bright in Thy Deeds" (1815, *Prayer Book Collection,* 1826), "The Hebrew Mourner" (m. Peter K. Moran).

EASTMAN, LUKE

b. 1790 Hollis, New Hampshire, d. 1847 Lowell, Massachusetts. Compiler. Graduated Dartmouth, Hanover, N.H. (1812); lawyer in Sterling, Mass. (1820); later in Dracut, Mass.; wrote *Masonick Melodies* (1818).

EBERHARD, ERNST

b. 1839 Hanover, Germany, d. 1913.
Baritone, organist, and conductor. Studied under Heinrich Enckhausen, H. Marshner and H. Lahmeyer; organist in St. Ann's Church, Brooklyn after 1864; then Church of Paulists, New York City; conductor of St. Cecilia mixed chorus, of Flora mixed chorus, and of the Harmonic and Philharmonic Societies in Newark, N.J.; founded the Grand Conservatory of Music in New York City (1876).

EBERHART, NELLE RICHMOND

b. 1871 Detroit, Michigan, d. 1944 Kansas City, Missouri. Lyricist. Taught school in Nebraska; collaborated with composer Charles Wakefield Cadman; wrote "At Dawning" (1906), "Four American Indian Songs," "Morning of the Year" (song cycle).

ECKHARD, JACOB, SR.

b. 1757 Eschewege, Hesse Cassel, Germany, d. 1833 Charleston, South Carolina. Composer. Came to America in 1776 as an organist in Richmond, Va., then at St. John's Lutheran Church, Charleston, S.C. (1786), then St. Michael's (1809); composed several tunes in *The Book of Common Prayer . . . and Hymns* (1799, W. P. Young) and in the *Choral Book* (1816, J. Loring) which included his tune "St. Michael's Newest."

ECKSTINE (ECKSTEIN), BILLY ("MR. B.")

b. 1914 Pittsburgh, Pennsylvania.
Black singer and bandleader. Sang with Earl Hines; organized his own band (1944), took with him Dizzy Gillespie, trumpeter and Budd

Johnson, tenor saxist; featured Sarah Vaughan, singer; later Dizzy left him to organize his own band; became a vocalist (1948), sang as "Mr. B."; his hit records were "My Foolish Heart" and "My Destiny" (1950); guest star on Tony Bennett's "This Is Music" program, London, England (1972); at the Newport Jazz Festival, New York City (1972).

EDDY, DANIEL C.

b. 1823 Salem, Massachusetts, d. 1896 Martha's Vineyard, Massachusetts. Hymnist. Became a Baptist minister in 1846; wrote "Maker of Land and Rolling Sea"; was the Know Nothing speaker of the Massachusetts House of Representatives in 1854.

EDDY, HIRAM CLARENCE

b. 1851 Greenfield, Massachusetts, d. 1937 Chicago, Illinois. Organist. Pupil of J. G. Wilson and Dudley Buck, then studied in Berlin; toured Europe; organist in Chicago (1874); director of Hershey School of Musical Art (1876); conducted the Chicago Philharmonic Vocal Society, then after 1910 in San Francisco; wrote *The Church and Concert Organist* and *The Organ in the Church.*

EDDY, MARY (BAKER)

b. 1821 Bow, New Hampshire, d. 1910 Chestnut Hill, Massachusetts. Hymnist. Wrote *Science and Health* (1875); formed the Christian Science Association (1876), the Church of Christ, Scientist, chartered 1879, the monthly *Christian Science Journal* (1883), first Christian Science Reading Room (1888), and the daily *Christian Science Monitor* (1908); wrote the hymns "Saw Ye My Saviour?" (1896), "Shepherd, Show Me How to Go" (1887), "O'er Waiting Harpstrings of the Mind" (1887), "Brood O'er Us with Thy Shelt'ring Wing" (1896), "O Gentle Presence, Peace and Joy and Power" (1896), "Blest Christmas Morn, Though Murky Clouds" (1903), and "It Matters Not What Be Thy Lot" (1910).

EDDY, NELSON

b. 1901 Providence, Rhode Island, d. 1967. Baritone. Pupil of David Bispham and William Vilonat; debut in Philadelphia (1922); sang with Savoy Opera Company and Philadelphia Civic Opera; New York debut in *Wozzeck* (1931); later featured in musical films with Jeanette MacDonald.

EDISON, HARRY ("SWEETS")

b. 1915 Columbus, Ohio.
Black trumpeter. Played in Count Basie's orchestra (1937-50); later in Hollywood film studios; organized his own quintet and toured with Joe Williams (1960-61); in Europe (1964); numerous engagements again with Count Basie; played at the Newport Jazz Festival, New York City (1972).

EDMUNDSON, GARTH

b. 1895 Prospect, Pennsylvania.
Composer. Studied at the Cincinnati Conservatory and was organist-choirmaster in the First Baptist Church, New Castle, Pa. (1918-40), then at the Presbyterian Church there after 1941; composed over 200 organ and choral works.

EDSON, LEWIS, JR.

b. 1771 Bridgewater, Massachusetts, d. 1845 near Catskill, New York. Composer and compiler. Son of Lewis Edson; singing master in Cooperstown, N.Y. (1795-97), Middlefield, N.Y. (1797), Danbury, Conn. (1798-1800), New York City after 1800, Shady, near Catskill, N.Y. (1830); compiled *The Social Harmonist* (1800), which included his tunes "Solitude," "Harlem," and "Friendship," also two tunes of his father's.

EDSON, LEWIS, SR.

b. 1748 Bridgewater, Massachusetts, d. 1820, near Catskill, New York. Composer and teacher. Blacksmith by trade and prominent singer; at age thirteen served in British army (1761-63); taught singing in Bridgewater (1763-69), in Halifax, N.S. (1769-71), Bridgewater (1771-76), Lanesborough, Mass. (1776-79), chorister in Church of England there; moved to New York State (1791); his tunes "Greenfield," "Lenox," and "Bridgewater" appeared in Simeon Jocelin and Amos Doolittle's *Chorister's Companion*, New Haven (1782); tunes "Resurrection" and "Dominion" in Lewis Edson, Jr.'s *The Social Harmonist* (1800); his tune "Lenox" used for two hymns by Charles Wesley—"Blow Ye the Trumpet, Blow!" and "Arise, My Soul, Arise."

EDWARDS, EDWIN BRANFORD (EDDIE)

b. 1891 New Orleans, Louisiana, d. 1963 New York City. Trombonist. With Original Dixieland Jazz Band organized by Nick La Rocca (1917); later led his own band in New York City.

EDWARDS, GUS

b. 1879 Hohensalza, Germany, d. 1945 Los Angeles, California. Songwriter. Wrote "All I Want Is My Black Baby Back" (1898, w. Tom Daly), "I Couldn't Stand to See My Baby

Lose" (1899, w. Will Cobb), "I Can't Tell Why I Love You But I Do" (1900, w. Cobb), "In My Merry Oldsmobile" (1905, w. Vincent Bryan), "School Days" (1907, w. Cobb), "By the Light of the Silvery Moon" (1907, w. Edward Madden).

EDWARDS, JULIAN

b. 1855 Manchester, England, d. 1910 Yonkers, New York. Conductor and producer. Born D.H. Barnard and used the stage name Julian Edwards; conductor of the Royal English Opera Company (1877); came to the U.S. (1889) where he produced several comic operas in Boston and New York City; composed the grand opera *Elfinella*, symphonies, overtures.

EDWARDS, THEODORE MARCUS (TEDDY)

b. 1924 Jackson, Mississippi.
Black tenor saxist. Played in Los Angeles bands during 1940s and '50s; some time with Benny Goodman in 1960s; played at Disneyland; at Monterey Jazz Festival (1963); on TV, "Jazz Scene USA."

EGAN, RAYMOND B.

b. 1890 Windsor, Ontario, Canada, d. 1952 Westport, Connecticut. Lyricist. Came to U.S. (1892); educated at the University of Michigan; staff writer for Grinnells Music Co., Detroit; with composer Richard A. Whiting wrote the lyrics for "And They Called It Dixieland" (1916), "Mammy's Little Coal Black Rose" (1916), "Some Sunday Morning" (also with Gus Kahn), "Till We Meet Again" (1918), "Sleepy Time Gal" (also with Ange Lorenzo and Joseph R. Alden).

EHLERS, ALICE

b. 1890 Vienna, Austria.
Harpsichordist. Taught in Berlin for a number of years, then came to America, where she joined the faculty of the University of Southern California, Los Angeles.

EICHBERG, JULIUS

b. 1824 Dusseldorf, Germany, d. 1893 Boston, Massachusetts. Violinist, composer, and teacher. Studied under F.W. Eichler and Julius Rietz; also at Royal Conservatory at Brussels, first prize for violin playing and composition; taught at Geneva Conservatory; came to New York City (1857); to Boston (1859); founded Boston Conservatory of Music; wrote *The Doctor of Alcantara* (operetta produced 1862), *To Thee, O Country, Great and Free* (chorus), *Lebensfruhling* (set of piano pieces), *Rose of Tyrol, A Night in Rome.*

EICHHEIM, HENRY

b. 1870 Chicago, Illinois, d. 1942 Santa Barbara, California. Violinist and composer. Graduated Chicago Music College; played first violin in Boston Symphony (1890-1912); toured America and Europe as a soloist; composed orchestral works based on native folk songs of the Orient, also piano pieces, chamber music and songs.

EINECKE, C. HAROLD

b. 1904 Quincy, Illinois.
Organist. Educated at Columbia University and Westminster Choir College; organist-choirmaster in Rye, N.Y., Quincy, Ill. (1925), Grand Rapids, Mich. (1930), St. Louis, Mo. (1945), Santa Ana, Calif. (1948), and at the First Methodist Church, Santa Barbara, Calif. after 1950.

EINSTEIN, ALFRED

b. 1880 Munich, Germany, d. 1952 El Cerrito, California. Teacher and writer. Music critic on the *Munchener Post*, then the *Berliner Tageblatt* (1927-32); the rise of Hitlerism forced him to flee Germany to England, Italy, and then the United States; taught at Smith College, Northampton, Mass.; edited musical encyclopedias, wrote *Mozart, His Character, His Work, Schubert—A Musical Portrait, Greatness in Music, Music in the Romantic Area*, and *A Short History of Music.*

ELDRIDGE, DAVID ROY ("LITTLE JAZZ")

b. 1911 Pittsburgh, Pennsylvania.
Black jazz trumpeter and singer. With Speed Webb and Zach Whyte in 1920s; McKinney's Cotton Pickers, Teddy Hill, and Fletcher Henderson in 1930s; with Sammy Kaye, Gene Krupa, and Artie Shaw in 1940s; own quintet in 1950s and with small bands; made many successful recordings with Anita O'Day; at Berlin Jazz Festival (1965); with Count Basie after 1966; at the Newport Jazz Festival, New York City (1972).

ELECTRIC FLAG (rock group)

Mike Bloomfield, guitar, (replaced by Hoshal Wright); Harvey Brooks, bass; Buddy Miles, vocals and drums; Herbie Rich, organ; John Simon, piano; Terry Clements, tenor; Marcus Doubleday, trumpet; Nick Gravenites, vocals and rhythm guitar; Virgil Gonsalves, sax and flute; Stemsy Hunter, vocals and sax; debut at Monterey Pop Festival (1967); albums—*Electric Flag, Long Time Coming.*

ELECTRIC PRUNE (rock group)

Ron Morgan, guitar; Mark Kincaid, vocals and guitar; Richard Whetstone, lead vocals, drums, and guitar; Brett Wade, vocals, bass guitar, and flute; group from South Carolina; albums—*Electric Prunes* (1967), *Just Good Old Rock and Roll, Mass in F Minor, Release of an Oath, Underground.*

ELEPHANT'S MEMORY (rock group)

Stan Bronstein, clarinet, flute, and soprano sax; Richard Frank, drums; Michael Shapiro, vocals; Richard Sussman, piano and organ; John Ward, bass guitar; Myron Yules, bass trombone; New York group; albums—*Elephant's Memory, Midnight Cowboy.*

ELGART, LARRY

b. 1922 New London, Connecticut.
Alto and soprano saxist, and bandleader. Formed own band with his brother, Les Elgart (1953); Les dropped out (1958), but rejoined (1963).

ELGART, LES

b. 1918 New Haven, Connecticut.
Trumpeter and bandleader. Co-leader with his brother, Larry, in their band (1953-58); rejoined the band (1963).

ELIRAN, RON

b. 1940 Haifa, Israel.
Singer, guitarist, violinist, and songwriter. Combat photographer in the Israeli-Egyptian war of 1957; came to New York and studied TV and motion picture directing at New York University; toured the states with the Ford Motor Company show "Jazz and Folk Wing-Ding"; served in the short war of 1967 and wrote the song "Sharm El Sheikh"; LP records include *Golden Songs of Israel, Ladino*, and *New Sounds of Israel.*

ELIZABETH (folk-jazz group)

Steve Weingarten, lead guitar and organ; Jim Dahme, lead vocals, flute, and guitar; Bob Patterson, vocals and guitar; Steve Bruno, bass, organ, and piano; Hank Ransome, drums, bass, and guitar; started in Philadelphia (1967); albums—*Elizabeth, Yo, Elizabeth.*

ELKUS, ALBERT ISRAEL

b. 1884 Sacramento, California, d. 1946 Oakland, California. Composer. Pupil of Oscar Weil, Robert Fuchs, Harold Bauer, et. al.; composed chamber music and choral works.

ELLINGTON, EDWARD KENNEDY ("DUKE")

b. 1899 Washington, D.C, d. 1974.
Famous black jazz bandleader, pianist, and composer of popular songs. Organized his jazz band (1918) in Washington, D.C., and again in New York City (1922); wrote "I Got It Bad and That Ain't Good" (w. Paul Wesber), "Don't Get Around Much Anymore" (w. Bob Russell), "Indigo Echoes" (w. Irving Mills), also piano suites *Black, Brown and Beige, Liberian Suite* (1947), *Harlem* (1951), *Blue Bells of Harlem* (1953); made successful tour of Europe including the Soviet Union in 1971.

ELLINGTON, MERCER KENNEDY

b. 1919 Washington, D.C.
Black trumpeter and bandleader. Son of Duke Ellington; organized his own band (1939); disc jockey on WLIB, New York City (1962-65); then played in his father's band.

ELLINGTON'S ORCHESTRA, DUKE

In 1971 consisted of Paul Gonsalves, tenor sax; Harry Carney, baritone sax; Russell Procope, alto sax and clarinet; Norris Turney, tenor sax, flute, alto sax, and clarinet; Harold "Money" Johnson, trumpet; Harold Ashby, tenor sax and clarinet; Joe Benjamin, bass; Rufus "Speedy" Jones, drums; Harold Minerve, alto sax; Tony Watkins, singer; Miss Mel Brookshire, singer.

ELLIOTT, ALONZO (ZO)

b. 1891 Manchester, New Hampshire, d. 1964 Wallingford, Connecticut. Composer and lyricist. Graduated Yale, Trinity College, Cambridge, England, Columbia Law School, and American Conservatory at Fontainebleau, France; studied with Nadia Boulanger in Paris, also with Leonard Bernstein and others; wrote "There's a Long, Long Trail A-winding" (1914, Joseph Vernon prize, w. Stoddard King); opera, *El Chivato.*

ELLIOTT, DON

b. 1926 Somerville, New Jersey.
Singer, musician, and composer. With Benny Goodman, and others during 1940s and '50s; wrote music for Broadway shows *A Thurber Carnival* (1960), *Happiest Man Alive* (1962), *The Beast in Me* (1963); also scores for films.

ELLIOTT, JOHN M. (JACK)

b. 1914 Gowanda, New York, d. 1972 Los Angeles, California. Composer, singer, and writer. Singer in vaudeville, night clubs, theatres and on radio; wrote songs for films; wrote background score for *Toot, Whistle, Plunk and Boom* (Walt Disney cartoon) which won Academy Award (1953); wrote "It's So Nice to Have a Man Around the House," "Elmer's Tune," "Sam's Song," "I Don't Want to Be Kissed"; died of a heart attack.

ELLIOTT, RAMBLIN' JACK

b. 1931 Brooklyn, New York.
Singer and guitarist. Real name—Elliott Charles Adnopoz; attended the University of Connecticut, Storrs, and Adelphi College, Garden City, New York; moved to Los Angeles where he played the guitar, then toured Europe (1956-59); LP records are *Guthrie Songs* (1961), *Country Style and Ramblin' Jack Elliott* (1962), *Hootenanny and Jack Elliott* (1964), *Bull Durham Sacks and Railroad Tracks, Jack Elliott, Ramblin', Young Brigham.*

ELLIS, DONALD JOHNSON (DON)

b. 1934 Los Angeles, California.
Trumpeter. Studied at Boston University; played with Ray McKinley, Charlie Barnet, and Maynard Ferguson in 1950s; also in U.S. Army jazz band; led own trio at Newport Jazz Festival (1961); also at First International Jazz Festival in Washington, D.C.; later on TV shows; took graduate work at the University of California at Los Angeles (1964); then taught there.

ELLIS, MITCHELL HERBERT (HERB)

b. 1921 Farmersville, Texas.
Guitarist and composer. With Oscar Peterson Trio during 1950s; with Donn Trenner's band on Steve Allen's TV show and with Terry Gibbs during 1960s; wrote "Detour Ahead."

ELMAN, MISCHA

b. 1891 Talnoi, South Russia, d. 1967.
Violinist. Debut as a concert violinist in Berlin (1904), and became world famous; came to America (1909); soloist with Philadelphia Orchestra (1909-17).

ELMAN, ZIGGY

b. 1914 Philadelphia, Pennsylvania, d. 1968.
Trumpeter. Born Harry Finkelman; raised in Atlantic City, N.J.; played with Benny Goodman, Tommy Dorsey, Charlie Barnet and others.

ELSON, ARTHUR B.

b. 1873 Boston, Massachusetts, d. 1940 New York City. Writer. Son and pupil of Louis C. Elson; graduated Harvard University and Massachusetts Institute of Technology; author of books on music.

ELSON, LOUIS CHARLES

b. 1848 Boston, Massachusetts, d. there 1920. Teacher and music critic. Pupil of Kreissmann in Boston and Gloggner-Castelli in Leipzig; critic on the *Boston Courier*, then the *Advertiser*; teacher at the New England Conservatory, Boston (1881); composed songs, operettas, and instrumental works; wrote *The History of German Song, Curiosities of Music, The Theory of Music, The Realm of Music.*

ELWELL, HERBERT

b. 1898 Minneapolis, Minnesota, d. 1974.
Noted composer. Studied in New York with Ernest Bloch, then in Paris with Nadia Boulanger (1922); won fellowship at American Academy in Rome (1926); music critic for Cleveland *Plain Dealer* after 1932; taught at Cleveland Institute of Music 1928-45; composed *The Happy Hypocrite* (ballet), *Pastorale* (for soprano and orchestra), *Divertimento* (for string quartet), *Lincoln, Requiem Aeternam* (won Paderewski Prize, 1946), *Orchestral sketches*, Sonata for violin and piano, choruses, songs.

ELWES, GERVASE CARY

b. 1866 Northampton, England, d. 1921 Boston, Massachusetts. Tenor. Studied in Vienna, then Paris; debut (1903); sang in Europe and America; killed by a locomotive.

EMERSON, BILLY

b. 1846 Belfast, Ireland, d. 1902 Boston, Massachusetts. Singer and popular composer. Born William E. Redmond; minstrel showman; promoted "Polly Wolly Doodle" (1883, *see* W.H. Hills) and "The Big Sunflower"; wrote the words and music "Could I only Back the Winner."

EMERSON, LUTHER ORLANDO

b. 1820 Parsonsfield, Maine, d. 1915 Hyde Park, Massachusetts. Composer. Studied medicine, but became an organist and composer; organist-choirmaster of the Bulfinch Street Church, Boston; compiled more than 70 books of hymns and conducted over 300 musical conventions in America; composed the tunes "Sessions" (1847, "Lord, I Am Thine, Entirely Thine," w. Samuel Davies) while living in Salem, Mass.

EMERSON, RALPH WALDO

b. 1803 Boston, Massachusetts, d. 1882 Concord, Massachusetts. Hymnist and essayist. Graduated Harvard (1821); wrote "The Concord Hymn"—"By the Rude Bridge That Arched the Flood," tune "Old Hundred" by Guillaume le Franc (of Rouen, France, d. 1570 Lausanne, Switzerland); in 1829 he became pastor of the Second Unitarian Church, Boston.

EMERY, STEPHEN ALBERT

b. 1841 Paris, Maine, d. 1891 Boston, Massachusetts. Teacher and composer.

Taught harmony and composition in Boston; was assistant editor of the *Musical Herald*; wrote *Foundation Studies in Pianoforte Playing, Op. 35, Elements of Harmony.*

EMMET, JOSEPH KLEINFELTER (EMMETT)

b. 1841 St. Louis, Missouri, d. 1891.
Vaudeville actor and yodeler. Wrote the words and music "Emmet's Lullaby" (1878, introduced in *Fritz, Our German Cousin*), "Climb Up the Mountain High" (1879), "Castle Bells" (1879), "Cuckoo Song" (1879), and "Sweet Violets" (1882, introduced in *Fritz Among the Gypsies*).

EMMETT, DANIEL D.

b. 1815 Mount Vernon, Ohio, d. there 1904.
Popular composer. Worked in the print shops of the *Huron Reflector*, Norwalk, Ohio, and the *Western Aurora*, Mt. Vernon, until he was seventeen; joined the army as a fifer and drummer and was stationed at Newport Barracks, Kentucky, and Jefferson Barracks, Missouri; organized the Virginia Minstrels (1843) which presented two songs by Emmett—"Old Dan Tucker" and "De Boatman's Dance"; wrote "Blue Tail Fly or Jim Crack Corn" (1846), "Jordan Am a Hard Road to Trabble" (1853), "Dixie" (1859), "Three Cheers for Our Jack Morgan" (1863, w. J.H. Hewitt); in 1895 he toured the country with the Al Fields Minstrels, and was a sensation in the southern states when he sang his own song, "Dixie."

ENDER, EDMUND SERENO

b. 1886 New Haven, Connecticut.
Teacher. Educated at Yale, University of Berlin, and Oxford University; taught music at South Dakota State College, Brookings (1910-12); organist-choirmaster of Gethsemane Church, Minneapolis, Minn. (1912-18); professor of music at Carleton College, Northfield, Minn. (1918-21), then at St. Paul's Baltimore, Md.; director of music at Goucher College, Towson, Md., and instructor at the Peabody Conservatory.

ENEVOLDSEN, ROBERT MARTIN

b. 1920 Billings, Montana.
Trombonist, saxist, and arranger. With various groups in Los Angeles and Las Vegas during 1950s; arranger and musician on Steve Allen's TV show (1962-64); arranger for Lionel Hampton, Billy Eckstine, and Bobby Troup.

ENGEL, A. LEHMAN

b. 1910 Jackson, Mississippi.
Composer. Studied at Cincinnati (Ohio) College of Music and at Conservatory, also Juilliard School, New York City; founder and conductor of Madrigal Singers; taught at Neighborhood Playhouse School, New York City; composed the operas *Pierrot of the Minute* and *Medea*, *Phobias* (ballet), *Jungle Dance, Introduction and Allegretto, Scientific Creation* (for orchestra), choral works.

ENGEL, CARL

b. 1883 Paris, France, d. 1944 New York City.
Musicologist. Studied in Strasbourg and Munich, then came to America (1905), where he became lector and editor of the Boston Music Company; became director of the music division of the Library of Congress, Washington, D.C. (1922); one of the founders of the American Musicological Society, and became editor in chief of *The Musical Quarterly* (1929).

ENGLANDER, LUDWIG

b. 1859 Vienna, Austria, d. 1914 Far Rockaway, New York. Popular composer. Came to New York City (1882); with librettist H.B. Smith wrote the music for the operettas *The Caliph* (1896), *Half a King* (1896), *The Rounders* (1899), *The Cadet Girl* (1900), *The Belle of Bohemia, When Knighthood Was in Flower* (1905, book—Charles Major) and many others; with Sydney Rosenberg wrote a musical review, *The Passing Show*, which was produced by George W. Lederer at the Casino Theatre, New York City (1894).

ENGLISH, THOMAS DUNN

b. 1819 near Philadelphia, Pennsylvania, d. 1902 Newark, New Jersey. Lyricist, editor, and playwright. Wrote "Ben Bolt" (m. Nelson Kneass), published in the *New York Mirror* (1848).

ENNIS, ETHEL

b. 1934 Baltimore, Maryland.
Black singer. Sang in night clubs in New York, Boston and other cities; also on TV shows; at Newport Jazz Festival (1964); very popular singer; Frank Sinatra, Danny Thomas and Ethel sang Gladys Shelley's hit tunes "Show's on Me Tonight" and "Does It Hurt to Love?" at the National Governor's banquet, 1972.

EPHROS, GERSHON

b. 1890 Serosk, Poland.
Cantor and compiler. After he came to America, he was appointed cantor in Norfolk, Va., then New York City, and at Temple Beth Mordecai, Perth Amboy, N.J. (1929); compiled *Cantorial Anthology of Traditional and*

Modern Synagogue Music; compiled a second edition for *Yom Kippur* (1949), *Shalosh R'golim Chants* (3rd edition), *Shabat* (4th edition, 1953), *Y'Mot Hachol* (5th edition, 1957).

EPPEL, JOHN VALENTINE

b. 1871 Iowa City, Iowa, d. 1931 California. Orchestra leader and composer. With Frederick K. Logan wrote, or arranged (from an old tune) "The Missouri Waltz" about 1916.

EPPERT, CARL

b. 1882 Carbon, Indiana, d. 1961 Milwaukee, Wisconsin. Noted composer. Studied in Europe with Hugo Kaun and others; founded Milwaukee Civic Orchestra; composed *A Symphony of the City* (symphonic cycle in four parts, first part performed by NBC orchestra under Goossens, 1932, and Hollywood Bowl Orchestra under Stock, balance by Rochester Philharmonic under Hanson, 1935), *Escapade* (musical satire, Indianapolis Symphony under Sevitzky, 1941), *Symphonic Suite I* (Chicago Symphony, 1941), *Symphonic Suite II* (Detroit Symphony, 1942), *Kaintuckee* (opera), *A Cameo Symphony, Symphony of the Land.*

ERB, JOHN LAWRENCE

b. 1877 Reading, Pennsylvania, d. 1950 Eugene, Oregon. Teacher, organist, and composer. Studied at Metropolitan College, New York, and Virgil School; taught at Wooster University, Ohio, University of Illinois, and Connecticut College, New London (1922); composed organ, piano and vocal music.

ERBEN, PETER

b. 1769 New York City, d. 1861 Brooklyn, New York. Organist and compiler. Organist for many years, and organist at Trinity Church, New York City (1820-39); in 1806 he published *Select Psalm and Hymn Tunes*; was a music publisher in New York City (1801-19).

ERICSON, LEIF

b. 1911 Alameda, California.
Baritone and actor. Started as a vocalist in Ted Fio Rito's band; later a film and TV actor of note.

ERRANI, ACHILLE

b. 1823 Italy, d. 1897 New York City.
Tenor and teacher. Sang in opera, then became a singing teacher in New York City.

ERSKINE, JOHN

b. 1879 New York City, d. there 1951.
Pianist, teacher, and librettist. President of the Juilliard School of Music until 1937; professor of English literature at Columbia University; piano soloist with leading orchestras; wrote the librettos to the operas *Jack and the Beanstalk* (Gruenberg) and *Helen Retires* (Antheil).

ERVIN, BOOKER TELLEFERRO, JR.

b. 1930 Denison, Texas.
Black tenor saxist. With Charlie Mingus after 1958; at Newport Jazz Festival with Mingus (1960 and 1962); played at Negro Arts Festival in Lagos, Nigeria in 1960; toured Europe after 1964.

ERWIN, GEORGE ("PEE WEE")

b. 1913 Falls City, Nebraska.
Trumpeter and bandleader. Played with Benny Goodman and Tommy Dorsey in 1930s; led his own bands in 1940s and '50s; staff musician for CBS during 1960s; on weekly radio jazz show with Ed Joyce; appeared with Lou McGarity at Carnegie Hall, New York City (1967).

ESLING, CATHERINE HARBISON (WATERMAN)

b. 1812 Philadelphia, Pennsylvania, d. there 1897. Hymnist. Miss Waterman married Capt. George Esling in 1840 and lived in Rio de Janeiro until he died in 1844; wrote the lyrics "Come Unto Me" (1839, m. Lowell Mason, tune "Henley"), and the lyrics "Thou'st Ever at My Side" (m. W.R. Dempster).

ESTABROOK, LIZZIE S. (TOURJEE)

b. 1858 Providence, Rhode Island, d. 1913. Composer. Daughter of Dr. Eben Tourjee; composed the tune "Wellesley" (1877-78, while a student at Wellesley College, Wellesley, Mass.) used for "There's a Wideness in God's Mercy" (w. F.W. Faber, there is a second tune by S.J. Vail).

ESTES, JOHN ("SLEEPY JOHN")

b. 1904 Lauderdale County, Tennessee.
Black singer and guitarist. Played in Memphis (1928-32) with harmonica player Hammie Nixon; played in Chicago (1935-41); became blind in 1957; was rediscovered in 1962 by David Blumenthal.

ESTY, JACOB

b. 1814 Hinsdale, New Hampshire, d. 1890. Organ maker. After 1850 developed his small shop into a major manufacturer of organs.

ETIENNE, DENIS GERMAIN

b. 1781 France, d. 1859.
Pianist and composer. Studied piano at the

Paris Conservatory; came to the United States about 1814; composed *The Battle of New Orleans* for the pianoforte (1815).

ETTING, RUTH

b. 1896 David City, Nebraska.
Torch singer. Introduced "Shaking the Blues Away" in the Ziegfeld Follies of 1927 (m. Irving Berlin); revived "Shine on, Harvest Moon" (by Nora Bryce and Jack Norworth) in the Ziegfeld Follies of 1930, originally sung by Nora Bryce in the Follies of 1908.

EUREKA BRASS BAND (New Orleans jazz band) *see* PERCY G. HUMPHREY

EUROPE, JAMES REESE (JIM)

b. 1881 Mobile, Alabama, d. 1919 Boston, Massachusetts. Black bandleader. Raised in Washington, D.C.; studied piano there, also violin with Enrico Hurlei; assistant director of United States Marine Band; joined Nashville Students, played at Proctor's, New York City (1905); toured Europe as Tennessee Students; musical director for Cole-Johnson musical show in New York City—*The Shoo Fly Regiment* (1906-08); then with *Mr. Lode of Kole;* organized the Clef Club Orchestra (1910), played at Carnegie Hall (1912); later organized the Tempo Club Orchestra;leader of the 169th Infantry band, formerly the 15th New York; trained in Spartanburg, South Carolina, played in Aix-les-Bains, France and in Paris (1918); leader of the "Hell Fighters"; stabbed in his dressing room in Boston and died shortly thereafter.

EVANS, DALE (MRS. ROY ROGERS)

b. 1912 Uvalde, Texas.
Singer, songwriter, and actress. Attended high school in Osceola, Arkansas; sang on radio in Memphis, Dallas, Louisville, and Chicago, then she went into the movies (1943); married Roy (1947); wrote "The Bible Tells Me So" (based on the hymn by Anna Warner and W.B. Bradbury), "Aha San Antone" and "Happy Birthday Gentle Savior"; she and Roy adopted and raised a number of children.

EVANS, FREDERICK SHAILER

b. 1863 Haddam, Connecticut, d. 1954.
Pianist and teacher. Graduated Leipzig Conservatory (1886); studied under Carl Reinecke and Jadassohn; concert pianist; taught piano in Cincinnati, Ohio; director of music at the Cincinnati Conservatory (1930-32).

EVANS, GEORGE

b. 1870 Wales, d. 1915 Baltimore, Maryland.
Minstrel showman, vaudeville actor, and composer. Known as "Honey Boy"; brought to U.S. at age seven; wrote "In the Good Old Summertime" (1902, w. Ren Shields).

EVANS, GIL

b. 1912 Toronto, Ontario, Canada.
Pianist and composer. Born Ian Ernest Gilmore Green; led his own band in Stockton, Calif. (1933-38); then led by Skinnay Ennis; arranger for Claude Thornhill (1941-43); in U. S. Army (1943-46); then with Thornhill again until 1948; arranged "Boplicity" and "Moondreams" for *Birth of the Cool* for nine-man group led by Miles Davis; also with Miles Davis "Miles Ahead" (1957), "Porgy and Bess" (1959), "Sketches of Spain" (1960); recorded with various top musicians.

EVANS, HERSCHEL

b. 1909 Denton, Texas, d. 1939 New York City. Black tenor saxist. Played with Count Basie; killed in an automobile crash.

EVANS, RAYMOND B. (RAY)

b. 1915 Salamanca, New York.
Lyricist. Attended Wharton School, University of Pennsylvania, Philadelphia; joined with Jay Livingston, composer, to write songs; they wrote three songs which won Academy Awards—"Buttons and Bows" (1948), "Mona Lisa" (1950), and "Whatever Will Be, Will Be" (1956); also "To Each His Own," "Copper Canyon," "Home Cookin'," "Tammy."

EVANS, REDD LOUIS

b. 1912 Meridian, Mississippi, d. 1972 New Rochelle, New York. Composer and lyricist. Educated at University of Arizona and Kent college; saxophonist and clarinetist with Teddy Wilson and Horace Heidt; with David Mannes wrote "There I've Said It Again," "No Moon at All," "Don't Go to Strangers," "American Beauty Rose"; wrote the lyrics for President Kennedy's campaign song "Walking Down to Washington."

EVANS, STOMP

b. 1900, d. 1930 Denver, Colorado.
Black jazz saxophonist. Played in King Oliver's band.

EVANS, WILLIAM EDWIN

b. 1851 Baltimore, Maryland, d. 1915 Richmond, Virginia. Hymnist. Educated at Randolph-Macon College, Ashland, Va.; became a Methodist minister in the Baltimore Conference (1872) then transferred to the Virginia Conference; then became an Episcopal minister and rector of the Church of the Advent, Birmingham, Alabama (1892);

wrote the hymn "Come, O Thou God of Grace" (tune "Italian Hymn"—Trinity).

EVANS, WILLIAM JOHN (BILL)

b. 1929 Plainfield, New Jersey.
Pianist. Led his own trio, then with Tony Scott and Miles Davis during 1950s; trio with drummer Paul Motian and bass player Scott La Faro on Riverside records (1961-62); won Grammy Award (1970) for best jazz performance, *The Bill Evans Album.*

EVEREST, CHARLES WILLIAM

b. 1814 East Windsor, Connecticut, d. 1877 Waterbury, Connecticut. Composer and hymnist. Graduated Trinity College, Hartford, Conn.; Episcopal pastor, serving as the rector at Hamden, Conn. for thirty-one years; wrote the hymn "Take Up Thy Cross" (1861, tune "Germany" from William Gardner's *Sacred Melodies*, 1815); also wrote the words and music "The Soldier's Vision" (1862), and "Toll the Bell Mournfully" (1865, on the death of President Lincoln).

EVERETT, ASA BROOKS

b. 1828 Virginia, d. 1875 near Nashville, Tennessee. Composer. Studied music in Boston, taught in the south, then studied in Leipzig, Germany for four years; joined his brother's firm, L.C. Everett Company, song book publishers in Richmond, Va.; composed the tune "Richmond" (1859, used for "Jesus, My Strength, My Hope," w. Charles Wesley); best-known work was *The Sceptre,* published by Bigelow and Main, New York City.

EVERETT, L. C.

b. 1818, d. 1867.
Publisher. Song book publisher in Richmond, Virginia.

EVERLY, DONALD (DON)

b. 1937 Brownie, Kentucky.
Singer. Appeared on radio station KMA, Shenandoah, Kentucky (1945) with his brother, Phil; moved to Nashville after schooling; recorded "Bye, Bye Love" (1957, by Boudleaux Bryant) which became a hit; later toured America, Europe, Canada, Australia, and New Zealand.

EVERLY, PHILIP (PHIL)

b. 1939 Brownie, Kentucky.
Singer. Appeared with his brother, Don, as a vocal duo; their albums—*Beat 'n Soul, Chained to a Memory, Date with the Everly Brothers, Both Sides of an Evening, Featuring Wake Up Little Susie, Sing, Sing Great Country Hits, It's Everly Time, Rock 'n Soul, Roots, Very Best of the Everly Brothers, Golden Hits of the Everly Brothers, Hit Sounds of the Everly Brothers.*

EVERY MOTHER'S SON (rock group)

Lary Larden, lead vocals and guitar; Dennis Larden, vocals and lead guitar; Bruce Milner, vocals, piano, and organ; Christopher Augustine, drums; Don Kerr, bass; New York group started in 1967; albums—*Every Mother's Son, Every Mother's Son's Back.*

FABIAN

b. 1943 Philadelphia, Pennsylvania.
Singer. Born Fabian Forte; debut in Philadelphia (1958); his first record was a flop, but by Christmas 1958 "Turn Me Loose" became a best-seller, followed by "Tiger" (1959); appeared in film *Hound Dog Man*, this title tune and "This Friendly World" were hits among the teenagers.

FABRAY, NANETTE

b. 1920 San Diego, California.
Singer. Sang in a number of musical comedies, including *Let's Face It* (1941, m. Cole Porter), and *High Button Shoes* (1947, m. Jule Styne).

FACES (rock band)

Rod Stewart featured singer; at Madison Square Garden, New York City in November 1971 and September 1972.

FAELTEN, CARL

b. 1846 Ilmenau, Thuringia, East Germany, d. 1925 Readfield, Maine. Pianist and teacher. Attended the Stadtpfeifereien orchestra school at Arnstadt; played in an orchestra in Frankfort-on-Main; served in Franco-Prussian War, where his fingers became stiff from handling a musket, and forced him to practice all over again; came to America (1882); taught at Peabody Institute, Baltimore; then later at New England Conservatory in Boston.

FAGERQUIST, DONALD A. (DON)

b. 1927 Worcester, Massachusetts.
Jazz trumpeter. Played in Gene Krupa's band (1944-45 and 1948); with Anita O'Day and his own combo; with Artie Shaw, Woody Herman and others.

FAIN, SAMMY

b. 1902 New York City.
Songwriter. Father was a cantor; appeared in vaudeville with Artie Dunn; wrote "Wedding Bells Are Breaking Up That Old Gang of Mine" (w. Irving Kahal and Willie Raskin), "I Can Dream, Can't I" (w. Kahal), "I'll Be Seeing You" (1938, w. Kahal), "Love Is a Many Splendored Thing" (1955, w. P. Webster), "That Old Feeling" (1938, w. Lew Brown), "Dear Hearts and Gentle People" (w. Bob Hilliard).

FAIRCHILD, BLAIR

b. 1877 Belmont, Massachusetts, d. 1933 Paris, France. Composer. Studied with Paine and W. Spaulding at Harvard University, then in Florence with Buonamici; served in the diplomatic corps in Turkey and Iran; composed *Dame Libellule* (Paris Opera Comique, 1921), orchestral works, vocal and piano pieces.

FAIRCLOTH, CHARLIE RAIFORD ("PEANUTS")

b. 1927 Pelham, Georgia.
Singer and songwriter. Wrote "It's Always Time for Love," "I Know How Lonesome, Lonesome Can Be," "Don't Use in Vain, the Name of Jesus."

FAIRLAMB, JAMES REMINGTON

b. 1838 Philadelphia, Pennsylvania, d. 1908 New York City. Organist, composer, and teacher. Organist in Philadelphia (1852-59); became U.S. consul at Zurich; organist and teacher in Washington, D.C. and New York (1872-1908); composed four operas, his opera *Treasured Tokens* was given its first performance in Philadelphia; wrote *Song of April*, and *Across the Eastern Hilltops*.

FAITH, PERCY

b. 1908 Toronto, Ontario, Canada.
Conductor and composer. Studied at the Toronto Conservatory; piano debut at Massey Hall, Toronto, at age fifteen; burned his hands severely in an accident; conducted his own string ensemble on Toronto radio; conducted Music by Faith on CBC (1933-40); conductor of the "Carnation Contented Hour," New York City after 1940; musical director of the Coca-Cola show after 1947; wrote "My Heart Cries for You" (recorded by Guy Mitchell); wrote the score for the film *Love Me or Leave Me* (1955).

FALCONS *see* EDDIE FLOYD

FALLEN SPARROWS (band) *see* SONNY WHITE

FARBERMAN, HAROLD

b. 1930 New York City.
Percussionist, conductor, and composer. Studied at Juilliard School, New York City; with Radio City Music Hall orchestra (1949); with Boston Symphony (1950-62); conductor of Orchestra U.S.A. after 1962; wrote *Saxophone Concerto, Then Silence.*

FARINA, RICHARD

b. 1936, d. 1966.
Singer and songwriter. Team of Richard and Mimi Baez Farina; half Cuban and half Irish; married Carolyn Hester, folk singer, later divorced; wrote "Pack Up Your Sorrows" (recorded by Johnny Cash, June Carter and others); married Mimi Baez, Joan's sister; their albums—*Celebrations for a Grey Day* (1965), *Reflections in a Crystal Wind* (1966), *Memories* (released after his death, 1968); he was killed in a motorcycle accident.

FARJEON, HARRY

b. 1878 Ho Ho Kus, New Jersey. d. 1948.
Composer. Educated at the Royal Academy of Music (1895-1901), became a teacher there (1903); composed the orchestral suite *Hans Anderson,* symphonic poems *Mowgli* and *Summer Vision,* a piano concerto, chamber music, songs.

FARLANDER, ARTHUR WILLIAM

b. 1898 Germany.
Hymnist. Came to America (1919) and studied at James Millikin University, Decatur, Illinois, the Divinity School of the University of Chicago, the Evangelical Theological Seminary, Chicago, and the Church Divinity School of the Pacific; rector in churches in San Francisco and Fresno and after 1936 at the Church of the Incarnation, Santa Rosa, Calif.; translated a number of European hymns into English.

FARLOW, TALMADGE HOLT (TAL)

b. 1921 Greensboro, North Carolina.
Guitarist. With Marjorie Hyams Trio (1948); then with Buddy De Franco Sextet, Red Norvo Trio and Artie Shaw's Gramercy Five during 1950s; won DB critics' poll New Star Award in 1954; played only occasionally during 1960s.

FARMER, ADDISON GERALD

b. 1928 Council Bluffs, Iowa, d. 1963 New York City. Black bass player. Twin brother of Art Farmer, trumpeter; with Art Farmer-Benny Golson Jazztet (1959-60); with other groups (1960-62).

FARMER, ARTHUR STEWART (ART)

b. 1928 Council Bluffs, Iowa.
Black jazz trumpeter. With Horace Henderson and Benny Carter (1945-50); played in Lionel Hampton's band; had his own quartet; played with Horace Silver and Gerry Mulligan in 1950s; organized a sextet (1959) with Benny Golson, the Jazztet, active until 1962; later played the flügelhorn in a quartet with guitarist Jim Hall (1962-64); with pianist Steve Kuhn (1965-66); also toured Europe; twin brother of bass player Addison Gerald Farmer.

FARMER, BESS ("MISS BESS")

b. 1919 Hegira, Kentucky.
Organist, accordianist, arranger, and songwriter. Graduated Tennessee Tech, Cookeville, Tenn. (1956), and Eastern Kentucky State College, Richmond, Ky. (M.A. degree, 1959); with "Renfro Valley Barn Dance," Renfro Valley, Ky. since 1953; arranger for "Renfro Valley Barn Dance"; wrote "For I Love You."

FARNIE, HENRY BROUGHAM

b. (?), d. 1889.
Lyricist. Wrote "The Stirrup Cup" (m. Luigi Arditi), "The Scout" (m. Fabio Campana), "Among the Lilies" (m. Alphonse Czibulka), "Up in a Balloon" (m. G.W. Hunt); with music by Charles Francois Gounod: "Bethlehem," "The Guardian Angel," "Ring on Sweet Angelus."

FARNON, ROBERT

b. 1917 Toronto, Ontario, Canada.
Conductor and composer. Played the violin at age seven; studied composition at age fifteen; served in Canadian army in World War II; composed two symphonies and light orchestral music; wrote *Candlelight and Vino, Portrait of a Flirt, Jumping Bean, The Westminster Waltz, Canadian Caravan, Derby Day, Manhattan Playboy.*

FARNUM, W. LYNNWOOD

b. 1885 Sutton, Quebec, d. 1930 New York City. Organist. Studied at the Royal College of Music and was organist-choirmaster in Montreal (1904-13), then of the Emmanuel Church, Boston (1913-18); then went into the Canadian army for a year; played at the San Francisco Exposition (1915) and won national attention; served the Church of the Holy Communion, New York City (1920-30).

FARRAR, GERALDINE

b. 1882 Melrose, Massachusetts, d. 1967 Ridgefield, Connecticut. Noted soprano. Studied with J.H. Long in Boston, then with Lilli Lehmann; operatic debut as Marguerite in *Faust* at the Royal Opera House in Berlin, Germany (1901); sang with Metropolitan Opera Company, New York City (1906-22); created the role of Goose Girl with live geese in Humperdinck's *Die Königskinder.*

FARRELL, EILEEN

b. 1920 Willimantic, Connecticut.
Noted soprano. Concert singer (1940-60); Metropolitan Opera debut (1960) in title role of Gluck's *Alceste;* sang at concerts in Paris (1962); also sang the title role in Cherubini's *Medea* with the American Opera Society and the San Francisco Opera; soloist with Milwaukee Symphony Orchestra at Carnegie Hall, New York City (1972).

FARRINGTON, HARRY WEBB

b. 1880 Nassau, Bahama Islands, d. 1931. Hymnist. Educated at Syracuse University, Harvard, and the Boston University School of Theology; organized the Week Day Church School, Gary, Indiana (1914); Methodist minister of the New York East Conference; wrote the hymns "I Know Not How That Bethlehem's Babe" (1910, tune "Shirleyn"—E.E. Harper) and "O God Creator, in Whose Hand" (1928, tune "Byrd"—R.R. Peery).

FARROW, MILES

b. 1871 Charleston, South Carolina, d. 1953 Catonsville, Maryland. Organist and writer. Organist and choirmaster of the Boys' School of St. Paul's Parish, Baltimore (1894-1909), then at the choir school of the Cathedral of St. John the Divine, New York City (1909-31); wrote *About the Training of Boys' Voices* (1898).

FARWELL, ARTHUR

b. 1872 St. Paul, Minnesota, d. 1952 New York City. Composer. Studied with H.A. Norris (Boston), and later with Humperdinck; established the American Music Society (1905); directed concerts in New York City (1910-13); director of Music School Settlement, New York (1915-18); taught at the University of California, Berkeley (1918-19); composed for orchestra, *Dawn, The Domain of Hurakan, Navajo War Dance, Cornell* (overture), *Love Song.*

FATOOL, NICHOLAS (NICK)

b. 1915 Milbury, Massachusetts.
Drummer. Played in various Dixieland bands; later with Benny Goodman, Artie Shaw, Bob Crosby and others; toured Japan, the Philippines, and Okinawa (1964); later played in Los Angeles and Hollywood.

FAUCHALD, NORA

b. 1898, d. 1971 New York City.
Soprano and teacher. Graduated Institute of Musical Art (now Juilliard School), New York City; won Juilliard scholarship for study in Europe; taught at the Juilliard School for twelve years; soloist at Town Hall, New York City (1930); with her husband, pianist George Morgan at Town Hall (1941); taught voice at St. Margaret's School, Waterbury, Conn.

FAULKNER, SANDFORD C.

b. 1803, d. 1874.
Composer. Lived on a ranch in Arkansas and was known as Colonel Sandy Faulkner; wrote "The Arkansas Traveller," based on old folk music, which was introduced by Joseph Tosso.

FAURE, JEANNE

b. 1863 New Orleans, Louisiana, d. 1950.
Singer. Graduated Dresden Conservatory (1887), with honors; sang in New Orleans theaters.

FAWKES, WALLY

b. 1924 Vancouver, B.C., Canada.
Clarinetist. Played with George Webb during 1940s; then with Humphrey Lyttleton; led the Troglodytes, his own group (1956-65); then formed a group with Johnny Parker.

FAY, AMY

b. 1844 Bayou Goula, Louisiana, d. 1928. Concert pianist. Granddaughter of John Henry Hopkins, P.E. Bishop of Vermont; studied in Berlin with Tausig, Deppe, and Kullak, and then in Weimar with Liszt (1873); debut in a concert at Mendelssohn Glee Club, New York City (1875); played in Theodore Thomas' orchestra at Sanders Theatre in Cambridge, Mass.; taught in Chicago after 1878; wrote *Music Study in Germany.*

FAY, STEPHEN

b. ca. 1870, d. after 1900.

Composer. Born David Stephens; wrote "The Levee Song" (1894), "Oh, I Was Bo'n in Mobile Town" (the tune was subsequently used for "I've Been Workin' on the Railroad"), "Chow Song," "Get Away from dis Co'nfiel'," "Ring On, Christmas Bells," "Overwork," "Red, White and Blue."

FAYE, ALICE

b. 1915 New York City.
Contralto. At age fourteen toured with the Chester Hale Dance Group; in chorus of *George White's Scandals;* on Rudy Vallee's radio show; appeared in films, *In Old Chicago* (1937), *Alexander's Ragtime Band* (1938), *Hello 'Frisco Hello* (1943); married briefly to singer Tony Martin; then married Phil Harris.

FAYE, RITA

b. 1944 Whitesboro, Texas.
Autoharpist. Album—*The Vibrant Tones of Rita Faye's Autoharp.*

FAZOLA, IRVING

b. 1912 New Orleans, Louisiana, d. there 1949. Clarinetist. In Bob Crosby's orchestra in Chicago in the 1930s; later played in Glenn Miller's band.

FEARIS, JOHN S.

b. 1867 Richland, Iowa, d. 1932 Chicago, Illinois. Popular composer. Senior member of J.S. Fearis and Bros., music publishers, Chicago; wrote "Little Sir Echo" (w. Laura Smith), "An Autumn Lullaby," "The Feast of the Lanters," "The Feast of Roses" (w. Thomas Moore), "Beautiful Isle of Somewhere" (1897, w. Jessie B. Pounds); also composed the operetta *Treasure Hunters.*

FEDERLEIN, GOTTFRIED HEINRICH

b. 1883 New York City, d. 1952 Flushing, New York. Organist. Pupil of his father, also of Goetschius and Saar.

FEIST, LEO

b. 1870, d. 1930.
Publisher and composer. Wrote "Does True Love Ever Run Smooth?"

FELD, MOREY

b. 1915 Cleveland, Ohio, d. 1971.
Jazz drummer. Played with Eddie Condon and others; at Newport Jazz Festival (1965); started school for drummers (1966).

FELDER, WILTON LEWIS

b. 1940 Houston, Texas.
Tenor saxist and composer. Educated at Texas Southern University; debut at age twelve; with The Swingers after 1951; later became the Jazz Crusaders; wrote "Turkish Black," "Deacon Brown."

FELDMAN, MORTON

b. 1926 New York City.
Noted composer. Studied composition with Wallingford Riegger and Stefan Wolpe; wrote *Projections* and *Projection 2* (for flute, trumpet, violin and cello 1951, drawn from the concept of indeterminacy and using graphic notation), *Intersection 1, Marginal Intersection* (1951), *Extension No. 4* (for three pianos), *Piece for Four Pianos* (1957), *Durations* (for chamber sextet, 1961), *Four Instruments* (1965), *Three Pieces for String Quartet, Vertical Thoughts 2* (1968), *The Rothko Chapel* (in memory of artist Mark Rothko, under conductor Maurice Peress, Corpus Christi Symphony, in Houston, Texas, 1972).

FELDMAN, VICTOR STANLEY (VIC)

b. 1934 London, England.
Pianist and vibraharpist. Came to New York (1955); with the Cannonball Adderley Quintet (1960-61); played in Hollywood film studios; in London and Monte Carlo (1961) with Peggy Lee; played vibes on Soviet Russian tour with Benny Goodman (1962); with June Christy in London (1965); recorded with Miles Davis.

FELEKY, LESLIE

b. 1912 Hungary, d. 1971 New York City.
Pianist and composer. Studied at the Budapest Conservatory; composed operettas in Hungary; came to America; composed music for films in Hollywood; later music director for Chez Vito, New York City.

FELICIANO, JOSE

b. 1945 Puerto Rico.
Singer and electric guitarist. Blind from birth; recorded "Light My Fire" (by Jim Morrison), also recorded "Wild World" by Cat Stevens; gave a concert at the Academy of Music, Philadelphia (1971); albums—*Alive, Alive-O; Bag Full of Soul; Feliciano; Fantastic Feliciano; Feliciano 10 to 23; Fireworks; MacKenna's Gold; Mas Exitos De Jose Feliciano; Sombras..Una Voz, Una Guitarra; Souled;* in concert at the Palace Theatre, New York City (1972).

FELIX, HUGO

b. 1866 Vienna, Austria, d. 1934 Los Angeles, California. Composer. Composed the operettas *Husarenblut* (Vienna, 1894), *Rhodope* (Berlin, 1900), *Mme. Sherry* (Berlin, 1902 and New York City, 1910).

FENSTED, E.A.

b. 1870 Trondheim, Norway, d. 1941 Washington, D.C. Bandmaster and composer. Came to U.S. (1888); was a bandmaster in the U.S. Army; wrote the "Maine Stein Song" (1901, w. Lincoln Colcord) popularized by Rudy Vallee.

FERGUSON, ALLYN M.

b. 1924 San Jose, California.
Pianist and conductor. Studied under Nadia Boulanger in Paris, and at Berkshire School with Aaron Copland; Stanford University, Palo Alto, California (Ph.D.); professor of music there; conducted symphony orchestra; organized jazz sextet; wrote arrangements for the King Sisters and Johnny Mathis; also for TV and films.

FERGUSON, MAYNARD

b. 1928 Montreal, P.Q., Canada.
Jazz trumpeter. Came to America (1948); played in Boyd Raeburn's band, also with Jimmy Dorsey, Charlie Barnet, then Stan Kenton (1950-53); played in Los Angeles and New York City; organized his own band (1957); later a sextet (1965); in England (1967-72); back in New York (1972) with his all-English orchestra at Town Hall.

FERGUSON, ROBERT B.

b. 1927 Willow Springs, Missouri.
Singer and songwriter. Known as "Eli Possumtrot"; wrote "Taos, New Mexico," "Natividad," "The Golden Years," "Wings of a Dove," "Have Faith in Me," "When You Are Here," "This Gun," "Eli's Blue."

FERRARI-FONTANA, EDOARDO

b. 1878 Rome, Italy, d. 1936 Toronto, Ontario, Canada. Tenor. Opera debut as Kurwenal in *Tristan und Isolde* (Turin, 1910); sang in Europe, South America, then with the Metropolitan Opera, New York after 1914.

FERRIS, THEODORE PARKER

b. 1908 Port Chester, New York.
Composer. Educated at Harvard University and General Theological Seminary (1933); rector of Emmanuel Church, Baltimore (1937-42), then at Trinity Church, Boston; composed the tune "Weymouth" (1941, for his summer home in Weymouth, Nova Scotia, for "And Have the Bright Immensities," w. H.C. Robbins), and "Behold a Sower, from Afar" (w. Washington Gladden).

FEUERMANN, EMANUEL

b. 1902 Kolomea, Poland, d. 1942 New York City. Cellist. Studied with Anton Walter and Julius Klengel; concert debut at age eleven; taught at Cologne Conservatory (1919-23) soloist with New York Philharmonic (1935-36); collaborated with Heifetz and Rubinstein in chamber music concerts; died following an operation.

FEVER TREE, THE (rock group)

Dennis Keller, vocals; John Tuttle, percussion; Rob Landes, piano, harp, flute, etc.; E.E. Wolfe III, bass; Michael Wolfe, guitar; albums—*Another Time, Another Place; Creation; Fever Tree; What Time Did You Say It Is in Salt Lake City* (1968).

FICKENSCHER, ARTHUR

b. 1871 Aurora, Illinois, d. 1954.
Pianist and composer. Graduated Royal Conservatory, Munich, Germany; head of music department at the University of Virginia at Charlottesville after 1920; invented the Polytone, an instrument with sixty tones to the octave, devised for research in pure intonation; works—*Willowwave and Wellaway* (for full orchestra, 1925), *Day of Judgment* (1927), *Out of the Gay Nineties* (1934); performed in New York City, Berkeley, Calif., Richmond, Va.

FIDLER, JACK

b. 1936 Webb City, Missouri.
Singer and songwriter. Leader of the Moonshiners (1963-67).

FIEDLER, ARTHUR

b. 1894 Boston, Massachusetts.
Noted violinist and conductor. He was studying in Berlin (1914) when the war forced his return to America; violinist and later violist of the Boston Symphony Orchestra; conducted Boston Sinfonietta (1924); conducted Cecilia Society (1926-49); Boston Pops (summer concerts) after 1930; albums—*All the Things You Are, American in Paris, Best of Arthur Fiedler and the Boston Pops, Duke At Tanglewood, Up, Up and Away with Arthur Fiedler and Boston Pops;* conducted Boston Pops at Carnegie Hall, New York City (1972).

FIELD, EUGENE

b. 1850 St. Louis, Missouri, d. 1895 Chicago, Illinois. Lyricist. Raised by a cousin in Amherst, Mass.; attended Williams College, Williamstown, Mass., Knox College, Galesburg, Illinois, and the University of Missouri, Kansas City; newspaper reporter in St. Joseph, Missouri, Kansas City, Mo., Denver and Chicago; wrote the lyrics "Little Boy Blue" (1891, m. Ethelburt Nevin) and "Wynken, Blynken and Nod."

FIELD, MICHAEL

b. 1915 New York City, d. there 1971.
Pianist. Raised by William L. Calhoun, piano teacher; studied at the Juilliard School, New York City; formed the duo-piano team of Vera

Appleton and Field, debut at Town Hall (1943); toured the U.S. and Europe; later became interested in food and cooking and wrote a number of books on cooking.

FIELD, WILLIAM H.

b. 1915, d. 1971 Philadelphia, Pennsylvania. Producer and director. Graduated University of Illinois; master's from Goodman School of Theater at University of Chicago; producer and director of New York City Opera Company.

FIELDS, CARL DONNELL ("KANSAS")

b. 1915 Chapman, Kansas.
Drummer. Played with Charlie Barnet, Dizzy Gillespie and others; served in navy in World War II; later with Cab Calloway, Sidney Bechet and others.

FIELDS, DOROTHY

b. 1905 Allenhurst, New Jersey, d. 1974.
Lyricist and librettist. Daughter of Lew Fields of the vaudeville team of Weber and Fields; wrote lyrics for Jimmy McHugh, Jerome Kern, Cole Porter (with her brother Herbert), Irving Berlin (with Herbert), Albert Hague, Arthur Schwartz, and Sigmund Romberg; with McHugh—"Diga, Diga, Doo," "I Can't Give You Anything but Love" (1928), "I'm in the Mood for Love" (1935); with Kern—"Lovely to Look At" (1935), "The Way You Look Tonight" (Academy Award, 1936).

FIELDS, GRACIE

b. 1898 Rochdale, England.
Singer and comedienne. Noted in New York night clubs; records—"Now Is the Hour," "Come Back to Sorrento."

FIELDS, HERBERT

b. 1919 Elizabeth, New Jersey, d. 1958 Miami, Florida. Bandleader and librettist. Studied at Juilliard, New York City; formed his own band (1946); wrote librettos for numerous Richard Rodgers shows—*Dearest Emmy* (1925), *The Girl Friend* (1926), *A Connecticut Yankee* (1927), *Present Arms* (1928), *Spring Is Here* (1929), *Simple Simon* (1930), *America's Sweetheart* (1931); all with Lorenz Hart as lyricist.

FIELDS, JAMES THOMAS

b. 1820 Portsmouth, New Hampshire, d. 1881 Boston, Massachusetts. Hymnist. Editor of the *Atlantic Monthly* (1862-70); wrote "Thou Who Has Called Our Being Here"; when Julia Ward Howe submitted her poem, "The Battle Hymn of the Republic," Fields paid her five dollars and published the poem in the February 1862 issue of the *Atlantic Monthly* without listing her name as poetess.

FIELDS, SHEP

b. 1910 Brooklyn, New York.
Saxophonist and bandleader. Replaced Jack Denny at the Hotel Pierre, New York City (1934); led the "Veloz and Yolande Orchestra" (top dance team of the era), opened at the Palmer House, Chicago; later led his own band; became famous by blowing through a straw into a glass of water thus making bubbling sounds; known for his "Rippling Rhythm."

FIFTH DIMENSION, THE (black rock group)

Vocals—Ron Towson, Lamonte McLemore, Marilyn McCoo, Florence La Rue Gordon; Billy Davis Jr., vocals and guitar; started in 1967, known as the Versatiles or the Hi-Fi's; their album *Age of Aquarius* was no. 1 on the hit list and sold 1.5 million disks the first six weeks; "Up, Up and Away" (by Jim Webb) won four Grammy awards; at the Riviera, Las Vegas (1972).

FIFTH ESTATE (rock group)

Rik Engler, vocals, bass guitar, etc.; Duck Ferrar, vocals, guitar, etc.; Wads Wadhams, electric harpsichord, etc.; Furvus Evans, drums and combine; D. William Shute, electric mandolin, etc.; album—*Ding Dong the Witch Is Dead.*

FILLMORE, JAMES H.

b. 1849, d. 1941.
Publisher. The Fillmore Music House, Cincinnati, Ohio, published "I Know That My Redeemer Liveth" (1893), words credited to J.H. Fillmore and music by Jessie B. Pounds, but the hymn was originally published in *Psalmodia Evangelica* (1789).

FILLMORE, JOHN COMFORT

b. 1843 Franklin, Connecticut, d. 1898 Taftville, Connecticut. Teacher and writer. Educated at Oberlin College, Ohio, and Leipzig Conservatory; founder and director of School of Music in Milwaukee (1884-95); musical director of Pomona College, Claremont, California.

FINCK, HENRY THEOPHILUS

b. 1854 Bethel, Missouri, d. 1926 Rumford Falls, Minnesota. Critic and writer. Taken to Aurora, Oregon, as a child, where his father organized the Aurora Band in the 1860s; graduated Harvard (1876); studied in Munich; was music editor of the *New York Evening Post* for forty years; published

Wagner and His Works (1893), *Songs and Song Writers* (1901), *Adventures in the Golden Age of Music,* and biographies of other European composers.

FINE, IRVING GIFFORD

b. 1914 Boston, Massachusetts, d. there 1962. Composer. Graduated from Harvard University and studied with Nadia Boulanger in Paris; composed *The Choral New Yorker, Toccata Concertante,* and music for a woodwind quintet.

FINE, VIVIAN

b. 1913 Chicago, Illinois.
Composer. Studied composition with Roger Sessions, et al.; musical director of Baron de Rothschild Foundation (1953-60); taught at Bennington College, Vermont after 1964; wrote *The Great Wall of China* (1947), *A Guide to the Life Expectancy of a Rose* (1956), *Valedictions* (1959), *Morning* (1962), *The Song of Persephone* (1964), *Dreamscope* (1964), *Paean* (1969), *The Race of Life* (1937), *Opus 51* (1938), *My Son, My Enemy* (1965).

FINEGAN, WILLIAM (BILL)

b. 1917 Newark, New Jersey.
Pianist, trumpeter, and arranger. Studied composition under Stephen Wolpe; at Paris Conservatory (1949-50); arranger for Glenn Miller (1938-42); for Tommy Dorsey (1942-52); formed a band with Ed Sauter (1952).

FINN, WILLIAM JOSEPH

b. 1881 Boston, Massachusetts, d. 1961 Bronxville, New York. Organist and writer. Studied at St. Charles College, St. Thomas College, The Catholic University of America, and the New England Conservatory; ordained a Roman Catholic priest (1906); organist-choirmaster in Washington, D.C., Boston, then Old Saint Mary's, Chicago (1906), where he organized the Paulist Choristers; wrote *A Manual of Church Music* (1905), *An Epitome of Some Principles of Choral Technique* (1935), *The Art of the Choral Conductor* (1939), *Child Voice Training* (1944), and *The Conductor Raises His Baton* (1944).

FINNEY, ROSS LEE

b. 1906 Wells, Minnesota.
Noted composer. Educated at University of Minnesota, Minneapolis, and Carleton College, Northfield, Minn. (1927); studied in Paris with Nadia Boulanger; attended Harvard (1929), then taught at Smith College, Northampton, Mass. (1929-48); set eight poems of Archibald MacLeish to music, introduced by Mabel Garrison (1935); *Slow Piece* (for strings, 1942), first symphony (1943), *Hymn, Fuguing and Holiday* (introduced in Los Angeles by Alfred Wallenstein, 1947); served in the Office of Strategic Services in World War II; his fourth string quartet was introduced in Cambridge, Mass. (1948); joined the faculty of the University of Michigan (1948); his second symphony was introduced by Eugene Ormandy and the Philadelphia Orchestra at Ann Arbor, Michigan (1960), and his third symphony by Ormandy (1964).

FIORILLO, DANTE

b. 1905 New York City.
Composer. Composed *Prelude* for string orchestra (Chamber Orchestra, Philadelphia, 1934), the *Prelude and Fugue* (New York Civic Orchestra, 1935), *Partita for Orchestra, Concerto, Introduction and Passacaglia;* also chamber music, songs.

FIORITO (FIO RITO), TED

b. 1900 Newark, New Jersey, d. 1971.
Bandleader and composer. Pianist in a dancing school at age thirteen; formed band to play at the Oriole Terrace, Detroit, then moved to Chicago; wrote "Love Bird" (1921, w. Mary Earl), "Doo Dah Blues" (1922, Fred Rose), "Lips" (1922, Fred Elwood), "No, No Nora" (1923, with Ernie Erdman, w. Gus Kahn), "Charley Boy" (1924, Kahn), "When Lights Are Low" (1924, Kahn and Ted Koehler), "I Never Knew I Could Love Anybody" (1925, Kahn), "Laugh, Clown, Laugh" (w. Sam Lewis and Joe Young), "King for a Day" (1928, Lewis and Young), "Now That You've Gone" (1931, Kahn); played in San Francisco and Los Angeles in the 1930s; died of a heart attack.

FIRST NATURAL HAIR BAND *see* GALT MAC DERMOT

FISCHER, CLARE

b. 1928 Durand, Michigan.
Pianist, organist, and composer. Graduated Michigan State University, earned master's in music; musical director in Los Angeles after 1957; conductor and arranger for Dizzy Gillespie's *A Portrait of Duke Ellington, Surging Ahead, Extensions* (with Jerry Coker); also toured Europe and South America.

FISCHER, JACOBO

b. 1896 Odessa, Russia.
Composer. Emigrated to Buenos Aires, Argentina; composed three symphonies (the third won a state prize), a ballet with chorus,

concertos for violin and piano, and chamber music.

FISCHER, WILLIAM

b. 1935 Mississippi.
Black composer. Educated at Xavier University, New Orleans, Colorado College, Colorado Springs, Academy of Music, Vienna, Austria; received Rockefeller Foundation and Fulbright grants; wrote *Time I* (1966, for saxophone, viola, cello, percussion and tape), *Batucada Fantastica* (1968, for two tape recorders and two percussionists), *Gift of Lesbos* (1968, for cello, piano, and tape recorder).

FISCHER, WILLIAM GUSTAVUS

b. 1835 Baltimore, Maryland, d. 1912 Philadelphia, Pennsylvania. Composer. Taught at Girard College, Philadelphia (school for orphans, 1858-68), then he was a piano dealer in the firm of Gould & Fischer, Philadelphia; composed the music for "I Love to Tell the Story" (1869, w. Katherine Hankey, 1866, and harmonized (1870) by Hubert P. Main), "I Am Coming to the Cross" (1872, w. William McDonald), "The Rock of Refuge" (1873, w. E. Johnson), "Whiter Than Snow," "A Little Talk with Jesus," and "I Am Trusting Lord, in Thee."

FISHER, EDDIE

b. 1928 Philadelphia, Pennsylvania.
Singer. Album—*Best of Eddie Fisher.*

FISHER, FRED

b. 1875 Cologne, Germany, d. 1942 New York City. Songwriter. Came to Chicago (1900); wrote "Come, Josephine, in My Flying Machine" (1910, w. Alfred Bryan), "Peg o' My Heart" (1913, w. Bryan), "Oui, Oui, Marie" (1918, w. Bryan and Joe McCarthy), "Dardanella" (1919, piano rag, Chicago, 1922), "Whispering Grass" (1941).

FISHER, WILLIAM ARMS

b. 1861 San Francisco, California, d. 1948 Boston, Massachusetts. Composer and writer. Studied with J.P. Morgan, H.W. Parker, and Antonin Dvořák in New York, then in London; editor and manager of Oliver Ditson Co., Boston; wrote "I Heard a Cry" (w. Sara Teasdale), "Seek Ye First the Kingdom of God."

FISHER, WILLIAM H.

b. 1913 New York City, d. 1972 Greenwich, Connecticut. Arranger. Prior to 1953 played the saxophone and clarinet; was arranger for "The Ed Sullivan Show" on TV for twenty-three years; also arranged for "The Jackie Gleason Show"; arranged music for the 26th annual Antoinette Perry (Tony) Awards program (1972).

FITCH, CLYDE

b. 1865 Schenectady, New York, d. 1909 France. Lyricist and producer. Graduated Amherst College, Amherst, Mass. (1887); produced fourteen plays between 1890 and 1900; wrote the lyrics "Love Makes the World Go 'Round" (1896, arr. William Furst) which was introduced in *Bohemia* (operetta).

FITCH, ELEAZER THOMPSON

b. 1791 New Haven, Connecticut, d. 1871. Hymnist. Graduated Yale University (1810); professor of divinity at Yale (1817-63); wrote three hymns which were included in *Connecticut Congregational Psalms and Hymns* which he compiled with Dr. Leonard W. Bacon.

FITELBERG, JERZY

b. 1903 Warsaw, Poland, d. 1951 New York City. Composer. Son of Gregory Fitelberg, composer and conductor of the Warsaw Philharmonic Orchestra; studied in Berlin; with the rise of Hitlerism he emigrated to Paris (1933), then to America (1940); composed two violin concertos, two piano concertos, and chamber music.

FITZGERALD, ELLA

b. 1918 Newport News, Virginia.
Noted black singer. Raised by an aunt in Harlem, New York City; joined Chick Webb's band at age sixteen; became the bandleader after Chick died; toured Europe, Canada, South America, Japan and Australia during 1950s and '60s; won three Grammy Awards (1958); "A-Tisket, A-Tasket" was arranged for her by Van Alexander (Al Feldman).

FIVE PENNIES (band) *see* RED NICHOLS

FLACK, ROBERTA

b. 1940.
Black singer. Her performance at the 1971 Newport (R.I.) Jazz Festival was a sensation with her rendition of "Reverend Lee"; first album was *First Take*; at Newport Jazz Festival, New York City (1972); in concert at Carnegie Hall, New York City (1972).

FLAGG, JOSIAH

b. 1737 Woburn, Massachusetts, d. 1794.
Bandleader and compiler. Compiled *A Collection of the Best Psalm Tunes* (1764, the plates were engraved by Paul Revere), and *Sixteen Anthems* (1766); established a band,

of which he was leader, and gave concerts in Faneuil Hall, Boston; conducted a concert by the 64th Regimental Band in Boston (1771).

FLAGLER, ISAAC VAN VLECK

b. 1842 Albany, New York, d. 1909.
Organist, editor, composer, and teacher. Studied in Europe; organist at First Presbyterian Church in Albany, then at Plymouth Church, Chicago, and First Presbyterian Church, Auburn, N.Y.; taught at Auburn Theological Seminary; also at Utica Conservatory of Music, Utica, N.Y.; composed comic opera, *Paradise* (1889), and *Variations on American Airs* (played by Eddy in Paris, 1889).

FLAGSTAD, KIRSTEN

b. 1895 Oslo, Norway, d. 1962.
Noted soprano. She made her debut in Oslo (1913); sang for Gothenburg Opera Company, Bayreuth (1933-34), then with Metropolitan Opera Company, New York City, and became famous; also a noted concert singer.

FLANAGAN, TOMMY LEE

b. 1930 Detroit, Michigan.
Pianist. Played with Miles Davis, J.J. Johnson, O. Pettiford, and Kenny Burrell during 1940s and '50s; with Coleman Hawkins, Jim Hall, Ella Fitzgerald, and Tony Bennett during 1960s; toured Europe and South America; at Juan-les-Pins Jazz Festival (1964).

FLANAGAN, WILLIAM

b. 1923 Detroit, Michigan. d. 1969.
Composer. Studied composition with Burrill Phillips, et al.; wrote *Divertimento for String Quartet* (1947), *Piano Sonata* (1950), *Song for a Winter Child* (1950, w. Edward Albee), *The Weeping Pleiades* (song cycle, 1953, w. A.E. Housman), *The Lady of Tearful Regret* (1958, w. Albee), *Narrative for Orchestra* (1964), *Another August* (1967).

FLATT, LESTER RAYMOND

b. 1914 Overton County, Tennessee.
Singer, guitarist, and songwriter. Started with radio station WDBJ, Roanoke, Virginia (1939); later joined Grand Ole Opry, Nashville (1944); teamed with Earl Scruggs, banjoist; their hit records were "Cabin in the Sky" (1959), "Go Home" (1961), "The Ballad of Jed Clampett" (1962, theme song of "The Beverly Hillbillies"), "Pearl, Pearl, Pearl" (1963), "Petticoat Junction" (1964), "California Uptight Band" (1967), "Nashville Cats" (1967).

FLEISCHER, LEON

b. 1928.
Pianist and conductor. Concert pianist (1952-64); then numbness struck his right hand which became partially paralyzed (1965); conducted New York Chamber Orchestra in Philharmonic Hall (1970) in a program of Haydn, Mozart, and Schubert; concert pianist at New York Philharmonic (1972).

FLETCHER, ALICE CUNNINGHAM

b. 1838 Cuba, d. 1923.
Writer. While a resident of Omaha, Nebraska, she made a study of Indian music; published *A Study of Omaha Music* (1893).

FLETCHER, DOUGLAS

b. 1884 Wiltshire, England.
Composer. Graduated Cooper Union, New York City, as a chemist, which became his livelihood, but he was also an organist and composer; composed the tune "Molleson" (1924, "My God, I Love Thee, Not Because," w. anonymous).

FLETCHER, JOHN GOULD

b. 1886, d. 1950.
Poet and critic. His poems were set to music in *Choral Suite* by Peggy Glanville-Hicks (1937).

FLOOD, RICHARD E. (DICK)

b. 1932 Philadelphia, Pennsylvania.
Singer and bandleader. Leader of the Country Lads (1956-58), The Searchers (1960-64), and The Pathfinders after 1964.

FLORENCE, ROBERT C. (BOB)

b. 1932 Los Angeles, California.
Pianist. Studied at Los Angeles City College; organized his own band in Hollywood; arranger for Si Zentner's band after 1959; his arrangement of "Lazy River" was a Zentner hit in 1961.

FLORIDA BOYS QUARTET

Organized (1947) by J.G. Whitfield; Les Beasley, second tenor and manager; Coy Cook, first tenor; Gein Allred, baritone; Billy Todd, bass; Derrell Stewart, pianist.

FLORIDA PLAYBOYS *see* RAY CHARLES

FLORIDIA, PIETRO

b. 1860 Modica, Sicily, Italy, d. 1932 New York City. Noted composer, pianist, and teacher. Baron Napolino di San Silvestro; wrote opera *Maruzza*, (Venice, 1894); came to America (1904); taught at Cincinnati Conservatory, Ohio; wrote the opera *Paoletta* (1910); conducted Italian Symphony of New

York City after 1913; composed (with Luigi Illica), *La Colonia Libera, Festouverture, The Scarlet Letter* (opera), *Madrigal* for baritone and orchestra, songs.

FLOYD, CARLISLE

b. 1926 Latta, South Carolina.
Composer. Studied at Converse College, Spartanburg, South Carolina, and Syracuse University, N.Y.; became an instructor at Florida State University, Tallahassee (1955); composed the operas *Slow Dusk* (1949), and *Fugitives* (1951), then *Susannah* (musical drama, 1954) and *Wuthering Heights,* (introduced in Santa Fe, New Mexico, 1958), *Of Mice and Men* (1970, based on John Steinbeck's book).

FLOYD, EDDIE

b. (?)
Black soul singer and songwriter. Started in Memphis, Tenn. with the Falcons (1955-62); wrote "634-5789" (recorded by Wilson Pickett); albums—*I've Never Found a Girl, Knock on Wood, Rare Stamps, You've Got to Have Eddie, California Girl, Down to Earth.*

FLYING BURRITO BROTHERS (country and western group)

Gram Parsons, vocals and guitar; Chris Hillman, guitar and mandolin; Sneeky Pete, steel guitar; Chris Ethridge, bass and piano; albums—*The Gilded Palace of Sin* (1969), *Burrito Deluxe.*

FOERSTER, ADOLPH MARTIN

b. 1854 Pittsburgh, Pennsylvania, d. 1927.
Composer and teacher. Studied at the Leipzig Conservatory; became a teacher at the Fort Wayne (Indiana) Conservatory, (1875-76); then a teacher in Pittsburgh; composed orchestra and chamber music, and songs.

FOGGY MOUNTAIN BOYS *see* LESTER FLATT and EARL SCRUGGS

FOLEY, CLYDE JULIAN ("RED")

b. 1910 Berea, Kentucky, d. 1968 Fort Wayne, Indiana. Singer, guitarist, and songwriter. Attended Georgetown College, Georgetown, Kentucky; with John Lair, started the "Renfro Valley Barn Dance" radio show(1938); wrote "Blues in My Heart"; appeared in Grand Ole Opry in the 1940s, and had his own show, "Ozark Jubilee," Springfield, Mo., in the '50s; top hits were "Foggy River," "Chattanooga Shoeshine Boy," "Just a Closer Walk with Thee," "Midnight, Tennessee Saturday Night."

FOLLEN, ELIZA LEE CABOT

b. 1787 Boston, Massachusetts, d. 1860 Brookline, Massachusetts. Hymnist. Daughter of Samuel Cabot; wrote *Hymns for Children* (Boston, 1825), *Poems* (1839), *The Lark and the Linnet* (1854).

FONTANA, CARL CHARLES

b. 1928 Monroe, Louisiana.
Trombonist. Played with Lionel Hampton, Woody Herman, and Stan Kenton in 1950s; at Las Vegas Jazz Festival (1962); later with Benny Goodman and again with Woody Herman.

FOOTE, ARTHUR WILLIAM

b. 1853 Salem, Massachusetts, d. 1937 Boston, Massachusetts. Noted composer. Graduated Harvard; organist of the First Unitarian Church, Boston (1878-1910); composed Suite in E Major (for string orchestra, introduced by the Boston Symphony under Max Fiedler, 1909), *A Night Piece* (1918, for flute and string quartet played by the Boston Symphony for his eightieth birthday party in 1933); composed twenty-five anthems, including "Still, Still with Thee," "God Is Our Refuge," "And There Were Shepherds," and "Awake Thou That Sleepest."

FORD, BENJAMIN FRANCIS ("WHITEY")

b. 1901 DeSoto, Missouri.
Banjoist and mandolin player. Raised in Little Rock, Arkansas; served in the navy (1918-22), then started his own Dixieland jazz band; played on WLS, Chicago, then KWK, St. Louis, when he became known as the "Duke of Paducah"; during World War II he traveled overseas entertaining servicemen, after which he joined Grand Ole Opry for sixteen years; his films were *Country Farm* and *Country Music on Broadway,* (1963).

FORD, ERNEST JENNINGS ("TENNESSEE ERNIE")

b. 1919 Bristol, Tennessee.
Singer and songwriter. Studied at the Cincinnati Conservatory of Music; served in the air corps during World War II; announcer on several radio stations, but first sang on station KXLA, Pasadena, California; had his own show on CBS and ABC (1950-55), then NBC-TV (1955-61); wrote "Smokey Mountain Boogie" (1949), "Shotgun Boogie" (1950), "Blackberry Boogie" (1951); his top hits were "Mule Train" (1949), "River of No Return" (1954), "Ballad of Davy Crockett" (1955), and "Sixteen Tons" (1955, Merle Travis).

FORD, HARRY

b. 1900 Brooklyn, New York, d. 1971 New York City. Pianist and conductor. Born Harry Moskowitz; in the 1920s he was road conductor for Sam Lanin and his Ipana Troubadors, and in the 1930s pianist and conductor with the Indiana Five, a Dixieland music group; from 1951-71 he was musical director of the Tuesday night shows at Roseland Dance City in New York City.

FORD, LENA GUILBERT

b. (?), d. 1918 London, England.
Lyricist. Raised in Elmira, N.Y.; wrote "Keep the Home Fires Burning" (1914, m. Ivor Novello); she was killed in a German Zeppelin raid on London.

FORMES DE VARAZ, CARL

b. 1810 Muhlheim on Rhine, Germany, d. 1889 San Francisco, California. Celebrated basso. Debut (1832) in opera at Cologne; studied under Basodowa in Vienna; sang as Sarastro in *Zauberflote* (1849) at Drury Theatre, London; as Caspar in *Der Freischutz* at Covent Garden (1850); came to America (1857); sang at New York Academy of Music; at Philadelphia Academy of Music (1858); married Pauline Greenwood, his pupil; later taught in San Francisco; Gustav Hinrichs stated in his *Memoirs* that Formes was the greatest basso of the nineteenth century.

FORNIA, RITA P. NEWMAN

b. 1879 San Francisco, California, d. 1922 Paris, France. Soprano. Pupil of Jean de Reszke and Frau Kempner; debut (1901) Hamburg Stadttheatre; sang at Covent Garden, London; then at the Metropolitan Opera, New York City.

FORRESTER, HOWARD WILSON ("HOWDY")

b. 1922 Vernon, Tennessee.
Singer and fiddler. With Bill Monroe's Blue Grass Boys; Roy Acuff's Smokey Mountain Boys after 1951; with Grand Ole Opry, Nashville, after 1951.

FORST, RUDOLF

b. 1900 New York City.
Violinist and composer. Studied at Columbia University, New York City, with Mason; composed *Music for Strings,* a string quartet (NBC by Gordon String Quartet, 1937, won NBC Music Guild Prize); *Aubade Mexicaine* (Greenwich Orchestra under Maganini, 1938); "Pastorale and Tempo di Valse" from *Divertimento* for chamber orchestra (Yaddo Festival, 1938); and *Toccata-Prelude* (WOR Symphonietta).

FOSDICK, HARRY EMERSON

b. 1878 Buffalo, New York, d. 1969.
Hymnist. Educated at Colgate University, Hamilton, N.Y., Union Theological Seminary, and Columbia University, New York City; became pastor of the first Baptist Church, Montclair, N.J. (1904), then taught at Union Theological Seminary, New York City (1915-46); served with the YMCA in France during World War I; pastor of the First Presbyterian Church (1919-25) and the Riverside Church, both New York City (1925-46); wrote the hymn "God of Grace and God of Glory" (1930, tune "Cwm Rhondda"—John Hughes).

FOSDICK, WILLIAM WHITEMAN

b. 1825 Cincinnati, Ohio, d. there 1862.
Lyricist. Wrote "Aura Lee" (1861, m. George R. Poulton), which was rewritten in 1865 with a new title, "Army Blue," and was adopted as the graduating class song at the United States Military Academy, West Point, New York; "Love Me Tender" by Elvis Presley and Vera Matson is based on the tune "Aura Lee."

FOSS, LUKAS

b. 1922 Berlin, Germany.
Composer. Studied in Paris and then came to America (1937) and studied at the Curtis Institute of Music, Philadelphia; staff pianist with the Boston Symphony, then became a professor at the University of California, Los Angeles (1953); composed *The Prairie* (cantata, 1943), *The Song of Anguish* (cantata, 1945) and *The Song of Songs* (cantata, 1946, introduced by the Boston Symphony Orchestra under Serge Koussevitzky, 1947, with the black soprano, Ellabelle Davis).

FOSTER, FAY

b. 1886, Leavenworth, Kansas, d. 1960 Bayport, New York. Pianist, organist, composer, and teacher. Wrote "The Nightingales of Flanders."

FOSTER, FRANK BENJAMIN

b. 1928 Cincinnati, Ohio.
Tenor saxist. Arranger for Count Basie after 1953, also played tenor sax in his band; toured Europe with Basie (1962-63); also Japan and Hawaii (1963); at Newport Jazz Festival (1960-61); formed his own band (1965).

FOSTER, GEORGE MURPHY ("POPS")

b. 1892 McCall, Louisiana, d. 1969.
Black double bass player. Powerful player using the slap bass technique; played in Fate Marable's band on the Mississippi River boats between St. Louis and New Orleans before 1920; joined Charles Creath's band (1924); with Bunk Johnson (1945); toured England (1966) with the New Orleans All-Stars.

FOSTER, LAWRENCE

b. 1941 Los Angeles, California.
Conductor. Guest conductor of Romanian Royal Philharmonic Orchestra; conductor of Houston (Texas) Symphony after 1971.

FOSTER, STEPHEN COLLINS

b. 1826 Lawrenceville, Pennsylvania, d. 1864 New York City. Popular composer. Lived in Harmony, Pa. for a time, then the family moved to Allegheny (annexed by Pittsburgh, 1909); attended Athens Academy, Tioga Point, Pa., Towanda Academy, Towanda, Pa., and Jefferson College, Cannonsburg, Pa. where he became homesick after one week. He visited his sister, Henrietta Wick, in Youngstown, Ohio (1842). About 1847 he went to work as a bookkeeper in his brother Dunning's commission house in Cincinnati, Ohio, where he could hear the blacks sing Negro spirituals as they unloaded the boats on the Ohio River. These songs made an everlasting impression on him. In 1849 he visited his sister, Henrietta, in Warren, Ohio. In 1850 he married Jane McDowell of Pittsburgh. In 1852 Stephen and Jane took a trip to New Orleans on a Mississippi River steamboat. They visited Federal Hill, the home of Judge John Rowan, a relative, in Bardstown, Kentucky, said to be Foster's inspiration for "My Old Kentucky Home." They had one daughter, Marion, born 1851. Stephen and Jane had many quarrels over liquor and money, and they separated several times. He died in January 1864. (*See* George Cooper.) Foster composed the music "Open Thy Lattice Love" (1844, w. G.P. Morris), "We Are Coming, Father Abraham, 300,000 More" (w. J.S. Gibbons), "Bring Back My Brother to Me" (1863, w. George Cooper), "There Was a Time" (1863, w. J.D. Byrne), "All Day Long" (1864, Clara Morton). His better known songs were "The Louisiana Belle" (1847), "Old Uncle Ned" (1848), "Oh Susanna" (1848), "Nelly Bly" (1849), "De Camptown Races" (1850), "Laura Lee" (1851), "Old Folks at Home" (1851, "Swanee River"), "Massas in de Cold, Cold Ground" (1852), "My Old Kentucky Home" (1853), "Jeannie with the Light Brown Hair" (1854), "Come Where My Love Lies Dreaming" (1855), "Gentle Annie" (1856), "Old Black Joe" (1860), "Better Times Are Coming" (1862), and "Beautiful Dreamer, Wake Unto Me" (1863, but published after his death in 1864). Upon examining his clothing, a slip of paper was found on which was written "Dear hearts and gentle people." (*See also* Bob Hilliard, Horace Waters, Thomas D. Rice, William C. Peters, Silas J. Vail.)

FOUNTAIN, PETER DEWEY, JR. (PETE)

b. 1930 New Orleans, Louisiana.
Clarinetist and bandleader. With Lawrence Welk's TV show (1957-59); organized his own combo at his club in New Orleans; also played in Las Vegas; albums—*Pete Fountain's New Orleans, The Blues, Best of Pete Fountain, Both Sides Now, Darktown Strutter's Ball, Dixieland, For the First Time, New Orleans at Midnight.*

FOUR BROTHERS *see* WOODY HERMAN

FOUR GRADUATES *see* THE HAPPENINGS

FOUR GUYS (vocal group) *see* HAROLD B. BURKETT

FOUR SEASONS, THE (modern group)

Frankie Valli, vocals; Bob Gaudio, vocals; Tommy De Vitto, vocals; Joe Long, vocals; albums—*Born to Wander* (1964), *Dawn, Edizione D'Oro* (Gold Edition), *Four Seasons—Gold Vault of Hits, Four Seasons—Looking Back, Four Seasons—2nd Vault of Golden Hits, Four Seasons—Sing Big Hits, Genuine Imitation Life Gazette, Half and Half.*

FOUR SOUNDS (jazz group) *see* GENE HARRIS

FOUR TOPS, THE (black blues-rock group)

Levi Stubbs, Jr., lead vocals; Renaldo "Obie" Benson, vocals; Abdul "Duke" Fakir, vocals; Lawrence Payton, vocals; American group first successful in England; albums—*Four Tops* (1965), *Four Tops' Greatest Hits, Four Tops Live, Four Tops No. 2, Four Tops Now, Four Tops on Broadway, On Top, Reach Out, Soul Spin, Still Waters Run Deep, Yesterday's Dreams.*

FOURNIER, VERNAL ANTHONY

b. 1928 New Orleans, Louisiana.
Drummer. With Ahmad Jamal Trio after 1956; also toured with George Shearing and

Larry Novak during 1960s; also toured with Nancy Wilson.

FOUTS, TOM C. ("CAPTAIN STUBBY")

b. 1918 Carroll County, Indiana.
Singer and bandleader. Leader of Captain Stubby and the Buccaneers after 1937; with "Don McNeill's Breakfast Club," ABC, Chicago after 1965; in the U.S. Navy Entertainment Section, all over the world, during World War II.

FOWLER, WALLY

b. 1917 Bartow County, Georgia.
Singer and bandleader. Leader of Oak Ridge Quartet; also leader of the Georgia Clodhoppers; wrote "I'm Sending You Roses," "That's How Much I Love You Baby."

FOWLER, WILLIAM L.

b. 1917 Salt Lake City, Utah.
Guitarist and teacher. Organized his own combo; directed military bands in World War II; studied at American Conservatory, Eastman School of Music, Rochester, N.Y., and Academia Chigiana, Siena, Italy; University of Utah, doctorate in music (1954); then taught there; directed university jazz workshops.

FOWLKES, CHARLES BAKER (CHARLIE)

b. 1916 Brooklyn, New York.
Baritone saxist. With Tiny Bradshaw, then Lionel Hampton (1944-48); married singer Wini Brown; with Count Basie after 1953.

FOX, ANCELLA M. (MRS. ORVIN L.)

b. 1847 Boston, Massachusetts, d. 1920.
Soprano, teacher, and writer. Studied in Boston under Mrs. J.H. Long; debut (1870) with Chicago Orpheus Society under Hans Balatka; soprano at Second Presbyterian Church, Chicago (1869-71); after the great fire left for Boston and sang at Fourth Presbyterian Church; taught at Chicago Musical College after 1884; music critic for *The Indicator.*

FOX, DELLA MAY

b. 1870 St. Louis, Missouri, d. 1913 New York City. Singer, dancer, and actress. Joined Dickson Sketch Club in St. Louis and toured the Midwest and Canada with actress Nellie Page (1883-85); studied under Heinrich Conried; New York debut (1890) in Adolf Muller's *The King's Fool;* with DeWolf Hopper in the operetta *Castles in the Air* (1890), *Wang* (1891) and *Panjandrum;* in *The Lady or the Tiger* (1894); starred in the operetta *The Little Trooper* (1894); *Fleur-de-Lis* (1895); with Lillian Russell and Jefferson de Angelis in *Wedding Day* (1897); *The Little Host* (1898-99); in a sanatorium (1900); married diamond broker Jack Levy; died of an intestinal obstruction.

FOX, SAM

b. 1882, d. 1971 San Francisco, California. Publisher. Borrowed $300 to start the Sam Fox Publishing Company in Cleveland, Ohio in 1906; in 1917 became the exclusive publisher for John Philip Sousa, the march king; published the score of *Brigadoon* (1947); also *Man of La Mancha.*

FOY, EDDIE

b. 1856 New York City, d. 1928 Kansas City, Missouri. Vaudeville actor and singer. Born Edward Fitzgerald; starred in the operetta *Little Robinson Crusoe* (1899, m. Gustav Luders) and introduced *Hamlet Was a Melancholy Dane* (1902) in Chicago.

FRANCIS, CONNIE

b. 1938 Newark, New Jersey.
Singer. Born Constance Franconero; played the accordian on "George Scheck's Startime," juvenile variety show, New York City at age eleven; at twelve on "Arthur Godfrey's Talent Scouts" show; recorded "Who's Sorry Now?" (1957, by Harry Ruby, Bert Kalmar, and Ted Snyder) which became a hit; appeared on "The Ed Sullivan Show" (1958); turned out eight gold records.

FRANK, J.L.

b. 1900 Rossal, Alabama, d. 1952 Chicago, Illinois. Songwriter. Producer on WLS, Chicago (1928-35), then he moved to Louisville, Ky. (1935), then to Nashville (1939); wrote "Chapel on the Hill," "Sundown and Sorrow," and "My Main Trail Is Yet to Come."

FRANKLIN, ARETHA

b. 1942 Memphis, Tennessee.
Noted black singer. As a youth, she sang in her father's church in Detroit; known as "Lady Soul" herself; won a 1971 Grammy award of the National Academy of Recording Arts and Sciences for the "best rhythm and blues vocal performance for "Don't Play That Song"; married Ted White; won Grammy Award (1972) for fifth straight year; albums—*Aretha Arrives, Aretha in Paris, Aretha Now, Aretha's Gold, Aretha Franklin, Aretha Franklin's Greatest Hits, Incomparable Aretha, Lady Soul, Laughing on the Outside, Once in a Lifetime, Queen of Soul, Runnin'*

Out of Fools, Soft and Beautiful, Songs of Faith, Soul Sister, Soul (1969), *Take a Look, Take It Like You Give It, Tender, Moving Swinging, Aretha Franklin; This Girl's in Love with You, Today I Sing the Blues, Unforgettable* (Tribute to Dinah Washington), and *Yeah.*

FRANKLIN, ERMA

b. 1940 Memphis, Tennessee.
Black singer. Sister of Aretha Franklin; album—*Soul Sister.*

FRANKO, NATHAN

b. 1861 New Orleans, Louisiana, d. 1930 Amityville, New York. Violinist and conductor. At age eight he toured the world with Adelina Patti; later joined the Metropolitan Opera Company orchestra, New York City; concertmaster after 1893; later conducted his own orchestra.

FRANKO, SAM

b. 1857 New Orleans, Louisiana, d. 1937 New York City. Violinist. Toured with Adelina Patti; conducted concerts on ancient music, New York City.

FRAZIER, DALLAS

b. 1939 Spiro, Oklahoma.
Singer, guitarist, trumpeter, and composer. His family moved to Bakersfield, Calif. when he was young; started with Ferlin Husky's touring troupe, then "Cliffie Stone's Hometown Jamboree" TV show; hit record was "Alley Oop" (1957); wrote "Georgia," "Elvira," "Hawg Jaw," "Soakin' Up the Suds," "Timber I'm Fallin'."

FRED, JOHN AND HIS PLAYBOY BAND (rock group)

John Fred, vocals and harmonica; Andrew Bernard, baritone sax; Ronnie Goodson, trumpet; Charlies Spin, trumpet; Jimmy O'Rouke, guitar; Harold Cowart, bass; Tommy De Generes, organ; Joe Micely, drums; started in Baton Rouge, Louisiana; albums—*John Fred and His Playboys* (1968), *Agnes English, Love My Soul, 34:40, Permanently Stated.*

FREED, ARTHUR

b. 1894 Charleston, South Carolina, d. 1973. Lyricist. Vaudeville actor with Gus Edwards and also Louis Silvers; wrote "Broadway Melody" (m. Nacio Herb Brown), "The Wedding of the Painted Doll" (1928, m. Brown), "This Heart of Mine" (m. Harry Warren), "Here Comes the Sun" (m. Harry Woods).

FREED, ISADORE

b. 1900 Brest Litovsk, Russia, d. 1960 Rockville Centre, New York. Composer. Parents brought him to America (1903); studied in Paris with Vincent d'Indy and in New York with Ernest Bloch; organist and conductor in synagogues; composed the opera *The Princess and the Vagabond* (first performed in Hartford, Conn., 1948), the oratorio *Micah* (written for the tenth anniversary of the State of Israel, 1958).

FREEMAN, ENOCH WESTON

b. 1798 Minot, Maine, d. 1835.
Hymnist. Became pastor of the First Baptist Church, Lowell, Mass. (1828); wrote "Hither We Come, Our Dearest Lord" which he included in his *Selection of Hymns* (1829-31).

FREEMAN, HARRY LAWRENCE

b. 1875 Cleveland, Ohio, d. 1943.
Noted black organist and composer. Music director for the Pekin Theatre, Chicago; composed opera, *The Martyr,* produced in Denver, Colorado, 1893 (repeated at Carnegie Hall, New York City, 1947); opera, *Valdo,* in Cleveland, Ohio (1906); music director for Cole and Johnson Brothers in New York; wrote operas, *The Tryst,* New York City (1911), and *Vendetta* at Lafayette Theatre in Harlem, New York City (1928); won Harmon Award (1930); wrote ballet, *The Zulu King* (1934); symphonic poem, *The Slave.*

FREEMAN, JAMES

b. 1759 Charlestown, Massachusetts, d. 1835 Newton, Massachusetts. Compiler. Graduated Harvard (1777); reader in Kings Chapel (1778) and minister of Kings Chapel, Boston (1787-1826); compiled the *Kings Chapel Collection of Psalms and Hymns* (1799).

FREEMAN, LAWRENCE ("BUD")

b. 1906 Chicago, Illinois.
Tenor saxist. Played with Tommy Dorsey, Benny Goodman, and Ray Noble; at the Newport and Monterey Jazz Festivals; toured Australia, New Zealand, and Japan (1963); at International Jazz Festival (1964); at the Newport Jazz Festival, New York City (1972).

FREEMAN, PAUL

b. 1935.
Black conductor. Graduated Eastman School, Rochester, New York (Ph.D.); studied in Berlin, Germany; associate conductor of Dallas Symphony Orchestra, Texas.

FREEMAN, RUSSELL DONALD (RUSS)

b. 1926 Chicago, Illinois.
Pianist. With Shelly Manne's group; toured Europe (1960); organized his own publishing firm (1962).

FREER, ELEANOR EVEREST

b. 1864 Philadelphia, Pennsylvania, d. 1942 Chicago, Illinois. Composer and operatic soprano. Daughter of Cornelius Everest, musical director of the Girl's Normal School, Philadelphia (1865-86); taught in Philadelphia until her marriage in 1891; composed the operas *The Legend of the Piper, Massimilliano, Little Women* (Louisa M. Alcott), *The Court Jester,* which were produced in Chicago and other cities in the Middle West.

FREMSTAD, OLIVE

b. 1872 Stockholm, Sweden, d. 1951 New York City. Soprano. Brought to America by her parents (1884); soloist at St. Patrick's Cathedral, New York City (1890); pupil of Lilli Lehmann, Berlin (1893-94); debut (1895); sang at Bayreuth (1896); with Vienna Royal Opera, later in Munich, then at Metropolitan Opera, New York (1903-14); later toured as a concert singer.

FRENCH, EDWARD

b. 1761 Stoughton, Massachusetts, d. 1845. Composer. Brother of Jacob French; composed the tune "New Bethlehem."

FRENCH, JACOB

b. 1754 Stoughton, Massachusetts, d. after 1802. Composer and compiler. Brother of Edward French; wrote *The New American Melody,* Medway, Mass. (1789), *The Psalmodist's Companion,* Worcester, (1793), and *The Harmony of Harmony,* Northampton, Mass. (1802); wrote the anthem "The Heavenly Vision" published in the *Worcester Collection* (1791).

FRIAR'S SOCIETY ORCHESTRA *see* NEW ORLEANS RHYTHM KINGS

FRICKER, SYLVIA

b. 1940 Chatham, Ontario, Canada.
Vocal duo of Ian and Sylvia. Married Ian Tyson in 1964; wrote "You Were on My Mind" and jointly with her husband, "Mr. Spoons."

FRIEDHEIM, ARTHUR

b. 1859 St. Petersburg, Russia, d. 1932 New York City. Composer. Studied under Franz Liszt; lived in England, Canada, then came to the United States; wrote a piano concerto and the opera *Die Taenzerin* (1897, *The Dancer,* performed at Karlsruhe).

FRIEDLAND, ANATOLE

b. 1881 St. Petersburg, Russia, d. 1938 Atlantic City, New Jersey. Songwriter. Studied music at the Moscow Conservatory, came to New York City and studied architecture at Columbia University; operated the Club Anatole on West 44th Street during Prohibition days; with the lyricist L. Wolfe Gilbert he wrote "My Sweet Adair," "Are You from Heaven," "Shades of the Night," "Singapore," "Who Believed in You?"

FRIEDMAN, DONALD ERNEST (DON)

b. 1935 San Francisco, California.
Pianist and composer. Played in San Francisco jazz groups during late 1950s; then in New York City; with Attila Zoller at Newport Jazz Festivals (1965-66); composed piano pieces.

FRIEDMAN, LEO

b. 1869 Elgin, Illinois, d. 1927 Chicago, Illinois. Composer and publisher. Wrote "Let Me Call You Sweetheart" (1910, w. Beth Slater Whitson).

FRIEND, CLIFF

b. 1893 Cincinnati, Ohio, d. 1974.
Popular composer and lyricist. Played the piano at age ten; later joined Buddy de Sylva in a vaudeville act; wrote "I Wish I Had a Girl Like You" (1921), "Lovesick Blues" (1922, w. Irving Mills), "Mama Loves Papa" (1924, with Abel Baer), "South American Joe" (1934, w. Irving Caesar), "When My Dream Boat Comes Home" (1936, with Dave Franklin), "The Merry-go-round Broke Down" (1937, with Franklin), "You Can't Stop Me from Dreaming" (1937, Franklin), "Don't Sweetheart Me" (1944, Charles Tobias).

FRIGO, JOHN VIRGIL

b. 1916 Chicago, Illinois.
Bass player and violinist. With Soft Winds Trio (1947-52); led his own trio at Mr. Kelly's Club, Chicago, after 1962; married singer Mara Lynn Brown; composed two tunes for her record, *My Way.*

FRIML, RUDOLF

b. 1879 Prague, Czechoslovakia, d. 1972, Hollywood, California. Popular composer. Studied at Prague Conservatory and became a concert pianist with Jan Kubelik, the violinist, in Europe and America; settled in New York City (1906); composed the scores for *The*

Firefly (1912, w. Harbach), *High Jinks* (1913), *Katinka* (1915), *Rose Marie* (1924, w. Otto Harbach and Hammerstein), *The Vagabond King* (1925), *The Three Musketeers* (1928), *Launa* (1930), *Anina* (1934); wrote "The Donkey Serenade (1937, introduced by Allan Jones), and "Indian Love Call."

FRISHBERG, DAVID L. (DAVE)

b. 1933 St. Paul, Minnesota.
Pianist and composer. Educated at the University of Minnesota; in air force (1955-57); with Carmen McRae and Kai Winding in late 1950s; with Dick Haymes, Odetta, Gene Krupa, Wild Bill Davison, Bud Freeman, Ben Webster, and Al Cohn-Zoot Sims group after 1963; wrote "Wallflower Lonely," "Cornflower Blue," "I'm Hip," "Peel Me a Grape."

FRISKIN, JAMES

b. 1886 Glasgow, Scotland, d. 1961.
Pianist. Studied at the Royal College of Music (1900-05); later taught at the Institute of Musical Art, New York City; composed a piano quintet in C minor, cello sonatas.

FRIZZELL, WILLIAM ORVILLE ("LEFTY")

b. 1928 Corsicana, Texas.
Singer, guitarist, and songwriter. Started with radio station KELD, El Dorado, Texas, on a children's program, then the family moved to Greenville, Texas; tried boxing, and became known as "Lefty"; hit records were "Always Late," "I Want to Be with You Always," "Don't Stay Away," and "I'm an Old, Old Man" (1952), "Travelin' Blues," "Long Black Veil" (1959), "Saginaw, Michigan" (1964).

FROMM, HERBERT

b. 1905 Kitzingen, Bavaria.
Composer. Became choirmaster at Temple Israel, Boston, Mass. (1935); composed *Adath Israel*, for the Friday evening service, *Psalm No. 23, Song of Miriam, Shofar Service.*

FROTHINGHAM, OCTAVIUS BROOKS

b. 1822 Boston, Massachusetts, d. there 1895.
Hymnist. Graduated Harvard (1843), theology (1846); pastor in Salem, Mass. (1847), Jersey City, N.J. (1855), Unitarian Society, N.Y. (1860); wrote "Thou Lord of Hosts, Whose Guiding Hand" (Samuel Longfellow and Samuel Johnson's *Book of Hymns*, 1846).

FRUIT JAR DRINKERS
Featured Uncle Dave Macon.

FRY, HENRY S.

b. 1875 Pottstown, Pennsylvania, d. 1946 Philadelphia, Pennsylvania. Organist, composer, and writer. Organist at several Philadelphia churches after 1900; president of the National Association of Organists for many years; gave over 600 organ recitals, more than 125 at the opening of new organs.

FRY, WILLIAM HENRY

b. 1815 Philadelphia, Pennsylvania, d. 1864 Santa Cruz, West Indies. Noted composer. Wrote an opera *Aurelia the Vestal* (1838, libretto—Henry Fry, his brother), but could not get it produced; his opera *Leonora* (libretto—Joseph R. Fry, his brother) was the first opera written and produced by a native-born American at the Chestnut Street Theatre, Philadelphia, on June 4, 1845 and conducted by Leopold Meignen; it was later produced at the Academy of Music in New York City (1858); his opera *Notre Dame de Paris* (libretto—J.R. Fry) was produced May 9, 1864 and conducted by Theodore Thomas; wrote considerable music for the Catholic church, including a *Stabat Mater;* in 1853 Jullien's orchestra in Philadelphia played four symphonies by Fry: *Childe Harold, A Day in the Country, The Breaking Heart* and *Christmas.*

FUGITIVES, THE *see* BOB PORTER

FUGS, THE (pop-rock group)

Ed Sanders, vocals; Ken Weaver, vocals and drums; Tuli Kupferberg, vocals; Ken Pine, vocals and guitar; Bill Wolf, bass; Bob Mason, drums; Doug Franklin, conductor; plus a chorus; albums—*Belle of Avenue A; Golden Filth; It Crawled into My Hand, Honest; Tenderness Junction;* known for their antiwar songs like "Kill for Peace," "The Evil Spirits from the Pentagon," "October 21, 1967."

FULEIHAN, ANIS

b. 1900 Kyrenia, Cyprus, d. 1970.
Composer. Came to U.S. (1915); studied piano with Alberto Jonas; debut as pianist; won Guggenheim Fellowship; composed *Mediterranean* (suite for orchestra, Cincinnati Symphony-Goossens, 1935), Concerto no. 1 for piano and string orchestra (Saratoga Spa Festival under F. Charles Adler, composer, soloist, 1937), Symphony no. 1 (New York Philharmonic under Barbirolli, 1936), *Fiesta and Invocation* (Indianapolis Symphony under Sevitzky, 1939), *Epithalamium* (Philadelphia String Simfonietta, 1941).

FULLER, BLIND BOY

b. 1903 Rockingham, North Carolina, d. 1940 Durham, North Carolina. Black singer. Born

Fuller Allen; his eyesight was lost when his jealous girl friend put a dose of lye in his washing water; played in the towns of North Carolina with Brownie McGhee; recorded with Sonny Terry after 1934.

FULLER, CURTIS DUBOIS

b. 1934 Detroit, Michigan.
Black trombonist. With Dizzy Gillespie, Lester Young, and Gil Evans during 1950s; later led own quartet; toured Europe with Quincy Jones; on South American tour with Coleman Hawkins (1961); with Art Blakey's Jazz Messengers (1961-65).

FULLER, JESSE ("LONE CAT")

b. 1896 Jonesboro, Georgia.
Singer, guitarist, and songwriter. Raised by a family named Wilson in Macedonia, Georgia, but ran away when he was only ten, and later worked in a chair factory in Brunswick, Georgia; wrote "San Francisco Bay Blues" (1954), "Drop Out Song" (1964); his LP records are *Jesse Fuller Working on the Railroad, Frisco Bound with Jesse Fuller, Jesse Fuller the Lone Cat, San Francisco Bay Blues* and *Jesse Fuller's Favorites.*

FULLER, OSCAR ANDERSON

b. 1904 Marshall, Texas.
Black singer and composer. Studied at Iowa State, Ames, Iowa (doctorate, 1942); first Negro to earn Ph.D. in music in U.S.; taught at North Carolina A&T College, Greensboro, Prairie View A&M, Texas, and Lincoln University, Jefferson City, Missouri after 1942.

FULLER, WALTER GILBERT (GIL)

b. 1920 Los Angeles, California.
Black bandleader and composer. Graduated in engineering; arranger for Les Hite (1940-42); in army during World War II; wrote for Woody Herman, Charlie Barnet, Count Basie and others; wrote music for Dizzy Gillespie and Neophonic Orchestra, conducted by Stan Kenton (1965); leader of house orchestra at Monterey Jazz Festival (1965); wrote "Things to Come."

FULLER, WALTER ("ROSETTA")

b. 1910 Dyersburg, Tennessee.
Black trumpeter. Played in Earl Hines' orchestra; later formed his own group (1941); led his own combo in San Diego, California after 1946.

FULSOM (FULSON), LOWELL

b. 1921 Oklahoma.
Black singer. Father was part Indian; went to Texas in his teens; accompanied Texas Alexander, blues singer; served in the navy in World War II; went to Oakland, California; his accompanists were Jay McShann (pianist) and Lloyd Glenn; top records were "Blue Shadows" (1951), "Old Time Shuffle," and "Every Day I Have the Blues"; albums—*Lowell Fulsom, Now; Soul; The Tramp.*

FUNICELLO, ANNETTE

b. 1942 Utica, New York.
Singer, dancer, and actress. Known as "Annette"; sang in numerous Walt Disney film productions; also on Disney's "Golden Horseshoe Revue" TV series and a member of his Mouseketeers on TV.

FURNESS, WILLIAM HENRY

b. 1802 Boston, Massachusetts, d. 1896.
Hymnist. Graduated Harvard (1820); Unitarian pastor in Philadelphia after 1825; several of his hymns appeared in Samuel Longfellow and Samuel Johnson's *Book of Hymns* (1846) and their *Hymns of the Spirit* (1864).

FURSCH-MADI, EMMY

b. 1847 Bayonne, France, d. 1894 Warrenville, New Jersey. Opera singer. She studied at the Paris Conservatory; debut in Paris; came to America (1874) and sang with the New Orleans French Opera Company; at Covent Garden, London (1879-81); sang in New York until her death.

FURST, WILLIAM WALLACE

b. 1852 Baltimore, Maryland, d. 1917.
Popular composer. Became musical director of the Tivoli Theatre, San Francisco (1884); composed the music for several comic operas; arranged the music "Love Makes the World Go 'Round" (1896, w. Clyde Fitch) from *Bohemia;* also composed "My Geraldine" (1880), "Babbie Waltzes" (1897); wrote *The Isle of Champagne,* early American operetta (1892), with lyrics by Charles A. Byrne.

GABRILOWITSCH, OSSIP SALOMONOWITSCH

b. 1878 St. Petersburg, Russia, d. 1936 Detroit, Michigan. Noted conductor. Studied with Anton Rubinstein and was a piano soloist in Berlin (1896); became conductor of the Detroit Symphony Orchestra (1918); married Clara Clemens, the daughter of Mark Twain.

GABURO, KENNETH

b. 1926 Somerville, New Jersey.
Composer. Studied at Eastman School of Music, Rochester, N.Y. (M.M.); wrote *Three Interludes for String Orchestra* (1949), *On a Quiet Theme* (1951), *Antiphony I* for three string groups and tape (1957), *Shapes and Sounds* for full orchestra (1960), *The Snow Queen* (1952, opera), *The Widow* (1959, one-act opera).

GAINES, SAMUEL RICHARDS

b. 1869 Saginaw, Michigan, d. 1945 Boston, Massachusetts. Organist, conductor, and composer. Wrote *The Mother-Heart.*

GALAJIKIAN, FLORENCE GRANDLAND

b. 1900 Maywood, Illinois.
Pianist and composer. Studied piano at age six; graduated Northwestern University School of Music and Chicago Musical College; taught at Chicago Conservatory of Music; her *Symphonic Intermezzo* won the National Broadcasting Company's orchestral award (1932); *Tragic Overture* (1934).

GALBRAITH, JOSEPH BARRY

b. 1919 Pittsburgh, Pennsylvania.
Guitarist. With Claude Thornhill during 1940s; later studio musician in New York City.

GALES, LAWRENCE BERNARD (LARRY)

b. 1936 New York City.
Bass player. Studied at Manhattan School of Music, (1956); played with J.C. Heard, Herbie Mann, Junior Mance, Thelonious Monk and others during 1960s.

GALLAUDET, THOMAS HOPKINS

b. 1787 Philadelphia, Pennsylvania, d. 1851. Hymnist. Graduated Yale (1805); established an institute for deaf-mutes in Hartford, Conn. (1814), superintendent there (1817-30); then chaplain of the Insane Asylum, Hartford (1838-51); wrote "Jesus, in Sickness and Pain" (*Connecticut Congregational Psalms and Hymns,* 1845).

GALLI-CURCI, AMELITA

b. 1882 Milan, Italy, d. 1963.
Noted coloratura soprano. Studied piano, harmony, and composition at the Royal Conservatory in Milan; won first prize (1903); taught herself singing by recording her voice on phonograph records; debut in Rome (1909) as Gilda; toured Europe and South America (1910-15); debut in Chicago (1916) as Gilda; at Metropolitan Opera in New York (1920) as Violetta; married Luigi Curci, Marchese de Simeri in Rome (1910); divorced (1920) and married her accompanist pianist Homer Samuels (1921); retired from the Metropolitan (1930).

GALLION, ROBERT H. (BOB)

b. 1922 Ashland, Kentucky.
Singer and songwriter. Wrote "I Miss You," "Love Pains," "Your Wild Life's Gonna Get You Down," "Him and Her," "Sweethearts Again," "Baby, Love Me."

GALLOP, SAMMY

b. 1915 Duluth, Minnesota, d. 1971 Van Nuys, Califorina. Lyricist. As a young man he went to New York City and wrote songs for various musicals; wrote the lyrics "There Must Be a Way," "Wake the Town and Tell the People," "Elmer's Tune," "Holiday for Strings," "Maybe You'll Be There," "Somewhere Along the Way," "Autumn Serenade," "Shoofly Pie and Apple Pan Dowdy," "Forgive My Heart" and many others; lived in retirement in Encino, Calif., but was hospitalized in Van Nuys, where he hanged himself.

GALLOWAY, CHARLES ("HAPPY")

b. ca. 1865, d. 1914.
Black guitarist.

GALSTON, GOTTFRIED

b. 1879 Vienna, Austria, d. 1950 St. Louis, Missouri. Pianist. Studied at the Vienna Conservatory; toured Australia and the United States (1913-14); taught at the Stern Conservatory, Berlin; toured Europe; wrote *Studienbuch.*

GANNETT, WILLIAM CHANNING

b. 1840 Boston, Massachusetts, d. 1923 New York City. Hymnist and compiler. Educated at Harvard and the Divinity School; became pastor of the Unitarian Church in Rochester, N.Y. (1889); wrote the lyrics "Sleep My Little Jesus" (m. Adam Geibel), "The Lord Is in His Holy Place" (1875, tune "Old 44th," 1558—unknown); with F.L. Hosmer and J.V. Blake published *Unity Hymns and Carols* (1880); with Hosmer published *The Thought of God in Hymns and Poems* (1885).

GANTVOORT, MARY GRETCHEN MORRIS

b. 1894, d. 1971 New York City.
Soprano. Dramatic soprano in concert, oratorio, and opera; soloist with the Cleveland Orchestra; after retirement she lived in Queens, New York; widow of Herman L. Gantvoort.

GANZ, RUDOLPH

b. 1877 Zurich, Switzerland, d. 1972 Chicago, Illinois. Pianist, conductor, and teacher. Debut as cellist at age ten and as pianist at age twelve; studied in Switzerland and Germany; mature debut with Berlin Philharmonic Orchestra (1899); with same orchestra conducted his own Symphony in E-flat (1900); married Mary Forrest, American concert singer; headed piano department of Chicago Musical College after 1901; conductor of St. Louis Symphony (1921-27); president of the Musical College (1933-54).

GARCIA, JERRY

b. 1941.
Guitarist. Lead guitarist for the Grateful Dead, rock group; while on a hunting trip, as a boy, accidently severed a large portion on his middle finger of his right hand with an ax while chopping wood; an excellent guitar player, plays twice as well to compensate for his missing finger.

GARCIA, MANUEL DEL POPOLO VINCENTE

b. 1775 Seville, Spain, d. 1832.
Tenor and composer. Came to New York City (1825); composed *Ebor Nova* (w. Stedman Whitwell of New Jersey) while aboard ship enroute to America; introduced Italian opera to New York City (1825) with his own company.

GARCIA, RUSSELL (RUSS)

b. 1916 Oakland, California.
Trumpeter, French horn player, and composer. Studio musician in Hollywood during 1950s; wrote for films, TV, etc. in Munich, Germany (1962-64); wrote *Adventure in Emotions* performed and recorded by Los Angeles Neophonic Orchestra (1965), and *Abstract Realities,* performed at Monterey Jazz Festival (1965).

GARDEN, MARY

b. 1877 Aberdeen, Scotland, d. 1967.
Noted soprano. Parents brought her to America when she was a child; debut as Louise at the Opera-Comique (1900); sang for Oscar Hammerstein at the Manhattan Opera House, New York City (1907-10); then she went with the Chicago Opera Company; retired in 1930.

GARDNER, NEWPORT

b. 1746, d. after 1826 Africa.
Black composer and teacher. Studied in Newport, Rhode Island, under Andrew Law; conducted singing school in Newport; wrote *Crooked Shanks* (1803), also an anthem performed at the Boston Concert (1825); left for Africa (1826) as a missionary.

GARDNER, ROBERT ALEXANDER (BOB)

b. 1897 Oliver Springs, Tennessee.
Singer. Attended the Kentucky School for the Blind, Louisville (1915-18); with Mac McFarland and Bob after 1922.

GARDNER, SAMUEL

b. 1891 Elizabethgrad, Russia.
Violinist and composer. Came to America (1912), where he made his debut; toured the states, and was guest conductor for his own compositions with leading orchestras.

GARFUNKEL, ART

b. 1942 New York City.
Singer and instrumentalist. Raised in Queens, N.Y.; graduated Columbia University, New York City; joined with Paul Simon; their albums are *Bookends, Bridge Over Troubled*

Water, The Graduate, Parsley, Sage, Rosemary, and Thyme, Sounds of Silence, Wednesday Morning 3 AM.

GARLAND, EDWARD B. ("MONTUDI")

b. 1895 New Orleans, Louisiana.
Black double bass player. Played in Kid Ory's Band in New Orleans (1911-19); went to Los Angeles (1919) with Kid Ory; was a close friend of Ory and spent most of his time playing in bands with him.

GARLAND, JOSEPH COPELAND

b. 1903 Norfolk, Virginia.
Black tenor saxist. Studied at Aeolian Conservatory in Baltimore; with Lucky Millinder, Don Redman, Louis Armstrong and others.

GARLAND, JUDY

b. 1922 Grand Rapids, Michigan, d. 1969 London, England. Singer and actress. Born Frances Ethel Gumm; at age two was singing on the stage with her two older sisters; Gumm Sisters were a hit in Chicago (1934); appeared in numerous films, including *The Wizard of Oz* (1939); was ill (1950-51), but made a comeback; *A Star Is Born* (1954); ill again (1958-59), but staged another comeback; moved to England with her producer husband, Sid Luft; *I Could Go on Singing* (1963); sang with her daughter, Liza Minnelli (1964).

GARNER, ERROLL LOUIS

b. 1921 Pittsburgh, Pennsylvania.
Black jazz pianist and composer. Developed a unique style of stride-piano playing; played with Georgie Auld and others; noted jazz pianist in 1940s, '50s and '60s; toured Europe (1962, '64 and '66); appeared on "Bell Telephone Hour" and other TV shows; wrote "Misty" and other tunes; albums—*Campus Concert, Concert by the Sea, Erroll Garner, Erroll Garner and Billy Taylor, Greatest Garner, Laura, One More Time, Other Voices;* at the Maisonette, St. Regis-Sheraton Hotel, New York City (1972).

GARNES, SHERMAN

b. 1941.
Black singer. Member of the Teen Agers, vocal group in New York City, first recorded (1956).

GARRISON, JAMES EMORY (JIMMY)

b. 1934 Miami, Florida.
Bass player. Played in Philadelphia; then New York City after 1958; with John Coltrane combo (1961-66); toured Europe.

GARRISON, MABEL

b. 1888 Baltimore, Maryland, d. 1963.
Coloratura soprano. Studied at Peabody Conservatory, Boston; made her debut as Filina in *Mignon*, Boston (1912); sang with the Metropolitan Opera, New York City (1914-20), then toured the Orient; married conductor George Siemonn; introduced eight poems of Archibald MacLeish set to music by Ross Lee Finney (1935); taught singing at Smith College, Northampton, Massachusetts.

GARY, JOHN

b. 1932 Watertown, New York.
Singer. Albums—*Best of John Gary, Catch a Rising Star, Especially for You, John Gary at Carnegie Hall Concert, John Gary on Broadway, Heart Filled with Song, Little Bit of Heaven, One and Only John Gary.*

GASKIN, RODERICK VICTOR (VIC)

b. 1934 Bronx, New York City.
Black bass player. Studied guitar with father; then studied at New York School of Music; served in U.S. Marines; played guitar in San Diego; then played bass in Los Angeles with Paul Horn Quintet; with the Jazz Crusaders, Shelly Manne, Les McCann Trio and others during 1960s.

GATES, ELLEN (HUNTINGTON)

b. 1835 Torrington, Connecticut, d. 1920 New York City. Hymnist. Youngest sister of Collis P. Huntington; wrote the lyrics "Your Mission" (1862, m. S.M. Grannis 1864, "If You Cannot on the Ocean"), the song was sung by Philip Phillips at the meeting of the Christian Commission in the Senate Chamber, Washington, D.C., February, 1865, attended by President Lincoln and Secretary of State William H. Seward, the Commission Chairman; also wrote "Come Home" (m. W.H. Doane), "The Prodigal Child" (1869), "Eternity" (m. P.P. Bliss), "O the Clanging Bells of Time!," "I Will Sing You a Song of That Beautiful Land" (1865, m. Philip Phillips).

GATEWAY SINGERS, THE

Jerome Walter, Elmerlee Thomas, Ernie Sheldon, and Travis Edmondson.

GATTI-CASAZZA, GIULIO

b. 1869 Udine, Italy, d. 1940 Ferrara, Italy.
Director. Director of the Municipal Theatre at Ferra (1894-1898); director at La Scala, Milan (1898-1909); director of the Metropolitan Opera House, New York (1910-35).

GAUL, HARVEY BARTLETT

b. 1881 New York City, d. 1945 Pittsburgh, Pennsylvania. Organist. Organist-choirmaster of Emmanuel Church, Cleveland, Ohio (1900-08); then went to Paris; then from 1910-45 served the Calvary Church, Pittsburgh; taught at Carnegie Institute; composed *Prayer of Thanksgiving* and many other works.

GAUNT, PERCY

b. 1852 Philadelphia, Pennsylvania, d. 1896 Palenville, New York. Popular composer. Became musical director for Charles H. Hoyt (1883) and directed Hoyt's farces; composed the songs "The Bowery" (w. Charles H. Hoyt), "Reuben, Reuben," and "Push dem Clouds Away" which were introduced by Harry Connor in *A Trip to Chinatown* in San Francisco in 1892; during Gaunt's funeral services, a reporter heard an organ grinder outside playing "Push dem Clouds Away."

GAUTHIER, EVA

b. 1886 Ottawa, Canada, d. 1958 New York City. Soprano. Debut in *Carmen*, Pavia, Italy; later came to America and was well known as soloist and recitalist of modern music.

GAY, MARIA

b. 1879 Barcelona, Spain, d. 1943 New York City. Contralto. Debut in *Carmen* in Brussels, Belgium (1902); pupil of Madame Adiny in Paris; sang at Covent Garden, London (1906) as Carmen; with Metropolitan Opera, N.Y. (1908-09), Boston Opera (1910-12), Chicago Opera (1913); married Giovanni Zenatello, tenor.

GAYE, MARVIN

b. 1939.
Black singer. Raised in Washington, D.C. where his father was a preacher; played the guitar; spotted in a black club in Detroit in 1961 by Berry Gordy, mogul behind Motown; first gold record was "Stubborn Kind of Fellow"; married Gordy's sister, Anna; in 1970 his album *What's Going On* and singles "Mercy, Mercy Me" (The Ecology) and "Inner City Blues" sold a combined 4,000,000 records.

GAYNOR, JESSIE LOVEL SMITH

b. 1863, d. 1921.
Composer and writer. She wrote "Thanksgiving Song," "Shepherd of Tender Youth."

GEDDA, NICOLAI

b. 1925 Stockholm, Sweden.
Tenor. Debut in Stockholm; with Paris Opera for three years; later with Metropolitan Opera, New York City; has recorded over forty complete operas; his 100th record was *Massenet's Manon*, recorded with Beverly Sills.

GEHOT, JEAN

b. 1756 Belgium, d. after 1803.
Violinist. Came to America (1792) with James Hewitt and associated with him in New York City; went to Philadelphia (1793); played in the orchestra of Thomas Wignell and Alexander Reinagle at the New Theatre on Chestnut Street, Philadelphia (1793-1803).

GEHRKENS, KARL WILSON

b. 1882 Kelleys Island, Ohio.
Teacher. Graduated Oberlin College, Ohio, later taught there; served as president of the Music Teachers National Association and editor of *School Music*, the association's magazine.

GEIB, ADAM

b. 1780 London, England, d. 1849 New York City. Pianist, composer, publisher, and piano maker. Came to New York City (1797) with his father, John, and brother, George; with his father, built pianos after 1800; John and Adam were music publishers in New York City (1816-21), with son, William (1822-29), Geib and (Darriel) Walker (1829-43), William H. Geib (1844-47); wrote "Governor Tompkins' March of Salute" (1808).

GEIB, GEORGE

b. 1782 London, England, d. 1842.
Pianist, organist, composer, teacher, and publisher. Came to New York City (1797) with his father and brother, Adam; debut in New York City (1811); played in concerts there until 1823; then was organist at St. Matthews Church, New York City; composed *A Grand Waltzer*, for the pianoforte (1816), *How to Choose a Wife* (1807), *Major Ross' March* (1822, piano), *God Save America* (1822).

GEIBEL, ADAM

b. 1855 near Frankfort-au-Main, Germany, d. 1933 Philadelphia, Pennsylvania. Popular composer. Came to America as a child; formed his own company, the Adam Geibel Company, now Hall-Mack Company in Philadelphia; he was blind, but composed music and for many years was organist at the Stetson Mission in Philadelphia; wrote "Joys of Spring" (w. George Cooper), "Elsie Moore" (1883), "The Last Voyage" (1885), "Little Cotton Dolly," "Kentucky Babe" (1896, w. R.H. Buck), "Sleep My Little Jesus" (w. W.C.

Gannett) and "Stand Up, Stand Up for Jesus" (w. George Duffield, 2nd tune—G.J. Webb).

GELLER, HERBERT (HERB)

b. 1928 Los Angeles, California.
Alto saxist. Played with Joe Venuti, Claude Thornhill, and Lucky Millinder during late 1950s; played in Los Angeles (1952-58); later in New York with Benny Goodman and Louis Bellson; then in Berlin, Germany on radio; in Hamburg after 1966.

GEMUNDER, AUGUST MARTIN LUDWIG

b. 1814 Wurtemberg, Germany, d. 1895 New York City. Violin maker. Made very fine violins; started with Vuillaume in Paris; came to America (1847); borrowed $25 to start in business in Boston; sent instruments to London (1851) for the exposition, won first prize; moved to New York City where he continued making violins.

GEMUNDER, GEORGE

b. 1816 Wurtemberg, Germany, d. 1899.
Violin maker. Came to America with his brother, August, and made violins in Boston; after 1852 they operated in New York City.

GENTLEMEN, THE *see* SONNY JAMES

GENTRY, BOBBIE LEE

b. 1942 Chickasaw County, Mississippi.
Singer, guitarist, and songwriter. Born Bobbie Street; she was raised in Greenwood, Miss., and Palm Springs, Calif.; studied at the Los Angeles Conservatory of Music; wrote "Ode to Billie Joe" (1967), "Chickasaw County Child," "Lazy Willie," "Papa Won't Let Me Go into Town with You," and "Tuesday's Child."

GEORGE, GRAHAM

b. 1912 Norwich, England.
Composer. Went to Canada (1928); educated at the University of Toronto, (D.Mus., 1939); served overseas with the Canadian armed forces in World War II; became a teacher at Queens University (1946) and also served as organist-choirmaster at St. James' Church, Kingston, Ontario; composed several anthems and other works including *Variations for Strings* (1943); wrote "If Ye Love Me" (1937), *Benedictus es, Domine* (1940), "Lord of All Power and Might" (1939), "Ride On, Ride On in Majesty" (1941), and "Unto Us a Son Is Born" (1945).

GEORGIA CLODHOPPERS *see* WALLY FOWLER

GEORGIA MINSTRELS (all black group) *see* BILLY KERSANDS

GEORGIA WILDCATS *see* SLIM BRYANT, CLAYTON MC MICHEN

GERARD, RICHARD H.

b. 1876 New York City, d. there 1948.
Composer and lyricist. Educated at Eclectic Medical College and New York College of Dental and Oral Surgery; with American Red Cross overseas; wrote the lyrics for "Sweet Adeline" (1903, m. Henry W. Armstrong).

GERICKE, WILHELM

b. 1845 Gratz, Austria, d. 1925.
Conductor. Director and conductor of the Boston Symphony Orchestra (1884-89 and 1898-1906).

GERLACH, FRED

b. 1925 Detroit, Michigan.
Singer, guitarist, and pianist. Mastered the twelve-string guitar; served in the army in Germany and the Philippines during World War II; then went to New York City where he worked as a draftsman and boogie-woogie pianist; his LP records are *Gallows Pole and Other Folk Songs,* and *Twelve-String Guitar.*

GERSCHEFSKI, EDWIN

b. 1909 Meriden, Connecticut.
Composer. Graduated Yale School of Music, also Tobias Matthay Pianoforte School, London, England; his *Streamline,* symphonic work for band (1936), presented in Chicago, Interlochen, and by U.S. Navy Band at Annapolis, Md.; *Symphony in Style of the Eighteenth Century* presented over NBC (1931) by several orchestras.

GERSHWIN, GEORGE

b. 1898 Brooklyn, New York, d. 1937 Hollywood, California. Noted composer. Took piano lessons with Charles Hambitzer and studied harmony with Rubin Goldmark; song plugger at Remick's, music publishers in New York City; he wrote "Swanee" (1919), *Rhapsody in Blue,* for piano and orchestra (1924), Concerto in F, for piano and orchestra (1925), *Three Preludes* for piano (1926), *An American in Paris,* tone-poem for orchestra (1928), and the opera *Porgy and Bess* (libretto by DuBose Heyward and Ira Gershwin), introduced in Boston in 1935 by Alexander Smallens.

GERSHWIN, IRA

b. 1896 New York City.
Librettist and lyricist. Older brother of George Gershwin. With DuBose Heyward, he

wrote the libretto for *Porgy and Bess* (1935); also wrote "Highland Fling" (m. Harry Warren), "My One and Only" (m. Warren), "Lady in the Dark" (m. Kurt Weill), "Two Little Girls in Blue" (m. V.M. Youmans and Paul Lannin).

GERVILLE-REACHE, JEANNE

b. 1882 Orthez, France, d. 1915 New York City. Contralto. She sang at the Paris Opera Comique after 1900, Manhattan Opera Company, New York (1907-10), Chicago Opera (1911-12), and Grand Opera of Canada (1913-14).

GETZ, STANLEY (STAN)

b. 1927 Philadelphia, Pennsylvania.
Jazz saxophonist and bandleader. Played in the Dick Rogers orchestra at age fifteen; later played with Jack Teagarden, Bob Chester, Stan Kenton, Jimmy Dorsey, Benny Goodman, Randy Brooks, and Herbie Fields; with Woody Herman's Herd (1947-49); toured Europe; lived in Copenhagen, Denmark (1958-61); his album *Jazz Samba* with Charlie Byrd started the bossa-nova craze in the United States; at the Newport Jazz Festival, New York City (1972).

GIANNEO, LUIS

b. 1897 Buenos Aires, Argentina.
Composer. Composed *Obertura para una Comedia Infantil*, for chamber orchestra of winds and percussion (NBC Symphony under Juan Jose Castro in New York City, 1941); *Violin Concerto*.

GIANNINI, DUSOLINA

b. 1902 Philadelphia, Pennsylvania.
Soprano. Studied with Marcella Sembrich; debut in New York concert (1923); toured Europe, then in the title role in *Aïda* at the Metropolitan Opera, New York (1935-36).

GIANNINI, VITTORIO

b. 1903 Philadelphia, Pennsylvania, d. 1966.
Composer. Brother of Dusolina Giannini; pupil of Rubin Goldmark; composed the operas *Lucedia* (Munich, 1934), *The Scarlet Letter;* also *Symphony in Memoriam Theodore Roosevelt*, and songs.

GIBBS, HAROLD BECKET

b. 1868 England, d. 1956.
Organist. Came to America (1903); organist-choirmaster of the Roman Catholic Cathedral, Covington, Kentucky, then in Cincinnati, Ohio; moved to New York City (1918).

GIBBS, TERRY

b. 1924 Brooklyn, New York.
Bandleader. Born Julius Gubenko; played vibes during 1940s and '50s and rated a top performer; leader of his own group recording after 1959; led his band at Monterey Jazz Festival (1961); on Regis Philbin's TV show (1964) and Steve Allen's show in Las Vegas (1965).

GIBSON, DONALD

b. 1928 Shelby, North Carolina.
Singer, guitarist, and songwriter. Started with radio station WNOX, Knoxville, Tennessee; wrote "Sweet Dreams," "Give Myself a Party" (1958), "Blue, Blue Day" (1958), "Oh, Lonesome Me" (1958), "Just One Time" (1960), "I Can't Stop Loving You" (1962), "Day into Night" (1962); LP records include *That Gibson Boy* (1959), *Look Who's Blue* (1960), *Girls, Guitars* (1961), *Some Favorites* (1962), *I Wrote a Song* (1963), *God Walks Hills* (1964), *Blue Million Tears* (1965), *The Best of Don Gibson* (1966), *All My Love* (1967), *King of Country Soul* (1968).

GIBSON, ROBERT (BOB)

b. 1931 New York City.
Singer and guitarist. Appeared on TV in Cleveland, Ohio, at New York's Carnegie Hall, and at folk festivals; his albums and LP records are *Folksongs of Ohio*, *Offbeat Folk Songs*, *I Come to Sing*, *Ski Songs* (1959), *Yes I See* and *Bob Gibson and Bob Camp* (1961), *Where I'm Bound* (1964).

GIDEON, MIRIAM

b. 1906 Greeley, Colorado.
Composer. She studied composition in the school of Roger Sessions; composed *Five Sonnets from Shakespeare*, *The Hound of Heaven* (for voice, oboe and string trio), *Fortunato* (opera), *Adon Olam* (synagogue music), *May the Words of My Mouth*, *Psalm 84*, *How Goodly Are Thy Tents*.

GIGLI, BENIAMINO

b. 1890 Recanati, Italy, d. 1957.
Tenor. Studied at Rome Liceo di Santa Cecilia; debut as Enzo (Rovigo, Italy, 1914); sang in opera houses in Europe and South America; with Metropolitan Opera, New York (1920-34, again in 1939); farewell concert tour (1955).

GILBERT, DAVID

b. 1936 Pennsylvania.
Conductor. Studied at Eastman School, Rochester, N.Y.; studied with Jonel Perlea for three years; assistant conductor of New York Philharmonic (1970); with Endo Akira, co-conductor of American Ballet Theater (1971).

GILBERT, HENRY FRANKLIN BELKNAP

b. 1868 Somerville, Massachusetts, d. 1928 Cambridge, Massachusetts. Composer. Studied at the New England Conservatory, Boston, then under Edward MacDowell; worked as a printer, engraver, and arranger; composed *Americanesque* (1903, symphony), *Dance in the Place Congo* (1906, tone-poem for orchestra, ballet in 1918), *Comedy Overture on Negro Themes* (for orchestra, 1910), *American Dances* (for piano, 1910).

GILBERT, LOUIS WOLFE

b. 1886 Odessa, Russia, d. 1970.
Lyricist. Brought to U.S. when only a year old; vaudeville actor; toured with John L. Sullivan; wrote for Eddie Cantor's radio show; wrote "Lucky Lindy" (1927, m. Abel Baer), "Don't Wake Me Up, Let Me Dream" (1925, m. Abel Baer and Mabel Wayne). (*See also* Anatole Friedland, Lewis F. Muir, Ed Sauter).

GILBERT, WALTER BOND

b. 1829 Exeter, England, d. 1910 Oxford, England. Composer and compiler. Received the B.Mus. from Oxford (1854), D.Mus. from the University of Toronto (1886), and Oxford (1888); came to Boston (1867), where he was an organist, then was organist at Trinity Chapel, New York City (1869-99); composed the tune "Maidstone" (1862), the anthem "A Great Multitude" (1885), the oratorio *St. John* (1857), *The Restoration of Israel* (1859), *Organ Preludes and Fugues* (1880); while in America he published *Hymnal and Canticles of the Protestant Episcopal Church* (1875), and *The Psalter* (1882).

GILBERTO, ASTRUD

b. 1940 Bahia, Brazil.
Singer. Raised in Rio de Janeiro; married singer Joao Gilberto, later divorced; toured with Stan Getz's combo.

GILBERTO, JOAO

b. 1931 Juaseiro, Bahia, Brazil.
Singer and guitarist. Sang with the Garotos da Lua group; popular during 1950s as a bossa nova player; came to New York (1962); recorded with Stan Getz.

GILCHRIST, WILLIAM WALLACE

b. 1846 Jersey City, New Jersey, d. 1916 Easton, Pennsylvania. Composer and compiler. Educated at the University of Pennsylvania, Philadelphia; organist-choirmaster in Episcopal churches in Philadelphia (1873-82), then at the Swedenborgian Church there; after 1882 also taught at the Academy of Music, Philadelphia; composed three oratorios *The Easter Idyll, The Lamb of God* (1909), and *The Christmas Oratorio* (1911); with James A. Moore, he edited *The Hymnal Companion to the Prayer Book* for the Reformed Episcopal Church (1885) and a Presbyterian hymnal (1895, with L.F. Benson); composed several symphonies.

GILDER, RICHARD WATSON

b. 1844 Bordentown, New Jersey, d. 1909 New York City. Hymnist. Served as a soldier in the Civil War; wrote the hymns "To Thee, Eternal Soul, Be Praise" (tune "Worship"—K.P. Harrington), "God of the Strong, God of the Weak" for a memorial service for Dr. J.L.M. Curry, Richmond, Va. (1903, tune "Godwin" by W.G. Blanchard), and "Through Love to Light! O Wonderful the Way" (tune "Finlandia" by Jean Sibelius).

GILES, CHARLES

b. 1783 near Fort Griswold, Connecticut. d. 1867 Syracuse, New York. Hymnist. Became a Baptist minister (1805); wrote "The Fading World Promiscuous Flows" ("Heaven Anticipated"), published in James Gallagher's *New Selection*, Cincinnati, Ohio (1835); from it the hymn "This World Is Poor from Shore to Shore," is taken.

GILFERT, CHARLES

b. 1787 New York City, d. 1829 New York City. Pianist, composer, and publisher. Gave concerts in New York City (1800-05); publisher in New York City after 1806; publisher in Charleston, South Carolina (1813-17); came to New York City for concerts (1812-15); married singer Agnes Holman (1815); manager of Charleston Theatre (1817-25); manager of Bowery Theatre, New York City (1826-29); wrote *The Steerman's Song* (1804, w. T. Moore), *Hibernias Tears* (1816, w. S. Woodworth), *The Minstrel* (1816, w. Woodworth); also the operas *Freedom Ho, The Spanish Patriots* and *The Virgin of the Sun.*

GILFERT, GEORGE

b. ca. 1764, d. ca. 1814.
Harpsichordist and publisher. Opened music

store in New York City (1787); president of Musical Society of City of New York (1789); played in John Street Theatre; music publisher in New York (1795-1814); published "Hymn to the Creator" (1795, w. Rev. Merrick, m. Friedrich Rausch).

GILIBERT, CHARLES

b. 1866 Paris, France, d. 1910 New York City. Baritone. Studied at the Paris Conservatory; sang in Brussels, Belgium; then with the Metropolitan Opera, New York (1900-03), and the Manhattan Opera, New York (1906-10).

GILKYSON, HAMILTON HENRY ("TERRY")

b. ca. 1919 Phoenixville, Pennsylvania.
Singer, guitarist, and songwriter. Studied at the University of Pennsylvania, Philadelphia; during World War II he did a weekly program on folk music for the Armed Forces Radio Service; wrote "The Cry of the Wild Goose"; his albums are *The Solitary Singer* (1950-51), *Golden Minutes of Folk Music, Remember the Alamo* (1961) and *Wild Goose* (1963).

GILLES, HENRI NOEL

b. 1778 Paris, France, d. 1834.
Oboist, guitarist, composer, and teacher. Son of Peter Gilles, Sr. (oboist), and brother of Peter Gilles, Jr. (cellist); studied at Paris Conservatory (1797-99); came to New York City (1815); lived in Baltimore (ca. 1818-30); composed *Soirée donée au Gl. La Fayette*, published by G. Willing, Baltimore.

GILLES, PETER, JR.

b. 1776 Paris, France, d. 1839.
Violoncellist and publisher. Came to America with his father, Peter Gilles, Sr. (oboist) and his brother, Henri Noel Gilles (1815); published music in New York City (1817), and in Philadelphia (1822); one of the twelve directors of the Musical Fund Society; composed *Air with Variations*, presented at the second performance of the First Concert at the Musical Fund Society, Philadelphia (1821).

GILLESPIE, HAVEN

b. 1888 Covington, Kentucky.
Songwriter. Wrote "Santa Claus Is Coming to Town" (m. J. Fred Coots), "Drifting and Dreaming" (m. Egbert van Alstyne), "Honey" (m. Richard A. Whiting).

GILLESPIE, JOHN BIRKS ("DIZZY")

b. 1917 Cheraw, South Carolina.
Black trumpet player and bandleader. First jazz musician to take his band on an overseas tour sponsored by the U.S. Department of State (1956); co-founder with Bird Parker of the "be-bop" movement; recorded with Zutty Singleton in the 1940s; played at the Metropole bar on Seventh Avenue, off Times Square, New York City during the 1950s; at the Newport Jazz Festival, New York City (1972).

GILLETTE, ABRAM DUNN

b. 1807 Cambridge (Washington County), New York, d. 1882. Hymnist. Became a Baptist minister (1807); wrote "Far Off Beyond the Sea, I Love" which appeared in *Hymns for Social Meetings* (1843).

GILLINGHAM, GEORGE

b. 1770 England, d. 1826 Philadelphia, Pennsylvania. Violinist, pianist, conductor, and composer. Came to America before 1792; with Benjamin Carr, conducted the *Battle of Prague* at Oeller's Hotel on Chestnut Street, Philadelphia (1792); leader of the Chestnut Street Theatre until 1818; one of the founders of the Musical Fund Society; teacher of music in New York City (1819-24); father of Miss A. Gillingham, piano teacher in Philadelphia; wrote *Anacreontic Glee* (1820), *The Victory of Trenton* (1812, w. Major William Jackson).

GILLIS, DON

b. 1912 Cameron, Missouri.
Composer. Graduated Texas Christian University, Fort Worth, North Texas Teachers College, Denton (M.Mus.); with Fort Worth radio station, then Chicago network; musical director of NBC Symphony; composed symphonies—*Symphony Five and a Half* (NBC Symphony under Toscanini), *The Panhandle, The Alamo, The Raven, Citizen Tom Paine, To an Unknown Soldier*, all for orchestra; *Music for Tonight; The Crucifixion* (cantata for radio).

GILMAN, CAROLINE HOWARD

b. 1794 Boston, Massachusetts, d. 1888 Washington, D.C. Hymnist. Daughter of Samuel Howard; married Dr. Samuel Gilman (1819); after his death in 1858 she lived in Cambridge, Mass. and later in Tiverton, Long Island, N.Y.; wrote "Is There a Lone and Dreary Hour?" and "We Bless Thee for This Sacred Day" (both appeared in Sewall's *Unitarian Collection*, New York, 1820).

GILMAN, LAWRENCE

b. 1878 Flushing, New York, d. 1939 Franconia, New Hampshire. Music critic. Music critic for *Harper's Weekly* (1901-13), then with the *North American Review*, and the *New York Herald-Tribune* after 1923; composed *A Dream of Youth*, and wrote a number of books on music including a biography of Edward A. MacDowell.

GILMAN, SAMUEL

b. 1790 Gloucester, Massachusetts, d. 1858 Kingston, Massachusett. Lyricist. Graduated Harvard (1811), tutor there (1817-19); Unitarian pastor in Charleston, South Carolina (1819-58); wrote the lyrics "Fair Harvard" (1836) based on the tune "Believe Me if All Those Endearing Young Charms" (Irish tune, 1808). (*See also* S.G. Bulfinch).

GILMORE, JOHN

b. 1931 Summit, Mississippi.
Black tenor saxist. Raised in Chicago; played in Air Force Band as clarinetist (1948-52); toured with Earl Hines and the Harlem Globetrotters; played with Sun Ra during 1950s; with Art Blakey and others during 1960s.

GILMORE, JOSEPH HENRY

b. 1834 Boston, Massachusetts, d. 1918 Rochester, New York. Hymnist. Educated at Brown University, Providence, R.I., and Newton Theological Seminary; his father was the Civil War Governor of New Hampshire; pastor in Baptist churches in Fisherville, N.H. and Rochester, N.Y.; became professor of English literature at Rochester University; wrote the hymn "He Leadeth Me" (1864, m. W.B. Bradbury). Dr. Gilmore enjoyed writing verses. His wife especially liked one poem which she sent to *The Watchman and Reflector.* Three years later he was called upon to preach at the Second Baptist Church in Rochester. After he entered the chapel, he wondered what the choir would sing. He picked up a hymnal, and the book opened at "He Leadeth Me."

GILMORE, PATRICK S.

b. 1829 Ballyar, Galway County, Ireland, d. 1892 St. Louis, Missouri. Popular composer. Came to America via Canada; conducted a band in Salem, Mass. (1848); organized his own band (1859); wrote "Good News from Home" (1854), "Oh Let Me Dream of Former Years" (1855), and the lyrics "Music Fills My Soul with Sadness" (1856, m. J.P. Ordway). He arranged the music "John Brown's Body" and introduced the song to the public at the presentation of colors in Boston on July 18, 1861, by the 12th Massachusetts Regiment. Gilmore and his band enlisted in the 24th Massachusetts Infantry in Boston in September, 1861, and were mustered out August, 1862, at New Bern, North Carolina. While the Union Forces occupied New Orleans in 1863, General Nathaniel Banks appointed Gilmore Bandmaster of the Union Forces in the Department of the Gulf. In 1863 he composed "When Johnny Comes Marching Home," giving credit to Father Louis Lambert, who may have written the lyrics. Gilmore conducted a band festival in New Orleans in 1864. He wrote "Freedom on the Old Plantation" (1866, w. W.D. Smith, Jr.). He organized the National Peace Jubilee in 1869 in Boston (*see* John S. Dwight), the World Peace Jubilee (1872), and the Third World Peace Jubilee (1873). In 1872 he became Bandmaster of the 22nd Regiment of the New York State National Guard, and led the band until his death. He composed two anthems, "Columbia" (1892), and "Ireland to England." He wrote a song, "The Voice of the Departing Soul, or Death at the Door," which was sung at his funeral services. (*See also* Henry K. Oliver).

GILSON, LOTTIE *see* CHARLES B. LAWLOR, JOSEPH W. STERN

GINASTERA, ALBERTO

b. 1916 Buenos Aires, Argentina.
Noted composer. Studied at the Conservatorio Williams and the National Conservatory; his ballet, *Panambi,* with choreographer Margarita Wallmann, was introduced at the Theatro Colon (1940); *Danzas Argentinas,* piano piece (Buenos Aires, 1937); *Canto del Tucuman* (Buenos Aires, 1938); *Malambo* for piano (Montevideo, Uruguay, 1940); ballet *Estancia* (Buenos Aires, 1952); symphony *Sinfonia Portena* (Buenos Aires, 1942); operas *Don Rodrigo* (Theatro Colon, 1964 and New York Opera, 1966), and *Homarzo* (Washington, D.C., 1967), which was banned in Argentina by the president on the grounds it was "obsessed with sex and violence"; married pianist Mercedes de Toro; the Opera Society of Washington produced his "bloodthirsty" *Beatrix Cenci,* conducted by Julius Rudel at the John F. Kennedy Center for the Performing Arts (1971).

GIORNI, AURELIO

b. 1895 Perugia, Italy, d. 1938 Pittsfield, Massachusetts. Pianist and composer. Studied at the St. Cecilia Academy, Rome; made his debut in Rome (1912), toured Europe, and came to America (1914); taught at the Institute of Musical Art, New York, and later in Philadelphia; composed chamber music, orchestral, choral and piano works.

GIORZA, PAOLO

b. 1837 Milan, Italy, d. 1914 Seattle, Washington. Composer and director. Son of

Luigi Giorza, painter; graduated Royal Conservatory at Milan at age seventeen; studied composition with La Croix; taught at the Metropolitan Conservatory of New York; composed music for over fifty ballets which he produced in New York City; wrote solos, duets, trios.

GIRLS OF THE GOLDEN WEST *see* DOLLY and MILLIE GOOD

GITTLESON, FRANK

b. 1896 Philadelphia, Pennsylvania.
Violinist and teacher. Studied in Philadelphia, New York, and Berlin; toured Europe and America (1913); taught at Peabody Conservatory, Baltimore after 1919; first American appearance with Philadelphia Orchestra (1914).

GIUFFRE, JAMES PETER (JIMMY)

b. 1921 Dallas, Texas.
Jazz clarinetist and composer. Popular during 1950s and '60s; toured Europe; formed trio with pianist Paul Bley and Steve Swallow, bass player; later formed a trio with Don Friedman and Barre Phillips which toured Europe (1965); then with bassist Richard Davis and drummer Joe Chambers; wrote *Four Brothers* for Woody Herman, *Composition for Trio and String Orchestra* (New York Chamber Orchestra at Town Hall, New York, 1961), *Hex* (Orchestra USA, 1965); the Jimmy Giuffre Three played at a jazz concert at Town Hall, New York City (1972).

GLADDEN, WASHINGTON

b. 1836 Pottsgrove, Pennsylvania, d. 1918 Columbus, Ohio. Hymnist. Raised in Oswego, N.Y.; educated at Williams College, Williamstown, Mass.; Congregational minister in churches in Brooklyn, N.Y., North Adams and Springfield, Mass., and pastor of the First Congregational Church, Columbus, Ohio (1883-1918); wrote the lyrics "The Mountains, The Mountains!" (1859, a traditional song at Williams College), the lyrics "O Master, Let Me Walk with Thee" (1879, m. H.P. Smith, tune "Maryton"), and "Behold a Sower, from Afar" (1897, m. T.P. Ferris, tune "Weymouth").

GLANVILLE-HICKS, PEGGY

b. 1912 Melbourne, Australia.
Music critic and composer. Studied at Melbourne Conservatory with Fritz Hart, Royal College of Music (1931), then in Vienna and Paris; became U.S. citizen (1948); music critic of *New York Herald-Tribune* (1948-58); wrote *Choral Suite* (1937, based on the poems of John G. Fletcher), *Concertino da Camera* (Amsterdam, 1943), *Letters from Morocco* for voice and chorus (1952), opera *Nausicaa* (Athens, 1961, book Robert Graves' *Homer's Daughter*).

GLASER, CHARLES (CHUCK)

b. 1936 Spaulding, Nebraska.
Singer and guitarist. Joined with his brothers in Tompall and the Glaser Brothers; their albums are *Country Folk, Now Country, This Land, Through the Eyes of Love, Tick, Tick Tick, Tompall and the Glaser Brothers, Wonderful World of the Glaser Brothers.*

GLASER, JAMES (JIM)

b. 1937 Spaulding, Nebraska.
Singer and songwriter. Joined with his brothers in Tompall and the Glaser Brothers; wrote "Thanks a Lot for Trying Anyway," "Sitting in an All Night Cafe"; with his brothers, he wrote "Let Me Down Easy," "A Girl Like You,""She Loves the Love I Give Her."

GLASER, TOMPALL

b. 1933 Spaulding, Nebraska.
Singer and songwriter. With his brothers Charles and James, formed Tompall and the Glaser Brothers, vocal and instrumental trio; he wrote "Stand Beside Me" (recorded by Jimmy Dean), "Streets of Baltimore" (1966, recorded by Bobby Bare), "You're Making a Fool Out of Me" (recorded by Jimmy Newman).

GLAZER, THOMAS

b. 1914 Philadelphia, Pennsylvania.
Singer, string bass, tuba player, and songwriter. Attended City College, New York City; had a show on ABC radio (1945-47); wrote "On Top of Spaghetti," "Skokiaam," "Old Soldiers Never Die," "A Dollar Ain't a Dollar Anymore," "Till We Two Are One," "More," "Ballad for the Babe," "A Worried Man," "Mama Guitar," "Care," "Melody of Love," and "Don't Weep, Don't Mourn, Don't Worry."

GLEASON, FREDERICK GRANT

b. 1848 Middletown, Connecticut, d. 1903 Chicago, Illinois. Music critic and composer. Studied with Dudley Buck, then in Leipzig, Berlin, and London; taught at the Hershey School of Music, Chicago (1877); then music critic of the *Chicago Tribune;* wrote the grand operas *Otho Visconti* and *Montezuma;* a cantata, *The Culprit Fay,* with orchestra, symphonic poems, and symphonic cantatas.

GLENN, EVANS TYREE

b. 1912 Corsicana, Texas, d. 1974.
Black trombonist. Played with Benny Carter, Cab Calloway, Don Redman, and Duke Ellington; formed his own quartet and played in New York City night clubs.

GLOVER, WILLIAM HENRY

b. 1819 London, England, d. 1875 New York City. Violinist, singer, and critic. Sang in opera.

GLUCK, ALMA

b. 1884 Bucharest, Rumania, d. 1938 New York City. Noted soprano. Born Reba Fierson; sang with Metropolitan Opera, New York City; second husband was Efrem Zimbalist, the violinist; third husband was Max Pallenberg, famous comedian, who was killed in a plane crash (1934); early successful Victor record was Louise Homer and Alma singing "Whispering Hope" (m. Septimus Winner); her daughter, Marcia Davenport, wrote *Of Lena Geyer* (1936), the story of an opera singer.

GLYNN, FRANKLIN

b. 1885 Rudstone, England.
Composer. Served with the Royal Air Force for four years during World War I; emigrated to Canada (1922), then to the United States (1925), where he was an organist-choirmaster in Worcester, Mass., and Memphis, Tenn., then after 1937 at St. John's Church, Roanoke, Virginia; composed the tunes "Scarborough" (1941, "The Great Creator of the Worlds" w. F.B. Tucker), "Maxon" (1941, "Sing, Men and Angels, Sing," w. John Masefield) and "Woking" (1941, "O Sometimes Gleams Upon Our Sight" w. J.G. Whittier).

GOBEL, GEORGE LESLIE

b. 1919 Chicago, Illinois.
Singer and comedian. Started singing on radio station WLS in the children's choir of the Chicago Episcopal Church (1931); sang as "The Little Cowboy" on WLS "National Barn Dance" (1932-40), when he left to serve in the air force during World War II; became a comedian and had his own TV shows starting in 1954 on NBC and CBS.

GODFREY, ARTHUR

b. 1903 New York City.
Producer and announcer. Famous as an announcer on CBS radio; later produced "The Arthur Godfrey Show," which started numerous artists on the road to stardom, including Pat Boone.

GODOWSKY, LEOPOLD

b. 1870 Vilna, Lithuania, d. 1938 New York City. Concert pianist. Studied in Berlin, then came to the United States and was giving concerts when only fourteen years old; wrote *The Progressive Series of Piano Lessons* and fifty-three studies on Chopin's Etudes; composed *Java* (piano suite), Sonata in E Minor for piano, and numerous other piano suites.

GOEPFART, CHRISTIAN H.

b. 1835 Weimar, Germany, d. 1890 Baltimore, Maryland. Organist and composer.

GOEPP, PHILIP HENRY

b. 1864 New York City, d. 1936 Philadelphia, Pennsylvania. Composer and teacher. Graduated Harvard University; studied composition with Paine; wrote program notes for the Philadelphia Orchestra after 1900; professor of theory at Temple University, Philadelphia; composed chamber music, orchestral and choral works, and songs.

GOETSCHIUS, PERCY

b. 1853 Paterson, New Jersey, d. 1943 New York City. Organist and teacher. Studied at the Stuttgart Conservatory, then taught there; professor at Syracuse (N.Y.) University (1890-92), New England Conservatory, Boston (1892-96), at the Institute of Musical Art, New York City (1905-25); composed songs and piano pieces.

GOETZ, E. RAY

b. 1886 Buffalo, New York, d. 1954 Greenwich, Connecticut. Producer and lyricist. With Sam M. Lewis and Edgar Leslie, wrote "For Me and My Gal" (1917, m. George W. Meyer); produced *Paris* (1928, m. Cole Porter), *Fifty Million Frenchmen* (1929, m. Porter).

GOGGIN, DAN

b. 1934.
Composer and tenor. Raised in Alma, Michigan; studied at Manhattan School of Music (1962), left for a singing part in *Luther* on Broadway, New York City (1963); with Marvin Solley wrote the music for the musical *Hark!* (lyrics Bob Lorick) at the Mercer Arts Center, New York City (1972).

GOLDBECK, ROBERT

b. 1839 Potsdam, Germany, d. 1908 St. Louis, Missouri. Conductor and teacher. Taught in New York (1857-67); founded a conservatory in Chicago (1868), director of same to 1873;

then conducted the St. Louis Harmonic Society.

GOLDBERG, RICHARD (RICHIE)

b. 1928 New Orleans, Louisiana.
Drummer. With Amos Milburn, Lightnin' Hopkins, and Eddie Vinson in 1940s; with Illinois Jacquet, Dinah Washington, Ray Charles and others in 1950s; played in Los Angeles; then with his wife, alto saxist Vi Redd, in San Francisco after 1965; co-led quartet there.

GOLDBERG, SZYMON

b. 1909 Wlokawek, Poland.
Concert violinist. Became concertmaster of the Berlin Philharmonic after Tossy Spivakowsky, but with the rise of Hitlerism, he was forced to flee Germany; debut as a solo violinist in New York City (1938), then toured the world; interned by the Japanese when he was caught in the Netherlands East Indies, but when the war ended he returned to New York City; conductor and violinist at Mostly Mozart and Bach Festival, New York City (1972).

GOLDEN WEST COWBOYS *see* REM WALL

GOLDFADEN, ABRAHAM

b. 1840 Konstantinovka, Russia,d. 1908 New York City. Composer. Founded a Yiddish theater in Iasi, Romania (1877); toured Eastern Europe, then came to New York City where he established a Yiddish theater (1882); composed the scores for the operettas *Di Zoiberin* and *Sulamith* (w. Henry Russotto); his theater was very successful.

GOLDKETTE, JEAN

b. 1899 Valenciennes, France, d. 1962 Santa Barbara, California. Pianist and bandleader. Played with McKinney's Cotton Pickers and Casa Loma; led his own band in Detroit after the late 1920s; also recorded in New York City with Bix Beiderbecke and other musicians; died of a heart attack.

GOLDMAN, EDWIN FRANKO

b. 1878 Louisville, Kentucky, d. 1956 New York City. Composer of marches. His mother had been a child prodigy pianist and his uncles Sam and Nathan Franko were violinists and conductors; studied at the National Conservatory, New York City; became a cornet player with the Metropolitan Opera (1895); founded and conducted his first band (1911); wrote "On the Mall," "Children's March," "On the Farm," "Central Park," "Emblem of Freedom," "Young America," "On the Campus," "On Parade," "Sunapee," "Indian March."

GOLDMARK, RUBIN

b. 1872 New York City, d. there 1936.
Composer and teacher. Studied in Vienna, then with Antonin Dvořák in New York City; taught at the Juilliard School, New York City; known for his *Requiem* inspired by Lincoln's *Gettysburg Address, Samson* a symphonic poem, and the *Negro Rhapsody;* one of his students was George Gershwin.

GOLDOVSKY, BORIS

b. 1908 Moscow, Russia.
Teacher. Son of Lea Luboshutz, the violinist; studied at the Moscow Conservatory, in Berlin, the Liszt Academy in Budapest, and at the Curtis Institute in Philadelphia; later he headed the opera department of the Cleveland Institute of Music, then became director of the opera school of the New England Academy in Boston; founded The New England Opera Company (1946).

GOLDSWORTHY, WILLIAM A.

b. 1878 Cornwall, England, d. (?).
Composer. Came to America (1888) but returned to England to study; organist-choirmaster in churches in Kingston, N.Y., St. Andrew's, N.Y. City (1912-26), then St. Mark's-in-the-Bouwerie (1926-46); composed the tune "Bouwerie" (1941, "The Great Creator of the Worlds," w. F.B. Tucker, "I Know Not How That Bethlehem's Babe,"w. H.W. Farrington); also composed the oratorio *The Vision in the Wilderness.*

GOLSCHMANN, VLADIMIR

b. 1893 Paris, France, d. 1972.
Conductor. Trained as a violinist; came to America as musical director of the Diaghilev Ballet; became conductor of the St. Louis Symphonic Orchestra (1931).

GOLSON, BENNY

b. 1929 Philadelphia, Pennsylvania.
Black tenor saxist and composer. Co-leader with Art Farmer of the Jazztet (1960-63); conducted international band and recorded *Stockholm Sojourn* (1964); in Europe (1964-66) on writing assignments; wrote "I Remember Clifford," "Whisper Not," "Little Karin," "Are You Real," "Just by Myself."

GOMEZ, EDGAR (EDDIE)

b. 1944 Santurce, Puerto Rico.
Bass player. Member of Marshall Brown's Newport Youth Band (1959-61); studied at

Juilliard; with Rufus Jones, Marian McPartland, Paul Bley, Gary McDonald and others during 1960s.

GONEKE, JOHN F.

b. ca. 1790, d. ca. 1844.
Pianist and composer. Resided in Raleigh, North Carolina (1813-26), in Columbia, Tennessee (about 1831), Athens, Georgia (about 1841); wrote "General Calvin Jones' Grand March" (1812), "Governor Miller's Grand March" (1814).

GONSALVES, PAUL

b. 1920 Boston, Massachusetts, d. 1974.
Jazz saxophonist. Played tenor sax with Count Basie and Dizzy Gillespie during 1940s; with Duke Ellington after 1950.

GONZALES, GUILLERMO JOSE

b. 1892 Mexico, d. 1971 Cordoba, Mexico.
Cellist. Studied at age three under his parents, both musicians; then at Conservatoria Nacional de Musica de Mexico; a founder of the Victor Talking Machines Company (later RCA-Victor); married Luz Pinental, soprano; they made many records for Victor; joined San Carlo Opera Company, later Metropolitan Opera, New York City; retired in 1955 to teach and translate Spanish classics.

GOOD, DOLLY

b. 1915 Muleshoe, Texas, d. 1967.
Singer. Born Dorothy Laverne Goad; attended school in Mt. Vernon, Illinois; sang with her sister Millie as Girls of the Golden West; died of a heart attack.

GOOD, MILLIE

b. 1913 Muleshoe, Texas.
Singer. Born Mildred Fern Goad; sang with her sister Dolly as Girls of the Golden West; resided in Cincinnati, Ohio.

GOODALE, EZEKIEL

b. 1780 West Boylston, Massachusetts, d. (?).
Printer. In 1802 he moved to Hallowell, Maine, opened a bookstore, then a printing shop in 1813; in 1817 he printed *The Hallowell Collection of Sacred Music* which was the product of the Handel and Haydn Society of Maine. (*See* Supply Belcher)

GOODE, JACK

b. 1908 Columbus, Ohio, d. 1971 New York City. Musical comedy performer. Born Irwin Thomas Whittridge; made his debut in *Of Thee I Sing* (1933); appeared in over ninety musicals; spent two years in the army in World War II, mostly overseas, and was discharged with an arthritic condition; with Lt. Governor George D. Nye of Ohio, another sufferer, he served as a guinea pig for an experimental serum; he recovered, and appeared opposite Ethel Merman in *Hello Dolly!* in New York.

GOODING, CYNTHIA

b. 1924 Rochester, Minnesota.
Singer and guitarist. Attended private schools in Cleveland, Ohio, Lake Forest, Ill., and Branksome Hall, Toronto, Ontario, Canada; first appeared on radio station XEW, Mexico City, Mexico (1945) and later on WNYC, New York City; her LP records are *Faithful Lovers and Other Phenomena, Italian Folk Songs, Mexican Folk Songs, Turkish, Spanish and Mexican Folk Songs, Queen of Hearts* (early English folk songs), and *A Young Man and a Maid* (with Theodore Bikel).

GOODMAN, ALFRED (AL)

b. 1890 Nikopol, Russia, d. 1972 New York City. Conductor, pianist, and composer. His father, a cantor, smuggled five-year-old Alfred out of Russia; studied at Peabody Conservatory, Baltimore; with Earl Carrol, wrote the score and book for *So Long Letty* (1916); Al conducted the show; also conducted for Al Jolson's shows; made many records, principally for motion picture themes, for RCA Victor.

GOODMAN, BENJAMIN DAVID (BENNY)

b. 1909 Chicago, Illinois.
Noted clarinetist and bandleader. Learned to play the clarinet at Hull-House, Chicago; joined Ben Pollack's band at age sixteen; formed his own band (1934); using Fletcher Henderson arrangements and playing his clarinet before his band, became nationally famous in 1935, known as the "King of Swing"; appeared on "Bell Telephone Hour" (1962); on "Vibrations," TV Channel 13 in 1972.

GOODRICH, ALFRED JOHN

b. 1847 Chile, Ohio, d. 1920 Paris, France.
Teacher and writer. Pupil of his father; taught at the Grand Conservatory, N.Y. (1876), Fort Wayne (Indiana) Conservatory, with the vocal department of Beethoven Conservatory, St. Louis, and Martha Washington College, Virginia; wrote *Complete Musical Analysis* (1889), *Analytical Harmony* (1894), *Theory of Interpretation* (1898), and *Counterpoint*.

GOODRICH, EBENEZER

b. ca. 1780 Templeton, Massachusetts, d. 1841. Clarinetist, violinist, teacher, organ and piano maker. Brother of William M. Goodrich; took over his brother's organ manufacturing business in Templeton, Mass. in 1833; later went into business with Thomas Appleton.

GOODRICH, JOHN WALLACE

b. 1871 Newton, Massachusetts, d. 1952 Boston, Massachusetts. Organist. Organist in Baptist and Congregational churches in Newton (1886-94), then studied in Munich and Paris; taught at the New England Conservatory of Music, Boston, and became its director (1930-42); also organist-choirmaster at Episcopal churches in Boston (1901-09); in 1902 he founded the Choral Art Society of Boston; conductor of the Cecilia Society (1907-10).

GOODRICH (GOODRIDGE), WILLIAM MARCELLUS

b. 1777 Templeton, Massachusetts, d. 1833 Boston, Massachusetts. Organ maker. He made organs which sold throughout the United States from 1805 until his death in 1833; his brother, Ebenezer Goodrich, succeeded him in business.

GOODWIN, J. CHEEVER

b. 1856 Boston, Massachusetts, d. 1912 New York City. Lyricist and librettist. Wrote the lyrics "Love Will Find a Way" (1890, m. Woolson Morse), and "When Reuben Comes to Town"; wrote the librettos for over forty musical comedies, including *Evangeline* (1874).

GOODWIN, WILLIAM R. (BILL)

b. 1942 Los Angeles, California.
Drummer. Son of an actor; studied piano at age five; played drums with Charles Lloyd, Mike Melvoin, Bud Shank, Art Pepper, Paul Horn and others during 1960s.

GORDON, ADONIRAM JUDSON

b. 1836 New Hampton, New Hampshire, d. 1895 Boston, Massachusetts. Composer. Educated at Brown University, Providence, R.I. and Newton Theological Seminary; pastor of the Baptist Church, Jamaica Plains, Mass., then the Clarendon Street Baptist Church, Boston; composed the tune "Gordon" ("Lord Jesus, I Love Thee," w. William Ralf Featherstone, 1842-78, a Canadian), and the words and music "Good Morning in Glory" and "O Holy Ghost Arise"; all of these hymns were included in his compilation *Coronation Hymnal.*

GORDON, DEXTER

b. 1923 Los Angeles, California.
Black tenor saxist. Played in Billy Eckstine's band and other bands in 1940s; led his own combo in 1950s; resided in Copenhagen, Denmark (1962-65); toured Europe and appeared at jazz festivals; at the Newport Jazz Festival, New York City (1972).

GORDON, GEORGE ANGIER

b. 1853 Oyne, Aberdeenshire, Scotland, d. 1929 Boston, Massachusetts. Hymnist. Came to America (1871); educated at the Congregational Theological Seminary at Bangor, Maine, and Harvard University; pastor of Old South Church, Boston, for forty-three years; wrote the hymn "O Will of God Beneath Our Life" (1915, tune "St. Magnus" by Jeremiah Clark).

GORDON, JOSEPH HENRY (JOE)

b. 1928 Boston, Massachusetts, d. 1963 Santa Monica, California. Trumpeter. With Charlie Parker, Dizzy Gillespie, Lionel Hampton, and Herb Pomeroy in 1950s; then with the Shelly Manne Quintet (1958-60); died after being severely burned in a fire.

GORDON, MACK

b. 1904 Warsaw, Poland, d. 1959 New York City. Lyricist. Brought to America as a child; attended school in Brooklyn and the Bronx, New York City; vaudeville actor and singer; wrote lyrics for Harry Revel—"Did You Ever See a Dream Walking?"; with Harry Warren—"Down Argentine Way," "Chattanooga Choo Choo," "Springtime in the Rockies" (1942), "You'll Never Know" (Oscar award, 1943); also wrote lyrics for James V. Monaco, Alfred Newman and Vincent M. Youmans.

GORE, CHARLIE MANSFIELD

b. 1930 Chapmanville, West Virginia.
Singer and songwriter. Wrote "Daddy-O," (1956, won Writer's Award) "Do You, Don't You," "I'm Gonna Tell You Something," "If God Can Forgive You," "Baby-O"; resided in Logan, West Virginia.

GORE, LESLEY

b. 1946 Tenafly, New Jersey.
Singer. Albums—*I'll Cry If I Want To* (1963), *Girl Talk, Golden Hits of Lesley Gore, Sound of Young Love.*

GORME, EYDIE

b. 1931 Bronx, New York City.
Singer. Attended City College of New York; sang with Ken Greenglass' band; with Tommy Tucker; with Tex Beneke, successor to Glenn Miller; on "Steve Allen's Tonight Show" (1953); at the Copacabana, New York City (1956); at the Palace Theatre, N.Y., on the Jerry Lewis show (1957); married singer Steve Lawrence (1957); appeared with Steve at the Eden Roc, Miami; at the Sands and Sahara, Las Vegas, and Cocoanut Grove, Los Angeles.

GORNEY, JAY

b. 1896 Bialystok, Russia.
Popular composer. His family fled Russia to escape the pogrom of 1906 and emigrated to Detroit, Michigan; studied law at the University of Michigan, Ann Arbor, and also music there; wrote the scores for *Top Hole* (1924), *Merry Go Round* (1927), *The Sketch Book* (1929), *Earl Carroll Vanities* (1930), *Americana* (1932), *Meet the People* (1939); E.Y. Harburg wrote the lyrics for many of his songs.

GORNO, ALBINO

b. 1859 Cassalmorano, Italy, d. 1944 Cincinnati, Ohio. Pianist, teacher, and composer. Studied at the Milan Conservatory; accompanied Adelina Patti on her American tour (1881-82), then taught at the Cincinnati (Ohio) Conservatory of Music; composed the cantata *Garibaldi*, an opera, and other works.

GOSPEL SINGING CARAVAN *see* JAMES E. JONES

GOTTLIEB, LOUIS

b. 1923 Los Angeles, California.
Bassist. Member of the "Gateway Singers" (1955); Ph.D. in Musicology at the University of California at Los Angeles (1958); with Alex Hassilev and Glenn Yarbrough formed "The Limeliters" (1959) in Hollywood; LP records are *The Limeliters* (1960); *Tonight in Person, Slightly Fabulous* (1961); *Sing Out, Children's Eyes, Folk Matinee* (1962); *Our Men in San Francisco, Makin' a Joyful Noise, 14K Folk Songs* (1963); *Best of the Limeliters* (1964).

GOTTSCHALK, L. GASTON

b. 1847 New Orleans, Louisiana, d. after 1889. Singer and teacher. Brother of Lcuis M. Gottschalk, composer; studied with Ronconi and Rizzo, then with Francesco Lamperti in Italy; debut at Theatre Della Concordia in Cremona; played five years in Genoa; later accompanist for Minne Hauk, Kellogg and Brignoli on their American tours; at Covent Garden, London; in St. Petersburg, Russia; accompanied with Saint Saëns and Gounod at soirées in Paris; taught at Chicago Musical College (1886-89).

GOTTSCHALK, LOUIS MOREAU

b. 1829 New Orleans, Louisiana, d. 1869 Rio de Janeiro, Brazil. Famous composer. At the age of eight he gave a concert in New Orleans, and entered the Paris Conservatory at thirteen; composed *Bananier and Bamboula* when he was only fifteen; composed *Le Banjo, La Morte, Radreuse, Tarantella, Tremole Etude, The Last Hope*, and the tune "Mercy" used for "Softly Now the Light of Day" (w. G.W. Doane) and "Holy Spirit, Truth Divine" (w. Samuel Longfellow).

GOULD, HANNAH FLAGG

b. 1792 Lancaster, Vermont, d. 1865.
Hymnist. She moved to Newburyport, Mass. as a child; wrote "O Thou Who Hast Spread Out the Skies" (1832, "For Use at Sea"), "O Father to the Fields That Are Ripe" ("Harvest"), and "Who, When Darkness Gathered O'er Us" (1841, "God Save the Queen").

GOULD, JOHN EDGAR

b. 1822 Bangor, Maine, d. 1875 Algiers, Africa. Composer. Piano dealer with the firm of Gould and Fischer, Philadelphia; composed the tunes "Pilot" ("Jesus, Saviour, Pilot Me," w. Edward Hopper, 1871), "Bera" used for "Behold! A Stranger at the Door" (1849, w. Joseph Grigg) and "O Thou, to Whose All-Searching Sight" (w. Nicolaus L. Zinzendorf, translated by John Wesley); arranged "Spohr" by Louis Spohr for "Another Six Days' Work Is Done" (w. Joseph Stennett); also composed the music for "Calm on the Listening Ear of Night" (w. E.H. Sears); with Edward S. White he compiled *The Modern Harp* (1846), and *Harmonia Sacra* (1851).

GOULD, MORTON

b. 1913 Richmond Hill, New York.
Noted composer. Studied at the Institute of Musical Art and at New York University; staff pianist for Radio City Music Hall; composed *Chorale and Fugue in Jazz* (1932) played by the Philadelphia Orchestra under Stokowski, *Spirituals* for string, choir and orchestra (1942), *Interplay* (American Concertette) for piano and orchestra (1943), *Fall River Legend*, ballet (1947), *Philharmonic Waltzes* for orchestra (1947), and Symphony no. 3 (1947).

GOULD, NATHANIEL DUREN

b. 1781 Chelmsford, Massachusetts, d. 1864 Boston, Massachusetts. Teacher and writer. Music teacher in Reading, Mass.; wrote the first *History of Church Music in America*, Boston (1853).

GOULD, WALTER

b. 1875 Philadelphia, Pennsylvania, d. 1955. Black pianist. Had a wooden leg; was known as "One-Leg Shadow"; early ragtime pianist; moved to Albany, N.Y.

GOULET, ROBERT

b. 1933 Lawrence, Massachusetts.
Singer and actor. Family moved to Canada when he was fourteen; disk jockey on station CKCA, Edmonton, Alberta; studied at Royal Conservatory of Music, Toronto, Ontario; on CBC-TV "Showtime"; appeared in *Camelot* (by Lerner and Loewe) in Toronto and New York City (1960); appeared on the "Ed Sullivan Show" and "Gary Moore Show"; married Carol Lawrence.

GOURLEY, JAMES PASCO, JR. (JIMMY)

b. 1926 St. Louis, Missouri.
Guitarist. Played in Chicago during 1940s; lived in Paris (1951-54, then again after 1957); played at Blue Note in Paris with Kenny Clarke; formed his own quartet; later formed trio with Kenny Clarke and organist Lou Bennett.

GOW, GEORGE COLEMAN

b. 1860 Ayer, Massachusetts, d. there 1938. Teacher and composer. Graduated Brown University, Providence, R.I. (1884) and Newton Theological Seminary (1889); taught at Smith College, Northampton, Mass.; then professor of music at Vassar College, Poughkeepsie, N.Y. (1895).

GOWER, JOHN HENRY

b. 1855 Rugby, England, d. 1922 Denver, Colorado. Composer. Graduated Oxford (1876) and received his D.Mus. there (1883); came to Denver (1887) and became organist and choirmaster of the Cathedral of St. John in the Wilderness; wrote *Original Tunes* (1890); composed the tune "Meditation" used for "O God, Unseen Yet Ever Near" (w. Edward Osler) and "There Is a Green Hill Far Away" (w. C.F. Alexander); composed the music for Rudyard Kipling's *Recessional.*

GOZZO, CONRAD JOSEPH

b. 1922 New Britain, Connecticut, d. 1964 Los Angeles, California. Trumpeter. Played with Benny Goodman, Claude Thornhill, Woody Herman, and Boyd Raeburn during 1940s; later with Bob Crosby in Los Angeles on radio; died of a heart attack.

GRAAS, JOHN

b. 1924 Dubuque, Iowa, d. 1962 Van Nuys, California. French horn player and composer. French horn soloist in Los Angeles during 1950s; with Eddie Fisher in Las Vegas, Nevada after 1961; wrote *Jazz Symphony No. 1, Jazz Chaconne No. 1;* died of a heart attack.

GRABLE, BETTY

b. 1916 St. Louis, Missouri, d. 1973.
Singer and actress. She got her start as a vocalist in Ted Fiorito's band during the 1930s; later appeared in many films.

GRADY'S COMMANDERS, EDDIE
(jazz band) *see* LYLE JOSEPH RITZ

GRAF, HERBERT

b. 1903 Vienna, Austria, d. 1973.
Director and writer. Son of Max Graf, the musicologist; stage director at the Frankfurt Opera, then came to America where he joined the Philadelphia Opera Association, and a year later the Metropolitan Opera in New York City; wrote *The Opera and Its Future in America* and *Opera for the People.*

GRAFF, GEORGE, JR.

b. 1886 New York City, d. 1973 East Stroudsburg, Pennsylvania. Lyricist. Wrote the lyrics for songs in *Isle O' Dreams* (1912, m. Ernest R. Ball) sung by Chauncey Olcott; Olcott asked for another song, and Graff wrote "When Irish Eyes Are Smiling" (1912), revival by Irish tenor John McCormack in 1929 made the song an everlasting hit; Graff became an investment counselor; later retired to live in Stroudsburg, Pa. in the Poconos.

GRAFF, JOHANN MICHAEL

b. 1714 Hayna, near Romhied, Schse-Meiningen, d. 1782 Salem, Massachusetts. Hymnist. Moravian minister in Pennsylvania and North Carolina; his hymns appeared in Moravian hymnals.

GRAHAM, ROGER

b. 1885 Providence, Rhode Island, d. 1938 Chicago, Illinois. Lyricist and publisher. Educated at Dental College; founded his own publishing company in New York City; wrote "I Ain't Got Nobody" (1908, m. Spencer Williams).

GRAINGER, PERCY ALDRIDGE

b. 1882 Brighton, Australia, d. 1961 White Plains, New York. Composer and pianist.

Studied in Melbourne and Frankfort; toured Europe after 1900; became a U.S. citizen (1917); taught at New York University until 1934; composed choral pieces, piano and orchestral works based on folk music.

GRAMMER, BILLY

b. 1925 Benton, Illinois.
Singer and guitarist. Started with radio station WARL, Arlington, Virginia (1947) on Connie B. Gay's "Radio Ranch"; joined Jimmy Dean (1955), then went with Grand Ole Opry (1959); his hit records were "Gotta Travel On" (1958), "Kissing Tree," and "Bonaparte's Retreat"; his LP records include *Gospel Guitar Album* and *Billy Grammer Hits* (1964).

GRANADE, JOHN ALEXANDER

b. (?), d. 1807.
Composer. Lived in North Carolina, Kentucky and Tennessee; known as the Western poet who composed the "Pilgrim Songs" (gospel hymns) and also as the "Wild Man of the Woods"; wrote "The Bold Pilgrim," "Apollyon's Lions," and "Sweet Rivers of Redeeming Love"; held a great revival meeting at Desha's Creek in 1799; became a Methodist minister in 1802.

GRAND FUNK RAILROAD (pop band)

Terry Knight, leader; also Mark Farner, Don Brewer, and Mel Schacher; in 1972 Knight filed suit to prevent a new manager and producer taking over.

GRAND OLE OPRY

Variety show on radio station WSM, Nashville, Tennessee. Organized (1925) by George D. Hay as the "WSM Barn Dance"; after 1941 shows were held in the Ryman Auditorium.

GRANELLI, GERALD JOHN (JERRY)

b. 1940 San Francisco, California.
Drummer and pianist. Studied drums with his father and with Joe Morello; with Vince Guaraldi (1962); formed the Jazz Ensemble (1964).

GRANGER, FREDERICK

b. ca. 1795 Germany, d. 1830 Boston, Massachusetts. Clarinetist, violinist, conductor, composer, and teacher. Music teacher in Boston after 1785; leader of the Federal Street Theatre Orchestra there until 1828, succeeded by his son, Thomas Granger; compiled the *Gentlemen's Pocket Companion* (1802); wrote "Massachusetts March" (1812), "The Star of Bethlehem" (1821, w. Henry Kirke White).

GRANNIS, SIDNEY MARTIN

b. 1827 Geneseo, New York, d. after 1884. Singer and composer. Lived in Leroy, N.Y., from 1831 to 1884, when he moved to Los Angeles; wrote the songs "Do They Miss Me at Home," "Only Waiting," "Cling to the Union," and "People Will Talk You Know"; composed the music for "Your Mission" (1864, w. Helen H. Gates).

GRANT, EARL

b. 1933 Oklahoma City, Oklahoma.
Singer, pianist, and organist. Raised in Kansas City, Missouri; graduated University of Southern California in music; studied at Kansas City Conservatory of Music, New Rochelle (N.Y.) Conservatory, and DePaul Conservatory, Chicago; served in U.S. Army; appeared on Ed Sullivan's show; toured Canada, Mexico, Japan, and Australia.

GRANT, MARSHALL GARNETT

b. 1928 Flats, North Carolina.
Singer and guitarist. Member of Johnny Cash's Tennessee Three, with Luther Perkins and W.S. Holland.

GRANT, RUPERT

b. 1914 Trinidad, West Indies, d. 1961 New York City. Calypso singer. Known as "Lord Invader" in Port au Spain, Trinidad; wrote "Rum and Coca-Cola" (1943, m. Lionel Belasco, 1906), later arranged by Jeri Sullavan, Paul Baron and Morey Amsterdam.

GRANT, WILLIAM PARKS

b. 1910 Cleveland, Ohio.
Noted composer. Studied composition and harmony at age fourteen under Davidson in Columbus and organ under Mayer; graduated Capital University in music (1932), M.A. from Ohio State University (1933); later taught in Stephenville, Texas at the agriculture college there; his *Poeme Elegiaque* (1928), *Symphonic Fantasia, Scherzo from the Symphony in D Minor*, presented by the Columbus Symphony Orchestra.

GRANZ, NORMAN

b. 1918 Los Angeles, California.
Impresario. Produced concerts at Los Angeles Philharmonic Auditorium during 1940s; staged jazz shows in the USA and overseas after 1957; sold his Verve Record Company to MGM (1961); arranged for overseas tours for Duke Ellington, Ella Fitzgerald, and Oscar Peterson.

GRASSE, EDWIN

b. 1884 New York City, d. 1954 New York City. Violinist, pianist, and composer. He was blind; studied with Carl Hauser, N.Y., then at the Brussels Conservatory; debut in Berlin (1902) and in New York (1903); gave many concerts in the United States.

GRATEFUL DEAD, THE (blues-rock group)

Jerry Garcia, lead guitar; Phil Lesh, bass; Ron "Pig Pen" McKernan (d. 1973), conga drums and harp; Bob Weir, guitar; Mikey Hart, drums; Bill Kruetzmann, drums; Tom Constanten, organ; started in San Francisco (1966); albums—*Anthem of the Sun, Aoxomoxoa, Grateful Dead, Live/Dead.*

GRAU, MAURICE

b. 1849 Brunn, Austria, d. 1907.
Theatrical and operatic manager. Manager of the Metropolitan Opera, New York City (1898-1903).

GRAUDAN, NICOLAI

b. 1896 Libau, Russia, d. 1964.
Cellist. Cellist with the St. Petersburg State Orchestra and teacher at the Conservatory; also played in Riga, Latvia, Duesseldorf, and the Berlin Philharmonic (1926); with the rise of Nazism, he came to the United States (1935); with his wife, Joanna, a pianist, he played in a number of American cities.

GRAUMAN, MAX

b. 1871, d. 1933.
Composer and compiler. Known as the "American Sulzer"; compiled *Song of Prayer* for Friday evening and *Musical Service* for New Year and Day of Atonement.

GRAUPNER, CATHERINE HILLIER

b. ca. 1777, Charleston, South Carolina, d. 1821. Singer. Wife of J.C. Gottlieb Graupner; sang in the Boston theater (1799).

GRAUPNER, JOHANN CHRISTIAN GOTTLIEB

b. 1767 Verden, Germany, d. 1836 Boston, Massachusetts. Oboist, teacher, and publisher. Arrived in Boston (1796); his wife, a noted singer, sang in the Boston theater (1799); with Francis Mallet and Filippo Trajetta (Traetta), founded the Conservatorio there (1801); organized the Boston Philharmonic Society (1810); helped organize the first Handel and Haydn Society in America in Boston (1815); was in the publishing business there (1803-25).

GRAVES, MILFORD

b. 1941 Jamaica, New York.
Black drummer. Played with New York Arts Quartet at the October Revolution (1964); with Jazz Composer's Orchestra at Town Hall (1964); Newport Jazz Festival (1965); taught at Black Arts Repertory Theater, Harlem, New York City.

GRAY, CLAUDE

b. 1932 Henderson, Texas.
Singer and guitarist. Called "The Tall Texan" (6 feet 5 inches); moved to Nashville, then toured the nation; formed "The Graymen" band (1966); top hits include "Family Bible" (1960), "I'll Just Have a Cup of Coffee, Then I'll Go" (1961), "My Ears Should Burn" (1961, by Roger Miller), "Mean Ole Woman," "I Never Had the One I Wanted," "Night Life" (1968).

GRAY, D. VINCENT

b. 1889 Blunt, South Dakota, d. 1950.
Composer. Studied at Grove City College of Music, Pa., Wooster College, Ohio (1914), and General Theological Seminary (1917); organist in Wooster, Ohio, and Sewickley, Pa.; became rector at St. Clement's Church, Seattle, Washington (1943); composed the tune "Holy Innocents" (1941, "When Christ Was Born in Bethlehem," w. Laurence Housman).

GRAY, GLEN ("SPIKE")

b. 1906 Roanoke, Illinois, d. 1963 Plymouth, Massachusetts. Saxophonist and orchestra leader. Born Glen Gray Knoblaugh; leader of the Casa Loma Orchestra during 1930s and '40s; recorded with various groups after 1956.

GRAY, JOHN W. (JOHNNY)

b. 1924 Vinita, Oklahoma.
Guitarist. Studied in Washington, D.C. (1944); played with Ray McKinley; later staff musician with ABC in Chicago; toured with George Shearing (1962); played with various combos in Hollywood.

GRAY, THOMAS

b. 1803 Roxbury, Massachusetts, d. 1849 Boston, Massachusetts. Hymnist. Graduated Harvard (1823, M.D. 1827); wrote several hymns which appeared in Gray's *Sunday School Collection* (1844).

GRAY, WARDELL

b. 1921 Oklahoma City, Oklahoma, d. 1955 Las Vegas, Nevada. Jazz saxophonist. With

Earl Hines, Benny Carter, Billy Eckstine, Benny Goodman Sextet and others.

GRAY, WILLIAM B.

b. (?), d. 1932.
Popular composer. Under the pseudonym Glenroy, he composed the music for "The Face on the Barroom Floor" (1893, w. Hugh D'Arcy), "She Is More to Be Pitied Than Censured," "The Volunteer Organist" (1893, w. Henry Lamb), "Old Jim's Christmas Hymn," "The Church Across the Way" (1894), "Oh What a Beautiful Ocean" (1897), and "Just When I Need You Most" (1900).

GRAYMEN, THE *see* CLAUDE GRAY

GRAYSON, KATHRYN

b. 1923 Winston-Salem, North Carolina.
Singer and actress. Starred in the film *Anchors Aweigh* (screen play—Isobel Lennart).

GREAT SOCIETY *see* GRACE SLICK AND THE GREAT SOCIETY

GREATOREX, HENRY WELLINGTON

b. 1811 Burton-on-Trent, England, d. 1858 Charleston, South Carolina. Compiler and arranger. In 1839 he came to Hartford, Conn., as organist of the Center Church, then became organist of St. Paul's, New York City (1846), Calvary Church (1851); in 1853 he moved to Charleston, where he died of yellow fever; arranged the tune for "Softly Now the Light of Day" (w. G.W. Doane, 1851); published a *Collection of Sacred Music* (1851), which included many tunes arranged by him.

GRECO, ARMANDO ("BUDDY")

b. 1926 Philadelphia, Pennsylvania.
Singer. His father had a record shop in Philadelphia; Mario Lanza often visited the shop; had a record hit (1952) with "Ooooh, Looka There, Ain't She Pretty," which sold a million and a half copies; wrote "For a Little While She's Mine" (w. Gladys Shelly), about a man's little daughter, recorded by Mike Douglas; sang at the St. Regis Maisonette, New York City (1972).

GREEN, ADOLPH

b. 1915 New York City.
Lyricist and librettist. Attended New York University; with Betty Comden wrote book and lyrics for *On the Town* (1944, m. Leonard Bernstein); with composer Jule Styne, wrote the lyrics for *High Button Shoes* (1947), *Two on the Aisle* (1951), *Peter Pan* (1954), *Bells Are Ringing* (1956, starring Judy Holliday), *Say Darling* (1958), *Wonderful Town* (1952, m. Leonard Bernstein), film song "It's Always Fair Weather" (m. Andre Previn).

GREEN, BENNIE

b. 1923 Chicago, Illinois.
Black trombonist. With 343rd Army Band in World War II; with Earl Hines, Charlie Ventura and others; at the Newport Jazz Festival, New York City (1972).

GREEN, BUD

b. 1897 Austria.
Lyricist. Brought to U.S. as an infant; wrote for Broadway shows; wrote "Away Down South in Heaven" (m. Harry Warren), "Alabamy Bound" (1925, with Buddy De Sylva, m. Ray Henderson), "That's My Weakness Now" (1928, m. Sammy Stept).

GREEN, CHARLIE ("BIG")

b. 1900 Omaha, Nebraska, d. 1935 New York City. Black trombonist. Played in Fletcher Henderson's band; also was accompanist for Bessie Smith.

GREEN, FREDERICK WILLIAM (FREDDIE)

b. 1911 Charleston, South Carolina.
Black guitarist. With Count Basie after 1937.

GREEN, GRANT

b. 1931 St. Louis, Missouri.
Black guitarist. Played with Jimmy Forrest, Jack Murphy, and Sam Lazar in St. Louis; played in New York City after 1960; first recorded in 1960; albums—*Am I Blue; Carryin' On; Feelin' the Spirit; Goin' West; Grantstand; Grant's First Stand; Green Street; His Majesty, King Funk; I Want to Hold Your Hand; Idle Moments; The Latin Bit; Street of Dreams; Sunday Mornin'.*

GREEN, JOHN W. (JOHNNY)

b. 1908 New York City.
Popular composer. Graduated Harvard; composed "I'm Yours" (w. E.Y. Harburg), "Body and Soul" (w. Edward Heyman and Robert Sour), "I Cover the Waterfront" (w. Heyman), "I Wanna Be Loved" (w. Heyman and Billy Rose); became conductor of the Promenade Concerts of the Los Angeles Philharmonic (1958); wrote *Night Club: Six Impressions* (for three pianos and orchestra); conductor at the Salute to Richard Rodgers at the Imperial Theater, New York City (March, 1972).

GREEN MINSTRELS, SILAS *see* IDA COX

GREEN, RAY

b. 1908 Cavendish, Missouri.
Composer. Studied with Bloch, Elkus, Milhaud, and Monteux; scholarship at San Francisco Conservatory; Carnegie Foundation Scholarship; University of California George Ladd Paris Prize; taught in San Francisco; wrote *Casey Jones,* for percussion and piano (1936); choral works—*Sea Calm* and *Hey Nonny No* (1934).

GREEN, URBAN CLIFFORD (URBIE)

b. 1926 Mobile, Alabama.
Trombonist. Played with Woody Herman and Benny Goodman during 1950s; later studio musician in New York City; formed own band after 1966.

GREEN VALLEY BOYS *see* REM WALL

GREEN, VERNICE, JR. ("BUNKY")

b. 1935 Milwaukee, Wisconsin.
Jazz saxist. Studied at Roosevelt University, Chicago; played alto sax, tenor sax, baritone sax, and clarinet with various groups in Milwaukee; after 1960 in Chicago with Red Saunders, Louis Bellson and others.

GREEN, WILLIAM EARNEST

b. 1925 Kansas City, Kansas.
Saxist and clarinetist. Played with WPA band in Kansas City; later with various groups in Los Angeles; with Nelson Riddle after 1960; also taught in Los Angeles; at 1965 Monterey Jazz Festival with Gil Fuller's orchestra.

GREENBRIAR BOYS

Bob Yellin, Eric Weissberg, and John Herald; Ralph Rinzler, Dian Edmondson; Frank Wakefield.

GREENE, HERBERT WILBUR

b. 1851 Holyoke, Massachusetts, d. 1924. Editor and teacher. With C.B. Hawley, founded the Metropolitan Conservatory of Music, New York City (1885), with Dudley Buck, Samuel P. Warren, H.R. Shelley, et al. as teachers.

GREENE, JACK HENRY

b. 1930 Maryville, Tennessee.
Singer, drummer, and guitarist. Played with bands in Atlanta, Georgia, then served in the army (1950-52); joined Grand Ole Opry (1967); hit records were "The Last Letter" (1967), "Don't You Ever Get Tired of Hurting Me," "Ever Since My Baby Went Away," "There Goes My Everything," "All the Time," "What Locks the Door," "You Are My Treasure" (1968).

GREENFIELD, ELIZABETH TAYLOR

b. 1809 Natchez, Mississippi, d. 1876 Philadelphia, Pennsylvania. Black singer. Known as the "Black Swan"; debut at Buffalo Musical Association, Buffalo, New York (1851); toured northern states and Canada (1851-53); toured England (1854) and gave command performance for Queen Victoria.

GREER, WILLIAM ALEXANDER ("SONNY")

b. 1903 Long Branch, New Jersey.
Drummer. With Duke Ellington (1919-51); later played with Johnny Hodges, Red Allen, and Tyree Glenn.

GREGORY, BOBBY C.

b. 1900 Staunton, Virginia.
Singer and songwriter. Attended schools in Staunton, Virginia, and Reno, Nevada; he wrote "She's Somebody's Darlin' Once More," "Ridin' Along Singin' a Song," "Three Women to Every Man," "Maggie Get the Hammer," "Gay Nineties Polka."

GRENVILLE, LILLIAN

b. 1888 New York City, d. 1928 Paris, France. Soprano. Debut as Juliette in Nice (1906); sang in Europe, then with the Chicago Opera (1910-11).

GRETCHANINOFF, ALEXANDER

b. 1864 Moscow, Russia, d. 1956 New York City. Composer. Educated at the Moscow Conservatory and at the St. Petersburg Conservatory under Rimsky-Korsakov; his opera *Dobrinya Nikitich* was introduced at the Bolshoi Theatre, Moscow (1903) and *Sister Beatrice* (w. Maurice Maeterlinck, 1912); came to New York City (1939); also composed *Missa Oecumencia* (Ecumenical Mass) for soloists, chorus, orchestra and organ (1936), and Symphony no. 5 introduced by the Philadelphia Orchestra under Stokowski (1939).

GREY, ALBERT THORNTON (AL)

b. 1925 Aldie, Virginia.
Trombonist. Played with Benny Carter, Lionel Hampton, Jimmie Lunceford, and Dizzy Gillespie during 1940s and '50s; with Count Basie (1957-61); then formed own combo with tenor saxist Billy Mitchell; with Count Basie again after 1964.

GREY, CLIFFORD

b. 1887 Birmingham, England, d. 1941 Ipswich, England. Lyricist. Wrote lyrics for numerous Broadway musicals after 1924; with Leo Robin wrote "Hallelujah" (m. Vincent

Youmans) for the musical *Hit the Deck* (1927), "Dream Lover" and "Paris Stay the Same" (1929, both m. Victor Schertzinger).

GRIFFES, CHARLES TOMLINSON

b. 1884 Elmira, New York, d. 1920 New York City. Composer. Studied in Berlin under Humperdinck; taught at the Hackley School in Tarrytown, N.Y. (1907-20); composed *The White Peacock*, for piano and orchestra (1915), and *The Pleasure Dome of Kubla Khan*, symphonic poem for orchestra introduced by the Boston Symphony under Monteux (1919).

GRIFFIN, JOHN ARNOLD, III (JOHNNY)

b. 1928 Chicago, Illinois.
Tenor saxist. Played with Art Blakey, Thelonious Monk and others during 1950s; formed a quintet with Eddie Lockjaw Davis (1960-62); resided in Paris after 1962; toured Europe.

GRIFFIS, ELLIOT

b. 1893 Boston, Massachusetts.
Composer. Studied at Ithaca, N.Y., New England Conservatory, Boston, Yale School of Music, and Mannes School, N.Y.; won Pulitzer Fellowship; N.Y. College of Music (Mus.D.); composed *Colossus* (symphonic poem), *Fantastic Pursuit* (symphony for string orchestra), *Montevallo* (concerto for strings, piano and organ, based on Southern mountain tunes), and songs.

GRIMES, ANNE (LAYLIN)

b. 1912 Columbus, Ohio.
Singer, banjoist, and guitarist. Graduated Ohio Wesleyan, Delaware, Ohio, and studied music at Ohio State, Columbus; elected president of the Ohio Folklore Society (1957); her LP record *Folk Songs of Ohio* (1957) included "Old Dan Tucker" and "De Boatman's Dance" (both written by Daniel D. Emmett, 1843) and "Darling Nellie Gray" (by Benjamin R. Hanby, 1856).

GRIMES, HENRY ALONZO

b. 1935 Philadelphia, Pennsylvania.
Bass player. With Gerry Mulligan, Tony Scott, and Sonny Rollins in late 1950s; with Cecil Taylor, Perry Robinson, and Mose Allison during 1960s.

GRIMES, TAMMY

b. 1934 Lynn, Massachusetts.
Singer and actress. Lead in *The Unsinkable Molly Brown* (1960, book—Richard Morris, m. Meredith Willson).

GRISWOLD, ALEXANDER VIETS

b. 1766 Simsbury, Connecticut, d. 1843 Boston, Massachusetts. Hymnist. Episcopal rector in Litchfield, Conn. (1795), Bristol, R.I. (1804), Salem, Mass. (1830-35); elected Bishop of the Eastern Diocese in 1811, and was Presiding Bishop (1836-43); wrote the lyrics "Holy Father, Great Creator" (1835, m. Henry Smart, tune "Regent Square"), which appeared in *Hymns for the Church and Home* (Philadelphia, 1860).

GRISWOLD, PUTNAM

b. 1875 Minneapolis, Minnesota, d. 1914 New York City. Bass opera singer. Debut at Covent Garden (1901); with Berlin Royal Opera (1906-11), then with the Metropolitan Opera, New York after 1912.

GROFÉ, FERDINAND RUDOLF VON (FERDE)

b. 1892 New York City, d. 1972 Santa Monica, California. Noted composer and pianist. Studied at the Leipzig Conservatory, Germany, then played the viola with the Los Angeles Symphony (1909-19); became pianist and arranger for Paul Whiteman (1919-33); wrote *Broadway at Night* (1924), *Mississippi Suite* (1925), *Grand Canyon Suite* for orchestra (1931), *Three Shades of Blue, Death Valley Suite, Tabloid Suite, Hollywood Suite, Metropolis, Kentucky Derby, Aviation Suite, Wheels, Symphony in Steel.*

GROSZ, WILHELM

b. 1894 Vienna, Austria, d. 1939 New York City. Popular composer. Composed chamber music, songs, music for the stage and arranged Jewish folk songs.

GROVE, RICHARD DEAN (DICK)

b. 1927 Lakeville, Indiana.
Pianist and arranger. Studied at Denver University Music School; organized own band in Los Angeles (1962); with John Graas Quintet (1964); staff arranger for King Family TV show.

GRUBER, EDMUND L.

b. 1879 Cincinnati, Ohio, d. 1941 Fort Leavenworth, Kansas. Composer. Wrote "The Caissons Go Rolling Along" (1907) for the 5th Artillery while in the Philippine Islands.

GRUENBERG, LOUIS

b. 1883 Brest-Litovsk, Russia, d. 1964.
Pianist and composer. His family brought him to America (1886); studied at the Vienna Conservatory under Busoni (1903); became a

concert pianist and returned to America (1919); composed *The Hill of Dreams* (1919, symphonic poem), the opera *The Emperor Jones* (play—Eugene O'Neill) introduced at the Metropolitan Opera House, New York City (1933), *Concerto for Violin and Orchestra* introduced by Heifetz and the Philadelphia Orchestra under Eugene Ormandy (1944).

GRUSIN, DAVE

b. 1934 Denver, Colorado.
Pianist and composer. Studied at the University of Colorado; served in U.S. navy; studied in New York City after 1956; with Andy Williams on part-time basis (1959-66); wrote arrangements for Mel Torme and Peggy Lee; then with Ruth Price in Los Angeles; also with Caterina Valente in Amsterdam (1966).

GUARALDI, VINCENT ANTHONY (VINCE)

b. 1928 San Francisco, California.
Pianist and composer. With Woody Herman and Cal Tjader during 1950s; led his own trio in San Francisco during 1960s; wrote "Cast Your Fate to the Wind," which won Grammy award for best jazz composition (1962); at Monterey Jazz Festival (1964); wrote *Charlie Brown's Christmas*, on TV (1965); also jazz mass performed at Grace Cathedral in San Francisco (1965).

GUARD, DAVE

b. 1934 near San Francisco, California.
Singer. With Bob Shane and Nick Reynolds, formed the Kingston Trio (1957); later Guard was replaced by John Stewart.

GUARNERI STRING QUARTET

Arnold Steinhardt, violin; John Dalley, violin; David Soyer, cello; Michael Tree, viola; in concert at Carnegie Hall, New York City (1972).

GUARNIERI, CAMARGO

b. 1907 Tieté, Brazil.
Composer. Studied at the Sao Paulo Conservatory and became a professor there after graduation; visited the United States in 1946; composed *Albertura Concertante* for orchestra, introduced by the Sao Paulo Orchestra (1942), and Symphony no. 1 introduced in Sao Paulo (1944) and by the Boston Symphony Orchestra directed by the composer (1946).

GUARNIERI, JOHN A. (JOHNNY)

b. 1917 New York City.
Jazz pianist and composer. With Jimmy Dorsey, Benny Goodman, and Artie Shaw (1940-41); played in New York City, then in Hollywood after 1962; wrote the musical show, *What a Perfect Business* (libretto—Martin Silberston).

GUESS WHO (Canadian rock group)

At Carnegie Hall, New York City concert (1972).

GUILBEAU, PHILLIP (PHIL)

b. 1926 Lafayette, Louisiana.
Trumpeter. Served in navy (1942-45); then with Paul Williams and Big Joe Turner; with Ray Charles (1960-65); toured with the Count Basie band after 1965.

GUILBERT, ANDRE LOUIS EUGENE

b. ca. 1780 France, d. ca. 1835 Charleston, South Carolina. Harpist and composer. Came to Charleston before 1809; published music in Charleston between 1817-26; wrote *Arbre Charmont* (ca. 1819, w. De Florian), *President Monroe's March* (1817), *Twelve English Songs* (1823); composed sonatas and a concerto for the harp.

GUILLOU, VICTOR

b. ca. 1790 Dominican Republic, d. ca. 1843 Philadelphia, Pennsylvania. Pianist, compiler, and dancing master; taught in Philadelphia (1811-43); compiled a *Select Collection of New Cotillions* (ca. 1819).

GUION, DAVID WENDELL DE FENTRESSE

b. 1892 Ballinger, Texas.
Composer. Studied at Polytechnic College, Fort Worth, Texas, and in Vienna with Leopold Godowsky; became a teacher and composer; his orchestral works were *Prairie Suite, Mother Goose Suite, Alley Tunes, Texas* (1952), the ballets—*Western Ballet* and *Shingandi*, also *My Cowboy Love Song* (1936).

GUIRAUD, ERNEST

b. 1837 New Orleans, Louisiana, d. 1892 Paris, France. Teacher. Son of Jean Baptiste Guiraud, the composer.

GUITERMAN, ARTHUR

b. 1871 Vienna, Austria, d. 1943.
Lyricist. Educated at the College of the City of New York (1891); wrote the lyrics "Bless the Four Corners of This House" (1916, tune "Home"—Van Denman Thompson).

GUMINA, THOMAS JOSEPH (TOMMY)

b. 1931 Milwaukee, Wisconsin.
Accordionist. Studied accordion at age eleven in Milwaukee; then under Andy Rizzo in

Chicago (1944-49); with Harry James (1951-54); formed his own combo in Las Vegas, Nevada; then with Buddy De Franco after 1960.

GUNN, GLENN DILLARD

b. 1874 Topeka, Kansas, d. 1963.
Pianist and teacher. Studied in Leipzig; debut as pianist (1896); taught at American Conservatory, Chicago (1900-01), Chicago Music College (1901-06), then his own school after 1906; music editor of *Chicago Herald Examiner.*

GUNTER, SIDNEY LOUIE, JR. ("HARDROCK")

b. 1925 Birmingham, Alabama.
Singer and songwriter. Wrote and recorded in 1950—"Birmingham Bounce," "Lonesome Blues," "How Can I Believe You Love Me," "Maybe Baby You'll Be True," "Dad Gave My Hog Away," "Rifles, Belts and Bayonets"; in 1951—"Honky Tonk Blues," "Don't You Agree," "Boogie-Woogie on a Saturday Night," "Hesitation Boogie," "I Believe That Mountain Music Is Here to Stay."

GURNEY, HENRY B.

b. 1873, d. 1956.
Singer. Soloist with Roxborough Symphony Orchestra, Philadelphia (1932); taught at Temple University School of Music, Philadelphia.

GUTHRIE, ARLO

b. 1947 Brooklyn, New York.
Singer, guitarist, and songwriter. Son of Woody Guthrie; played at the Gaslight in New York City, Club 47 in Cambridge, Mass., and the Second Fret in Philadelphia; wrote "Alice's Restaurant" which was a hit song at the 1967 Newport Folk Festival, Newport, Rhode Island; wrote "Coming into Los Angeles, Bringing in a Couple of Keys* Don't Touch My Bags, if You Please, Mister Customs Man" (1970). (*Keys means kilograms of illegal narcotics.)

GUTHRIE, WOODROW WILSON (WOODY)

b. 1912 Okemah, Oklahoma, d. 1967.
Singer, guitarist, and songwriter. At age fourteen, after his father's business failed, his sister Clara died in a fire, his mother was committed to the State Asylum at Norman, and his father was injured in a fire, he ran away from home; played on radio stations KFVD, Los Angeles, and XELO, Tijuana, Mexico; served with the Merchant Marine in World War II; wrote "This Land Is My Land," "Goin' Down This Road," "Jack Hammer John," "Pretty Boy Floyd," "Sharecropper Song," "Pastures of Plenty."

GUY, BUDDY

b. 1936 Lettsworth, Louisiana.
Black guitarist. Considered by some as the greatest blues guitarist in the world; accompanist for Junior Wells; also recorded with Muddy Waters, Howlin' Wolf, and Willie Dixon; raised in Louisiana; started in Chicago; albums—*Man and the Blues* (1968), *This Is Buddy Guy, Light My Blues in San Francisco.*

GUY, HARRY P.

b. 1870, d. 1950.
Black singer. Raised in Zanesville, Ohio; sang with the Fisk Jubilee Singers; later with Fred S. Stone's band in Detroit, Michigan.

GUY, JOSEPH LUKE

b. 1920 Birmingham, Alabama.
Black trumpeter. With Fats Waller, Coleman Hawkins, Charlie Barnet, Billie Holiday and others.

GWALTNEY, THOMAS O. (TOMMY)

b. 1921 Norfolk, Virginia.
Clarinetist. Studied with E. Caceres and P. Hucko; played with Sol Yaged in New York (1946-47); at Newport and Randall's Island Jazz Festivals (1956-57) with Bobby Hackett; with Charlie Byrd (1962); produced Virginia Beach Jazz Festivals (1959-61 and 1965); opened his own jazz club, Blues Alley, in Washington, D.C.

HACKELY, E. AZALIA

b. (?), d. 1923.
Black soprano. She resided in Philadelphia; made concert tours; held Folksong Festivals throughout the United States.

HACKETT, ARTHUR

b. 1884 Portland, Maine.
Tenor. Brother of Charles Hackett; sang in the Paris opera, then recital tours in Great Britain and the United States; later taught voice at the University of Michigan, in Ann Arbor.

HACKETT, CHARLES

b. 1889 Worcester, Massachusetts, d. 1942 New York City. Tenor. Debut in the opera *Mignon,* Genoa (1916); sang in Europe and South America; debut in New York at Metropolitan Opera as Almaviva (1919); sang with Metropolitan Opera (1919-22), then with Chicago Opera (1923-34), and the Metropolitan again after 1935.

HACKETT, KARLETON SPAULDING

b. 1867 Brookline, Massachusetts, d. 1935 Chicago, Illinois. Teacher and music critic. Graduated Harvard University (1891); with John J. Hattstaedt founded the American Conservatory of Music, Chicago (1886) and served as vice-president and head of the vocal department; was music critic of *Chicago Evening Post*; later president of the Chicago City Opera Company.

HACKETT, ROBERT LEO (BOBBY)

b. 1915 Providence, Rhode Island.
Jazz trumpeter and cornetist. Played in Will Bradley's band; also with Horace Heidt; with Glenn Miller (1941-42) on guitar; led various jazz combos; with Benny Goodman in Mexico (1963); also recorded with Tony Bennett; recorded *Rhapsody in Blue* while in Glenn Miller's band; at the Newport Jazz Festival, New York City (1972).

HACKH, OTTO CHRISTOPH

b. 1852 Stuttgart, Germany, d. 1917 Brooklyn, New York. Pianist and teacher. Studied at the Stuttgart Conservatory; taught there (1872-75), then at the German Conservatory, New York (1880-89); composed a number of piano pieces.

HADEN, CHARLES EDWARD (CHARLIE)

b. 1937 Shenandoah, Iowa.
Bass player. Played with Art Pepper, Paul Bley and Hampton Hawes during late 1950s; with Ornette Coleman and Denny Zeitlin in 1960s; rehabilitated at Synanon, the narcotics center (1963) and has since supported the center.

HADLEY, HENRY KIMBALL

b. 1871 Somerville, Massachusetts, d. 1937 New York City. Conductor and composer. Violinist with the Mapleson Opera Company (1893); taught music at St. Paul's Episcopal School, Garden City, N.Y. (1896); debut as conductor in New York (1900); conductor of Seattle Symphony (1909-11), San Francisco Symphony (1911-15), N.Y. Philharmonic after 1920; wrote the operas *Safie* (Mainz, 1909), *Azora* (Chicago, 1917), *Bianca* (N.Y., 1918), *Cleopatra's Night* (Metropolitan Opera, 1920); symphonies—*Youth and Life* (Seidl, 1897), *The Four Seasons* (1901), *North, East, South and West* (London Philharmonic and Boston Symphony); numerous overtures, musical dramas, piano quintets, cantatas, ballet suites for orchestra, violin sonatas, songs; married Inez Barbour, soprano.

HADLEY, JAMES F. (JIM)

b. 1922 Hamilton, Alabama.
Singer and songwriter. Wrote "Nobody Knows but Mommy" (1956), "Walked the Floor a Thousand Miles" (1956), "Honky Tonk Girl" (1957), "Foolish Ways" (1957), "Wanted" (1958).

HAFER, JOHN RICHARD (DICK)

b. 1927 Wyomissing, Pennsylvania.
Tenor saxist, flutist, etc. Played with Charlie Barnet after 1949; with Woody Herman, Claude Thornhill, Bobby Hackett, Elliot Lawrence during 1950s; with Charles Mingus, Benny Goodman, on Merv Griffin's TV show during 1960s.

HAGAN, HELEN EUGENIA

b.1893 Portsmouth, New Hampshire, d. 1964. Black pianist. Graduated Yale University, School of Music, New Haven, Conn.; won Lockwood and Samuels Simmons Sanford Fellowship awards for study abroad; debut in Aeolian Hall, New York City.

HAGEN, PETER ALBRECHT, JR., VAN
see VAN HAGEN

HAGEN, PETER ALBRECHT, SR., VAN
see VAN HAGEN

HAGGARD, MERLE

b. 1937 Bakersfield, California.
Guitarist, singer, and songwriter. Married Bonnie Owens, singer; his hit records were the LP, *Strangers*, which included his own song, "I'm Gonna Break Every Heart I Can" (1965), "Just Between the Two of Us" (with Bonnie Owens, 1966), "Swinging Doors" (1966, his own composition), "I'm a Lonesome Fugitive" (1967); played in the White House for President and Mrs. Nixon (1973).

HAGGART, ROBERT SHERWOOD (BOB)

b. 1914 New York City.
Bass player and composer. Double bass player in Bob Crosby's band after 1935; later TV staff musician in 1960s; wrote "Big Noise from Winnetka," "South Rampart Street Parade," "What's New?"

HAGUE, ALBERT

b. 1920 Berlin, Germany.
Popular composer. Studied with Arthur Perleberg, then with Darile Alderighi in Rome on a scholarship; at the College of Music at the University of Cincinnati, Ohio (1939-42), then went into the U.S. Air Force during World War II; wrote the music for *Reluctant Lady* (w. Maurice Valency), "The Mercer Girls" (1953, TV), *Plain and Fancy* (1955, book—Joseph Stein and William Glickman), *Redhead* (1959, lyrics Dorothy Fields).

HAGUE, WILLIAM

b. 1808 Pelham, New York, d. 1887.
Hymnist. Became a Baptist minister (1829); wrote "Hark, Sinner, Hark! God Speaks to Thee," which appeared in Cutting's *Hymns for the Vestry and Fireside* (1841).

HAHN, EMILIE

b. 1891 Germany, d. 1971 New York City. Teacher. She was raised in Yokohama, Japan, where her father was in the import-export business; educated at the University of Kiel, Germany, and came to America (1914); taught at the Overbrook (Pa.) School for the Blind, the N.Y. Institute for the Education of the Blind and the preparatory department of the Juilliard School of Music, N.Y. City; pupil of Emile Jaques-Dalcroze, Swiss musician and educator.

HAHN, JACOB H.

b. 1847 Philadelphia, Pennsylvania, d. 1902. Organist, manager, and teacher. Studied with Florenz Ziegfeld in Chicago, then three years at Leipzig Conservatory; founded the Detroit Conservatory of Music, Detroit, Michigan (1875).

HAHN, JERRY DONALD

b. 1940 Alma, Nebraska.
Guitarist. Studied guitar with his father; at Wichita University, Kansas; played in studio bands in San Francisco after 1962; with John Handy at Monterey Jazz Festival (1965).

HAIEFF, ALEXEI

b. 1914 Blagoveshchensk, Siberia.
Noted composer. Came to U.S. (1931) and studied at Juilliard School of Music, New York City and in Paris; professor of music at University of Buffalo, N.Y. (1962-68) and composer in residence at University of Utah, Salt Lake City after 1968; wrote a symphony (1942), a divertimento, introduced by Barone Little Symphony (1946), *Eclogue* for cello and piano (1947), *Piano Concerto* (N.Y. City, 1952), second symphony (Boston Symphony, 1958).

HAIG, ALAN W. (AL)

b. 1923 Newark, New Jersey.
Pianist. Played with Charles Barnet, Dizzy Gillespie, and Charlie Parker in 1940s; later with Chet Baker and Stan Getz; later played in clubs in New York City.

HAINES, NAPOLEON J.

b. 1824 London, England, d. 1900 New York City. Piano maker. Founded the Haines Brothers Piano Manufacturers, New York City.

HAKIM, SADIK

b. 1922 Duluth, Minnesota.
Pianist. Born Argonne Dense Thornton; played with Charlie Parker, L. Young, and Slam Stewart; with Buddy Tate (1955-60); formed own group.

HALE, EDWARD EVERETT

b. 1822 Boston, Massachusetts, d. 1909.
Hymnist and writer. Graduated Harvard (1840); pastor of the Unitarian Church,

Worcester, Mass. (1846-56) and the South Congregational Church, Boston (1856-99); his short story "The Man Without a Country" (1863) was made into an opera by Walter J. Damrosch; he wrote "O Father, Take the New Built Shrine" (1858) which appeared in Samuel Longfellow and Samuel Johnson's *Hymns of Spirit* (1864).

HALE, MARY WHITWELL

b. 1810 Boston, Massachusetts, d. 1862. Hymnist. Taught in Boston, Taunton, Mass., and Keane, N.H.; several of her hymns appeared in the *Cheshire Collection* (1844).

HALE, PHILIP

b. 1854 Norwich, Vermont, d. 1934 Boston, Massachusetts. Organist and music critic. Graduated Yale University (1876); pupil of Dudley Buck (1876); organist at St. Peter's, Albany, N.Y. (1879-82); studied organ (1882-87); organist at St. John's, Troy, N.Y. (1887-89) and conductor of Schubert Club, Albany, N.Y.; then critic on the *Boston Home Journal, Post, Musical Record* (1897-1901), *Musical World*, then *Boston Herald* (1903-34); program annotator of Boston Symphony Orchestra (1901-34).

HALE, SARAH JOSEPHA BUELL

b. 1788 Newport, New Hampshire, d. 1879. Hymnist. Wrote "Our Father in Heaven, We Hallow Thy Name" (Mason and Greene's *Church Psalmody*, 1831); wrote "Mary Had a Little Lamb" (1830), set to music about 1868 by H.R. Waite.

HALEY, BILL

b. 1925 Highland Park, Michigan.
Bandleader. Leader of Bill Haley and the Comets; originated rock 'n roll when he recorded "Rock Around the Clock" (1954), which became the theme song of the film *Blackboard Jungle* (1955); albums—*Bill Haley and His Comets, Bill Haley—Scrapbook, Bill Haley's Greatest Hits, Rock Around the Clock, Rock'n Roll Revival;* at the "Legend of Rock 'n Roll" show at Hollywood Bowl, California (1972).

HALEY, WILLIAM D'ARCY

b. 1828 London, England, d. 1890 San Jose, California. Compiler. Attended Harvard and Meadville Theological School, Meadville, Pa. (1853); pastor of the First Congregational Church, Alton, Ill. (1853-56), then the First Unitarian Church, Washington, D.C. (1858-61); chaplain of the 7th Massachusetts Volunteer Infantry (1861-62), and 1st Lieutenant, 2nd North Carolina Infantry (1863-64); compiled *A Manual of the Broad Church* (1859) which included 110 hymns.

HALL, ADELAIDE

b. 1909 Brooklyn, New York.
Black singer. Sang in *Shuffle Along*, and *Blackbirds* and other revues in 1920s; Art Tatum was her accompanist in 1930s.

HALL, ALBERT WESLEY

b. 1915 Jacksonville, Florida.
Black double bass player. Raised in Philadelphia; with Teddy Wilson, Mildred Bailey and others.

HALL, ALFRED ("TUBBY")

b. 1855 Sellers, Louisiana, d. 1946 Chicago, Illinois. Black drummer. Brother of Minor Hall; raised in New Orleans; played in Frank Dusen's Eagle Band; later with Jimmie Noone, Louis Armstrong and others.

HALL, AMARIAH

b. 1785 Raynham, Massachusetts, d. there 1827. Composer. Kept a tavern, manufactured straw bonnets and taught singing; composed the tune "All Saints New" ("Why Should We Start and Fear to Die?," w. Isaac Watts, other tunes William Boyd's "Pentecost" and W.B. Bradbury's "Zephyr," "Rest").

HALL, CONNIE

b. 1929 Walden, Kentucky.
Singer. Raised in Cincinnati, Ohio, but started singing over radio station WZIP, Covington, Kentucky, then joined the "Jimmie Skinner Show" on WNOP, Newport, Ky. (1954); her Decca LP records were *Connie Hall* and *Country Songs with Connie Hall.*

HALL, EDMOND

b. 1901 New Orleans, Louisiana, d. 1967.
Black clarinetist. Played in New Orleans bands during 1920s; with Claude Hopkins and others during 1930s; with Red Allen, Teddy Wilson and own groups during 1940s and '50s; toured England and Scandinavia (1962); with Dukes of Dixieland on tour of Japan (1964); recorded with Harry Belafonte.

HALL, FREDERICK DOUGLASS

b. 1898 New York City, d. there 1964.
Black organist and teacher. Studied at Morehouse College, Atlanta, Georgia, Chicago Musical College, Columbia University, N.Y. City, and Royal College of Music, London; doctorate in music (1952) Columbia University; taught at Jackson State, Jackson, Mississippi, Clark College, Atlanta,

Georgia, Alabama A&M, Normal, Alabama, Dilliard University, New Orleans, La.

HALL, JAMES STANLEY (JIM)

b. 1930 Buffalo, New York.
Guitarist. Played in Los Angeles in early 1950s; recorded in Cleveland (1955) with Chico Hamilton; then with Jimmy Guiffre trio; duo with Lee Konitz, Sonny Rollins, Art Farmer quartet, Red Mitchell and Colin Bailey in 1960s; toured South America with Ella Fitzgerald and Roy Eldridge (1960); on Ralph Gleason TV show (1962 and 1963); at Newport (1962-63); toured Europe with Art Farmer; at The Guitar, New York City (1972); guest of Symphony Sid program.

HALL, MINOR ("RAM")

b. 1897 Sellers, Louisiana, d. 1959.
Black jazz drummer. Brother of Tubby Hall; played in Lawrence Duhe's orchestra in Chicago (1918); joined King Oliver's band; in Kid Ory's band after 1944.

HALL, VERA

b. 1905 Livingston, Alabama, d. there 1964. Singer. Spent her early life as a domestic servant; John Lomax recorded a number of her songs for the American Archive of Folk Song of the Library of Congress, including "Soon One Mornin' Death Came Creepin'."

HALL, WALTER HENRY

b. 1862 London, England, d. 1935 Brooklyn, New York. Teacher, organist, and conductor. Studied at the Royal Academy of Music and came to America in 1883; organist of St. Luke's Episcopal Church, Germantown, Philadelphia (1883-90), St. Peter's Church, Albany, N.Y. (1890-96), then St. James' Church, N.Y. City; in 1893 he founded and conducted the Brooklyn Oratorio Society, until 1935; became professor of choral music at Columbia University, N.Y. City (1913).

HALL, WENDELL WOODS

b. 1896 St. George, Kansas.
Singer, guitarist, and composer. Educated at the University of Chicago Preparatory School; served in World War I; known as "Red-Headed Music Maker" on radio; made world radio tour (1924-27); played ukulele; wrote "It Ain't Gonna Rain No Mo' " (1923) based on an old Negro spiritual.

HALL, WILLIAM

b. 1796, d. 1884.
Lyricist and publisher. Music publisher in New York City with the firm of Firth & Hall (1823-48), William Hall and Son (1848-54); wrote "O Lady Love Awake" (m. James W. Perossier).

HALLAM, LEWIS

b. (?) England, d. 1755 Jamaica, B.W.I.
Singer and manager. Came to America as leader of the Hallam Company (1752), sent here by his brother, William Hallam; later called Old American Company, performed stage shows and operas; performed in Williamsburg, Va. (1752), in New York City and Philadelphia (1754), but met much opposition from the Society of Friends (Quakers) and the governor of Pennsylvania.

HALLAM, LEWIS, JR.

b. ca. 1741 England, d. 1808 Philadelphia, Pennsylvania. Manager. With his brother, Henry, partner of the Old American Company, after the death of their father (1755); later known as the Old American Opera Company; produced operas in Philadelphia (1787-94); William Dunlap became the manager in 1796.

HALLSTROM, HENRY

b. 1906 Hernosand, Sweden.
Composer. Came to California (1913); graduated the University of California, Berkeley (1929); organist-choirmaster in Morristown, N.J. (1930-37), Bard College, Annandale-on-Hudson, N.Y. (1937-38), then at St. John's, Lynchburg, Virginia; taught at Randolph-Macon College, Ashland, Va; composed the tune "Lynchburg" (1941, "Give Peace, O God, the Nations Cry," w. J.W. Norris).

HAMBLEN, CARL STUART

b.1908 Kellerville, Texas.
Singer, bandleader, and songwriter. Attended McMurray College, Abilene, Texas; went to California to sing on station KFI, Los Angeles; ran for President of the U.S. on the Prohibition Party ticket in 1952; wrote "But I'll Be Chasin' Women" (1949), "This Old House" (1954, made famous by Rosemary Clooney), "Mainliner" (1955, sung by Hank Snow), "The Lord Is Counting on You."

HAMBOURG, BORIS

b. 1884 Woronesch, Russia, d. 1954 Toronto, Ontario, Canada. Cellist. Studied at Hoch Conservatory, Frankfort; debut in Pyrmont (1903); toured Australia, Europe, then the U.S.; lived in Pittsburgh then opened a school in Toronto, Ontario, Canada (1911) with his father and brother.

HAMER, GEORGE FREDERICK

b. 1862 Lawrence, Massachusetts, d. 1945. Organist, composer, and teacher. Graduated Royal Academy of Music, Munich, Germany; taught piano, organ, and composition in Lawrence; organist of Trinity Church there; composed Overture in C Minor for small orchestra and Overture in E Minor for large orchestra, piano pieces, songs.

HAMILTON, CLARENCE GRANT

b. 1865 Providence, Rhode Island, d. 1935. Teacher and composer. Educated at Brown University, Providence; organist in the Congregational Church, a composer, and became professor of music at Wellesley College; wrote *Outlines of Music History* (1908) and composed the tune "Wallace" (1914, "The Kings of the East Are Riding," w. Katherine Lee Bates).

HAMILTON, FORESTSTORN ("CHICO")

b. 1921 Los Angeles, California.
Black drummer. With Lionel Hampton, Lena Horne and others in 1940s; with Gerry Mulligan quartet and led his own quartet during 1950s; led a new group in 1960s; toured Japan; accompanied Lena Horne again after 1965.

HAMILTON, GEORGE, IV

b. 1937 Winston-Salem, North Carolina.
Guitarist, singer, and songwriter. Attended the University of North Carolina at Chapel Hill, and American University, Washington, D.C.; sang on WMAL-TV, Washington, 1956; his own show on ABC-TV (1959); hit records were "Before This Day Ends" (1960), "Three Steps to a Phone" (1961), "Abilene" (1963), "Fort Worth, Dallas and Houston" (1964); wrote "If You Don't Know I Ain't Gonna Tell You" (1961), "I've Got a Secret, Sam," and "Everybody's Baby."

HAMILTON, JAMES (JIMMY)

b. 1917 Dillon, South Carolina.
Black clarinetist and tenor saxist. Played with Teddy Wilson, Benny Carter and others during 1930s; with Duke Ellington after 1942.

HAMILTON, ROY

b. 1929 Leesburg, Georgia, d. 1969.
Black baritone. Raised in Jersey City, New Jersey; sang in church choirs; his hit records were "If I Loved You" and "You'll Never Walk Alone" (no. 1 on rhythm and blues lists of 1954), "Angelica" (1969); he died of a stroke.

HAMLIN, ANNA

b. 1902 Chicago, Illinois.
Soprano. Daughter of George John Hamlin; debut in Albenga, Italy (1926); then sang with the Chicago Opera Company.

HAMLIN, GEORGE JOHN

b. 1868 Elgin, Illinois, d. 1923 New York City. Tenor. Sang in concerts after 1895; with the Chicago Opera after 1911.

HAMMER, HOWARD ROBERT (BOB)

b. 1930 Indianapolis, Indiana.
Pianist and composer. Studied at Michigan State University, and Manhattan School of Music, N.Y. City; with Gene Krupa, Lionel Hampton, Charles Mingus, Tommy Dorsey, Red Allen, Woody Herman and others; wrote the *Hammerhead Waltz* for Clark Terry; *Dear John C.* and *Doin' the Snake* for Charlie Mingus.

HAMMERSTEIN, OSCAR

b. 1847 Stettin, Germany, d. 1919 New York City. Popular composer and producer. Came to New York City (1863) and invented a cigar making machine which netted him a fortune; wrote the scores for three shows produced at the Stadt Theatre, New York City; built the Harlem Opera House (1890) and the Manhattan Opera House (1906) where performed Luisa Tetrazzini, Nellie Melba, and Mary Garden, with Cleofonte Campanini, conductor; in 1910 he sold out to the Metropolitan Opera Company.

HAMMERSTEIN, OSCAR, II

b. 1895 New York City, d. 1960 Doylestown, Pennsylvania. Librettist and lyricist. Grandson of Oscar Hammerstein; graduated from Columbia University (1916); wrote the book and lyrics for *Show Boat* (1927, m. Jerome Kern), *Rose Marie* (1924, m. Rudolf Friml, also Otto Harbach), *The Student Prince* (1924, with Harbach and Mandel, m. Sigmund Romberg), and with Richard Rodgers—*Oklahoma* (1943), *Carousel* (1945), *South Pacific* (1949), *The King and I* (1951), *Flower Drum Song* (1958), and *The Sound of Music* (1959). (*See also* Vincent M. Youmans)

HAMMOND, EDWARD PAYSON

b. 1831 Ellington, Connecticut, d. 1910 Hartford, Connecticut. Hymnist. Wrote "Christian Go and Tell Jesus" and "I Feel Like Singing All the Time," which appeared in his compilation *Hymns of Prayer and Praise.*

HAMMOND, JOHN, JR.

b. 1943 New York City.
Black guitarist and singer. Father was a singer; John Jr. sang at the Newport Folk Festival, Newport, R.I. (1963); at the Ash Grove in Los Angeles, (1968); his Vanguard LP records were *John Hammond* (1963), *Big City Blues* (1964), *So Many Roads* (1965), *Country Blues* (1966), *Mirrors* (1967); at the Apollo Theater, Harlem, New York City (1972).

HAMMOND, JOHN PAUL

b. 1942 New York City.
Singer and guitarist. Son of John Henry Hammond, Jr., record executive and critic; played in New York City; toured England (1965).

HAMMOND, RICHARD

b. 1896 Kent, England.
Composer. Graduated Yale University; studied music with Mortimer Wilson and Nadia Boulanger in Paris; composed the ballet *Fiesta*, also piano pieces, chamber works, songs, orchestral works.

HAMMOND, SAMUEL LEROY

b. (?), d. 1864.
Lyricist. Resided in Augusta, Georgia; served in the Confederate army, killed 1864; wrote "The South" (m. John H. Hewitt), published by Dunn and Selby.

HAMMOND, WILLIAM CHURCHILL

b. 1860 Rockville, Connecticut, d. 1949 Holyoke, Massachusetts. Teacher and organist. Taught organ at Smith College, Northampton, Mass. (1890-1900), then was head of the music department at Mount Holyoke College, South Hadley, Mass. (1900-37); organist-choirmaster of the Second Congregational Church, Holyoke, Mass. (1885-1949).

HAMPTON, LIONEL

b. 1913 Louisville, Kentucky.
Black jazz vibraphonist and bandleader. Raised in Birmingham, Alabama, then Chicago; attended the University of Southern California; drummer with Les Hite's band; vibraphonist with Benny Goodman; organized his own band, played piano and drum solos; wrote "Flying Home" (1939); broke ground (1971) for the $13 million Lionel Hampton Houses (apartments) built in West Harlem, New York City, with Federal funds; played at Newport Jazz Festival, N.Y. City (1972).

HAMPTON, LOCKSLEY WELLINGTON ("SLIDE")

b. 1932 Jeannette, Pennsylvania.
Trombonist and tuba player. Raised in Indianapolis; played with Lionel Hampton, Buddy Johnson, and Maynard Ferguson during 1950s; formed own octet (1959); later musical director of Lloyd Price band.

HANAFORD, PHOEBE A. (COFFIN)

b. 1829 Nantucket Island, Massachusetts, d. 1921 Rochester, New York. Lyricist. She wrote "The Empty Sleeve" (1862) about a Civil War amputee case, which was set to music by John W. Dadmun, published in the *Southern Literary Messenger* by George W. Bagby; first woman ordained a Universalist minister in New England.

HANBY, BENJAMIN R.

b. 1833 Rushville, Ohio, d. 1867 Chicago, Illinois. Popular composer. Graduated Otterbein University, Westerville, Ohio (1858); minister of the United Brethern Church in New Paris, Ohio (1861-63); worked for a time with the John Church Company in Cincinnati, then in 1865 joined Root & Cady, music publishers in Chicago; composed "Adoration" (1866), and "Lowliness"; best known for "Darling Nellie Gray" (1856); also composed "Santa Claus, or Up on the House Top" and "Ole Shady: The Song of the Contraband" (1861, w. D.B. Durant); Hanby sent his song "Darling Nellie Gray" to a music publisher in Boston, but heard nothing from them; when the song swept the nation, he wrote for the usual royalties, and they replied that he had the fame and they had the money and that balanced the account!

HANBY, WILLIAM

b. 1808 Washington County, Pennsylvania, d. 1880. Compiler. At age sixteen he was apprenticed to a saddler, but ran away to Ohio because of the bad treatment he received; became a minister of the United Brethern Church in 1831 and treasurer of "The Telescope," the church paper at Circleville, Ohio in 1836; his home there became the underground railway station for runaway slaves; compiled *The Church Harp* (1841), *Hymns for the Sunday School* (1842), and a hymnal; elected the fifteenth bishop in 1845; his eldest son was Benjamin R. Hanby, the composer.

HANCHETT, HENRY GRANGER

b. 1853 Syracuse, New York, d. 1918 Siasconset, Massachusetts. Pianist, organist, composer, teacher, and writer. Studied music privately, then medicine; teacher of piano (1876-84); also active medical doctor; active in musical societies in the New York area; his father, M.W. Hanchett, invented the "Sostenuto" or "tone-sustaining pedal" for the piano.

HANCOCK, HERBERT JEFFREY (HERBIE)

b. 1940 Chicago, Illinois.
Black composer and pianist. Studied piano at age seven; with Donald Byrd, Phil Woods, Oliver Nelson, and Miles Davis combo during 1960s; wrote "Watermelon Man," popularized by Mongo Santamaria.

HANDY, GEORGE

b. 1920 Brooklyn, New York.
Pianist and composer. Born George Joseph Hendleman; arranger for Alvino Rey and Boyd Raeburn during 1940s; wrote *New York Suite* and three saxophone quartets for New York Saxophone Quartet (1964-65); also wrote for Kay Thompson.

HANDY, JOHN

b. 1890 Pass Christian, Mississippi, d. there 1971. Jazz bandleader. Moved to New Orleans (1918) where he formed his own bands, the Original Tuxedo Orchestra and the Young Tuxedo Brass Band.

HANDY, JOHN RICHARD, III

b. 1933 Dallas, Texas.
Saxophonist and clarinetist. Musician and teacher in San Francisco during 1940s; with Charles Mingus and Randy Weston in New York in late 1950s; formed own group (1959); toured Europe for State Department (1961); with Santa Clara (Calif.) Symphony Orchestra; at Monterey Jazz Festival with Mingus (1964); organized own quintet in San Francisco (1965) with violinist Michael White.

HANDY, WILLIAM CHRISTOPHER

b. 1873 Florence, Alabama, d. 1958 New York City. Noted black musician and composer. Graduated Teachers A & M College, Huntsville, Alabama (1892); played the cornet at the Columbian Exposition in Chicago (1893); in 1896 he joined Mahara's Minstrels, then formed his own band (1903); composed *The Memphis Blues* (1909), *St. Louis Blues* (1914), *The Beale Street Blues, John Henry Blues, The Harlem Blues, Joe Turner Blues, Careless Love*, several marches and the *Afro-American Hymn*.

HANLON, BERT

b. 1890 New York City, d. there 1972.
Lyricist and actor. Appeared in vaudeville, films, and Broadway musicals; wrote the lyrics "M-i-s-s-i-s-s-i-p-p-i" with Benny Ryan (m. Harry Tierney), also "Far Far Away in Rockaway," "I'd Like to Be a Monkey in the Zoo," "Omaha."

HANNA, JAKE

b. 1931 Roxbury, Massachusetts.
Drummer. Raised in Dorchester, Mass.; served in Air Force Band; with Tommy Reed, Maynard Ferguson, Marian McPartland Trio and others in 1950s; with Woody Herman and others in 1960s.

HANNA, ROLAND

b. 1932 Detroit, Michigan.
Pianist. Played in Detroit in 1940s; in U.S. Army Band (1950-52); studied at Eastman School, Rochester, N.Y. and at Juilliard, N.Y. City; with Benny Goodman and Charles Mingus in late 1950s; also had own trio after 1959.

HANNUM, LEWIS

b. (?), d. 1884.
Violin maker. Started making violins in 1876; one of his violins was played for many years by Professor Schultz of the Mendelssohn Quintette Club.

HANSEN, CHARLES F.

b. 1867 Lafayette, Indiana, d. 1947 Indianapolis, Indiana. Organist. Blind from birth; served as organist in churches in Indianapolis (1885-98), then at the Second Presbyterian Church there (1898-1947).

HANSON, HOWARD HAROLD

b. 1896 Wahoo, Nebraska.
Noted composer. Studied at Luther College, Decorah, Iowa, the Institute of Musical Art, N.Y. City, and Northwestern University, Evanston, Ill.; taught at the College of the Pacific, San Jose, Calif. (1915-18), was dean of its Conservatory (1918-21); then he won the Prix de Rome and studied there (1921-24); became director of the Eastman School of Music, Rochester, N.Y. (1924); composed Symphony no. 1 (1922), *The Lament for Beowulf* (1925), Symphony no. 2 (1930), *Merry Mount* (opera, 1933), Symphony no. 3 (1936), Symphony no. 4 (introduced by the Boston Symphony Orchestra with the composer conducting, 1943), Symphony no. 5, "Sinfonia Sacra" (1954); his choral piece, *Three Songs*

from "Drum-Taps" for baritone solo, mixed chorus, and orchestra is based on three poems of Walt Whitman written in 1861, 1865 and 1871.

HAPPENINGS (vocal group)

Ralph De Vito, vocals; Bob Miranda, vocals; Tom Guiliano, vocals; Dave Libert, organ; started as the Four Graduates; albums—*The Happenings* (1966), *Back to Back, Happenings Golden Hits, Piece of Mind, Psycle.*

HARBACH (HAUERBACH), OTTO

b. 1873 Salt Lake City, Utah, d. 1963 New York City. Lyricist and librettist. Attended Collegiate Institute, Salt Lake City; graduated Knox College, Galesburg, Illinois; taught in Walla Walla, Washington; wrote lyrics for Rudolf Friml, George Gershwin, Louis Hirsch, Karl Hoschna, Jerome Kern, Alfred Newman, Sigmund Romberg, Herbert Stothart, Harry Tierney, and Vincent M. Youmans; wrote the lyrics for "Indian Love Call," "Rose Marie," "The Desert Song," "Smoke Gets in Your Eyes."

HARBAUGH, HENRY

b. 1817 near Waynesborough, Pennsylvania, d. 1867 Mercersburg, Pennsylvania. Hymnist. Attended Marshall College, Mercersburg, but was unable to graduate due to lack of funds; ordained a minister in the German Reformed Church and served in Lewisburg, Lancaster, and Lebanon, Pa.; professor of theology at Mercersburg (1863-67); wrote the hymn "Jesus, I Live to Thee" (1850, tune "Lake Enon," I.B. Woodbury).

HARBURG, EDGAR YIPSEL ("YIP")

b. 1898 New York City.
Lyricist and librettist. Attended City College of N.Y.; wrote lyrics for Harold Arlen, Vernon Duke, Jay Gorney, John W. Green, and Burton Lane; wrote the lyrics "April in Paris" (1932), "It's Only a Paper Moon" (1933), "Over the Rainbow" (Academy Award, 1939), "How Are Things in Glocca Morra?"

HARDEN, ARLEEN

b. 1945 England, Arkansas.
Singer and guitarist. On "American Swingaround," Chicago (1966); WLW "Midwestern Hayride," Cincinnati (1967-68); member of the Harden Trio; albums—*Arleen Harden Sings Roy Orbison, with Harden Trio, Great Country Hits, Sing Me Back Home, Tippy Toeing.*

HARDEN TRIO (vocal group)

Robbie, Arleen, and Bobby Harden; all born in England, Arkansas; sang over radio stations in Little Rock, Arkansas, Springfield, Missouri, Shreveport, Louisiana, then in Grand Old Opry, Nashville; trio split in 1968.

HARDIN, LILIAN (LIL)

b. 1898 Memphis, Tennessee, d. 1971 Chicago, Illinois. Black jazz pianist. Known as a barrelhouse player; played in King Oliver's band; married to Louis Armstrong (1924-38); she was playing the St. Louis Blues at a Memorial for Armstrong at the Civic Center Plaza, Chicago, when she collapsed and died.

HARDING, LAVERE ("BUSTER")

b. 1917 Ontario, Canada, d. 1965 New York. City. Arranger. Arranger for Artie Shaw, Dizzy Gillespie, Cab Calloway, Glenn Miller, Tommy Dorsey and others.

HARDWICKE, OTTO ("TOBY")

b. 1904 Washington, D.C.
Jazz saxophonist. Played with Duke Ellington's band.

HARDY, HAGOOD

b. 1937 Angola, Indiana.
Vibraphonist. Educated at the University of Toronto, Canada; led his own group there (1956-58); with Gigi Gryce Sextet, Herbie Mann, Martin Denny, and George Shearing Quintet during 1960s.

HAREWOOD, ALPHONSE (AL)

b. 1923 Brooklyn, New York.
Drummer. Played with J.J. Johnson, Gigi Gryce, Art Farmer, Curtis Fuller, Benny Goodman and others during 1950s; with Lou Donaldson, Mary Lou Williams, Stan Getz and others in 1960s; at Monterey Jazz Festival (1963).

HARLEM CHORALE (vocal group)

Featured black mezzo-soprano Betty Allen in the *St. Matthew Passion* by Bach at Salem United Methodist Church, New York City (1972).

HARLEM DICTATORS *see* JAMES OSIE JOHNSON

HARLING, WILLIAM FRANKE

b. 1887 London, England, d. 1958.
Composer. Studied at Grace Church Choir

School, New York, Academy of Music, London, and in Brussels; organist at U.S. Military Academy, West Point, N.Y.; composed the opera, *A Light from St. Agnes* (Chicago Opera, 1925), lyric drama *Deep River* (New York, 1926), *Jazz Concerto, Venetian Fantasy*, and with Richard A. Whiting "Beyond the Blue Horizon" (w. Leo Robin).

HARLOW, SAMUEL RALPH

b. 1885 Boston, Massachusetts, d. 1972. Hymnist. Educated at Harvard and Columbia University, Union and Hartford Theological Seminaries; ordained a Congregational minister; became chaplain and head of the Department of Sociology at International College, Smyrna, Turkey (1912-22), then after 1923 at Smith College, Northampton, Mass.; wrote the hymn "O Young and Fearless Prophet of Ancient Galilee" (tune "Blairowrie" by J.B. Dykes).

HARMATI, SANDOR

b. 1892 Budapest, Hungary, d. 1936 Flemington, New Jersey. Conductor and composer. Studied at Budapest Academy of Music; concertmaster of State Orchestra, Budapest (1912-14); led Lenox String Quartet in U.S.; conducted New York Women's String Orchestra; Omaha Symphony Orchestra (1924-28); composed *Symphonic Poem* (Pulitzer Prize, 1923), *String Quartet* (Philadelphia Chamber Music Association Prize, 1925).

HARMON, JOEL, JR.

b. 1773 Suffield, Connecticut, d. 1833 York, Pennsylvania. Composer and compiler. Moved to Pawlet, Vermont in 1808 where he was a merchant and taught music; his original tunes were published in *The Columbian Sacred Minstrel* (1809), and he issued *A Musical Primer* (ca. 1814); lived for a time in Richland, N.Y.; major in the War of 1812.

HARNEY, BENJAMIN ROBERTSON

b. 1871 Middleborough, Kentucky, d. 1938. Philadelphia, Pennsylvania. Composer of ragtime tunes. Played piano rags in Kansas City, Missouri, St. Louis, and New York City; accompanist for "Strap" Hill, the singer, at Tony Pastor's in New York City; composed "Mister Johnson Turn Me Loose" (ragtime) introduced by May Irwin in the musical *Courted in Court* (1895), "You've Been a Good Old Wagon, but You've Done Broke Down" (1895), "Tell It to Me" and "The Black Man's Kissing Bug"; wrote *B.R. Harney's Ragtime Instructor* (1897) which was published by Isadore Whitmark, New York City.

HARNICK, SHELDON

b. 1924 Chicago, Illinois.
Lyricist and composer. Studied violin; graduated Northwestern University in music; wrote "Boston Beguine" for *New Faces of 1952* produced by Leonard Sillman; "Merry Minuet" (1953) for the *Almanac of John Murray Anderson*; teamed with Jerry Bock, composer, on *Fiorello!* (1959, story about New York's mayor, Fiorello LaGuardia, book by George Abbott and Jerome Weidman), which won the Pulitzer Prize; song "Fiddler on the Roof" (1964, m. Jerry Bock).

HARPER, EARL ENYEART

b. 1895 Craig, Missouri, d. 1967.
Composer and compiler. Educated at Nebraska Wesleyan University, Lincoln, Nebr., Boston University School of Theology, Harvard University and the University of Chicago; Methodist minister in the Nebraska and New England Conferences; composed the tune "Shirleyn" for "I Know Not How That Bethlehem's Babe" (1928, w. H.W. Farrington); compiled *The Abingdon Hymnal* (1928) and the *Junior-Intermediate Anthem Book* (1924).

HARPER, M. C. ("REDD")

b. 1903 Nocona, Texas.
Gospel singer and songwriter. Attended University of Oklahoma, Norman (1923-26); wrote "Lord Keep Your Hand on Me," "Each Step of the Way," "Until We Meet Again," "A Quiet Time," "I Walk the Glory Road," "Just Smile and Praise the Lord."

HARPER'S BIZARRE (folk-rock)

Ted Templeman, drums and trumpet; Dickie Scoppettone, guitar; Eddie James, guitar; John Peterson, drums; Dick Yount, guitar and bass drums; started in California (1963); albums—*Feelin' Groovy* (1967), *Anything Goes, Harper's Bizarre, Harper's Bizarre 4, Secret Life of Harper's Bizarre.*

HARRELD, KEMPER

b. 1885 Muncie, Indiana.
Black violinist and educator. Studied at Chicago Musical College and Stern Conservatory of Music, Berlin, Germany; head of music department at Morehouse College, Atlanta, Georgia (1911); one of founders of the National Association of Negro Musicians (1919); at Spelman College, Atlanta, Georgia after 1927.

HARRELL, MACK

b. 1909 Celeste, Texas, d. 1960.
Baritone. Studied at Juilliard School in New York City; later taught there; debut at Metropolitan Opera, N.Y. City (1940) as Biterolf in *Tannhauser*; as Nick Shadow in Stravinsky's *The Rake's Progress* (1953); last performance there (1958) as Amfortas in *Parsifal.*

HARRIGAN, EDWARD ("NED")

b. 1845 New York City, d. there 1911.
Lyricist and vaudeville actor. Harrigan and Tony Hart were a vaudeville team; David Braham composed the music and Harrigan wrote the lyrics for "The Mulligan Guard" (1873), "The Skidmore Guard" (1874), "Patrick's Day Parade" (1874), "Sweet Mary Ann" (1878) and the *Skidmore Fancy Ball* (1879) which included the song "The Babies on Our Block."

HARRINGTON, CALVIN S.

b. 1826, d. 1886.
Composer. Professor at Wesleyan University, Middletown, Conn.; composed the music "Homeward Bound" (w. W.F. Warren), "Softly, Now Tenderly, Lift Him with Care" (1862, about a wounded Civil War soldier), "In Some Way or Other the Lord Will Provide" (1873, w. Mrs. Martha A.W. Cook, arranged by Eben Tourjee).

HARRINGTON, KARL POMEROY

b. 1861 Somersworth, New Hampshire, d. 1953. Composer. Graduated Wesleyan University Middletown, Conn. (1882); composed the tunes "Worship" (for "To Thee, Eternal Soul, be Praise," w. R.W. Gilder), "Christmas Song" (for "There's a Song in the Air," w. J.G. Holland), "Weihnacht" (for "Long Years Ago O'er Bethlehem's Hills," w. L.R. Brewer, 1892), "Evanston," and the tune "Copeland" (for "Christ's Life Our Code, His Cross Our Creed," w. Benjamin Copeland, 1900); while he was teaching at the University of North Carolina, Chapel Hill, he wrote the college song "Mrs. Winslow's Soothing Syrup"; later he was professor of Latin at Wesleyan University.

HARRIOTT, ARTHURLIN ("JOE")

b. 1928 Jamaica, B.W.I.
Alto saxist. Played with small groups after emigrating to England (1951); formed his own combo in 1960; composed variations of jazz.

HARRIS, BARBARA

b. 1935 Evanston, Illinois.
Singer and actress. Starred in *The Apple Tree* (1966, m. Jerry Bock).

HARRIS, BARRY DOYLE

b. 1929 Detroit, Michigan.
Black pianist. Played in Detroit during 1950s; then with Cannonball Adderley, Yusef Lateef, Coleman Hawkins and others during 1960s; also led his own trio.

HARRIS, BENJAMIN ("LITTLE BENNY")

b. 1919 New York City, d. 1975.
Black jazz trumpeter and composer. With Tiny Bradshaw (1939), Earl Hines (1941), John Kirby (1943); wrote "Little Benny," "Lion's Den," "Craze-ology and Ornithology."

HARRIS, CHARLES KASSELL

b. 1867 Poughkeepsie, New York, d. 1930 New York City. Popular composer. Lived in Milwaukee, Wisconsin, and published his early songs there; wrote "After the Ball" (1892), "Can Hearts Soon Forget" (1892), "There'll Come a Time" (1895), "Break the News to Mother" (1897), " 'Mid the Green Fields of Virginia" (1898), "Night in June" (1899), "For Old Times' Sake" (1900), "I've a Longing in My Heart" (1900); "After the Ball" became a hit after Harris paid J.A. Libby $500 to sing the song in *A Trip to Chinatown*, while performing in Chicago (*see also* Percy Gaunt); John Philip Sousa featured the song along with his band at the Columbian Exposition in Chicago in 1893.

HARRIS, EDDIE

b. 1934 Chicago, Illinois.
Black tenor saxist. Served with 7th Army Symphony Orchestra in Europe; recorded "Exodus" while in Chicago; led his own combo in Chicago; albums—*Best of Eddie Harris; Come on Down; Cool Sax, Warm Heart; Exciting Eddie Harris; Explosive Eddie Harris; Here Comes the Judge; High Voltage; The "In" Sound; Mean Greens; Plug Me In.*

HARRIS, GENE

b. 1933 Benton Harbor, Michigan.
Pianist. Formed his own quartet, The Four Sounds, which later became a trio, The Three Sounds (1956); played in New York City after 1958; later featured arrangements by Julian Lee; albums—*Black Orchid, Blue Hour, Bottoms Up, Coldwater Flat, Elegant Soul, Feelin' Good, Good Deal, Here We Come,*

Hey There, Introducing the Three Sounds, It Just Got to Be Fun, LD Plus 3, Moods.

HARRIS, PHIL

b. 1906 Linton, Indiana.
Drummer and bandleader. Co-leader of the Lofner-Harris band during the 1920s and '30s; later took over the band; played at the Waldorf-Astoria, N.Y. City (1935); his singer, Leah Ray, later married Sonny Werblin of the N.Y. Jets football team; Phil married Alice Faye; became conductor for Jack Benny on his radio series.

HARRIS, RICHARD

b. 1929 England.
Singer and actor. Sang the part of King Arthur in film *Camelot* (1967); hit record "MacArthur Park" (1968); in concert at Philharmonic Hall, New York City (1972).

HARRIS, ROY

b. 1898 Lincoln County, Oklahoma.
Noted composer. Studied at the University of California, Los Angeles, then in Paris with Nadia Boulanger; taught at the Westminster Choir School, Princeton, N.J. (1934-38); chief of the Music Section for the Office of War Information during World War II; composed *Concerto for Piano, Clarinet and String Quarter* (1927), *String Sextet* (1932), Symphony no. 1 (1933), *Quartet for Strings* (1937), *Quintet for Piano and Strings* (1937), Symphony no. 3 (1938), Symphony no. 4 (1939), no. 5 (1942), no. 6 (1944).

HARRIS, TASSO

b. 1918 Pittsburgh, Pennsylvania.
Trombonist and educator. Played with Tommy Dorsey, Artie Shaw, Claude Thornhill and others during 1940s; later taught music at the University of Denver, Colorado; trombonist with Denver Symphony Orchestra; also taught privately.

HARRIS, THORO

b. 1874 Washington, D.C.
Composer. Moved to Chicago (1903); owned the Windsor Music Company there, music publishers; his tune "Crimea" was included in *The Methodist Hymnal.*

HARRIS, WILL J.

b. 1900 New York City.
Composer, lyricist, and director. Vaudeville director (1921-34); staged musical productions, USO shows; wrote the lyrics "Sweet Sue—Just You" (1928, m. Victor Young).

HARRIS, WILLARD PALMER (BILL)

b. 1916 Philadelphia, Pennsylvania.
Trombonist. Played with Woody Herman and others during 1940s, recorded *Bijou;* toured with Jazz at the Philharmonic during 1950s; later with Benny Goodman, Charlie Teagarden, and Red Norvo in Las Vegas.

HARRIS, WILLIAM VICTOR

b. 1869 New York City, d. there 1943.
Conductor and composer. Pupil of Charles Blum, Anton Seidl and others; coach at Metropolitan Opera, N.Y. (1892-95); conductor of Cecilia Chorus; composed an operetta *Mlle. Mai et M. de Septembre;* cantata, piano suite, songs.

HARRIS, WILLIE (BILL)

b. 1925 Nashville, North Carolina.
Guitarist. Led his own group in 1960; graduated Washington Junior College of Music; taught in Washington, D.C.

HARRISON, HAZEL

b. 1881 La Porte, Indiana.
Black pianist. Studied with Victor Heinze in Chicago; later with Ferruccio Busoni and Egon Petri in Germany; with Berlin Philharmonic Orchestra (1903-06); toured United States in 1920s; appeared with Los Angeles Symphony, Minneapolis Symphony, and Chicago Symphony orchestras; later taught at Howard University, Washington, D.C.

HARRISON, JAMES HENRY (JIMMY)

b. 1900 Louisville, Kentucky, d. 1931 New York City. Black jazz trombonist. Played in small combos in Detroit and throughout the Midwest (1916-21); with Billy Fowler, Duke Ellington, and Fletcher Henderson during 1920s; rated one of the first truly great trombonists.

HARRISON, LOU

b. 1917 Portland, Oregon.
Conductor and composer. Conductor of New York Little Symphony Orchestra; composed *Canticle, Fifth Simfony,* for percussion ensemble; *Concerto for Flute.*

HARRISON, NOEL

b. 1933 London, England.
Singer and actor. Son of actor Rex Harrison; sang in London night clubs; came to America before 1966; recorded Leonard Cohen's "Suzanne" and "So Long, Marianne"; albums—*Collage, Great Electric Experiment Is Over, Noel Harrison, Santa Monica Pier.*

HARROLD, ORVILLE

b. 1878 Muncie, Indiana, d. 1933 Darien, Connecticut. Tenor. Pupil of Oscar Saenger (1909-12); debut with Manhattan Opera Company, N.Y. (1910); sang with Mme. Trentini in comic opera; with Hammerstein's London Opera (1911); with Metropolitan Opera, New York after 1919.

HART, FREDDIE

b. 1933 Lochapoka, Alabama.
Singer and songwriter. Served in the U.S. Marines; albums—*Big Hits, Country's Best*; wrote "Easy Lovin' " which was selected Song of the Year at the 1971 Country Music Association awards presentations, Nashville.

HART, FREDERIC

b. 1898 Aberdeen, Washington.
Composer. Studied at American Conservatory in Chicago; served in army in France in World War I; studied with Boulanger, Wilson, and Goldmark; taught at Diller-Quaile School after 1923, and at Sarah Lawrence College after 1929; wrote *The Romance of Robot*, one-act opera, presented at Federal Music Theatre in New York City (1937).

HART, LORENZ MILTON

b. 1895 New York City, d. there 1943.
Lyricist. Attended Columbia University; joined with Richard Rodgers to write songs for Lew Fields (1920); with Rodgers they wrote many successful Broadway shows and songs including "With a Song in My Heart" (1929), "Blue Moon" (1934), "This Can't Be Love" (1938); on opening night of their *A Connecticut Yankee*, Hart disappeared; after a two-day search, he was found suffering with pneumonia, and died three days later.

HART, MOSS

b. 1904 New York City, d. 1961.
Playwright and librettist. Librettist for *Face the Music* (1932, m. Irving Berlin), *I'd Rather Be Right* (1937, with George S. Kaufman, m. Richard Rodgers), *Lady in the Dark* (1941, m. Kurt Weill), *Winged Victory* (1943, m. David Rose).

HART, OLIVER

b. 1723 Warminster, Pennsylvania, d. 1795 Hopewell, New Jersey. Hymnist. Became a Baptist minister (1749); wrote "My Father, I Come to Thee," which appeared in the *Sunday School Union Hymn Book* (1835).

HARTE, ROY

b. 1924 New York City.
Drummer. Played with Dizzy Gillespie, Lucky Millinder and others in 1940s; president of Hollywood Drum City after 1950; also record executive.

HARTFORD, JOHN

b. 1937 New York City.
Singer and songwriter. Raised in St. Louis, Missouri; played the banjo and guitar; wrote "Tall, Tall Grass," "Jack's in the Sack," "When the Sky Begins to Fall," "I Shoulda Wore My Birthday Suit," "Corn Cob Blues," "Today," "Front Porch," "Like Unto a Mocking Bird" (all 1966); "Gentle on My Mind" (1967); his RCA-LPs were *John Hartford Looks at Life* (1966), *Earthwords and Music* (1967), *The Love Album* (1968); at Philadelphia Folk Festival, Upper Salford Township, Pa. (1972).

HARTMANN, ARTHUR MARTINUS

b. 1881 Mate Szalka, Hungary, d. 1956 New York City. Violinist and teacher. Brought to Philadephia by his parents (1887); studied with Van Gelder, then Loeffler; made over 250 appearances as concert violinist (1890-1916); composed orchestral work, violin music and songs.

HARTSOUGH, LEWIS

b. 1828 Ithaca, New York, d. 1919 Mount Vernon, Iowa. Composer and compiler. First superintendent of the Utah Mission of the Methodist Episcopal Church; wrote "Let Me Go" (1862) and "I Hear Thy Welcome Voice" (1872, "I Am Coming Lord"); musical editor of *The Revivalist* (1868), compiled by Joseph Hillman; assisted John W. Dadmun in compiling *The Sacred Harmonium* (1864).

HASAAN IBN ALI

b. 1931 Philadelphia, Pennsylvania.
Pianist and composer. With Joe Morris' band in late 1940s; also played in concerts in Philadelphia; his compositions were recorded on *The Max Roach Trio Featuring the Legendary Hasaan.*

HASCHE, WILLIAM EDWIN

b. 1867 New Haven, Connecticut, d. 1929 Roanoke, Virginia. Composer. Studied with Parker and others; director of New Haven Symphony Orchestra; taught at Yale (1903); conducted New Haven Choral Union; composed the symphonic poems *Waldidylle, Fridjof*, and *Ingeborg*; cantata *The Haunted Oak*; a symphony.

HASSARD, JOHN ROSE GREENE

b. 1836 New York City, d. 1888.
Critic. Graduated Fordham, N.Y. City (1855); music critic of *New York Tribune* (1866-88).

HASSELMANS, LOUIS

b. 1878 Paris, France, d. 1957 San Juan, Puerto Rico. Conductor. Married Minnie Egener, soprano; studied at Paris Conservatory; debut as conductor at Lamoureaux Concerts, Paris (1905); founded Hasselmans' Orchestra (1907); conductor at Opera-Comique (1909-11), Montreal Opera (1911-13), Marseilles Concerts (1913-14), Chicago Opera (1918-20), Metropolitan Opera, New York (1921-36).

HASSILEV, ALEX

b. 1932 Paris, France.
Singer and banjoist. His parents brought him to America as a boy; sang at the Cosmo Alley coffee house, Hollywood (1959), then joined Glenn Yarbrough at the Limelite Club in Aspen, Colorado; then Alex and Glenn joined with Louis Gottlieb in 1959 to form "The Limeliters."

HASSLER, MARK

b. 1834 Germany, d. 1906 Philadelphia, Pennsylvania. Conductor. Came to Philadelphia (1842) with his father, Henry Hassler, violinist and conductor, and with his brother, Simon; conducted society orchestras in Philadelphia (1850-94); also played at the "hops" in Congress Hall, Cape May, New Jersey; his daughter, Harriet, vocal teacher in N.Y. City; Rosalie, pianist; son Herbert, music director at Chestnut Street Opera House; Arthur, management of dance and concert orchestras.

HASSLER, SIMON

b. 1832 Germany, d. ca. 1900 Philadelphia, Pennsylvania. Conductor. Came to Philadelphia (1842) with his father, Henry Hassler, conductor, and his brother, Mark Hassler; conducted orchestra at Walnut Street Theatre (1865-72), Chestnut Street Theatre (1872-82), Chestnut Street Opera House (1882-99).

HAST, LOUIS H.

b. ca. 1830, Upper Palatinate, Germany, d. 1890 Louisville, Kentucky. Organist. Taught music in Bardstown, Kentucky, then settled in Louisville (1851); organist-choirmaster of the Christ Church Cathedral (1878-89); organized many concerts in Louisville.

HASTINGS, FRANCIS H.

b. 1834, d. 1916.
Piano maker. Employed by Elias and George G. Hook in 1855 making organs and pianos in Boston; became member of firm of Hook & Hastings in 1865.

HASTINGS, THOMAS

b. 1784 Washington, Connecticut, d. 1872 New York City. Composer. When he was twelve the family moved to Clinton, N.Y.; he moved to Geneva, N.Y. (1818) where he taught music, then to Utica (1828) where he edited a religious paper; in 1832 became choirmaster of the Bleecker Street Presbyterian Church, New York City; he was a perfect albino, very near-sighted, yet had the ability to read music from a book held upside-down by someone else; wrote "Rock of Ages" (1830, w. A.M. Toplady), "Majestic Sweetness Sits Enthroned" (1830, w. Samuel Stennett), "Veni Sancte Spiritus," "O'er the Gloomy Hills of Darkness" (1830, w. William Williams), "On the Mountain Top Appearing," "Guide Me O Thou Great Jehovah" (w. William Williams) and "From Every Stormy Wind That Blows" (1840, w. H. Stowell). (*See* Solomon Warriner)

HATFIELD, EDWIN FRANCIS

b. 1807 Elizabethtown, New Jersey, d. 1883 Summit, New Jersey. Hymnist and compiler. Educated at Middlebury College, Vermont, and Andover; pastor of the 2nd Presbyterian Church, St. Louis, Missouri (1832-35), then in New York City (1835-63); published *Freedom's Lyre*, New York, which included many of his orginal hymns, *The Church Hymn Book for the Worship of God* (Presbyterian, 1872) and *Chapel Hymns* (1884).

HATTON, ANN JULIA (KEMBLE) CURTIS

b. ca. 1757 England, d. after 1795.
Librettist and playwright. Sister of the great English actress, Mrs. Sarah Kemble Siddons (1755-1831); first husband named Curtis; she was a large woman with a squint and of much annoyance to her famous sister, called herself "Anne Siddons"; read lectures at Dr. Graham's Temple of Health in London; attempted to poison herself in Westminster Abbey to attract public attention; came to New York City in 1793; wrote the libretto for the opera *Tammany, or the Indian Chief* (m. James Hewitt), produced in New York City on March 3, 1794, this was the first opera composed by an American; also wrote the lyrics for "The Patriot" (ca. 1795, "While Europe Strives with Mad Career").

HATTSTAEDT, JOHN JAMES

b. 1851 Monroe, Michigan, d. 1931 Chicago, Illinois. Teacher. With Karleton Hackett, he founded the American Conservatory of Music, Chicago, in 1886, with courses in all branches of music, and degrees in teaching.

HAUBIEL, CHARLES

b. 1892 Delta, Ohio.
Pianist and composer. Studied piano with Lhevinne and others; toured with Kocian; teacher at Oklahoma City Musical Art Institute; later at New York University; composed *Karma*, symphonic variations (Schubert Centenary prize); also piano works, chamber music and orchestral works.

HAUFRECHT, HERBERT

b. 1909 New York City.
Composer. Studied at Juilliard School of Music, New York City; composed *Suite for String Orchestra* (Juilliard Graduate School String Orchestra under Edgar Schenkman, 1934), *Overture for an American Mural* (WNYC Concert Orchestra, composer conducting, 1939), *Three Fantastic Sketches* (NBC Symphony Orchestra, under Frank Black, 1941), choruses, songs.

HAUK, MINNIE

b. 1852 New York City, d. 1929 Lucerne, Switzerland. Noted soprano. Born Minnie Hauck; pupil of Errani and Moritz Strakosch; debut as Nora, New York (1866); with Vienna Opera (1868-72); after 1872 in Europe and the United States.

HAUSER, WILLIAM

b. 1812, d. 1880.
Compiler. Published *The Olive Leaf* (1878), at Wadley, Georgia, one of the last shape-note tune books of spiritual folk songs.

HAVENS, RICHARD P. (RITCHIE)

b. 1941 Brooklyn, New York.
Black singer and electric sitar player. Raised in the Bedford Stuyvesant black ghetto of Brooklyn; one of nine children; his father started out as a professional pianist but spent twenty years in metal plating; played in Greenwich Village coffee houses, New York City (1962); albums—*Mixed Bag* (1967), *Richard P. Havens (1983), Somethin' Else Again*; at the Westbury, Long Island Music Fair (1972).

HAVENS, ROBERT L. (BOB)

b. 1930 Quincy, Illinois.
Trombonist. Studied trombone at age seven; played with Ralph Flanagan, George Girard, and Al Hirt in 1950s; on Lawrence Welk's TV show after 1960.

HAVER, JUNE

b. 1926 Rock Island, Illinois.
Singer and actress. She got her start as a vocalist in Ted Fiorito's band; later became famous as a film actress.

HAWES, BALDWIN ("BUTCH")

b. 1919 Cambridge, Massachusetts.
Singer, guitarist, and songwriter. Butch and his brother Pete sang with the Almanac Singers during the 1940s; later Butch moved to Santa Monica, California; wrote "UAW-CIO" and "Going Away to Sea, Baby Mine."

HAWES, BESS LOMAX

b. 1921 Austin, Texas.
Singer and teacher. Daughter of John Lomax; attended University of Texas (1936-37), later Bryn Mawr College (Pa.); served with Office of War Information in World War II; taught at San Fernando Valley State College, Los Angeles; sang at Newport Folk Festivals, Berkeley, and UCLA Folk Festivals during the 1960s.

HAWES, HAMPTON

b. 1928 Los Angeles, California.
Pianist. With Shorty Rogers, Red Mitchell, and Howard Rumsey in 1950s; named Arrival of the Year by Metronome (1956); appeared on Steve Allen's TV show; with Jackie McLean, Harold Land and others during 1960s.

HAWKINS, COLEMAN ("BEAN")

b. 1904 St. Joseph, Missouri, d. 1969.
Noted black tenor saxophonist. Played in Fletcher Henderson's band (1923-34); in Europe (1934-39); his solo record *Body and Soul* is a jazz classic; played in small combos during 1960s.

HAWKINS, ERSKINE

b. 1914 Birmingham, Alabama.
Black jazz trumpeter and bandleader. He brought his Alabama State Collegians out of the Deep South in 1936; Wilbur Bascomb played "Tuxedo Junction" on the trumpet; Hawkins made a hit with "After Hours" (by Avery Parrish); Della Reese sang with his band.

HAWKINS, HAROLD F. ("HAWKSHAW")

b. 1921 Huntington, West Virginia, d. 1963 Camden, Tennessee. Singer and guitarist. Served in the armed forces in World War II in the Pacific, and when the war ended sang over station WUTM in Manila, the Philippines; then on WWVA, Wheeling, West Virginia (1946); with Grand Old Opry, Nashville (1955); his King records were "Slow Poke" (1952), "Lonesome 7-7203" (1953), *From Our Vaults, Hawkshaw Hawkins* (1958); *All New Hawkshaw Songs* (1963); killed in a plane crash.

HAWKINS, JOHN ISAAC

b. 1772 Taunton, England, d. 1855 Elizabeth Town, New Jersey. Pianist, inventor and composer. Came to United States as a child; attended College of New Jersey, Princeton; resided in Bordentown, N.J.; obtained first patent on an upright piano (1800) (which he mailed to his father in England for the English patent—also patented by Thomas Loud in England, 1802); his cottage piano used coiled strings for bass tones; advertised in *Claypoole's American Daily Advertiser* Feb. 19, 1800; piano attracted Thomas Jefferson and Hawkins gave a demonstration for Jefferson; composed "Mark the Beauties of Creation" and "Ode on the Death of Titian Peale" (1800, w. Rembrandt Peale), "People's March" (1801); left for England (1802) but returned to New Jersey (1848); also composed "The People's Friend" (1801, w. Rembrandt Peale).

HAWKINS, MICAH

b. 1777 Stony Brook, Long Island, New York, d. 1825 New York City. Pianist and composer. Wrote the *Saw Mill, or A Yankee Trick,* a musical, performed at Chatham Theatre, New York City (1824).

HAWKS, ANNIE (SHERWOOD)

b. 1835 Hoosick, New York, d. 1918 Bennington, Vermont. Hymnist. Wrote "I Need Thee Every Hour" (1872, m. Robert Lowry), which first appeared in a small collection prepared by Lowry and W.H. Doane for the National Baptist Sunday School Association which met in Cincinnati, Ohio in 1872; longtime resident of Brooklyn, New York.

HAWLEY, CHARLES BEACH

b. 1858 Brookfield, Connecticut, d. 1915. Singer, organist, composer, and teacher. Wrote "Ah! 'Tis a Dream," "Bedouin Love Song," "Daisies," "Greeting," "My Little Love," "The Nightingale and the Rose"; with H.W. Greene, founded the Metropolitan Conservatory of Music, New York City (1885).

HAWORTH, C. E.

b. 1860, d. 1929.
Composer. He lived in Huntington, West Virginia; wrote *Te Deum* and *Jubilate.*

HAY, GEORGE D.

b. 1895 Attica, Indiana, d. 1968.
Impresario. Started "The National Barn Dance" on radio station WLS, Chicago, Illinois (1924); started "Grand Ole Opry" on radio station WSM, Nashville, Tennessee (1925).

HAY, JOHN

b. 1838 Salem, Indiana, d. 1905 Newport, New Hampshire. Hymnist and statesman. Educated at Brown University, Providence, R.I., and studied law in the office of Abraham Lincoln in Springfield, Illinois, being admitted to the bar in 1861; served as a private secretary to President Lincoln; later served as Ambassador to the Court of St. James and as Secretary of State; wrote the hymn "Not in Dumb Resignation" (tune "Llangloffan"—Welsh).

HAYDEN, SCOTT

b. 1882 Sedalia, Missouri, d. 1915 Chicago, Illinois. Black pianist and arranger. Played in St. Louis night clubs; Scott Joplin married his cousin; wrote "Sunflower Slow Drag" (1901, with Scott Joplin), "Felicity Rag" (1911), and "Kismet Rag" (1913), both published by John Stark; died of tuberculosis.

HAYES, CLARENCE LEONARD (CLANCY)

b. 1908 Caney, Kansas, d. 1972 San Francisco, California. Jazz singer. Appeared with such bands as Turk Murphy's and Bob Scobey's in 1940s; later led his own band; his biggest hit was "A-Huggin' and A-Chalkin' " (1945).

HAYES, ISAAC

b. 1942 near Memphis, Tennessee.
Black soul singer. Known as the "Black Moses"; also great organist; raised in Memphis; received his fourth consecutive platinum record, signifying more than two million in sales; albums—*Isaac Hayes Movement, Hot Buttered Soul, Presenting Isaac Hayes*; appeared at Philharmonic Hall, New York City (1971); appears at his concerts with a shaved head; won Grammy Award (1972) for best motion picture score, *Shaft.*

HAYES, LOUIS SEDELL

b. 1937 Detroit, Michigan.
Black drummer. With Horace Silver (1956-59); then with Cannonball Adderley (1959-65); with Oscar Peterson Trio after 1965; at Newport Jazz Festival (1965).

HAYES, ROLAND

b. 1887 Curryville, Georgia.
Black tenor. Family moved to Chattanooga, Tennessee (1900); graduated Fisk University, Nashville; after graduation joined Fisk Jubilee Singers in Boston; studied there with Arthur Hubbard (1911); gave recital at Symphony Hall, Boston (1917); toured Europe (1920-23); gave command performance for King George V; in Berlin (1924); taught at Boston University after 1950.

HAYES TRIO (black group)

Organized (1917) by Roland Hayes, tenor; William Richardson, baritone; William Lawrence, pianist.

HAYMES, DICK

b. 1918 Buenos Aires, Argentina.
Singer. Records—"It Can't Be Wrong," "You'll Never Know."

HAYNES, FRANK

b. 1931 San Francisco, California, d. 1965. Tenor saxist. Played with Walter Bishop, Randy Weston and others at various New York night spots; died of cancer.

HAYNES, HENRY D. ("HOMER")

b. 1920 Knoxville, Tennessee, d. 1971 Hammond, Indiana. Singer and guitarist. Partner with Kenneth C. Burns in the team "Homer & Jethro"; they joined the "Renfro Valley Square Dance," Mt. Vernon, Kentucky (1939); Homer served in the medical corps in the Pacific in World War II; sang over radio stations in Cincinnati, Springfield, Missouri, Chicago; they became famous in 1962 for a commercial for Kellogg's cornflakes, sitting around a table in country clothes.

HAYNES, JOHN C.

b. 1830 Brighton, Massachusetts, d. 1907. Publisher. Entered employ of Oliver Ditson in 1845 at $1.50 per week; later made a partner of the Boston firm; president of the corporation after the death of Ditson in 1888.

HAYNES, ROY OWEN

b. 1926 Roxbury, Massachusetts.
Drummer. With Charlie Parker, Lester Young, and Sarah Vaughan during 1950s; also led own trio; with Stan Getz in 1960s; also led own quartet; played at the Newport Jazz Festival, New York City (1972).

HAYS, LEE

b. 1914 Little Rock, Arkansas.
Bass. Sang with the Almanac Singers with Pete Seeger; after World War II with The Weavers; with Pete Seeger wrote "If I Had a Hammer."

HAYS, WILLIAM SHAKESPEARE (WILL)

b. 1837 Louisville, Kentucky, d. there 1907. Popular composer. Attended three colleges—at Hanover, Indiana, Clarksville, Tenn., and Georgetown, Kentucky, but never graduated; during the Civil War he traveled through the Confederate lines as a war correspondent, was captured in New Orleans in 1862, charged with writing seditious songs, and thrown into prison by General Ben Butler, the Union Commander; wrote "The Drummer Boy of Shiloh" (1862), "My Southern Sunny Home," "We Parted by the River" (1866), "Nora O'Nea" (1866), "Write Me a Letter" (1866), "Little Log Cabin in the Lane" (1871), "Molly Darling" (1871), "Number Twenty-Nine" (1871), "Roll Out! Heave Dat Cotton" (1877), "Early in de Mornin' " (1877), "Walk in de Middle of de Road" (1880). (*See also* A.E. Blackmar and Septimus Winner)

HAYTON, LEONARD GEORGE (LENNIE)

b. 1908 New York City, d. 1971 Palm Springs, California. Pianist and popular composer. Played in jazz groups including those of Frankie Traumbauer, Bix Beiderbecke, and Red Nichols; music director for MGM (1940-53), then with 20th Century Fox; husband of Lena Horne, singer and actress; wrote the scores for the films *Star* (Julie Andrews), *On the Town* (1949), *The Harvey Girls*, and *Singin' in the Rain*; his instrumental pieces were *Flying Fingers, Mood Hollywood*, and *Midnight Mood.*

HAZARD, RICHARD P. (DICK)

b. 1921 Trenton, New Jersey.
Pianist and arranger. Studied piano at age eight; on Hoagy Carmichael radio series in Hollywood after 1946; accompanist and conductor for Herb Jeffries in 1950s; wrote arrangements for Judy Garland, Peggy Lee and others.

HAZELWOOD, LEE

b. 1929 Mannford, Oklahoma.
Singer and songwriter. Raised in Oklahoma and Texas; albums—*World of Lee Hazelwood* (1966), *Hazelwoodism—Its Cause and Cure, Houston, Love and Other Crimes, Nancy and Lee.*

HEAP, JAMES ARTHUR (JIMMY)

b. 1922 Taylor, Texas.
Singer and songwriter. Served in U.S. Army Air Corps during World War II; leader of The Melody Masters (1947-64); the Jimmy Heap Show after 1964; he wrote "Haunted Hungry Heart," "Make Me Live Again," "Ethyl in My Gas Tank," "When They Operated on Papa."

HEARD, JAMES CHARLES ("J.C.")

b. 1917 Dayton, Ohio.
Black jazz drummer. Played with Teddy Wilson; recorded with Sidney Bechet in the 1930s and '40s.

HEATH, ALBERT ("TOOTIE")

b. 1935 Philadelphia, Pennsylvania.
Black drummer. Brother of Percy Heath; with

J.J. Johnson in late 1950s; in trio with Cedar Walton and Reggie Workman in New York City in early 1960s; with George Russell in Stockholm, Sweden, after 1965.

HEATH, JAMES EDWARD (JIMMY)

b. 1926 Philadelphia, Pennsylvania.
Black flutist and tenor saxist. Brother of Percy Heath; played with Dizzy Gillespie, Miles Davis and others during 1950s; with Donald Byrd, Art Farmer and others during 1960s.

HEATH, LYMAN

b. 1804 Bow, New Hampshire, d. 1870.
Singer and composer. Composed the music "The Burial of Mrs. Judson" (a Baptist missionary), "Mournfully, Tenderly, Bear On the Dead" (w. H.S. Washburn).

HEATH, PERCY

b. 1923 Wilmington, North Carolina.
Black bass player. Older brother of Jimmy and Tootie Heath; played with Miles Davis, Howard McGhee and others during 1940s; with Dizzy Gillespie (1950-52); member Modern Jazz Quartet (1952); at the Newport Jazz Festival, New York City (1972).

HEATH, WILBUR F.

b. 1843 Corinth, Vermont, d. 1915.
Bandmaster, composer, and writer. Leader of an Illinois regimental band which led the procession of the burial of President Lincoln in Springfield, Ill.; taught in Iowa City and Marengo, Iowa; superintendent of music in the public schools in Ft. Wayne, Indiana after 1873; wrote *Vocal Exercise Charts* and *Common School Music Readers.*

HEATHERTON, JOEY

b. 1944 New York City.
Singer and dancer. Popular in New York City night clubs; with her group of dancers at the Empire Room in the Waldorf-Astoria Hotel (1972).

HECKMAN, DONALD J. (DON)

b. 1932 Reading, Pennsylvania.
Alto saxist, clarinetist, and writer. Educated at the University of Miami, Coral Gables, Florida; played in college band (1948); toured Venezuela with band (1951); with John Benson Brooks trio, Don Ellis, and Ed Summerlin during 1960s; jazz reviewer for *American Record Guide.*

HEDGE, FREDERICK HENRY

b. 1805 Cambridge, Massachusetts, d. there 1890. Hymnist. Graduated Harvard University; minister of the Unitarian Church in Bangor, Maine; translated *Ein feste burg* by Martin Luther; wrote the hymn "It Is Finished," ("Man of Sorrows!", 1843, tune "Christi Mutter"); with Dr. F.D. Huntington, edited *Unitarian Hymns for the Church of Christ* (Boston, 1853).

HEERINGEN, ERNEST VON *see* VON HEERINGEN

HEFTI, NEAL

b. 1922 Hastings, Nebraska.
Trumpeter, pianist, and composer. With Earl Hines, Charlie Barnet, Harry James, and Woody Herman during the 1940s; led own group during 1950s; wrote *The Good Earth* and *Wildroot* for Woody Herman; also *Li'l Darlin'* for Count Basie; *Batman Theme*; wrote scores for films.

HEGNER, ANTON

b. 1861 Copenhagen, Denmark, d. 1915 New York City. Cellist and composer. Studied at the Copenhagen Conservatory; debut in 1875; later taught in New York City; composed two concertos for the cello; four quartets.

HEIDEN, BERNHARD

b. 1910 Frankfurt-on-Main, Germany.
Composer. Student of Paul Hindemith; became a music teacher at the University of Indiana, Bloomington (1946); composed two symphonies, stage music for *Henry IV* and *The Tempest*, and chamber music.

HEIFETZ, JASCHA

b. 1901 Vilna, Lithuania.
Famous concert violinist. Accepted at the Vilna Conservatory at the age of five, and graduated when eight years old; then studied with Leopold Auer; received a tremendous reception as a violinist in Berlin, Vienna, and Leipzig; his family fled the Russian Revolution by way of Siberia, China, Japan, then finally landed in San Francisco; became a U.S. citizen (1925).

HEILNER, IRWIN

b. 1908.
Composer. Wrote *The Tide Rises* (w. Henry W. Longfellow).

HEIN, SILVIO

b. 1879 New York City, d. 1928.
Composer. With Chris Smith, wrote "He's a Cousin of Mine" (1906).

HEINRICH, ANTHONY PHILIP

b. 1781 Schoenbuchel, Bohemia, d. 1861 New York City. Composer. Settled in Philadelphia (1818) where he directed music in the Southwick Theatre, then taught violin lessons in Louisville and Bardstown, Ky.; while in Boston in 1832 he composed *Antonia*, and in 1838 he was giving piano recitals in New York City; his symphonic and choral works contained music of the Kentucky Indians, and once he played before President John Tyler at the invitation of John H. Hewitt, who called Heinrich the "maniac musician."

HEINRICH, MAX

b. 1853 Chemnitz, Germany, d. 1916.
Baritone. Came to America (1873); sang at concerts and German festivities.

HEINS, FRANCIS DONALDSON

b. 1878 Hereford, Herefordshire, England.
Composer. Studied at the Royal Conservatorium, Leipzig, Germany, then went to Ottawa, Canada, in 1902 to teach; in 1927 he went to teach at the Toronto Conservatory of Music; composed the tune "Hereford"—"There's a Voice in the Wilderness Crying" (w. J.L. Milligan).

HELD, ANNA

b. 1865 Warsaw, Poland, d. 1918 New York City. Noted singer and actress. Family moved to Paris (1871); debut in Jacob Adler's Yiddish Theatre, London (1885); Paris debut (1893); came to America (1896) with Florenz Ziegfeld as her common-law husband; New York debut (1896) in *A Parlor Match*; became famous singing "Won't You Come and Play Wiz Me?"; in *La Poupée* (1897), *Papa's Wife* (1899), *The Little Duchess* (1901), *Follies of 1907*; divorced Ziegfeld (1913); in *Follow Me* (1916).

HELFER, WALTER

b. 1896 Lawrence, Massachusetts, d. 1959 New Rochelle, New York. Composer. Graduated Harvard University; awarded fellowship at American Academy in Rome; studied with Mason and Respighi; taught at Hunter College, New York City; composed *Symphony on Canadian Airs, Fantasie on Children's Tunes, Prelude to A Midsummer Night's Dream* (Paderewski Prize, 1938), *String Quartet.*

HELLER, JAMES GUTHEIM

b. 1892 New Orleans, Louisiana, d. 1971.
Composer. Studied with Stillman-Kelley and Durst; graduated Hebrew Union College as a rabbi; taught at Cincinnati Conservatory of Music; his *Four Sketches for Orchestra* (1934) played by the Cincinnati Symphony Orchestra.

HELLERMAN, FRED

b. 1927 New York City.
Singer and songwriter. Served in the Coast Guard in World War II; attended New York University, Columbia, and graduated from Brooklyn College (1949); sang with The Weavers; wrote or arranged "Kisses Sweeter Than Wine," "I'm Just a Country Boy," "Delia," "Come Away Melinda," "The Honey Wind Blows," "Healing River."

HELMS, BOBBY LEE

b. 1933 Bloomington, Indiana.
Singer. His song hits were "Fraulein" (1957), "My Special Angel" (1957), "Jacqueline" (1958), "Jingle Bell Rock"; wrote "I Don't Owe You Nothin' " (1956), and "Tonight's the Night" (1957); his LP records were *Bobby Helms Sings, Best of Bobby Helms* (1963); *Sorry, My Name Isn't Fred; I'm the Man.*

HEMMENWAY, JAMES

b. 1800, d. 1849 Philadelphia, Pennsylvania.
Black conductor and composer. Leader of Hemmenway's Military Band in Philadelphia (1827), played at Washington Hall, Philadelphia; wrote *Miss Billing's Waltz* (1819), *The Washington Gray's Bugle Quick Step* (1821), *Washington Gray's Grand March* (1823), *General La Fayette's Trumpet March and Quick Step* (1824).

HEMPHILL, SHELTON ("SCAD")

b. 1906 Birmingham, Alabama, d. 1959.
Black trumpeter. Played in Duke Ellington's band.

HENDERS, HARRIET

b. 1904 Marengo, Iowa, d. 1972 Carmel, New York. Soprano. Born Harriet Henderson; graduated Simpson College; studied with Bernhardt Bronson there and with Ragna Linne in Los Angeles; operatic debut in Graz, Austria (1931); with the German Opera in Prague; at Salzburg Festival (1937) under Arturo Toscanini; joined Metropolitan Opera, New York City (1939); married Dr. Ferdinand G. Kojis (1942) and retired; died of injuries following an auto accident.

HENDERSON, HORACE

b. 1904 Cuthbert, Georgia.
Black composer. Brother of Fletcher Henderson, bandleader; composed *Rug Cutter's Swing* recorded by Red Allen (originated by Allen); toured as pianist for Lena Horne.

HENDERSON, JAMES FLETCHER ("SMACK")

b. 1897 Cuthbert, Georgia, d. 1952 New York City. Black bandleader, arranger, and pianist. Graduated Atlanta University, Atlanta, Ga.; with W.C. Handy (1920); later accompanied Ethel Waters; led his own band after 1923; arranger for Isham Jones, Jimmy and Tommy Dorsey, and others during 1930s; later arranger for Benny Goodman; pianist for Ethel Waters on tour (1948-49); suffered a stroke in 1950.

HENDERSON, JOSEPH A. (JOE)

b. 1937 Lima, Ohio.
Black tenor saxist. With Sonny Stitt in late 1950s; with Jack McDuff, Horace Silver and others in 1960s; at Juan-les-Pins Jazz Festival (1964), also Monterey Jazz Festival that year.

HENDERSON, LYLE CEDRIC ("SKITCH")

b. 1918 England.
Pianist, bandleader, and conductor. Brought to U.S. at age seven; raised in Halstad, Minnesota, and Blackwell, Okla.; studied with Fritz Reiner, Schoenberg, and Ernst Toch; organized a band and played at Pennsylvania Hotel, New York City, with Nancy Read, singer; later musical director for Frank Sinatra; conductor of NBC "Tonight" TV show after 1962; conductor of Tulsa (Okla.) Philharmonic (1972).

HENDERSON, RAY

b. 1896 Buffalo, New York, d. 1971 Greenwich, Connecticut. Popular composer. Staff pianist and arranger for Shapiro-Bernstein; composed "That Old Gang of Mine" (1923 w. Billy Rose and Mort Dixon), "Alabamy Bound" (1925, w. Bud Green and Buddy De Sylva), "Bye, Bye Blackbird" (Dixon), "Five Foot Two, Eyes of Blue" (Sam Lewis and Joe Young), and with lyricists Buddy De Sylva and Lew Brown—"The Best Things in Life Are Free" (1927), "Button Up Your Overcoat," "You Are My Lucky Star," "Sonny Boy" (1928, written for Al Jolson), "Keep Your Sunny Side Up" (1929).

HENDERSON, WAYNE MAURICE

b. 1939 Houston, Texas.
Trombonist. Studied trombone at age eleven; with the Jazz Crusaders; appeared on Steve Allen's "Jazz Scene U.S.A."

HENDERSON, WILLIAM JAMES

b. 1855 Newark, New Jersey, d. 1937 New York City. Librettist and music critic. Graduated Princeton University (1876); critic for *New York Times* (1887-1902), and *New York Sun* (1902-37); wrote the librettos for Damrosch's operas *The Scarlet Letter* and *Cyrano de Bergerac*; committed suicide (shooting).

HENDERSON, WILLIAM RANDALL (BILL)

b. 1930 Chicago, Illinois.
Singer. Vocalist on Horace Silver record, *Señor Blues* (1958); with Count Basie and others during 1960s.

HENDRICKS, JOHN CARL (JON)

b. 1921 Newark, Ohio.
Black singer and songwriter. Formed a vocal trio with Dave Lambert and Annie Ross (1958); won several polls as the no. 1 vocal group in jazz; later Yolande Bavan replaced Annie Ross (1962); Hendricks went solo after 1964; wrote "Yeh! Yeh!," "Gimme That Wine."

HENDRICKSON, ALTON REYNOLDS (AL)

b. 1920 Eastland, Texas.
Singer and guitarist. Played with Dizzy Gillespie; at Monterey Jazz Festival (1962); recorded on Artie Shaw's Gramercy 5; also on bossa nova albums (1962-65).

HENDRIX, JAMES MARSHALL ("JIMI")

b. 1942 Seattle, Washington, d. 1970 London, England. Black singer and guitarist. Rock superstar; died of an apparent overdose of drugs; his albums were *Are You Experienced; Axis, Bold as Love; Electric Ladyland; Flashing; Get That Feeling; Smash Hits.*

HENDRIX EXPERIENCE, THE JIMI (rock group)

Jimi Hendrix, guitar; Mitch Mitchell, drums; Noel Redding, bass.

HENNIG, RUDOLPH

b. 1850 Germany, d. 1904 Philadelphia, Pennsylvania. Cellist. Came to Philadelphia ca. 1867; cellist at Walnut Street Theatre; one of the founders of the Philadelphia Musical Academy (1869); first cellist in Theodore Thomas' orchestra (1872-79); taught in Philadelphia after 1880.

HENSCHEL, LILLIAN BAILEY

b. 1860 Columbus, Ohio, d. 1901 London, England. Soprano. Wife of George Henschel, who conducted the Boston Symphony Orchestra (1881-84); she was his pupil, and married him (1881); she and her husband, who was also a baritone and pianist, gave concerts.

HENSLER, ELSIE

b. 1836, d. 1929.
Soprano. Sang at the Musical Fund Society Concerts, Philadelphia (1855); member of Mme. La Grange's opera company after 1856.

HENSLEY, HAROLD GLENN

b. 1922 Whitetop, Virginia.
Singer and fiddler. Attended high school in Grundy, Virginia, and studied at Valley Conservatory of Music, Studio City, Calif.; with Home Town Jamboree, Hollywood (1946-59), Billy Liebert's Jamboree Band (1946-59), Doye O'Dell's Western Varieties (1959-60), and Noel Bogg's Western Spring Band after 1961; headed country and western group that entertained Prince Philip of England on his visit to 20th Century-Fox Studios, Hollywood (1966).

HENSON, HERBERT LESTER ("COUSIN HERB")

b. 1925 East St. Louis, Illinois.
Singer and songwriter. Sang on radio in Bakersfield, Calif.; wrote "Board of Education" (1951), "I Miss You So" (1951), "Easy Going Kisses" (1952), "Uncertain Feeling" (1952), "I Wrote My Heart a Letter" (1953), "Rose to a Redhead" (1953), "Hurry Back" (1954), "Man Hold Lightning" (1956), "Space Command," "Up Yaander," "Goodbye Baby, Goodbye" (1959), "Uncle Ned" (1959).

HERBERT, VICTOR

b. 1859 Dublin, Ireland, d. 1924 New York City. Popular composer. Married Theresa Foerster, prima donna of the Stuttgart (Germany) Opera (1886), then they came to America; he became director of the Boston Festival Orchestra (1891), bandmaster of the 22nd Regiment of the New York National Guard (1893), and was conductor of the Pittsburgh Symphony (1898-1904); with librettist Harry B. Smith wrote the comic operas *The Serenade* which opened in Cleveland, Ohio (1897) with "I Love Thee, I Adore Thee" introduced by W.H. MacDonald and Jessie Bartlett Davis; *The Idol's Eye* (1897) with "The Cuban Song" introduced by Will Danforth; *The Fortune Teller* at the Grand Opera House in Toronto (1898) with "Gypsy Love Song" introduced by Eugene Cowles and the quintet Romany Life; *Cyrano de Bergerac* (book—Stuart Reed) in the Academy of Music in Montreal (1899); *The Singing Girl* (book—S. Strange) at Her Majesty's Theatre in Montreal (1899) with "If You Were Only Mine" sung by Alice Nielsen, who then became known as "The Singing Girl"; *The Ameer* opened at the Lyceum Theatre, Scranton, Pa. (1899) (book—Frederick Ranken and lyrics—Kirk LaShelle); *Babes in Toyland* appeared in 1903 and *It Happened in Nordland* (1904); "Kiss Me Again," with lyrics by Henry Blossom, appeared in *Mlle. Modiste* (1905) and "The Streets of New York, or In Old New York," lyrics by Henry Blossom, featured Fred Stone and David Montgomery in *The Red Mill* (1906); "Ah, Sweet Mystery of Life" and "Italian Street Song" were sung by Emma Trentini in *Naughty Marietta* (1910); "Sweethearts" (w. Robert B. Smith) was introduced by Christine MacDonald in 1913; *My Dream Girl,* lyrics by Rida Johnson Young, and introduced by Walter Woolf in 1924, was Victor Herbert's last song and last operetta; died of a heart attack in 1924 in New York City.

HERBST, JOHANNES

b. 1734 Germany, d. 1812.
Composer. Came to Pennsylvania (1786); Moravian pastor in Lancaster, later in Lititz, then pastor and bishop in Salem; composed about 125 sacred songs and anthems.

HERD, THE *see* WOODY HERMAN

HERD, THE (English rock group)

HERITAGE, RICHARD ABRAHAM

b. 1852 Bryan, Ohio, d. 1929.
Conductor, singer, and teacher. Studied under George F. Root, L. Gaston Gottschalk, Louis Falk, et al.; graduated Chicago Musical College; taught at the State Normal School in Valparaiso, Indiana; published *The Musical Ideal,* monthly magazine, after 1881.

HERMAN, JERRY

b. 1933 New York City.
Composer. Wrote the scores for *Milk and Honey* (1961), and *Hello Dolly!* (1964, book—Michael Stewart, based on Thornton Wilder's "Matchmaker," with Carol Channing in the lead).

HERMAN, WOODROW CHARLES (WOODY)

b. 1913 Milwaukee, Wisconsin.
Singer, clarinetist, saxophonist, and bandleader. Started as an entertainer at age six; formed his own band (1936); Stan Getz played the saxophone as one of the Four Brothers with Woody Herman's Herd (1947-49); his explosive *Caledonia* included on RCA's album *Big Bands' Greatest Hits* (1971); at Roseland

Dance City, New York (1972); at Newport Jazz Festival, New York City (1972).

HERRICK, JOSEPH

b. (?), d. 1807 Milford, New Hampshire. Clarinetist, flutist, and composer. Compiled *The Instrumental Preceptor* (1807) which included thirteen of his marches and several songs.

HERRMANN, BERNARD

b. 1911 New York City.
Composer. Studied at the Juilliard School, New York City; founded the New Chamber Orchestra (1931); went to work for CBS radio (1934); composed the cantata *Moby Dick* (book—Herman Melville) premiered by the New York Philharmonic (1940); then became a film composer; his *London Phase 4 Stereo* disk (he conducted the London Philharmonic) contains excerpts from his film scores *Psycho, Vertigo, North by Northwest, Citizen Kane* and *Jane Eyre.*

HERTZ, ALFRED

b. 1872 Frankfurt, Germany, d. 1942 San Francisco, California. Conductor. Became conductor at the Metropolitan Opera, New York City (1902), then was a conductor in San Francisco (1915-30).

HESS, DAVID

b. 1936 New York City.
Composer and writer. With Aaron Schroeder wrote "I Got Stung" for Elvis Presley; "Speedy Gonzales" for Pat Boone; with John Corigliano, Jr. wrote *The Naked Carmen*, rock extravaganza (Mercury Records, 1970).

HESS, FREDERICK

b. 1863 Mannheim, Germany, d. 1941.
Cellist. Brought to America at age three; at age eight studied cello under his father; later graduated from Dr. Hoch's Conservatory at Frankfort, Germany; studied under Bernhard Cossmann and Joachim Raff; located in Chicago (1885); played in Theodore Thomas' orchestra; taught at American Conservatory of Music and Apollo School of Music, Chicago.

HESSELIUS, MONS GUSTOFF (GUSTAVUS)

b. 1682 Folkarna, Sweden, d. 1755 Philadelphia, Pennsylvania. Organ maker. Came to Philadelphia (1711); maker of virginals and spinets (1742); built the organ installed in the Moravian Church, Bethlehem, Pa. (1746); also a portrait painter.

HESTER, CAROLYN

b. ca. 1937 Waco, Texas.
Soprano. Sang at college concerts at the University of Texas, University of Virginia, Yale, Harvard; Edinburgh Festival, Scotland (1962); toured England and U.S.; her Columbia LP record was *Carolyn Hester* (1962) and Dot Records, *That's My Song* (1965); married Richard Farina, singer, later divorced.

HEWITT, HORATIO DAWES

b. (?), d. 1894.
Critic and composer. Wrote "Suffer Little Children to Come to Me."

HEWITT, JAMES

b. 1770 Dartmoor, England, d. 1827 Boston, Massachusetts. Composer and publisher. Came to America (1792) with Jean Gehot, B. Bergmann, and William Young; opened a music store in New York City (1793); published music there (1797-1817); also in Boston after 1812; composed first American opera, *Tammany* (1794, w. Ann Julia Hatton), also *The Patriot, or Liberty Asserted* (1794, story of the Swiss patriot, William Tell), *Governor Jay's March* (1795), *Major Morton's March* (1795), *The New York Rangers March* (1795), six sonatinas for the harpsichord or pianoforte; many songs—"Primroses" (*see* Mrs. Pownall); in 1821 conducted a grand oratorio in Augusta, Georgia.

HEWITT, JAMES LANG

b. 1807, d. 1853.
Publisher. Son of James Hewitt; music publisher in Boston (1824-25), and in New York City (1826-35); published *The Sylviad* (1825, A.P. Heinrich), *Overture de la cour, Polonaise de la cour, Fantasia alla Polonese.*

HEWITT, JOHN HILL

b. 1801 New York City, d. 1890 Baltimore, Maryland. Popular composer. Son of James Hewitt; sometimes used the pseudonym Eugene Raymond; known as the "Father of the American Ballad"; attended West Point, but left the academy for music (1822); lived in Augusta, Georgia (1822-25), Greenville, South Carolina (1825-27), moved to Boston (1827) when his father died there, then moved to Baltimore, where he edited *The Clipper*; became editor of *The Capitol* in Washington, D.C. (1840) and taught in Hampton, Virginia, (1841-50); between 1842-45 Hewitt made weekly visits to the White House where he gave piano lessons to Alice Tyler, daughter of President John Tyler; in 1861 he became drillmaster of Confederate troops in Richmond, Virginia; later editor of the *Evening Mirror* in Savannah, Georgia; lived in Baltimore (1870-90); wrote the lyrics "The South" (1860, m. Arnaud Preót), and composed the music for "The South" (1861, w. Charles Woodward); wrote "The Minstrel's Return from the War" (1827), "Hark, Brothers Hark" (1837), "Flag of the Sunny South" (1861, w. E.V. Sharp), "The Young Volunteer" (1861), "All Quiet Along the Potomac Tonight" (1861, w. Ethel Lynn Beers), "We Are Going to the Wars Billy Boy," "I Will Meet Thee," "Somebody's Darling" (w. Marie LaCoste), "Dreaming of Thee" (w. John D. Burns), "Once More at Home" (1865), "Our Native Land," "The Mountain Bugle," "Take Me Home Where the Sweet Magnolia Blooms," "Dear Land of the South" (1860), and "Carry Me Back to the Sweet Sunny South."

HEWS, GEORGE

b. 1806 Weston, Massachusetts, d. 1873 Boston, Massachusetts. Composer. After 1830 music teacher and counter-tenor in the Handel and Haydn Society, where he served as vice president (1854-58); organist of the Battle Street Church; composed the tune "Holley" in 1835, for "Softly Fades the Twilight Ray" (1843, w. S.F. Smith), and "Softly Now the Light of Day" (1835, w. G.W. Doane).

HEYMAN, EDWARD

b. 1907 New York City.
Lyricist. Educated at the University of Michigan; wrote for Broadway shows; wrote "Body and Soul" (with Robert Sour—m. Johnny Green), "I Cover the Waterfront" (m. Green), "I Wanna Be Loved" (with Billy Rose—m. Green). (*See also* Vincent M. Youmans and Victor Young.)

HEYMAN, KATHERINE RUTH

b. 1877 Sacramento, California, d. 1944 Sharon, Connecticut. Pianist. Debut in Boston (1899); became known as an interpreter of the works of Alexander N. Scriabine, the eminent Russian composer.

HEYWARD, LELAND

b. 1902 Nebraska City, Nebraska, d. 1971 Yorktown Heights, New York. Producer. Attended Princeton University, but flunked out as a freshman; went to work as a reporter for the *Sun*, which soon fired him; made a fortune as an actor's agent, then became a producer; produced *South Pacific, Call Me Madam*, and *Sound of Music*; married five time; his wives included Margaret Sullavan and Pamela Digby Churchill, divorced wife of Randolph Churchill.

HEYWOOD, EDDIE, JR.

b. 1915 Atlanta, Georgia.
Pianist, bandleader, and composer. Son of Eddie Heywood, Sr., famous jazz pianist; accompanied Billie Holiday; organized own band (1943); wrote "Sleep," "Fish Fry," " 'Tain't Me," "Canadian Sunset," "I'm Saving Myself for You."

HIBBLER, AL

b. 1915 Little Rock, Arkansas.
Black singer. Born blind; sang in Jay McShann's Kansas City Band; then with Duke Ellington; his top records were "He" (1954) and "Unchained Melody" (1955); sang "Nobody Knows the Touble I've Seen" at Louis Armstong's funeral (1971).

HI-FI'S *see* THE FIFTH DIMENSION

HIGGINBOTHAM, JACK ("J. C.")

b. 1906 Social Circle, Georgia, d. 1973.
Black trombonist. Played in Lucky Millinder's Blue Rhythm Band; with Fletcher Henderson, Red Allen and others in 1940s; with Louis Armstrong; played in New York night spots in 1950s and '60s; toured Scandinavia (1963) and also at Norfolk, Va. Jazz Festival; in Copenhagen, Denmark after 1965; played at the Newport Jazz Festival, New York City (1972).

HIGGINS, BILLY

b. 1936 Los Angeles, California.
Drummer. Played with Ornette Coleman (1959); then with various groups during 1960s.

HIGGINS, HAYDN ("EDDIE")

b. 1932 Cambridge, Massachusetts.
Pianist. Studied piano under his mother; educated at Northwestern University School of Music in Chicago; with Jimmy Ille's Dixieland group and formed own trio in Chicago during 1950s; with Jack Teagarden and others during 1960s.

HIGGINSON, THOMAS WENTWORTH

b. 1823 Cambridge, Massachusetts, d. there 1911. Hymnist. Pastor of Unitarian churches in Newburyport, Mass. (1847-50) and Worcester, Mass. (1852-58); during the Civil War he was a colonel of the first Negro regiment raised in South Carolina; wrote several hymns which appeared in Samuel Longfellow and Samuel Johnson's *Book of Hymns* (1846).

HIGLEY, BREWSTER M.

b. 1823 Rutland, Vermont, d. 1911 Swanee, Oklahoma. Lyricist. Was a country medical doctor in Beaver Creek, Kansas, when he wrote the lyrics "Home on the Range," which first appeared in the December 1873 issue of *The Smith County Pioneer* (Kansas) magazine; Daniel E. Kelly composed the music; it is now the official state song of Kansas.

HILL, ALEX

b. 1907 Little Rock, Arkansas, d. 1937.
Black jazz pianist. Known as a barrelhouse player, also a fine arranger and composer; arranged for Fats Waller, Claude Hopkins, Benny Carter and others; composed "Baby Brown," "Dixie Lee," "Anything for You," " 'Long About Midnight."

HILL, ANDREW

b. 1937 Port au Prince, Haiti.
Black pianist and composer. Born Andrew Hille; brought to U.S. at age four; raised in Chicago; with Paul Williams and accompanist to Dinah Washington during 1950s; played in various combos in Los Angeles and New York City during 1960s; married organist Laverne Gillette; also toured Europe.

HILL, BERTHA ("CHIPPIE")

b. 1905 Charleston, South Carolina, d. 1950 New York City. Black singer. Debut in Harlem, New York City; toured with Ma Rainey; known as a classic blues singer; recorded with Louis Armstrong's band (1925-26); recorded "Trouble in Mind" (m. Richard M. Jones); took part in the memorial concert for Bessie Smith at Town Hall, New York City (1948); killed in an auto accident (1950).

HILL, EDWARD BURLINGAME

b. 1872 Cambridge, Massachusetts, d. 1960. Composer. Graduated Harvard (1894); studied with Lang, Whiting and others; taught piano in Boston (1887-1902); at Harvard University after 1908; composed the pantomime for orchestra *Jack Frost in Midsummer* (Chicago Orchestra, 1907), women's chorus with orchestra *Nuns of the Perpetual Adoration* (Musical Art Society, 1907), symphonies *Sinfonietta* and *Lilacs, Stevensonia Suites* nos. 1 and 2, chamber music, sonatas, songs.

HILL, FREDERICK ROOSEVELT (FREDDY)

b. 1932 Jacksonville, Florida.
Black pianist. Studied with Percy Mills; educated at Florida A & M College, Tallahassee; served in U.S. Army (1953); resided in Los Angeles after 1957; played with Gerald Wilson and Earl Bostic.

HILL, GOLDIE

b. 1933 Karnes County, Texas.
Singer. Sang on "Louisiana Hayride," station KWKH, Shreveport, La. (1952); Grand Ole Opry, Nashville (1953); married Carl Smith, singer; her hit records were "I Let the Stars Get in My Eyes" (1953), "Say, Big Boy" (1953), "Yesterday's Girl"; featured on Decca LP records *According to My Heart, Hit Parade, Heartaches* (1961).

HILL, JAMES VAUGHN

b. 1930 Portsmouth, Ohio.
Gospel singer and songwriter. Attended Ohio University, Athens, Ohio; with Stamps Quartet; wrote "Each Step I Take," "What a Day That Will Be," "For God So Loved," "I Walked Today with the Lord," "Road of No Return," "No One Cared So Much."

HILL, JOHN LEUBRIE

b. 1873, d. 1916.
Black composer. Wrote and arranged instrumental rags, musical comedies, and popular songs; wrote the *Darktown Follies* (1913), presented at the Lafayette Theatre, Harlem, New York City, which included "At the Ball," later used by Florenz Ziegfeld in his Follies.

HILL, MABEL WOOD

b. 1891 Brooklyn, New York, d. 1954 Stamford, Connecticut. Composer. Studied under Rothwell and Rubner (1917); first recital of her songs given in 1918; helped found the Brooklyn Music School Settlement and the Hudson River Music School; her ballet pantomime, *Pinocchio*, was on tour throughout the U.S. (1936-37); *The Jolly Beggars* was presented at the Banff Festival, Canada.

HILL, MILDRED J.

b. 1859 Louisville, Kentucky, d. 1916 Chicago, Illinois. Organist and concert pianist. Composed, or rather arranged, the music "Good Morning to All" (1893), which later became "Happy Birthday to You" (w. Patty Smith Hill, her sister); actually the song "Happy Greetings to All" first appeared in *The Anniversary and Sunday School Music Book No. 2*, issued by Horace Waters in 1858 (per ad in the *New York Times* of October 6, 1858).

HILL, STEPHEN P.

b. 1806 Salem, Massachusetts, d. 1884 Washington, D.C. Composer. Became a

Baptist minister (1832); wrote "Come, Saints, Adore Your Saviour God," which appeared in his compilation *Christian Melodies* (Baltimore, 1836).

HILL, TEDDY

b. 1909 Birmingham, Alabama.
Black bandleader. Played tenor sax with Luis Russell; organized his own band (1934).

HILL, THOMAS

b. 1818 New Brunswick, New Jersey, d. 1891 Waltham, Massachusetts. Hymnist. Graduated Harvard (1843) and Cambridge Divinity School (1845); President of Antioch College, Yellow Springs, Ohio (1859); later President of Harvard; pastor in Portland, Maine (1873); wrote "All Holy, Ever Living One."

HILL, URELI CORELLI URIAH

b. 1802 Northampton, Massachusetts, d. 1875 Paterson, New Jersey. Conductor, violinist, organist, and trumpeter. Son of Uri K. Hill, composer and publisher; brother of George Handel "Yankee" Hill, noted actor; director of the Sacred Music Society; organized and conducted the Philharmonic Society of New York (1842) with an orchestra of sixty-one players.

HILL, URI K.

b. 1780 Rutland, Vermont, d. 1844 Philadelphia Pennsylvania. Violinist, composer, compiler, and publisher. Son of Frederick Hill, publisher and father of Uri Corelli Hill, conductor; resided in Northampton, Mass. (1800-05); organist at Brattle Street Church (1805-10); taught in New York City (1810-22); published music in New York City with his father (around 1815); engraved plates for Adam Geib, Peter Erben and others; taught in Philadelphia after 1822; compiled *The Vermont Harmony* (1801), *Sacred Minstrel* (1806), *The Handelian Repository* (1814), *Solfeggio Americano* (1820); composed *Governor Sullivan's March* (1807), "The Heroes of the Ocean" (1813).

HILL, WILLIAM JOSEPH (BILLY)

b. 1899 Boston, Massachusetts, d. 1940 New York City. Composer. Known as Billy Hill; studied the violin at New England Conservatory in Boston; played in a band in a Chinese restaurant in Salt Lake City, Utah, then went to New York (1930); composed *The Last Roundup* (1931, based on folk music), *The Old Spinning Wheel, Empty Saddles* (1936), *In the Chapel in the Moonlight, There's a Home in Wyoming;* wrote the lyrics for songs of Peter De Rose—"Wagon Wheels" (1934), "In a Mission by the Sea," "Down the Old Oregon Trail."

HILLER, LEJAREN ARTHUR

b. 1924 New York City.
Composer. Attended Princeton University, New Jersey (Ph.D., 1947), University of Illinois (M.M., 1958); professor of music at University of Illinois after 1958; New York State University, Buffalo, N.Y. after 1969; wrote *Music for Time of the Heathen* (1961), *Amplification for Tape Recorder and Band* (1962), *Music for Man with the Oboe* (1962), *Music for Spoon River Anthology* (1962).

HILLHOUSE, AUGUSTUS LUCAS

b. 1792 New Haven, Connecticut, d. 1859 Paris, France. Hymnist. Brother of James Hillhouse, the poet; graduated Yale (1810); wrote "Trembling before Thine Awful Throne" (1822 in *Christ in Song,* 1870); conducted a school in Paris.

HILLIARD, BOB

b. 1918 New York City, d. 1971 Hollywood, California. Lyricist. Wrote the lyrics for "Dear Hearts and Gentle People" (m. Sammy Fain), "Our Day Will Come," "Mention My Name in Sheboygan," "Civilization," "Bongo Bongo Bongo," "Big Brass Band from Brazil," "Au Revoir," "Don't You Believe It"; succumbed to a heart attack soon after returning from an "Alice in Wonderland Day" at Disneyland; wrote the lyrics for a Disney animated *Alice* film in 1951.

HILLMAN, JOSEPH

b. 1833 Schoharie County, New York, d. 1890. Compiler. Superintendent of the Congress Street Methodist church, Troy, N.Y., for fifteen years; organized the Troy Praying Band (1858) and in 1868 conducted camp meetings at Round Lake, N.Y.; while living in Utica, N.Y., he compiled, with Lewis Hartsough, *The Revivalist* (1868); also issued *Sunday School Hymns, Sacred Hymns,* and a *History of Methodism in Troy.*

HILLS, WILLIAM H.

b. 1859 Somerville, Massachusetts, d. there 1930. Compiler of popular songs. Published *Student Songs* (1881) which included "My Bonnie"; his third edition published in 1883 contained "Polly Wolly Doodle" and "There Is a Tavern in the Town."

HILLTOPPERS (vocal group) *see* BILLY VAUGHN

HILLYER, LONNIE

b. 1940 Monroe, Georgia.
Trumpeter. Raised in Detroit; studied with Larry Teal, Barry Harris, and Bill Horner, Jr.; played with World Stage and Yusef Lateef during 1950s; with Slide Hampton, Barry Harris, and Charles Mingus in early 1960s; formed quintet with Charles McPherson (1966).

HILSBERG, IGNACE

b. 1894 Warsaw, Poland.
Pianist and teacher. Studied at the St. Petersburg Conservatory; soloist with orchestras in Europe, the United States, and the Far East; later taught at the Institute of Musical Art, New York City and the Juilliard School, New York City.

HINCKLEY, ALLEN CARTER

b. 1877 Boston, Massachusetts, d. 1954 Yonkers, New York. Bass. Pupil of Carl Schachner and Oscar Saenger; debut with Boston Light Opera (1901); opera debut as King Henry in *Lohengrin*, Hamburg, Germany (1903); sang in Europe, then with Metropolitan Opera, New York (1908-11); later with the Chicago Opera Company.

HINDEMITH, PAUL

b. 1895 Hanau, Germany, d. 1963 Frankfurt, Germany. Noted composer. Studied at the Frankfurt Conservatory; in 1933 he went to Turkey, and then came to the United States where he became a citizen and taught at Yale University; in 1953 he went to Zurich, Switzerland to live; composed the operas *Cardillac* (1926) and *Neues vom Tage* (1929), chamber music (Kammermusik, 1922-30), *Mathis Der Maler* (symphony, 1934), *Der Schwanendreher* (1935), *Nobilissima Visione* (1938), and many other compositions.

HINES, EARL ("FATHA")

b. 1903 Pittsburgh, Pennsylvania.
Black pianist and bandleader. Played with Louis Armstrong's band; later his own band in 1920s; developed the "trumpet-style" piano solos featuring hard-hit octaves played by the right hand; his style influenced other jazz pianists such as Jess Stacy and Joe Sullivan; considered by some as the greatest of jazz pianists.

HINES, JEROME

b. 1921 Hollywood, California.
Singer. Albums—*Great Moments of Sacred Music, Holy City, I Love to Tell the Story.*

HINES, MIMI

b. 1933 Vancouver, B.C., Canada.
Singer. Albums—*Mimi Hines Is Happening, Mimi Hines Sings.*

HINRICHS, GUSTAV

b. 1850 Ludwigslust, Germany, d. 1942 Mountain Lakes, New Jersey. Conductor and composer. Came to America (1870) and lived in San Francisco; conductor of American Opera Company; assisted Theodore Thomas (1885-86); his own opera company (1886-96); with Columbia University (1899-1906); conducted at Metropolitan Opera (1903-08); composed operas, choral pieces, orchestral works, songs.

HINSHAW, WILLIAM WADE

b. 1867 Union, Iowa, d. 1947 Washington, D.C. Bass and director. Studied with L.G. Gottschalk and others; debut with Savage Opera, St. Louis (1899); organized school of opera in Chicago (1903); founded International Grand Opera Company (1909); sang at Metropolitan Opera (1910-13); later directed his own touring opera company.

HINTON, MILTON J. (MILT)

b. 1910 Vicksburg, Mississippi.
Black bass player. With Cab Calloway (1936-51); with Louis Armstrong, Teddy Wilson, and Benny Goodman in 1950s; appeared in concerts and on TV shows during 1960s with Sammy Davis, Jr., Judy Garland and others.

HINTON, SAM

b. 1917 Tulsa, Oklahoma.
Singer. Attended Texas A & M College, and graduated University of California at Los Angeles (1940); his LP records are *Folk Songs of California and the Old West* (1952), Decca LPs *Singing Across the Land* (1955), *A Family Tree of Folk Songs* (1956), *The Real McCoy* (1957); others—*American Folk Songs and Balladeers* (1964).

HIRED HANDS *see* SLIM WILLET

HIRSCH, GODFREY M.

b. 1907 New Orleans, Louisiana.
Vibraphonist. Percussionist at Saenger Theater, New Orleans during 1930s; with Dave Roberts Trio; in U.S. Navy during World War II; with WWL radio band (1945-60); then with Pete Fountain's combo.

HIRSCH, LOUIS ACHILLE

b. 1887 New York City, d. there 1924.
Popular composer. Studied at the City College of New York and the piano at the Stern

Conservatory in Berlin (1906); staff pianist for Shapiro-Bernstein; wrote the score for the musical shows *He Came from Milwaukee* (1910), *Revue of Revues* (1911), *Vera Violetta* (1911), *The Whirl of Society* (1912), *Going Up* (1917, with Otto Harbach), *Mary* (1920), *O'Brien Girl* (1921); among his songs were "Come Dance with Me" (1911, w. Harold Atteridge), "Garden of Your Dreams" (1918), "Tickle Toe" (1917), "Love Nest" (1920).

HIRT, ALOIS MAXWELL (AL)

b. 1922 New Orleans, Louisiana.
Trumpeter. Studied trumpet at age six; later at Cincinnati (Ohio) Conservatory; in army during World War II; later with Jimmy and Tommy Dorsey, Ray McKinley, and Horace Heidt; formed a combo with Pete Fountain during 1960s; albums—*Best of Al Hirt, Cotton Candy, Pete Fountain and Al Hirt—Bourbon Street, Here in My Heart, Al Hirt at Dan's Pier 600, Al Hirt at the Mardi Gras, Al Hirt Live at Carnegie Hall, Al Hirt Now.*

HIRT, GERALD P.

b. 1924 New Orleans, Louisiana.
Trombonist. Younger brother of Al Hirt; with New Orleans Symphony; served in army bands during World War II; later joined his brother's combo.

HITE, LES

b. 1903 DuQuoin, Illinois, d. 1962 Santa Monica, California. Black alto saxist and bandleader. Played in Los Angeles during 1920s and '30s; led his own band (1940-45), which at one time included Lionel Hampton and Dizzy Gillespie; died of heart disease.

HODES, ARTHUR W. (ART)

b. 1904 Nikoliev, Russia.
Jazz pianist. Played with Benny Goodman, Wingy Manone, Bix Beiderbecke and others; later disc jockey and writer for *Down Beat* and *The Reporter.*

HODGES, EDWARD

b. 1796 Bristol, England, d. there 1876.
Composer. In 1835 he went to Toronto, Ontario, Canada, then to New York City in 1839 where, for many years, he was director of music at Trinity Church; returned to England upon his retirement; composed the tune "Antioch"—"Joy to the World" (w. Isaac Watts—2nd tune by Lowell Mason), and the tune "Habbakek"—"Happy Is the Pilgrim's Lot" (w. John Wesley).

HODGES, JOHN CORNELIUS (JOHNNY)

b. 1906 Cambridge, Massachusetts, d. 1970.
Black alto saxist. Studied saxophone with Sidney Bechet; with Duke Ellington (1928-51 and again after 1955); recorded with Wild Bill Davis after 1961; also with Ellington's band and Lawrence Welk's orchestra; albums—*Back to Work, Big Sound, Blue Hodge, Blue Notes, Blue Pyramid, Blue Rabbit, The Blues, Con-Soul and Sax, Creamy, Don't Sleep in the Subway, Eleventh Hour.*

HODGES, JOHN G.

b. 1915, d. 1971 New York City.
Jazz pianist. Son of Dr. Gladys Hodges, music teacher; graduated University of Texas; studied under Fats Waller; pianist for Jack Teagarden's band; also Eddie Dunsmore and Eddie Condon at Nick's in Greenwich Village.

HODGES, JOHN SEBASTIAN BACH

b. 1830 Bristol, England, d. 1915 Baltimore, Maryland. Composer. Son of Edward Hodges. Graduated from Columbia (1850) and General Theological Seminary (1854); became an Episcopal rector and served in Pittsburgh (1854); taught at Nashotah House, Wisc. (1856); rector of Grace Church, Newark, N.J. (1860), then St. Paul's, Baltimore (1870-1905); composed the tune "Eucharistic Hymn" (1868)—"Bread of the World, in Mercy Broken" (w. R. Heber).

HODGES, LEIGH MITCHELL

b. 1876 Denver, Colorado, d. 1954.
Hymnist. Reporter on the *Evening Ledger,* Mexico, Missouri, *Kansas City Star,* Kansas City, Mo., with the *Ladies Home Journal,* New York City after 1899, then the *North American,* Philadelphia, and the *Evening Bulletin,* Philadelphia; resided in Doylestown, Pa.; wrote the hymn "As When, in Far Samaria" (tune "Ellacombe"—German tune).

HODGKINSON, JOHN

b. 1767 Manchester, England, d. 1805 near Bladensburg, Maryland. Singer and actor. Born John Meadowcraft; debut in Philadelphia (1792); joined Old American Company orchestra (1792); sang leading role of William Tell in *The Archers* (1796, w. William Dunlap, m. Benjamin Carr); founder and president of Columbian Anacreontic Society, New York City (1795-99); sang and played in Charleston, S.C. (1803-04); wrote *The Launch, or Huzzah for the (Frigate) Constitution* (m. Victor Pelissier), one act pasticcio, performed in 1797 in New York, Boston, and Portsmouth.

HODGKINSON, MRS. JOHN (née BRETT)

b. ca. 1770 England, d. 1803.
Singer and actress. Sister of Arabella Brett

and Mrs. William King; taught to sing and play the violin by her father, actor Mr. Brett; married singer and actor John Hodgkinson; American debut in Philadelphia (1792); New York debut in concert (1793).

HOFFMAN, AL

b. 1902 Minsk, Russia, d. 1960 New York City. Songwriter. Came to U.S. (1908); raised in Seattle, Wash.; led his own band there; drummer in night club bands; in England (1934-37); with Clem Watts and Bob Merrill wrote "If I Knew You Were Comin' I'd 've Baked a Cake" (1950); and with Mabel Wayne and Maurice Sigler, "Little Man You've Had a Busy Day."

HOFFMAN, CHARLES FENNO

b. 1806 New York City, d. 1884 Harrisburg, Pennsylvania. Lyricist. First editor of *The Knickerbocker* magazine (1833); wrote the lyrics for "Monterey."

HOFFMANN, RICHARD

b. 1831 Manchester, England, d. 1909 Mt. Kisco, New York. Pianist, teacher, and composer. Pupil of Liszt and others; came to New York City (1847); pianist for Jenny Lind on her tours in America; also played with von Bulow in New York City (1875); composed piano pieces, anthems.

HOGAN, ERNEST

b. 1865, d. after 1910.
Black composer and pianist. Born Reuben Crowder; wrote "All Coons Look Alike to Me" (1896); it was a ragtime song in Negro dialect and became very successful, but his popular song left Hogan with a feeling of guilt for many years thereafter; played at Proctor's, New York City (1905) with Nashville Students; starred in *The Oyster Man* (1910).

HOIBY, LEE

b. 1926 Madison, Wisconsin.
Composer. Wrote the music for *Summer and Smoke* (book—Tennessee Williams, libretto—Lanford Wilson) produced by St. Paul, Minnesota Opera Company (1971), and New York City Opera (1972); also score for *After Eden*, produced by Harkness Ballet, also by City Center Joffrey Ballet under John Butler in New York City (1972).

HOLBROOK, JOSEPH PERRY

b. 1822 near Boston, Massachusetts, d. 1888. Composer. One of the editors of *The Hymnal of the Methodist Episcopal Church* (1878); composed the tune "Refuge" for "Jesus, Lover of My Soul" (w. Charles Wesley, second tune "Whitman" by Lowell Mason), "Truman"—"I Heard the Voice of Jesus Say" (w. Horatius Bonar, second tune "Vox Dilecti" by J.B. Dykes), "Greek Hymn"—"Christian! Dost Thou See Them" (w. Andrew of Crete, second tune "St. Andrew of Crete" by J.B. Dykes).

HOLCOMB, ROSCOE

b. 1913 Daisy, Kentucky.
Singer. Worked in the coal mines near Hazard, Kentucky, then at odd jobs after the mines closed down; his LP records are *Mountain Music of Kentucky, The High Lonesome Sound, The Music of Roscoe Holcomb and Wade Ward.*

HOLDEN, ALBERT JUNOS

b. 1841 Boston, Massachusetts, d. 1916.
Organist, composer, and compiler. Wrote "O Salutaris Hostia," "Soul of My Savior."

HOLDEN, OLIVER

b. 1765 Shirley, Massachusetts, d. 1844 Charlestown (Boston), Massachusetts. Composer. Carpenter and self-taught musician. His pipe organ is in the Old State House in Boston; donated the land on which a Baptist church was built in Charlestown; representative in the Massachusetts House for eight annual terms between 1818 and 1833; composed the tunes "Coronation"—"All Hail the Power" (1793, w. Edward Perronet), "Cowper," "Confidence," "Concord," and a patriotic anthem "Mt. Vernon."

HOLIDAY, BILLIE ("LADY DAY")

b. 1915 Baltimore, Maryland, d. 1959 New York City. Black singer. Born Eleanor Fagan Gough; stepdaughter of Clarence Holiday, banjoist, who played in Fletcher Henderson's band; sang in Fifty-second Street (New York City) clubs during the 1930s; sang with Count Basie's band; also with Artie Shaw, Benny Carter, Paul Whiteman and others; for a time Eddie Heywood, Jr. was her accompanist; known for her torch ballads "My Man," "Mean to Me," "I Cried for You and You Let Me Down"; Diana Ross played Billie in the film of her life story, *Lady Sings the Blues* (1973).

HOLLAND, JOSIAH GILBERT

b. 1819 Belchertown, Massachusetts, d. 1881 New York City. Hymnist. Graduated from Berkshire Medical College and became a physician in Springfield, Mass., but later became an editor; editor of *Scribner's Magazine* (1870) until his death; wrote the hymn "There's a Song in the Air" (1879, tune "Christmas Song" by K.P. Harrington), also

"For Summer's Bloom, and Autumn's Blight" (*Hymn Book for the Church and Home*, 1868).

HOLLAND, JUSTIN

b. 1819 Norfolk County, Virginia, d. 1886. Black guitarist and writer. Settled in Boston (1833); then in Chelsea, Mass.; attended Oberlin College, Oberlin, Ohio (1841); taught in Cleveland, Ohio after 1845; wrote *Holland's Comprehensive Method for the Guitar* (1874), and *Holland's Modern Method for the Guitar* (1876).

HOLLANDA, CHICO BUARQUE DE

b. 1942 Brazil.
Singer, guitarist, and composer. His first success was *A Band* (1966); toured Italy (1969-71); Brazilian government rejected two out of three of his songs; confiscated his hit record "Apesar de Voce" in May, 1971; played at Canecao night club, Rio de Janiero (1971); Rio's Sight and Sound Museum named him Composer of the Year (1971).

HOLLEY, MAJOR QUINCY, JR. ("MULE")

b. 1924 Detroit, Michigan.
Bass player. With Charlie Parker, Woody Herman, Kenny Burrell Trio, Quincy Jones, Duke Ellington and others.

HOLLOWAY, JAMES L. ("RED")

b. 1927 Helena, Arkansas.
Tenor saxist. Studied at Chicago Conservatory; with Gene Wright (1943-46); then in 5th Army band; with Roosevelt Sykes; organized own quartet (1952); with Lloyd Price, Jack McDuff and others in 1960s; at Antibes Jazz Festival (1964).

HOLLY, CHARLES HARDIN ("BUDDY")

b. (?), d. 1959 Fargo, North Dakota.
Singer. Raised in Lubbock, Texas; started as a country singer (1956); turned to rock (1957); killed in a plane crash from Mason City, Iowa, enroute to Fargo; albums—*Buddy Holly Story* (1957), *Buddy Holly* (1958), *Best of Buddy Holly, Giant, Great Buddy Holly, Buddy Holly and the Crickets, Buddy Holly's Greatest Hits, Buddy Holly Showcase, Holly in the Hills, Love Is Strange, Reminiscing.*

HOLM, CELESTE

b. 1919 New York City.
Singer and actress. Appeared in numerous films; sang at the Salute to Richard Rodgers at the Imperial Theater, New York City in March 1972.

HOLMAN, LIBBY

b. 1906 Cincinnati, Ohio, d. 1971 Stamford, Connecticut. Torch singer. Born Elspeth Holtzman. Educated at the University of Cincinnati and Columbia University; sang "Moanin' Low" in *The Little Show* (1929) and introduced "Body and Soul" and "Give Me Something to Remember You By" in *Three's a Crowd* (1930, m. Arthur Schwartz); married Zachary Smith Reynolds, the twenty-year-old tobacco heir in November 1931, and he was found shot to death July, 1932, on the family's estate in Winston-Salem, N.C.; she was charged with his murder, but later the charges were dropped; she died by inhaling carbon monoxide fumes from her car parked in her garage with the doors shut on her estate in Stamford.

HOLMAN, WILLIS ("BILL")

b. 1927 Olive, California.
Tenor saxist and composer. Played with Charlie Barnet and Stan Kenton during 1950s; arranger for Gerry Mulligan, Terry Gibbs, Stan Kenton, and Woody Herman during 1960s; wrote *Trilogy*, performed by Los Angeles Neophonic Orchestra (1965); with Gerry Mulligan, wrote *Music for Baritone Saxophone and Orchestra*, produced by Neophonic Orchestra (1966).

HOLMES, CHARLIE

b. 1910 Boston, Massachusetts.
Black alto and soprano saxophonist. Played with Luis Russell and Louis Armstrong.

HOLMES, EDWARD

b. 1797 near London, England, d. 1850 United States. Piano teacher and music critic.

HOLMES, HENRY

b. 1839 London, England, d. 1905 San Francisco, California. Violinist and composer. Son of Thomas and brother of Alfred Holmes of London; taught at the Royal College of Music, London, and composed four symphonies.

HOLMES, JOHN HAYNES

b. 1879 Philadelphia, Pennsylvania, d. 1964. Hymnist. Graduated Harvard (1902); became a Unitarian minister in Dorchester, Mass. (1904), then at the Community Church, New York City (1907); wrote the hymn "The Voice of God Is Calling" (1913, tune "Meirionydd"—Welsh).

HOLMES, OLIVER WENDELL

b. 1809 Cambridge, Massachusetts, d. 1894 Boston, Massachusetts. Poet and lyricist.

Graduated Harvard University (1829); studied medicine in Europe, then returned to America (1835); practiced medicine for eleven years, then taught it; wrote the lyrics for "Keller's American Hymn" (1872, m. Matthias Keller), "The Wonderful One Hoss Shay" (m. Max Brand), "O Love Divine, That Stooped to Share" (tune "Hesperus"—Henry Baker) and "Lord of All Being, Throned Afar" (tune "Louvan"—V.C. Taylor, 2nd tune "Keble" by John B. Dykes).

HOLMES, RICHARD ARNOLD ("GROOVE")

b. 1931 Camden, New Jersey.
Black organist. Played in clubs in the Los Angeles area; recorded after 1961; albums—*After Hours, Best of Richard Groove Holmes, Come Together, Get Up and Get It, The Groover, Groovin' with Jug, Jazz Milestones, Living Soul, Misty, Somethin' Special, Soul Message, Soul Mist.*

HOLT, BENJAMIN

b. 1774, d. 1861 Lancaster, Massachusetts. Compiler and composer. Music teacher in Boston; issued *The New England Sacred Harmony* (1803), which included twenty-two of his original tunes; in 1802 he assisted Nahum Mitchell and Bartholomew Brown in compiling *The Columbian and European Harmony* (Bridgewater Collection); the third edition (1810) was called *Songs of the Temple* or *Templi Carmina.*

HOLT, ISAAC ("RED")

b. 1932 Rosedale, Mississippi.
Black drummer. With Ramsey Lewis and El Dee Young, formed the Ramsey Lewis Trio (1956); went solo (1966).

HOLY MODAL ROUNDERS (rock group)

John Wesley Annis, bass; Steve Weber, guitar; Richard Tyler, piano; Sam Shepard, drums (also an off-Broadway playwright); Peter Stampfel, banjo; albums—*Moray Eels Eat the Holy Modal Rounders, Holy Modal Rounders.*

HOLYOKE, SAMUEL ADAMS

b. 1762 Boxford, Massachusetts, d. 1820 Concord, Massachusetts. Composer and compiler. Graduated Harvard (1789); composed the tune "Arnheim"; with Hans Gram and Oliver Holden, compiled the *Massachusetts Compiler* (Boston, 1795); also issued *The Columbian Repository of Sacred Harmony* (Exeter, N.H., 1802) which included several tunes of Jacob B. Moore; *The Christian Harmonist* (1804) and *The Instrumental Assistant* (1807); published the song, "Washington," (1790, in praise of General Washington).

HOMBURG, AL

b. 1937 Ellis, Kansas.
Singer, guitarist, and songwriter. Graduated Oklahoma City University in music (1958); teacher; wrote "Voice of Love," "Ladder of Love," "Tomorrow Is Now," "Baby Doll"; taught in Cumberland, Maryland.

HOMER AND JETHRO *see* HENRY D. HAYNES and KENNETH C. BURNS

HOMER, LOUISE DILWORTH BEATTY

b. 1871 Pittsburgh, Pennsylvania, d. 1947 Winter Park, Florida. Contralto. Studied in Paris with Fidele Koenig; debut at Vichy, France (1898); sang in Europe, then with Metropolitan Opera, New York City (1900-1919); married Sidney Homer; early successful record with Alma Gluck was "Whispering Hope" (m. Septimus Winner).

HOMER, SIDNEY

b. 1864 Boston, Massachusetts, d. 1953 Winter Park, Florida. Composer. Pupil of G.W. Chadwick and others, taught theory in Boston (1888-96); composed songs.

"HOMETOWN JAMBOREE" *see* CLIFFIE STONE and JIMMY BRYANT

HOMETOWNERS *see* PAT PATTERSON and BUDDY ROSS

HOOD, GEORGE

b. 1807 Topsfield, Massachusetts, d. 1882. Composer and compiler. Taught music, then became a Presbyterian minister; wrote *The History of Music in New England* (1846), *The Southern Melodist* (1846, which contained two of his tunes and two by Jacob Hood, his brother), and a *Musical Manual* (1864).

HOOD, WILLIAM H. (BILL)

b. 1924 Portland, Oregon.
Baritone saxist. Conductor for G.I. shows in Pacific area after World War II; with Benny Goodman, Terry Gibbs and others during 1960s; at Monterey Jazz Festivals (1958, 1962, and 1965).

HOOK, ELIAS

b. 1805, d. 1881.
Organ maker. Learned the art of organ making as an apprentice to William M. Goodrich of Templeton, Mass.; went into the business with his brother, George in 1827 in Salem, Mass.; moved their plant to Boston

(1832); F.H. Hastings became a partner (1865), under the name of Hook & Hastings.

HOOK, GEORGE G.

b. 1807, d. 1880.
Organ maker. Made organs with his brother, Elias, in Salem, Mass. after 1827, and in Boston after 1832.

HOOKER, BRIAN, JR.

b. 1880 New York City, d. 1946 New London, Connecticut. Lyricist and librettist. Educated at Yale (M.A.); taught at Columbia and at Yale; with Porter Steele wrote "Don't Tell Me What You Dreamed Last Night" (w. Franklin Pierce Adams); lyrics for "Song of the Vagabonds" (1925, m. Rudolf Friml).

HOOKER, JOHN LEE

b. 1917 Clarksdale, Mississippi.
Black singer and guitarist. Raised in Memphis, Tenn.; worked as a janitor in Detroit in the daytime (1943), and played in small clubs at night; cut his first record 1946; his LP records include *John Lee Hooker Sings the Blues* (1952), *Burnin', I'm John Lee Hooker, Travelin'* (1961), *Folklore* (1962), *Big Soul, Don't Turn Me from Your Door* (1963), *John Lee Hooker, Great Blues Album* (1963).

HOOPER, NESBERT ("STIX")

b. 1938 Houston, Texas.
Drummer and bandleader. Educated at Texas Southern University, Houston; organized The Swingsters (1952), later known as the Modern Jazz Sextet, The Nite Hawks, finally the Jazz Crusaders; appeared on Steve Allen's TV show, "Jazz Scene USA."

HOPKINS, CLAUDE

b. 1903 Alexandria, Virginia.
Black bandleader. Graduated Howard University; musical director for Josephine Baker in Paris (1925-27); played in the Savoy Ballroom in Harlem, New York City.

HOPKINS, EDWARD JEROME

b. 1836 Burlington, Vermont, d. 1898 Athenia, New Jersey. Organist and editor. Wrote "Spirit of God" (Benediction), "Calm on the Listening Ear of Night."

HOPKINS, HARRY PATTERSON

b. 1873 Baltimore, Maryland.
Organist, teacher, and composer. Graduated Peabody Institute, Baltimore (1896); studied with Dvořák; organist and teacher in Baltimore after 1899; composed a symphony, songs.

HOPKINS, JOHN HENRY

b. 1861 Burlington, Vermont, d. 1945 Grand Isle, Vermont. Composer. Nephew of J.H. Hopkins, Jr.; studied at the University of Vermont, Burlington (1883, D.D., 1906), and General Theological Seminary (B.D., 1893); became rector of the Church of the Redeemer, Chicago (1910-29); composed the tunes "Westerly" (1941) for "God the Father, God the Son" and "Grand Isle" (1940) for "I Sing a Song of the Saints of God" (w. Lesbia Scott).

HOPKINS, JOHN HENRY, JR.

b. 1820 Pittsburgh, Pennsylvania, d. 1891 Troy, New York. Composer. Son of the Episcopal Bishop of Vermont; graduated the University of Vermont, Burlington, and served as a rector in Williamsport, Pa.; wrote the Christmas carol, "We Three Kings of Orient Are" (1863) and "Gather Around the Christmas Tree"; resigned his position in Williamsport in 1887 to work for the General Theological Seminary, but when he arrived in New York City, the position was given to someone else; at 67 he could not find work, and when his funds were depleted, he had to give his landlord his collection of over 500 books to pay for his rent; when all his funds and all his books were gone, a friend took him into his home in Troy where Hopkins died a broken and disappointed man.

HOPKINS, JOSIAH

b. 1786 Pittsford, Vermont, d. 1862 Geneva, New York. Hymnist. Pastor of a Congregational Church in New Haven, Vermont (1809-30), then at the First Presbyterian Church, Auburn, N.Y. (1830-48); several of his hymns appeared in *Christian Lyre* (New York, 1830).

HOPKINS, LINDA

b. 1925 New Orleans, Louisiana.
Black singer. Baptist singer; sang in New Orleans, Honolulu, and Oakland, Calif.; with Allen and Rossi's night club act; lead in the musical, *Inner City* at Ethel Barrymore Theatre, New York City (1972); acclaimed for her song, "It's My Belief"; in *Soul* at the Center at Alice Tully Hall, New York City (1972).

HOPKINS, SAM ("LIGHTNIN' ")

b. 1912 Leon County, Texas.
Black singer and guitarist. His LP records include *Lightnin' Hopkins* (1950), *Lightnin' Hopkins and the Blues, Lightnin' Strikes, Lightnin' Hopkins* (1959), *Goin' Away, Gotta Move Your Baby, Autobiography in Blues,*

County Blues (1960), *Lightnin'* (1961), *Walkin' This Road by Myself, Blues in My Bottle* (1962), *Lightnin' and Co., Smokes Like Lightnin'* (1963), *Hootin' the Blues* (1964), *Early Recordings* (1964), *First Meetin'* (1964).

HOPKINSON, FRANCIS

b. 1737 Philadelphia, Pennsylvania, d. there 1791. Composer. Received his M.A. (1760) from the College of Philadelphia (now the University of Pennsylvania); was a lawyer, judge, signed the Declaration of Independence, was the first Secretary of the Navy under Washington, poet, harpsichordist, organist and composer; lived in Bordentown, N.J. (1773-91); wrote "My Days Have Been So Wondrous Free" (1759), "The Battle of the Kegs" (1778), and the opera *The Temple of Minerva* (1781); published *A Collection of Psalm Tunes* (1763 for Christ and St. Peter's Church, Philadelphia, *The Psalms of David* for the Reformed Dutch Church of N.Y. (1767), and *Seven Songs for the Harpsichord or Forte Piano* (1788).

HOPKINSON, JOSEPH

b. 1770 Philadelphia, Pennsylvania, d. there 1843. Lyricist. Son of Francis Hopkinson; wrote the lyrics "Hail Columbia" (1798) to the tune "The President's March" (m. Philip Phile), which was introduced at a concert in Philadelphia in 1798 by Gilbert Fox, singer and actor.

HOPKIRK, JAMES

b. 1908 Toronto, Ontario, Canada.
Composer. Educated at the University of Toronto and was organist-choirmaster at St. Matthias' Church, Toronto (1929-37), then at churches in Hamilton, Ontario and Vancouver, B.C. until 1942 when he resigned to join the Canadian Army; composed the tune "Bellwoods" (1938, "O Day of God, Draw Nigh").

HOPPER, EDWARD

b. 1816 New York City, d. there 1888.
Hymnist. Graduated Union Theological Seminary (1843) and was licensed to preach by the Third Presbytery of New York; served as pastor of the Mariner's Church in New York Harbor, and later he was minister of a Presbyterian Church in Sag Harbor, N.Y.; wrote the hymns "Jesus, Savior, Pilot Me" (1871, tune "Pilot"—J.E. Gould), "They Pray the Best Who Pray and Watch" (1874), and "Wrecked and Struggling in Midocean" (1874).

HOPPER, WILLIAM DE WOLF

b. 1858 New York City, d. 1935 Kansas City, Missouri. Singer and comedian. Performed with McCaull Opera Company in the 1880s; later headed his own company in Gilbert and Sullivan operettas; sang "A Pretty Girl" in *Wang* (1891, m. Woolson Morse); starred in *The Pied Piper* (1908, m. Manuel Klein); his wife was Hedda Hopper (1890-1966), the noted columnist.

HORENSTEIN, JASCHA

b. 1898 Kiev, Russia, d. 1973.
Conductor. First conductor in Düsseldorf, but lost his position (1933) when Hitler came to power; came to America to live, but continued working as a guest conductor in Europe and South America.

HORN, CHARLES EDWARD

b. 1786 London, England, d. 1849 Boston, Massachusetts. Conductor and composer. Son of Karl Friedrich Horn; wrote "On the Lake Where Drooped the Willow" (1858, w. G.P. Morris) and the oratorio *The Remission of Sin* (1835, w. John Milton's *Paradise Lost*); the greatest performance was in 1839 at the New York Sacred Music Society with 1,000 voices; conductor of Boston Handel and Haydn Society (1847-49).

HORN, PAUL

b. 1930 New York City.
Flutist and composer. With Chico Hamilton Quintet (1956-58); leader of his own quintet in Hollywood during 1960s; albums—*Cosmic Consciousness, Cycle, Here's That Rainy Day, Paul Horn in India, Inside, Jazz Suite on the Mass Texts* (m. Lalo Schifrin).

HORN QUINTET *see* LYNN BLESSING

HORN, SHIRLEY

b. 1934 Washington, D.C.
Black singer and pianist. Studied at Howard University Jr. School of Music; organized her own trio (1954); gave concerts in New York City and Washington, D.C.

HORNE, LENA

b. 1917 Brooklyn, New York.
Black singer. Sang with Noble Sissle's band; then with Charlie Barnet; appeared in Lew Leslie's *Blackbirds* (1939); sang at the Little Trocadero, Los Angeles; appeared in films; toured for the USO during World War II; toured Europe (1947-50, and between 1952-59); married Lennie Hayton.

HORNE, MARILYN

b. 1934 Bradford, Pennsylvania.
Soprano. Sang with the opera company in Gelsenkirchen, Germany in 1960s; married Henry Lewis, conductor of New Jersey Symphony Orchestra; sang in concert version of Wagner's *Die Walküre* at Carnegie Hall with William Steinberg and the Pittsburgh Symphony Orchestra (1972).

HORNER, ANTON

b. 1877 Austria, d. 1971 Springfield, Pennsylvania. Horn player. Came to America (1895); joined Pittsburgh Symphony under Victor Herbert (1899); toured Europe with Sousa band (1900); with Philadelphia Orchestra (1902-46); solo horn player for twenty-eight years; called "one of the greatest horn players of all time" by Eugene Ormandy; also taught at Curtis Institute of Music in Philadelphia.

HOROWITZ, VLADIMIR

b. 1904 Kiev, Russia.
Famous concert pianist. Married Wanda Toscanini, the daughter of Arturo Toscanini, the conductor; became world famous, but became ill from nervous exhaustion in 1935; resumed his career in 1939, but later became ill again; won Grammy Award (1972) for the "Classical Album of the Year," *Horowitz Plays Rachmaninoff.*

HORSLEY, CHARLES EDWARD

b. 1822 London, England, d. 1876 New York City. Organist and composer. Son of William Horsley, the English organist and composer; pupil of his father.

HORTON, JOHNNY

b. 1929 Tyler, Texas, d. 1960 en route to Nashville, Tennessee. Guitarist and singer. Played basketball at Baylor University, Waco, Texas, and at the University of Seattle, Washington; known as "The Singing Fisherman"; his hit records include "I'm Just a One Woman Man" (1957), "All Grown Up" (1958), "Johnny Reb," "When It's Springtime in Alaska," and "The Battle of New Orleans" (1959), "Sink the Bismark" (1960, which he wrote with Tillman Franks), and "North to Alaska" (1960) (his own); killed in an auto accident.

HORTON, VAUGHN

b. 1911 Broad Top, Pennsylvania.
Popular composer. Graduated Pennsylvania State College, University Park, Pa.; wrote "Mockin' Bird Hill," "Till the End of the World," "Teardrops in My Heart," "Blossoms in the Springtime," "Sugarfoot Rag," "Small World," "Plantation Boogie," "Bar Room Polka," "Heartbreak Trail," "Home Sweet Homesick Blues," "After the Hangover's Over," "Big Wheel Cannonball," "Pennsylvania Turnpike, I Love You" (1967).

HORVATH, CECILE AYRES DE

b. 1889 Boston, Massachusetts.
Pianist. Daughter of Eugene E. Ayres; studied with her father, Gabrilowitsch and others; concert pianist in Europe after 1910, and in the United States; later taught in Chicago; wife of Zoltan de Horvath.

HORVATH, ZOLTAN DE

b. 1886 Chicago, Illinois.
Pianist and teacher. Taught in Philadelphia.

HOSCHNA, KARL

b. 1877 Kuschwarda, Bohemia (Czechoslovakia), d. 1911 New York City. Popular composer. Studied the oboe at the Vienna Conservatory, then joined the Austrian army band; came to America (1896) and played the oboe in Victor Herbert's orchestra, later went to work for Isadore Witmark, music publisher; with Otto Harbach, lyricist, wrote *The Belle of the West* (1905), *Three Twins* (1908), *Madame Sherry* (1910), and the songs "Cuddle Up a Little Closer" (1908), "Girl of My Dreams" (1910), and "The Birth of Passion" (1910).

HOSMER, FREDERICK LUCIAN

b. 1840 Framingham, Massachusetts, d. 1929 Berkeley, California. Hymnist. Educated at Harvard and was a Unitarian minister in Northboro, Mass., Quincy, Ill., Cleveland, St. Louis and Berkeley; wrote the lyrics "O Light, from Age to Age the Same" (1890, m. W. Croft, "Eatington"), "O Beautiful, My Country!" (1884, m. B. Helder, "Helder"), "Father, to Thee We Look in All Our Sorrow" (1881, m. L. Bourgeois, "L'Omnipotent"), "Made Lowly Wise" (1879, m. J. Fish "Blackbourne"), "O Thou in All Thy Might So Far" (1876, tune "Irish," 1749), "Thy Kingdom Come, on Bended Knee" (1891, tune "St. Flavian," 1562). (*See* William C. Gannett)

HOT FIVE AND SEVEN (stop chorus)
Louis Armstrong, leader.

HOUGH, WILL M.

b. 1882 Chicago, Illinois, d. 1962 Carmel, California. Lyricist. Educated at the University of Chicago; wrote material for vaudeville shows and also for Broadway shows; with Frank R. Adams wrote "I

Wonder Who's Kissing Her Now" (1909, m. Joe E. Howard and Harold Orlob).

HOUSE, EDDIE JAMES, JR. ("SON")

b. 1902 Clarksville, Mississippi.
Black singer and guitarist. Raised in Tallulah, Louisiana, moved back to Clarksville, then on to Rochester, N.Y. where he worked for a time as a sleeping car porter on the New York Central System out of Buffalo; his records include "Death Letter Blues," "Empire State Express," and "Pearline."

HOUSELEY, HENRY

b. 1851 Sutton-in-Ashfield, England, d. 1925 Denver, Colorado. Composer. Became organist at St. John's Cathedral, Denver, in 1888 and served for thirty-seven years; composed cantatas, operas, and works for orchestra, string quartet and organ.

HOUSTON, DAVID

b. 1938 Shreveport, Louisiana.
Singer and guitarist. Appeared on the "Louisiana Hayride" program, Shreveport, when he was twelve; his hit records include "Mountain of Love" (1963), "Livin' in a House Full of Love" (1965), "Almost Persuaded" (1966), "Loser's Cathedral" (1967), "Already It's Heaven" (1968).

HOUSTON, GILBERT VANDINE ("CISCO")

b. 1918 Wilmington, Delaware, d. 1961 San Bernardino, California. Ballad singer. Toured with Woody Guthrie during the 1930s and '40s; served in the Merchant Marine in World War II; later sang in Town Hall and Madison Square Garden, New York City; his LP records include *Railroad Songs, Cowboy Songs, Songs of the Open Road, Cisco Special* (1961), *I Ain't Got No Home* (1962), *Legacy of Cisco Houston* (1964); died of cancer.

HOUSTON, JOHN CHARLES

b. 1933 Philadelphia, Pennsylvania.
Pianist and trombonist. Played in Philadelphia; then in Los Angeles with various combos.

HOVEY, RICHARD

b. 1864 Normal, Illinois, d. 1900 New York City. Lyricist. Wrote "A Stein Song" (1898, m. Frederick Bullard) and "We Are Adventurers Who Come" (m. Bliss Carmen).

HOVHANESS, ALAN

b. 1911 Somerville, Massachusetts.
Noted composer. Born Alan Chakmakjian; studied at New England Conservatory, Boston, with Frederick Converse; known for his Symphony no. 1 performed by BBC Symphony under Leslie Howard (1939), *Armenian Rhapsody no. 2* (1944), *Lousadzak* (concerto for piano and orchestra, Boston Symphony, 1945), *Elibris* (concerto for flute and orchestra, San Francisco, 1950), eighth symphony *Arjuna* (Madras, India, 1960), *Meditation on Zeami* (American Symphony under Leopold Stokowski, 1964), 19th Symphony (New York Philharmonic under Andre Kostelanetz, 1967).

HOWARD, AVERY ("KID")

b. 1908 New Orleans, Louisiana, d. there 1966. Trumpeter. Drummer and cornetist in New Orleans during 1920s; later led his own band; played trumpet in George Lewis' band.

HOWARD, DARNELL

b. 1892 Chicago, Illinois, d. 1966.
Black clarinetist, saxophonist, and violinist. Played with King Oliver's orchestras.

HOWARD, FANNIE

b. 1885.
Black pianist. Graduated Atlanta University, Atlanta, Georgia; studied at Oberlin Conservatory, Oberlin, Ohio; married Joseph Douglass, violinist; toured with her husband.

HOWARD, FRANK

b. 1823 England, d. after 1880.
Organist, pianist, and composer. Studied in Bristol, England, under James Montrie, also John Lockey of St. Paul's, London; organist of King's Chapel, Boston (1849-65); moved to Duxbury, Mass. (1880); composed piano pieces, church music, and songs.

HOWARD, FRANK

b. 1833, d. ca. 1900.
Composer. Born Delos Gardner Spalding; also used pseudonym "Frank Martindale"; wrote "Only a Pansy Blossom" (w. Eben E. Rexford), "When the Robins Nest Again."

HOWARD, HARLAN

b. 1929 Harlan County, Kentucky.
Popular composer. Raised in Detroit; served four years with the paratroopers at Ft. Benning, Ga.; wrote "Pick Me Up on Your Way Down," "Heartaches by the Number" (1959), "Above and Beyond" (1960), "Heartbreak USA" (1960), "Busted" (1963), "Your Heart Turned Left" (1964), "I've Got a Tiger by the Tail" (1965), "Streets of Baltimore" (1966), "Evil on Your Mind" (1966, sung by Jan Howard, his wife).

HOWARD, JAN

b. 1932 West Plains, Missouri.
Singer. Member of Carter Sisters group; sang with Wynn Stewart.

HOWARD, JOHN TASKER

b. 1890 Brooklyn, New York, d. 1964.
Composer and writer. Educated at Williams College, Williamstown, Mass.; studied composition with Howard Brockway and Mortimer Wilson; author of *Our American Music, Stephen Foster* and other books; composed vocal, piano and orchestral works.

HOWARD, JOSEPH E.

b. 1878 New York City, d. 1961 Chicago, Illinois. Popular composer. Vaudeville actor; "Hello, Ma Baby" was written by Howard and Ida Emerson, his wife (1899); he also composed "On a Saturday Night" (1902, w. A.J. Sterling), "Goodbye, My Lady Love" (1904), "What's the Use of Dreaming" (1906), "Blow the Smoke Away" (1906, w. Will M. Hough), "I Wonder Who's Kissing Her Now" (1909, w. Harold Orlob, W. Hough, and F.R. Adams), introduced by Howard in *The Prince of Tonight* in Chicago.

HOWARD, PAUL JACK

b. 1908 Midland, Arkansas.
Bandleader and songwriter. Leader of Arkansas Cotton Pickers after 1941; wrote "Oklahoma City," "Rootie Tootie," "Lazy Morning," "Texas Boogie" (1948), "With Tears in My Eyes."

HOWARD, ROLLIN

b. 1840 New York, d. 1879 Boston, Mass.
Minstrel showman and songwriter. Born Ebenezer G.B. Holder; active in minstrel shows (1869-79); wrote "You Never Miss the Water 'Til the Well Runs Dry" (1874, w. Harry Linn); arranged the music and plugged "Shew Fly! Don't Bother Me" (1869, Billy Reeves and Frank Campbell), and "Shew Fly Gallop" (1869, George Thorne).

HOWE, ELIAS

b. 1820 Framingham, Massachusetts, d. 1895.
Violin maker, compiler, and publisher. Published *The Ethiopian Glee Book* (under the pseudonym "Gumbo Chaff") for Christy's Minstrels (Boston, 1849).

HOWE, JULIA WARD

b. 1819 New York City, d. 1910 Middletown, Rhode Island. Lyricist. Lived in Boston where her husband, Dr. Samuel G. Howe, edited the antislavery paper the *Boston Commonwealth.* She was visiting in Washington, D.C. in November, 1861, where she heard soldiers singing "John Brown's Body." The Rev. James F. Clarke, who was with her, suggested she write more appropriate words. After she returned to her room in the Willard Hotel, she wrote the stirring lyrics "The Battle Hymn of the Republic," which was published in the *Atlantic Monthly* in February, 1862. The verses made her world famous. (*See* Patrick S. Gilmore, also James T. Fields)

HOWE, MARY

b. 1882 Richmond, Virginia, d. 1964 Washington, D.C. Composer. Studied piano with Harold Randolph and composition in Paris with Nadia Boulanger and others; graduated Peabody Conservatory, Baltimore; lived in Washington, D.C.; married Walter Bruce Howe; composed the orchestral works *Dirge, Sand, Stars, Poema, Coulennes, Mists; Cards,* ballet; violin sonata; quintet suite; *Habanera,* for two pianos; choruses, songs.

HOWE, SOLOMON

b. 1750 North Brookfield, Massachusetts, d. 1835 New Salem, Massachusetts. Compiler. Graduated Dartmouth College, Hanover, N.H. (1777) and moved to Greenwich, Mass.; published *The Worshiper's Assistant* (1779), *The Farmers' Evening Entertainment* (1804), and *Divine Hymns on the Suffering of Christ* (1805).

HOWLIN' WOLF *see* CHESTER A. BURNETT

HOYT, CHARLES H.

b. 1860 Concord, New Hampshire, d. 1900 Charlestown, New Hampshire. Lyricist and playwright. First job was with the *St. Albans Advertiser,* St. Albans, Vermont; then he went with the *Boston Post*; wrote the farces *A Brass Monkey, A Rag Baby, A Hole in the Ground, A Tin Soldier, A Midnight Belle, A Trip to Chinatown, A Runaway Colt, A Contented Woman, A Texas Steer, A Black Sheep;* wrote the lyrics "The Bowery" (1892, m. Percy Gaunt).

HUBBARD, FREDERICK DEWAYNE (FREDDIE)

b. 1938 Indianapolis, Indiana.
Black trumpeter. With Slide Hampton, J.J. Johnson, Quincy Jones, Art Blakey's Jazz Messengers, Max Roach and others during 1960s; at Berlin Jazz Festival (1965); at the CTI Summer Jazz Festival, New York City (1972).

HUBBARD, JOHN

b. 1759 Townsend, Massachusetts, d. 1810 Hanover, New Hampshire. Composer and compiler. Graduated Dartmouth College, Hanover, N.H. (1785); taught in Ipswich and Deerfield, Mass., then at Dartmouth College (1804-10); issued *Harmonica Selecta* (1789), and *Thirty Anthems*, one of which was original, (1814) at Newburyport, Mass.

HUBBELL, RAYMOND

b. 1879 Urbana, Ohio, d. 1954 Miami, Florida. Composer. Arranger and pianist for Charles K. Harris, publishing house; wrote the music for *Chow Chow* (1902, later called *The Runaways*), *Fantana* (1905), *Mexicana* (1906), *A Knight for a Day* (1907), *Hip Hip Hooray* (1915), *The Bid Show* (1916), *Cheer Up* (1917), *The Kiss Burglar* (1918), *The Elusive Lady* (1922), *Yours Truly* (1927), *The Girl from Cooks'* (1927), and *Three Cheers* (1928) starring Will Rogers and Dorothy Stone.

HUBBLE, JOHN EDGAR (ED)

b. 1928 Santa Barbara, California.
Trombonist. Played with Billy Maxted, Phil Napoleon, and Don Ewell; organized own quartet (1964).

HUBERDEAU, GUSTAVE

b. 1878 Paris, France, d. there 1945.
Operatic bass. Studied at the Paris Conservatory; sang at Opera Comique, Manhattan Opera Company, New York (1908); with Chicago Opera Company after 1910.

HUCKO, MICHAEL ANDREW ("PEANUTS")

b. 1918 Syracuse, New York.
Clarinetist and tenor saxist. Played with Glenn Miller's Army Air Force band, Jack Teagarden, and Louis Armstrong; at Newport Jazz Festival (1963-64); Aspen Jazz Festival (1964-66); organized his own quintet (1963).

HUDSON DUSTERS *see* DAVE VAN RONK

HUDSON, WILL

b. 1908 Barstow, California.
Composer, conductor, and arranger. Studied music in Detroit; organized his own band (1931); joined with Eddie de Lange (1934) and wrote songs with him; studied classical composition at Juilliard School, New York City after 1948; with de Lange, wrote—"Moonglow" (1934, w. Irving Mills), "Don' Kiss Me Again" (Mills), "By the Great Hornspoon" (Mills); also "Organ Grinder's Swing" (w. Mitchell Parish and Mills), "Midnight at the Onyx" (Parish).

HUEHN, JULIUS M.

b. 1910 Melrose, Massachusetts, d. 1971 Rochester, New York. Teacher and opera singer. Attended Carnegie-Mellon Institute, Pittsburgh, Pa. and the Juilliard Graduate School, New York City; sang with the Metropolitan Opera Company (1935-46), except for a period when he served as a captain in the Marines in World War II; later became chairman of the vocal department at the Eastman School of Music, Rochester, New York.

HUERTER, CHARLES

b. 1885 Brooklyn, New York.
Composer and teacher. Wrote *Pirate Dreams*.

HUGHES, EDWIN

b. 1884 Washington, D.C. d. 1965.
Pianist and teacher. Studied with Leschetizky and others; concert pianist in Europe and the United States; taught at the Institute of Musical Art, New York City (1916-22).

HUGHES, LANGSTON

b. 1902 Joplin, Missouri, d. 1967.
Black librettist and lyricist. Spent his childhood with his grandmother in Lawrence, Kansas, then with his mother in Lincoln, Illinois, and in Cleveland, Ohio; attended Columbia University, New York City; graduated Lincoln University; wrote the poem "The Negro Speaks of Rivers" (1921), the play *The Barrier* (opera—Jan Meyerowitz), a libretto *Street Scene* (1947, book—Elmer Rice, m. Kurt Weill), with Russell Atkins wrote *In Memorium—Beryl Rubenstein* (1953, m. Hale Smith) presented at Karamu House, Cleveland, Ohio, and "Backlash Blues" (m. Nina Simone).

HUGHES, WILLIAM HENRY (BILL)

b. 1930 Dallas, Texas.
Black bass trombonist. Educated at Howard University, Washington, D.C.; played with Andy Kirk, Frank Wess, and Count Basie.

HUHN, BRUNO

b. 1871 London, England, d. 1950 New York City. Pianist, choral conductor, and composer. Pupil of Sophie Taunton, then in New York with S.B. Mills and L. Alberti; concert pianist in Europe, choral conductor and accompanist in New York; composed a *Te Deum*, with orchestra and songs.

HULETT, WILLIAM C.

b. (?), d. 1785.
Violinist, conductor, dancer, singer, and

manager. Orchestra leader of Old American Company; with Alexander Dienval, founded a series of subscription concerts in New York City (1760).

HULSTEYN, JOAI'N C. VAN *see* VAN HULSTEYN

HUME, PAUL

b. 1916.
Critic. Music critic for the *Washington Post*; in review of Margaret Truman's concert 12/6/50 in Washington, D.C. wrote:"Yet Miss Truman cannot sing very well. She is flat a good deal of the time—more last night than at any time we have heard her"; received a handwritten note from President Truman: "I never met you, but if I do you'll need a new nose and plenty of beefsteak and perhaps a supporter below."

HUMES, HELEN

b. 1913 Louisville, Kentucky.
Black singer. Vocalist with Count Basie (1938-42); with Red Norvo in 1950s; toured Australia with Norvo; at Monterey Jazz Festival (1962); then in Australia again (1964-65); albums—*Helen Humes Sings, Songs I Like to Sing, Swingin' with Humes.*

HUMISTON, WILLIAM HENRY

b. 1869 Marietta, Ohio, d. 1923 New York City. Pianist and conductor. Graduated Lake Forest College, Illinois; studied with MacDowell and others; conductor of opera companies on tour; editor of program notes of New York Philharmonic after 1912; assistant conductor after 1916; composed orchestral works and songs.

HUMPERDINCK, ENGELBERT

b. 1936 India.
Singer. Born Gerry Dorsey; his father was in the army in India; met Gordon Mills, manager, in London; Mills changed Dorsey's name to Humperdinck; with Tom Jones and Mills, formed Management Agency and Music, Ltd. (1967); their share now worth over $25 million; appeared on television shows in New York City; albums—*Release Me* (1967), *Engelbert, Engelbert Humperdinck, Last Waltz.*

HUMPHREY, JIM

b. ca. 1870.
Black cornetist. Many of his children and grandchildren became well-known musicians, including trumpeter Percy Humphrey, clarinetist Willie Humphrey, Jr., and trombonist Earl Humphrey.

HUMPHREY, PAUL NELSON

b. 1935 Detroit, Michigan.
Black drummer. In U.S. Navy band (1955-57), toured the world; with Wes Montgomery, Gene Ammons, Lee Konitz, Ernie Andrews, Les McCann and others during 1960s; at Newport Jazz Festival (1965) with McCann.

HUMPHREY, PERCY G.

b. 1905 New Orleans, Louisiana.
Black trumpeter. Brother of trombonist Earl and clarinetist Willie Humphrey; leader of Eureka Brass Band after 1947.

HUMPHREY, WILLIAM J., JR. (WILLIE)

b. 1901 New Orleans, Louisiana.
Black clarinetist and saxophonist. Brother of trombonist Earl and trumpeter Percy Humphrey; played in Eureka Brass Band; also with Paul Barbarin at Dixieland Hall, New Orleans.

HUMPHRIES, ROGER

b. 1944 Pittsburgh, Pennsylvania.
Drummer. Nephew of trumpeter Frank Humphries; organized own group (1960); played at Carnegie Music Hall, Pittsburgh; with Horace Silver Quintet after 1964.

HUNEKER, JAMES GIBBONS

b. 1860 Philadelphia, Pennsylvania, d. 1921 Brooklyn, New York. Music teacher and critic. Taught piano at the National Conservatory in New York City (1881-91); published *Mezzotints in Modern Music* (1899) and *Chopin, the Man and His Music* (1900).

HUNT, G. W.

b. 1854 near Ionia, Michigan, d. 1940.
Organist, pianist, composer, and teacher. Studied with Mason and Sternberg; taught piano, organ, and theory in Erie, Pa. after 1882; wrote "Awfully Clever," "The Bold Fisherman," "Up in a Balloon" (w. H.B. Farnie).

HUNTER, CHARLES H.

b. 1878 Columbia, Tennessee, d. 1906 St. Louis, Missouri. Composer. Born blind; attended the School for the Blind in Nashville; worked for the Jesse French Piano Company in Nashville and taught himself to play the piano; wrote his first rag in 1899, "Tickled to Death," and "A Tennessee Tantalizer" (1900); in 1901 wrote—" 'Possum and 'Taters," "Cotton Bolls" and "Queen of Love"—two-step; moved to St. Louis (1902); wrote "Just Ask Me" and "Why We Smile" (1903), "Back to Life" and "Seraphine

Waltzes" (1905) published by John S. Stark; died of tuberculosis.

HUNTER, "IVORY" JOE

b. 1911 Kirbyville, Texas, d. 1974.
Black singer and songwriter. Sang in church choirs as a youth; had his own radio show on station KFDM, Beaumont, Texas; wrote and recorded "Blues at Sunrise" (1944); also "I Need You So" and "I Almost Lost My Mind" (1950, also recorded by Pat Boone); recorded "Since I Met You Baby" (1956).

HUNTER, WILLIAM

b. 1811 Ballymoney, Country Antrim, Ireland, d. 1877 Alliance, Ohio. Hymnist. Came with his parents to York, Pa. (1817); educated at Madison College, Hamilton, N.Y.; professor at Allegheny College, Meadville, Pa. (1855), and later minister of the Methodist church in Alliance, Ohio; wrote "Joyfully, Joyfully Onward I Move" (1842, m. A.D. Merrill), "Rest for the Weary" (m. J.W. Dadmun, "In the Christian's Home in Glory") and "Land of Beulah" (ca. 1862, m. J.W. Dadmun, "I Am Dwelling on the Mountain"); many of his hymns appeared in his compilations—*Minstrel of Zion* (1845), *Select Melodies* (1851), and *Songs of Devotion* (1859).

HUNTINGTON, DE WITT CLINTON

b. 1830 Townshend, Vermont, d. 1912.
Lyricist. Graduated Syracuse University, Syracuse, N.Y. and received D.D. and LL.D. degrees from Genesee College; resided in Lincoln, Nebraska; wrote the lyrics "O Think of the Home Over There" (m. T.C. O'Kane).

HUNTINGTON, FREDERICK DAN

b. 1819 Hadley, Massachusetts, d. there 1904. Hymnist. Graduated Amherst (1839) and Cambridge Divinity School (1842); Unitarian minister in Boston (1842-55); professor at Harvard after 1855; ordained Episcopal minister (1859) and became Bishop of Central New York (1869); with Dr. F.H. Hedge edited *Unitarian Hymns for the Church of Christ*, (Boston, 1853), which included three of his hymns.

HUNTINGTON, JONATHAN

b. 1771 Windham, Connecticut, d. 1838 St. Louis, Missouri. Compiler. Sang and taught music in Windham, Conn. (1797-1804), Troy, N.Y. (1806-07), Northampton, Mass. (1808-13), and then Boston and St. Louis; compiled *The Apollo Harmony* (1807) and *Classical Sacred Music* (1812); with William Cooper, of Boston, published *The Beauties of Church Music and Sure Guide to the Art of Singing* (1804).

HUPFELD, CHARLES FREDERICK

b. 1788 Germany, d. 1864 Philadelphia, Pennsylvania. Violinist. Came to America (1801) with his brother, John Hupfeld, also a violinist; settled in Philadelphia; gave concerts (1816-20); joined in forming the Musical Fund Society (1820); principal conductor of the Society (1828-45); wrote *A Concerto Militaire* played by the noted flutist Francis Blondau in concerts between 1810-20.

HUPFELD, HERMAN

b. 1894 Montclair, New Jersey, d. there 1951. Composer and singer. Served in navy in World War I; sang his own songs in Ziegfeld's *Midnight Frolic* (1912); wrote "Sing Something Simple," "As Time Goes By" (1931).

HUPFIELD (HUPFELD), CHARLES

b. (?), d. 1819 Philadelphia, Pennsylvania. Violinist and publisher. Gave concerts at Bush Hill, Philadelphia (1797); music publisher in Philadelphia (1801-04) and with the firm of Charles Hupfield and F. Hammer, Baltimore (1805-12); gave concerts in Philadelphia (1812-18).

HURLBURT, WILLIAM HENRY

b. 1827 Charleston, South Carolina, d. 1895 Cadenabbia, Italy. Hymnist. Educated at Harvard; three of his hymns appeared in Samuel Longfellow and Samuel Johnson's *Book of Hymns* (1848); editor of the *New York World* (1876-83).

HUROK, SOLOMON ISAIEVICH (SOL)

b. 1888 Russia, d. 1974 New York City.
Impresario. Booking agent for Russian cultural groups after 1950; brought Russian musicians, singers, and ballet dances to America; his office damaged by an incendiary device, New York City (1972).

HURT, "MISSISSIPPI" JOHN

b. 1892 Teoc, Mississippi, d. 1966 Grenada, Mississippi. Black singer and guitarist. Raised in Avalon, Miss., where he worked picking cotton, and was a railroad hand for a while; his LP records were *Presenting Mississippi John Hurt: Folk Songs and Blues* (1963), and *Worried Blues* (1964).

HUSBAND, JOHN JENKINS

b. 1760 Plymouth, England, d. 1825 Philadelphia, Pennsylvania. Composer and teacher. Came to America (1807); taught music in Philadelphia; clerk of St. Paul's P.E. Church; composed the tune "English Melody" ("Rejoice and Be Glad," w. H. Bonar, also used for "We Praise Thee, Oh God," w. W.P. Mackay, 1866), "We Are on Our Journey Home"; issued a revised edition of *Philadelphia Harmony* (by Andrew Adgate) published by M. Carey, (Philadelphia, 1807 and 1811); also wrote "Revive Us Again" (known to the public as "Hallelujah, I'm a Bum").

HUSKY, FERLIN

b. 1927 Flat River, Missouri.
Singer and guitarist. Disc jockey in Bakersfield, California (1949); sang under the names "Terry Preston" and "Simon Crum"; his LP records include *Ferlin Husky* (1959), *Ferlin Husky and His Hush Puppies, Born to Lose, Ferlin Husky Favorites* (1959), *Gone Home* (1960), *Walkin' and Hummin', Memories of Home* (1961), *Some of My Favorites* (1962), *Heart and Soul of Ferlin Husky* (1963), *By Request* (1964), *I Could Sing All Night.*

HUSS, HENRY HOLDEN

b. 1862 Newark, New Jersey, d. 1953 New York City. Composer. Studied at the Munich Conservatory, then taught piano and composition in New York; with his wife, soprano Hildegard Hoffman, gave joint recitals in the United States and Europe; composed Piano Concerto in B Major (New York Philharmonic), *Recessional* for mixed chorus, organ and orchestra (Worcester, Mass. Festival, 1911), *Violin Sonata* (Kneisel, Spiering, et al.), String Quartet in E Minor (Kneisel Quartet), songs.

HUTCHENRIDER, CLARENCE BEHRENS

b. 1908 Waco, Texas.
Clarinetist. Played with the Glen Gray Casa Loma Orchestra (1931-43); organized own trio (1958), played at Gaslight Club, New York City.

HUTCHERSON, ROBERT (BOBBY)

b. 1941 Los Angeles, California.
Black vibraphonist. Brother of singer Renee Robin; with Curtis Amy, Charles Lloyd and others in Los Angeles; with Al Grey-Billy Mitchell combo in San Francisco; in New York after 1961 with Jackie McLean, Archie Shepp, Hank Mobley and others; later returned to west coast; at Monterey Jazz Festival (1965).

HUTCHESON, ERNEST

b. 1871 Melbourne, Australia, d. 1951 New York City. Teacher and composer. Studied at the Leipzig Conservatory; became a teacher at the Peabody Conservatory, Baltimore (1900); Chautauqua Institute (1911); dean of Juilliard Graduate School of Music, New York (1926); composed the symphonic poem, *Merlin and Vivien* (Berlin, 1899), a symphony, piano concerto (1899), two-piano concerto, violin concerto.

HUTCHINSON, ABIGAIL JEMIMA (ABBY)

b. 1829 near Milford, New Hampshire, d. 1892 New York City. Singer. Professional debut with brothers John, Judson, and Asa (1841) in *The Aeolian Vocalists,* toured New England; at Niblo's Garden, New York City (1843); toured England (1845); married Ludlow Patton (1849) and retired from the stage; rejoined the group (1860) to support Lincoln and the Civil War; with her brother John sang at funeral of poet John Greenleaf Whittier (1892).

HUTCHINSON, ASA

b. 1823, d. 1884.
Singer. Member of the singing Hutchinson Family.

HUTCHINSON FAMILY

Abby, Joshua, Jesse, Judson, John, and Asa were a popular singing group from Milford, N.H.; there were thirteen brothers and sisters in all; toured England (1846); in January, 1862, sang in the White House for President Lincoln; sang the "Battle Cry of Freedom" (George F. Root) at a War Rally (1863) in Union Square, New York City, and were so successful in raising funds, they repeated the song often during the duration of the war; another favorite of theirs was "Tenting on the Old Camp Ground" (Walter Kittredge).

HUTCHINSON, JOHN WALLACE

b. 1821, d. 1908.
Singer. Member of the singing Hutchinson Family.

HUTTON, BETTY

b. 1921 Battle Creek, Michigan.
Singer, comedienne, and actress. Started with Vincent Lopez's orchestra; later appeared in many films.

HUTTON, INA RAY

b. 1918 Chicago, Illinois.
Bandleader. She started with an all-girl orchestra; in 1940 added men—Jack Purcell, guitarist, George Paxton, tenor saxophonist and arranger, trumpeter Randy Brooks (she married Brooks), Stuart Foster, baritone, Hal Schaefer, pianist.

HYDE, ABBY BRADLEY

b. 1799 Stockbridge, Massachusetts, d. 1872 Andover, Massachusetts. Hymnist. Married Rev. Lavius Hyde of Salisbury, Mass. (1818); two of her hymns appeared in Dr. L. Bacon's *Hymns and Sacred Songs for the Monthly Concert* (Andover, 1823), nine in Asahel Nettleton's *Village Hymns* (1824, plus thirty-four in the revised edition, 1851), and one hymn in Nason's *Congregational Hymn Book* (1857).

HYDE, WILLIAM DE WITT

b. 1858 Winchendon, Massachusetts, d. 1917. Hymnist. Educated at Harvard (1875) and Andover Theological Seminary; pastor of the Congregational Church, Paterson, N.J. (1882-85), then president of Bowdoin College, Brunswick, Maine (1885-1917); wrote the hymn "Creation's Lord, We Give Thee Thanks" (1903, tune "Seabury"—Claude Means).

HYER SISTERS COLORED MINSTRELS *see* SAM LUCAS and ANNA and EMMA HYERS

HYERS, ANNA MADAH

b. 1854 Sacramento, California, d. ca. 1924. Black contralto. Sister of Emma Louise Hyers; sisters made their debut at the Metropolitan Theatre in Sacramento, California (1867); toured U.S.; sang airs from *Il Trovatore* and *La Traviata* in Boston (1869); formed the Hyer Sisters Colored Minstrels which included Wallace King, John Luca of the Luca Family Singers, Tom Fletcher, and Sam Lucas; produced *Out of Bondage, The Underground Railway* and *The Princess Orelia of Madagascar.*

HYERS, EMMA LOUISE

b. 1853 Sacramento, California, d. ca. 1916. Black soprano. Sister of Anna Madah Hyers; with the Hyer Sisters Colored Minstrels.

HYLLESTED, AUGUST

b. 1856 Stockholm, Sweden, d. 1946 Blairmore, Scotland. Pianist and teacher. Played in public in Stockholm at age eight; toured Scandinavia at age eleven; studied at Royal Conservatory at Copenhagen under Edmund Neupert and Neils W. Gade; in Berlin with Theodor Kullak; toured England (1883); came to America (1885); toured eastern U.S. and Canada; taught at the Chicago Musical College.

HYMAN, DICK

b. 1927 New York City.

Pianist and organist. Musical director for Arthur Godfrey's radio show in late 1950s; later arranger for Bobby Hackett, Al Hirt, J.J. Johnson, Ethel Ennis, Cozy Cole and others; composed musical settings for Shakespeare's poems, recorded by Earl Wrightson as *Shakespeare's Greatest Hits* (1964); at Newport Jazz Festival, New York City (1972).

IAN, JANIS

b. 1951.
Singer and songwriter. At sixteen she wrote "Society's Child" (about a white girl and a black boy); introduced on a TV rock show by Leonard Bernstein (1967); albums—*Janis Ian* (1967), *For All the Seasons of Your Mind, Secret Life of J. Eddy Fink, Who Really Cares.*

IDE, GEORGE BARTON

b. 1806 Coventry, Vermont, d. 1872.
Hymnist and compiler. Educated at Middlebury College, Vermont; pastor in Boston, Philadelphia, and Springfield, Mass.; edited *The Baptist Harp,* (Philadelphia, 1849) which included nine of his hymns.

IKE AND TINA *see* IKE AND TINA TURNER

IKETTES (dancers) *see* TINA TURNER

IMBER, NAPHTALI HERZ

b. 1856 Galicia, Poland, d. 1909.
Lyricist. In Palestine (1882-88); came to America (1892); wrote "Ha-Tikvah" (The Hope), Zionist song (1886, m. arranged by Samuel Cohen from the tune "Cart and Oxen," a Moldavian-Rumanian folk song); became unofficial national anthem of Israel after 1947.

IMBRIE, ANDREW WELSH

b. 1921 New York City.
Composer. Graduated Princeton University (1942); M.A. at the University of California at Berkeley (1947); taught there after 1947; wrote three string quartets, trios, sonatas, one symphony, Ballad in D (1947), *Legend* (1959), *On the Beach at Night* (1948), *Three Against Christmas* (opera).

IMPERIALS *see* HENRY T. SLAUGHTER

IMPRESSIONS, THE (rock group)

Curtis Mayfield, lead vocals and songwriter; Samuel Gooden, bass vocals; Fred Cash, tenor vocals; Jerry Butler, formerly with the group; started in Chicago (1958) as the Roosters; albums—*Best Impressions, Best of the Impressions, Impressions, Impressions' Greatest Hits, Keep on Pushing, Never Ending Impressions, One by One, People Get Ready, Ridin' High, This Is My Country, We're a Winner, Young Mods' Forgotten Story;* Curtis Mayfield replaced by Leroy Hutson.

INCH, HERBERT REYNOLDS

b. 1904 Missoula, Montana.
Composer. Graduated Eastman School of Music, Rochester, N.Y.; won fellowship at American Academy in Rome; Ernest Bloch award; University of Rochester Travelling Fellowship; Montana State University, Bozeman (Ph.D.); composed *Variations on a Modal Theme* (1927), *Three Pieces for Small Orchestra* (1930), Symphony no. 1 (Rochester Philharmonic Orchestra under Hanson, 1932), *Serenade* (for string orchestra, Eastman School, Rochester Civic Orchestra under Hanson, 1939).

INCREDIBLE STRING BAND, THE (Scotch group)

INDIANA FIVE (Dixieland Band) *see* HARRY FORD

INFLUENCE (Canadian rock group)

INGALLS, JEREMIAH

b. 1764 Andover, Massachusetts, d. 1828 Hancock, Vermont. Composer. Choirmaster at the Congregational Church in Newberry, Vt., moved to Rochester, N.Y., then to Hancock, Vt.; composed the tunes "Fillmore" ("And Can It Be That I Should Gain," w. Charles Wesley), "Kentucky" ("A Charge to Keep I Have," w. Charles Wesley), "Garden Hymn" ("The Lord into His Garden Comes," 1800, w. Rev. Campbell), "New Jerusalem" ("Lo! What a Glorious Sight Appears," w. Isaac Watts), and "Northfield" ("How Long, Dear Saviour," w. Isaac Watts—last stanza); published *Christian Harmony* (Exeter, N.H. 1804).

INGRAM, FRANCES

b. 1888 Liverpool, England.
Contralto. She studied with Maurel; sang with Chicago Opera Company (1911-13); with Montreal Opera after 1913.

INMAN, ROBERT AUTREY

b. 1929 Florence, Alabama.
Singer and songwriter. Attended Kinzer College, Florence, Alabama; wrote "Mr. Moon," "Town That Never Sleeps," "Blues in Advance," "I Don't Believe You've Met My Baby," "Blue Monday," "She's Looking Good."

IRELAND, GEORGE THOMAS ("G. TOM")

b. 1865 Louisville, Kentucky, d. 1963.
Black clarinetist. Educated at Central Tennessee College (Walden University), Nashville, Tenn.; settled in Sedalia, Missouri; reported for the *Democrat* for fifty years; played in the Queen City Concert Band; died at age ninety-eight.

IRON BUTTERFLY (rock group)

Erik Brann, lead guitar; Lee Dorman, bass; Ron Bushy, drums; Doug Ingle, vocals and organ; started in Los Angeles (1967); albums—*Ball, In-A-Gadda-Da-Vida, Iron Butterfly.*

IRVINE, JESSIE S.

b. 1836, d. 1887.
Composer. She wrote the music "The Lord Is My Shepherd" (ca. 1890, this title has been used by other composers).

IRVIS, CHARLIE

b. 1899 New York City, d. there 1939.
Black trombonist. Played in Duke Ellington's band (1924-26); with Charlie Johnson (1927-28); with Charlie Johnson and others in 1930s.

IRWIN, MAY

b. 1862 Whitby, Ontario, Canada, d. 1938 New York City. Black singer and actress. Born Georgia Campbell; debut with sister Ada "Flo Irwin" (1875) in Buffalo, N.Y.; joined Tony Pastor's vaudeville show, New York City (1877); introduced "Mister Johnson Turn Me Loose" (m. B.R. Harney) in the musical *Courted in Court* (1895); sang "I'm Lookin' for de Bully" (1896, by Charles Trevathan); popularized "When You Ain't Got No Money, Well, You Needn't Come Around" (w. C.S. Brewster and m. A. Baldwin Sloane).

ISHAM'S ORIENTAL AMERICA COMPANY (black minstrels) *see* SIDNEY WOODWARD

ISHKABIBBLE (MERWYN BOGUE) *see* KAY KYSER

ISLEY BROTHERS (black group)

Ronald Isley, Rudolph Isley, and O'Kelly Isley; also Marvin Isley plays bass and Ernest Isley plays several instruments and arranges; there was a sixth brother in the group, Vernon, who was killed in a car crash; albums—*Take Some Time Out for the Isley Brothers* (1964), *Isley Brothers, Doin' Their Thing, Isley Brothers Do Their Thing, Isley Brothers Live at Yankee Stadium, It's Your Thing, Soul on the Rocks, This Old Heart of Mine, Twist and Shout.*

ISRAELS, CHARLES H.

b. 1936 New York City.
Bass player. Studied at MIT and Brandeis University, Waltham, Mass.; with Billie Holiday, Max Roach and others in 1950s; then with the Bill Evans trio after 1961; toured Europe (1964-65) with Evans; also recorded with his own group after 1965.

ISTOMIN, EUGENE

b. 1925 New York City.
Virtuoso pianist. His parents were born in Russia; studied together at Curtis Institute in Philadelphia with Leonard Bernstein; double debut (1943) with Philadelphia Orchestra under Eugene Ormandy and New York Philharmonic under Rodzinski; played for Presidents Truman and Kennedy; has toured six continents.

ITURBI, JOSE

b. 1895 Valencia, Spain.
Famous pianist and conductor. Studied at the Valencia Conservatory, and Paris Conservatory; taught at Geneva Conservatory (1919-23); toured Europe as concert pianist; American debut (1928); conducted in Mexico City, led various American orchestras, then became conductor of the Rochester (N.Y.) Philharmonic Orchestra (1936).

IVES, BENONI I.

b. 1822, d. 1912 Auburn, New York.
Singer. Methodist minister in New York State, and a fine singer; chaplain of the state prison at Auburn, N.Y. for ten years; *The Revivalist* (1868) makes reference to his singing.

IVES, BURL

b. 1909 Hunt, Illinois.
Ballad singer and actor. Attended Eastern Illinois University, Charleston, Ill., Indiana State, Terre Haute, Ind., and New York University; served in the army in World War II; concert debut in Town Hall, New York City (1945); appeared in films and Broadway musical shows; his albums include *The Wayfarin' Stranger, Ballads and Folk Songs* (1949), *Captain Burl Ives' Ark* (1952), *Down to*

the Sea in Ships, Folk Songs Dramatic and Humorous, Versatile Burl Ives, Best of Burl Ives (1961), *Songs of the West* (1962), *My Gal Sal* (1965).

IVES, CHARLES EDWARD

b. 1874 Danbury, Connecticut, d. 1954 New York City. Noted composer. Studied under his father, George E. Ives, who was a bandmaster in the Civil War; also with Dudley Buck, Rowe Shelly, and Horatio Parker; was an insurance broker; composed his Symphony no.3 for orchestra which was introduced by the New York Little Symphony Orchestra under Lou Harrison (1946) and won the Pulitzer Prize; *Three Places in New England* for orchestra (1914), Sonata no. 2 for Piano (1915).

IVES, ELAM, JR.

b. 1802, d. 1864.
Compiler. With Deodatus Dutton, Jr., issued the *American Psalmody* (1830), called *The Hartford Collection;* New York musical reporter for *The Harbinger* (1847).

IZENZON, DAVID

b. 1932 Pittsburgh, Pennsylvania.
Bass player. Worked with various groups in 1950s; played with Archie Shepp, Sonny Rollins, Mose Allison, Ornette Coleman and others during 1960s; in Europe with Coleman (1965-66).

J

JACKSON, AL, JR.

b. (?) Memphis, Tennessee.
Black drummer. As a youth was a member of his father's sixteen-piece orchestra; educated at A.M. and N. College, Pine Bluff, Arkansas; member of Booker T & the M.G.s (Memphis group).

JACKSON, CALVIN

b. 1919 Philadelphia, Pennsylvania.
Pianist and composer. Leader of his own orchestra in Canada during late 1940s and '50s; played with small groups in Los Angeles after 1961; composed *Profile of an American* (dedicated to President John F. Kennedy), performed by the Hollywood Symphony Orchestra (1966); scored the TV series "The Asphalt Jungle" (1962) and the Hollywood film *The Unsinkable Molly Brown.*

JACKSON, CLIFTON LUTHER (CLIFF)

b. 1919 Culpepper, Virginia, d. 1970.
Black jazz pianist. Popular pianist in night clubs in New York City.

JACKSON FIVE (black vocal group)

Michael (b. 1958), lead singer; Jackie (b. 1951); Tito (b. 1954); Jermaine (b. 1955); Marlon (b. 1957); five brothers; their father, Joseph Jackson, was a crane operator in Gary, Indiana; after their success, bought a home in Encino, Calif.; album—*Jackson 5.*

JACKSON, FRANZ

b. 1912 Rock Island, Illinois.
Tenor saxist, clarinetist, and bandleader. Played with David Eldridge, Fats Waller, Earl Hines and others during 1930s and '40s; organized Original Jass (Jazz) All-Stars (1956).

JACKSON, GEORGE K.

b. 1745 Oxford, England, d. 1823 Boston, Massachusetts. Composer and compiler. Educated at Saint Andrews College (1791); in 1796 came to Norfolk, Va. where he taught and played the organ; played in churches in Alexandria, Virginia, Baltimore, Philadelphia, and Elizabeth, N.J.; while organist in St. George's Chapel, New York City, wrote *David's Psalms* (set to music, 1804); in 1812 went to Boston to live, where he organized a series of oratorio concerts in Boston and Salem; in 1816 published *A Choice Collection of Chants.*

JACKSON, GREIG STEWART ("CHUBBY")

b. 1918 New York City.
Bass player. With Woody Herman during 1940s; in Chicago during 1950s; led his own band and later combos in New York City during 1960s; album—*Chubby Jackson Sextet and Big Band;* at the Newport Jazz Festival, New York City (1972).

JACKSON, MAHALIA

b. 1911 near New Orleans, Louisiana, d. 1972 Evergreen Park, Illinois. Noted black singer. Leading American gospel singer; after both parents died, went to Chicago at age fifteen; sang in gospel tours in the Midwest; first recorded "God Gonna Separate the Wheat from the Tares" (1934); "Move On Up a Little Higher" (1954), her first hit record; sang at concerts at Carnegie Hall, New York City (1950-56); sang at inauguration of President Kennedy (1961); at the March on Washington (1963); sang "Precious Lord, Take My Hand" at Morehouse College, Atlanta, Georgia, following the funeral of the Rev. Dr. Martin Luther King (1968); toured Europe (1971) and hospitalized in Munich, Germany, for coronary heart disease; albums—*Abide with Me, Best of Mahalia Jackson, Bless This House, Garden of Prayer, Gospel World of Mahalia Jackson, Great Gettin' Up Morning, Great Songs of Love and Faith, I Believe, I Lift My Voice, In the Upper Room, My Faith, Just As I Am.*

JACKSON, MIKE

b. 1888 Louisville, Kentucky, d. 1945 New York City. Black pianist and songwriter. Lived in Terre Haute, Indiana; played in night spots in East St. Louis, Illinois, and in Harlem, New York City; wrote "Man, Knock Me a Drink."

JACKSON, MILTON (MILT, "BAGS")

b. 1923 Detroit, Michigan.
Black vibraharpist. Played with Dizzy Gillespie, Thelonious Monk, Woody Herman and others; also singer, pianist, and guitarist; with John Lewis, founded the Modern Jazz Quartet (1952); at the Newport Jazz Festival, New York City (1972).

JACKSON, OLIVER, JR.

b. 1934 Detroit, Michigan.
Drummer. Played with Yusef Lateef, Buck Clayton, Lionel Hampton, Earl Hines, Charlie Shavers and others.

JACKSON, PRESTON (JAMES P. McDONALD)

b. 1903 New Orleans, Louisiana.
Black trombonist. Played with Louis Armstrong, Erskine Tate and others; organized his own combo and played in Chicago.

JACKSON, QUENTIN LEONARD ("BUTTER")

b. 1909 Springfield, Ohio.
Black trombonist. Played in Duke Ellington's band (1948-59); toured Europe with Quincy Jones.

JACKSON, SAMUEL P.

b. 1818 Manchester, England, d. 1885 New York City. Composer. Son of James J. Jackson, organ builder.

JACKSON, STONEWALL

b. 1932 Tabor City, North Carolina.
Singer and guitarist. Served in the submarine service in the navy during the Korean War; his hit records include "Life to Go" (1958), "Waterloo" (1959), "Why I'm Walkin' " (1960), "A Wound Time Can't Ease" and "Leona" (1962), "Old Showboat" (1963), "B.J. the D.J.," also "Don't Be Angry" (which he wrote, 1964), "Trouble and Me" (1965), "Stamp Out Loneliness" (1967), "All's Fair in Love and War" (1967).

JACKSON, TONY

b. 1876 New Orleans, Louisiana, d. 1921 Chicago, Illinois. Black pianist, singer, and composer. Wrote the rag tunes "The Naked Dance" (1902), "Michigan Water" (1912), "Pick-it Boy" (1917), and the songs "Pretty Baby" (1916, with Egbert Van Alstyne, w. Gus Kahn), "Miss Samantha Johnson's Wedding Day" (1916), "Waiting at the Old Church Door" (1916), "Some Sweet Day" (1917, with Abe Olman and Ed Rose), "Why Keep Me Waiting So Long" (1917).

JACKSON, WANDA

b. 1937 Maud, Oklahoma.
Singer and popular composer. Took piano lessons in Bakersfield, Calif. at age nine; had her own show on station KLPR, Oklahoma City, at age fourteen; toured as a singer with Elvis Presley (1955-56); appeared in Las Vegas, Nevada, night spots in the 1960s; married Wendell Goodman, who arranged her tours; wrote "Kicking Our Hearts Around," "Right or Wrong," "In the Middle of a Heartache" (1961); she was a hit singing "Fujiyama Mamma" in Japan and "Santo Domingo" in Germany.

JACOBI, FREDERICK

b. 1891 San Francisco, California, d. 1952 New York City. Composer. Studied at the Juilliard School, New York City with Rubin Goldmark, in Berlin with Paul Juon, and with Ernest Bloch; composed *Indian Dances, California Suite, The Pied Piper, The Eve of St. Agnes, The Poet in the Desert,* also piano concertos and cello concertos, *Sabbath Evening Service* (Jewish), *Three Excerpts from the Prophet Nehemiah* and *Hagiographa.*

JACOBI, VICTOR

b. 1883 Budapest, Hungary, d. 1921 New York City. Composer. Came to New York City (1913); wrote the score for *The Proud Princess* (1912), *The Marriage Market* (1913, adapted from a German play), *Sibyl* (1916, Harry Graham and H.B. Smith), *Rambler Rose* (1917), *Apple Blossoms* (1919, with Fritz Kreisler and lyrics by William Le Baron), *The Half Moon* (1920), *The Love Letter* (1921, based on Ferenc Molnar's *The Phantom Rival*).

JACOBSOHN, SIMON E.

b. 1839 Milau, Russia, d. 1902 Chicago, Illinois. Violinist. Studied at the Leipzig Conservatory; conductor of the Bremen Orchestra (1860), Theodore Thomas Orchestra, New York (1872); later taught at the Cincinnati (Ohio) Conservatory and in Chicago.

JACQUET, JEAN BAPTISTE ("ILLINOIS")

b. 1922 Broussard, Louisiana.
Black jazz tenor saxist. Played with Lionel Hampton, Cab Calloway, Count Basie and others during 1940s and '50s; also led his own quartet; studied the bassoon with Manuel Zegler of the New York Philharmonic and later played in New York City; at Newport Jazz Festival, New York City (1972).

JACQUET, ROBERT RUSSELL

b. 1917 Broussard, Louisiana.
Black trumpeter and singer. Brother of Illinois and Linton Jacquet; studied at Wiley College and the University of Southern California at Los Angeles; played with his brother Illinois Jacquet, Gerald Wilson, Benny Carter and others.

JAGEL, FREDERICK

b. 1897 Brooklyn, New York.
Tenor. Pupil of Portanova and Castaldi; debut in *La Boheme*, Livorno, Italy; sang in Italy and California; debut at Metropolitan Opera, New York (1927); with Metropolitan (1927-50); later taught at the New England Conservatory, Boston.

JAMAL, AHMAD

b. 1930 Pittsburgh, Pennsylvania.
Black pianist and composer. Formed trio with bassist Jamil Nasser and drummer Vernel Fournier; later drummer Frank Grant (1966); wrote *Minor Moods, Extensions, One for Miles;* albums—*All of You, Bright, the Blue and the Beautiful, Chamber Music of New Jazz, Count 'Em 88, Cry Young, Extensions, Happy Moods, Heat Wave, Ahmad Jamal at Pershing, Jamal at the Penthouse.*

JAMES, CORNELIUS ("PINOCCHIO")

b. 1927 Macon, Georgia.
Singer. Studied at Cosmopolitan School of Music, Cincinnati, Ohio; with Lionel Hampton after 1957; toured Europe with Hampton (1957-58); at Essen Jazz Festival (1961); tour of Far East (1963).

JAMES, DOROTHY

b. 1901 Chicago, Illinois.
Composer. Pupil of Weidig and Gruenberg; studied at Chicago Musical College; master's at American Conservatory of Music; taught at Michigan State University, East Lansing, Mich.; choral works—*Christmas Night* (1933), *The Jumblies* (1934), *The Little Jesus Came to Town* (1935); also orchestral works, and chamber music.

JAMES, ELMER

b. 1910 Yonkers, New York, d. 1954.
Black tuba and bass player. Played with Chick Webb, Fletcher Henderson, Lucky Millinder and others.

JAMES, ELMORE

b. ca 1920, d. 1963 Chicago, Illinois.
Black guitarist. Blues guitarist in the bottleneck style; formed his own group called the Broomdusters; played in Chicago night spots; died of complications of asthma and the flu; albums—*Anthology of the Blues—Legend of Elmore James, Elmore James, Whose Muddy Shoes.*

JAMES, HARRY HAAG

b. 1916 Albany, Georgia.
Jazz trumpeter and bandleader. Father led a circus band; played the trumpet in the Christy Brothers Circus Band at age nine, leader of the band at age twelve; family moved to Beaumont, Texas; joined Ben Pollack's band (1936); later formed his own band; formed new band, the Music Makers (1963); his recording of "All or Nothing at All" with Frank Sinatra was included in RCA's *Big Bands' Greatest Hits* (1971); at Roseland Dance City, New York (1972).

JAMES, NEHEMIAH ("SKIP")

b. 1902 Yazoo County, Mississippi, d. 1969.
Black singer. Sharecropper in Yazoo County, Mississippi; strip miner in Birmingham; sawmill worker in Arkansas; sang the blues; due to his religious feelings, could not accept the profane blues, entered the church (1932) and did not record for thirty-two years; albums—*Skip James Today, Devil Got My Woman.*

JAMES, PERCY EDWARD, JR.

b. 1929 St. Louis, Missouri.
Black drummer. Educated at Lincoln University, Jefferson City, Mo.; played bongos and conga drums; played with Quartette Trés Bien in St. Louis and on tour.

JAMES, PHILIP FREDERICK WRIGHT

b. 1890 Jersey City, N.J.
Composer. Educated at City College of New York; served in France in World War I; organist-choirmaster in Montclair, N.J. and New York City (1919-23); conducted the New Jersey Symphony Orchestra (1922-29); became head of the music department of New York University (1933); composed the tune "Tregaron" (1941, "And Have the Bright Immensities," w. H.C. Robbins).

JAMES, SONNY

b. 1929 Hackleburg, Alabama.
Singer. Born Jimmy Loden; served in Korea during the Korean War; toured all fifty states as a singer; his LP records include *Young Love* (1962), *The Minute You're Gone* (1964), *You're the Only World I Know* (1965), *Behind the Tear* and *True Love's Blessing* (1966), *I'll Never Find Another You* (1967), *Only the Lonely* (1969); featured with The Gentlemen.

JAMES, WILLIAM (BILLY)

b. 1936 Pittsburgh, Pennsylvania.
Drummer. With Lionel Hampton, Booker Ervin and others in 1950s; with Sonny Stitt, Gene Ammons and others in 1960s.

JAMES, WILLIS LAURENCE

b. 1909 Montgomery, Alabama.
Black educator and musicologist. Graduated Morehouse College, Atlanta, Georgia; studied at Chicago Musical College; consultant to the Institute of Jazz Studies, New York City; Library of Congress survey committee on American music; specialized in studies of Negro folk music and jazz.

JAMISON, SAMUEL W.

b. 1855 Washington, D.C. d. 1930 Boston, Massachusetts. Black pianist. Graduated New England Conservatory, Boston; concert pianist.

JAN AND DEAN (vocal duo)

Jan Berry and Dean Torrence; started in California (1963); albums—*Jan and Dean Take Linda Surfin', Surf City and Other Swingin' Cities, Drag City, Dead Man's Curve, Ride the Wild Surf, The Little Old Lady from Pasadena, Jan and Dean, Jan and Dean's Golden Hits, Popsicle.*

JANIS, CONRAD

b. 1928 New York City.
Trombonist and bandleader. Led his own combo during 1950s and '60s; also acted in Broadway shows; appeared on Steve Allen's show and other TV shows.

JANSSEN, WERNER

b. 1900 New York City.
Conductor and composer. Graduated Dartmouth College, Hanover, N.H., and Mus. D., University of California (1923); studied with Converse, Chadwick and others, American Academy in Rome (1930); with New York Symphony Orchestra (1934); conducted Baltimore Symphony (1937-39), Janssen Symphony, Los Angeles (1940); composed a symphony; symphonic poem, *New Year's Eve in New York;* musical comedies and songs.

JANUS CHORALE, THE

Robert Hickok, conductor; in concert at the Metropolitan Museum of Art, New York City (1972).

JANUSCHOWSKY, GEORGINE VON *see* VON JANUSCHOWSKY

JARBORO, CATERINA (YARBOROUGH)

b. 1903 Wilmington, North Carolina.
Black opera singer. Raised in Wilmington, North Carolina; studied voice in Paris and Milan; debut in title role in Verdi's opera *Aïda* at Puccini Opera House, Milan, Italy (1930); later sang *Aïda* with Chicago Opera Company (1933).

JARRETT, KEITH

b. 1945 Allentown, Pennsylvania.
Pianist and composer. Studied piano at age three; studied at Berklee School, Boston; played with Roland Kirk, Tony Scott, and Art Blakey in New York during 1960s.

JARVIS, CHARLES H.

b. 1837 Philadelphia, Pennsylvania, d. there 1895. Pianist and teacher. Son of Charles W. Jarvis, his teacher; piano debut at age seven; studied theory with Leopold Meignen; organized and played in the Classical Soirées, Philadelphia (1862-95).

JARVIS, CHARLES W.

b. ca. 1809 England, d. 1871 Philadelphia, Pennsylvania. Pianist and composer. Came to Philadelphia (ca. 1835); published the opera *Luli, or the Switzer's Bride* (1846); *Here Let Me Dream of Days Now Vanished* (1846, w. T.S. Sullivan); the sea chanty "Three Bells" (1853, w. Rose Hughes), and *Eugene's Farewell* (waltz); published an instruction book (1852).

JASPAR, ROBERT B.

b. 1926 Liege, Belgium, d. 1963 New York City. Flutist, tenor saxist, and clarinetist. Came to New York (1956); played with J.J. Johnson, Donald Byrd, Miles Davis and others; died following an operation for heart surgery.

JAY AND THE AMERICANS (vocal group)

Jay Black, Kenny Vance, Sandy Deane; Marty Sanders, guitar; started in Brooklyn, New York with a hit in 1963; albums—*She Cried, Blockbusters, Come a Little Bit Closer, Early American Hits, Jay and the Americans, Jay and the Americans' Greatest Hits, Livin' Above Your Head, Sunday and Me, Try Some of This, Wax Museum.*

JAY AND THE TECHNIQUES (vocal group)

Jay Proctor, black singer; Karl Landis, black singer; Ronnie Goodly, John Walsh, George Lloyd, Chuck Crowl; Dante Dancho, guitar; albums—*Apples, Peaches, Pumpkin Pie* (1967), *Love, Lost and Found.*

JAY, PENNY

b. 1930 Monteagle, Tennessee.
Singer and songwriter. Attended schools in Knoxville, Tenn.; leader of the Jay Penny Show after 1965; wrote "Another Heaven" (1959), "Second Wedding Day," "Just Over the Line," "After It's Over," "Convict's Angel," "Gravy Train" (1967).

JAYNE, MITCH

b. 1930 Hammond, Indiana.
Singer and banjoist. Disk jockey on radio station KSMO, Salem, Missouri, when he joined the group known as "The Dillards"; their LP records were *Bluegrass* (1963) and *The Dillards Live* (1964).

JAZZ COMPOSERS ORCHESTRA

Organized in 1955; Timothy F. Marquand, President (1969); Michael Mantler, director, conductor, and composer; Cecil Taylor, pianist; Don Cherry, cornetist; Gato Barbieri, tenor saxist; Pharoah Sanders, tenor saxist; Larry Coryell, guitarist; Roswell Rudd, trombonist; recorded "Escalator Over the Hill," by Carla Bley, conducted by her husband, Michael Mantler (1971).

JAZZ CORP, THE (jazz group)
see WILLIAM PLUMMER

JAZZ CRUSADERS (jazz group) *see*
WILTON LEWIS FELDER and STIX HOOPER

JAZZ ENSEMBLE *see* JERRY GRANELLI

JAZZ MESSENGERS (band) *see*
ART BLAKEY and HORACE SILVER

"JAZZ SCENE USA" (TV series)

Produced by Steve Allen.

JEAN, NORMA (BEASLER)

b. 1938 Wellston, Oklahoma.
Singer. Own show on station KLPR, Oklahoma City, at age thirteen; joined Red Foley's "Ozark Jubilee," Springfield, Missouri (1958); Grand Ole Opry, Nashville, Tenn. (1960); her hit records include "Let's Go All the Way" (1963), "Go Cat Go" (1964), "I Wouldn't Buy a Used Car from Him" (1965), "Game of Triangles" (1966, duet with Bobby Bare), "Norma Jean Sings Porter Wagoner" (1967), "Heaven's a Prayer Away" (1968).

JEFFERS, JOHN

b. 1860 Massillon, Ohio, d. 1939.
Editor, composer, and teacher. Studied in Chicago (1886); then taught there; co-editor of *The Musical Journal.*

JEFFERSON AIRPLANE (rock group)

Jorma Kaukonen, lead guitar; Jack Cassidy, bass; Skip Spence, drums; Paul Kantner, guitar; Marty Balin, vocals; Signe Andersen, vocals; started in San Francisco; first big hit (1967); Spencer Dryden replaced Spence on the drums and Grace Slick replaced Signe Andersen; albums—*After Bathing at Baxter's, Bless Its Pointed Little Head, Crown of Creation, Jefferson Airplane Takes Off, Surrealistic Pillow, Volunteers.*

JEFFERSON, BLIND LEMON

b. 1897 Couchman, Texas, d. 1930 Chicago, Illinois. Black guitarist and singer. Born blind; illiterate; sang on the streets of Wortham, Texas; country-blues singer of the 1920s; considered one of the greats; joined with Huddie Leadbelly playing in the red-light district of East Dallas; first recorded with Paramount (1926); album—*Blind Lemon Jefferson: 1926-29* (issued in 1968); his frozen body was found in the snow in Chicago.

JEFFERSON, HILTON

b. 1903 Danbury, Connecticut, d. 1968.
Black jazz saxophonist. Played with King Oliver's orchestras; also with Cab Calloway.

JEFFERSON, JOSEPH

b. 1774 Plymouth, England, d. 1832 Harrisburg, Pennsylvania. Baritone and actor. Grandfather of Joseph Jefferson the noted actor; came to Boston (1795) where he made his debut with the Old American Company; New York City debut (1796); sang in the opera, *Sterne's Maria,* New York Ctiy (1799, w. William Dunlap, m. Benjamin Carr).

JEFFREY, JOHN ALBERT

b. 1855 Plymouth, England, d. 1929 Brookline, Massachusetts. Composer. Came to America (1876) and settled in Albany, N.Y. where he organized a choral society, and later became organist in All Saint's Cathedral; in 1893 became organist of the First Presbyterian Church, Yonkers, N.Y.; later moved to Boston where he taught at the New England Conservatory until his death; composed the tune "Albany" (1886, "Ancient of Days," w. W.C. Doane).

JENKINS, FREDDY ("POSEY")

b. 1906 New York City.
Black trumpeter. Played with Duke Ellington's band (1928-34 and again in 1937).

JENKINS, GORDON

b. 1910 Webster Groves, Missouri.
Bandleader, arranger, and composer. Arranger for Andre Kostelanetz, Benny Goodman, and Paul Whiteman; orchestra leader accompanying Judy Garland, Dick Haymes and others; wrote *San Fernando Valley* (1943), *P.S. I Love You, Manhattan Tower* (1946), *Blue Prelude, California, Seven Dreams*.

JENKINS, MARVIN LEE

b. 1932 Aultman, Ohio.
Pianist. Played in his brother's band (Obie Jenkins) (1946-54); in U.S. Army band (1954-56); played flute with Barney Kessel, with Gloria Lynne and others in 1960s, also led own trio; wrote *Big City, Next Spring, Rainy Day in Los Angeles*.

JENKS, ABRAHAM S.

b. 1820, d. 1895 Philadelphia, Pennsylvania. Compiler. Dry goods merchant interested in music, and taught a Bible class at the Wharton Street Methodist Episcopal Church of Philadelphia; published a *Choral Hymn Book* (1858), *Devotional Melodies* (1859), and *The Heart and Voice* (1865); his *Devotional Melodies* included eighty-six tunes by William J. Kirkpatrick, thirteen by Josiah Lowe, twelve by J.H. Van Nardoff and the hymn "Say Brothers, Will You Meet Us?" which is the "John Brown Song."

JENKS, STEPHEN

b. 1772 New Canaan, Connecticut, d. 1856 Thompson, Ohio. Composer and compiler. Resided in Ridgefield, Conn. (1800), later moved to Providence, R.I. then to Thompson, Ohio (1829); compiled *The New England Harmony* (1800, *The Musical Harmonist*), *The Delights of Harmony* (1805, *The Norfolk Compiler*), *The Hartford Collection of Sacred Harmony* (1807), *Laus Deo*, the *Harmony of Zion* (1818, *The Union Compiler*); his tunes were "Communion" (also called "St. Stephen"), "Bartimaus," and "Sellick" (after a miserly but the richest farmer in the church).

JENNINGS, WAYLON

b. 1937 Littlefield, Texas.
Singer and disk jockey. Disk jockey at age twelve on the local station in Littlefield; toured with Buddy Holly's group as electric bass player (1958-59) until Holly was killed in a plane crash; then formed his own band; his hit records include "Stop the World and Let Me Off" (1965), "Anita You're Dreaming," "That's the Chance I'll Have to Take," "Where I Went Wrong," "Look into My Tear Drops," "That's What You Get for Loving Me"; at Max's Kansas City, New York City (1973).

JEPSON, HARRY BENJAMIN

b. 1870 New Haven, Connecticut, d. 1952 Groton, Connecticut. Organist, teacher, and composer. Graduated Yale University; studied with Stoeckel, Parker, and Widor; assistant professor at Yale (1899); professor and organist after 1906.

JEPSON, HELEN

b. 1907 Titusville, Pennsylvania.
Noted soprano. Studied at Curtis Institute of Music, Philadelphia; sang with Chautauqua, New York Opera Association, Philadelphia Grand Opera Company, then with Metropolitan Opera, New York City (1935) and Chicago Opera (1936).

JEREMY AND THE SATYRS (band)

Jeremy Steig, leader; album—*Jeremy and the Satyrs* (1968).

JEROME, WILLIAM

b. 1865 Cornwall-on-Hudson, New York, d. 1932 New York City. Lyricist, actor, and singer. Appeared in minstrel shows; later a publisher; married singer Maude Nugent; wrote "Back Home in Tennessee" (1915, m. Walter Donaldson); and with music by Andrew Mack—"The Little Bunch of Whiskers on His Chin," "The Same Old Mother Loves Me" (1895), "My Pearl Is a Bowery Girl" (1894); "Row, Row, Row" (1912, m. James V. Monaco). (*See also* Jean Schwartz)

JESSYE, EVA

b. 1895 Coffeyville, Kansas.
Black choral conductor. Studied at Western University, Kansas, and Langston University, Langston, Oklahoma (1916); taught music at Morgan State College, Baltimore; later studied with Will Marion Cook; went to New York about 1922; organized Original Dixie Jubilee Singers in New York City (1926), later called Eva Jessye Choir; appeared on "Major Bowes Family Radio Hour" and the "General Motors Hour"; choral director for *Four Saints in Three Acts* (m. Virgil Thompson, w. Gertrude Stein); with Edward Matthews, lead singer; choir director for *Porgy and Bess* (m. George Gershwin).

JETER, LEONARD

b. 1881 Newport, Rhode Island, d. 1970.
Black cellist and teacher. Concert player in New York City and also a teacher there.

JEWELL, LUCINA

b. 1874, d. (?).
Composer and teacher. She wrote "In My Father's House Are Many Mansions" ("And Jesus said, let not your heart be troubled," w. Bible).

JIM AND JESSE (vocal and instrumental duo) *see* JIM and JESS MC REYNOLDS

JOBIM, ANTONIO CARLOS

b. 1927 Rio de Janeiro, Brazil.
Pianist, guitarist, and composer. Founded the bossa nova movement in Brazil with singer and composer Joao Gilberto; wrote "Chega de Saudade," recorded by Gilberto: "Corcovado," "Desafinado," "The Girl from Ipanema," "One Note Samba," "Jazz Samba," "Meditation"; resided in Los Angeles after 1965.

JOCELYN, SIMEON

b. 1746 Branford, Connecticut, d. 1823 New Haven, Connecticut. Publisher. Jocelyn and Amos Doolittle opened a music shop and publishing business in New Haven in 1782; they published *The Chorister's Companion.*

JOHN, "LITTLE" WILLIE

b. (?), d. 1968 Walla Walla, Washington.
Black singer. Recorded "Fever" (1956) and "Talk to Me, Talk to Me" (1958); sent to prison (1966) for manslaughter committed in Seattle; died of pneumonia in the Washington State Penitentiary in Walla Walla; James Brown released a memorial album, *Thinking About Little Willie John and a Few Nice Things.*

JOHNNY AND JACK (vocal duo)

Johnny Wright and Jack Anglin; albums—*All the Best of Johnny and Jack, Here's Johnny and Jack, Johnnie and Jack Sing Poison Love, Sincerely.*

JOHNS, CLAYTON

b. 1857 New Castle, Delaware, d. 1932 Boston, Massachusetts. Pianist, teacher, and composer. Pupil of J.K. Paine and W.H. Sherwood in Boston, then with Kiel and others in Berlin; concert-pianist and teacher in Boston, then at New England Conservatory, Boston, after 1912; composed a *Berceuse* and *Scherzino* for orchestra played by the Boston Symphony Orchestra, and numerous songs.

JOHNS, EMILE

b. (?) France, d. 1842 New Orleans, Louisiana. Composer, publisher, and teacher. Came to New Orleans (1823) as a music teacher; published a collection of original pieces of music in *Album Louisianais* (ca. 1825); established E. Johns & Co., music publishers in New Orleans (1837).

JOHNSON, ALBERT J. ("BUD")

b. 1910 Dallas, Texas.
Black tenor saxist and arranger. With Earl Hines (1934-42); with Woody Herman, Billy Eckstine, Dizzy Gillespie and others in 1940s; with Benny Goodman, Tony Pastor, Earl Hines and others in 1950s and'60s; at Newport Jazz Festival (1961) with Count Basie.

JOHNSON, ARTEMAS NIXON

b. 1817, d. after 1865.
Compiler. With Josiah Osgood and Sumner Hill, compiled *The Bay State Collection of Church Music* (Boston, 1850); he also compiled *The United States Collection of Church Music* (1865).

JOHNSON, BILL

b. 1872 New Orleans, Louisiana, d. (?).
Black double bass player and bandleader. Organized the Original Creole Ragtime Band before 1912; later known as That Creole Band; band broke up (1918).

JOHNSON, "BLIND" WILLIE

b. 1902 Marlin, Texas, d. 1949 Beaumont, Texas.Black singer and guitarist. Blind; sang Negro spirituals, gospel songs, and ballads.

JOHNSON, CHARLES L.

b. 1876 Kansas City, Missouri, d. there 1950. Ragtime composer. Wrote "Sweet and Low" (1919, w. J. Stanley Royce), "It Takes a Coon to Do the Ragtime Dance" (1899, w. Robert Penick), "Iola" (1906, w. James O'Dea), "Tobasco" (1909, ragtime waltz), "Doc Brown's Cakewalk" (1899), "Black Smoke" (1902), "Dill Pickles Rag" (1906), "Porcupine Rag" (1909), "Golden Spider Rag" (1910), "Barber Pole Rag" (1911), "Tar Babies Rag" (1911), "Swanee Rag" (1912), "Hen Cackle Rag" (1912), "Crazy Bone Rag" (1913), "Alabama Slide" (1915), "Fun on the Levee" (1917).

JOHNSON, EDWARD

b. 1878 Guelph, Ontario, Canada, d. there 1959. Tenor and manager. Studied at University of Toronto; sang with Lombardi in Florence; concerts in New York; opera debut at Padua; with Chicago Opera (1920), Metropolitan Opera, New York after 1921, manager of same (1935).

JOHNSON, ERASTUS

b. 1826 Lincoln, Maine, d. 1909 Waltham, Massachusetts. Hymnist. As a young man he embarked on the ship Gold Hunter for California. Just before rounding Cape Horn, the crew mutinied, and pressed him into service to pilot the ship, which he sailed to California without mishap. He lived there and in Washington as a rancher for nineteen years, then returned east. In 1873 he attended a YMCA convention in Carlisle, Pa., as a delegate from Pittsburgh, and John Wanamaker, prominent Philadelphia merchant, was the president. At the close of the first session a telegram was received announcing the failure of Jay Cooke, in whose bank Wanamaker had deposited $70,000, which greatly upset Wanamaker. Soon panic spread over the nation, throwing a pall of gloom on the convention. It was then he wrote his hymn "O Sometimes the Shadows Are Deep" (tune—"The Rock of Refuge," William G. Fischer, who was also at the convention with Johnson).

JOHNSON FAMILY SINGERS

Gospel singers on radio, Charlotte, North Carolina; "Pop" Johnson, "Mom" Johnson, Betty (later a pop singer), Kenneth, Jim, and Bob; best-selling album—*Shall We Gather at the River?*

JOHNSON, FRANCIS (FRANK)

b. 1792 Philadelphia, Pennsylvania, d. there 1844. Black trumpeter, bandleader, and composer. Organized a band of Negroes, The Washington Guards, Company Three, in Philadelphia (1815-40); composed a *Collection of Cotillions* published by Willig (1818); *General Cadwalader's March* (1819); presented Mrs. Ann Rush with eighty-seven of his piano arrangements (1821); played at grand ball for General Lafayette (1825); toured Europe (1837); gave command performance for Queen Victoria (1838); composed *Quick Step* for the State Fencibles, the Philadelphia Grays.

JOHNSON, GEORGE W.

b. 1839 Binbrook, Canada, d. 1917 Pasadena, California. Lyricist. Schoolteacher in Canada, then taught school in Cleveland, Ohio; later a newspaper editor in Detroit; became a professor at the University of Toronto, Ontario, Canada, but came back to America to retire; as a young man he courted Maggie Clark, but she died a year after their marriage; wrote "When You and I Were Young Maggie," which appeared in his book of poems, *Maple Leaves;* it was set to music by James A. Butterfield.

JOHNSON, GUS

b. 1913 Tyler, Texas.
Drummer. Played with Jay McShann, Earl Hines, and Count Basie in 1940s; with Count Basie, Ella Fitzgerald, Woody Herman, Gerry Mulligan and others in 1950s.

JOHNSON, HALL

b. 1888 Athens, Georgia, d. 1970.
Black choir director and violinist. Raised in Atlanta, Georgia; studied at Knox Institute, Ga., Atlanta University, Atlanta, Ga., Allen University, Columbia, S.C.; Hahn School of Music, and Institute of Musical Art, New York City; played in Jim Europe's 169th Infantry band, formerly the 15th New York in France in World War I; organized the Hall Johnson Choir (1925); recorded for RCA Victor (1928); wrote play with singing parts, *Run Little Chillun,* staged in New York City (1933) and Los Angeles (1935); choir appeared in *The Green Pastures* (1936) and other films; wrote *Son of Man* (Easter cantata), *Fi-Yer* (operetta), *The Green Pastures Spirituals.*

JOHNSON, HERBERT

b. 1857, d. 1904.
Singer and composer. Wrote "I'm a Pilgrim, I'm a Stranger" (w. S.B. Dana).

JOHNSON, HORACE

b. 1893 Waltham, Massachusetts, d. 1964 Tucson, Arizona. Composer. Studied with Bainbridge Crist and John P. Marshall; composed piano pieces, orchestral suites, songs.

JOHNSON, HOWARD E.

b. 1887 Waterbury, Connecticut, d. 1941 New York City. Lyricist. Wrote the lyrics "Where Do We Go from Here" (1918, m. Percy Wenrich), "When the Moon Comes Over the Mountain" (1931, m. H.M. Woods), "Ireland Must Be Heaven," and other songs.

JOHNSON, HUNTER

b. 1906 Benson, North Carolina.
Composer. Graduated Eastman School of Music, Rochester, N.Y.; taught at University of Michigan, Ann Arbor; won Guggenheim Fellowship (1941); studied in Europe (1933-35); composed a symphony; *Concerto for Piano and Small Orchestra* (Greenwich Concert Orchestra, New York under Lehman Engel, Harry Cumpson, soloist, 1937).

JOHNSON, JAMES LOUIS ("J.J.")

b. 1924 Indianapolis, Indiana.
Black trombonist and composer. Played with

Benny Carter, Count Basie and Illinois Jacquet in 1940s; with Kai Winding and others in 1950s; composed a six-part work, *Perceptions*, recorded (1961) with an orchestra conducted by Gunther Schuller and later performed at Monterey Jazz Festival (1961); during 1960s led a quartet and later a sextet with Clark Terry and Sonny Stitt which toured Japan (1964).

JOHNSON, JAMES OSIE

b. 1923 Washington, D.C.
Black drummer. Played with Harlem Dictators, Willie Smith, Clark Terry, Earl Hines and others.

JOHNSON, JAMES PRICE (JIMMY)

b. 1891 New Brunswick, New Jersey, d. 1955 New York City. Black jazz pianist. Known for his Harlem style; also a talented composer; taught Fats Waller; wrote *Charleston, South Carolina* (1923, using the distinctive Charleston rhythm), and *Charleston* (w. Cecil Mack) which was introduced by Ned Wayburn in October, 1923 in the "Follies" at the Amsterdam Theatre, New York City; it was 1925 before the Charleston was taken up by the dance bands.

JOHNSON, JAMES WELDON

b. 1871 Jacksonville, Florida, d. 1938 Wiscasset, Maine. Black lyricist, singer, and vaudeville actor. Brother of J. Rosamond Johnson; member of the vaudeville team of Bob Cole and the Johnson Brothers (1901-06); left the group (1906) to become U.S. Consul in Venezuela; with his brother, composer, wrote "Since You Went Away" and "Lift Every Voice and Sing," called the "Negro National Anthem"; wrote *Passionale* (four songs for tenor, m. H.T. Burleigh); "The Creation," poem (m. Louis Gruenberg); *The Last Judgment* (m. Noel Da Costa).

JOHNSON, JOHN

b. 1759 England, d. 1819.
Singer and actor. Successful on London stage; came to America (1795) for Old American Company; sang in *The Archers* (w. William Dunlap, m. Benjamin Carr) performed in New York City (1796); with Joseph Tyler managed the Old American Company after 1805.

JOHNSON, JOHN ROSAMOND

b. 1873 Jacksonville, Florida, d. 1954 New York City. Black composer. Brother of lyricist James Weldon Johnson; studied at New England Conservatory of Music, Boston; traveled with Oriental America, minstrel show; with team of Cole and the Johnson Brothers (1901-06); wrote "Walk Together Children" for chorus and orchestra (1915), "Florida Cakewalk" (piano), "De Chain Gang," "Them Lonesome Moanin' Blues," "My Baby's in Memphis, Layin' Around"; with Bob Cole—"Under the Bamboo Tree," "The Maiden with the Dreamy Eyes," "Lazy Moon," "Li'l Gal" (w. P.L. Dunbar); with Bob Cole and lyricist J.W. Johnson, the musical shows *The Shoo-Fly Regiment* (1906) and *The Red Moon* (1908), produced on Broadway, New York City; with J.W. Johnson—"Since You Went Away," and "Lift Every Voice and Sing," called the "Negro National Anthem."

JOHNSON, LONNIE

b. 1889 New Orleans, Louisiana, d. 1970.
Black violinist and guitarist. Played in duets with Joe Venuti, Eddie Lang and others; albums—*Losing Game, Tomorrow Night.*

JOHNSON, MANZIE ISHAM

b. 1906 Putnam, Connecticut, d. 1971.
Jazz drummer. Played with Fats Waller, Don Redman, Louis Armstrong and others.

JOHNSON, OLLIE ("DINK")

b. 1892 Biloxi, Mississippi, d. 1954 Portland, Oregon. Black pianist. Raised in Biloxi, Miss; played with Jelly Roll Morton, Kid Ory and others.

JOHNSON, PETE K.H.

b. 1904 Kansas City, Missouri, d. 1967.
Black pianist. Considered by some as the greatest "boogie-woogie" pianist; teamed with Albert Ammons, singer Joe Turner, Meade Lux Lewis; appeared at Newport Jazz Festival (1958); later suffered a heart attack and became inactive; various benefits were held for him.

JOHNSON, PLAS JOHN, JR.

b. 1931 New Orleans, Louisiana.
Tenor saxist. Played in small groups in Los Angeles during 1950s; with Henry Mancini after 1962; also recorded under the name Johnny Beecher.

JOHNSON, REGINALD VOLNEY

b. 1940 Owensboro, Kentucky.
Bass player. Played trombone in U.S. Army bands (1957-61); played with Archie Shepp, Bill Baron, Roland Kirk, Sun Ra and others during 1960s; with Art Blakey after 1965.

JOHNSON, ROBERT

b. 1913 near Clarksdale, Mississippi, d. 1937 San Antonio, Texas. Black singer. Around 1933 met Johnny Shines and Walter Horton in Arkansas (both were Memphis musicians who had gone to Chicago), and played in various night spots with them for two years; recorded in San Antonio, Texas, and also in Dallas; known for "Hellhound on My Trail" and "Me and the Devil Blues"; he was murdered, apparently by a jealous lady friend.

JOHNSON, SAMUEL

b. 1822 Salem, Massachusetts, d. 1882 North Andover, Massachusetts. Hymnist and compiler. Educated at Harvard and Cambridge Divinity School; in 1853 formed a Free Church at Lynn, Mass., where he remained until 1870; wrote the lyrics "City of God, How Broad and Far" (1864, m. tune "Richmond," 1792—unknown) and "Life of Ages, Richly Poured" (1864, m. German, 1657); collaborated with Samuel Longfellow in publishing *A Book of Hymns* (1846) and *Hymns of the Spirit* (1864).

JOHNSON, THOR

b. 1913 Wisconsin Rapids, Wis., d. 1975. Conductor. Graduated University of North Carolina, Chapel Hill; studied with Walter, Malko, and Weingartner; conducted the Ann Arbor (Mich.) Festival; conductor of Cincinnati (Ohio) Symphony after 1946.

JOHNSON, WALTER

b. 1904 New York City.
Black jazz drummer. Played in Fletcher Henderson's band off and on between 1928-40; later with Lucky Millinder and others.

JOHNSON, WILLIE GEARY ("BUNK")

b. 1879 New Orleans, Louisiana, d. 1949 New Iberia, Louisiana. Black cornetist and trumpeter. Joined Adam Oliver's Creole Orchestra at age sixteen; then with Buddy Bolden until 1898; said to have led an army band in the Spanish-American War; then played in Storyville honky-tonks in New Orleans; first recorded in 1940; played in San Francisco (1943); recorded again in 1947 but disks were not released until 1952; had his first stroke in 1948.

JOHNSTON, THOMAS

b. ca. 1708 Boston, Massachusetts, d. 1767. Organ maker and publisher. Built an organ (1752) for Christ Church, Boston; also an organ (1754) for the Episcopal church in Salem, Mass.

JOLLY, PETE

b. 1932 New Haven, Connecticut.
Pianist, accordianist, and songwriter. Born Peter A. Ceragioli; played with Buddy De Franco, Shorty Rogers, and Georgie Auld during 1950s; also led own groups in Los Angeles; wrote "El Yorke," "Little Bird."

JOLSON, AL

b. 1886 Russia, d. 1950 San Francisco, California. Jazz singer. Born Asa Yoelson; he sang "Mammy" in the film *The Jazz Singer* (1927); sang again in *The Singing Fool* (1928); sang "Sonny Boy" (1928, m. Ray Henderson); died soon after returning from Korea, where he had entertained American troops.

JONAS, ALBERTO

b. 1868 Madrid, Spain, d. 1943 Philadelphia, Pennsylvania. Concert pianist in Europe and the United States. For a time he taught at the Detroit Conservatory in Michigan; wrote *The Master School of Modern Piano-Virtuosity,* published in six volumes.

JONES, ALLAN

b. 1907 Scranton, Pennsylvania.
Singer. Introduced "The Donkey Serenade" by Rudolf Friml (1937).

JONES, ALTON

b. 1899 Fairfield, Nebraska, d. 1971 New York City. Concert pianist and teacher. Studied at Drake University, Des Moines, Iowa; gave his first recital at Aeolian Hall, New York City (1925); taught at the Juilliard School, New York City, for almost fifty years, having joined the faculty in 1921.

JONES, BOOKER T.

b. 1944 Memphis, Tennessee.
Black organist. Graduated Indiana University, Bloomington, in music; also played baritone sax, guitar, and tuba; with Booker T and the M.G.s; recorded "Green Onions" (1962) with the M.G.'s (Memphis group); top instrumental group on Billboard's 1967 poll.

JONES, CARMELL

b. 1936 Kansas City, Kansas.
Trumpeter. Educated at Kansas University; played with combos in Kansas City, Missouri; later in Los Angeles; with Horace Silver Quintet; played in Berlin, Germany after 1965.

JONES, CHARLES

b. 1910 Tamworth, Ontario, Canada.
Teacher and composer. Taught at Mills

College, Oakland, Calif.; composed symphonies, *Suite for String Orchestra, Concerto for Small Orchestra,* chamber works, songs.

JONES, CLAUDE

b. 1901 Boley, Oklahoma, d. 1962 New York City. Trombonist. Played with Fletcher Henderson, Cab Calloway, Duke Ellington and others.

JONES, CURTIS

b. 1906 Naples, Texas.
Black singer and pianist. Played in Dallas, Kansas City, and Chicago during 1930s; active again in Chicago in 1960s; in Europe after 1962.

JONES, DARIUS ELIOT

b. 1815 Carroll, New York, d. 1881 Davenport, Iowa. Composer and compiler. Son of Abner Jones; choir leader at the Plymouth Church when he issued *Temple Melodies* (1861, New York City); later entered Iowa College, Davenport, Iowa, and was ordained a Congregational minister (1858); served in churches in Columbus City and Newton Center, Iowa; while agent for Grinnell College, Grinnell, Iowa, he issued *Songs for the New Life* (1869); composed the tune "Stockwell" (1850, "Silently the Shades of Evening," w. C.C. Cox).

JONES, ELVIN RAY

b. 1927 Pontiac, Michigan.
Black drummer. Brother of Hank and Thad Jones; played in Detroit (1952-56); later with Pepper Adams-Donald Byrd Quintet in New York City; later with the John Coltrane Quartet and others during 1960s; at Slug's, New York City (1972).

JONES, FLOYD

b. 1917 Arkansas.
Black guitarist and songwriter. Played in Chicago night spots; first recorded in 1947; wrote and recorded "On the Road" (1953), which became a favorite of the Canned Heat Blues Band.

JONES, GEORGE

b. 1931 Saratoga, Texas.
Singer and guitarist. Served in the marines during the Korean War; resided in Vidor, Texas; hit records include "Treasure of Love" (1958), "White Lightnin' " (1959), "She Thinks I Still Care" (1962), "Aching, Breaking Heart" (1962), "Take Me," "Love Bug," "Things Have Gone to Pieces" (1965), "I'm a People" (1966), "You Can't Get There from Here" (1967).

JONES, HENRY (HANK)

b. 1918 Pontiac, Michigan.
Black jazz pianist. With various groups during 1940s; pianist for Ella Fitzgerald (1948-53); later a studio musician in New York City; also with his brother Thad in the Thad Jones-Mel Lewis Orchestra; appeared on various TV shows; albums—*Blue Bird, Happenings, Have You Met Hank Jones, Hank Jones Quintet, Hank Jones Trio.*

JONES, HERBERT ROBERT

b. 1923 Miami, Florida.
Black trumpeter. Educated at Florida A&M University, Tallahassee; with Lucky Millinder, Andy Kirk, Budd Johnson and others in 1950s; with Duke Ellington and others in 1960s.

JONES, ISHAM

b. 1894 Coalton, Ohio, d. 1956 Hollywood, California. Jazz bandleader and composer. Wrote "You're in the Army Now" (1917, w. Tell Taylor and Ole Olson), "On the Alamo" (1922, w. Gilbert Keyes and Joe Lyons), "It Had to Be You" (w. Gus Kahn), "I'll See You in My Dreams" (1924, w. Kahn), "There Is No Greater Love" (w. Marty Symes), "My Best to You" (Symes); retired to a ranch in Colorado.

JONES, JACK

b. 1938 Los Angeles, California.
Singer. Son of singer Alan Jones and actress Irene Hervey; sang with his father in night clubs in Elko, Nevada, Las Vegas, and Los Angeles; then sang on his own; won Grammy award (1962) for his record "Lollipops and Roses," also (1963) award for "Wives and Lovers"; married actress Jill St. John, model Lee Lawrence, and airline stewardess Gretschen Roberts, all divorces.

JONES, JAMES EDWARD (JIMMY)

b. 1921 Scottsville, Kentucky.
Singer and songwriter. With Gospel Singing Caravan (1962-66); New Gospel Singing Caravan after 1966; also LeFevres after 1957; wrote "Lord It's Me Again," "Shake the Master's Hand," "Peace in My Heart," "What Heaven Means to Me," "Sing," "My Soul Belongs to Jesus."

JONES, JAMES HENRY

b. 1918 Memphis, Tennessee.
Pianist. Raised in Chicago; played with Stuff Smith, J.C. Heard, Sarah Vaughan and others; arranger for Harry Belafonte and Duke Ellington; also led his own trio.

JONES, JONATHAN (JO)

b. 1911 Chicago, Illinois.
Black jazz drummer. Played with the Count Basie band off and on between 1935-48, having served in the army in World War II; later with Illinois Jacquet and others.

JONES, JOSEPH RUDOLPH ("PHILLY JOE")

b. 1923 Philadelphia, Pennsylvania.
Black drummer. With Miles Davis, Tony Scott, Gil Evans and others in 1950s; in Los Angeles and San Francisco during 1960s with various groups; toured Japan (1965).

JONES, LINDLEY A. ("SPIKE")

b. 1911 Long Beach, California, d. 1964 Los Angeles, California. Drummer and bandleader. Was a Hollywood studio drummer; organized his own band; performed crazy comedy antics which delighted the audience.

JONES, LOUIS MARSHALL ("GRANDPA")

b. 1913 Niagra, Kentucky.
Singer and banjoist. Joined Bradley Kincaid's country singers on station WLS, Chicago (1935); dressed up as "grandpa"; had his own band in Wheeling, West Virginia (1937); on WLW, Cincinnati (1938-44); served in the army in Germany in World War II; with Grand Ole Opry after 1946; hit tunes include "Good Ole Mountain Dew," "Eight More Miles to Louisville," "Old Rattler," "Going Down in Town."

JONES, LOUIS VAUGHN

b. 1893 Cleveland, Ohio.
Black violinist and teacher. Served in World War I; studied in Paris and played in jazz orchestras in Paris; returned to the United States (1929); taught at Howard University, Washington, D.C., after 1931.

JONES, QUINCY, JR.

b. 1933 Chicago, Illinois.
Black bandleader and composer. Vice-president of Mercury Records (1964); wrote film scores—*The Boy and the Tree, The Pawnbroker, Mirage, Walk, Don't Run, The Silver Thread;* also wrote TV scores: "Ironsides," "It Takes a Thief"; wrote *Soundpiece for String Quartet and Contralto* (1962, performed at Lincoln Center, New York City), *Soundpiece for Jazz Orchestra* (1964, performed in Stuttgart, Germany, during "Light Music Week"); in concert at Carnegie Hall, New York City (1972).

JONES, REUNALD, SR.

b. 1910 Indianapolis, Indiana.
Trumpeter. With Count Basie (1953-59); with Nat King Cole (1961-65); toured Pacific with Cole (1965); later in France with Diahann Carroll.

JONES, RICHARD MYKNEE

b. 1889 Donaldsville, Louisiana, d. 1954 Chicago, Illinois. Black jazz pianist and composer. Known as a barrelhouse player; played for Clarence Williams; composed "Jazzin' Babies Blues," "Riverside Blues," "Trouble in Mind," "Southern Stomps," "Red Wagon"; "Trouble in Mind" was first recorded by "Chippie" Hill and became one of the most recorded blues of all time.

JONES, ROBERT ELLIOTT ("JONAH")

b. 1909 Louisville, Kentucky.
Black trumpeter. Played in Cab Calloway's band and with others; led his own quartet in late 1950s and '60s; played at Rainbow Grill, New York City.

JONES, RUFUS ("SPEEDY")

b. 1936 Charleston, South Carolina.
Black drummer. Educated at Florida A&M University, Tallahassee; with Lionel Hampton in New York City (1958), Maynard Ferguson (1959-63), and Count Basie (1964-66); led own group after 1966.

JONES, SAMUEL

b. 1924 Jacksonville, Florida.
Black bass player and cellist. Played with Les Jazz Modes, Illinois Jacquet, Cannonball Adderley, and Dizzy Gillespie during 1950s; with Adderley combo (1959-65); with Oscar Peterson Trio after 1966.

JONES, SHIRLEY

b. 1934 Smithton, Pennsylvania.
Singer and actress. Album—*Maggie Flynn.*

JONES, SISSIERETTA

b. 1868 Portsmouth, Virginia, d. 1933.
Black soprano. Raised in Providence, Rhode Island; studied at the New England Conservatory, Boston; sang at the Jubilee and Cakewalk, Madison Square Garden, New York City (1892); known as the "Black Patti"; sang at the White House for President Benjamin Harrison; at the Pittsburgh Exposition (1892-93); toured England (1893); leader of Black Pitt's Troubadours (1893-1910).

JONES, THADDEUS JOSEPH (THAD)

b. 1923 Pontiac, Michigan.
Black trumpeter and cornetist. Played in Count Basie's band in the "battle of the bands," Count Basie vs. Stan Kenton in

Detroit (1956); Thad Jones-Mel Lewis band played in the Village Vanguard night club, New York City after 1966, with Roland Hanna, piano, Richard Davis, bass, Eddie Daniels, sax; album—*Consummation;* toured Soviet Russia with band (1972) under auspices of the State Department; at Newport Jazz Festival, New York City (1972).

JONES, TOM

b. 1940 Wales.
Rock and ballad singer. Born Thomas Jones Woodward (name changed by his manager, Gordon Mills); came to America and sang in Las Vegas night clubs; also at Copacabana in New York City; albums—*A-Tom-ic Jones, Fever Zone, Funny, Familiar, Forgotten Feeling, Green, Green Grass of Hope* (1967), *Help Yourself, It's Not Unusual, Tom Jones Live, Tom Jones Live in Las Vegas, This Is Tom Jones, Tom, What's New Pussy Cat.*

JOPLIN, JANIS

b. 1943 Port Arthur, Texas, d. 1970 Los Angeles, California. Rock singer. Went to San Francisco at age seventeen and sang in coffee houses; returned home (1965) and attended college; joined Big Brother and the Holding Company rock band in San Francisco (1966); in Monterey Pop Festival (1967); went out on her own (1969) and became a top rock singer; claimed she had kicked the heroin habit before she died; albums—*I Got Dem Ol' Kozmic Blues Again Mama, Pearl.*

JOPLIN, SCOTT

b. 1868 Texarkana, Texas, d. 1917. New York City. Noted black composer and pianist. Known as the "King of Ragtime"; pianist in night spots in St. Louis; then at Columbian Exposition in Chicago (1893); settled in Sedalia, Missouri, as pianist in the Maple Leaf Club; wrote "Maple Leaf Rag" (1899), "Original Rag" (1899), "Peacherine Rag" (1901), "The Easy Winners" (1901), "Palm Leaf Rag" (1903), "Slow Drag" (1903), "Rose Leaf Rag" (1907), "Fig Leaf Rag" (1908), "Stoptime Rag" (1910).

JORDAN, CLIFFORD LACONIA

b. 1931 Chicago, Illinois.
Black tenor saxist. Played with Horace Silver, Max Roach and others in 1950s; with Kenny Dorham, also led own quartet; with Max Roach, Charles Mingus and others in 1960s; toured Europe (1964); albums—*Soul Fountain, These Are My Roots.*

JORDAN, IRVING SIDNEY ("DUKE")

b. 1922 Brooklyn, New York.
Pianist. Played in Steve Pulliam combo at New York World's Fair (1939); later played with Charlie Parker, Stan Getz, Roy Eldridge, and Oscar Pettiford; in Paris after 1959; wrote *Flight to Jordan.*

JORDAN, JAMES TAFT

b. 1915 Florence, South Carolina.
Black trumpeter and singer. With Chick Webb, Ella Fitzgerald (1933-42), Duke Ellington (1943-47); later with Benny Goodman and others.

JORDAN, JOE

b. 1882 Cincinnati, Ohio, d. 1971 Tacoma, Washington. Black pianist, violinist, drummer, and composer. Raised in St. Louis, Mo.; attended Lincoln University, Jefferson City, Mo.; played in the Taborin Band; in Chicago (1903); wrote and orchestrated the music for the Nashville Students at their concert at Proctor's, New York City (1905), first public concert of syncopated music in America; music director of Pekin Theatre, Chicago (1906-13); Samuel Coleridge-Taylor, black violinist and composer, gave a concert there (1906); pianist and arranger for Jelly Roll Morton, Louis Armstrong, and Eddie Duchin; also wrote for Ginger Rogers and Ethel Merman; wrote "Nappy Lee—A Slow Drag" (1903), "Pekin Rag" (1904), "J.J.J. Rag" (1905); with Cole and Johnson—"The Red Moon" (1909), "Lovey Joe" (with Will M. Cook) for Fanny Brice in the *Ziegfeld Follies* of 1910; "Morocco Blues," "Teasin' Rag," which Blossom Seely used as her theme song.

JORDAN, JULES

b. 1850 Willimantic, Connecticut, d. 1927 Providence, Rhode Island. Choirmaster and composer. Studied with Osgood in Boston, Shakespeare in London, and Sbriglia in Paris; choirmaster of Grace Church, Providence; conductor of Arion Club (1880); composed the comic opera, *Rip Van Winkle* (1898, book—Washington Irving), cantata with orchestra, songs.

JORDAN, LOUIS

b. 1908 Brinkley, Arkansas, d. 1975.
Black singer and alto saxist. With Chick Webb (1936-38); then formed his own group, Tympany Five; his hits were "Ain't Nobody Here But Us Chickens" and "Open the Door, Richard" (1947), "Saturday Night Fish Fry" (1950), also "Choo Choo Ch'Boogie"; toured England with Chris Barber (1962); album—*Louis Jordan's Greatest Hits.*

JORDAN, SHELIA

b. 1929 Detroit, Michigan.
Singer. Raised in Summerhill, Pa.; married pianist Duke Jordan (1952), later divorced; sang in night clubs in Greenwich Village, New York City; first recorded in 1963; album—*Portrait of Shelia.*

JORDANAIRES

Vocal group which varied over the years after it was founded in Springfield, Mo. (1948); among the early members were Gordon Stoker, Hoyt Hawkins, and Neal Matthews.

JOSÉ, DICK

b. 1873 Cornwall, England, d. 1941 San Francisco, California. Tenor. Came to America as a child; was a blacksmith in Reno, Nevada; ballad singer with the Lew Dockstader Minstrels, Charlie Reed's Minstrels; toured eight years with Denman Thompson in "The Old Homestead" and later appeared in Keith vaudeville; plugged the songs of H.P. Danks, John W. Bratton, Paul Dresser, M.H. Rosenfeld and others.

JOSEFFY, RAFAEL

b. 1852 Miskolcz, Hungary, d. 1915 New York City. Pianist. Studied at the Leipzig Conservatory and later with Liszt; toured Europe, lived in Vienna; later taught at the National Conservatory; composed a number of piano pieces.

JOSTEN, WERNER

b. 1885 Elberfeld, Germany, d. 1963 New York City. Composer. Became professor of music at Smith College, Northampton, Mass. (1923); composed *Concerto Sacro* for strings and piano, *Jungle* for orchestra, *Crucifixion* for bass solo and mixed chorus, *Ode for St. Cecilia's Day* for soprano, baritone, mixed chorus and orchestra, *A Une Madone* for tenor and orchestra, the ballet *Joseph and His Brethern* produced by the Juilliard School of Music (1936).

JOURNEYMEN, THE (singing group) *see* SCOTT MC KENZIE, JOHN PHILLIPS

JOYS OF COOKING

Organized in Los Angeles (1967) by two women—Terry Garthwaite (b. 1938) vocals and guitar, and Toni Brown (b. 1938) vocals, electric piano, organ (also songwriter); and three men—Fritz Kasten (b. 1943) drums, Ron Wilson (b. 1933) congas, and Jeff Neighbor (b. 1942) bass.

JUCH, EMMA

b. 1865 Vienna, Austria, d. 1939 New York City. Noted soprano. Studied in New York with Mme. Murio-Celli; concert debut in London (1882); with Her Majesty's Theatre, London (1882-86); American Opera Company under Thomas (1886-87); sang in the United States and Mexico with her own opera company.

JUDSON, ADONIRAM

b. 1788 Malden, Massachusetts, d. 1850 at sea. Hymnist. Graduated Brown University, Providence, R.I. (1807); went to India (1815) as a Congregational missionary, then to Burma, where he was captured and imprisoned by the natives in Rangoon (1824-26); wrote "Come, Holy Spirit Love Divine" (*Winchell's Collection,* 1832).

JUDSON, ARTHUR

b. 1881 Dayton, Ohio, d. 1975.
Violinist, conductor, and manager. Manager of the Philadelphia Orchestra after 1907; Robin Hood Dell concerts in Fairmount Park, Philadelphia, were organized by Judson and Mrs. Abbott (1930).

JUDSON, SARAH HULL BOARDMAN

b. 1803 New Haven, Connecticut, d. 1845 St. Helena. Hymnist. First married Rev. George D. Boardman, then became the second wife of Dr. Adoniram Judson; wrote "Proclaim the Lofty Praise" (*W. Urwick's Dublin Collection,* 1829).

JUG STOMPERS (black band)
see GUS CANNON

JUILLIARD STRING QUARTET, THE

Violinists Robert Mann and Earl Carlyss, violist Samuel Rhodes, and cellist Claus Adam; at Tully Hall, New York City, in all-Mozart program (1972).

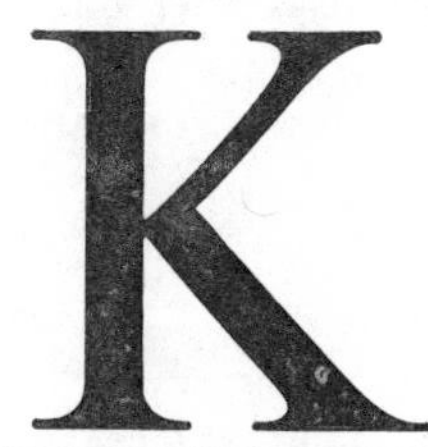

KAAIHUE, JOHNNY ("JOHNNY UKELELE")

b. 1901 Hawaii, d. 1971 Los Angeles, California. Bandleader. Started as a boxer and baseball player; formed the Royal Hawaiians (1921), disbanded (1955); later acted in the "Hawaiian Eye" TV program; also recorded on Capitol Records.

KAHAL, IRVING

b. 1903 Houtzdale, Pennsylvania, d. 1942 New York City. Lyricist. Wrote the lyrics for a number of songs composed by Sammy Fain: "Wedding Bells Are Breaking Up That Old Gang of Mine" (with Willie Raskin), "I Can Dream, Can't I?," "I'll Be Seeing You" (1938).

KAHN, ERICH ITOR

b. 1905 Rimbach, Odenwald, d. 1956 New York City. Composer. Composed *Giaconna dei Tempi di guerra* for piano, *Three Madrigals* for mixed choir, *Music for Ten Instruments and Soprano;* died from injuries suffered in an automobile accident.

KAHN, GUS

b. 1886 Coblenz, Germany, d. 1941 Beverly Hills, California. Lyricist. Family came to Chicago (1891); with Egbert Van Alstyne wrote "Sunshine and Roses" (1913), "Memories" (1915), "Pretty Baby" (1916, also with Tony Jackson); wrote "Carolina in the Morning" (1922, m. Walter Donaldson); also wrote lyrics for Nacio Herb Brown, Ted Fiorito, Isham Jones, Victor Schertzinger, Richard A. Whiting, and Vincent M. Youmans.

KAISER, ALOIS

b. 1840 Szobotist, Hungary, d. 1908.
Cantor and composer. Studied under Solomon Sulzer in Vienna; came to Baltimore (1866); cantor of the Oheb Shalom synagogue there.

KALEIDOSCOPE, THE (rock group)

David Lindley, vocals and lead guitar; Soloman Feldthouse, lead vocals, guitar, clarinet; Templeton Parcely, vocals, lead violin, and organ; Stuart A. Brotman, vocals and bass; Paul Lagos, vocals and drums; Maxwell Buda, harmonica; started in San Francisco (1966); sensation at 1968 Folk Festival in Newport, R.I.; albums—*Beacon from Mars, Bernice, Kaleidoscope, Side Trips.*

KALMAR, BERT

b. 1884 New York City, d. 1947 Los Angeles, California. Lyricist and librettist. Vaudeville comedian; met Harry Ruby, and they wrote "He Sits Around" for Belle Baker, singer; wrote "Who's Sorry Now?" (1923, m. Ted Snyder); with Harry Ruby wrote the book and lyrics for several Broadway shows; the songs, "Thinking of You" (1927), "I Wanna Be Loved by You" (1928); then in films, *Three Little Words* (1950).

KAMINSKY, MAX

b. 1908 Brockton, Massachusetts.
Jazz trumpeter. Played in Tommy Dorsey's band; also with Tony Pastor and Artie Shaw (1941); made first TV appearance in "Jazz" (1942) with Eddie Condon's group which included Bill Taylor, bass player; played at the Newport Jazz Festival, New York City (1972).

KAMUCA, RICHARD

b. 1930 Philadelphia, Pennsylvania.
Tenor saxist. Played with Stan Kenton, Woody Herman, and Maynard Ferguson in 1950s; with Gerry Mulligan, Gary McFarland and own quintet with Roy Eldridge during 1960s.

KANE, HELEN

b. 1910, d. 1966.
Singer. Known as the "Boop-boop-a-doop" girl; sang "I Wanna Be Loved by You" in *Good Boy* (1928, w. Bert Kalmar and m. Harry Ruby).

KANGAROO (rock group)

John Hall, bass; Teddy Speleos, lead guitar; Norman Dow Smart II, drums; Barbara Keith, vocals; album—*Kangaroo* (1968).

KANSAS CITY BAND

Led by Jay McShann in the 1940s. (*See* Al Hibbler)

KANSAS KLODHOPPERS, DOC MC CAULLY's *see* DOC WILLIAMS

KAPELL, WILLIAM

b. 1922 New York City, d. 1951 San Francisco, California. Concert pianist of great promise, but was killed in an airplane crash.

KARL, THOMAS (TOM)

b. 1846 Dublin, Ireland, d. 1916 Rochester, New York. Tenor. Studied with H. Phillips and others; sang in Italian opera; came to America with Parepa-Rosa; then with Henry C. Barnabee organized "The Bostonians," a comic opera group (1887, until 1896).

KARP, RICHARD

b. 1904 Vienna, Austria.
Conductor. Settled in Pittsburgh where he conducted opera and trained opera singers.

KASENETZ-KATZ SINGING ORCHESTRAL CIRCUS (rock circus)

Consists of the 1910 Fruitgum Company, Lieutenant Garcia's Magic Music Box, Music Explosion, 1989 Musical Marching Zoo, Ohio Express, JCW Rat Finks, St. Louis Invisible Band, and Teri Nelson group; albums—*Kasenetz-Katz Singing Orchestral Circus, Kasenetz-Katz Super Circus.*

KATIMS, MILTON

b. 1909 Brooklyn, New York.
Conductor. First violist with the NBC Symphony Orchestra, New York City; later a conductor; conducted the Seattle (Washington) Symphony (1954-55).

KATZ, FREDERICK

b. 1919 Brooklyn, New York.
Cellist, pianist, and composer. Played in concerts in New York City; then with Chico Hamilton Quintet (1955-56); taught anthropology at Valley State College; wrote *Cello Concerto* (1961), *Toccata* (1963), Jewish liturgical service for cantor, choir, and jazz groups, performed at Redlands University, Redlands, California, and in various temples.

KATZ, RICHARD AARON

b. 1924 Baltimore, Maryland.
Pianist. Studied at Manhattan School of Music and at Juilliard, New York City; played with various groups in New York City during 1950s and '60s; with Delaware Symphony Orchestra; toured Europe with Helen Merrill; with Orchestra U.S.A. after 1964.

KAUFMAN, GEORGE S.

b. 1889 Pittsburgh, Pennsylvania, d. 1961. Playwright and librettist. Wrote many successful plays; also sketches for *The Band Wagon* (1931, m. Arthur Schwartz, lyrics Howard Dietz); librettist for *I'd Rather Be Right* (1937) with Moss Hart (m. Richard Rodgers), *Helen of Troy* (1926) with Marc Connelly (m. Harry Ruby), *Strike Up the Band* (1930) with Morrie Ryskind (m. George Gershwin).

KAY, CONNIE

b. 1927 Tuckahoe, New York.
Black drummer. Born Conrad Henry Kirnon; played with Cat Anderson, Miles Davis, Lester Young, Stan Getz and others; with Modern Jazz Quartet after 1955.

KAY, HERSHY

b. 1919 Philadelphia, Pennsylvania.
Composer. Studied at Curtis Institute, Philadelphia (1936-40); orchestrator of scores for Broadway shows—*On the Town* (1944), *A Flag Is Born* (1947), *Peter Pan* (1950), *Golden Apple* (1954), *Sand Hog* (1955), *Candide* (1956), *Once Upon a Mattress* (1958), *Juno* (1957), *Livin' the Life* (1959), *Milk and Honey* (1961), *110 in the Shade* (1963), *Kelly* (1965), *Coco* (1969); also arranged ballet scores, and orchestrated film scores.

KAY, ULYSSES

b. 1917 Tucson, Arizona.
Noted black composer. Graduated Eastman School of Music; received Alice M. Ditson Fellowship, and American Composers Alliance Prize, Rosenwald Fellowship, Fulbright Scholarship, Prix de Rome prize, and Guggenheim Fellowship; served in a navy band in World War II; composed *Sinfonietta* (Rochester Civic Orchestra under Hanson, 1939), *Five Mosaics* for orchestra, *Oboe Concerto* (1940), *Piano Sonata* (Phi Mu Alpha Award, 1940), *Danse Calinda* (ballet, book—Ridgely Torrence, 1941), *Of New Horizons* (1944, American Composers Prize), *A Short Overture* (Gershwin Memorial Prize, 1947), *The Juggler of Our Lady* (opera performed at Xavier University, New Orleans, La., 1962), *Fantasy Variations* (1963), *Umbrian Scene* (1964), *Theatre Set* (1968); sent to Russia (1965) on a State Department cultural mission; taught at Lehman College of City University of New York after 1968.

KAYE, DANNY

b. 1913 Brooklyn, New York.
Actor and patter singer. Sang the "Patter Song" made up almost entirely of names of

Russian composers, "Tchaikovsky" (w. Ira Gershwin, m. Kurt Weill) in *Lady in the Dark* (1941); also in *Let's Face It* (1941, m. Cole Porter), and several films.

KAYE (KUNATZ), PETER

b. 1918 Chicago, Illinois.
Singer. Attended the Chicago Conservatory (1938); on radio station WBBM, Chicago after 1946; wrote "Apple of My Eye," "The Caller," "Teasin' Teasin'."

KAYE, SAMMY

b. 1910 Rocky River, Ohio.
Clarinetist and bandleader. His parents came from Czechoslovakia. Graduated Ohio University, Athens, Ohio, in civil engineering; formed his band in the 1930s; in 1941 played at Frank Dailey's Meadowbrook; band included Gene Krupa, Roy Eldridge, and Teddy Wilson; Marty Oscard played the lead sax for several years; his motto was "Swing and Sway with Sammy Kaye."

KAZEE, BUELL HILTON

b. 1900 Burton Fork, Kentucky.
Singer and banjoist. Graduated Georgetown College, Georgetown, Kentucky; pastor of First Baptist Church, Morehead, Kentucky (1928-50); professor at Lexington Baptist College after 1950; his records include "Rock Island Line," "Hobo's Last Ride," "East Virginia," "Darling Cora," "The Roving Cowboy," "Yellow Pups," "John Henry"; LP record—*Buell H. Kazee, His Songs and Music.*

KEANE, ELLSWORTH MC GRANAHAN

b. 1927 St. Vincent, British West Indies.
Black trumpeter. Educated at London University, England; with Mike McKenzie's Harlem Allstars; with Joe Harriott after 1959-65; later with Kurt Edelhagen Orchestra in Cologne, Germany; featured soloist on trumpet and flügelhorn.

KEELER, RUBY

b. 1910 Halifax, Nova Scotia.
Singer and actress. Appeared in films; lead in the revival of *No, No Nanette* (1972).

KEELY, HENRY J.

b. 1839 Reading, Pennsylvania, d. 1926 Philadelphia, Pennsylvania. Choirmaster. Studied organ with Michael Cross; directed Gethsemane Baptist Church choirs, Philadelphia (1872-1908); also directed the Lyric Choral Society; taught piano, organ, and voice for about fifty years; his daughter, Abbie Keely, noted soprano in Philadelphia between 1890-1920.

KEENE, ARTHUR F.

b. ca. 1798 Ireland, d. after 1830 Nashville, Tennessee. Singer, composer, and teacher. Debut in New York City (1818); later taught in New York City; later moved to Nashville; wrote "Fancy's Vision" (1818), "Farewell but Whenever You Welcome the Hour" (1824, w. Thomas Moore).

KEENE, BOB

b. 1922 Manhattan Beach, California.
Bandleader. Born Robert Kuhn; played clarinet with Ray Bauduc and Eddie Miller in 1940s; led his own band.

KEENE, CHRISTOPHER

b. 1947.
Conductor. Studied piano; history major at the University of California at Berkeley; formed own opera company at age eighteen and produced Britten's *Rape of Lucretia;* assistant conductor of San Francisco Opera at eighteen; conducted the New York City Opera at twenty-three; engaged for both the City Opera and Metropolitan Opera, New York City at age twenty-four.

KEFER, PAUL

b. 1875 Rouen, France, d. 1941 Rochester, New York. Cellist. Studied at Verviers Music School and the Paris Conservatory; played in Paris orchestras after 1900, then with the New York Symphony (1908-13).

KELBERINE, ALEXANDER

b. 1903 Kiev, Russia, d. 1940 New York City.
Concert pianist. Studied with Busoni and Siloti; toured Europe; debut in New York (1928); later taught with the Sternberg Conservatory, Philadelphia.

KELLAWAY, ROGER

b. 1939 Waban, Massachusetts.
Pianist. Studied piano at age seven; studied at New England Conservatory, Boston (1957-59); bass player with Jimmy McPartland and Ralph Marterie in 1950s; with Kai Winding, Mark Murphy, Al Cohn-Zoot Sims and others as pianist; formed own trio; albums—*Roger Kellaway Trio, Spirit Feel, Stride.*

KELLER, GRETA

b. 1901 Vienna, Austria.
Singer. Came to America before 1928; appeared in the musical show *Broadway* (1928, George Abbott production); sang in various musical shows, at supper clubs, on radio, and TV; recorded (1971) Greta Keller-Rod McKuen, "An Evening in Vienna" and "Love Is a Daydream" and other songs by Yula

(Russian-American composer, lyricist, and singer); lives in New York City.

KELLER, MATTHIAS

b. 1813 Ulm, Wurtemberg, Germany, d. 1883 Boston, Massachusetts. Composer. Came to Boston as a young man; composed the music "Keller's American Hymn" (1866, w. O.W. Holmes); the original song had words by Keller, and was a failure, but Dr. Holmes wrote new lyrics for the song for the great Peace Jubilee of 1872 in Boston when it became successful; "Father Almighty, We Bow at Thy Feet" (w. Theron Brown) is sung to the same tune.

KELLEY, EDGAR STILLMAN

b. 1857 Sparta, Wisconsin, d. 1944 New York City. Composer. Pupil of F.W. Merriam, Clarence Eddy and others; taught at the New York College of Music; critic for the *San Francisco Examiner* (1893-95); at Yale (1901-02); taught in Berlin (1902-10); then with Cincinnati Conservatory and Western College, Oxford, Ohio; composed *Gulliver* (humorous Symphony), *Chinese Suite for Orchestra, Aladdin, Puritania* (comic opera, Boston, 1892), "Phases of Love," "Eldorado," "Israfel" and other songs.

KELLOGG, CLARA LOUISE

b. 1842 Sumter, South Carolina, d. 1916 New Hartford, Connecticut. Famous soprano. Studied in New York (1856-61); debut at the Academy of Music (1861); debut in London at His Majesty's Theatre (1867); married Max Strakosch, her manager.

KELLY, DANIEL E.

b. 1843 Kingston, Rhode Island, d. 1905 Waterloo, Iowa. Popular composer and vaudeville entertainer. Lived in Gaylord, Smith County, Kansas; wrote the music for "Home on the Range" (w. Dr. B.M. Higley, 1873), which is now the state song of Kansas.

KELLY, GENE

b. 1912 Pittsburgh, Pennsylvania.
Singer and actor. Starred in the screen musical *Anchors Aweigh* (screen play—Isobel Lennart).

KELLY, GUY

b. 1906 Scotlandville, Louisiana, d. 1940.
Jazz trumpeter. Kelly and Red Allen were rivals among the younger New Orleans trumpeters.

KELLY, THOMAS RAYMOND ("RED")

b. 1927 Shelby, Montana.
Bass player. With Woody Herman and Stan Kenton in 1950s; with Harry James (1961-66).

KELLY, WYNTON

b. 1931 Jamaica, West Indies.
Black pianist. With Lester Young, Dizzy Gillespie and others in 1950s; toured with Miles Davis (1959-63); formed his own trio with bassist Paul Chambers and drummer Jimmy Cobb; trio played at the World Jazz Festival in Japan (1964).

KELPIUS, JOHANNES

b. 1673 Sweden, d. 1708 Philadelphia, Pennsylvania. Organist and composer. Came to Philadelphia (1694); leader of the Hermits in Wissahickon Valley, Philadelphia; supplied music for the Swedish Gloria Dei Church, Philadelphia (1703); published a book of nineteen hymns (1708).

KELTERBORN, LOUIS

b. 1891 Boston, Massachusetts, d. 1933 Neuchatel, Switzerland. Conductor, organist, teacher, and composer. Studied at the Basel and Geneva Conservatories; taught at Wolff Conservatory, Basel (1917-19); organist in Burgdorf after 1919; taught at Neuchatel Conservatory after 1927; composed a symphony, choral and organ works.

KEMP, HAL

b. 1905 Marion, Indiana, d. 1940.
Bandleader. Organized his band while a student at the University of North Carolina, Chapel Hill, N.C., in early 1930s; toured England; played at Hotels Taft and Pennsylvania, New York City after 1934; also played the clarinet; Skinnay Ennis sang and doubled on the drums; Earl Geiger was lead trumpeter; Eddie Kusborski, trombonist; Janet Lafferty, singer (Janet Blair); on December 19th he was injured in a head-on car crash, and died two days later.

KEMP, ROBERT C.

b. 1820 Wellfleet, Cape Cod, Massachusetts, d. 1897 Charlestown, Massachusetts. Conductor and compiler. Organized public concerts in Reading, Mass. (1854), Lynn, and Boston, known as the "Old Folks Concert" group; they went to Washington, D.C., and sang for President James Buchanan; he compiled the *Faneuil Hall Temperance Song Book* (1876) and *Father Kemp's Old Folks Concert Music* (1889); in 1857 assisted in the revised edition of *The Continental Harmony.* (*See* William Billings)

KENDIS, JAMES

b. 1883 St. Paul, Minnesota, d. 1946 Jamaica, New York. Composer and lyricist. Formed Kendis Music Corp.; also associated with James Brockman; with Nat Vincent and James Brockman wrote "I'm Forever Blowing Bubbles" (m. John William Killette), sung by June Caprice in *The Passing Show* of 1918.

KENNAN, KENT

b. 1913 Milwaukee, Wisconsin.
Composer. Graduated Eastman School of Music, Rochester, N.Y.; won fellowship at American Academy in Rome; composed *Promenade* (Santa Cecilia Orchestra, Rome, 1938), *Air de Ballet* (Detroit Symphony under Kolar, 1941), *Nocturne* for viola and small orchestra, *Lament* (NBC Symphony Orchestra under Black, 1941), *Andante* for solo oboe and small orchestra (Rochester Civic Orchestra, 1941), *Concertino for an American Going to War.*

KENNEDY, JOSEPH J., JR.

b. 1923 Pittsburgh, Pennsylvania.
Violinist, conductor, and composer. Studied violin at age ten under his grandfather; with Ahmad Jamal (1949); Duquesne University, master's degree in music (1960); taught in Richmond, Virginia public schools; played in Richmond Symphony Orchestra; composed *Suite for Trio and Orchestra,* which he conducted with Cleveland Summer Symphony (1965); also wrote *Surrealism, You Can Be Sure, Tempo for Two.*

KENSINGTON MARKET (Canadian rock group)

KENTON, STANLEY NEWCOMB (STAN)

b. 1912 Wichita, Kansas.
Bandleader and composer. His albums include *Adventures in Jazz, Artistry in Rhythm, Ballad Style of Stan Kenton, Finian's Rainbow, Hair, Kenton Plays Wagner, Stan Kenton Conducts Jazz Compositions of Dee Barton, Stan Kenton Conducts the Los Angeles Neophonic Orchestra, Stan Kenton Deluxe Set, Stan Kenton's Greatest Hits, Stan Kenton Plays for Today, Road Show, Romantic Approach, Sophisticated Approach, Standards in Silhouette, West Side Story* and *The World We Know;* his band appeared at the 1971 Newport Jazz Festival, but Stan was recuperating from a recent operation, so the band was led by Dick Shearer, a trombonist and by Mike Vax, a trumpeter; they played *The Macumba Suite* (m. Ken Hanna); also at Newport Jazz Festival, New York City (1972).

KENTUCKIANS

Featured Goober Buchanan.

KENTUCKY PARDNERS (vocal group) *see* CHARLIE MONROE

KENTUCKY RAMBLERS *see* GABE TUCKER

KENWORTHY, RUTH DEWOLFE

b. 1889, d. 1971 New York City.
Chorus manager. Daughter of Kate Kenworthy, an opera singer; joined the Schola Cantorum (1909); sang the soprano obligato of Verdi's *Te Deum* with the New York Philharmonic under Toscanini; chorus manager of the Schola Cantorum (1942-71).

KEPPARD, FREDDY

b. 1889 New Orleans, Louisiana, d. 1933 Chicago, Illinois. Black cornetist and bandleader. Organized his Olympia Orchestra about 1905 with Alphonse Picou on clarinet; joined Bill Johnson's Original Creole Ragtime Band (1912); played at Orpheum Theatre, San Francisco (1913); then at Winter Garden, New York City (1915) as That Creole Band.

KERKER, GUSTAVE A.

b. 1857 Herford, Westphalia, Germany, d. 1923 New York City. Popular composer. The family settled in Louisville, Kentucky (1867); he wrote the music for the operettas *The Pearl of Pekin* (1888), *Castles in the Air* (1889, w. C.A. Byrne), and with Hugh Morton, lyricist: *In Gay New York* (1896), *The Belle of New York* (1897, Edna May had the lead as a Salvation Army lassie), *The Whirl of the Town* (1897), *The Telephone Girl,* and *The American Beauty* (1897, starring Lillian Russell).

KERN, JEROME DAVID

b. 1885 New York City, d. there 1945.
Noted composer. Studied at New York City College of Music (1902); pianist with music publishers in Tin Pan Alley, and later became vice president of T.B. Harms, music publisher; wrote the scores for *La Belle Paree* (1911), arranged *The Girl from Utah* (1914), *Nobody Home* (1915), *Oh Boy* (1917, lyrics by P.G. Wodehouse), *Show Boat* (1927, libretto-Oscar Hammerstein II from Edna Ferber's

book), *The Cat and the Fiddle* (1931), *Music in the Air* (1932), *Roberta* (1933), *Very Warm for May* (1939); best-known songs from his shows include "Ol' Man River" (1927), "Smoke Gets in Your Eyes" (1933), "Why Do I Love You," "Make Believe," and "The Last Time I Saw Paris" (1940, w. Oscar Hammerstein II). (*See* Billie Burke, Marilyn Miller).

KERNOCHAN, MARSHALL RUTGERS

b. 1880 New York City, d. 1955 Edgartown, Massachusetts. Editor and composer. Studied with Wetzler, Knorr, and Goetschius; musical editor of *The Outlook;* later president of Galaxy Music Corp., music publishers in New York City; composed *The Foolish Virgins* (cantata), *The Sleep of Summer* (for women's chorus and orchestra), and many songs.

KERR, ANITA

b. 1927 Memphis, Tennessee.
Pianist, singer, and composer. She studied piano at age four; staff pianist on a Memphis radio station at fourteen; organized the "Anita Kerr Singers" (1949); appeared on many shows; also "Anita Kerr Quartet"; made arrangements for top performers; composed the music for the albums *The Sea* (1966, w. Rod McKuen), *The Earth* (1967, using a seventy-piece orchestra), *The Sky;* score for the film *Limbo* (1972).

KERR, HARRISON

b. 1899 Cleveland, Ohio.
Composer. Taught at University of Oklahoma, Norman, Okla.; with Civil Affairs Division, Dept. of Army; on UNESCO International Music Council; composed *Dance Sonata* for two pianos and percussion instruments (Bennington College Festival, 1938), *Dance Suite* (Rochester Symphony under Hanson, 1942), Symphony in D Minor.

KERSANDS, BILLY

b. ca. 1840, d. ca. 1915.
Black singer, dancer, and minstrel showman. Joined the Georgia Minstrels (1865); later led the show; for a time James A. Bland was a member of the all-black troupe.

KERSEY, KENNY

b. 1916 Harrow, Ontario, Canada.
Black jazz pianist. Known for his stride-piano style with leaping left hand; played in Red Allen's band (1941); joined Andy Kirk's band (1942).

KERSHAW, DOUGLAS JAMES (DOUG)

b. 1936 Tiel Ridge, Louisiana.
Singer and songwriter. Attended high school in Lake Arthur, La. and Jennings, La., McNeese State College, Lake Charles, La.; wrote "Look Around," "So Lovely Baby," "Blue Mood," "Mr. Love," "Hey Mae," "Never Love Again," "Sad Face," "Hardly Anymore."

KESSEL, BARNEY

b. 1923 Muskogee, Oklahoma.
Guitarist. Played in various bands in 1950s; later staff musician in Hollywood studios.

KEY, FRANCIS SCOTT

b. 1779 Frederick, Maryland, d. 1843 Baltimore, Maryland. Lyricist. Educated at St. John's College, Annapolis, Md., and became an attorney; wrote the lyrics "The Star Spangled Banner" (1814, tune "Anacreon in Heaven," John S. Smith), "The Warrior's Return" and "Lord with a Glowing Heart I'd Praise Thee" (1819, tune "St. Chad," Richard Redhead); wrote his inspired words, "The Star Spangled Banner," while a prisoner on a British ship which was bombarding Fort McHenry, Baltimore, in 1814; at daybreak, when the bombing stopped, Key saw the flag still waving over the fort.

KIEFER, RICHARD

b. 1939 Cleveland, Ohio.
Trumpeter. Played with Buddy Morrow, Benny Goodman, and Urbie Green during 1950s; with Maynard Ferguson (1957-63); later with Max Gregor Orchestra in Munich, Germany; at Berlin Jazz Festival (1964); Recklinghausen Jazz Festival (1965).

KILGORE, WYATT MERLE

b. 1934 Chickasha, Oklahoma.
Popular composer. Raised in Shreveport, La.; disc jockey on station KENT, Shreveport, at sixteen; later in Monroe and Springhill, La.; attended Louisiana Tech, Ruston, La.; wrote "More and More" (1952), "Dear Mama" (1959), "Johnny Reb" (1959), "Love Has Made You Beautiful" (1960), "Wolverton Mountain" (1962, with Claude King); his LP records include *Merle Kilgore* (1964) and *Nevada Smith.*

KIMBALL, JACOB, JR.

b. 1761 Topsfield, Massachusetts, d. there 1826. Musician, composer, and compiler. In 1775 he was a drummer in Captain Baker's company of Little's Regiment, Massachusetts Militia; graduated Harvard (1780) and was admitted to the bar in Strafford, N.H. but taught music instead; issued *The Rural Harmony* (Boston, 1793), and *The Essex Harmony* (Exeter, N.H., 1800, different book from the one issued by D. Bayley, 1770).

KINCAID, BRADLEY

b. 1895 Point Leavell, Kentucky.
Singer. Served in the army in France in World War I; graduated George Williams College, Downers Grove, Illinois (1928); toured the U.S. (1928-48); recorded four albums entitled *The Kentucky Mountain Boy.*

KINCAIDE, DEANE

b. 1911 Houston, Texas.
Saxist, clarinetist, and arranger. Arranger for Bob Crosby, Ben Pollack, Muggsy Spanier, Jimmy and Tommy Dorsey in 1930s and '40s; member of NBC "Tonight" orchestra (1963-65); also arranger for "Jackie Gleason" TV series.

KINDER, RALPH

b. 1876 England, d. 1952.
Organist. Came to America as a boy; studied in Providence, R.I., and England; organist at Holy Trinity Protestant Episcopal Church, Philadelphia (1899-1937), then at St. Thomas', Whitemarsh, Pa.; composed anthems, songs, and organ pieces.

KINDLER, HANS

b. 1893 Rotterdam, Netherlands, d. 1949 Watch Hill, Rhode Island. Cellist. Studied at the Rotterdam Conservatory; later with Mossel, Casals, and Gerardy; taught at Scharwenka Conservatory, Berlin; toured Europe and the United States; organized and conducted National Symphony Orchestra, Washington, D.C. (1930); also soloist in Europe.

KING, BERTIE

b. 1912 Colon, Panama.
Black alto saxophonist. Raised in Jamaica, British West Indies; played with Benny Carter and others; in London after 1936; played in Leonard Feather's Olde English Swing Band; served in British Navy (1939-43); later with Leslie Hutchinson; toured Europe, United States, and the Caribbean.

KING, CAROLE

b. 1944 Brooklyn, New York.
Singer, pianist, and songwriter. Married and divorced lyricist Gerry Goffin; they wrote "Will You Love Me Tomorrow" (1961, recorded by the Shirelles) and "Up on the Roof" (1963, recorded by the Drifters); she wrote "So Far Away," "Where You Lead," "Child of Mine"; album—*Tapestry;* married Charles Larkey, bass player; won four Grammy Awards (1972) for "It's Too Late" (single), *Tapestry* (album), song "You've Got a Friend" (recorded by James Taylor), and best female vocal performance for *Tapestry.*

KING, CLAUDE

b. 1933 Shreveport, Louisiana.
Singer. Attended the University of Idaho, Moscow, Idaho; later sang in night spots in Shreveport; top records include "Big River, Big Man" (1961), "The Commancheros" (1961), "The Burning of Atlanta" (1962), "Wolverton Mountain" (1962), "Tiger Woman" (1965, written by King and Merle Kilgore), "Laura" (1967); album—*Meet Claude King* (1962).

KING, DENNIS

b. 1897 Coventry, England, d. 1971 New York City. Baritone. Born Dennis Pratt; resided in Great Neck, L.I., N.Y.; became an American citizen (1953); appeared in *Rose Marie, The Three Musketeers, Show Boat, I Married an Angel,* and *The Vagabond King* (1925, Rudolph Friml) with Jeanette MacDonald.

KING, E.J.

b. (?), d. 1844.
Compiler. With Benjamin F. White compiled *The Sacred Harp* (1844).

KING, FRANK ("PEE WEE")

b. 1914 Milwaukee, Wisconsin.
Popular composer and bandleader. Played on radio stations in Racine, Green Bay, and Milwaukee (1933); with "Gene Autry Show," Louisville, Ky. (1934); formed the Golden West Cowboys (1936); wrote "Bonaparte's Retreat" (1946, with Redd Stewart), "Tennessee Waltz" (1948, with Redd Stewart), "Slow Poke" (1951), "Bimbo" (1954); his LP records include *Pee Wee King and Redd Stewart* (1964), *Country Barn Dance.*

KING, FREDDIE

b. 1934 Gilmer, Texas.
Black guitarist. Played in Chicago night spots; first recorded in 1956; albums—*Hide Away, Freddie King Is a Blues Master, My Feeling for the Blues.*

KING, HENRY

b. 1896 Christianburg, Virginia.
Pianist and bandleader. Considered among the best of the society bands in the 1930s; played only in the plushest hotel rooms.

KING, KARL

b. 1890, d. 1971 Fort Dodge, Iowa.
Composer. Best-known marches were "Emblem of Freedom," "Fidelity," "Post of Freedom," "Loyal Americans," "Our Heritage," "Roll of Honor," and "Trombone King."

KING, MORGANA

b. 1930 Pleasantville, New York.
Singer. Sang in New York City night spots after 1956; albums—*Gemini Changes, I Know How It Feels to Be Lonely, It's a Quiet Thing, Miss Morgana King, More Morgana, Wild Is Love, With a Taste of Honey.*

KING, RILEY B. ("B.B.")

b. 1925 Itta Bena, Mississippi.
Black guitarist. Started in 1962; became a sensation at the Cafe Au Go Go in New York City (1968); among the top of the blues guitarists; albums—*Best of B.B. King, Blues Is King, Blues on Top of Blues, Boss of the Blues, Completely Well, Confessin' the Blues, From the Beginning, His Best—the Electric B.B. King, The Jungle, B.B. King's Greatest Hits, Let Me Love You, Live and Well, Live at the Regal, Mr. Blues, Rock Me Baby;* at the Mar y Sol, Puerto Rican Pop Festival (1972); played at the Newport Jazz Festival, New York City (1972).

KING, ROBERT A.

b. 1862 New York City, d. there 1932.
Songwriter. Born Robert Keiser; songwriter for Shapiro-Bernstein, music publishers; wrote "Beautiful Ohio" (1918, w. Ballard Smith), "Dreamy Alabama" (1919), "Beautiful Hawaii," "I Ain't Nobody's Darling," "Ain't My Baby Grand?," "I Scream, You Scream, We All Scream for Ice Cream," "Moonlight on the Colorado," "When the Boys Come Home," "Lafayette We Hear You Calling" (1918).

KING SISTERS (singers)

Alyce, Donna, Louise, and Yvonne King sang with Horace Heidt and Alvino Rey.

KING, STODDARD

b. 1889 Jackson, Wisconsin, d. 1933 Spokane, Washington. Lyricist. Educated at Yale; columnist for *Washington Spokesman-Review;* 3rd Washington Infantry, National Guard in World War I; wrote lyrics for "There's a Long Long Trail A-Winding" (1914, m. Alonzo Elliott).

KING, WAYNE

b. 1901 Savannah, Illinois.
Bandleader. Graduated Valparaiso University, Indiana; formed his own band (1927); played in the Aragon Ballroom, Chicago (1927-35); served as a major in the Special Services in World War II; became known as The Waltz King.

KING, WILLIAM

b. (?) England, d. 1796.
Singer and actor. Sang in the opera, *The Archers* (1796, w. William Dunlap, m. Benjamin Carr); his wife was the sister of Arabella Brett and Mrs. Hodgkinson.

KINGS OF DIXIELAND (jazz band) *see* SHARKEY BONANO

KINGS OF RHYTHM *see* IKE TURNER

KINGSLEY, GEORGE

b. 1811 Northampton, Massachusetts, d. there 1884. Composer. Music teacher in Boston and organist at the Hollis Street Church; later professor of music at Girard College, Philadelphia, then organist at Dr. Storrs' Church of the Pilgrims, Brooklyn; composed the tune "Ware" ("Now to the Lord a Noble Song," w. Isaac Watts), the tune "Heber" ("Jesus the Very Thought of Thee," translated by Edward Caswall), "By Cool Siloam's Shady Hill" (w. R. Heber, second tune by I.B. Woodbury), the tune "Frederick" ("I Would Not Live Alway," (1833, w. W.A. Muhlenberg), "Messiah" ("Brethern While We Sojourn Here," w. Joseph Swain), "Far O'er the Sea" (w. Felicia D.B. Hemans), tune "Tappan" ("The Lord Our God Is Clothed with Might," w. Henry Kirke White).

KINGSTON TRIO (vocal group)

Bob Shane, Nick Reynolds, and Dave Guard; later Guard replaced by John Stewart; albums—*Kingston Trio* (1958), *Best of the Kingston Trio, Children of the Morning, College Concert, The Folk Era, Kingston Trio at Large, Once Upon a Time, Stay Awhile, Stereo Concert.*

KINKELDEY, OTTO

b. 1878 New York City, d. 1966.
Teacher. Graduated New York University, Columbia (M.A.), University of Berlin (Ph.-D.); studied with MacDowell and others; choir director and teacher in New York (1898-1902); University of Breslau (1909-14); chief of music division, New York Public Library (1915-23); wrote on music.

KINNEY, ELIZABETH CLEMENTINE (DODGE) STEDMAN

b. 1810 New York City, d. 1889.
Hymnist. Married first E.C. Stedman and second W.B. Kinney; wrote "Jesus, Saviour, Pass Not By," which appeared in *Songs of Christian Praise* (1880, N.Y. City).

KINNEY, RAY

b. 1900, d. 1972 Honolulu, Hawaii.
Singer and songwriter. Entertainer who wrote and sang songs of the Hawaiian Islands for more than fifty years; composed his most popular song, "Across the Sea," at only fifteen years of age; performed at the opening of the Roxy Theater; later for the opening of the Hawaiian Room of the Lexington Hotel, New York City.

KIPNIS, ALEXANDER

b. 1891 Zhitomir, South Russia.
Opera singer. Opera star in Hamburg, Wiesbaden, then with the Berlin State Opera; but the rise of Hitler forced him to flee Germany, and he came to the United States.

KIRBY, JOHN

b. 1908 Baltimore, Maryland, d. 1952 Hollywood, California. Black double bass player. Played for Fletcher Henderson, Chick Webb, and Lucky Millinder; organized a sextet (1937) including Charlie Shavers (trumpeter), Buster Bailey (clarinetist), Billy Kyle (pianist), O'Neill Spencer (drummer), and Russell Procope (saxophonist); played at the Waldorf-Astoria, New York City; Maxine Sullivan, vocalist, was Kirby's wife.

KIRCHNER, LEON

b. 1919 Brooklyn, New York.
Composer. Studied at University of California at Los Angeles with Arnold Schoenberg, and University of California at Berkeley (1940), then with Ernest Bloch, Roger Sessions and others; served in the army in World War II; lectured and taught at Berkeley (1946-51), Mills College, Oakland, Calif., then Harvard (1961); known for *Daun* (choral piece, 1943, text—Garcia Lorca, *String Quartet* (received Music Critics Circle Award, 1950), *Sonata Concertante* (1952).

KIRK, ANDREW D. (ANDY)

b. 1898 Newport, Kentucky.
Black bandleader. Don Byas, saxophonist, played in Kirk's band.

KIRK, EDDIE

b. 1919 Greeley, Colorado.
Singer and yodeler. Joined Glen Rice's Beverly Hillbillies in the 1930s; with Larry Sunbrock's band (1935); won National Yodeling Championship (1935 and 1936); served in the navy in World War II; his records include "Candy Kisses" (1949), "The Gods Were Angry with Me" (1949), "Born to Lose," "Petals from a Faded Rose."

KIRK, RONALD T. ("RAHSAAN ROLAND")

b. 1936 Columbus, Ohio.
Black musician and composer. Educated at Ohio State School for the blind; played saxophone and clarinet with Boyd Moore band in 1950s; learned to play three instruments simultaneously, the tenor sax, stritch (alto sax), and manzello (soprano sax); recorded for Cadet Records (1960) in Chicago, for Prestige (1961); toured Europe (1961-64); wrote *From Bechet, Byas and Fats, Three for Dizzy, Lonesome August Child, Mystical Dreams, No Tonic Pres;* at Newport Jazz Festival, New York City (1972).

KIRKPATRICK, WILLIAM JAMES

b. 1838 Duncannon, Pennsylvania, d. 1921 Germantown, Philadelphia, Pennsylvania. Composer and compiler. Carpenter in Philadelphia, Methodist, and a composer; composed the tune "Cradle Song" ("Away in a Manger" 1888, *see* J.R. Murray); in 1858 he assisted A.S. Jenks in the publication of *Devotional Melodies,* and subsequently with J.R. Sweney, they published forty-seven books of songs; after the death of Sweney, Kirkpatrick published an additional forty song books.

KIRSTEN, DOROTHY

b. 1919 Montclair, New Jersey.
Noted soprano. Studied with Astolfo Pescia; debut in Italy; sang with Metropolitan Opera, New York City, after 1945; appeared in Broadway shows and films; sang with Gordon MacRae; albums (with MacRae)—*Desert Song, New Moon, Student Prince.*

KITT, EARTHA

b. 1928 Columbia, South Carolina.
Black singer. Appeared in films and on numerous TV shows; albums—*Fabulous Eartha Kitt, Eartha Kitt in Person at the Plaza, New Faces of 1952, That Bad Eartha, Eartha Kitt Revisited.*

KITTREDGE, GEORGE LYMAN

b. 1860 Boston, Massachusetts, d. 1941.
Writer. Taught at Harvard University for forty-eight years; wrote books on English and Scottish ballads and folk songs.

KITTREDGE, WALTER

b. 1834, d. 1905.
Popular composer. Lived in Merrimack, New Hampshire; wrote the words and music of the popular Civil War song, "Tenting on the Old Camp Ground."

KLAUDT INDIAN FAMILY

Arikara Indian Gospel Singers, Dakota Badlands; Dad and Mom Klaudt and sons Vernon, Melvin, Raymond, and Kenneth; Vernon's wife Betty; Mel Stewart, pianist.

KLAUSER, JULIUS

b. 1854 New York City, d. 1907 Milwaukee, Wisconsin. Teacher. Studied at the Leipzig Conservatory with Wenzel, then became a music teacher in Milwaukee; wrote *The Septonate and the Centralization of the Tonal System* (1890).

KLAUSER, KARL

b. 1823 St. Petersburg, Russia, d. 1905 Farmington, Connecticut. Teacher and editor. Taught in New York City after 1850; music director of the Farmington Conservatory after 1856.

KLEIN, BRUNO OSCAR

b. 1856 Osnabruck, Germany, d. 1911 New York City. Organist. Son of Carl K. Klein, organist at the Osnabruck Cathedral, in Hanover; Bruno was the pupil of his father; made concert tour of the United States (1878-83); settled in New York City (1884); organist and teacher there; wrote the opera *Kenilworth;* composed piano pieces and church music.

KLEIN, MANUEL

b. 1876 London, England, d. there 1919. Composer. Came to New York about 1900; wrote the score for *Mr. Pickwick* (1903, book—Charles Klein, his brother), *A Society Circus* (1905), *Pioneer Days* (1906), *The Pied Piper* (1908, starring De Wolf Hopper), *A Trip to Japan* (1909), *America* (1913), *Hop o' My Thumb* (1913), *The Wars of the World* (1914); after a quarrel with J.J. Shubert over some trumpets he needed, he resigned as producer at the Hippodrome and returned to England.

KLEINSINGER, GEORGE

b. 1914 San Bernardino, California. Composer. Studied at New York University (B.A. in music); fellowship at Juilliard Graduate School, New York City (1938-40); composed *I Hear America Singing* (St. Louis Symphony), *Street Corner* (concerto for harmonica and orchestra, Cleveland Orchestra), *Tubby the Tuba* (New York Philharmonic under Stokowski), *Overture on American Folk Themes* (Boston Pops Orchestra), *Pan the Piper* (Cincinnati Symphony under Thor Johnson), *Peewee the Piccolo* (Philadelphia Symphony), *Western Rhapsody* (Buffalo).

KLEMM, JOHANN GOTTLOB

b. 1690 Saxony, Germany, d. 1762 Bethlehem, Pennsylvania. Organ maker. Came to Philadelphia (1726); then went to New York City, where he built the Trinity Church organ (1740); then went to Bethlehem, Pa., where he built pipe organs after 1757.

KLEMM, JOHN G.

b. ca. 1797, d. ca. 1867. Dealer, publisher, and organ maker. The firm of John G. Klemm & Brother was active in Philadelphia from 1818-1880; they published "The Campbells Are Comin' " (G.F.C.), "Grand March" (Klemm), "Home Sweet Home" (1823, John Howard Payne and Henry Bishop).

KLEMPERER, OTTO

b. 1885 Breslau, Germany-Poland. d. 1973. Conductor. Studied at Hoch's Conservatory, Frankfort-on-Main, and at the Klindworth-Scharwenka Conservatory, Berlin; conducted opera in several cities in Germany during the 1920s and '30s; while in Leipzig, his protective railing gave way and he struck his head on the stage, suffering a severe concussion; when the Nazis came to power in 1933, he was forced to resign his position, and fled to America, where he was musical director of the Los Angeles Philharmonic (1933-39).

KLINK, AL

b. 1915 Danbury, Connecticut. Tenor saxist and flutist. Played with Glenn Miller, Tommy Dorsey, Benny Goodman and others; staff musician with NBC after 1954.

KNABE, ERNEST

b. 1837, d. 1894. Piano maker. Son of William Knabe, Sr.

KNABE, VALENTINE WILHELM LUDWIG

b. 1797 Kreuzburg, Prussia, Germany, d. 1864 Baltimore, Maryland. Piano manufacturer. Founder of the piano factory in Baltimore, and was succeeded by his sons William and Ernest; the business was merged with the American Piano Company of New York (1908).

KNABE, WILLIAM, JR.

b. 1841, d. 1889.
Piano maker. Son of William Knabe, Sr.

KNAPP, PHOEBE PALMER

b. 1839 New York City, d. 1908 Poland Spring, Maine. Composer. Her husband, Joseph F. Knapp, founded the Metropolitan Life Insurance Company; with her mother, Phebe (or Phoebe) Palmer, hymnist, she composed the music for the "Cleansing Wave" (or "Stream") and "Welcome to Glory" which appeared in *The Revivalist* (1868); she also wrote the music "Blessed Assurance" (1873, w. Fanny Crosby, "Lo! He Comes, Lo!"), "My Body, Soul and Spirit" (w. Mary D. James).

KNEELAND, ABNER

b. 1774 Gardner, Massachusetts, d. 1844 near Farmington, Iowa. Hymnist. Contributed 147 hymns to *American Universalists Hymns* (1808); edited the *Philadelphia Hymn Book* (1819) and *Hymns for the Use of Those Who Are Slaves to No Sect* (1834); went on trial for blasphemy in Boston (1836).

KNEELAND, LEVI

b. 1803 Masonville, New York, d. 1834 Packerville, Connecticut. Hymnist. Became a Baptist minister (1828); wrote "Christian Worship, How Inviting," which appeared in Linsley and Davis' *Select Hymns* (1836).

KNEISEL, FRANZ

b. 1865 Bucharest, Romania, d. 1926 Boston, Massachusetts. Violinist and teacher. Pupil of Grun and Hellmesberger in Vienna; concertmaster in Berlin; Boston Symphony Orchestra (1885-1903); founded the "Kneisel Quartet," active 1887-1917; taught at the Institute of Musical Art, New York City after 1905.

KNEISEL, MARIANNE

b. 1897 Boston, Massachusetts, d. 1972 Blue Hill, Maine. Violinist and patron. Daughter of Franz Kneisel; sister of violinist Frank Kneisel; married banker Felix Kahn, brother of Otto Kahn; studied at Institute of Musical Art in New York (now Juilliard School) at age nine; taught there after 1922; formed the Marianne Kneisel String Quartet which toured for more than twenty-five years; in 1952 she turned her home, Kneisel Hill, into a school of music.

KNEPPER, JAMES M. (JIMMY)

b. 1927 Los Angeles, California.
Trombonist. Played with Charles Mingus and other bands during 1950s; with Benny Goodman on tour of Soviet Russia (1962); played in New York City night clubs and Broadway shows in 1960s; then joined Thad Jones-Mel Lewis at Village Vanguard, New York City.

KNIGHT, EDWARD, JR.

b. ca. 1795 England, d. 1833 New Orleans, Louisiana. Pianist and compiler. Son of Edward Knight, English singer; husband of Mary Anne Povey, singer; debut in New York City (1826) with his wife; compiled *Canadian Airs, Collected by Lieutenant Beck, R.N. on Arctic Expedition of Captain Franklin* (1823).

KNIGHT, GLADYS

b. 1944 Atlanta, Georgia.
Black singer. Won first place on the "Ted Mack Amateur Hour" at age four; formed Gladys Knight and the Pips (1958) locally; national recordings (1966); appeared on the "Ed Sullivan Show"; sang at the Copacabana, New York City.

KNIGHT AND THE PIPS, GLADYS (vocal group)

Gladys Knight, Merald Knight, Edward Patten, and William Guest; started in 1966; later appeared at the Copacabana, New York City; albums—*Everybody Needs Love, Feelin' Bluesy, Greatest Hits, Gladys Knight and the Pips, Nitty Gritty, Silk 'n Soul.*

KNIGHT, TERRY

b. 1943.
Manager. Disc jockey; became manager and producer for the Grand Funk Railroad (pop band); replaced in 1972, and Knight filed suit for $5 million damages.

KNOWLES, JAMES DAVIS

b. 1798 Providence, Rhode Island, d. 1838. Hymnist. Educated at Columbian College; pastor of the Second Baptist Church, Boston (1825); professor at Newton Theological Institute (1832); wrote "O God, Through Countless Worlds of Light" (*Baptist Psalmist,* 1843).

KNOWLES, JOHN HARRIS

b. 1832 Cork, Ireland, d. 1908 New York City. Singer and choral leader. Educated at General Theological Seminary; sang in Trinity (Episcopal) Church choir, Chicago;

Episcopal rector in Aurora, Illinois, Naperville, Ill., St. Clement's, Chicago (1884), then in New York City.

KOBBE, GUSTAV

b. 1857 New York City, d. 1918 Bay Shore, New York. Music critic and teacher. Pupil of Adolf Hagen in Wiesbaden and Joseph Mosenthal in New York; graduated Columbia College (1877), Law School (1879); music critic in New York and a teacher, also published some songs; wrote *Wagner's Life and Works, The Ring of the Nibelung.*

KOCHANSKI, PAUL

b. 1887 Odessa, Russia, d. 1934 New York City. Violinist. Pupil of Cesar Thomson at the Brussels Conservatory; debut with Musical Society, Warsaw (1898); toured Europe and the United States; taught at the Juilliard School, New York, until 1934.

KOEHLER, TED

b. 1894 Washington, D.C., d. 1973.
Lyricist. Raised in New York City and Newark, N.J.; played the piano and became a song plugger; with composer Harold Arlen wrote "Get Happy" (1930), "Kicking the Gong Around" and "I Love a Parade" (1931), "Stormy Weather" (1933); wrote for films in Hollywood; also wrote lyrics for Burton Lane and Ted Fiorito.

KOEMMENICH, LOUIS

b. 1866 Elberfeld, Germany, d. 1922 New York City. Conductor and vocal teacher. Pupil of Anton Krause and Barmen; teacher and conductor at Kullak's Academy, N.Y. (1890); conductor of the Brooklyn Sangerbund (1894), the New York Oratorio Society (1912-17), Mendelssohn Glee Club (1913-19), and New York Beethoven Society (1917-22); composed a cantata, choruses.

KOFLER, LEO

b. 1837 Brixen, Austria, d. 1908 New Orleans, Louisiana. Organist and composer. Became choirmaster and organist of St. Paul's Chapel, New York City (1877).

KOLAR, VICTOR

b. 1888 Budapest, Hungary, d. 1941 Detroit, Michigan. Conductor and composer. Studied at the Prague Conservatory (1904); violinist with the New York Symphony (1907-19); associate conductor of the Detroit Symphony after 1919; composed symphonic and chamber music.

KONITZ, LEE

b. 1927 Chicago, Illinois.
Alto saxophonist. Played with Miles Davis, Claude Thornhill, Stan Kenton and others; toured Europe (1965-66).

KONRAD, WILLIAM

b. 1869 Fulton, Illinois, d. 1942.
Violinist, composer, and teacher. Studied under Fischer, Fehl, and S.E. Jacobson; debut at age thirteen; first theatrical performance at age fifteen; played first violin at Academy of Music after 1889; taught violin at Western Musical School, Fulton; wrote *Largo for String Quartet, Duet for Zither and Piano.*

KORNGOLD, ERICH WOLFGANG

b. 1897 Brno, Moravia, d. 1957 Hollywood, California. Composer. Son of Julius Korngold, a music critic in Vienna; composed *The Showman,* at only eleven years of age, which was presented in thirty theaters, *Schauspieloverture,* op. 4 and *Sinfonietta,* op. 5 at the age of fourteen, then the one-act operas *Der Ring des Polykrates* and *Violanta;* the opera *Die tote Stadt* (*The Dead City*); settled in Hollywood in 1934 and composed music for moving pictures.

KORNGOLD, JULIUS

b. 1860 Brno, Moravia, Czechoslovakia, d. 1945 Hollywood, California. Critic. Studied law, then became music critic of the *Neue Freie Presse* in Vienna, Austria.

KOSAKOFF, REUVEN

b. 1898 New Haven, Connecticut.
Composer. Composed a number of songs, chamber music, and *Concerto Palestine* for piano.

KOSTELANETZ, ANDRE

b. 1901 St. Petersburg, Russia.
Famous conductor, pianist, and composer. Piano debut at age eight; studied at St. Petersburg Academy; chorus master of Petrograd Opera (1920); came to New York City (1922) as accompanist and coach for Metropolitan Opera; conducted for CBS after 1931; married Lily Pons, opera singer; toured Pacific playing for servicemen in World War II; composed the *Music for Tomorrow* for the New York World's Fair (1939).

KOTZSCHMAR, HERMANN

b. 1829 Finsterwalde, Germany, d. 1909 Portland, Maine. Organist and conductor. Studied with Julius Otto in Dresden; came to

America (1848), and settled in Portland, Maine (1849) where he was an organist and conductor of the Haydn Association.

KOUGUELL, ARKADIE

b. 1897 Simferopol, Crimea, Russia.
Composer. Director of the State Music School in the Crimea, then at the American University in Beirut, Lebanon, later in Tel Aviv, Paris, and then New York City; composed *Hora Rhapsody, Hebrew Rhapsody, Jacob and Rachel* (ballet), and *Melodie et Danse Hebraique.*

KOUSSEVITZKY, SERGE

b. 1874 Vishny-Volotchok, Russia, d. 1951 Boston, Massachusetts. Famous conductor. Both of his parents, who were Orthodox Jews, were also musicians; studied in Moscow, Berlin, and Vienna with Nikisch and Mahler; moved to Paris (1920), then to America where he became conductor of the Boston Symphony Orchestra (1924), and of the Berkshire Music Festival at Tanglewood, Lenox, Mass. (1936).

KOUTZEN, BORIS

b. 1901 Uman, Russia, d. 1966.
Violinist and composer. Came to U.S. (1924); with Philadelphia Orchestra; composed *Solitude* (nocturne, Philadelphia Orchestra under composer, 1927), *Concerto for Five Solo Instruments and String Orchestra* (1935) *Valley Forge* (symphonic poem, National Orchestra Association, New York, under Barzin, 1940), Symphony in C, *Mouvement Symphonique* for violin and piano; String Quartet no. 2 (Society for Publishers of American Music Award).

KRAL, IRENE

b. 1932 Chicago, Illinois.
Singer. Sister of Roy Kral; sang with Woody Herman, Maynard Ferguson, Stan Kenton, Herb Pomeroy and other bands; married to trumpeter Joe Burnett.

KRAL, ROY JOSEPH

b. 1921 Chicago, Illinois.
Singer and pianist. Sang with his wife, Jackie Cain, in the Charlie Ventura combo (1948-49); the duo sang in Las Vegas night clubs during 1950s; in New York City after 1962.

KRAMER, ARTHUR WALTER

b. 1890 New York City, d. 1969.
Editor and composer. Studied with his father, Maximilian Kramer, James Abraham, and others; on the editorial staff of *Musical America* (1916-21), editor (1929-36); vice-president of Galaxy Musical Corp., New York music publishers; composed *Rococo Romance* (choral cycle), *Interlude for a Drama* (wordless, for solo, oboe, cello, and piano), *The Hour of Prayer* (for chorus), two symphonic sketches.

KREHBIEL, HENRY EDWARD

b. 1854 Ann Arbor, Michigan, d. 1923 New York City. Critic. Graduated the University of Cincinnati, Ohio; music critic of *Cincinnati Gazette;* later editor of *Music Review,* New York, then critic on *New York Tribune* (1880-1923); wrote *How to Listen to Music, Music and Manners in the 18th Century, Chapters of Opera, Studies in the Wagnerian Drama, Afro-American Songs, The Pianoforte and Its Music, A Book of Operas, A Second Book of Operas, More Chapters of Operas.*

KREISLER, FRITZ

b. 1875 Vienna, Austria, d. 1962 New York City. Famous violinist. Pupil of Massart and Delibes; debut in Paris; toured Europe and America; composed a string quartet, operettas, violin pieces, etc. which he attributed to composers of the past, having obtained the original manuscripts; then in 1935 he announced that they were his own compositions, astounding the musical world.

KRENEK, ERNST

b. 1900 Vienna, Austria.
Composer. Came to America (1933) and taught at Vassar College, Poughkeepsie, N.Y., Hamline University, St. Paul, Minn., and the Chicago Musical College; composed the opera *Jonny Spielt Auf* introduced by the Leipzig Opera (1927), Concerto no. 3 for Piano and Orchestra (1946, introduced by the Minneapolis Symphony Orchestra under Dimitri Mitropoulos), Symphony no. 4 (1947) and Symphony no. 5 (1950, introduced by the Albuquerque Symphony under Kurt Frederick), and the cantata *Die Zwingburg* (w. Franz Werfel).

KRESS, CARL

b. 1907 Newark, New Jersey, d. 1965 Reno, Nevada. Guitarist. Played with Red Nichols, Jimmy and Tommy Dorsey during late 1920s; recorded with Nichols and the Dorsey Brothers; later with Eddie Lang; died of a heart attack.

KREUTZ, ARTHUR

b. 1906 La Crosse, Wisconsin.
Composer. Studied at Brussels Conservatory,

the University of Wisconsin, Madison, Columbia University, N.Y. (M.A.); won Guggenheim Fellowship and American Prix de Rome; composed *Music for Symphony Orchestra* (NBC Symphony under Frank Black, 1940), *American Dances* (WOR Sinfonietta under Katims, 1941), *Symphonic Sketch on Three American Folk Tunes* (ISCM Festival, Berkeley, Calif. 1942), *Long May Our Land Be Bright* (University Symphony under composer, Austin, Texas).

KRIENS, CHRISTIAAN

b. 1881 Amsterdam, Netherlands, d. 1934 West Hartford, Connecticut. Conductor and composer. Studied at Hague Conservatory; debut with his father's orchestra in Amsterdam (1895); conductor of his own orchestra; toured Europe; conductor of French Opera Company, New Orleans, La. (1906); teacher and conductor in New York after 1907.

KRIPS, JOSEPH

b. 1902 Vienna, Austria, d. 1974.
Conductor. Studied at the Vienna Academy under Felix Weingartner; became music director in Karlsruhe, Germany (1926), then at the Vienna State Opera in the 1930s; when the Nazis came to power he was forbidden to participate in any musical performances, and was a day laborer for eight years; conductor of the London Symphony (1949-53), Buffalo (N.Y.) Philharmonic (1953-57), and became conductor of the San Francisco Symphony in 1963.

KROEGER, ERNEST RICHARD

b. 1862 St. Louis, Missouri, d. there 1934. Pianist, teacher, and composer. Taught at Forest Park University, then had his own music school in St. Louis after 1904; composed *Lalla Rookh* (orchestral suite), overtures, piano pieces, Piano Sonata op. 33.

KRONOLD, SELMA

b. 1866, d. 1920.
Soprano. With the Hinrichs Opera Company (1889-93); at the Academy of Music, Philadelphia.

KRUEGER, KARL

b. 1894 New York City.
Conductor. Studied with Fuchs and others; cellist and organist; toured Europe and South America; conductor of Seattle Symphony Orchestra (1926-31), Kansas City Philharmonic after 1933, and Detroit Symphony after 1943.

KRUPA, GENE

b. 1909 Chicago, Illinois, d. 1973.
Jazz drummer. With Benny Goodman's band; left in 1938 after a blow-up with Goodman at the Earle Theater in Philadelphia; formed his own band and opened at the Steel Pier in Atlantic City, N.J.; with Anita O'Day, singer, and Roy Eldridge, trumpeter, the band enjoyed its greatest success; Gene was arrested in California on a marijuana possession charge but later released; on "Vibrations" (1972), TV Channel 13 program.

KUBELIK, RAFAEL

b. 1914 Batchory, Czechoslovakia.
Music director. Son of violinist Jan Kubelik (*see* Rudolf Friml); graduated Prague Conservatory; conducted Czech Philharmonic (1936-48); music director of Chicago Symphony Orchestra after 1950, then appointed music director of Metropolitan Opera Company, New York for the 1973-74 season; stood 6'4" tall; first married violinist Ludmila Bertlova, she died; then married Elsie Morison, Australian soprano.

KUBIK, GAIL T.

b. 1914 South Coffeyville, Oklahoma.
Composer. Graduated Eastman School, Rochester, N.Y.; won Guggenheim Fellowship; composer for Army films (1943); composed *Whoopee-Ti-Yi-Yo* (for small orchestra based on cowboy tunes, CBS Concert Orchestra under Bernard Herrmann, 1941), *Men and Ships* (symphonic piece), Concerto in D for Violin and Orchestra (won Carl Fischer Prize), *American Caprice* (for piano and small orchestra), *Puck* (for chamber orchestra); won Sinfonia National Award.

KUERTI, ANTON

b. 1934 Vienna, Austria.
Pianist. Studied in America; opposed U.S. involvement in Vietnam and went to Canada; became pianist in residence at University of Toronto, Ontario (1965); albums—*Beethoven, Schubert, Mendelssohn, Chopin Etudes, Mozart Fantasia, Scriabin Sonatas, Alban Berg, Schumann.*

KUHN, STEPHEN LEWIS

b. 1938 Brooklyn, New York.
Pianist. Studied piano at age five; graduated Harvard (1959); with John Coltrane, Stan Getz, Art Farmer and others during 1960s; at Newport Jazz Festival (1963) with Getz, and Monterey Jazz Festival (1964) with Farmer; appeared on Steve Allen's TV show.

KULLMANN, CHARLES

b. 1903 New Haven, Connecticut.
Tenor. Studied at Juilliard School of Music, New York City and at Fontainebleau; toured Europe as a soloist with Yale Glee Club; debut with American Opera Company (1929); debut with Metropolitan Opera, New York City (1935); with Metropolitan (1935-50, and again 1954-60).

KUNITS, LUIGI VON *see* VON KUNITS

KUPFERMAN, MEYER

b. 1926 New York City.
Composer. Graduated Queens College, N.Y.; won first La Guardia Award; taught at Sarah Lawrence College after 1951; wrote film background scores; his Symphony no. 4 was commissioned by the Louisville Orchestra and no. 5 by Samuel Rudofker; wrote *Chamber Symphony, Concerto for Six Instruments, Divertimento for Orchestra, Partita for Piano, Six String Quartets, Four Pieces for Cello and Piano.*

KURT, MELANIE

b. 1880 Vienna, Austria, d. 1941 New York City. Opera singer and violinist. Studied at Vienna Conservatory and with Leschetizky; toured as a pianist; sang with Lilli Lehmann; in German opera (1905-12); then sang Wagnerian roles with Metropolitan Opera, New York City (1915-17).

KURTZ, EDWARD FRAMPTON

b. 1881 New Castle, Pennsylvania.
Composer. Graduated State University of Iowa (M.A.); studied at Pittsburgh Conservatory, Cincinnati and Detroit Conservatories; studied with Ysaye, Clapp, Stillman-Kelley, and Goetschius; taught at Iowa State; his March in D (1919) played by Cincinnati, Cleveland, St. Louis, and Minneapolis Symphonies, *Scherzo* from the Symphony in A minor (1927) by Rochester Philharmonic.

KWARTIN, ZAVEL

b. 1874 Nowo Archangelks, d. 1953 Brooklyn, New York. Baritone and composer. Cantor in Vienna, St. Petersburg, Budapest, then at the Temple Emanu-El in Brooklyn, N.Y.; one of the finest interpreters of chazzanuth.

KWESKIN JUG BAND, THE JIM (jug band)

Jim Kweskin, vocals and guitar; Geoff Muldaur, vocals, washboard, etc.; Richard Greene, fiddle; Maria d'Amato, vocals and tambourine; Bill Keith, banjo and guitar; Fritz Richmond, jug and washboard bass; started in Cambridge, Mass. (1963); albums—*Best of Jim Kweskin and the Jug Band, Garden of Joy, Jug Band Music, Jump for Joy, Jim Kweskin and the Jug Band, Relax Your Mind, Whatever Happened to Those Good Old Days.*

KYLE, WILLIAM OSBORNE (BILLY)

b. 1914 Philadelphia, Pennsylvania, d. 1966 Youngstown, Ohio. Black jazz pianist. Played in Lucky Millinder's band; with the John Kirby Sextet (1938-42); with Louis Armstrong (1953-66); died following an ulcer attack.

KYNARD, CHARLES E.

b. 1933 St. Louis, Missouri.
Organist. Studied piano in Kansas City, Mo. (1942); graduated the University of Kansas in music education; toured world with U.S. Army show (1956-57); with Kansas City Philharmonic (1961); later played in Hollywood studio orchestras.

KYSER, KAY

b. 1905 Rocky Mount, North Carolina.
Bandleader. Formed his band at the University of North Carolina, Chapel Hill, N.C.; opened at the Blackhawk Restaurant, Chicago (1934); on the American Tobacco Company radio program; famous for his "College of Musical Knowledge"; also his trumpeter "Ishkabibble" (Merwyn Bogue); married Georgia Carroll, his singer; later retired to North Carolina where he became a Christian Science healer.

LA BELLE, PATTI (black vocal group)

Sarah Dash and Nona Hendryx (with organist Andre Lewis); record—"Moon Shadow" (1972).

LACHMUND, CARL VALENTINE

b. 1857 Booneville, Missouri, d. 1928 Yonkers, New York. Pianist, conductor, teacher, and composer. Studied in Cologne with Heller, Jensen, and Seiss (1870); also four years with Liszt at Weimar; composed *Japanese Overture* (performed by Thomas and Seidl), trio (played by Berlin Philharmonic Orchestra).

LACIAR, SAMUEL LINE

b. 1874 Mauch Chunk, Pennsylvania, d. 1943 Philadelphia, Pennsylvania. Critic, editor, and composer. Music editor of *The Press* (1900-05), the Curtis Publishing Company (1905-12), and the *Evening Ledger*, Philadelphia, after 1912; composed chamber music.

LACY, STEVE

b. 1934 New York City.
Soprano saxist. Born Steven Lackritz; played with Cecil Taylor, Gil Evans, and Jimmy Giuffre during 1950s; led own quartet with Roswell Rudd and Dennis Charles; in Copenhagen, Denmark (1963) with Kenny Drew; at Bologna, Italy Jazz Festival; in Europe after 1965 with Carla Bley in Jazz Realities; also led his own group there with trumpeter Enrico Rava.

LADNIER, TOMMY

b. 1900 Mandeville, Louisiana, d. 1939 New York City. Black cornetist. Joined Fletcher Henderson's band (1926); Panassie came to America in 1938 and persuaded Ladnier and Mezz Mezzrow to cut some records, also with Ladnier and Sidney Bechet, which records became jazz classics.

LA FARGE, PETER

b. 1931 Fountain, Colorado, d. 1965 New York City. Popular composer. An American Indian, he was the adopted son of Oliver LaFarge, the novelist; served in the Korean War and won five battle stars; wrote "Ira Hayes," "Black Stallion," "Coyote," "As Long as the Grass Shall Grow."

LA FARO, SCOTT

b. 1936 Newark, New Jersey, d. 1961 Geneva, New York. Bass player. Played with Chet Baker, Barney Kessel, and Howard Rumsey during 1950s; led his own trio in New York City (1960-61); killed in an auto accident.

LA FORGE, FRANK

b. 1877 Rockford, Illinois, d. 1953 New York City. Pianist and voice teacher. Pupil of Harrison M. Wild of Chicago and Leschetizky in Vienna (1900-04); accompanist for Gadski and Sembrich on tours; then was a voice teacher in New York City; composed piano pieces and songs—"Like the Rosebud," "Song of the Open" (w. J.H. Lowell), "Retreat or Schlupfwinkel" (w. Princess Gabriele Wrede); died while giving a concert.

LA HACHE, THEODOR VON *see*
VON LA HACHE

LAINE, FRANKIE

b. 1913 Chicago, Illinois.
Singer. Born Frank Lo Vecchio; sang for Joe Kayser's band (1930); then the depression hit, and there was little work; joined Fred Croyole's band (1937); had other odd jobs; sang in Hollywood night clubs (1946); toured England (1954); had his own show on CBS-TV (1955-56).

LAINE, GEORGE VITELLE ("PAPA JACK")

b. 1873 New Orleans, Louisiana, d. 1966.
Drummer and bandleader. Organized first white and black jazz band in New Orleans (1888) called the Reliance Brass Band for parades and the Ragtime Band for dances; players included Achille Baquet, black clarinetist, and Dave Perkins, black trombonist.

LAIR, JOHN LEE

b. 1894 Livingston, Kentucky.
Manager, songwriter, and producer.

Produced WLS "National Barn Dance," Chicago (1927-28); with Red Foley started "Renfro Valley Barn Dance" (1938); wrote "Freight Train Blues," "The Man That Comes Around," "Win or Lose," "Take Me Back to Renfro Valley," "Little Birdie."

LAMARE, HILTON ("NAPPY")

b. 1907. New Orleans, Louisiana.
Guitarist. banjoist, and singer. Played with Ben Pollock and Bob Crosby in 1930s; later with various groups in Los Angeles; with Bob Crosby in Las Vegas (1962); with Eddie Miller in Cleveland (1963); with other groups in Los Angeles.

LAMB, ARTHUR J.

b. 1870 Somerset, England, d. 1928 Providence, Rhode Island. Lyricist. Wrote the lyrics "Asleep in the Deep" (1897, m. H.W. Petrie), "Dreaming of Mother and Home" (1898, m. J.S. May), "At the Bottom of the Deep Blue Sea" (1899, m. Petrie), "A Bird in a Gilded Cage" (1900, m. Harry von Tilzer).

LAMB, JOHN LEE

b. 1933 Vero Beach, Florida.
Bass player. Studied at Lincoln Park Academy; Air Force School of Music; with U.S. Air Force dance bands; studied at Philadelphia Musical Academy; led his own sextet in Philadelphia (1957-59); with Paul Currey Trio, Johnny Walker Trio, and Duke Ellington in 1960s.

LAMB, JOSEPH FRANCIS

b. 1887 Montclair, New Jersey, d. 1960 Brooklyn, New York. Ragtime pianist and composer. Wrote "Sensation" (1908), "Excelsior Rag" (1909), "Ethiopia Rag" (1909), "Champagne Rag" (1910), "American Beauty Rag" (1913); also the songs "Love in Absence" (1909, w. Mary O'Reilly), "I'll Follow the Crowd" (1913, w. G. Satterlee), "I Want to Be a Birdman" (1913, Satterlee).

LAMBERT, ALEXANDER

b. 1862 Warsaw, Poland, d. 1929 New York City. Pianist. Son of Henry L. Lambert; studied at Vienna Conservatory under Julius Epstein, later under Liszt at Weimar; concert pianist in Germany; came to New York to live (1884); appeared at Steinway Hall with Remenyi; played at concerts conducted by Franz van der Stucken; later head of the New York College of Music; killed by a taxicab.

LAMBERT, DAVID ALDEN

b. 1917 Boston, Massachusetts.
Singer and vocal arranger. With the Lambert-Hendricks-Ross vocal trio after 1958; later Yolande Bavan replaced Annie Ross; settled in New York City (1964) as disc jockey and vocal leader.

LAMBERT, DONALD

b. 1904 Princeton, New Jersey, d. 1962.
Black pianist. In duo piano act with Paul Seminole; recorded for Bluebird and Circle.

LAMBERT, LOUIS

b. 1835 Charleroi, Pennsylvania, d. 1910 Newfoundland, New Jersey. Lyricist. Ordained a Roman Catholic priest (1859) for the diocese of Alton, Illinois; chaplain of the 18th Illinois Infantry during the Civil War; wrote the lyrics "When Johnny Comes Marching Home" (1863, m. credited to Patrick S. Gilmore); wrote *Chants et Chansons* published in Paris (1880).

LAMBERT, LUCIEN

b. 1828 New Orleans, Louisiana, d. (?) Brazil. Black pianist. Brother of Sydney Lambert; studied piano at the Paris Conservatory; returned to the United States; made successful concert tours here; later became court musician to Dom Pedro, Emperor of Brazil; his son, Lucian Lambert (1858-1945) was a noted composer.

LAMBERT, SYDNEY

b. 1823 New Orleans, Louisiana, d. (?) France. Black pianist and teacher. Brother of Lucian Lambert; studied at the Paris Conservatory; became a teacher in Paris, France.

LAMOND, FELIX

b. 1864 London, England, d. 1940 New York City. Organist-choirmaster at Trinity Chapel, New York City (1897-1918); with the American Red Cross in World War I, then director of musical composition at the American Academy, Rome, Italy (1918-40).

LAMONT, FORREST

b. 1885 Athelsyan, Canada, d. 1937 Chicago, Illinois. Tenor. Studied in the United States and Europe; made his opera debut in Rome; toured the West Indies and South America; sang with the Chicago Opera Company after 1917; later with the Cincinnati and Philadelphia Opera Companies.

LAMP OF CHILDHOOD (Jim Hendricks) *see* MUGWUMPS

LAND, HAROLD DE VANCE

b. 1928 Houston, Texas.
Tenor saxist. Played with Max Roach-Clifford

Brown Quintet, and Curtis Counce during 1950s; with Gerald Wilson at Monterey Jazz Festival (1963); led own groups in San Francisco, Los Angeles, and Vancouver, B.C., during 1960s.

LANDON, CHARLES W.

b. 1856 Lakeville, Connecticut, d. 1918. Composer, teacher, and writer. Studied with William Mason and William H. Sherwood; established the Claverack College Conservatory, Claverack, N.Y.; president of the New York State Music Teachers' Association (1889).

LANDSBERG, MAX

b. 1845 Berlin, Germany, d. 1928 Rochester, New York. Compiler. Jewish rabbi who studied at the Jewish seminary at Breslau; in 1871 called to the Temple Berith Kodesh in Rochester, which post he held for twenty-four years; with Newton Mann translated *Praise to the Living God* (1885) setting for the *Yigdal*, the thirteen articles of the Jewish creed; there are seven tunes for the *Yigdal*, the second being "Leoni," transcribed by Meyer Lyon, chief singer of the Great Synagogue.

LANDSHOFF, LUDWIG

b. 1874 Stettin, Poland, d. 1941 New York City. Editor and compiler of early music, and musicologist; wrote *Alte Meister des Bel Canto* in two volumes.

LANE, BURTON

b. 1912 New York City.
Pianist and composer. With Remick's in Tin Pan Alley, then with Irving Berlin; wrote the Broadway reviews *Three's a Crowd* (1930), *Third Little Show* (1931), *Hold On to Your Hats* (1940), *Laughing Room Only* (1944, Olsen and Johnson production), *Finian's Rainbow* (1947, w. E.Y. Harburg); best-known songs were "Swing High, Swing Low" (w. Ralph Freed), "You're Breaking My Heart" (w. Ted Koehler), "Moments Like This" (w. Frank Loesser), "How Are Things in Glocca Mora?" (1947), "On a Clear Day You Can See Forever" (1966, w. Alan Jay Lerner).

LANE, SPENCER

b. 1843 Tilton, New Hampshire, d. 1903 Reedville, Virginia. Composer. Served four years in the army during the Civil War; organist and choirmaster at St. James' (Episcopal) Church, Woonsocket, R.I. for thirteen years; at Monson, Mass., Richmond, Va., then All-Saints Church, Baltimore; composed the tune "Penitence" (1875, in Woonsocket, "In the Hour of Trial," *J. Montgomery's Original Hymns*, 1835).

LANG, BENJAMIN JOHNSON

b. 1837 Salem, Massachusetts, d. 1909 Boston, Massachusetts. Conductor. Studied in Europe under Liszt, then became organist in the Old South Church and later the South Congregational Church in Boston, then to King's Chapel (1885); organist for the Handel and Haydn Society (1859-95) and its director (1895-97); founded and directed the Boston Apollo Club (1871-1901) and the Cecilia Club (1874-1907); composed the oratorio *David.*

LANG, EDDIE

b. 1902 Philadelphia, Pennsylvania, d. there 1933. Jazz guitarist. Born Salvatore Massaro; played with the Dorsey brothers in the Scranton Sirens, later the Mound City Blue Blowers; with Joe Venuti and others in 1920s; later with Paul Whiteman and Bing Crosby; died following a tonsillectomy.

LANG, HENRY ALBERT

b. 1854 New Orleans, Louisiana, d. 1930 Philadelphia, Pennsylvania. Pianist, teacher, and composer. Studied in Germany; came to Philadelphia (1891); headed department of theory at Philadelphia Conservatory (1913-30); composed two symphonies, violin concerto, piano pieces, songs.

LANG, MICHAEL ANTHONY

b. 1941 Los Angeles, California.
Pianist. Son of film producer Jennings Lang; studied piano at age five; studied under Pearl Kaufman; graduated the University of Michigan (1963); played with Bob Pozar Trio, Paul Horn Quintet, and Los Angeles Neophonic Orchestra during 1960s.

LANGDON, CHAUNCEY

b. 1763 Farmington, Connecticut, d. 1830 Castleton, Vermont. Compiler. Graduated Yale (1787), then studied law in Hebron, Conn.; settled in Castleton, Vt. and became a member of Congress (1815-17); in 1786, while a junior at Yale, published *The Beauties of Psalmody.*

LANGFORD, FRANCES

b. 1913 Lakeland, Florida.
Singer and actress. She sang with Louis Armstrong on several records; appeared in films; albums—*The Bickersons, The Bickersons Fight Back.*

LANGSTROTH, IVAN

b. 1887 Alameda, California, d. 1971 New York City. Composer and teacher. Toured the Scandinavian countries (1917-20) as a concert pianist; taught theory and composition in

Vienna until 1939 when he returned to the United States to teach at the Chatham Square Music School, New York City.

LANIER, SIDNEY

b. 1842 Macon, Georgia, d. 1881 Lynn, North Carolina. Lyricist. Poet; had been a soldier in the Confederate army in Virginia and a flute player in Baltimore; wrote the lyrics "The Centennial Meditation of Columbia" (1876, m. Dudley Buck), and "Into the Woods My Master Went" (1880, tune—"Lanier," P.C. Lutkin, which appeared in *The Methodist Hymnal*, 1905), "Ballad of the Trees and the Master" (m. Arthur Shepherd).

LANZA, MARIO

b. 1921 Philadelphia, Pennsylvania, d. 1959. Noted tenor. Born Alfredo Arnold Cocozza; studied with Irene Williams in Philadelphia, Grant Garnell, and Enrico Rosati; scholarship at Tanglewood, Mass. (1942); in Special Services in World War II as a singer; debut at Grant Park, Chicago (1946); Hollywood Bowl (1946); appeared in several films after 1947; lead in *The Great Caruso* (1951).

LAPETINA, F. M.

b. 1858 Naples, Italy, d. 1943.
Violinist and mandolin player. Studied in Italy; later teacher of violin and mandolin in Philadelphia; composed a number of pieces for the violin and mandolin; author of a mandolin method.

LAPHAM, CLAUDE

b. 1890 Fort Scott, Kansas, d. 1957.
Composer. His compositions were based on Japanese themes; composed *Japanese Concerto* for piano and orchestra, *Miharayama* (tone poem for orchestra, Tokyo Symphony under Klaus Pringsheim, 1935), song cycles.

LA PORTA, JOHN D.

b. 1920 Philadelphia, Pennsylvania.
Saxist and clarinetist. Played with Woody Herman, Charles Mingus, Leonard Bernstein, Igor Stravinsky and others during 1950s; later taught at Berklee School of Music; directed Boston Youth Band after 1964.

LARCOM, LUCY

b. 1826 Beverly, Massachusetts, d. there 1893. Hymnist. Worked in the cotton mills of Lawrence, Mass., then became a school teacher; she wrote the lyrics "I Learned It in the Meadow Path" (1885, m. J.A. Lloyd, 1844), and "Draw Thou My Soul, O Christ" (1892, tune—"St. Edmund," A.S. Sullivan).

LA ROCA, PETER SIMS (PETE)

b. 1938 New York City.
Drummer. Played with Sonny Rollins, Tony Scott, and Slide Hampton in 1950s; with John Coltrane, Art Farmer Quartet, Charles Lloyd and own groups in 1960s.

LA ROCCA, DOMINIC JAMES (NICK)

b. 1889 New Orleans, Louisiana, d. there 1961. Cornetist and bandleader. Son of an Italian immigrant shoemaker; played in New Orleans bars (1908); went to Chicago (1914) and joined the Dixie Jass Band; leader of the Original Dixieland Band, played at the Paradise Club, New York City (1915); recorded "Tiger Rag" (1917, based on J.P. Sousa's "National Emblem March") with Larry Shields; played at Rector's Cafe in London (1919); gave command performance for King George V.

LAROQUE, PHILIP

b. ca. 1780, d. ca. 1838.
Violinist, pianist, composer, and teacher. Played his pastorale at a concert in New Orleans with Louis H. Desforges, violinist (1805); had three operas of his produced in 1810 at the St. Peter Street Theater, New Orleans—*La Jeune Mére, Nicodeme dans la Lune*, and *Pauvre Jacques;* wrote *Masonic March* (1813); his *Battle of the Memorable 8th of January 1815* was introduced at a concert in New Orleans on January 31, 1816.

LA ROSA, JULIUS

b. 1930 Brooklyn, New York.
Singer. Popular with the teenage group; sang "Lipstick and Candy," "Rubber Sole Shoes" (1956).

LASHA, WILLIAM B. ("PRINCE")

b. 1929 Fort Worth, Texas.
Black saxist and flutist. Played with Ornette Coleman during late 1940s; with Sonny Simmons, alto saxophonist, during 1950s and '60s; toured Europe (1965).

LATEEF, YUSEF

b. 1921 Chattanooga, Tennessee.
Black flutist, saxist, and writer. Born William Evans; played in night spots in Detroit during 1950s; with Charles Mingus, Babatundi Olatunji, Cannonball Adderley and leader of his own combo during 1960s; wrote *Yusef Lateef's Flute Book of Blues.*

LATHBURY, MARY ARTEMISIA

b. 1841 Manchester, New York, d. 1913 East Orange, New Jersey. Hymnist. Wrote the hymn "Day Is Dying in the West" (1877) for the Chautauqua, N.Y. Methodist camp meeting (tune "Chautauqua" or "Evening Praise" by W.F. Sherwin), also "Break Thou the Bread of Life" (1877, tune "Bread of Life," W.F. Sherwin).

LATOUCHE, JOHN

b. 1917 Richmond, Virginia, d. 1956 Calais, Vermont. Lyricist and librettist. Attended Columbia University, New York City; with composer Earl Robinson wrote "Ballad for Uncle Sam" for the WPA revue *Sing for Your Supper* (1939), the song later renamed "Ballad for Americans"; wrote the lyrics for "Cabin in the Sky" (1940, m. Vernon Duke); with Harold Adamson, wrote the lyrics for Eddie Cantor's show *Banjo Eyes* (1941, m. Duke); also book and lyrics for *The Golden Apple* (m. Jerome Moross, produced 1954); libretto for *The Ballad of Baby Doe* (m. Douglas Moore), produced at the Central City Opera House, Central City, Colorado (1956).

LAUFER, CALVIN WEISS

b. 1874 Brodheadsville, Pennsylvania, d. 1938. Composer. Educated at Franklin and Marshall College, Lancaster, Pa., and Union Theological Seminary, N.Y.; Presbyterian minister serving in Long Island City, N.Y., and West Hoboken, N.J.; then became an editor of church publications and resided in Philadelphia; wrote the words and music of the hymns "O Thou Eternal Christ of God" (tune—"Percival-Smith," 1933) and "We Thank Thee, Lord" (tune—"Field," 1919).

LAVALLEE, CALIXA

b. 1842 Vercheres, Canada, d. 1891 Boston, Massachusetts. Pianist. Toured the United States as a concert pianist; composed two operas, a symphony, an oratorio.

LA VALLEY, DOUG LOUIS

b. 1934 Boston, Massachusetts.
Singer and songwriter. Attended school in Mooers, N.Y., and Plattsburgh, N.Y.; on station CKCW, Moniton, New Brunswick, Canada, after 1959; wrote "When I Stop Loving You," "Have You Seen Suzie" (1959), "I Want To," "Alone with You," "Unwanted Stranger, How Reckless Can You Be" (1959).

LA VIOLETTE, WESLEY

b. 1894 St. James, Minnesota.
Composer. Graduated Northwestern University, Evanston, Ill., Chicago Music College (Mus.D.); composed *The Spook Hour* (scherzino for orchestra, National Chamber Orchestra, N.Y., under Ganz, 1931), *Collegiana* (festival rhapsody for orchestra, Chicago Philharmonic under Czerwonky, 1936), *Chorale* (American Concert Orchestra, Chicago, under composer, 1936), *First Symphony* (Rochester Civic Orchestra under Hanson, 1938), *San Francisco* (overture, San Francisco Symphony under composer, 1941).

LAW, ANDREW

b. 1748 Milford, Connecticut, d. 1821 Cheshire, Connecticut. Compiler. Graduated Brown University, Providence, R.I. (1775), with M.A. (1778); the Rev. Law was a teacher of music; published *Plain Tunes* (1767), *Select Harmony* (1779), *Musical Primer* (1780), *Christian Harmony* (1805), *A Collection of the Best and Most Approved Tunes* (1779), *A Collection of Hymns for Social Worship* (1782), *Rudiments of Music* (1783), *The Harmonic Companion* and *The Art of Playing the Organ* (1807).

LAWATSCH, ANNA MARIA DEMUTH

b. 1712 Karlsdorf, Moravia, Czechoslovakia, d. 1759 Bethlehem, Pennsylvania. Hymnist. Her hymns appeared in Moravian (United Brethren) hymnals.

LAWLOR, CHARLES B.

b. 1852 Dublin, Ireland, d. 1925 New York City. Popular composer. Lawlor and Jim Thornton were a vaudeville team; with lyricist Thornton wrote "The Irish Jubilee" (1890), "Upper Ten, Lower Five"; he wrote the lyrics "Pretty Jenny Slattery" (1896, m. J.W. Blake) and "Best in the House" (1896, m. J.W. Bratton); with lyricist J.W. Blake wrote "Daisy McIntyre" (1897), and "The Sidewalks of New York" which was introduced by Lottie Gilson in the Old London Theatre in the Bowery, New York City (1894), and which became the theme song of Al Smith when he ran for Governor of New York and then for the Presidency in 1928.

LAWRENCE, ELLIOTT

b. 1925 Philadelphia, Pennsylvania.
Pianist, bandleader, and composer. Organized his own band in late 1940s; at one time Gerry Mulligan was his arranger; musical director and arranger for Broadway musical shows in 1960s.

LAWRENCE, STEVE

b. 1935 Brooklyn, New York.
Singer. Appeared on "Steve Allen's Tonight Show" (1955); married Eydie Gorme, singer; joined army (1958) as vocalist for the Army Band-Orchestra at Fort Myer, Virginia; later appeared on the "Gary Moore Show"; starred in the Broadway musical *What Makes Sammy Run?* (1964, libretto—Budd and Stuart Schulberg).

LAWS, HUBERT

b. 1939 Houston, Texas.
Flutist and musician. Played saxophone with Jazz Crusaders (1954-60); with Mongo Santamaria, Orchestra USA, Sergio Mendes and others in 1960s; at the CTI Summer Jazz Festival, New York City (1972).

LAWSON, JOHN R. ("YANK")

b. 1911 Trenton, New Jersey.
Trumpeter. Played with various bands during late 1930s, '40s and '50s; with Louis Armstrong, Bob Crosby and others in 1960s, at Eddie Condon's club in New York City (1963-65); with trombonist Vic Dickenson at the Newport Jazz Festival, New York City (1972).

LAWSON, WARNER

b. 1903 Hartford, Connecticut.
Black pianist and teacher. Graduated Fisk University, Nashville, Tenn., Yale (B.Mus., 1929); taught at North Carolina A&T College, Greensboro, and Fisk University; head of music department at Howard University, Washington, D.C. after 1942; directed the Howard University Choir with National Symphony Orchestra, Washington, D.C.

LAYTON, JOHN TURNER

b. 1849, d. 1916 Washington, D.C.
Black composer and compiler. Taught in the public schools in Washington, D.C. (1883-1916); compiled a *Hymnal for Use by the African Methodist Episcopal Church*, which included some of his tunes and two tunes by Henry F. Grant, who was also black; Grant taught in the public schools there also.

LAYTON, TURNER

b. 1894 Washington, D.C.
Black singer, pianist, and composer. Teamed with Henry Creamer in the vaudeville act of Layton & Johnson; later they settled in England and were popular entertainers there; with lyricist Creamer wrote "After You've Gone" (1918), "Way Down Yonder in New Orleans" (1922), "Dear Old Southland" (1921).

LAZARUS, EMMA

b. 1849 New York City, d. 1894.
Lyricist. She was of Sephardic ancestry; wrote *The New Colossus* (1883), which was inscribed on a tablet on the Statue of Liberty, New York Harbor (1903); her *Songs of a Semite* (1883) included "The Banner of the Jew" which later became a popular Zionist anthem.

LEACH, ROWLAND

b. 1885 Haverhill, Massachusetts.
Composer. Educated at Beloit College, Beloit, Wisconsin, and at Yale (1910); taught violin and theory in New Haven, Conn., Rockford College, Ill., Calgary, Alberta, Can., Bush Conservatory of Music, Chicago, De Pauw University, Greencastle, Indiana, and the University of Redlands, Calif.; composed the tune "Welcome" ("Welcome, Day of the Lord," w. Percy Dearmer).

LEADBELLY (HUDDIE LEDBETTER)

b. 1885 Mooringsport, Louisiana, d. 1949 New York City. Popular black composer. He picked cotton, sang, and played the guitar; got in brawls, spent 1918-25 in prison in Texas, 1930-34 in prison in Louisiana; recorded for John A. Lomax (1932) while in prison; wrote "Goodnight Irene," "Easy Rider," "Rock Island Line," "Gray Goose," "Good Morning Blues," "The Midnight Special," "Whoa Back Buck," "Keep Your Hands Off Her," "Fannin Street, New York City," (some adaptations of folk music).

LEAMONT, ROBERT

b. ca. 1760, d. ca. 1810.
Violinist, conductor, composer, and teacher. Leader of a theater orchestra in Boston (1795-99); then taught in Charleston, South Carolina until 1807; wrote *Le Rosier* (1810).

LEAR, EVELYN

b. 1929 New York City.
Soprano. "The Jewish-American Princess"; studied at Juilliard, New York City; debut in Alban Berg's *Lulu* in Vienna (1962); debut at Metropolitan Opera, New York City (1967); second marriage to baritone Thomas Stewart (1955); joint recital with husband at Hunter College (1972); also soloist at Town Hall and Carnegie Hall, New York City (1972).

LEAVITT, JOSHUA

b. 1794 Heath, Massachusetts, d. 1873.
Compiler. Graduated Yale (1814); became a Congregational minister; compiled *Christian Lyre* (1830) which included eight hymns of Jared Bell Waterbury.

LED ZEPPELIN (blues group)

Jimmy Page, formerly with the Yardbirds; John Paul Jones; Robert Plante; John Bonham; albums—*Led Zeppelin* (1969), *Led Zeppelin Volume II.*

LEE, BRENDA

b. 1944 Atlanta, Georgia.
Singer. Born Brenda Mae Tarpley; had her own TV show at age six; later on Springfield, Missouri TV show; on New York network TV (1956); later toured Europe and South America.

LEE, DAI KEONG

b. 1915 Honolulu, Hawaii.
Composer. Studied with Roger Sessions and others; won Guggenheim Fellowship; Juilliard Graduate School, N.Y.; composed two symphonies, *Prelude and Hula, Hawaiian Festival Overture, Golden Gate* (overture), *Pacific Prayer.*

LEE, JEANNE

b. 1939 New York City.
Singer. Studied singing with her father, a concert singer; also studied piano; formed trio (1962) which included pianist Ran Blake; at Monterey Jazz Festival (1962); toured Europe (1963).

LEE, JULIAN

b. 1923 Dunedin, New Zealand.
Pianist and arranger. Educated at New Zealand Foundation for Blind and Auckland University; arranger for New Zealand Broadcasting Company (1947-56); pianist and arranger in Sidney, Australia (1956-63); came to Los Angeles (1963); arranger for George Shearing and Gene Harris.

LEE, PEGGY

b. 1920 Jamestown, North Dakota.
Singer and songwriter. Born Norma Jean Engstrom; sang on a Fargo, N.D. radio station at age sixteen; sang for Will Osborne's band; recorded "Elmer's Tune" for Benny Goodman; married guitarist Dave Barbour; appeared in films; she wrote "Manaña," "It's a Good Day," "I Don't Know Enough About You" (with her husband, Dave Barbour, guitarist); sang at the Waldorf Hotel, New York City (1972).

LEE, ROSE

b. 1922 Baltimore, Maryland.
Singer and banjoist. She had her own radio program in Hagerstown, Maryland at age fifteen; married Joe Maphis and formed a very successful singing and instrumental duo.

LEEMAN, CLIFFORD

b. 1913 Portland, Maine.
Drummer. Played with Artie Shaw, Charlie Barnet, Jimmy and Tommy Dorsey and others in 1930s and '40s; with Bob Crosby, Red Nichols, Dukes of Dixieland and others in 1960s; toured Japan, Australia, and New Zealand (1964).

LEES, BENJAMIN

b. 1924 Harbin, Manchuria.
Composer. Family settled in Los Angeles when he was a child; served in armed forces in World War II; educated at the University of Southern California, Los Angeles; studied with George Antheil and others; known for *Profile for Orchestra* (string quartet, 1952), *Sonata for Two Pianos* (N.Y., 1952), *First Symphony Declamations* for piano and string orchestra (1955), Symphony no. 2 (Louisville, Ky. Orchestra, 1958), *Concerto for Violin and Orchestra* (1958, Boston Symphony, 1963, Henryk Szerying, soloist).

LEFEBVRE, CHANNING

b. 1895 Richmond, Virginia, d. 1967.
Composer. Studied at Peabody Conservatory, Baltimore, and at the Institute of Musical Art, New York City; served in the U.S. Navy in World War I; organist-choirmaster at St. Luke's, Montclair, N.J., then Trinity Church, New York City (1922-41), when he became director of music at St. Paul's School, Concord, N.H.; composed the music for "Fishermen's Night Hymn" (1941, w. Edith Clayton).

LE FEVRE, PIERCE AVON

b. 1936 Kannapolis, North Carolina.
Conductor. Attended high school in Atlanta, Ga.; graduated Tennessee Tech., Cookeville (1958); leader of Le Fevres after 1963 and with the Gospel Singing Caravan after 1962.

LE FEVRE, URIAS

b. 1910 Roosevelt, Oklahoma.
Conductor. Attended high school in Smithville, Tenn., and Lee College, Cleveland, Tenn. (1929-32); leader of Le Fevres (1921-63); group included his wife, Eva Mae Whittington, sons Alphus, Mylon Rae, and Pierce Avon.

LEFT BANKE (rock group)

Rick Brand, banjo and mandolin; Steve Martin, vocals; Tom Finn, bass; Mike Brown, organ, piano, and harp; George Cameron, vocals; started in New York City (1966); albums—*The Left Banke Too, Walk Away Renee/Pretty Ballerina.*

LEGGE, WADE

b. 1934 Huntington, West Virginia, d. 1963 Buffalo, New York. Pianist. Played with Dizzy Gillespie, Johnny Richards and others in 1950s.

LEGINSKA, ETHEL

b. 1886 Hull, England, d. 1970.
Pianist and conductor. Born Ethel Liggins; studied at the Frankfort Conservatory, and with Leschetizky; toured Europe as a concert pianist; New York debut (1913); conducted Boston Philharmonic, and Chicago Women's Symphony; composed a one-act opera, *Gale* (Chicago Opera Company, 1935), orchestral and other works.

LEHMANN, LILLI

b. 1848 Wurzburg, Germany, d. 1929 Berlin. Noted soprano. Daughter of opera singers August Lehmann and soprano T. Marie Loewe Lehmann; studied piano in Prague at age six; studied singing at age ten with her mother; debut as the First Boy in *The Magic Flute* (1865); debut at Berlin Opera (1870) as Vielka in *L'Etoile du Nord;* London debut (1880) as Violetta in *La Traviata;* debut at Metropolitan Opera in New York (1885) as Carmen; sang Wagnerian roles there (1885-89 and again 1891-92 and 1898); toured Europe after 1899; married tenor Paul Kalisch (1888); later divorced.

LEHMANN, LOTTE

b. 1886 Perleberg, Germany.
Soprano. Studied at Berlin Royal Academy of Music and with Mathilde Mallinger; debut in Hamburg (1910); with the Vienna State Opera; with Chicago Opera (1930) and the Metropolitan Opera, New York City (1934-45); gave concerts until 1951; taught in Santa Barbara, Calif.

LEHMANN, OTTO

b. 1906 Munich, Germany, d. 1971 New York City. Conductor and teacher. Studied at the University of Munich and was director of the Munich Opera; with the rise of Nazism, he came to America; conductor of the Hartford Opera Company for a time, and also of the New York City Center Opera, and taught at the Manhattan School of Music.

LEHRER, THOMAS

b. 1928 New York City.
Pianist and popular composer. Graduated Harvard with M.A. in math; taught there; toured U.S. part of each year in the 1950s; wrote "The Irish Ballad," "Pollution," "We Will All Go Together When We Go," "Poisoning Pigeons in the Park," "Be Prepared."

LEICHTENTRITT, HUGO

b. 1874 Pleschen, Poland, d. 1951 Cambridge, Massachusetts. Composer, teacher, and writer. Student at Harvard University, then returned to Poland; composer and musicologist; after the rise of Hitlerism, he came to the United States (1934), where he taught at Harvard College, Radcliffe College, and New York University; wrote *Music, History and Ideas* (1938), *Formenlehre*, and biographies of Handel and Chopin.

LEIGHTON, JAMES ALBERT ("BERT")

b. 1877 Beecher, Illinois, d. 1964 San Francisco, California. Composer, vaudeville singer, and lyricist. With his brother Frank, formed the vaudeville team the Leighton Brothers; wrote "Steamboat Bill" (1910, w. Ren Shields).

LEINSDORF, ERICH

b. 1912 Vienna, Austria.
Conductor. Came to America and became conductor at the Metropolitan Opera, New York City, for German repertoire; later in Cleveland, then in Rochester, New York, then with the Metropolitan Opera again; became musical director of the Boston Symphony (1961); later at Metropolitan Opera, New York City; conducted with Jess Thomas and Birgit Nilsson in *Tristan and Isolde* at the Met (1971).

LE JEUNE, GEORGE FITZ CURWOOD

b. 1841 London, England, d. 1904 Staten Island, New York. Composer. First came to Montreal, then directed music in the Pearl St. Church, Hartford, Conn., and St. Luke's (Episcopal) Church, Philadelphia; in 1871 went to the Anthon Memorial Church, New York City; became organist at St. John's Chapel of Trinity Parish (1876-1904); tune "Love Divine" was published in his book *Twenty-four Hymns with Original Tunes* (1887), set to "Love Divine, All Loves Excelling" (w. Charles Wesley).

LELAND, JOHN

b. 1754 Grafton, Massachusetts, d. 1841 North Adams, Massachusetts. Hymnist. Baptist elder; wrote the lyrics "Christians, If Your Hearts Are Warm" (1805, m. Amzi Chapin); in 1801 the farmers in Cheshire, Mass. decided to send the largest cheese in America to President Jefferson, and Elder

Leland carried the cheese, weighing 1,450 lbs., in his oxcart to Washington, preaching along the way; became known nationally as the "Cheshire Cheese Preacher."

LEMAN, J. WILLIAM F.

b. 1880, d. 1953.
Violist and conductor. Directed Women's Symphony Orchestra, Philadelphia, after 1921; also conducted Frankford Symphony Orchestra (1925-35).

LEMARE, EDWIN H.

b. 1865 Isle of Wight, British Isles, d. 1934 Los Angeles, California. Organist and composer. Organist in various churches; composed Andantino in D-flat.

LENER, JENO

b. 1871 Szabadka, Hungary, d. 1948 New York City. Violinist. Studied at the Budapest Academy of Music; debut there (1913); with Budapest Philharmonic until 1918; led his own string quartet, London, after 1920; came to New York City (1929).

LENNON SISTERS (vocal group)

Dianne (b. 1939 Los Angeles); Peggy (b. 1941 Los Angeles); Kathy (b. 1943 Santa Monica, Calif.); Janet (b. 1946 Culver City, Calif.); albums—*Best Loved Catholic Hymns, Diary of Favorites, Lennon Sisters with Lawrence Welk, On the Groovy Side, Pop Country, Somethin' Stupid, Twelve Great Hits.*

LEONARD, CLAIR

b. 1901 Newton, Massachusetts.
Composer. Graduated Harvard; studied with Nadia Boulanger; taught at Vassar College; wrote music for *My Country Right or Left* and for *Dance of Death* (1935), both presented at Adelphi Theatre in New York City.

LEONARD, EDDIE

b. 1875 Richmond, Virginia, d. 1941 New York City. Singer, actor, lyricist, and composer. Born Lemuel Gordon Toney; singer and actor in minstrel shows; served in Spanish-American War; sang at Tony Pastor's in New York City; with Primrose and West Minstrel Show (1902); wrote lyrics for "Ida Sweet as Apple Cider" (1903, m. Eddie Munson).

LERMAN, JOSEPH W.

b. 1865, d. 1935.
Composer. Wrote the tune "Corwin" ("God's Trumpet Wakes the Slumb'ring World," w. Samuel Longfellow, 1864).

LERNER, ALAN JAY

b. 1918 New York City.
Lyricist and librettist. Son of the founder of the Lerner women's clothing shops; studied piano at the Juilliard School, New York City; graduated Harvard University (1940); joined with composer Frederick Loewe to write musical shows, including: *Brigadoon* (1947), *Paint Your Wagon* (1951), *My Fair Lady* (1956, won the Pulitzer Prize), *Gigi* (won Academy Award, 1958); also wrote lyrics for Burton Lane and Andre Previn.

LERT, ERNST JOSEPH MARIA

b. 1883 Vienna, Austria, d. 1955 Baltimore, Maryland. Teacher and director. Changed his name from Levi to Lert; studied at the University of Vienna with Guido Adler; then became stage director of the Breslau Opera; later at Leipzig (1912), at Frankfort (1920), at La Scala in Milan (1923-29); came to America and was with the Metropolitan Opera, New York City (1929-31), and taught at the Peabody Conservatory, Baltimore, (1931-55); wrote *Mozart auf dem Theater.*

LERT, RICHARD

b. 1885 Vienna, Austria.
Conductor. Brother of Ernst Levi (Lert); conductor in Germany, then at Berlin State Opera (1929-32); with the rise of Nazism, he came to America and resided in Los Angeles; conducted at the Hollywood Bowl.

LES JAZZ MODES *see* SAMUEL JONES

LESBERG, JACK

b. 1920 Boston, Massachusetts.
Bass player. Played with various bands in 1950s; with Georgie Auld, Doc Severinsen, Eddie Condon, Louis Armstrong and others in 1960s; at Newport Jazz Festival (1965) with George Wein.

LESLIE, EDGAR

b. 1885 Stamford, Connecticut.
Songwriter. Educated at Cooper Union, New York City; wrote songs for films; also a publisher; wrote "Lonesome" (1909, m. Kerry Mills and G.W. Meyer), "My Mother's Rosary" (1915, m. Meyer), "When Ragtime Rosie Ragged the Rosary" (1911, m. Lewis F. Muir), "Moonlight on the Rhine" (with Bert Kalmar, m. Ted Snyder), "Moon Over Miami" (1936, m. Joe Burke); with E. Ray Goetz wrote "For Me and My Gal" (1917, m. George W. Meyer).

LESTER, KETTY (REVOYDA FRIERSON)

b. 1934 Hope, Arkansas.
Singer. Educated at San Francisco City College; studied voice there with Myrtle Leonard; sang in night clubs in San Francisco and Los Angeles; toured South America (1958) with Cab Calloway; toured Europe (1962).

LETMAN, JOHN BERNARD

b. 1917 McCormick, South Carolina.
Trumpeter. Played with Cab Calloway, Count Basie and others during 1940s; led own groups in New York City in 1950s; at Cincinnati Jazz Festival (1963) and Connecticut Jazz Festival (1965).

LEVANT, OSCAR

b. 1906 Pittsburgh, Pennsylvania, d. 1972 Beverly Hills, California. Pianist and composer. Studied with Stokowski, Schonberg, and Schillinger; pianist for jazz bands; his *Piano Sonatina* (1931) played at Festival of American Music at Yaddo; *String Quartet* (1937) at Denver; *Nocturne,* orchestral work (1936) in Los Angeles; appeared in films; gave numerous concerts of works by George Gershwin; averaged forty concerts yearly before 1972.

LEVETT, DAVID MAURICE

b. 1844 New York City, d. 1914.
Pianist, composer, and teacher. Taught piano at New York College of Music.

LEVEY, STAN

b. 1925 Philadelphia, Pennsylvania.
Drummer. Played with Dizzy Gillespie, Stan Kenton and others during 1940s and '50s; toured Europe (1962-63) with Peggy Lee and Ella Fitzgerald; with Pat Boone in Japan (1964).

LEVINE, JAMES

b. 1943 Cincinnati, Ohio.
Conductor. Great-grandfather was a cantor, his father a violinist and bandleader; studied piano at age four; debut with Cincinnati Symphony Orchestra at age ten; studied with Rudolf Serkin at the Marlboro Festival and with Rosina Lhevinne at Juilliard, New York City; student and later assistant conductor of Cleveland Orchestra (1964-70); guest conductor in Philadelphia, Chicago, Atlanta; named principal conductor of Metropolitan Opera, New York City (1972).

LEVINE, MARKS

b. 1890 New York City, d. there 1971.
Lyricist and manager. Brother of Mischa Levitzki, pianist; attended high school in Russia; graduated Cooper Union, New York City (1914); wrote the lyrics "When I Love You," "Spring Came," "We Love and Dream," "I Looked at a Tulip"; manager of concert division of National Broadcasting Company (1930-41); later president and director of the National Concert and Artists Corp.; managed Serge Rachmaninoff, Fritz Kreisler, Ignace Jan Paderewski, Ezio Pinza and others.

LEVITSKI, MISCHA

b. 1898 Krementchug, Russia, d. 1941 Avon, New Jersey. Pianist. Brother of Marks Levine; studied in New York and Berlin; debut in Berlin (1914); New York debut (1916); toured America, Europe and the Orient; composed piano works.

LEVITT, RODNEY CHARLES

b. 1929 Portland, Oregon.
Trombonist and bandleader. Played with Dizzy Gillespie (1956-57); with New York City Radio City Orchestra (1957-63); led own orchestra after 1960; at Newport Jazz Festival (1960 and 1964).

LE VOE, SPIVY

b. 1906 Brooklyn, New York, d. 1971 Los Angeles, California. Nightclub entertainer. She was a stout, deep-voiced woman who played the piano and sang risqué songs; operated Spivy's Roof on East 57th Street, New York City (1940-51), then Spivy's Club in Paris.

LEVY, ERNST

b. 1895 Basel, Switzerland.
Composer. Resided in Paris, then came to America when the Nazis came to power in Germany; became a teacher in Boston; composed nine symphonies, songs, choral and chamber music with Hebraic overtones.

LEVY, LOUIS A.

b. 1928 Chicago, Illinois.
Pianist. Played with Boyd Raeburn, Woody Herman and others in 1950s; with Ella Fitzgerald, Peggy Lee, Stan Getz and others in 1960s; toured Europe and Pacific area with Ella Fitzgerald.

LEWIS, AL

b. 1901 New York City.
Songwriter. Educated at the University of Michigan; wrote "Rose O'Day" (1942, with Charles Tobias), "Why Don't You fall in Love with Me?" (1937, m. Mabel Wayne).

LEWIS, ALLIE MAY

b. 1859 Des Moines, Iowa, d. 1930.
Pianist, organist, and teacher. Taught piano,

organ, guitar, and harmony in Washington, Iowa.

LEWIS, FRANK

b. ca. 1868, d. 1924.
Black clarinetist. Played in Buddy Bolden's band in New Orleans in the 1890s.

LEWIS, FREEMAN

b. 1780, d. 1859.
Composer and compiler. Resided in Uniontown, Pennsylvania, where he was a surveyor; compiled *The Beauties of Harmony* (1813), which included his tune "Beloved" ("O Thou, in Whose Presence My Soul Takes Delight," w. Joseph Swain).

LEWIS, GARY

b. 1945.
Bandleader. Son of actor Jerry Lewis; rose to prominence with his rock band, Gary Lewis and the Playboys; second marriage to dancer Kay Elaine Poorboy (1972).

LEWIS, GEORGE (ZENO)

b. 1900 New Orleans, Louisiana, d. 1968.
Black clarinetist. Played in Black Eagle Band in 1920s; also with Red Allen; with Evan Thomas in Rayne, Louisiana (1931); recorded with Jim Robinson and Bunk Johnson in 1940s; led his own groups in 1950s; toured Europe (1959) and Japan in 1960s.

LEWIS, HENRY

b. 1933.
Black conductor. Guest conductor of the San Francisco Opera, the Vancouver Opera, Boston Opera, American Opera Society and major symphony orchestras; first black music director of a leading American orchestra when appointed to that post by the New Jersey Symphony (1968); first black conductor engaged by Metropolitan Opera, New York City (1972); married Metropolitan soprano Marilyn Horne.

LEWIS, H. MERRILLS

b. 1908 Meriden, Connecticut.
Composer. Studied at Yale School of Music with Smith and Donovan; received a fellowship at Juilliard Graduate School, studied under Goldmark; taught at Furman University, Greenville, S.C.; wrote Symphony in A (1936), *Three Serenades for Orchestra* (1937), *Lake Song* for women's voices and piano (1936).

LEWIS, HUGH X.

b. 1932 Yeaddiss, Kentucky.
Singer. Attended schools in Cumberland, Kentucky, and Kansas City, Missouri; wrote "B.J. the D.J.," "If This House Could Talk," "Thought I'd Let You Know," "I Just Wasted the Rest."

LEWIS, JERRY LEE

b. 1935 Ferriday, Louisiana.
Singer, pianist, and popular composer. His group was voted the Best Small Combo of 1957; wrote "End of the Road" (1956), "High School Confidential" (1958, with R. Hargrave), "Lewis Boogie" (1958); his hit singles were "Another Time, Another Place" (1968), "What's Made Milwaukee Famous" (1968).

LEWIS, JESSICA

b. 1890 New York City, d. 1971 Los Angeles, California. Opera singer. She sang briefly with the Metropolitan Opera, New York City, but spent most of her career with the Chicago Opera Company; sang at the White House with Mary Garden at a musicale given by President William H. Taft.

LEWIS, JOHN AARON

b. 1920 La Grange, Illinois.
Black jazz pianist, composer, and arranger. Joined Dizzy Gillespie's band (1945) as pianist and arranger; with Illinois Jacquet (1948); founded the Modern Jazz Quartet (1952) with Milt Jackson; wrote *Toccata for Trumpet and Orchestra* (1947), *Ulysses* (1949), *Afternoon in Paris* (1949), *Period Suite* (1950), *Delaunay's Dilemma* (1953), *Vendome* (1953), *Fontessa* (1955), *Versailles* (1955), *Concorde* (1956), *A Fugue for Music Inn* (1956), *Two Degrees East, Three Degrees West* (1957).

LEWIS, MARY

b. 1900 Hot Springs, Arkansas, d. 1941 New York City. Opera singer. Sang in musical comedies in New York City; opera debut in Vienna (1923); sang in Europe (1924-25); with Metropolitan Opera Company, New York (1926-30), debut in the title role in *Mimi*; married to Michael Bohnen, bass, divorced; then to Robert Hague.

LEWIS, MEADE LUX

b. 1905 Louisville, Kentucky, d. 1964 Minneapolis, Minnesota. Black boogie-woogie pianist. Played in New York City night clubs; at Jimmy Ryan's Club on 52nd Street, New York City (1941); often teamed with Albert Ammons and Pete Johnson; killed in an auto accident.

LEWIS, MEL

b. 1929 Buffalo, New York.
Drummer and bandleader. Born Melvin Sokoloff; name changed by Ray Anthony,

whose band he joined (1949); had own group with Bill Holman in 1950s; with Mulligan band, Dizzy Gillespie, Stan Kenton and others in 1960s; played at Village Vanguard, New York City, in Thad Jones-Mel Lewis band after 1964; toured Soviet Russia with band (1972) under auspices of State Department; at Newport Jazz Festival, New York City (1972).

LEWIS, RAMSEY E., JR.

b. 1935 Chicago, Illinois.
Black pianist. Formed a trio (1956); their record "The In Crowd" sold over one million copies (1965) and won a Grammy award; later played at Carnegie Hall; albums—*Another Voyage, Bach to the Blues, Barefoot Sunday Blues, Best of Ramsey Lewis, Bossa Nova, Choice, Country Meets the Blues, Dancing in the Street, Down to Earth, Goin' Latin*; played at the Maisonette, St. Regis Hotel, New York City (1972).

LEWIS, SAMUEL M.

b. 1885 New York City, d. there 1959.
Lyricist. Sang in night clubs in New York City; collaborated with Joe Young in writing lyrics; they wrote "How Ya Gonna Keep 'em Down on the Farm?" (m. Walter Donaldson), "My Mammy" (m. Donaldson, made famous by Al Jolson), "When You're a Long Way from Home" (1914, m. G.W. Meyer), "There's a Cradle in Caroline" (m. Fred Ahlert), "In a Little Spanish Town" (1926, m. Mabel Wayne), "Dinah" (1925, m. Harry Akst), "Daddy Long Legs" (m. Harry Ruby), "Five Foot Two, Eyes of Blue" (m. Ray Henderson), "Laugh, Clown Laugh" (m. Ted Fiorito), "King for a Day" (1928, m. Fiorito), "A Night in Spain" (1927, m. Jean Schwartz), "Absence Makes the Heart Grow Fonder for Someone Else" (m. Harry Warren).

LEWIS, TED

b. 1891 Circleville, Ohio, d. 1971 New York City. Clarinetist, bandleader, and entertainer. Born Theodore Leopold Friedman; joined a trio at Hammerstein's Theatre (1911); led his first band at Coney Island, N.Y. (1916); won his first top hat in a dice game with a New York cab driver (1919), and it became his trademark, though worn and battered, but never replaced over the years; his opening line was "Is ev'rybody happy?"

LHEVINNE, JOSEF

b. 1874 near Moscow, Russia, d. 1944 New York City. Pianist. Studied at the Moscow Conservatory with W. Safonoff (1885); won Rubinstein prize (1895); taught at Moscow Conservatory (1902-06); toured Europe and the U.S. (1905 and 1912); then resided in New York; with his wife, Rosina, gave two-piano programs.

L'HULIER, JOHN B.

b. ca. 1780 France, d. 1848 Philadelphia, Pennsylvania. Violinist, teacher, and compiler. Taught in Philadelphia (1802-48); compiled *The Minstrel*, a collection of airs, waltzes, and marches, published by George Willig (1829).

LIBERACE, WALTER VALENTINO

b. 1919 West Allis, Wisconsin.
Pianist and composer. Concert debut at age eleven; studied at Wisconsin College of Music; soloist with Chicago Symphony Orchestra in Milwaukee; entertainer in night clubs; TV debut (1952) station KLAC, Los Angeles; at Carnegie Hall (1953), Madison Square Garden (1954); appeared in films; instrumentals—*Rhapsody by Candlelight, Boogie-Woogie Variations*; known for his flashy costumes and candelabra on his piano.

LICHTENBERG, LEOPOLD

b. 1861 San Francisco, California, d. 1935 Brooklyn, New York. Violinist. Debut at age eight; studied with Beaujardin and Wieniawski; toured Europe and America; member of Boston Symphony Orchestra; then taught at the National Conservatory, New York after 1899.

LICHTENWANGER, WILLIAM

b. 1915 Asheville, North Carolina.
Librarian. Educated at the University of Michigan (B.M., 1937, M.M., 1940); Head of the Reference Section, Music Division, Library of Congress, Washington, D.C.; editor and contributor, *Collier's Encyclopedia* (1949-51); associate editor and contributor, *Notes* (1946-61); editor of *Notes* (1961-63); music consultant and contributor, *Notable American Women* (Harvard University Press, 1971).

LIEBLING, EMIL

b. 1851 Pless, Poland, d. 1914 Chicago, Illinois. Pianist. Studied in Berlin, Vienna, then with Liszt; came to America (1867); taught in Chicago after 1872; composed a number of piano pieces and songs.

LIEBLING, ESTELLE

b. 1880 New York City, d. 1970.
Soprano. She sang in opera in Europe and the United States; then taught at the Curtis Institute of Music, Philadelphia.

LIEBLING, GEORG

b. 1865 Berlin, Germany, d. 1945 New York City. Pianist. Studied with Liszt and others; taught in Kullak's Academy (1880-85); then toured Germany and Austria; concert-pianist to Duke of Coburg (1890); resided in Munich (1908-23), then came to Los Angeles to live.

LIEBLING, LEONARD

b. 1880 New York City, d. there 1945. Pianist and editor. Graduated City College of New York; studied in Berlin; taught piano in Berlin and then in New York City; on staff of *Musical Courier* (1902), then editor (1911); music critic of *New York American* until 1936.

LIEURANCE, THURLOW

b. 1878 Oskaloosa, Iowa, d. 1963 Boulder, Colorado. Composer. Wrote *Hail! Wichita.*

LIGHT, BEN

b. 1893, d. 1965 Pacific Palisades, California. Pianist. Debut in Denver, Colorado (1909); played on the West Coast and in the Rockies.

LILIUOKALANI, QUEEN OF HAWAII

b. 1838 Honolulu, Hawaiian Islands, d. there 1917. Composer. She became Queen in 1891 and reigned until 1893 when deposed by the Americans under Sanford B. Dole, who became the first and only President of the Hawaiian Republic; under orders of President Dole, she was arrested in January, 1895, and sentenced to life in prison, but was kept guarded in Iolani Palace until she was released in September, 1895; while a princess, she composed the "Hawaiian National Anthem" (ca. 1868), which was played at official functions for twenty years until a new anthem was written; wrote "Aloha Oe!" (1884).

LIMELITERS, THE *see* LOUIS GOTTLIEB, ALEX HASSILEV, and GLENN YARBROUGH

LINCOLN, ABBEY

b. 1930 Chicago, Illinois.
Black singer. Sang in Hawaii and California as Gaby Lee; later known as Abbey Lincoln; married Max Roach, drummer and composer; later appeared in films.

LIND, JENNY

b. 1820 Stockholm, Sweden, d. 1887 England. Noted soprano. Studied with Croelius and Berg at the Court Theatre at age nine; debut in Stockholm Opera (1838) as Agatha in Weber's *Freischutz;* studied with Manuel Garcia in Paris (1841); Berlin Opera debut (1844) as Norma; toured Europe; London debut (1847) as Alice in *Robert le Diable;* toured America (1850-52) on a concert tour arranged by P.T. Barnum and was a tremendous success; known as the "Swedish Nightingale"; married composer-conductor Otto Goldschmidt (1852), toured Europe; settled in England (1856).

LINDA AND THE STONE PONEYS (folk group)

Linda Ronstadt, guitar; Bob Kimmel, rhythm guitar; Ken Edwards, lead guitar; started recording (1965) in Los Angeles; albums—*Stone Poneys, Evergreen—Volume 2, Stone Poneys—Volume 3,* and *Friends.*

LINDSAY, HOWARD

b. 1899 Waterford, New York, d. 1968.
Playwright and librettist. Attended Harvard University; with Russell Crouse wrote the libretto for *Anything Goes* (1934, m. Cole Porter), starring Ethel Merman; *Call Me Madam* (1950, m. Irving Berlin), also starring Ethel Merman, and *Sound of Music* (1959, m. Richard Rodgers), starring Mary Martin.

LINDSAY, JOHNNY

b. 1894 Algiers, Louisiana, d. 1950 Chicago, Illinois. Black double bass player. Played in Jelly Roll Morton's band in the 1920s; recorded "Black Bottom Stomp" with the band.

LINGLE, PAUL

b. 1902 Denver, Colorado, d. 1962 Honolulu, Oahu, Hawaiian Islands. Black pianist. Played in San Francisco night clubs; in Honolulu after 1952.

LINLEY, FRANCIS

b. 1771 Doncaster, England, d. 1800.
Composer. Composed a "Christmas Anthem" which was included in *The Book of Common Prayer and Selection of Psalms with Occasional Hymns,* published (1799) by W.P. Young, Charleston, S.C.

LINN COUNTY BLUES BAND (blues band)

Fred Walk, guitar and electric sitar; Larry Easter, soprano sax and woodwinds; Dino Long, bass; Stephen Miller, vocals and organ; Snake McAndrew, drums; albums—*Linn County* (1968), *Fever Shot, Linn County Blues Band, Till the Break of Dawn.*

LIPTON, PEGGY

b. 1947 New York City.
Singer. Album—*Peggy Lipton.*

LIST, KURT

b. 1913 Vienna, Austria.
Composer. Studied with Alban Berg and Anton Webern; composed the opera *The Wise and the Foolish*, two symphonies, a woodwind quintet; music editor of the magazine *Commentary*, devoted to Jewish cultural life.

LISTEMANN, BERNARD FRIEDRICH WILHELM

b. 1841 Schlotheim, East Germany, d. 1917 Chicago, Illinois. Violinist. Brother of Fritz Listemann; pupil of Ullrich and others; came to America (1867) with his brother; leader of Thomas' Orchestra (1871-74); founded Philharmonic Club (1874) and toured the states; founded Boston Philharmonic Orchestra (1878) and was its conductor (1878-81); leader of New Symphony Orchestra (1881-85); also founded Listemann Quartet and Listemann Concert Company (1883); professor at Chicago College of Music after 1893.

LISTEMANN, FRANZ

b. 1873 New York City, d. 1930 Chicago, Illinois. Cellist. Son of Bernard and brother of Paul Listemann; studied with Fries and Giese in Boston, then in Leipzig and Berlin; first cellist with Pittsburgh Orchestra; then a concert performer and teacher in New York City.

LISTEMANN, FRITZ

b. 1839 Schlotheim, East Germany, d. 1909 Boston, Massachusetts. Violinist. Pupil of his uncle, Ullrich, and at Leipzig Conservatory (1858); came to New York (1867); first violinist with Thomas' Orchestra (1871), then Philharmonic Orchestra (1878), Symphony Orchestra (1881-85); composed violin concertos.

LISTEMANN, PAUL

b. 1871 Boston, Massachusetts, d. 1950.
Concertmaster. Son of Bernard Listemann, violinist; studied with his uncle, Fritz Listemann, also in Leipzig and Berlin; with Listemann Quartet and Concert Company (1890-93); concertmaster of Pittsburgh Orchestra, and American Orchestra, New York (1896); soloist with Redpath Concert Company.

LISTON, MELBA DORETTA

b. 1926 Kansas City, Missouri.
Black trombonist and composer. Arranger and trombonist with Billie Holiday, Dizzy Gillespie, Count Basie, Quincy Jones and others in 1940s and '50s; arranger for Charles Mingus, Duke Ellington, Eddie Fisher and others in 1960s; wrote *Melba's Blues, Just Waiting, All Deliberate Speed.*

LITTA, MARIE VON ELSNER

b. 1856, d. 1883 Bloomington, Illinois.
Singer. Sang in Steinway Hall, New York City at age nine; sang in the German Theatre, Cleveland (1869); studied under John Underner in Cleveland; with Mme. Viardot in Paris; debut in Col. Mapleson's company at Drury Lane, London (1876); sang in McVicker's theatre, Chicago (1878) as Lucia in Donizetti's opera; died of spinal meningitis.

LITTLE, BOOKER, JR.

b. 1938 Memphis, Tennessee, d. 1961 New York City. Black trumpeter. Played with Max Roach, Mal Waldron, and John Coltrane in late 1950s; co-led quintet (1961) with Eric Dolphy; died of uremia.

LITTLE, DUDLEY ("BIG TINY")

b. 1930 Worthington, Minnesota.
Pianist, singer, and bandleader. Led own Japanese jazz group in Tokyo (1952-54); with Irving Ashby Trio, and Lawrence Welk band in 1950s; organized his own combo.

LITTLE RICHARD

b. 1935 Macon, Georgia.
Black pianist and singer. Born Richard Penniman; blues and black rhythm singer; raised in Macon, Georgia; sang solos in local gospel choir at age fourteen; played piano in a Seventh Day Adventist Church of Times Square, New York City (1957); albums—*Fabulous Little Richard; Here's Little Richard; Little Richard; His Biggest Hits; Greatest Hits; Grooviest Seventeen Original Hits; Our Significant Hits.*

LITTLE WALTER

b. 1930, d. 1969.
Black harpist and harmonica player. Born Walter Jacobs; played in Muddy Water's band; the band recorded "Walkin' Blues" and "Rollin' Stone" (the name later adopted by the British rock group); album—*Hate to See You Go.*

LITTLEFIELD, MILTON SMITH

b. 1864 New York City, d. 1934.
Hymnist. Educated at Johns Hopkins, Baltimore, Union Theological Seminary, and received his D.D. from Washburn College; Presbyterian clergyman; wrote the hymn "Come, O Lord, Like the Morning Sunlight" (tune—"Trust," Mendelssohn), included in

The Hymnal for Young People (1928); president of the Hymn Society (1927-28).

LITTLEJOHN, JOHN

b. (?), d. (?).
Black guitarist. Born John Funchess; Chicago slide guitarist known for his delta bottleneck style; albums—*John Littlejohn's Chicago Blues Stars* (1969), *Catfish Blues, Shake Your Money Maker.*

LIVERMORE, ABIEL ABBOT

b. 1811 Wilton, New Hampshire, d. there 1892. Compiler. Graduated Harvard (1833), Divinity (1836); Unitarian pastor in Keane, N.H. (1836), Cincinnati (1850), Yonkers, N.Y. (1857), then president of the Theological School in Meadville, Pa. (1863); editor of *Christian Hymns* (1844, Cheshire Pastoral Association).

LIVERMORE, SARAH WHITE

b. 1789 Wilton, New Hampshire, d. there 1874. Hymnist. Taught in Wilton; her hymns appeared in *Christian Hymns* (1844) and *Putnam's Singers and Songs of the Liberal Faith* (1875).

LIVINGSTON, JAY HAROLD

b. 1915 McDonald, Pennsylvania.
Pianist and composer. Studied piano in Pittsburgh with Harry Archer and became a pianist and vocal arranger; served in the armed forces in World War II; with lyricist Raymond B. Evans wrote "To Each His Own" (1946), "Buttons and Bows" (1948), "Mona Lisa" (1949), "Whatever Will Be, Will Be" ("Qué Será," 1956); with Ray Evans the lyrics "Golden Earrings" (m. Victor Young).

LIVINGSTON, JERRY

b. 1909 Denver, Colorado.
Composer. For a time he was a pianist with small bands in New York City; with lyricists Marty Symes and Al Neiberg wrote "When It's Darkness on the Delta" (1932), "Sunday Down in Caroline" (1933), "It's the Talk of the Town" (1933), "In a Blue and Pensive Mood" (1934); also with Mack David "Haven't We Met Before?" (1934), "Just a Kid Named Joe," "That's All Brother" (w. Clyde Hager and David), "My Destiny" (1950, David).

LLOYD, CHARLES

b. 1938 Memphis, Tennessee.
Tenor saxist, flutist, and bandleader. Educated at the University of Southern Calif., Los Angeles; played with Chico Hamilton, Cannonball Adderley and others; then formed his own quartet (1965); albums—*Best of Charles Lloyd, Discovery, Dream Weaver, Forest Flower, Journey Within, Charles Lloyd in London, Love-In, Nirvana, Of Course, Of Course.*

LOCATELLI, JOSEPH J.

b. 1934 Boston, Massachusetts.
Drummer. Played with Billy May, Jackie Cain, Roy Kral, Red Norvo and others in 1960s.

LOCKLIN, HENRY (HANK)

b. 1918 McLellan, Florida.
Singer and guitarist. Sang on station KWKH, Shreveport, La.; toured U.S., Canada, and Europe; became mayor of McLellan in the 1950s; his LP records are *Best of Hank Locklin, Encores, Hank Locklin Favorites, Foreign Love* (1958), *Please Help Me* (1960), *Happy Journey* (1962), *Ways of Life* (1963), *Irish Songs* (1964).

LOCKWOOD, NORMAND

b. 1906 New York City.
Composer. Won Fellowship at American Academy in Rome (1929); studied with Nadia Boulanger in Paris; taught at Oberlin College, Ohio; composed *Fragments from Sappho* (for girl's voices), *Drum Taps* (choir and orchestra), *Requiem* (for chorus, tenor, and orchestra), *Dirge for Two Veterans* (mixed choir), six string quartets.

LOCKWOOD, ROBERT, JR.

b. 1915 Marvell, Arkansas.
Singer and guitarist. Played in various night spots in St. Louis and Chicago; with Little Walter, Muddy Waters and others in 1950s.

LOEFFLER, ARTHUR

b. 1894 New York City.
Concert pianist; taught at the Institute of Music in Cleveland, Ohio; wrote *Men, Women and Pianos—A Social History.*

LOEFFLER, CHARLES MARTIN

b. 1861 Mulhouse, Alsace, d. 1935 Medfield, Massachusetts. Composer. As a boy he lived in Kiev, Russia; studied in Berlin and Paris; came to Boston (1881), played with the Boston Symphony (1882-1903); composed *A Pagan Poem* (1906), *Music for Four Stringed Instruments* (1917), *Memories of My Childhood,* (tone poem for orchestra, 1924), and *Evocation* (1930, w. T.W. Mackail, introduced by the Cleveland Orchestra, 1931).

LOESSER, FRANK HENRY

b. 1910 New York City, d. there 1969.
Composer and lyricist. Attended City College

of N.Y.; wrote the lyrics "In Love with the Memory of You" (1931, m. William Schuman); with music by Hoagy Carmichael, "Small Fry" and "Two Sleepy People"; wrote the words and music "Praise the Lord and Pass the Ammunition" (1942); served in the Special Forces in World War II; also wrote "Baby, It's Cold Outside" (1949), "On a Slow Boat to China" (1948), "Once in Love with Amy" (1948), "My Darling, My Darling" (1948, from *Where's Charley?*); also wrote the scores for *Guys and Dolls* (1950), *The Most Happy Fella* (1956), *How to Succeed in Business Without Really Trying* (1961).

LOEWE, FREDERICK

b. 1904 Berlin, Germany.
Pianist and composer. Studied in Vienna, then came to New York City (1924); with Earle Crooker wrote the score for *Salute to Spring* (1937) and *Great Lady* (1938); with lyricist Alan Jay Lerner wrote *Life of the Party* (1942, *Salute to Spring* revised), *What's Up?* (1943), *The Day Before Spring* (1945), *Brigadoon* (1947), *Paint Your Wagon* (1951), *My Fair Lady* (1956, based on G.B. Shaw's play), *Camelot* (1960, book—T.H. White); the hit song in *My Fair Lady* was "With a Little Bit of Luck," which was based on "Listen to the Mocking Bird" (by Septimus Winner, 1855).

LOFTON, CLARENCE

b. 1896 Kingsport, Tennessee, d. 1956 Chicago, Illinois. Boogie-woogie pianist. Known as "Cripple Clarence"; played in Chicago night spots after 1917.

LOFTON, LAWRENCE ("TRICKY")

b. 1930 Houston, Texas.
Trombonist. Played in small combos in Los Angeles; served in the army in the Korean War; played again with various groups in Los Angeles.

LOGAN, FREDERICK KNIGHT

b. 1871 Oskaloosa, Iowa, d. 1928.
Pianist, composer, and conductor. Studied privately; music director with theater companies; with John Valentine Eppel, wrote or arranged (from an old tune) "The Missouri Waltz" (about 1916).

LOGAN, GIUSEPPI

b. 1935 Philadelphia, Pennsylvania.
Saxist and oboe player. Studied at New England Conservatory, Boston; also with Dennis Sandole and others; played at Town Hall, New York City in concert with string ensemble.

LOGAN, JOSHUA LOCKWOOD

b. 1908.
Librettist. With Oscar Hammerstein II wrote the libretto for *South Pacific* (1949, m. Richard Rodgers, adapted from the book by James A. Michener).

LOGAN, WENDELL MORRIS

b. 1940 Thonson, Georgia.
Black composer. Graduated Southern Illinois University, Carbondale, master's 1964; State University of Iowa, Ph.D.; taught at Ball State University, Muncie, Ind., and Florida A&M College, Tallahassee, Florida.

LOMAX, ALAN

b. 1915 Austin, Texas.
Singer and folklorist. Son of John A. Lomax; attended Harvard, graduated the University of Texas (1936); assistant curator of Archive of American Folk Song, Library of Congress, Washington, D.C. (1937-42); with Office of War Information in World War II; lectured on folk music at numerous colleges; his LP record is *Texas Folk Songs* (1958); with Sidney R. Cowell compiled *American Folk Song and Folk Lore* (1942); wrote *The Folk Songs of North America in the English Language* (1960).

LOMAX, JOHN AVERY

b. 1875 Goodman, Mississippi, d. 1948 Greenville, Mississippi. Folklorist. Graduated University of Texas, Austin (1897, M.A. 1906, Harvard, 1907); taught at Texas A&M College (1903-10); secretary of the University of Texas at Austin (1910-17); curator of Archive of American Folk Song, Library of Congress, Washington, D.C. after 1934; wrote *Cowboy Songs and Other Frontier Ballads* (Sturgis and Walton, 1910), and *American Ballads and Folk Songs* (The Macmillan Company, N.Y., 1934).

LOMBARDO, CARMEN

b. 1903 London, Ontario, Canada, d. 1971 North Miami, Florida. Saxophone player in his brother Guy's band, the Royal Canadians; wrote several popular songs, including "Seems Like Old Times," "Sailboat in the Moonlight," "Powder Your Face with Sunshine," and "Boo Hoo"; his sister, Mrs. Elaine Lombardo Gardner, married Kenny Gardner, the band's vocalist; resided in Woodmere, Long Island, New York.

LOMBARDO, GUY

b. 1902 London, Ontario, Canada.
Bandleader. Started his own band and played

in Cleveland, Ohio, then came to New York City; band included his three brothers Carmen, Lebert, and Victor; they were known as the Royal Canadians with the trademark "the sweetest music this side of heaven"; since 1929 they have played "Auld Lang Syne" (w. Robert Burns—Scotch tune, 1799) every New Year's Eve over radio and later TV from the Roosevelt Grill to 1962, then from the Waldorf-Astoria.

LONDON, GEORGE

b. 1920 Montreal, P.Q., Canada.
Baritone. Born Burnstein; educated at Los Angeles City College (1937-39); debut in *La Traviata*, Hollywood Bowl (1941); with San Francisco Opera after 1943; sang in European opera (1949-52); debut at Metropolitan Opera, New York City (1951) in *Aïda*; appointed court singer by President of Austria (1955); title role in *The Lost Savage* (1963-64); taught opera at the University of Cincinnati; president of American Guild of American Artists (1968).

LONDON, JULIE

b. 1926 Santa Rosa, California.
Singer and actress. Sang on radio at age three; attended school in San Bernardino, Calif.; appeared in films; married Jack Webb, actor (1947), of "Dragnet" fame; later separated; her recording of "Cry Me a River" was a smash hit of 1956; appeared in films and TV shows.

LONE PINE MOUNTAINEERS *see* HAROLD BREAU

LONGACRE, LINDSAY BARTHOLOMEW

b. 1870 Pottsville, Pennsylvania, d. 1952.
Composer. Educated at the School of Mines, Columbia University, Drew Theological Seminary, the University of Jena, Germany, and New York University, (Ph.D., 1908); Methodist minister in New York State, when he became professor of Old Testament literature and religion at Iliff School of Theology, Denver, Colorado (1910); composed the tune "Deeper Life" ("Dear God, Our Father, at Thy Knee Confessing," w. Katharine Lee Bates).

LONGFELLOW, HENRY WADSWORTH

b. 1807 Portland, Maine, d. 1882 Cambridge, Massachusetts. Lyricist. Graduated Bowdoin College, Brunswick, Maine; professor of belles lettres at Harvard University for over forty years; when he visited London, he was received by Queen Victoria; wrote the lyrics "Rainy Day" (1847, m. W.R. Dempster and also I.B. Woodbury), "I Heard the Bells on Christmas Day" (m. Henry Bishop), "Day Is Done" (m. Michael Balfe), "Tell Me Not in Mournful Numbers" (m. I. Conkey), "The Blind Boy" (m. W.R. Dempster), "The Death of Minnehaha" (1856, m. C.C. Converse), "Stars of the Summer Night" (1856, m. I.B. Woodbury), "Beware" (1865, m. Charles Moulton), "The Golden Legend" (1880, m. Dudley Buck), "The Tide Rises" (m. Irwin Heilner).

LONGFELLOW, SAMUEL

b. 1819 Portland, Maine, d. there 1892.
Hymnist. Younger brother of Henry Wadsworth Longfellow; educated at Harvard and became a Unitarian minister in Fall River, Mass., Brooklyn, N.Y., and Germantown, Philadelphia; wrote the hymns "Again as Evening's Shadow Falls" (tune—"Abends," H.S. Oakley), "Now on Land and Sea Descending" (1859, tune—"Vesper Hymn," D.S. Bortniansky), "Holy Spirit, Truth Divine" (1864, tune—"Mercy," L.M. Gottschalk, also "Harts," 1769), "God's Trumpet Wakes the Slumb'ring World" (1864, "Corwin," J.W. Lerman), "O Still in Accents Sweet and Strong" ("Mt. Calvary," R.P. Stewart), "Go Forth to Life, O Child of Earth" (1864, "Rhys," Rhys Thomas), "I Look to Thee in Every Need" ("O Jesu," 1747), "The Summer Days Are Come Again" ("Soll's Sein," 1658) and " 'Tis Winter Now, the Fallen Snow" (m. old English air); with Samuel Johnson compiled *A Book of Hymns* (1846) and *Hymns of the Spirit* (1864).

LONZO AND OSCAR *see* JOHN and ROLLIN SULLIVAN, and KEN MARVIN

LOOMIS, HARVEY WORTHINGTON

b. 1865 Brooklyn, New York, d. 1931 Roxbury, Massachusetts. Composer. Studied at the National Conservatory, New York with Dvořák (1892); resided in New York; composed music to poems, pantomimes, piano pieces, and songs.

LOPATNIKOFF, NIKOLAI

b. 1903 Revel (Tallinn), Estonia.
Composer. Studied at the St. Petersburg Conservatory, Russia, at Helsingfors, and Heidelberg, Germany; came to America (1939) and became a citizen (1944); taught in Hartford, Conn., White Plains, N.Y., Carnegie, Pittsburgh, Pa., and at the Berkshire Music Center; composed Concerto for Violin and Orchestra, op. 26 (introduced by the

Boston Symphony under Serge Koussevitsky, 1942) and *Sinfonietta* (for orchestra, 1942).

LOPEZ, TRINI

b. 1937 Dallas, Texas.
Singer. Recorded "La Bamba" (by Ritchie Valens and Bob Keene); albums—*Folk Album, It's a Great Life, Trini Lopez at PJ's, Trini Lopez Live at Basin St. East, Now, Second Latin Album, Trini, Welcome to Trini Country.*

LOPEZ, VINCENT

b. 1895 Brooklyn, New York.
Orchestra leader and pianist. Popular in the 1920s; discovered Betty Hutton; broadcast from the Grill Room of the Hotel Taft, New York City.

LORD, BOBBY

b. 1934 Sanford, Florida.
Singer. Attended the University of Tampa, Florida; had his own show in TV; featured on Red Foley's show, Springfield, Mo., late 1950s; joined Grand Ole Opry, Nashville, Tenn., in 1960s; then the "Bobby Lord Show" there; hit records include "Hawkeye," "Without Your Love, Life Can Have Meaning," and the LP record, *Best of Bobby Lord* (1965).

LORENZO, ANGE

b. 1894 near West Branch, Michigan, d. 1971 Saginaw, Michigan. Pianist, singer, and composer. Played the piano with a group called the Tunesters during the 1930s; with Richard A. Whiting and Joseph R. Alden, wrote "Sleepy Time Gal" (1925); also wrote "Dreamy Dream Gal" and "Watching for Your Shadow"; collaborated with Raymond Egan and Gus Kahn also.

LORIMER, MICHAEL

b. 1946.
Classical guitarist. Formal debut at age fourteen; studied six summers with Andres Segovia in Italy and Spain; New York debut at Alice Tully Hall at Lincoln Center (March, 1971).

LOS ANGELES NEOPHONIC ORCHESTRA (jazz orchestra) *see* RUSS GARCIA and BILL HOLMAN

LOTHAR AND THE HAND PEOPLE (rock group)

John Emelin, lothar-theremin (electronic wand which makes shrieking sounds); Tom Flye, drums; Kim King, lead guitar; Paul Conly, rhythm guitar; Rusty Ford, bass guitar; popular in Denver, Colorado (1966); albums—*Lothar and the Hand People, Space Hymn.*

LOTTO, ALBERT

b. 1947 Los Angeles, California.
Pianist. Gave a recital for Princess Grace of Monaco (1971); at the Brooklyn Academy of Music.

LOUD, THOMAS, JR.

b. ca. 1792 England, d. ca. 1866 Philadelphia, Pennsylvania. Organist, pianist, piano maker, and writer. Came to Philadelphia (1812) where he studied music with George Pfeffer; became organist of St. Andrew's (Episcopal) Church; published *The Psalmist* (1824) and *The Organ Study* (1853); his father, Thomas Loud, Sr. patented an upright piano in England (1802), came to New York (1816); Thomas, Jr. founded his piano business in Philadelphia (1816); his brother John Loud became a partner (1818), brother Philologus Loud (1822), then the fourth brother Joseph Loud.

LOUD, THOMAS, SR.

b. ca. 1770 England, d. 1833 New York City. Inventor. Patented an upright piano in England (1802) (John Hawkins had patented an upright piano in America, 1800); came to New York (1816).

LOUDERMILK, JOHN D.

b. 1934 Durham, North Carolina.
Songwriter. Wrote "A Rose and a Baby Ruth" (recorded by George Hamilton IV), "Sittin' on the Balcony" (recorded by Eddie Cochran).

"LOUISIANA HAYRIDE"

Variety show on radio station KWKH, Shreveport, Louisiana; first director was Horace Logan in 1948.

LOUISIANA HAYRIDERS *see* NAT STUCKEY

LOUVIN, CHARLIE

b. 1927 Rainesville, Alabama.
Singer and songwriter. Raised on a farm in Henegar, Alabama; served in World War II; joined his brother Ira in a duo; on station WNOX, Knoxville, Tenn.; served in the Korean War; then teamed with his brother on a Memphis, Tenn. show; they wrote "When I Stop Dreaming," "The Weapon of Prayer," and "I Take the Chance"; after Ira was killed, Charlie's LP record, *I'll Remember Always,* became a best seller in 1967.

LOUVIN, IRA

b. 1924 Rainesville, Alabama, d. 1965 near Jefferson City, Missouri. Singer. Served in

World War II, then joined his brother, Charlie, in a duo; their LP records were *Ira and Charlie* and *Family Who Prays* (1958), *Love Ballads* and *Satan Is Real* (1959), *My Baby's Gone* (1960), *Encore* (1961), *The Weapon of Prayer* (1962), *Keep Your Eyes on Jesus* (1963), *Current Hits* (1964); Ira and his wife, singer Anne Young, were killed in a head-on collision near Jefferson City.

LOVE (rock group)

Arthur Lee, black singer, also on guitar, piano, drums, etc.; John Echols, lead guitar; Bryan Maclean, vocals and guitar; Ken Forssi, electric bass; Michael Stuart, percussion; started in Los Angeles (1965); Alban "Snoopy" Pfisterer and Tjay Cantrelli in the group; albums—*Forever Changes, Love, Love (Da Capo), Love Four Sail, Out Here.*

LOVECRAFT, H. P. (folk-rock group)

George Edwards, vocals and guitar; Dave Michaels, vocals, organ, etc.; Tony Cavallari, vocals and guitar; Mike Tegza, vocals and drums; Jeffrey Boyan, vocals and bass; started in Chicago (1967); albums—*H.P. Lovecraft, H.P. Lovecraft II.*

LOVIN' SPOONFUL (rock group)

Steve Boone, bass; John Sebastian, lead vocals and autoharp; Jerry Yester, lead guitar; Joe Butler, drums; Zal Yanovsky, lead guitar, formerly in the group; started in New York City (1965); group split (1970); albums—*Do You Believe in Magic, Day Dream, What's Up, Tiger Lily, Very Best of the Lovin' Spoonful.*

LOWE, MUNDELL

b. 1922 Laurel, Mississippi.
Guitarist. Played with various bands in 1940s; staff musician with NBC (1950-58); wrote scores for several TV shows; later with ABC-TV in Los Angeles.

LOWELL, JAMES RUSSELL

b. 1819 Cambridge, Massachusetts, d. there 1891. Lyricist. Graduated Harvard (1821) and succeeded Henry Wadsworth Longfellow as professor of belles lettres at Harvard University; wrote "The Concord Hymn" ("By the Rude Bridge That Arched the Flood," 1836, tune—"Old Hundred"), "Men Whose Boast It Is That Ye" (1844, tune—"Ives"), "Once to Every Man and Nation" (1849, tune—"Ton-y-Botel" or "Ebenezer" by T.J. Williams).

LOWRY, ROBERT

b. 1826 Philadelphia, Pennsylvania, d. 1899 Plainfield, New Jersey. Composer. Educated at Bucknell University, Lewisburg, Pa. (B.A., 1854, M.A., 1857); Baptist minister, serving as pastor in Westchester, Pa., New York City, Brooklyn, Lewisburg, Pa., and Plainfield, N.J.; composed the music for "I Need Thee Every Hour" (1872, tune—"Need," w. Annie S. Hawks), "Shall We Gather at the River?" (1864, w. and m.), "All the Way My Savior Leads Me" (1875, w. Fanny Crosby), "Christ Arose!," "Something for Jesus," "One More Day's Work for Jesus" (w. Anna Warner), "Savior, Thy Dying Love" (1879, w. S.D. Phelps); wrote the words and music for the songs "Where Is My Wandering Boy Tonight" (1877) and "Our Boys Are Coming Home" (1865); his collection of gospel songs, *Bright Jewels*, sold over one million copies; with W.H. Doane edited *Pure Gold for the Sunday School* (1871) and *Good as Gold* (1881); with I.D. Sankey, *The Royal Hymnal for the Sunday School* (1898).

LOY, MATTHIAS

b. 1828 Cumberland County, Pennsylvania, d. 1915 Columbus, Ohio. Translator. Became a professor at the Evangelical Lutheran Theological Seminary, Columbus, Ohio (1865); President of Capital University, Columbus (1880); translated several German hymns which were included in the *Evangelical Lutheran Hymnals* of 1858, 1863, and 1880.

LUBOSHUTZ, LEA

b. 1887 Odessa, Russia, d. 1965.
Violinist and teacher. Sister of Pierre Luboshutz and mother of Boris Goldovsky; studied at Moscow Conservatory; soloist with orchestras in Europe and U.S., then became a teacher at Curtis Institute of Music, Philadelphia.

LUBOSHUTZ, PIERRE

b. 1894 Odessa, Russia, d. 1971 Rockport, Maine. Concert pianist. Studied at the Moscow Conservatory (1912); with his sisters Lea, violinist, and Anna, cellist, he toured Europe; married pianist Genia Nemenoff, and they made their debut in a two-piano concert at Town Hall, New York (1937); they taught at Michigan State University, East Lansing, Michigan (1962-68).

LUCA, ALEXANDER C.

b. 1805 Milford, Connecticut, d. 1872 Monrovia, Liberia. Black tenor. Toured with the Hutchinson Family; formed his own group, the Luca Family Singers, which also included John Luca, bass-baritone; Cleveland Luca, pianist; later John Luca joined the Hyer Sisters Colored Minstrels, headed by Anna M.

Hyers and Emma L. Hyers; emigrated to Liberia about 1860.

LUCAS, CLARENCE

b. 1866 Niagara, Ontario, Canada, d. 1947. Conductor, critic, and composer. Studied at the Paris Conservatory; composed operas.

LUCAS, SAM

b. 1840 Washington, Ohio, d. 1916 New York City. Black singer, vaudeville performer, and songwriter. Born Samuel Lucas Milday; joined the Union Army during the Civil War; member of the Hyer Sisters Colored Minstrels; wrote "Daffney, Do You Love Me" (1875, m. Henry Hart), "Thankful Every Time," "Carve Dat 'Possum" ("De possum meat am good to eat"); first sang "Grandfather's Clock" in New Haven, Conn. (1876) which he claimed he sold to Henry C. Work; toured England and gave a command performance for Queen Victoria.

LUCKSTONE, ISIDORE

b. 1861 Baltimore, Maryland, d. 1941 New York City. Teacher. Pupil of P. Scharwenka; accompanist for noted artists on tours; teacher of singing in New York City (1897); also head of vocal department of New York University.

LUDDEN, WILLIAM

b. 1823 Williamsburg, Massachusetts, d. 1912. Organist, conductor, teacher, and editor. Graduated Yale Medical College (1850); studied music in Boston with Lowell Mason and George J. Webb; later in Paris; taught singing in New Haven, Conn.; later in Chicago; then moved to Savannah, Georgia (1896) where he established a publishing house, later known as Ludden & Bates Southern Music House; after retirement lived in Brooklyn, New York.

LUDERS, GUSTAV

b. 1865 Bremen, Germany, d. 1913 New York City. Composer. Wrote *Little Robinson Crusoe* (1899) starring Eddie Foy; with Frank Pixley, book and lyrics, he wrote *The Prince of Pilsen* (1903), *Woodland* (1904), *The Grand Mogul* (1907), *Marcelle* (1908), *The Gipsy* (1912); with George Ade—*The Sho Gun* (1904) and *The Fair Co-Ed* (1909), *Somewhere Else* (1913).

LUENING, OTTO

b. 1900 Milwaukee, Wisconsin.
Composer. Studied at Munich Academy; won Guggenheim Fellowship; studied with Busoni and others; taught at Columbia University, New York City; composed *Concertino* (for flute with strings, harp, and celesta, Philadelphia Chamber Orchestra under Isadore Freed, composer-soloist, 1935), *Two Symphonic Sketches* (New York Philharmonic under Hans Lange, 1936), *Suite for String Orchestra* (Saratoga Spa Festival under F. Charles Adler, 1937), *Evangeline* (opera, Columbia University, 1947).

LULU BELLE

b. 1913 Boone, North Carolina.
Singer. Born Myrtle Eleanor Cooper; on the "National Barn Dance" program, Chicago (1932); married Scotty Wiseman, became the team of Lulu Belle and Scotty, had their own program on WLS, Chicago (1933-58); they retired to Spruce Pine, N.C. (1958); their hit records included "Home Coming Time," "Whippoorwill Time," "Mountain Dew," "Empty Christmas Stocking," "Time Will Tell," "In the Doghouse Now."

LUMAN, BOBBY GLYNN

b. 1937 Nacogdoches, Texas.
Singer. Attended high school in Kilgore, Texas; became a regular on the "Louisiana Hayride" program, Shreveport, La.; Grand Ole Opry, Nashville, Tenn. (1964); his hit records were "Let's Think About Living" (1960), "Ain't Got Time to Be Unhappy" (1968).

LUNCEFORD, JIMMIE

b. 1902 Fulton, Missouri, d. 1947 Seaside, Oregon. Black bandleader. Graduated Fisk University, Nashville, Tenn.; took graduate courses at City College of N.Y.; athletic director in a Memphis, Tenn. high school; organized his band in late 1920s; summer engagements in Lakeside, Ohio; opened at Cotton Club, New York City (1933); became one of the great jazz bands; on the road when he suffered a fatal heart attack.

LUNSFORD, BASCOM LAMAR

b. 1882 Mars Hill, North Carolina, d. 1973. Singer and banjoist. Attended Rutherford and Trinity Colleges; law degree (1913); organized the Mountain Dance and Folk Festival at Asheville, N.C. (1928); sang over 400 songs for the Archive of American Folk Song of the Library of Congress; brought his troupe to the White House (1939) at the request of President F.D. Roosevelt to sing for the King and Queen of England; organized the annual Folk Festival at Renfro, Kentucky (1946); LP records are *Minstrel of the Appalachians*, *Smoky Mountain Ballads.*

LUNT, JOHN REINHOLD

b. 1859 Hamburg, Germany, d. 1925 Buffalo, New York. Conductor and composer. Studied at Leipzig Conservatory; conductor of chorus of Bremen Opera (1880-83); assistant conductor of German Opera Company (1884-87); conductor of Buffalo Orchestra and Orpheus Society (1887-1903); toured as conductor of Victor Herbert operettas; then again in Buffalo after 1914.

LUNT, WILLIAM PARSONS

b. 1805 Newburyport, Massachusetts, d. 1857 Aqaba, Jordan. Hymnist and compiler. Graduated Harvard (1823), Cambridge Divinity (1828); Unitarian pastor in Quincy, Mass. (1835); seven of his hymns appeared in Putnam's *Singers and Songs of the Liberal Faith;* compiled *The Christian Psalet* (1841) which contained seventeen hymns by President John Quincy Adams.

LUTKIN, PETER CHRISTIAN

b. 1858 Thompsonville, Wisconsin, d. 1931 Evanston, Illinois. Composer. Studied music in Europe (1881-84); organist and choirmaster at St. Clement's (Episcopal, 1884-91, Chicago), then St. James' (1891-96), when he became dean of music at Northwestern University, Evanston, Ill.; composed the tune "Carman" (1895, "Come My Soul Thou Must Be Walking," w. F.R.L. von Canitz), and Sanctus in F Minor, "Lanier" (1905, "Into the Woods My Master Went" w. Sidney Lanier), "Theodore" ("Our Father's God, to Thee We Raise" w. Benjamin Copeland, 1903, and "O God of Love, O King of Peace" w. H.W. Baker, 1861), "Patten" ("Almighty Lord, with One Accord," w. M.W. Stryker, 1896).

LUTOSLAWSKI, WITOLD

b. 1913 Warsaw, Poland.
Composer. Studied at Warsaw Conservatory (1934-37); served in Polish army in World War II; became composer-in-residence at Dartmouth College, Hanover, N.H. (1966); known for *Symphonic Variations* (Polish Radio Symphony, 1939), *Variations on a Theme of Paganini* (1914), *Twelve Folk Melodies* for piano (1945), First Symphony (1948), *Triptych Silesien* for soprano and orchestra (Warsaw, 1951), Concerto for Orchestra (Warsaw, 1954), *Miniature Suite* (Warsaw, 1956 and Hartford, Conn., 1958), *Jeux Venitiens*, chance music (Venice, 1961, and Tanglewood, Mass., 1965), *Postludium* for orchestra (1963), *Paroles Tissees* for tenor and orchestra (1965).

LYMON, FRANKIE

b. 1943 Detroit, Michigan, d. 1968.
Black singer and songwriter. Leader of Frankie Lymon and the Teenagers; wrote and recorded "Why Do Fools Fall in Love?" (1956) when only thirteen; his record sold over one million copies; records—"ABC's of Love," "Creation of Love," "Goody Goody," "I Promise to Remember," "I Want You to Be My Girl"; died of an overdose of drugs.

LYNN, JUDY

b. 1936 Boise, Idaho.
Singer and songwriter. At sixteen crowned Queen of the Snake River Stampede, Nampa, Idaho; Miss Idaho (1955) and runner-up Miss America; married John Kelly, promoter; wrote "My Father's Voice," "Antique in My Closet," "Honey Stuff," "The Calm Before the Storm."

LYNN, LORETTA

b. 1935 Butchers Hollow, Kentucky.
Singer. Born Loretta Webb; lived in Wabash, Indiana, then Custer, Washington; formed her own band for night club spots; toured the United States, Canada, and Europe during the 1960s; her hit records were "I'm a Honky Tonk Girl," "Success" (1962); "Before I'm Over You" (1963); "Wine, Women and Song" (1964); "Blue Kentucky Girl," "Happy Birthday," and "The Home You're Tearing Down" (1965); "Dear Uncle Sam," "You Ain't Woman Enough" (1966); "Don't Come Home a-Drinkin' " (1967); at Grand Ole Opry, Nashville, Tenn. (1972).

LYON, GEORGE WASHINGTON

b. 1825, d. 1894.
Instrument maker and dealer. Went to Chicago (1864) with P.J. Healy and established the firm of Lyon & Healy, manufacturers of harps.

LYON, JAMES

b. 1735 Newark, New Jersey, d. 1794 Machias, Maine. Composer. Educated at Princeton, where he composed a graduation ode (1759); Presbyterian minister in Philadelphia (1762-64), then Newark, N.J. (1764), Onslow, Nova Scotia (1765-71), and Machias, Maine (1771-82), then a Congregational minister there (1782-94); in 1761 published *Urania*, a collection of his psalm tunes, anthems and hymns, and in 1792 *Directions for Singing, Keys in Music and Rules of Transposition.*

LYONS, JAMES

b. 1932 Jersey City, New Jersey.
Black alto saxist. Raised in Harlem, New

York City; served in Korea in army during Korean War; played with Cecil Taylor after 1960 in New York City and Copenhagen, Denmark.

LYTELL, JIMMY (JAMES SARRAPEDE)

b. 1906 Brooklyn, New York, d. 1973 Kings Point, New York. Jazz clarinetist and bandleader. Played professionally by age fourteen; formed own Dixieland jazz band in 1920s; had radio show in 1940s.

LYTLE, JOHN DILLARD

b. 1932 Springfield, Ohio.
Black vibraphonist. Played drums at age nine in his father's band; with Ray Charles, Gene Ammons, Boots Johnson and others in 1950s; played vibes in his own trio after 1957.

MC ALLISTER, D.C.

b. 1853 Battle Creek, Michigan, d. 1920. Singer, conductor, composer, and teacher. Raised in Kalmazoo, Mich.; studied singing under his parents; prominent tenor and choir director in Kalamazoo; wrote *Bye and Bye Is Surely Coming* (duet and chorus), *Centennial Anthem* (quartet and chorus), "I Will Lift Up Mine Eyes" (octavo anthem, 121st Psalm), *Hail, Festival Day* (octavo).

MAC ARTHUR, MARGARET (CROWL)

b. 1928 Chicago, Illinois.
Singer and autoharpist. Raised in Licking, Mo., Salinas, Calif., Napoleonville, La., Moncks Corner, South Carolina; attended University of Chicago; married and moved to Marlboro, Vermont; LP record is *Folk Songs of Vermont* (1963).

MC AULIFFE, WILLIAM LEON

b. 1917 Houston, Texas.
Popular composer. Raised in Houston; member of a local band at age sixteen; with Pappy O'Daniel (1933-35); with Bob Wills and the Texas Playboys (1935-42); flight instructor in navy in World War II; organized the Western String Band, Tulsa, Okla. (1946), later changed to the Cimarron Boys; wrote "Steel Guitar Rag," "Redskin Rag," "Panhandle Rag," "Cozy Inn" (1961), "Faded Love" (1962), "I Don't Love Nobody" (1963).

MACBETH, FLORENCE

b. 1891 Mankato, Minnesota.
Coloratura soprano. Studied with Yeatman Griffith; opera debut at Darmstadt (1913); with Chicago Opera Company after 1914; with Ravinia Opera and in concerts.

MC BRIDE, ROBERT GUYN

b. 1911 Tucson, Arizona.
Composer. Taught at the University of Arizona, Tucson, and Bennington College, Vermont; composed *Prelude to a Tragedy* (New York Philharmonic under Hans Lange, 1935), *Fugato on a Well Known Theme* (University Chamber Orchestra, Tucson, 1935), *Mexican Rhapsody* (for orchestra), *Show Piece* (ballet, Ballet Caravan, 1937—orchestra suite by Philadelphia Orchestra under Stokowski, 1937), *Workout* (for oboe and piano).

MC BROWNE, LEONARD LEWIS

b. 1933 Brooklyn, New York.
Black drummer. Played with Pete Brown, Buster Bailey, and Paul Bley in 1950s; led own combo, The Four Souls (1959-61); with Sarah Vaughan, Randy Weston, Teddy Wilson and others in 1960s.

MC CABE, CHARLES C.

b. 1836 Athens, Ohio, d. 1906 New York City. Singer. Graduated Ohio Wesleyan University, Delaware, Ohio; in 1862 appointed chaplain of the 122nd Ohio Infantry and became known as the "Singing Chaplain" of the Civil War; captured in June, 1863, at Winchester, Virginia, and imprisoned in Libby Prison, Richmond, Va.; in 1896 elected bishop of the Methodist Episcopal Church; with D.T. MacFarlan compiled *Winnowed Hymns* (1873). At the Christian Meeting in Washington, D.C., February, 1864, attended by President Lincoln, McCabe sang "The Battle Hymn of the Republic," and the President requested McCabe to sing it again. In January, 1865, at another meeting of the Commission, McCabe again sang "The Battle Hymn," and President Lincoln joined in the chorus.

MC CANN, LESLIE COLEMAN (LES)

b. 1935 Lexington, Kentucky.
Black pianist, singer, and composer. Served in U.S. Navy in 1950s; with singer Gene McDaniels (1959); organized his own trio (1959); at Antibes Festival (1962); toured Europe (1963) with Zoot Sims and Charles Byrd; wrote "The Shout," "The Shampoo," "The Truth," "It's Way Past Suppertime"; at the Newport Jazz Festival, New York City (1972).

MACARTHY, HARRY

b. 1834 England, d. 1888 Oakland, California. Singer and entertainer in Arkansas. Came to

America (1849); composed "The Bonnie Blue Flag" (1860, the original Confederate flag of South Carolina was blue; based on the melody "The Irish Jaunting Car"), "Missouri," "A Voice from the South" (1861), "The Origin of the Stars and Bars, Our Flag," "The Volunteer," and "It Is My Country's Call" which was dedicated to the New Orleans Cadets. "The Bonnie Blue Flag" was sung in Jackson, Mississippi, at the Mississippi Convention which passed the secession act on January 9, 1861. Later, as other states seceded, additional verses were added to "The Bonnie Blue Flag" to cover each state in the Confederacy.

MC CARTHY, JOSEPH

b. 1885 Somerville, Massachusetts, d. 1943 New York City. Lyricist. With various publishers; wrote "Rambling Rose" (1918, m. Joe Burke), "I'm Always Chasing Rainbows" (1918, m. Harry Carroll), "Oui, Oui Marie" (1918, with Alfred Bryan, m. Fred Fisher). (*See also* James V. Monaco, Al Piantadosi, Harry Tierney, Percy Wenrich)

MACARTY, EUGENE VICTOR

b. 1821 New Orleans, Louisiana, d. after 1880. Black composer. Active in New Orleans after the Civil War.

MC CLURE, RONALD DIX

b. 1941 New Haven, Connecticut.
Bass player. Graduated Julius Hartt Conservatory, Hartford, Conn. (1962); with Maynard Ferguson, Marian McPartland Trio, Wynton Kelly Trio and others during 1960s.

MAC COLL, HUGH FREDERICK

b. 1885 Pawtucket, Rhode Island, d. 1953 Providence, Rhode Island. Composer. Graduated from Harvard College in music; studied under Converse and Spaulding; his *Arabs* (symphonic illustration, 1932) performed by Boston, Providence, and Rochester Symphony Orchestras, *Ballad for Orchestra and Piano* (1934), and *Romantic Suite in Form of Variations* (1935) also performed by Providence Symphony Orchestra and other orchestras.

MC COLLIN, FRANCES

b. 1892 Philadelphia, Pennsylvania, d. there 1960. Composer. She composed four works for string orchestra: *Adagio; Two Chorale Preludes; Scherzo Heavenly Children at Play; Prayer;* all performed by the Philadelphia Chamber String Simfonietta; also other orchestra works and chamber music.

MC CONATHY, OSBOURNE

b. 1875 Pitts Point, Kentucky, d. 1949. Conductor. Studied with Luther Mason and others; director of Louisville Festivals (1900-03); conductor in Boston (1904-12); associate conductor of North Shore Festivals, Evanston, Illinois (1913-25); president of Music Teachers National Association.

MC CORMACK, JOHN

b. 1884 Athlone, Ireland, d. 1945 Dublin, Ireland. Noted tenor. Studied under Sabbatini; won Gold Medal at the National Irish Festival (1902); sang in the Dublin Catholic choir; debut at Convent Garden, London (1907); New York debut at Manhattan Opera House (1910); with the Boston Opera (1910-11) and the Chicago Opera (1912-14); became an American citizen (1917); became famous singing Irish songs.

MC COY, FREDERICK ALLAN

b. 1932 New York City.
Vibraphonist. Played with Kenny Burrell, Philly Joe Jones and others in 1960s; formed own combo.

MC COY, SETH

b. 1928 Sanford, North Carolina.
Black tenor. Graduated North Carolina Agricultural and Technical College at Greensboro (1950); served in the Korean War; studied with Pauline Tesmacher at the Music School Settlement in Cleveland; with the Robert Shaw Chorale (1963-65); soloist at Philharmonic Hall, New York (1972); debut at Tully Hall with the Bach Aria Group, New York (1973); at Carnegie Hall, New York (1973); at Mostly Mozart Festival at Philharmonic Hall (1973).

MC COY, WILLIAM J.

b. 1848 Crestline, Ohio, d. 1926.
Composer and writer. Composed the song, "May."

MC COYS (rock group)

Rick Zehringer, vocals and guitar; Randy Zehringer, drums; Randy Hobbs, bass; Bobbie Peterson, organ; first recorded in 1965; albums—*Hang on Sloopy, Human Ball, You Make Me Feel So Good.*

MC CRACKEN, ROBERT EDWARD

b. 1904 Dallas, Texas.
Clarinetist and tenor saxist. With Trumbauer

and Venuti in 1930s; with Benny Goodman, Russ Morgan and others in 1940s; with Louis Armstrong, Ben Pollack, Kid Ory and others in 1950s; played in various night spots in California during 1960s.

MC CREE, JUNIE

b. 1865 Toledo, Ohio, d. 1918 New York City. Lyricist and actor. Wrote "Put Yours Arms Around Me Honey, Hold Me Tight" (1910, m. Albert von Tilzer).

M'CREERY, JOHN

b. ca. 1780 Ireland, d. 1825.
Composer and arranger. Settled in Petersburg, Virginia; wrote *The American Star* (1812); arranged *A Selection of the Ancient Music of Ireland* (published in 1824) which contained 204 tunes.

MC CREERY, JOHN LUCKEY

b. 1835 Sweden, New York, d. 1906 Washington, D.C. Hymnist. Learned the printer's trade in Dixon, Ill., then published the *Delaware County Journal*, Delhi, Iowa; wrote the hymn "There Is No Death," which first appeared in *Arthur's Home Magazine*, (July, 1863); moved to Washington, D.C. in 1880, where he worked for the government in different positions.

MC CURDY, ED

b. 1919 Willow Hill, Pennsylvania.
Ballad singer. Raised in Shippensburg, Pa.; attended Panhandle A&M College in Goodwell, Okla., and Oklahoma Central State; debut on Canadian Broadcasting System (1946); moved to New York City (1954); hit albums—*The Ballad Record, Ballad Singer's Choice, Barroom Ballads, Ed McCurdy, Songs of the Old West, Blood, Booze 'n Bones, Ed McCurdy's Treasure Chest.*

MC CURDY, ROY WALTER, JR.

b. 1936 Rochester, New York.
Drummer. Studied at Eastman School in Rochester at age ten; played in Air Force band; with Art Farmer, Cannonball Adderley and others in 1960s; toured Europe (1962) and Japan (1963); at Newport Jazz Festival (1963).

MC CUTCHAN, ROBERT GUY

b. 1877 Mount Ayr, Iowa, d. 1958 Claremont, California. Composer. Educated at Park College, Parkville, Mo., Simpson College, Indianola, Iowa, and in Berlin and Paris; taught music at Baker University, Baldwin City, Kansas (1904-10), and DePauw University, Greencastle, Indiana, from 1911; composed the tune "Fowler" for "My God, I Thank Thee" (w. Adelaide A. Procter, second tune, "Wentworth"), "Oxnam" (1929, used for "Rise Up, O Men of God," w. W.P. Merrill), "DePauw" at Lake Winona, Ind. (1930, for "Thou Rulest, Lord, the Lights on High," w. Theodore Williams), "Responses to the Beatitudes of Our Lord" (1932), and "Thy Testimonies Are Very Sure"; musical editor of *Standard Hymns* and *The Methodist Hymnal* (1935).

MAC DERMOT, GALT

b. 1928 Montreal, Quebec, Canada.
Composer. Composed the rock opera *Hair* (libretto—Gerome Ragni and James Rado) opened (1968) at Joe Papp's Public Theater, New York City, moved later to the Biltmore Theater, 47th St. West of Broadway; his Mass in F premiered at Cathedral Church of St. John the Divine (1971); albums—*Hairpieces, Galt MacDermot's First Natural Hair Band.*

MACDONALD, BALLARD

b. 1882 Portland, Oregon, d. 1935 Forest Hills, New York. Lyricist. Educated at Princeton University; wrote "Play That Barber Shop Chord" (1910, m. Lewis F. Muir), "The Trail of the Lonesome Pine" (1913, m. Harry Carroll), "Back Home Again in Indiana" (1917, m. James F. Hanley).

MC DONALD, ENOS WILLIAM ("SKEETS")

b. 1915 Greenway, Arkansas, d. 1968 Inglewood, California. Singer and songwriter. Sang on Royal Oak, Flint, and Pontiac, Michigan, radio stations; later sang with the Lonesome Cowboys; wrote "Bless Your Little Old Heart," "A Big Family Trouble," "I'm Hurtin'," "Baby Brown Eyes."

MC DONALD, HARL

b. 1899 Boulder, Colorado, d. 1955 Princeton, New Jersey. Composer. Educated at the University of Southern California, Los Angeles, University of Redlands, Calif., and Leipzig Conservatory, Germany; taught at the University of Pennsylvania, Philadelphia; became manager of the Philadelphia Orchestra (1939); composed *Rhumba* (for orchestra, 1935), *Three Hebrew Poems* (for orchestra, 1936), and *Saga of the Mississippi* (for orchestra, 1947, introduced by the Philadelphia Orchestra, Eugene Ormandy conducting, 1948).

MAC DONALD, JEANETTE

b. 1907 Philadelphia, Pennsylvania, d. 1965. Singer. New York debut (1920) in the chorus of *The Demi-Tasse Revue;* appeared in films after 1925; made a concert tour of Europe (1931); starred with Nelson Eddy in the films *Naughty Marietta* (1935), *Rose Marie* (1936), *Maytime* (1937), *The Girl of the Golden West* (1938), *Sweethearts* (1938); married Gene Raymond; sang in grand opera with Ezio Pinza in *Romeo and Juliet* in Montreal and in *Faust* in Chicago.

MC DONALD, WILLIAM

b. 1820 Belmont, Maine, d. 1901 Monrovia, California. Hymnist and compiler. Methodist minister in the Maine Conference (1843), Wisconsin Conference (1855), and the New England Conference (1859); issued *The Western Minstrel* (1840) and *Beluh Songs* (1870); wrote the hymn "I Am Coming to the Cross" (1872, m. W.G. Fischer).

MAC DONOUGH, GLEN

b. 1870 Brooklyn, New York, d. 1924 Stamford, Connecticut. Lyricist. Educated at The Gunnery and Manhattan College; wrote "White Light Alley" (1920, m. A.B. Sloane), "Toyland" (m. Victor Herbert) for the operetta *Babes in Toyland,* produced at Chicago Opera House (1903).

MAC DOWELL, EDWARD ALEXANDER

b. 1861 New York City, d. there 1908. Famous composer and pianist. Studied piano with Teresa Carrena, then in France and Germany; head of the music department of Columbia University, New York City (1896-1904); best-known for his piano suites *To a Wild Rose* and *To a Water Lily;* also wrote an *Indian Suite* (for orchestra), two concertos for piano and orchestra, four sonatas for piano, and several symphonic poems.

MC DOWELL, FREDERICK ("MISSISSIPPI FRED")

b. 1904 Rossville, Tennessee, d. 1972 Memphis, Tennessee. Gospel singer and composer. Resided in Como, Miss.; sang in a concert at the New School, directed by Alan Lomax (ca. 1965); at the Gaslight Cafe, New York City (1970); toured Europe; at Newport Jazz Festival and the Ann Arbor Blues Festival in 1969 and 1970; wrote "You Got to Move" (recorded by the Rolling Stones), "I Do Not Play No Rock and Roll," nominated for a Grammy Award.

MC DUFF, BROTHER JACK

b. 1926 Champaign, Illinois.
Organist and composer. Born Eugene McDuffy; led his own group in Cincinnati, Ohio in 1950s and toured the Midwest; at Nice, France Jazz Festival (1964-65); in Stockholm, Sweden (1965); wrote *Dink's Blues, Sanctified Waltz, Rock Candy.*

MC ENERY, DAVE ("RED RIVER DAVE")

b. 1914 San Antonio, Texas.
Singer and songwriter. Leader of Swift Cowboys; wrote "The Blind Boy's Dog," "A Sinner's Prayer," "I Won't Care a Hundred Years from Now," "I Bought a Rock for a Rocky Mountain Gal," "It's for God and Country and You Mom."

MC FARLAND, GARY

b. 1933 Los Angeles, California, d. 1971 New York City. Vibraharpist, conductor, and composer. Studied at Berklee School of Music; at the University of Oregon, Eugene, Oregon; awarded Best New Composer by *Downbeat Magazine* (1963); musical director of Downbeat Jazz Festival, Chicago (1965); conductor of the University of California at L.A. Jazz Festival (1967); wrote jazz ballet *Reflections in the Park* (1964); conducted eleven of his own compositions at the "Profiles" concert at Philharmonic Hall, New York City (1966).

MC FARLAND, JOHN THOMAS

b. 1851 Mount Vernon, Indiana, d. 1913 Maplewood, New Jersey. Hymnist. Attended Iowa Wesleyan University, Mt. Pleasant, Iowa, Simpson College, Indianola, Iowa, and Boston University School of Theology; served as a minister in several areas, then Secretary of the Sunday School Union; in 1904 became editor of *Sunday School Literature* for the Methodist Church; wrote the third verse for "Away in a Manger." (*See* J.E. Spilman)

MC FARLAND, LESTER ("MAC")

b. 1902 Gray, Kentucky.
Singer and songwriter. Attended the Kentucky School for the Blind (1913-18); concert pianist; Mac and Bob Gardner after 1922; wrote "Orphan Girl," "Kentucky Bride's Fate," "Hut on the Back of the Lot," "Go and Leave Me if You Wish To," "Does True Love Live Today."

MC 5 (rock group)

Rob Tyner, vocals and sax; Fred Smith, guitar; Michael Davis, bass; Dennis Thompson, drums; Wayne Kramer, lead guitar; group from Detroit (1968); album—*MC 5.*

MC GARITY, ROBERT LOUIS (LOU)

b. 1917 Athens, Georgia, d. 1971 Alexandria, Virginia. Trombonist. At nineteen he appeared with Kirk Devore in Atlanta, Ga., and at twenty with Nye Mayhew at Glen Island Casino, N.Y.; with Ben Bernie (1938-40); then with Benny Goodman; toured Japan with Bob Crosby (1964) and in 1967 appeared with Pee Wee Erwin at Carnegie Hall.

MC GEE, KIRK

b. 1899 Franklin, Tennessee.
Singer and guitarist. Member of Sam and Kirk McGee from Sunny Tennessee after 1923; Fruit Jar Drinkers after 1937.

MC GEE, SAM FLEMING

b. 1894 Franklin, Tennessee.
Singer and banjoist. Member of Sam and Kirk McGee from Sunny Tennessee after 1923; Fruit Jar Drinkers after 1937.

MC GHEE, ANDY

b. 1927 Wilmington, North Carolina.
Tenor saxist, flutist, and clarinetist. Studied at New England Conservatory, Boston (1949); with Lionel Hampton (1957-63), then with Woody Herman.

MC GHEE, HOWARD

b. 1918 Tulsa, Oklahoma.
Black trumpeter. Played with Lionel Hampton, Charlie Barnet, Andy Kirk and others in 1940s; also with Count Basie, Billy Eckstine; with J.J. Johnson and Sonny Stitt in 1960s; organized his own band (1966); Howard McGhee's Big Band and the John Oddo Trio on "Jazz on the River" boat cruises, New York City (1972).

MC GHEE, WALTER BROWN ("BROWNIE")

b. 1915 Knoxville, Tennessee.
Black singer, pianist, and guitarist. Stricken with poliomyelitis at age four; raised in Kingsport, Lenoir City, and Marysville, Tenn.; with Sonny Terry after 1939 and Harry Belafonte after 1959; also toured Europe with Terry (1962-64); at Newport Jazz Festivals (1961-62); his hit records include *Traditional Blues* (1958), *On the Road with Burris* (1959), *Brownie's Blues* (1960), *Blues in My Soul* (1961), *Blues and Shouts* (1962), *Down Home Blues* (1963).

MC GRANAHAN, JAMES

b. 1840 Adamsville, Pennsylvania, d. 1907.
Composer. Resided in Kinsman, Ohio; composed the music for "He Will Hide Me" (w. Mary E. Servoss), "Revive Thy Work, O Lord" (w. Albert Midlane, 1860) and "Come" ("O, Word of Words the Sweetest," w. Mrs. James Gibson Johnson) published in *Gospel Hymns.*

MC GREGOR, ERNEST FRANK

b. 1879 Alexandria, New Hampshire, d. 1946.
Hymnist. Educated at the University of Minnesota, Minneapolis, and at Yale, where he received his Ph.D. (1910); held pastorates at Avon and Clinton, Conn., then went to the Congregational Church in Norwalk, Conn. (1912); wrote the hymn "Lift High the Triumph Song Today" (1931, tune "Suomi"—Finnish calvary march from the Thirty Year's War).

MC GRIFF, JIMMY

b. 1936 Philadelphia, Pennsylvania.
Organist. Formed his own trio; played at the Antibes Jazz Festival.

MC GUIRE SISTERS (vocal group)

Christine (b. 1928); Dorothy (b. 1930); Phyllis (b. 1931); all three born in Middletown, Ohio; albums—*Best of the McGuire Sisters, McGuire Sisters, Our Golden Favorites.*

MC HUGH, JIMMY

b. 1894 Boston, Massachusetts, d. 1969 Beverly Hills, California. Composer. Attended Staley College, Boston; came to New York City and wrote songs for the Cotton Club in Harlem (1921); with lyricist Dorothy Fields wrote "I Can't Give You Anything but Love, Baby" (1928), "On the Sunny Side of the Street" (1928), "Cuban Love Song," "Don't Blame Me," "I'm in the Mood for Love"; with Harold Adamson—"It's a Most Unusual Day"; also wrote "South American Way" (1939) and "Comin' in on a Wing and a Prayer" (1943).

MC INTOSH, RIGDON M.

b. 1836, d. 1899.
Composer. Associated with L.C. Everett Company, song book publishers in Richmond, Virginia; the firm was very active in the South prior to the Civil War; composed music under the pseudonym Emilius Laroche; wrote the tune "The Kingdom Coming" ("From All Dark Places," w. Mary B.C. Slade).

MC INTOSH, THOMAS S.

b. 1927 Baltimore, Maryland.
Trombonist and composer. Studied at Peabody Conservatory in Baltimore; played in U.S. Army band; graduated Juilliard School, New York City (1958); with Art Farmer-Benny Golson Jazztet, James Moody, New York Jazz Sextet, Mel Lewis-Thad Jones

and others in 1960s; wrote *Something Old, Something New* for Dizzy Gillespie (1963). Gillespie (1963).

MC INTYRE, HAL

b. 1914 Cromwell, Connecticut, d. 1959 Los Angeles, California. Saxophonist and bandleader. Joined Glenn Miller's band in Cromwell, Conn. (1937); left the band (1941); formed his own band; played at President Franklin D. Roosevelt's Birthday Ball at the Statler Hotel, Washington, D.C. (1945); entertained the U.S. troops overseas; a carelessly discarded lighted cigarette caused a bedroom fire which snuffed out his life.

MC INTYRE, KENNETH ARTHUR

b. 1931 Boston, Massachusetts.
Alto saxist. Studied piano at age nine; served in U.S. Army during Korean War; graduated Boston Conservatory of Music; organized his own group in New York City; at Newport Jazz Festival (1963); taught in New York public schools.

MACKAY, CHARLES

b. 1814 Perth, Scotland, d. 1889.
Lyricist. Known as "The People's Singer and Friend"; came to America (1857), and from 1862-65 was a war correspondent for the *London Times;* wrote the lyrics "If I Were a Voice, a Persuasive Voice" (m. I.B. Woodbury), and the words and music "The Voice of the Crowd," "There's a Good Time Coming," "Cheer Boys, Cheer" (1861, m. Henry Russell).

MC KAY, GEORGE FREDERICK

b. 1899 Harrington, Washington.
Composer. Graduated Eastman School of Music, Rochester, N.Y.; composed *From a Mountain Town* (sinfonietta, People's Symphony, Boston, under Sevitzky, 1934), *Fantasy on a Western Folk Song* (for chamber orchestra, Seattle Symphony, 1935), *To a Liberator* (symphonic poem, Indianapolis Symphony under Sevitzky, 1940), *Organ Sonata* (first prize of American Guild of Organists), *Violin Concerto* (honorable mention, Jascha Heifetz Contest).

MACKELLER, THOMAS

b. 1812 New York City, d. 1899.
Hymnist. Worked for Harper Bros., publishers, when he was fourteen, then joined a type foundry in Philadelphia (1833), which later became Mackeller, Smiths & Jordan; several of his hymns appeared in *Lyra Sacra Americana* (1868) and *Hymns and Songs of Praise* (1874); wrote *Hymns and a Few Metrical Psalms* (Philadelphia, 1883).

MC KENNA, DAVID J.

b. 1930 Woonsocket, Rhode Island.
Pianist. Played with Woody Herman, Charlie Ventura, Bobby Hackett and others in 1950s; later with Buddy Morrow.

MAC KENZIE, GISELLE

b. 1927 Winnipeg, Manitoba, Canada.
Singer and entertainer. Singer in night clubs in New York City; album—*Gisele MacKenzie in Person at the Empire Room.*

MC KENZIE, SCOTT

b. (?).
Singer. Started in San Francisco (1967); made a hit with his single, "San Francisco—Wear Some Flowers in Your Hair"; formed the Smoothies, with Papa Phillips; later The Journeymen; made his mistake by not joining the Mamas and the Papas; album—*Voice of Scott McKenzie.*

MC KENZIE, WILLIAM ("RED")

b.1899 St. Louis, Missouri, d. 1948 New York City. Singer and bandleader. Leader of the Mound City Blue Blowers.

MC KIBBON, ALFRED BENJAMIN (AL)

b. 1919 Chicago, Illinois.
Bass player. With Dizzy Gillespie and others in 1940s; with George Shearing Quintet and Cal Tjader in 1950s; later played with various groups in Los Angeles area; played at Newport Jazz Festival, New York City (1972).

MC KINLEY, CARL K.

b. 1895 Yarmouth, Maine.
Composer and teacher. Graduated Knox College, Galesburg, Ill., and Harvard University; studied with Goldmark, Nadia Boulanger and others; Guggenheim Fellowship (1927-29); taught at the New England Conservatory, Boston; composed *The Blue Flower* (symphonic poem, Flager Prize), also conducted his *Masquerade* at the New York Stadium Concerts (1926).

MC KINLEY, RAY

b. 1910 Fort Worth, Texas.
Drummer and bandleader. Played with Jimmy Dorsey and others in 1930s; co-led band with trombonist Will Bradley (1939-42); then led own band; co-leader with Jerry Gray of Glen Miller's band after Miller's death; led new Glen Miller band after 1957; toured

Japan (1964-65); resigned from band (1966); for a time Ed Sauter was his arranger; at Roseland Dance City, New York City (1972).

MC KINNEY'S COTTON PICKERS

Led by William McKinney, black drummer, originally a quartet from Paducah, Kentucky.

MACKINNON, HUGH A.

b. 1891 St. Johnsbury, Vermont.
Organist and teacher. Educated at Dartmouth College, Hanover, N.H. (1914), and Trinity School of Church Music, New York City (1916); organist-choirmaster in St. Johnsbury, Vt. (1906), Hanover, N.H. (1911), Newark, N.J. (1914), New York City (1915), East Hampton, Long Island (1917), Utica, N.Y. (1918), Laramie, Wyoming (1929), San Francisco, Calif. (1942); became a teacher at the University of Wyoming, Laramie (1946).

MC KUEN, ROD

b. 1933 Oakland, California.
Singer and composer. Served in the army in Japan and Korea during the Korean War; sang for President Rhee of Korea, Queen Elizabeth of England, and for President John F. Kennedy at White House dinners; won Grand Prix du Disc, Paris, and eleven ASCAP awards; his works include *The Sea, Something Beyond,* First and Second Piano Concertos, *Structures in Jazz,* and over 100 popular songs; in concert at Carnegie Hall, New York City (1972).

MC KUSICK, HAROLD WILFRED (HAL)

b. 1924 Medford, Massachusetts.
Saxist, flutist, and clarinetist. With Claude Thornhill, Woody Herman, Boyd Raeburn and others in 1940s and '50s; after 1958 staff musician with CBS.

MC LEAN, DON

b. 1945.
Folk singer and guitarist. Worked with Josh White and Pete Seeger; performed in coffee houses in New York City and at folk clubs; recorded "Tapestry" (1971), "American Pie," hit record (1972).

MC LEAN, JOHN LEONARD (JACKIE)

b. 1932 New York City.
Alto saxist. Played with Art Blakey, Charles Mingus and others in 1950s; toured Europe (1960-63); Japan (1965); played in New York City night clubs; albums: *'Bout Soul, Action Action Action, Bluesnik, Capuchin Swing, Destination Out, Fickle Sonance, Inta Somethin', It's Time, Jackie's Bag, Jazz Interplay, Let Freedom Ring, Lights Out, New and Old Gospel, New Soil, One Step Beyond.*

MAC LEISH, ARCHIBALD

b. 1892 Glencoe, Illinois.
Poet and author. Eight of his poems were set to music by Ross Lee Finney and introduced by Mabel Garrison (1935).

MC LELLAN, C.M.S.

b. 1892 Bath, Maine, d. 1916 London, England. Lyricist and playwright. Lived in London after 1897; wrote "My Beautiful Lady" for *The Pink Lady* (m. Ivan Caryll), New York City (1911) and in London (1912).

MACLENNAN, FRANCIS

b. 1870 Bay City, Michigan, d. 1935 Port Washington, New York. Tenor. Studied in New York, London, and Berlin; sang in London (1902); with Savage Opera Company in the States after 1904; Royal Opera, Berlin (1907); Hamburg Opera (1913); Chicago Opera (1915-17); then again in Berlin; married soprano Florence Easton; they were divorced.

MC LEOD, ALICE

b. 1937 Detroit, Michigan.
Pianist. Half-sister of bass player Ernie Farrow; with Terry Gibbs Quartet (1961-62); joined John Coltrane combo (1966); married Coltrane (1966).

MC MICHEN, CLAYTON

b. 1900 Allatoona, Georgia.
Singer and songwriter. Leader of the Georgia Wildcats (1932); wrote "My Carolina Home," "Dear Old Dixie Land," "Corn Licker Still in Georgia," "When I Lived Up in Arkansaw," "McMichen's Breakdown," "Giving Everything Away."

MAC MILLAN, ERNEST CAMPBELL

b. 1893 Mimico, Ontario, Canada, d. 1973. Conductor, organist, and teacher. Studied in Toronto and Edinburgh, Mus.D. at Oxford (1918); principal of Toronto Conservatory (1926) and dean of music at University of Toronto; knighted (1935); conducted Toronto Symphony Orchestra; composed orchestral and chamber music.

MC NAIR, HAROLD

b. 1931 Kingston, Jamaica, B.W.I.
Flutist and saxist. Played with Kenny Clarke in Paris (1960-61); later with Quincy Jones; in Bahamas (1962); played in New York City after 1965.

MC PARTLAND, JAMES DUGALD

b. 1907 Chicago, Illinois.
Cornetist and trumpeter. Played with Ben Pollack in 1920s; also with Jack Teagarden, the Wolverines and others; served in World War II; married pianist Marian Page (1945); led his own groups; also appeared with his wife; later with Tony Parenti in 1960s; album—*Dixieland;* Jimmie MacPartland Dixieland Band at City Hall, New York City (1972).

MC PARTLAND, MARIAN PAGE

b. 1918 Slough, Buckinghamshire, England.
Pianist and composer. Toured with USO during World War II; married Jimmy McPartland (1945); played with her husband (1946-50); formed own trio (1951); wrote "There'll Be Other Times" (recorded by Sarah Vaughan), "Twilight World" (played on "Tonight" show; albums—*Marian McPartland, "Great" Britains—McPartland and Shearing.*

MC PEAKE, WILLIAM CURTIS ("BIG RED")

b. 1927 Scotts Hill, Tennessee.
Singer and banjoist. With Grand Ole Opry, Nashville, Tenn. after 1956.

MC PHATTER, CLYDE L.

b. 1931, d. 1972 Bronx, New York.
Black rhythm and blues singer. Pioneer rock 'n roll singer; formed the Drifters and was the lead singer; later replaced by Ben E. King; the Drifter sound was notable for the sweep of violins in the background; group remained popular in the 1960s; he recorded the million-seller, "A Lover's Question"; died of a heart attack.

MC PHEE, COLIN

b. 1901 Montreal, Quebec, Canada, d. 1964.
Composer. Composed *Sea Chanty* (suite for baritone and unison male chorus), *Sarabande* (for orchestra), piano concerto with orchestra, piano concerto with orchestra and wind octet, sonatina for two flutes, clarinet, trumpet, and piano, symphony in one movement, songs; taught at University of California, Los Angeles (1958-64).

MC PHERSON, CHARLES

b. 1939 Joplin, Missouri.
Black alto saxist. Played with Barry Harris, Lonnie Hillyer and others in late 1950s; with Charles Mingus, Barry Harris and others in 1960s; formed own group with Hillyer; albums—*Bebop Revisited, Con Alma, From This Moment On, Horizons, Charles McPherson—The Quintet Live, McPherson's Mood.*

MC RAE, CARMEN

b. 1922 New York City.
Black singer and pianist. Played and sang with Benny Carter, Mercer Ellington and others in 1940s; later she went solo and became famous; at Monterey Jazz Festival (1962); World Jazz Festival, Japan (1964); later accompanied by Norman Simmons Trio; albums—*Alfie, For Once in My Life, Haven't We Met, "Live" and Wailing, Carmen McRae in Person, San Francisco, My Foolish Heart, Portrait of Carmen, Second to None, Woman Talk;* at Alice Tully Hall, New York City (1972).

MAC RAE, GORDON

b. 1921 East Orange, New Jersey.
Singer. Sang with Jo Stafford, their first hit record was "Whispering Hope" (1949, m. Septimus Winner, 1868); sang in Broadway shows with Dorothy Kirsten; appeared in twenty-one films; sang in New York City night clubs, at Maisonette, St. Regis Hotel (1972); albums—*Carousel, Desert Song* (with Kirsten), *New Moon* (with Kirsten), *Oklahoma, Student Prince* (with Kirsten), *There's Peace in the Valley* (with Jo Stafford), *Whispering Hope* (with Stafford).

MC REYNOLDS, JAMES MONROE (JIM)

b. 1927 Coeburn, Virginia.
Singer and guitarist. Partner with his brother in the duo "Jim & Jesse"; radio debut on WNVA, Norton, Virginia (1947); station WVLK, Lexington, Kentucky (1952); WNOX, Knoxville, Tenn. (1954); "Swanee River Jamboree," Live Oak, Florida (1955); "Lowndes County Jamboree," Valdosta, Georgia (1957); their records were *Jim & Jesse* (1963), *Bluegrass* (1963), *Country Church* (1964), *Diesel by the Trail* (1966), *Thunder Road* (1967), *Tijuana Taxi* (1967).

MC REYNOLDS, JESSE

b. 1929 Coeburn, Virginia.
Singer and mandolinist. Partner with his brother in the duo "Jim & Jesse"; served in the armed forces in Korea (1952-54).

MC SHANN, JAY ("HOOTIE")

b. 1909 Muskogee, Oklahoma.
Black pianist and bandleader. Led his own band in 1930s and '40s; saxophonist Paul Quinichette and Charlie Parker played in his bands; Al Hibbler sang in his bands; played in Kansas City night clubs in 1950s and '60s; at the Kansas City Jazz Festival (1964).

MC WHOOD, LEONARD BEECHER

b. 1870 Brooklyn, New York, d. 1939 Hanover, New Hampshire. Teacher.

Graduated Columbia University, New York City (1893) and remained there as a graduate student for five years under Edward A. MacDowell; taught music in Newark, N.J., Columbia University, N.Y., Vassar, Poughkeepsie, N.Y. and after 1918 at Dartmouth College, Hanover, N.H.; composed the tune "Hymn of Nations" for his words "All People of the Earth" (1933).

MAAS, LOUIS

b. 1852 Wiesbaden, Germany, d. 1889 Boston, Massachusetts. Pianist. conductor, and composer. Graduated King's College, London, at age fifteen, with high honors; studied at the Leipzig Conservatory under Reinecke and Papperitz; his first overture performed (1868) in Gewandhaus Hall, Leipzig; conducted his first symphony (1872) at Gewandhaus; came to America (1880) and taught at the New England Conservatory, Boston.

MAAZEL, LORIN

b. 1930 Paris, France.
Conductor. His parents were musicians from Los Angeles, and were studying in Paris; they returned to Los Angeles (1932); at the age of nine he conducted at a music festival at Interlochen, Michigan, and at the New York's World Fair; in 1940 he conducted in Lewisohn Stadium, N.Y., and with the NBC Symphony; a guest conductor in Europe and America, then became musical director of the West Berlin Opera (1965) and conductor of Berlin's Radio Symphony Orchestra; after the death of George Szell, Maazel became conductor of the Cleveland (Ohio) Orchestra (1971).

MABERN, HAROLD

b. 1936 Memphis, Tennessee.
Pianist. With Walter Perkins and his MJT Plus Three combo (1958); with Lionel Hampton, the Art Farmer-Benny Golson Jazztet, Miles Davis, J.J. Johnson, Joe Williams and others during 1960s.

MACK, ANDREW

b. 1863 Boston, Massachusetts, d. 1931 New York City. Irish tenor and popular composer. Wrote "Heart of My Heart" (1899, "The Story of the Rose," w. "Alice"), "Always Together" (1891, w. Thomas Le Mack, his brother), "The Wedding of the Lily and the Rose" (w. Le Mack), "Little Johnny Dugan" (1893); with lyrics by William Jerome—"The Little Bunch of Whiskers on His Chin," "The Same Old Mother Loves Me" (1895), and "My Pearl Is a Bowery Girl" (1894).

MACK, CECIL

b. 1883 Norfolk, Virginia, d. 1944 New York City. Black lyricist. Born Richard C. McPherson; educated at Norfolk Mission College, Lincoln University, and the University of Pennsylvania; associated with the vaudeville team of Williams and Walker; also Chris Smith and Cecil Mack; wrote lyrics for "Charleston" (1923, m. James P. Johnson), with composer Chris Smith wrote "Never Let the Same Bee Sting You Twice" (1900), "Good Morning, Carrie" (with Tim Brymm),"He's a Cousin of Mine" (with Silvio Hein).

MACK, TED

b. 1904 Greeley, Colorado.
Manager. "The Ted Mack Amateur Hour" on radio gave many a budding artist an early start, such as Gladys Knight and others.

MACK, WARNER

b. 1938 Nashville, Tennessee.
Singer and songwriter. Born Warner MacPherson; raised in Vicksburg, Miss.; sang on "Louisiana Hayride" and Red Foley's "Ozark Jamboree"; wrote "Last Night," "Then a Tear Fell," "Surely," "Is It Wrong," "My Love for You," "If You See Me Cry," "Memory Mountain," "I Wake Up Crying," "The Least Little Thing," "This Little Hurt," "Blue Mood."

MACON, "UNCLE" DAVE

b. 1870 Smartt Station, Tennessee, d. 1952 Readyville, Tennessee. Singer, banjoist, and songwriter. Raised in Nashville, Tenn.; debut at Loew's Theatre, Birmingham, Alabama (1916); toured the country; later bought a farm in Readyville; wrote "The Dixie Bee Line," "Cumberland Mountain Deer Race," "When the Train Comes Along," "From Earth to Heaven," "They're After Me," "Rock About Sara Jane."

MAD RIVER, THE (blues-rock group)

David Roberts, lead guitar; Lawrence Hammond, lead singer and bass; Rick Bochner, vocals and twelve-string guitar; Thomas Manning, vocals, twelve-string guitar, and bass; Gregory LeRoy Dewey, vocals, drums, etc.; formed at Antioch College, Yellow Springs, Ohio; first recorded in 1968; albums—*Mad River, Paradise Bar and Grill.*

MADDEN, EDWARD

b. 1878 New York City, d. 1952 Hollywood, California. Lyricist. Educated at Fordham University, New York City; wrote for Fanny

Brice and other singers; wrote for Broadway shows; wrote "By the Light of the Silvery Moon" (1907, m. Gus Edwards), "Moonlight Bay" (1912, m. Percy Wenrich).

MADDOX, ROSE

b. 1926 Boaz, Alabama.
Singer and guitarist. The "Maddox Brothers and Rose" consisted of the four brothers, Cal, Henry, Fred, and Don, plus their sister Rose; they were raised in Bakersfield, Calif.; their hit records were "Philadelphia Lawyer," "Tramp on the Street," "Tall Man"; Rose's hit records were "One Rose" (1960), "Bluegrass" (1962), "Along with You" (1963), "Sing a Little Song of Heartaches" (1963), "We're the Talk of the Town" (with Buck Owens) and other records with Buck.

MADDY, JOSEPH EDGAR

b. 1891 Wellington, Kansas, d. 1966 Traverse City, Michigan. Conductor and teacher. Studied with Ludwig Becker and others; with Minneapolis Symphony (1909-14); later at the University of Michigan; organized and conducted the National High School Orchestra after 1926; president of Music Educators National Conference (1936); author of books on teaching and instructional techniques.

MADEIRA, JEAN (BROWNING)

b. 1918 Christopher Illinois, d. 1972 Providence, Rhode Island. Contralto. Debut as piano soloist with St. Louis Symphony (1941); studied piano at Juilliard (1941) but switched to voice; debut with San Carlo Opera; graduated Juilliard (1945); at the Chautauqua Opera; joined the Metropolitan Opera, New York City (1948); at Vienna State Opera (1955) in the title role in *Carmen,* as Amneris in *Aïda,* Azucena in *Il Trovatore;* sang leading roles at the Metropolitan Opera (1956-71); also sang at Royal Opera, Covent Garden, La Scala, and others.

MADI, KALIL

b. 1926 Cleveland, Ohio.
Drummer. Played with Erskine Hawkins, Cootie Williams, Lucky Thompson and others during late 1940s and '50s; with Randy Weston, Three Sounds, and others in 1960s.

MADRIGAL SINGERS *see* LEHMAN ENGEL

MAGANINI, QUINTO

b. 1897 Fairfield, California, d. 1974.
Flutist and conductor. Pupil of Barrere and Nadia Boulanger; won Pulitzer Prize (1927) and Guggenheim Fellowship; flutist in San Francisco Symphony Orchestra, and New York Symphony; conducted his own Little Symphony Orchestra; composed vocal works, chamber music, and orchestral works.

MAGHETT, "MAGIC SAM"

b. 1937 Grenada, Mississippi.
Black singer and guitarist. Played in Chicago night spots; first recorded in 1957; hit record was "I Feel So Good, I Want to Boogie."

MAGIDSON, HERBERT

b. 1906 Braddock, Pennsylvania.
Songwriter. Educated at the University of Pittsburgh, Pa.; wrote songs for Hollywood films after 1929; wrote "The Continental" (1934, m. Con Conrad), "Music, Maestro Please" (1938, m. Allie Wrubel).

MAGNOLIA BAND (black band)

Active in New Orleans, La. (ca. 1910); King Oliver, cornet; Lorenzo Tio, Sr., clarinet; George "Pops" Foster, bass; Johnny St. Cyr, guitar and banjo; George Baquet, clarinet.

MAGRATH, GEORGE

b. 1857 New York City, d. 1938.
Pianist. Graduated Stuttgart Conservatory (1877); concert pianist and teacher; principal of piano department of Miss Bauer's Conservatory, Cincinnati, Ohio after 1883.

MAHAL, TAJ

b. 1942 New York City.
Singer and guitarist. Born Henry Sainte Claire Fredericks-Williams; raised in Springfield, Mass.; graduated the University of Massachusetts; first recorded in 1967; at Newport Folk Festival (1968); albums—*Giant Step, Live at Bill Graham's Fillmore West, Natch'l Blues, Taj Mahal;* at Alice Tully Hall, New York City (1972); appeared in film, *Sounder* (1972).

MAHARA'S MINSTRELS *see* WILLIAM C. HANDY

MAHAVISHNU ORCHESTRA, THE (transcendental jazz)

John McLaughlin, double-neck six-string twelve-string electric guitar, and acoustic guitar (studied under Miles Davis); Jerry Goodman, electric violin; Jan Hammer, keyboards and Moog synthesizer; Billy Cobham, percussion (also played with Miles Davis); Rick Laird, bass; albums—*Inner Mounting Fire* (1971), and *Birds of Fire* (1973).

MAHLER, FRITZ

b. 1901 Vienna, Austria, d. 1973. Conductor. Came to America and became conductor of the Symphony Orchestra in Hartford, Conn.

MAHLER, GUSTAV

b. 1860 Kalischt, Bohemia, d. 1911 Vienna, Austria. Composer. Educated at the Vienna Conservatory; conducted at the Metropolitan Opera House and with the New York Philharmonic Symphony Orchestra (1908-11), when he suffered a collapse in New York City, and was treated in Paris and Vienna, where he died; his Symphony no. 1 was introduced in Budapest (1889), no. 2 conducted by Richard Strauss in Berlin (1895), but both were greeted with hostility; his Symphony no. 9, written in 1909 in New York City, was introduced by the Vienna Philharmonic (1912).

MAHONEY, JACK

b. 1882 Buffalo, New York, d. 1945 New York City. Lyricist. Wrote "When You Wore a Tulip and I Wore a Big Red Rose" (1914, m. Percy Wenrich).

MAHR, EMIL

b. 1851 Wiesbaden, Germany, d. 1914 Brookline, Massachusetts. Violinist and teacher. Studied in Berlin (1870) under Joachim; went to Bayreuth (1876) with Wilhelmj as one of first violins at the Wagner Festival; came to America (1887) and taught at the New England Conservatory, Boston.

MAIER, GUY

b. 1892 Buffalo, New York, d. 1956 Santa Monica, California. Pianist. Studied at the New England Conservatory; debut in Boston (1915); toured as solo pianist and also with Lee Pattison in two-piano programs; taught at the University of Michigan, Ann Arbor.

MAIN, HUBERT PLATT

b. 1839 Ridgefield, Connecticut, d. 1925. Composer and compiler. Became music editor of Bigelow & Main in 1868 and supervised the publication of over 500 books on music; wrote "We Shall Meet Beyond the River" (1867, w. John Atkinson) and arranged or harmonized "O Do Not Be Discouraged" (w. J.A. Grenade), "Land Ahead!" (m. J.M. Evans), "I Love to Tell the Story" (m. W.G. Fischer), "In the Sweet Bye and Bye" (m. J.P. Webster). (*See* M.W. Stryker)

MAINER, JOSEPH E.

b. 1898 Asheville, North Carolina. Singer and fiddle maker. Leader of Mainer's Mountaineers, WBT, Charlotte, North Carolina (1934-65); wrote "Johnson's Old Gray Mule," "Maple on the Hill," "Roan Mountain," "Take Me in the Life Boat," "Train III," "Hard Times in Cotton Mill."

MAINIERI, MICHAEL, JR.

b. 1938 Bronx, New York. Vibraphonist. Appeared on Paul Whiteman show with his own group at age fourteen; toured with Buddy Rich; later formed his own trio (1965).

MAITLAND, ROLLO FRANCIS

b. 1884 near Williamsport, Pennsylvania, d. 1953 Philadelphia, Pennsylvania. Organist, composer, and critic. Came to Philadelphia for schooling (1897); studied under David Wood; organist in Philadelphia after 1901; organist at the Swedenborgian Church after 1920; his daughter, S. Marguerite Maitland, was an organist and composer.

MALLET, FRANCIS

b. 1750 France, d. 1834 Boston, Massachusetts. Pianist, organist, composer, teacher, and publisher. Arrived in Philadelphia (1793); moved to Boston, organist there (1798); with Filippo Trajetta (Traetta) and Gottlieb Graupner, organized the Conservatorio, Boston (1801); taught there (1801-13); music publisher in Boston with Mallet & Graupner (1802-04) and in business for himself (1805-07); taught music in New York City (1813-23) and in Boston after 1827; wrote "The Flowing Tear" (w. John H. Nichols), and "Rule New England" (1802, w. Thomas Paine, another tune by F. Schaffer).

MALO (rock group)

Under leadership of Jorge Santana, brother of Carlos Santana, based in San Francisco; album—*Malo.*

MALOTTE, ALBERT HAY

b. 1895 Philadelphia, Pennsylvania, d. 1964 Los Angeles, California. Organist and composer. Studied privately; concert organist in U.S. and Europe; founded school for theater organists in Los Angeles (1927); musical director of Walt Disney Studios for four years; composed the music for *The Lord's Prayer* (1935).

MAMAS AND THE PAPAS (rock group)

Denny Doherty, vocals; Cass Elliot, vocals; John Phillips, vocals and guitar; Michelle

Phillips, vocals; started in the Virgin Islands where a piece of piping fell on Cass Elliot and changed her voice; sang in California (1965); known as the "Royal Family of American Rock"; group split (1968); albums—*Crashon Screamon All Fall Down, Farewell to the First Golden Era, Gathering of Flowers, Mamas and the Papas, Deliver, Golden Era, 16 of Their Greatest Hits, Papas and Mamas;* Cass Elliot went out on her own.

MANA-ZUCCA (ZUCKERMAN)

b. 1894 New York City.
Singer and pianist. She studied in New York and in Europe; sang in light opera and also toured as a pianist; composed orchestral works, chamber music, and a number of songs; her husband, Irwin M. Cassel, wrote the lyrics to her songs.

MANCE, JULIAN C. ("JUNIOR")

b. 1928 Chicago, Illinois.
Black pianist. Played with Dizzy Gillespie in 1950s; formed his own trio (1961); album—*Harlem Lullaby.*

MANCINI, HENRY

b. 1924 Cleveland, Ohio.
Composer and arranger. Studied music at Carnegie Institute, Pittsburgh, and the Juilliard School, New York City; served in World War II; pianist in Ted Beneke's band; wrote the score for *The Glenn Miller Story* (1951); won Academy Award for *Breakfast at Tiffany's* (1961) and the song "Moon River" (w. Johnny Mercer); won Academy Award for "Days of Wine and Roses" (1962, w. Mercer).

MANCUSO, RONALD BERNARD ("GUS")

b. 1933 Rochester, New York.
Baritone horn and bass player. With Carl Fontana; later formed own group (1964).

MANDALA (Canadian gospel group)

MANDEL, JOHN ALFRED (JOHNNY)

b. 1925 New York City.
Trumpeter and composer. Played trumpet and was arranger for Boyd Raeburn; wrote film scores; wrote "The Shadow of Your Smile" for *The Sandpiper,* which won an Academy Award (1966); also arranger for Frank Sinatra, Mel Torme and others.

MANGIONE, CHARLES FRANK (CHUCK)

b. 1940 Rochester, New York.
Composer and teacher. Studied piano at age eight; studied at Eastman School of Music, Rochester; later taught there; directed school's twenty-six-piece jazz ensemble; played piano and flügelhorn ("pregnant" trumpet) in his own quartet; conducted Rochester Philharmonic on occasions (1971); wrote *Hill Where the Lord Hides,* and *Feel of a Vision;* albums—*Kaleidoscope* (performed at Eastman), *Together* (with Rochester Philharmonic).

MANINI, JOSEPH, JR.

b. 1930 Providence, Rhode Island, d. 1964 Los Angeles, California. Saxist. Played alto and tenor saxophones with Gerald Wilson, Terry Gibbs, Shelly Manne, Louis Bellson and others; he shot himself.

MANN, DAVID

b. 1916 Philadelphia, Pennsylvania.
Composer and lyricist. Educated at the University of Pennsylvania, Villanova University (M.A.), and Curtis Institute of Music; pianist with Charlie Spivak and Jimmy Dorsey; served in the army in World War II; with Redd L. Evans wrote "There! I've Said It Again," "No Moon at All," "Don't Go to Strangers."

MANN, ELIAS

b. 1750 Weymouth, Massachusetts, d. 1825 Northampton, Massachusetts. Compiler. Lived in Worcester (1789-96), then moved to Northampton where he joined the First Congregational Church and taught singing there; published *The Northampton Collection of Sacred Harmony* (1778 and 1797), and *The Massachusetts Collection of Sacred Harmony* (1807).

MANN, HERBIE

b. 1930 Brooklyn, New York.
Black flutist and bandleader. With Matt Matthews Quintet and others in 1950s; formed his Afro-Jazz sextet (1959); toured Africa (1960) under auspices of U.S. State Department; in Brazil (1961-63); toured Japan (1964); Herbie Mann Quintet played at Newport Jazz Festival, New York City (1972).

MANN, HERMAN

b. 1771 Walpole, Massachusetts, d. 1833 Dedham, Massachusetts. Music publisher. Assisted Amos Albee and Oliver Shaw in compiling and printing *The Columbian Sacred Psalmonist* (1808); printer and music publisher in Dedham, Mass. (1797-1811), in Providence, R.I. (1812-15), then in Dedham after 1815.

MANN, NEWTON M.

b. 1836 Cazenovia, New York, d. 1926 Chicago, Illinois. Translator. Unitarian minister, serving as pastor at churches in Kenosha, Wisc., Troy and Rochester, N.Y., and Omaha, Nebr.; working with Max Landsberg, a Jewish rabbi, they translated *Praise to the Living God* (1885), the setting for the *Yigdal,* the thirteen articles of the Jewish Creed; there are seven tunes for the *Yigdal.*

MANNE, SHELDON (SHELLY)

b. 1920 New York City.
Drummer. Played with Bobby Byrne, Stan Kenton, Woody Herman and others in 1940s; in Los Angeles in 1950s; opened Shelly's Manne Hole in Hollywood (1960).

MANNES, DAVID

b. 1866 New York City, d. there 1959.
Violinist, conductor, and teacher. Studied in New York, Berlin, and Brussels; concertmaster of New York Symphony (1898); conductor of Symphony Club (1902); taught at Music School Settlement, New York City; founded the David Mannes Music School, New York (1916); married pianist Clara Damrosch who served as co-director of the school.

MANNES, LEOPOLD DAMROSCH

b. 1899 New York City, d. 1964.
Pianist and composer. Son of Clara Damrosch and David Mannes; graduated Harvard University, pupil of Guy Maier and others; won Pulitzer Prize for composition and Guggenheim Fellowship; taught at David Mannes School, New York City, and at the Institute of Musical Art, New York City; composed suite for orchestra, suite for two pianos, string quartet, songs.

MANNEY, CHARLES FONTEYN

b. 1872 Brooklyn, New York, d. 1951 New York City. Composer. Studied with William Arms Fisher and J. Wallace Goodrich in Boston.

MANONE, JOSEPH ("WINGY")

b. 1904 New Orleans, Louisiana.
Trumpeter and bandleader. Appeared at Arcadia Ballroom, St. Louis (1924); recorded with Zutty Singleton (1938); played in Los Angeles during 1940s; in Las Vegas in 1950s and '60s; album—*Wingy Manone.*

MANSKI, DOROTHEE

b. 1895 New York City, d. 1967 Bloomington, Indiana. Soprano. Debut as the Witch in *Hansel und Gretel* (1927); at the Metropolitan Opera, New York City (1927-41); taught at Indiana University; daughter, Inge Manski, sang at the Metropolitan.

MANTLER, MIKE

b. 1943 Vienna, Austria.
Trumpeter and composer. Studied at Vienna Academy of Music; came to Boston (1962), played there with Lowell Davidson; after 1964 in New York City with Davidson, Cecil Taylor, Paul Bley, Carla Bley; in Jazz Composer's Orchestra at Newport Jazz Festival (1965); composed *Communications III, IV.*

MAPHIS, OTIS W. ("JOE")

b. 1921 Suffolk, Virginia.
Singer and banjoist. Debut on station WBRA, Richmond, Virginia at age ten; later on Chicago's "National Barn Dance"; married Rose Lee, singer, and formed successful singing duo; toured the United States, Europe, and the Pacific area; their hit records include *Twin Banjo Special, Joe and Rose Lee Maphis, Flying Fingers, Your Old Love Letters, Randy Lynn Rag, Honky Tonk Down Town.*

MAPLE CITY FOUR

Organized at La Porte, Indiana (1926); on WLS "Barn Dance" (1928-53); Fritz Meissner, first tenor; Bob Bender, second tenor; Art James, baritone; Leroy Pat Patterson, bass; Al Rice; later Chuck Kerner, second tenor; Arwin Schweig, bass.

MARABLE BAND, FATE (black band)

Played on the Streckfus Riverboats on the Mississippi from St. Louis to New Orleans after 1920 on Monday nights (reserved for Negroes); Fate Marable, piano; Baby Dodds, drums; Pops Foster, bass; Johnny St. Cyr, banjo and guitar; later Zutty Singleton, drums; Johnny Dodds, clarinet; Red Allen, trumpet; Boyd Atkins, sax; Louis Armstrong, cornet (later trumpet).

MARABLE, FATE

b. 1890 Paducah, Kentucky, d. 1947 St. Louis, Missouri. Black pianist and bandleader. Played on Mississippi River boats after 1907; formed his own band (1917); later a pianist in St. Louis night clubs

MARAIS, MIRANDO

b. 1912 Amsterdam, The Netherlands.
Singer and pianist. Born Rosa Lily Odette Baruch de la Pardo; studied at Muziek Lyceum; debut in piano duo with Marcel Baruch de la Pardo (1928); toured Europe with Marcel (1928-35); came to America (1939) to

escape Nazism; met singer Joseph Marais; both became U.S. citizens (1945); debut for Mirando and Joseph at Town Hall, New York City (1946); married Joseph (1947), made concert tours of the U.S.; lived in Idyllwild, California.

MARANATHA (Jesus rock group)

Name is Greek-Aramaic for "O Lord, come!"; at Carnegie Hall, New York City (1972).

MARCH, DANIEL

b. 1816 Millbury, Massachusetts, d. 1909. Hymnist. Educated at Yale and served as pastor in several Congregational and Presbyterian churches; wrote the hymn "Hark, the Voice of Jesus Calling" (1868, tune "Ellesdie"—W.A. Mozart).

MARES, PAUL

b. 1900 New Orleans, Louisiana, d. 1949 Chicago, Illinois. Jazz trumpeter. Organized the New Orleans Rhythm Kings (1920); *Farewell Blues* was composed in 1923 by Mares, Leon Rappolo, and Elmer Schoebel.

MARETZEK, MAX

b. 1821 Brunn, Moravia (Czechoslovakia), d. 1897 Staten Island, New York. Composer and teacher. Well-known impresario; wrote the opera, *Ricco;* wrote three ballets while in London; came to New York (1848) and became an operatic director there; conducted opera for thirty-five years.

MARGULIES TRIO *see* ALWIN SCHRODER, LEO SCHULZ

MARIANO, CHARLES HUGO

b. 1923 Boston, Massachusetts.
Alto saxist. Played with Stan Kenton, Shelly Manne and others in 1950s; toured Japan (1960-64) in own quartet with his wife, Toshiko Akiyoshi; later taught at Berklee School of Music, Boston.

MARIO, QUEENA

b. 1896 Akron, Ohio, d. 1951 New York City. Soprano. Born Tillotson; studied with Oscar Saenger and Sembrich; sang with Metropolitan Opera Company (1923); married Wilfred Pelletier; divorced.

MARIOTINI, CAYETANO

b. (?), d. 1817 New Orleans, Louisiana.
Impresario. Brought his circus from Cuba to New Orleans before 1816; produced Kreutzer's opera, *Paul and Virginia,* at Olympic Theatre (1817); produced five operas there; filed a petition in bankruptcy (1817); then died shortly thereafter.

MARKS, JOHN D. (JOHNNY)

b. 1909 Mt. Vernon, New York.
Composer, lyricist, and publisher. Graduated Colgate University, and Columbia University; studied music in Paris; Captain of the 26th Special Service Company in World War II; produced army shows in U.S. and overseas; formed St. Nicholas Music (1949); wrote "Rudolph the Red Nosed Reindeer" (1949), "I Heard the Bells on Christmas Day."

MARLATT, EARL BOWMAN

b. 1892 Columbus, Indiana.
Hymnist. Educated at DePauw University, Greencastle, Indiana, Harvard, Oxford in England, and the University of Berlin; worked for a newspaper in Kenosha, Wisconsin, for a year, then served as a lieutenant in World War I; became professor of philosophy at Boston University (1925); wrote the hymn "Spirit of Life, in This New Dawn" (tune "Maryton"—H.P. Smith), " 'Are Ye Able,' Said the Master" (1926, "Beacon Hill"—H.S. Mason).

MARLIN, MORRIS WAYNE ("SLEEPY")

b. 1915 Maunie, Illinois.
Fiddler. Won International Fiddle Championship at Kentucky Fair (1949, 1951, and 1955-59).

MARQUAND, TIMOTHY F.

b. 1941.
Trumpeter and manager. Son of John P. Marquand, novelist, and Adelaide Hooker, composer (wrote a symphony); attended Harvard University; member of Jazz Composers Orchestra, organized in 1955, President in 1969.

MARSALA, JOSEPH

b. 1907 Chicago, Illinois.
Clarinetist, bandleader, and publisher. Led his own combo (1936-45); later became a music publisher and record executive.

MARSCHAUSEN, THEODORE

b. 1773 Germany, d. 1843 New York City. Organist, composer,and teacher. Came to New York City about 1811; organist at St. Peter's Church; wrote *The Harvest Rose, The Harp* (w. Walter Scott); *New York Water Music* (piano); *Te Deum Laudamus* (ca. 1811).

MARSH, SIMEON BULKLEY

b. 1798 Sherburne, New York, d. 1875 Albany, New York. Composer. From 1818 to 1837 choirmaster in a Presbyterian church in Albany, N.Y.; in 1837 he founded the *Intelligencer* which later became the *Recorder* in Amsterdam, N.Y.; from 1846-59 taught music in Schenectady and gave free instruction to children; in 1859 he returned to Sherburne to teach music; composed the tune "Martyn" (1834, used for "Jesus, Lover of My Soul," w. Charles Wesley); composed the cantatas *The Savior* and *The King of the Forest.*

MARSH, WARNE MARION

b. 1927 Los Angeles, California.
Tenor saxist. Served in U.S. Army (1945-47); played with Lennie Tristano in New York City during 1950s and '60s.

MARSHALL, ARTHUR

b. 1881 Saline County, Missouri, d. 1956.
Black pianist and arranger. Moved to Sedalia, Mo. (1885); protege of Scott Joplin; played in the Maple Leaf night club; arranged "Pan-Am Rag" (1914, for Tom Turpin); wrote "Kinklets, Ham and the Peach," "The Pippin"; from 1907-08 wrote "Silver Arrow," "National Prize Rag," and "Missouri Romp—A Slow Drag," which he recorded (1950).

MARSHALL, CHARLES

b. 1887 Waterville, Maine, d. 1951 Lake George, New York. Tenor. Pupil of William Whitney, Vannucini, and Lombardi; debut in Florence (1901), sang in Italian opera houses; later in Russia, Greece, and Turkey; with Chicago Opera (1921-31).

MARSHALL, JACK WILTON

b. 1921 El Dorado, Kansas.
Guitarist, conductor, and arranger. Arranger for various jazz artists; album (with Shelly Manne)—*Sounds Unheard Of.*

MARSHALL, JOHN PATTON

b. 1877 Rockfort, Massachusetts, d. 1941 Boston, Massachusetts. Teacher and composer. Studied with MacDowell and others; professor of music at Boston University (1903); composed piano pieces and songs.

MARSHALL, JOSEPH ("KAISER")

b. 1902 Savannah, Georgia, d. 1948 New York City. Black jazz drummer. Played in Fletcher Henderson's band.

MARSHALL, WENDELL

b. 1920 St. Louis, Missouri.
Black jazz bass player. Played with Lionel Hampton, Duke Ellington and others in 1940s and '50s.

MARSTON, GEORGE W.

b. 1840 Sandwich, Massachusetts, d. 1901.
Organist, pianist, composer, and teacher. Studied in Munich, Florence, and London; teacher of piano and harmony in Portland, Maine; composed anthems, piano pieces, German songs.

MARTHA AND THE VANDELLAS (black vocal group)

Martha Reeves, Rosalind Ashford, Betty Kelly; later Lois Reeves (sister of Martha) replaced Betty Kelly; Martha Reeves was a secretary for Motown in Detroit; recorded for Motown (1962); albums—*Dance Party, Greatest Hits, Heat Wave, Martha and the Vandellas—Live, Ridin' High, Sugar 'n Spice, Watch Out.*

MARTIN, DEAN

b. 1917 Steubenville, Ohio.
Singer and actor. Born Dino Crocetti; family moved to Long Beach, Calif. (1937); sang in night clubs (1943); met Jerry Lewis while at the 500 Club in Atlantic City, N.J. (1946); later Martin and Lewis appeared in many films; broke up (1957); later appeared in more films; "Dean Martin Show" on NBC-TV in early 1970s.

MARTIN, FREDDY

b. 1906 Springfield, Ohio.
Bandleader. Raised in an orphanage in Springfield; played the saxophone and organized his own band; played with Eddy Hodges and his Band of Pirates; then with Jack Albin's band at the Hotel Bossert, Brooklyn; started his own band again (1932) at the Roosevelt Grill, New York City; at the St. Francis Hotel, San Francisco (1941); then at the Cocoanut Grove in the Ambassador Hotel, Los Angeles.

MARTIN, GRADY

b. 1929 Marshall County, Tennessee.
Singer and bandleader. Attended schools in Chapel, Tenn.; Grady Martin and Slew Foot Five; albums—*Big City Lights, Hot Time Tonight, Instrumentally Yours, Songs Everybody Knows, Touch of Country.*

MARTIN, HUGH

b. 1914 Birmingham, Alabama.
Composer. Studied at the Birmingham Conservatory and attended Birmingham-Southern College; with lyricist Ralph Blane wrote "Buckle Down, Winsocki" (*Best Foot Forward,* 1941), "The Trolley Song" (*Meet Me in St. Louis,* 1944 film); served in Europe in

World War II; they also wrote "Love" and "Pass that Peace Pipe"; he wrote the score for *Look Ma, I'm Dancin'* (1948, starring Nancy Walker), and *Make a Wish* (1951).

MARTIN, JAMES HENRY (JIMMY)

b. 1927 Sneedville, Tennessee.
Singer and songwriter. Leader of Sunny Mountain Boys after 1953; wrote "It's Not Like Him," "She Left Me Again," "I'll Never Take No for an Answer."

MARTIN, MARY

b. 1913 Weatherford, Texas.
Singer. Made her stage debut in *Leave It to Me* (1938, m. Cole Porter), where she sang "My Heart Belongs to Daddy"; also sang in *One Touch of Venus* (1943, m. Kurt Weill), *South Pacific* (1949, m. Richard Rodgers) and *Sound of Music* (1959, m. Rodgers); married Richard Halliday, and moved to Anapolis, Brazil, to live; at the Celebration for Richard Rodgers, Imperial Theater, New York City (1972).

MARTIN, RICARDO (HUGH WHITFIELD)

b. 1881 Hopkinsville, Kentucky, d. 1952 New York City. Tenor. Pupil of Escalais and others; debut in Nantes, France (1904); sang in Italy; with French Opera Company, New Orleans, La., Metropolitan Opera (1907-15), Boston Opera (1915-17), then Covent Garden, London; with Chicago Opera after 1920.

MARTIN, TONY

b. 1914 San Francisco, California.
Singer. Born Alvin Morris, Jr.; played saxophone and sang with a band at Palace Hotel, San Francisco, at age sixteen; radio debut on the "Lucky Strike Hour" (1932); attended St. Mary's College; appeared in several films after 1933; served in the Air Force in the China-Burma-India area as a technical sergeant (1942-46); married Cyd Charisse, dancer; appeared with her in night club shows in Las Vegas.

MARTINELLI, GIOVANNI

b. 1885 Montagnana, Italy, d. 1969 New York City. Noted tenor. Debut in *La Tosca* at Covent Garden, London (1912); member of Metropolitan Opera, New York after 1913; also sang in Europe and South America; became artistic director of Chicago Opera Company (1941); with Kirsten Flagstad in *Tristan and Isolde* at the Chicago Opera (1948).

MARTINO, DONALD

b. 1931.
Composer. Studied with Milton Babbitt at Princeton; also with Roger Sessions.

MARTINU, BOHUSLAV

b. 1890 Policka, Bohemia, d. 1959 Liestal, Switzerland. Composer. Educated at the Prague Conservatory, and played the violin in the Czech Philharmonic Orchestra; lived in Paris (1923-41), then came to America to live; composed the ballet *Istar* (1921), *Concerto Grosso* (for chamber orchestra, 1937), *Double Concerto* (1938), Symphony no. 1 (Boston Symphony, directed by Koussevitsky, 1942), *Concerto for Violin and Orchestra* (1943), Symphony no. 2 (Cleveland Orchestra under Erich Leinsdorf, 1943).

MARTIRANO, SALVATORE

b. 1927.
Composer. Wrote "O, O, O, O, That Shakespearian Rag" (1958, for chorus and instrumental ensemble), *Ballad* (1966, for amplified singer and chamber ensemble).

MARVELETTES (black vocal group)

Wanda Rogers, Katherin Schaffner, Gladys Horton; later Ann Bogan replaced Gladys Horton; recorded for Motown, Detroit (1961); albums—*Please Mr. Postman, In Full Bloom, The Marvelettes, The Marvelettes' Greatest Hits, Sophisticated Soul.*

MARVIN, KEN ("LONZO")

b. 1924 Haleyville, Alabama.
Singer. Member of the duo of "Lonzo and Oscar" with Rollin "Oscar" Sullivan over station WTJS, Jackson, Tenn., after 1939.

MARX, WILLIAM WOOLLCOTT

b. 1937 Los Angeles, California.
Pianist and composer. Son of harpist and comedian Arthur "Harpo" Marx; studied at Juilliard, New York City (1955-57); led his own trio in Hollywood; wrote scores for TV films and shows.

MARZO, EDUARDO

b. 1852 Naples, Italy, d. 1929 New York City. Organist, composer, and teacher. Came to the United States (1869); director of concerts and of opera companies on tour; organist and voice teacher in New York City after 1882.

MASI, FRANCESCO

b. ca. 1786 Italy, d. 1853 Washington, D.C. Pianist, organist, composer, and teacher. Came to Boston (1807); gave recitals at Boylston Hall (1814); music publisher in Boston (1815-18); publisher in Alexandria, Virginia (1818-22); wrote the (Boston) "Càdets March" (1815), "The Battles of Lake Champlain and Plattsburg," "I Love Thee Dearly" (1818, w. William H. Benton), " 'Tis Love of Woman Born" (w. D.M. Black).

MASON, DANIEL GREGORY

b. 1820 Savannah, Georgia, d. 1869. Publisher. Son of composer Lowell Mason; with his brother, Lowell Mason, founded the publishing house of Mason Brothers, which was dissolved upon the death of Daniel.

MASON, DANIEL GREGORY

b. 1873 Brookline, Massachusetts, d. 1953 Greenwich, Connecticut. Composer. Nephew of William and grandson of Lowell Mason; graduated Harvard (1905), then taught music at Columbia University, New York City (1909-42); known for his Symphony no. 3 (*Lincoln* Symphony, New York Philharmonic under John Barbirolli, 1937), Op.32 *Suite after English Folksongs*, Op.19 *Quartet on Negro Themes*, Op.23 *Songs of the Countryside;* wrote *Music in My Times and Other Reminiscences* (1938).

MASON, EDITH BARNES

b. 1893 St. Louis, Missouri, d. 1973. Soprano. Pupil of Clement and Maurel; with Boston Opera (1913), Metropolitan Opera (1915-17), Paris Opera and Opera Comique (1918-21), Chicago Opera (1921-30); also in Europe, Havana, and Mexico City; with Metropolitan Opera, New York City after 1935; married conductor Giorgio Polacco, later divorced.

MASON, FRANK STUART

b. 1883 Weymouth, Massachusetts, d. 1929 Boston, Massachusetts. Teacher. Taught at the New England Conservatory in Boston.

MASON, HARRY SILVERNALE

b. 1881. Composer. Educated at Boston University School of Theology and became an instructor in fine arts in religion at Auburn Theological Seminary, Auburn, N.Y.; composed the tune "Beacon Hill" (1924, for " 'Are Ye Able,' Said the Master," w. Earl Marlatt).

MASON, HENRY

b. 1831 Brookline, Massachusetts, d. 1890 Boston, Massachusetts. Organ and piano maker. With his brother, Lowell Mason, Jr., manufactured organs in the firm of Mason & Hamlin.

MASON, LOWELL

b.1792 Westborough, Massachusetts, d. 1872. Orange, New Jersey. Noted composer. Went to Savannah, Georgia, in 1815 to work in a bank, and also became organist and choirmaster of the First Presbyterian Church there in 1824; in 1827 moved to Boston where he again worked in a bank and became choirmaster of Dr. Lyman Beecher's Church; in 1832 with George J. Webb and others he founded the Boston Academy of Music, then the New York Normal Institute for training teachers in 1853; in 1858 he organized the Worcester (Mass.) Musical Festivals; arranged the music for "Joy to the World" (1839, using two themes from *The Messiah* by Handel; there is a second tune by Edward Hodges), "From Greenland's Icy Mountains" (1824), "Watchmen Tell Us of the Night" (1830, w. J. Browning), "My Soul Be on Thy Guard" (1830, w. George Heath), "Safely Through Another Week" (1824, w. John Newton), "Blest Be the Tie That Binds" (1832, w. John Fawcett, also arranged second tune by J.G. Nageli), "My Faith Looks Up to Thee" (1832, w. Ray Palmer), "Hail to the Brightness" (1833, w. Thomas Hastings), "Come Unto Me" (1839, w. Catherine W. Esling), "O Day of Rest and Gladness" (1839, w. C. Wordsworth), "Jesus, Where'er Thy People Meet" (1847, w. William Cowper, 1779), "Hark! Ten Thousand Harps and Voices" (1840, w. T. Kelly), "Along the Banks" (w. Joel Barlow, 1799), "Go Labor On!" (1850, w. H. Bonar), "O Could I Speak the Matchless Worth" (w. S. Medley, 1789), "Let All on Earth Their Voices Praise" (w. Isaac Watts, 1719), "Work for the Night Is Coming" ("Work Song," w. Annie L. Walker), and "Nearer My God to Thee" (1859, w. Sarah F. Adams); when the oceanliner *Titanic* struck an iceberg in 1912, the band members played "Nearer My God to Thee" as the great ship sank into the sea.

MASON, LOWELL, JR.

b. 1823 Westboro, Massachusetts, d. 1885. Publisher. Son of composer Lowell Mason; with his brother, Daniel Gregory, founded the publishing house of Mason Brothers; after the death of Daniel in 1869, Lowell joined his brother, Henry, in the manufacture of organs.

MASON, LUTHER WHITING

b. 1828 Turner, Maine, d. 1896 Buckfield, Maine. Teacher and writer. Wrote *Die neue Gesangschule* and the *National System of Music Charts*.

MASON, WILLIAM

b. 1829 Boston, Massachusetts, d. 1908 New York City. Pianist and composer. Son of Lowell Mason; studied in Leipzig (1849) and at Weimar under Liszt; with Theodore Thomas started chamber music concerts in 1854; married Mary Webb, the daughter of composer George J. Webb; he composed "God Moves in a Mysterious Way" (w. William Cowper, 1773); compiled *The Social Glee Book*

(1848); wrote *Memories of a Musical Life* (1901).

MASTERSOUNDS (jazz group) *see* BUDDY MONTGOMERY

MATHER, COTTON

b. 1663 Boston, Massachusetts, d. there 1728. Hymnist and compiler. Son of Increase Mather and grandson of Richard Mather; followed his father as pastor of the Second (or North Congregational) Church, Boston (1723); wrote and compiled hymns; wrote more than 450 books; published his *Psalterium Americanum* (1718). (*See also* Thomas Walter)

MATHER, RICHARD

b. 1596 Lancashire, England, d. 1669 Dorchester, Massachusetts. Hymnist and compiler. His Puritan beliefs led him into difficulties with leaders of the Church of England and he was suspended from the ministry (1633); came to Massachusetts (1635); pastor of the Congregational Church in Dorchester (1645-69); principal author of the *Bay Psalm Book* (1640), with Rev. Thomas Weld and Rev. John Eliot; with Richard Lyon and Rev. Henry Dunster edited and revised the third edition (1650).

MATHES, DAVID WAYNE

b. 1933 Steubenville, Ohio.
Singer, guitarist, and songwriter. Attended high school in Fairborn, Ohio; attended the Florida Institute of Technology, Orlando, and the University of Tennessee, Nashville (1966); wrote "Sleepy Head," "A Friend in Need," "When We Meet Jesus," "Joann," "Oh Sinner Won't You Listen," "No One but Jesus," "His Love Is Real."

MATHEWS, RONALD ALBERT

b. 1935 Brooklyn, New York.
Pianist and composer. Graduated Manhattan School of Music, New York City (1959); wrote music for TV shows and films.

MATHEWS, WILLIAM SMITH BABCOCK

b. 1837 New London, New Hampshire, d. 1912 Denver, Colorado. Editor and music critic. Studied in Lowell, Mass., and Boston; taught piano in Macon, Georgia (1860-63); organist in Chicago (1867-93); edited the *Musical Independent* (1868-72); critic of the *Chicago Times* (1878), also *Morning News & Tribune* until 1886; founded and edited the magazine *Music* (1891).

MATHIS, JOHNNY

b. 1933 Maud, Texas.
Singer. Member of the Jimmy Lee and Johnny Mathis duo; album—*Great Country Hits.*

MATHIS, JOHNNY

b. 1935 San Francisco, California.
Black singer. Studied with Connie Cox in San Francisco; attended San Francisco State College where he was a high jumper; sang in night clubs; recorded "Wonderful Wonderful" (1956) which was a hit; toured the U.S. and Europe; appeared in numerous films.

MATLOCK, JULIAN CLIFTON ("MATTY")

b. 1907 Paducah, Kentucky.
Clarinetist. Played with Ben Pollock, Bob Crosby and others in 1930s; with Red Nichols and others in 1940s; later led his own groups in California and Las Vegas.

MATTHEWS, HARRY ALEXANDER

b. 1879 Cheltenham, England.
Composer. Came to Philadelphia (1900) and was organist in churches there, then directed music at the University of Pennsylvania; organist at the Church of St. Luke and The Epiphany (1916-37), then at St. Stephen's Church; composed the cantata *The City of God,* also *Introits and Graduals of the Church Year.*

MATTHEWS, ONZY D., JR.

b. 1936 Fort Worth, Texas.
Pianist, bandleader, and singer. Raised in Los Angeles; studied voice at Westlake College of Music, Hollywood (1952); organized his own band (1961) and played in Los Angeles night spots.

MATTHEWS, WILLIAM SMYTHE BABCOCK

b. 1837 Loudon, New Hampshire, d. 1912 Denver, Colorado. Teacher. Taught music in Chicago, Illinois (1867-1910).

MATTIOLI, LINO

b. 1853 Parma, Italy, d. 1949 Cincinnati, Ohio. Cellist and composer. Graduated Parma Royal Music School (1869); taught at College of Music in Cincinnati, Ohio; wrote *Habanera* (for cello), *Barcarolle* (for piano), *Gavotte* (for string quartet).

MATTISON, HIRAM

b. 1811 Herkimer County, New York, d. 1868 Jersey City, New Jersey. Composer and compiler. Methodist minister; assisted Isaac

B. Woodbury in preparing the *Lute of Zion* (1853) and in 1859 he compiled *Sacred Melodies for Social Worship;* his tunes are "Go, Let the Angels In" and "Heaven at Last."

MATZ, PETER

b. 1928 Pittsburgh, Pennsylvania.
Pianist and composer. Played with Maynard Ferguson (1951); later arranger for Kay Thompson, Diahann Carroll, Andy Williams, Perry Como, and Barbra Streisand.

MATZENAUER, MARGARETE

b. 1881 Temesvar, Hungary, d. 1963.
Contralto. Studied with Franz Emerich and others; debut in Strasbourg (1901); then with Munich Opera (1904-11); with Metropolitan Opera, New York City (1911-30); married tenor Edoardo Ferrari-Fontana; later divorced.

MAUBOURG, JEANNE

b. 1875 Namur, Belgium.
Soprano. Pupil of Mmes. Labarre and Jouron-Duvernay; at La Monnaie, Brussels (1897-1907); at Metropolitan Opera, New York City (1909-14); then a teacher in New York.

MAUREL, VICTOR

b. 1848 Marseilles, France, d. 1923 New York City. Baritone. Studied in Marseilles and at Paris Conservatory; debut at the Grand Opera (1868); sang at La Scala, Milan (1870); then in London, Egypt, Russia, New York; taught in New York after 1909; his reputation was world renowned.

MAXIM, ABRAHAM

b. 1773 Carver, Massachusetts, d. 1829 Palmyra, Maine. Popular composer and compiler. Had an unfortunate love affair, and went into the woods to meditate, whereupon he saw a bird on the roof of a logger's hut. The bird, a sparrow, made sorrowful sounds to him, which he set to music for the lyrics "As on Some Lonely Building's Top" (w. Nahum Tate). Compiled *The Oriental Harmony* (1802) and *The Northern Harmony* (1805); his brother, John Maxim, composed over 100 tunes and political songs between 1840 and 1848.

MAXSON, FREDERICK

b. 1862 Beverly, New Jersey, d. 1934 Philadelphia, Pennsylvania. Organist, composer, and teacher. Studied with D.D. Wood and Guilmont; organist of Central Congregational Church in Philadelphia (1884-1902), then at First Baptist Church there until 1934; wrote organ pieces—Romance in C, Madrigal in G, Festive March in E-flat, *A Spring Time Fantasy.*

MAXWELL, MARY HAMLIN

b. 1814, d. 1853.
Hymnist. Wrote "God Hath Said, 'For Ever Blessed'," which first appeared in her *Original Hymns* (New York, 1849), and included in the *Methodist Episcopal Hymnal* (1878).

MAY, E. WILLIAM

b. 1916 Pittsburgh, Pennsylvania.
Composer. Arranger for Charlie Barnet and others; arranged "Cherokee" for Barnet; also arranger for Frank Sinatra; music for TV shows.

MAY, EARL CHARLES BARRINGTON

b. 1927 New York City.
Bass player. Accompanist for Gloria Lynne, Carmen McRae, Sarah Vaughan and others during 1960s.

MAYFIELD, CURTIS

b. 1942 Chicago, Illinois.
Black tenor and guitarist. Sang in a group called the Northern Jubilees which included Jerry Butler; in group the Roosters, organized in Chicago (1958), which later was known as The Impressions; for a time was guitarist for Jerry Butler; co-authored "He Will Break Your Heart" and "Find Another Girl"; wrote "Gypsy Woman"; at the Bitter End, New York City (1972).

MAYHEW, STELLA

b. 1875, d. 1934.
Singer. Sang in night spots in New York City and in Broadway reviews; popularized "Down Among the Sugar Cane" (by Chris Smith, Avery and Hart).

MAYNOR, DOROTHY

b. 1910 Norfolk, Virginia.
Black soprano. Raised in Greensboro, North Carolina; graduated Hampton Institute, Hampton, Virginia (1933); studied at Westminster Choir School, Princeton, N.J.; sang at Berkshire Music Festival (1939); sang in the United States and Europe; founded Harlem School of Arts, New York City (1966); when Serge Koussevitzky heard her at the Berkshire Festival in Tanglewood, he exclaimed, "A miracle! A native Flagstad!"

MEACHAM, FRANK W.

b. ca. 1850 Buffalo, New York, d. after 1895. Popular composer. Composed the march "The American Patrol" (1885), and the song "There Is No Place Like New York After All" (1895, w. George Cooper).

MEAD, GEORGE

b. 1902 New York City.
Composer. Educated at Trinity School and Columbia University (M.A. 1925); organist-choirmaster of churches in Brooklyn and New York City, and Director of Music at Hofstra College, Hempstead, N.Y. (1936-40); composed the organ piece *Fantasy* and the one-act *Broker's Opera.*

MEANS, CLAUDE

b. 1912 Cincinnati, Ohio.
Composer. Organist-choirmaster at All-Saint's Church, Denver, Colorado (1933), then studied with David McK.Williams in New York City; organist-choirmaster at Christ Church, Greenwich, Conn. (1934-72); during World War II served in the armed forces (1942-46) and spent over a year in France; composed the tune "Seabury" ("Creation's Lord, We Give Thee Thanks," w. W.D. Hyde), and the anthems "Lord of All Power and Might," "The King Rides Forth" and "O Come and Mourn."

MEES, ARTHUR

b. 1850 Columbus, Ohio, d. 1923 New York City. Conductor. Studied in Berlin; assistant conductor of Thomas Orchestra (1896); conducted Mendelssohn Glee Club, New York (1898-1904); wrote program notes for the New York Philharmonic Orchestra (1887-96); also conducted choruses of various societies in New York City and Albany, N.Y.; wrote *Choirs and Church Music.*

MEETZ, RAYMOND (RICHARD)

b. ca. 1785 France, d. after 1837.
Pianist, composer, teacher, and publisher. Debut in New York City (1806); teacher and publisher in New York City (1818-26); wrote "General Montgomery's Dead March" (1818, General Richard Montgomery killed in Quebec, 1775, reburied in New York City, 1818).

MEGERLIN, ALFRED

b. 1880 Antwerp, Belgium.
Violinist. Studied at the Antwerp and Brussels Conservatories; came to America (1914); concertmaster of the New York Philharmonic Orchestra after 1917.

MEHTA, ZUBIN

b. 1936 Bombay, India.
Conductor. His father, Mehli Mehta, was conductor of the Bombay Orchestra; he is Parsee (of Persian descent); studied at the Academy of Music in Vienna; became conductor of the Los Angeles Philharmonic (1962), and also conductor of the Montreal Symphony simultaneously; before the age of thirty he was a guest conductor of the Vienna Philharmonic, the Berlin Philharmonic, the Salzburg Festival, the Philadelphia Orchestra, and the Metropolitan Opera in New York City; also guest conductor of the Israel Philharmonic in Rio de Janeiro to celebrate the 150th anniversary of Brazil's independence (1972).

MEIGNEN, LEOPOLD

b. 1793 France, d. 1873 Philadelphia, Pennsylvania. Teacher and arranger. Studied at the Paris Conservatorie; came to America (ca. 1827); taught music in Philadelphia, among his students were William H. Fry and Septimus Winner; arranged *Chimes of the Monastery* from a melody by Winner (published in Macon, Ga.); with John Winebrenner compiled *The Seraphina or Christian Library of Church Music.*

MEINECKE, CHRISTOPHER

b. 1782 Germany, d. 1850 Baltimore, Maryland. Composer. Came to Baltimore (1800); organist at St. Paul's Episcopal Church there; his *Messe Lateinisch* Op.25 was published in Leipzig (ca. 1817); composed a "Te Deum" produced at St. Paul's (1821); sixty-two of his tunes were published in *Music for the Church* in 1844 by John Cole and N.C. Burt, including "Gloria Patri."

MEISLE, KATHRYN

b. 1895 Philadelphia, Pennsylvania, d. 1970. Contralto. Studied at Philadelphia Conservatory; debut as soloist with Minneapolis Symphony; noted concert singer; debut in opera as Erda, Chicago Opera (1923); with Metropolitan Opera, New York City after 1934; married Calvin Franklin, concert manager.

MELBA, NELLIE

b. 1859 near Melbourne, Australia, d. 1931 Sydney, Australia. Noted soprano. Born Helen Porter Mitchell; studied piano, organ and theory; married Captain Charles Nesbit Armstrong (1882); toured Australia as a concert singer; studied in Paris with Mathilde Marchesi; debut in Brussels (1887) as Gilda; at

Covent Garden, London (1888) as Lucia; in Paris (1889) as Ophelie; as Lucia at La Scala, Milan (1893) and at the Metropolitan Opera in New York (1893); sang Brunnhilde in *Siegfried* at the Metropolitan (1896) straining her voice and requiring a rest; toured the United States (1897-98); at the Manhattan Opera in New York after 1907; last appearance in the United States (1920) and at Covent Garden, London (1926).

MELCHIOR, LAURITZ LEBRECHT HOMMEL

b. 1890 Copenhagen, Denmark, d. 1973.
Noted tenor. Studied at Royal Opera School in Copenhagen; debut as baritone as *Pagliacci* (1913); appeared as a tenor (1918); sang in famed Wagner festival at Bayreuth, Germany (1924); with Metropolitan Opera, New York City (1926-50); excelled in Wagnerian roles; also sang in San Francisco; sang and conducted the "Radetzky March" (J. Strauss) at the 50th anniversary of the San Francisco Opera (1972).

MELDONIAN, RICHARD A.

b. 1930 Providence, Rhode Island.
Saxist and flutist. Played with Stan Kenton, Charlie Barnet and others in 1950s; at Newport Jazz Festival (1964); played alto sax, tenor sax, and soprano saxophone.

MELINE, FLORANT

b. 1790 France, d. 1827 Albany, New York.
Clarinetist, conductor, composer, and teacher. Came to New York City (1812); served as an officer in the War of 1812; performed at concerts with his wife (vocals); moved to Albany (1824) where he became conductor of the 89th Regimental Band (New York Militia); wrote twelve divertimentos for two flutes, N.Y. (1821), "Governor DeWitt Clinton's March" (1817), "Governor Joseph C. Yates Grand March" (1822), "Madison's March" (ca. 1813).

MELIS, CARMEN

b. 1885 Cagliari, Sardinia, Italy, d. 1967.
Soprano. Sang at Manhattan Opera House, New York (1909), Boston Opera (1911), and Metropolitan Opera, New York City after 1913.

MELMOTH, MRS.

b. 1749 Ireland, d. 1823.
Singer and actress. Played in Dublin, Edinburgh, Drury Lane, and Covent Garden, London; came to New York City (1792); sang in concerts in New York City.

MELODY KNIGHTS (band) *see* SONNY WHITE

MELODY MASTERS, THE *see* JIMMY HEAP

MELODY RANCH BAND *see* CARL B. COTNER

MELROSE BAND (black band)

Active in New Orleans (ca. 1910); included King Oliver, cornet; Honore Dutrey, trombone.

MELROSE, WALTER

b. 1889 Sumner, Illinois, d. 1968.
Songwriter and publisher. Served in U.S. Air Force in World War I; wrote "Sweetheart o' Mine" (1918, m. Jelly Roll Morton).

MELTON, JAMES

b. 1904 Moultrie, Georgia, d. 1961.
Noted tenor. Radio debut (1927); operatic debut as Lt. Pinkerton in Puccini's *Madame Butterfly* in Cincinnati, Ohio (1932); debut with Metropolitan Opera, New York City, as Tamino in *Die Zauberflote* (1942).

MELTZER, CHARLES HENRY

b. 1853 London, England, d. 1936 New York City. Critic. Studied at the Sorbonne in Paris; later a music critic and journalist in New York City.

MELVOIN, MICHAEL

b. 1937 Oshkosh, Wisconsin.
Pianist and organist. Studied piano at age three; graduated Dartmouth College (1959); played with Gerald Wilson, Paul Horn Quintet, Terry Gibbs combo and others during 1960s; toured New Zealand (1964) with Gene McDaniels.

MEMPHIS SLIM

b. 1915 Memphis, Tennessee.
Black pianist, singer, and songwriter. Born Peter Chatman; in Chicago (1939-42) with Big Bill Broonzy; recorded for Miracle (1949); recorded in Houston and Cleveland (1952); Chicago (1953); concert at Carnegie Hall, New York City (1959); in London (1960); wrote "The Comeback" and "Everyday I Have the Blues" (popularized by Joe Williams).

MEMPHIS STUDENTS (black orchestra)

Early players of syncopated music; organized in 1908.

MENASCE, JACQUES DE

b. 1905 Bad Ischl, Austria, d. 1960 Gstaad, Switzerland. Pianist. Studied at Vienna State

Academy; with Sauer and others; debut as pianist at Salzburg Festival (1933); toured in concerts with Angel Reyes in Europe and U.S.; came to America (1941) and later became a U.S. citizen; composed three piano sonatinas, two piano concertos, chamber music.

MENDEL, ARTHUR

b. 1905 Boston, Massachusetts.
Conductor and writer. Associate editor of *The Musical Quarterly;* conductor of the Cantata Singers of New York; chairman of the music department at Princeton University; with Hans T. David compiled and edited *The Bach Reader.*

MENDELSSOHN QUINTETTE CLUB OF BOSTON *see* THOMAS RYAN

MENDES, SERGIO

b. 1941 Niteroi, Brazil.
Pianist. Studied at Niteroi Conservatory (1950); early bossa nova pianist; played in France and Italy (1963); Japan (1964); came to U.S. (1965); toured with Brazil combo and Tijuana Brass.

MENNIN, PETER

b. 1923 Erie, Pennsylvania.
Composer. Studied at Oberlin College; served in World War II; graduated Eastman School, Rochester, N.Y. (Ph.D.); taught at Juilliard School, N.Y. after 1947; composed four symphonies, no. 3 (New York Philharmonic 1947), no. 4 (*The Cycle,* for chorus and orchestra, N.Y. 1949); *Folk Overture: Fantasia* for string orchestra, *Concertino* (for flute, strings, and percussion), *Divertimento and Partita* (for piano), *Sinfonia* (for chamber orchestra), *The Christmas Story* (cantata).

MENOTTI, GIAN-CARLO

b. 1911 Cadigliano, Italy.
Famous composer. Came to America (1928), studied at the Curtis Institute, Philadelphia, then taught there; composed the operas *Amelia Goes to the Ball* (1934), *The Old Maid and the Thief* (1939), *The Medium* (1945), *The Telephone* (1946), *The Consul* (musical drama, 1949), *Amahl and the Night Visitors* (1951), *The Saint of Bleeker Street* (1954), *The Unicorn, The Gorgon and The Manticore* (chamber opera, 1956), *Maria Golovin* (musical drama, 1958), *The Most Important Man* (1971, the New York City Opera).

MENUHIN, YEHUDI

b. 1917 New York City.
Famous concert violinist. The family moved to San Francisco when he was only a year old; when he was ten years old he played a violin concerto by Beethoven in Carnegie Hall, New York City, with flawless precision; retired from the concert stage in 1935, but resumed giving concerts two years later; in Beethoven concert with pianist Hephzibah Menuhin at the Metropolitan Museum of Art Concert (1973).

MERCER, JOHN H. (JOHNNY)

b. 1909 Savannah, Georgia.
Lyricist and singer. Contract writer for Miller Music, New York City (1929-33); wrote for Lew Leslie's *Blackbirds* (1935-36); sang for Paul Whiteman (1938-39), then with Benny Goodman; wrote "Blues in the Night" (1941, m. Harold Arlen), "Dearly Beloved" (1942, m. Jerome Kern), "That Old Black Magic" (1945, Arlen), "Ac-cen-tchu-ate the Positive" (1945, Arlen), "On the Atchison, Topeka and Santa Fe" (1946, w. Harry Warren); also wrote lyrics for Hoagy Carmichael, Victor Schertzinger, and R.A. Whiting.

MERCHANT, JIMMY

b. 1941.
Black singer. Member of the Teen Agers, vocal group in New York City.

MERCIER, CHARLES

b. (?), d. after 1818.
Composer and teacher. Came to Philadelphia about 1807; taught there (1811-18); wrote "General Harrison's March" (1813).

MEREDITH, ISAAC HICKMAN

b. 1872 Norristown, Pennsylvania, d. 1962 Orlando, Florida. Singer and composer. Gospel singer at the age of nineteen; became the musical editor and later president of Tullar-Meredith Company, New York City; composed the tune "Stowell" ("Lord of All Power and Might," w. Hugh Stowell).

MERMAN, ETHEL

b. 1909 Astoria, Queens, New York.
Singer. Born Ethel Agnes Zimmerman; in the musicals *Girl Crazy* (1930, m. George Gershwin), *George White Scandals* (1932, m. Richard A. Whiting), played Annie Oakley in *Annie Get Your Gun* (1946, Berlin), *Call Me Madam* (1950, Berlin), *Gypsy* (1959, m. Jule Styne).

MERO-IRION, YOLANDA

b. 1887 Budapest, Hungary, d. 1963.
Pianist. She studied at Budapest Conservatory; debut as soloist with Dresden Philharmonic (1907); toured Europe, Central and South America; recitalist in New York City; com-

posed *Capriccio Ungharese,* for piano and orchestra; married Herman Irion, of Steinway & Sons.

MEROLA, GAETANO

b. 1881 Naples, Italy, d. 1953 San Francisco, California. Conductor. Studied at Naples Conservatory; assistant conductor of the Metropolitan Opera, New York City (1899); then Savage Opera Company, Manhattan Opera Company, then with San Francisco Opera as general manager; died while conducting a concert in San Francisco.

MERRILL, ABRAHAM DOW

b. 1796 Salem, New Hampshire, d. 1878. Composer. Methodist minister; composed the music for "Joyfully, Joyfully Onward I Move" (1842, w. William Hunter, tune "Triumph").

MERRILL, HELEN

b. 1929 New York City.
Singer. Sang with Earl Hines Sextet and others in 1950s; in Europe after 1959.

MERRILL, ROBERT

b. 1919 Brooklyn, New York.
Noted baritone. Born Moishe Miller; debut at the Metropolitan Opera (1945) as Germont in *La Traviata;* leading baritone at the Metropolitan for twenty-five years; also well-known concert artist and radio singer; with Richard Tucker at Carnegie Hall, New York City (1973).

MERRILL, ROBERT (BOB)

b. 1921 Atlantic City, New Jersey.
Composer. Served in the cavalry and Special Services (1940-42); with Columbia Pictures (1943-48); wrote "If I Knew You Were Comin' I'd've Baked a Cake" (1950, with Al Hoffman and Clem Watts), "Sparrow in the Tree Top" (1951), "Doggie in the Window," "Mambo Italiano," "Honeycomb," "Love Makes the World Go Round" (1961); wrote the scores for *New Girl in Town* (1957, based on *Anna Christie*), *Take Me Along* (1959, based on *Ah Wilderness*), *Carnival* (1961, Lili).

MERRILL, WILLIAM PIERSON

b. 1867 Orange, New Jersey, d. 1954.
Hymnist. Educated at Rutgers, New Brunswick, N.J., and Union Theological Seminary; Presbyterian minister in Philadelphia, Chicago, then of the Brick Presbyterian Church, New York City; wrote the hymn "Rise Up, O Men of God" (1911, tune "Festal Song"—W.H. Walter and "Oxnam"—R.G. McCuthan).

MERRITT, JAMES

b. 1926 Philadelphia, Pennsylvania.
Bass player. With B.B. King, Chris Powell and others in 1950s; with Art Blakey, Max Roach and others in 1960s.

MERZ, KARL

b. 1836 Bensheim, Germany, d. 1890 Wooster, Ohio. Composer, teacher, and writer. Studied under his father, an organist, also under F.J. Kunkel; came to Philadelphia (1854); organist at South Presbyterian church there; later in Salem, Va., and Harrisonburg; then at Oxford Female College, Oxford, Ohio (1861-82); at the University of Wooster, Wooster, Ohio, after 1882; chief editor of *Musical World* after 1873; wrote a sonata, *Bitter Tears* (nocturne), *Tranquillity* (andante), *Caprice* (for piano and violin).

MESSITER, ARTHUR HENRY

b. 1834 Somersetshire, England, d. 1916 New York City. Composer. Came to America (1863) where he spent some time in Poultney, Vermont, and in Philadelphia; in 1866 became choirmaster in Trinity Church (Episcopal), New York City; composed the tune "Marion" (1883, "Rejoice, Ye Pure in Heart," w. E.H. Plumptre, 1865); music editor of the *Episcopal Hymnal* of 1893.

METCALF, LOUIS

b. 1905 St. Louis, Missouri.
Black trumpeter. Played with Duke Ellington's band (1927-29); later with King Oliver and others; then formed his own band; worked in vaudeville in Montreal; on Mississippi riverboats during 1930s; in Canada (1944-51); played in New York City night spots after 1951.

METCALF, SAMUEL LYTLER

b. 1798 Winchester, Virgina, d. 1856 Cape May, New Jersey. Compiler. The family moved to Shelbyville, Kentucky, when he was a boy; when he was only nineteen he published at his own expense *The Kentucky Harmonist* (1817), which netted him the funds to enter Transylvania University, Lexington, Ky., where he earned his Doctor of Medicine degree; practicing physician in New Albany, Indiana, and later became professor of chemistry at Transylvania; wrote *Indian Wars in the West, Terrestrial Magnetism,* and *Calorie* (1845).

METTOME, DOUGLAS VOLL

b. 1925 Salt Lake City, Utah, d. there 1964. Trumpeter. Played with Billy Eckstine, Benny Goodman, Woody Herman and others in 1940s and '50s.

METZ, JULIUS

b. ca. 1798 France, d. after 1857.
Singer, pianist, composer, and teacher. Debut in New York City (1819); with New York Philharmonic (1842); taught in New York City (1819-57); wrote the *Clermont Waltz* (1820), *Spanish Waltz* (1818) "West Point March" (1825) *The Primrose*, a ballad (1818).

METZ, THEODORE A.

b. 1848 Hanover, Germany, d. 1936 New York City. Popular composer. Bandmaster in the minstrel troupe of McIntyre and Heath; wrote the music "There'll Be a Hot Time in the Old Town Tonight" (1896, w. Joe Hayden, a singer in the troupe); the song was adopted by the Rough Riders under Colonel Theodore Roosevelt as their official song.

MEYER, GEORGE W.

b. 1884 Boston, Massachusetts, d. 1959 New York City. Composer. Wrote "Lonesome" (1909, with Kerry Mills, w. Edgar Leslie), "When You're a Long Way from Home" (1914, w. Sam M. Lewis), "My Mother's Rosary" (1915, Leslie), "For Me and My Gal" (1917, w. Lewis and E. Ray Goetz), "Tuck Me to Sleep in My Old 'Tucky Home" (w. Lewis and Joe Young), "If I Only Had a Match" (w. Art Johnston and Lee Morris).

MEYER, JOSEPH

b. 1894 Modesto, California.
Composer. Studied the violin in Paris; served in the army in World War I; wrote "California Here I Come" (1922, w. Buddy De Sylva), "If You Knew Susie" (1925, De Sylva), "Falling in Love with You" (w. Benny Davis), "Crazy Rhythm" (1928, with Roger Wolf Kohn and w. Irving Caesar); wrote the scores for *Big Boy* (1925, starring Al Johnson) and *Lady Fingers* (1929).

MEYER, LUCY (RIDER)

b. 1849 New Haven, Vermont, d. 1922 Chicago, Illinois. Composer. Educated at Oberlin College, Ohio; at various times she taught in Brandon, Vermont, Greensboro, N.C., Poultney, Vermont, McKendree College, Lebanon, Ill., then at Northfield Seminary (1885), when she married the Rev. Josiah S. Meyer; became principal of the Chicago Training School (1885-1917); composed "The Lord Bless Thee and Keep Thee" (w. from the Old Testament).

MEYEROWITZ, JAN

b. 1913 Breslau, Poland.
Composer. Studied in Berlin and Rome, then came to the United States; wrote the operas *The Barrier* (play by Langston Hughes), *Herodiade, Simoon, Bad Boys in School, The Glory Around His Head, The Five Foolish Virgins, Missa Rachel Plorans; King Caspar's Voyage* (orchestral), *Remembrance of a Former Life* (orchestral), and oratorio *Esther* which was performed at the Spring Festival of the University of Illinois (1957).

MEZZROW, MILTON (MEZZ)

b. 1899 Chicago, Illinois, d. 1972 Paris, France. Clarinetist and composer. Panassie came to America in 1938 and persuaded Mezz and Tommy Ladnier to cut some records which became jazz classics; wrote *Swingin' with Mezz, Dissonance, Sendin' the Vipers, Blues in Disguise, Gone Away Blues, My Thoughts* (with Stuff Smith), *If You See Me Comin'* (with Teddy Bunn), *Revolutionary Blues;* played with Louis Armstrong, Django Reinhardt, Eddie Condon, Sidney Bechet and others; lived in Paris after 1951.

"MIDDAY MERRY-GO-ROUND" *see* RICHARD L. BLANCHARD

MIDDLEBROOKS, WILFRED ROLAND

b. 1933 Chattanooga, Tennessee.
Bass and tuba player. With Eric Dolphy, Ella Fitzgerald and others during 1950s; with Fitzgerald, Carol Lawrence, Kay Starr, Paul Smith and others in 1960s.

MIDDLETON, VELMA

b. 1917 St. Louis, Missouri, d. 1961 Sierra Leone, Africa. Black singer and dancer. With Louis Armstrong's band after 1942; on tour in Africa where she died.

"MIDWESTERN HAYRIDE"

Variety show on radio station WLW, Cincinnati, Ohio; started in 1938; hosted by Dean Richards.

MIERSCH, CARL ALEXANDER JOHANNES

b. 1865 Dresden, Germany, d. 1916 Cincinnati, Ohio. Violinist. Studied at Dresden Conservatory; with Boston Symphony Orchestra (1891); court violinist and artistic director of Athens Conservatory (1894-98); returned to U.S. (1902); at Cincinnati College of Music after 1910.

MIERSCH, PAUL FRANCIS

b. 1868 Dresden, Germany, d. 1956.
Cellist. Brother of Carl Miersch; studied at Royal Academy, Munich; came to New York (1892); soloist with New York Symphony Orchestra (1892-97); then with the

Metropolitan Opera, New York after 1908; composed cello and violin concertos, *Indian Rhapsody for Orchestra.*

MIGNONE, FRANCISCO

b. 1897 Sao Paulo, Brazil.
Composer. Studied at the Sao Paulo Conservatory, where he later became professor of harmony and piano; composed *Congada, dansa Afrobrasileira* (for orchestra, from his opera *Contratador de Diamantes,* 1920), *Four Churches* (symphonic poem for orchestra, 1940).

MILBURN, RICHARD

b. ca. 1845, d. ca. 1900.
Black singing barber. One day he was walking down the streets of Philadelphia whistling a tune and Septimus Winner, the composer, heard him. From the melody, Winner composed "Listen to the Mocking Bird" in 1855, and on the first copy published he gave credit to Dick Milburn for the melody. Later Milburn became a barber in Philadelphia and sang in church choirs there.

MILDENBERG, ALBERT

b. 1878 Brooklyn, New York, d. 1918 Raleigh, North Carolina. Composer. Pupil of Joseffy, Bruno Oskar Klein, and C.C. Muller; composed operas and orchestral suites.

MILES EXPRESS, THE BUDDY (jazz-rock group)

Jim McCarty, guitar; Herbie Rich, organ; Virgil Gonsalves, baritone sax; Terry Clements, tenor sax; Marcus Doubleday, trumpet; Billy Rick, bass; Bob McPherson, tenor sax; Ron Woods, drums; Buddy Miles (black), vocals and drums; four of the group were from the Electric Flag; started in Hollywood in 1968; albums—*Electric Church; Expressway to Your Skull;* at the Schaefer Music Festival, New York City (1972).

MILES, LIZZIE

b. 1895 New Orleans, Louisiana, d. 1963.
Black singer. Born Elizabeth Mary Landreaux; sang in King Oliver's orchestra; recorded with Jelly Roll Morton and Clarence Williams; known as a classic blues singer.

MILES, LUKE ("LONG GONE")

b. 1925 Lachute, Louisiana.
Black singer. With Lightnin' Hopkins after 1952; later sang in Los Angeles night clubs.

MILEY, JAMES ("BUBBER")

b. 1903 Aiken., South Carolina, d. 1932 Welfare Island, New York. Black trumpeter and composer. Played with Duke Ellington's orchestra (1926-29); wrote a number of jazz songs with Ellington, such as, "Black and Tan Fantasy," "East St. Louis Toodle-oo," "Blues I Love to Sing," "Blue Bubbles," "Doin' the Voom Voom," "Creole Love Call."

MILLARD, HARRISON

b. 1830 Boston, Massachusetts, d. there 1895. Tenor and popular composer. Studied in Italy; toured England as tenor concert-singer; settled in New York City (1856) as a teacher, singer, and composer; composed an opera, grand mass, and numerous popular songs including "The Pilot Brave" and "Ship Ahoy!" (both to the lyrics of George Cooper).

MILLER, ANNE LANGDON

b. 1908 New York City.
Composer. Studied at the Institute of Musical Art and the David Mannes School of Music in New York City; entered the Community of Poor Clares (1948); composed the tune "Vermont" (1941, "Give Peace, O God, the Nations Cry," w. John W. Norris).

MILLER BAND, STEVE (rock group)

Steve Miller, lead vocals and lead guitar; William Bozz Scraggs, rhythm guitar; Tim Davis, drums; Lonnie Turner, bass; Jim Peterman, organ; Curley Cooke, guitar, former member; started in Chicago in 1968; toured England and Europe; returned to San Francisco; albums—*Brave New World, Children of the Future, Sailor, Your Saving Grace;* in concert at the Academy of Music, New York City (1972).

MILLER, BOB

b. 1895 Memphis, Tennessee, d. 1955 Nyack, New York. Singer, songwriter, and publisher. Studied at the Chicago Conservatory of Music and the Southern Conservatory of Music; wrote "There's a Star Spangled Banner Waving Somewhere," "Chime Bells," "Twenty-one Years," "Eleven Cent Cotton," "Dry Voters and Wet Drinkers," "Seven Years with the Wrong Woman," "When the White Azaleas Start Blooming," "Rockin' Alone in an Old Rockin' Chair," "Missouri Joe," "Duck Foot Sue," "Hurry Johnnie, Hurry."

MILLER, CLARENCE H.

b. 1923 Sioux City, Iowa.
Bass player and singer. With Jay McShann (1949-54); at Monterey Jazz Festival (1960) with Jon Hendricks; singer in Honolulu, Hawaii after 1964.

MILLER, EDDIE

b. 1891, d. 1971 Amityville, New York. Baritone. Sang in Broadway shows and in night spots in New York City; later a voice teacher.

MILLER, EDWARD R. (EDDIE)

b. 1911 New Orleans, Louisiana. Tenor saxist and clarinetist. Played with Bob Crosby band in 1940s and '50s; played with Crosby at 1964 Olympics in Japan.

MILLER, EMILY (HUNTINGTON)

b. 1833 Brooklyn, Connecticut, d. 1913 Northfield, Minnesota. Hymnist. Graduated Oberlin College, Ohio; married John E. Miller (1860); Dean of Women at Northwestern University, Evanston, Ill.; wrote the hymn "Angel's Story" (1879, m. G.F. Root "I Love to Hear the Story Which Angel Voices Tell"), and "Tell the Blessed Tydings" (tune "Deva," E.J. Hopkins).

MILLER, ERNEST ("PUNCH")

b. 1894 Raceland, Louisiana. Black trumpeter and singer. Played in military band under Willie Humphrey during World War I; played with Jack Carey, Kid Ory, Erskine Tate and others.

MILLER, FRANKIE

b. (?) Victoria, Texas. Singer and songwriter. Wrote "Blackland Farmer."

MILLER, GLENN

b. 1904 Clarinda, Iowa, d. 1944 in an airplane crash over the English Channel. Bandleader and trombonist. Joined Ben Pollack's band (1927); attended the University of Colorado at Boulder; studied in New York with Joseph Schillinger; joined Ray Noble's band; later formed his own band which included Bob Price and Irving Fazola; enlisted in the army (1942); organized the A.E.F. band in England; wrote "Moonlight Serenade," which became his theme song.

MILLER, HENRY NED

b. 1925 Raines, Utah. Singer and songwriter. Attended schools in Murray, Utah, West Jordan, Utah, and Salt Lake City (1952); wrote "From a Jack to a King," "Do What You Do, Do Well," "Dark Moon," "Snowflake."

MILLER, JODY

b. 1941 Phoenix, Arizona. Singer. She attended high school in Blanchard, Oklahoma; sang in night clubs; also sang at San Remo (Italy) Song Festival; hit albums were *He Walks Like a Man* (1964), *Queen of the House* (1965), *Jody Miller* (1965), *Great Hits of Buck Owens* (1966), *Silver Threads and Golden Needles, Nashville Sound of Jody Miller.*

MILLER, MARILYN

b. 1898, d. 1936. Singer and dancer. Introduced "Look for a Silver Lining" in *Sally* (1920, w. Guy Bolton and P.G. Wodehouse, m. Jerome Kern, produced by Florenz Ziegfeld); with Clifton Webb and the chorus she sang "Easter Parade" in *As Thousands Cheer* (1933, m. Irving Berlin).

MILLER, MITCH

b. 1911 Rochester, New York Chorus leader, conductor, and oboist. Studied at Eastman School of Music, Rochester; joined CBS orchestra (1936); with Columbia Records (1950); started the "Sing Along with Mitch" (1958).

MILLER, REED

b. 1880, d. 1923. Tenor. Married Nevada Van Der Veer, contralto.

MILLER, ROGER DEAN

b. 1936 Fort Worth, Texas. Popular composer. Raised in Erick, Oklahoma; served in the army in Korea during the Korean War; wrote "When Two Worlds Collide" (1961, with Bill Anderson); "Chug a Lug" (1963); "Dang Me" (1964); "King of the Road," "Engine, Engine No. 9," "Kansas City Star," "One Dyin' and 'A-Buryin'," "England Swings" (1965); "Husbands and Wives" (1966); "In the Summer Time" (sung by Andy Williams); since he couldn't write music, he sang or played his tunes for friends to write down.

MILLER, RUSSELL KING

b.1871 Philadelphia, Pennsylvania, d. 1939. Organist, composer, and teacher. Studied on a J.C.B. Standbridge organ installed (1852) at Calvary Presbyterian Church, Philadelphia; director of music at Hollond Presbyterian Church, Philadelphia (1893-98); also taught at the Pennsylvania Institute for Instruction of the Blind.

MILLER, WILLARD DARNELL

b. 1937 Bland County, Virginia. Singer and songwriter. Attended schools in Hollybrook, Va., and Bland, Va.; wrote

"Back to You," "One Never Knows," "I Stopped Living."

MILLIGAN, HAROLD VINCENT

b. 1888 Astoria, Oregon, d. 1951 New York City. Organist and composer. Graduated Guilmant Organ School, New York City; studied with T.T. Noble and A.E. Johnstone; organist and choirmaster at various churches, then at Riverside Church, New York City; toured U.S. as organ soloist; president of the National Association of Organists; wrote *Pioneer American Composers*, edited *Colonial Love Lyrics;* composed organ works, operettas, songs.

MILLIGAN, JAMES LEWIS

b. 1876 Liverpool, England. d. (?).
Hymnist. Emigrated to Canada (1911) and became a lay preacher in a Methodist circuit in Hastings County, Ontario; later became editorial writer for the *Toronto Globe* and then the *Stafford Beacon-Herald;* wrote the hymn "There's a Voice in the Wilderness Crying" (tune "Hereford"—F.D. Heins) which appeared in *The Hymnary of the United Church of Canada* (1930).

MILLINDER, LUCIUS ("LUCKY")

b. 1900 Anniston, Alabama, d. 1966.
Black bandleader. Singer and front man for the Blue Rhythm Band (1934) which recorded a "Tiger Rag" variant entitled "Ride, Red Ride."

MILLS BROTHERS (black vocal group)

Herbert (b. 1912), Harry F. (b. 1913), Donald F. (b. 1915); all born in Piqua, Ohio; John Jr. died in 1935 and was replaced by his father, John Mills (b. 1889 Bellefonte, Pa.), he retired (1957) after one of his legs was amputated; brothers continued numerous appearances; debut on radio (1925) in Cincinnati, Ohio; with CBS in New York City (1929), first known blacks on national radio; in Los Angeles (1934); gave command performance for King George V and Queen Mary at the Paladium (1934); guitarist Norman Brown with the group (1936-69); their record "Lazy River" (1931) sold three million disks; "Paper Doll" (1942) sold five million; "Glow Worm" (1952) over one million disks; brother active and recording in 1972.

MILLS, FLORENCE

b. 1895 Washington, D.C., d. 1927.
Black singer. While singing in a theater in Harlem, New York City, her accompanist was Fats Waller.

MILLS, FREDERICK A. ("KERRY")

b. 1869 Philadelphia, Pennsylvania, d. 1948 Hawthorne, California. Popular composer. For a time he taught the violin in Ann Arbor, Michigan; wrote "Rastus on Parade" (1895, cakewalk), "Happy Days in Dixie" (1896), "Let Bygones Be Bygones" (1897, w. C. Shackford), "Whistling Rufus" (1899, w. M. Lind), "At a Georgia Camp Meeting" (1899, popularized by the song and dance team of Genaro and Bailey, with a strut or cakewalk before each chorus, which made the song famous), and "Meet Me in St. Louis" (1904, revived in the 1944 movie with Judy Garland).

MILLS, GORDON

b. 1935 India.
Manager. His father was a sergeant in the British army in India; after he returned to London he discovered Gerry Dorsey, whom he renamed Engelbert Humperdinck; also Thomas Jones Woodward, whom he renamed Tom Jones; and Raymond O'Sullivan whom he renamed Gilbert O'Sullivan; formed a company with Jones and Humperdinck.

MILLS, HENRY

b. 1786 Morristown, New Jersey, d. 1867 Auburn, New York. Hymnist. Graduated Princeton (1802); pastor of the Presbyterian Church, Woodbridge, N.J. (1816); professor at Auburn Theological Seminary (1821-54); published *Horae Germanical; A Version of German Hymns* (1845).

MILLS, IRVING

b. 1894 New York City.
Songwriter and publisher. President of American Academy of Music and American Recording Artists; vice-president of Mills Music; wrote "Indigo Echoes" (m. Duke Ellington), "Lovesick Blues" (1922, m. Cliff Friend), "Moonglow" (1934, m. Will Hudson).

MILLS, JACKIE

b. 1922 Brooklyn, New York.
Drummer. With Harry James during 1940s and '50s; with Harry Edison combo in 1960s; also a record company executive.

MILLS, SEBASTIAN BACH

b. 1838 Cirencester, Gloucester, England, d. 1898 Wiesbaden, Germany. Pianist and teacher. Studied under his father, an organist; at Royal Academy, London, then at Leipzig (graduated 1859); came to New York City (1859); became a noted concert pianist in New York; also taught in New York City.

MILNES, SHERRILL

b. 1935 Downers Grove, Illinois.
Baritone. Studied pre-med. at Drake University, Des Moines, Iowa; sang Marlboro, Kelloggs and Falstaff beer commercials on TV; debut at Metropolitan Opera, New York City, in Gounod's *Faust* (1965); European debut (1970) in Verdi's *Macbeth* at the Vienna Staatsoper; sang Iago in *Otello* in Mexico City (1965) and at the Metropolitan Opera, New York City (1972).

MILSTEIN, NATHAN

b. 1904 Odessa, Russia.
Concert violinist. Studied under Ysaye and Auer, and then as a lad of nine, and a violinist, toured with Vladimir Horowitz, the pianist, who was the same age; later came to America.

MINGUS, CHARLES

b. 1922 Nogales, Arizona.
Black bass player, bandleader, and composer. Played in Los Angeles and San Francisco during 1940s; with Red Norvo, Charlie Parker, Stan Getz and others in 1950s; formed his own combo in New York City; composed *Meditations on Integration,* performed by his group at Monterey Jazz Festival (1964); known as a "hard bop" jazz player; *The Mingus Dances* (ballet) presented by Alvin Ailey and City Center Joffrey Ballet, New York City (October, 1971).

MINNELLI, LIZA

b. 1946 California.
Singer. Daughter of Judy Garland; sang on the Liza Minnelli-Norm Crosby Riviera show; often with Johnnie Ray; starred in the film *Cabaret* (1972), with the only singing role.

MIRACLES, THE (black singers)

Smokey Robinson, leader and songwriter. Albums—*Flying High Together, Make It Happen, Miracles' Greatest Hits, One Dozen Roses, Pocket Full of Miracles, Smokey Robinson and the Miracles.*

MIRANDA, CARMEN

b. 1909 Marco Canavezes, Portugal, d. 1953.
Singer and dancer. Taken to Brazil as a child; night club entertainer, with her own band and radio show in Brazil; New York debut in the Shuberts' Broadway show *The Streets of Paris* (1939), sang "South American Way"; appeared in film of same name with Betty Grable and Don Ameche (1940) and other films; later in night clubs and personal appearances; at the London Palladium (1948).

MISSOURIANS, THE (band) *see* CAB CALLOWAY

MITCHELL, ABBIE

b. 1884 New York City, d. 1960.
Black soprano. Studied voice with Harry T. Burleigh and Emilia Serrano in New York City; later in Paris; sang with the Nashville Students, black orchestra, which played at Proctor's, New York City (1905), first public concert of syncopated music in America; became a concert singer; married Will Marion Cook.

MITCHELL, BILLY

b. 1926 Kansas City, Missouri.
Black tenor saxist. Played with Woody Herman, Lucky Millinder and others in 1940s; with Dizzie Gillespie, Count Basie and others in 1950s; led his own group in 1960s with trombonist Al Grey; with Clarke-Boland orchestra in Eurcpe (1963).

MITCHELL, DWIKE

b. 1930 Jacksonville, Florida.
Pianist. With Lionel Hampton in 1950s; then formed duo with Willie Ruff; first modern jazzmen to tour Soviet Russia; with President Johnson on his goodwill trip to Mexico City (1966).

MITCHELL, GEORGE

b. 1899 Louisville, Kentucky.
Black jazz trumpeter. Played in Jelly Roll Morton's band; with Jimmy Noone's band (1928).

MITCHELL, GORDON B. ("WHITEY")

b. 1932 Hackensack, New Jersey.
Bass player. Brother of Red Mitchell; led his own group during 1950s; with Benny Goodman and others in 1960s; studio musician in Los Angeles.

MITCHELL, GROVER

b. 1930 Whatley, Alabama.
Black trombonist. Played with Duke Ellington, Lionel Hampton, and Count Basie in 1960s; toured Europe and Japan with Count Basie.

MITCHELL, GUY

b. 1925 Detroit, Michigan.
Singer. Won a gold record for "My Heart Cries for You" (m. Percy Faith).

MITCHELL, KEITH MOORE ("RED")

b. 1927 New York City.
Bass player. With Hampton Hawes and Andre Previn in 1950s; co-led own group with Harold

Land (1961-62); later with MGM studio orchestra.

ΙITCHELL, NAHUM

b. 1769 East Bridgewater, Massachusetts, d. 1853 Plymouth, Massachusetts. Compiler. Graduated Harvard (1789) and studied law in Plymouth, Mass.; State Representative (1803-05), judge (1811-21), State Senator (1813-14), Representative to the 8th Congress in Washington, D.C., and State Treasurer (1822-27); assisted Bartholomew Brown and Benjamin Holt in compiling *The Bridgewater Collection of Sacred Music* (1802).

ΊITCHELL, PRISCILLA

b. 1941 Marietta, Georgia.
Singer. Made her debut at age four on station WFOM, Marietta; married Jerry Reed Hubbard, singer and songwriter; they settled in Nashville; her hit records were "Yes, Mr. Peters" (1965), "Slippin' Around"; LP record, *We Belong Together.*

MITCHELL, RICHARD ALLEN ("BLUE")

b. 1930 Miami, Florida.
Black trumpeter. Played with Horace Silver Quintet (1958-64); toured Japan with George Wein show (1965); later formed his own quintet.

MITCHELL, WILLIAM

b. 1907 New York City, d. 1971 Binghamton, New York. Teacher. Graduated Columbia University, New York City, (M.A.); taught music there (1932-68), then at State University, Binghamton; professor (1952); president of American Musicological Society; wrote *Elementary Harmony* (1939).

MITROPOULOS, DMITRI

b. 1896 Athens, Greece, d. 1960 Milan, Italy. Noted conductor. Graduated Athens Conservatory (1919); also studied in Brussels; repetiteur at Berlin Opera until 1925; later conductor in Athens; conductor of the Minneapolis Symphony Orchestra after 1937; musical director of the New York Philharmonic after 1950.

MIZE, BILLY

b. 1932 Kansas City, Kansas.
Singer and songwriter. Debut on station KERO-TV, Bakersfield, Calif. (1953); wrote "I Saw Her First," "Who Will Buy the Wine," "It Could Happen," "Solid Slender"; album—*This Time and Place.*

MOBLEY, HENRY (HANK)

b. 1930 Eastman, Georgia.
Black tenor saxist. With Max Roach, Horace Silver, Dizzy Gillespie, Thelonious Monk and others during 1950s; with Miles Davis and others in 1960s; also formed his own group.

MOBY GRAPE (pop group)

Jerry Miller, lead guitar; Peter Lewis, guitar; Bob Mosley, bass; Don Stevenson, drums; Skip Spence, rhythm guitar (left the group to go solo); Miller, Stevenson, and Mosley were previously with a group called the Frantics; Peter Lewis had been with Peter and the Wolves; Skip Spence was with the Jefferson Airplane; they released five singles and an album (1967); albums—*Moby Grape, Wow, Grape Jams, Truly Fine Citizen;* group disbanded in 1969.

MODERN JAZZ QUARTET *see* JOHN A. LEWIS, MILT JACKSON, PERCY HEATH

MODERN JAZZ SEXTET *see* STIX HOOPER

MOER, PAUL

b. 1916 Meadville, Pennsylvania.
Pianist and composer. Played with various bands in 1940s and '50s; with Benny Carter, Paul Horn Quintet and others in 1960s; wrote *Tall Polynesian* and *Short Politician,* both recorded by the Paul Horn Quintet.

MOFFETT, CHARLES MACK

b. 1929 Fort Worth, Texas.
Drummer and composer. Served in U.S. Navy in Pacific; welterweight boxing champion in the navy; graduated in music education at the University of Texas, Austin; later taught in high schools in Texas; played with Ornette Coleman, Sonny Rollins and others in 1960s; toured Europe with Coleman (1965-66).

MOFFO, ANNA

b. 1935 Wayne, Pennsylvania.
Soprano. Attended Radnor High School; studied four years at Curtis Institute, Philadelphia; went to Italy on Fulbright Scholarship; married Mario Lanfranchi, Italian film producer; starred in *Madame Butterfly* (1956) and many other Italian films; with the Metropolitan Opera, New York City for twelve years; also sang opera in Hamburg, Germany.

MOHR, HERMANN

b. 1830 Nienstedt, Germany, d. 1896 Philadelphia, Pennsylvania. Teacher and composer. Graduated Royal Church Music Institute, Berlin (1855); taught at

Philadelphia Musical Academy after 1886; composed *Bergmannsgruss* (a cantata), *Saengerchor* (with orchestra and solo), *Der Orakelspruch* (opera); compositions for mixed choruses, also male choruses, female choruses, songs.

MOLE, IRVING MILFRED ("MIFF")

b. 1898 Roosevelt, Long Island, New York, d. 1961 New York City. Trombonist. Played with Original Memphis Five; later with Red Nichols, Paul Whiteman, and Benny Goodman in 1940s; died following a stroke.

MOLLENHAUER, EDWARD

b. 1827 Erfurt, East Germany, d. 1914 Owatonna, Minnesota. Violinist. His brother, Friedrich, was a violinist and composer; another brother, Heinrich, a cellist; studied with Ernst and Spohr; founded a violin school in New York (1853); composed two operas, *Passion* (a symphony), two other symphonies, violin pieces, string quartets.

MOLLENHAUER, EMIL

b. 1855 Brooklyn, New York, d. 1927 Boston, Massachusetts. Conductor. Son of Friedrich Mollenhauer, violinist, and nephew of Edward; at only nine years of age he was a violinist; then with Boston Symphony Orchestra; conducted Boston Handel and Haydn Society (1899-1927); Apollo Club (1901-27); also conducted Boston Symphony at festivals.

MOLLER, JOHN CHRISTOPHER

b. (?), d. 1803 New York City.
Composer. Came to New York City about 1790; published music in New York (1797); wrote *Favorite La Chasse* (1803, w. Thomas Moore), *The Chase* (1811), *Sinfonia* (for piano).

MONACO, JAMES V.

b. 1885 Genoa, Italy, d. 1945 Beverly Hills, California. Popular composer. Came to Chicago (1891), then went to New York City (1910); wrote "Row, Row, Row" (1912, w. William Jerome), "You Made Me Love You" (1912, w. Joseph McCarthy), "Six Lessons from Madame La Zonga" (w. Charles Newman), "Crying for Joy" (w. Billy Rose), "An Apple for the Teacher" (w. Johnny Burke), "I Can't Begin to Tell You" (w. Mack Gordon).

MONCUR, GRACHAN, JR.

b. 1915 Miami, Florida.
Black double bass player and bandleader. Played bass with The Savoy Sultans; also led his own band in Newark, N.J.

MONCUR, GRACHAN, III

b. 1937 New York City.
Black trombonist. Son of bass player Grachan Moncur; studied music at Laurinburg Institute, Laurinburg, North Carolina; also at Manhattan School of Music and at Juilliard, New York City; with Ray Charles, Art Farmer-Benny Golson Jazztet, Jackie McLean and others in 1960s.

MONK, THELONIOUS SPHERE

b. 1917 Rocky Mount, North Carolina.
Black jazz pianist. Played in Dizzy Gillespie's band; also with Red Allen; played in Minton's Playhouse, Harlem, New York City during the 1940s with Charlie Christian, pianist; Gillespie, trumpeter; Kenny Clarke, drummer; and developed what was called "bebop," later simply "bop"; appeared at Philharmonic Hall and Carnegie Hall, New York City during 1960s; at Newport Jazz Festival, New York City (1972).

MONKEES (rock group)

Mickey Dolenz, lead vocals, guitar, and drums; Davy Jones, vocals and tambourine; Michael Nesmith, bass; Peter Tork, guitar, left the group; Mickey had been a child actor and on TV; Davy had played on Broadway in *Oliver;* recorded "Last Train to Clarksville" (1966); albums—*Birds, The Bees and The Monkees, Head* (soundtrack), *Instant Reply, The Monkees, Greatest Hits, Headquarters, Present Mickey, David and Michael, Pisces, Aquarius, Capricorn and Jones, Ltd., More of the Monkees.*

MONOD, THEODORE

b. 1836 Paris, France, d. there 1921.
Hymnist. Educated at the Western Theological Seminary, Pittsburgh, Pa.; pastor of the Second Presbyterian Church, Kankakee, Illinois (1861-64); returned to France (1864) and became pastor of the Chapelle du Nord, then the Reformed Church in Paris; wrote the hymn "O the Bitter Shame and Sorrow" (1874, tune "St Jude"—C.J. Vincent).

MONROE, CHARLES PENDLETON (CHARLIE)

b. 1903 Rosine, Kentucky.
Singer. The Monroe Brothers, Charlie and Bill started in radio in 1927; Charlie organized the "Kentucky Pardners" (1938); retired in the 1950s; their albums include *Early Blue Grass Music by the Monroe Brothers, Bill and Charlie Monroe;* Charlie's record album—*Who's Calling You Sweetheart Tonight.*

MONROE, VAUGHN

b. 1911 Akron, Ohio, d. 1973.
Singer, trumpeter, and bandleader. His band a hit in Boston, then brought to New York (1941), with a big-time debut at the Meadowbrook; later played on radio advertising Camel cigarettes.

MONROE, WILLIAM (BILL)

b. 1911 Rosine, Kentucky.
Popular composer. He and his brother Charlie made their debut on radio in 1927; Bill organized "The Bluegrass Boys"; he wrote "Kentucky Waltz" (1934, later he added lyrics), "Blue Grass Ramble," "Blue Moon of Kentucky," "Cheyenne," "On the Kentucky Shore," "Scotland," "Uncle Pen," "Memories of Mother and Dad"; at Grand Ole Opry, Nashville, Tenn. (1972).

MONTANA, PATSY

b. 1914 Hot Springs, Arkansas.
Singer and songwriter. Born Rubye Blevins; attended the University of Western Louisiana; lead singer for the "Prairie Ramblers" (1934); married Paul Rose; wrote "I'm a Little Cowboy Girl," "The Buckaroo," "Me and My Cowboy Sweetheart," "The Moon Hangs Low," "I've Found My Cowboy Sweetheart," "My Baby's Lullaby," "Cowboy Rhythm," "My Poncho Pony."

MONTAND, YVES

b. 1921 Monsummarro, Italy.
Singer. Albums—*Extraordinaire, French Popular and Folk Songs.*

MONTANI, NICOLA ALOYSIUS

b. 1880 Utica, New York, d. 1948 Philadelphia, Pennsylvania. Composer and compiler. Organist of the Church of St. John the Evangelist, Philadelphia (1906-23), then the Paulist Church, New York City (1923-24); editor of *The Catholic Choirmaster* for twenty-five years and edited the *St. Gregory Hymnal* and *The Catholic Choirbook;* composed eight masses.

MONTEUX, PIERRE

b. 1875 Paris, France, d. 1964.
Conductor. Conducted the Boston Symphony Orchestra (1919-24), later the San Francisco Symphony Orchestra, then became a guest conductor; moved to Hancock, Maine, where he held summer conducting classes.

MONTGOMERY, CHARLES F. ("BUDDY")

b. 1930 Indianapolis, Indiana.
Black pianist and vibraphonist. Brother of Monk and Wes Montgomery; with Slide Hampton and the Mastersounds in 1950s; formed Montgomery Brothers Quartet in San Francisco (1960); at Monterey Jazz Festival (1961).

MONTGOMERY, JOHN LESLIE ("WES")

b. 1925 Indianapolis, Indiana, d. 1968.
Black guitarist. Brother of Buddy and Monk Montgomery; with the Mastersounds, Montgomery Brothers Quartet, and Wynton Kelly Trio during 1960s; also toured Europe.

MONTGOMERY, MARION

b. 1934 Natchez, Mississippi.
Singer. Sang in Chicago night clubs; then in New York and other cities; toured England (1965); married pianist Laurence Holloway.

MONTGOMERY, MELBA JOYCE

b. 1938 Iron City, Tennessee.
Singer. She won the Pet Milk amateur contest, Nashville, Tenn. (1958) which started her career; later toured overseas for the USO; hit albums were *Being Together, Big Wonderful Country World of Melba Montgomery, Blue Moon of Kentucky, Close Together, Country Girl, Don't Keep Me Lonely Too Long, Hallelujah Road, I'm Just Living, Let's Get Together, Melba Toast, What's in Our Hearts.*

MONTGOMERY, WILLIAM HOWARD ("MONK")

b. 1921 Indianapolis, Indiana.
Black bass player. Brother of Buddy and Wes Montgomery; played with Mastersounds (1957-60); with Montgomery Brothers Quartet after 1960; also Jack Wilson Quartet, Cal Tjader Quintet and others in 1960s.

MOODY, CLYDE

b. 1915 Cherokee, North Carolina.
Singer and bandleader. Leader of The Woodchoppers; known as "The Hillbilly Waltz King."

MOODY, JAMES

b. 1925 Savannah, Georgia.
Alto and tenor saxist and flutist. Played with Dizzy Gillespie in 1940s; later led his own groups; rejoined Gillespie in 1960s; with Gene Ammons and Sonny Stitt in the "Battle of the Saxophones"; played at the Newport Jazz Festival, New York City (1972).

MOOG SYNTHESIZERS, GERSHON KINGSLEY AND HIS

Recital at the Jewish Museum, New York City (1972).

MOONSHINERS *see* JACK FIDLER

MOORE, CAROLINE RUDY

b. 1943 Nashville, Tennessee.
Singer, pianist, organist, and teacher. Attended Free Will Baptist College, Nashville, George Peabody College, Nashville, and R.I.P., Richmond, Va.; with her sister, Patricia Rudy Woods, member of the Rudy Sisters, gospel singers.

MOORE, CHARLES B., JR. (CHARLIE)

b. 1935 Piedmont, South Carolina.
Singer. Leader of the Carolina Mountaineers (1953-55); Dixie Partners after 1959; albums (with Bill Napier) *Gospel and Sacred, Grand Ole Opry Hymnal, Songs by Moore and Napier for Lonesome Truck Drivers* (co-writers of "Truck Driver's Queen").

MOORE, CLEMENT CLARKE

b. 1779 New York City, d. 1863 Newport, Rhode Island. Hymnist and poet. Educated at Columbia, New York City; became a professor at the General Theological Seminary, New York City (1821); wrote "Lord of Life, All Praise Excelling" ("Harvest") which appeared in the *American Prayer Book Collection* (1808); best known for "Twas the Night Before Christmas."

MOORE, DOROTHY LOUISE SUTTON (DOTTIE)

b. 1930 Humphrey, Arkansas, d. 1967 Flushing, Michigan. Singer. Attended school in Flint, Michigan; leader of the Countrymen (1964-67); album—*The Golden Voice* (1967); died of a heart attack.

MOORE, DOUGLAS STUART

b. 1893 Cutchogue, Long Island, New York, d. 1969. Composer. Studied at Yale University; with Vincent d'Indy and Nadia Boulanger in Paris and Ernest Bloch in Cleveland; became a teacher at Columbia University (1928); composed *The Pageant of P.T. Barnum* (1924, suite for orchestra), *Quartet* (1933, for strings), *The Devil and Daniel Webster* (1938, folk opera, w. Stephen V. Benet), Symphony no.2 in A Major (1945), *The Ballad of Baby Doe*, (1957, opera, book—John LaTouche); received the Pulitzer Prize in music (1951).

MOORE, FRANCIS JOHN

b. 1885 Derby, England.
Hymnist. Educated at Trinity College, Toronto, Ontario, Canada, and was curate in St. James' Cathedral, Toronto; chaplain with the Canadian Overseas Forces (1914-18); in 1931 he became curate of Christ Church, Cincinnati, Ohio, then rector of the Church of the Advent, Cincinnati in 1938; wrote the hymn "Father of Mercy" (1935, tunes "Fairest Lord Jesus" and "St. Elisabeth" from Franz Liszt).

MOORE, GARY

b. 1915 Baltimore, Maryland.
Producer. Many singers and musicians have appeared on the popular "Gary Moore Show" on television.

MOORE, GRACE

b. 1901 Jellico, Tennessee, d. 1947 Copenhagen, Denmark. Noted soprano. Studied at Ward-Belmont School, Nashville, Tenn., and Wilson-Greene School, Washington, D.C.; sang in musical comedies in New York; debut at the Metropolitan Opera, New York City (1928); also at Paris Opera Comique (1929); later left grand opera for musical comedies; died in an airplane crash.

MOORE, JOHN WEEKS

b. 1807 prob. Andover, New Hampshire, d. 1889 Manchester, New Hampshire. Compiler. Son of Jacob B. Moore, Sr., hymnist (*see* Sam Adams Holyoke) and brother of Jacob Bailey Moore; editor of music journals and collections; published a *Cyclopedia of Music* (1852).

MOORE, MELVIN

b. 1923 Chicago, Illinois.
Trumpeter. With Jimmie Lunceford, Lucky Millinder and others in 1940s; with Duke Ellington and others in 1950s; at Monterey Jazz Festival (1964) with Charles Mingus and Thelonious Monk; also at Monterey (1965) with Gil Fuller.

MOORE, MILTON A. ("BREW")

b. 1924 Indianola, Mississippi.
Tenor saxist. Played with Claude Thornhill, Gerry Mulligan and others in 1940s; later at San Francisco night clubs; toured Europe after 1961.

MOORE, OSCAR FRED

b. 1912 Austin, Texas.
Black guitarist. With Nat King Cole Trio (1943-47); later with various groups in Los Angeles.

MOORE, PHIL, III

b. 1939.
Black pianist. Son of singer-teacher Phil Moore, Jr.; raised in San Francisco; studied piano at age six with his mother; later at Berklee School in Boston; with Gerald Wilson

and organized his own group in 1960s in Los Angeles.

MOORE, RUSSELL ("BIG CHIEF")

b. 1913 Komatke, near Sacaton, Arizona. Trombonist. With Noble Sissle, Louis Armstrong and others in 1940s; rejoined Armstrong in 1960s; member of the Pima tribe; at American Indian Festival in Boston (1965).

MOORE, WILLIAM, JR. (BILLY)

b. 1916 Parkersburg, West Virginia. Pianist and arranger. Arranger for Jimmie Lunceford; pianist-arranger for the Peters Sisters (1953-60); then staff arranger for Berliner Rundfunk Radio, Berlin, Germany (1960-63); toured Europe after 1964 with Delta Rhythm Boys.

MORALES, NORO

b. 1911 San Juan, Puerto Rico, d. 1964. Pianist and composer. Joined his father's orchestra when he was fifteen; took it over on his father's death; came to New York at the peak of the rumba craze with his brother, where they formed their own band; later the mambo craze helped his popularity.

MORAN, PETER K.

b. (?) Ireland, d. 1831 New York City. Pianist, cellist, composer, and teacher. Came to New York (1817); taught in New York City (1818-30); organist at Grace Church (1823); organist at first concert of New York Choral Society (1824); cellist with Garcia Opera Company in New York City (1825); later organist at St. John's Church; his wife was a singer on the New York stage (1818-26); wrote "Adieu My Native Land Adieu" (1820), "The Carrier Pigeon" (1822, w. Percival—sung by Mrs. Holman), "The Hebrew Mourner" (1822, w. by late Rev. J.W. Eastburn), "Her Smiling Eyes" (1818, sung by Mr. Keene), "President Monroe's Inauguration March" (1821).

MOREHOUSE, HENRY LYMAN

b. 1834 Stanfordville, New York, d. 1917 Brooklyn, New York. Hymnist. Became a Baptist minister (1864); wrote "Friend of Sinners, Hear My Plea" ("Pardon Desired") which was included in *Good as Gold* (1883).

MORELLO, JOSEPH A.

b. 1928 Springfield, Massachusetts. Drummer. With Marian McPartland, Stan Kenton, and Dave Brubeck Quartet in 1950s; continued with Brubeck in 1960s.

MORGAN, AL

b. 1908 New Orleans, Louisiana. Black double bass player. Played on Mississippi River boats in 1920s with Fate Marable; later with Cab Calloway, Les Hite and others.

MORGAN, BILLIE

b. 1922 Nashville, Tennessee. Singer and songwriter. She wrote "Life to Live" (1959), "Move Over," "Thinking All Night," "Treating Me the Way You Do," "Too Weak to Go Home," "Country Girl at Heart" (1959), "I'll Accept What I Can't Change" (1960), "I Had to Talk to Someone."

MORGAN, GEORGE THOMAS

b. 1924 Waverly, Tennessee. Singer and songwriter. Attended high school in Barberton, Ohio; sang on radio stations in Akron and Wooster, Ohio, and Wheeling, West Virginia; wrote "Candy Kisses" (1948), "I'm in Love Again" (1959); albums—*Barbara, Best of George Morgan, Candy Kisses, Country Hits by Candlelight, Like a Bird, Room Full of Roses, Sounds of Goodbye, Steal Away.*

MORGAN, GEORGE WASHBOURNE

b. 1822 Gloucester, England, d. 1892 Tacoma, Washington. Organist and conductor. Played the organ in the Gloucester cathedral at age eight; later organist at St. Paul's and Westminster Abbey; organist at St. Thomas' Church, New York City (1853), then at Grace Church (1854-67); later at St. Ann's Roman Catholic Church and Dr. Talmadge's Brooklyn Tabernacle for twelve years; played at Centennial Exhibition in Philadelphia (1876); played in concerts with his daughter, Maude Morgan, harpist.

MORGAN, HAROLD LANSFORD ("LANNY")

b. 1934 Des Moines, Iowa. Alto saxist. Studied at Los Angeles City College; played in band there; with Charlie Barnet and others in 1950s; with Maynard Ferguson and own quartet in 1960s; with Ferguson at Newport Jazz Festivals (1960-61 and 1963).

MORGAN, HELEN

b. 1900 Danville, Illinois, d. 1941 Chicago, Illinois. Singer and actress. Born Helen Riggins, took name of her stepfather Thomas Morgan; studied singing in New York City with Edward Petri; debut (1920) in chorus of *Sally,* in *George White's Scandals* (1925), *Americana* (1926), *Grand Guignal* reviews (1927), *Show Boat* (1927), *Sweet Adeline*

(1929), *The Ziegfeld Follies* (1931), *George White's Scandals* (1936), *A Night at Moulin Rouge* (1939); also in films; known for singing "My Bill."

MORGAN, JANE

b. 1920 Boston, Massachusetts.
Singer. Albums—*Fascination, Fresh Flavor, In Gold, In My Style, Jane Morgan in Nashville, Sounds of Silence, Traces of Love.*

MORGAN, JAYE P.

b. 1929.
Singer. Sang in West Coast night spots; arrested (1972) in New Orleans while changing planes for an engagement in San Juan, Puerto Rico, on a marijuana charge, released on bond.

MORGAN, JOHN PAUL

b. 1841 Oberlin, Ohio, d. 1879 Oakland, California. Organist and composer. Wrote organ music.

MORGAN, JUSTIN

b. 1747 West Springfield, Massachusetts, d. 1798 Randolph, Vermont. Composer. Horse breeder; in 1788 he moved to Randolph, Vt.; composed the hymn tune "Montgomery" and an anthem called "The Judgement Anthem."

MORGAN, LEE

b. 1938 Philadelphia, Pennsylvania, d. 1972 New York City. Black trumpeter. Played with Dizzy Gillespie and Art Blakey Jazz Messengers in 1950s; then with Jimmy Heath and Art Blakey in 1960s; later formed his own quintet, which was playing at Slugs, an East Village, New York City night club, in February, 1972, when in walked his wife who shot and killed him.

MORGAN, RUSS

b. 1904 Scranton, Pennsylvania, d. 1969.
Trombonist and bandleader. Started as a coal miner in Pennsylvania; played the piano, but after breaking his arm took up the slide trombone to strengthen it; also played sax, guitar, vibes, and organ; by 1925 was arranging for John Philip Sousa and Victor Herbert; member of the Detroit Symphony; trombonist in Jean Goldkette's orchestra; musical head of Lifebuoy and Philip Morris radio series; his band played in the Biltmore Hotel, New York City (1936).

MOROSS, JEROME

b. 1913 Brooklyn, New York.
Composer. Composed *Paeans* (Chamber Symphony Orchestra, New York, under Hermann, 1932), *Beguine* (CBS under Green, 1934), *A Tall Story* (CBS Orchestra under Barlow, 1938); ballets: *American Pattern, American Saga, Frankie and Johnny* (Ruth Page, choreographer, 1938); *Symphony* (Seattle Symphony under Beecham, 1943); *Paul Bunyan,* (ballet suite for orchestra), *Suite* for chamber orchestra.

MORR, SKIP

b. 1912 Chicago, Illinois, d. 1962 Ross, California. Trombonist and drummer. Born Charles William Coolidge; played in various bands in 1930s; studio musician in Hollywood in 1940s; played with Muggsy Spanier and others in 1950s.

MORRIS, GEORGE P.

b. 1802 Philadelphia, Pennsylvania, d. 1864 New York City. Lyricist. In 1823 Morris and Samuel Woodworth founded the *New York Mirror;* he compiled *National Melodies of America;* wrote the lyrics "Open Thy Lattice Love" (1844, m. Stephen Foster), "Woodman, Spare That Tree" (m. Henry Russell), "The Star of Love" (1850, m. M.V. Wallace), "On the Lake Where Drooped the Willow" (1858, m. C.E. Horn), "Down by the River Side I Stray" (1861, m. J.R. Thomas), "The Union Right or Wrong" (1861, m. William Plain), "The American Standard" (1861, m. A. Bagioli), "Take Your Harps from the Silent Willows" (m. T.M. Towne).

MORRIS, HAROLD

b. 1890 San Antonio, Texas, d. 1964 New York City. Composer. Piano soloist with leading American orchestras playing his compositions; composed *Poem* (after Tagore's "Gitanjali," for orchestra), a symphony, piano concerto, string quartet, violin and piano concerto, rhapsody for piano, violin and cello.

MORRIS, LEE

b. 1916 Boston, Massachusetts.
Songwriter. Graduated Colby College, Waterville, Maine, and Boston Teachers College (M.Ed.); with Art Johnston wrote "If I Only Had a Match" (m. George W. Meyer).

MORRIS, MARION (LONGFELLOW)

b. 1849 Portland, Maine, d. 1924.
Hymnist. Married W. F. Morris of Boston (1826); wrote "He Knows the Bitter, Weary Way" (1874, "Times of Trial").

MORRIS, MARLOWE

b. 1915 Bronx, New York City.
Organist and pianist. With Sid Catlett,

Coleman Hawkins and others in 1940s; later played in various night spots in New York City and Boston.

MORRIS, ROBERT

b. 1818 near Boston, Massachusetts, d. 1888 La Grange, Kentucky. Lyricist and hymnist. Published *Poetry of Free Masonry;* in 1868 commissioned by the United Order to undertake historic and archeological exploration in Palestine (Israel); while sitting on the ruins of Capernaum by Lake of Gennesaret wrote the lyrics "Oh, Galilee, Sweet Galilee" (m. H.R. Palmer); also wrote "When the Boys Come Home" (1865, m. J.A. Butterfield).

MORRISON, GEORGE

b. 1891 Fayette, Missouri, d. 1974.
Black bandleader. Led a band in Denver, Colorado.

MORRISON, HAROLD RALPH

b. 1931 Highlonesome, Missouri.
Singer and banjoist. Member of the Wilburn Brothers Show (1963-68); wrote "Hunt the Coon Tonight," "Flat Top Hop," "Scotland 5," "Briar Patch," "Little Dobie," "Acre of Banjos."

MORRISON, JAMES DOUGLAS (JIM)

b. 1944 Melbourne, Florida, d. 1971 Paris, France. Rock singer. Son of Rear Admiral George Morrison; lead singer of the Doors, and after recording the Doors' first album, threw sand into the console board, ruining it; in March, 1969, in Miami he was arrested for exposing himself before an audience of 12,000 at the Dinner Key Auditorium; became an instant success with the group's first single, "Light My Fire"; wrote "The End" and "Break on Through" ("to the Other Side").

MORSE, ANNA JUSTINA

b. 1893 Haverhill, Massachusetts.
Composer. Educated at Wellesley College (1919), Yale, and Northwestern University, Evanston, Ill.; taught in New Haven, Conn., and after 1925 at Kemper Hall, Kenosha, Wisconsin; composed the tunes "Consecration" (1941, "O Love That Wilt Not Let Me Go," w. George Matheson) and "Kemper" (1941, "God Be with You 'till We Meet Again," w. J.E. Rankin).

MORSE, CHARLES HENRY

b. 1853 Bradford, Massachusetts, d. 1927 Boston, Massachusetts. Organist and teacher. Graduated New England Conservatory, Boston (1873); taught there (1873); musical director at Wellesley College, Wellesley, Mass. (1875-84); organist at Plymouth Church, Brooklyn, New York, after 1891; composed the tune "Stowe" for "Still, Still with Thee" (w. Harriet Beecher Stowe).

MORSE, ROBERT

b. 1931 Newton, Massachusetts.
Singer and actor. Starred in the musical *How to Succeed in Business Without Really Trying* (1961, m. Frank Loesser).

MORSE, THEODORA ("DOLLY")

b. 1890 Brooklyn, New York, d. 1953 White Plains, New York. Lyricist. Used pseudonyms Dorothy Terris and D.A. Estrom; wife of Theodore F. Morse; wrote the words "Hail, Hail the Gang's All Here" (1917, m. T.F. Morse), "Three O'Clock in the Morning" (1919, m. Julian Robledo), "Siboney" (m. Ernesto Lecuona).

MORSE, THEODORE F.

b. 1873 Washington, D.C., d. 1924 New York City. Popular composer. Wrote "Dear Old Girl" (1903, w. R.H. Buck), "Hurry for Baffin's Bay" (1903, w. Vincent Bryan), "It's Great to Be a Soldier" (w. Jack Drislane), "Hail, Hail the Gang's All Here" (1917, w. Theodora Terris, his wife), based on *The Pirates of Penzance.*

MORSE, WOOLSON

b. 1858, d. 1897.
Popular composer. Wrote "Love Will Find a Way" (1890, w. J.C. Goodwin); wrote the comic operas *Merry Monarch* (1890), *Panjandrun* (1893), *Dr. Syntax* (1894), *Wang* (1891, w. Goodwin, New York cast included De Wolf Hopper, songs included "A Pretty Girl" and "Every Rose Must Have Its Thorn").

MORTON, HENRY STERLING ("BENNY")

b. 1907 New York City.
Black jazz trombonist. Played in Count Basie's band; soloist for Fletcher Henderson; also with Raymond Scott; played in Eddie Condon's group when jazz made its first TV appearance in 1942, which featured Max Kaminsky, Pee Wee Russell, Joe Sullivan, Bill Taylor and Zutty Singleton; played at Newport Jazz Festival, New York City (1972).

MORTON, JELLY ROLL

b. 1885 New Orleans, Louisiana, d. 1941 Los Angeles, California. Black pianist, bandleader, and composer. Born Ferdinand Joseph La Menthe; brother-in-law of Dink Johnson; first great composer and orchestrator of jazz; joined Buddy Bolden's

Band before 1907; played in the Storyville (red light) district of New Orleans; toured southern states after 1904; played at Barron Wilkins' place in Harlem, New York City (1908); worked in San Diego and Los Angeles (1917-22); went to Chicago (1922); made his first recordings (1923); organized his own group, the Red Hot Peppers; wrote "Superior Rag" (1915), "The Original Jelly Roll Blues" (1915), "Frog-i-more" (1918, later known as "Sweetheart o' Mine," w. Walter Melrose), "Wolverine Blues" (1923), "London Blues" (1923), "Kansas City Stomp" (1923), "King Porter Stomp" (1924), "Shreveport Stomp" (1925), "New Orleans Blues" (1925).

MOSENTHAL, JOSEPH

b. 1834 Kassel, Germany, d. 1896 New York City. Violinist, organist, conductor, and composer. Conducted the Mendelssohn Glee Club, New York, after 1867.

MOST, SAMUEL

b. 1930 Atlantic City, New Jersey.
Flutist, clarinetist, and alto saxist. Brother of clarinetist Abraham Most; played with Mat Mathews, Teddy Wilson and others in 1950s; later with Buddy Rich, Louis Bellson, Red Norvo and others.

MOTEN, BENNIE

b. 1894 Kansas City, Missouri, d. there 1935. Black bandleader. Organized his own band in Kansas City about 1922; first recorded in 1923; at one time Count Basie played the piano in his band; album—*Count Basie in Kansas City.*

MOTHER EARTH (soul band)

Tracy Nelson, vocals; Lonnie Castille, drums; Powell St. John, harp; Martin Fierro, saxophone; started in Texas, first recorded in 1968; albums—*Revolution* (soundtrack), *Living with the Animals, Make a Joyful Noise, Mother Earth Presents Tracy Nelson Country.*

MOTHERS OF INVENTION (rock group)

Frank Zappa, lead guitar; Ray Collins, vocals; Roy Estrada, bass; Jimmy Carl Black, rhythm guitar; Ian Underwood, piano and sax; Don Preston, piano; Motorhead Sherwood, sax and tambourine; Bunk Gardner, sax and drums; first album in 1966; played in Greenwich Village, New York City; albums—*Absolutely Free, Burnt Weeny Sandwich, Freak Out, Mothermania—Best of the Mothers, Mothers, We're Only in It for the Money, Cruisin' with Ruben and the Jets.*

MOTIAN, STEPHEN PAUL

b. 1931 Providence, Rhode Island.
Drummer. Served in army in Korean War; played with Oscar Pettiford, George Wallington, Al Cohn-Zoot Sims and others in 1950s; later with Bill Evans, Paul Bley and others.

MOUND CITY BLUE BLOWERS (jazz group)
see EDDIE LANG, RED MC KENZIE

MUDGE, ENOCH

b. 1776 Lynn, Massachusetts, d. there 1850. Compiler. Methodist minister, having joined the New England Conference (1793); preached in New Bedford, Mass. (1837-50); compiled *The American Camp Meeting Hymn Book* (1818).

MUGWUMPS (rock group)

Cass Elliot, Denny Doherty, Zal Yanovsky, James Hendricks; started in 1964; later Cass joined the Mamas and the Papas and Jim Hendricks, her husband, headed Lamp of Childhood and later went solo; Zal left to join the Lovin' Spoonful and Denny joined the Mamas and the Papas; album—*The Mugwumps.*

MUHLENBERG, WILLIAM AUGUSTUS

b. 1796 Philadelphia, Pennsylvania, d. 1877 New York City. Hymnist. Great-grandson of Dr. Henry M. Muhlenberg, founder of the Lutheran Church in America; in 1817 became an Episcopal priest, and served as rector of St. James' Church, Lancaster, Pa.; wrote the lyrics "I Would Not Live Alway" (1833, m. George Kingsley), "Shout the Glad Tidings, Exultingly Sing" (1826, m. tune "Avison"—Charles Avison, 1766) (*See* H.U. Onderdonk); organized a boys' choir at the Flushing Institute on Long Island (1828) and a boys' choir in the Church of the Holy Communion, New York City (1846).

MUIR, LEWIS F.

b. 1884, d. 1950.
Pianist and ragtime composer. Played ragtime at honky-tonks in St. Louis (1904) and in New York City (1910); later a success in London; wrote "Play That Barber Shop Chord" (1910, w. Ballard MacDonald), "When Ragtime Rosie Ragged the Rosary" (1911, w. Edgar Leslie); with lyrics by L. Wolfe Gilbert—"Waiting for the Robert E. Lee," "Here Comes My Daddy Now," and "Mississippi River Steamboat" (1912); with Maurice Abrahams—"Cowboy Joe" and "Hitchy-Koo" (1912).

MULLER, WILLIAM

b. 1834 Brunswick, Germany, d. 1897 New York City. Cellist. Son of Karl Friedrich Muller, konzertmeister of the Brunswick Orchestra; with his three brothers, Hugo, Bernhard, and Karl, Jr., organized a concert quartet (1855).

MULLICAN, AUBREY WILSON ("MOON")

b. 1909 near Corrigan, Texas, d. 1967 Beaumont, Texas. Pianist, singer, and songwriter. Debut on radio station KPBX, Beaumont, Texas; wrote "Sweeter Than the Flowers" (1948), "Cherokee Boogie" (1951, with W.C. Redbird); hit records were "I'll Sail My Ship Alone," "Mona Lisa," "Moon Mullican Show," "New Jole Blon," "Sweeter Than the Flowers."

MULLIGAN, GERALD JOSEPH (GERRY)

b. 1927 New York City.
Baritone saxist and composer. Wrote arrangements for Gene Krupa, Claude Thornhill, and Elliott Lawrence; organized a jazz quartet; later a thirteen-piece band in 1960s; toured Europe (1960), and Japan (1964); wrote *Disc Jockey Jump* (recorded by Gene Krupa, 1947), *Venus de Milo* (pianist in the performance was John Lewis); with Bill Holman—*Music for Baritone Saxophone and Orchestra* (produced by the Neophonic Orchestra, 1966); in concert with Dave Brubeck and Paul Desmond at Carnegie Hall, New York City (1972); with the Dave Brubeck Trio at the Newport Jazz Festival, New York City (1972).

MULLINS, BASCOM THEODORE (TED)

b. 1934.
Singer and songwriter. Attended schools in Weeksbury, Kentucky, Elkhorn, Kentucky, and Cincinnati, Ohio; wrote "I'm Old Kentucky Bound," "I'm a Stranger in This World," "Are You Coming Back to Me," "Find Them," "Sunshine on the Other Side," "Sermon on the Mount," "New Star in Heaven Tonight," "Where Jesus Lives."

MUMLER, FREDERICK

b. 1772 Germany, d. 1807 Boston, Massachusetts. Violoncellist and composer. Resided in Boston; appeared in concerts there; wrote "Ah! Fatal Was the Morning" (1806), "Massachusetts Quick Step" (1806).

MUMMA, GORDON

b. 1935 Framingham, Massachusetts.
Composer. With Merce Cunningham Dance Company Studio after 1966; composed *Hornpieces* (1964, for French horn), *Home* (unmultiplexed polyphase radio communication array), *Second Horn* (1969), *Runway* (1969, with David Behrman).

MUNCH, CHARLES

b. 1891 Strasbourg, Alsace (Germany-France), d. 1968. Conductor. Studied at the Strasbourg Conservatory, then the violin under Lucien Capet in Paris; visiting his family in Strasbourg when World War I began; mustered into the German army and was wounded at Verdun; later conductor of the Paris Conservatory Orchestra for eight years; became the conductor of the Boston Symphony Orchestra (1948).

MUNDY, JIMMY

b. 1907 Cincinnati, Ohio.
Black composer. Played tenor sax with Erskine Tate, Earl Hines and others; arranger for Hines, Benny Goodman, and Count Basie; works—*Queer Street, Blue Skies.*

MUNSEL, PATRICE

b. 1925 Spokane, Washington.
Coloratura soprano. Pupil of William Pierce Herman, N.Y.; debut at the Metropolitan Opera, N.Y. (1943); with the Metropolitan (1943-57); appeared in Broadway musical shows and operettas.

MURANYI, JOSEPH PAUL

b. 1928 Martins Ferry, Ohio.
Clarinetist. Played with Red Allen, Max Kaminsky, Bobby Hackett, Jimmy McPartland, Eddie Condon and others; led Village Stompers after 1963.

MURDEN, ELIZA CRAWLY

b. ca. 1790, d. ca. 1851 Charleston, South Carolina. Composer and poet. Resided in Charleston, S.C.; published her poems in *Miscellaneous Poems;* wrote *March,* composed and dedicated to the United States Marine Corps (1814).

MURPHY, HENRY LAMBERT

b. 1885 Springfield, Massachusetts, d. 1954 Hancock, New Hampshire. Tenor. Graduated Harvard University; pupil of Thomas Cushman and others; with the Metropolitan Opera, New York (1911-15); also soloist with various orchestras.

MURPHY, LYLE ("SPUD")

b. 1908 Salt Lake City, Utah.
Composer and saxophonist. Wrote the scores

for the films *The Tony Fontaine Story* (1963) and *God's Country.*

MURPHY, MARK HOWE

b. 1932 Syracuse, New York.
Singer and pianist. Studied piano at age seven; sang in various night spots in New York City; appeared on "Steve Allen's Jazz Scene USA" and other TV shows; at Newport Jazz Festival (1962); toured Europe.

MURPHY, MELVIN E. ("TURK")

b. 1915 Palermo, California.
Trombonist and composer. With Peter Clute, established their own night club in San Francisco, Earthquake McGoon's; played the trombone there; wrote *Ballad of Marie Brizzard, Something for Annie.*

MURPHY, STANLEY

b. 1875 Dublin, Ireland, d. 1919 New York City. Lyricist. Brought to U.S. at age eight; became a U.S. citizen; wrote the lyrics for "Put on Your Old Grey Bonnet" (1909, m. Percy Wenrich).

MURRAY, JAMES ARTHUR ("SUNNY")

b. 1927 Philadelphia, Pennsylvania.
Drummer. Played with Willie "The Lion" Smith, Red Allen and others; later with Cecil Taylor, Albert Ayler, and Archie Shepp.

MURRAY, JAMES RAMSEY

b. 1841 Andover, Massachusetts, d. 1905 Cincinnati, Ohio. Composer and compiler. Studied with Lowell Mason, Root, Bradbury, and Webb; for a time he was editor with Root & Cady, Chicago, then with John Church, Cincinnati; wrote "How Strong and Sweet My Father's Care," "Cling to the Bible," "Thanks for the Sabbath School," and "A Tear for a Comrade That's Gone" (w. T.F. Winthrop); edited *Dainty Songs for Little Lads and Lassies* (1887) which contained the words "Away in a Manger" and was credited for composing the music for same, but other tunes were composed by J.B. Herbert, W.J. Kirkpatrick, and J.E. Spilman for this Christmas carol.

MUSIC EXPLOSION, THE (black group)

Jamie Lyons, lead vocals; Don (Tudor) Atkins, lead guitar; Rick Nesta, rhythm guitar; Butch Stahl, bass guitar and organ; Bob Avery, drums and harmonica; started in Ohio; first recorded in 1967; album—*Little Bit O' Soul.*

MUSIC MAKERS (band) *see* HARRY JAMES

MUSICA AETERNA ORCHESTRA

Frederic Waldman, conductor; in concert at the Metropolitan Museum of Art, New York City (1972).

MUSICAL RAMBLERS *see* GABE TUCKER

MUSIN, OVIDE

b. 1854 Liege, Belgium, d. 1929 Brooklyn, New York. Violinist. Studied at Liege Conservatory; at age eleven took violin prize; studied at Paris Conservatory; at fourteen won gold medal; toured Europe, America, then the world; taught at Liege Conservatory after 1897; then directed his own school in New York City after 1908.

MUSSO, VIDO WILLIAM

b. 1913 Carrini, Sicily.
Tenor saxist. Played with Benny Goodman, Stan Kenton and others; led his own group; played in Las Vegas after 1957.

MYER, EDMUND JOHN

b. 1846 York Springs, Pennsylvania, d. 1934. Singer, teacher, and writer. Taught voice culture and singing in New York City; also wrote books on singing.

MYRICK, WELDON MERLE

b. 1938 Jayton, Texas.
Singer and songwriter. Attended high school in Girard, Texas; wrote "Hiding Alone," "He's My Baby," "Hanging Around," "I'm Surely Dying."

NABOKOV, NICHOLAS

b. 1903 Lubcha, Novogrudok, Russia. Noted composer. Studied with Rebikov in Yalta, Stuttgart Conservatory (1920-22), Berlin Hochschule, and Sorbonne (1926); taught at Wells College, Aurora, N.Y. (1936-41); U.S. citizen (1939); taught at Peabody Conservatory, Baltimore (1947-52); with Berlin Festival (1964-68); with Teheran (Iran) Festival (1969); composed *Ode, or Meditation at Night* (Ballet Russe, Paris, 1928), *Symphonie Lyrique* (Paris, under Monteux, and Boston, under Koussevitzky, 1930), *Job* (oratorio, Mexico City, under Iturbi, 1934), *Union Pacific* (ballet, Philadelphia, 1934), *Sinfonia Biblica* (New York Philharmonic under Mitropoulos, 1941), *The Return of Pushkin* (three-part elegy for voice and orchestra, Boston, under Koussevitzky, 1948), *Vita Nova* (for soprano, tenor, and orchestra, Boston, 1951), *Les Hommages* (cello concerto, Philadelphia, 1953), *Symboli Chorestiani* (Venice Festival, 1956), *The Holy Devil* (opera, libretto—Stephen Spender, Kentucky Opera Association, Louisville, 1958), *A Prayer* (symphony, New York Philharmonic under Bernstein, 1968).

NABORS, JAMES (JIM)

b. 1932 Sylacuga, Alabama. Singer and actor. Started on the "Andy Griffith Show"; famous as "Gomer Pyle"; later had own singing show on CBS-TV; sang on Bob Hope's Christmas show for GIs overseas (1971); at York, Pa. fair (1972).

NAGINSKI, CHARLES

b. 1909 Cairo, Egypt, d. 1940 Lenox, Massachusetts. Composer. His parents brought him to America as a youth; studied at American Academy in Rome on Walter Damrosch Fellowship; composed *Suite* for small orchestra (Greenwich Sinfonietta, N.Y., under Charles Lichter, 1935), *Suite* for orchestra (1936), *Sinfonietta* (CBS Concert Orchestra under Victor Bay, 1938), *Five Pieces from a Children's Suite* (Boston Pops Orchestra under Fiedler,1940), *The Minotaur, Nocturne and Pantomine,* a symphony.

NANCE, WILLIS ("RAY")

b. 1913 Chicago, Illinois. Black trumpeter and violinist. Played with Earl Hines and Horace Henderson in late 1930s; with Duke Ellington in 1940s and '50s; with Ellington, Paul Lavalle and others in 1960s; album—*Body and Soul.*

NANTON, JOE ("TRICKY SAM")

b. 1904 New York City, d. 1948 San Francisco, California. Black trombonist. Played in Duke Ellington's band (1926-48).

NAPOLEON, MARTY

b. 1921 Brooklyn, New York. Pianist. Nephew of trumpeter Phil Napoleon; played with Louis Armstrong (1952-54); then formed his own group; returned to Armstrong's band (1966).

NAPOLEON, PHIL

b. 1901 Boston, Massachusetts. Trumpeter and bandleader. Led Original Memphis Five in 1920s; later with various bands; opened his own club, near Miami, Florida (1966).

NAPOLEON, TEDDY GEORGE

b. 1914 Brooklyn, New York, d. 1964 Elmhurst, New York. Pianist. Brother of Marty Napoleon; played with Gene Krupa during 1940s and '50s; died of cancer.

NASH, FREDERICK OGDEN

b. 1902 Rye, New York, d. 1971 Baltimore, Maryland. Lyricist. Attended Harvard for one year, class of 1924; taught for a year at St. George's School, Newport, R.I.; editor for Doubleday, Doran & Co., publishers; with S.J. Perelman wrote the words, and Kurt Weill the music for "One Touch of Venus" (1943); Nash wrote the lyrics and Weill the music of the songs "How Much Do I Love You?," "Speak Low," and "That's Him"; wrote the words for the musical *Two's Company* (1952, m. Vernon Duke); also known for his lines "Candy is dandy, but liquor is quicker," to which he added in the 1960s "Pot is not," and also "The Bronx? No thonx."

NASHVILLE BRASS

Danny Davis; this group won the 1969, 1970 and 1971 awards as the Instrumental Group of the Year at the Country Music Association presentations in Nashville, Tennessee.

NASHVILLE STUDENTS (black orchestra)

Played at Proctor's, New York City (1905), first public concert of syncopated music in America, written and orchestrated by Joe Jordan; starred Ernest Hogan (pianist), Abbie Mitchell (soprano), Ida Forsyne (dancer), James Reese Europe (pianist and violinist); later toured Europe as the Tennessee Students; another group formed (1908) called the Memphis Students, also early players of syncopated music.

NASON, ELIAS

b. 1811 Wrentham, Massachusetts, d. 1887. Compiler. Graduated Brown University, Providence, R.I.; taught in Newburyport, Massachusetts (1840-49), then became a Congregational minister; published *Songs for the School Room* (1855), *Congregational Hymn Book* (1857), and with Dr. Edward Kirk, *Songs for Social and Public Worship* (1863).

NASSER, JAMIL SULIEMAN

b. 1932 Memphis, Tennessee.
Bass player. Born George Leon Joyner; educated at Arkansas State University; in army band (1953-55); with B.B. King (1955-56); later with Teddy Charles, Sonny Rollins, and Sonny Stitt in 1950s; led his own trio (1962-64); later with Ahmad Jamal Trio and others.

NAT KING COLE TRIO

Cole, pianist; Oscar Moore, guitarist; Wes Prince, bass player.

"NATIONAL BARN DANCE, THE "

Variety show on radio station WLS, Chicago, Illinois; started in 1924 by George D. Hay.

NAU, MARIA DOLORES BENEDICTA JOSEFINA

b. 1818 New York City, d. 1891 Paris, France. Soprano. Studied at the Paris Conservatory, won first prize in 1834; debut in opera (1836) in Paris; sang in Paris Opera (1836-53); sang in Europe; retired in 1856.

NAVARRO, THEODORE ("FATS")

b. 1923 Key West, Florida, d. 1950 New York City. Black jazz trumpet player. Played in Billy Eckstine's band; also with Andy Kirk.

NAZZ (rock group)

Robert "Stewkey" Antoni, lead vocals, organ, and piano; Todd Rundgren, guitar; Carson van Osten, bass guitar; Thom Mooney, drums; started in Philadelphia; first recorded in 1968; albums—*The Nazz; Nazz, Nazz.*

NEFF, HILDEGARDE (HILDEGARD KNEF)

b. 1925 Ulm, Germany.
Singer. Albums—*Germany's Hildegard Neff, New Knef.*

NEGRONI, JOE

b. 1940.
Black singer. Member of the Teen Agers, vocal group in New York City; the group appeared in the film *Rock, Rock, Rock.*

NEIDLINGER, BUELL

b. 1936 Westport, Connecticut.
Bass player. With Cecil Taylor in late 1950s; with Jimmy Giuffre, Freddie Red, Cecil Taylor and others in 1960s.

NEIDLINGER, WILLIAM HAROLD

b. 1863 Brooklyn, New York, d. 1924.
Conductor, composer, and teacher. Wrote "The Birthday of a King" (1890) and "Spirit of God" (w. George Croly); also a cantata, *Prayer, Promise and Praise.*

NELON, REX LOYD

b. 1932 Asheville, North Carolina.
Singer. With the Gospel Singing Caravan (1962-66); with The Le Fevres (1957-68).

NELSON, DAVID

b. 1793 Jonesboro, Tennessee, d. 1844 Oakland, Illinois. Lyricist. Graduated Washington College, Lexington, Va. (1810), M.D. in Philadelphia (1812); surgeon in War of 1812; then became a Presbyterian minister; founded two colleges at Greenfields, near Quincy, Illinois; wrote "My Days Are Gliding Swiftly By" (1835, tune "Lord Ullin's Daughter").

NELSON, ERIC HILLIARD ("RICKY")

b. 1940 Teaneck, New Jersey.
Singer and actor. Son of Ozzie and Harriet Nelson; appeared on the "Ozzie and Harriet" show at age eight; starred on his parents' show for many years; later appeared in films; sang on his own.

NELSON, LOUIS ("BIG EYE")

b. 1885 New Orleans, Louisiana, d. there 1949. Black clarinetist. Born Louis De Lisle;

resided in New Orleans; played in the Original Creole Orchestra (ca. 1917); recorded in 1949.

NELSON, OLIVER EDWARD

b. 1932 St. Louis, Missouri.
Black composer. Played saxophone with Wild Bill Davis, Louis Bellson and others during 1950s; works—*Woodwind Quintet* (1960), *Song Cycle for Contralto and Piano* (1961), *Dirge for Chamber Orchestra* (1962), *Soundpiece for String Quartet and Contralto* (1963), *Soundpiece for Jazz Orchestra*, conducted by the composer at the Light Music Week in Stuttgart, Germany (1964).

NELSON, OSWALD GEORGE (OZZIE)

b. 1906 Jersey City, New Jersey.
Singer and bandleader. Graduated Rutgers University, New Brunswick, N.J.; attended New Jersey Law School; his band played at Glen Island Casino (1932); New Yorker Hotel, New York City (1935); married his singer, Harriet Hilliard (1935); started the "Ozzie and Harriet" show on radio (1943), later on TV (1951); "Ozzie's Girls" on NBC-TV (1972).

NELSON, WILLIE

b. 1933 Fort Worth, Texas.
Singer and songwriter. Raised in Abbott, Texas; attended Baylor University, Waco, Texas; wrote "Crazy" (1961, sung by Patsy Cline), "Hello Fool" (1961, with Jim Coleman, sung by Ralph Emery), "Hello Walls" (1961, sung by Faron Young), "Three Days" (1962, with Faron Young), "Touch Me" (1962); LP records—*Willie Nelson* (1963), *Make Way for Willie Nelson* (1967), *Country Willie, His Own Songs* (1967).

NEOPHONIC ORCHESTRA *see* FRANK L. CARLSON, GIL FULLER

NERO, PETER

b. 1934 Brooklyn, New York.
Pianist. Born Bernard Nierow; played in symphony concerts at age fourteen; studied at the Juilliard School, New York City; studied composition at Brooklyn College; appeared on "Arthur Godfrey's Talent Scouts" at age nineteen; played with Paul Whiteman; appeared in night clubs; in concert celebrating George Gershwin's 75th anniversary at Philharmonic Hall, New York City (1972).

NESBIT, JOHN

b. 1900, d. 1938.
Black trumpeter. Played with McKinney's Cotton Pickers.

NESBITT, EDWARD KERR (EDDIE)

b. 1919 Norfolk, West Virginia.
Singer and songwriter. Leader of the Country Drifters (1958-64); member of The Moonshiners after 1967; wrote "Doubting Heart," "Outside Your Picture Frame," "Unwanted," "You Pass Me By," "Borrowing."

NETTL, PAUL

b. 1889 Hohenelbe, Czechoslovakia, d. 1972 Bloomington, Indiana. Teacher and writer. Studied law, then turned to music, and became a lecturer at the University of Prague (1920); his study of Jewish musical life was published as *Alte judische Spielleute und Musiker;* after he came to America, he became a professor at the University of Indiana, Bloomington; also wrote *The Story of Dance Music, Forgotten Musicians, The Book of Musical Documents, Beethoven Encyclopedia* and *Mozart 1756-1956.*

NETTLES, BILL

b. ca. 1902 Natchitoches, Louisiana, d. 1967 West Monroe, Louisiana. Singer. With The Nettles Family and Dixie Blue Boys; wrote "Just Before We Say Goodbye" (1943), "God Bless My Darling, He's Somewhere," "If You're Sorry," "Change Your Sadness to a Smile"; died of a heart attack.

NETTLETON, ASAHEL

b. 1783 North Killingworth, Connecticut, d. 1844 East Windsor, Connecticut. Compiler. Graduated Yale (1809) and was ordained a Congregational minister (1817); held revival meetings in Conn., Mass. and New York; compiled *Village Hymns* (1824), with 600 hymns without tunes; the tunes were published separately in *Zion's Harp* (1824).

NEUENDORFF, ADOLF HEINRICH ANTON MAGNUS

b. 1843 Hamburg, Germany, d. 1897 New York City. Pianist, violinist, conductor, and composer. His parents brought him to America in 1855; composed comic operas; conductor of the New York Philharmonic Orchestra in 1878, and again after 1880.

NEVADA, EMMA

b. 1859 Alpha, California, d. 1940 Liverpool, England, Noted soprano. Born Emma Wixom; debut at the Academy of Music in New York City (1884); appeared in the title role of *Rose of Sharon* in 1884 at Covent Garden, London. When she gave a concert in the Academy of Music in Philadelphia on

November 17, 1899, she sang "Listen to the Mocking Bird," and Septimus Winner, the composer, was in the audience. He went backstage to meet her and she received him in the Green Room with a kiss.

NEVEU, PIERRE NICOLAS

b. (?) France, d. after 1805.
Composer and teacher. Came to Philadelphia about 1803; taught there; wrote *A Vocal Romance, op. XII* in French and English (1804), and *General Principles* (instruction in music).

NEVIN, ARTHUR F.

b. 1871 Edgeworth, Pennsylvania, d. 1943 Sewickley, Pennsylvania. Composer. Brother of Ethelburt Nevin; studied in Boston and Berlin; spent two summers in Montana with the Blackfeet Indians (1903-04); composed the Indian opera *Poia* (libretto—Randolph Hartley) produced by Pittsburgh Orchestra in concert and by the Berlin Royal Opera, *Twilight* (opera), *Lorna Doone* (orchestral suite), *Love Dreams* (Pittsburgh Orchestra), songs.

NEVIN, EDWIN HENRY

b. 1814 Shippensburg, Pennsylvania, d. 1889. Hymnist. Graduated Jefferson College (1833), Princeton Theological Seminary (1836); became a Presbyterian minister, later minister of the Reformed Dutch Church, Lancaster, Pa., then in Philadelphia; several of his hymns appeared in Nason's *Congregational Hymn Book* (1857) and in *Lyra Sacra Americana* (1868).

NEVIN, ETHELBURT WOODBRIDGE

b. 1862 Edgeworth, Pennsylvania, d. 1901 New Haven, Connecticut. Noted composer. Fifth of eight children, all talented musicians; debut as a pianist in Pittsburgh (1886); moved to Boston (1887); his *Water Scenes,* a piano suite published in 1891 contained the piece "Narcissus"; his other suites include *In Arcady* (1892), *May in Tuscany* (1895), *A Day in Venice* (1897). One day in 1898 Nevin received in the mail a poem entitled "The Rosary," by Robert C. Rogers, which Nevin liked so well he composed music for it. *The Rosary* was introduced by Francis Rogers at a concert at Madison Square Garden. He also wrote *Little Boy Blue* (1891, w.—poem by Eugene Field). Nevin also liked another poem, "Mighty Lak' a Rose," by Frank L. Stanton, and set the words to music, but it was not published until after his death in 1901.

NEVIN, GEORGE BALCH

b. 1859 Shippensburg, Pennsylvania, d. 1933 Easton, Pennsylvania. Composer. Wrote "Song of the Armourer" (w. Frances V. Hubbard), and "O Little Mother of Mine."

NEVIN, GORDON BALCH

b. 1892 Easton, Pennsylvania, d. 1943 New Wilmington, Pennsylvania. Organist and composer. Studied with Charles Maddock, J. Warren Andrews, and J. Fred Wolle; organist in Pennsylvania and Cleveland, Ohio; taught at Westminster College (1932-43); wrote "God of Our Fathers, Let Thy Face."

NEVINS, NATALIE

b. 1943 Philadelphia, Pennsylvania.
Gospel singer. Album—*I Believe (and Other Great Inspirational Songs).*

NEVIUS, JOHN W.

b. 1774 Somerville, New Jersey, d. 1854 Sunbeam, Illinois. Teacher and compiler. Carpenter by trade but also taught music; bandleader while living in New Brunswick, N.J.; with Cornelius Van Deventer and John Frazee compiled *The New Brunswick Collection of Sacred Music* (1817).

NEW CHRISTY MINSTRELS

Vocal and instrumental group organized by Randy Sparks in 1961.

NEW LOST CITY RAMBLERS

Vocal and instrumental group. (*See* Mike Seeger, Tracy Schwarz, John Cohen, Tom Paley.)

NEW ORLEANS ALL STARS (jazz band) *see* POPS FOSTER

NEW ORLEANS RHYTHM KINGS (jazz band)

Organized in Chicago (1920) as Friar's Society Orchestra at Friar's Inn; Paul Mares, cornet; Louis Black, banjo; George Brunis (Brunies), trombone; Jack Pettis, sax; Leon Rappolo, clarinet; Elmer Schoebel, pianist; Frank Snyder, drums; Arnold Loyocano, bass; later Ben Pollock, drums; Mel Stitzel, piano; first recorded in 1922 by Gennett Records; Jelly Roll Morton often played with the group, making it the first racially integrated group on record.

NEW YORK ROCK AND ROLL ENSEMBLE (rock group)

Dorian Rudnytsky, guitar, piano, cello, and trumpet; Michael Kamen, piano, English horn, oboe, etc.; Martin Fulterman, drums; Brian Corrigan, lead vocals and guitar; Clifford Nivison, lead guitar; started in New York City in 1967; albums—*New York Rock and Roll Ensemble, Faithful Friends, Reflections.*

NEW YORK SAXOPHONE QUARTET *see* JOHNNY CARISI

NEW YORK SYNCOPATED ORCHESTRA (black band)

Will Marion Cook, bandleader.

NEWBORN, PHINEAS, JR.

b. 1931 Whiteville, Tennessee.
Pianist and composer. Debut in New York City (1956); later played with Charles Mingus; became mentally ill in the 1960s and was confined to Camarillo State Hospital; later released and led his own trio in Los Angeles; wrote *New Blues, Theme for Basie;* albums—*Great Jazz Piano, Here Is Phineas, Newborn Touch, World of Piano.*

NEWCOMB, ETHEL

b. 1879 Whitney Point, New York, d. 1959.
Pianist. Studied with Leschetizky in Vienna, and later was his assistant; debut in Vienna (1903); toured England, Germany, and the United States after 1908.

NEWHALL, CHARLES STEDMAN

b. 1842 Boston, Massachusetts, d. 1935 Berkeley, California. Hymnist. Educated at Amherst College, Mass., and Union Theological Seminary; served as a soldier in the Civil War; became a Congregational minister; joined the U.S. Forestry Service in California in 1898; wrote the hymn "O Jesus, Master, When Today" (1913, tune "Beloit" by C.G. Reissiger).

NEWLEY, ANTHONY

b. 1931 England.
Composer and actor. Albums—*Doctor Doolittle* (songs from), *Roar of the Greasepaint* (*The Smell of the Crowd*); *Stop the World, I Want to Get Off; Tony; Genius of Anthony Newley.*

NEWMAN, ALFRED

b. 1901 New Haven, Connecticut, d. 1970.
Pianist and popular composer. Studied at the Von Ende School of Music, directed shows on Broadway, then went to Hollywood where he was general music director of 20th Century-Fox (1939-60); wrote "Concentrate" (w. Otto Harbach), "Voodoo Man" (Harbach), "Moon of Manakoora" (w. Frank Loesser), "Blue Tahitian Moon" (w. Mack Gordon); with lyrics by Sammy Cahn: "The Girl Next Door," "Lovely Lover," "The Pleasure of His Company,"

NEWMAN, ANTHONY (TONY)

b. 1941 Los Angeles, California.
Harpsichordist and organist. Studied at Ecole Normale de Musique in Paris; student of Pierre Cochereau and Alfred Cortot; with Edith Oppens at Mannes School, New York City (B.A., 1963); master's degree in composition at Harvard (1967); D.M.A. in organ from Boston University; taught at Juilliard and at State University in Purchase, N.Y.; at the Mostly Mozart Festival at Philharmonic Hall, New York City (1972).

NEWMAN, CHARLES

b. 1901 Chicago, Illinois.
Lyricist. Wrote "Six Lessons from Madame La Zonga" (m. James V. Monaco), "I Met Her on Monday" (1942, m. Allie Wrubel).

NEWMAN, DAVID ("FATHEAD")

b. 1933 Dallas, Texas.
Black alto and tenor saxist. Played with Ray Charles (1954-64); toured world (1964); albums—*Bigger and Better, Fathead, Fathead Comes On, Many Facets of David Newman, Straight Ahead.*

NEWMAN, JIMMY

b. 1927 Big Mamou, Louisiana.
Singer and songwriter. Own show on KPLC radio and TV, Lake Charles, La.; later on "Louisiana Hayride," Shreveport; wrote "Cry, Cry Darling" (1954, with J. Miller); LP records—*Songs of Jimmy Newman* (1962), *Folk Songs of the Bayou* (1963), *Artificial Rose* (1966), *Cry, Cry Darling, Fallen Star, Crossroads* (1966), *Born to Love You, Jimmy Newman Sings Country Songs, World of Music* (1967).

NEWMAN, JOSEPH DWIGHT (JOE)

b. 1922 New Orleans, Louisiana.
Black trumpeter. Played with Count Basie in 1940s and again from 1952-61; then led his own combos; toured Soviet Russia with Benny Goodman (1962); also played with pianist Roger Kellaway; played in various TV shows; album—*Main Stem* (with Oliver Nelson); at Newport Jazz Festival, New York City (1972).

NEWMAN, RANDY

b. 1944.
Singer and composer. Wrote "Mama Told Me Not to Come" (introduced by the Three Dog Night rock group), "I Think It's Gonna Rain Today" (recorded by Judy Collins); lives in Los Angeles; first recorded himself (1968); albums—*Randy Newman, Performance* (soundtrack); in concert at Philharmonic Hall, New York City (1972).

NEWSOM, THOMAS PENN

b. 1929 Portsmouth, Virginia.
Tenor saxist, clarinetist, and flutist. Graduated Peabody Conservatory, Baltimore; M.A. from Columbia Teachers College, New York City; with USAF dance band toured Europe and North Africa (1955); toured South America (1961) and Soviet Russia (1962) with Benny Goodman; later NBC staff musician.

NEWTON, FRANKIE

b. 1906 Emory, Virginia, d. 1954 New York City. Black jazz trumpeter. Joined Charlie Barnet's band (1937); also with Teddy Hill; played in Mezz Mezzrow's second big band.

NEWTON, HENRY JOTHAM

b. 1823 Hazelton, Pennsylvania, d. 1895 New York City. Piano maker. Manufactured pianos in New York.

NICHOLAS, ALBERT

b. 1900 New Orleans, Louisiana, d. 1973. Black clarinetist and saxophonist. Played in Kid Ory's band; with King Oliver (1924); with Zutty Singleton (1940).

NICHOLL, HORACE WADHAM

b. 1848 Tipton, England, d. 1922 New York City. Organist, writer, and composer. Son of John N. Nicholl, musician; pupil of Samuel Prince; organist in Pittsburgh (1871); editor in New York (1878); taught in Farmington, Conn. (1888-95); published a book on harmony; composed *Tartarus* (a symphonic poem), *Hamlet* (a psychic sketch), two symphonies, twelve symphonic preludes and fugues for organ, suite for full orchestra, a cycle of four oratorios with orchestra.

NICHOLS, ERNEST LORING ("RED")

b. 1905 Ogden, Utah, d. 1965 Las Vegas, Nevada. Cornetist and bandleader. Formed his own band, Red Nichols and His Five Pennies (1926); played at the Famous Door, New York City (1940); later starred, with Ruth Etting, on radio for Kellogg's Corn Flakes; played with Casa Loma orchestra; toured Japan with World Jazz Festival (1964); was playing in a casino when he died of a heart attack.

NICHOLS, GEORGE WARD

b. 1831 Tremont, Maine, d. 1885 Cincinnati, Ohio. Educator. Served in the Civil War; founded the College of Music of Cincinnati (1878) with the financial assistance of Reuben R. Springer.

NICHOLS, HERBERT HORATIO

b. 1919 New York City, d. there 1963.
Pianist. Played with various groups in New York City.

NIEHAUS, LEONARD

b. 1929 St. Louis, Missouri.
Alto saxist and arranger. With Stan Kenton in 1950s; with Lalo Schifrin in 1960s; later formed his own groups; albums—*Lennie Niehaus Octet no.2, Lennie Niehaus Quintet, Lennie Niehaus Quintet and Strings, Lennie Niehaus Sextet, Zounds.*

NIELSEN, ALICE

b. 1876 Nashville, Tennessee, d. 1943 New York City. Singer. Of Swedish and Irish extraction; first professional appearance was as Yum Yum in *The Mikado* in Oakland, Calif. (1893); sang in Victor Herbert's *The Serenade* (1897), the *Fortune Teller* (1898), and *The Singing Girl* (1899), and sang "If You Were Only Mine," "Love Is a Tyrant," and "Lovely Nature, Fare Thee Well"; became known as the "singing girl"; left operetta for grand opera, much to the disappointment of Herbert, and sang in Naples, London, Paris, and other cities.

NILES, JOHN JACOB

b. 1892 Louisville, Kentucky.
Singer, dulcimer player, and composer. Served in the U.S. Army Air Corps in France (1918) and was partially paralyzed in a plane crash; studied at the Schola Cantorum, Paris, and the Cincinnati Conservatory of Music (1919); toured U.S. with contralto Marion Kerby; composed the oratorio, *Lamentations* (performed at Indiana State Teachers College, Terre Haute, 1951), *Rhapsody for the Merry Month of May, Mary the Rose;* published numerous books on folk music and ballads.

NILSSON, BIRGIT

b. 1918 Karup, Sweden.
Soprano. Born Birgit Svenson. Debut at the Metropolitan Opera, New York City (1959) as Isolde in *Tristan and Isolde;* debut in

Stockholm (1947); has sung the part of Isolde over 167 times; sang in *Tristan and Isolde* at the Metropolitan Opera, New York City (1971) with Erich Leinsdorf conducting.

NILSSON, CHRISTINE

b. 1843 Wederslof, Sweden, d. 1921 Stockholm, Sweden. Noted soprano. Studied in Stockholm and in Paris under Masset, Sedie, and Wartel; debut in Paris (1864) as Violetta; sang in Paris (1864-70); also at engagements in London during this period; toured the United States (1870-72) under Strakosch; American tours also 1873-74 and in 1884; farewell concert in London (1891); married (1872) to Auguste Rouzaud (d. 1882) and to Count Angel Vallejo y Miranda (d. 1902).

NILSSON, HARRY

b. 1942 Brooklyn, New York.
Jazz-rock singer. Resides in Los Angeles; first recorded "Ten Little Indians" (1941) m. Septimus Winner, 1868); does two-, three-and four-part harmonies in a range of about three octaves; albums—*Pandemonium Shadow Show* (1967), *Aerial Ballet, Harry, Nilsson Sings Newman, Spotlight on Nilsson, Nilsson Schmilsson* (winner of 1972 Grammy Award).

NIMITZ, JACK JEROME

b. 1930 Washington, D.C.
Saxist and clarinetist. With Stan Kenton in late 1950s; formed quintet with Bill Hood (1964) and played in Los Angeles night spots; with Monterey Jazz Festival orchestra (1964-65).

NIMMONS, PHILLIP RISTA

b. 1923 Kamloops, B.C., Canada.
Clarinetist and saxist. Graduated the University of British Columbia; studied at Juilliard, New York City, and the Royal Conservatory, Toronto, Ontario; wrote scores for Canadian radio and TV shows; organized own group; taught in Toronto.

1910 FRUITGUM COMPANY

Frank Jeckell, lead vocals and rhythm guitar; Pat Karwan, lead guitar and vocals; Mark Gutkowski, vocals and organ; Floyd Marcus, vocals and drums; first recorded in 1968; appealed to the teenybopper group; albums—*Checkmate, Goody Goody Gumdrops, Hard Ride, Indian Giver, Juiciest Fruitgum, 1, 2, 3, Red Light, Simon Says.*

NITE HAWKS *see* CAL SMITH, STIX HOOPER

NITSCHMANN, DAVID

b. 1696 Zauchtenthal, Moravia, Czechoslovakia, d. 1772 Bethlehem, Pennsylvania. Hymnist. Missionary in St. Thomas, Virgin Islands (1732), then Bishop of the Brethren's Church (1735); his hymns appeared in Moravian hymnals.

NITTY GRITTY DIRT BAND, THE (jug band)

Ralph Barr, guitar, banjo, and clarinet; Chris Darrow, guitar, banjo, etc.; Jimmie Faddenn drums, jug, washtub bass, etc.; Jeffrye Hanna, lead vocals, guitar, washboard, etc.; John McEuen, piano, guitar, etc.; Les Thompson, guitar, mandolin, etc.; former members were Bruce Kunkel and Jackson Browne; started in 1966; played in the film *Paint Your Wagon* (1968); albums—*Nitty Gritty Dirt Band, Rare Junk, Ricochet;* group split up in 1968.

NOBLE, RAY

b. 1907 Brighton, Sussex, England.
Bandleader and composer. Wrote "Love Is the Sweetest Thing," "Cherokee," "Comanche War Dance," "I Hadn't Anyone 'till You," "Good Night Sweetheart, 'till We Meet Tomorrow" (with Jimmy Campbell and Reg Connelly, w. Rudy Vallee).

NOBLE, THOMAS TERTUIS

b. 1867 Bath, England, d. 1953 Rockport, Massachusetts. Composer. Won a scholarship to the Royal College of Music, London (1886); in 1913 came to New York City to become organist at St. Thomas Church; composed the anthems "Fierce Was the Wild Billow," "O Wisdom, Spirit of the Living God," and "Souls of the Righteous"; wrote the tune "New England" ("O Who Shall Roll Away the Stone," w. Marion F. Ham).

NOLCINI, CHARLES

b. (?) Italy, d. 1844 near Boston, Massachusetts. Composer and teacher. Taught from 1821-44; appeared at concerts in Boston; wrote "A Military Waltz" (1821), "The Grasshoppers' Waltz" (1839), "The Tear of Gratitude Waltz" (1840).

NOONE, JIMMY

b. 1895 near New Orleans, Louisiana, d. 1944 Los Angeles, California. Black clarinetist. Studied with Lorenzo Tio, Jr.; joined Buddy Petit in New Orleans; with Jelly Roll Morton in Los Angeles (1917); with Freddie Keppard (1918); then joined King Oliver, with Bill Johnson; with pianist Earl Hines (1927); recorded "Apex Blues" (1923), "Sweet Lorraine" (1927), "Body and Soul" (1941),

"Shag" (1932); played with Charles "Doc" Cook and his Seventeen Interns; with Zutty Singleton (1943); died of a heart attack.

NORDEN, N. LINDSAY

b. 1887 Philadelphia, Pennsylvania, d. 1956 Philadelphia, Pennsylvania. Organist, conductor, composer, teacher, and editor. Graduated Columbia University; studied with Spicker, Rybner, Weld, and F.W. Robinson in New York; chapel organist at St. Bartholomew's, New York City, and St. Mary's and All Saints' in Brooklyn; organist at Second Presbyterian Church, Philadelphia (1916-27); conducted Mendelssohn Club there (1916-26).

NORDICA, LILLIAN

b. 1857 Farmington, Maine, d. 1914 Batavia, Java. Opera singer. Born Lillian Norton; pupil of John O'Neill in Boston (1871); soloist with Patrick S. Gilmore's band (1878), toured U.S. and Europe; studied in Paris and Milan; debut in Milan (1879); learned the part of Isolde (*Tristan and Isolde*) in French (1910) for a single performance; while on a world tour, her ship struck a reef off Thursday Island, she caught pneumonia and died four months later.

NORDOFF, PAUL

b. 1909 Philadelphia, Pennsylvania.
Composer. Studied at the Juilliard School of Music, N.Y.; won Bearns Prize of Columbia University; awarded Guggenheim Fellowship; taught at Philadelphia Conservatory; composed *Prelude and Three Small Fugues* (last by the Philadelphia Orchestra under Stokowski, 1937; complete by the Pennsylvania Orchestra under Sabatini, 1940), *Suite* (St. Louis Symphony under Golschmann, 1940), *Piano Concerto* (National Symphony, Washington, D.C., under Kindler, composer soloist, 1939), *Violin Concerto*, songs.

NORENA, EIDE (KAJA HANSEN)

b. 1884 Horten, Norway.
Soprano. Studied in Oslo; sang at La Scala, Milan; also Covent Garden, London (1924-25) then at Paris Opera; American debut in New York (1926); at Chicago Opera (1926-27); at Metropolitan Opera, New York after 1933.

NORMAN, FRED

b. 1910 Leesburg, Florida.
Black composer. Arranger for Claude Hopkins, Gene Krupa, Dorsey Brothers and others; wrote music for the stage show *Ol' Man Satan* (1959).

NORMAN, JESSYE

b. 1946.
Black soprano. Created a stir when she appeared at Tanglewood singing the "Liebestod" and the *Wesendonck Lieder* with Colin Davis conducting the Boston Symphony Orchestra (1972); recorded Mozart's *Le Nozze di Figaro* with the Boston Symphony (1972).

NORRIS, HOMER ALBERT

b. 1860 Wayne, Maine, d. 1920 New York City. Composer. Studied in Boston and in Paris; taught in Boston; composed *Zoroaster* (an overture), *Nain* (cantata), and songs; published *Harmony* and *Counterpoint* on French basis.

NORRIS, JOHN WYATT

b. 1893 Sioux City, Iowa.
Hymnist. Educated at the University of Pennsylvania, Philadelphia, and the Philadelphia Divinity School (1925); rector in Philadelphia (1925-37), then a teacher at the Divinity School there (1937-41), at Lawrence Hall, Chicago (1941-45), rector of St. John's, Poultney, Vermont (1945-48), then at St. Michael's, Brattleboro, Vt.; wrote the hymn "Give Peace, O God, the Nations Cry" (1940, tune "Vermont"—Anne L. Miller and "Lynchburg"—Henry Hallstrom).

NORTH, FRANK MASON

b. 1850 New York City, d. 1935 Madison, New Jersey. Hymnist. Graduated Wesleyan University, Middletown, Conn.; became a Methodist minister in the New York Conference (1873), the N.Y. East Conference (1887) where he preached in Middletown, Conn. for five years; made Secretary of the New York Missionary (1892) then the Board of Foreign Missions (1912); wrote the hymns "Where Cross the Crowded Ways of Life" (1903, tune, "Germany"), "The World's Astir! The Clouds of Storm" (tune, "All Saints New").

NORTON, ANDREW

b. 1786 Hingham, Massachusetts, d. 1853 Newport, Rhode Island. Hymnist. Educated at Harvard University, became librarian there, then professor at the Theological School (1819-30); his hymns appear in *Martineau's Hymns* (1873) and Putnam's *Singers and Songs of the Liberal Faith* (Boston, 1875).

NORTON, GEORGE A.

b. 1880 St. Louis, Missouri, d. 1923 Tucson, Arizona. Pianist and lyricist. Studied at the

Peabody Conservatory, Baltimore; pianist in vaudeville; wrote lyrics for "My Melancholy Baby" (1911, m. Ernie Burnett).

NORVO, RED

b. 1908 Beardstown, Illinois.
Jazz vibraphonist. Born Kenneth Norville; his arranger was Ed Sauter; soloist for Paul Whiteman; formed his own band (1936) in Syracuse, N.Y.; married Mildred Bailey, his vocalist, and were billed as "Mr. and Mrs. Swing"; played at the Hotel Commodore, New York City (1938); played at Murray's in Tuckahoe, N.Y. (1939); later broke up his band and joined Benny Goodman; later played in casinos in Las Vegas; at the Newport Jazz Festival, New York City (1972).

NORWORTH, JACK

b. 1879 Philadelphia, Pennsylvania, d. 1959 Laguna Beach, California. Composer, lyricist, and vaudeville comedian. Toured in vaudeville with his wife, Nora Bayes; wrote songs for the Ziegfeld Follies; wrote the music for "Shine On, Harvest Moon" (1908, w. Nora Bayes); lyrics for "Take Me Out to the Ball Game" (1908, m. Albert von Tilzer).

NOTO, SAM

b. 1930 Buffalo, New York.
Trumpeter. With Stan Kenton, Louis Bellson and others during 1950s; later with Count Basie; formed own quintet with Joe Romano (1965).

NOTTINGHAM, JAMES EDWARD, JR.

b. 1925 Brooklyn, New York.
Trumpeter. Played with leading bands in late 1950s; played on various CBS-TV shows; formed own quintet (1962) with Budd Johnson; with Thad Jones-Mel Lewis band after 1966.

NOVACEK, OTTOKAR

b. 1866 Fehertemplom, Hungary, d. 1900 New York City. Violinist. Studied at the Leipzig Conservatory where he won the Mendelssohn Prize (1899); member of Boston Symphony (1891); Damrosch Orchestra, New York (1892-1903); forced into retirement by heart trouble; composed violin pieces, chamber music, and Bulgarian dance music.

NOVAES, GUIOMAR

b. 1895 Sao Paulo, Brazil.
Pianist. She studied piano at age five with Chiafarelli; graduated Paris Conservatory, won first prize; debut in Paris (1907); toured Europe; debut in New York (1915); married Octavio Pinto, composer; retired for a few years; then returned to New York (1934).

NUGENT, MAUDE

b. 1873 Brooklyn, New York, d. 1958 New York City. Singer, actress, and popular composer. Married lyricist William Jerome; wrote "Sweet Rosie O'Grady" which she introduced at The Abbey, Johnny Reilly's place on Eighth Avenue, New York City (1896); other songs were "Mamie Reilly" (1897), "I Can't Forgive You Honey," "Mary from Tipperary," "There's No Other Girl Like My Girl," "Somebody Wants You," "Down at Rosie Reilly's Flat," and "My Pretty Little China Maid."

NULL, CECIL A.

b. 1927 East War, West Virginia.
Singer and guitarist. Attended schools in Warriormine, W. Va., and Grundy, Virginia; music teacher; member of Tennessee Serenaders (1951); Cecil Null and Annette after 1964; album—*Instrumental Country Hymns.*

NUNO, JAIME

b. 1824 San Juan de las Abadesas, Spain, d. 1908 Bayside, New York. Conductor. Came to the United States (1856); conducted opera in New York and abroad; taught singing in Buffalo, N.Y., after 1869; also conductor of the Buffalo Symphony Orchestra; wrote the "Mexican National Hymn" (adopted, 1854).

NYE, HERMES

b. 1908 Chicago, Illinois.
Ballad singer. Attended Washburn College, Topeka, Kansas, and the University of Kansas, Lawrence (Bachelor of Laws, 1933); attorney in Dallas, Texas; albums—*Anglo-American Folk Songs* (1952), *Ballads of the Civil War, Texas Folk Songs, War Songs, U.S.A., Reliques from Percy and Child.*

NYRO, LAURA

b. 1949.
Singer. Resides in New York; white soul singer; wrote "Stoned Soul Picnic," recorded by the Fifth Dimension; first recorded in 1967; albums—*More Than a New Discovery, Eli and the Thirteenth Confession, New York Tendaberry.*

OAK RIDGE QUARTET *see* WALLY FOWLER

OAKEY, EMILY SULLIVAN

b. 1829 Albany, New York, d. there 1883. Hymnist. Wrote the lyrics and Philip P. Bliss the music for "Sowing the Seed by the Daylight Fair" (1850), and "I Am So Glad" (1870).

OAKUM *see* SAMSON OCCUM

OBERHOFFER, EMIL JOHANN

b. 1867 Munich, Germany, d. 1933 San Diego, California. Conductor. Studied with Kistler and I. Philipp; conducted Philharmonic Club in Minneapolis, Minn.; from 1905-22 conducted Minneapolis Symphony Orchestra; composed church music, songs.

O'BRIEN, FLOYD

b. 1905 Chicago, Illinois, d. there 1968.
Jazz trombonist. Played in Bob Crosby's band; also with Gene Krupa, Phil Harris and others.

O'BRYANT, JIMMY

b. 1928 Chicago, Illinois.
Jazz saxophonist. Played with King Oliver's orchestras.

O'BRYANT, JOAN

b. 1923 Wichita, Kansas, d. 1964.
Ballad singer. Attended the University of Wichita, and National University, Mexico City, Mexico; M.A. at Wichita (1949); taught at the University of Wichita; LP records—*American Ballads and Folksongs* (1957), *Folksongs and Ballads of Kansas* (1957); died in an automobile accident in Colorado.

OCCUM (OAKUM), SAMSON

b. 1722 Mohegan, New York, d. 1779 Stockbridge, New York. Hymnist and compiler. American Indian; educated at Moore's Indian Charity School, Lebanon, Conn. (origin of Dartmouth College); ordained (1759) by the Presbytery of Suffolk County, N.Y., to minister to the Indians; wrote the lyrics "Awaked by Sinai's Awful Sound" (m. S. Chandler, tune—"Ganges"); *The Indian Philosopher,* songs (w. Dr. Watts) published in Northampton, Mass. (1802).

OCHS, PHILIP DAVID

b. 1940 El Paso, Texas.
Popular composer and singer. Attended Staunton Military Academy (Virginia) and Ohio State University, Columbus; many of his songs are of political protest; wrote "The Cuban Invasion" (1961), "Draft Dodger Rag," "Cops of the World," "There But for Fortune," "State of Mississippi"; albums—*All the News That's Fit to Sing, Greatest Hits, I Ain't Marching Anymore, Phil Ochs in Concert, Pleasures of the Harbor, Tape from California.*

O'DANIEL, WILBERT LEE ("PAPPY")

b. 1890 Malta, Ohio, d. 1969.
Singer. Raised in Kingman, Kansas; moved to Fort Worth, Texas (1925), was a flour salesman; with Bob Wills formed the "Light Crust Doughboys," sang on station KFJZ, Fort Worth (1932); on WBAP (1933); formed Hillbilly Flour Company (1935); served as Governor of Texas; his group's records were "Beautiful Texas," "On to Victory, Mr. Roosevelt," "Texas Rose," "Bluebonnet Waltz," "Alamo Waltz," "Kelly Waltz," "Texas Breakdown."

O'DAY, ANITA

b. 1919 Chicago, Illinois.
Singer. With Gene Krupa, Stan Kenton and others in 1940s; later made many successful records with Roy Eldridge, Oscar Peterson Trio, Gary McFarland, Cal Tjader and others; albums—*Incomparable, Anita O'Day Sings the Winners, This Is Anita, Time for Two.*

O'DEA, ANNE CALDWELL

b. 1867 Boston, Massachusetts, d. 1936 Hollywood, California. Singer, actress, and lyricist. Singer with Juvenile Opera Company, N.Y.; wrote the libretto for *Take the Air;* wrote the lyrics "I Know That You Know" (1926, m. Vincent M. Youmans), "A Night in Spain" (1927, m. Jean Schwartz).

O'DELL, ALLEN DOYE

b. 1912 Plainview, Texas.
Singer and songwriter. Wrote "Dear Okie," "I Miss You Already," "Castle of My Dreams"; albums—*Crossroads; Valley o' Tears.*

O'DELL, MAC

b. 1916 Roanoke, Alabama.
Singer and songwriter. Wrote "Blessed Lord"; "That Judgment Day"; "Wolves in Sheep's Clothing"; "Sign on the Highway"; "Banking with My Lord"; "Thirty Pieces of Silver"; album—*Hymns for the Country Folks.*

ODENHEIMER, WILLIAM HENRY

b. 1817 Philadelphia, Pennsylvania, d. 1879 Burlington, New Jersey. Compiler. Episcopal Bishop of New Jersey (1859-74) and of Northern New Jersey (later Newark) (1874-79); with Frederic Mayer Bird (b. 1838, Philadelphia) compiled *Songs of the Spirit* (New York, 1872).

ODETTA (HOLMES-FELIOUS)

b. 1930 Birmingham, Alabama.
Black singer. Raised in Los Angeles; attended Los Angeles City College; sang in night clubs there; debut at Town Hall, New York City (1959); at Carnegie Hall (1960); her albums are *Odetta, Best of Odetta, Odetta at Carnegie Hall, Odetta at the Gate of Horn, Odetta at Town Hall, Odetta Sings Ballads and Blues, Odetta Sings Dylan, Odetta Sings Folk Songs, One Grain of Sand.*

OEHMLER, LEO CARL MARTIN

b. 1867 Pittsburgh, Pennsylvania, d. 1930 Pasadena, California. Pianist, composer, and teacher. Teacher of Charles W. Cadman.

O'FARRILL, ARTURO ("CHICO")

b. 1921 Havana, Cuba.
Bandleader and arranger. Came to New York City (1948); arranger for Benny Goodman and Dizzy Gillespie in 1950s; organized his own band; played in New York and in Mexico City (1962-65); later in New York City.

O'GWYNN, JAMES LEROY

b. 1928 Winchester, Mississippi.
Singer and songwriter. Attended school in Hattiesburg, Miss.; wrote "I Won't Love You Anymore," "Talk to Me Lonesome Heart."

O'HARA, GEOFFREY

b. 1882 Chatham, Ontario, Canada, d. 1967. Composer. Came to U.S. (1914); educated at Chatham Collegiate Institute; Armed Forces song leader in World War I; became U.S. citizen; honorary Mus.D. from Huron College; wrote "K-K-K-Katy" (1918), "Give a Man a Horse He Can Ride."

O'HARA, JOHN

b. 1905 Pottsville, Pennsylvania, d. 1970. Writer and librettist. Wrote many successful stories; librettist for *Pal Joey* (1940, m. Richard Rodgers).

OHIO EXPRESS (rock group)

Douglas Grassel, rhythm guitar; Tim Corwin, drums; Dean Kastran, bass guitar; Jim Pfayler, organ; Dale Powers, lead guitar; started their group while still in high school in Ohio; first recorded in 1968; albums—*Beg, Borrow and Steal, Chewy, Chewy, Mercy, Very Best of Ohio Express, Yummy, Yummy, Yummy, Zig Zag.*

OHLSSON, GARRICK

b. 1948.
Pianist. Resides in White Plains, N.Y.; won three major world piano competitions—Italy's Busoni Prize, Montreal's International Competition, and the International Chopin Competition held in Warsaw, Poland (1970); American debut with Philadelphia Orchestra under Eugene Ormandy at Philharmonic Hall; also performed with New York Philharmonic under Seiji Ozawa.

O'HORGAN, THOMAS

b. 1926 Chicago, Illinois.
Singer, harpist, producer, and composer. Studied music at De Paul University, Chicago (earned M.A. and Ph.D.); wrote scores for The Playwrights Theatre Club, Chicago, renamed Second City and came to New York; produced shows at Caffe Cinco, at Judson Church, *Big Me,* pop musical at Frankie's Tropical Bar on 8th Street; at Ellen Stewart's Cafe La Mama (1961-68); produced *Hair, Lenny, Jesus Christ Superstar.*

O'KANE, TULLIUS CLINTON

b. 1830 Delaware, Ohio, d. 1912.
Composer. Composed the music "O Think of the Home Over There" (w. D.C. Huntington).

OKUN, MILT

b. 1923 Brooklyn, New York.
Ballad singer. Studied music at College of City of New York and Oberlin Conservatory (Ohio); taught in Queens; LP records—*Adirondack Folk Songs and Ballads, I Sing of Canada, Every Inch a Sailor, Fo'c'sle Songs and Shanties, Traditional American Love*

Songs, Merry Ditties, America's Best Loved Folk Songs, We Sing of the Sea.

OLCOTT, CHAUNCEY

b. 1858 Buffalo, New York, d. 1932 Monte Carlo, Monaco. Noted singer and popular composer. Wrote "Olcott's Home Song" which he sang in the *Minstrel of Clare* (1896); "Sweet Inniscarra," "Kate O'Donahue," and "Old Fashioned Mother" in *Sweet Inniscarra* (1897), "My Wild Irish Rose" (1899) and "Olcott's Lullaby" which appeared in *A Romance of Athlone*, and "Mother Machree" (1910, w. Rita Johnson Young); with George Graff, Jr. wrote the lyrics, and Ernest Ball the music, "When Irish Eyes Are Smiling" (1912).

"OLD DOMINION BARN DANCE"

Variety show on radio station WRVA, Richmond, Virginia; started in 1946 with "Sunshine Sue" Workman, director.

OLDBERG, ARNE

b. 1874 Youngstown, Ohio, d. 1962.
Teacher and composer. Played piano at age five; then at six played Haydn symphonies with his father in duet; studied in Chicago, Vienna, and Munich; taught at Northwestern University, Evanston, Illinois, after 1899; composed *Paola and Francesca* (overture, Thomas Orchestra), Symphony in F Minor (won National Federation Prize 1911), *Festival* Overture, horn concerto, piano sonata, chamber music.

OLIPHANT, GRASSELLA

b. 1929 Pittsburgh, Pennsylvania.
Drummer. With Ahmad Jamal, Sarah Vaughan and others in 1950s; with Gloria Lynne and others in 1960s; at Newport Jazz Festival (1961) with Lynne.

OLIVER, HENRY KEMBLE

b. 1800 Beverly, Massachusetts, d. 1885 Salem, Massachusetts. Composer. Graduated Dartmouth (1818); became a schoolmaster and church organist; lived in Lawrence, Mass. (1848-58), then to Salem, Mass.; Treasurer of Massachusetts during the Civil War and first chief of the Bureau of Labor for ten years; composed the tunes "Federal Street," "Bosworth," "Harmony Grove," "Hudson," "Merton," "Morning," "Salisbury Plain," and "Walnut Grove"; his tune "Federal Street" was used for "Lord, How Mysterious Are Thy Ways" (w. Anna Steele), "God Calling Yet, Shall I Not Hear?" (w. G. Tersteegen), and "Jesus, and Shall It Ever Be" (w. Joseph Grigg); at Pat Gilmore's Peace Jubilee in Boston (1872), Oliver conducted as the chorus of ten thousand voices sang his hymn; with Bancroft and S.P. Tuckerman published *National Lyre* (1848).

OLIVER, JOSEPH ("KING")

b. 1885 New Orleans, Louisiana, d. 1938 Savannah, Georgia. Black cornetist, bandleader and composer. Many leading black musicians started with King Oliver's Creole Jazz Band, including Louis Armstrong (1922); wrote "Snake Rag" (1923), "The Chimes" (1923), "Canal Street Blues" (1923), "Working Man's Blues" (1923), "Chattanooga Stomp" (with Alphonse Picou), "New Orleans Stomp" (with Picou), "Dixieland Blues" (1925), "Doctor Jazz" (w. Walter Melrose), "Tack Annie" (1927, with Paul Barbarin), "Showboat Shuffle" (1927, with Barney Bigard).

OLIVER, LYNN

b. 1921 Brooklyn, New York.
Teacher. Studied at Manhattan School of Music; served as a radio operator in the South Pacific during World War II; studied piano, vibes, and tympani at the Manhattan School after the war; established a school for jazz musicians in New York City, the Lynn Oliver Studios (1953); played in big bands during the 1940s and '50s, with Art Mooney, Bobby Byrne, Tommy Reynolds, and Jose Melis.

OLIVER, MELVIN JAMES ("SY")

b. 1910 Battle Creek, Michigan.
Black trumpeter, arranger, and composer. Played in Zach White's band; then joined Jimmie Lunceford's band, where he was also arranger; he wrote "Dream of You" and "Yes, Indeed!" which became a big hit after it was recorded by Tommy Dorsey; then played and arranged for Tommy Dorsey; at the Newport Jazz Festival, New York City (1972).

OLIVERO, MAGDA

b. 1913 Italy.
Soprano. Debut in Italy (1935); came to United States (1967); New York debut in Philharmonic Hall with the Little Orchestra Society (1971), singing Poulenc's *La Voix Humaine* and Puccini's *Manon Lescaut*.

OLIVIER, ADAM

b. ca. 1870, d. after 1900.
Black bandleader. Leader of Adam Olivier's Creole Orchestra in New Orleans (1895).

OLMAN, ABE

b. 1888 Cincinnati, Ohio.
Pianist and composer. Office manager for Gus Edwards productions; wrote songs for

London revue; pianist in Paris night club; publisher in 1914; wrote music for "Oh Johnny, Oh Johnny, Oh" (1917, w. Ed Rose).

OLMSTEAD, TIMOTHY

b. 1759 Phoenix, Oswego Country, New York, d. 1848. Composer. Served as a musician in the Revolutionary War in the 7th and 9th Connecticut Regiments, and was at the Battle of White Plains, N.Y.; moved to Hartford in 1785; during the War of 1812 served in the First Regiment of the Connecticut Militia (1814); his tunes were published in *The Musical Olio* (1805, Northampton, Mass.) with a second edition (1811, New London, Conn.)

OLSEN, GEORGE

b. 1893 Portland, Oregon, d. 1971 Paramus, New Jersey. Bandleader. His record "Who" sold over a million copies in 1926; RCA released an album *Vintage Years* with included "Who," "Varsity Drag," "Doin' the Racoon," "The Girl Friend" and "Makin' Whoopee"; his signature song was "Beyond the Blue Horizon."

OLYMPIA BAND (black band)

Buddy Bolden, leader. (*See* Buddy Bolden)

OLYMPIA ORCHESTRA (black jazz band) *see* FREDDY KEPPARD

ONDERDONK, HENRY USTICK

b. 1789 New York City, d. 1858 Philadelphia, Pennsylvania. Hymnist. Educated at Columbia where he received his B.A. (1805) and D.D. (1827); also received an M.D. from Edinburgh University in 1810; rector of St. Ann's (Episcopal), Brooklyn (1815-27), when he was elected bishop co-adjutor of Pennsylvania and bishop diocesan in 1836; his weakness for alcohol forced his resignation in 1844, but he was restored to his position in 1856; wrote the lyrics "How Wondrous and Great Thy Works, God of Praise" (tune "Old Hundred Fourth," 1621, Thomas Ravenscroft or "Lyons," 1815); with W. A. Muhlenberg edited *The Plain Music for the Book of Common Prayer* (1854).

O'NEILL, EUGENE F.

b. 1888 Boston, Massachusetts, d. 1972 Cambridge, Massachusetts. Irish tenor. Joined Keith's and Loew's vaudeville circuits as a young man; later in Broadway musicals; introduced "Trees" and "Sweethearts" from the musical *Maytime.*

OPERTI, LE ROI

b. 1895 Boston, Massachusetts, d. 1971 New York City. Singer and actor. Debut at the age of twelve as Gottfried in the opera *Lohengrin* at the Park Theatre; spent thirteen years in opera, musical comedy and stock in Boston, then came to New York.

ORANGE, JOSEPH

b. 1941 New York City.
Black trombonist. Nephew of J.C. Higginbotham; played in Marshall Brown's Newport Youth Band; with Lionel Hampton, Archie Shepp, Herbie Mann and others during 1960s.

ORBISON, ROY

b. 1936 Wink, Texas.
Popular composer and singer. Attended North Texas State College, Denton; sang on station KVWC, Vernon, Texas; toured Europe, the United States, and Canada; resided in Hendersonville, Tenn.; wrote "Claudette," "Blue Angel," "Only the Lonely," "Dream Baby," "Running Scared," "It's Over," "Candy Man," "Crying," "Pretty Woman," "Mean Woman Blues."

ORCHESTRA U.S.A. *see* RICHARD KATZ

ORDWAY, JOHN P.

b. 1824 Salem, Massachusetts, d. 1880 Boston, Massachusetts. Popular composer. Leader of Ordway's Aeolians (minstrels); wrote "Music Fills My Soul with Sadness" (1850, w. P.S. Gilmore) and arranged the music "Home Again" (1851, words and music—M.S. Pike); wrote the words and music "Galloping Sleigh Ride" (1844), "Home Delights" (1855), "Twinkling Stars Are Laughing" (1855), "Silvery Midnight Moon" (1856), "Witching Love by Moonlight" (1857), "Give Me Your Hand" (1858), "Silver Moonlight Winds" (1858), "Still He Kept · Thinking" (1862), "Somebody's Darling Slept Here" (1862).

ORE, JOHN THOMAS

b. 1933 Philadelphia, Pennsylvania.
Bass player. With Ben Webster, Bud Powell, George Wallington and others in 1950s; with Thelonious Monk, Teddy Wilson and others in 1960s.

OREM, PRESTON WARE

b. 1862 Philadelphia, Pennsylvania, d. there 1938. Organist. Organist at the Walnut Street Presbyterian Church, Philadelphia (1901-10); taught at the Philadelphia Conservatory and

Combs Conservatory; editor of the Presser Company (1900-31).

ORIENTAL AMERICA (black minstrel show) *see* JOHN ROSAMOND JOHNSON

ORIGINAL CREOLE RAGTIME BAND (black jazz band)

Organized in New Orleans (1912) by Bill Johnson, bass player; Freddy Keppard, cornet; Eddie Vinson, trombone; George Baquet, clarinet; Leon Williams, guitar; Dink Johnson, drums; Jimmy Palao, violin; later Bab Frank, piccolo player; "Big Eye" Louis Nelson; later called the Creole Band; broke up in 1918.

ORIGINAL DIXIE JUBILEE SINGERS (black group) *see* EVA JESSYE

ORIGINAL DIXIELAND JAZZ BAND (white jazz band)

Organized by Nick La Rocca, cornetist in Chicago; played in New York City (1917); recorded with Columbia and Victor; Eddie Edwards, trombone; Henry Ragas, piano; Larry Shields, clarinet; Tony Spargo (Sbarbaro), drummer; later Emil Christian, trombone; J. Russell Robinson, piano; Jimmy Lytel, clarinet; Frank Signorelli, piano.

ORIGINAL JAZZ ALL-STARS (jazz band) *see* FRANZ JACKSON

ORIGINAL MEMPHIS FIVE (white jazz band)

Phil Napoleon, trumpeter; Miff Mole, trombonist; Jimmy Lytel, clarinetist; Frank Signorelli, pianist.

ORLOB, HAROLD

b. 1885 Logan, Utah.
Composer. Educated at the University of Utah, and the Michigan Conservatory; director of the Detroit Opera House; wrote Broadway stage scores; with Joe E. Howard wrote "I Wonder Who's Kissing Her Now" (1909, w. Will M. Hough and Frank R. Adams).

ORMANDY, EUGENE

b. 1899 Budapest, Hungary.
Famous conductor. At the age of five he was accepted as a student at the Budapest Academy and studied under Jeno Hubay; became conductor of the Minneapolis Symphony Orchestra (Minn.) (1931) and the Philadelphia Orchestra (1936); conducted weekly series of the Philadelphia Orchestra at Philharmonic Hall, New York City (1972).

ORNSTEIN, LEO

b. 1895 Krementchug, Russia.
Composer. His parents brought him to America (1907); known for *Wild Men's Dance* (1915), *Poems,* a concerto for two pianos.

ORTEGA, ANTHONY ROBERT

b. 1928 Los Angeles, California.
Saxist and clarinetist. With Lionel Hampton, Dizzy Gillespie, Luis Rivera and others in 1950s; with Quincy Jones, Don Ellis, Gerald Wilson and others in 1960s; formed own quartet.

ORTMANN, OTTO RUDOLPH

b. 1889 Baltimore, Maryland, d. 1956.
Pianist and teacher. Graduated Baltimore City College and Peabody Institute, Baltimore; taught there after 1913 and later became director; published *The Physical Basis of Piano Touch and Tone,* and *The Physiological Basis of Touch and Tone.*

ORY, EDWARD ("KID")

b. 1886 Laplace, Louisiana, d. 1973 Honolulu, Hawaii. Black-creole trombonist and bandleader. Played in Dixie Part in New Orleans; formed his own band (1911); band included, at various times—King Oliver and Louis Armstrong; left New Orleans for Los Angeles (1919); formed an orchestra there; recorded the first known jazz records by a black musician—*Ory's Creole Trombone* and *Society Blues* (both 1921); joined King Oliver in 1924 with the Oliver Syncopators; wrote and recorded "Muskrat Ramble" (1926) with Armstrong Hot Five and Hot Seven; joined Orson Wells' radio show with new band on CBS network from Los Angeles (1944).

ORY'S BAND, KID (black jazz band)

Organized in 1911 in New Orleans; played until 1919; Kid Ory, trombone; at various times—Johnny Dodds, clarinet; Ed Garland, bass; Mutt Carey, cornet; Lawrence Duhé, clarinet; Theodore Bonner, sax; Fred Washington, piano; Sidney Bechet, clarinet; Albert Nicholas, clarinet; King Oliver, cornet; Louis Armstrong, cornet; organized new band in Los Angeles (1944) for the Orson Wells radio show on CBS network for Standard Oil—Kid Ory, trombone; Mutt Carey, trumpet; Ed Garland, bass; Bud Scott, guitar; Jimmy Noone, clarinet; Buster Wilson, pianist; Zutty Singleton, drums; Jimmy Noone died and was replaced by Wade Whaley, cornet.

OSBORN, DAVID ROMAINE (DAVE)

b. 1941 Great Barrington, Massachusetts. Singer and songwriter. Attended schools in Hillsdale, N.Y.; wrote "Little Darlin' " (1959), "Shake It," "Please Say No," "Cryin'," "You're Gone," "You Treat Me Mean."

OSBORNE, BOBBY VAN

b. 1931 Hyden, Kentucky.
Tenor. The "Osborne Brothers," trio of Bob and Sonny Osborne and Benny Birchfield; started singing (1953) on radio stations in Knoxville, Tenn., Detroit, Mich., Wheeling, West Va.; joined by Benny (1959); albums—*Bluegrass Instrumentals, Cuttin' Grass Osborne Brothers Style, Favorite Hymns, Modern Sounds of Bluegrass Music, Up This Hill and Down, Up to Date and Down to Earth, Voices in Bluegrass.*

OSBORNE, JIMMY

b. 1923 Winchester, Kentucky, d. 1957 Louisville, Kentucky. Singer and songwriter. Wrote "Song of Kathy Fiscus."

OSBORNE, SONNY

b. 1937 Hyden, Kentucky.
Baritone. Joined with his brother Bob, and later Benny Birchfield, as the "Osborne Brothers"; at the 1971 Country Music Association awards in Nashville, Tenn., they won the title of the Group of the Year; sang in the White House for President and Mrs. Nixon (1973).

OSGOOD, GEORGE LAURIE

b. 1844 Chelsea, Massachusetts, d. 1922 Godalming, England. Singer, conductor, composer, teacher, and writer. Composed "My Little Woman"; organized and conducted the Boston Singers' Society (1890); wrote a *Guide to the Art of Singing* (1874).

OSSOLI, SARAH MARGARET (FULLER)

b. 1810 Cambridgeport, Massachusetts, d. 1850 at sea. Hymnist. Edited the *Dial* (1840); married the Marchese Ossoli in Rome (1847); lost in a shipwreck off New York City (1850); wrote "Jesus, a Child His Course Began," which appeared in the *Christian Union Hymnal.*

OSTERBERG, JIM ("IGGY STOOGE")

b. (?).
Drummer. Known as "Iggy Stooge"; leader of the Stooges, psychedelic rock band; started at Ann Arbor, Michigan (1968), college dropouts; later teamed up with James Williamson, guitarist and songwriter; toured England (1971-72); albums—*Stooges, Funhouse.*

OSTINELLI, SOPHIE HENRIETTE HEWITT

b. (?), d. 1846.
Organist and singer. Her husband was Louis Ostinelli, music publisher in Boston (1824-25).

O'SULLIVAN, DENIS

b. 1868 San Francisco, California, d. 1908 Columbus, Ohio. Baritone. Studied with Talbo and others; debut in concert (1895); in opera with Carl Rosa Company; sang title role in Stanford's *Shamus O'Brien* (1896) in England and America.

O'SULLIVAN, GILBERT

b. 1947 Ireland.
Singer. Born Raymond O'Sullivan; named changed by his promoter Gordon Mills; album—*Gilbert O'Sullivan Himself;* no. 1 single hit in the U.S. "Alone Again (Naturally)" (1972).

OUDIN, EUGENE (ESPERANCE)

b. 1858 New York City, d. 1894 London, England. Baritone, pianist, and composer.

OUSLEY, HAROLD LOMAX

b. 1929 Chicago, Illinois.
Tenor saxist. With Miles Davis in late 1950s; toured Europe in 1960s; in Paris with Clark Terry; in concert at Jazz Vespers, St. Peter's Church, New York City (1972).

OVERTON, HALL F.

b. 1920 Bangor, Michigan, d. 1972.
Composer and teacher. Studied piano; taught at Juilliard after 1960; works—*Symphony for Strings* (1956), *Second Symphony* (1962), *Dialogues for Chamber Orchestra* (1964, commissioned by Clarion Orchestra and performed on State Department sponsored tour of Soviet Russia).

OWENS, ALVIS E., JR. ("BUCK")

b. 1929 Sherman, Texas.
Popular composer. Joined Bill Woods' band in Bakersfield, Calif. (1950); later formed his own band, The Buckaroos; wrote "Excuse Me (I Think I've Got a Heartache)" (1960, with Harlan Howard); also with Howard—"Foolin' Around" and "Under the Influence of Love" (1961), "Love's Gonna Live Here" (1963), "I Don't Care" and "My Heart Skips a Beat" (1964), "Together Again" (1964), "Think of Me" (1966, with D. Rich), "Open Your Heart" (1966).

OWENS, BONNIE

b. 1933 Blanchard, Oklahoma.
Singer. Sang on station KTYL, Mesa, Arizona, with her husband, Buck Owens; later divorced; sang in Bakersfield, Calif.; married Merle Haggard; their LP record *Just Between the Two of Us* (1965) contained original songs written by them; her other records are "Hi-Fi to Cry By," "Lead Me On," "Philadelphia Lawyer," "That Little Boy of Mine."

OWENS, JAMES ROBERT

b. 1943 New York City.
Black trumpeter and flügelhorn player. With Newport Youth Band, Slide Hampton, Charles Mingus, Herbie Mann and others in 1960s.

OXFORD, VERNON

b. 1941 near Rogers, Arkansas.
Singer. Leader of the Tonemasters.

OZARK QUARTET *see* HENRY T. SLAUGHTER

OZAWA, SEIJI

b. 1935.
Conductor. Studied with Leonard Bernstein and was his protege; conductor of San Francisco Symphony Orchestra.

P

PACHE, JOSEPH

b. 1861 Friedland, Czechoslovakia, d. 1926 Baltimore, Maryland. Director. Studied at Royal Akademy, Munich, and Scharwenka Conservatory; founded an oratorio society in New York (1903); director of oratorio society in Baltimore after 1904.

PACHELBELL, CHARLES THEODOR

b. 1690 Nurenberg, Germany, d. 1750 Charleston, South Carolina. Organist. Came to Boston about 1730; became organist of Trinity Church, Newport, R.I. (1733); in 1737 gave a benefit concert in Charleston, S.C., then became organist at St. Philip's Church there in 1738; wrote *Magnificat*, for two choirs and organ.

PACK, MARSHALL THOMAS

b. 1922 Belton, South Carolina.
Singer and songwriter. Attended schools in Pelzer, S.C., and Clinton, S.C.; wrote "Say It Now," "My Precious Old Dad," "Home Is Where I Want to Be," "Mother Is Old," "Precious Love," "The Best Is Yet to Come."

PADEREWSKI, IGNACE JAN

b. 1860 Kurilovka, Poland, d. 1941 New York City. Famous pianist. Studied at Warsaw Conservatory, and in Berlin and Vienna; taught at the Warsaw Conservatory (1878-83); toured Europe, America and the world; elected Premier of Poland (1919); toured America again in 1922; composed the opera *Manru* (Dresden, 1901, and the Metropolitan Opera), opera *Sakuntala* (text—C. Mendes), *Symphony to Revolution of 1864* (Boston Symphony, 1909), *Second Symphony* (1912), *Chants du voyageur* (a violin sonata), and numerous other works.

PAFF, MICHAEL

b. (?), d. ca. 1810 New York City.
Music publisher. John and Michael Paff were music publishers in New York City (1799-1810), then John Paff (1811-14); among their publications were "The Willow" (1799, J.L. Dussek), "Myra of the Vale" (1799, J. Bayley), "The Maid of the Rock" (1799, Charles Dignum), "The Beggar Boy" (1802, J.D. Winter), "Emma" (1802, John Worgan), "Crazy Henry to Crazy Jane" (1802, T. Welsh), "The Sweet Little Girl of the Lakes" (ca. 1803, W. Ware).

PAGE, NATHANIEL CLIFFORD

b. 1866 San Francisco, California, d. 1956 Philadelphia, Pennsylvania. Composer. Pupil of E.S. Kelley; music editor in New York after 1895; composed an opera, *The First Lieutenant* (1889); orchestral suites, piano pieces, songs.

PAGE, ORAN ("HOT LIPS")

b. 1908 Dallas, Texas, d. 1954 New York City. Black trumpeter. Played in the Count Basie and Artie Shaw orchestras.

PAGE, PATTI

b. 1927 Claremore, Oklahoma.
Singer. Raised in Tulsa, Okla.; had her own show on a Tulsa radio station; Jack Rael, a bandleader, heard her sing and became her manager; appeared on the "Breakfast Club" show, Chicago; promoted the "Tennessee Waltz"; later appeared on many guest shows.

PAGE, RONNIE

b. 1938 Mulkeytown, Illinois.
Tenor. Member of the Oak Ridge Quartet, Rangers Trio, and Chuck Wagon Gang.

PAGE 7, THE *see* WALTER PAGE CAVANAUGH

PAGE, WALTER SYLVESTER

b. 1900 Gallatin, Missouri, d. 1957 New York City. Black double bass player. Played in Count Basie's band (1935-43 and 1946-48).

PAICH, MARTIN LOUIS

b. 1925 Oakland, California.
Pianist, arranger, and composer. Arranger for Dinah Shore, Andy Williams, Mel Torme, Ray Charles, Sammy Davis, Jr., Lena Horne and others; arranged and composed works for the Los Angeles Neophonic Orchestra.

PAINE, JOHN KNOWLES

b. 1839 Portland, Maine, d. 1906 Cambridge, Massachusetts. Composer. Music teacher and composer, and became professor of music at Harvard in 1873; composed "The Centennial Hymn" (w. J.G. Whittier), conducted by Theodore Thomas at the opening of the Centennial in Philadelphia (1876); composed a cantata, *Christmas Ode to the Nativity* (ca. 1868, w. John Milton); with Uzziah C. Burnap, he was musical editor of *Hymns and Songs of Praise* (1874).

PAINE, THOMAS (ROBERT TREAT)

b. 1773 Taunton, Massachusetts, d. 1811 Boston, Massachusetts. Lyricist. Born Thomas Paine, son of Robert Treat Paine, a signer of the Declaration of Independence; changed his name to Robert Treat Paine (1801); wrote the lyrics "Rise Columbia" (1796, m. "Rule Brittannica"—Thomas A. Arne), "Adams and Liberty" (1798, m. "Anacreon in Heaven"—Joseph S. Smith, "To Arms, Columbia" (1799, m. P.A. von Hagen, Jr.), "Rule New England" (1800, m. F. Schaffer, another tune by Francis Mallet).

PALEY, THOMAS

b. 1928 New York City.
Singer and banjoist. Graduated City College of New York (1950), Yale (M.A., 1952, later Ph.D.); taught math at the University of Connecticut at Storrs; original member of the "New Lost City Ramblers" (1958) with Mike Seeger and John Cohen; later he left the group and was replaced by Tracy Schwarz.

PALLISER, ESTHER WALTERS

b. 1872 Philadelphia, Pennsylvania, d. (?).
Soprano. Daughter of B. Frank Walters, organist at St. Luke's Church, Philadelphia (1868-84); she sang in Philadelphia (1885-95) and later in Europe.

PALMER, EARL C., SR.

b. 1924 New Orleans, Louisiana.
Drummer. Studied at Gruenwald's School of Music in New Orleans; with Buddy Collette, Red Callender, Benny Carter and others.

PALMER, HORATIO RICHMOND

b. 1834 Sherburne, New York, d. 1907 Park Hill-on-Hudson, New York. Composer. Educated at Rushford Academy of Music, New York City, later in Berlin and Florence; published the musical magazine *Concordia* (Chicago, 1861-74), then headed the Church Choral Union, New York City; composed the tune "Vincent" for "Lord, for Tomorrow and Its Needs" (w. Sybil F. Partridge), music for "Come, Sinner, Come" (1878, w. W.E. Witter), "Triumph By and By" (w. C.B. Blackall), "Oh Galilee, Sweet Galilee" (1874, w. Robert Morris), the anthem "All My Heart This Night Rejoices" (ca. 1894).

PALMER, PHOEBE

b. 1807, d. 1874.
Hymnist. Wife of Walter C. Palmer and mother of Phoebe Palmer Knapp; wrote "Blessed Bible, How I Love Thee," "The Cleansing Stream" (m. Mrs. Knapp), "Welcome to Glory" (m. Mrs. Knapp, appeared in *The Revivalist*, 1868), and "O When Shall I Sweep Through the Gates," which appeared in Ira D. Sankey's *Songs and Solos* (1878).

PALMER, RAY

b. 1808 Little Compton, Rhode Island, d. 1887 Newark, New Jersey. Hymnist. Taught in a school for girls in New York City and later in New Haven, Conn.; graduated from Yale (1830) and became a Congregational minister in Bath, Maine, for fifteen years and in Albany, N.Y. for fifteen years; retired in 1878 to live in Newark; wrote the hymns "My Faith Looks Up to Thee" (1831, m. Lowell Mason) and "Come, Holy Ghost, in Love" (1859, m. Mason). Mason asked Palmer to furnish him with some verses for a hymn book he was about to publish, and Palmer did so. Several days later Mason met Palmer on a street in Boston and said to him: "Mr. Palmer, you may live many years and do many things, but I think you will be best known to posterity as the author of 'My Faith Looks Up to Thee.' "

PALMER, ROBERT M.

b. 1915 Syracuse, New York.
Composer. Graduated Eastman School of Music, Rochester, N.Y.; awarded MacDowell Colony Fellowship; won American Academy of Arts and Letters cash award; composed *Poem* (for violin and small orchestra, Rochester Civic Orchestra under Hanson, with John Celantano, soloist, 1938), a symphony, chamber works, songs.

PALMER, ROLAND FORD

b. 1891 London, England.
Hymnist. Educated at Grove School, Lakefield, Ontario; Peterborough Collegiate Institute, and Trinity College, Toronto (1916); served as a novice in the Society of St. John the Evangelist, Cambridge, Mass., and as superior of the society's house in San Francisco; in 1927 sent to Canada to open a house there; wrote the hymn "Sing of Mary Pure and Lowly" (1938) based on an earlier

anonymous poem, 1914 (tune "Pleading Saviour" from the *Plymouth Collection*, 1855).

PALMER, ROY

b. 1892 New Orleans, Louisiana, d. 1964. Jazz trombonist. Played in Lawrence Duhé's group at the Dreamland Cafe in New Orleans in the 1920s.

PANIZZA, ETTORE

b. 1875 Buenos Aires, Argentina, d. 1967. Conductor. Studied at the Milan Conservatory; conductor in Italian theaters after 1899; at Covent Garden, London (1907-13); at La Scala, Milan (1916); at the Metropolitan Opera, New York, after 1934 as conductor of Italian works; composed an opera, *Il fidanzeto del mare* (Buenos Aires, 1897), *Medioevo latino* (Geneva, 1900), *Aurora* (Buenos Aires, 1908).

PANKEY, AUBREY

b. 1905 Pittsburgh, Pennsylvania, d. 1971 East Berlin, East Germany. Black concert singer. Studied in Paris; returned to the U.S. during World War II, but settled in Paris again in 1948; expelled from Paris in 1953 for defending Ethel and Julius Rosenberg, convicted atom bomb spies; went to East Germany where he sang Negro spirituals and classical music; killed in an automobile accident.

PARAY, PAUL

b. 1886 Treport, France.
Conductor. Studied at Paris Conservatory; Prix de Rome winner; conducted Lamoureux Concerts, Paris, after 1931; conducted Detroit Symphony after 1952.

PARENTEAU, ZOEL

b. 1883 Northampton, Massachusetts, d. 1972 Englewood, New Jersey. Composer and arranger. Music director of radio station KDKA in Pittsburgh; wrote stage scores for *The Amber Empress* and *Follow the Girl*, also songs for *Kiki*, the anthems "The Lord Is My Shepherd," "I See His Blood Upon a Rose," "Do I Love Thee."

PARENTI, ANTHONY

b. 1900 New Orleans, Louisiana, d. 1972 Queens, New York City. Clarinetist and saxist. Played with Ben Pollack, Ted Lewis, Dukes of Dixieland and others; also led own combos in New York City.

PARHAM, CHARLES VALDEZ ("TRUCK")

b. 1913 Chicago, Illinois.
Double bass player. Played in Jimmie Lunceford's band (1942-47).

PARIS, JACKIE

b. 1926 Nutley, New Jersey.
Singer and guitarist. Played with Lionel Hampton and others; married singer Anne Marie Moss, later vocal team in New York City night clubs.

PARISH, MITCHELL

b. 1900 Shreveport, Louisiana.
Lyricist. Attended Columbia University and New York University; became a staff writer for a New York publisher (1919); wrote "Star Dust" (1927, m. Hoagy Carmichael), "Deep Purple" (1939, m. Billy de Rose, 1934), with Irving Mills, "Organ Grinder's Swing" (m. Will Hudson).

PARK, JOHN EDGAR

b. 1879 Belfast, North Ireland, d. 1956. Hymnist. Educated at New College, Edinburgh, Royal University, Dublin, and Princeton Theological Seminary; pastor of churches in New York and Massachusetts; became president of Wheaton College, Norton, Mass. (1926); wrote the hymn "We Would See Jesus, Lo! His Star Is Shining" (tune "Cushman," Rev. H.B. Turner).

PARK, ROSWELL

b. 1807 Lebanon, Connecticut, d. 1869 Chicago, Illinois. Hymnist. Educated at Union College, Schenectady, N.Y., and West Point Military Academy; served in the Corps of Engineers, U.S. Army, then was professor of chemistry at the University of Pennsylvania; ordained an Episcopal minister and served as president of Racine College, Wisconsin (1852-63); then established a school in Chicago; wrote the hymn "Jesus Spreads His Banner O'er Us" (1836, tune "Autumn," arranged from F.H. Barthelemon).

PARKER, CHARLES CHRISTOPHER ("BIRD")

b. 1920 Kansas City, Missouri, d. 1955 New York City. Black alto saxophonist. Joined Dizzy Gillespie in making recordings; cofounder with Gillespie of the "bop" movement; Parker became one of the most imitated musicians of the 1940s and 1950s; played at Minton's Playhouse, Harlem, New York City during the 1940s.

PARKER, EDWIN POND

b. 1836 Castine, Maine, d. 1926 Hartford, Connecticut. Composer. Educated at Bowdoin College, Brunswick, Maine, and Bangor Theological Seminary; became a Congregational minister and served the Center Church, Hartford, Conn. for half a century; wrote the hymn "Lord, As We Thy Name Profess" (1890, tune, "Savannah"); also arranged the tune "Mercy" by L.M. Gottschalk for "Softly Now the Light of Day" (w. G.W. Doane); wrote the words and music "Master, No Offering" (1888).

PARKER, GEORGE ALBERT

b. 1856 Kewanee, Illinois, d. 1939.
Pianist, organist, and teacher. Studied under Clarence Eddy and Frederic Grant Gleason of Chicago; also at Royal Conservatory, Stuttgart, Germany; taught at Syracuse University, Syracuse, New York after 1882.

PARKER, HENRY TAYLOR

b. 1867 Boston, Massachusetts, d. there 1934. Music critic. Critic of the *Boston Transcript* after 1905 until his death.

PARKER, HERMAN ("JUNIOR")

b. 1927 West Memphis, Arkansas.
Black harmonica player. Toured with Sonny Boy Williamson; played with Howlin' Wolf (1949); first recorded in Memphis (1952); hit record, "Feelin' Good" (1954); toured with Willie Mae Thornton and Johnny Ace; recorded "Annie Get Your Yo-Yo" (1962).

PARKER, HORATIO WILLIAM

b. 1863 Auburndale, Massachusetts, d. 1919 Cedarhurst, New York. Noted composer and organist. Studied under Stephen A. Emory, John Orth, and George W. Chadwick, and in Munich (1882-85); taught in Garden City, N.Y. (1885-93); wrote oratorio *Hora Novissima* (1893); awarded M.A. by Yale; professor of music there (1894-1919); his *A Wanderer's Psalm* presented at Hereford Festival (1900); Mus.D. from Cambridge University, England (1902); "A Star Song" won the Paderewski Prize (1901); won prizes for operas *Mona* by Metropolitan Opera House, and *Fairyland* by the National Federation of Women's Clubs.

PARKER, JAMES CUTLER DUNN

b. 1828 Boston, Massachusetts, d. 1916 Brookline, Massachusetts. Composer. Educated at Harvard (1848), studied law, then music in Leipzig, Germany (1851-54); organist-choirmaster at Trinity Church, Boston (1864-91); published *A Manual of Harmony* (1855 and 1870); wrote the cantata *Redemption Hymn* (1877) and the oratorio *Life of Man* (1895).

PARKER, LEO

b. 1925 Washington, D.C., d. 1962 New York City. Baritone saxist. Played with Benny Carter, Billy Eckstine, and Dizzy Gillespie in 1940s; died of a heart attack; album—*Let Me Tell You 'bout It.*

PARKER, THEODORE

b. 1810 Lexington, Massachusetts, d. 1860 Florence, Italy. Hymnist. Educated at Harvard and Divinity School (1836); minister of Unitarian Church in West Roxbury, Mass. (1837), Boston (1846-59); several of his hymns appeared in Putnam's *Singers and Songs of the Liberal Faith* (Boston, 1875); died of tuberculosis.

PARKINSON, ELIZABETH ("PARKINA")

b. 1882 Kansas City, Missouri, d. 1922 Colorado Springs, Colorado. Soprano. Pupil of Mrs. Lawton in Kansas City and others; debut in Paris (1902); Covent Garden, London (1904-07); toured Australia.

PARKINSON, WILLIAM

b. 1774 Frederick County, Maryland, d. 1848. Hymnist. Became a Baptist minister (1798); wrote "Come, Dear Brethren in the Saviour" ("Prayer Meeting"), which appeared in his *A Selection of Hymns and Sabbath Songs* (1809, known as *Parkinson's Collection*) and later in the *Christian Union.*

PARLAN, HORACE LOUIS

b. 1931 Pittsburgh, Pennsylvania.
Pianist. With Charles Mingus (1957-60); with Booker Ervin, George Tucker, Roland Kirk and others in 1960s; later formed own trio; album—*Up and Down.*

PARLOW, KATHLEEN M.

b. 1890 Calgary, Alberta, Canada, d. 1963. Violinist. Her parents took her to California in 1895; pupil there of Conrad and Holmes; debut at age six; appeared with London Symphony at fifteen; pupil of Auer; toured after 1907.

PARRY, JOSEPH

b. 1841 Merthyr Tydfil, Wales, d. 1903 Cartref, Penarth. Composer. His family came to Danville, Pa. (1854), where he became an organist in 1865; gave concerts in N.Y., Ohio, and Pennsylvania, then went to England where he received his B.Mus. from Cambridge (1871); taught music in Danville (1871-73), but in 1881 returned to Wales to teach at University College, Cardiff; composed the tune "Aberystwyth" (1879), two oratorios *Emmanuel* (1880) and *Saul of Tarsus* (1892).

PARSONS, ALBERT ROSS

b. 1847 Sandusky, Ohio, d. 1933 Mt. Kisco, New York. Organist and teacher. Studied with F.K. Ritter in New York, then in Leipzig and Berlin; organist at Fifth Avenue Presbyterian Church, N.Y. (1885); taught at Metropolitan College of Music (1885); president of Music Teachers' National Association (1890); president of American College of Musicians (1893-95), when it closed; composed vocal quartets, songs.

PARSONS, ERNEST J.

b. 1882 Revelstoke, England.
Composer. In 1906 settled in Morristown, New Jersey, and became a master plumber; served as tenor and assistant organist at St. Peter's Church, Morristown, and carillonneur at Princeton, N.J.; composed the tune "Sturgis" (1936, "Christ Leads Me Through No Darker Rooms," w. Richard Baxter).

PARTCH, HARRY

b. 1901 Oakland, California, d. 1974.
Composer. Has designed new instruments; formulated new theory of music to a forty-three-tone scale; wrote *By the Rivers of Babylon* (1930), *Barstow* (1941), *The Letter* (1943), *U.S. Highball* (1943), *Intrusions* (1949-59), *Plectra and Percussion Dances* (1949-52), *Oedipus* (1951), *The Bewitched* (1955), *Windsong* (1958), *Rotate the Body in All Its Planes* (1961), *Water, Water* (1962), *And on the Seventh Day Petals Fell in Petaluma* (1963-64).

PARTON, DOLLY REBECCA

b. 1946 near Sevierville, Tennessee.
Singer. Attended schools in Locust Ridge, Tenn.; with Porter Wagoner syndicated TV Show; wrote "Dumb Blonde," "Something Fishy."

PARTY TIMERS, THE

Featured Wanda Jackson. (*See* Wanda Jackson)

PASATIERI, THOMAS

b. 1943.
Composer. Wrote the opera, *The Trial of Mary Lincoln* (libretto—Anne Howard Bailey) presented on TV Channel 13 in 1972, with mezzo-soprano Elaine Bonazzi singing the role of Mary Lincoln and baritone Wayne Turnage as Robert Lincoln; based on the insanity trial of Mrs. Lincoln in 1875.

PASMORE, HENRY BICKFORD

b. 1857 Jackson, Wisconsin, d. 1944 San Francisco, California. Organist, composer, and teacher. Wrote *A Northern Romance*, "My Love Dwelt in a Northern Land."

PASS, JOE

b. 1929 New Brunswick, New Jersey.
Guitarist. Born Joseph Anthony Passalaqua; toured with Tony Pastor; later arrested on a narcotics charge, later spent three and a half years in a U.S. Public Health Service Hospital in Fort Worth, Texas; restored to health and productive activity by joining the Synanon Foundation in Santa Monica, Calif.; albums—*Brasamba, Catch Me, Simplicity, Twelve-String Guitar.*

PASTERNACK, JOSEPH A.

b. 1881 Czentochowa, Poland, d. 1940 Chicago, Illinois. Conductor. Studied at the Warsaw Conservatory; violist in the Metropolitan Opera (1909-10); conducted Century Opera Company, Philadelphia Philharmonic, Boston "Pops" (1916); conductor in radio programming for NBC after 1927.

PASTOR, ANTONIO (TONY)

b. 1837 New York City, d. 1908 Elmhurst, New York. Impresario. Opened his first variety (vaudeville) theater in Paterson, N.J. (1865); opened his famous Music Hall on 14th Street in New York City in 1881; all the great variety artists appeared there—Ben Harney played his piano rags; singers were Bonnie Thornton, Lottie Gilson, May Irwin, Sophie Tucker; and Irving Berlin plugging the songs of Harry Von Tilzer.

PASTOR, TONY

b. 1907 Middletown, Connecticut, d. 1969. Singer, tenor saxist, and bandleader. Born Antonio Pestritto; played in John Cavallaro's band (1927); with Artie Shaw (1936-39); formed his own band (1940); played in the Blue Room of the Hotel Lincoln, New York City; Rosemary Clooney sang in his band (1947); disbanded and formed small group (1957) which included his two sons, vocalists Guy Pastor and Tony Pastor, Jr.

PASTORIUS, FRANZ DANIEL

b. 1651 Germany, d. 1719 Germantown, Pennsylvania. Lyricist. Came to Philadelphia (1683); wrote "Come Corinna."

PATHFINDERS, THE *see* DICK FLOOD

PATTERSON, DON

b. 1936 Columbus, Ohio.
Black organist. Played with Sonny Stitt, Gene Ammons, Wes Montgomery, Kenny Burrell and others; later on his own; albums—*Best of Don Patterson, Boppin' and Burnin', Boss Men, Brothers 4, Exciting New Organ, Four Dimensions, Funk You, Hip Cake Walk, Mellow Soul, Oh Happy Day, Opus De Don, Patterson's People, Satisfaction, Soul Happening.*

PATTERSON, FRANKLIN PEALE

b. 1871 Philadelphia, Pennsylvania, d. (?).
Composer. Descendant of Charles and Rembrant Peale; studied with Stoll, Schmidt, Clark, and Fach; also at Munich Conservatory of Music; his *Beggar's Love* (1918) won Chamber Opera Guild Prize; *The Echo,* one-act opera (1920), produced by National Federation of Music Clubs; *Overture to Opera* "Mountain Blood" (1925) given by Cleveland, Rochester, and San Diego orchestras.

PATTERSON, JIMMY DALE ("PAT")

b. 1935 Lewisburg, West Virginia.
Singer and songwriter. Leader of the Hometowners after 1960; wrote "Lonesome Soldier," "The Letter" (1968), "Just a Minute."

PATTERSON, SAM

b. 1881 St. Louis, Missouri.
Black singer, dancer, and lyricist. Formed a singing and tap dancing duo with Louis Chauvin in St. Louis and toured the states; joined the Musical Spillers, variety act (1906); wrote "The Moon Is Shining in the Skies" (1903, m. Louis Chauvin), the musical revue *Dandy Coon* (1903, m. Chauvin).

PATTI, ADELINA

b. 1843 Madrid, Spain, d. 1919 Wales.
Noted soprano. Born Adela Juana Maria Patti; both parents were singers; brought to New York as a child; New York debut at age seven at a concert directed by Max Maretzek; sang in Maurice Strakosch's concerts (1851-55); studied voice with Strakosch and with her half-brother Ettore Barili and piano with her sister, soprano Carlotta Patti (1835-1889); toured the West Indies with L.M. Gottschalk; New York opera debut (1859) as Lucia; Covent Garden (1861); Paris (1862); sang at Covent Garden, London, for twenty-three years; extremely successful on European, North and South American tours; made numerous tours of the United States; farewell concert in London (1906); her singing career spanned fifty-six years; married three times; second husband (1886) was tenor Nicolini (Ernest Nicolas, 1834-1898).

PATTI, CARLO

b. 1842 Madrid, Spain, d. 1873 St. Louis, Missouri. Violinist. Brother of Adelina Patti, world-famed opera singer.

PATTISON, JOHN NELSON

b. 1845 Niagara Falls, New York, d. 1905 New York City. Pianist. Pupil of Liszt and others; toured U.S. as pianist with Parepa Rosa; composed *Niagara* (symphony for orchestra and military band), and chamber music.

PATTISON, LEE MARION

b. 1890 Grand Rapids, Wisconsin.
Pianist and composer. Graduated New England Conservatory, Boston, with honors; debut in Boston (1913); toured in duo-piano recitals with Guy Maier; also in double concertos with American orchestras; composed piano pieces, songs.

PATTON, JOHN ("BIG JOHN")

b. 1936 Kansas City, Missouri.
Black organist. Played piano as accompanist to Lloyd Price; first recorded in 1963; albums—*Along Came John, Got a Good Thing Goin', Let 'em Roll, Oh Baby, That Certain Feeling, Understanding, Way I Feel.*

PAUL, LES

b. 1906 Waukesha, Wisconsin.
Singer and guitarist. Born Lester Polsfuss; music director of station WJJD, Chicago; albums—with the Les Paul Trio—*Guitar Artistry of Les Paul* and *Les Paul Now*; with Mary Ford—*Fabulous Les Paul and Mary Ford, Hits of Les and Mary.*

PAUPERS, THE (Canadian rock group)

PAUR, MARIA BURGER

b. 1862 Gengenbach, Germany, d. 1899 New York City. Pianist. Studied at Stuttgart Conservatory and with Leschetizky and Essipoff in Vienna; married Emil Paur, conductor of the Boston Symphony Orchestra (1893-1906).

PAVAROTTI, LUCIANO

b. 1935 Modena, Italy.
Tenor. Bel canto opera singer; debut (1961) in Teatro Municipale in *Reggio Emilia*; came to America and sang with Joan Sutherland in *Lucia di Lammermoor* in Miami; toured

Australia with Joan and her husband, conductor Richard Bonynge; Metropolitan Opera debut in *La Boheme* (1968); sang with Beverly Sills in Bellini's *I Puritani* in Philadelphia (1972); at the Metropolitan Opera, New York City (1972) with Sutherland in Donizetti's *Daughter of the Regiment.*

PAXTON, TOM

b. 1937 Chicago, Illinois.
Popular composer. Raised in Bristol, Oklahoma; graduated the University of Oklahoma, Norman; served in the army; sang in night clubs in New York City; wrote "The Marvelous Toy," "Ramblin' Boy" (sung by the Weavers at Carnegie Hall, 1963), "Bottle of Wine," "Every Time," "The Man Who Built the Bridges," "Brand New Baby," "The Willing Conscript," "Whose Garden Was This?"

PAYCHECK, JOHNNY

b. 1941 Ohio.
Singer and songwriter. Wrote "Don't Start Counting on Me" (1964), "The Girl They Talk About," "A-11" (1965); albums—*Country Soul, Gospel Time, Jukebox Charlie, Lovin' Machine, Johnny Paycheck at Carnegie Hall, Johnny Paycheck's Greatest Hits, Wherever You Are.*

PAYNE, CECIL MC KENZIE

b. 1922 Brooklyn, New York.
Black saxist. Played baritone and alto saxophone; with Dizzy Gillespie, Randy Weston and others; toured Europe with Lionel Hampton (1963-64); with Randy Weston at Paris Jazz Festivals (1964 and 1966).

PAYNE, DONALD RAY

b. 1933 Amarillo, Texas.
Bass player. With Herbie Mann, Tony Bennett and others; also led his own trio in New York City.

PAYNE, JIMMY

b. 1936 Leachville, Arkansas.
Singer and guitarist. Raised in Malden, Missouri; sang in St. Louis night clubs; served in the army; his records are "Tallahassee," "Woman, Woman—What Does It Take to Keep a Woman Like You Satisfied," "Worst That Love Can Give," "Ladder to the Sky," "Every Pretty Girl."

PAYNE, JOHN HOWARD

b. 1791 New York City, d. 1852 Tunis, North Africa. Famous librettist and singer. While in London he wrote the libretto for the opera *Clari* (1823, m. H.R. Bishop), of which "Home, Sweet Home" was part of the score; it was a great success in London, and then throughout the United States. Payne was writing a history of the tribal customs and legends of the Cherokee Indians and visited Chief John Ross near Spring Place, Georgia, in 1835, when Payne was arrested by the Georgia Guard. He was accused of sedition and imprisoned for twelve days in a log cabin there. He was tried and acquitted in the Chief Joseph Vann House near Spring Place. In 1850 Payne was a guest of President Millard Fillmore in the White House for a special Jenny Lind concert. At the end of the concert, she turned to Payne and sang to him, "Home, Sweet Home." On June 28, 1851, the U.S. steam frigate *Mississippi* arrived in Tunis bringing the new Consul General, John Howard Payne.

PAYNE, LEON ROGER

b. 1917 Alba, Texas.
Singer and one-man band. Blind from childhood; attended the Texas School for the Blind (1924-35); played the piano, organ, guitar, trombone, and drums; debut on radio station KWET, Palestine, Texas (1935); joined Bob Wills and his Texas Playboys (1938); records—"Lost Highway," "Blue Side of Lonesome," "Things Have Gone to Pieces," "I Love You Because," "Doorstep to Heaven."

PAYNE, PERCIVAL ("SONNY")

b. 1926 New York City.
Drummer. Played in Count Basie's band; also with Frank Sinatra; led his own trio.

PCHELLAS, JOHN F. W.

b. ca. 1795, d. after 1835.
Composer, teacher, and publisher. Teacher and publisher in Philadelphia (1820-24) and in New York City (1825-35); composed *Three Sonatas for Pianoforte and Violin* (1820), "Mary I Believ'd Thee True" (ca. 1820, w. Thomas Moore).

PEABODY, WILLIAM BOURNE OLIVER

b. 1799 Exeter, New Hampshire, d. 1847 Springfield, Massachusetts. Hymnist. Educated at Harvard (1817), Cambridge Divinity School (1819); pastor of Unitarian Church, Springfield, Mass. (1820-47); his hymns appeared in his *Poetical Catechism for the Young* (1823) and the *Springfield Collection of Hymns for Sacred Worship* (1835) which he edited.

PEACHES AND HERB (black soul group)

Herb Fame and Francine Barker; former member—Marlene Mack; first recorded in 1967; albums—*Let's Fall in Love, For Your Love, Golden Duets, Peaches and Herb's Greatest Hits.*

PEACOCK, GARY

b. 1935 Burley, Idaho.
Bass player. Served in army in Germany, played piano in army band (1956); later with Tony Scott, Bud Shank, Jimmy Woods, Terry Gibbs, Paul Bley and others; with Albert Ayler and Don Cherry in Europe (1965).

PEANUT BUTTER CONSPIRACY (blues-rock group)

Al Brackett, bass; Bill Wolff, guitar; John Merrill, rhythm guitar; Sandi Robinson, vocals; Jim Voight, drums; former member—Lance Fent; started in California in 1967; albums—*The Peanut Butter Conspiracy Is Spreading, The Great Conspiracy.*

PEARCE, STEPHEN AUSTEN

b. 1836 Brompton, Kent, England, d. 1900 Jersey City, New Jersey. Organist. Received D.Mus., Oxford, England (1864); came to New York City (1872); organist in churches there.

PEARL, MINNIE

b. 1912 Centerville, Tennessee.
Singer and comedienne. Born Sarah Ophelia Colley; known as the "Queen of Country Comedy from Grinder's Switch" (which was three miles from her home); attended Ward-Belmont College, Nashville; debut on "Grand Ole Opry," Nashville (1940); albums—*Minnie Pearl, Monologue, How to Catch a Man, Cousin Minnie, Giddyup Go-Answer.*

PEARLS BEFORE SWINE (folk-rock group)

Tom Rapp, vocals and guitar; Jim Bohannon, organ, piano, etc.; Wayne Harley, banjo, autoharp, etc.; Lane Lederer, bass and guitar; group started in Florida; first recorded in 1967; albums—*One Nation Underground, Balaklava, These Things Too.*

PEARSON, COLUMBUS CALVIN, JR. ("DUKE")

b. 1932 Atlanta, Georgia.
Pianist and composer. With John Peck, Donald Byrd and others; with Golson-Farmer Jazztet at Newport Jazz Festival (1960); accompanist for Nancy Wilson and Dakota Staton; albums—*Dedication, Honey Buns, Introducing Duke Pearson's Big Band, Now Hear This, The Phantom, Prairie Dog, Right Touch, Sweet Honey Bee, Wahoo.*

PEASE, ALFRED HUMPHRIES

b. 1838 Cleveland, Ohio, d. 1882 St. Louis, Missouri. Pianist and composer. Wrote "Stars of the Summer Night," "Hush Thee, My Baby."

PECK, NAT

b. 1925 New York City.
Trombonist. With Glenn Miller, Don Redman, Roy Eldridge, Coleman Hawkins and others in 1940s; studied at Paris Conservatory after 1950; with various small groups in New York City during 1950s; in France (1958) and in Germany (1962); later in England.

PEEK, EARL H.

b. 1921 Fort Payne, Alabama.
Gospel singer. Presents gospel concerts with the Senators Quartet.

PEEL AND THE LOWER EAST SIDE, DAVID (folk-rock group)

Started in New York City in 1968; first recorded in 1969; albums—*Have a Marijuana, American Revolution.*

PEERCE, JAN

b. 1906 New York City.
Noted tenor. Born Jacob Pearlman; studied violin at age nine; formed a jazz combo in his teens and toured summer camps; soloist at Radio City Music Hall for six years; debut (1937) in Baltimore with Columbia Opera Company as the Duke in *Rigoletto* with Robert Weede in the lead; debut (1941) at the Metropolitan Opera, New York City as Alfredo in *La Traviata*; sang at the Metropolitan with his brother-in-law, Richard Tucker; took the part of Tevye in *Fiddler on the Roof* (December, 1971).

PEERY, ROB ROY

b. 1900 Saga, Japan, d. 1973 Dayton, Ohio. Composer. His parents were missionaries in Japan, and came to Denver, Colorado (1903), then to Atchinson, Kansas; graduated from Midland College (1920, now at Fremont, Nebr.), taught in Omaha, then Lenoir-Rhyne College, Hickory, N.C.; studied at Oberlin Conservatory (Mus.Bac., 1925), and taught at Catawba College, Salisbury, N.C.; in 1931 became chief music critic for the Theodore Presser Company, Philadelphia; composed the tune "Byrd" ("O God Creator, in Whose Hand" w. Harry W. Farrington).

PEIFFER, BERNARD

b. 1922 Epinal, France.
Pianist and bandleader. Came to America (1954); played with various groups in Philadelphia; at Montreal Jazz Festival (1962); became U.S. citizen (1965); organized the Bernard Peiffer Jazz Trio with Al Stauffer (bass player), James Paxson (percussion), Miss Crader (singer).

PELISSIER, VICTOR

b. 1760 France, d. 1820 Philadelphia, Pennsylvania. Composer and French horn virtuoso. Played in Philadelphia (1792); first horn player in Old American Company, New York City (1793); his comic operas produced in New York City—*Edwin and Angelina, or The Banditti* (1796, book—Elihu H. Smith), *The Launch, or Huzzah for the (Frigate) Constitution* (1797, book—John Hodgkinson), *Sterne's Maria, or the Vintage* (book—William Dunlap); also the music for the shows *The Fourth of July, Temple of American Independence; Ariadne Abandoned by Theseus in the Isle of Naxos* (1797); published music in Philadelphia (1811-14), and in New York City (1815-17); went blind; wrote "Ah Why on Quebec's Bloody Plain" (1812), "Allemande" (1812), "Believe Me Sir" (as sung by Miss Arabella Brett), *Hornpipe* (dance), "March to Canada."

PELLETIER, WILFRED

b. 1896 Montreal, P.Q., Canada.
Conductor. Won a Quebec Government scholarship (1914) and studied in Europe; conducted Metropolitan Opera, New York after 1932; also Ravinia in Los Angeles, San Francisco Opera, and Canadian orchestras; married soprano Queena Mario, divorced; then Rose Bampton.

PENA, RALPH RAYMOND

b. 1927 Jarbidge, Nevada.
Bass player and composer. Played with Jimmy Giuffre, Shorty Rogers and others in 1950s; duo with Pete Jolly (1958-62); also with Frank Sinatra; led his own band in Los Angeles; wrote *Serendipity.*

PENFIELD, SMITH NEWELL

b. 1837 Oberlin, Ohio, d. 1920.
Organist, conductor, composer, and teacher. Studied at Leipzig with Moscheles, Papperitz, and Reinecke; then in Paris under Delioux; returned to America and resided in Rochester, N.Y.; later moved to Savannah, Georgia, and established the Savannah Conservatory of Music and the Mozart Club there; received degree of Doctor of Music from the University of New York (1883).

PENNINGTON, LILY MAY

b. 1917 Pilot, Kentucky.
Singer. Attended schools in Clear Branch, Ky., and Walnut, Ky.; with "Renfro Valley Barn Dance" (1939-57); leader of Coon Creek Girls (1937-57); wrote "Little Birdie," "Pretty Polly," "Uncle Doodie," "Lonesome Lulu Lee," "Flower Blooming in the Wildwood."

PENNINGTON, RAY

b. 1933 Clay County, Kentucky.
Singer and songwriter. Sang on TV in Cincinnati, Ohio at age sixteen; formed his own band (1952); wrote "Three Hearts in a Tangle" (1961, Roy Drusky record), "Who's Been Moving the Lawn," "Walking on New Grass" (1966, Kenny Price record), "Happy Tracks" (1967, Kenny Price record).

PENNSYLVANIANS (band) *see* FRED WARING

PENNY, GEORGE BARLOW

b. 1861 Haverstraw, New York, d. 1934.
Organist, conductor, composer, and teacher. Wrote the *Crimson and the Blue.*

PEPPER, ARTHUR EDWARD

b. 1925 Gardena, California.
Jazz saxophonist. With Stan Kenton (1943-52); played alto and tenor saxophones; served time in jail on a narcotics charge; albums—*Gettin' Together, Intensity, Modern Jazz Classics, Art Pepper Meets the Rhythm Section, Smack Up, Surf Ride.*

PERABO, JOHANN ERNST

b. 1845 Weisbaden, Germany, d. 1920 Boston, Massachusetts. Pianist and teacher. His parents brought him to New York in 1853; studied with Moscheles and others; at Leipzig Conservatory; returned to Boston (1865), resided there as a teacher and concert pianist.

PERAHIA, MURRAY

b. 1947 Bronx, New York City.
Pianist. Studied at age four; with Jeanette Haien after age six; won $1,000 Kosciuszko scholarship (1965); debut recital under auspices of Young Concert Artists (1966); majored in conducting at Mannes College of Music, New York City with Carl Bamberger; later taught there; played with Rudolf Serkin and others; concerts at Carnegie Hall, also with the New York Philharmonic (1972).

PERAZA, ARMANDO

b. 1924 Havana, Cuba.
Congo drums and bongo player. With George Shearing Quintet (1954-64); later with Cal Tjader; album—*Wild Thing.*

PERCIFUL, JACK T.

b. 1925 Moscow, Idaho.
Pianist. Played with Harry James after 1958; toured Latin America with James (1961) and Japan (1964).

PERCY, WILLIAM ALEXANDER

b. 1885 Greenville, Mississippi, d. there 1942. Hymnist. Studied at the University of the South, Sewanee, Tenn., and Harvard (LL.B., 1908); practiced law and was a captain in the 37th Division (1918-19); wrote the hymn "They Cast Their Nets in Galilee" (1924, tune "Georgetown"—David Mc. K. Williams).

PEREZ, MANUEL

b. 1879 New Orleans, Louisiana, d. 1946.
Black cornetist, trumpeter, and bandleader. Had his own band in New Orleans; later went to Chicago about 1917.

PERKINS, CARL LEE

b. 1932 Jackson, Tennessee.
Singer. Joined the "Big D Jamboree" in Dallas, Texas; formed his own group; wrote "Blue Suede Shoes" and "Boppin' the Blues" (with C. Griffin); albums—*Introducing Carl Perkins, On Top, Original Golden Hits.*

PERKINS, CHARLES CALLAHAN

b. 1823 Boston, Massachusetts, d. 1886 Windsor, Vermont. Composer and critic. Graduated Harvard University (1843); studied painting in Rome (1843-46); in Paris (1846-49) and composed music there (without training); returned to Boston (1849); president of Handel and Haydn Society (1850); studied in Leipzig under Moscheles (1851); his quartet performed by Mendelssohn Quartette Club (1853); in Europe (1857-69) as painter and sculptor; back in Boston (1869); killed by a runaway horse while driving.

PERKINS, EMILY SWAN

b. 1866 Chicago, Illinois, d. 1941.
Composer. Organized the Hymn Society (1922) and became its corresponding secretary; for many years she lived in Riverdale-on-Hudson, N.Y.; composed the tune "Laufer" (1925, "The Light of God Is Falling," w. L.F. Benson).

PERKINS, HENRY SOUTHWICK

b. 1833 Stockbridge, Vermont, d. 1914.
Conductor and teacher. Studied under his father, a singing teacher; taught at the University of Iowa, Iowa City (1867-69); then at Iowa Academy of Music, Iowa City, for five years; conducted choral societies; edited over thirty singing books; taught sight reading at Chicago Musical College.

PERKINS, JULIUS EDSON

b. 1845 Stockbridge, Vermont, d. 1875 Manchester, England. Bass singer. Studied under Delle Sadie (1867); debut (1869); also studied in Italy; sang in operas; married Marie Roze in London (1874).

PERKINS, LUTHER MONROE

b. 1928 Memphis, Tennessee, d. 1968 Hendersonville, Tennessee. Singer and guitarist. Member of Johnny Cash's Tennessee Three, with Marshall Grant and W.S. Holland; he died of burns.

PERKINS, ORSON

b. 1802 Hartland, Vermont, d. 1882 Taftsville, Vermont. Composer and teacher. Taught singing for over forty years; composed church music.

PERKINS, WALTER

b. 1932 Chicago, Illinois.
Drummer. Played with Ahmad Jamal; formed own combo; with Carmen McRae, Sonny Rollins, Art Farmer, Teddy Wilson and others in 1960s.

PERKINS, WILLIAM OSCAR

b. 1831 Stockbridge, Vermont, d. 1902.
Teacher and compiler. Studied music in Boston; taught voice and harmony; moved to New York City; compiled singing books.

PERKINS, WILLIAM REESE

b. 1924 San Francisco, California.
Piccolo player, flutist, and tenor saxist. Played with Woody Herman and Stan Kenton in 1950s; later with Los Angeles Neophonic Orchestra and others; formed his own quintet; album—*Quietly There.*

PERKINSON, COLERIDGE-TAYLOR

b. 1932 New York City.
Black composer. Studied at Manhattan School of Music (B.A., 1953, master's, 1954), Berkshire Music Center, the Mozarteum, and Nederland Radio Union Hilversum; wrote music for "Song of the Lusitanian Bogey" (w. Peter Weiss), "God Is a Guess What?" (w. Ray McIver), "Man Better Man" (w. Errol Hill), all for Negro Ensemble Company, New York City; associate conductor of the Symphony of New World (1965); wrote *Concerto for Viola and Orchestra,* performed by the

Symphony of the New World; concert piece, *Attitudes*, sung by George Shirley at the Metropolitan Museum of Art, New York City (1964), commissioned by the Ford Foundation.

PEROSSIER, JAMES W.

b. ca. 1785 France, d. after 1822.
Composer, singer, cellist, flutist, guitarist, and teacher. Taught in New York City (1809-15); moved to Charleston, South Carolina; wrote "O Lady Love Awake" (1822, w. William Hall), "Too Late I Staid" (1813).

PERRY, EDWARD BAXTER

b. 1855 Haverhill, Massachusetts, d. 1924 Camden, Maine. Pianist. Blinded when young; pupil of J.W. Hill in Boston, later with Liszt and others; played before the German emperor; toured America and gave over 12,000 concerts in ten years; composed *Loreley* (fantasia), *The Lost Island* (for piano).

PERRY, JULIA

b. 1927 Akron, Ohio.
Black composer. Studied at Westminster Choir School, Princeton, N.J., at Juilliard, at Berkshire Music Center, with Nadia Boulanger in Paris and with Luigi Dallapiccola in Florence, Italy; conducted a series of concerts in Europe sponsored by the U.S. Information Service; wrote *Stabat Mater* (for solo voice and string orchestra, 1951), *A Short Piece for Orchestra* (1952), *The Cask of Amontillado* (performed at Columbia University, New York City, 1954), *Pastoral* (for flute and strings, 1959), *Homunculus, C. F.* (for soprano and percussionists, 1969); her *Violin Sonata* won the Boulanger Grand Prix.

PERRYMAN, RUFUS

b. 1892 Monroe, Louisiana, d. 1973.
Black boogie-woogie pianist. Known as "Speckled Red"; wrote "The Dirty Dozens," the well-known talkin' dirty and insult song.

PERSICHETTI, VINCENT

b. 1915 Philadelphia, Pennsylvania.
Composer. Studied at Combs College of Music, Curtis Institute and the Philadelphia Conservatory (Mus.D.); taught there after 1942; later at Juilliard School of Music, New York City; composed *Dance Overture* (won Juilliard Award, 1943), three piano sonatas (no. 3 won Colorado College Fine Arts Festival award), two string quartets (no. 2, Blue Network Prize, 1945), *The Hollow Men* (for trumpet and string orchestra), three symphonies, chamber music.

PERSINGER, LOUIS

b. 1888 Rochester, Illinois, d. 1967.
Violinist. Pupil of Becker, Ysaye and others; toured Europe; led Chamber Music Society in San Francisco, known as the Persinger Quartet (1916-28); taught at Cleveland Institute of Music (1929-30); then at Juilliard School, New York City after 1930.

PETER, JOHANN FRIEDRICH

b. 1746 Hernndyck, Netherlands, d. 1813 Bethlehem, Pennsylvania. Composer, organist, and teacher. Came to Nazareth, Pa. (1769); organist at Brethren's House in Bethlehem (1770); composed about 100 works for the Moravian Church, mostly anthems and arias; six string quintets, Salem (1789); under his direction, Haydn's *Creation* first performed in America (1811).

PETER, PAUL AND MARY *see* PETER YARROW, NOEL PAUL STOOKEY, MARY ELLIN TRAVERS

PETERS, ROBERTA

b. 1930 New York City.
Noted soprano. Debut at Metropolitan Opera as Zerlina in *Don Giovanni* (1950); also appeared in *Rigoletto, The Barber of Seville, The Marriage of Figaro*; appeared in films; at Covent Garden, London (summers, 1951-60); at Salzburg Festival (1963-64); Vienna (1963) and Munich Festivals (1964); soloist at Carnegie Hall (March, 1972).

PETERS, WILLIAM CUMMING ("W. C.")

b. 1805 Woodbury, England, d. 1866 Cincinnati, Ohio. Clarinetist, composer, and publisher. Taught music in Pittsburgh (1825-29); opened music stores in Louisville, Ky. (1829), Pittsburgh (1830), Cincinnati (1839), then a fourth store and publishing house in Baltimore; wrote "They Are Come" (1839), "General Scott's Artillery March" (1847), "The Picket" (1861), "The Marching Song of Sherman's Army" (1864); compiled the *Catholic Harmonist* (Baltimore, 1851); when Stephen Foster was an unknown in 1848, he gave copies of "Oh Susannah" and "Old Uncle Ned" to Peters, which Peters published in his *Songs of the Sable Harmonists* without giving credit to Foster.

PETERSILEA, CARLYLE

b. 1844 Boston, Massachusetts, d. 1903 near Los Angeles, California. Pianist and teacher. Studied at Leipzig Conservatory where he won the Helbig Prize; toured Germany; studied with Liszt at Weimar (1884); taught at the New England Conservatory, Boston (1886); resided in California after 1894.

PETERSON, OSCAR EMMANUEL

b. 1925 Montreal, Quebec, Canada.
Black pianist. Came to U.S. (1949); played with Norman Granz during 1950s; toured Europe with Ella Fitzgerald in 1960s; also led his own trio after 1959; albums—*Affinity, Louis Armstrong Meets Oscar Peterson, At Newport, At the Opera House, Blues Etude, Bursting Out with the All-Star Big Band, Canadiana Suite, Easy Walker, Eloquence, Fiorello, Stan Getz and the Oscar Peterson Trio, Great Oscar Peterson, In a Romantic Mood.*

PETIT, BUDDY

b. 1887 New Orleans, Louisiana, d. 1931.
Black cornetist. Born Buddy Crawford; raised by Joseph Petit, New Orleans bandleader; founded Young Olympia Band with Sidney Bechet in New Orleans (ca. 1911); joined Jelly Roll Morton in Los Angeles for a short time in 1917; then returned to New Orleans where he continued playing.

PETRAK, RUDOLF

b. 1917 Sucany, Czechoslovakia, d. 1972 Greenwich, Connecticut. Tenor. Began his career with the Bratislava Opera and Prague Opera; American debut (1948) at New York City Center as Rodolfo in the City Opera's production of *La Boheme*; with City Opera Company (1948-56); sang at the Philadelphia Orchestra's presentation of Carl Orff's *Carmina Burana* in Carnegie Hall, New York City (1960); died of a heart ailment.

PETRIE, HENRY W.

b. 1857 Bloomington, Illinois, d. 1925 Paw Paw, Michigan. Popular composer. Wrote "I'm Mamma's Little Girl" (1894), "The Tramp's Dream" (1895), "Will You Love Me Sweetheart When I'm Old" (1895), "I Don't Want to Play in Your Yard," "Asleep in the Deep" (w. A.J. Lamb, introduced by Jean Early in Chicago in 1898 while touring with Haverly Minstrels), "Just to Remind Me of You" (1900) and "At the Bottom of the Deep Blue Sea" (w. A.J. Lamb).

PETTICOLAS, PHILIPPE ABRAHAM

b. 1760 France, d. 1841.
Pianist, teacher, and artist. Teacher of pianoforte and harpsichord with his son, August Petticolas, in Richmond, Virginia (1804-19).

PETTIFORD, OSCAR

b. 1922 Okmulgee, Oklahoma, d. 1960 Copenhagen, Denmark. Black bass player and composer. Played with Charlie Barnet, Duke Ellington, and Woody Herman in 1940s; toured Europe (1958); injured in an automobile accident in Vienna, Austria (1958), but recovered; played in Copenhagen with Stan Getz; also played cello; album—*My Little Cello*; works—*Black-eyed Peas and Collard Greens, Swingin' Till the Girls Come Home, Tricrotism.*

PETZET, WALTER

b. 1866 Breslau, Germany, d. 1941 Dresden, Germany. Pianist and teacher. Raised in Augsburg; pupil of Arnokleffel, Rheinberger, and Abel; graduated Royal School of Music, Munich (1886); at Frankfort-au-Main under Hans von Bulow; came to America (1887); taught at Northwestern Conservatory, Minneapolis, Minn.; composed a trio played at National Music Teachers' Association in Chicago (1888), also a symphony, two overtures, songs.

PFEIFFER, GEORGE

b. ca. 1790, d. after 1827.
Pianist, composer, and teacher. Taught in Philadelphia (1814-20); settled in New Orleans, La. (1822); Thomas Loud, Jr. was a pupil of Pfeiffer; later jealousy arose between the men; a public performance was held, and decided in favor of the pupil; Pfeiffer wrote *Canadian Dance* (1817), *The Chaplet of Fame* (w. M. Fortune).

PHELPS, AUSTIN

b. 1820 West Brookfield, Massachusetts, d. 1890 Bar Harbour, Maine. Hymnist. Professor at Andover (1848-79); wrote "Father! If I May Call Thee So," which appeared in the *Sabbath Hymn Book* (1858).

PHELPS, ELLSWORTH C.

b. 1827 Middletown, Connecticut, d. 1913 Brooklyn, New York. Teacher and composer. Organist, self-taught; resided in Brooklyn, N.Y. after 1857; taught for thirty years in public schools; composed two comic operas, two symphonies—*Hiawatha* and *Emancipation, Psalm 145* with orchestra, four symphonic poems.

PHELPS, SYLVANUS DRYDNE

b. 1816 Suffield, Connecticut, d. 1895 New Haven, Connecticut. Hymnist. Pastor of the First Baptist Church in New Haven for twenty-nine years; wrote the lyrics "Something for Jesus" (1862, m. Robert Lowry, "Saviour, Thy Dying Love Thou Gavest Me"), first published in *Pure Gold*

(1871), and later in the early *Baptist Hymn and Tune Book.*

PHILBURN, AL

b. 1902 Newark, New Jersey, d. 1972 Glen Cove, L.I., New York. Jazz trombonist. Played with Paul Specht, Cass Hagen, Ed Kirkeby, and Red Nichols during 1920s and '30s.

PHILE, PHILIP

b. 1734 Germany, d. 1793 Philadelphia, Pennsylvania. Violinist, orchestra leader, and composer. Born Philip Pfeil; leader of Theatre Royal orchestra, John Street, New York City (1779); leader of Old American Company orchestra, Philadelphia (1785); soloist at first Uranian Concert (April, 1787); taught violin and German flute in New York City after 1787; later returned to Philadelphia; composed *Harmony Music* for wind instruments; "The President's March," also known as "The Washington March" played in the presence of General George Washington at the John Street Theatre on November 24, 1789; same tune used by Joseph Hopkinson for "Hail Columbia" (1798); Phile also composed under the pseudonym John Roth; composed and played his violin concertos between 1787-91.

PHILIPP, ISIDOR EDMOND

b. 1863 Budapest, Hungary, d. 1958.
Pianist. Studied at Paris Conservatory, won first prize (1883); studied with Saint-Saëns and others; toured Europe; president of the Society d'Art; taught at Paris Conservatory (1913); taught in Boston and New York (1934-35); settled in U.S. (1941); composed *Reverie melancolique* a suite fantastique, and *Serenade humoristique* for orchestra.

PHILLIPS, BARRE

b. 1934 San Francisco, California.
Bass player. With Don Ellis, Jimmy Giuffre, Archie Shepp, Peter Nero, George Russell and others in 1960s; in Europe (1964) with Russell and Giuffre (1965); at Newport Jazz Festival (1965) with Shepp.

PHILLIPS, BURRILL

b. 1907 Omaha, Nebraska.
Noted composer. Graduated Eastman School of Music, Rochester, N.Y.; won Guggenheim Fellowship (1942-43) and American Academy of Arts and Letters Award; taught at Eastman School; composed *Selections from McGuffey's Readers* (suite, Rochester Philharmonic under Hanson, 1934), *Symphony Concertante* (Eastman Little Symphony under Van Hoesen, 1935), *Play Ball* (Eastman School Festival under Hanson with Rochester Civic Orchestra, 1938), *Music for Strings* (Rochester Civic Orchestra, 1939) *Dance* (overture, Rochester Civic Orchestra under Hanson, 1940), *Three Satiric Fragments* (Rochester Civic Orchestra under Hanson, 1941), *Scena* (for small orchestra), *Three Divertimenti* (for piano).

PHILLIPS, CHARLES DON (CHARLIE)

b. 1937 Clovis, New Mexico.
Singer and songwriter. Attended schools in Farwell, Texas; wrote "Sugartime" (BMI award, 1958), "By My Bride," "One Faded Rose."

PHILLIPS, ESTHER MAE JONES

b. 1935 Galveston, Texas.
Black singer. Toured with Johnny Otis (1949-52) as "Little Esther"; later soloist; in England (1965), sang with Beatles on BBC-TV; at Newport Jazz Festival (1966); albums—*And I Love Him, Country Side of Esther Phillips, Esther*; at the CTI Summer Jazz Festival, New York City (1972).

PHILLIPS, JOHN ("PAPA")

b. 1941 Parris Island, South Carolina.
Singer. Attended University of Virginia and George Washington University (basketball player); formed the "Smoothies" with Scott McKenzie; later John and Scott joined with Richard Weissman to form "The Journeymen"; later was Papa John of the "Mamas and the Papas"; their albums include the *Mamas and the Papas, Mamas and Papas Deliver, Mamas and Papas Golden Era, Papas and Mamas, Crashon Screamon All Fall Down.*

PHILLIPS, JOSEPH EDWARD (FILIPELLI)

b. 1915 Brooklyn, New York.
Tenor saxist. With Woody Herman and others in 1940s; toured Europe with Benny Goodman (1959); later formed own quartet in Pompano Beach, Florida; album—*Perdido*; at the Newport Jazz Festival, New York City (1972).

PHILLIPS, PHILIP

b. 1834 Jamestown, New York, d. 1895 Delaware, Ohio. Singer and composer. Known as the "Singing Pilgrim" and toured Europe, Australia, and the United States; compiled twenty-nine collections of sacred music and a *Methodist Hymn and Tune Book* (1866); wrote "O, Why Should the Spirit" (w. William Knox), which he sang before the

Christian Meetings in Washington, D.C. in February, 1863, and January, 1865, both attended by President Lincoln; among his hymnals were *Early Blossoms* (1860), *Musical Leaves* (1862), and the *Singing Pilgrim* (1866). (*See also* Martha Ann Cook and Ellen H. Gates)

PHILLIPS, WILLIAM CLARENCE (BILL)

b. 1936 Canton, North Carolina.
Singer and songwriter. With the "Old South Jamboree" on station WMIL, Miami, Florida (1955); later on WLAC-TV in Nashville, Tenn; wrote "My Heartache" and "Falling Back to You" (1958), "It's Best This Way" (1959), "There's a Change in Me"; LP records—*Country Action, Little Boy Sad, Bill Phillips Style.*

PIANTADOSI, AL

b. 1884 New York City, d. 1955 Encino, California. Popular composer. Wrote "My Mariuccia Take a Steamboat" (1906, w. George Ranklyn), "That's How I Need You" (1912, w. Joseph McCarthy and Joe Goodwin), "The Curse of an Aching Heart" (1913, w. Henry Fink), "Baby Shoes" (1916, Goodwin and Ed Rose), "I'm Tired of Making Believe" (1928, w. George A. Kelly).

PIATIGORSKY, GREGAR

b. 1903 Ekaterinoslaw, Russia.
Cellist. Studied at Imperial Conservatory of Moscow (1911-16); debut (1916); with Imperial Opera, Moscow (1916-19); Berlin Philharmonic (1923-28); came to U.S. (1929); taught at Curtis Institute, Philadelphia; later professor at the University of Southern California School of Music, Los Angeles; U.S. citizen (1942); toured world as virtuoso; in concert at the New York Philharmonic (1972).

PICKARD, OBEY ("DAD")

b. (?), d. 1958.
Guitarist. Member of the Pickard Family, consisting of Dad on guitar; Mom on autoharp; Bubb—Obey, Jr.; Charlie; Ruth Pickard Colwell; Ann Pickard Rhea.

PICKETT, JESS

b. ca. 1860, d. ca. 1922.
Black pianist and composer. Wrote *The Dream*, based on the *Habanera*, of African origin, recorded in *The Digah's Stomp* by Fats Waller on a 1926 Victor record.

PICKETT, WILSON

b. 1941 Prattville, Alabama.
Black singer and songwriter. Started as a gospel singer and Negro spirituals singer; then with the Falcons in Detroit; wrote and recorded "If You Need Me" (1963); albums—*Best of Wilson Pickett, Exciting Wilson Pickett, Greatest Wilson Pickett Hits, Hey Jude, I'm in Love, In the Midnight Hour, Midnight Mover, Right On, Sound of Wilson Pickett, Wicked Pickett*; at the Apollo, New York City (1972).

PICOU, ALPHONSE FLORISTAN

b. 1878 New Orleans, Louisiana, d. there 1961. Black clarinetist. Played in Freddy Keppard's Olympia Orchestra (1905); later in King Oliver's Band; with Oliver, wrote "Chattanooga Stomp" (1923), "New Orleans Stomp" (1923); recorded with Kid Rena (1940) and Papa Celestin (1947).

PIED PIPERS (Tommy Dorsey's group) *see* JO STAFFORD

PIERCE, JOSEPH DE LACROIS ("DÉDÉ")

b. 1904 New Orleans, Louisiana, d. 1973.
Black trumpeter and cornetist. Played with Paul Barnes, Albert Burbank and others; led his own group; married Billie, younger sister of Sadie Gootson, who sang in Buddy Petit's band; Dédé and Billie accompanied Ida Cox on tours; later became blind.

PIERCE, NAT

b. 1925 Somerville, Massachusetts.
Black pianist and composer. Arranger for Woody Herman, Carmen McRae and others; wrote "Poor House Blues," "Dr. Wong's Bag," "Tunin' In," "Stingray," "Kissin' Cousins"; played in the Savoy Ballroom in Harlem, New York City.

PIERCE, WEBB

b. 1926 West Monroe, Louisiana.
Singer and songwriter. Started with radio station KLMB in Monroe; later Shreveport; formed his own band; wrote "Wondering" and "That Heart Belongs to Me" (1952), "Last Waltz" (with M. Freeman), "Slowly" (1954, with T. Hill), "Even Tho' " (with W. Jones and C. Peeples), "You're Not Mine Anymore" (1954, with Teddy and Doyle Wilburn), "I Don't Care" (1955, with Cindy Walker), "Teen-age Boogie" (1956), "A Thousand Miles Ago" (1959, with Mel Tillis).

PIERPONT, JAMES S.

b. 1822 Boston, Massachusetts, d. 1893 Winter Park, Florida. Popular composer. Arranged the music "The Little White Cottage" (or "Gentle Nettie Moore" 1857, w. Marshall Pike and m. G.S. Pike) and "Strike for the South" (1863, w. Carrie Bell Sinclair);

wrote the words and music "Jingle Bells" (or "One Horse Open Sleigh," 1857), "Wake, Lady Wake!" and "We Conquer or Die" (1861).

PIERPONT, JOHN

b. 1785 Litchfield, Connecticut, d. 1866 Medford, Massachusetts. Lyricist. Graduated Yale in 1804, took a course in theology, and became the Unitarian minister of the Hollis St. Church, Boston, for thirty-six years; wrote the lyrics "Warren's Address at the Battle of Bunker Hill" (ca. 1823), "Stand! The Ground's Your Own, My Braves," based on the Scotch tune "Bruce's Address," (w. Robert Burns); published *Airs of Palestine* and the poem "The Yankee Boy."

PIERSON, ARTHUR TAPPAN

b. 1837 New York City, d. 1911 Brooklyn, New York. Hymnist. Educated at Hamilton College, Clinton, N.Y.; became a Presbyterian minister (1860) and served in Binghamton and Waterford, N.Y., Detroit, Mich., and Philadelphia, Pa.; his hymns appeared in *Hymns and Songs of Praise* (New York, 1874), and *Laudes Domini* (New York, 1884).

PIERSON, ROBERT MOREY

b. 1930 Detroit, Michigan.
Tenor saxist. Played with Lionel Hampton, Johnny Long, Quincy Jones, Woody Herman and others.

PIKE, ALBERT

b. 1809 Boston, Massachusetts, d. 1891 Washington, D.C. Poet and lyricist. Attended Harvard (1826); settled in Little Rock, Arkansas (1832); editor of *Advocate* (1835); served in Mexican War (1846); Brigadier General in Confederate Army in Missouri expedition (1862), commanded brigade of Cherokee and Creek Indians, defeated at Battle of Pea Ridge, Arkansas, and sent back to Indian territory; wrote "Southrons, Hear Your Country Call You" (1861, m. "Dixie"—Daniel D. Emmett), "The War Song of Dixie" (1861, m. J.C. Vierick).

PIKE, DAVID SAMUEL

b. 1938 Detroit, Michigan.
Vibraphonist and marimba player. Played with Paul Bley, Herbie Mann and others; also led his own group; albums—*Doors of Perception; Jazz for the Jet Set.*

PILLOIS, JACQUES

b. 1877 Paris, France, d. 1935 New York City. Composer. Studied at Paris Conservatory; taught music history at Fontainebleau School (1921), New York University (1927-30), and Smith College, Northampton, Mass. (1929-30); laureate of French Institute; won Trement, Nicolo, and Rousseau Prizes; composed vocal works and chamber music.

PILLOW, RAY

b. 1937 Lynchburg, Virginia.
Singer. Served in the U.S. Navy; later toured in the Martha White Road Show; LP records—*I'll Take the Dog, People Music.*

PINKETT, WILLIAM WARD

b. 1906 Newport News, Virginia, d. 1937 New York City. Black jazz trumpeter. With White Brothers in Washington, D.C. after 1926; later with King Oliver, Jelly Roll Morton and others.

PINZA, EZIO

b. 1892 Rome, Italy, d. 1957 Stamford, Connecticut. Noted basso. Studied at Ravenna and Bologna; debut at La Scala, Milan; New York debut at Metropolitan Opera in Spotini's *La Vestale* (1926); with the Metropolitan Opera until 1948; sang in the musical comedy *South Pacific* (1949).

PIRSSON, WILLIAM

b. ca. 1780, d. after 1810.
Composer and teacher. Came to New York City (1799); student there of George K. Jackson; teacher and choral conductor in New York City; wrote "Glide Gently On, Thou Murm'ring Brook" (1804), *Twelve Anthems for Dr. George K. Jackson* (organist at St. George's Chapel) *by His Late Pupil* (1809).

PISK, PAUL A.

b. 1893 Vienna, Austria.
Teacher and composer. Professor at the University of Redlands, California (1937).

PISTON, WALTER

b. 1894 Rockland, Maine.
Noted composer. Graduated from the Massachusetts Normal Art School; enlisted in the navy in World War I, where he was a member of the band; afterwards graduated from Harvard University in music, then studied with Nadia Boulanger; became a professor of composition at Harvard; composed a *Concerto for Orchestra* (1933), *Concertino* for piano and orchestra (1937), seven symphonies (the first in 1937 and the seventh in 1960; the third, in 1937, won the Pulitzer Prize).

PITTS, WILLIAM S.

b. 1830 Orleans County, New York, d. 1918 Brooklyn, New York. Popular composer. When he was seventeen the family moved to Union, Wisc.; composed the tunes "Princethorpe," "Wildwood," (Church in the Wildwood" or "Little Brown Church in the Vale," 1857, but not published until 1865). In 1857 he first saw the wooded site where the church now stands, imagined a church there, and wrote the song. When he returned to the spot in 1863, to his surprise he found a little brown church there. Graduated Rush Medical College, Chicago (1868) and became a practicing physician in Fredericksburg, Iowa until 1906; in 1863 wrote "I've Been Dreaming of You Jessie," "On Such a Night as This," "Home on Furlough," "Our Brave Boys in Blue" (w. Hattie S. Aldrich) and "Kiss Me Goodby for Mother" (w. M.J. Million).

PLAINSMEN QUARTET

Organized in Dallas, Texas (1956); Jerry Redd, tenor; Thurman Bunch, first tenor; Jack Mainord, second tenor; Rusty Goodman, bass; Howard Welborn, baritone and manager; Larry Denham, pianist.

PLATER, ROBERT

b. 1914 Newark, New Jersey.
Alto saxist, clarinetist, and flutist. With Lionel Hampton (1946-64); then with Count Basie.

PLATTERS, THE (black vocal group)

1955 hits were "The Great Pretender" and "Only You."

PLAYBOYS *see* GARY LEWIS

PLEASANT VALLEY BOYS, THE *see* CARSON ROBISON, JERRY L. BYRD

PLIMPTON, JOB

b. 1784 Medway, Massachusetts, d. 1864 Brookline, Massachusetts. Organist, compiler, and organ maker. Student of George K. Jackson; taught in New York City (1806-20); moved to Brookline, Mass. (1820); first to build reed organs in America; built the Apollino, his own invention (1820); built an organ with eight stops (1836), exhibited at Mechanics Fair, Boston; wrote *The Washington Choir*, collection of music (1843); his *Universal Repository of Music* (1808) contains thirty-eight marches, waltzes, and ballads.

PLUMMER, WILLIAM

b. 1938 Boulder, Colorado.
Bass player. With Buddy De Franco, George Shearing and others in 1950s; with The Jazz Corp, Paul Horn and others in 1960s.

POE, ELIZABETH (ARNOLD)

b. 1787 London, England, d. 1811 Richmond, Virginia. Singer and actress. Mother of Edgar A. Poe; daughter of actor Henry Arnold and actress Elizabeth Smith; came to Boston (1795); debut as singer (1796) in Boston; gave concerts in Portsmouth, N.H., and Newport, R.I. (1796); married comedian C.D. Hopkins (1802), he died (1805); married actor David Poe (1805); she died of tuberculosis.

POINDEXTER, NORWOOD ("PONY")

b. 1926 New Orleans, Louisiana.
Saxophonist and clarinetist. Played alto and tenor sax with Billy Eckstine and others in 1940s; later took up the soprano sax and formed his own quartet; in Europe after 1964.

POLACCO, GIORGIO

b. 1875 Venice, Italy, d. 1960 New York City. Conductor. Opera conductor in Buenos Aires, Argentina, Rio de Janeiro, Brazil, Brussels, Belgium, Warsaw, Poland, St. Petersburg, Russia, and London, England; became Toscanini's assistant (1911) and later conductor of the Metropolitan Opera, New York City; then artistic director at the Chicago Civic Opera Company after 1923.

POLLACK, BEN

b. 1903 Chicago, Illinois, d. 1971 Palm Springs, California. Drummer and jazz bandleader. Benny Goodman joined Pollack's band in 1925; Glenn Miller joined the band in 1927; Pollack married Doris Robbins, a singer in his band, divorced (1957); opened Easy Street North, a night club in Palm Springs in the 1960s; he hanged himself.

POMEROY, HERB

b. 1930 Gloucester, Massachusetts.
Trumpeter and bandleader. Played with Stan Kenton, Lionel Hampton, Charlie Parker and others in 1950s; later director of Radio Malaya Orchestra, Malaysia (1962); director of MIT Concert Jazz Band, Cambridge, Mass., after 1963; also instructor at Summer Jazz Clinics.

POND, SYLVESTER BILLINGS

b. 1792 near Worcester, Massachusetts, d. 1871 New York City. Composer. Piano maker in Albany, New York (1820), then joined Firth & Hall, music publishers, New York City (1832); the firm became William A. Pond & Company (1863); compiled the *United States Psalmody* (1841); composed the tune "Armenia" ("All Praise to Our Redeeming Lord," w. Charles Wesley).

PONS, LILY

b. 1904 Cannes, France.
Celebrated coloratura soprano. Studied piano at Paris Conservatorie at age thirteen; voice at twenty-one; American debut in *Lucia de Lammermoor* (Gaetano Donizetti) at the Metropolitan Opera House, New York City (1931); in 1956 the Metropolitan Opera held a celebration in honor of her 25th anniversary with the opera; became a U.S. citizen in 1940.

PONSELLE, ROSA

b. 1897 Meriden, Connecticut.
Noted soprano. Born Rosa Ponzillo; pupil of William Thorner and Romano Romani; opera debut at the Metropolitan Opera, New York City (1918) as Leonora in *Forza del Destino*; sang with the Metropolitan Opera (1918-36); appeared at Covent Garden, London, and in Italy.

POOLE, HENRY WARD

b. 1825 Salem, Massachusetts, d. 1890.
Organ maker and writer. Entered Yale at age fifteen; after graduation was a mining engineer in Pottsville, Pa.; later assistant astronomer in Dudley Observatory, Albany; the first organ he constructed did not have perfect tone, devised a new system of pedals; had Joseph Alley of Newburyport, Mass., construct the organ which was installed in the church of Dr. James F. Clarke, Indiana Place, Boston; wrote articles on piano making for the *American Journal of Science* (1850, 1867-68).

PORCINO, AL

b. 1925 New York City.
Trumpeter. Played with Tommy Dorsey, Gene Krupa, Count Basie, Woody Herman, Stan Kenton and others in 1950s; later with Frank Sinatra, Vic Damone, Eddie Fisher and others.

PORTER, COLE

b. 1892 Peru, Indiana, d. 1964 Santa Monica, California. Popular composer. Graduated Yale (1913) where he wrote the "Bulldog" song, then attended Harvard; joined the French Foreign Legion and became a French officer in World War I; after the war he studied with Vincent d'Indy in Paris; injured riding horseback, hospitalized for two years, confined to a wheelchair for five years, then finally his right leg was amputated in 1958; wrote the songs for the musical shows *Fifty Million Frenchmen* (1929), *The New Yorkers* (1930), *The Gay Divorcee* (1932), *Anything Goes* (1934), *Leave It to Me* (1938), *Du Barry Was a Lady* (1939), *Panama Hattie* (1940), *Let's Face It* (1941), *Something for the Boys* (1943), *Mexican Hayride* (1944), *Kiss Me Kate* (1948, book—Bella and Sam Spewack), *Can-Can* (1953), *Silk Stockings* (1955); his hit songs were "Let's Do It" (1928), "You Do Something to Me" (1929), "What Is This Thing Called Love" (1929), "Love for Sale" (1930), "Night and Day" (1932), "I Get a Kick Out of You" (1934), "Begin the Beguine" (1935), "My Heart Belongs to Daddy" (1938), "Don't Fence Me In" (1944), "Wunderbar" (1948), "I Love Paris" (1953), "I've Got You Under My Skin," "In the Still of the Night," "You'd Be So Nice to Come Home To," "True Love."

PORTER, QUINCY C.

b. 1897 New Haven, Connecticut, d. 1966.
Composer. Studied music at Yale University, in Paris with Vincent d'Indy and in Cleveland with Ernest Bloch; became a teacher at the Cleveland Institute of Music (1923), later at Vassar College, Poughkeepsie, N.Y., the New England Conservatory, Boston, then professor of music at Yale (1946); composed Quartet no. 4 (for strings, 1931), Quartet no. 7 (for strings, 1943), *Concerto for Viola and Orchesta* (1948, introduced by the CBS Symphony Orchestra, Dean Dixon conducting).

PORTER, ROBERT DOUGLAS (BOB)

b. 1932 Ballinger, Texas.
Singer and songwriter. Attended schools in Mason, Texas, and Watsonville, Calif.; leader of The Fugitives after 1965; wrote "Thanks to Heaven," "Remember Me," "You're a Fool," "Stockade," "My Broken Heart Knows."

POTTER, CHARLES THOMAS (TOMMY)

b. 1918 Philadelphia, Pennsylvania.
Black bass player. Played with Charlie Parker and others; with Harry Edison, Al Cohn-Zoot Sims and others in 1960s.

POUNDS, JESSIE BROWN

b. 1861, d. 1921.
Hymnist. She wrote the hymns "Beautiful Isle

of Somewhere" (1897, m. J.S. Fearis), "O Scatter the Seeds," "Preach Through the Cross," and "We Are Going Down the Valley"; "Beautiful Isle of Somewhere" was a favorite of President William McKinley.

POWELL, ALMA WEBSTER

b. 1874 Elgin, Illinois, d. 1930 Mahwah, New Jersey. Soprano. Sang in operas; also teacher of voice.

POWELL, BENJAMIN GORDON (BENNY)

b. 1930 New Orleans, Louisiana.
Black trombonist. With Count Basie (1951-63); lead his own combo; played in orchestras for various Broadway shows; appeared on TV with Sammy Davis, Jr.

POWELL, DICK

b. 1904 Mountain View, Arkansas, d. 1963. Singer. Educated at Little Rock (Ark.) College; vocalist with small bands; emcee at Stanley and Enright Theatres in Pittsburgh; appeared in films with Ruby Keeler, Marion Davis, Joan Blondell and others; died of cancer.

POWELL, EARL ("BUD")

b. 1924 New York City, d. 1966 Brooklyn, New York. Black jazz pianist. Played with Cootie Williams, Dizzy Gillespie, Don Byas and others; in Paris (1959-62); stricken with tuberculosis; returned to New York (1964); considered by many as one of the greatest jazz pianists; albums—*The Amazing Bud Powell, Bud Powell Trio, The Scene Changes, Time Waits.*

POWELL EVERARD STEPHEN, SR. ("RUDY")

b. 1907 New York City.
Black clarinetist and alto saxist. Played with Fats Waller, Fletcher Henderson, Cab Calloway, Teddy Wilson and others in 1950s; later with Ray Charles.

POWELL, JOHN

b. 1882 Richmond, Virginia, d. 1963.
Pianist and composer. Pupil of Leschetizky and others; debut in Vienna (1907); toured Europe, then America after 1912; composed *Negro Rhapsody* and *Natchez-on-the-Hill* for orchestra; *Virginiesque*, violin sonata; *Psychologique*, and *Noble and Teutonica*, piano sonatas; *At the Fair* and *In the South*, piano suites; piano and violin concertos, string quartets.

POWELL, MAUD

b. 1868 Peru, Illinois, d. 1920 Uniontown, Pennsylvania. Violinist. Studied in Paris and Leipzig; debut with Berlin Philharmonic (1885); in America with Theodore Thomas Orchestra (1885); toured Europe and America; married H. Godfrey Turner.

POWELL, SHELDON

b. 1928 Lawrenceville, Virginia.
Tenor saxist and flutist. Played with Sy Oliver, Lucky Millinder, Louis Bellson, Erskine Hawkins, Benny Goodman and others in 1950s; with Clark Terry, Louis Bellson and others in 1960s.

POWELL, VIRGINIA (GINNY)

b. (?), d. 1959.
Singer. Sang in Boyd Raeburn's band; married Boyd Raeburn.

POWNALL, MRS. MARY ANN

b. 1751 England, d. 1796 Charleston, South Carolina. Singer and songwriter. Known as Mrs. Wrighten in England; came to New York City before 1794; first song plugger for a publishing house in America; plugged "Primroses" and other songs of James Hewitt, New York City; female lead in *Tammany*, first opera composed by an American (1794, m. James Hewitt, libretto—Ann Julia Hatton); with Old American Opera Company, Philadelphia; wrote the song, "Washington" (in praise of General Washington) and sang it at a concert in Boston on August 1, 1794; sang "Washington and Liberty" at the City Theatre in Charleston, S.C., on February 22, 1796, and "Address to the Ladies," then died there.

PRATT, CHARLES E.

b. 1841 Hartford, Connecticut, d. 1902 New York City. Popular composer. Wrote the lyrics "We'll Fight for Uncle Abe" (m. Fred Buckley), a Civil War song; composed the music "Walking Down Broadway" (w. W.H. Lingard) and "When Jamie Comes Over the Sea" (1879, w. John Kenyon); wrote the words and music "Bring Back My Bonnie to Me," (or "My Bonnie Lies Over the Ocean" 1882), and "Don't Go Out Tonight, Boy" (1895).

PRATT, HENRY

b. 1777, d. 1849.
Organ maker. Resided in Winchester, N.H.; constructed over fifty instruments, including small church organs and chamber organs.

PRATT, SILAS GAMALIEL

b. 1846 Addison, Vermont, d. 1916 Pittsburgh, Pennsylvania. Noted composer. Studied with Kullak and others; organized Apollo Club, Chicago (1871); studied with H. Dorn in Berlin (1875); produced *Anniversary*

Overture there (1876); gave symphonic concerts in Chicago (1878); produced his opera *Zenobia* (1882); gave concerts of his own composition at Crystal Palace, London, in 1885; piano teacher at the New York Metropolitan Conservatory, N.Y. (1890); composed *Lucille* (lyric opera, Chicago, 1887), *The Last Inca* (cantata with orchestra) *Prodigal Son* (symphony), *Magdalena's Lament* (for orchestra), *The Tempest* (symphonic suite), *Columbus* (cantata).

PRAY, LEWIS GLOVER

b. 1793 Quincy, Massachusetts, d. after 1873. Hymnist and compiler. In business in Boston (1815-38); compiled the *Sunday School Hymn Book* (Unitarian, 1833), *Sunday School Hymn and Service Book* (1847), *The Sylphide's School* (1862), and *Autumn Leaves* (1873); the last two included his poems and hymns.

PRENTISS, ELIZABETH (PAYSON)

b. 1818 Portland, Maine, d. 1878 Dorset, Vermont. Hymnist. In 1845 married George L. Prentiss, a Congregational minister of New Bedford, Mass.; in 1851 they moved to New York City; she wrote the lyrics "More Love to Thee, O Christ" (ca. 1856, tune "Propior Deo"—A.S. Sullivan, 1872); published *Golden Hours: Hymns and Songs of the Christian Life* (1874); also tune "More Love to Thee" by W.H. Doane; her hymns appeared in Schaff's *Christ in Song* (1869) and Hatfield's *Church Hymn Book* (New York, 1872).

PRESBREY, OTIS F.

b. 1820 Livingston County, New York, d. 1901. Composer. Graduated Berkshire Medical College in 1847 and was a medical doctor for four years; then worked for the Department of Internal Revenue in Buffalo, N.Y., and Richmond, Va.; later lived in Washington, D.C., and New York City where he published the *New York Evangelist;* composed the music "Not Half Has Ever Been Told" (1877, w. J.B. Atchison, and arranged by J.W. Bischoff); with Bischoff and Rev. J.E. Rankin published *Gospel Bells* (1883).

PRESLEY, ELVIS AARON

b. 1935 Tupelo, Mississippi.
Celebrated singer. Raised in Memphis, Tenn.; appeared on "Louisiana Hayride," Shreveport, La. (1954); in moving pictures (1956); served in U.S. Army in Germany (1958-60); LP records—*Any Way You Want Me, Blue Hawaii, Date with Elvis, Easy Come, Easy Go, Elvis, Elvis' Golden Records, Follow That Dream, From Elvis in Memphis, Fun in Acapulco, G.I. Blues, Girl Happy, Girls, Girls, Girls, Heartbreak Hotel, His Hand in Mine, How Great Thou Art, Jailhouse Rock, Just for You, Kid Galahad, King Creole, Kissin' Cousins, Let's Be Friends, Love Me Tender, Loving You, On Stage, Paradise, Hawaiian Style, Peace in the Valley, Potluck, Elvis Presley, Real Elvis, Roustabout, Something for Everybody, Speedway, Strictly Elvis, Tickle Me, Touch of Gold, Viva Las Vegas;* Jerry Lieber and Mike Stoller wrote many songs for Presley, including "Hound Dog" and "Jailhouse Rock."

PRESS, MICHAEL

b. 1872 Vilna, Lithuania, d. 1938 Lansing, Michigan. Violin soloist, chamber-music player, teacher, and conductor.

PRESSER, THEODORE

b. 1848 Pittsburgh, Pennsylvania, d. 1925 Philadelphia, Pennsylvania. Publisher. Studied at the New England Conservatory, Boston (1872) and the Leipsig Conservatory (1878); taught at Ohio Wesleyan, Delaware, Ohio, Xenia College, Ohio, and Hollins Institute, Va.; founded *The Etude* in Lynchburg, Va. (1883); moved to Philadelphia (1884); founded the Music Teachers National Association (1876); established the Presser Foundation (1916); endowed the Presser Home for Retired Music Teachers (1907).

PREVIN, ANDRE

b. 1929 Berlin, Germany.
Composer. Studied at the Berlin Conservatory, then came to Los Angeles (1938); composer-director for MGM pictures (1948-60); wrote symphonies and numerous compositions for the piano, a string quartet, a cello sonata, and a flute quintet; wrote the complete scores for the screen musicals *It's Always Fair Weather* (w. Betty Comden and Adolph Green), *Pepe* (song lyrics by Previn's wife, Dory Langan), *Coco* (w. Alan Jay Lerner); lived with Mia Farrow.

PREVOST, EUGENE PROSPER

b. 1809 Paris, France, d. 1872 New Orleans, Louisiana. Conductor and composer. Studied at the Paris Conservatory, won first and second grand prizes in composition; came to New Orleans (1837); conductor of French Opera Company there for almost thirty years; his opera, *Cosimo,* produced at Orleans Theatre (1839); also his opera, *Le Bon Garçon* (1839); later a singing teacher there.

PRICE, CARL F.

b. 1881 New Brunswick, New Jersey, d. 1948. Composer. Served as president of the Methodist Social Union and of the Hymn Society, and composed over 200 hymn tunes and cantatas; composed the tune "The Morning Watch" ("Awake, My Soul, and with the Sun" w. Thomas Ken).

PRICE, FLORENCE B.

b. 1888 Little Rock, Arkansas, d. 1953 Chicago, Illinois. Black pianist and composer. Graduated New England Conservatory, Boston; studied at Chicago Musical College and American Conservatory of Music, Chicago; wrote Symphony in E Minor (Wanamaker Award, 1925), *Concert Overture on Negro Spirituals, Symphonic Tone Poem, Negro Folksongs for Counterpoint* (for string quartet); soloist with Chicago Symphony under Frederick Stock (1932) playing own works.

PRICE, KENNY

b. 1931 Florence, Kentucky.
Singer and guitarist. Served in Korea during the Korean War; started with radio station WLW, Cincinnati, Ohio (1954); had two hits written by Ray Pennington—"Walking on New Grass" (1966) and "Happy Tracks" (1967); then "Pretty Girl, Pretty Clothes, Pretty Sad" (1967); LPs—*Heavyweight, One Hit Follows Another.*

PRICE, LEONTYNE

b. 1927 Laurel, Mississippi.
Black soprano. Graduated Central State College, Miss. (1949); studied at Juilliard; debut in *Four Saints in Three Acts* (1952); sang in *Porgy and Bess;* in Puccini's *Tosca* on TV (1955); Poulenc's *Dialogue of the Carmelites* with San Francisco Opera; with the Metropolitan Opera, New York City after 1961.

PRICE, LLOYD

b. 1932 New Orleans, Louisiana.
Black singer. Auditioned by Art Rupe in New Orleans (1952); sang "Lawdy Miss Clawdy," which was recorded with Fats Domino on the piano, became a hit record; albums—*Mr. Personality, Mr. Personality's Big 15*; at Brandy's II, New York City (1972).

PRICE, RAY NOBLE

b. 1926 Perryville, Texas.
Singer and songwriter. Attended high school in Dallas, Texas; served in the armed forces in World War II; attended North Texas Agriculture College, Arlington; radio debut on station KRBC, Abilene, Texas; wrote "I'm Tired," "Give Me More of Your Kisses," "Soft Rain" (1961); LP records—*Ray Price Sings Heart Songs* and *Talk to Your Heart* (1958), *Faith* (1960), *Greatest Hits* (1961), *San Antonio Rose* (1962), *Night Life* (1963), *Love Life* (1964), *Burning Memories* (1965), *The Other Woman* (1966).

PRICE, RUTH

b. 1938 Phoenixville, Pennsylvania.
Singer and dancer. Sang in Charlie Ventura's combo, with Red Garland, Harry James and others in 1960s; album—*Ruth Price with Shelly Manne and His Men at the Manhole.*

PRIDE, CHARLEY

b. 1938 Sledge, Mississippi.
Black singer and guitarist. Played baseball in Helena, Montana league and sang in night clubs there; then signed with RCA-Victor (1964); LP records—*Best of Charley Pride, Country Charley Pride, Country Way, Just Plain Charley, Make Mine Country, Charley Pride in Person—Live at Panther Hall, Pride of Country Music, Sensational Charley Pride, Songs of Pride—Charley, That Is;* at the 1971 Country Music Association awards in Nashville won two awards—Male Vocalist of the Year and Entertainer of the Year; won Grammy Award (1972) for "Did You Think to Pray?" and also for "Let Me Live."

PRIMA, LOUIS

b. 1911 New Orleans, Louisiana.
Singer, trumpeter, and bandleader. Played with Red Nichols (1930); organized his own band (1933); his female vocalist was Martha Raye; married singer Keely Smith (1953); she sang in his band; also featured Sam Butera and the Witnesses; Keely went out on her own (1961).

PRINCE, ROBERT

b. 1929 New York City.
Composer. Composed ballets, staged by choreographer Jerome Robbins, *New York Export; Opus Jazz and Events,* (performed by Ballets USA in New York City and Europe, 1961), *Meet the Band* (for Benny Goodman's tour of Soviet Russia, 1962); also dance music for Broadway shows and TV—*Dr. Faustus* (1964), *Half a Sixpence* (1965).

PRINCE, THOMAS

b. 1687 Sandwich, Massachusetts, d. 1758 Boston, Massachusetts. Compiler. Graduated Harvard (1709); associate minister of Old South Church, Boston (1718-58); published (1758) a revised Bay Psalm Book, entitled *The Psalms, Hymns and Spiritual Songs.*

PROBY, P. J.

b. 1938 Texas.
Singer. Born James Marcus Smith; went to

Hollywood; wrote songs; went to England and became a success there; albums—*Phenomenon, P.J. Proby, Somewhere, What's Wrong with My World.*

PROCOPE, RUSSELL

b. 1908 New York City.
Black clarinetist and saxist. With Fletcher Henderson, Chick Webb and John Kirby; with Duke Ellington after 1945.

PROFFITT, FRANK

b. 1913 Laurel Bloomery, Tennessee, d. 1965 Vilas, North Carolina. Singer. Raised in Reese, N.C.; later bought his own farm in Pick Britches Valley, N.C.; in 1938 Anne and Frank Warner visited Proffitt and recorded his folk songs, including "Tom Dooley," which they introduced, but which didn't become famous until the 1950s.

PROPHETS, THE (gospel singers)

Organized in Knoxville, Tennessee (1959); Roy McNeal, lead singer; Ed Hill, emcee and baritone; Duane Allen, baritone; Lew Garrison, tenor; Jay Berry, second tenor; Dave Rodgers, bass; Jim Boatman, bass; Rancil Taylor, bass; Joe Moscheo, pianist and composer; Gary Trusler, piano; Jim Wesson (gospel singers); albums—*Love Like the Sun, The Prophets, Vital and Vibrant, Upward and Onward.*

PROTHEROE, DANIEL

b. 1866 Wales, d. 1934 Chicago, Illinois.
Popular composer. Founded the Lyric Glee Club in Milwaukee, Wisc. in 1896, and later became director of the Arion Club; after 1900 composed numerous songs.

PRUETT TWINS (black singers) *see* IDA COX

PRUEVER, JULIUS

b. 1874 Vienna, Austria, d. 1943 New York City. Teacher and conductor. From 1924-33 directed Philharmonic concerts in Berlin, but was forced to flee Germany with the rise of Hitlerism; came to New York and became a teacher training young opera singers.

PRYOR, ARTHUR

b. 1870 St. Joseph, Missouri, d. 1942 West Long Branch, New Jersey. Trombonist, bandleader, and composer. Soloist in Sousa's band at the Chicago Fair (1893); later formed his own band; introduced "Swanee" (m. George Gershwin) at the Capital Theatre, New York City (1919); wrote "Southern Hospitality" (1899, a ragtime cakewalk), "A Coon Band Contest," "Mr. Black Man," "Razzazza Mazzazza" (a trombone extravaganza), "The Whistler and His Dog" (1905).

PRYSOCK, ARTHUR

b. 1929 Spartanburg, South Carolina.
Black singer. Joined Buddy Johnson's orchestra in Harlem, New York City (1945); later a soloist; sang in concerts at the Academy of Music, Philadelphia, Symphony Hall, Newark, N.J., and Carnegie Hall, New York City; albums—*Art and Soul, Best of Arthur Prysock, Country Side of Arthur Prysock, Fly My Love, Funny Thing, I Must Be Doing Something Right, Lord Is My Shepherd, Love Me, Mister Prysock, Prysock/Basie.*

PUCKETT, GARY *see* UNION GAP

PUCKETT, GEORGE RILEY

b. 1890 Alpharetta, Georgia, d. 1946 College Park, Georgia. Singer. Joined with Gid Tanner in forming the Skillet Lickers and was lead singer of the band (1924).

PUENTE, GIUSEPPE DEL

b. 1845 Naples, Italy, d. 1900 Philadelphia, Pennsylvania. Baritone and teacher.

PURCELL, HENRY

b. 1742, d. 1802.
Composer. Dr. Purcell was rector of St. Michael's Episcopal Church, Charleston, S.C. (1782-1802) and contributed some tunes to the *Choral Book* (J. Loring, 1816) including "St. Michael's New"; with his organist, Samuel Rodgers, established a boy's choir in the church (1791), recruited from the local orphanage just founded in Charleston. (Not to be confused with the English composer, Henry Purcell, 1659-1695).

PURNELL, WILLIAM ("KEG")

b. 1915 Charleston, West Virginia, d. 1965. Drummer. With Benny Carter, Eddie Heywood and others in 1940s and '50s.

PURVIS, RICHARD IRVEN

b. 1915 San Francisco, California.
Organist. Studied at Peabody Conservatory, Baltimore, Curtis Institute of Music, Philadelphia, the Royal School of Music, London, and at Quarr Abbey on the Isle of Wight; organist-choirmaster at churches in Philadelphia and taught at Episcopal Academy, Overbrook, Pa. (1937-41); bandmaster of the 28th Infantry Division in Europe

in World War II and spent six months in a German prison; became organist-choirmaster in churches in San Francisco after the war.

PUTNAM, CURLY

b. 1930 Princeton, Alabama.
Singer and songwriter. Attended Southern Union College, Wadley, Alabama (1950); wrote "Green, Green Grass of Home" (Gold Record, 1967, and BMI award), "Set Me Free," "Jail Birds Can't Fly," "Right Straight in the Eye," "My Elusive Dreams," "Untouchable You."

PYNE, JAMES KENDRICK

b. 1852, d. 1938 England.
Organist and choirmaster at St. Mark's (Episcopal) Church, Philadelphia (1873-75); organist at Manchester Cathedral, England (1876-1938); Minton Pyne was choirmaster at St. Mark's (1881-1905), (brother of James).

QUARLES, JAMES THOMAS

b. 1877 St. Louis, Missouri, d. 1954 Saugus, California. Organist and teacher. Studied with Widor in Paris and others; founded Choral Art Society in St. Louis; taught at Cornell University, Ithaca, N.Y., after 1913; professor of music at University of Missouri, Columbia, after 1923; wrote "Alma Mater"—University of Missouri.

QUARTETTE TRÉS BIEN (jazz quartet) *see* PERCY EDWARD JAMES, JR.

QUEBEC, IKE ABRAMS

b. 1918 Newark, New Jersey, d. 1963 New York City. Black tenor saxist. Played with Roy Eldridge, Benny Carter, Coleman Hawkins, and Cab Calloway in the 1940s; died of lung cancer; albums—*Angry Tenors, Blue and Sentimental, Heavy Soul, It Might as Well Be Spring, Soul Samba.*

QUEEN CITY CONCERT BAND (black band)

Organized in Sedalia, Missouri before 1896; Ed Gravitt, cornet and leader; W.H. Carter, trombone; G. Tom Ireland, clarinet; Nathaniel Diggs, clarinet; Al Wheeler, tenor horn; James Scott, alto horn; James Chisholm, alto horn; R.O. Henderson, baritone horn; A.H. Hickman, tuba; C.W. Gravitt, bass drum; Emmett Cook, snares; Henry Martin, drum major.

QUEENER, CHARLES CONANT

b. 1921 Pineville, Kentucky.
Pianist. Played with Muggsy Spanier, Harry James, Benny Goodman and others in 1940s; later in his own trio.

QUICKSILVER MESSENGER SERVICE (rock group)

John Cipollina, guitar; Gary Duncan, guitar; David Freiberg, bass; Gregory Elmore, drums; started in San Francisco in 1965; first recorded in 1967; albums—*Happy Trails, Quicksilver Messenger Service, Shady Grove.*

QUILL, DANIEL EUGENE (GENE)

b. 1927 Atlantic City, New Jersey.
Alto saxist and clarinetist. Played with Buddy De Franco, Claude Thornhill, Gene Krupa, Phil Woods and others in 1950s; later formed his own combo; album—*Quill.*

QUIMBY, HELEN SHERWOOD

b. 1870 Rochester, New York.
Violinist, pianist, and teacher. Graduated Nansemond Seminary (1888); teacher of violin and piano in Suffolk, Virginia.

QUINCHETTE, PAUL

b. 1921 Denver, Colorado.
Tenor saxist. Studied at Denver University, then Tennessee State College; played with Jay McShann, Louis Jordan, Lucky Millinder and others in 1940s; with Count Basie, Benny Goodman and led his own combo in 1950s.

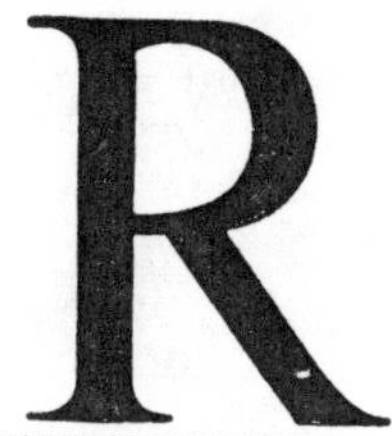

RABBIT FOOT MINSTRELS *see* MA RAINEY, IDA COX

RABIN, MICHAEL

b. 1936 New York City, d. there 1972. Violinist. Son of George Rabin, violinist with New York Philharmonic and Jeanne Seidman, pianist; studied piano at age five with his mother, then violin with his father; between nine and twelve years of age studied under Ivan Galamian at Lake Placid, N.Y.; at age thirteen won Edgar Stillman Kelley contest; debut (1950) as soloist with National Orchestral Association at Carnegie Hall; gave concerts on six continents; died after an epileptic seizure.

RACHMANINOFF, SERGEI

b. 1873 Onega, Novgorod, Russia, d. 1943 Beverly Hills, California. Noted composer. Studied at the St. Petersburg Conservatory and the Moscow Conservatory; left Russia for Switzerland in 1917, then came to America; known for his Concerto no. 2 in C Minor for Piano and Orchestra (1901), Symphony no. 2 in E Minor (1907), *The Isle of the Dead* (tone-poem for orchestra, 1908), Concerto no. 3 in D Minor for Piano and Orchestra (1909), *Preludes*, (for piano, opp. 23, 32, 1903-1910), Concerto no. 4 in G Minor for Piano and Orchestra (1926), *Rhapsody on a Theme of Paganini* (for piano and orchestra, 1934), Symphony no. 3 in A Minor (1936, introduced by the Philadelphia Orchestra under Leopold Stokowski), and *Symphonic Dances* (for orchestra, 1940, introduced by the Philadelphia Orchestra under Eugene Ormandy, 1941).

RADER, DONALD ARTHUR

b. 1935 Rochester, Pennsylvania.
Trumpeter and flügelhorn player. Played with Woody Herman, Maynard Ferguson, Count Basie and others; wrote arrangements for Herman, Ferguson, Basie, and Terry Gibbs.

RAE, JOHN

b. 1934 Saugus, Massachusetts.
Drummer. Born John Anthony Pompeo; with George Shearing, Herbie Mann and others in 1950s; later with Cal Tjader; formed his own quartet.

RAEBURN, BOYD ALBERT

b. 1913 Faith, South Dakota, d. 1966 Lafayette, Indiana. Bass saxophonist and bandleader. Started his band in the 1930s; played the tenor sax first, then baritone, and finally the bass sax; a fire at Palisades Amusement Park in N.J. (1944) destroyed the band's music and some of its instruments; he organized a new band; his arranger Johnny Mandel also played the trombone; later Johnny Richards was arranger; retired in 1959; died of a heart attack.

RAGAN, BRONSON

b. 1915 Rome, New York, d. 1971 Elizabeth, New Jersey. Organist and teacher. Studied organ at Juilliard, New York City with Gaston Dethier and David McK. Williams; organist at Holy Trinity, New York City (1946-71) and at Temple Beth-El in Jersey City, N.J.; joined the faculty at Juilliard (1938) and the Manhattan School of Music (1962), also the summer faculty of the Pius X School of Liturgical Music (1950); died of a heart attack.

RAGAS, HENRY

b. (?), d. 1919.
Pianist. Played in Nick La Rocca's Original Dixieland Jazz Band (1915-19); died of pneumonia.

RAGLIN, ALVIN (REDRICK)

b. 1917 Omaha, Nebraska, d. 1955 Boston, Massachusetts. Double bass player. With Duke Ellington (1941-45).

RAGTIME BAND (jazz band) *see* PAPA LAINE

RAGTIME JUG STOMPERS *see* DAVE VAN RONK

RAGTIMERS *see* MUGGSY SPANIER

RAIDERS, THE *see* REVERE, PAUL AND THE RAIDERS

RAIMONDI, RUGGERO

b. 1942 Bologna, Italy.
Tenor. Debut in Bologna (1965); debut at Metropolitan Opera, New York City (1970) in Verdi's *Ernani.*

RAINEY, GERTRUDE MALISSA NIX PRIDGETT ("MA")

b. 1886 Columbus, Georgia, d. 1939 Rome, Georgia. Black singer. Star of the Rabbit Foot Minstrels; appeared in tent shows in the south; her accompanist was Lovie Austin (Cora Calhoun, pianist); first blues singer to record for Paramount; became known as the "Mother of the Blues"; married actor Will Rainey; discovered Bessie Smith.

RAINGER, RALPH

b. 1901 New York City, d. 1942 Beverly Hills, California. Pianist and popular composer. Studied at the Institute of Musical Art, New York City and later became an attorney, which he left for music; wrote "Moanin' Low" (1929, w. Howard Dietz); with lyrics by Leo Robin—"Love in Bloom," "June in January," "Thanks for the Memory" (1938); also "Blue Hawaii," "Sweet Is the Word for You" (w. Harry Owen); died in an airplane crash.

RAINS, LEON

b. 1870 New York City, d. 1954 Los Angeles, California. Basso. Pupil of Saenger and Bouhy; sang with Damrosch Opera Company (1897-99), Dresden Opera (1899), and the Metropolitan Opera, New York City (1908); later taught in New York City.

RAINWATER, MARVIN

b. 1925 Wichita, Kansas.
Singer and songwriter. Attended Washington State University, Walla Walla, Wash.; served in the navy in World War II; radio debut on "Arthur Godfrey's Talent Scouts" on CBS-TV; later on station WWVA, Wheeling, West Virginia; wrote "Gonna Find Me a Bluebird," "Albino Stallion," "Sticks and Stones," "I Gotta Go Get My Baby," "I Miss You Already."

RAISA, ROSA

b. 1893 Bialystok, Poland, d. 1963.
Noted soprano. Discovered by conductor Cleofonte Campanini (1860-1919) and his wife soprano Eva Tetrazzini (1862-1938); studied under Eva and at the Naples Conservatory with Barbara Marchisio; debut at Parma, Italy (1913); American debut in Chicago (1913) as Aïda; in Europe (1914-15); with the Chicago Opera after 1916; sang leading role in Franke Harling's *A Light from St. Agnes* (1925); Leah in Ludovico Rocca's opera *The Dybbuk* in Detroit (1938); married baritone Giacomo Rimini.

RALPH, JAMES

b. 1698 Philadelphia, Pennsylvania, d. 1762 Chiswick, England. Librettist. Went to London, England (1724); wrote the libretto for the comic opera *The Fashionable Lady,* produced in London (1730, it ran nine performances) and in New York City (1750); this was the first opera for which the words were written by a native-born American; became a character in Alexander Pope's *Duncaid,* attained notoriety, and returned to Philadelphia; friend of Benjamin Franklin.

RAMBLING MOUNTAINEERS *see* CARL M. STORY

RAMBOS, THE SINGING

Of Nashville, Tennessee; Buck Rambo, lead singer and guitarist; his wife, Dottie, lead guitarist and soloist; Reba Rambo, bassist; Pat Jones, pianist and organist; albums—Buck—*Country Boy Gospel;* Dottie—*The Good Ole Days, It's the Soul of Me, Sunshine Shine On, Dottie Rambo and Imperials.*

RAMEY, EUGENE GLASCO

b. 1913 Austin, Texas.
Bass player. With Countess Johnson, Jay McShann, Luis Russell and others in 1940s; with Count Basie, Art Blakey and others in 1950s.

RANDALL, JAMES RYDER

b. 1839 Baltimore, Maryland, d. 1908 Augusta, Georgia. Lyricist. He was teaching at Poydras College, Pointe Coupee Parish, Louisiana, when he read in the newspapers that Union troops were marching through the streets of Baltimore (1861). Saddened, although inspired, he wrote the lyrics "Maryland, My Maryland" (now the state song of Maryland), based on the German Christmas carol, "Tannenbaum, O Tannenbaum."

RANDI, DON

b. 1937 New York City.
Pianist. Born Don Schwartz; studied at the Los Angeles Conservatory; played in night spots in Hollywood; also played harpsichord and organ; wrote "Mexican Pearls" (1966); album—*Love Theme from Romeo and Juliet.*

RANDOLPH, HAROLD

b. 1861 Richmond, Virginia, d. 1927 Northeast Harbor, Maine. Pianist. Studied at

Peabody Institute, Baltimore; director of the conservatory after 1898; later played with Boston Symphony Orchestra.

RANDOLPH, INNES

b. 1837 Winchester, Virginia, d. 1887.
Poet and lyricist. Wrote for the *Baltimore American;* wrote "I'm a Good Old Rebel," shortly after General Lee's surrender in 1865; the poem later became a cowboy song and was included in *Cowboy Songs* by John A. Lomax (1910).

RANDOLPH, IRVING ("MOUSE")

b. 1909 St. Louis, Missouri.
Black trumpeter. Played with Fate Marable on the Mississippi river boats; with Andy Kirk, Benny Carter, Fletcher Henderson, Cab Calloway and others in 1940s; with Ella Fitzgerald, Don Redman, Edmond Hall and others in 1950s.

RANDOLPH, ZILMER TRENTON

b. 1899 Dermott, Arkansas.
Trumpeter and composer. Played in Milwaukee, Wisc., with Bernie Young (1927-31); trumpeter and arranger for Louis Armstrong (1931-35); wrote "Ol' Man Lose"; later arranger for Duke Ellington, Woody Herman and others.

RANEY, JAMES ELBERT

b. 1927 Louisville, Kentucky.
Guitarist. Played with Woody Herman, Buddy De Franco, Terry Gibbs, Artie Shaw, Stan Getz and others in 1950s; later with Red Norvo, Stan Getz and others; album—*Two Jim and A Zoot.*

RANEY, WAYNE T.

b. 1921 Wolf Bayou, Arkansas.
Singer, harmonica player, and songwriter. With the Raney Family Gospel Singers; wrote "Why Don't You Haul Off," "A Gathering in the Sky," "Book of Revelations," "Lonesome Wind Blues."

RANGERS TRIO *see* RONNIE PAGE

RANKIN, JEREMIAH EAMES

b. 1828 Thornton, New Hampshire, d. 1904 Cleveland, Ohio. Hymnist. Graduated Middlebury College, Middlebury, Vermont (1848); Congregational minister and President of Howard University, Washington, D.C. for four years; compiled *The Auld Scotch Mither, Ingleside Rhymes, Hymns Pro Patria,* and with Bischoff and Presby, *Gospel Bells* (1883); wrote the hymn "God Be with You" (1860, m. W.G. Tomar); *Gospel Bells* included one tune by his son, Walter N. Rankin (d. 1877 Washington, D.C.).

RAPEE, ERNO

b. 1891 Budapest, Hungary, d. 1945 New York City. Conductor. Graduated Budapest Conservatory with honors; director of the Hungarian Opera company, New York City (1913); musical director of Capitol and Roxy Theatres; also guest appearances in Berlin, Vienna, and Budapest; then with film studios in Hollywood; musical director of NBC; conductor of General Motors Symphony Orchestra; musical director of Radio City Music Hall, New York City (1933-45).

RAPPOLD, MARIE WINTEROTH

b. 1880 Brooklyn, New York, d. 1957 Los Angeles, California. Soprano. Sang in London at only ten years of age; studied with Oscar Saenger; sang in concert; with the Metropolitan Opera, New York after 1905.

RAPPOLO, JOSEPH LEON

b. 1902 Lutcher, Louisiana, d. 1943 Jackson, Louisiana. Clarinetist. Studied violin, then clarinet; ran away from home at age fourteen, but the police nabbed him in Hattiesburg, Mississippi; played with Friar's Society Orchestra, later known as the New Orleans Rhythm Kings; *Farewell Blues* was composed in 1923 by Rappolo, Paul Mares, and Elmer Schoebel; confined to a mental institution at age twenty-five.

RASBACH, OSCAR

b. 1888 Dayton, Kentucky, d. 1975.
Pianist, composer, and teacher. Studied under Ludwig Thomas, Julius Jahn, Jode Anderson, A.J. Stamm, and Hans Thornton; also choral director; wrote operettas, *Dawn Boy* and *Open House;* composed music for "Trees" (1922, w. Joyce Kilmer, 1913).

RASCALS, THE (rock group)

Eddie Brigati, vocals; Felix Cavaliere, organ; Gene Cornish, guitar; Dino Danelli, drums; started in Garfield, N.J., in 1965 as the Young Rascals; played at James Brown's Madison Square Garden debut (1966); toured England; first recorded in 1965; albums—*Collections, Freedom Suite, Groovin', Once Upon a Dream, Rascal's Greatest Hits, See, Young Rascals.*

RASKIN, MILTON WILLIAM

b. 1916 Boston, Massachusetts.
Pianist. Played with Wingy Manone and Gene Krupa in 1930s; with Tommy Dorsey, Teddy Powell, Alvino Rey and others in 1940s; staff musician with MGM in 1950s.

RATHAUS, KAREL

b. 1895 Ternopol, Poland, d. 1954 New York City. Composer. Studied at the University of Vienna and with Franz Schreker, then settled in Berlin; with the rise of Hitler, he fled to London, then New York City; taught at Queens College, New York City; composed chamber music, piano pieces, and much orchestral music.

RAUSCH, EDGAR LEON

b. 1927 Springfield, Missouri.
Singer and bandleader. Served in the navy in World War II; in Bob Wills' band; organized the New Texas Playboys, Fort Worth, Texas (1964).

RAUSCH, FRIEDRICH

b. 1755 Erfiert, Germany, d. 1823 New York City. Pianist, organist, and composer. Resident musician at the Court of St. Petersburg, Russia; went to London, then New York City about 1793; music publisher in New York City (1794-97) in joint venture with George Gilfert and James Hewitt; vice president of St. Cecilia Society (1799); in London (1804-06); returned to New York City (1806); wrote *Prince Kutusoff* (1820), "Hymn to the Creator" (1795, w. Rev. Merrick, published by George Gilfert).

RAVAN, GENYA

b. 1941 Poland.
Singer. Born Goldie Zelkowitz; debut in a Brooklyn, New York, club (1963); with the Escorts (1963-64); led the band Goldie and the Gingerbreads (1964-70); lead singer for the hard rock group the Ten Wheel Drive; her lead guitarist is Mitch Styles who helps her write songs; she was arrested in Cherry Hill, N.J., for using an obscenity over the microphone (1971).

RAWLS, LOU

b. 1935 Chicago, Illinois.
Black singer. Started as a gospel singer; debut at Hollywood Bowl (1959) with Dick Clark; first recorded in 1961; soulful blues singer; albums—*Best of Lou Rawls, Black and Blue, Carryin' On, Close Up, Feelin' Good, Nobody But Lou, Lou Rawls and Strings, Lou Rawls Live, Soulin', Too Much, Tobacco Road, Your Good Thing, You're Good for Me, You've Made Me So Very Happy;* at the Maisonette, St. Regis Hotel, New York City (1972); won Grammy Award (1972) for best male rhythm and blues performance for "Natural Man"; at the Newport Jazz Festival, New York City (1972).

RAY, DANNY ("BIG BLACK")

b. 1934 Georgia.
Black conga drummer. Played in Lord Flea's Calypso Band in the Bahamas; then with Calypso Eddy Trio for three years; formed group with Jamaican trumpeter Billy Cook in Nassau, Bahamas; played in New York City in 1960s with Randy Weston's group and others; with Dizzy Gillespie at Newport Jazz Festival (1965).

RAY, JOHNNIE

b. 1927 Dallas, Oregon.
Singer. Tossed high in a blanket at age ten, fell hard on his head, and became about half deaf; recorded (1952) "The Little White Cloud That Cried," which became a sensation; his records sold in the millions; charged with soliciting a man in a bar in Detroit in 1959, but acquitted; albums—*Mr. Cry, Johnnie Ray's Greatest Hits;* at Rainbow Grill, New York City (1972).

RAY, WADE

b. 1913 Evansville, Indiana.
Violinist and singer. Debut as violinist in Boynton, Arkansas at age five; on station KMOX, St. Louis (1931-43); served in the army in World War II; later on "Cowtown," Los Angeles; LP record—*Down Yonder.*

RAYE, MARTHA

b. 1916 Butte, Montana.
Singer and comedienne. Sang with Louis Prima's band at the Famous Door, New York City (1935); Louis and Martha appeared on Rudy Vallee's variety show "The Fleischmann Hour" on radio; she appeared in many films; album—*Together Again for the First Time* (with Carol Burnett).

RAYMOND, GENE

b. 1908 New York City.
Singer. Appeared in many films with Jeannette MacDonald.

RAZAF, ANDY

b. 1895 Washington, D.C., d. 1973.
Black lyricist. Born Andreamenentania Paul Razafinkeriefo; nephew of Queen Ranavalona III of Madagascar; with Harry Brooks, wrote "Ain't Misbehavin" (m. Fats Waller) and other songs for *Hot Chocolate* (1929); also lyrics for Lew Leslie's *Blackbirds of 1930* (m. Eubie Blake), which starred Ethel Waters and the Berry Brothers.

READ, DANIEL

b. 1757 Rehoboth, Massachusetts, d. 1836 New Haven, Connecticut. Composer and compiler. Brother of Joel and William Read, composers; published *The American Singing Book* (New Haven, 1785); with Amos Doolittle, *The American Musical Magazine* (May, 1786 to September, 1787); *An Introduction to Psalmody* (New Haven, 1790), *The Columbian Harmonist* (New Haven, 1793), *The New Haven Collection* (Dedham, Mass., 1818); composed the tunes "Windham," "Russia," "Lisbon," "Stafford," and "Sherburne," which was first used for "While Shepherds Watched Their Flocks" (second tune "Christmas," by Handel).

READ, GARDNER, JR.

b. 1913 Evanston, Illinois.
Composer. Graduated Eastman School, Rochester, N.Y.; won Berkshire Music Centre Fellowship, Cromwell European Fellowship, Juilliard Prizes (1938 and 1941), MacDowell Fellowship; composed *Sketches of the City* (suite, poems of Carl Sandburg, Rochester Civic Orchestra under Hanson, 1934), Symphony no. 1 (New York Philharmonic under Barbirolli, 1937), *Passacaglia and Fugue* (Ravinia, under Rodzinski, 1938), Symphony no. 2 (Boston Symphony under composer, 1943, won Paderewski Prize), *Night Flight* (Eastman Orchestra, 1944).

READ, JOEL

b. 1753 Attleboro, Massachusetts, d. there 1837. Compiler, singing teacher, and choir leader. Brother of Daniel Read and William Read, and all three were composers; in 1808 published *The New England Selection, or Plain Psalmodist*, which included fifteen tunes credited to "Read," some of which are known to have been written by Daniel.

REARDON, CASPER

b. 1907 Little Falls, New York, d. 1941 New York City. Harpist. Played in symphony orchestras; recorded with Jack Teagarden (1934).

REBELS QUARTET (gospel singers)

Organized in 1949; with WFLA-TV, Tampa, Florida; John Matthews, manager and baritone; Horace Parrish, tenor; London Parris, bass; Jimmy Taylor, lead and pianist; songs recorded include "How Great Thou Art," "The Bible Tells Me So," "Rock of Ages," "Oh What a Friend We Have in Jesus," "The Old Rugged Cross," "Whispering Hope."

RECORD BOYS (band) *see* SAMMY STEPT

RECTOR, WILLIAM EUGENE ("RED")

b. 1929 Marshall, North Carolina.
Banjoist and mandolin player. With "Walker's Fun Time," WNOX-TV, Knoxville, Tenn. (1959-67).

RED HOT PEPPERS (black jazz group)

Organized in Chicago (1923) for Victor recordings by Jelly Roll Morton; Andrew Hilaire, drums; Kid Ory, trombone; George Mitchell, trumpet; Johnny Lindsay, bass; Johnny St. Cyr, banjo; Omer Simeon, clarinet.

REDD, FREDDIE

b. 1928 New York City.
Pianist. Served in U.S. Army (1946-49); played with Cootie Williams, Oscar Pettiford, Art Blakey and others in 1950s; later led his own quartet; wrote the score for the off-Broadway play, *The Connection* (1959); album—*The Connection.*

REDDING, OTIS

b. 1941 Dawson, Georgia, d. 1967 Lake Monona, Wisconsin. Black singer. Raised in Macon, Georgia; became a top soul-rock singer; left a concert in Madison, Wisconsin in his private plane and crashed enroute to Cleveland; 4,500 people attended his funeral in Macon; albums—*Dictionary of Soul, Dock of the Bay, Great Otis Redding Sings Soul Ballads, Immortal Otis Redding, In Person at the Whiskey A-Go-Go, King and Queen, Live in Europe, Love Man, Otis Blue, Pain in My Heart, Soul Album.*

REDMAN, DONALD MATTHEW

b. 1900 Piedmont, West Virginia, d. 1964. Black jazz bandleader, arranger, and saxophonist. Studied at the Boston Conservatory and the Detroit Conservatory; played alto-saxophone in Fletcher Henderson's band; also with McKinney's Cotton Pickers; started his own band in the 1930s; wrote "Chant of the Weed," his theme song; later wrote arrangements for radio and the theater; led first black band to play on a sponsored radio series, "Chipso" (1932).

REDNER, LEWIS H.

b. 1831 Philadelphia, Pennsylvania, d. 1908 Atlantic City, New Jersey. Composer. Real estate broker in Philadelphia and organist of the Church of the Holy Trinity, when Rector Phillips Brooks asked him to compose the music for a Christmas carol Brooks had written, "Oh Little Town of Bethlehem" (1868).

REECE, ALPHONSO SON ("DIZZY")

b. 1931 Kingston, Jamaica.
Black trumpeter. Played in Paris (1949-50) with Don Byas, also Jay Cameron; later in Germany, and in England with Tony Crombie's band; came to New York (1959).

REED, LUCY

b. 1921 Marshfield, Wisconsin.
Singer. Born Lucille DeRidder; with Woody Herman, Charlie Ventura and others in 1950s.

REED, SUSAN KAREN

b. 1927 Columbia, South Carolina.
Harpist and singer. Daughter of Daniel Reed, actor and playwright; debut at Town Hall, New York City (1946); LP records—*Susan Reed, Susan Reed Sings Old Airs, Old Airs from Ireland, Scotland and England.*

REESE, DELLA

b. 1932 Detroit, Michigan
Black singer. Born Dellareese Taliaferro, one of five children; sang with Mahalia Jackson's troupe at age thirteen; attended Wayne State University, Detroit; sang at the Flame Club, Detroit; sang with Erskine Hawkins' band; toured England, Germany, Scandinavia, Chile, Uruguay, Israel, and Australia.

REESE, LIZETTE WOODWORTH

b. 1856 Baltimore, Maryland, d. 1935.
Poetess. Wrote the lyrics "Glad That I Live Am I" from her book of poems *A Handful of Lavender* (1891) (m. Geoffrey Shaw, tune "Water-End," 1925).

REEVES, DELANO (DEL)

b. 1933 Sparta, North Carolina.
Singer. Sang in night clubs in Las Vegas in the 1960s; also appeared in motion pictures; LP records—*Best of Del Reeves, Big Daddy Del, Country Concert Live, Doodle-oo-Doo-Doo, Down at Good Time Charlie's, Gettin' Any Feed for Your Chickens, Girl on the Billboard, Little Church in the Del, Looking at the World Thru a Windshield, Our Way of Life, Running Wild, Special Delivery, Struttin' My Stuff.*

REEVES, JAMES TRAVIS (JIM)

b. 1924 Panola County, Texas, d. 1964 in a plane crash. Singer and songwriter. Attended school in Carthage, Texas; University of Texas at Austin; later on station KWKH, Shreveport, La.; toured for the USO; wrote "Am I Losing You," "I Know One," "I'm Getting Better" (all 1960); albums—*According to My Heart, Best of Jim Reeves, Blue Side of Lonesome, Country Side of Jim Reeves, Distant Drums, Gentleman Jim, Girls I Have Known, God Be With You, Good 'n Country, Have I Told You Lately That I Love You, He'll Have to Go, International Jim Reeves, Intimate Jim Reeves, Kimberly Jim, Moonlight and Roses, My Cathedral, Jim Reeves, and Some Friends, J.R. on Stage, J.R. Up Thru the Years, J.R. Way, Songs to Warm the Heart, Talkin' To Your Heart, Tall Tales and Short Tempers, Touch of Velvet, Touch of Sadness, We Thank Thee, Yours Sincerely, Jim Reeves.*

REHAK, FRANK JAMES

b. 1926 Brooklyn, New York.
Trombonist. Served in the navy during World War II; with Gene Krupa, Art Mooney, Claude Thornhill, Woody Herman, Dizzy Gillespie and others.

REICH, STEVE

b. 1936.
Composer. Graduated Cornell University, Ithaca, N.Y.; studied music at Juilliard, New York City and at Mills College; while trying to control two tape recorders, found he could not control them exactly, thus creating out-of-phase and overlapping rhythms, part of his early work; his *Phase Patterns* presented at the Public Theatre, New York City (1971).

REID, DON S.

b. 1945 Staunton, Virginia.
Singer. Member of the Statler Brothers quartet, with his brother Harold, also Philip E. Balsley and Lew C. DeWitt; he served as master of ceremonies; their albums—*Flowers on the Wall, Oh Happy Day, Statler Brothers Sing the Big Hits.*

REID, HAROLD W.

b. 1939 Augusta County, Virginia.
Bass. Member of the Statler Brothers, vocal quartet, with his brother Don.

REILLY, DEAN EDWIN

b. 1926 Auburn, Washington.
Bass player. His father led a dance band in the 1920s; played in various San Francisco night spots.

REINAGLE, ALEXANDER

b. 1756 Portsmouth, England, d. 1809 Baltimore, Maryland. Noted composer. Studied in England under Raynor Taylor; came to New York (1786); in Philadelphia gave music lessons to Nellie Custis, adopted daughter of George Washington; with Thomas Wignall opened Chestnut Street Theatre in Philadelphia (1793); composed the music for the opera, *The Sicilian Romance* (w. Henry Siddons) produced at the theater May 6, 1795; *A Sonata to George Washington* (1789) for Washington's reception in Trenton, N.J.; *Columbus* (1799, historical play) which included "When Columbus Sought This Strand" (w. Alexander Martin).

REINECKE, ABRAHAM

b. 1712 Stockholm, Sweden, d. 1760 Bethlehem, Pennsylvania. Hymnist. Came to America (1744) as a Moravian minister; his hymns appeared in Moravian hymnals.

REINER, FRITZ

b. 1888 Budapest, Hungary, d. 1963.
Conductor. Conductor of the Budapest Opera, the Dresden Opera (1914-22), then came to America as conductor of the Cincinnati Symphony Orchestra (1923-31); became conductor in Pittsburgh (1938-48), then was with the Metropolitan Opera, New York City (1948-49); with the Chicago Symphony (1953).

REINHARDT, MAX

b. 1873 Baden, Austria, d. 1943.
Producer and director. Born Max Goldman; was an actor, and started directing shows in Berlin (1903); in 1920 founded the theatre festival in Salzburg, Austria; when the Nazis came to power he emigrated to the United States; directed *The Eternal Road* (1937, m. Kurt Weill and book—Franz Werfel).

REISER, ALOIS

b. 1884 Prague, Czechoslovakia.
Composer. Studied with Dvořák; resided in Los Angeles; composed *Summer Evening* (Prague Philharmonic, 1911), *Slavic Rhapsody* (Los Angeles Philharmonic under composer, 1931), *Concerto for Cello and Orchestra* (Los Angeles Philharmonic under Rodzinski, with Ilya Bronson, soloist, 1933), *Erewhon* (Los Angeles Federation Orchestra under composer, 1936).

RELIANCE BRASS BAND (jazz band) *see* PAPA LAINE

REMAINS, THE (rock group)

Barry Tashian, lead guitar and vocalist; Chip Damiani, drums; Vern Miller, Jr., trumpet, tuba, etc.; William Henry Briggs III, electric organ and piano; started in Boston in 1965; all four were dropouts from Boston University; group disbanded; album—*The Remains* (1967).

REMENYI, EDUARD

b. 1830 Heves, Hungary, d. 1898 San Francisco, California. Violinist. Fought in the insurrections against the Austro-Hungarian Empire (1848), but fled to America when the revolt was put down; returned to Europe and toured with Brahms (1852-53); on the concert stage in San Francisco when he suffered a fatal stroke.

REMICK, JEROME H.

b. (?), d. 1931.
Publisher. Among his song pluggers and songwriters were Burton Lane, Harry Tierney, and Richard A. Whiting.

REMINGTON, EMORY

b. 1892, d. 1971 Rochester, New York.
Trombonist and teacher. Taught trombone at the Eastman School of Music, Rochester, N.Y., for fifty years (1921-71); his daughter, Janet Remington, harpist with the Pittsburgh Symphony Orchestra.

RENA, HENRY ("KID")

b. 1898 New Orleans, Louisiana, d. there 1949. Black trumpeter and bandleader. Played in Kid Ory's band (1918); later with Bob Lyons; led his own band; recorded on Delta Records.

"RENFRO VALLEY BARN DANCE" *see* BESS FARMER, RED FOLEY, JOHN LAIR

REPPER, CHARLES BRASHEAR

b. 1889 Alliance, Ohio.
Pianist and composer. Wrote "Heigho," "Oleander Time," "Where Is Spring"; operettas—*The Dragon of Wu Foo, Penny Buns and Roses.*

RESNIK, REGINA

b. 1923 Brooklyn, New York.
Soprano. Studied with Rosalie Miller; debut at Metropolitan Opera, New York City (1944), as Leonora in *Il Trovatore;* sang as Carmen (1970) at the Metropolitan Opera celebrating her 25th anniversary there.

RETI, RUDOLF

b. 1885 Ucize, Yugoslavia, d. 1957.
Teacher and writer. Music critic for *Das Echo* in Vienna and composed the symphonic suite *David and Goliath;* rise of Nazism caused him to flee to Palestine, then the United States, where he became a teacher and pianist in Montclair, N.J.; wrote the books *The Thematic Process in Music* (1951) and *Tonality-Atonality-Pantonality* (1958).

REUSS, ALLAN

b. 1915 New York City.
Guitarist. Played with Benny Goodman, Paul Whiteman, and Jack Teagarden in 1930s; with Ted Weems, Jimmy Dorsey, Benny Goodman, and Harry James in 1940s.

REUSS, EDUARD

b. 1851 New York City, d. 1911 Dresden, Germany. Teacher. Studied with Edward Kruger and Liszt; taught at Carlsruhe (1880), Wiesbaden (1896), director of conservatory at Wiesbaden (1902), then in Dresden and later as teacher in Berlin; his wife, Louise Belce Reuss, was an operatic soprano.

REUTER, FLORIZEL VON *see* VON REUTER

REVEL, HARRY

b. 1905 London, England, d. 1958 New York City. Pianist and popular composer. Studied in Germany and Austria; came to America (1929); with Mack Gordon, lyricist and vaudeville actor, he wrote "Underneath the Harlem Moon" (1932), "An Orchid to You" (1933), "Did You Ever See a Dream Walking" (1933), "Goodnight My Love," "Paris in the Spring" (1935), "Never in a Million Years"; during World War II supervised the USO unit in Hollywood; wrote the music for the show *Are You with It?* (1945, w. Arnold B. Horwitt).

REVELATOR QUARTET (gospel singers)

Organized in 1959; Jack R. Bryson, first tenor; Kenneth R. Briggs, second tenor; Dale Baker, baritone; Scranton Ark Hall, bass; Jerry Evans, pianist; Bobby Burks, guitarist; Sanford Williams, bass player; Bobby Ball.

REVERE, PAUL

b. 1735 Boston, Massachusetts, d. there 1818. Engraver, patriot, and manufacturer of church bells. Son of Apollos De Rivoire, a French Huguenot; engraved the plates for *A Collection of the Best Psalm Tunes* compiled by Josiah Flagg (1764) and the frontispiece and over 100 tunes on copper plates for *The New England Psalm Singer* of William Billings; set up a bell foundry in 1792 with his son, Joseph, and cast church bells.

REVERE AND THE RAIDERS, PAUL (rock group)

Mark Lindsay, lead vocals and sax; Paul Revere, piano and organ; Freddie Weller, lead guitar; Joe Junior Correro, drums; Charlie Coe, bass guitar; former members—Michael "Smitty" Smith, Jim "Harpo" Valley, Drake Levin, Philip "Fang" Volk; started as the Downbeats in Portland, Oregon (1962); appeared on Dick Clark's TV show (1965); albums—*Alias Pink Puzz, Hard and Heavy with Marshmallow, Here They Come, Just Like Us, Midnight Ride, Paul Revere and the Raiders, Greatest Hits, Revolution.*

REVOLUTIONARY ENSEMBLE, THE (improvisational group)

Violinist Leroy Jenkins, bassist Sirone, and drummer Jerome Cooper; played in the Oscar Wilde Room of the Mercer Art Center, New York City (March, 1972).

REVUELTAS, SILVESTRE

b. 1899 Durango, Mexico, d. 1940 Mexico City, Mexico. Noted composer. Studied at the National Conservatory in Mexico City and at the Chicago Musical College; concert violinist, then assistant conductor with the Orquesta Sinfonica in Mexico City; composed *Esquinas* (1931), *Caminos* (tone picture for orchestra 1934, introduced by the Orquesta Sinfonica under Carlos Chavez), *Sensemaya* (tone poem for orchestra, 1937, w. Nicolas Guillen).

REXFORD, EBEN E.

b. 1841 Johnsburg, New York, d. 1916 Green Bay, Wisconsin. Lyricist. Lived for a time in Shiocton, Wisc.; well known for his books on horticulture—*Home Floriculture, Grandmother's Garden, Flowers—How to Grow Them,* and *Four Seasons in a Garden;* wrote, with music by George F. Root—"My Beau That Went to Canada" (1865) and "O Where Are the Reapers?"; also "Only a Pansy Blossom" (m. Frank Howard), "Silver Threads Among the Gold" (1873, m. H.P. Danks), and "Linger Near Me, Little Treasure" (1877, m. W.T. Keefer).

REY, ALVINO

b. ca. 1918 Cleveland, Ohio.
Guitarist and bandleader. Born Al McBurney; formed his band when he and the King sisters left Horace Heidt (1938); played on radio station KHJ, Los Angeles; featured Yvonne, Donna, Louise, and Alyce King; married Louise King; played at the Hotel Biltmore, New York City; at Meadowbrook (1942); George Handy was arranger (1943); Alvino entered the navy (1944-45); later appeared on TV shows; known as an electric guitarist.

REYNOLDS, MALVINA

b. 1900 San Francisco, California.
Popular composer and singer. Graduated the University of California, Berkeley (Ph.D.);

wrote the words for "Sally, Don't You Grieve" (1957, m. Woody Guthrie), and composed "Turn Around" (with Alan Greene); "From Way Up Here" (1960, with Pete Seeger), "Let It Be" (1960), "Temptation" (1961), "Little Boxes" (1962), "What Have They Done to the Rain" (1963, sung by Joan Baez and Bob Dylan).

REYNOLDS, NICK

b. 1933 Coronado, California.
Singer. With Bob Shane and Dave Guard, formed the Kingston Trio (1957).

REYNOLDS, ROGER

b. 1934.
Composer. Places the performers in different areas, the scores of his compositions show the movement from one part of the stage to another; wrote *The Emperor of Ice Cream* (1963), *Blind Men* (1966).

REYNOLDS, THOMAS A.

b. 1917 Akron, Ohio.
Clarinetist and producer. Studied at Ohio State University; played with Isham Jones in late 1930s; led his own band (1939-55); then a radio program producer, including "Bandstand USA" on Mutual network.

RHINOCEROS (blues-rock group)

John Finley, vocals; Michael Fonfara, organ; Alan Gerber, piano; Doug Hastings, guitar; Billy Mundi, drums; Danny Weis, guitar; Jerry Penrod, bass; started playing in Central Park, New York City (1968); first recorded in 1968; albums—*Rhinoceros, Satin Chickens.*

RHODES, TODD WASHINGTON

b. 1900 Hopkinsville, Kentucky, d. 1965.
Black pianist. Studied at Springfield School of Music, Springfield, Ohio (1915-17), and at Erie Conservatory, Erie, Pa. (1917-21); organized The Cotton Pickers, with William McKinney as drummer-manager; later known as McKinney's Cotton Pickers; organized his own band in Detroit (1947).

RHYTHM BOYS

Paul Whiteman, Harry Barris, Bing Crosby and Al Rinker (1928-29).

RICCI, RUGGIERO

b. 1920 San Francisco, California.
Violinist. Studied with his father, a bandmaster; then with Louis Persinger; debut in San Francisco at age eight; played Beethoven concerto in Chicago and New York at eleven; toured Europe.

RICCIO, PATRICK JOSEPH

b. 1918 Port Arthur, Ontario, Canada.
Alto saxist. Musical director and arranger for RCAF Streamliners (1941-46); in London during the war; later formed his own band; at Canadian Jazz Festival in Toronto (1959).

RICE, FENELON BIRD

b. 1841 Greensburg, Ohio, d. 1901 Oberlin, Ohio. Organist and teacher. Studied in Boston and Leipzig; organist in Boston for three years; director at Oberlin College after 1871; Mus.D. at Hillsdale (Michigan) College.

RICE, JOHN

b. ca. 1720 England, d. 1795.
Organist at Trinity Church, New York City (1744-61).

RICE, THOMAS DARTMOUTH (DADDY)

b. 1808 New York City, d. there 1860.
Early minstrel showman. Know as "Daddy" or "Jim Crow" Rice; wrote the words to "Jim Crow" (ca. 1828), "Lucy Long, Gich a Gittin' Upstairs" and "Clare de Kitchen"; plugged "Shinbone Alley" (1836) by William Clifton; plugged his lifetime hit "Jim Crow" in Louisville, Cincinnati, Pittsburgh and other cities. Stephen Foster approached Rice in Cincinnati in 1851 and sold Rice his song "Long Ago Day." Later Foster saw Rice again, and Rice asked Foster to compose some music to a poem by G. Mellon, so Foster wrote "This Rose Will Remind You."

RICH, BERNARD ("BUDDY")

b. 1917 Brooklyn, New York.
Jazz drummer and bandleader. Played with Bunny Berigan's band; with Artie Shaw; with Tommy Dorsey; considered by some critics as the greatest drummer of all time; fought with Frank Sinatra, the band's singer; so cocky, rash, and outspoken that the band players almost had to stand in line to "take a sock at him" (Bob Bach in *Metronome*); formed his own band; joined Harry James in 1950s; formed another band (1967).

RICH, DAVID EARL (DAVE)

b. 1936 Briar Creek, Kentucky.
Singer and songwriter. Attended high school in Breman, Kentucky; wrote "Your Pretty Blue Eyes," "Our Last Night Together," "I Forgot," "Didn't Work Out Right," "Ain't It Fine," "Red Sweater."

RICH, THADDEUS

b. 1885 Indianapolis, Indiana, d. 1969.
Violinist. Studied violin with his father,

William S. Rich, violinist; debut at age nine; studied at Leipzig Conservatory, graduated with honors at age fifteen; joined Gewandhaus Orchestra, Leipzig (1900); pupil of Joachim in Berlin (1902); returned to America (1905); concertmaster for Philadelphia Orchestra after 1906; also dean of music at Temple University, Philadelphia.

RICHARDS, ANN

b. 1935 San Diego, California.
Singer. Born Margaret Ann Borden; with Charlie Barnet and George Redman; with Stan Kenton, then married him (1955).

RICHARDS, CHARLES ("RED")

b. 1912 Brooklyn, New York.
Black pianist. With Bobby Hackett, Roy Eldridge, Sidney Bechet, Tab Smith and others in 1940s; with Muggsy Spanier, Wild Bill Davison and others in 1950s.

RICHARDS, CHARLES HERBERT

b. 1839 Meriden, New Hampshire, d. 1925 New York City. Hymnist. Attended Amherst, Yale, Union Seminary, and Andover Theological Seminary where he graduated (1865); Congregational minister at churches in Madison, Wisc., and Philadelphia; assisted in the compilation of *Songs of Christian Praise* (1880), *Songs of Prayer and Praise* (1883), and *Songs of Christian Life* (1912); wrote the hymn "Our Father, Thy Dear Name Doth Show" (1910, tune "Bethlehem" or "Evangel"—German).

RICHARDS, EMIL

b. 1932 Hartford, Connecticut.
Vibraphonist. Born Emilio Joseph Radocchia; studied at Hartford School of Music (1949-52); with Hartford and New Britain Symphony Orchestras, also the Connecticut Pops Orchestra (1952-54); in Japan with U.S. Army band; later with George Shearing; then formed his own quintet.

RICHARDS, GEORGE

b. ca. 1755 Newport, Rhode Island, d. 1816 Philadelphia, Pennsylvania. Hymnist and compiler. Chaplain in the U.S. Navy; Universalist preacher in Portsmouth, N.H., and New Haven, Conn. (1793-1809), then in Philadelphia; committed suicide; with S. Lane edited the *Universalist Hymn Book* (Boston, 1792) which included forty-nine of his hymns, *A Collection of Hymns* (Dover, N.H., 1801) including six of his, also a second edition (1806) which included twenty-six of his hymns.

RICHARDS, JOHNNY

b. 1911 Schenectady, New York d. 1968.
Arranger. Born John Cascales; played violin, banjo, and trumpet in a vaudeville act, "The Seven Wonders of the World" at age ten; played saxophone at seventeen and was writing scores for films in London at age twenty; then in Hollywood during 1930s; led his own dance band in 1940s; later arranger for Boyd Raeburn, Stan Kenton, and Dizzy Gillespie.

RICHARDSON, CHARLOTTE SMITH

b. 1775 d. after 1806.
Hymnist. Published her *Poems Written on Different Subjects* (1806); her hymn "O God, to Thee We Raise Our Eyes," was taken from her poems.

RICHARDSON, JAMES

b. 1817 Dedham, Massachusetts, d. 1863 Washington, D.C. Hymnist. Graduated Harvard (1837), Divinity School (1845); Unitarian pastor in Southington, Conn., and Haverhill, Mass.; served the Washington, D.C. hospitals during the Civil War; two of his hymns appeared in Samuel Longfellow and Samuel Johnson's *Book of Hymns* (1848).

RICHARDSON, JEROME C.

b. 1920 Oakland, California.
Black singer and saxist. Studied at San Francisco State College; served in navy in World War II; with Lionel Hampton, Earl Hines, Lucky Millinder, Cootie Williams and others in 1950s; with Quincy Jones and others in 1960s; album—*Groove Merchant.*

RICHARDSON, J.P.

b. 1935, d. 1959 Fargo, North Dakota.
Singer and songwriter. Known as "Big Bopper" rock singer; wrote and recorded "Chantilly Lace" (1958); album—*Chantilly Lace;* was disc jockey and singer on station KTRM, Beaumont, Texas; appeared before 1,100 fans at the Surf Ballroom in Mason City, Iowa; next morning chartered a plane with Buddy Holly and Ritchie Valens, the plane crashed and all three were killed.

RICHINGS, PETER

b. 1798 England, d. 1871 Media, Pennsylvania. Opera singer and actor. Came to New York City (1821); debut there at the Park Theatre; singer and actor for forty-six years; retired in 1867.

RICHMAN, ABRAHAM SAMUEL ("BOOMIE")

b. 1921 Brockton, Massachusetts.
Saxist, flutist, and clarinetist. With Muggsy Spanier, Jerry Wald, and Tommy Dorsey (1946-52); recorded with Benny Goodman and others.

RICHMOND, CHARLES DANIEL (DANNIE)

b. 1935 New York City.
Drummer and tenor saxist. With Charles Mingus and others in 1950s; album—*"In" Jazz for the Cultural Set.*

RICHMOND, MILES C.

b. 1930 Wilsonville, Georgia.
Singer and songwriter. Wrote "Cajun Wheel," "U.S. Government Blues," "Downhill Pull," "Lorena," "Far Place," "God's Radio Station."

RICKETTS, FREDERICK J.

b. 1881, d. 1945 New York City.
Composer. Wrote "Colonel Bogey" (1916, under the pseud. Kenneth J. Alford), which was included in the film *The Bridge on the River Kwai* (1957).

RICKSECKER, PETER

b. 1791 Bethlehem, Pennsylvania, d. there 1873. Composer and teacher. Taught in Nazareth Hall after 1811; then Graceham, Ind., and Lancaster, Pa.; sent to the West Indies as a deacon (1822-43); pastor in Hopedale, Pa. (1849-54); missionary to the Indians in Kansas (1856-57); wrote *The Battle of New Orleans* (1816).

RIDDLE, NELSON

b. 1921 Oradell, New Jersey.
Bandleader. Studied piano and trombone; arranger for Jerry Wald, Charlie Spivak, and Tommy Dorsey; played in army band; later with Bob Crosby, Nat King Cole and others; formed own band; albums—*Best of Nelson Riddle, Bright and Beautiful, Contemporary Sound of Nelson Riddle, Music for Wives and Lovers, Oscar Peterson and Nelson Riddle, Riddle of Today, Riddle Touch, Wonderful Nat King Cole Songs.*

RIDER-KELSEY, CORINNE

b. 1880 Le Roy, New York, d. 1947 Toledo, Ohio. Soprano. Pupil of L.A. Torrens in Chicago and Mr. and Mrs. Toedt in New York; opera debut at Covent Garden, London; also sang in concert and oratorio.

RIEGGER, WALLINGFORD

b. 1885 Albany, Georgia, d. 1961.
Noted composer. Graduated Institute of Musical Art, New York City; studied in Berlin; taught at Drake University, Des Moines, Iowa, and Ithaca (N.Y.) Conservatory; composed *Rhapsody for Orchestra* (New York Philharmonic), *Study in Sonority* (Philadelphia Orchestra), Piano Trio in B Minor (Paderewski Prize, 1922), *La Belle Dame sans Merci* (chamber work, Coolidge Prize, 1924), *Dichotomy, Divertissement, Chromatic Quartet,* suite for flute solo.

RIEMENSCHNEIDER, ALBERT

b. 1878 Berea, Ohio, d. 1950 Akron, Ohio. Organist, conductor, and teacher. Studied with Reinhold and others; director of Baldwin-Wallace Conservatory, Berea; also conducted annual Bach festivals there.

RIESENFELD, HUGO

b. 1879 Vienna, Austria, d. 1939 Hollywood, California. Musical director and composer. Violinist in Vienna Opera; concertmaster at Manhattan Opera House, New York City; later director of Rialto, Rivoli, and Criterion Theatres in New York City; then musical director of film productions in Hollywood; composed operettas, orchestral works, and songs.

RIGHTEOUS BROTHERS, THE (white soul group)

Bobby Hatfield; Jimmy Walker; formerly, Bill Medley; started in 1962; broke up in 1968; albums—*Go Ahead and Cry, One for the Road, Re-Birth, Righteous Brothers, Greatest Hits, Standards, Sayin' Somethin', Soul and Inspiration, Souled Out.*

RIKER, FRANKLIN WING

b. 1876, d. 1958.
Singer and composer. Wrote "A Gentle Hint."

RILEY, EDWARD

b. 1769 England, d. 1829 Yonkers, New York. Pianist, singer, composer, teacher, and publisher. Came to New York City (1806); music publisher there (1811-29), continued by his sons Edward C. and Frederick Riley until 1851; wrote "La Fayette's Grand March and Quick Step" (1824).

RILEY, EDWARD C.

b. ca. 1800 England, d. 1871 New York City. Flutist, composer, teacher, and publisher. Son of Edward Riley; debut in New York City (1821); publisher in his father's business (1832-42); wrote "The Grand Canal March" (1823), *Riley's Easy Flute Duets* (1819, thirty-one airs for two flutes), "The President of Haiti's March" (Jean Pierre Boyer, 1825).

RING, BLANCHE

b. 1872, Boston, Massachusetts, d. 1961. Singer and actress. Appeared on the New York stage; sang "Bedelia" (m. Jean Schwartz) in *The Jersey Lily* (1903).

RIO, ANITA

b. 1873 Alameda, California, d. 1971 Old Saybrook, Connecticut. Soprano. Concert debut in *The Messiah* in Boston (1901) and her operatic debut at Covent Garden, London, England (1909); sang at the Handel and Haydn Centennial; married A.P. Cole; lived in Lyme, Conn. and taught singing until her 95th birthday.

RIPLEY, THOMAS BALDWIN

b. 1795 Boston, Massachusetts, d. 1876 Portland, Maine. Hymnist. Became a Baptist minister (1816); published *A Selection of Hymns for Conference and Prayer Meetings* (1821, also 1829).

RITCHIE, JEAN

b. 1922 Viper, Kentucky.
Singer and songwriter. Youngest of fourteen children, all musically minded; her father Balis was one of ten children, all singers; her grandfather Austin, also one of ten children, all singers; her great grandfather John was one of eleven children, all singers; her great great grandfather Crockett one of eleven children, all singers; graduated the University of Kentucky, Lexington; wrote "A Tree in the Valley-O," Let the Sun Shine on Me," "What'll I Do With Baby-O," "The Cuckoo She's a Pretty Bird"; albums—*American Folk Tales and Songs, Appalachian Dulcimer* (Instruction), *Brand, Oscar and Jean Ritchie, Carols of All Seasons, Clear Waters Remembered, Jean Ritchie Sings.*

RITCHINGS-BERNARD OLD FOLKS COMPANY *see* WILLIAM L. TOMLINS

RITTER, FREDERIC LOUIS

b. 1834 Strasbourg, France, d. 1891.
Conductor, composer, and writer. Studied under Schletterer and Hauser; also in Paris; came to Cincinnati, Ohio (ca. 1855), founded the Cecilia Society and Philharmonic Society there; went to New York (1862), conductor of Sacred Harmonic Society; taught at Vassar College, Poughkeepsie, N.Y. (1867); composed piano pieces; wrote *Music in England.* and *Music in America* (New York, 1883).

RITTER, MAURICE WOODWARD ("TEX")

b. 1906 Panola County, Texas, d. 1974.
Singer and songwriter. Attended the University of Texas, and Northwestern University, Evanston, Ill.; on radio in New York during the 1930s; movie star in Hollywood in the 1940s and '50s; wrote "I Dreamed of a Hillbilly Heaven" (1961, with Eddie Dean and H. Sothern); albums—*Best of Tex Ritter, Blood on the Saddle, Hillbilly Heaven, Just Beyond the Moon, Tex Ritter's Wild West;* at Nashville's Grand Ole Opry (1972).

RITZ, LYLE JOSEPH

b. 1930 Cleveland, Ohio.
Bass and tuba player. Studied at Occidental College and Carnegie Institute in Pittsburgh; later with Los Angeles Community Symphony Orchestra; later with Eddie Grady's Commanders and others.

RIVARDE, SERGE ACHILLE

b. 1865 New York City, d. 1940 London, England. Violinist. Studied at the Paris Conservatory with Dancla; divided first prize with Ondricek (1879); solo violinist with Lamoureux orchestra after 1899; professor at Royal College of Music, London.

RIVE-KING, JULIE

b. 1857 Cincinnati, Ohio, d. 1937 Indianapolis, Indiana. Noted pianist. Daughter of Caroline Rivé, pianist and teacher; studied in New York under William Mason, S.B. Mills, and Pruckner; in Europe (1872-74) under Reinecke at Leipzig, and Liszt at Weimar; debut (1874) in Leipzig with Reinecke conducting, in Cincinnati (1874), Liszt's E-flat Concerto with the New York Philharmonic (1875), Beethoven's Fifth Concerto in Philadelphia; toured the world; married Frank H. King, her manager; wrote *On Blooming Meadows,* piano waltz.

RIZZI, TREFONI ("TONY")

b. 1923 Los Angeles, California.
Guitarist. Played trumpet in army band; later with Boyd Raeburn, Les Brown and others; joined NBC as a staff musician in Los Angeles.

ROACH, MAXWELL (MAX)

b. 1925 Brooklyn, New York.
Black drummer. Played with Charlie Parker, Dizzy Gillespie, Benny Carter and others in

1940s; at Paris Jazz Festival (1949) with Charlie Parker; later formed his own quintet; albums—*Best of Max Roach and Clifford Brown in Concert, Bitter Sweet Percussion, Clifford Brown and Max Roach at Basin Street, Deeds Not Words, Drums Unlimited, It's Time, Members, Don't Get Weary, Charlie Mingus Quintet Plus Max Roach, Study in Brown;* played at the Newport Jazz Festival, New York City (1972).

ROADRUNNERS (vocal group) *see* JIM ROBERTS

ROBARGE, JOHN F. *see* TEX ROE

ROBBINS, CHANDLER

b. 1810 Lynn, Massachusetts, d. 1882 Westport, Massachusetts. Hymnist and compiler. Educated at Harvard (1829) and Cambridge Divinity School (1833); pastor of the Second Unitarian Church, Boston (1833); edited *The Social Hymn Book* (1843) and *Hymns for Christian Worship* (1854); his hymns "Lo, the Day of Rest Declineth" (tune "Bedfort Street"—L.B. Barnes) and "While Thus Thy Throne of Grace We Seek," appeared in Dr. G.E. Ellis' *Psalms and Hymns for the Sanctuary* (1845); published the *Hymns of Henry Ware, Jr.* in four volumes (1847).

ROBBINS, HOWARD CHANDLER

b. 1876 Philadelphia, Pennsylvania, d. 1952. Hymnist. Educated at Yale and Episcopal Theological Seminary (1903); rector in Morristown, N.J., Englewood, N.J., and Church of the Incarnation, New York City (1911-17), dean of the Cathedral of St. John the Divine (1917-29), then taught at General Theological Seminary (1929-41); wrote the hymns "Now Yield We Thanks and Praise" (1929, tune "Darmstadt"), "The Sabbath Day Was By" (tune "Dexter Street"—Winfred Douglas), "And Have the Bright Immensities" (1931, tune "Tregaron"—P. James).

ROBBINS, MARTY

b. 1925 Glendale, Arizona.
Singer and songwriter. Attended high school in Phoenix, Arizona; served in the Pacific in the navy in World War II; sang in Phoenix night clubs; wrote "I'll Go on Alone" and "I Couldn't Keep from Crying" (1953); "White Sport Coat" (1957); "She Was Only Seventeen" (1958); "El Paso" (1959); "It's Your World" and "Don't Worry" (1961); "Devil Woman" (1962); "Beggin' to You" (1963); "One of These Days" and "The Cowboy in the Continental Suit" (1964); "My Woman, My Woman, My Wife" (Grammy Award, 1971).

ROBBS, THE (vocal group)

Dee Robb, Joe Robb, Bruce Robb, and Craig Robb; started in Florida in 1961; appeared on Dick Clark's TV show, "Where the Action Is" (1966); album—*The Robbs* (1967).

ROBERTS, CHARLES LUCKEYETH ("LUCKEY")

b. 1890 Philadelphia, Pennsylvania, d. 1968. Black pianist, bandleader, and composer. Led his own band in the 1920s; played at Carnegie Hall (1939); later owned his own club in Harlem, New York City; wrote "Junk Man Rag" (1913), "Pork and Beans" (1913), "Music Box Rag" (1914), "Palm Beach" (1914), "Shy and Sly" (1915), "Helter Skelter" (1915), "Spanish Venus" (1915), "Railroad Blues" (1920), "M'lasses" (1923), "Park Avenue Polka" (1949), also *Whistlin' Pete,* miniature syncopated rhapsody for piano and orchestra (1939), and a Spanish suite (1939).

ROBERTS, DANIEL CRANE

b. 1841 Bridgehampton, L.I., New York, d. 1907 Concord, New Hampshire. Hymnist. Graduated Kenyon College, Gambier, Ohio (1857) and enlisted in the 84th Ohio volunteers (1862); became an Episcopal rector in 1866 and served in churches in Montpelier, Vt., Lowell, Mass., Brandon, Vt., then Concord, N.H. (1878-1907); wrote the lyrics "God of Our Fathers" (1876) for a Fourth of July Centennial celebration in Brandon, Vt. (tune "National Hymn"—G.W. Warren, 1892).

ROBERTS, HOWARD MANCEL

b. 1929 Phoenix, Arizona.
Guitarist. Formed his own group in Los Angeles; albums—*All Time Great Instrumental Hits, Color Him Funky, Goodies, Howard Roberts Is a Dirty Guitar Player, Januty-Jolly, Out of Sight—But "In" Sounds, Howard Roberts Guilty, Whatever's Fair.*

ROBERTS, J. HENRY

b. 1856 Pittston, Pennsylvania, d. 1920. Pianist and teacher. Educated at Beaver College and Musical Institute in Beaver, Pa.; concert pianist; taught piano, organ, and vocal music in Cleveland, Ohio.

ROBERTS, JIM

b. 1933 Atlanta, Georgia.
Singer and bandleader. Born James Robert Caudle; attended schools in East Point, Ga., and Middle Georgia College, Cochran, Ga. (1952-53); leader of the RR Ranch Boys (1961-

65) and the Roadrunners after 1966; albums—*Beautiful Saviour, Faith Unlocks the Door, How Great Thou Art, Whispering Hope.*

ROBERTS, KENNY

b. 1927 Lenoir City, Tennessee.
Singer and yodeler. Member of the Down Towners; albums—*Country Music Singing Sensation, Incredible Kenny Roberts, Indian Love Call, Yodelin' Kenny Roberts Sings Country Songs.*

ROBERTS, LEE S.

b. 1884 Oakland, California, d. 1949 San Francisco, California. Pianist and composer. In the piano manufacturing business (1911); developed QRS artist-recorded music rolls for the player-piano (1912); wrote "Smiles" (1917, "There are smiles that make us happy," w. J. Will Callahan).

ROBERTSON, DONALD IRWIN

b. 1922 Peking, China.
Popular composer. His father was a professor at Peking Union Medical College; returned to U.S. (1927); attended the University of Chicago; moved to Los Angeles (1945); wrote "I Really Don't Want to Know" (1954, sung by Eddy Arnold), "I Don't Hurt Anymore" (1954, sung by Hank Snow), "Please Help Me, I'm Falling" (sung by Hank Locklin), "The Happy Whistler" (1956); sung by Elvis Presley—"Anything That's a Part of You," "I'm Yours," "There's Always Me," "They Remind Me Too Much of You."

ROBERTSON, WALTER

b. 1928 Omaha, Nebraska.
Ballad singer. Had his own show on station KING-TV, Seattle, Washington; albums—*American Northwest Ballads* (1955), *Walt Robertson* (1959).

ROBESON, LILA P.

b. 1880 Cleveland, Ohio, d. 1960.
Contralto. Studied with Burnham and others; sang in concerts after 1905; at Metropolitan Opera, New York after 1912; then taught in Cleveland.

ROBESON, PAUL BUSTILL

b. 1898 Princeton, New Jersey.
Noted black bass singer. Graduated Rutgers University, New Brunswick, N.J. (1919) and Columbia University, New York City; debut (1925) at a recital in Greenwich Village Theatre, New York City; Town Hall, New York City concert (1926); appeared in *Show Boat* (1928, 1930, and 1932); appeared as Othello in London, England; in *Emperor Jones;* recipient of the Whitney M. Young Memorial Award (1972).

ROBIN, LEO

b. 1900 Pittsburgh, Pennsylvania.
Lyricist. Educated at the University of Pittsburgh Law School and Carnegie Technical Drama School; wrote the lyrics for "Hallelujah" (1927, with Clifford Grey, m. Vincent Youmans), "Louise" (1929, m. R.A. Whiting), "Prisoner of Love" (m. Con Conrad); with music by Ralph Rainger—"Love in Bloom," "June in January," "Thanks for the Memories" (1938); "Just in Love" (m. David Rose); songs for *Gentlemen Prefer Blonds* which included "Diamonds Are a Girl's Best Friend" (m. Jule Styne).

ROBINSON, ALVAN, JR.

b. 1802 Raynham, Massachusetts, d. 1865. Compiler and publisher. Compiled *Massachusetts Collection of Martial Musick* (Hallowell, Maine, 1818) containing over fifty-five marches and airs; published music in Exeter, New Hampshire (1820); later lived near Durham, Maine.

ROBINSON, CHARLES SEYMOUR

b. 1829 Bennington, Vermont, d. 1899 New York City. Hymnist and compiler. Educated at Williams College, Williamstown, Mass. (1849), Union Seminary (1853), Princeton (1855); Presbyterian minister in Troy, N.Y. (1855), Brooklyn, N.Y. (1860), American Chapel in France (1868), Memorial Presbyterian Church, New York City (1870); compiled *Songs of the Church* (1862) and *Songs for the Sanctuary* (1865) (both included some of his hymns), *Spiritual Songs* (1878) and *Laudes Domini* (1884).

ROBINSON, EARL

b. 1910 Seattle, Washington.
Composer. Attended the University of Washington, Seattle (1928); toured U.S. as a singer and guitarist; graduated the University of Washington in music (1938); taught at Elisabeth Irwin High School, New York City after 1957; wrote *Ballad for Americans* (cantata, over CBS radio, 1939), score for the Paramount picture, *California;* cantatas—*Battle Hymn, Tower of Babel, The Town Crier, The Lonesome Train, In the Folded and Quiet Yesterdays, Preamble to Peace;* folk opera, *Sandhog;* ballet, *Bouquet for Molly;* songs.

ROBINSON, ELI

b. 1908 Greensville, Georgia.
Black trombonist. Played with Frank Terry, Zach White, McKinney's Cotton Pickers, Lucky Millinder, and Count Basie in 1940s; later with small groups.

ROBINSON, FRANKLIN WHITMAN

b. 1875 New York City, d. 1946 Northeast Harbor, Maine. Organist and teacher. Studied music at Columbia University, New York, with MacDowell and Rubner; graduated City College of New York; taught at the Institute of Musical Art, N.Y., after 1908; taught harmony through ear-training system which he devised; author of *Aural Harmony.*

ROBINSON, FREDERICK L.

b. 1901 Memphis, Tennessee.
Black trombonist. Studied at Dana's Musical Institute, Warren, Ohio; played with Louis Armstrong, Benny Carter, Andy Kirk and others in 1930s; later with Noble Sissle and others.

ROBINSON, JAMES

b. 1892 Deeringe, Louisiana.
Black trombonist. Played in army band in France in World War I; with Kid Rena, Tuxedo Band in New Orleans and with others in 1920s; worked as a longshoreman during the depression years; with Bunk Johnson and George Lewis during 1940s.

ROBINSON, J. RUSSELL

b. 1892 Indianapolis, Indiana, d. 1963 Palmdale, California. Pianist and composer. Played with the Original Dixieland Jazz Band; wrote "Sappho Rag" (1909), "Dynamite Rag" (1910), "The Minstrel Man" (1911), "Whirlwind Rag" (1911), "Erratic Rag" (1911), "That Eccentric Rag" (1912), "On the Eight O'Clock Train" (1912, w. M. Kendall), "Te-na-na" (1912, Kendall), "Margie" (1920, with Benny Davis and Con Conrad), "Aggravatin' Papa" (w. Roy Turk), "St. Louis Gal" (1923).

ROBINSON, PRINCE

b. 1902 Portsmouth, Virginia, d. 1960.
Black clarinetist and tenor saxist. With Duke Ellington, then McKinney's Cotton Pickers (1927-34); with Blanche Calloway, Roy Eldridge and others in later 1930s; with Louis Armstrong (1940-44); later with Claude Hopkins combo.

ROBISON, CARSON J.

b. 1890 Oswego, Kansas, d. 1957 Pleasant Valley, New York. Singer and songwriter. Radio debut in Kansas City, Mo. (1920), New York City (1924); formed the Buckaroos (1932); wrote "Life Gets Tee-Jus, Don't It" (1948), "Barnacle Bill the Sailor," "Goin' Back to Texas," "Settin' by the Fire," "My Blue Ridge Mountain Home," "Left My Gal in the Mountains," "There's a Bridle Hangin' on the Wall," "Little Green Valley," "New River Train."

ROBYN, ALFRED GEORGE

b. 1860 St. Louis, Missouri, d. 1935 New York City. Pianist, organist, and popular composer. Son of William Robyn, conductor; played organ at age ten in St. John's Church; solo-pianist at sixteen with Emma Abbott's company; produced comic opera *Jacinta;* composed piano pieces and popular songs, including "Answer."

ROCCO, MAURICE JOHN

b. 1915 Oxford, Ohio.
Pianist and singer. Studied piano under his mother, a teacher; played the piano while standing up; appeared in films.

ROCHE, MARY ELIZABETH

b. 1920 Wilmington, Delaware.
Black singer. Sang with the Savoy Sultans (1941-42); later with Duke Ellington; performed the "Blues" sequence in *Black, Brown and Beige* with Duke at Carnegie Hall (1944).

ROCKEFELLER, MARTHA BAIRD

b. 1895, d. 1971 New York City.
Concert pianist. Debut in 1926 with the London Symphony Orchestra under Sir Thomas Beecham; later appeared with the Boston Symphony under Serge Koussevitsky; second wife of John D. Rockefeller, Jr.; in 1962 she created the Martha Baird Rockefeller Fund for Music to help young musicians of unusual promise.

RODEHEAVER, HOMER ALVAN

b. 1880 Union Furnace, Ohio, d. 1955 Winona Lake, Indiana. Publisher. Published Sunday School music; in 1936 the Rodeheaver Company of Chicago combined with the Hall-Mack Company of Philadelphia (founded in 1895 by J. Lincoln Hall and Irvin H. Mack) to become the Rodeheaver Hall-Mack Company with offices in Philadelphia, Chicago, and agencies in England, Australia, and New Zealand.

RODGERS, JAMES FREDERICK (JIMMIE)

b. 1933 Camas, Washington.
Singer and guitarist. His mother was a piano teacher and gave him lessons; attended Clark College, Vancouver, Washington; served in the Army Air Force in World War II; sang in Vancouver and Portland, Oregon night clubs; recorded "Honeycomb," which became a sensation in 1957; appeared in films.

RODGERS, JIMMIE CHARLES

b. 1897 Meridian, Mississippi, d. 1933 New York City. Singer and yodeler. Worked as a railroad brakeman, and became known as the "Singing Brakeman"; cut his first records with the Victor Talking Machine Company, Bristol, Tenn. (1927); albums—*Best of the Legendary Jimmie Rodgers, Country Music Hall of Fame, Jimmie the Kid, My Rough and Rowdy Ways, My Time Ain't Long, Never No Mo' Blues, Short But Brilliant Life of Jimmie Rodgers, Train Whistle Blues;* he died of tuberculosis.

RODGERS, RICHARD CHARLES

b. 1902 Hammels Station, Long Island, New York. Popular composer. Attended Columbia University and the Institute of Musical Art (1922-24); with Herbert Fields as librettist and Lorenz Hart as lyricist, wrote the shows *Dearest Enemy* (1925), *The Girl Friend* (1926), *A Connecticut Yankee* (1927), *Present Arms* (1928), *Spring Is Here* (1929), *Simple Simon* (1930), *America's Sweetheart* (1931); with Lorenz Hart—*On Your Toes* (1936) (and George Abbott), *Babes in Arms* (1937), *I'd Rather Be Right* (1937, book—George Kaufman and Moss Hart), *I Married an Angel* (1938, play—John Vaszary), *The Boys from Syracuse* (1938), *Pal Joey* (1940, book—John O'Hara), *By Jupiter* (1942); with Oscar Hammerstein II—*Oklahoma!* (1943, play—Lynn Riggs), *Carousel* (1945, play "Liliom"—F. Molnar), *South Pacific* (1949, book—James A. Michener, adapted by Hammerstein and Joshua Logan), *The King and I* (1951, book—Margaret Landon), *Flower Drum Song* (1958, book—C.Y. Lee), and *The Sound of Music* (1959); Salute to Richard Rodgers held at the Imperial Theater, New York City in March, 1972.

RODIN, GILBERT A.

b. 1906 Chicago, Illinois, d. 1974.
Trumpeter and flutist. Played with Ben Pollack's band (1927-35); later musical director and arranger for Bob Crosby's band.

RODNEY, RED

b. 1927 Philadelphia, Pennsylvania.
Trumpeter. Born Robert Chudnick; studied at the Mastbaum School; played with Jimmy Dorsey, Tony Pastor, Claude Thornhill, Woody Herman and others in 1940s; later with Charlie Ventura, Sammy Davis Jr. show, Oscar Pettiford and others.

RODZINSKI, ARTUR

b. 1894 Split, Dalmatia, d. 1958 Boston, Massachusetts. Conductor. Studied law, then switched to music; conductor in Warsaw, Poland, then became an assistant to Leopold Stokowski of the Philadelphia Orchestra (1926), also taught at the Curtis Institute there; went to Los Angeles (1929), Cleveland, Ohio (1933), then to the New York Philharmonic (1943); resigned this position, however, due to disagreements with the Society, and became conductor of the Chicago Symphony Orchestra (1947).

ROE, TEX

b. 1922 Oswego, New York.
Singer and songwriter. Born John F. Robarge; leader of the Travellers, from Cortland, N.Y., after 1955; wrote "Rest Awhile," "All the Time," "Stop Trying to Tell Me," "Treasure Chest," "Santa Claus," "Rocket Ship."

ROEDER, MARTIN

b. 1851 Berlin, Germany, d. 1895 Boston Massachusetts. Composer and librettist. Studied at Berlin Hochschule; taught singing in Boston; conductor in Dublin and Boston; wrote essays, librettos; music critic and writer under pseudonym Raro Miedtner; composed three operas, a symphony, two symphonic poems.

ROGERS, BERNARD

b. 1893 New York City, d. 1968.
Composer. Studied with Ernest Bloch at the Institute of Musical Art, New York City; won Guggenheim Fellowship and Pulitzer Prize; taught composition at Eastman School of Music, Rochester, N.Y.; composed *Adonais,* prelude to *Hamlet, Fairy Tales* (New York Philharmonic, 1936), a symphony for orchestra, *Soliloquy* for strings, *Pastorale, Nocturne, The Raising of Lazarus* (choral work), *The Warrior* (opera, Metropolitan Opera, New York, 1947).

ROGERS, CLARA KATHLEEN BARNETT

b. 1844 Cheltenham, England, d. 1931 Boston, Massachusetts. Singer and teacher. Daughter of John Barnett, "The father of English Opera"; studied at the Leipzig Conservatory and in Milan; debut in Turin (1863); sang under name "Clara Doria" in Italy and England; with Parepa-Rosa

Company in America (1871); lived in Boston as a singer and teacher; wrote *The Philosophy of Singing* (New York, 1893); married Henry M. Rogers, an attorney in Boston (1878); composed a sonata for piano and violin, and songs.

ROGERS, FRANCIS

b. 1870 Roxbury, Massachusetts, d. 1951 New York City. Baritone. Graduated Harvard University; taught singing at Yale and at the Juilliard School of Music, New York City; appeared as a recitalist; friend of Ethelburt Nevin, and introduced Nevin's *The Rosary* at a concert at Madison Square Garden, New York City (1898).

ROGERS, GINGER

b. 1911 Independence, Missouri.
Singer and dancer. Introduced "Embraceable You" and "But Not for Me" in *Girl Crazy* (1930, m. George Gershwin); appeared in numerous films with Fred Astaire.

ROGERS, JAMES HOTCHKISS

b. 1857 Fairhaven, Connecticut, d. 1940 Pasadena, California. Music critic. Studied music in Chicago, Berlin, and Paris; church-organist in Cleveland, Ohio; music critic for the *Cleveland Plain Dealer.*

ROGERS, MILTON ("SHORTY")

b. 1924 Great Barrington, Massachusetts.
Jazz trumpeter and arranger. Studied at the Los Angeles Conservatory and under Dr. Wesley LaViolette; played with Red Norvo; served in army in World War II; then with Woody Herman as trumpeter and arranger in 1940s; with Stan Kenton and others in 1950s; album—*Shelly Manne's The 3 and The 2.*

ROGERS, ROBERT C.

b. 1862 Buffalo, New York, d. 1912 Santa Barbara, California. Lyricist and poet. Wrote "The Rosary" (m. Ethelburt Nevin, 1898); the poem appeared in *The Wind in the Clearing and Other Poems* by Rogers; someone mailed the poem to Nevin, who composed music for it.

ROGERS, ROY

b. 1912 Cincinnati, Ohio.
Singer and actor. Born Leonard Slye; attended school in Duck Run, Ohio; worked in a shoe factory in Cincinnati; formed the Sons of the Pioneers in Los Angeles in the 1930s with Tim Spencer and Bob Nolan; albums with Dale Evans—*The Bible Tells Me So, Jesus Loves Me, Lore of the West, Peter Cottontail, Sweet Hour of Prayer.*

ROGERS, TIMMIE

b. 1915 Detroit, Michigan.
Black singer and songwriter. Had his own band in 1950s; wrote "Back to School Again," "Bring Enough Clothes for Three Days," "If You Can't Smile and Say Yes," "Fla-ga-la-pa."

ROITMAN, DAVID

b. 1884 Doroshinke, Podolia, d. 1944 New York City. Tenor. Officiated at St. Petersburg, Vilna, Odessa, then came to America; associated with the Shaare Zedek Temple, New York City (1943); had a fine tenor voice and his recordings are good examples of Eastern European chazzanuth.

ROLAND, GENE

b. 1921 Dallas, Texas.
Trumpeter, trombonist, and songwriter. Studied at North Texas State Teachers College; in Eighth Air Force band with Jimmy Giuffre; with Stan Kenton (1944-55); with Woody Herman and others after 1956; wrote "Tampico," and "Sittin' and Rockin'," recorded by June Christy; "Are You Livin' Ol' Man," recorded by Anita O'Day.

ROLAND, JOSEPH ALFRED

b. 1920 New York City.
Black vibraphonist. Studied clarinet at the Juilliard School, New York City (1937-39); served in the Aleutians in the Air Corps in World War II; played with Oscar Pettiford, George Shearing and others in 1950s; led his own combo; album—*Jolting with Joe Roland.*

ROLLER COASTERS *see* DUKE DUMAS

ROLLING STONES (English rock group)

Leader Mick Jagger; toured thirty-one cities in U.S. (1972).

ROLLINI, ADRIAN

b. 1904 New York City, d. 1956 Homestead, Florida. Bass saxist and vibraphonist. Active with bands after 1920.

ROLLINS, THEODORE WALTER ("SONNY")

b. 1929 New York City.
Black tenor saxist. Played with Art Blakey, Bud Powell, later with Max Roach Quintet and others; formed his own quartet with pianist Al Daley, bassist Larry Ridley, and drummer David Lee at the Village Vanguard (1972).

ROLLINS, WALTER E. ("JACK")

b. 1907, d. 1973 Cincinnati, Ohio.
Country and western lyricist. Wrote popular children's songs—"Peter Cottontail,"

"Smokey the Bear," and "Frosty the Snowman."

ROMA, CARO

b. 1866, d. 1937.
Singer and composer. Wrote "Can't Yo' Hear Me Callin' Caroline" (w. W.H. Gardner).

ROMBERG, SIGMUND

b. 1887 Szegedin, Hungary, d. 1951 New York City. Noted composer. Studied engineering in Vienna, then served in the 19th Hungarian Infantry Regiment, and came to New York City (1909); went to work for J.J. Shubert as a staff composer (1914); wrote the music for *Maytime* (1917), *Blossom Time* (1921), *The Student Prince* (1924, book and lyrics—Otto Harbach, Oscar Hammerstein II, and Frank Mandel), *The New Moon* (1928), *Up in Central Park* (1945); wrote "Auf Wiedersehen" (1915, w. Herbert Reynolds), "Will You Remember" (1917, w. Rida J. Young),"Song of Love" (1921, w. Dorothy Donnelly), "Drinking Song" in *The Student Prince* (w. Dorothy Donnelly), "Lover Come Back to Me" (1928, w. Hammerstein), "When I Grow Too Old to Dream." (*See* Vivienne Segal)

ROME, HAROLD JACOB

b. 1908 Hartford, Connecticut.
Popular composer. Attended Trinity College and Yale (1929), then Yale School of Architecture (1934); wrote the songs for the shows *Pins and Needles* (1937, which included "Sunday in the Park"), *Sing Out the News* (1938, "Franklin D. Roosevelt Jones"), *Streets of Paris* (1940), *Let Freedom Ring* (1942); served in the Special Forces in World War II; then wrote the scores for *Call Me Mister* (1946), *Wish You Were Here* (1952, play—Arthur Kober), *Fanny* (1954, play—Marcel Pagnal), *Destry Rides Again* (1959, book—Max Brand), *I Can Get It for You Wholesale* (1961, book—Jerome Weidman).

RONCONI, GIORGIO

b. 1810 Milan, Italy, d. 1890.
Baritone and composer. Son of Domenico Ronconi; taught at Cordova, Spain (1863); then in New York City after 1867.

RONSTADT, LINDA

b. 1946 Tucson, Arizona.
Singer. Recorded "We Need a Lot More of Jesus" ("and a Lot Less Rock and Roll"); album—*Silk Purse.*

ROOFTOP SINGERS *see* ERIK DARLING

ROOSEVELT, BLANCHE (TUCKER)

b. 1853, d. 1898.
Singer, writer, and journalist. First met Giuseppe Verdi in 1875 and then wrote about him.

ROOSEVELT, HILBOURNE LEWIS

b. 1849 New York City, d. 1886.
Organ maker. A Roosevelt organ was in the New York section of the main building at the Centennial exhibition in Philadelphia (1876), with two echo organs, one connected by a wire cable two hundred feet long, both hydraulic and electric engines provided the power for the organ; the Roosevelt organ installed in the Swedenborgian Church (1882) had adjustable combination positions.

ROOSTERS *see* THE IMPRESSIONS

ROOT, E. TOWER

b. 1822 Sheffield, Massachusetts, d. 1896. Publisher. Brother of George F. Root; with firm of Root & Cady, Chicago music publishers; at one time or another, Benjamin R. Hanby, James R. Murray, and George F. Root worked for the firm.

ROOT, FREDERIC WOODMAN

b. 1846 Boston, Massachusetts, d. 1916 Chicago, Illinois. Organist and teacher. Son of George F. Root, popular composer; studied with his father, also with Blodgett and Mason in New York; studied in Europe (1869-70); then organist, teacher of vocal classes, writer, and lecturer; taught in Chicago; composed choral works and songs; editor of the *Song Messenger.*

ROOT, GEORGE FREDERICK

b. 1820 Sheffield, Massachusetts, d. 1895 Bailey's Island, Maine. Popular composer. When he was six the family moved to North Reading, Mass.; taught in Boston (1841) and was a close associate of Lowell Mason, Bradbury, and Webb; in 1844 went to New York City as musical instructor at the New York Institution for the Blind; here he met Fanny Crosby who wrote the lyrics for his songs "The Hazel Dell" (1853), "There's Music in the Air" (1854), and "Rosalie, the Prairie Flower" (1855); in 1859 he joined the firm of Root and Cady, Chicago music publishers; composed the first Civil War song to be published, "The First Gun Is Fired," copyrighted April 18, 1861; composed "Can the Soldier Forget" (w. Charles Boynton), "Brother Tell Me of the Battle" (w. Thomas

Manahan), "The Vacant Chair" (1862, w. H.S. Washburn), "God Save Our Nation, A Battle Hymn" (w. T. Tilton), "The Battle Cry of Freedom" (or "Rally 'Round the Flag Boys," 1863, first sung by Jules Lombard at a Civil War Rally in Chicago), "Tramp, Tramp the Boys Are Marching" (1864), "Goodby Old Glory" (1865, w. L.J. Bates), "My Beau That Went to Canada" (1865, w. E.E. Rexford), "Where Are the Reapers?" (w. E.E. Rexford); the tune "Ellon" (1871, "Angel's Story," w. Emily H. Miller); the cantata *Under the Palms* (*Captive Judah in Babylon*, w. H. Butterworth).

ROREM, NED

b. 1923 Richmond, Indiana.
Noted composer. Studied at Northwestern University, Evanston, Ill., Curtis Institute, Philadelphia (1947), Juilliard School, New York City (1949), then in Paris (1949-55); lived in U.S. after 1955; taught at the University of Buffalo, N.Y. (1959-61); composer in residence at Utah University, Salt Lake City (1965-66); composed Overture in C (won Gershwin award, New York Philharmonic, 1949), First Symphony (Vienna, 1951), *Six Irish Poems* for voice and orchestra (Paris radio), *Melos* (ballet, Prix de Biarritz), *Dorian Gray* (ballet, Barcelona, 1952), *Designs for Orchestra* (Louisville Orchestra, 1955), Second Symphony (La Jolla, Calif., 1956), Third Symphony (New York Philharmonic under Bernstein, 1959), *Eagles* (tone poem, Philadelphia Orchestra, 1959), *Miss Julie* (opera, book—August Strindberg, libretto—Kenward Elmslie, N.Y., 1965).

ROSE, DAVID

b. 1910 London, England.
Conductor and popular composer. His family came to Chicago (1914); studied at the Chicago Musical College, then was a pianist on radio and for the Ted Fiorito orchestra; served in the air force in World War II; composed the music for *Winged Victory* (1943, Moss Hart) and the instrumental works *Holiday for Strings* (1943), *Our Waltz, Dance of the Spanish Onion, Nostalgia* and *Holiday for Trombones;* served as musical director of "The Red Skelton Show," Fred Astaire shows, Bob Hope show and "Dean Martin Show"; wrote "One Love," "Once Upon a Lullaby" and "Just in Love" (w. Leo Robin).

ROSE, ED

b. 1875 Chicago, Illinois, d. 1935 Evanston, Illinois. Lyricist. Educated at Valparaiso University; wrote lyrics for "Oh Johnny, Oh Johnny, Oh" (1917, m. Abe Olman).

ROSE, FRED

b. 1897 Evansville, Indiana, d. 1954 Nashville, Tennessee. Popular composer. Joined Paul Whiteman's band in the 1920s; sang over radio in Chicago and New York; with Roy Acuff founded Acuff-Rose Publications, music publishers, Nashville, Tenn. (1943); wrote "Be Honest With Me" (won Academy Award), "Tears on My Pillow," "Foggy River," "Texarkana Baby," "Waltz of the Wind," "Sweet Kind of Love," "Doo Dah Blues" (with Ted Fiorito).

ROSE, LEONARD

b. 1918 Washington, D.C.
Cellist. Solo cellist with the New York Philharmonic, but later became a soloist on the concert stage.

ROSE, VINCENT

b. 1880 Palermo, Italy, d. 1944 Rockville Center, New York. Director, composer, pianist, and violinist. Came to U.S. (1897); became a U.S. citizen; educated at the Palermo School of Music; studied with Liberati; formed own orchestra (1904) on West Coast; with John Schonberger wrote "Whispering" (1920, w. Richard Coburn).

ROSE, WILLIAM (BILLY)

b. 1899 New York City, d. 1966 Montego Bay, Jamaica, West Indies. Lyricist and producer. Stenographer to Bernard Baruch during World War I; wrote "Barney Google"; staged *Jumbo* featuring Jimmy Durante at the New York Hippodrome (1936); musical water spectacular *Aquade* at the Great Lakes Exposition (1937), also at the New York World's Fair (1939) and San Francisco (1940); wrote the lyrics for many popular songs, largest single stockholder of the American Telephone and Telegraph Company. (*See* Harold Arlen, Con Conrad, John W. Green, Ray Henderson, James V. Monaco, Thomas "Fats" Waller, Harry Warren, Mabel Wayne and Vincent M. Youmans)

ROSEN, MAX

b. 1900 Rumania, d. 1956.
Violinist. Studied in New York and in Europe; debut in Dresden (1915); appeared in U.S. after 1918 with success.

ROSENBLATT, JOSEPH

b. 1882 near Kiev, Russia, d. 1933 Jerusalem, Israel. Tenor and cantor. Came to America (1912); concert tenor after 1926; died on a visit to Palestine (Israel).

ROSENFELD, MAURICE

b. 1867 Vienna, Austria, d. 1939 Chicago, Illinois. Teacher and critic. Studied at Columbia University, N.Y., graduated Chicago Music College; later taught there, then became director; established his own school in Chicago (1916); critic for the *Chicago Examiner* and then the *News* after 1917.

ROSENFELD, MONROE H.

b. 1861 Richmond, Virginia, d. 1918 New York City. Composer. Wrote "Johnny Get Your Gun" (1886) under the pseudonym F. Belasco.

ROSENSTOCK, JOSEPH

b. 1895 Cracow, Poland.
Conductor in Stuttgart, Darmstadt, Mannheim, then became musical director of the Jewish Kulturbund in Berlin, but due to the rise of Nazism, he fled to Japan, where he conducted the Nippon Philharmonic Orchestra, Tokyo; then came to America where he became director of the New York City Opera Company until 1955.

ROSENTHAL, MORIZ

b. 1862 Lemberg, Poland, d. 1946 New York City. Pianist. Studied piano; left Vienna (1933) when Hitler came to power, and settled in New York City; with Ludwig Schuette wrote *Die Schule des hoeheren Klavierspiels* (*The School of Piano Mastery*); popular pianist in recitals at Carnegie Hall, New York City, in early 1900s.

ROSEWIG, ALBERT H.

b. 1846 Germany, d. 1929 Philadelphia, Pennsylvania. Composer and publisher. Came to Philadelphia (1855); wrote "Maid of Athens Here We Part" at age twelve, published by William R. Smith; employed as pirate-copyist for Lee & Walker, transcribed Gilbert and Sullivan operettas during performances in Philadelphia; directed music at Church of St. Borromeo (Catholic) for thirty-five years; also published music.

ROSOWSKY, SALOMON

b. 1878 Riga, Latvia, d. 1962.
Teacher. Son of cantor Baruch Leib Rosowsky; wrote *The Cantillation of the Bible* (*The Five Books of Moses*); familiar with the folk songs of the Eastern Jews, and after he came to the United States, lectured at the New School for Social Research, and later taught at the Cantors Institute of the Jewish Theological Seminary of America, in New York City.

ROSS, BEVERLY MORGAN ("BUDDY")

b. 1914 Oshkosh, Wisconsin.
Singer. Leader of the Hometowners, station WLWT, Cincinnati, Ohio.

ROSS, JEROLD (JERRY)

b. 1926 New York City, d. there 1955.
Singer and lyricist. With composer Richard Adler wrote "Rags to Riches" (1953); the musicals *The Pajama Game* (1954) which included "Hernando's Hideaway," and *Damn Yankees* (1955).

ROSSINI, CARLO

b. 1890 Osimo, Italy.
Compiler. Became a priest in 1913 and served as a chaplain in the Italian Army in World War I; studied at the Pontifical Institute of Sacred Music in Rome (1920); served as organist-choirmaster in Catholic churches in Pittsburgh, Pa. (1921-26), then at St. Paul's Cathedral (1926-49), when he became secretary of the St. Caecilia Association in Rome; compiled *The Parochial Hymnal* (1936).

ROTHIER, LEON

b. 1874 Rheims, France, d. 1951 New York City. Bass. Studied at the Paris Conservatory, won first prizes in three years; with Paris Opera and then tlie Metropolitan Opera, New York, after 1910.

ROTHMUELLER, ARON MARKO

b. 1918 Trnjani, Croatia.
Composer and musicologist. Composed a symphony, two ballet suites and chamber music; wrote *Die Musik der Juden;* after he came to the United States, he taught at Indiana University, Bloomington, Indiana.

ROTHWELL, WALTER HENRY

b. 1872 London, England, d. 1927 Los Angeles, California. Conductor. Studied at Vienna Royal Academy; conducted Amsterdam Royal Opera; conducted first performance of *Parsifal* in America (1903); conductor of the St. Paul, Minnesota Orchestra (1908-15); New York Stadium concerts (1916); guest conductor in Cincinnati and Detroit (1917-18); Los Angeles Philharmonic Orchestra (1919-27).

ROTOLI, AUGUSTO

b. 1847 Rome, Italy, d. 1904 Boston, Massachusetts. Conductor, teacher, and composer. Pupil of Lucchesi; singing-master to Princess Margherita (1876); taught at New England Conservatory, Boston, after 1885; composed *Salmo elegiaco,* with orchestra (1878), *Mass for the Funeral of King Victor Emmanuel* (1878).

ROURKE, M.E.

b. 1867 Manchester, England, d. 1933 New York City. Lyricist. Wrote under the pseudonym Herbert Reynolds; wrote the lyrics for "They Didn't Believe Me" (1914, m. Jerome Kern) for *The Girl from Utah.*

ROWLES, JOHN

b. 1947 New Zealand.
Baritone. Came to New York City; sang in various night clubs and hotels in New York and other cities; sang in the Plaza Persian Room, New York City (1971); album—*Exciting John Rowles.*

ROWSON, SUSANNAH (HASWELL)

b. 1762 Portsmouth, England, d. 1824 Boston, Massachusetts. Lyricist, librettist, and actress. Brought to America at age five by her lieutenant father; returned to England (1778); married William Rowson, musician (1786); wrote the novel *Charlotte Temple* (1790); came to America with her husband to work for Thomas Wignell (1793); on stage in Annapolis, Baltimore, Philadelphia, and Boston; wrote lyrics for songs by James Hewitt, Benjamin Carr, and Peter A. Van Hagen; wrote lyrics for "Slaves in Algiers" (1794, m. Alexander Reinagle), *The Volunteers* (comic opera, m. Reinagle).

ROYAL, ERNIE

b. 1921 Los Angeles, California.
Jazz trumpeter. Played in Lionel Hampton's band; also with Elliot Lawrence.

ROYAL HAWAIIANS *see* JOHNNY KAAIHUE

ROYCE, EDWARD

b. 1886 Cambridge, Massachusetts, d. 1963. Composer. Taught at the Eastman School of Music, Rochester, N.Y.; composed *The Fire-Bringers* (Rochester Philharmonic under Hanson, 1926), *Far Ocean* (tone poem for orchestra, Rochester Philharmonic under Hanson, 1929, won Eastman Award), songs.

RR RANCH BOYS (vocal group) *see* JIM ROBERTS

RUBEN AND THE JETS *see* MOTHERS OF INVENTION

RUBIN, RUTH ROSENBLATT

b. 1906 Montreal, Quebec, Canada.
Singer and writer. Attended Hunter College, New York City, in 1920s; married Harry Rubin (1932), lived in New York City; wrote *Treasury of Jewish Folk Song* (1950), *The Story of Yiddish Folksong;* albums—*Jewish Children's Songs and Games* (1954), *Yiddish Love Songs, Ruth Rubin Sings Yiddish Folk Songs.*

RUBINSTEIN, ARTUR

b. 1886 Lodz, Poland.
Concert pianist. Became a world-famous pianist. Lived in Paris, but fled to America when the German armies overran France; settled in Hollywood.

RUBINSTEIN, BERYL

b. 1898 Athens, Georgia, d. 1953 Cleveland, Ohio. Pianist and composer. Pupil of Alexander Lambert and others; with the Metropolitan Opera at age thirteen; played in London (1925) and with leading American orchestras; taught at the Cleveland Institute of Music, dean after 1932, and later director; composed an opera, piano pieces, orchestral works.

RUBY, HARRY

b. 1894 New York City, d. 1974.
Popular composer. Pianist and song plugger, along with Walter Winchell, for Gus Edwards, music publisher, New York City, then for Harry von Tilzer; performed with Harry Cohn in an act called Edwards & Ruby; wrote "Daddy Long Legs" (w. Sam Lewis and Joe Young), "And He'd Say Oo-La-La Wee-Wee" (w. George Jessel), "Timbuctoo" (w. Bert Kalmar), "The Vamp from East Broadway" (with Irving Berlin and introduced by Fanny Brice in the *Ziegfeld Follies,* 1920), "My Sunny Tennessee" (w. Kalmar); with Kalmar wrote the shows *Helen of Troy, New York* (book—George S. Kaufman and Marc Connelly), *The Ramblers* (1926, starring Clark and McCullough), *Five O'Clock Girl* (1927), *Animal Crackers* (1928), *High Kickers* (1941, starring George Jessel and Sophie Tucker); their songs were "I Wanna Be Loved by You" (1928, from *Good Boy,* sung by Helen Kane, the "boop-boop-a-doop" girl), "Watching the Clouds Roll By" (1928), "Hooray for Captain Spaulding" (theme song of Groucho Marx), "Three Little Words," and "Nevertheless."

RUDEL, JULIUS

b. 1921.
Conductor. Came to U.S. from Vienna, Austria; studied at Mannes College of Music,

New York City; joined New York City Opera (1943), conductor after 1957; music director at the John F. Kennedy Center, Washington, after 1971; conducted Alberto Ginastera's opera, *Beatrix Cenci* at the Center (1971).

RUDERSDORFF, HERMINE

b. 1822 Ivanowsky, Ukraine, d. 1882 Boston, Massachusetts. Soprano and teacher.

RUDHYAR, DANE

b. 1895 Paris, France.
Composer. Came to America (1916); his symphonic poem, *Surge of Fire,* won Los Angeles Orchestra prize (1920); author of book on Debussy; composed *Desert Chants, Ouranos, Five Stanzas, To the Real, Hero Chants, Three Dance Poems,* sinfonietta, and a symphony.

RUDY SISTERS, THE (singers) *see* CAROLINE RUDY MOORE, PATRICIA RUDY WOODS

RUEGGER, ELSA

b. 1881 Lucerne, Switzerland, d. 1924 Chicago, Illinois. Cellist. Studied at the Lucerne Conservatory, took first prize at age thirteen; toured Europe and America; taught at Scharwenka Conservatory, Berlin (1908-14); then resided in San Francisco; married Edmund Lichtenstein, violinist.

RUFF, ALBERT E.

b. 1851 Glasgow, Scotland, d. 1948.
Teacher. Studied in Mannheim, Germany, at age eleven; played in Theatre Royal orchestra, Glasgow, from ages sixteen to eighteen; then graduated Leipzig Conservatory (1873), studied voice culture; taught in Chicago after 1880; founded the Chicago College of Vocal and Instrumental Art (1885).

RUFTY, HILTON

b. 1909 Richmond, Virginia.
Composer. Educated at the University of Richmond, Hampden-Sydney College, Va., and the University of Virginia, Charlottesville, Va.; became organist-choirmaster of St. Stephen's Church, Richmond (1936), and professor of music at the University of Richmond in 1946; with John Powell and Annabel M. Buchanan, published *Twelve Folk Hymns* (1934) and with Reed Smith, *American Anthology of Old World Ballads* (1937); composed the operetta *The Twelve Dancing Princesses.*

RUGGLES, CARL

b. 1876 Marion, Massachusetts, d. 1971 Bennington, Vermont. Noted composer. Studied at Harvard University; founded and conducted the Winona (Minn.) Symphony; composed *Portals* for string orchestra, *Men and Angels, Sun-Treader, Men and Mountains;* several of his works were performed at the International Society for Contemporary Music festivals in Europe, and were highly original.

RUNCIE, CONSTANCE FAUNT LE ROY

b. 1836 Indianapolis, Indiana, d. 1911 Winnetka, Illinois. Composer. Wife of James Runcie, Episcopal minister in Madison, Indiana (1861-71); later in St. Joseph, Missouri; wrote "Hear Us, O Hear Us," "Round the Throne," "Silence of the Sea," "Take My Soul, O Lord," "I Never Told Him," "Dove of Peace," "I Hold My Heart So Still," "My Spirit Rests."

RUNKEL, KENNETH E.

b. 1882 Lisbon, Iowa.
Composer. Studied at Cornell College, Mt. Vernon, Iowa, MacPhail College of Music, Minneapolis, Minn., McGill University, Montreal, Quebec, and Trinity College of Music, London (1937); taught in Alliance, Ohio, Waco, Texas, and Jacksonville, Texas; organist-choirmaster in St. Paul and Minneapolis, then after 1943 at the First Methodist Church, Russell, Kentucky; composed the tune "Eternal Light" (1941, w. Thomas Binney) and the cantata *The Good Samaritan.*

RUSH, TOM

b. 1941 Portsmouth, New Hampshire.
Singer. Graduated Harvard University (1964); toured U.S. and made major appearances in leading cities; albums—*Blues, Songs, Ballads, Circle Game, Mind Ramblin', Tom Rush, Take a Little Walk with Me.*

RUSHING, JAMES ANDREW (JIMMY)

b. 1902 Oklahoma City, Oklahoma, d. 1972 New York City. Black singer. Taught himself to play the violin; debut (1925) in night spots in Hollywood; singer with Walter Page's Blue Devils (1927) in Oklahoma City; with Bennie Moten (1929), Count Basie (1935-50); formed own septet; his short and squat appearance was the inspiration for the song "Mr. Five by Five"; led seven-piece band at Savoy Ballroom in Harlem, New York City (1950-52); later toured U.S. and Europe; Australia (1964); at the Half Note, New York City (1972).

RUSSELL, CHARLES ELLSWORTH ("PEE WEE")

b. 1906 Maplewood, Missouri, d. 1969.
Clarinetist. Played in Jean Goldkette's band;

with the Louis Prima group at the Famous Door on 52nd Street (1935); played in Frankie Trumbauer's orchestra in the Arcadia Ballroom, St. Louis (1925); recorded with Zutty Singleton (ca. 1938); played at Jimmy Ryan's Club on 52nd Street, New York City in the 1940s.

RUSSELL, ELLA

b. 1864 Cleveland, Ohio, d. 1935.
Soprano. Studied under John Underner in Cleveland; then in Paris with Anna de la Grange; debut as Leonora in *Il Trovatore* (1882) in Prato, Tuscany; sang at La Scala in Milan; toured Spain with Tamberlik, tenor; debut at Covent Garden, London (1886) as Gilda in Verdi's *Rigoletto;* sang at state concerts in Buckingham Palace for Queen Victoria.

RUSSELL, HENRY

b. 1812 Sheerness, England, d. 1900 London, England. Popular composer. Of Jewish ancestry; was a concert singer in the United States from 1833 to 1841; for a time organist in the First Presbyterian Church in Rochester, N.Y.; composed the music "Woodman Spare That Tree" (1837, w. G.P. Morris), "A Life on the Ocean Wave" (1838, w. Epes Sargent), "The Old Arm Chair" (w. and m.), "The Ivy Green" (w. Charles Dickens, sung by William Morgan in Oregon City, Oregon, 1849); wrote the lyrics "Buffalo Gals" (1848, "Girls won't you come out tonight?" based on the tune "Lubly Fan," m. John Hodges); also wrote the "War Song of the Texas Rangers" (1861), and the music for "Traitor, Spare That Flag" (1861, w. W.J. Wetmore), "Cheer Boys, Cheer" (1861, w. Charles McKay) and "To the West" (McKay).

RUSSELL, LILLIAN

b. 1861 Clinton, Iowa, d. 1922 Pittsburgh, Pennsylvania. Noted singer. Born Helen Louise Leonard; debut in *H.M.S. Pinafore* (1879); during the 1880s she sang in Tony Pastor's Theatre, New York City; starred in the operetta *The American Beauty* (1897, m. G. A. Kerker); introduced "When Chloe Sings a Song" from *Whirl-i-gig* (1899, m. John Stromberg) at the Music Hall in New York City.

RUSSELL, LOUIS ARTHUR

b. 1854 Newark, New Jersey, d. there 1925. Conductor and teacher. Pupil of Warren and others in New York; conducted Schubert Vocal Society, Newark, after 1879; Easton (Pa.) Choral Society after 1885; founded and became director of Newark College of Music (1885); organized Newark Symphony Orchestra (1893); composed *A Pastoral Rhapsody,* cantata with orchestra.

RUSSELL, LUIS CARL

b. 1902 Careening Cay, off Panama, d. 1963. Black pianist and bandleader. Son of Alexander Russell, pianist and organist; won lottery prize in 1919 and came to New Orleans where he played in various bars; joined Charles Cook's orchestra in Chicago (1924); then joined King Oliver; took over Oliver's band (1927).

RUSSELL, WILLIAM

b. 1798 Glasgow, Scotland, d. 1873 Lancaster, Massachusetts. Hymnist. Educated at the University of Glasgow; came to Savannah, Georgia (1817); wrote "O'er the Dark Wave of Galilee," which appeared in the *Unitarian Christian Examiner* (1826).

RYAN, FATHER ABRAM J.

b. 1838 Hagerstown, Maryland, d. 1886 Louisville, Kentucky. Lyricist. Studied at Niagara and Vincentian novitiate in Germantown, Philadelphia, and was ordained a priest in 1861; served as a chaplain in the Confederate Army during the Civil War; after the war served parishes in Biloxi, Mississippi, Nashville and Knoxville, Tennessee, and Macon, Georgia; wrote the lyrics "The Sword of Robert E. Lee" (m. A.E. Blackmar and others).

RYAN, THOMAS

b. 1827 Ireland, d. 1903 New Bedford, Massachusetts. Clarinetist. Came to America (1844); studied in Boston (1849); toured America with Mendelssohn Quintet Club of which he was co-founder; also played viola; wrote *Recollections of an Old Musician* (New York, 1890); composed quartets, quintets and songs.

RYBNER, PETER MARTIN CORNELIUS

b. 1855 Copenhagen, Denmark, d. 1929 New York City. Pianist and teacher. Studied with Reinecke and others; conducted Carlsruhe Philharmonic Society (1892); professor of music at Columbia University, New York (1904-19), succeeding MacDowell; gave piano recitals with his daughter Dagmar Rybner, pianist; composed *Prinz Ador,* three-act dance legend (Carlsruhe, 1903).

RYDELL, BOBBY

b. 1942 Philadelphia, Pennsylvania.
Singer. Born Robert Ridarelli; sang with Paul Whiteman's band at age nine; played the drums and with Frankie Avalon on the trumpet, joined Rocco and the Saints (1959);

sang at the Copacabana, New York City at age nineteen; appeared in films; at "The Legend of Rock 'n Roll" show at the Hollywood Bowl, Calif. (1972).

RYDER, NOAH F.

b. 1914 Nashville, Tennessee, d. 1964 Norfolk, Virginia. Black composer and teacher. Attended Hampton Institute, Hampton, Virginia, and the University of Michigan (M.Mus.); taught at Palmer Memorial Institute, Sedalia, N.C. (1936-38), Winston-Salem Teachers College, N.C. (1938-41), and Virginia State College, Norfolk, Va. after 1947; wrote *Five Sketches for Piano, Sea Suite for Male Voices;* song "Haul Away Mateys We're Almost Home," awarded grand prize in Navy War Writers Contest (1944).

RYDER, THOMAS PHILANDER

b. 1836 Cohasset, Massachusetts, d. 1887. Organist, conductor, composer, teacher, and organmaker. Pupil of Gustav Satter; organist at Tremont Temple, Boston, after 1879; composed piano pieces—*Chanson des Alpes* (1880), *A Dainty Morsel, Lida, Rustic Maiden, Sounds from the Glen.*

S

SAAR, LOUIS VICTOR FRANZ

b. 1868 Rotterdam, Netherlands, d. 1937 St. Louis, Missouri. Composer. Studied at the Munich Conservatory, then with Brahms; won Mendelssohn Prize for a piano suite and songs (1891); operatic accompanist in New York (1892-95); taught at the National Conservatory, N.Y. (1896-98), College of Music (1898), Cincinnati College of Music after 1906, Chicago Music College after 1917; composed a piano quartet, string quartet, choral pieces, sonatas for violin sonatas for cello and for horn, numerous songs.

SAENGER, GUSTAV

b. 1865 New York City, d. there 1935. Violinist and conductor. Played in the Metropolitan Opera orchestra, with the New York Philharmonic, and the New York Symphony Orchestra; conducted at the Empire Theatre after 1893; editor of *The Metronome* and *The Musical Observer;* composed. instrumental pieces and songs.

SAENGER, OSCAR

b. 1868 Brooklyn, New York, d. 1926 Washington, D.C. Baritone and teacher. Studied with Bouhy; sang with Hinrichs American Opera Company; taught at the National Conservatory, New York.

ST. CYR, JOHN ALEXANDER (JOHNNY)

b. 1890 New Orleans, Louisiana, d. 1966. Black banjoist and guitarist. Played in Fate Marable's Band on the Mississippi River boats after 1920; played in Jelly Roll Morton's band in the 1920s; recorded with Morton; played with Zutty Singleton and Louis Armstrong.

SAINTE-MARIE, BUFFY

b. 1941 prob. Sebago Lake, Maine.
Singer and songwriter. A Cree Indian, she was adopted and raised in Wakefield, Mass.; attended the University of Massachusetts, Amherst; sang at The Gaslight Cafe, New York City in 1960s; wrote "Cod'ine," "The Universal Soldier" (1963), "Now That the Buffalo's Gone," "Incest Song," "It's My Way"; albums—*Fire and Fleet and Candlelight, Illuminations, I'm Gonna Be a Country Girl Again, It's My Way, Little Wheel Spin and Spin, Many a Mile.*

SALTER, MARY TURNER

b. 1856 Peoria, Illinois, d. 1938 Orangeburg, New York. Soprano. Studied with Max Schilling and others; sang at Broadway Tabernacle, N.Y. (1877), and Trinity Church, New Haven, Conn. (1879); taught at Wellesley College, Wellesley, Mass. (1881); married Sumner Salter.

SALTER, SUMNER

b. 1856 Burlington, Iowa, d. 1944 New York City. Organist and musical director. Studied at Amherst College, Amherst, Mass.; taught at Cornell University, Ithaca, N.Y. (1900-02); musical director at Williams College, Williamstown, Mass. (1905); edited *The Pianist and Organist* (New York City); composed church music.

SALZEDO, CARLOS

b. 1885 Arcachon, France, d. 1961 Waterville, Maine. Harpist and composer. Studied at the Paris Conservatory; came to U.S. (1909); U.S. citizen (1923); solo harpist at the Metropolitan Opera, New York City; served in the French Army in World War I; taught at Curtis Institute, Philadelphia after 1924; toured U.S. with Horace Britt; works—*Ballade, Scintillation, Desirade, Dances for Harps.*

SALZMAN, ERIC

b. 1933 New York City.
Composer. Graduated Columbia University, New York City (1954); M.F.A. from Princeton University (1956); studied with Sessions, Babbitt and others; Fulbright Scholarship to Rome (1956-58); music critic for the *New York Times,* then with *Stereo Review;* director of Hunter College concerts; wrote *In Praise of the Owl and Cuckoo* for voice, guitar, and chamber ensemble (1963), *Foxes and Hedgehogs* (1967, w. John Ashbery), *The Peloponnesian War Dance* (1968, with Daniel Negrin), *The Nude Paper Sermon Tropes for Actor.*

SAM AND DAVE (soul singers)

Sam Moore and Dave Prater; albums—*Best of Sam and Dave, Double Dynamite, Hold on I'm Comin', Soul Men.*

SAMAROFF, OLGA HICKENLOOPER

b. 1882 San Antonio, Texas, d. 1948 New York City. Pianist. Pupil of Von Sternberg when she was only nine; studied at the Paris Conservatory; studied with Ernest Hutcheson and others; debut in N.Y. (1905); London (1906); married Leopold Stokowski, divorced; injured her wrist in a fall and retired from concert tours; taught at the Juilliard School of Music, New York City and at the Philadelphia Conservatory of Music.

SAMINSKY, LAZARE

b. 1882 Vale-Gotzulovo, near Odessa, Russia, d. 1959 Rye, New York. Composer. Studied at the University of St. Petersburg and the conservatory there; settled in America (1920) and became musical director of Temple Emanu-El, New York City; known for his Symphony no. 4 (1926) and *The Daughter of Jephtha* (opera-ballet, 1928), the operas *Julian Aposta* and *The Plague's Galliard,* the choral works *By the Rivers of Babylon* and *Lament of Rachel,* rooted in Jewish themes.

SAMPSON, EDGAR MELVIN

b. 1907 New York City.
Black jazz saxophonist, violinist, composer, and arranger. Played with Duke Ellington (1927), with Arthur Gibb's orchestra (1927-28), Charles Johnson's orchestra (1928-30), with Fletcher Henderson (1931-33), with Chick Webb after 1933; formed his own band (1949); wrote "If Dreams Come True" (1937), "Stompin' at the Savoy" (1934, with Benny Goodman and Chick Webb), "Lullaby in Rhythm" (1938, with Clarence Profit), "I'll Be Back for More" (with Candido Camero, w. Sammy Gallop), "Happy and Satisfied" (w. Walter Bishop), "Light and Sweet" (w. Bill Hardy).

SANBORN, JOHN PITTS

b. 1879 Port Huron, Michigan, d. 1941 New York City. Critic. Attended Harvard, M.A. (1902); music editor of the *New York Globe* (1905-25); later with the *New York Daily Mail* and the *New York World Telegram;* also wrote magazine articles and program annotations; director of the Institute of Audible Arts.

SANDBURG, CARL

b. 1878 Galesburg, Illinois, d. 1967 Flat Rock, North Carolina. Poet and singer. Compiled *The American Songbag;* Frederick S. Converse composed *American Sketches* (1935), based on Sandburg's *Songbag;* also wrote *Lost* and *Prairie Waters by Night,* both of which were set to music by Jacques Wolfe; Richard Donovan based his symphonic poem, *Smoke and Steel,* on Sandburg's poem; albums—*Great Carl Sandburg Folk Songs, Carl Sandburg Sings His American Songbag;* also wrote *Rootabaga Stories, How to Tell Corn Fairies When You See Them, Poems for Children.*

SANDERS, ROBERT L.

b. 1906 Chicago, Illinois, d. 1974.
Composer. Studied at the Bush Conservatory, Chicago; won fellowship at American Academy in Rome; also studied in Paris; assistant conductor of Chicago Civic Orchestra (1933-38); composed a suite for orchestra (Augusteo Orchestra, Rome, composer conducting, 1929), *The Tragic Muse* (Chicago Symphony under DeLamarter, 1936), Little Symphony in G (New York Philharmonic Prize, 1938, split award), and songs.

SANDERSON, SIBYL

b. 1865 Sacramento, California, d. 1903 Paris, France. Soprano. Studied with de la Grange and Massenet, who wrote his *Thais and Esclarmonde* for her; debut at Opera Comique, Paris (1889); at the Metropolitan Opera, New York City after 1898.

SANDS, TOMMY

b. 1937 Chicago, Illinois.
Singer and actor. Played *The Singing Idol* (1958) in the NBC play; married Nancy Sinatra, later divorced; recorded "Teenage Crush," "Cutie Wootie."

SANGER, ZEDEKIAH

b. 1771 Framingham, Massachusetts, d. 1821 Boston, Massachusetts. Compiler. Lived in Albany, N.Y., and Boston (1813-21); compiled *The Meridian Harmony* (1808).

SANJUAN, PEDRO

b. 1886 San Sebastian, Spain.
Conductor and composer. Conductor of the Havana (Cuba) Philharmonic Orchestra; then conductor of the Spartanburg (S.C.) Symphony Orchestra and Festivals; composed *Rondo Fantastico,* on Basque theme (Havana Philharmonic under composer, 1926; won Spanish National Prize, 1934), *Castilla* (Havana Philharmonic, 1927), *Liturgia Negra.*

SANKEY, IRA DAVID

b. 1840 Edinburg . Pennsylvania, d. 1908 Brooklyn, New York. Singer and composer. When he was seventeen he joined the Methodist Episcopal Church; singing partner of Dwight L. Moody, the evangelist; joined Moody in 1861 and was with him until 1899; then became president of the YMCA in Newcastle, Pa.; composed the music for "There Were Ninety and Nine" (1868, w. Elizabeth C. Clephane), "I Am Praying for You" (1874, w. S.O. Clough), "Only Remembered" (w. H. Bonar), "A Soldier of the Cross" and "Shine On, O Star!" and "There Are Lonely Hearts to Cherish" (w. George Cooper). He was writing the stories of the gospel hymns when double tragedy struck. He went blind and his completed manuscript was destroyed in a fire. Undaunted, he rewrote the entire book with the help of a friend, and the book was published in 1905. Compiled *Sacred Songs and Solos* (1881) known as *Sankey and Moody's Songs.*

SANTANA BLUES BAND

Organized in San Francisco (1966) by Carlos Santana, guitar; Gregg Rolie, piano and organ; Dave Brown, bass guitar; later Jose Areas, conga drums and trumpet; Mike Carrabello, conga drums; Mike Shrieve, drums; albums—*Santana, Abraxas* (1970).

SANTIAGO, HERMAN

b. 1940.
Black singer. Member of the Teen Agers, vocal group in New York City.

SAPERTON (SAPERSTEIN), DAVID

b. 1889, d. 1970.
Pianist. Taught piano at Curtis Institute, Philadelphia.

SAPIO, ROMUALDO

b. 1858 Palermo, Italy, d. 1943 New York City. Conductor and teacher. Studied at the Naples Conservatory; conductor for Patti, Albani, and Nordica on American tours after 1888; taught at the National Conservatory, New York, after 1892; married Clementine de Vere, soprano.

SASLAVSKY, ALEXANDER

b. 1876 Kharkov, Russia, d. 1924 San Francisco, California. Violinist. Studied with Gorsky and Gruen; concertmaster of the New York Symphony Orchestra (1903), of Russian Symphony, N.Y. (1904-08), of Los Angeles Philharmonic after 1919.

SATTER, GUSTAV

b. 1832 Vienna, Austria, d. 1879 Savannah, Georgia. Composer. Studied in Vienna and Paris; composed *Washington* (a symphonic tone-picture), two symphonies, opera *Olanthe,* overtures *Lorelei, Julius Caesar* and *An die Freude.*

SAUNDERS, OTIS

b. 1872 Springfield, Missouri.
Black pianist. Toured with Scott Joplin (1894-96); went to Sedalia, Mo., with Joplin; claimed to have helped Joplin with his ragtime compositions.

SAUTER, EDWARD E. (ED)

b. 1914 Brooklyn, New York.
Drummer, trumpeter, and arranger. Studied at the Juilliard Conservatory (1935); worked with Archie Bleyer to 1931; then as arranger for Red Norvo and Mildred Bailey; with Benny Goodman (1939-44); arranger for Tommy Dorsey, Artie Shaw, Woody Herman, and Ray McKinley; formed a band with Bill Finegan (1952); wrote "All the Cats Join In" (w. L.W. Gilbert and Joe Wilder) from *Make Mine Music.*

SAVAGE, HENRY WILSON

b. 1859 Alton, New Hampshire, d. 1927. Producer. Graduated Harvard; organized a stock company which gave light and serious operas at the Castle Square Theatre, Boston; also produced operas in New York City; his productions included *Parsifal* and *Madame Butterfly* in English, by the Savage Opera Company while touring the United States.

SAVITT, JAN

b. 1908 Russia, d. 1948 near Sacramento, California. Violinist and bandleader. His father was a drummer in the Imperial Regimental Band of the Czar; came to America (1923); won three scholarships for playing and conducting at the Curtis Institute, Philadelphia; became youngest member ever to play in the Philadelphia Symphony; later concertmaster for Leopold Stokowski; organized his own string quartet (1926), won Philharmonic Society's Gold Medal Award; hired as musical director of station WCAU, Philadelphia; organized his Top Hatters (1939) and appeared at the Hotel Lincoln, New York City; his star singer was "Bon Bon" George Tunnell, who previously led his own vocal trio, The Three Keys, and was one of the first blacks ever to work in a white band; later Gloria DeHaven sang for his band; died of a cerebral hemorrhage while traveling to an engagement in Sacramento.

SAVO, JIMMY

b. 1896, d. 1960.
Singer. Popular in night clubs and Broadway shows in New York City; introduced "River Stay Away from My Door" (1931, w. Mort Dixon and m. Harry Woods).

SAVOY SULTANS (jazz group) *see* GRACHAN MONCUR, JR.

SAWYER, CHARLES CARROL

b. 1833 Mystic, Connecticut, d. after 1890. Lyricist. Son of Captain Joshua Sawyer, ship builder; moved to New York City at age twelve; wrote the Civil War song, "Weeping Sad and Lonely" (m. Henry Tucker).

SAYERS, HENRY J.

b. 1854 Toronto, Ontario, Canada, d. 1932 New York City. Popular composer. Wrote the words and music "Ta-ra-ra-bom-der-e" which was introduced in London (1891) by Lottie Collins, where it became a sensation; she then introduced the song in the United States in 1892 where it also became tremendously successful.

SCALA, FRANCIS

b. 1819 Italy, d. 1903.
Composer and bandleader. Joined the U.S. Marine Band in 1842 and became the bandleader in 1855 and served until 1871: the band gave weekly concerts in the Capitol starting in 1838 and in the 1840s in the White House; composed the "President's March" and "Mrs. Lincoln's Polka," which the band played in the White House in February, 1862; his "Lincoln's Union March" was played in the Capitol in June, 1862.

SCALERO, ROSARIO

b. 1870 near Turin, Italy, d. 1954 Settimo Vittone, Italy. Violinist and teacher. Studied in Turin, London, and Leipzig; taught at St. Cecilia Liceo, Rome; founded Societa del Quartetto in Rome (1913); taught composition in New York City after 1919; composed choral, orchestral, and chamber music.

SCANLAN, WILLIAM J.

b. 1856 Springfield, Massachusetts, d. 1898 White Plains, New York. Popular composer. Singer and an actor and appeared in a number of musicals; wrote "Peek-a-Boo" (1881), "My Nellie's Blue Eyes" (1883), "Peggy O'Moore" (1885), "My Maggie" (1888) and "Molly O!" (1891); from 1891-92 appeared in *Kathleen Mavourneen,* but suffered a breakdown and was committed to the Bloomingdale Asylum in White Plains, where he died.

SCHAEFER, MARY CHERUBIN

b. 1886 Slinger, Wisconsin.
Teacher and writer. Educated at Marquette University, Milwaukee, Wisc. (1922) and joined the Sisters of St. Francis (1903); organist-choirmaster at St. Lawrence's Church, Milwaukee (1904-09), director of music at St. Joseph's Convent (1909-24), St. Joseph's Conservatory of Music (1924-33), and the Alverno College of Music (1933-38); wrote *Music Appreciation for Schools* (1936), *The Liturgical Choir Book* (1939), and *The Organist's Companion* (1945).

SCHALIT, HEINRICH

b. 1886 Vienna, Austria, d. 1943.
Composer. Studied at the State Academy for Music in Vienna; became organist at the Great Synagogue in Rome (1933), then came to the United States where he served congregations in Providence, R.I., and Denver, Colorado; composed *Hebrew Song of Praise* and *Friday Night Liturgy.*

SCHARFENBERG, WILLIAM

b. 1819 Kassel, Germany, d. 1895 Quogue, New York. Pianist, editor, and teacher. With Ureli Corelli Hill and Henry Christian Timm, founded the New York Philharmonic Society (1842).

SCHEEL, FRITZ

b. 1852 Lubeck, Germany, d. 1907 Philadelphia, Pennsylvania. Conductor. Pupil of his father, a musician and in Leipzig; conductor in Bremerhaven (1869); then other German cities; at Columbian Exposition, Chicago (1894); founded and conducted the San Francisco Symphony (1895-99), founded and conducted the Philadelphia Orchestra (1900-07); also conducted Orpheus and Eurydice Clubs after 1905.

SCHEHL, J. ALFRED

b. 1882 Cincinnati, Ohio, d. 1937.
Director and compiler. Educated at Xavier University, Cincinnati, and the Cincinnati Conservatory; violinist in the Cincinnati Symphony Orchestra (1898-1908); director of the May Music Festival (1906-12); organist-choirmaster in Cincinnati churches after 1899; editor of the (Catholic) *St. Caecilia Hymnal* (1929).

SCHELLING, ERNEST HENRY

b. 1876 Belvidere, New Jersey, d. 1939 New York City. Pianist and composer. Studied at the Paris Conservatory, later with Paderewski and others; toured Europe and America as a recitalist and soloist with leading orchestras;

guest conductor in New York, Boston, Philadelphia, and Los Angeles; conductor of the Baltimore Symphony after 1935; composed *Fantastic Suite* for piano and orchestra (Amsterdam, 1907), Symphony in C Minor, *Symphonic Legend, A Victory Ball* (New York Philharmonic, 1923), *Morocco,* (tone-poem, New York Philharmonic, 1927).

SCHERMERHORN, KENNETH

b. 1930 Schenectady, New York.
Musical director. Studied at the New England Conservatory; with Leonard Bernstein at Tanglewood; in Italy on Beebe Fellowship; with American Ballet Theater (1957-68); musical director of the Milwaukee Symphony Orchestra after 1968; at Carnegie Hall, New York City (1972).

SCHERTZINGER, VICTOR

b. 1890 Mahanoy City, Pennsylvania, d. 1941 Hollywood, California. Popular composer. Conducted theater orchestras in Los Angeles (silent movies); wrote "Marcheta, My Wonderful Dream Girl" (w. Oliver Morosco); with lyrics by Clifford Grey—"Dream Lover" and "Paris Stay the Same" (1929); lyrics by Gus Kahn—"Love Me Forever 'nd "One Night of Love" (starring Grace Moore); with Johnny Burke—"I Don't Cry Any More" and "Willow Tree"; "I'll Never Let a Day Pass By" (w. Frank Loesser), "I Remember You" (w. Johnny Mercer).

SCHETKY, JOHN GEORGE

b. 1776 Edinburgh, Scotland, d. 1831 Philadelphia, Pennsylvania. Singer, cellist, composer, and publisher. Came to Philadelphia (1787); violinist for Raynor Taylor's benefit concert (1796); arranged Kotzwara's *Battle of Prague* for full band; music publisher in Philadelphia with firm of Carr and Schetky (1803-11); published "O Had I the Wings of an Eagle I'd Fly" (1801, m. S. Webbe).

SCHEVE, EDWARD BENJAMIN

b. 1865 Westphalia, Germany, d. 1924 Longmont, Colorado. Teacher. Came to America (1888); professor of music at Grinnell College in Iowa after 1906.

SCHIFRIN, LALO

b. 1932 Argentina.
Composer. Came to Hollywood and wrote the scores for motion pictures, including *I Love My Wife;* wrote the theme music for television's "Mission Impossible," "Rock Requiem" (1971, dedicated to the dead in the Southeast Asia War).

SCHILLINGER, JOSEPH

b. 1895 Kharkov, Russia, d. 1943 New York City. Composer. Studied at the Imperial Conservatory in St. Petersburg, then became a conductor; directed the Ukrainian Symphony Orchestra, then was a composer in Leningrad; after he came to America he taught at the New School for Social Research, New York City, and at Columbia University; composed the ballet *The People and the Prophet, Symphonic Rhapsody for Piano, North Russian* Symphony and *The Twelve,* a symphonic cantata.

SCHINDLER, KURT

b. 1882 Berlin, Germany, d. 1935 New York City. Conductor. Studied at Berlin University and Munich University; with Thuille and others; conducted Stuttgart Opera (1902); then in other German cities; at the Metropolitan Opera, N.Y. (1905-08); founded MacDowell Chorus, N.Y. (1909) which became the Schola Cantorum (1912); collector of Spanish, Russian, and Finnish folk music.

SCHIPPERS, THOMAS

b. 1930 Kalamazoo, Michigan.
Conductor. Conducted the Metropolitan Opera, New York City at age twenty-five; also guest conductor at the New York Philharmonic; appointed Musical Director of Cincinnati Symphony Orchestra (1971).

SCHIRMER, RUDOLF ERNEST

b. 1859 New York City, d. 1919 Santa Barbara, California. Publisher. Rudolph and Gustav (b. New York 1864-1907) were sons of Gustav Schirmer (b. Germany 1829-1893) who founded Beer and Schirmer, New York City (1837), and which became G. Schirmer (1866); the firm published the *Musical Quarterly* after 1915.

SCHLESINGER, DANIEL

b. 1799 Hamburg, Germany, d. 1839 New York City. Composer. Came to America (1836); composed a Grand Overture, a Quartet in C Minor, and orchestral work; after his death, a memorial service was held in the Broadway (Jewish) Tabernacle, New York City, featuring the works mentioned.

SCHLESINGER, SIGMUND

b. 1835 Uhlen, Wurttemberg, Germany, d. 1906 Mobile, Alabama. Composer. During the Civil War he wrote "Camp Moore Polka," "Fort Morgan Gallopade," "Trio Waltz," "The Old House by the Bay" (w. Harry A. Barclay); also compiled *Musical Services for American Jewish Temples.*

SCHLIEDER, FREDERICK WILLIAM

b. 1873.
Organist, composer, and teacher. Taught at the Philadelphia Conservatory, and headed the department of theory.

SCHMIDT, ARTHUR PAUL

b. 1846 Altona, Germany, d. 1921.
Publisher. Came to America about 1866; founded music publishing firm in Boston (1876).

SCHMITZ, E. ROBERT

b. 1889 Paris, France, d. 1949 San Francisco, California. Pianist and director. Studied at the Paris Conservatory; won first prize in piano; toured America (1919); formed Franco-American Musical Society, New York (1920), later became Pro Musica, Inc. (1923) devoted to French composers, presenting concerts of their works.

SCHMUCKER, BEALE MELANCHTHON

b. 1827 Gettysburg, Pennsylvania, d. 1888 near Phoenixville, Pennsylvania. Compiler. Son of Samuel S. Schmucker; became a Lutheran clergyman in the present West Virginia and Pennsylvania; with Frederic Mayer Bird, compiled *Pennsylvania Hymns for Use of the Evangelical Lutheran Church* (1865).

SCHNEIDER, ALEXANDER

b. 1908 Vilna, Lithuania.
Violinist, conductor, and teacher. Came to New York City; taught there; conductor of New York String Orchestra, composed of his students.

SCHNEIDER, EDWARD FABER

b. 1872 Omaha, Nebraska, d. 1950.
Composer and teacher. Wrote *Fires of Wisdom.*

SCHNITZER, GERMAINE

b. 1889 Paris, France.
Pianist. Graduated the Paris Conservatory at age fourteen; toured Europe (1904); then America (1906); married Dr. Leo Burger (1913) and made New York City her home.

SCHOEBEL, ELMER

b. 1896 East St. Louis, Illinois, d. 1970 St. Petersburg, Florida. Popular composer. Played with the Isham Jones band in New York City and with Louie Panico; wrote "Bugle Call Rag," "Farewell Blues" (1923, with Leon Rappolo and Paul Mares) while a member of the New Orleans Rhythm Kings; also wrote "Nobody's Sweetheart."

SCHOENEFELD, HEINRICH

b. 1857 Milwaukee, Wisconsin, d. 1936 Los Angeles, California. Conductor and composer. Studied with his father, a musician, then at the Leipzig Conservatory; won a prize for composition; pianist, teacher, and conductor of the Germania Mannerchor, Chicago, after 1879; conducted the Pacific Sangerfest, Los Angeles, after 1915; composed the symphonies—*Rural* and *Springtime,* overtures—*In the Sunny South* and *The American Flag, The Three Indians* (ode with orchestra), violin sonatas, piano pieces.

SCHOMACKER, JOHANN HEINRICH

b. 1800 Schleswig-Holstein, Germany, d. 1875 Philadelphia, Pennsylvania. Piano maker. Started making pianos in Philadelphia (1837), firm continued active until 1935 under his son Henry C. Schomacker and H.W. Gray.

SCHÖNBERG (SCHOENBERG), ARNOLD

b. 1874 Vienna, Austria, d. 1951 Brentwood, California. Famous composer. Studied under Alexander von Zemlinsky in Vienna and married Zemlinsky's sister; served in the Austrian Army in World War I; with the rise of Hitlerism in Europe, he came to America and taught at the University of Southern California and the University at Los Angeles; known for *Gurre-Lieder* (1901), *Pierrot Lunaire* (1912), *Verklaerte Nacht* (1899-1917), Quartet no. 3 for strings (1926), no. 4 for strings (1937), *Concerto for Piano and Orchestra* (1942), *Ode to Napoleon* (1942).

SCHONBERG, HAROLD C.

b. 1915 New York City.
Critic. Educated at Brooklyn College (A.B. cum laude), New York University (A.M., 1938), D.Lit. at Temple University, Philadelphia (1964); associate editor of *Music Lover* (1939-41); First Lt. Army Airborne Signal Corps in World War II; critic of the *New York Sun* (1946-50); the *New York Times* after 1950; wrote *The Great Pianists* (1963), *Great Conductors* (1967) and other books on music.

SCHONBERGER, JOHN

b. 1892 Philadelphia, Pennsylvania.
Violinist and composer. With Vincent Rose wrote "Whispering" (1920, w. Richard Coburn).

SCHORR, FRIEDRICH

b. 1888 Navyvarad, Hungary, d. 1953 Farmington, Connecticut. Opera singer. Son of cantor Baruch Schorr, sang in Wagner operas in Graz, Prague, Cologne, then was with the Berlin State Opera (1923-32), but the rise of Hitler forced him to flee Germany and come to the United States.

SCHRADICK, HENRY

b. 1846 Hamburg, Germany, d. 1918 Brooklyn, New York. Violinist. Studied with his father, a musician, and others, also at the Brussels Conservatory; taught at the Moscow Conservatory (1864-68); conductor in Germany; taught violin at the Cincinnati Conservatory (1883-89); then at the National Conservatory, N.Y., the Broad Street Conservatory, Philadelphia, and the American Institute of Applied Music, N.Y., after 1912.

SCHRODER, ALWIN

b. 1855 Neuhaldensleben, Germany, d. 1920 Detroit, Michigan. Cellist and teacher. Pupil of his father, Hermann, his three brothers, and others; first cellist in Hamburg and Leipzig (1881); with Boston Symphony (1886-1903); with Kneisel Quartet (1903); taught at the New York Institute of Musical Art (1905-07); with Boston Symphony (1910-12); went on concert tours; with Margulies Trio and Boston String Quartet.

SCHUBERT, CHRISTIAN JOHN

b. 1870 Chicago, Illinois, d. 1953.
Pianist and teacher. Graduated the Royal Conservatory in Munich, Germany (1889); taught at Western Musical Academy, Chicago; resided in Hyde Park, Illinois.

SCHULLER, GUNTHER

b. 1925 New York City.
Noted composer. His father, Arthur Schuller, was a violinist with the New York Philharmonic; studied at Manhattan School of Music (1942); first horn of Cincinnati Symphony (1943-45); teacher at Cincinnati College of Music; with Metropolitan Opera, N.Y. (1945-59); also taught at Manhattan School of Music after 1950; associate professor at Yale (1964); president of New England Conservatory, Boston, after 1966; composed *Symphony for Brass and Percussion* (Cincinnati Symphony, 1950), *Dramatic Overture for Orchestra* (Darmstadt, Germany, 1951), *Symphonic Tribute to Duke Ellington* (1955), *String Quartet* (Festival at University of Illinois at Urbana, 1957), *Concertino for Jazz Quartet and Orchestra* (Baltimore Symphony, 1959), *Variants* (ballet, New York, 1961, under George Balanchine, choreographer), *Spectra* for orchestra (New York Philharmonic under Mitropoulos, 1960), *The Visitation* (opera, Hamburg Opera, 1966).

SCHULTZE, WILLIAM

b. 1827 Hanover, Germany, d. 1888 Syracuse, New York. Violinist and teacher.

SCHULZ, LEO

b. 1865 Posen, Germany, d. 1944 Crescenta, California. Cellist. Studied at Berlin Hochschule; soloist with Berlin Philharmonic; with the New York Philharmonic (1890-1931); member of Margulies Trio (1904-15).

SCHUMAN, WILLIAM HOWARD

b. 1910 New York City.
Noted composer. Studied at Columbia University, New York City, and at the Mozarteum in Salzburg; taught at Sarah Lawrence College (1935-45); later became president of the Juilliard School of Music, New York City; known for his *American Festival Overture* (1943), Quartet no. 3 (1939), Symphony no. 3 (introduced by the Boston Symphony under Koussevitzky, 1941) *A Free Song* (1942), Symphony no. 5 (1943), *Undertow* (ballet, 1945), *Concerto for Violin and Orchestra* (1947), and Symphony no. 6 (Dallas Symphony, 1949).

SCHUMANN, ELIZABETH

b. 1891 Merseburg, Germany, d. 1952 New York City. Soprano. Sang at Hamburg Opera (1909-15); then with Vienna State Opera after 1919; toured U.S. in 1921; sang at the Metropolitan Opera, N.Y.

SCHUMANN-HEINK, ERNESTINE ROSSLER

b. 1861 Lieben, Czechoslovakia, d. 1936 Hollywood, California. Famous contralto. At age fifteen she signed with the Royal Opera in Dresden for a pittance, and lived on sausages and beer to "make her strong"; her husband left her and she signed with the Hamburg Opera for ten dollars a month, and had to support three children; came to America (1898) and sang for the Metropolitan Opera House, New York City; during World War I her eldest son fought for Germany and was killed in action, and her other four boys fought for America; made her farewell appearance at the Metropolitan (1932).

SCHUSTER, JOSEPH

b. 1905 Istanbul, Turkey, d. 1969.
Cellist. Cellist with the Berlin Philharmonic Orchestra, but was forced to flee Germany when Hitler came to power; came to the United States where he was solo cellist with the New York Philharmonic, but later became a soloist.

SCHWARTZ, ARTHUR

b. 1900 Brooklyn, New York.
Popular composer. Graduated Columbia Law School, N.Y. (1924); with lyricist Howard Dietz wrote the scores for the musical shows—*Little Show* (1929), *Three's a Crowd* (1930, including "Something to Remember You By" sung by Libby Holman), *The Bandwagon* (1931, including "Dancing in the Dark"), *Flying Colors* (1932), *At Home Abroad* (1935), *Inside USA* (1948); also *A Tree Grows in Brooklyn* (1951, book—Betty Smith), *By the Beautiful Sea* (1951, book—Herbert and Dorothy Fields); with Dietz—*The Gay Life* (1961, book—Michael and Fay Kanin, play—Arthur Schnitzler's *Anatol*, 1911); also wrote the song "They're Either Too Young or Too Old" (w. Frank Loesser).

SCHWARTZ, JEAN

b. 1878 Budapest, Hungary, d. 1956 Los Angeles, California. Popular composer. The family came to New York City (1891); pianist and song plugger for Shapiro and Bernstein, Tin Pan Alley; with lyricist William Jerome wrote "Don't Put Me Off at Buffalo Any More" (1901), "Hamlet Was a Melancholy Dane" (1902, introduced by Eddie Foy in Chicago), "Bedelia" (1903, sung by Blanche Ring in *The Jersey Lily*), "My Irish Molly-O" (Blanche Ring in *Sergeant Blue*, 1905); also wrote with lyrics by Grant Clarke—"Back to the Carolina," "You Love and I Love Angels"; with Harold Atteridge—songs for *The Passing Show* (1913 and 1921); with Anne Caldwell—"A Night in Spain" (1927); with Sam M. Lewis and Joe Young—"Why Do They All Take the Night Boat to Albany" and "Rock-a-bye Your Baby with a Dixie Melody"; "Au Revoir, Pleasant Dreams" (w. Jack Meskill); "Trust in Me" (1937, w. Milton Ager); married Rosika Dolly, one of the Dolly Sisters.

SCHWARTZ, STEPHEN

b. 1948.
Lyricist and librettist. Wrote *Godspell*, also the words for Leonard Bernstein's *Mass*, performed at the John F. Kennedy Center for the Performing Arts, Washington, D.C. (1971).

SCHWARZ, JOSEPH

b. 1883 Odessa, Russia, d. 1945 New York City. Concert pianist.

SCHWARZ, TRACY

b. 1938 New York City.
Singer and guitarist. Attended college in Washington, D.C.; in 1962 joined the "New Lost City Ramblers" with Mike Seeger and John Cohen, replacing Tom Paley.

SCOLLARD, CLINTON

b. 1860 Clinton, New York, d. 1932 Kent, Connecticut. Lyricist. Wrote the lyrics for "Sylvia" (1914, m. Oley Speaks).

SCOTT, ARTHUR ("BUD")

b. 1890 New Orleans, Louisiana, d. 1949 Los Angeles, California. Black banjoist and guitarist. Played both banjo and guitar at different times in King Oliver's band (1924); guitarist in Kid Ory's band on "Orson Welles' Southwest" CBS program (1944); recorded with Kid Ory's band (1944).

SCOTT, CLEMENT

b. 1841 England, d. 1904 London, England. Lyricist. Drama critic in New York City for a number of years, then returned to London; wrote the lyrics "Oh Promise Me" (m. Reginald de Koven) which was sung by Jessie Barlett Davis in *Robin Hood* (libretto by H.B. Smith).

SCOTT, HAZEL

b. 1920 Port of Spain, Trinidad.
Noted black pianist and singer. In Broadway show *Sing Out the News* (1938) sang "FDR Jones"; popular in New York City night clubs during 1940s, '50s and '60s; married Rep. Adam Clayton Powell Jr. (1945); at Danny Mazur's, Huntington, Long Island, New York (1972).

SCOTT, HENRI GUEST

b. 1876 Coatesville, Pennsylvania, d. 1942 Hagerstown, Maryland. Operatic bass. Studied in Philadelphia and New York; sang in Europe and America; with the Metropolitan Opera Company, New York after 1915.

SCOTT, JACOB RICHARDSON

b. 1815 Boston, Massachusetts, d. 1861. Hymnist. Graduated Brown University, Providence, R.I. (1836), Newton Theological College (1842); Baptist preacher in Petersburg, Va., Portland, Me., Fall River, Mass., then Yonkers, N.Y.; wrote "To Thee This Temple We Devote" (*The Psalmist*, 1843).

SCOTT, JAMES SYLVESTER

b. 1886 Neosho, Missouri, d. 1938 Kansas City, Missouri. Noted black pianist and composer. Studied with John Coleman, black pianist; moved to Carthage, Mo., played the piano in a music store there (1902); taught in Kansas City, Mo. (1914), played in theaters there; his rags—"A Summer Breeze" (1903), "On the Pike" (1904), "Frog Legs Rag" (1906), "Kansas City Rag" (1907), "Great Scott Rag" (1909), "Hilarity Rag" (1910), "The Ragtime Oriole" (1911), "Climax Rag" (1914), "Evergreen Rag" (1915), "Honeymoon Rag" (1916), "Pegasus—A Classic Rag" (1920), "Broadway Rag—A Classic" (1922); his waltzes—"Hearts Longing" (1910), "Suffragette" (1914), "Springtime of Love" (1919); his songs—"She's My Girl from Anaconda" (1909, w. Henry Dumars), "Sweetheart Time" (1909, Dumars), "Take Me Out to Lakeside" (1914), w. Ida Miller), "The Shimmie Shake" (1920, w. Cleota Watson).

SCOTT, JOHN PRINDLE

b. 1877 Norwich, New York, d. 1932.
Baritone and composer. Also wrote hymns.

SCOTT, NORMAN

b. 1921 New York City, d. 1968.
Bass-baritone. Born Norman Schultz; operatic debut (1946); sang with New England Opera Company, Boston; with New York Opera Company (1948-51); Metropolitan debut (1951) as Monterone in *Rigoletto;* with Vienna State Opera (1956).

SCOTT, ORANGE

b. 1800 Brookfield, Vermont, d. 1847 Newark, New Jersey. Compiler. Methodist minister, having joined the New England Conference in 1822; became active in the antislavery movement and broke away from the church in 1842 and formed the Wesleyan Methodist Connection at Utica, N.Y.; compiled *A New and Improved Camp Meeting Hymn Book* (1829).

SCOTT, RAYMOND

b. 1909 Brooklyn, New York.
Popular composer. Born Harry Warnow; studied at the Institute of Musical Art, New York City; house pianist for CBS radio (1930-36); wrote "Christmas Night in Harlem" (1932) introduced on radio by his brother, Mark Warnow, and his orchestra; in 1936 joined Jerry Colona and Bunny Berigan (trumpet player) on "Saturday Night Swing"; organized his own jazz band (1937); wrote "Toy Trumpet" (1937, sung by Shirley Temple), "Mountain High, Valley Low" (w. Bernard Harrighen), the instrumental pieces *Twilight in Turkey, In an 18th Century Drawing Room, All Around the Christmas Tree, War Dance of the Wooden Indians, In a Magic Garden, In a Subway Far from Ireland,* and the score for the ballet, *The Gremlins.*

SCOTT, ROBERT BALGARNIE YOUNG

b. 1899 Toronto, Ontario.
Hymnist. Graduated Knox College and the University of Toronto (Ph.D.); minister of the United Church in Long Branch, Ontario, then taught at Union College, Vancouver, B.C., then since 1931 at the United Theological College in Montreal; chaplain in the Royal Canadian Air Force during World War II; wrote the hymn "O Day of God, Draw Nigh" (tune "Bellwoods"—James Hopkirk).

SCOTT, TONY

b. 1921 Morristown, New Jersey.
Clarinetist. Born Anthony Sciacca; studied at the Juilliard School, New York City (1940-42); played with Claude Thornhill, Charlie Ventura and others.

SCOTTI, ANTONIO

b. 1866 Naples, Italy, d. there 1936.
Famous baritone. Debut in Malta (1889); sang at the Metropolitan Opera, New York City (1899-1933); died in poverty and suffered ill health in his declining years.

SCRANTON SIRENS (jazz group) *see* EDDIE LANG

SCRUGGS, EARL EUGENE

b. 1924 Cleveland County, North Carolina.
Songwriter and banjoist. Attended school in Boiling Springs, N.C.; joined Bill Monroe and his Bluegrass Boys, Nashville, Tenn. (1944); joined with Lester Flatt to form the Foggy Mountain Boys (1951); wrote "Foggy Mountain Special," "Foggy Mountain Chimes," "Flint Hill Special," "Randy Lynn Rag," "Earl's Breakdown," "Rocky Mountain Rock"; their albums—*Bonnie and Clyde, Changin' Times, Fabulous Sound of Flatt and Scruggs, Final Fling, Foggy Mountain Banjo, Nashville Airplane, Songs of Glory.*

SCUDDER, ELIZA

b. 1821 Boston, Massachusetts, d. 1896 Salem, Massachusetts. Hymnist. Wrote the lyrics "Thou Long Disowned, Reviled, Oppressed" (1873, m. Robert Wainwright, tune "Manchester," 1774); niece of Dr. E.H. Sears, but she joined the Episcopal church; contributed to *Hymns of the Spirit* (1864), edited by Samuel Longfellow and Samuel Johnson.

SCUDDER, MOSES L.

b. 1814 Huntington, Long Island, N.Y., d. 1891 Washington, D.C. Compiler. Graduated Wesleyan University, Middletown, Conn. (1837); Methodist minister serving churches in

Worcester, Mass. and Boston, later in Troy, N.Y. and New York City; compiled *The Wesleyan Psalmist, or Songs of Canaan* (1842), which was one of the first camp meeting song books to include tunes.

SEA TRAIN (rock group)

Andy Kulberg, bass and flute; Roy Blumenfeld, drums; Richard Greene, violin and viola; John Gregory, vocals and lead guitar; Don Kretmar, sax and bass; Jim Roberts, vocals; former member—Andy Musar; debut at the Cafe Au Go Go, New York City (1968); later moved to Mill Valley, Calif.; album—*Sea Train.*

SEARCHERS, THE *see* DICK FLOOD

SEARS, EDMUND HAMILTON

b. 1810 Sandisfield, Berkshire County, Massachusetts, d. 1876 Weston, Massachusetts. Hymnist. Educated at Union College, Schenectady, N.Y. and at Harvard Divinity School; became pastor of the Unitarian Church in Wayland, Mass. (1838); wrote the lyrics "Calm on the Listening Ear of Night" (1835, m. J.E. Gould) and the Christmas carol "It Came Upon a Midnight Clear" (1857, m. R.S. Willis).

SEBALD, ALEXANDER

b. 1869 Pest, Hungary, d. 1934 Chicago, Illinois. Violinist. Studied with Saphir and C. Thomson; toured with Gewandhaus Quartet in Germany; taught in Chicago and also Berlin; composed violin pieces.

SEEBOECK, WILLIAM CHARLES ERNEST

b. 1859 Vienna, Austria, d. 1907 Chicago, Illinois. Pianist and composer. Studied under Johannes Brahms; at the St. Petersburg Conservatory (1877); came to America (1879); pianist of the Apollo Club, Chicago, also taught there; organist and choirmaster of Jefferson Park Presbyterian Church; his opera, *The Missing Link,* performed at Central Music Hall (1889); wrote *Minuet Antique No. 1 and 2, Bourret No. 1 and 2, Berceuse* for piano and violin, concert etudes, caprices, quartets.

SEEDS, THE (SKY SAXON'S BLUES BAND)

Sky Saxon, lead vocals; Daryl Hooper, piano and organ; Jan Savage, guitar; Rick Andridge, drums; started in Los Angeles, Calif. (1966); disbanded in 1968; albums—*The Seeds, Future, Merlin's Music Box, Web of Sound, Full Spoon of Seedy Blues.*

SEEGER, CHARLES LOUIS, JR.

b. 1886 Mexico City, Mexico.
Teacher and writer. Graduated Harvard (1908); professor of music at the University of California, Berkeley (1912-19); at the Institute of Musical Art, New York City (1921-33); in Washington, D.C. after 1935; Chief of Music Division, Pan American Union (1941-53); with the Lomaxes he wrote *Folk Song USA;* later he wrote *Army Song Book* (1941), *Cancionero Popular Americano* (1950). (See Mike, Peggy and Peter Seeger, his children)

SEEGER, MARGARET (PEGGY)

b. 1935 New York City.
Singer. Daughter of Charles L. Seeger, Jr.; attended Radcliffe College, Cambridge, Mass.; sang in England (1933); married Ewan MacColl, Scotch folk singer and songwriter; sang with her sisters Barbara and Penny on the LP record, *Three Sisters;* her albums—*Bothy Songs of Scotland, Classic Scots Ballads, Female Frolic, Folk Songs of Courting and Complaint, Paper Stage;* with E. MacColl *Long Harvest* and *Now Is the Time for Fishing.*

SEEGER, MICHAEL (MIKE)

b. 1933 New York City.
Singer, banjoist, and guitarist. Son of Charles L. Seeger, Jr.; joined with John Cohen and Tom Paley to form the New Lost City Ramblers (1958); their albums—*Modern Times, New Lost City Ramblers, "New" New Lost City ramblers;* his albums—*Old Time Country Music, Tipple, Loom and Rail.*

SEEGER, PETER R. (PETE)

b. 1919 New York City.
Popular composer and singer. Son of Charles L. Seeger, Jr.; attended Harvard University (1936-38); founded The Almanac Singers (1940); served in the army in the Pacific theater in World War II; organized The Weavers (1948); took the Fifth Amendment before a House Committee (1955), indicted on ten counts of contempt of Congress, dismissed by U.S. Court of Appeals (1962); wrote "Kisses Sweeter Than Wine," "Where Have All the Flowers Gone," "If I Had a Hammer" (with Lee Hays).

SEELY, MARILYN JEANNE (JEANNIE)

b. 1940 Titusville, Pennsylvania.
Singer and songwriter. With WSM Grand Ole Opry, Nashville, Tenn. after 1966; wrote "Enough to Live," "Between Today and

Tomorrow"; albums—*I'll Love You More, Little Things, Jeannie Seely, Seely Style, Thanks Hank;* with Jack Greene—*Jack Greene and Jeannie Seely.*

SEGAL, VIVIENNE

b. 1897 Philadelphia, Pennsylvania. Singer. Introduced "Auf Wiedersehen" in *The Blue Paradise* (1915, w. Herbert Reynolds and m. Sigmund Romberg).

SEGO BROTHERS AND NAOMI (gospel singers)

Formed in Macon, Georgia (1946); James Sego; Naomi (wife of James); Rev. W.R. Sego; Lamar Sego; Eddie Cook, pianist.

SEGUIN, ARTHUR EDWARD S.

b. 1809 London, England, d. 1852 New York City. Bass. His wife, Ann Childe Seguin, was an opera singer; made her debut in 1828; his sister, Elizabeth, was the mother of Parepa-Rosa who married violinist Carl Rosa (1842-1889) in 1867, who organized an English opera company; his brother, William H. (1814-50) was a bass singer.

SEIDL, ANTON

b. 1850 Pest, Hungary, d. 1898 New York City. Conductor. Studied at the Leipzig Conservatory; with Wagner (1872-79) and assisted in score of *The Ring of the Nibelung;* conducted Neumann's Wagner troup (1879-83); Bremen Opera (1883-85), Metropolitan Opera, New York (1885-91), New York Philharmonic Orchestra (1895-97); also at Bayreuth and Covent Garden, London; married Frl. Krauss, soprano.

SEIFERT, M.J.

b. 1864 Chicago, Illinois, d. 1947. Composer and teacher. Studied under Florenz Ziegfeld, Gaston Gottschalk, et.al.; organist at St. Aloysius church, Chicago (1885-87); established Western Musical Academy, Chicago (1888); wrote *Veni Creator,* three chorals, and a waltz for piano.

SELBY, WILLIAM

b. ca. 1739 England, d. 1798 Boston, Massachusetts. Organist, choral director, and composer. Came to Boston (1771); organist at King's Chapel; organized and conducted choral concerts in Boston (1782, 1786, and 1787).

SEMBRICH, MARCELLA

b. 1858 Wisniewszyk, Galicia, Russia, d. 1935 New York City. Noted coloratura soprano. Born Praxede Marcelline Kochanska, Sembrich being her mother's maiden name; studied piano with William Stengel, whom she later married; also with Victor Rokitansky and others; debut in Athens (1877); sang in Europe (1878-98); with the Metropolitan Opera, New York (1898-1909); later taught at the Juilliard School of Music, New York, and Curtis Institute of Music, Philadelphia.

SEMINOLE, PAUL

b. 1904 Philadelphia, Pennsylvania, d. 1932 Asbury Park, New Jersey. Black American Indian guitarist, pianist and xylophonist. Vaudeville actor with his father, who was from Florida; did a specialty act playing the piano with his right hand and the guitar with his left hand; later played in Luckey Roberts' society bands; also played piano duo with Don Lambert.

SENATORS QUARTET *see* EARL H. PEEK

SENDREY, ALFRED

b. 1884 Budapest, Hungary. Conductor and teacher. Conductor at German and Austrian opera houses, then musical director of the Leipzig broadcasting station; came to the United States and taught at Westlake College of Music, Los Angeles; wrote *Bibliography of Jewish Music.*

SENKRAH, ARMA LEORETTE HOFFMAN HARKNESS

b. 1864 New York City, d. 1900 Weimar, Germany. Violinist. Studied with Arno Hilf at the Leipzig Conservatory; also with Wieniawski, and Massart at Paris Conservatory; toured as concert violinist; she committed suicide.

SERKIN, RUDOLF

b. 1903 Eger, Austria. Noted pianist and teacher. Debut with Philadelphia Orchestra under Eugene Ormandy (1937); instructor at Curtis Institute, Philadelphia after 1939; married the daughter of violinist Adolf Busch; established a summer school at his vacation home in Marlboro, Vermont; soloist with Philadelphia Orchestra under Ormandy at Philharmonic Hall, New York City (1972); head of the Marlboro Music Festival (1972).

SERLY, TIBOR

b. 1900 Losonc, Hungary. Composer and arranger. Came to America after 1935; arranged Mozart's *Fantasia and Fugue,* composed for organ in musical clock

(Budapest Philharmonic under Serly, 1935); arranged *Mikrokosmos,* from Bartok, for orchestra (St. Louis Symphony under Golschmann); also completed Bartok's last piano concerto and viola concerto.

SESSIONS, ROGER HUNTINGTON

b. 1896 Brooklyn, New York.
Famous composer. Studied at Harvard, Yale, and privately with Ernest Bloch; taught at the Cleveland Institute of Music (1921-25), later at Columbia University, Princeton, and the University of California at Berkeley; known for his Symphony in E Minor introduced by the Boston Symphony under Koussevitzky (1927), Concerto in B Minor for Violin and Orchestra (1935), Symphony no. 2 introduced by the San Francisco Symphony under Pierre Monteux (1947).

SEVENTEEN INTERNS (black band)

Organized by Charles "Doc" Cook at Dreamland, Chicago (1918); band included (at various times) Zutty Singleton, drums; Freddy Keppard, cornet; Jimmy Noone, clarinet; Luis Carl Russell, pianist.

SEVERINSEN, CARL H. ("DOC")

b. 1927 Arlington, Oregon.
Played in the Tommy Dorsey and Benny Goodman bands; music director of the "Tonight Show" on TV after 1967; formed his own band, the New Generation Brass, and company of singers and dancers, Today's Children; at the Copacabana, New York (1971); at Philharmonic Hall, New York, (1972).

SEVILLE, DAVID

b. 1919 Fresno, California, d. 1972 Beverly Hills, California. Composer. Born Ross Bagdasarian; served in the air force in World War II; grew grapes; wrote "Come On-a My House" (recorded by Rosemary Clooney) which became a great success; he couldn't read or write music, so he whistled into a tape recorder; wrote "The Witch Doctor" (1958) by recording his own voice at half speed, then playing it back at normal speed, the effect was like a small animal singing, so he wrote "Alvin and the Chipmunks" (1958).

SEVITZKY, FABIAN

b. 1893 Volotchek, Russia, d. 1967.
Conductor. Nephew of Serge Koussevitzky; studied at the St. Petersburg Conservatory, won gold medal; after coming to America, founded the Chamber String Sinfonietta, Philadelphia; conductor of Boston People's Symphony (1933-46); then of Indianapolis Symphony after 1937; married Maria Koussevitzky, singer.

SEWALL, FRANK

b. 1837 Bath, Maine, d. 1915 Washington, D.C. Composer and compiler. Graduated Bowdoin College (1858); president of Urbana University, Urbana, Ohio, for sixteen years; then became pastor of the Swedenborgian Church, Washington, D.C. (1890); compiled *The Christian Hymnal* (1867, including twenty-two of his tunes), *The Welcome* (1868, for Sunday Schools), *A Daily Psalter and Hymnal* (1884), and *The Hosanna* (1878, including twelve of his tunes).

SEWARD, THEORDORE FRELINGHUYSEN

b. 1835 Florida, New York, d. 1902 East Orange, New Jersey. Organist, conductor, and compiler. With George L. White compiled *Jubilee Songs* (1884), compilation of Negro spirituals; studied under George F. Root and Lowell Mason; edited *Musical Pioneer* and *Musical Gazette,* New York City, after 1860; taught in Orange, New Jersey, after 1877.

SEYMOUR, JOHN LAURENCE

b. 1893 Los Angeles, California.
Composer. Composed *In the Pasha's Garden,* a one-act opera, performed at the Metropolitan Opera (1935).

SEYMOUR, JOHNNY

b. 1865, d. 1942 Chicago, Illinois.
Black pianist. Played in the Cairo Street concession at the Chicago Fair (1893); played in various night spots in Chicago.

SHANE, BOB

b. 1934 Hawaii.
Singer. With Nick Reynolds and Dave Guard, started the Kingston Trio (1957); played in the Purple Onion, San Francisco, Mr. Kelly's in Chicago, Blue Angel and Village Vanguard in New York City.

SHANNON, JAMES ROYCE

b. 1881 Adrian, Michigan, d. 1946 Pontiac, Michigan. Actor, composer, and lyricist. Organized own theatrical company, toured U.S. and Europe; director of weekly shows at the Majestic Theatre, Detroit (1919); drama critic of *Detroit Free Press;* wrote "Too-Ra-Loo-Ra-Loo-Ra, That's an Irish Lullaby" (1913) for musical *Shameen Dhu* produced in New York City (1914) and other songs.

SHAPERO, HAROLD SAMUEL

b. 1920 Lynn, Massachusetts.
Composer. Became an instructor at Brandeis University, Waltham, Mass.; composed the *Nine-Minute Overture* which received the Prix de Rome (1941); composed the ballets *Pocohontas* and *The Minotaur, The Defense of Corinth* for narrator, men's chorus and piano four hands, *Emblems* (w. Allan Tate) for men's chorus and piano, and a symphony.

SHAPEY, RALPH

b. 1921 Philadelphia, Pennsylvania.
Composer. Studied violin with Emanuel Zetlin and composition with Stefan Wolpe; received various awards; assistant conductor of the Philadelphia National Youth Orchestra (1938-42); taught at the University of Chicago after 1964; wrote *Challenge—The Family of Man* for orchestra (1955), *Mutations* for piano (1956), *Ontogeny* for orchestra (1958), *Dimensions* for soprano and twenty-three instruments (1960), *Convocation* for chamber group (1962), *Sonance* for carillon (1964).

SHATTUCK, ARTHUR

b. 1881 Neenah, Wisconsin, d. 1951 New York City. Pianist. Studied with Leschetizky; debut as soloist with Copenhagen Philharmonic; toured Europe and America.

SHAVERS, CHARLIE JAMES

b. 1917 New York City, d. there 1971.
Black trumpeter and song writer. Played in New York City with Tiny Bradshaw and Lucky Millinder (1936); trumpet soloist in the John Kirby Sextet (1938-44), Raymond Scott Quintet, then with Tommy Dorsey's orchestra (1945-49); hit songs included "Undecided" (1938) and "Pastel Blue"; led his own groups during the 1950s and 1960s, toured America and Europe.

SHAVITCH, VLADIMIR

b. 1888 Russia, d. 1947 West Palm Beach, Florida. Conductor. Pupil of Godowsky and others; conducted Syracuse (N.Y.) Symphony after 1924; guest conductor in Moscow, London, Berlin, etc.; also in Detroit, San Francisco, and Los Angeles.

SHAW, ARTIE

b. 1910 New York City.
Clarinetist and bandleader. Born Arthur Arshawsky; raised in New Haven, Conn.; played the clarinet in Irving Aaronson's band, the Commanders; became a staff musician for CBS; formed his own band (1936); recorded "Begin the Beguine" (1936, m. Cole Porter) which sold over two million disks; bandleader in the navy in the Pacific area in World War II; later appeared as guest clarinet soloist for symphony orchestras.

SHAW, OLIVER

b. 1779 Middleborough, Massachusetts, d. 1848 Providence, Rhode Island. Composer and compiler. As a boy he accidently stuck a knife in his right eye, and lost his sight in that eye; later he was observing the sun when partially recovered from yellow fever, and at twenty-one became totally blind; studied music under Gottlieb Graupner of Boston (1803); in 1807 moved to Providence, R.I., where he became organist of the First Congregational Church; his tunes were "Taunton," "Bristol," "Dighton," "Weybosset," "Meeting," "Benevolent," "Pleasant," and "Planet"; wrote *The Gentleman's Favorite Selection of Instrumental Music* (Dedham, Mass., 1805); in 1808 he assisted Amos Albee and Herman Mann in compiling *The Columbian Sacred Harmonist;* he issued *The Musical Olio* (1814), *Providence Selection of Psalms and Hymns* (1815), *The Melodia Sacra* (1819), *Original Melodies* (1823 and 1832), and *The Social Sacred Melodist* (1835); his tune "Gentleness" ("There's Nothing True but Heaven") was played at his funeral.

SHAW, ROBERT

b. 1916 Red Bluff, California.
Conductor. Educated at Pomona College, Claremont, Calif.; received numerous honorary degrees; director of Fred Waring Glee Clubs (1938-45); choral director at Berkshire Music Center and at Juilliard, New York City (1946-49); founder and director of Robert Shaw Chorale (1948); San Diego (Calif). Summer Symphony (1953-58); associate director of the Cleveland Orchestra (1956-67); conductor of Atlanta (Georgia) Symphony Orchestra after 1966.

SHEA, GEORGE BEVERLY

b. 1909 Winchester, Ottawa, Canada.
Gospel singer. Attended Houghton College, Houghton, N.Y.; member of evangelist Billy Graham's crusade, "The Hour of Decision"; considered by many as America's outstanding singer of sacred songs.

SHEARING, GEORGE

b. 1919 London, England.
Pianist and composer. Born blind, attended the Shillington Street School for the Blind, then the Linden Lode School; appeared on the British Broadcasting System both as a pianist and accordianist; came to New York in 1947

and 1949; played in New York night clubs; then settled in the U.S.; composed "Lullaby of Birdland" (1952).

SHELLEY, GLADYS

b. (?) Lawrence, New York.
Dancer, actress, and lyricist. Educated at Columbia University, New York City; wrote lyrics for Broadway musicals; wrote "For a Little While She's Mine" (1972, m. Buddy Greco), about a man's little daughter; Frank Sinatra, Danny Thomas, and Ethel Ennis sang her hit songs, "Show's on Me Tonight" and "Does It Hurt to Love?" at the National Governors' banquet (1972).

SHELLEY, HARRY ROWE

b. 1858 New Haven, Connecticut, d. 1947 Short Beach, Connecticut. Composer and compiler. Educated at Yale and was an organist in Brooklyn churches (1878-99), the Fifth Avenue Baptist Church (1899-1914), and the Central Congregational Church, Brooklyn, N.Y. (1914-36); compiled *The Modern Organist* and *Gems for the Organ;* wrote the cantatas *Verilla Regis* and *Death and Life.*

SHENANDOAH BOYS *see* JIM EANES

SHEPARD, FRANK HARTSON

b. 1863 Bethel, Connecticut, d. 1913 Orange, New Jersey. Organist. Studied with Thayer in Boston; then in Leipzig (1886-90); established a school in Orange, N.J. (1891).

SHEPARD, JEAN

b. 1933 Pauls Valley, Oklahoma.
Singer and bass player. Attended school in Visalia, Calif.; sang with Ferlin Husky and later on the Red Foley show; albums—*Best By Request, Best of Jean Shepard, Heart, We Did All That We Could, I'll Fly Away, I'll Take the Dog, Real Good Woman, Seven Lonely Days.*

SHEPARD, THOMAS GRIFFEN

b. 1848 Madison, Connecticut, d. 1905 Brooklyn, New York. Organist and conductor. Studied with G.W. Morgan and J.P. Morgan; instructor of Yale Glee Club, conductor of the Oratorio Society and director of the Apollo Club; teacher and critic; composed a comic opera, and a Christmas cantata.

SHEPHERD, ARTHUR

b. 1880 Paris, Idaho, d. 1958 Cleveland, Ohio. Teacher and composer. Studied at the New England Conservatory, Boston; taught in Salt Lake City, Utah, after 1897; conducted Salt Lake City Symphonic Orchestra; taught at the New England Conservatory after 1909, later at Case-Western Reserve University, Cleveland Ohio; composed *Ouverture Joyeuse* (Paderewski Prize, 1902), piano sonata and song *The Lost Child* (National Federation prizes, 1909), piano pieces, baritone solo with chorus and orchestra, songs.

SHEPP, ARCHIE

b. 1937 Ft. Lauderdale, Florida.
Black tenor saxophonist. One of his early pieces was "Rufus" (short for "Rufus Swung His Face at Last to the Wind, Then His Neck Snapped"—a lynching).

SHEPPARD, FRANKLIN LAWRENCE

b. 1852 Philadelphia, Pennsylvania, d. 1930 Germantown, Philadelphia, Pennsylvania. Composer. Played the organ and was editor of *Alleluia* (1915) a Sunday school songbook; composed the tune "Terra Beata" (1915, for "This Is My Father's World," w. M.D. Babcock), from an old melody.

SHERWIN, MANNING

b. 1902 Philadelphia, Pennsylvania.
Composer. Wrote "A Nightingale Sang in Berkeley Square" (1940); also the music for—*Fun and Games* (1941 revue, Princess Theatre, London, England), *Rise Above It* (1941, Comedy Theatre, London), *Get a Load of This* (1941, Hippodrome Theatre, London), *Fine and Dandy* (1942, Saville Theatre, London).

SHERWIN, WILLIAM FISKE

b. 1826 Buckland, Massachusetts, d. 1888 Boston, Massachusetts. Composer and compiler. Organized the choruses for the Chautauqua, N.Y. Methodist camp meetings; at one time a student of Lowell Mason and later taught vocal music at the New England Conservatory of Music, Boston; composed the tune "Chautauqua" or "Evening Praise" (1877) for "Day Is Dying in the West" (w. Mary A. Lathbury); with Silas J. Vail compiled *Songs of Grace and Glory* (1874), which included Vail's tune "Close to Thee."

SHERWOOD, WILLIAM HALL

b. 1854 Lyons, New York, d. 1911 Chicago, Illinois. Pianist. Son and pupil of Rev. M.A. Sherwood, founder of Lyons Music Academy; studied with others; debut in Berlin; toured U.S. (1876); taught at the New England Conservatory, Boston, and at Chicago Conservatory (1889); founded Sherwood Piano School (1897); married his pupil, Estella F. Adams, a pianist; composed piano pieces.

SHIELDS, LARRY

b. 1893 New Orleans, Louisiana, d. 1953 Hollywood, California. Clarinetist. Played in the Original Dixieland Band with Nick La Rocca at the Paradise Club in New York City (1915); recorded "Tiger Rag" with Nick (1917); played with the band in London (1919); gave command performance for King George V; collapsed from overwork (1925).

SHIELDS, REN

b. 1868 Chicago, Illinois, d. 1913 Massapequa, New York. Lyricist and vaudeville actor. Wrote "In the Good Old Summertime" (1902, m. George Evans); with Max Million in vaudeville until 1897; later in *Gay Paree* in Chicago.

SHILKRET, NATHANIEL

b. 1895 New York City.
Conductor and songwriter. Brother of pianist-conductor-composer Jack Shilkret (1896-1964); educated at Bethany College (Mus. D.); studied with Floridia, Henius, and Hambitzer; clarinetist with the New York Philharmonic and the New York Symphony; wrote "The First Time I Saw You" (1937, m. Allie Wrubel); with L.W. Gilbert wrote "Jeannine, I Dream of Lilac Time."

SHINES, JOHNNY

b. 1915 Memphis, Tennessee.
Black guitarist and bandleader. Played with Robert Johnson (1933-35); later organized his own band; recorded in Testament's *Masters of Modern Blues,* Volume 1.

SHIRELLES, THE (rock 'n roll group)

Played at the show, "The Legend of Rock 'n Roll," at the Hollywood Bowl, Calif. (1972).

SHIRLEY, DONALD

b. 1927 Kingston, Jamaica, B.W.I.
Black pianist. Studied at the Leningrad Conservatory at age nine; graduated Harvard University, also earned Ph.D.; soloist with various symphony orchestras.

SHIRLEY, GEORGE

b. 1934.
Black tenor. Graduated Wayne State University, Detroit; served in U.S. Army; debut (1959) with Turnau Opera Players, Woodstock, N.Y. in Strauss' *Die Fledermaus;* sang in opera in Milan (1960), Florence (1960), Spoleto, Italy (1961); debut at the Metropolitan Opera, New York City (1961) in Mozart's *Cosi fan tutte;* sang *Attitudes,* concert piece (m. Coleridge-Taylor Perkinson) at the Metropolitan Museum of Art, New York City (1964).

SHOOK, BEN

b. 1874 Cleveland, Ohio.
Black composer. Studied in Leipzig; played in Fred S. Stone's band in Detroit, Michigan; wrote "Dat Gal of Mine" (1902).

SHORE, DINAH

b. 1920 Winchester, Tennessee.
Singer. Born Frances Rose Shore; stricken with polio at age eighteen months, received Sister Kenny treatment; sang on radio stations WNEW and WSM, Nashville; became a sensation singing "Dinah" on radio jazz show "The Chamber Music Society of Lower Basin Street" and on Eddie Cantor program; her record "Yes, My Darling Daughter" sold a million disks; prominent in films; married to actor George Montgomery (1943-62); her "Dinah Shore Show" on NBC and "Dinah's Place" on NBC-TV after 1970 made her a national figure.

SHORTALL, HARRINGTON

b. 1895 Chicago, Illinois.
Composer. Educated at Thacher School in Ojai, Calif., and Harvard University; served in army in World War I; pupil of Boulanger; taught music in Chicago; wrote *Symphonia Brevis* (1937), chamber music; *Choral Memorial* won Westminster Choir Award in 1936.

SHOWALTER, A.J.

b. 1858 Cherry Grove, Virginia, d. 1929.
Editor and dealer. Studied with his father; then with P.J. Merges of Philadelphia, H.R. Palmer of New York, and George F. Root of Chicago, et.al.; with firm of A.J. Showalter & Co., Dalton, Georgia; editor and publisher of *The Music Teacher.*

SHULMAN, HARRY

b. 1916 Rochester, New York, d. 1971 New York City. Oboist and teacher. Studied at the Curtis Institute of Music, Philadelphia, M.A. from Hunter College, New York City; debut at age nineteen as first oboe with Pittsburgh Symphony; with NBC Symphony under Toscanini (1938); served in World War II; then with ABC; played in the annual Puerto Rico Festival since 1957; also with Aspen (Colorado) Music Festival and School.

SHURTLEFF, ERNEST WARBURTON

b. 1862 Boston, Massachusetts, d. 1917 France. Hymnist. Educated at Harvard and

Andover Theological Seminary (1883); Congregational minister in Palmer and Plymouth, Mass., and Minneapolis, Minn.; did relief work during World War I when he died in France; wrote the hymn "Lead On O King Eternal" (1887, tune "Lancashire"—Henry Smart, 1836) published in *Hymns of the Faith.*

SHUTTA, ETHEL

b. 1896 New York City.
Singer. Born Ethel Schutte; debut at age five at Madison Square Garden doing the cakewalk and singing "Won't You Come Home, Bill Bailey"; first Broadway performance in *The Passing Show* of 1922, produced by the Schuberts; married George Olsen, bandleader, later divorced; appeared with Eddie Cantor in *Whoopie* (1928) and in many other Broadway shows; appeared in various editions of the Ziegfeld Follies.

SIEGMEISTER, ELIE

b. 1909 New York City.
Composer. Graduated Columbia University (1927); studied with Nadia Boulanger in Paris and at the Juilliard Graduate School, New York City (1935-38); with Olin Downes edited *A Treasury of American Song;* known for *Ozark Set* for orchestra (1943), *Wilderness Road* for orchestra (1944), and Symphony no. 1 introduced by the New York Philharmonic under Leopold Stokowski (1947).

SIEVEKING, MARTINUS

b. 1867 Amsterdam, Netherlands, d. 1950 Pasadena, California. Pianist. Studied at the Leipzig Conservatory; debut in London (1890); came to Boston, Mass. (1895); toured United States after 1896; taught music in New York City after 1915; composed piano pieces, suite (played by Lamoureux in Paris).

SIGOURNEY, LYDIA HOWARD HUNTLEY

b. 1791 Norwich, Connecticut, d. 1865 Hartford, Connecticut. Noted poetess and hymnist. Married Charles Sigourney, Hartford, Conn. (1819); wrote *Fill the Font with Roses* (cantata by G.W. Warren, 1878); her hymns appeared in Nettleton's *Village Hymns* (1824), Ripley's *Selection* (1829), Cheever's *Common Place Book* (1831), *Baptist Additional Hymns* by Winchell (1832), *Christian Lyre Supplement* (1833), Linsley and Davis' *Selected Hymns* (1836), *Connecticut Psalms and Hymns* (1845), *Universalist Hymns for Christian Devotion* by Adams and Chapin (Boston, 1846), and *Lyra Sacra Americana* (London, 1868).

SILL, EDWARD ROWLAND

b. 1841 Windsor, Connecticut, d. 1887 Cleveland, Ohio. Hymnist. Educated at Yale; professor of English literature at the University of California, Berkeley (1874-82); wrote the hymn "Send Down Thy Truth, O God" (tune "Garden City"—H.W. Parker).

SILLS, BEVERLY

b. 1929 Brooklyn, New York.
Noted soprano. Born Belle Silverman; married Peter Greenough; skyrocketed to fame in Handel's *Giulio Cesare* with New York City Opera (1966, revived 1971); their daughter Meredith (Muffy) suffered hearing loss; son Peter, Jr., mentally retarded and epileptic died at age ten; she was named 1972 chairman of the National Foundation-March of Dimes Mothers' March on Birth Defects.

SILOTI, ALEXANDER

b. 1863 Charkov, Russia, d. 1945 New York City. Pianist. Studied at the Moscow Conservatory, won gold medal; debut in Moscow (1880); pupil of Liszt; professor at the Moscow Conservatory (1887-90); toured Europe; taught at the Juilliard School of Music, New York City, after 1922; composed piano pieces.

SILVER APPLES (rock duo)

Dan Taylor, drums; Simeon, simeon; debut at Max's Kansas City, New York (1968); the simeon is an electronic instrument Simeon made himself; albums—*Silver Apples, Contact.*

SILVER, FRANK

b. 1896 Boston, Massachusetts, d. 1960 Brooklyn, New York. Drummer, conductor, and lyricist. Drummer in Bowery music hall, New York City (1911); toured in Raymond Hitchcock's *Hitchy-Koo;* wrote "Yes! We Have No Bananas" (1923, m. Irving Conn).

SILVER, HORACE

b. 1928 Norwalk, Connecticut.
Black pianist. Pianist and musical director of the Jazz Messengers of drummer Art Blakey; played "hard bop" or "funky" jazz.

SILVERS, LOUIS

b. 1889 New York City, d. 1954 Hollywood, California. Composer, pianist, and conductor. Pianist in vaudeville; music director for Gus Edwards' vaudeville shows for ten years; wrote the film scores *The Jazz Singer* and *One Night of Love* (1934); wrote "April Showers" (w. Buddy de Sylva).

SIMEON, OMER VICTOR

b. 1902 New Orleans, Louisiana, d. 1959 New York City. Black clarinetist. Played in Jelly Roll Morton's band; recorded "Dead Man Blues" on Victor (ca. 1924) with George Mitchell, trumpeter, and Kid Ory, trombonist, considered by some as the masterpiece of jazz on Victor; played also with the Syncopators.

SIMMONDS, KIM

b. 1947 England.
Guitarist. Leader of the Savoy Brown Blues Band; first recorded in 1968; albums—*Getting to the Point, Blue Matter, Raw Sienna, Step Further.*

SIMMONS, JOHN JACOB

b. 1918 Haskell, Oklahoma.
Double bass player. Played with Louis Armstrong, Illinois Jacquet, Erroll Garner and others.

SIMON, CARLY

b. 1945.
Singer. Educated at Sarah Lawrence College, Bronxville, N.Y.; organized Simon Sisters, vocal duo, with her sister, Lucy; recorded "One More Time," "That's the Way I've Always Heard It Should Be"; married singer James Taylor (1972); won Grammy Award (1972) as the "Best New Artist."

SIMON, ERNEST ARTHUR

b. 1862 London, England, d. 1950 Louisville, Kentucky. Organist. First settled in Chicago, and later became organist-choirmaster at Christ Church Cathedral, Louisville, Kentucky (1901-46).

SIMON, PAUL

b. 1942 Newark, New Jersey.
Singer, guitarist, and songwriter. Raised in Queens, N.Y.; graduated Queens College; joined with Art Garfunkel, sang at Gerde's Folk City, N.Y., and at the Hollywood Bowl, Calif. (1967); their first hit was "Sounds of Silence"; Simon wrote "Mrs. Robinson" for *The Graduate;* they won several Grammy Awards (1971), record of the year, album of the year, song of the year, and best contemporary song, for "Bridge Over Troubled Water"; Simon wrote "Richard Cory" (w. E.A. Robinson).

SIMON, STEPHEN

b. 1937 New York City.
Musical director. Musical director of Handel Society of New York (1971); also Orchestral Society of Westchester, N.Y.; resides in Scarsdale, N.Y.

SIMONE, NINA

b. 1933 Tyron, North Carolina.
Black singer, pianist, and songwriter. Born Eunice Kathleen Wayman; studied at Juilliard in New York City with Carl Friedberg, and at the Curtis Institute, Philadelphia with Vladimir Sokoloff; pianist at Arlene Smith's Studio, Philadelphia; singer and pianist in Atlantic City, N.J. night spot (1954); sang at the Apollo Theatre, Harlem, New York City; wrote black protest songs—"Backlash Blues" (w. Langston Hughes), "Turning Point," "I Wish I Knew How It Would Feel to Be Free," "Go Limp" (with Alex Comfort); albums—*Best of Nina Simone, High Priestess of Soul, I Put a Spell on You, Let It All Out, Little Girl Blue, 'Nuff Said, Pastel Blues, Nina Simone and Piano, Nina Simone in Concert, Nina Simone Sings the Blues, To Love Somebody, Wild Is the Wind;* at the Newport Jazz Festival, New York City (1972).

SIMPSON, J.D. (JIMMY)

b. 1928 Ashland City, Tennessee.
Singer. Leader of the Oilfields Boys (1953-56).

SIMS, JACK ("ZOOT")

b. 1925 Inglewood, California.
Jazz saxophonist. Started with Bobby Sherwood; played in Woody Herman's band; albums—*Inter-Action, Waiting Game;* at the Newport Jazz Festival, New York City (1972).

SINATRA, FRANCIS ALBERT (FRANK)

b. 1915 Hoboken, New Jersey.
Singer. Worked for the *New Jersey Observer;* with three instrumentalists formed the Hoboken Four which appeared on "Major Bowes Original Amateur Hour" (1937); sang for Harry James' band (1939); then with Tommy Dorsey; when Frank would start singing, the girls in the audience would scream and swoon; went on his own (1942); then made many films; made guest appearances on many shows; married Nancy Barbato (divorced), actress Ava Gardner, (divorced), actress Mia Farrow, 1965 (divorced).

SINATRA, NANCY

b. 1941 Hoboken, New Jersey.
Singer. Daughter of Frank Sinatra, singer; made a sensation with her recording of "These Boots Are Made for Walkin' " (1966);

albums—*Boots, Country My Way, How Does That Grab You, Movin' with Nancy, Nancy, Nancy and Lee* (with Lee Hazelwood), *Nancy in London, Speedway, Sugar.*

SINGENBERGER, JOHN BAPTIST

b. 1848 Kirchberg, Switzerland, d. 1924 Milwaukee, Wisconsin. Conductor. Founded the Caecilian Society (1873) at St. Francis, Wisc.; early meetings were held in Milwaukee (1874) and Dayton, Ohio (1875); founded the magazine *Caecilia* in 1874, published in German and mostly for Catholic parishes.

SINGER, OTTO

b. 1833 Sora, Saxony, Germany, d. 1894 New York. Pianist, conductor, teacher, and composer. Studied at the Leipzig Conservatory (1852-55) under Richter, Moscheles, and Hauptmann; came to New York City (1867); taught in N.Y. (1867-73); then taught at Cincinnati College of Music; wrote *The Landing of the Pilgrim Fathers* (a cantata for the festival of 1876), *Festival Ode* (cantata for the opening of the music hall in Cincinnati, 1878).

SINGER, RICHARD

b. 1879 Budapest, Hungary, d. 1940 New York City. Pianist. Studied with Leschetizky and Busoni; toured Europe and the United States.

SINGING RAMBOS, THE *see* RAMBOS

SINGLETON, ARTHUR JAMES ("ZUTTY")

b. 1898 Bunkie, Louisiana.
Black jazz drummer. Raised in New Orleans; joined Fate Marable, pianist, on riverboat excursions on Monday nights (reserved for Negroes) in 1923; recorded (1924) with Fate Morable (Marable); joined Charles Creath, cornetist and bandleader in St. Louis, Mo. (1924); married Majorie Creath, sister of Charles; with Louis Armstrong (1925); played in Paris (1951); considered by some as the greatest jazz drummer of all time.

SINGLETON, MARGARET LOUISE (MARGIE)

b. 1935 Coushatta, Louisiana.
Singer and songwriter. Attended high school in Shreveport, La.; wrote "Not What He's Got" (1956), "My Picture of You" (1957), "Love Is a Treasure," "Take Time Out for Love," "Shattered Kingdom," "Moonlight Music" (1958).

SIR DOUGLAS QUINTET (blues group)

Doug Sahm, guitar and fiddle; George Rains, drums; Whitney "Hershey" Freeman, bass; Bill Atwood, horn; Terry Henry, horn; Mel Martin, horn; Frank Morin, horn; Martin Ferrio, horn; Wayne Talbert, piano; started in Texas; in San Francisco (1955-56); albums—*Best of Sir Douglas Quintet* (1966), *Mendocino, Sir Douglas Quintet Plus Two Equals Honky Blues, Together After Five.*

SISSLE, NOBLE

b. 1889 Indianapolis, Indiana.
Black bandleader and lyricist. Toured with Thomas Jubilee Singers; teamed with composer Eubie Blake (1915) in song writing; wrote the lyrics for "I'm Just Wild About Harry" and "Love Will Find a Way" in *Shufflin' Along* (1921-24, m. Blake), "Dixie Moon" in *Chocolate Dandies* (1924, m. Blake); formed his own band, Sidney Bechet and Charlie Parker played in the band; young singer named Lena Horne joined the band (1937); drum major in Jim Europe's 369th Infantry Band (formerly the 15th New York) during World War I, played in Aix-les-Bains, France (1918) and in Paris.

SIZEMORE, ASHER

b. 1906 Manchester, Kentucky.
Singer and songwriter. Attended schools in Ashland, Ky.; wrote "Memories of Kentucky" (1934), "My Kitty Kat," "Girl of My Dreams," "Cowboy's Last Ride," "Prisoner's Lament," "My Tennessee Rose," "My Pony" (1936).

SIZEMORE, GORDON

b. 1909 Endee, Kentucky.
Singer and songwriter. Attended schools in Richmond, Ky.; wrote "Wrinkled and Old," "You Dirty Dog," "Norma," "Grandma's Mini-skirt."

SKELLY, JOSEPH P.

b. ca. 1850, d. after 1890.
Plumber by trade and wrote about 400 popular songs. Composed the music "Twinkle, Twinkle Little Star" (w. George Cooper) and "Strolling on the Brooklyn Bridge" (1883, w. Cooper); also wrote "Little Darlin'," "Down by the Old Stream" (1874), "My Pretty Red Rose" (1877), "The Gentleman from Kildare" (1879), and "If My Dreams Would All Come True" (1879).

SKILLET LICKERS (vocal and string group) *see* GID TANNER, GEORGE R. PUCKETT

SKILTON, CHARLES SANFORD

b. 1868 Northampton, Massachusetts, d. 1941 Lawrence, Kansas. Organist and composer. Studied at Berlin Hochschule and with Dudley Buck in New York City; professor at the State University of Kansas, Lawrence , Kansas, after 1903; many of his compositions were based on Indian themes.

SKINNER, EDWARD

b. 1891, d. 1971 San Francisco, California. Manager. Rancher and miner, then manager of the San Francisco Symphony Orchestra (1936-64), and the added job of manager of the San Francisco Opera (1951-71).

SKY, PATRICK (PAT)

b. 1940 Liveoak Gardens, Georgia.
Singer and songwriter. Served in the army; later sang in Greenwich Village, New York City coffee houses; wrote "Many a Mile," "Hangin' Round," "Nectar of God," "Separation Blues," "Love Will Endure."

SLADE, MARY BRIDGES (CANEDY)

b. 1826 Fall River, Massachusetts, d. there 1882. Hymnist. Teacher, assistant editor of *The New England Journal of Education* and the founder of *Wide Awake;* wrote the hymn "From All the Dark Places" (tune "The Kingdom Coming"—Emilius Laroche).

SLAUGHTER, HENRY T.

b. 1927 Roxboro, North Carolina.
Singer and songwriter. Member of the Ozark Quartet (1946-58), Wetherford Quartet (1958-64), and Imperials (1964-67); wrote "If the Lord Wasn't Walking," "Then the Answer Came," "What a Precious Friend He Is," "I've Never Loved Him Better," "Keep on Holding," "I'll Be There."

SLENCZYNSKI, RUTH

b. 1925 Sacramento, California.
Pianist. Her father was a violinist; debut in Oakland, Calif. at age four; gave concert at Bach Saal, Berlin at age six; concert in Paris at age seven; then came back to America as concert pianist with great success.

SLEZAK, WALTER

b. 1902 Vienna, Austria.
Singer and actor. Son of tenor Leo Slezak (1875-1946, born Leo Schonberg); studied at the University of Vienna; sang in operettas in Europe; became an actor in the U.S. on the stage and in films.

SLICK, GRACE (WING)

b. 1940.
Singer. Raised in Palo Alto, Calif.; with Grace Slick and the Great Society; albums—*Conspicuous Only in Its Absence, How It Was* (1968); the group broke up and Grace joined the Jefferson Airplane; married Jerry Slick, film maker, when she was twenty-one; had a highly publicized daughter by Paul Kantner, of the Jefferson Airplane, since divorced from Slick.

SLOANE, A. BALDWIN

b. 1872 Baltimore, Maryland, d. 1926 Red Bank, New Jersey. Popular composer. Wrote "When You Ain't Got No Money, Well You Needn't Come Around" (w. C.S. Brewster) popularized by May Irwin; wrote the scores for many musicals, featured songs were "Susie Ma Sue" (1900, w. George V. Hobart), "My Tiger Lily" (1900, w. Clay M. Greene), "There's a Little Street in Heaven Called Broadway" (1902, w. Sidney Rosenfeld), "What's the Matter with the Moon Tonight" (1902, w. Rosenfeld); wrote the music for *The Wizard of Oz* (book and lyrics by L. Frank Baum) starring Fred Stone and David Montgomery (later movie featuring Judy Garland); wrote "Heaven Will Protect the Working Girl" (1909, w. Edgar Smith), "Life Is Only What You Make It After All" (1909, w. Smith), "On the Boardwalk" (1920), "White Light Alley" (1920, w. Glen MacDonough), "Just Sweet Sixteen" (1920, w. Arthur Swanstrom).

SLONIMSKY, NICOLAS

b. 1894 St. Petersburg, Russia.
Pianist, conductor, and composer. Came to America (1923); wrote *Music Since 1900* and *Lexicon of Musical Invective,* which presented the hostile opinions of music critics over the ages; conductor of the Apollo Club of Boston (1927-49).

SLY AND THE FAMILY STONE (black and white soul-rock group)

Sly Stone, vocals and organ; Rose Stone, vocals and electric piano; Freddie Stone, vocals and guitar; Larry Graham, Jr., vocals and bass; Greg Errico, drums; Jerry Martini, sax, flute, piano, etc.; Cynthia Robinson, vocals and trumpet; started in San Francisco; first recorded in 1967; albums—*Dance to the Music, Life, Stand, Whole New Thing, Woodstock.*

SMALLENS, ALEXANDER

b. 1889 St. Petersburg, Russia, d. 1972. Conductor. His parents brought him to

America (1890); studied in Paris, then became conductor of various opera companies in America; conducted George Gershwin's opera *Porgy and Bess* at its introduction in Boston (1935).

SMATHERS, BEN

b. 1928 Jackson County, North Carolina. Singer. Attended high school in Hendersonville, N.C.; leader of Stoney Mountain Cloggers.

SMILEY, ARTHUR LEE, JR. ("RED")

b. 1925, d. 1972 Richmond, Virginia. Guitarist. Country music performer.

SMIT, LEO

b. 1921 Philadelphia, Pennsylvania.
Composer. As a gifted child, he was accepted by the Curtis Institute, Philadelphia, when he was only nine years old; became a pianist; also is known for his compositions—the overture *The Parcae* (1953, *The Three Fates*), Symphony no. 1 performed by the Boston Symphony Orchestra (1957).

SMITH, ALFRED MORTON

b. 1879 Jenkintown, Pennsylvania, d. (?).
Composer. Graduated the University of Pennsylvania, Philadelphia, and the Philadelphia Divinity School (1905); assistant rector in Long Beach, Calif., then at St. Matthias' Church, Los Angeles (1906-16); served as a chaplain in France and Germany in World War I; joined the Episcopal City Mission, Philadelphia (1919); composed the tunes "Assisi," "Sursum corda," and "Labor."

SMITH, ARTHUR ("GUITAR BOOGIE")

b. 1921 Clinton, South Carolina.
Bandleader and songwriter. Organized the Smith Brothers; radio debut in 1937; served in the Navy Band in World War II; organized the "Arthur Smith Show" on WBT-TV, Charlotte, North Carolina; wrote "Guitar Boogie," "Banjo Buster," "Foolish Questions," "I Saw a Man," "Shadow of the Cross."

SMITH, BESSIE

b. 1895 Chattanooga, Tennessee, d. 1937 Clarksdale, Mississippi. Black singer. She was the most famous of the blues singers; at one time Thomas "Fats" Waller was accompanist for her; her mournful recordings as "The Empress of the Blues" became famous in jazz history; died in an automobile accident; albums—*Bessie Smith Story, Vol. 1, Vol. 2, Vol. 3, Vol. 4.*

SMITH, BLAINE

b. 1915 Dickens, Iowa.
Singer. Attended high school in Macedonia, Ohio; leader of Boys from Iowa (1936-39); most popular songs recorded—"Big Blue Eyes," "Golden River," "Sweet Fern," "Wonder Valley," "Whispering Hope."

SMITH, CAL

b. 1932 Sallisaw, Oklahoma.
Singer. Born Grant Calvin Shofner; member of Ernest Tubb's Texas Troubadours after 1962; leader of Nite Hawks; albums—*All the World Is Lonely Now, At Home with Cal, Drinking Champagne, Goin' to Cal's Place, Cal Smith Sings, Travelin' Man.*

SMITH, CARL

b. 1927 Maynardville , Tennessee.
Singer and guitarist. Radio debut on station WROL, Knoxville, Tenn.; served in the navy; joined Grand Ole Opry, Nashville, Tenn. (1950); married Goldie Hill, singer; toured the U.S., Europe, and the Far East; albums—*Country Gentleman Sings, Country on My Mind, Deep Water, Faded Love and Winter Roses, Gentleman in Love, I Love You Because, I Want to Live and Love, Kisses Don't Lie, Man with a Plan, Satisfaction Guaranteed.*

SMITH, CAROLINE LOUISA SPRAGUE

b. 1827 Salem, Massachusetts, d. 1886.
Hymnist. Married the Rev. Charles Smith, pastor of the South Congregational Church, Andover, Mass.; wrote "Tarry with Me, O My Saviour" (*Plymouth Collection*, 1855).

SMITH, CHRIS

b. 1879 Charleston, South Carolina, d. 1949 New York City. Black popular composer. Started as an actor with Elmer Bowman; with lyricist Cecil Mack wrote "Never Let the Same Bee Sting You Twice" (1900), "Good Morning Carrie" (and with J. Tim Brymm), "He's a Cousin of Mine" (and with Silvio Hein), "You're in the Right Church but the Wrong Pew," "Down Among the Sugar Cane" (Avery and Hart, popularized by Marie Cahill and Stella Mayhew), "Ballin' the Jack" (1913, ragtime, w. Jim Burris, revived by Danny Kaye), "Jasper Johnson Shame on You" (w. John Larkins), "After All That I've Been to You" (w. Jack Drislane), and "Beans, Beans, Beans" (w. Elmer Bowman).

SMITH, CLADYS ("JABBO")

b. 1908 Claxton, Georgia.
Black jazz trumpeter. Played in Claude Hopkins' band; also led his own group.

SMITH, CLARENCE ("PINETOP")

b. 1904 Troy, Alabama, d. 1929 Chicago, Illinois. Black pianist and composer. Generally credited for originating the word boogie-woogie in his "Pinetop's Boogie-Woogie."

SMITH, CONNIE

b. 1941 Elkhart, Indiana.
Singer. After entering an amateur contest in Ohio (1963), she was signed by RCA Victor; albums—*Back in Baby's Arms, Best of Connie Smith, Born to Sing, Connie in the Country, Connie's Country, Cute 'n Country, Downtown Country, I Love Charley Brown, Miss Smith Goes to Nashville, Connie Smith, Connie Smith Sings Bill Anderson, Connie Smith Sings Great Sacred Songs, Soul of Country Music, Sunshine and Rain.*

SMITH, DAVID STANLEY

b. 1877 Toledo, Ohio, d. 1949 New Haven, Connecticut. Conductor and teacher. Educated at Yale and in Germany; conductor of the New Haven (Conn.) Symphony; became professor of music at Yale (1925); composed the *Prince Hal Overture,* the tune "Fortitude" for "Be Strong! We Are Not Here to Play" (w. M.D. Babcock), *The Fallen Star* for chorus and orchestra (Paderewski Prize, 1909), *Darkness and Dawn* (symphonic poem), anthems, songs.

SMITH, DEXTER

b. 1839 Peabody, Massachusetts, d. 1909.
Lyricist, editor, and publisher. Wrote the lyrics for about fifty songs set to music by Mathias Keller of Boston, between 1860-75; editor of *Ditson's Musical Record.*

SMITH, ELIHU HUBBARD

b. 1771 Litchfield, Connecticut, d. 1798 New York City. Librettist. Educated at Yale and the College of Philadelphia (medicine, 1791); practiced medicine in Wethersfield, Conn., and in New York City (1796); wrote libretto *Edwin and Angelina, or The Banditti* (1791-93, ballad by Oliver Goldsmith, m. Victor Pelissier), produced by John Hodgkinson, manager of Old American Company in New York City (1796); died in the yellow fever epidemic of 1798.

SMITH, ELIZABETH LEE ALLEN

b. 1817 Hanover, New Hampshire, d. 1877. Hymnist. Daughter of William Allen, President of Dartmouth College; married Dr. H.B. Smith (1843), who was a professor at Union Theological Seminary, New York City (1850); her hymns appeared in *Schaff's Christ in Song* (1869 and 1870).

SMITH, ETHEL

b. 1921 Pittsburgh, Pennsylvania.
Singer. Albums—*At the End of a Perfect Day, Hollywood Favorites, Make Mine Hawaiian.*

SMITH, GERRIT

b. 1859 Hagerstown, Maryland, d. 1912. Organist, composer, and teacher. Wrote "Dreaming."

SMITH, HALE

b. 1925.
Black composer. Attended the Cleveland Institute of Music, Cleveland, Ohio (M.Mus., 1952); at Karamu House, Cleveland (1955); with E.B. Marks Music Corp. after 1959; later with Sam Fox music publisher; taught at C.W. Post College, Long Island, N.Y., after 1968; wrote *In Memorium—Beryl Rubinstein* (1953, w. Langston Hughes and Russell Atkins, for chorus and chamber orchestra, presented at Karamu House), *Epicedial Variations* for violin and piano (1956), *Contours for Orchestra* (1962, recorded by Louisville (Kentucky) Orchestra), *Music for Harp and Orchestra* (1967), *Faces of Jazz* (1968).

SMITH, HARRY B.

b. 1860 Buffalo, New York, d. 1936 Atlantic City, New Jersey. Lyricist and librettist. Wrote the librettos for a number of the romantic operas of Reginald de Koven and Victor Herbert; wrote the lyrics and Herbert the music "I Love Thee, I Adore Thee" (1897), "Romany Life" (1897), "Gypsy Love Song" (1898), and "If You Were Only Mine" (1899); wrote the lyrics and John Stromberg the music *The Kissing Bug* (1899), *My Josephine* (1899), and *De Cake Walk Queen* (1900). (*See also* Ludwig Englander)

SMITH, HEZEKIAH LEROY GORDON ("STUFF")

b. 1909 Portsmouth, Ohio, d. 1967.
Black jazz violinist and songwriter. With Mezz Mezzrow wrote "My Thoughts"; he also wrote "Desert Sands," "Time and Again" (recorded by Sarah Vaughan).

SMITH, JOE

b. 1902 Ripley, Ohio, d. 1937 New York City. Black jazz trumpeter. Played in McKinney's Cotton Pickers.

SMITH, JULIA

b. 1911 Denton, Texas.
Composer. Studied at the Juilliard School of Music, New York City under Goldmark and Jacobi; composed *Liza Jane* (CBS orchestra, 1940), *Cynthia Parker* (opera, produced by Texas State College), *The Stranger of Manzano* and *The Gooseherd and the Goblin,* (work for children, Hartt Opera Guild, Hartford, Conn., 1949), suites for orchestra, two pieces for viola and piano, chamber music, songs.

SMITH, KATE

b. 1909 Greenville, Virginia.
Noted singer. Introduced "When the Moon Comes Over the Mountain" (1931, m. Harry M. Woods) and "God Bless America" (1938, m. Irving Berlin); albums—*Best of Kate Smith, How Great Thou Art, Just a Closer Walk with Thee, May God Be with You, Songs of the Now Generation, Kate Smith Anniversary Album, Kate Smith at Carnegie Hall, Kate Smith the One and Only, Kate Smith Today.*

SMITH, KEELY

b. 1932 Norfolk, Virginia.
Singer. Married Louis Prima; sang in his band after 1953; went out on her own (1961); albums—*I Wish You Love, That Old Black Magic.*

SMITH, MARY LOUISE (RILEY)

b. 1843 Brighton, New York, d. 1927.
Hymnist. Wrote the lyrics "Scatter Seeds of Kindness" (m. S.J. Vail, "Let Us Gather Up the Sunbeams").

SMITH, MAYBELLE

b. 1924 Jackson, Tennessee, d. 1972 Cleveland, Ohio. Black singer. Member of the Blues Hall of Fame; known as "Big Maybelle"; best known for her recordings of "Candy," "96 Tears," and "So Long"; sang at Newport Jazz Festival of 1958; toured most of Western Europe; after the drug-related death of Jim Hendrix in 1970, she gave up a twenty-seven-year narcotics habit, but became recurrently ill after withdrawal.

SMITH, OCIE LEE ("O.C.")

b. 1937 Louisiana.
Black singer. Attended Los Angeles City College; served in U.S. Air Force; was singing in a New York City club when he met trumpeter Sy Oliver who introduced him to Sid Bernstein, manager of the Beatles; became a vocalist in Count Basie's band; albums—*Dynamic O.C. Smith, For Once in My Life, Hickory Holler Revisited, O.C. Smith at Home.*

SMITH, ROBERT BACHE

b. 1875 Chicago, Illinois, d. 1951 New York City. Lyricist. Reporter on the *Brooklyn Eagle;* wrote for vaudeville and burlesque shows; brother of Harry B. Smith; wrote lyrics for "Sweethearts" (m. Victor Herbert) introduced by Christine MacDonald (1913).

SMITH, SAMUEL FRANCIS

b. 1808 Boston, Massachusetts, d. 1895 Newton, Massachusetts. Lyricist. Graduated Harvard University (1829) and Andover Theological Seminary; pastor of Baptist churches in Waterville, Maine, and Newton, Mass.; taught at Waterville College, now Colby College; wrote the lyrics "America" (1832, tune—"God Save the King"), "The Morning Light Is Breaking" (1833, m. G.J. Webb), "Softly Fades the Twilight Ray" (1843, m. George Hews), and "Lord of Our Life, God Whom We Fear" (1893, m. V.C. Taylor).

SMITH, SAMUEL J.

b. 1771, d. 1835.
Hymnist. Resided in Burlington, N.J.; wrote "Arise, My Soul, with Rapture Rise" (*Priscilla Gurney's Hymns,* London, 1818, also *American Prayer Book Collection,* 1826).

SMITH, WILLIAM

b. 1754 Scotland, d. 1821.
Compiler. Rector of Trinity Church, New York City; published *The Churchman's Choral Companion to His Prayer Book* (1809, which included tunes by Benjamin Carr and Raynor Taylor); with William Little published *The Easy Instructor, or a New Method of Teaching Sacred Harmony* (1801); resided in New York City before 1802; in Hopewell, N.J. (1803-06); compiled *The Easy Instructor Part II.*

SMITH, WILLIAM HENRY JOSEPH BERTHOL BONAPARTE BERTHLOFF ("WILLIE THE LION")

b. 1897 Goshen, New York, d. 1973.
Black jazz pianist, bass player, composer, and comic. Educated at Howard University, Washington, D.C.; studied music theory with Hans Steinke; played in Newark, N.J. (1914) and night clubs in Atlantic City, N.J., and New York City before 1917; drum major in Tim Brymm's "Seventy Black Devils" of the 350th Infantry (formerly the 8th Illinois Infantry) during World War I; toured Europe,

Canada, and Africa (1949-50); considered one of the great characters of jazz; piano pieces include *Echoes of Spring, Morning Air, Passionette, Concentratin', Sneak Away, Ripplin' Waters, I'm Gonna Ride the Rest of the Way, Cuttin' Out, Here Comes the Band, Conversation on Park Avenue;* gave concert with Eubie Blake (aged eighty-nine) at the Whitney Museum, New York City (1972).

SMITH, WILLIAM MC LEISH (WILLIE)

b. 1908 Charleston, South Carolina, d. 1967. Black alto-saxophonist. Played with the Jimmie Lunceford band (1930-41); served in navy (1942-44); with Harry James (1944-51); later with Duke Ellington and others.

SMITH, WILSON GEORGE

b. 1855 Elyria, Ohio, d. there 1929.
Composer. Studied with Otto Singer in Cincinnati, then in Berlin (1880-82); taught in Cleveland, Ohio, after 1882; wrote *Octave Studies;* composed piano pieces and songs.

SMOKEY MOUNTAIN BOYS

Featured Roy Acuff. (*See* Roy Acuff)

SMOTHERS, RICHARD (DICK)

b. 1938 New York City.
Singer and bass fiddle player. With his brother, Tommy, as the "Smothers Brothers"; their albums are *Curb Your Tongue, Knave, Golden Hits of the Smothers Brothers, It Must Have Been Something I Said, Mom Always Liked You Best, Smothers Brothers Play It Straight, Smothers Brothers Comedy Hour, Think Ethnic, Tour de Farce American History, Two Sides of the Smothers Brothers.*

SMOTHERS, THOMAS (TOMMY)

b. 1937 New York City.
Singer and guitarist. With brother Dick as the "Smothers Brothers"; family moved to Philippines before 1941 where their father, Major Thomas B. Smothers, Jr. was stationed, later imprisoned and died on a Japanese prison ship; boys raised in Redondo Beach, Calif., both attended San Jose State College; played at The Limelite in Aspen, Colorado in the 1950s; later at Basin Street East, New York City, and the Flamingo Hotel, Las Vegas; appeared on CBS-TV on their own program (1965).

SNAËR, SAMUEL

b. 1833 New Orleans, Louisiana, d. (?).
Black pianist, composer, and teacher. Active in New Orleans concerts and the theater after the Civil War; wrote instrumental works, a mass, dance suites, and ballads.

SNOW, CLARENCE EUGENE ("HANK")

b. 1914 Liverpool, Nova Scotia, Canada. Singer and guitarist. Radio debut on station CHNS, Halifax, Nova Scotia (1934); U.S. debut in Dallas, Texas (1944); albums—*C.B. Atkins and C.E. Snow by Special Request, Best of Hank Snow, Big Country Hits, Gloryland March, Guitar Stylings of Hank Snow, Heartbreak Trail, Highest Bidder, Hits Covered by Snow, Hits, Hits and More Hits, I Went to Your Wedding, I've Been Everywhere, More Hank Snow Souvenirs, My Nova Scotia Home, Railroad Man, Southern Cannonball;* at Grand Ole Opry, Nashville, Tenn. (1972).

SNOW, ELIZA ROXEY

b. 1804 Becket, Massachusetts, d. 1887. Hymnist. Mormon leader; sister of Lorenzo Snow, fifth president of the Mormon Church in Utah; polygamous wife of Joseph Smith and Brigham Young.

SNYDER, TED

b. 1881 Freeport, Illinois, d. 1965 Woodland Hills, California. Popular composer. Raised in Boscobel, Wisconsin; with lyricist Irving Berlin wrote "Sweet Italian Love," "Kiss Me Honey, Kiss Me," "That Beautiful Rag" (1910), "That Mysterious Rag" (1911), "Take a Little Tip from Father" (1912), "My Wife's Gone to the Country" (1913); also wrote "In the Land of Harmony" (w. Bert Kalmar), "Moonlight on the Rhine" (w. Kalmar and Edgar Leslie), "The Sheik of Araby" (1921, w. H.B. Smith and Francis Wheeler), "Who's Sorry Now" (1923, Kalmar and Harry Ruby).

SOBOLEWSKI, J. FREDRICH EDUARD

b. 1808 Konigsberg, East Germany, d. 1872. Conductor and composer. Came to Milwaukee, Wisc. (1859); conductor of St. Louis Philharmonic (1860-66); wrote opera *Mohega* produced in Milwaukee (1859).

SODERO, CESARE

b. 1886 Naples, Italy, d. 1947 New York City. Conductor. Studied at Naples Conservatory; conducted Aborn and Savage Opera Companies in the United States; with NBC; later with the Metropolitan Opera, New York City.

SOKOLOFF, NICOLAI GRIGOROVITCH

b. 1886 Kiev, Russia, d. 1965.
Conductor. Directed the Cincinnati Symphony Orchestra (1918); founded and conducted the Cleveland Symphony Orchestra

(1919-34); became National Director of the Federal Works Progress Administration for music projects (1935); later became conductor of the Seattle Symphony Orchestra (Washington).

SOLLEY, MARVIN

b. 1937 Louisville, Tennessee.
Composer and baritone. Received master's degree in voice from Indiana University; taught voice in Louisiana; sang in *Luther* on Broadway, New York City (1963); with Dan Goggin, formed the Saxons; with Goggin wrote the musical *Hark!* (lyrics Bob Lorick) produced at the Mercer Arts Center, New York City (1972).

SOLOMON, IZLER

b. 1910 St. Paul, Minnesota.
Conductor. Conductor in Columbus, Ohio, then of the Music Festival in Aspen, Colorado.

SONDHEIM, STEPHEN

b. 1930 New York City.
Composer, lyricist, and librettist. Graduated Williams College, Williamstown, Mass., in Music; studied at Princeton University with Milton Babbitt; wrote lyrics for *West Side Story* (1957, m. Leonard Bernstein), also *Gypsy* (1959, m. Jule Styne); wrote words and music for *A Funny Thing Happened on the Way to the Forum* (1962); lyrics for *Do I Hear a Waltz?* (1962, m. Richard Rodgers, book—Arthur Laurents); score for *Company* (book—George Furth, which won a Tony, 1971); score for the *Follies of 1971.*

SONNECK, OSCAR GEORGE THEODORE

b. 1873 Jersey City, New Jersey, d. 1928 New York City. Editor and writer. Studied in Heidelberg (1893), also Munich and Italy; music librarian at Library of Congress, Washington, D.C. (1899), director of music division after 1902; editor of *The Musical Quarterly* (1915).

SONNY AND CHER *see* SALVATORE BONO, CHERYL BONO

SONS OF THE PIONEERS *see* ROY ROGERS

SOUL STIRRERS (gospel singers) *see* SAM COOKE, JOHNNIE TAYLOR

SOUL SURVIVORS (white soul group)

Kenneth Jeremiah, vocals; Richard Ingui, vocals; Charles Ingui, vocals; Paul Venturini, organ; Edward Leonetti, guitar; Joey Forgione, drums; started in New York City (1966); first recorded in 1967; albums—*When the Whistle Blows Anything Goes, Take Another Look.*

SOUR, ROBERT

b. 1905 New York City.
Lyricist. With Edward Heyman wrote the lyrics for "Body and Soul" (m. Johnny Green).

SOUSA, JOHN PHILIP

b. 1854 Washington, D.C., d. 1932 Reading, Pennsylvania. Noted composer. Led the U.S. Marine Corps Band from 1880 until 1892 when he organized his own band, which held its first concert in Plainfield, N.J.; his marches include "Semper Fidelis" (1888), "The Thunderer" (1889), "The Washington Post March" (1889), "Liberty Bell" (1893), "High School Cadets," "King Cotton" (1895), "El Capitan" (1896), "The Stars and Stripes Forever" (1897), and "Hands Across the Sea" (1899).

SOUTH, EDDIE

b. 1904 Louisiana, Missouri, d. 1962.
Black violinist. Studied at the Chicago College of Music; also in Paris and Budapest; toured Europe (1927-31 and 1937-38).

SOUTHARD, LUCIEN H.

b. 1827 prob. Sharon, Vermont, d. 1881 Augusta, Georgia. Organist, composer, teacher, and compiler. Served as a Union soldier in the Civil War; first director of the Peabody Conservatory, Baltimore; composed an opera, *The Scarlet Letter* (1855); compiled a book of piano and organ pieces, *Morning and Evening* for church services (1865).

SOUTHERN SYNCOPATED ORCHESTRA (black band)

Led by Will Marion Cook, violinist; toured Europe (1919); band included soprano-saxist and clarinetist Sidney Bechet.

SOUTHERNERS, THE *see* AL TERRY

SOUTHGATE, CHARLES

b. (?), d. 1818.
Violoncellist, singer, editor, and compiler. Printer with Lynch in Richmond, Virginia (1806-18); editor of *The Visitor* (1809-10) which published "President Madison's March" (1809, m. Peter Weldon) and "Cotillions" (1810, arranged by August Peticolas); compiled and published *Harmonica Sacra* (1818).

SOUTHGATE, THOMAS

b. 1814, d. 1868.
Publisher.

SOVINE, WOODROW W. ("RED")

b. 1918 Charleston, West Virginia.
Singer and songwriter. Radio debut on station

WCHS, Charleston with Jim Pike; formed his own group, the Echo Valley Boys; later on KWKH, Shreveport, La.; with Webb Pierce wrote "Little Rosa" and "Why Baby Cry" (1956); his own compositions are—"Too Much," "I Think I Can Sleep Tonight," "Don't Be the One," "Missing You," "Long Night," "Class of '49"; albums—*Closing Time 'Til Dawn; Giddy Up Go; Girl Named Sam; Nashville Sound of Red Sovine; Phantom 309.*

SOWERBY, LEO

b. 1895 Grand Rapids, Michigan, d. 1968 Port Clinton, Ohio. Composer. Educated at the American Conservatory of Music, Chicago (1918); bandmaster of the 332nd Field Artillery Regiment in France in World War I; studied at the Academy in Rome on a fellowship (1921-24); then taught at the American Conservatory, Chicago, and was also organist-choirmaster of St. James', Chicago, starting in 1927; composed the oratorio *The Canticle of the Sun* (1946), also *Forsaken of Man* (1940).

SPACH, BARRETT

b. 1898 Chicago, Illinois.
Organist and teacher. Educated at the University of Chicago and the David Mannes School, New York City (1924); taught at the Cincinnati Conservatory (1924-26), then studied in Paris; then became organist at the Fourth Presbyterian Church, Chicago (1929); in 1946 became professor of organ at Northwestern University, Evanston, Illinois.

SPAETH, SIGMUND

b. 1885 Philadelphia, Pennsylvania, d. 1965 New York City. Critic and author. Graduated Haverford College, Pa.; Ph.D. at Princeton University (1910); critic for the *New York Evening Mail* (1914-18); executive of Community Concerts Corp., New York City; published *American Mountain Songs, The Facts of Life in Popular Song, The Common Sense of Music, Barber Shop Ballads.*

SPAFFORD, HORATIO GATES

b. 1829 Lawrenceburg, New York, d. 1888 Jerusalem. Hymnist. Lawyer when, in the financial crises of 1873 he lost his fortune, his home in a fire, and his four daughters drowned when the French packet *Ville-du-Havre* sank in a collision with another steamer, but his wife was saved; but in his anguish he wrote the hymn "It Is Well with My Soul" (1873, m. P.P. Bliss); in 1881, with his followers, established a colony in Jerusalem to await the second coming of Christ, and died there.

SPALDING, ALBERT

b. 1888 Chicago, Illinois, d. 1953 New York City. Violinist. Studied in New York, Paris, and Florence; debut in Paris (1905); soloist with the New York Symphony Orchestra (1908); played with leading orchestras in the United States and Europe; composed violin pieces.

SPANIER, FRANCIS ("MUGGSY")

b. 1906 Chicago, Illinois, d. 1966.
Jazz trumpeter and band leader. Made some recordings in 1939 with his Ragtimers and his muted cornet; led a fifteen piece band in 1941 acclaimed by many; his arrangements provided by Deane Kincaide; played at the Arcadia Ballroom, New York City.

SPANKY AND OUR GANG (folk group)

Elaine "Spanky" McFarlane, lead vocals, electric jug, washboard, etc.; Nigel Pickering, guitar and bass; Malcolm Hale, vocals, guitar, and trombone; John Seiter, drums; Kenny Hodges, vocals and bass guitar; Lefty Baker, tenor vocals and lead guitar; Geoffrey Myers, former member; started in 1967; named after the silent film comedies; albums—*Like to Get to Know You, Spanky and Our Gang, Spanky's Greatest Hits.*

SPANN, OTIS

b. 1931 Jackson, Mississippi.
Black pianist. Half-brother of Muddy Waters; played in Muddy Waters' band; cut his first album in 1960; recorded in Copenhagen, London, and Chicago; Muddy Waters accompanied him on his Bluesway LP of 1966; albums—*Blues Is Where It's At, Blues Never Die, Bottom of the Blues, Cryin' Time, Cracked Spanner Head, Otis Spann.*

SPARKS, RANDY

b. 1933 Leavenworth, Kansas.
Singer and songwriter. Attended school in Oakland, Calif.; University of California at Berkeley; formed the "New Christy Minstrels" (1961) named after Christy's Minstrels formed in 1846; sold the name and group for $2,500,000; wrote "Saturday Night," "Today," "Green, Green" (with Barry McGuire); his minstrels sang on the steps of the White House, Washington, D.C. (1964) at the invitation of President Lyndon B. Johnson.

SPEAKS, OLEY

b. 1874 Canal Winchester, Ohio, d. 1948 New York City. Baritone and popular composer. Sang in churches in Columbus, Ohio, and New York City; wrote the music for "On the Road to Mandalay" (1907, w. Rudyard

Kipling), "Morning" (1910, w. Frank L. Stanton), "Sylvia" (1914, w. Clinton Scollard), "When the Boys Come Home," a popular song of World War I.

SPEAR, THOMAS TRUMAN

b. 1803 Massachusetts, d. 1882 Boston, Massachusetts. Pianist, arranger, and artist. Pupil of George K. Jackson in Boston (1820); taught in Boston after 1824; portrait painter after 1832; arranged the song "The Charming Portrait" (1821).

SPECTOR, PHIL

b. 1941 Bronx, New York City.
Singer and songwriter. His father died when he was nine, and his mother took him to California to live; wrote "To Know Him Is to Love Him," at age seventeen; recorded from 1960-64 and became a millionaire; wrote songs for Ike and Tina Turner.

SPEER, GEORGE THOMAS ("G.T.")

b. 1891 Fayetteville, Georgia, d. 1966.
Singer. Member of the Speer Family—G.T., Leana"Mom" (his wife), Brock Speer and his wife Faye, Ben Speer, Ann Sanders, Harold Lane, Rosa Nell, Mary Tom; organized in 1920; Speer Trio, Gadsden, Alabama (1934); died of a heart attack.

SPEER, LENA BROCK ("MOM")

b. (?), d. 1967.
Singer. Member of the Speer Family, gospel singers.

SPELMAN, TIMOTHY MATHER

b. 1891 Brooklyn, New York.
Composer. Studied with Spalding and Hill at Harvard University, later with Courvoisier; wrote *Saints' Days* (symphonic suite, given by the Boston Symphony), Symphony in G Minor, and *Litany of the Middle Ages* (presented in Rochester, N.Y., and in Paris).

SPENCER, ALLEN HERVEY

b. 1870 Fair Haven, Vermont, d. 1950 Chicago, Illinois. Pianist, composer, teacher, and writer. Studied under William H. Sherwood and Edgar Sherwood; taught piano in Toledo, Ohio.

SPENCER, ELEANOR

b. 1890 Chicago, Illinois, d. 1973.
Pianist. Studied with Leschetizky; debut with London Philharmonic (1912); debut in New York (1913); soloist with orchestras in Europe and United States.

SPENCER, ROBERT NELSON

b. 1877 Tunnel, New York, d. (?).
Hymnist. Educated at Wyoming Seminary, Dickinson College, Carlisle, Pa. (D.D., 1931), and Kansas Theological School; preacher at Fort Riley, Kan., Junction City, Kan., Springfield, Mo., then Grace and Holy Trinity, Kansas City, Missouri (1909-30), when he became bishop of West Missouri; wrote the hymn "O Heavenly Grace in Holy Rite Descending" (1939, tune "Charterhouse"—David Evans).

SPENCER, TIM

b. 1908 Webb City, Missouri, d. 1974.
Singer and publisher. Joined with Roy Rogers and Bob Nolan to form the Sons of the Pioneers (1930); later appeared in moving pictures; formed Manna Music, publishers (1954); wrote "Room Full of Roses" (1949); leader of Tim Spencer Family and Pioneer Trio.

SPENCER, WILLIAM O'NEILL

b. 1909 Springfield, Ohio, d. 1944 New York City. Black jazz drummer. Played in Lucky Millinder's band; also with John Kirby.

SPENSER, WILLARD

b. 1852 Cooperstown, New York, d. 1933 Wayne, Pennsylvania. Composer. Composed a waltz at age fifteen, published by Lee and Walker (1867); wrote *The Little Tycoon*, first successful comic opera by an American, Temple Theatre (1885); also wrote *The Princess Bonnie*, Chestnut St. Theatre, Philadelphia (1894), *Miss Bob White*, Chestnut St. Theatre (1901), *Rosalie*, *The Wild Goose*; *The Little Tycoon* passed 10,000 professional and amateur performances; *The Princess Bonnie*, 3000 performances.

SPEWACK, BELLA COHEN

b. 1899 Hungary.
Librettist and playwright. Married Sam Spewack (1922); with her husband wrote many Broadway comedies, also librettos for the musicals *Leave It to Me* (1938) and *Kiss Me Kate* (1948, which won the Antoinette Perry (Tony) Award and the Page One Award for 1949).

SPEWACK, SAMUEL

b. 1899 Ukraine, Russia, d. 1971 New York City. Librettist and playwright. Brought to New York as a child; attended Columbia University for three years; newspaper reporter and foreign correspondent; with his wife,

Bella, wrote numerous comedies for Broadway; wrote libretto for *Kiss Me Kate* (1948, m. Cole Porter); also *Leave It to Me* (1938, in which Mary Martin made her Broadway debut).

SPICKER, MAX

b. 1858 Koenigsberg, Germany, d. 1912 New York City. Compiler. Compiled *Services for Sabbath Evening and Morning* for synagogues, which included works by William Sparger, H. Zoellner, Gounod, Attenhofer, F.v.d. Stucken, and Will C. Macfarlan.

SPIERING, THEODOR

b. 1871 St. Louis, Missouri, d. 1925 Munich, Germany. Violinist. Studied with H. Schradieck in Cincinnati, then in Berlin; founded the Spiering Quartet, Chicago; concertmaster of the New York Philharmonic (1909), conductor in 1911; later guest conductor in Europe.

SPILMAN, JONATHAN E.

b. 1812 Freenville, Kentucky, d. 1896.
Popular composer. Graduated Illinois College, Jacksonville, Ill., and Transylvania College of Law, Lexington, Ky.; practiced law for eighteen years, then became a Presbyterian minister in Illinois; married Elizabeth Taylor, a niece of Zachary Taylor; composed a tune for "Flow Gently, Sweet Afton" (another tune by Alex Hume); Spilman's tune was used for "Away in a Manger" (there are other tunes by J.B. Herbert and W.J. Kirkpatrick).

SPIRIT (rock group)

Mark Andes, vocals and bass; Randy California, lead guitar; Ed Cassidy, drums; Jay Ferguson, vocals; John Locke, piano; group started in California (1967) with the help of Lou Adler, who backed the Mamas and the Papas; albums—*Spirit* (1968), *Family That Plays Together, Clear.*

SPITALNY, PHIL

b. 1890 Romanoff, Russia, d. 1970.
Bandleader. Leader of a dance and radio orchestra; then hired female musicians in the 1930s; with Arlene Francis as Mistress of Ceremonies on his "Hour of Charm" radio series.

SPIVAKOWSKY, TOSSY

b. 1907 Odessa, Russia.
Violinist. Concertmaster of the Berlin Philharmonic Orchestra when only eighteen years old; with the rise of Nazism, he fled to Australia, then to the United States; became a concertmaster in Cleveland, Ohio, then a violin soloist.

SPRINGFIELD, DUSTY

b. (?) England.
Singer. Born Mary O'Brien; became a top female vocalist in England; specialized first in country and western music, then black soul; left England for America; settled in Memphis, Tenn.; first recorded in 1966; albums—*Dusty Springfield's Golden Hits, Stay Awhile/I Only Want to Be with You, Dusty in Memphis/Brand New Me, Look of Love, Something Special.*

SPROSS, CHARLES GILBERT

b. 1874 Poughkeepsie, New York, d. 1962 Poughkeepsie, New York. Pianist and composer. Studied with Carl Lachmund and others; accompanist for noted artists; composed choral works, songs.

STACH, MATTHAUS

b. 1711 Mankendorf, Moravia (Czechoslovakia), d. 1787. Hymnist. Moravian missionary in Greenland (1733) and in Pennsylvania (1771); his hymns appeared in Moravian hymnals.

STACY, JESS

b. 1904 Cape Girardeau, Missouri.
Jazz pianist. Played in Benny Goodman's band; previously recorded with Paul Mares (1935); played at Jimmy Ryan's Club on 52nd Street, New York City, in the 1940s.

STAFFORD, JO

b. 1918 Coalinga, California.
Singer. Raised in Long Beach, Calif.; formed the Stafford Sisters Trio with her two sisters on KNK, Hollywood (1935); joined Tommy Dorsey and the Pied Pipers group; with "Johnny Mercer Show" (1944); had her own radio show (1945-49); with Gordon MacRae, her hit record was "Whispering Hope" (1949, m. Septimus Winner, 1868); "Jo Stafford Show" in Luxembourg (Europe) in 1950 was beamed to major cities throughout Europe; married Paul Weston.

STAHL, WILLY

b. 1896 New York City, d. 1963.
Composer. Graduated the Vienna Conservatory of Music (1913); played violin with New York and St. Paul, Minn. orchestras; later taught at the Pacific Institute in

Hollywood, Calif.; his *Dead Forest,* tone poem (1932) presented by National Symphony Orchestra, New York City; also composed chamber music.

STAIR, PATTY

b. 1869 Cleveland, Ohio, d. 1926.
Organist, conductor, composer, and teacher. Born Martha Greene; wrote "The Interrupted Serenade."

STAIRS, LOUISE E.

b. 1892.
Organist, composer, and teacher. Composed under the pseudonym Signey Forest; wrote "Lord, Speak to Me" (w. Frances R. Havergal).

STAMMERS, EDWARD

b. (?), d. 1802 Philadelphia, Pennsylvania. Compiler. With William Little compiled *The Easy Instructor, or a New Method of Teaching Sacred Harmony* (1798), published by William Little and William Smith (Philadelphia, 1801), first note-shaped tune book published in America; also compiled *The Philadelphia Chorister,* published posthumously (1803, Philadelphia).

STAMPER, DAVID

b. 1883 New York City, d. 1963 Poughkeepsie, New York. Popular composer. Accompanied Nora Bayes in vaudeville; with lyricist Gene Buck wrote songs for *Ziegfeld Follies*—"Daddy Has a Sweetheart and Mother Is Her Name" (1912), "Just You and I and the Moon," "Without You," "Everybody Sometime Must Love Somebody" (1913); with Raymond Hubbell, the score for the *Follies* (1914); with Louis A. Hirsch (1915); with Hirsch—"My Rambler Rose," " 'Neath the South Sea Moon" (1922), "Some Sweet Day" (1923); "Ain't Love Grand" (1927, w. Cyrus Wood).

STAMPER, WALLACE LOGAN ("PETE")

b. 1930 Russellville, Kentucky.
Singer and songwriter. Attended school in Charleston, Ky.; with WRVK and "Renfro Valley Barn Dance" after 1958; wrote "Kiss Me One More Time," "I Should Be with You," "Car Song," "Dear Maw," "Hey Maw," "Stranger's Story."

STAMPS QUARTET (singers) *see* JAMES W. BLACKWOOD, JR.

STANLEY, ALBERT AUGUSTUS

b. 1851 Manville, Rhode Island, d. 1932 Ann Arbor, Michigan. Organist, teacher, and composer. Studied in Providence, R.I., and in Leipzig; professor of music at the University of Michigan, Ann Arbor (1888-1922); conducted Choral Union at Ann Arbor Festivals after 1893; composed *The City of Freedom* (ode with orchestra, Boston, 1883), *Chorus triumphalis, Commemoration Ode* with orchestra, *Altis* (symphonic poem), *The Awakening of the Soul* (symphony).

STANLEY, CARTER GLEN

b. 1925 McClure, Virginia, d. 1966 Bristol, Virginia. Singer and guitarist. With his brother Ralph; their albums—*Angels Are Singing, For the Good People, Sacred Songs, Good Old Camp Meeting Songs, Greatest Country and Western Show on Earth, Hard Times, How Far to Little Rock, Hymns of the Cross, Jacob's Vision, Live and Out of Sight, Mountain Music Sound, Old Time Camp Meeting, Sacred Songs from the Hills, Sunday Morning Meeting.*

STANLEY, RALPH EDMOND

b. 1927 Straton, Virginia.
Singer and banjoist. Joined with his brother, Carter, as the "Stanley Brothers"; radio debut on WCYB, Bristol, Virginia (1945); toured Europe in the 1960s; formed the Clinch Mountain Boys; their albums—*Brand New Country Songs, Hills of Home, Over the Sunset Hill.*

STANTON, EDMUND C.

b. (?), d. 1901.
Manager. In charge of the Metropolitan Opera House, New York City, from its opening (1883).

STANTON, FRANK LIBBY

b. 1857 Charleston, South Carolina, d. 1927. Lyricist. Poet and journalist for the *Atlanta Constitution,* Atlanta, Georgia; wrote the lyrics "Mighty Lak' a Rose" (1900, m. Ethelburt Nevin), "Morning" (1910, m. Oley Speaks).

STAPLE SINGERS, THE (black gospel-rock singers)

"Pop" Roebuck Staples, vocals and guitar; and daughters—Cleo Staples, vocals; Pervis Staples, vocals; Mavis Staples, contralto; recorded Bob Dylan's "John Brown" (1962), and his "Hard Rain's Gonna Fall"; known as gospel singers; appeared at a Fillmore East, New York City rock show (1968); albums—*Amen, For What It's Worth, Freedom Highway, Best of the Staple Singers, Gospel Program, Pray On, Staple Singers, We'll Get Over, What the World Needs Is Love.*

STARCHER, BUDDY EDGAR

b. 1910 Ripley, West Virginia.
Guitarist and bandleader. Leader of Buddy Starcher's All-Star Band (1937-67); wrote "I'll Still Write Your Name in the Sand," "Sweet Thing," "The Fire in My Heart," "Song of the Waterwheel," "History Repeats Itself."

STARK, BOBBY

b. 1906 New York City, d. there 1945.
Black jazz trumpeter. Played in Chick Webb's band.

STARK, EDWARD JOSEF

b. 1858 Hohenems, Austria, d. 1918.
Cantor and composer. Brought to America as a boy; studied in New York City and abroad; cantor in Brooklyn, N.Y., and in San Francisco in Reform Jewish temples.

STARK, JOHN STILLWELL

b. 1841 Shelby County, Kentucky, d. 1927. Publisher. Joined 1st Regiment of the Indiana Heavy Artillery Volunteers as a bugler, on New Year's Day, 1864, served in the occupation of New Orleans; opened a music store in Sedalia, Mo. (1885); published *Original Rag* (1899) and *Maple Leaf Rag* (1899), both by Scott Joplin, the black composer; also published the songs of James S. Scott, black composer, and Scott Hayden.

STARR, KAY

b. 1922 Dougherty, Oklahoma.
Singer. Had her own show on station WRR, Dallas, Texas at age eleven; staff vocalist on station WREC, Memphis, Tenn. at thirteen; sang on "Grand Ole Opry," Nashville, Tenn. at fifteen; sang in Joe Venuti's band (1939-41), and Charlie Barnet's band (1943-45); then suffered a throat infection and her voice became lower and huskier; signed with Capital Records (1946).

STATESMAN QUARTET (gospel singers)

Roland "Rosie" Rozell, first tenor; Jake Toney, lead; Doy Ott, baritone; "Big Chief" Weatherington, bass; Hovie Lister, pianist and emcee.

STATLER BROTHERS (quartet) *see* DON S. REID, HAROLD W. REID, PHILIP E. BALSLEY, LEW C. DE WITT

STATON, DAKOTA

b. 1932 Pittsburgh, Pennsylvania.
Black singer. Studied at the Filion School of Music in Pittsburgh; named "Most promising newcomer of the year" (1955) by *Downbeat;* albums—*Dakota* (1967), *Late, Late Show, My Funny Valentine.*

STAUGHTON, WILLIAM

b. 1770 Coventry, England, d. 1829 Washington, D.C. Composer. Came to Charleston, S.C., in 1793, then went to New York and Philadelphia; first president of Columbian College (now George Washington University) (1821-29); wrote the lyrics "Strike the Cymbal" (1812, Italian tune); five of his tunes were in the *Baptist Hymn Book* (1825), and several in the 1819 and 1826 edition of John Rippon's *Hymns.*

STAUNTON, WILLIAM

b. 1803 Cheshire, England, d. 1889 New York City. Composer. Came to America (1818); graduated Hobart College, Geneva, New York; ordained (1833), pastor until 1859; wrote *Voluntaries for the Organ and Piano Forte* (ca. 1856), *Te Deum Laudamus* (1858), *Songs and Prayers for the Family Altar* (1860), *The Book of Common Praise* (1866).

STEAMBOAT FOUR, THE

Featured John Miles, Jr.

STEARNS, AGNES JUNE

b. 1939 Albany, Kentucky.
Singer. Attended schools in New Lisbon, Indiana; albums—*Back to Back, River of Regret.*

STEARNS, THEODORE

b. 1880 Berea, Ohio, d. 1935 Los Angeles, California. Critic and composer. Graduated Wurzburg University; music critic on the *New York Morning Telegraph* and *Chicago Herald Examiner;* conducted musical comedies; composed operas—*Snowbird* (Chicago Opera, 1922 and Dresden State Opera, 1927), *Atlantis* (both to his own librettos); also *Suite Caprese.*

STEBBINS, GEORGE COLES

b. 1846 East Carleton, New York, d. 1945 Catskill, New York. Composer. Choirmaster of the first Baptist Church, Chicago, then at the Clarendon St. Church, Boston (1874-76), and Tremont Temple (1876), when he became a gospel singer and composer for Dwight L. Moody; composed the tunes "Evening Prayer" for "Savior, Breathe an Evening Blessing" (w. James Edmeston), "Friend" for "I've Found a Friend" (1863, w. J.G. Small), "Holiness" for "Take Time to Be Holy" (w. W.D. Longstaff), "True-hearted, Whole-hearted" (1890, w. Frances R. Havergal), "We Speak of the Realms of the Blest" (w. Elizabeth Mills), "The Bird with the Broken Pinion" (w. Hezekiah Butterworth), and "There Is a Green Hill Far Away" (w. C.E.

Alexander, second tune by Charles Gounod, 1871).

STEBBINS, GEORGE WARING

b. 1869 Chicago, Illinois, d. 1930.
Organist, conductor, and teacher. Son of George C. Stebbins, singing evangelist.

STEBER, ELEANOR

b. 1916 Wheeling, West Virginia.
Noted soprano. Debut at the Metropolitan Opera, New York City (1940) as Sophie in *Der Rosenkavalier;* soloist on "The Voice of Firestone" on radio (1948); with the Metropolitan Opera (1940-63); European debut in concert with the Vienna Philharmonic (1953) and in opera as Elsa in *Lohengrin* at the Bayreuth Festival (1953).

STECK, GEORGE

b. 1829 Cassel, Germany, d. 1897 New York City. Piano manufacturer. Came to America (1853); made pianos in New York City.

STEEL, JOHN

b. 1900, d. 1971 New York City.
Tenor. Starred in the *Ziegfeld Follies;* Irving Berlin wrote "A Pretty Girl Is Like a Melody" for him.

STEELE, DANIEL

b. 1772, d. 1828.
Teacher and publisher. Published music in Albany, N.Y. (1806-25); taught there after 1817; published *The Easy Instructor, or a New Method of Teaching Sacred Harmony* (revised edition), having obtained the copyright from William Little.

STEELE, PORTER

b. 1880, d. 1966.
Pianist, conductor, and composer. With Brian Hooker, Jr. wrote "For I've Been Reading Freud" ("Don't tell me what you dreamed last night," w. Franklin Pierce Adams).

STEELE, TOMMY

b. 1937 London, England.
Singer. Born Thomas Hicks; sang in London coffee shops; made a hit with "Heartbreak Hotel" (1956); came to New York City; later film actor in Hollywood; co-starred with Petula Clark in *Finian's Rainbow;* albums—*Everything's Coming Up Broadway* (1967), *Finian's Rainbow* (soundtrack), *Half a Sixpence, Sixpenny Millionaire.*

STEFFE, EDWIN

b. 1907 Washington, D.C.
Baritone. Son of organist-pianist Charles Alexander Steffe (Baltimore Symphony) and grandson of William Steffe; studied voice under Frank Bibb at the Peabody Conservatory, Baltimore; concert artist for twelve years with Columbia artists; sang "The Battle Hymn of the Republic" (J.W. Howe and William Steffe) before 45,000 people in Australia under the Melbourne Symphony and before 100,000 under the Adelaide Symphony in a candlelight service festival at Christmas; also toured U.S.

STEFFE, WILLIAM

b. ca. 1830, d. ca. 1890.
Organist and choirmaster. Family name was di Stefano; resided in Philadelphia after 1856; organist-choirmaster of the Indian Fields Camp Meetings in the 1850s held annually by the Southern Methodists since 1801 at St. George, near Charleston, South Carolina; credited by some as having written "Say Brothers, Will You Meet Us?" tune for "John Brown's Body."

STEIN, LEON

b. 1910 Chicago, Illinois.
Composer. Studied at the American Conservatory; graduated in music from DePaul University (1931), master's degree (1935); later taught there; wrote *Suite Hebraic* (1933), *Fantasie* orchestral work (1936), *Liederkrantz of Jewish Folksongs* for children's chorus and piano (1936).

STEINBERG, WILLIAM

b. 1899 Cologne, Germany.
Conductor. Conducted in opera houses in Cologne, Prague, Frankfurt, was a guest conductor in Israel when he came to New York City to assist Toscanini in the direction of the NBC Symphony Orchestra; later conductor in Buffalo, New York, and Pittsburgh; conducted Pittsburgh Symphony Orchestra in concert version of Wagner's *Die Walküre* at Carnegie Hall (1972) with Marilyn Horne, soprano.

STEINDEL, BRUNO

b. 1896 Zwichau, Saxony, Germany, d. 1949 Santa Monica, California. Cellist. First cellist with Berlin Philharmonic; later with Chicago Orchestra.

STEINER, MAXIMILIAN RAOUL

b. 1888 Vienna, Austria, d. 1971 Hollywood, California. Popular composer. Studied at the Imperial Academy of Music in Vienna; at age fourteen wrote and conducted the operetta *Beautiful Greek Girl,* presented at the Orpheum Theatre in Vienna; came to New York

(1914) to conduct shows for Florenz Ziegfeld; wrote "It Can't Be Wrong" (1943, w. Kim Gannon) and the scores for dozens of motion pictures; won Academy Awards for film scores *The Informer* (1935), *Now, Voyager* (1942), and *Since You Went Away* (1945).

STEINERT, ALEXANDER LANG

b. 1900 Boston, Massachusetts.
Composer. Graduated Harvard; studied in Paris with D'Indy and others; fellowship at American Academy in Rome; pianist and conductor; composed *Nuit Meridionale* (Boston Symphony under Koussevitzky, 1926), *Concerto Sinfonico* for piano and orchestra (Boston Symphony with composer as soloist, 1935).

STEINWAY (STEINWEG), HEINRICH ENGELHARDT

b. 1797 Wolfshagen, Harz, Germany, d. 1871 New York City. Piano maker. Came to New York (1851) from Brunswick, Germany, with his sons C.F. Theodor (1825-89), Henry (1829-65), Wilhelm (1836-96), and Albert (1840-77); established business to manufacture pianos; by 1859 Steinway & Sons employed 800 men who produced sixty pianos a week; successors were Charles H. (1857-1919), Frederick T. (1860-1927), George A. (1865-?).

STEPPENWOLF (Canadian group)

Started in Los Angeles, Calif.; John Kay, lead singer; hit single was "Born to Be Wild."

STEPT, SAM H. (SAMMY)

b. 1897 Odessa, Russia, d. 1964 Los Angeles, California. Bandleader and popular composer. Family settled in Pitsburg, Ohio (1900); led his five-piece band at the Claremont Cafe, Cleveland (1920-25); organized the Record Boys, New York City, early singing team on radio; formed a publishing company with Bud Green; wrote "That's My Weakness Now" (1928, w. Bud Green), "Breaking in a Pair of Shoes" (1936, with Dave Franklin, w. Ned Washington), "I Came Here to Talk for Joe" (1941, with Charles Tobias and Lew Brown), "Don't Sit Under the Apple Tree" (1942, with Tobias and Brown), "Seems Like Yesterday" (1950).

STERLING, ANDREW B.

b. 1874 New York City, d. 1955 Stamford, Connecticut. Lyricist. Wrote the lyrics and Harry von Tilzer the music for "My Old New Hampshire Home" (1898), "I've Lost My Baby" (1899), "I Wonder if She's Waiting" (1899), "Where the Sweet Magnolias Grow" (1899), and "Wait 'Till the Sun Shines Nellie" (1905); with Max Dreyfus—"The Girl I Loved in Old Virginia" (1899), "The Lady with the Auburn Hair" (1899); with C.B. Ward—"Strike Up the Band," "Here Comes a Sailor" (1900); with Joe E. Howard—"On a Saturday Night" (1902).

STERLING, ANTOINETTE

b. 1850 Sterlingville, New York, d. 1904 Hampstead, England. Contralto. She studied with Mme. Marchesi and others; sang oratorios in Plymouth Church, Brooklyn, N.Y.; sang in concerts in London (1873); married John MacKinlay, London (1875).

STERLING, WINTHROP SMITH

b. 1859 Cincinnati, Ohio, d. there 1943. Organist and teacher. Studied at the Cincinnati Conservatory, also in Leipzig and London; professor at the Cincinnati College of Music after 1887; founded and was dean of the Metropolitan College of Music (1903).

STERN, CARL

b. 1902 Paterson, New Jersey, d. 1971 Bangor, Maine. Cellist. Studied with Wille, Willeke at the Institute of Musical Art, New York City; played in the NBC Symphony Orchestra under Arturo Toscanini (1937-44); cellist with the New York Philharmonic (1944-64) and first cellist after 1957; after 1964 taught at the Dalcroze School of Music, then retired to Brooksville, Maine.

STERN, ISAAC

b. 1920 Kriminesz, Russia.
Violinist. Brought to U.S. at age three; studied piano at age six and violin at age eight; studied with Louis Persinger in New York City, and at San Francisco Conservatory of Music; debut (1931) with San Francisco Symphony Orchestra; at Town Hall, New York City (1937) and in N.Y. again (1939); toured bases in South Pacific in World War II; toured Europe, Australia, and South America (1948-53); soloist at the National Symphony Orchestra, Washington, D.C., 41st season opening (9/9/71); soloist with the Philadelphia Orchestra in Philharmonic Hall, New York City (1972).

STERN, JOSEPH WILLIAM

b. 1870 New York City, d. 1934 Brightwater, L.I., New York. Popular composer. Composed the music and Edward B. Marks the lyrics for "The Little Lost Child" (1894, introduced by Della Fox), "His Last Thoughts Were of You" (1894), "No One Ever Loved More Than I" (1895), and "My Mother Was a Lady" (1895, introduced by Meyer Cohen at Tony Pastor's Music Hall and popularized later by Lottie Gilson).

STERNBERG, CONSTANTIN *see* VON STERNBERG

STEVENS, CAT

b. 1948 London, England.
Rock singer, guitarist, and songwriter. Born Stephen Giorgiou; dropped out of school at age seventeen and started playing the guitar in London and writing songs; came to America; sang at Philharmonic Hall, New York City (1971); wrote "Wild World," recorded by Jose Feliciano.

STEVENS, CONNIE

b. 1938 Brooklyn, New York.
Singer. Also appeared in films; album—*Songs of Hank Williams.*

STEVENS, RISË

b. 1913 Bronx, New York City.
Noted mezzo-soprano. Born Risë Steenberg; on the radio at age ten on "The Children's Hour"; sang with the New York Opera-Comique in Brooklyn as a teenager; studied with Anna Schön-René, later in Europe; debut in Prague (1936) in the title role in *Mignon;* later at the Staatsoper in Vienna; at the Metropolitan Opera, New York City debut (1938) in *Mignon;* with the Metropolitan Opera (1938-62); also appeared in films; with Michael Manuel, co-manager of the Metropolitan Opera National Company (1964).

STEWARD, REDD

b. (?) Ashland City, Tennessee.
Pianist, guitarist, and songwriter. Joined PeeWee King and his Golden West Cowboys; later on Grand Ole Opry, Nashville, Tenn.; with King wrote "Bonaparte's Retreat" (1946, sung by Kay Starr), and "Tennessee Waltz" (1948).

STEWART, HUMPHREY JOHN

b. 1856 London, England, d. 1932 San Diego, California. Organist. Settled in San Francisco (1886); gave recitals in Balboa Park at the San Diego Exposition (1915).

STEWART, LEROY ("SLAM")

b. 1914 Englewood, New Jersey.
Black bass player. Developed the humming technique with the baa playing; played in Benny Goodman's band; later joined Benny, Red Norvo, and Teddy Wilson in a quartet.

STEWART, N. COE

b. 1837 Hermitage, Pennsylvania, d. 1921. Conductor, teacher, and writer. Superintendent of singing in the schools in Cleveland, Ohio; one of the founders of the Music Teachers' National Association (1876).

STEWART, REX WILLIAM

b. 1907 Philadelphia, Pennsylvania, d. 1967. Black cornetist and trumpeter. Played in Duke Ellington's band; recorded with Sidney Bechet; also played in Fletcher Henderson's band.

STEWART, THOMAS

b. 1928 San Saba, Texas.
Baritone. Started singing at age ten; studied at Juilliard, New York City; met his wife there, soprano Evelyn Lear, married (1955); sang complete Wagnerian "Ring" in Vienna, Hamburg, and Berlin (1971); sang part of Golaud at the Metropolitan Opera, New York City in *Pelleas and Melisande;* also as Kurwenal in *Tristan and Isolde* at the Met; solo recital at Alice Tully Hall, New York City (1972).

STEWART, WYNN

b. 1934 Morrisville, Missouri.
Singer, bandleader, and songwriter. Radio debut on station KWTO, Springfield, Mo., at age thirteen; formed his own band at fifteen; opened his own club in Las Vegas; later organized The Tourists in Hacienda Heights, Calif.; albums—*It's Such a Pretty World Today, Let the Whole World Sing It with Me, Love's Gonna Happen to Me, Wynn Stewart and Jan Howard Sing Their Hits, You Don't Care What Happens to Me, Yours Forever.*

STICKLES, WILLIAM C.

b. 1882 Cohoes, New York, d. 1971 Queens New York. Pianist, composer, and arranger. Educated at Utica (N.Y.) Conservatory and Syracuse University, N.Y.; served as assistant to Isadore Braggiotti in Florence, Italy, for five years, teaching voice.

STICKNEY, JOHN

b. 1744 Stoughton, Massachusetts, d. 1827 South Hadley, Massachusetts. Compiler and composer. At the age of seven apprenticed to a shoemaker and butcher in Milton; enlisted as a private (1776) in Captain Hendricks' company at Castleton and was present at the taking of General Burgoyne at Saratoga, N.Y. (1777); in 1774 published *The Gentleman and Lady's Musical Companion,* printed and sold by Daniel Bayley of Newbury Port, Mass.

STIEDRY, FRITZ

b. 1883 Vienna, Austria, d. 1968.
Conductor and director. Conductor in opera houses in Dresden, Posen, Prague, Nuremberg, Kassel, and Berlin; became director of the New Friends of Music, New York City

(1938), then of the Metropolitan Opera, New York City (1948).

STILL, WILLIAM GRANT

b. 1895 Woodville, Mississippi.
Noted black composer. Attended Wilberforce University, Wilberforce, Ohio; studied at Oberlin (1916); served in the navy in World War I; with W.C. Handy in publishing in New York City; studied with Edgard Varese, French composer, in New York City, and George Chadwick in Boston (1923); composed *La Guiablesse* (ballet, performed in Rochester, N.Y., and also by the Chicago Opera Company), *Afro-American Symphony* (New York Philharmonic), *Africa, Darker America, From the Black Belt, Puritan Epic, From the Journal of a Wanderer, Levee Land, Log Cabin Ballads, Troubled Island* (opera, New York, 1949), *Highway No. 1 USA* (seventh opera, libretto by Verna Arvey, his wife, premiere in 1963 at Fourth Annual Festival of Music, University of Miami at Coral Gables, Florida); Leopold Stokowski wrote in 1945: "Still is one of our greatest American composers."

STILLMAN, MILDRED (WHITNEY)

b. 1890 San Francisco, California, d. 1950.
Hymnist. Educated at Barnard College, New York City; wrote the hymn "Now Once Again for Help That Never Faileth" (1934, tune "Welwyn"—Alfred Scott-Gatty).

STITT, EDWARD ("SONNY")

b. 1924 Boston, Massachusetts.
Black jazz saxophonist. Son of Edward Boatner, singer and choirmaster; played in Dizzy Gillespie's band; at the Newport Jazz Festival, New York City (1972).

STOCK, FREDERICK A.

b. 1872 Dulich, Germany, d. 1942 Chicago, Illinois. Violinist and conductor. His father was a military bandmaster; studied at the Cologne Conservatory; with Chicago Symphony Orchestra (1895); assistant conductor to Theodore Thomas (1899), conductor (1905-42); composed a symphony, symphonic poems, chamber music, songs.

STOCKING, JAY THOMAS

b. 1870 Lisbon, New York, d. 1936 Newton, Massachusetts. Hymnist. Educated at Amherst, Yale Divinity School, and the University of Berlin; Congregational minister at churches in New England, New Jersey, Missouri, and Washington, D.C.; wrote the hymn "O Master Workman of the Race" (tune "St. Michel's" also called "St. Maria," "Beulah," or "Woolrich Common" by William Gawler).

STOCKTON, JOHN HART

b. 1813 New Hope, Pennsylvania, d. 1877 Philadelphia, Pennsylvania. Composer. Became a Methodist preacher in 1846 and later received into the New Jersey Conference; wrote the words and music for the hymn "Come, Every Soul by Sin Oppressed" (tune "Stockton"); published *Salvation Melodies* (1874) and *Precious Songs* (1875).

STOCKTON, MARTHA MATILDA BRUSTAR

b. 1821, d. 1885.
Hymnist. Married the Rev. W.C. Stockton of Ocean City, N.J.; wrote "God Loved the World of Sinners Lost," which appeared in *Laudes Domini* (1884).

STOCKWELL, SAMUEL

b. 1788, d. 1816 New York City.
Singer, organist, composer, and teacher. On the New York stage between 1798-1805; taught in Boston after 1805; secretary of the Philharmonic Society (1809); also one of the founders and secretary of the Handel and Haydn Society; with James Hewitt, alternate conductor of the Musical Academy after 1811; wrote *Too Late for Redress* (1813); published the *Copenhagen Waltz* about 1815 (m. Samuel Webbe) with variations for the pianoforte.

STOESSEL, ALBERT FREDERICK

b. 1894 St. Louis, Missouri, d. 1943 New York City. Violinist and conductor. Studied at Berlin Hochschule; debut in Berlin; conducted the New York Oratorio Society (1921); also Westchester (N.Y.) and Worcester (Mass.) Festivals; director of music at New York University (1924); with Juilliard School, New York City, after 1930; composed *Suite Antique* for orchestra, a violin sonata, piano and orchestral works, songs.

STOJOWSKI, SIGISMOND

b. 1870 Strelce, Poland, d. 1946 New York City. Pianist. Studied at the Paris Conservatory, won first prize, studied with Paderewski; taught at the Institute of Musical Art, New York City (1905-11), and at the Von Ende School (1911-17); married Luisa Morales-Machado, pianist; composed a symphony (Leipzig, 1898), *Spring* for chorus and orchestra, *Polish Rhapsodie* for piano and orchestra, *A Prayer for Poland* (choral work), violin concerto (1908), two violin concertos, three piano concertos.

STOKES, BYRON D.

b. 1886 Jackson, Michigan, d. 1974.
Lyricist. Wrote the lyrics for "The Sweetheart of Sigma Chi" (1912, m. F. Dudleigh Vernor).

STOKOWSKI, LEOPOLD

b. 1882 London, England.
Famous conductor. Studied at the Royal College of Music in London and attended Queen's College at Oxford; came to New York (1905) and became organist-choirmaster at St. Bartholomew's Church, then was conductor of the Cincinnati Symphony (1909-12), and of the Philadelphia Orchestra (1912-38); during the 1950s conductor of the Houston (Texas) Symphony Orchestra; a special celebration was held for his ninetieth birthday (1972).

STOLZ, ROBERT

b. 1880 Graz, Austria.
Composer. Composed operettas and music for films.

STONE, CLIFFIE

b. 1917 Burbank, California.
Singer, bass violist, and songwriter. Born Clifford Gilpin Snyder; played in the bands of Anson Weeks and Freddy Slack; later comedian on CBS "Hollywood Barn Dance"; master of ceremonies on Western shows on radio; featured on "Hometown Jamboree"; albums—*It's Fun to Square Dance—With Calls, Square Dance U.S.A., Square Dance U.S.A. Volume 2.*

STONE COUNTRY (country rock)

Dan Barry, bass; Don Beck, five-string guitar, twelve-string guitar, etc.; Doug Brooks, rhythm guitar; Dennis Conway, drums; Steve Young, lead guitar; Richard Lockmiller, rhythm guitar; started in California (1968); album—*Stone Country.*

STONE, JOSEPH C.

b. 1758 Ward (now Auburn), Massachusetts, d. 1837 Auburn, Massachusetts. Composer. Forty-two of his tunes are included in *The Columbian Harmony* which he published jointly with Abraham Wood.

STONE PONEYS *see* LINDA AND THE STONE PONEYS

STONE, SLY

b. 1944 Denton, Texas.
Black singer. Born Sylvester Stewart; organized Sly and the Family Stone.

STONEMAN, ERNEST V. ("POP")

b. 1893 Monarat, Virginia, d. 1968 Nashville, Tennessee. Autoharpist and founder of the Stoneman Family. Recorded "Sourwood Mountain" for OKeh records (1926); formed The Stonemans with his wife and Uncle Eck Dunford; raised thirteen children; usually six of the children sang and played instruments with the group; their albums—*Dawn of the Stoneman's Age, Great Stonemans, It's All in the Family, Live, Stoneman Country, Stoneman Family, Those Singin', Stompin' Sensational Stonemans, Tribute to Pop Stoneman, White Lightning.*

STONEY MOUNTAIN CLOGGERS *see* BEN SMATHERS

STOOGES—IGGY STOOGE *see* JIM OSTERBERG

STOOKEY, NOEL PAUL

b. 1937 Baltimore, Maryland.
Singer. Graduated Michigan State University, East Lansing, Mich,; sang in night clubs in New York City; joined with Peter Yarrow and Mary Ellin Travers to form "Peter, Paul and Mary" (1962); with their help wrote "Puff the Magic Dragon" (also with Milton Okun), "A-Soulin," "On a Desert Island," "Early in the Morning," "It's Raining," "Talking Candy Bar Blues."

STORER, HENRY JOHNSON

b. 1860 Cambridge, Massachusetts, d. 1935 Belmont, Massachusetts. Composer. Teacher in Albany, N.Y., and in Boston; composed the tune "Patmos" (1891, "I Heard a Sound of Voices," w. Godfrey Thring, 1886).

STORER, MARIA

b. ca. 1750 England, d. 1795 Philadelphia, Pennsylvania. Singer and actress. Sisters (three) were all actresses; married Mr. Henry; elder sisters—Miss Storer who married Mr. Henry after Maria died, Ann (Mrs. Hogg), and Fanny (Mrs. Mechler); they all came to America (1767) from Jamaica, B.W.I.; Maria sang and acted with the Old American Company, Philadelphia (1768-92); William Dunlap wrote in 1797: "She was, until 1792, the best public singer America had known."

STORM, GALE

b. 1922 Bloomington, Texas.
Singer and actress. For a time Billy Vaughn was her arranger.

STORY, CARL MOORE

b. 1916 Lenoir, North Carolina.
Singer. Leader of the Rambling Mountaineers after 1945.

STOVALL, VERN

b. 1928 Altus, Oklahoma.
Singer, guitarist, and songwriter. Raised in Vian, Oklahoma, near Muskogee; joined Fred Maddox' group in Pomona, Calif. (1958); organized his own band (1961); later teamed with Janet McBride; with Bobby George wrote "The Long Black Limousine" (recorded by Bobby Bare and George Hamilton IV), "Who'll Be the One" (recorded by Ray Price), "One More Memory" (recorded by Wynn Stewart), "Also Dallas" (with Gene McCoslin).

STOW, BARON

b. 1801 Croyden, New Hampshire, d. 1869 Boston, Massachusetts. Compiler. Graduated Columbian College (now George Washington University), Washington, D.C. (1825); Baptist minister at two different churches in Boston for thirty-five years; with Samuel F. Smith compiled *The Psalmist* (1843), a hymn book for use in Baptist churches.

STOWE, HARRIET BEECHER

b. 1811 Litchfield, Connecticut, d. 1896 Hartford, Connecticut. Writer. Wrote the lyrics "Still, Still with Thee" (m. Charles H. Morse, tune "Stowe," Barnby's "Windsor," Mendelssohn's "Consolation," Mason's "Henley"); also wrote "When Purple Morning Breaketh" (1855); best known for her anti-slavery book *Uncle Tom's Cabin;* sister of the Rev. Henry Ward Beecher, who included "Still, Still with Thee" in *The Plymouth Collection* (1855).

STRACKE, WIN

b. 1908 Lorraine, Kansas.
Singer and guitarist. Raised in Chicago; attended Lake Forest College, Illinois; sang as soloist with symphony orchestras; soloist for "Hymns of All Churches" during the 1930s; served in the army in North Africa and Europe in World War II; sang American folk music under a program sponsored by the Renaissance Society of the University of Chicago (1947); on the NBC program "America's Music" (1952); toured USA in folk concerts.

STRAKOSCH, MAX

b. 1834 Lemberg, Galicia, Austro-Hungary, d. 1892 New York City. Impresario. Manager for Clara Louise Kellogg, soprano, whom he later married; wrote *Sea Serpent,* a polka, published (1850) in New Orleans by W.T. Mayo; brother-in-law of Adelina Patti.

STRANG, GERALD

b. 1908 Claresholm, Canada.
Composer. Composed a symphony (in part by the Federation Symphony, Los Angeles, composer conducting, 1937), *Percussion Music for Three Players* (Seattle, Washington under John Cage, 1938), piano works.

STRANGE, WILLIAM E. (BILLY)

b. 1930 Long Beach, California.
Singer and guitarist. Wrote "Limbo Rock"; albums—*Great Western Themes, In the Mexican Bag, James Bond Theme, King of the Road, Twelve-String Guitar, Billy Strange with the Challengers.*

STRANSKY, JOSEPH

b. 1872 Deutschbrod, Bohemia, d. 1936 New York City. Conductor. Studied medicine, but later switched to music; conductor in Prague, Hamburg, and Berlin, then came to America as conductor of the New York Philharmonic Orchestra (1911-23).

STRAUB, SOLOMON W.

b. 1842, d. 1899.
Conductor, writer, editor, and publisher. Studied under William Mason, Robert Goldbeck, Carlo Bassini, and Carl Zerrahan; editor of the *Song Friend.*

STRAVINSKY, IGOR

b. 1882 Oranienbaum, near St. Petersburg, Russia, d. 1971 New York City. Famous composer. Studied law at the University of St. Petersburg (1905), but then took private music lessons with Rimsky-Korsakov; came to America (1939); known for *The Fire-Bird* (ballet, 1910), *Petrushka* (ballet, 1911), *The Rite of Spring* (ballet, 1913), *The Song of the Nightingale* (1914), *The Soldier's Tale* (ballet, 1918), *Pulcinella* (ballet, 1919), *Mavra* (comic opera, 1922), *The Wedding* (cantata, 1923), *Oedipus Rex* (opera-oratorio, 1927), *Apollon Musagete* (ballet, 1927), *Capriccio* for piano and orchestra (1929), *Symphony of Psalms* (1930), Concerto in D Major for Violin and Orchestra (1931), *Persephone* (melodrama, 1933), *Card Game* (ballet, 1936), Concerto in

E-flat Major (1938), Symphony in C Major (1940), *Ode* (triptych for orchestra, 1943), *Symphony in Three Movements* (1945) Concerto in D Major for Strings (1946), *Mass* for mixed chorus and ten wind instruments (1948), *Orpheus* (ballet, 1948), *The Rake's Progress* (opera, 1951).

STRAWBERRY ALARM CLOCK (rock group)

Mark Weitz, organ; Lee Freeman, vocals, sax, etc.; Ed King, lead guitar; Gary Lovetro, bass; George Bunnell, bass; Randy Seol, drums; started in California (1967); albums—*Best of the Strawberry Alarm Clock, Good Morning Starshine, Incense and Peppermints, Wake Up, It's Tomorrow, World in a Sea Shell.*

STRAYHORN, WILLIAM (BILLY)

b. 1915 Dayton, Ohio. d. 1967.
Black pianist, composer, and arranger. Arranger for and collaborator with Duke Ellington after 1939; wrote "Tapioca" (1940), "Day Dream" (1940, with Ellington), "Take the 'A' Train" (1941), "Passion Flower" (1941), "Chelsea Bridge" (1941), "Overture to a Jam Session" (1946), "C Jam Blues" (1956), "A Drum Is a Woman" (1956, with Ellington), "Such Sweet Thunder," a suite (1957).

STREISAND, BARBRA

b. 1942 Brooklyn, New York.
Singer and actress. Appeared on "Mike Wallace's PM East" television show; appeared in the musical *I Can Get It for You Wholesale* produced by David Merrick; starred in *Funny Girl* (1964, book—Isobel Lennart), and *Hello Dolly.*

STRELEZKI, ANTON

b. 1859 Croyden, England, d. 1907.
Composer. Wrote *Dreams.*

STRICKLAND, LILY TERESA

b. 1887 Anderson, South Carolina, d. 1958 Hendersonville, North Carolina. Organist and composer. Wrote "Because of You," "At Eve I Heard a Flute," "My Lover Is a Fisherman," "My Shepherd, Thou," "The Road to Home."

STRINGBEAN (singer and banjoist) *see* DAVID AKEMAN

STRINGFIELD, LAMAR

b. 1897 Raleigh, North Carolina, d. 1959 Asheville, North Carolina. Composer. Served in army on Mexican border, then in France in World War I; studied at the Institute of Musical Art in New York City; pupil of Goetschius, Wedge, and Robinson; his *From the Southern Mountains,* orchestral suite (1927) won the Pulitzer Prize; composed *A Negro Parade* (symphonic patrol, 1931), *The Legend of John Henry* (symphonic ballad, 1932), *Moods of a Moonshiner* (symphonic suite in three parts, 1934); heard in the major cities of the United States.

STRINGHAM, EDWIN JOHN

b. 1890 Kenosha, Wisconsin, d. 1974.
Teacher and composer. Graduated Northwestern University, Evanston, Ill.; studied at St. Cecilia Academy in Rome; dean of the College of Music, Denver College, Colorado (1919-29); then at Teachers College, Columbia University, and Union Seminary, N.Y.; composed a symphony, orchestral suites, overtures.

STROHN, ALBERT J.

b. 1888 Evansville, Indiana.
Composer. Graduated Northwestern University School of Music, Evanston, Ill. (1916); became organist-choirmaster at St. Paul's-by-the-Lake, Chicago (1914); composed the tune "Stewart" (1933, "Brightest and Best of the Sons of the Morning," w. Reginald Heber), and the anthem "Great Peace Have They That Love Thy Law."

STROMBERG, JOHN ("HONEY")

b. 1853, d. 1902 New York City.
Popular composer. With lyricist Edgar Smith wrote a number of shows for Weber and Fields—*The Art of Maryland* (1896), *The Geezer* (1896), *The Glad Hand* (1897), *The Pousse-Cafe* (1897), *Hurly-Burly* (1898, which included "Dinah," or "Kiss Me Honey Do," introduced by Peter F. Dailey), *Helter-Skelter* (1899), *Whirl-i-gig* (1899, including "When Chloe Sings a Song," introduced by Lillian Russell), *Fiddle-dee-dee* (1900), *Twirly-Whirly* (1902); Harry B. Smith wrote the lyrics and Stromberg the music for *I'm Making a Bid for Popularity* (1899), *The Kissing Bug* (1899), *My Josephine* (1899), and *De Cake Walk Queen* (1900); died in 1902, apparently a suicide; Lillian Russell introduced "Come Down, Ma Evenin' Star" in *Twirly-Whirly* just after his death.

STRONG, GEORGE TEMPLETON

b. 1856 New York City, d. 1948 Geneva, Switzerland. Composer. Studied at the Leipzig Conservatory; composed *In den Bergen* (symphony), *Undine* (symphonic poem), *Gestrebt-Gewonnen-Gescheitert,* choral works with orchestra, piano pieces.

STRONG, NATHAN

b. 1748 Coventry, Connecticut, d. 1816. Hymnist and compiler. Graduated Yale (1769); pastor of First Congregational Church,

Hartford, Conn. (1774-1816); editor of *The Hartford Selection* (1799), which included eight of his hymns, six of which were reproduced in Nettleton's *Village Hymns* (1824).

STRONG, SUSAN

b. 1875 Brooklyn, New York.
Soprano. Pupil of Korbay; sang in Europe and U.S. opera, with companies under Damrosch and Mapleson; with the Metropolitan Opera, New York City (1899-1900).

STROUSE, CHARLES

b. 1928 New York City.
Popular composer. Studied at the Eastman School of Music, University of Rochester, N.Y., and with Aaron Copland and Nadia Boulanger in Paris; with lyricist Lee Adams of Mansfield, Ohio, wrote the musicals *Golden Boy, Bye Bye Birdie* (book—Michael Stewart), *Applause,* and *Six;* wrote the scores for the movies *Bonnie and Clyde* and *The Night They Raided Minsky's.*

STRUBE, GUSTAV

b. 1867 Ballenstedt, Germany, d. 1953. Violinist. Studied with his father; in Ballenstedt orchestra when only ten years of age; studied at the Leipzig Conservatory (1883); taught at the Mannheim Conservatory; with Boston Symphony Orchestra (1899); conductor of Worcester, Mass. Festivals (1909); taught at the Peabody Conservatory, Baltimore (1913); conducted the Baltimore Symphony (1916); composed overtures—*The Maid of Orleans, Puck, Fantastic;* symphonic poems—*Longing, Fantastic Dance;* two symphonies.

STRYKER, MELANCTHON WOOLSEY

b. 1851 Vernon, New York, d. 1929 Clinton, New York. Hymnist. Educated at Hamilton College, Clinton, N.Y., and at Auburn Theological Seminary; Presbyterian minister in Auburn and Ithaca, N.Y., Holyoke, Mass., and Chicago, Ill.; became president of Hamilton College (1892); with Hubert P. Main compiled *The New Alleluia* (1886); wrote the hymn "Almighty Lord, with One Accord" (1896, tune "Patten"—P.C. Lutkin).

STUBBS, GEORGE EDWARD

b. 1857 New Brunswick, New Jersey, d. 1937 New York City. Organist and writer. Educated at Rutgers, New Brunswick; became an organist in churches in Connecticut and New York City, then organist at St. Agnes Chapel, New York City (1892-1937); wrote *Practical Hints on the Training of Choir Boys* (1888) and compiled a *Choir Service Book* (1902).

STUCKEY, NATHAN WRIGHT (NAT)

b. 1937 Cass County, Texas.
Singer and songwriter. Leader of the Corn Huskers (1958-59), the Louisiana Hayriders (1962-66), and the Sweet Thangs after 1966; wrote "All My Tomorrows," "My Can Do," "Sweet Thang" (all three in 1967); sang with Connie Smith.

STUECKGOLD, GRETE

b. 1895 London, England.
Soprano. Pupil of Jacques Stueckgold; operatic debut in Nuremberg; with Berlin Stadtische Opera; with the Metropolitan Opera, New York City after 1929; she married Gustav Schuetzendorf, baritone.

STULTS, R.M.

b. 1861 Hightstown, New Jersey, d. 1923. Composer. Wrote "The Sweetest Story Ever Told" (1892, "Tell Me, Do You Love Me?").

STUTSMAN, GRACE MAY

b. (?) Melrose, Massachusetts.
Hymnist. Raised in Indianapolis, Indiana; attended Boston University and the New England Conservatory of Music, Boston; became a music critic for *The Christian Science Monitor,* Boston, and *Musical America,* New York City; wrote the words and music of the Christmas carol "In Bethlehem 'neath Star-lit Skies" (tune "Waits' Carol," 1927), which appeared in the *Methodist Hymnal* (1935).

STYNE, JULE

b. 1905 London, England.
Popular composer. His family came to Chicago (1913); studied at the Chicago Musical College, and formed his own band (1931), then went to Hollywood; with lyrics by Frank Loesser wrote "Since You," "Conchita, Marquita, Lolita," "I Don't Want to Walk Without You"; with Sammy Cahn—"I've Heard That Song Before" (introduced by Frank Sinatra, 1943), "I'll Walk Alone" (1944), "It's Been a Long, Long Time," "Poor Little Rhode Island," (state song), "Let It Snow, Let It Snow," "Five Minutes More," and "I Believe"; with Cahn wrote the musical *High Button Shoes* (1947) starring Phil Silvers and Nanette Fabray; with lyricist Leo Robin—*Gentlemen Prefer Blondes* (book—Anita Loos) starring Carol Channing singing "Diamond's Are a Girl's Best Friend"; *Bells*

Are Ringing (1956, w. Betty Comden and Adolph Green) starring Judy Holliday, *Gypsy* (1959, book—Gypsy Rose Lee, w. Stephen Sondheim) starring Ethel Merman; with Cahn also wrote the song "Three Coins in the Fountain" (1954) which won a Academy Award.

SUBOTNIK, MORTON

b. 1933 Los Angeles, California.
Electronic composer. Studied with Leon Kirchner and Darius Milhaud; co-founder of Mills College Performance Group, Oakland, Calif., and San Francisco Tape Music Center; associate dean of music at California School of Arts; wrote *Silver Apples of the Moon, The Wild Bull, Electronic Chamber* for electronic lights, sound consoles, and eight players.

SULLIVAN, BRIAN

b. 1915 Oakland, California, d. 1969.
Tenor. Studied at the University of California; debut as Count Almaviva in *Il Barbiere de Siviglia* in Long Beack, Calif.; with Central City Opera Association in Colorado; at the Berkshire Music Festivals; Metropolitan Opera, N.Y. debut (1948), in title role of *Peter Grimes;* sang at the Metropolitan for over ten years.

SULLIVAN, HENRY

b. 1893 Worcester, Massachusetts.
Composer. Wrote "I May Be Wrong (but I Think You're Wonderful") (1929, w. Harry Ruskin); also for *Bow Bells,* revue, Hippodrome Theatre, London (1932) which included the songs—(w. Desmond Carter) "All Roads Lead to Bow Bells," "Mona Lisa," "Love Keeps Out the Rain"; and *Fanfare,* revue, Prince Edward Theatre, London (1932), which included "Martinique," "Song of Heart's Desire," "Dreams That Don't Grow Old" (also w. Desmond Carter).

SULLIVAN, JOE

b. 1906 Chicago, Illinois, d. 1971 San Francisco, California. Jazz pianist. Born O'Sullivan; stride piano player; played with such greats as Bix Biederbecke, Louis Armstrong, Jack Teagarden, Benny Goodman, Russ Columbo, Ozzie Nelson, Bing Crosby, and Red Nichols; died of hepatic failure.

SULLIVAN, JOHN ("LONZO")

b. 1917 Edmonton, Kentucky, d. 1967 Nashville, Tennessee. Singer and comic. Served in World War II; joined his brother Rollin "Oscar" in the team of "Lonzo and Oscar" (1946) over station WAVE, Louisville, Kentucky; joined Grand Ole Opry, Nashville, Tenn. (1947-67); their LP records—*Country Comedy Time, Lonzo and Oscar* (1961), *Country Music Time* (1963).

SULLIVAN, MAXINE

b. 1911 Homestead, Pennsylvania.
Black singer. Born Marietta Williams; sang "Loch Lomond" while in Claude Thornhill's band, which made her famous; also sang in John Kirby's band; became John Kirby's wife.

SULLIVAN, ROLLIN ("OSCAR")

b. 1919 Edmonton, Kentucky.
Singer and comic. Joined with Ken Marvin "Lonzo" to form the team of "Lonzo and Oscar" over station WTJS, Jackson, Tenn. (1939); served in World War II; over WAVE, Louisville, Ky. (1946); his brother, John, replaced Marvin as "Lonzo"; Dave Hooten, of St. Claire, Missouri replaced John (1967).

SUMMERS, ANDREW ROWAN

b. 1912 Abington, Virginia, d. 1968.
Singer and dulcimer player. Graduated the University of Virginia, Charlottesville (LL.B., 1935); practiced law; folk song collector; LP records—*The Unquiet Grave* (1951), *The Faulse Ladye* (*Mary Hamilton*) *and The Lady Gay* (*Barbara Allen*) (1954), *Andrew Rowan Sings* (1957).

SUMMERS, THOMAS OSMOND

b. 1812 Dorsetshire, England, d. 1882.
Hymnist and compiler. Came to America and was admitted to the Baltimore Conference (1835); missionary in Texas (1840-43), Tuscaloosa, Ala. (1844), Charleston, S.C. (1846), later pastor at Vanderbilt University, Nashville, Tenn.; edited the *Methodist Episcopal Songs of Zion* (1851) and *Wesleyan Psalter* (1855); several of his children's hymns appeared in Stevenson's *Hymns for the Church and Home* (1873).

SUMNER, JOHN DAVID ("J.D.")

b. 1924 Lakeland, Florida.
Gospel singer and songwriter. With Sunny South Quartet, WFLA, Tampa, Fla. (1945-49), Sunshine Boys Quartet, WSB, Atlanta, Ga. (1948-54), Blackwood Brothers Quartet, Memphis, Tenn. (1954-65), and Stamps Quartet after 1965; wrote "Inside the Gate," "The Old Country Church," "Keep Me," "Lord Teach Me How to Pray."

SUNNY SOUTH QUARTET *see* J.D. SUMNER

SUNSHINE COMPANY, THE (pop group)

Mary Nance, lead vocals and tambourine; Maury Manseau, lead vocals, guitar, autoharp, and piano; Larry Sims, vocals and guitar; Merel Gregante, vocals, and drums; Douglas "Red" Mark, tenor vocals, lead guitar and violin; Dave Hodgkins, acoustical guitar; group started in California (1967); albums—*Happy Is the Sunshine Company, Sunshine and Shadows, Sunshine Company.*

SUNSHINE BOYS QUARTET *see* J.D. SUMNER

SUPREMES, THE

Black singers. The original trio consisted of Jean Terrell, Diana Ross, and Florence Ballard of Detroit, Michigan; by 1964 they racked up seven gold records in less than two years; first group to have five consecutive records reach the no. 1 spot on the best-selling charts; after Diana Ross and Florence Ballard dropped out, Mary Wilson and Cindy Birdsong of Camden, N.J. joined the group; Jean Terrell was born in Belzoni, Miss.

SURETTE, THOMAS WHITNEY

b. 1862 Concord, Massachusetts, d. there 1941. Organist and teacher. Graduated Harvard (1891); organist in Baltimore; later taught at Bryn Mawr (Pa.) College.

SURFARIS (surf and folk rock)

Pat Connolly, lead vocals and bass; Jim Fuller, lead guitar; Bob Berryhill, rhythm guitar; Ron Wilson, drums; Jim Pash, sax, clarinet, and guitar; started in California (1963); albums—*Wipe Out, It Ain't Me Babe, Surfaris Play Wipe Out.*

SUTHERLAND, JOAN

b. 1926 Australia.
Noted coloratura soprano. Studied in Sydney; debut there in Purcell's *Dido and Aeneas* (1947); studied at the Royal College of Music, London (1951); at Covent Garden, London as Lucia (Donizetti) (1959), which made her famous; Metropolitan Opera debut (1961) as Lucia; secured an international reputation as a singer of classical bel canto operas; married conductor Richard Bonynge; in Bellini's *Norma* at the San Francisco Opera (1972).

SUTRO, ROSE LAURA

b. 1870 Baltimore, Maryland, d. 1957.
Pianist. Studied at Berlin Hochschule; with her sister, Ottilie, gave two-piano concerts.

SUTTON, RALPH EARL

b. 1922 Hamburg, Missouri.
Jazz pianist. Known as a stride-piano player; played with Jack Teagarden; served in army in World War II; played with Joe Schirmer, Jack Teagarden and others; played "Honky-Tonk Train Blues" at the Newport Jazz Festival, New York City (1972).

SVECENSKI, LOUIS

b. 1862 Osijek, Yugoslavia, d. 1926 New York City. Violist and violinist. Studied at the Vienna Conservatory; with Boston Symphony (1885-1903); played viola with Kneisel Quartet (1885-1917); taught at the Institute of Musical Art, New York City; later at the Curtis Institute of Music, Philadelphia.

SWAIN, LEONARD

b. 1821 Concord, Connecticut, d. 1869. Hymnist. Educated at Dartmouth College, Hanover, N.H., and Andover; Congregational minister in Nashua, N.H. (1847) and at the Central Church, Providence, R.I. (1852); his hymns appeared in *The Sabbath Hymn Book* (1858).

SWAN, DOTTIE

b. 1916 Hundred, West Virginia.
Singer and songwriter. Wrote "Blue Eyes" (1955), "Contact," "Crying" (1956), "Red, White and Blue Christmas" (1965), "Aunt Hattie" (1967).

SWAN, JABEZ

b. 1800 Stonington, Connecticut, d. 1884. Hymnist. An elder and evangelist, and preached in New London, Conn.; wrote the lyrics "When for Eternal Worlds I Steer" (tune "Sonnet"—anonymous). Another older tune is credited to S. Arnold about 1790.

SWAN, TIMOTHY

b. 1758 Worcester, Massachusetts, d. 1842 Suffield, Connecticut. Publisher and composer. At sixteen apprenticed to a hatter in Northfield, Mass. and was self-taught in music; then moved to Boston where he was a publisher (1817-21); published *Federal Harmony* (same title by Asahel Benham); moved to Suffield and taught music; composed the tunes "Montague," "Poland," "Quincy," "London," "Spring," and "China" (published in the *New England Harmony,* 1801, "Why Do We Mourn Departed Friends," w. I. Watts).

SWANSON, HOWARD

b. 1909 Atlanta, Georgia.
Black composer. Won Rosenwald fellowship at the Cleveland Institute of Music; studied with Nadia Boulanger in Paris; returned to New York (1940); his songs performed by Marion Anderson in New York; his *Short*

Symphony conducted by Mitropoulos with the New York Philharmonic won the New York Music Critics' Circle award (1952); composed Symphony no. 1 (1945), *Night Music* for small orchestra (1950), *Suite for Cello and Piano* (1949), piano pieces, songs.

SWARTHOUT, DONALD MALCOLM

b. 1884 Pawpaw, Illinois, d. 1962.
Conductor and teacher. Studied in Chicago and at the Leipzig Conservatory; taught at Oxford College, Ohio and Millikin University, Decatur, Ill.; at the University of Kansas, Lawrence after 1923; conductor of Lawrence Choral Union.

SWARTHOUT, GLADYS

b. 1904 Deepwater, Missouri, d. 1969.
Noted contralto. Studied in Kansas City, Mo., and at the Busch Conservatory, Chicago; debut as soloist with Minneapolis (Minn.) Symphony (1923); with Chicago Civic Opera Company (1924-25), Ravinia Opera Company (1927-29), and the Metropolitan Opera, New York City after 1929; married Frank Chapman, baritone; also appeared in films.

SWEATMAN, WILBUR C.

b. 1882 Brunswick, Missouri, d. 1961.
Black clarinetist, bandleader, and actor. Played in W.C. Handy's Mahara's Minstrels before 1910; went to Chicago (1910).

SWEENEY, JOEL WALKER

b. 1810 Appomattox, Virginia, d. there 1860.
Banjoist and inventor. Entertainer and early minstrel showman; credited with having invented the five-string banjo (previous "banjars" from Africa had four strings).

SWEET INSPIRATIONS, THE (love-soul-gospel group)

Cissy Drinkard Houston, Myrna Smith, Sylvia Shemwell, Estelle Brown; started as a group in 1967; previously were gospel singers; albums—*Sweet Inspirations, Cissy Drinkard and the Sweet Inspirations Sing Songs of Faith and Inspiration, What the World Needs Now Is Love, Sweet, Sweet Soul, Sweets for My Sweet.*

SWEET, REGINALD LINDSAY

b. 1885 Yonkers, New York, d. 1950.
Composer. Studied with Noyes, Eisenberger, Koch, and Kaun; taught in Chautauqua, N.Y. and in New York City; composed *Riders to the Sea,* a one-act opera, and chamber music.

SWEET THANGS *see* NAT STUCKEY

SWEETSER, JOSEPH EMERSON

b. 1825 England, d. 1873.
Composer and compiler. Came to America as a young man and was organist at the Church of the Puritans, New York City; with George F. Root compiled what became known as the *Root and Sweetser Collection* of church music (1849); composed the tune "Greenwood" ("Lord, in the Strength of Grace," w. Charles Wesley).

SWEM, E. HEZ.

b. ca. 1860, d. after 1912.
Composer. Educated at DePauw University, Greencastle, Ind., and the Southern Baptist Theological School, Louisville, Ky.; became pastor of the Centennial Baptist Church, Washington, D.C. (1884); thirty-nine of his hymn tunes were included in the supplement of *The Baptist Hymnal* of 1883, and thirty-three of his tunes in *The Gospel Message* (1912).

SWIFT COWBOYS (vocal group) *see* DAVE MC ENERY

SWINGERS, THE (jazz group) *see* WILTON L. FELDER

SWINGSTERS, THE (jazz band) *see* STIX HOOPER

SYDEMAN, WILLIAM

b. 1928 New York City.
Noted composer. Studied at Duke University, Durham, N.C., Mannes College of Music, New York (1955), also with Roger Sessions and others, and Hartt College of Music at the University of Hartford, Conn. (1958, M.A.); lived in Hastings-on-Hudson, N.Y.; taught at Mannes College after 1959; composed *Concerto da Camera* (Pacifica Foundation Award, 1960), Study for Orchestra no. 2 (Boston Symphony under Erich Leinsdorf, 1963), no. 3 (same under Leinsdorf, 1965), *In Memoriam—John F. Kennedy* (same, 1966); *The Lament of Elektra* for contralto, chorus, and chamber orchestra (Tanglewood, 1964), *Music for Viola, Winds and Percussion* (Dartmouth College, Hanover, N.H., 1966).

SYMES, MARTY

b. 1904 Brooklyn, New York, d. 1953 Forest Hills, New York. Lyricist. With lyricist Al Neiberg and composer Jerry Livingston wrote "When It's Darkness on the Delta" (1932), "Sunday Down in Caroline" (1933), "In a Blue and Pensive Mood" (1934), "It's the Talk of the Town" (1947); with composer Joe

Burke—"By the River of Roses" (1944); with composer Isham Jones—"There Is No Greater Love" and "My Best to You."

SYMMES, THOMAS

b. 1678, d. 1725 Bradford, Massachusetts. Writer. Graduated Harvard (1698); minister in Bradford, Mass. (1708-25); wrote *The Reasonableness of Regular Singing* (Boston, 1720, an attack against those Puritans opposed to singing), *Utile Dulci, or a Joco-Serious Dialogue Concerning Regular Singing* (1723).

SYNCOPATED ORCHESTRA, NEW YORK (black band)

Will Marion Cook, leader.

SZELL, GEORGE

b. 1897 Budapest, Hungary, d. 1970. Noted conductor. Conducted opera in Strasbourg, Prague, Darmstadt, Dusseldorf, and Berlin; then came to New York City where he conducted the NBC Symphony Orchestra, the New York Philharmonic, the New Friends of Music Orchestra, the Metropolitan Opera, then the Cleveland Orchestra after 1946.

SZIGETI, JOSEPH

b. 1882 Budapest, Hungary, d. 1973. Concert violinist. Wrote the book *With Strings Attached.*

SZUMOWSKA, ANTOINETTE

b. 1868 Lublin, Poland, d. 1938 Rumson, New Jersey. Pianist. Studied with Paderewski and others; toured Europe and U.S.; married Joseph Adamowski and settled in Boston; member of Adamowski Trio.

TABARY, LOUIS

b. 1773 Provence, France, d. 1831 New Orleans, Louisiana. Impresario. Went to Cap Français, Saint-Domingue, West Indies (1803); then in New Orleans after 1804; director of theater on St. Peter Street (1806); at St. Philip Street theater (1808); produced several operas at both theaters; opened Orleans Street theater (1814), destroyed by fire (1816); alternated with Jean Baptiste Fournier as director of the two theaters at various times.

TALBOTT, HOWARD

b. 1865 Yonkers, New York, d. 1928 Reigate, England. Popular composer. Born Richard Munkittrick; in London, England after 1900; composed the music for the shows *A Chinese Honeymoon* (1901) Strand Theatre, London, which included the songs "I Want to Be a Lidy" and "A Paper Fan," *The Belle of Brittany* (1908) Queen's Theatre, London, songs—(w. Percy Greenbank) "Daffodil Time" and "Two Giddy Goats," *The Blue Moon* (1905) Lyric Theatre, London, songs—(w. Percy Greenbank and Paul Rubens) "Burmah," "Mother Dear."

TALLEY, MARION

b. 1907 Nevada, Missouri.
Noted coloratura soprano. Studied violin and piano; sang in church choir; debut in Kansas City concert; residents contributed funds for her study in New York and Italy; operatic debut as Gilda at the Metropolitan Opera, New York City (1926); later appeared with the Ravinia Opera Company and the Chicago Opera Company; also appeared in films.

TALMA, LOUISE J.

b. 1906 Arachon, France.
Composer. Graduated New York University, M.A. from Columbia University; studied piano with Isidor Philipp and in Paris with Nadia Boulanger; professor of music at Hunter College; wrote *Terre de France* (1925, song cycle), *Three Madrigals* (1929), *La Belle Dame Sans Merci* for baritone (1929), *Five Sonnets from the Portuguese* (1934, song cycle), *Piano Sonata* (1943), *Toccata for Orchestra* (1944), *The Alcestiad* (opera, libretto—Thornton Wilder, premiered in West Germany, 1962).

TANNEBERGER, DAVID

b. 1728 Berthelsdorf, Saxony, Germany, d. 1804 York, Pennsylvania. Organ builder. Came to Bethlehem, Pa. (1749) and assisted Johann G. Klemm in building organs; built organs in Lititz, Pa. after 1762.

TANNER, JAMES GIDEON ("GID")

b. 1885 Thomas Bridge, Georgia, d. 1960 Dacula, Georgia. Singer and bandleader. Born near Monroe, Ga; first records made by Gid and George Riley Puckett in New York City (1924); formed his Skillet Lickers; hit records—"Back Up and Push," "Down Yonder."

TAPPAN, WILLIAM BINGHAM

b. 1794 Beverly, Massachusetts, d. 1849 West Needham, Massachusetts. Hymnist. Apprenticed to a clockmaker when he was twelve years old; in 1815 went to Philadelphia where he made and repaired clocks; became a licensed Congregational minister in 1840, and was an evangelist preacher; died suddenly of cholera; wrote the hymn " 'Tis Midnight, and on Olive's Brow" (tune "Olive's Brow"—W.B. Bradbury); his hymns appeared in Nettleton's *Village Hymns* (1824) and *Lyra Sacra Americana* (1868).

TAPPER, BERTHA FEIRING

b. 1859 Christiania, Norway, d. 1915 Boston, Massachusetts. Pianist and teacher. Graduated the Leipzig Conservatory of Music (1878); came to America (1881); pianist with Kneisel Quartet; taught at the New England Conservatory of Music and also at the New York City Institute of Musical Art.

TARLETON, JOHNNY JAMES RIMBERT (JIMMIE)

b. 1892 Chesterfield County, South Carolina. Singer, banjoist, guitarist, and songwriter. With Tom Darby, singer-guitarist, made several records in Atlanta, Ga. (1927); later joined the Skillet Lickers and other bands; jailed for moonshining (1927); jailed in Atlanta for riding the rails (1932); wrote "Columbus Stockade Blues" and "Birmingham Jail" (1927), "Atlanta Prison Blues" (1932) which were best sellers.

TARRIERS, THE *see* ERIK DARLING

TATUM, ARTHUR (ART)

b. 1910 Toledo, Ohio, d. 1956 Los Angeles, California. Black jazz pianist. Almost blind from birth; became one of the most admired of jazz pianists of all time; named by Sidney Bechet as his favorite pianist.

TAUBMAN, HOWARD

b. 1907 New York City.
Music editor for the *New York Times*; wrote *Opera Front and Back, Music on My Beat.*

TAWS, JOSEPH CHARLES

b. 1763 Aberdeen, Scotland, d. 1833 Philadelphia, Pennsylvania. Composer, publisher, organ and piano maker. Came to New York (1786) and associated with J.J. Astor there in his music store; went to Philadelphia (1788); constructed the first barrel organ in America in St. Peter's P.E. Church, Philadelphia; music publisher there (1813-24); wrote *Air* with variations for the pianoforte (1820), *Bright Star of Evening* (1824), *Fantasie* (1824), *La Fauvette* (waltz, 1820), *Welcome La Fayette* (1824), *My Home* (1825).

TAYLOR, EDDIE

b. 1923 Beneard, Mississippi.
Black guitarist. Accompanist on Jimmy Reed's discs after 1952; also recorded under his own name (1955-57).

TAYLOR, JAMES

b. 1948.
Singer and guitarist. Raised in Chapel Hill, N.C.; attended Milton Academy, outside Boston; entered McLean Hospital, mental home in Belmont, Mass. at age seventeen; joined the Flying Machine, New York City band at eighteen; began using heroin; went to London (1968); recorded "Sweet Baby James" (1969); in mental hospital Austin Riggs in Stockbridge, Mass. (1969); in film *Two-Lane Blacktop* (1971); albums—*Sweet Baby James, Mud Slide Slim;* won Grammy Award (1972) as best pop male vocalist for "You've Got a Friend" (by Carole King); married singer Carly Simon (1972).

TAYLOR, JOE CARL

b. 1921 Portsmouth, Ohio.
Singer and songwriter. Attended high school in Fort Wayne, Indiana; known as "The Cowboy Auctioneer"; wrote "He's a Cowboy Auctioneer" (1949), "My Gal's a Square Dance Caller," "My Sweet Eleanor," "The Crickhopper Song."

TAYLOR, JOHNNIE

b. 1937 Crawfordsville, West Memphis, Arkansas. Black singer. Moved to Cleveland (1952); sang with the Five Echoes in Chicago; traveled with Mahalia Jackson and the Soul Stirrers, gospel group; recorded "Wanted: One Soul Singer" (1960); made a hit with "Who's Making Love?" (1969); albums—*Rare Stamps, Raw Blues, Soul Full of Blues, Johnnie Taylor—Philosophy Continues, Wanted, One Soul Singer.*

TAYLOR, JOSEPH DEEMS

b. 1885 New York City, d. there 1966.
Composer. Educated at New York University; music critic for the *New York World* (1921-25), then editor of *Musical America*, a journal; known for his *Through the Looking Glass* suite for orchestra, *The King's Henchman* (opera, 1927, libretto—Edna St. Vincent Millay) *Peter Ibbetson* (opera, 1930, book—Du Maurier), and *Elegy* for orchestra (1946).

TAYLOR, KATE

b. 1949.
Singer and pianist. Sister of James Taylor, singer and guitarist; brother Alex Taylor (b. 1947), singer and cellist; brother Livingston Taylor (b. 1950), singer and violinist, attended Quaker School in Westtown, Pa.; attended Cambridge School in Weston, Mass.; album—*Sister Kate* (1971).

TAYLOR, RAYNOR

b. 1747 England, d. 1825 Philadelphia, Pennsylvania. Organist and composer. Taught in England (Alexander Reinagle was his pupil); came to America (1792); organist in Baltimore and Annapolis, Md.; organist at St. Peter's Church in Philadelphia after 1793; wrote *An Anthem for Two Voices* (1793), *The Bells* for piano, songs—"The Waving Willow" (1800), "Cupid and the Shepherd," "The Wounded Soldier"; some of his tunes were included in *The Churchman's Choral Companion to His Prayer Book* (1809).

TAYLOR, TELL

b. 1876 Vanlue, Ohio, d. 1937 Chicago, Illinois. Composer. Resided near Findlay,

Ohio; wrote "Down by the Old Mill Stream" (1910); with Ole Olson wrote lyrics for "You're in the Army Now" (1917, m. Isham Jones).

TAYLOR, VIRGIL CORYDON

b. 1817 Barkhamstead, Connecticut, d. 1891 Des Moines, Iowa. Composer. Lived for awhile in Hartford, Conn., then moved to Poughkeepsie, N.Y. (1851) where he was organist of the Central Baptist Church, then organist in Brooklyn (1861), then Niagara Falls, N.Y., and finally Des Moines where he served St. Paul's Church; composed the tune "Louvan" (1846, "There's Nothing Bright Above, Below," w. Thomas Moore), "God Whom We Fear" (w. S.F. Smith, 1893), and "Lord of All Being, Throned Afar" (w. O.W. Holmes).

TAYLOR, WILLIAM (BILLY)

b. 1906 Washington, D.C.
Black double bass player. Tuba player who became a great bass player, also jazz pianist; played in Eddie Condon's group when jazz made its first TV appearance in 1942 which featured Max Kaminsky, Benny Morton, Pee Wee Russell, Joe Sullivan, and Zutty Singleton.

TAYLOR, WILLIAM, JR. (BILLY)

b. 1921 Greenville, North Carolina.
Black pianist. Graduated Virginia State College (1942); played with Dizzy Gillespie, Eddie South, Stuff Smith and others; later formed his own trio.

TCHEREPNIN, ALEXANDER

b. 1899 St. Petersburg, Russia.
Noted composer. Son of Nicholas Tcherepnin, conductor and composer; studied at the St. Petersburg Conservatory (1917), Tiflis Conservatory, Caucasus, and the Paris Conservatory with Isidor Philipp and others; piano recital in London (1922), and Monte Carlo (1923); toured U.S. (1927 and 1934), Orient (1934-37), then Paris; taught at De Paul University, Chicago (1949-64); became U.S. citizen (1958); composed *Ajanta Frescoes* (ballet, Covent Garden, London, 1923, for Anna Pavlova), *Rapsodie Georgienne* for cello and orchestra (Bordeaux, 1924, Andre Hekking, soloist), second piano concerto (Paris, 1924), first symphony (Paris, 1927), *Ol-Ol* (opera, Weimar, 1928), *The Farmer and the Fairy* (Aspen Festival, Colorado, 1952), fourth symphony (Boston Symphony, 1958, won Glinka Prize).

TEAGARDEN, CHARLES

b. 1913 Vernon, Texas.
Trumpeter. Brother of Jack Teagarden; played in his brother's band; also with Harry James, Jimmy Dorsey and others.

TEAGARDEN, WELDON J. ("JACK")

b. 1905 Vernon, Texas, d. 1964 New Orleans, Louisiana. Trombonist and bandleader. Starred in Ben Pollack's band (1929); later with Paul Whiteman; formed his own band (1939); at the Roseland Ballroom, New York City; Charlie Spivak, his partner, played the lead trumpet; later his brother, Charlie Teagarden, and Jimmy McPartland, both jazz trumpeters, joined the band; group disbanded in 1943; he made hundreds of famous recordings with outstanding jazz musicians such as Louis Armstrong and Red Nichols; found dead of a heart attack in his New Orleans hotel room.

TEASDALE, SARA

b. 1884 St. Louis, Missouri, d. 1933 New York City. Poetess and lyricist. Wrote "I Heard a Cry" (m. William Arms Fisher).

TEEN AGERS (black vocal group)

Frankie Lymon, lead singer; Joe Negroni, baritone; Herman Santiago, tenor; Jimmy Merchant, tenor; Sherman Garnes, bass; organized in Harlem, New York City; recorded (1956) six songs which made the charts; appeared in the film *Rock, Rock, Rock*.

TELVA, MARION

b. 1897 St. Louis, Missouri, d. 1965.
Contralto. Studied in New York City; debut there (1925) at the Metropolitan Opera as Dame Quickly in *Falstaff*; later as Adalgisa in *Norma*; as Mrs. Deane in Deems Taylor's *Peter Ibbetson* (1931); with the Metropolitan Opera (1925-31).

TEMPLE, SHIRLEY

b. 1928 Santa Monica, California.
Singer and child actress. Made her debut in films at age three in *Stand Up and Cheer; Little Miss Marker* (1934), *Dimples* (1936), *Heidi* (1937), *Rebecca of Sunnybrook Farm* (1938).

TEMPLETON, ALEC

b. 1910 Cardiff, Wales, d. 1963 Greenwich, Connecticut. Noted pianist and composer. Blind from birth; played piano from age two; wrote his first composition *Slow Movement* at age four; studied at the Royal College of Music, London; pianist in British Isles (1927-

35); came to America (1935) and became a U.S. citizen (1941); composed *Bach Goes to Town.*

TEMPO CLUB ORCHESTRA (black band) *see* JAMES R. EUROPE

TEMPTATIONS (soul group)

Mel Franklin, Otis Williams, Eddie Kendricks, Paul Williams, Dennis Edwards; David Ruffin, former member; recorded with Motown Corp., Detroit (1962); played at the Copacabana, New York (1968); albums—*Cloud Nine, Gettin' Ready, Meet the Temptations, On Broadway, Puzzle People, Diana Ross and the Supremes Join the Temptations, TCB, Temptations' Greatest Hits, In a Mellow Mood, Live, Live at the Copacabana, Sing Smokey, Wish It Would Rain, Temptin' Temptations, Together, With a Lot of Soul.*

"TENNESSEE BARN DANCE" *see* RICHARD L. BLANCHARD

TENNESSEE MOUNTAIN BOYS, THE

Featured Johnny Wright.

TENNESSEE STUDENTS (black orchestra) *see* NASHVILLE STUDENTS

TENNESSEE THREE, JOHNNY CASH'S (instrumental group)

Marshall Grant, Luther Perkins, and W.S. Holland.

TERRELL, MARY E. CHURCH

b. 1863 Memphis, Tennessee, d. 1954.
Black composer. Civil rights leader; member of the School Board in Washington, D.C. for a number of years; wife of Judge Robert H. Terrell; she composed one tune included in the *African Methodist Episcopal Hymnal* compiled by J. T. Layton.

TERRY, AL

b. 1922 Kaplan, Louisiana.
Singer and songwriter. Born Allison Joseph Theriot; leader of The Southerners (1946-52); Al Terry and Band after 1954; wrote "Hurricane Party," "Walking and Crying with the Blues," "A Dime's Worth a Lot of Teardrops," "Today's Another Day Like Yesterday."

TERRY, CLARK

b. 1920 St. Louis, Missouri.
Black trumpeter. Played in Duke Ellington's band; albums—*CT Meets Monk, Gingerbread Men, Happy Horns of Clark Terry, It's What's Happenin', Mumbles, Power of Positive Swinging, Soul Duo* (with Shirley Scott), *Spanish Rice, Tijuana Jazz, Together* (with Coleman Hawkins), *Tonight*; played at Newport Jazz Festival, New York City (1972).

TERRY, GORDON

b. 1931 Decatur, Alabama.
Singer and songwriter. Wrote "You'll Regret" (1954), "Keep Right on Talking," "I Lost Her" (1957); album—*Gordon Terry Way.*

TERRY, "SONNY"

b. 1911 near Durham, North Carolina.
Black singer and harmonica player. Born Saunders Teddell; blinded in an accident when young; toured with Leadbelly in 1930s, with Alec Stewart and Pete Seeger in the '40s; with Brownie McGee as Terry and McGee during the '50s; with Harry Belafonte during '60s; Terry and McGee's albums—*Back Country Blues, Best of Terry and McGee, Brownie and Sonny, Long Way from Home, Sonny and Brownie at Sugar Hill, Where the Blues Begin.*

TESCHEMACHER, FRANK

b. 1906 Kansas City, Missouri, d. 1932 Chicago, Illinois. Clarinetist. Started in a small band with Jimmy MacPartland, Bud Freeman, and Jim Lannigan.

TETRAZZINI, LUISA

b. 1871 Florence, Italy, d. 1940 Milan, Italy. Noted soprano. Studied under her sister, soprano Eva Tetrazzini (1862-1938); then at the Istituto Musicale in Florence with Contrucci and Ceccherini; debut in Florence (1890) as Inez in *L'Africaine;* then went to Argentina for several years and became a leading singer there in operettas and grand opera; with the Mexican Opera under Giorgio Polacco (1905); American debut in San Francisco at the Tivoli Theatre (1906); at Covent Garden, London (1907) as Violetta; New York debut as Violetta at the Manhattan Opera House (1908); became a sensational success; with the Manhattan Opera (1908-10); later at the Metropolitan Opera and the Chicago Opera; last appearance at the Paramount Theater in New York (1931).

TEXANS, THE *see* TED DAFFAN

TEXAS LONGHORNS, BILLIE WALKER'S *see* DOC WILLIAMS

TEXAS MEDLEY QUARTETTE (black vocal group)

Double quartet or octet organized by Scott Joplin in Sedalia, Missouri (1895); his brothers, Will Joplin (tenor) and Robert Joplin (baritone); John Williams, baritone; Leonard Williams, tenor; Emmett Cook (with the Queen City Concert Band) tenor; Richard Smith, bass; Frank Bledsoe, bass.

TEXAS PLAYBOYS, THE *see* BOB WILLS

TEXAS SLIM pseud. of JOHN LEE HOOKER

TEXAS SONS *see* JIMMY DOLLAR, JOHNNY DOLLAR

TEXAS TROUBADOURS

Featured Ernest Tubb.

THARPE, SISTER ROSETTA

b. 1921 Cotton Plant, Arkansas, d. 1973.
Black singer. Born Rosetta Nubin; sang in Cab Calloway's band; also with Lucky Millinder; recorded with Marie Knight and also solo; albums—*Precious Memories, Sister Rosetta Tharpe.*

THAYER, WHITNEY EUGENE

b. 1838 Mendon, Massachusetts, d. 1889 Burlington, Vermont. Organist, editor and composer.

THAYER, WILLIAM ARMOUR

b. 1874 Brooklyn, New York, d. there 1933. Organist, conductor, and composer. Wrote "My Laddie" (Adelphia field song).

THEBOM, BLANCHE

b. 1919 Monessen, Pennsylvania.
Mezzo-soprano. Operatic debut as Fricka in *Die Walkure* (1944); as Baba the Turk in Stravinsky's *The Rake's Progress* at the Metropolitan Opera (1953); with the Metropolitan Opera (1944-68); became director of the Civic Opera in Atlanta, Georgia (1968).

THIBAULT, CHARLES

b. ca. 1794 France, d. 1853.
Pianist and composer. Studied at the Paris Conservatory; won the Grand Prix; composed *The Greek March of Liberty* (1824).

THOBURN, HELEN

b. 1885 Union City, Pennsylvania, d. 1932 New York City. Hymnist. Educated at Leland Stanford University, Palo Alto, Calif.; spent eight years in China for the YMCA; with Elizabeth Wilson wrote the hymn "Father of Lights, in Whom There Is No Shadow" (tune "Welwyn"—Alfred Scott-Gatty).

THOMAS, CARLA

b. 1942 Memphis, Tennessee.
Black singer. Daughter of Rufus Thomas, singer; started on radio station WDIA with the Teen Town Singers; graduated Tennessee A&I State University, Nashville; wrote and recorded "Gee Whiz!" ("Look at His Eyes," 1961); recorded "The King and Queen" with Otis Redding; became known as the "Queen of Memphis Sound"; albums—*Best of Carla Thomas, Comfort Me, Carla, Gee Whiz, King and Queen, Queen Alone.*

THOMAS, CHRISTIAN FRIEDRICH THEODORE

b. 1835 Esens, Hanover, Germany, d. 1905 Chicago, Illinois. Famous conductor. Came to America (1845); toured the south (1851) as violin soloist; conducted concerts at Dodworth's Hall (1855-69); organized his own orchestra (1866) in New York City; concerts in Central Park, Irving Hall, and Steinway Hall after 1872; conductor at Centennial Exhibition in Philadelphia (1876) and conducted orchestra of 200 instruments and 1,000 voices; founded the Chicago Symphony Orchestra (1891). (*See also* William Mason)

THOMAS, DANNY

b. 1914 Deerfield, Michigan.
Singer and comedian. Popular entertainer on TV shows; with Frank Sinatra and Ethel Ennis sang Gladys Shelley's two big hits, "Show's on Me Tonight" and "Does It Hurt to Love?" at the National Governors' banquet (1972).

THOMAS, ISAIAH

b. 1749 Boston, Massachusetts, d. 1831 Worcester, Massachusetts. Publisher and compiler. With E.T. Andrews in firm of Thomas and Andrews; published *The Worcester Collection of Sacred Harmony* (1786), Abraham Wood's *Divine Songs* (1789), Samuel Holyoke's *Harmonia Americana* (1791), Oliver Holden's *American Harmony* (1792); compiled and published *Sacred Dirges, Hymns and Anthems* (1800, comprised of twenty-eight pages); founder of American Antiquarian Society.

THOMAS, JESS

b. 1927 Hot Springs, South Dakota.
Tenor. Graduated the University of Nebraska, Lincoln; master's degree from Stanford University, Palo Alto, Calif.; school counselor for six years, then studied singing with Otto Schulmann; sang at Baden State Opera in Karlsruhe, Germany; debut at the

Metropolitan Opera, New York City (1962); role of Caesar in *Antony and Cleopatra* at the Met (1966); with Birgit Nilsson in *Tristan and Isolde* at the Met (1971) with Erich Leinsdorf conducting.

THOMAS, JOHN CHARLES

b. 1892 Meyersdale, Pennsylvania, d. 1960. Noted baritone. Studied medicine, but won scholarship at Peabody Conservatory, Baltimore; debut (1912); sang in operettas in New York City; opera debut in *Aïda* in Washington, D.C. (1925); then with La Monnaie Opera, Brussels; Philadelphia Grand Opera after 1925; Chicago Opera (1930); Metropolitan Opera, New York City after 1933; later with San Francisco and Los Angeles opera companies.

THOMAS, JOHN R.

b. 1829 Newport, South Wales, d. 1896 New York City. Baritone and composer. Came to America with Sequin English Opera Company; later sang with Bryant's Minstrels; settled in New York City; composed the songs "Annie of the Vale" (1852), "Goodby, Farewell" (1853), "Eileen Alanna," "Beautiful Isle of the Sea," "In Heavenly Love Abiding," " 'Tis but a Faded Flower" (1860, w. Ellen C. Howarth), "Down by the Riverside I Stray" (1861, w. G.P. Morris), "The Patriot Flag" (1861, w. H.M. Addey), "Breathe It Softly to My Loved Ones" (w. W.D. Smith, Jr.), "Oh Let Me Shed One Silent Tear" (w. F.H. Norton); with lyrics by George Cooper—"Rose of Killarney" (1876), "Linger Not, Darling" (1863), "Our Noble Chief Has Passed Away" (1865, on the death of President Lincoln), "Must We Then Meet as Strangers" (1875), "Golden Hours" (1875).

THOMAS JUBILEE SINGERS (black group) *see* NOBLE SISSLE

THOMAS, MICHAEL TILSON

b. 1945 Hollywood, California.
Conductor. His grandparents, Boris and Bessie Thomashafsky, helped found the Yiddish Theater, New York City; spent summers of 1966-67 at Bayreuth as a coach at the Wagnerian festivals; conducted *Planh* (by Stanley Silverman) and *Elephant Steps* (multimedia opera by Silverman) in Los Angeles (1968); associate conductor of the Boston Symphony Orchestra (1969); musical director of Buffalo (N.Y.) orchestra (1971).

THOMAS, RUFUS

b. 1917.
Black singer. Disc jockey on station WDIA, Memphis, Tenn.; recorded " 'Cause I Love You" (1960, with his daughter Carla), "The Dog," "Can Your Dog Do the Monkey?," "Walkin' the Dog"; became the creator of the dance known as "the Dog."

THOMPSON, ELI ("LUCKY")

b. 1924 Detroit, Michigan.
Black jazz saxophonist. Played in Billy Eckstine's band; also with Count Basie and Lionel Hampton.

THOMPSON, H. S.

b. ca. 1825, d. after 1865.
Popular composer and lyricist. Wrote the original words and music "Clementine" (1863, "Down the river lived a maiden"); revised words were written by Percy Montrose (1884, "In a cavern, in a canyon"); wrote the lyrics "Homeward Bound" (m. M. Arne, same title G.F. Webb (1858), J.W. Dadmun, and C.S. Harrington); wrote the words and music "Lilly Dale" (1852), "Cousin Jedediah," "Ida Lee," "Annie Lisle" (1857), "Keep This Bible Near Your Heart" (1861), "The Soldier Lay on the Tented Field" (1862), "Kiss Me Goodnight Mother" (1862), "Kitty Alone," "Marion Lee," "Down by the River" (1863), "My Own Lover Home Again" (1863), "A Nation Mourns Her Chief" (1865, on the death of President Lincoln); "Annie Lisle" is the tune for "Far Above Cayuga's Waters," the alma mater of Cornell University, Ithaca, N.Y., and seven other universities.

THOMPSON, HENRY WILLIAM (HANK)

b. 1925 Waco, Texas.
Singer, bandleader, and songwriter. Had his own radio show on station WACO, Waco, at age seventeen; served in the navy in the Pacific in World War II; attended Princeton University; organized the Brazos Valley Boys (1947); wrote "Whoa Sailor!" and "Swing Wide Your Gate of Love" (1946), "A Lonely Heart Knows," "Humpty Dumpty Heart" and "Today" (1948), "Green Light" (1949), "Waiting in the Lobby of Your Heart" (1952, with Billy Gray), "Yesterday's Girl" (with Gray), "Rub-A-Dub-Dub" (1953), "Wildwood Flower" (1955).

THOMPSON, OSCAR

b. 1887, d. 1945 New York City.
Critic. With *New York Post* (1927-34); *New York Sun* after 1936; wrote *How to Listen to Music, Practical Music Criticism* and *Debussy.*

THOMPSON, RANDALL

b. 1899 New York City.
Composer. Graduated Harvard and studied at the American Academy at Rome (1922-25); taught at Wellesley College, the University of California, the University of Virginia, at Princeton, and Harvard, then became a director at the Curtis Institute; known for his Symphony no. 1 (1931), *The Peaceable Kingdom* for mixed chorus (1936), *Alleluia* (1940), *The Testament of Freedom* (1942), and Symphony no. 3 in A Minor (1948).

THOMPSON, SUE

b. 1926 Nevada, Missouri.
Singer and guitarist. Born Eva Sue McKee; attended high school in San Jose, California; appeared on TV in San Francisco; later appeared in Las Vegas night clubs; albums—*Country Side of Hugh Thompson, Golden Hits, Paper Tiger, This Is Sue Thompson, Sue Thompson—with Strings Attached.*

THOMPSON, VAN DENMAN

b. 1890 Potter Place, town of Andover, New Hampshire. Composer. Educated at Colby Academy, Harvard University, and the New England Conservatory of Music, Boston; taught at Woodland College, Jonesboro, Arkansas (1910) then in 1911 went to De Pauw University, Greencastle, Indiana; composed the oratorio *The Evangel of the New World* for the Methodist Sesqui-Centennial, Baltimore (1934), the tunes "Longden" for "Alleluia! Alleluia! Hearts to Heaven and Voices Raise" (w. C. Wordsworth and other tunes), and "Home" ("Bless the Four Corners of This House," Arthur Guiterman, 1916).

THOMPSON, WILL L.

b. 1847 Liverpool, Ohio, d. 1909 New York City. Popular composer. Educated at Mount Union College, Alliance, Ohio, and the Boston Conservatory of Music; wrote the words and music "Softly and Tenderly" (ca. 1900), "Gathering Shells from the Seashore" (1875), "Come Where the Lilies Bloom" (1878), "Golden Years Are Passing By" (1879), "I Am King" (1880), "Under the Moonlight Sky" (1881), "Goodnight Gentle Folks" (1882), "Moonlight Will Come Again" (1883), "If All Our Hearts Were Good and True" (1885), and "Razzle Dazzle" (1888). When Dwight L. Moody, the evangelist, lay very ill, visitors were forbidden. Thompson called to inquire about Moody, and hearing that Thompson was there, Moody asked the doctors to let him in. When Thompson greeted him, Moody said, "Will, I would rather have written 'Softly and Tenderly, Jesus Is Calling' than anything I have been able to do in my whole lifetime." At the memorial services for the Rev. Dr. Martin Luther King in Atlanta, Ga., on April 8, 1968, the Ebenezer Baptist Church choir sang "Softly and Tenderly."

THOMS, WILLIAM M.

b. 1850 New York City, d. 1913.
Publisher, editor, and critic. Studied singing, piano, and violin; when only seventeen became publisher of *American Art Journal*; published *The World of Art* (1877-78) which included sketches and portraits of George F. Bristow, Anton Rubinstein, Emma Albani, et. al.

THOMSON, MARY ANN

b. 1834 London, England, d. 1923 Philadelphia, Pennsylvania. Hymnist. Wife of John Thomson, librarian of the Free Library of Philadelphia; wrote the lyrics "O Zion, Haste, Thy Mission High Fulfilling" (1868, tune "Tidings" or "Angelic Songs"—James Walch, 1876).

THOMSON, VIRGIL GARNETT

b. 1896 Kansas City, Missouri.
Famous composer. Graduated Harvard University and studied in Paris with Nadia Boulanger; music critic of the *New York Herald-Tribune* (1940-54); known for his *Four Saints in Three Acts,* (opera, 1928, w. Gertrude Stein), *The Mother of Us All* (opera, 1947), *Louisiana Story* suite for orchestra (1948).

THORNHILL, CLAUDE

b. 1908 Terre Haute, Indiana, d. 1965 Caldwell, New Jersey. Pianist, arranger, and bandleader. Studied at the Cincinnati Conservatory and the Curtis Institute in Philadelphia; arranger and pianist for Andre Kostelanetz; arranged "Loch Lomond" which made Maxine Sullivan famous; formed his own band (1939); played at Glen Island Casino (1941); served in the navy (1942-45); formed a new band (1946); disbanded (1948); died of a heart attack.

THORNTON, JAMES

b. 1861 Liverpool, England, d. 1938 New York City. Popular composer. Partner in the vaudeville team with Charlie Lawlor; his wife, Bonnie Thornton (Lizzie Cox), was a singer who plugged his songs; he was an alcoholic, and Bonnie would be at the stage door every payday to collect his pay so Jim couldn't squander the money on liquor; wrote the words and music "When You Were Sweet Sixteen" (1898) and also the lyrics and Ward the music "The Irish Jubilee" and "Upper Ten and Lower Five"; also "My Sweetheart's the Man in the Moon" (1892), "Maggie Mooney" (1894), "Don't Give Up the Old Love for the New" (1896), "On the Benches in the Park" (1896), "It Don't Seem Like the Same Old Smile" (1896), "There's a Little Star Shining for You" (1897).

THREE DOG NIGHT (rock group)

Jimmy Greenspoon, keyboards; Joe Schermie, bass; Floyd Sneed, drums and percussion; Michael Allsup, vocals; Danny Hutton, vocals; Chuck Negron, vocals; Cory Wells, vocals; albums—*Seven Separate Fools, Naturally, Golden Bisquits, Harmony.* (*See* also Randy Newman)

THREE KEYS, THE (vocal trio)

Featured George Tunnell.

THREE SOUNDS, THE (jazz group) *see* GENE HARRIS

THUNDER, HENRY GORDON, JR.

b. 1865 Philadelphia, Pennsylvania, d. 1958. Organist and conductor. Son of Henry Gordon, Sr.; organized the Thunder Orchestra (1896) which was merged into the Philadelphia Orchestra (1899); conducted the Philadelphia Choral Society after 1897 into the 1940s; also organist at Tioga Methodist Church; organist at the Sesqui-Centennial Exhibition in Philadelphia (1926).

THUNDER, HENRY GORDON, SR.

b. 1832 Ireland, d. 1881 Philadelphia, Pennsylvania. Organist. Organist at St. Augustine's Church, Philadelphia (1855-81), except for five years (ca. 1871-76) organist at St. Stephen's Church, New York City; official organist at the Centennial Exhibition in Philadelphia (1876).

THURSBY, EMMA CECILIA

b. 1857 Brooklyn, New York, d. there 1931. Soprano. Studied in Brooklyn, Boston, and Milan; concert debut at Plymouth Church, Brooklyn (1875); famous concert singer; toured Europe and America; sang with Gilmore (1875).

TIBBETT, LAWRENCE

b. 1896 Bakersfield, California, d. 1960. Famous baritone. Studied with Frank La Forge and others; debut in Los Angeles (1917); Hollywood Bowl (1923); debut with the Metropolitan Opera, New York City (1923); also sang at Covent Garden, London (1937) and in other European cities.

TIERNEY, HARRY AUSTIN

b. 1890 Perth Amboy, New Jersey, d. 1965 New York City. Popular composer. Studied at the Virgil Conservatory of Music, New York City, and became a concert pianist; wrote "M-i-s-s-i-s-s-i-p-p-i" (w. Bert Hanlon and Benny Ryan, introduced by Frances White in the *Ziegfeld Follies*, 1916),"It's a Cute Little Way of My Own" (w. Alfred Bryan, sung by Anna Held in *Follow Me*, 1917); went to work for Jerome Remick, music publisher; wrote the score for *Irene* (1919, in which "Alice Blue Gown" was sung by Edith Day), *Up She Goes* (1922, play—Frank Craven), *Kid Boots* (1923, lyrics—Joseph McCarthy, starring Eddie Cantor), *Rio Rita* (1927, w. McCarthy); wrote the score for the ballet *Prelude to a Holiday in Hong Kong.*

TIETJEN, ANDREW

b. 1911 New York City, d. there 1953. Organist. Educated at Columbia University; organist-choirmaster at St. Thomas' Chapel, All Angels (1937-41), and Chapel of the Intercession (1941-43); served in the U.S. Army during World War II; organist-choirmaster at Trinity Church until 1953; directed the Trinity Choir of St. Paul's Chapel over CBS radio station.

TILL, GEORGE WILLIAM

b. 1866 Philadelphia, Pennsylvania, d. 1947. Organ builder. Worked for Odell Organ Company in New York City (1886-1900), Haskell Company in Philadelphia (1900-01), and with Odell (1901-05); with John Wanamaker Company, Philadelphia (1905-38) in charge of organ building and repairs; invented adjustable mutation stops, coupling expression pedals, divisional coloring of stops, humidified wind supply, master tremolo and adjustable tremolo, piano mechanism with organ case, with automatic sostenuto for all pedal keys.

TILL, JAKOB

b. 1713 Moravia (Czechoslovakia), d. 1783. Hymnist. Moravian minister in Pennsylvania (1771); his hymns appeared in Moravian hymnals.

TILLETT, WILBUR FISK

b. 1854 Henderson, North Carolina, d. 1936 Nashville, Tennessee. Hymnist. Educated at Randolph-Macon College, Ashland, Virginia, Princeton, and Princeton Theological Seminary; preached in Danville, Va. (1880-82), then went to Vanderbilt University where he taught theology; wrote the hymn "O Son of God Incarnate" (1921, tune "Incarnation"—

Alfred Wooler); assisted in compiling *The Methodist Hymnal* (1935).

TILLIS, FREDERICK CHARLES

b. 1930 Galveston, Texas.
Black composer. Graduated the State University of Iowa, Ames; earned Ph.D.; directed air force band; taught at Wiley College, Texas; Grambling College, La.; Kentucky State College, Frankfort after 1967; works—*Three Plus One* (1969, for violin, guitar, clarinet, and tape recorder), *Freedom: Memorial to Martin Luther King, Jr.*, for chorus (1968), also band music.

TILLIS, MEL

b. 1932 Pahokee, Florida.
Popular composer. Wrote "Honky Tonk Song" (1957, with B. Peddy and recorded by Webb Pierce), "I'm Tired" (1957, Webb Pierce record), "A Thousand Miles Ago" (1959, Pierce), "Ten Thousand Days" (1959, with Carl Smith), "One More Time" (recorded by Ray Price), "Heart Over Mind" (1961, Price record); also recorded by Webb Pierce in 1962—"Crazy Wild Desire" and "Take Time" (with Marijohn Wilkins); "The Violet and the Rose" (1962, with B. Ange and J. Reinfeld), "Detroit City" (1963, recorded by Bobby Bare).

TILLMAN, FLOYD

b. 1914 Ryan, Oklahoma.
Popular composer and singer. Raised in Post, Texas; joined the Blue Ridge Playboys; wrote "It Makes No Difference Now," "I Love You So Much It Hurts" (1948), "I'll Never Slip Around Again" (1949, recorded by Margaret Whiting and Jimmy Wakely), "Slipping Around with Joe Blow" (1950, Franklin-Messner recording), "Each Night at Nine," "I Gotta Have My Baby Back."

TIM, TINY

b. ca. 1930 New York City.
Singer. Born Herbert B. Khaury; sang in Greenwich Village, New York City spots (1962); sang duets in soprano as well as baritone; imitated Jeanette MacDonald and Nelson Eddy; first recorded in 1968; albums—*God Bless Tiny Tim, Tiny Tim's Second Album, For All My Little Friends, What the World Needs Now, You Are What You Eat* (soundtrack); married Vicky Budinger on the Johnny Carson TV show (1969); played at the Magic Mountain, Valencia, Calif. (1972).

TIMBERLINERS *see* HYLO BROWN

T.I.M.E., THE (rock group)

Larry Byrom, guitar; Bill Richardson, guitar; Pat Couchois, drums; Richard Tepp, bass; Steve Rumph and Nick St. Nicholas, former members; appeared at the Electric Circus, New York City (1968); albums—*T.I.M.E., Smooth Ball.*

TIMM, HENRY CHRISTIAN

b. 1811 Hamburg, Germany, d. 1892 Hoboken, New Jersey. Manager. With Ureli Corelli Hill and William Scharfenberg, founded the New York Philharmonic Society (1842); president of the society (1848-63).

TINY ALICE (rock group)

Seven-person Cleveland based group; album—*Tiny Alice.*

TIO, LORENZO, JR.

b. 1880, d. 1934.
Black clarinetist. Son of Lorenzo Tio, Sr.; resided in New Orleans.

TIO, LORENZO, SR.

b. ca. 1865 Mexico, d. 1920.
Black clarinetist. Graduated Mexican Conservatory, Mexico City; came to New Orleans before 1885 with his brother, Louis Tio; played in the Excelsior Band and the Magnolia Band in New Orleans; played at the New Orleans Exposition (1885); played in Jelly Roll Morton's band after 1917.

TIO, LOUIS

b. 1863 Mexico, d. 1927.
Black musician. Came to New Orleans before 1885 with his brother, Lorenzo Tio, Sr.

TIOMKIN, DIMITRI

b. 1899 St. Petersburg, Russia.
Popular composer. Studied at the St. Petersburg Conservatory and also in Berlin; came to Hollywood (1930) to write musicals for MGM; served in the Signal Corps during World War II as a musical director; wrote the scores for over 120 screen plays and won the Motion Picture Academy Award for *High Noon* (1952), *The High and the Mighty* (1954), *The Old Man and the Sea* (1958); wrote "Do Not Forsake Me" (1952, w. Ned Washington), "Friendly Persuasion" (1956, w. Paul Francis Webster), "The Ballad of the Alamo," "Strange Are the Ways of Love" (1960), and "Green Leaves of Summer" (1961).

TIPTON, CARL B.

b. 1925 Gate City, Virginia.
Singer and songwriter. Leader of the "Carl Tipton Show," WGNS, Murfreesboro, Tenn.

after 1946; wrote "Going Home," "Years Have Gone By," "Pray, Pray, Pray," "Beneath the Clay," "Won't You Kneel and Pray."

TITCOMB, H. EVERETT

b. 1884 Amesbury, Massachusetts.
Composer. Organist in Episcopal churches in Amesbury, Mass., Auburndale, and Andover, Mass., then Boston; taught at the New England Conservatory and the Boston University School of Music; composed *Victory Te Deum*; wrote *A Choirmaster's Notebook on Anglican Services and Liturgical Music.*

TIZOL, JUAN

b. 1900 San Juan, Puerto Rico.
Jazz trombonist and composer. Played with Duke Ellington (1929-44), with Harry James (1944-51), and with Ellington (1951-53); composed *Bakiff*, and with Duke Ellington—*Caravan, Pyramid, Conga brava, Perdido* (w. added by Harry Lenk and Ervin Drake, 1942).

TOBANI, THEODORE MOSES

b. 1855 Hamburg, Germany, d. 1933 Jackson Heights, New York. Composer. Brought to America as a boy; wrote the piano piece *Hearts and Flowers* (1893), long used in theaters for pathos.

TOBIAS, CHARLES

b. 1898 New York City, d. 1970.
Songwriter. Charles, Harry, and Henry Tobias were sons of a tailor of Worcester, Mass.; he wrote "Somebody Loves You" (1932, with Peter de Rose), "It's the Gipsy in Me" (1936, Cliff Friend), "Rose O'Day" (1942, Al Lewis), "Don't Sit Under the Apple Tree" (1942, Sammy Stept and Lew Brown), "Don't Sweetheart Me" (1944, Cliff Friend), "No Can Do" (1945, Nat Simon,) "The Old Lamplighter" (1949, Nat Simon), "A Million Miles Away" (1949, Nat Simon).

TOBIAS, HARRY

b. 1895 New York City.
Songwriter. Brother of Charles and Henry Tobias; wrote "Take Me to My Alabam'," "That Girl of Mine" (both Will Dillon, 1916); "Sweet and Lovely" (1931, with Gus Arnheim and Jules Lemare), "The Call of the Rockies" (1934, with Neil Moret), "No Regrets" (1936, with Roy Ingraham), "Sail Along Silv'ry Moon" (1937, with Percy Wenrich), "Without Your Love" (1950, with his brother Henry and Dave Oppenheim).

TOBIAS, HENRY

b. 1905 Worcester, Massachusetts.
Composer. Brother of Charles and Harry Tobias; wrote "Here Comes the Girl" (1937, with his brothers and Milton Berle), "You Walked Out of the Picture" (1938, with Little Jack Little and Dave Oppenheim), "Sorry Dear" (1939, with Dave Oppenheim), "Rolleo Rolling Along" (1942, with his brother Harry and Don Reid); wrote the music for *Earl Carroll's Vanities* of 1932 and 1935, which included "At Last" (w. Sam Lewis).

TOCH, ERNEST

b. 1887 Vienna, Austria, d. 1964 Los Angeles, California. Composer. Self-taught and won Frankfurt's Mozart Prize (1909) and Mendelssohn Prize (1910); then studied at the Hoch Conservatory; served in the Austrian army in World War I; graduated Mannheim School of Music (Ph.D., 1921); came to U.S. (1934) and taught at the New School for Social Research (1934-36); went to Hollywood (1937); wrote scores for films, choral and orchestral works, chamber music; wrote *Big Ben* (1934), *Pinocchio, A Merry Overture* (1936), *Hyperion* (1947); won Pulitzer Prize in music (1956).

TOLLEFSEN, AUGUSTA SCHNABEL

b. 1885 Boise, Idaho, d. 1955.
Pianist. Studied with Clara Schumann and others; toured with orchestras in Europe and U.S.; member of Tollefsen Trio; married Carl Tollefsen, violinist.

TOMER, WILLIAM GOULD

b. 1832 Finesville, Warren County, New Jersey, d. 1896 Phillipsburg, New Jersey. Composer. Soldier in the Union Army and detailed to the headquarters of General O.O. Howard, founder of Howard University; when he was in charge of music at the Grace Methodist Episcopal Church, Washington, D.C., composed the music for the hymn "God Be with You" (1880, w. J.E. Rankin); then taught in the New Jersey public schools and was editor of the *High Bridge Gazette.*

TOMKINS, EDDIE

b. 1908, d. 1943.
Black trumpeter. Played in Jimmie Lunceford's orchestra.

TOMLINS, WILLIAM LAWRENCE

b. 1844 London, England, d. 1930 Delafield, Wisconsin. Organist and conductor. Studied at the Royal Academy of Music in London; came to New York (1870); organist in churches for five years; with Ritchings-Bernard Old Folks Company; conductor of Apollo Club, Chicago (1875-98); trained children in singing after 1881; conducted Arion Musical Club of Milwaukee (1878-88).

TOMPALL AND THE GLASER BROTHERS (vocal and instrumental trio) *see* TOMPALL GLASER, CHARLES GLASER, JAMES GLASER

TONEMASTERS *see* VERNON OXFORD

TONNING, GERARD

b. 1860 Stavanger, Norway, d. 1940 New York City. Conductor and composer. Studied at the Munich Conservatory; choral conductor in Duluth, Minn. after 1887; in Seattle, Wash. after 1905; composed the opera *Leif Erikson*, instrumental works, songs.

TOP HATTERS (band) *see* JAN SAVITT

TORMÉ, MELVIN HOWARD (MEL)

b. 1925 Chicago, Illinois.
Singer and composer. Served in World War II; appeared in night clubs in Las Vegas and Los Angeles; wrote "Stranger in Town," "California Suite," "Christmas Song," "Ain't Gonna Be Like That"; at the Maisonette, St. Regis-Sheraton Hotel, New York City (1972).

TORREY, BRADFORD

b. 1843 Weymouth, Massachusetts, d. 1912 Santa Barbara, California. Hymnist. On the staff of *The Youth's Companion* (1886-1901); ornithologist and naturalist; edited *Thoreau's Journal* and wrote *Birds in the Bush* and *Nature's Invitation*; wrote the hymn "Not So in Haste, My Heart" (1875, tune "Dolomite Chant"—Austrian melody).

TORREY, MARY IDE

b. 1817, d. 1869.
Hymnist. Daughter of the Rev. Jacob Ide of Medway, Mass.; married the Rev. Charles T. Torrey (1837); wrote "When Silent Steal Across My Soul," which appeared in Nason's *Congregational Hymn Book* (1857).

TORRINGTON, FREDERICK HERBERT

b. 1837 Dudley, England, d. 1917 Toronto, Ontario, Canada. Organist and conductor. Pupil of James Fitzgerald; organist in St. James Church, Montreal, Quebec (1856-68); conducted his orchestra at the Boston Peace Jubilee (1869); taught at the New England Conservatory, Boston; organist at Metropolitan Church, Toronto after 1873; organized first Toronto musical festival (1886); conducted the Toronto Philharmonic Society; founded the Toronto College of Music (1888); composed music for church services.

TOSCANINI, ARTURO

b. 1867 Parma, Italy, d. 1957.
Famous conductor. Studied at the Parma Conservatory; cellist on concert tours; conductor of opera in Rio de Janeiro, Brazil (1886), in Turin, Italy (1887-98), La Scala, Milan (1898-1908), the Metropolitan Opera, New York City (1908-15); musical director at La Scala (1921-29), the New York Philharmonic (1926-36), and the N.B.C. Symphony Orchestra (1937-54); considered the most eminent conductor of his day.

TOSSO, JOSEPH

b. 1802 Mexico, d. 1887 Lexington, Kentucky. Violinist and entertainer. Introduced the instrumental piece *The Arkansaw Traveler* (1851, S.C. Faulkner).

TOUGH, DAVE

b. 1908 Oak Park, Illinois, d. 1948 Newark, New Jersey. Jazz drummer. With Artie Shaw and Woody Herman.

TOUREL, JENNIE

b. 1910 Montreal, Quebec, Canada, d. 1973. Mezzo-soprano. Sang with the Metropolitan Opera, New York City (1943-45); also in concerts; in concert with pianist Earl Wild at Town Hall, New York City (1973).

TOURJEE, EBEN

b. 1834 Warwick, Rhode Island, d. 1891 Boston, Massachusetts. Teacher. Founded the New England Conservatory of Music in Providence, R.I., but moved the school to Boston in 1870; later became Dean of the College of Music of Boston University; arranged the music "In Some Way or Other the Lord Will Provide" (1873, by C.S. Harrington, w. Martha A.W. Cook); music editor of the *Hymnal of the Methodist Episcopal Church with Tunes* (1878) and editor of *The Tribute of Praise* (1882).

TOWBIN, CYRIL

b. 1897 New York City, d. 1971 Los Angeles, California. Concert violinist and conductor. Studied at the Juilliard School, New York City; directed the Chamber Music Art Society, New York City; toured North America and Europe; taught in Seattle, Washington; conducted Hollywood Studio Symphony and the Los Angeles Community Symphony Orchestra.

"TOWN HALL PARTY"

Variety show on TV Channel 11, Compton, California; started in 1951; written by Johnny Bond and directed by Wesley Tuttle.

TOWNSON, RON

b. 1933 St. Louis, Missouri.
Black tenor. Originally planned a career in

opera; went to Hollywood and joined Nat King Cole's Merry Young Souls; formed group called the Versatiles, then the Hi-Fi's, then the Fifth Dimension; their record "Up, Up and Away" (m. Jimmy Webb) was a big hit and won four Grammy Awards in 1968; another hit was "Aquarius—Let the Sunshine In," from the musical *Hair* (m. Galt MacDermot, libretto—Gerome Ragni and James Rado).

TRAETTA (TRAJETTA), FILIPPO

b. 1777 Venice, Italy, d. 1854 Philadelphia, Pennsylvania. Composer and teacher. Son of Tomaso Traetta, composer of operas; studied in Venice and later with Piccinni; arrested and imprisoned for political activities, but escaped to America (1799); with Gottlieb Graupner and Francis Mallet founded the Conservatorio in Boston (1801); resided in Charleston, South Carolina (1802-08); in New York City (1809-22); founded the American Conservatorio in Philadelphia (1823), which was active until 1853; wrote a book on vocal methods; composed the oratorio *Peace* (1815); his *Two Marches for the Pianoforte* were published by Uri K. Hill (1815).

TRAUBEL, HELEN

b. 1903 St. Louis, Missouri, d. 1972 Santa Monica, California. Noted soprano. Studied with Vetta Karst in St. Louis after 1916; debut with the St. Louis Symphony; soloist with the New York Philharmonic concert in Lewisohn Stadium (1926); operatic debut with the Metropolitan Opera in New York City (1937) in *The Man Without a Country*; in *Die Walküre* at the Met (1939); at Teatro Colon in Buenos Aires, Argentina (1943); coached Margaret Truman (1955-58); married William Bass; later sang in night clubs; last engagement with Jimmy Durante at Lake Tahoe, Calif. (1964).

TRAVELERS 3

Vocal and instrumental group started by Pete Apo, Charles Oyama, and Dick Shirley (1959); Michael Gene Botta (1964); Joseph Ronald Lamonno replaced Shirley (1965).

TRAVELLERS *see* TEX ROE

TRAVERS, MARY ELLIN

b. 1936 Louisville, Kentucky.
Singer. Started singing with Noel Paul Stookey; later Peter Yarrow joined the act and they became the very successful "Peter, Paul and Mary."

TRAVIS, MERLE ROBERT

b. 1917 Rosewood, Kentucky.
Popular composer, singer, and guitarist. Radio debut in Evansville, Indiana (1935); later with the Georgia Wildcats over station WLW, Cincinnati, Ohio; served in the marines in World War II; wrote "Sixteen Tons" (recorded by Tennessee Ernie Ford, 1955); "Old Mountain Dew;" "Smoke, Smoke, Smoke" ("That Cigarette," w. Tex Ritter).

TREHARNE, BRYCESON

b. 1879 Merthyr Tydvil, Wales, d. 1948 New York City. Composer. Studied at the Royal College of Music, London; also in Paris, Milan, and Munich; taught at Adelaide University, Australia (1901-11); worked with Gordon Craig in Paris after 1912; imprisoned by Germans in World War I; later lived in Boston; he composed orchestral pieces and songs.

TRENKLE, JOSEPH

b. ca. 1840 Germany, d. 1878 San Francisco, California. Pianist. Came to Boston (1859); later active in San Francisco.

TREVILLE, YVONNE DE (LE GIERCE)

b. 1881 Galveston, Texas, d. 1954 New York City. Soprano. Studied with Marchesi; sang in Spain (1901); at Paris Opera Comique (1902); Boston Opera (1911-12); also in recitals.

TREVOR, VAN

b. 1940 Lewiston, Maine.
Singer, guitarist, and songwriter. Wrote "Guitar," "Our Side," "Born to Be with You," "You've Been So Good to Me," "He's Losing His Mind."

TRISTANO, LEONARD J. (LENNIE)

b. 1919 Chicago, Illinois.
Pianist and composer. Blind since age nine; bandleader in 1950s.

TROGLODYTES (jazz group) *see* WALLY FAWKES

TROWBRIDGE, JOHN ELIOT

b. 1845 Newton, Massachusetts, d. 1912.
Organist and composer. Studied under B.C. Blodgett of Smith College and Junius W. Hill of Wellesley College; organist in Newton and Boston; organist of Congregational Church, West Newton after 1881; wrote *Emmanuel* (oratorio, produced in Tremont Temple, Boston, 1887), *Lydia* (cantata), Mass in E

Major, *The Heros of '76* (secular operatic cantata), church music.

TRUMAN, MARY MARGARET

b. 1924.
Soprano. Daughter of President Harry S. Truman; studied voice with Mrs. Strickler, New York City (1946); debut on radio with Detroit Symphony, K. Krueger conducting (March, 1946); Hollywood Bowl Symphony Orchestra, Eugene Ormandy conducting (August, 1946); U.S. concert tours (1946-50); recital attended by Prime Minister Clement Atlee in Washington, D.C. (December 6, 1950); critic Paul Hume panned her singing; President Truman in letter to Hume intimated he would punch Hume in the nose; her career ended; married Clifton Daniel, newspaper editor (1956). (*See also* Paul Hume)

TRUMBAUER, FRANKIE

b. 1901 Carbondale, Illinois, d. 1956 Kansas City, Missouri. Jazz saxophonist. Had his own orchestra at the Arcadia Ballroom in St. Louis (1925) with Bix Beiderbecke and Pee Wee Russell.

TUBB, ERNEST DALE

b. 1914 Crisp, Texas.
Popular composer, singer, and guitarist. Radio debut on station KONO, San Antonio, Texas (1934); on KGKO, Fort Worth (1940); joined Grand Ole Opry, Nashville, Tenn. (1943); wrote "Walking the Floor Over You," "My Tennessee Baby" (1949); albums—*All Time Hits, Another Story, By Request, Country Dance Time, Country Hit Time, Country Hits Old and New, Great Country, If We Put Our Heads Together, Just Call Me Lonesome, On Tour, Stand By Me.*

TUBB, GLENN DOUGLAS

b. 1935 San Antonio, Texas.
Singer and songwriter. Attended schools in Donelson, Tenn., and Austin, Texas; wrote "Tell Her So," "Repeat After Me," "Memory Killer," "I Don't Want It," "Next Time," "I Don't Believe."

TUBB, JUSTIN WAYNE

b. 1935 San Antonio, Texas.
Popular composer, singer, and guitarist. Son of Ernest Tubb; attended the University of Texas at Austin; disc jockey on WHIN, Gallatin, Tenn. (1953); joined Grand Ole Opry, Nashville (1955); wrote "I'm a Big Boy Now," "Rock It Down to My House" (1958), "I Know You Do," and "Buster's Gang" (1959), "Lonesome 7-7203" (1963, recorded by Hawkshaw Hawkins), "Keeping Up with the Joneses" (Faron Young-Margie Singleton record), "Love Is No Excuse" (1964, Jim Reeves-Dottie West record).

TUBERT, ROBERT (BOB)

b. 1932 Worcester, Massachusetts.
Songwriter. Attended Arizona State College at Temple; graduated Southwest Missouri College at Springfield (1954); script writer for the "Ozark Jubilee," Springfield; wrote the lyrics "Our Winter Love" (m. Don Cowell), "Satin Pillows" (with Sonny James), "You're the Only World I Know" (1965, with Sonny James).

TUCKER, FRANCIS BLAND

b. 1895 Norfolk, Virginia.
Hymnist. Educated at the University of Virginia, Charlottesville, Va., and the Virginia Theological Seminary (1920); served as a private in the AEF in World War I; rector in Brunswick County, Va., Washington, D.C., then at old Christ Church, Savannah, Georgia (1945); wrote the hymns "All Praise to Thee, for Thou, O King Divine" (1938, tune "Engelberg"—C.V. Stanford) and "Our Father, by Whose Name" (1939, tune "Rhosymedre"—John Edwards).

TUCKER, GAYLORD BOB ("GABE")

b. 1915 Pierce, Kentucky.
Singer and songwriter. Attended high school in Greensberg, Ky.; Lindsey Wilson College, Columbia, Ky. (1933); with Kentucky Ramblers, Jackson, Tenn. (1937-39); then various other bands; leader of Musical Ramblers, Houston, Texas (1951-55); wrote "Lonely Broken Heart" (1944), "It'd Surprise You" (1952).

TUCKER, GREGORY

b. 1909, d. 1971 Cambridge, Massachusetts.
Pianist, composer, and teacher. Studied at the Combs Conservatory of Music and the Curtis Institute, both in Philadelphia; taught at the Edgewood School, Greenwich, Conn. (1929-33), and Bennington College, Bennington, Vermont (1933-47); professor at the Massachusetts Institute of Technology, Cambridge (1947-71); composed modern dance music and for the ballet.

TUCKER, JOHN IRELAND

b. 1819 Brooklyn, New York, d. 1895.
Compiler. Graduated Columbia College (1837); organized a boys' choir in the Church

of the Holy Cross, Troy, N.Y. (1844) and led the singing at the first Choral Eucharist at the Church of the Annunciation, New York City (1852); compiled *The Parish Hymnal* (1870), *Tunes Old and New, Adapted to the Hymnal* (1872), *The Service Book* (1873), and *The Children's Hymnal* (1874).

TUCKER, ORRIN

b. 1911 St. Louis, Missouri.
Singer and bandleader. Organized his band (1936); hit the big time when his singer, Bonnie Baker (née Evelyn Nelson of Orange, Texas) sang "Oh, Johnny, Oh, Johnny, Oh" in 1939 (old World War I tune); later his singers were Scottee Marsh and Helen Lee.

TUCKER, RICHARD

b. 1914 Brooklyn, New York, d. 1975.
Celebrated dramatic tenor. Born Reuben Tickel; brother-in-law of Jan Peerce; as a youth was an alto soloist in a synagogue choir in New York City; cantorial training (1931-36); studied with tenor Paul Althouse (1939); operatic debut in *La Traviata* and *Rigoletto* with Salmaggi company in New York (1944); Metropolitan debut (1945) as Enzo in *La Gioconda*; celebrated his twenty-fifth year with the Metropolitan Opera in 1970; with Robert Merrill at Carnegie Hall, New York City (1973).

TUCKER, SOPHIE

b. 1884 Russia, d. 1966.
Singer and entertainer. Sang in night clubs in New York City; J. Fred Coots and Spencer Williams composed material for Sophie; starred in *High Kickers* (1941, m. Harry Ruby) with George Jessel.

TUCKER, TOMMY

b. 1908 Souris, North Dakota.
Bandleader. His singers were baritone Don Brown, Kerwin Sommerville, and Amy Arnell; then he hit the big time (1941) with his record "I Don't Want to Set the World on Fire"; successful for a number of years; then disbanded; became assistant professor of fine arts at Monmouth College, in New Jersey.

TUCKERMAN, SAMUEL PARKMAN

b. 1819 Boston, Massachusetts, d. 1890 Newport, Rhode Island. Composer. Organist in Boston (1840-49), then studied in Europe; became organist of Trinity Church, New York City (1856); compiled *The National Lyre* (1848) with S.A. Bancroft (which included many tunes by Tuckerman), *Cathedral Chants* (1858), and *The Episcopal Harp* (1844).

TUCKEY, WILLIAM

b. 1708 Somersetshire, England, d. 1781 Philadelphia, Pennsylvania. Organist and composer. Organist of Trinity Church, New York City, after 1750; composed and directed *An Anthem on the Death of His Late Sacred Majesty* (George II) in Trinity Church (1761); composed an anthem on Psalm 34 (1762); his anthem "Liverpool" included in James Lyons' *Urania Collection* (1761); conducted first colonial performance of Handel's *Messiah* (in abbreviated form) in 1770; his tune "Psalm 97" included in *The Hallowell Collection of Sacred Music* published by Ezekiel Goodale (Hallowell, Maine, 1817).

TUFTS, JOHN

b. 1689 Medford, Massachusetts, d. 1750 Amesbury, Massachusetts. Singer and writer. Educated at Harvard (1708); became pastor of the Second Church, Newbury, Mass.; in 1737 accused of immorality by some women in his parish, and forced to resign, with only one dissenting vote of the congregation; published *Plain and Easy Introduction to the Art of Singing* (1712), *An Instruction to the Singing of Psalm Tunes* (1714).

TUFTS, JOHN WHEELER

b. 1825 Dover, New Hampshire, d. 1908.
Composer. Wrote "The American Flag," "Song for Arbor Day," "From Forest Wide and Free," "Song of the Flag."

TULL, JETHRO (rock group)

Ian Anderson, lead vocals and flutist; Barry Barlow, drummer; Martin Barre, guitarist; John Evan, organist; Jeffrey Hammond-Hammond, vocals and guitar; started in 1967; sensation at Madison Square Garden (1971) with their "bounce"; albums—*Benefit, This Was Jethro Tull, Stand Up, Aqualung.*

TULLAR, GRANT COLFAX

b. 1870, d. 1950 Ocean Grove, New Jersey.
Composer. Methodist minister; the firm of Meredith and Tullar published Methodist church hymnals; composed the music "Face to Face" (1899, w. Mrs. Frank A. Beck).

TUNESTERS *see* ANGE LORENZO

TUPPER, JAMES

b. 1819 Charleston, South Carolina, d. 1868 Summerville, South Carolina. Hymnist. Attorney and member of the state legislature; wrote "Dark Was the Hour When Jesus Bore," which appeared in *The Baptist Psalmody* (1850).

TURK, WILLIAM

b. ca. 1866, d. ca. 1911.
Black bass player. Lived in Baltimore, Md.; was six feet tall and weighed about 300 pounds; played one note with his right hand and four with his left, at the same time.

TURNAU, JOSEPH

b. 1888 Kolin, Czechoslovakia, d. 1954 New York City. Teacher. Stage director with the Vienna State Opera (1923-25), then at Breslau, then Frankfurt (1929-33); with the rise of Nazism he came to America (1933) and taught at Hunter College, New York City.

TURNER, ALFRED DUDLEY

b. 1854 St. Albans, Vermont, d. 1888 Boston, Massachusetts. Composer and teacher. Studied piano in Boston at age nine with J.C.D. Parker; later graduated from the New England Conservatory, Boston; then taught there; composed piano pieces; compositions reached op. 36.

TURNER, ANNIE MAE "TINA" (BULLOCK)

b. 1939 Brownsville, Tennessee.
Black singer. Raised in Knoxville, Tenn.; met Ike Turner in St. Louis (1956), and married him; in team of Ike and Tina Turner; with Tina and the Ikettes (dancers) after 1961; Ike and Tina reside in Los Angeles; toured Europe with Rolling Stones (1966), toured U.S. with them (1970); also toured Japan and Africa (1971), where they appeared in a film, *Soul to Soul.* (*See* Ike Turner for albums)

TURNER, HERBERT BARCLAY

b. 1852 Brooklyn, New York, d. 1927 Washington, Connecticut. Composer. Educated at Amherst College, Amherst, Mass. (1874); and Union Theological Seminary; pastor of the Congregational Church, Washington, Conn., when he became chaplain of Hampton Institute, Hampton, Virginia (1892-1925); composed the tune "Cushman" used for "We Would See Jesus, for the Shadows Lengthen" (w. Anna B. Warner) and "We Would See Jesus; Lo! His Star Is Shining" (w. J.E. Park).

TURNER, IKE

b. 1934 Clarksdale, Mississippi.
Black guitarist, pianist, and singer. Leader of Ike Turner and the Kings of Rhythm (1956); played the "chitlin' circuit" throughout the South; wrote "Fool in Love" (1959) recorded by Tina; formed team of Ike and Tina Turner; married Tina; toured Europe with Rolling Stones (1966) and the States (1970); albums—*Ike and Tina Turner—Revue "Live"* (1964), *Come Together, Fantastic Ike and Tina Turner, The Hunter, In Person, Live, Ooh Poo Pah Doo, Deep River—Mountain High, Soul of Ike and Tina;* won Grammy Award (1972) with Tina for best rhythm and blues vocal, "Proud Mary."

TURNER, JOE

b. 1907 Baltimore, Maryland.
Black jazz pianist. Known for his Harlem style; played in night clubs in New York City.

TURNEY, EDWARD

b. 1816 Easton, Connecticut, d. 1872 Washington, D.C. Hymnist and compiler. Graduated Madison University, N.Y.; pastor in Hartford, Conn., and Granville, Ohio (1842-47); professor at Madison (1850) and Fairmount Theological Seminary, Cincinnati, Ohio (1853-58), then in Washington, D.C.; published *Baptismal Hymns* (1862) and *Memorial Poems and Hymns* (1864, which included four of his hymns).

TURPIN, THOMAS MILLION

b. 1873 Savannah, Georgia, d. 1922 St. Louis, Missouri. Noted black composer. Owned a place called Rosebud in St. Louis, where he played the piano and composed music; the first ragtime song to be published by a black man was his "Harlem Rag" (1897); also wrote "The Bowery Buck" (1899), "A Ragtime Nightmare" (1900), "St. Louis Rag" (1903), and "The Buffalo Rag" (1904); became known as the "Father of St. Louis Ragtime."

TURTLES (rock group)

Howard Kaylan, lead vocals; Johnny Barbata, drums; Jim Pons, vocals and bass; Al Nichol, vocals and lead guitar; Mark Volman, vocals; Jim Tucker, former member; started in Los Angeles in 1965; toured U.S. and England; albums—*It Ain't Me Babe, Happy Together, Turtle Soup, Turtles' Golden Hits, Turtles' More Golden Hits, Turtles Present the Battle of the Bands, You Baby.*

TUTHILL, BURNET CORWIN

b. 1888 New York City.
Composer. His mother was an organist; graduated Columbia University (1909); manager of the Cincinnati Conservatory of Music (1922-30); director of the Memphis College of Music after 1937; his *Bethlehem* pastorale op. 8 (1934) performed by the Cincinnati, St. Louis, Rochester, and Cleveland Symphony Orchestras; also composed *Come Seven* (rhapsody, 1935), *Dr. Joe* (march, 1933).

TUXEDO BRASS BAND (black band)

Organized in New Orleans about 1910 by Oscar "Papa" Celestine.

TWAITS, WILLIAM

b. 1781 England, d. after 1811.
Singer and actor. Burletta singer; with Philadelphia Theater (ca. 1801); also sang and acted in New York City; manager of Charleston, S.C. theater after 1811.

TWEEDY, DONALD NICHOLS

b. 1890 Danbury, Connecticut, d. there 1948. Composer. Graduated Harvard University in music; pupil of Heilman, Spalding, and Hill; studied at the Institute of Musical Art with Goetschius (1912); first lieutenant in army in World War I; taught at the Eastman School of Music; later at Hamilton College; wrote *L'Allegro* (symphonic study, 1925), *Three Dances for Orchestra* (1934), chamber music.

TWEEDY, HENRY HALLAM

b. 1868 Binghamton, New York, d. 1953.
Hymnist. Educated at Yale, Union Theological Seminary, and the University of Berlin; held pastorates in Utica, N.Y., and Bridgeport, Conn., then became professor of practical theology at Yale Divinity School (1909); wrote the hymns "O Spirit of the Living God" (tune "St. Leonard"—Henry Hiles), and "O Gracious Father of Mankind."

TWITTY, CONWAY

b. 1935 Friars Point, Mississippi.
Singer, bandleader, and songwriter. Born Harold Jenkins; formed his own band; wrote songs and soundtrack for films; formed a new band, The Lonely Blue Boys, Oklahoma City, Okla. (1966); albums—*Darling You Know I Wouldn't Lie, Here's Conway Twitty and His Lonely Blue Boys, I Love You More Today, Look into My Teardrops, Next in Line, To See My Angel Cry, You Can't Take the Country Out of Conway.*

TYERS, WILLIAM H.

b. 1876 Richmond, Virginia, d. 1924.
Black composer. Raised in New York City; staff arranger for the Joseph Stern Company, music publishers; wrote dance music—*Maori, Trocha, Panama, The Call of the Woods* (waltz)

TYLER, JOSEPH

b. 1751 England, d. 1823 New York City. Singer and actor. American debut (1795); sang part of Arnold in *The Archers* (w. William Dunlap, m. Benjamin Carr, New York City, 1796); in *The Provoked Husband,* New York City (1796); opened Washington Gardens, restaurant (1798); managed Old American Company after 1805 with John Johnson; resembled George Washington and often played the part of General Washington.

TYLER, ROYALL

b. 1758 Boston, Massachusetts, d. 1826 Brattleboro, Vermont. Librettist. Educated at Harvard; soldier in American Revolution and Shay's Rebellion (1786); later elected Chief Justice of the Supreme Court of Vermont; wrote the libretto *May Day in Town, or New York in an Uproar* (composer unknown), produced by Thomas Wignell in New York City (1787); also wrote a play, *The Contrast,* produced in New York (1787).

TYLER, "T" TEXAS

b. 1916 near Mena, Arkansas, d. 1972 Springfield, Missouri. Singer, bandleader, and songwriter. Born David Luke Myrick; served in the armed forces in World War II; had his own show in Los Angles; appeared in several western films; wrote "Deck of Cards"; albums—*Deck of Cards, Hits of T. Texas Tyler.*

TYMPANY FIVE (black jazz group) *see* LOUIS JORDAN

TYSON, IAN

b. 1933 British Columbia, Canada.
Vocal duo of Ian and Sylvia. They sang in clubs in Toronto in 1960, then Ian married Sylvia [Fricker] (1964); they sang in Town Hall, New York City (1964) and at the Lindy Opera House, Los Angeles (1967); he wrote "Four Strong Winds," and with Sylvia, "Mr. Spoons"; their LPs—*Four Strong Winds, Northern Journey* (1964).

UGGAMS, LESLIE

b. 1943 New York City.
Black singer. Sang at the Apollo Theatre in New York City; became a star on TV; albums—*Hallelujah Baby, Just to Satisfy You, Leslie, So in Love, Time to Love, What's an Uggams.*

UKELELE, JOHNNY *see* JOHNNY KAAIHUE

ULTIMATE SPINACH (pop-rock group)

Ian Bruce-Douglas, lead vocals, bells, and chimes; Barbara Hudson, vocals, electric guitar, and kazoo; Keith Lahteinen, vocals, drums, etc.; Richard Nese, bass; Geoffrey Winthrop, vocals, lead guitar, and electric sitar; started in Boston in 1968; albums—*Ultimate Spinach, Behold and See.*

UNION GAP, GARY PUCKETT AND THE (pop group)

Gary Puckett, vocals; Dwight Bement, tenor sax; Kerry Chater, bass guitar; Paul Wheatbread, drums; Gary "Mutha" Withem, piano; started as The Union Gap in California (1967); group's members wear Union Civil War Uniforms; albums—*Incredible, Gary Puckett and the Union Gap, New Gary Puckett and the Union Gap, Union Gap, Young Girl.*

UNITED STATES OF AMERICA (rock group)

Joseph Byrd, synthesizer; Dorothy Moskowitz, vocals; Craig Woodson, tabla and African drums; Gordon Marron, vocals and electric violin; Rand Forbes, bass; started in California (1967); recorded in 1968; disbanded in 1968; album—*United States of America.*

UPTON, GEORGE PUTNAM

b. 1834 Roxbury, Massachusetts, d. 1919 Chicago, Illinois. Critic. Associated with the *Chicago Daily Tribune* (1862-1919); used pseudonym "Peregrine Pickle."

URSO, CAMILLA

b. 1842 Nantes, France, d. 1902 New York City. Violinist. Daughter of Salvator Urso, organist and flutist; studied with Massart; debut in America at age ten; with the Germania Society and the Musical Fund in Boston (1853-54); toured the world as a solo artist; later resided in Nashville.

USSACHEVSKY, VLADIMIR

b. 1911 Hailar, Manchuria.
Composer and teacher. Came to U.S. (1930); attended Pomona College, Calif., and the Eastman School of Music, Rochester, N.Y. (M.A. and Ph.D.); taught at Columbia University after 1947; composed electronic music; wrote *Underwater Valse* (1952), *Sonic Contours* (1952), *Piece for Tape Recorder* (1955), *Studies in Sound* (1955), *Wireless Fantasy* (1960), *Of Wood and Brass* (1965), *Computer Piece* (1968); also several pieces with Otto Luening—*Incantation for Tape Recorder* (1953).

VAGRANTS, THE (rock group)

Jay Storch, organ; Peter Sabatino, vocals; Leslie West, guitar; Roger Mansour, drums; Larry West, bass; started in New York; first recorded in 1967.

VAIL, SILAS JONES

b. 1818 Brooklyn, New York, d. there 1884.
Composer. Learned the haberdasher's trade in Danbury, Conn., then turned to music; composed the tune "Close to Thee" (1874, "Thou, My Everlasting Portion," w. Fanny Crosby); composed the music for "There's a Wideness in God's Mercy" (w. F.W. Faber), "Scatter Seeds of Kindness" (w. Mary Riley Smith), and "We Shall Meet Beyond the River" (1867, w. John Atkinson); compiled *The Athenaeum Collection* (1863) which included ten new songs of Stephen Foster, and with W.F. Sherwin, *Songs of Grace and Glory* (1874).

VALDA, GUILIA

b. 1855, d. 1925.
Singer. Born Julia Wheelock.

VALENS, RITCHIE

b. 1940 d. 1959 Fargo, North Dakota.
Singer, guitarist, and songwriter. Born Richard Valenzuela; his widowed mother mortgaged her house to rent a dance hall for her son to perform, where he held dances three times a month; with Bob Keene, bandleader; wrote "Come On, Let's Go," also "La Bamba," recorded by Trini Lopez; killed in an airplane crash with Buddy Holly and the "Big Bopper" J.P. Richardson; albums—*Ritchie Valens, Ritchie Valens Memorial Album.*

VALLEE, HERBERT PRIOR ("RUDY")

b. 1901 Island Pond, Vermont.
Singer. Graduated Yale; organized the Connecticut Yankees (his band); on the "Fleischmann Yeast" program for many years; during the 1930s starred in many Broadway reviews and films; made his debut in a musical show in *How to Succeed in Business Without Really Trying* (1961, m. Frank Loesser); with Leon Zimmerman wrote "I'm Just a Vagabond Lover."

VALLERIA, ALWINA

b. 1848 Baltimore, Maryland, d. 1925.
Singer. Married R.H.P. Hutchinson; first American to sing at the Metropolitan Opera, New York City (1883).

VALTON, PETER

b. (?) England, d. 1784.
Composer. Organist of St. Philip's Church, Charleston, S.C. (1764-81), then St. Michael's (1781-84); composed *Ode for the Festival of St. John the Evangelist*; some of his tunes were included in *The Choral Book* (J. Loring, 1816), including "St. Michaels."

VAN ALSTYNE, EGBERT

b. 1882 Chicago, Illinois, d. there 1951.
Popular composer. Attended the Chicago Musical College and Cornell College, Mt. Vernon, Iowa; went to New York City (1900); with Harry H. Williams, the vaudeville actor and lyricist, wrote "Navajo" (1903, introduced by Marie Cahill), and "In the Shade of the Old Apple Tree" (1905); they wrote the musicals *A Broken Doll* starring Alice York (1909), and *Girlies* with Ernest Truex and Maude Raymond (1910); wrote "That Old Gal of Mine" (1912, w. Earle C. Jones) and with lyricist Gus Kahn "Sunshine and Roses" (1913), "Memories" (1915), "Pretty Baby" (with Tony Jackson), "Your Eyes Have Told Me So" (with Walter Blaufuss, sung by Grace La Rue in vaudeville); also wrote "Drifting and Dreaming" (1925, w. Haven Gillespie).

VAN ALSTYNE, FRANCES C. *see* FANNY CROSBY

VAN CLEVE, JOHN SMITH

b. 1851 Maysville, Kentucky, d. 1917.
Composer, teacher, and writer. Lost his sight at age eight; attended the Institute for the Blind in Columbus, Ohio; graduated Boston University; taught music at the Institute for Blind, Columbus (1872-75); then at the institute in Janesville, Wisc.; resided in Cin-

cinnati after 1879; taught at the Conservatory there; wrote a commemoration ode and cantata (1878) for the unveiling of the Woodward Statute in Cincinnati; composed Piano and Violin Sonata in E, Sonata in G-sharp Minor.

VAN DER STUCKEN, FRANK VALENTIN

b. 1858 Fredericksburg, Texas, d. 1929 Hamburg, Germany. Conductor and composer. Studied in Antwerp, then with Grieg and others; conducted Breslau City Theatre (1881-82); musical director of the Arion Society, New York City (1884); dean of the Cincinnati College of Music (1897-1901); conducted the Cincinnati Symphony (1895-1907); conducted the Cincinnati May Festivals; composed *William Ratcliff* (symphonic prologue, Cincinnati, 1899), *Pagina d'amore* (orchestral episode), *Pax Triumphans.*

VAN DRESSER, MARCIA

b. 1880 Memphis, Tennessee, d. 1937 London, England. Soprano. Studied in Chicago, Munich, and Paris; sang in light opera in Europe after 1898; also in grand opera; returned to United States (1914).

VAN DYKE, HENRY

b. 1852 Germantown, Philadelphia, d. 1933 Princeton, New Jersey. Teacher and diplomat. Educated at Princeton and Princeton Theological Seminary (1877); pastor of the United Congregational Church, Newport, R.I. (1879-83), and the Brick Presbyterian Church, New York City (1883-99), when he became professor of English literature at Princeton, and lived in Princeton; wrote the lyrics "Jesus, Thou Divine Companion" (originally as "Toiling of Felix," 1898, tune "Pleading Savior," 1855, revised in 1910); also wrote the hymns "Joyful, Joyful We Adore Thee" (1911, tune "Hymn to Joy"—Beethoven) and "No Form of Human Framing" (1921, tune "Alford"—J.B. Dykes); served as United States Minister to the Netherlands and Luxembourg (1913-17).

VAN DYKE, LEROY FRANK

b. 1929 Spring Fork, Missouri.
Singer. Graduated the University of Missouri, Columbia (1952); wrote "Auctioneer"; albums—*Country Hits, Great Hits of Leroy Van Dyke, I've Never Been Loved, Just a Closer Walk with Thee, Lonesome Is, Walk on By.*

VAN GORDON, CYRENA

b. 1896 Camden, Ohio, d. 1967.
Contralto. Born Cyrena Procock; studied at the Cincinnati College of Music; debut as Amneris at the Chicago Opera (1915); with the Metropolitan Opera, New York City, as Amneris (1934).

VAN (or VON) HAGEN, PETER ALBRECHT, JR.

b. 1781 Netherlands, d. 1837 Boston, Massachusetts. Violinist, composer, and publisher. Debut in New York City (1786) and gave many concerts there; moved to Boston (1796); music publisher in Boston (1798-1803); organist at Trinity Church there until 1809; reported to be an alcoholic; composed *To Arms, Columbia* (1799, w. Thomas Paine), *Anna* (1802), *Gentle Zephyr* (1802), *May Morning* (1802), *Governor Eustis' March* (1824).

VAN (or VON) HAGEN, PETER ALBRECHT, SR.

b. 1750 Netherlands, d. 1803, Boston, Massachusetts. Publisher. Came to New York City (ca. 1789); father of Peter, the composer; went to Boston (1796); with Benjamin Crehore, published music in Boston (1798-1803).

VAN HEUSEN, JAMES

b. 1913 Syracuse, New York.
Popular composer. Born Edward Chester Babcock; attended Casanovia Seminary and Syracuse University; with lyricist Eddie De Lange wrote "Oh You Crazy Moon," "Darn That Dream" (1939), "Shake Down the Stars" (1940); with lyricist Johnny Burke wrote "Imagination" (1940), "Swinging on a Star" (1944, for Bing Crosby), "Suddenly It's Spring," "Just My Lück" (1946); with Sammy Cahn—"Incurably Romantic," "Come Dance with Me," and "Love and Marriage."

VAN HOOSE, ELLISON

b. 1869 Murfreesboro, Tennessee, d. 1936 Houston, Texas. Tenor. Studied with Jean de Reszke and others; sang with the Damrosch-Ellis Opera Company after 1897; with Mayence Opera; Chicago Opera (1911-12); also in concerts; later musical director in Houston.

VAN HULSTEYN, JOAI'N C.

b. 1869 Amsterdam, Netherlands, d. 1947 Baltimore, Maryland. Violinist. Studied at the Liege Conservatory; later taught at the Peabody Institute in Baltimore.

VANILLA FUDGE (rock group)

Carmine Appice, drums; Tim Bogert, bass; Vincent Martell, bass guitar; Mark Stein, organ; started on Long Island, New York (1967); albums—*Vanilla Fudge, Beat Goes On, Near the Beginning, Renaissance, Rock and Roll, While the World Was Eating.*

VAN RONK, DAVID (DAVE)

b. 1936 Brooklyn, New York.
Singer, bandleader, and songwriter. Performed with jazz groups in New York City; formed the Ragtime Jug Stompers with Sam Charters; wrote "Bambee," "Frankie's Blues," "Pretty Mama," "Bad Dream Blues," "If You Leave Me"; albums—*Inside Dave Van Ronk, Just Dave Van Ronk, No Dirty Names, Dave Van Ronk and the Hudson Dusters, Dave Van Ronk and the Ragtime Jug Stompers, Dave Van Ronk Folksinger.*

VAN VACTOR, DAVID

b. 1906 Plymouth, Indiana.
Conductor and composer. Conducted Knoxville (Tenn.) Symphony Orchestra; composed *Five Little Pieces* for orchestra (Chicago Symphony under DeLamarter, 1931), Symphony in D (New York Philharmonic, composer conducting, 1939, won first prize, 1938), *Symphony Suite* (Ravinia Festival, composer conducting, 1939), *Divertimento for Small Orchestra* (Ravinia Festival under composer, 1939), *Masque of the Red Death* for orchestra (after Poe), *Two Overtures to a Comedy* (no. 2 by Indianapolis Symphony under Sevitzky, 1941), *Gothic Impressions* (Chicago Symphony under composer, 1942).

VAN VECHTEN, CARL

b. 1880 Cedar Rapids, Iowa, d. 1964.
Writer. Graduated the University of Chicago; with the *New York Times*; edited program notes of the New York Symphony Orchestra (1910-11); wrote *Music and Bad Manners, The Merry-Go-Round, Music After the Great War, Interpreters and Interpretations, The Music of Spain.*

VAN ZANT, MARIE

b. 1861 New York City, d. 1920 Cannes, France. Opera singer. Daughter of Jeanie van Zandt, singer with Carl Rosa Company; studied in Milan; debut in Turin (1879); sang at Paris Opera Comique (1880-84); suffered temporary loss of voice, took leave of absence due to radical criticism; later sang in London.

VARDELL, CHARLES GILDERSLEEVE

b. 1893 Salisbury, North Carolina, d. 1958. Composer. Graduated the Eastman School of Music, Rochester, N.Y. (Ph.D.); composed *Joe Clark Steps Out,* (descriptive piece with jazz influence, Rochester Philharmonic under Hanson, 1937, also given as ballet at Eastman Festival), *Saturday Night* for orchestra.

VARÈSE, EDGARD

b. 1883 Paris, France, d. 1965 New York City. Noted composer. Studied at the Paris Conservatory; served in French Army (1914); came to New York (1915); founded the New York Symphony (1919); with Carlos Salzedo, founded the International Composers Guild (1922); U.S. citizen (1926); avant-garde prophet of organized sound; composed *Bourgogne* (tone poem, Berlin, 1910), *Hyperprism* for winds and percussion (New York, 1923), *Octandre* (New York, 1924), *Integrales* for small orchestra (New York, 1925), *Arcana* (Philadelphia Orchestra under Stokowski, 1927), *Ionisation* (New York, 1933), *Equatorial* (New York, 1934), *Poeme Electronique* (Paris, 1957), *Nocturnal* (New York, 1961).

VARNAY, ASTRID

b. 1918 Stockholm, Sweden.
Soprano. Debut at the Metropolitan Opera, New York City (1941).

VAUGHAN, SARAH LOIS

b. 1924 Newark, New Jersey.
Black singer and pianist. Vocalist and second pianist with Earl Hines' orchestra (1943); with Billy Eckstine's band; went out on her own (1945); married George Treadwell, trumpeter (1959); toured England and France; known as the "Divine Sarah" (after Sarah Bernhardt); guest star on Tony Bennett's "This Is Music" program, London, England (1972); at the Newport Jazz Festival, New York City (1972); Latin American tour (1972).

VAUGHN, BILLY

b. 1919 Glasgow, Kentucky.
Bandleader and arranger. Attended Western Kentucky, Bowling Green, and a school for barbers in Louisville; served in the army in World War II; formed a vocal group, the Hilltoppers, with Jimmy Sacca, singer; wrote "Trying" (1952); signed with Dot Records; wrote arrangements for Pat Boone, the Fontaine Sisters, and Gale Storm.

VEAZIE, GEORGE AUGUSTUS

b. 1835 Boston, Massachusetts, d. 1915.
Editor and teacher. Taught sight singing and vocal music at the New England Conservatory, Boston.

VEE, BOBBY

b. 1943 Fargo, North Dakota.
Singer. Born Bobby Velline; his older brothers, Sidney, Jr. and Bill had their own local band, The Shadows; in 1959 Buddy Holly was killed in a plane crash on his way to a Fargo show and The Shadows, with Bobby Vee, substituted; they were called in for a recording date and Bobby sang "Susie Baby"; the brothers wrote and recorded "Devil or Angel"; Bobby then appeared in films.

VELIKANOFF, IVAN

b. 1890 Russia, d. 1971 Simsbury, Connecticut. Tenor. Leading tenor with the Moscow Art Theatre; toured with the Russian troupe in America (1925-26); remained here and became a U.S. citizen; founded the West Hartford School of Music (Conn.) and taught at the school for twenty-one years; resided in Winsted, Conn.; appeared as a soloist with the New York Philharmonic, the Philadelphia Symphony, and the Cincinnati Symphony orchestras.

VELIS, ANDREA

b. ca. 1931 New Kensington, Pennsylvania. Tenor. His parents came from Greece and settled in New Kensington, Pa.; debut at the Metropolitan Opera (1961); sang a record of 106 roles in 1962-63 season; at All-Britten recital at Caramoor, England (1968); the Witch in Humperdinck's *Hansel and Gretel* at the Met (1971).

VELOZ AND YOLANDE ORCHESTRA *see* SHEP FIELDS

VELVET UNDERGROUND (rock group)

Lou Reed, vocals and lead guitar; Sterling Morrison, bass and rhythm guitar; Maureen Tucker, percussion; Doug Yule, vocals, guitar and organ; John Cale, previous member; discovered by Andy Warhol; toured in Warhol's show, The Exploding Plastic Inevitable; first recorded in 1967; albums—*Velvet Underground and Nico, White Light/White Heat, The Velvet Underground.*

VENGEROVA, ISABELLE

b. 1877 Minsk, Russia, d. 1956 New York City. Pianist and teacher. Studied with Joseph Dachs at the Vienna Conservatory and also with Leschetizky and Anna Essipoff; taught at the St. Petersburg Conservatory after 1906; came to U.S. (1923); American debut (1925) with the Detroit Symphony; taught at the Curtis Institute, Philadelphia, after 1924.

VENUTI, GIUSEPPE ("JOE")

b. 1903 aboard ship enroute to U.S. from Italy. Jazz violinist. Played in duets with Lonnie Johnson; also as a soloist; considered one of the greatest jazz violinists of all time; formed his own band; during the 1940s featured a young singer, Kay Starr; also drummer Barrett Deems; made some discs with guitarist Eddie Lang during the 1930s.

VERBRUGHEN, HENRI

b. 1873 Brussels, Belgium, d. 1934 Northfield, Minnesota. Conductor and violinist. Studied at the Brussels Conservatory; won first prize in violin; soloist with Lamoureux; concertmaster and assistant conductor of the Scottish Orchestra, Glasgow (1902); also of the Choral Union, Glasgow; State Orchestra in Sydney, Australia; guest conductor of the Russian Symphony, New York City (1918); Minneapolis (Minn.) Symphony (1922-31); taught at Carleton College, Northfield, until his death.

VERE, CLEMENTINE DE

b. 1864 Paris, France, d. 1954 Mt. Vernon, New York. Soprano. Studied with Mme. Albertini-Baucarde in Florence, Italy; debut in Florence at age sixteen; sang in concert in Europe and America, also in opera; toured U.S. with opera troupe (1899); at the Metropolitan Opera, New York City (1900-01), later at Covent Garden, London; married Romualdo Sapio, manager of an opera troupe of which she was a singer.

VERNOR, F. DUDLEIGH

b. 1892 Detroit, Michigan, d. there 1974.
Organist and composer. Wrote "The Sweetheart of Sigma Chi" (1912, w. Byron D. Stokes).

VERRALL, JOHN

b. 1908 Britt, Iowa.
Composer. Studied with Jacobi, Kodaly, and Copland; won Guggenheim Fellowship (1946); taught at the University of Washington, Seattle; composed *Concert Piece* for strings and horn, later revised (New York Philharmonic under Mitropoulos, 1941), *Portrait of a Man* for orchestra, *Serenade for Five Instruments, Sonata* for viola and piano, four string quartets, chamber music.

VERRETT, SHIRLEY

b. 1933 New Orleans, Louisiana.
Black mezzo-soprano. Debut at La Scala, Milan, Italy; guest singer on numerous TV shows; album—*Anna Bolena* (1973, featuring Beverly Sills and Shirley Verrett, London Symphony Orchestra, conducted by Julius Rudel).

VERSATILE SEXTET *see* IRVING AARONSON

VERY, JONES

b. 1813 Salem, Massachusetts, d. there 1880. Hymnist. Graduated Harvard University (1836); became a Unitarian missionary (1843); seven of his hymns appeared in Samuel Longfellow and Samuel Johnson's *Book of Hymns* (1846) and two in their *Hymns of the Spirit* (1864).

VERY, WASHINGTON

b. 1815 Salem, Massachusetts, d. there 1853. Hymnist. Brother of Jones Very; graduated Harvard (1843); one of his hymns appeared in Samuel Longfellow and Samuel Johnson's *Book of Hymns* (1846), and this hymn and two others in Putnam's *Singers and Songs* (1874).

VIANESI, AUGUSTE CHARLES LEONARD FRANÇOIS

b. 1837 Leghorn, Italy, d. 1908 New York City. Conductor. Studied in Paris (1859); conducted Drury Lane Theatre, London; then in New York; later at Covent Garden, London; Grand Opera, Paris (1887); in New York (1891-92).

VICARS, HAROLD

b. (?) London, England, d. 1922 Providence, Rhode Island. Composer, conductor, and arranger. Educated at King's College, London; studied music in Germany; conducted Daly's Theatre, London, for ten years; toured with the Moody Manners Opera Company; wrote the operas *49th Star* and *Zorema*; wrote under pseudonym "Moya"; wrote "The Song of Songs" (1914, w. Maurice Vaucaire).

VILLAGE STOMPERS *see* JOE MURANYI

VINCENT, GENE

b. 1935 Virginia, d. 1971 Newhall, California. Singer. Born Vincent Eugene Craddock; early rock 'n roll singer; his recording of "Be-Bop-A-Lulu" (1956) sold a million records; appeared in films; toured England (1961) in a black leather jacket and drew large crowds; died of hemorrhaging caused by a bleeding ulcer; albums—*Gene Vincent's Greatest, I'm Back and I'm Proud.*

VINCENT, NATHANIEL HAWTHORNE (NAT)

b. 1889 Kansas City, Missouri.
Composer, lyricist, and singer. Vaudeville actor in teams of Tracey and Vincent, also Franklyn and Vincent; member of The Happy Chappies with Fred Howard; wrote songs for Broadway shows; with James Brockman and James Kendis, wrote "I'm Forever Blowing Bubbles" (m. John W. Killette) in *The Passing Show* of 1918.

VINER, WILLIAM LETTON

b. 1790 Bath, England, d. 1867 Westfield, Massachusetts. Composer. Studied under Charles Wesley, then came to America in 1859; organist and composer; composed the tune "Dismissal" ("Lord, Behold Us with Thy Blessing," w. H.J. Buckoll); his tune appeared in Flood's *Harmonist* (1845).

VINTON, BOBBY

b. 1935 Canonsburg, Pennsylvania.
Singer and bandleader. His father was a bandleader; formed a band to play locally; signed with Epic Records, New York City (1960); organized the Bachelors, four-piece twist band (1962); also appeared as a soloist; recorded "Roses Are Red," his first gold record.

VIRGINIA BOYS

Jim McReynolds and Jess McReynolds, Alfred Donald McHan, Robert Clark Thompson, Vassar Clements, et al.

VIRGINIA MINSTRELS *see* DANIEL D. EMMETT

VIRGINIA SERENADERS *see* COOL WHITE

VOCES INTIMAE TRIO *see* MATITIAHU BRAUN

VODERY, WILL

b. 1885 Philadelphia, Pennsylvania, d. 1951 New York City. Black bandleader and composer. Graduated the University of

Pennsylvania, Philadelphia; music supervisor for the Florenz Ziegfeld *Follies* (1911-32); wrote the music for Joe Howard's *The Time, The Place, The Girl*; wrote the songs for *The Oyster Man* (1910) starring Ernest Hogan; leader of the 807th Infantry band in World War I, stationed at Fort Betev, France after the war.

VOGRICH, MAX WILLIAM CARL

b. 1852 Szeben, Hungary, d. 1916 New York City. Pianist. Debut at age seven; studied at the Leipzig Conservatory; toured Europe, Mexico, and South America (1870-78); toured U.S. with Wilhelmj; in Australia (1882-86); resided in New York City after 1886; composed *Wanda* (grand opera, Florence, Italy, 1875), two other operas, *The Captivity* (oratorio, Metropolitan Opera, 1891), *Missa Solemnis*, two symphonies, cantatas, violin concerto.

VOKES, HOWARD DEAN

b. 1931 Clearfield, Pennsylvania.
Singer and songwriter. Attended high school in Unity, Pa.; leader of The Country Boys after 1956; wrote "The Love I Once Knew Will Never Return," "Tears at the Grand Ole Opry," "Hank Williams Isn't Dead," "Death on the Highway," "Atom Bomb Heart."

VOLPE, ARNOLD

b. 1869 Kaunas, Lithuania, d. 1940 Miami, Florida. Manager. Founded the Volpe Symphony Orchestra, New York City (1898); helped organize the concerts in Lewisohn Stadium (1918); founded the Miami Symphony Orchestra (1926).

VON BONNHORST, CARL FRANZ WILHELM

b. ca. 1774 Westphalia, Germany, d. 1844 Pittsburgh, Pennsylvania. Composer. Settled in Philadelphia before 1808; moved to Pittsburgh (1821); wrote *The Shepherd's Feast*, symphony (performed in Pittsburgh, 1830).

VON DOHNÁNYI, ERNEST

b. 1877 Pressburg, Hungary (now Bratislava, Czechoslovakia). Composer. Studied at the Royal Academy, Budapest; concert pianist, and became an instructor at Florida State College, Tallahassee, Florida (1948); composed Suite in F-sharp Minor, for orchestra (1909), *Variations on a Nursery Theme* for piano and orchestra (1913), *Ruralia Hungarica* for piano, op. 32a (1924).

VON HAGEN, *see* VAN HAGEN

VON HEERINGEN, ERNEST

b. 1810 Grossmehlza, East Germany, d. 1855 Washington, D.C. Annotator. Rated unsuccessful as innovator in notation and scoring by some experts.

VON JANUSCHOWSKY, GEORGINE

b. 1859 Austria, d. 1914 New York City. Soprano. Sang in Austria and Germany (1877-80); Germania Theatre, New York (1880); again in Germany and Austria (1892-95).

VON KUNITS, LUIGI

b. 1870 Vienna, Austria, d. 1931 Toronto, Ontario, Canada. Conductor, violinist, and teacher. Graduated University of Vienna; studied with Kral, Gruen and others; taught in Chicago, Ill. (1893); concertmaster Pittsburgh Orchestra (1896-1910) and taught at the Pittsburgh Conservatory; after 1912 professor at Canadian Academy of Music, Toronto, and conductor of the Symphony Band.

VON LA HACHE, THEODOR

b. 1823 Dresden, Germany, d. 1867 New Orleans, Louisiana. Composer. Born von Hache; came to New Orleans before 1847; wrote the "Confederates' Polka March," "Carrie Bell" (w. Captain W.C. Capers), "The Free Market" (w. John Overall), "Genevieve's Doves" (w. Henry Clary McNairy); instrumental pieces—*Ever of Thee, Freedom's Tear, Rosey Thorn, Le Plage de Mer* (variations).

VON REUTER, FLORIZEL

b. 1890 Davenport, Iowa.
Violinist. Studied with Bendix in Chicago and later with Marteau in Berlin; toured America; composed operas, violin and orchestral works.

VON STERNBERG, IVANOVITCH CONSTANIN

b. 1852 St. Petersburg, Russia, d. 1924 Philadelphia, Pennsylvania. Pianist. Studied at the Leipzig Conservatory, at the Berlin Akademie, and with Liszt; toured widely, then settled in Philadelphia (1890) when he became director of the Sternberg School of Music.

VON TILZER, ALBERT

b. 1878 Indianapolis, Indiana, d. 1956 Los Angeles, California. Popular composer. Born Albert Gumm; brother of Harry von Tilzer; in 1899 went to work for the Chicago office of

Shapiro, Bernstein and von Tilzer, music publishers; wrote "The Absent Minded Beggar Waltz" (1900), "Take Me Out to the Ball Game" (1908, w. Jack Norton), and "Put Your Arms Around Me Honey, Hold Me Tight" (1910).

VON TILZER, HARRY

b. 1872 Detroit, Michigan, d. 1946 New York City. Popular composer. Born Harry Gumm; older brother of Albert; the family moved to Indianapolis when he was young; he changed his name to von Tilzer when he started writing music; wrote the music "A Bird in a Gilded Cage" (1900, w. A.J. Lamb), "On a Sunday Afternoon" (1902), "Wait 'Til the Sun Shines Nellie" (1905), "I Want a Girl Just Like the Girl That Married Dear Old Dad" (1911, with Will Dillon), and "And the Green Grass Grew All Around" (1912).

VON ZEMLINSKY, ALEXANDER

b. 1872 Vienna, Austria, d. 1942 Larchmont, New York. Conductor and composer. Studied at the Vienna Conservatory; conducted the Vienna Opera; also in other European cities; composed the operas *Sarema, Es War Einmal, Kleider Machen Leute,* and *Kreidekreis,* choral and orchestral works, piano pieces, and songs; married Schönberg's sister.

VON ZINZENDORF, NIKOLAUS LUDWIG

b. 1700 Saxony, Germany, d. 1760 Herrnhut, Saxony. Lyricist and Moravian bishop. Came to Bethlehem, Pa. (1741) and established a choir of eighty singers in the Moravian church there (1742); organized the Singstunden, which performed on Easter Sunday in Bethlehem (1744), the beginning of the Trombone Choirs; wrote "O Thou, to Whose All-searching Light" (translated by John Wesley, m. John E. Gould).

VOTICHENKO, SACHA

b. 1888 Russia, d. 1971 Scottsdale, Arizona. Royal tympanon player and teacher. Taught in New York City for many years; performed in concerts on the royal tympanon, made in 1705 by his ancestor, Pantaleon Hebenstreit; keyless instrument, predecessor of the harpsichord, struck with padded hammers, much like the dulcimer and the Hungarian czymbalom.

WAGENAAR, BERNARD

b. 1894 Netherlands, d. 1971 Kennebunkport, Maine. Composer. Came to America (1920); joined the New York Philharmonic as a violinist (1921); became a teacher at the Juilliard School, New York City (1927); composed symphonies and string quartets.

WAGLER, FREDERICK A.

b. (?), d. ca. 1830.
Composer. Music teacher and composer in Washington, D.C. (1822-30); composed "Commodore David Porter's March" (1816), "Monroe's Grand March" (ca. 1821), "President A. Jackson's Inauguration March" (1829), "General Jackson's Favorite March" (1829); with Charles K. Wagler arranged *Three Favourite Mazourkas* (introduced by the Russian Legation).

WAGNER, JOSEPH FREDERICK

b. 1900 Springfield, Massachusetts, d. 1974. Conductor and composer. Conducted the Boston Civic Orchestra (1925-44); later the Duluth (Minn.) Symphony; composed *Rhapsody for Orchestra* (Boston Civic Orchestra under composer, 1925), *Four Miniatures* (NBC Symphony under Black, 1941), *Hudson River Legend* (ballet, Boston Civic Orchestra under Arthur Fiedler, 1944, with Jan Veen Dancers), *Fugal Triptych* for piano, percussion, and string orchestra.

WAGONER, PORTER WAYNE

b. 1927 West Plains, Missouri.
Singer and guitarist. Radio debut on KWTO, Springfield, Mo. (1951); later on "Ozark Jubilee"; joined Grand Ole Opry, Nashville, Tenn. (1957); formed The Wagonmasters with Norma Jean; later with Dolly Parton; their hit albums—*Always, Always, Just Between You and Me, Just the Two of Us, Porter Wayne and Dolly Rebecca;* Wagoner and Dolly Parton were named Top Duo of the Year at the 1971 Country Music Association awards, Nashville, Tenn.

WAGONMASTERS, THE *see* PORTER WAGONER

WAINWRIGHT, JONATHAN MAYHEW

b. 1792 Liverpool, England, d. 1854 New York City. Composer and compiler. His parents were Americans visiting in England when he was born; graduated Harvard (1812); organist in college, and a composer; in 1818 became rector of Christ (Episcopal) Church, Hartford, Conn.; then Grace Church, New York City (1821-34), then Boston, then St. John's Chapel, New York (1837-54), and provisional Bishop (1852-54); issued *Music of the Church* (1828, revised edition 1852), and *Psalmodia Evangelica* (1830).

WAKELY, JIMMY

b. 1914 Mineola, Arkansas.
Singer. Radio debut on station WKY, Oklahoma City, Oklahoma; formed Wakely Trio with Johnny Bond and Scott Harrel (1937); appeared in numerous films; formed Saddle Pals Trio (1943); sang with Margaret Whiting (1949); albums—*Heartaches, Here's Jimmy Wakely, Now and Then, Show Me the Way.*

WALD, MAX

b. 1889 Litchfield, Illinois, d. 1954.
Composer. Studied in Chicago, later with d'Indy; composed *Retrospectives* (two orchestra pieces, Chicago Symphony under Stock, 1926), *The Streets of Spring* (overture), *The Dancer Dead* (poem for orchestra, NBC Symphony under Goossens, 1932, won NBC prize).

WALKER, AARON ("T-BONE")

b. 1910 Linden, Texas, d. 1975.
Black singer, guitarist, and songwriter. Sang with Les Hites' band (1939-40); later played the electric guitar in dance bands; wrote "Stormy Monday" and other great blues songs; albums—*Singing the Blues, Funky Town, Good Feelin', Stormy Monday Blues, The Truth.*

WALKER, BILLY

b. 1809 Enoree, South Carolina, d. 1875 Spartanburg, South Carolina. Compiler. Prominent singer and ardent Baptist; wrote

"Louisiana" (1835) and "Come Little Children"; published *Southern Harmony* (1835, last edition was 1854); often said "I prefer to have A.S.H. [author of *Southern Harmony*] after my name than President before it," so A.S.H. was carved on his tombstone.

WALKER, BILLY MARVIN

b. 1929 Ralls, Texas.
Singer, guitarist, and songwriter. Radio debut on station KICA, Clovis, New Mexico; joined Grand Ole Opry, Nashville, Tenn. (1960); wrote "Anything Your Heart Desires," "What Makes Me Love You Like I Do," "Pretend You Just Don't Know Me," "Make Believe," " 'Till We Can Make It Come True," "It's Doggone Tough on Me."

WALKER BROTHERS (pop rock group)

Gary Leeds, later known as Gary Walker, drums; Scott Engel, vocals and electric bass; John Maus, vocals and guitar; the group made it big in England, although all three are Americans; first recorded in 1966; album—*Introducing the Walker Brothers.*

WALKER, CHARLIE

b. 1926 Collin County, Texas.
Singer and disk jockey. Joined the Cowboy Ramblers (1943); sang at the Golden Nugget in Las Vegas; golf announcer; albums—*Born to Lose, Close All the Honky Tonks, Country Style, Don't Squeeze My Sharmon, He Is My Everything, Recorded Live in Dallas, Texas, Charlie Walker's Golden Hits, Charlie Walker's Greatest Hits, Wine, Women and Walker.*

WALKER, CINDY

b. (?) Mexia, Texas.
Composer. Wrote a song while a dancer at Billy Rose's Casa Mañana, Fort Worth, Texas; wrote "Lone Star Trail" (1942, recorded by Bing Crosby), "Take Me in Your Arms and Hold Me" (1950, recorded by Eddy Arnold), "Gold Rush Is Over" (1952, Hank Snow record), "Trademark" (1953, with Porter Wagoner, recorded by Carl Smith), "I Don't Care" (1955, with Webb Pierce), "You Don't Know Me" (Arnold record), "Leona" (1962, Stonewall Jackson record), "This Is It" and "Distant Drums" (both recorded by Jim Reeves).

WALKER, EDYTH

b. 1870 Hopewell, New Jersey, d. 1950 New York City. Contralto. Studied at the Dresden Conservatory; with the Vienna Opera, the Metropolitan Opera, New York City (1903-06), then sang in opera in Europe; taught at the American Conservatory, Fountainebleau, France, after 1933.

WALKER, GEORGE

b. (?), d. 1911.
Songwriter and vaudeville showman. Member of the team of Bert Williams and George Walker, vaudeville singers and actors. (*See* Egbert (Bert) Williams)

WALKER, GEORGE

b. 1922 Washington, D.C.
Black pianist and composer. Graduated Oberlin College (1941); studied at the Curtis Institute, Philadelphia (1945), and the Eastman School, Rochester, N.Y. (Doctor of Musical Arts, 1957); debut at Town Hall, New York City (1945); Fulbright Fellowship (1957); Whitney Fellowship (1958), Guggenheim Fellowship (1969), Rockefeller Grant (1970); taught at New School for Social Research, New York City, Smith College, Northampton, Mass., the University of Colorado, Boulder, and Rutgers University, New Brunswick, N.J. after 1969; wrote *Gloria in Memoriam* (1963), *Address for Orchestra* (1959), performed by Atlanta, Baltimore, and Minneapolis Symphonies and the Symphony of the New World.

WALKER, JAMES JOHN

b. 1881 New York City, d. there 1946.
Lyricist and mayor. Attended St. Francis Xavier College and New York Law School (1912); while a state Senator, wrote the lyrics "Will You Love Me in December as You Do in May" (1905, m. Ernest R. Ball); elected Mayor of New York City (1925); due to charges of graft and maladministration, he resigned (1932).

WALKER, WAYNE PAUL

b. 1925 Quapaw, Oklahoma.
Composer. Attended school in Kilgore, Texas; served in the Coast Guard in World War II; employed by the Cedarwood Publishing Company, Nashville, Tenn.; wrote "I've Got a New Heartache" (recorded by Ray Price), "Holiday for Love" (Webb Pierce record) and "Why, Why" (Carl Smith record), all 1957; "Fallen Angel" (1960, with Ben Weisman and B. Raleigh, recorded by Pierce); "Hello Out There" (Carl Belew record), "Pride" (Price record), "Unloved, Unwanted" (Kitty Wells record), and "A Little Heartache" (Eddy Arnold Record, all 1962); "Leaving on Your Mind" (1963, Patsy Cline record); "Memory No. 1" (Pierce record), "Burning Memories" (Price record), and "I Thank My Lucky Stars" (Arnold record), all 1964.

WALL, REM

b. 1918 West Frankfort, Illinois.
Leader and songwriter. Leader of Golden West Cowboys (1935-39); Green Valley Boys after 1948; wrote "Teardrops Keep Falling," "Trying," "Under the Old Oak Tree," "That's All She Left Me."

WALLENSTEIN, ALFRED

b. 1898 Chicago, Illinois.
Noted cellist and conductor. Studied with Julius Klengel; debut in Los Angeles (1912); solo cellist with the Chicago Symphony, then with the New York Philharmonic; conductor of radio orchestra; Mutual Network after 1935; conducted Los Angeles Philharmonic after 1943.

WALLER, CHARLES

b. 1935 Joinerville , Texas.
Singer and guitarist. The family moved to Los Angeles when he was young; started working in Baltimore when he met John Duffy, and they formed a team to sing and play on radio; later Eddie Adcock and Jim Cox joined the group, which became known as the "Country Gentlemen"; their LP records—*Bluegrass* (1962) and *Country Gentlemen* (1965).

WALLER, THOMAS ("FATS")

b. 1904 Waverly, New York, d. 1943 Kansas City, Missouri. Black composer. Played the organ for a theater in Harlem for the black singer Florence Mills, and later was accompanist for Bessie Smith, blues singer; wrote "Squeeze Me" (1925, w. Clarence Williams), "Honeysuckle Rose" (1929), "I've Got a Feelin' I'm Fallin' " (1929, with Harry Link, w. Billy Rose); wrote the scores for *Keep Shufflin'* (1928, with J.C. Johnson) and *Hot Chocolate* (1929) which included "Ain't Misbehavin" (with Harry Brooks, w. Andy Razaf); best piano solos were *Minor Drag, Viper's Drag, London Suite,* and *Handful of Keys;* traveling east on a train, suffering from pneumonia and drinking heavily; when the conductor tried to awaken him the next morning, found him dead in his berth.

WALTER, BRUNO

b. 1876 Berlin, Germany, d. 1962.
Noted conductor. Born Bruno Schlesinger; the rise of Hitlerism forced Walter to leave Germany for Austria (1933), then the Anschluss forced him to flee to America, where he accepted an engagment with the New York Philharmonic-Symphony Society, and later also with the Metropolitan Opera; published his autobiography *Theme and Variations* and wrote *Von der Musik und vom Musizieren.*

WALTER, CYRIL F.

b. 1915 Minneapolis, Minnesota, d. 1968 New York City. Pianist. Played in New York City supper clubs for thirty years; most recently at the Drake Hotel; died of cancer.

WALTER, LITTLE *see* LITTLE WALTER

WALTER, THOMAS

b. 1696 Boston, Massachusetts, d. 1725 Roxbury, Massachusetts. Singer and writer. Graduated Harvard (1713) when only seventeen; in 1718 became minister of the Roxbury Church, with the ordination sermon preached by his grandfather, Rev. Increase Mather; present was his uncle, Rev. Cotton Mather (son of Cotton Mather); in 1721 published *The Ground Rules of Musick Explained, or An Introduction to the Art of Singing by Note,* on the press of James Franklin, where Benjamin was an apprentice.

WALTER, WILLIAM HENRY

b. 1825 Newark, New Jersey, d. 1893 New York City. Composer. Organist in churches in Newark, then at three Episcopal churches in New York City until 1869; received a D.Mus. from Columbia (1864), and became organist there (1865); composed the tunes "Festival Song" (1894, "Awake and Sing the Song" William Hammond, 1745) and "Chant in Ab."

WALTERS, WAYNE D.

b. 1926 Van Buren, Arkansas.
Singer and bandleader. Leader of the Christian Troubadours after 1954.

WALWORTH, CLARENCE AUGUSTUS

b. 1820 Plattsburgh, New York, d. 1900 Albany, New York. Hymnist. Educated at Union College, Schenectady, N.Y. (1838); entered the General Theological Seminary (1842); originally a Presbyterian, became a Roman Catholic (1845); served thirty-four years as rector of St. Mary's, Albany, N.Y.; translated "Holy God, We Praise Thy Name" from the German (tune "Te Deum," 1774).

WARD, CHARLES B.

b. 1865 London, England, d. 1917 New York City. Popular composer. Composed the music "Picture 84" (w. Gussie Davis, 1894), "The Band Played On" (1895, w. J.F. Palmer), and "Strike Up the Band, Here Comes a Sailor" (1900, w. A.B. Sterling); introduced "The Band Played On" himself at Hammerstein's Harlem Opera House; the song was publicized and promoted by the *New York World,* resulting in the sale of one million copies of sheet music.

WARD, CLARA

b. 1924 Philadelphia, Pennsylvania, d. 1973. Black singer. The Clara Ward Singers, a hit at the Baptist Convention of 1943, included her mother, sister, and Marion and Henrietta Waddy; toured the country with the Big Gospel Cavalcade; appeared at the Newport Jazz Festival (1957); albums—*Gospel Concert, Heart, the Faith, the Soul of Clara Ward, I Feel the Holy Spirit, Lord Touch Me, Meeting Tonight, Packin' Up, Ward Singers.*

WARD, JUSTINE BAYARD (CUTTING)

b. 1879 Morristown, New Jersey.
Teacher. With Mother Stevens helped found the Pius X School of Liturgical Music (1918); studied at the Pontifical Institute of Sacred Music in Rome, Italy (1925).

WARD, ROBERT

b. 1917 Cleveland, Ohio.
Composer. Graduated the Eastman School of Music, Rochester, N.Y.; won Columbia University Fellowship, and MacDowell Fellowship; composed *Slow Music for Orchestra,* Movement from a Symphony in E Minor (Rochester Civic Orchestra under Hanson, 1938), Symphony no. 1 (Juilliard School Orchestra, 1941, won Juilliard Award, 1942), *A Yankee Overture,* Symphony no. 2; won American Academy of Arts and Letters Award (1946); opera, *The Crucible* (libretto—Bernard Stambler, based on Arthur Miller's play), produced by the New York City Opera Company (1961).

WARD, SAMUEL AUGUSTUS

b. 1848 Newark, New Jersey, d. there 1903. Composer. Dealer in musical instruments; for fourteen years conductor of the Newark Orpheus Club; composed the music "Oh Mother, Dear Jerusalem" which was first published in *The Parish Choir* (Boston, 1888); the tune became known as "Materna," which was used to the words "America, the Beautiful" (1895, w. Katherine Lee Bates).

WARD'S DOMINOES, BILLY *see* JACKIE WILSON

WARE, HARRIET

b. 1877 Waupun, Wisconsin, d. 1962 New York City. Composer. Graduated the Pillsbury Conservatory, Owatonna, Minn. (1895); pupil of William Mason and others; married Hugo M. Krumbhaar; composed *Sir Olaf* (cantata, New York Symphony, 1910), *The Fay Song,* piano pieces, and numerous songs.

WARE, HELEN

b. 1887 Woodbury, New Jersey.
Violinist and composer. Studied violin with Frederic Hahn in Philadelphia and composition with Hugh Clarke at the University of Pennsylvania; studied in Vienna and in Budapest with Hubay; played in many recitals in Europe and America after 1912; composer and arranger of Hungarian and Slavic music.

WARE, HENRY, JR.

b. 1794 Hingham, Massachusetts, d. 1843 Framingham, Massachusetts. Hymnist. Graduated Harvard (1812); taught at Exeter Academy in New Hampshire; pastor of the Second Unitarian Church, Boston (1817-30); professor in the Cambridge Theological School (1830-42); wrote the hymn "Happy the Home When God Is There" (tune "St. Agnes"—J.B. Dykes); his hymns were published in four volumes by Rev. Chandler Robbins (1847).

WARE, LEONARD

b. 1909 Richmond, Virginia.
Black guitarist. Studied at the Tuskegee Institute; organized his own trio; wrote "I Dreamt I Dwelt in Harlem," "Hold Tight."

WARFIELD, CHARLIE

b. 1883 Guthrie, Tennessee.
Black pianist and composer. Raised in Nashville, Tenn.; went to St. Louis (1897), then Chicago (1900); with Spencer Williams wrote "I Ain't Got Nobody" (1916) featured by Sophie Tucker and Bert Williams; with Clarence Williams wrote "Baby, Won't You Please Come Home?" (1919).

WARING, FRED

b. 1900 Tyrone, Pennsylvania.
Bandleader and arranger. Formed a dance band; later the Fred Waring Glee Club; graduated Pennsylvania State College; formed the Pennsylvanians; the Fred Waring radio show was popular in the 1940s and '50s.

WARNER, ANNA B.

b. 1820 Martlaer, West Point, New York, d. 1915 Highland Falls, New York. Hymnist. Sister of Sarah Warner; wrote the lyrics "Jesus Loves Me" (1859, m. W.B. Bradbury), "One More Day's Work for Jesus" (m. Robert Lowry); edited *Hymns of the Church Militant* (1858) and published *Wayfaring Hymns, Original and Translated* (1869).

WARNER, FRANK

b. 1903 Selma, Alabama.
Ballad singer. Graduated Duke University, Durham, N.C. (1925); joined YMCA, Greensboro, N.C. (1928); married Anne Locker, singer; they sang in concerts in the U.S. and overseas; his albums—*American Folk Songs and Ballads* (1952), *Songs and Ballads of America's Wars* (1954), *Songs of the Civil War.*

WARREN, GEORGE WILLIAM

b. 1828 Albany, New York, d. 1902 New York City. Composer. Organist in Episcopal churches in Albany, N.Y., Brooklyn, and New York City; composed the music "Behold the Lamb of God" (w. Matthew Bridges, 1848), "Heralds of Christ" (w. Laura S. Copenhaver), and "God of Our Fathers" (1892, w. D.C. Roberts, first played at a service at St. Thomas' Church in New York City, 1892); also composed the *First Easter Cantata,* "The Singing of the Birds" and the *Second Easter Cantata,* "Fill the Font with Roses" (1878, w. Mrs. Lydia Sigourney), and *The Magdalene* (1877).

WARREN, HARRY

b. 1893 Brooklyn, New York.
Popular composer. Started as a drummer in the John Victor Brass Band; served in the navy in World War I; then was a song plugger for Stark and Cowan music publishers; wrote "Away Down South in Heaven" (w. Bud Green), "Nagasaki" (Mort Dixon), "Absence Makes the Heart Grow Fonder for Someone Else" (Sam M. Lewis and Joe Young), "Would You Like to Take a Little Walk" (Mort Dixon and Billy Rose); composed the score for the Ed Wynn show *The Laugh Parade* (1931, w. Dixon and Young), score for Billy Rose's *Crazy Quilt* (1931, which included "I Found a Million Dollar Baby in a Five and Ten Cent Store," Dixon and Rose); also with Al Dubin—"Shuffle Off to Buffalo" (1932), "Lullaby of Broadway" (1935); with Mack Gordon—"The Chattanooga Choo Choo" (1941), "You'll Never Know" (1943); with Johnny Mercer—"Jeepers Creepers" (1938), "On the Atchison, Topeka and Santa Fe" (1945); with Harold Adamson—"A Love Affair to Remember," "The Legend of Wyatt Earp"; also wrote "You Wonderful You" (1950, Jack Brooks and Saul Chapin), "This Heart of Mine" (Arthur Freed), "The Stanley Steamer" (1947, Ralph Blane); with Ira Gershwin—"Highland Fling" and "My One and Only" (1927).

WARREN, HENRY C.

b. 1855 Killingly, Connecticut, d. 1934. Pianist, organist, and teacher. Taught piano, organ and theory in Danielsonville, Conn. after 1873.

WARREN, LEONARD

b. 1911 Bronx, New York City, d. 1960 New York City. Baritone. Born Leonard Varenoff; sang at Radio City Music Hall; studied in Italy; debut (1939) at the Metropolitan Opera, New York City as Paolo in *Simon Boccanegra;* died on the stage at the Metropolitan while singing the role of Don Carlo in *La Forza del Destino.*

WARREN, MARGIE ANN ("FIDDLIN' KATE")

b. 1922 Grand Junction, Colorado.
Fiddler, singer, and songwriter. Attended the Hollywood Conservatory of Music (1937-38), and Hartnell College, Salinas, Calif.; wrote "Tennessee Two-step," "Del Rio," "Isle of Sicily," "Katie Warren Breakdown."

WARREN, RICHARD HENRY

b. 1859 Albany, New York, d. 1933 South Chatham, Massachusetts. Organist. Organist-choirmaster in New York City churches (1880-1907), then at the Church of the Ascension; founded and conducted the Church Choral Society (1886-95) and again 1903-07).

WARREN, SAMUEL PROWSE

b. 1841 Montreal, Quebec, Canada, d. 1915 New York City. Organist. Studied in Berlin, Germany (1861-64); organist-choirmaster in New York City (1865-66), then at Grace Chapel, New York City (1868-94), and the Munn Avenue Presbyterian Church, East Orange, N.J., after 1894.

WARREN, SAMUEL RUSSELL

b. ca. 1815 Rhode Island, d. 1882 Montreal, P.Q., Canada. Organ maker. Moved to Canada (1837); made organs in Montreal, Quebec, Canada; his son, Samuel P. Warren, was a prominent organist.

WARREN, SMOKEY

b. 1916 Phoenix, Arizona.
Singer and bandleader. Leader of the Arizona Trailblazers.

WARREN, WILLIAM FAIRFIELD

b. 1833 Williamsburg, Massachusetts, d. 1929 Brookline, Massachusetts. Hymnist. Wrote the lyrics "Homeward Bound" (ca. 1858, m. J.W. Dadmun, also C.S. Harrington) and "I Worship Thee, O Holy Ghost" (m. A.J.

Abbey); graduated Wesleyan University, Middletown, Conn., in 1853, and Andover Theological Seminary; minister of the Methodist Episcopal Church; helped establish Boston University (1869) and was its first (acting) president.

WARRINER, SOLOMON

b. 1778 Wilbraham, Massachusetts, d. 1860 Springfield, Massachusetts. Compiler. Officer in an artillery regiment at Northampton in 1814; choirmaster in Pittsfield (1815-20), then in Springfield until his death; compiled *The Springfield Collection* (1813); founded the Handel and Haydn Society in Springfield; Thomas Hastings' *Utica Collection* was combined with Warriner's in *Musica Sacra, or the Springfield and Utica Collections United* (1816).

WARWICK, DIONNE

b. 1941 East Orange, New Jersey.
Black singer. Born Marie Dionne Warrick; played the organ and sang in her church choir; discovered by Burt Bacharach (1960); sang in Basin Street East (1964); first big record hit was "Don't Make Me Over"; "Valley of the Dolls" sold a million records; albums—*Anyone Who Had a Heart, Here, Where There Is Love, I'll Never Fall in Love Again, Make Way for Dionne Warwick, Presenting Dionne Warwick, Promises, Promises, Sensitive Sound of Dionne Warwick, Soulful.*

WASHBURN, EDWARD ABIEL

b. 1819 Boston, Massachusetts, d. 1881 Philadelphia, Pennsylvania. Hymnist. Graduated Harvard (1838), and Andover Theological Seminary; Congregational minister, then Episcopal rector of St. Paul's, Newburyport, Mass. (1844-51), rector of St. John's, Hartford, Conn. (1853-62), St. Mark's, Philadelphia (1865-81); his translations of hymns appeared in Schaff's *Christ in Song* (1869).

WASHBURN, HENRY S.

b. 1813 Providence, Rhode Island, d. 1903. Lyricist. Educated at Brown University, Providence; served in the Massachusetts legislature both as a representative and senator; wrote the lyrics "The Burial of Mrs. Judson (1846, a Baptist missionary, tune—"Mournfully, Tenderly, Bear on the Dead," m. Lyman Heath), "The Vacant Chair" (1862, m. G.F. Root).

WASHINGTON, DINAH

b. 1924 Tuscaloosa, Alabama, d. 1967.
Black singer. Born Ruth Jones; raised in Chicago; played piano for her church choir; sang in Lionel Hampton's band (1943-46) first recorded in 1947; albums—*Best of Dinah Washington, Dinah, Dinah Discovered, Dinah Jams, Dinah Washington Sings Bessie Smith, For Lonely Lovers, For Those in Love, Late Late Show, Two of Us, Unforgettable, Golden Hits, Dinah Washington Sings Fats Waller, What a Difference a Day Makes.*

WASHINGTON, NED

b. 1901 Scranton, Pennsylvania.
Lyricist and librettist. Wrote for the *Earl Carroll Vanities;* the *Blackbirds of 1934;* wrote "Sweet Madness" (1933, m. Victor Young), "Breaking in a Pair of Shoes" (1936, m. Sammy Stept), "The Nearness of You" (1940, m. Hoagy Carmichael), "When You Wish Upon a Star" (1940, Academy Award), "Do Not Forsake Me" (m. Dimitri Tiomkin, Academy Award, 1952).

WASSERMAN, DALE

b. 1921.
Composer. Wrote the musical, *Man of La Mancha,* which opened in New York City in November 1965, and ran for almost six years, originally starring Richard Kiley and Joan Diener.

WATERBURY, JARED BELL

b. 1799 New York City, d. 1876 Brooklyn, New York. Hymnist. Graduated Yale (1822); became a Congregational minister in Hudson, N.Y., and at the Bowdin Street Church, Boston; wrote the hymn "Soldiers of the Cross Arise!" (tune "Caledonia"—Scottish air); eight of his hymns appeared in Rev. J. Leavitt's *Christian Lyre* (1830) and one in *Songs for the Sanctuary* (1865).

WATERS, ETHEL

b. 1900 Chester, Pennsylvania.
Celebrated black singer. Sang in Lew Leslie's *Blackbirds of 1930* (w. Andy Razaf, m. Eubie Blake); sang in musical *As Thousands Cheer* (1933), and the film *Cabin in the Sky* (1940); sang in the White House (January 24, 1971) for President and Mrs. Nixon, and was introduced by the President as "the most outstanding gospel singer in the world today"; sang "His Eye Is on the Sparrow."

WATERS, HORACE

b. 1812 Jefferson, Maine, d. 1893 New York City. Composer and compiler. Piano dealer and publisher; composed the music for " 'Tis Religion That Can Give" (w. Mary Masters) published in his *Sabbath Bell;* published *The Anniversary and Sunday School Music Book No. 2* (1858) which contained "Homeward Bound" (*see* W.F. Warren, G.J. Webb, J.W. Dadmun, and C.S. Harrington) and "Happy Greetings to All" (*see* Mildred J. Hill); one of the founders of the Prohibition Party; his *Atheneum Collection of Hymns and Tunes for the Church and Sunday Schools* (1863) contained twenty-nine pieces by Stephen C. Foster.

WATERS, MUDDY

b. 1915 Rolling Fork, Mississippi.
Black singer, guitarist, and songwriter. Born McKinley Morganfield; raised in Clarksdale, Miss.; formed his own band; toured England (1958); albums—*After the Rain, Electric Mud, Folk Singer, Muddy, Brass and Blues, Sail On, Muddy Waters at Newport.*

WATSON, ARTHEL ("DOC")

b. 1923 Deep Gap, North Carolina.
Singer, banjoist, and guitarist. Attended the Raleigh (N.C.) School for the Blind; despite his handicap, mastered the banjo and guitar; joined Clarence Ashley's old-time string band; albums—*Home Again, Good Deal, Old Time Music at Clarence Ashley's, Progressive Bluegrass, Southbound, Doc Watson, Doc Watson and Son, Watson Family;* sang at the Village Gaslight, New York City (1972).

WATSON, FRANCES NASH

b. 1890 Omaha, Nebraska, d. 1971. Charlottesville, Virginia. Concert pianist. Studied in Europe; soloist with the Washington Symphony Orchestra; married Maj. Gen. Edwin M. Watson; played at the White House for President and Mrs. Franklin D. Roosevelt; organized the Watergate concerts of the National Symphony Orchestra, Washington, D.C.

WATSON, HENRY COOD

b. 1818 London, England, d. 1875 New York City. Critic and writer. His father, John Watson, was chorus master at Covent Garden; came to America (1840); art and music critic of the *New World,* New York City; critic of the *Albion;* editor of *Musical Chronicle* (1843-47); the *American Musical Times* after 1847; *New York Tribune* (1863-67); started the *American Art Journal* (1863); wrote the libretto, *Lurline* (m. William Vincent Wallace).

WATTERS, LU

b. 1911 Santa Cruz, California.
Bandleader. Led the Yerba Buena band in California during the 1940s.

WATTS, ANDRE

b. 1946 Nuremberg, Germany.
Black pianist. Father transferred to Germany; Hungarian mother; father transferred back to Philadelphia; studied at the Musical Academy; debut with the Philadelphia Orchestra at age nine; at sixteen played for the New York Philharmonic under Leonard Bernstein; Bernstein "flipped" when he first heard Watts; studied at the Peabody Conservatory, Baltimore; toured U.S. and Europe; with the Pittsburgh Symphony Orchestra at Carnegie Hall, New York City (1972).

WATTS, WINTTER

b. 1884 Cincinnati, Ohio, d. 1962 Brooklyn, New York. Composer. Studied singing in Florence, Italy; won Loeb Prize (1919); composed *Two Etchings* for orchestra, *Vignettes of Italy, Wings of Night, Like Music on the Water* (vocal cycles), incidental music for *Alice in Wonderland,* ballads, and songs.

WAYNE, MABEL

b. 1904 Brooklyn, New York.
Popular composer. Studied in Europe, entered vaudeville at age sixteen; wrote "Don't Wake Me Up, Let Me Dream" (1925, with Abel Baer, w. L. Wolfe Gilbert), "In a Little Spanish Town" (1926, w. Sam Lewis and Joe Young), "Ramona" (1927, Gilbert), "Chiquita" (1928, Gilbert), "Little Man You've Had a Busy Day" (1934, with Al Hoffman and Maurice Sigler), "Why Don't You Fall in Love with Me?" (1937, w. Al Lewis), "It Happened in Monterey" (1940, w. Billy Rose), "Dreamer's Holiday" (1949, w. Kim Gannon).

WAYNE, THOMAS

b. 1940 Panola County, Mississippi, d. 1971 Memphis, Tennessee. Singer. Born Thomas William Perkins; brother of Luther Perkins who backed up Johnny Cash, the singer; moved to Memphis as a young man; hit records were "Tragedy" (1959), "Laura," "No

One," "Kiss Away," and "This Time"; his brother died in a house fire in Nashville, Tenn. (1968); he died in a two-car collision in Memphis.

WEATHERFORD, TEDDY

b. 1903 Bluefield, West Virginia, d. 1945 Calcutta, India. Black jazz pianist. Known for his Harlem style; played with Erskine Tate, Earl Hines, and Jack Carter.

WEAVER, POWELL

b. 1890 Clearfield, Pennsylvania, d. 1951 Oakland, California. Composer. Studied at the Institute of Musical Art, New York City; church organist; his *The Vagabond* (symphonic poem, 1930) given by orchestras in Kansas City, St. Louis, and Minneapolis; composed *The Faun*, suite in three movements (1927).

WEAVERS, THE *see* PETER SEEGER

WEBB, CLIFTON

b. 1896 Indianapolis, Indiana, d. 1966.
Singer and actor. Sang in a number of musical comedies, including *As Thousands Cheer* (1933, m. Irving Berlin), in which he sang "Easter Parade" with Marilyn Miller.

WEBB, DEAN

b. 1937 Indianola, Missouri.
Singer and mandolin player. Member of the group known as "The Dillards"; their LP records—*Bluegrass* (1963) and *The Dillards Live* (1964).

WEBB, GEORGE JAMES

b. 1803 Wiltshire, Salisbury, England, d. 1887 Orange, New Jersey. Noted composer. Came to America (1830) and settled in Boston, where he became associate director of the Boston Academy of Music with Lowell Mason; lived in Orange, N.J. (1870-76 and 1885-87); during the summers held music festivals in Binghamton, N.Y.; composed the music "The Morning Light Is Breaking" (1837, w. S.F. Smith), which tune was later used for "Stand Up for Jesus" (w. George Duffield); wrote "Homeward Bound" (1858, *see also* J.W. Dadmun and C.S. Harrington), and "The Voice of God Is Calling"; composed the music "Hail to the Anointed" (w. J. Montgomery), "Our Country's Flag Forever" (1861, w. Henry Heine), "Oh Thou Whose Hand Hath Brought Us" (1879, w. F.W. Goodby); published *Children's Hosanna.*

WEBB, JUNE ELLEN

b. 1934 L'Anse, Michigan.
Singer and songwriter. Wrote "The Party Is Over" (1957), and "The Secret of Life" (1958).

WEBB, WILLIAM ("CHICK")

b. 1902 Baltimore, Maryland, d. there 1939. Black bass drummer and bandleader. Played in Harlem's Savoy Ballroom, New York City (1928); Ella Fitzgerald joined the band (1935); later played at the Park Central, New York City; the band was very popular to the end; Chick was taken ill while playing on a riverboat outside Washington, D.C., and rushed to Johns Hopkins Hospital in Baltimore; seven days later he called out, "I'm sorry, I gotta go!" and he was gone.

WEBER, ADAM

b. 1854 Cincinnati, Ohio, d. 1906.
Conductor and bandmaster. Conductor of orchestra at Heuck's Opera House, Cincinnati; manager of Weber's Military Band.

WEBER, ALBERT

b. 1828 Bavaria, Germany, d. 1879 New York City. Piano maker. Came to America about 1844; manufactured pianos in New York City after 1851.

WEBER, BEN BRIAN

b. 1916 St. Louis, Missouri.
Composer. Studied medicine at the University of Chicago, then switched to music; known for his *Sonata da Camera, Concerto for Piano, Cello and Five Wind Instruments*, the ballet *The Pool of Darkness, Concert Aria after Solomon* for soprano and orchestra, and a symphony on the poems of William Blake, the English poet and engraver.

WEBER, JOHN C.

b. 1856 Cincinnati, Ohio, d. 1938.
Clarinetist and conductor. Musical director and clarinet soloist in Cincinnati.

WEBER, JOSEPH M.

b. 1867 New York City, d. 1942 Los Angeles, California. Vaudeville actor. Joined Lew Fields in 1885; the vaudeville team of Weber and Fields became famous. (*See* John Stromberg for a list of shows produced for Weber and Fields)

WEBSTER, BENJAMIN FRANCIS

b. 1909 Kansas City, Missouri, d. 1973.
Black alto saxophonist. Played in Cab Calloway's band; also with Teddy Wilson.

WEBSTER, CHARLES R.

b. 1762, d. 1832.
Music dealer. With his twin brother, George Webster, were music dealers in Albany, New York; they issued *The Easy Instructor, or a New Method of Teaching Sacred Harmony*

(first note-shaped tune book), having acquired the copyright from William Little.

WEBSTER, FREDDIE

b. 1917 Cleveland, Ohio, d. 1947 Chicago, Illinois. Black trumpeter. Played with Lucky Millinder, Earl Hines and others; recorded with Sarah Vaughan.

WEBSTER, GEORGE

b. 1762, d. 1821.
Music dealer. With his twin brother, Charles R. Webster, were music dealers in Albany, N.Y.

WEBSTER, JOSEPH PHILBRICK

b. 1819 Manchester, New Hampshire, d. 1875 Elkhorn, Wisconsin. Organist, choirmaster, and popular composer. Moved to Madison, Ind. (1851), then to Racine, Wisc. (1856), then settled in Elkhorn (1857); composed the music and S.F. Bennett wrote the words "The Irish Volunteer" (1861), "The Soldier to His Mother" (1862), "Old Abe Has Gone and Did It Boys" (1862), "The Negro Emancipation Song" (1862), and "In the Sweet Bye and Bye" (1867, which tune is also used for "The Cowboy's Dream" w. Will C. Barnes); also composed the music "The New Star Spangled Banner" (1861, w. Edna Proctor), "Mother Can I Go" (1861, w. W.B. Tremaine), "There's a Cottage on the Hillside of the Noble Prairie State" (w. Minne Moore), "Lorena" (1863, w. Rev. H.D.L. Webster), "Our Soldier" (1863, w. E.B. Dewing), "Protect the Freedman" (1863, w. Luke Collins), "Our Soldier's Welcome Home" (1865, w. E.B. Dewing), "Little Maud" (1870, w. T.B. Aldrich), and words and music "Where the Little Feet Are Waiting" ("The Golden Stair").

WEBSTER, PAUL FRANK

b. 1909 Kansas City, Missouri, d. 1966.
Black trumpeter. Played in Jimmie Lunceford's orchestra.

WEEDE, ROBERT

b. 1903 Baltimore, Maryland, d. 1972 Walnut Creek, California. Baritone and musical comedy star. Born Robert Wiedefeld; debut in 1924, New York; debut in 1933 at Radio City Music Hall, with Jan Peerce as featured singer; Metropolitan debut (1937) as Tonio in *Pagliacci,* with the company until 1942 (and 1944-45); in the musicals *The Most Happy Fella* (1956), *Milk and Honey,* and *Cry for Us All* (1969); also sang with the San Francisco Opera, gave a special performance of *Pagliacci* there (1964).

WEIDIG, ADOLF

b. 1867 Hamburg, Germany, d. 1931 Hinsdale, Illinois. Teacher and composer. Studied at the Hamburg Conservatory; won Mozart cash award; taught in Chicago after 1892 and was co-director of the American Conservatory there; composed chamber music and orchestral works.

WEIGAND, LOUIS A.

b. 1856 Cincinnati, Ohio, d. 1912.
Violinist and teacher. Played first violin in orchestra at Heuck's Opera House, Cincinnati; also taught violin there after 1880.

WEIGL, KARL

b. 1881 Vienna, Austria, d. 1949 New York City. Composer. For his symphonic cantata, *Weltfeier,* the city of Vienna awarded him a prize (1924); composed four symphonies and many songs.

WEIL, OSCAR

b. 1840 Columbia County, New York, d. 1921. Composer, teacher, and critic. Wrote *Herbstfrühlengslied (Spring Song),* "In Autumn."

WEIL, HERMANN

b. 1877 Germany, d. 1949 Blue Mt. Lake, New York. Baritone. Studied with Mottl and Dippel; debut in Freiburg (1900); sang at Bayreuth; with the Metropolitan Opera, New York City (1911-17).

WEILL, KURT

b. 1900 Dessau, Germany, d. 1950 New York City. Popular composer. Studied at the Berlin Hochshule under Humperdinck and Krasselt (1918) and with Ferruccio Busoni (1921-24); wrote the operas *The Protagonist* (1924, play—Georg Kaiser), *The Royal Palace* (1927, Ivan Goll), *Mahogany* (1927, book—Bertolt Brecht), *The Three Penny Opera* (1928, w. Brecht, adapted from John Gay); *The Silver Lake* (book—Kaiser), opened in Berlin (February 18, 1933) and the next day the Reichstag was set aflame, so Weill left for Paris and London, coming to America (1935); wrote the musicals *Johnny Johnson* (1936, w. Paul Green), *The Eternal Road* (1937, book—Franz Werfel, directed by Max Reinhardt), *Knickerbocker Holiday* (1938, librettist—Maxwell Anderson, which included "September Song"), *Lady in the Dark* (1941, book—Moss Hart and lyrics—Ira Gershwin, starring Gertrude Lawrence and Danny Kaye), *One Touch of Venus* (1943, w. S.J. Perelman and Ogden Nash, book—F. Anstey, starred Mary Martin), *Street Scene* (1947, book—Elmer Rice, w. Langston Hughes), *Down in the Valley* (folk opera, 1947, book—

Arnold Sundgaard), *Lost in the Stars* (1949, libretto—Maxwell Anderson, book—Alan Paton, *Cry the Beloved Country*); also wrote the radio cantata *Lindbergh's Flight.*

WEIN, GEORGE

b. 1925 Boston, Massachusetts.
Singer, pianist, and manager. Toured U.S. and Europe with Thelonius Monk, jazz musician; organized the first Newport, R.I. Jazz Festival (1954); with Albert B. Grossman, organized the first Newport Folk Festival (1959), the first annual Ohio Valley Jazz Festival in Cincinnati, Ohio (1962), jazz festival in Berlin, Germany, and the World Jazz Festival in Japan; albums—*George Wein's Newport All Stars, That Newport Jazz, George Wein in Paris.*

WEINBERG, HENRY

b. 1931.
Composer. Studied with Milton Babbitt at Princeton; also with Roger Sessions.

WEINBERG, JACOB

b. 1879 Odessa, Russia, d. 1956 New York City. Composer. Emigrated to Palestine; wrote the national opera *Hechalutz,* (*The Pioneer*), then came to New York (1929); composed the oratorios *Isaiah* and *Life of Moses.*

WEINBERGER, JAROMIR

b. 1896 Prague, Czechoslovakia, d. 1967. Composer. Studied at the Prague Conservatory and then with Max Reger in Berlin; taught at the Ithaca Conservatory, Ithaca, N.Y. (1922-26); went back to Europe, but settled in the United States (1939); known for his *Schwanda, The Bagpipe Player* (opera, 1926), *Christmas Overture* for orchestra and organ (1929), *The Legend of Sleepy Hollow* suite for orchestra (1939), *Under the Spreading Chestnut Tree* for orchestra (1939).

WEINER, LAZAR

b. 1897 Cherkass, Russia.
Composer. Composed the cantatas *Legend of Toil,* and *O Thee, America;* the opera, *The Golem; Biblical Suite* for solo, chorus and piano; the ballet *Lag Baomer; Shiro Chadosho, Sabbath Evening Service, Shiro Chadosho, Sabbath Morning Service.*

WEINZWEIG, JOHN

b. 1913 Toronto, Ontario, Canada.
Composer. With Canadian Broadcasting Corp.; composed *The Enchanted Hill* (after poem by Walter de la Mare) and *Suite,* both for small orchestra (Rochester Civic Orchestra under Hanson, 1938); also *Spectre* for string orchestra and four tympani (CBC, Alexander Chuhaldin conducting, 1939), *A Tale of Tuamotu* for orchestra and solo bassoon, choruses, songs.

WEIR, MARY (BRINKLEY)

b. 1783, d. 1840 New York City.
Composer. Lived in New York City from 1802-40; composed *The Lord of the Castle.*

WEISGALL, HUGO

b. 1912 Eibenschultz, Czechoslovakia.
Composer. Came to U.S. to live; composed *Quest,* ballet for the Baltimore Ballet Company (orchestral suite—New York Philharmonic under Barbirolli, 1942); the musicals—*The Tenor* (1950, play—Wedekind), *The Stronger* (1952, play—Strindberg), *Six Characters in Search of an Author* (1956, play—Pirandello), *Purgatory* (1959, play—Yeats), *Athaliah* (1964, play—Racine).

WEISMAN, BENJAMIN (BEN)

b. 1921 Providence, Rhode Island.
Pianist and composer. Both his parents were singers; sang in a synagogue at age five; served in the Air Force band in World War II; composed for Elvis Presley after 1956—"Crawfish," "Wooden Heart," "Don't Leave Me Now," "Fame and Fortune," "Steppin' Out of Line," "Rock-a-hulu-twist"; with Wayne Walker wrote "Fallen Angel" (1960); "The Night Has a Thousand Eyes" (1962, w. Dotty Wayne).

WEISS, ADOLPH

b. 1891 Baltimore, Maryland, d. 1971 Van Nuys, California. Bassoonist and composer. At sixteen became first bassoonist of the Russian Symphony Orchestra in New York City, then with the New York Philharmonic, the New York Symphony, the Chicago Symphony, and the Rochester Orchestra; in 1925 studied with Arnold Schonberg, then played with the San Francisco Symphony; composed a *Rhapsody* for four French horns (1957), and *Vade Mecum* for wind instruments (1958).

WEISSENBERG, ALEXIS SIGISMUND

b. 1929 Sofia, Bulgaria.
Pianist. Studied piano at age three; later studied with Pantcho Vladigeroff; during the Soviet occupation in 1945 fled Bulgaria with his mother, they were stopped at the Turkish border and imprisoned for six months; escaped and fled to Israel; his mother sent him alone to study music in New York;

studied at the Juilliard School with Olga Samaroff; won Leventritt Award (1948) and appeared with the New York Philharmonic under George Szell.

WELD, ARTHUR CYRIL GORDON

b. 1862 Jamaica Plain, Massachusetts, d. 1914 West Point, New York. Musical director and composer. Musical director for productions of Henry W. Savage; conducted musical comedy orchestras.

WELDON, PETER

b. (?), d. after 1812.
Pianist, clarinetist, conductor, and composer. Active as a musician and conductor as various concerts in New York City (1797-1810); composed *The New York Serenading Waltz* (1802), "President Madison's March" (1809, published in Charles Southgate's *The Visitor*, Richmond, Virginia), *La Battalla de Baylen* for the pianoforte, *Favorita Waltz Brazilense* (1810), *El Sitio de Gerona* (1810), *The Brazilian Waltz* for the pianoforte, with an accompaniment for the flute, clarinet, flagiolet, and violin (1812).

WELITCH, LJUBA

b. 1912 Bulgaria.
Soprano. Debut in Sofia, Bulgaria (1934); later in Vienna; opera star in Europe during 1940s; debut at the Metropolitan Opera, New York City (1949) as Salome; sang at the Met (1949-53); retired from opera (1953) and became European film star; later came to New York to live; appeared on TV.

WELK, LAWRENCE

b. 1903 Strasburg, North Dakota.
Bandleader. Played the accordian; his six-man combo played on radio station WNAX, Yankton, South Dakota (1925); moved to Chicago in 1930s; called his playing "Champagne Music"; at the Aragon Ballroom, Santa Monica, Calif. (1951-61); moved to the Hollywood Palladium (1961); on radio and TV after 1953; on ABC network, with Mutual network after 1971.

WELLS, ARDIS ARLEE

b. 1917 Monterey, Minnesota.
Singer and songwriter. Wrote "That's What Makes the World GoRound," "I Don't Know Why," "Selling Chance," "Huddle Cuddle Boogie" (1956).

WELLS, GEORGE C.

b. 1819 Colchester, Connecticut, d. 1873 Minneapolis, Minnesota. Composer. Methodist minister united with the Troy Conference (1845), then the Wisconsin Conference, and later the Minnesota Conference; *The Revivalist* (1868) included one hymn of his, two tunes and three arranged by him, also "Tenting Again" (a paraphrase of the popular Civil War song) written by his wife, Elvenah Raymond Wells.

WELLS, JUNIOR

b. 1932 West Memphis, Arkansas.
Black singer and harpist. Known as a blues singer; played the harp for Muddy Waters; organized his own band in Chicago (1966); toured Europe; first recorded in 1966; albums—*Junior Wells' Chicago Blues Band (Hoo Doo Man Blues), It's My Life, Baby, Comin' at You, You're Tuff Enough.*

WELLS, KITTY

b. 1919 Nashville, Tennessee.
Singer and guitarist. Born Muriel Deason; known as the "Queen of Country Music"; radio debut on WSIX, Nashville (1936); married Johnny Wright, singer; sang on WCHS, Bluefield, West Va., WNOX, Knoxville, Tenn., WPTF, Raleigh, N.C., and WEAS, Decatur, Ga.; albums—*Bouquet of Country Hits, Burning Memories, Country All the Way, Country Heart, Country Music Time, Cream of Country Hits, Dust on the Bible, Especially for You, Guilty Street.*

WELLS, MARCUS MORRIS

b. 1815 Otego, New York, d. 1895 Hardwick, New York. Composer. Lived for a time in Buffalo, then Cooperstown, then became a farmer in Hardwick; wrote the tune "Guide," with the words "Holy Spirit, Faithful Guide," which was published in *The Musical Pioneer* (1858), and later in *The Psalm King* (1866).

WELLS, WILLIAM ("DICKIE")

b. 1910 Centerville, Tennessee.
Black jazz trombonist. Played in Count Basie's band; played at the Pleyel in Paris (1952).

WELS, CHARLES

b. 1825 Prague, Czechoslovakia, d. 1906 New York City. Pianist. Studied with Tomaschek; concert pianist (1847); in New York as teacher and concert pianist after 1849; composed a piano concerto, concert overture, and suite for orchestra.

WENDLING, PETE

b. 1888 New York City, d. 1974.
Composer. Wrote ragtime; wrote "Oh What a Pal Was Mary," and "Yacka Hula Hickey Dula" featured by Al Jolson.

WENRICH, PERCY

b. 1887 Joplin, Missouri, d. 1952 New York City. Popular composer. Studied at the Chicago Musical College; with his wife, Dolly Connolly, were vaudeville entertainers; wrote "Under a Tropical Moon" (1908, w. C.R. McDonald), "Rainbow" (1908, w. Alfred Bryan), "Up in a Balloon" (1908, w. Ren Shields), "Put on Your Old Gray Bonnet" (1909, w. Stanley Murphy), "Moonlight Bay" (1912, Edward Madden), "When You Wore a Tulip" (1914, Jack Mahoney), "Sweet Cider Time" (Joe McCarthy), "Where Do We Go from Here" (1918, Howard Johnson).

WERFEL, FRANZ

b. 1890 Prague, Czechoslovakia, d. 1945 Beverly Hills, California. Librettist. Married Alma Mahler, the composer's widow, in 1929; translated several operas of Verdi into German; wrote the libretto for the cantata *Die Zwingburg* by Ernst Krenek and the opera *Bolivar* by Milhaud; with the rise of Nazism, he left Germany for America; saddened by the persecution of the Jews in Germany, he wrote *The Eternal Road* (m. Kurt Weill), which had a successful run in New York City (1936); also wrote *Verdi,* a biographical novel.

WERNER, ERIC

b. 1901 Vienna, Austria.
Composer and musicologist; lecturer at the Institute of Religion and Sacred Music in New York; wrote *The Music of Post-Biblical Judaism* and *The Conflict between Hellenism and Judaism in the Music of the Early Christian Church.*

WERRENRATH, REINALD

b. 1883 Brooklyn, New York, d. 1953 Plattsburg, New York. Baritone. Graduated New York University; studied with Victor Maurel and others; debut in concert in New York City (1907); debut in opera as Silvio at the Metropolitan Opera, New York City (1919); noted oratorio singer; many recital tours in U.S. and England.

WERTHNER, PHILIP

b. 1858 Baraboo, Wisconsin, d. 1930.
Pianist and teacher. Studied under Scharwenka, of Berlin; piano teacher in Cincinnati, Ohio.

WESLEY, CHARLES, SR.

b. 1707 Epworth, England, d. 1788 London, England. Hymnist. Came to America (1735) to the colony of Georgia with his brother, John, but returned to England (1736); wrote numerous hymns, including "Jesus, Lover of My Soul" (tune "Whitman"—Lowell Mason, also "Refuge"—J.P. Holbrook), "Come, Sinners, to the Gospel Feast" (1747, m. Mason, 1830), "O Love Divine, How Sweet Thou Art," "Let Our Bodies Part," "A Charge to Keep I Have" (tune "Kentucky—Jeremiah Ingalls, 1832), "All Praise to Our Redeeming Lord" (m. S.B. Pond), "Lord in the Strength of Grace" (m. J. C. Sweetser); founder of the Methodist Church with his brother John.

WESLEY, JOHN

b. 1703 Epworth, England, d. 1791 London. Hymnist. Brother of Charles Wesley; studied at Oxford University; founded the Methodist church; wrote the hymn "How Happy Is the Pilgrim's Lot" (tune "Habbakuk"—Edward Hodges); came to America in 1735 to the colony of Georgia as a missionary, to 1738; compiled *The Collection of Psalms and Hymns* (Charlestown, 1737), altering Isaac Watts' poem to read "Before Jehovah's awful throne"; brought before a grand jury in Savannah, Georgia, and charged with "making alterations in the metrical psalms and introducing into the church and service at the altar compositions of psalms and hymns not inspected or authorized by any proper judicature."

WESSEL, MARK E.

b. 1894 Coldwater, Michigan, d. 1973.
Composer. Graduated Northwestern University, Evanston, Ill.; studied with Schonberg; won Guggenheim and Pulitzer Fellowships; composed *Scherzo Burlesque* for piano and strings (Rochester Little Symphony under Hanson, composer soloist, 1926), *Ballade* for violin, oboe, and string orchestra (Eastman School Festival under Belov, 1932), *Holiday* and *Song and Dance* (Eastman School Festival under Hanson, 1934).

WEST, DOROTHY MARIE (DOTTIE)

b. 1932 McMinnville, Tennessee.
Singer and songwriter. Married Bill West, guitarist; both Dottie and Bill graduated Tennessee Tech., Cookeville, Tenn.; they wrote "Here Comes My Baby" (1964, recorded by the Wests and also Perry Como), "Would You Hold It Against Me?" (1966, Wests' record); her albums—*Country Girl, Dottie Sings Eddie, Feminine Fancy, Here Comes My Baby, Makin' Memories, Queen of Country Music, Sound of Country Music, Suffer Time, Dottie West Sings Sacred Ballads.*

WEST, HEDY

b. 1938 Cartersville, Georgia.
Singer and banjoist. Sang in coffee houses in Chicago and New York; appeared with Pete Seeger at the Village Gate in New York; later gave recitals in the USA and Europe; album—*Hedy West.*

WEST, MAE

b. 1892 Brooklyn, New York.
Singer and actress. Appeared in films with W.C. Fields during the 1930s; became famous for her remark, "Come up and see me some time, tall, dark and handsome"; sang in New York City night clubs during the 1960s; became a blues, rock 'n roll singer; albums—*Fabulous Mae West, Way Out West, Ethel Merman, Mae West, Lydia Roberts, Side by Side/W.C. Fields.*

WEST, ROBERT ATHOW

b. 1809 Thetford, England, d. 1865 Washington, D.C. Hymnist. Came to America (1843); one of seven men who prepared *The Methodist Hymn Book* (1849); for a time editor of the *Commercial Advertiser,* New York City; wrote the hymn "Come, Let Us Tune Our Loftiest Song" (tune "Duke Street"—John Hatton).

WEST, WESLEY WEBB ("SPEEDY")

b. 1924 Springfield, Missouri.
Singer, guitarist, and songwriter. Member of Cliffie Stone's band (1948-59); wrote "Speedin' West," "Railroadin'," "Sunset," "Stealing Moonlight," "West of Samoa" (1956), "Tulsa Twist" (1964).

WESTENDORFF, THOMAS P.

b. 1848 Bowling Green, Virginia, d. 1923 Chicago, Illinois. Popular composer. Resident of Plainfield, Ind., when he wrote the words and music "I'll Take You Home Again Kathleen" (1879); also wrote "Bringing Pretty Blossoms" (1880), "My Bonnie Sweet Lassie" (1880), "Dar's One More Ribber for to Cross" (1881), "Kissing Papa Through the Telephone" (1899), and "Old Thompson's Mule"; "We Marched with Sherman's Army to the Sea" (1864) was published when he was only sixteen.

WESTERGAARD, PETER

b. 1931.
Composer. Studied with Milton Babbitt at Princeton; also with Roger Sessions.

WESTERN, JOHNNY

b. 1934 Two Harbors, Minnestoa.
Singer and songwriter. Attended schools in Northfield, Minn.; wrote "Ballad of Paladin"; appeared as an actor in western films.

WESTERN STRING BAND *see* LEON MC AULIFFE

WESTON, HORACE

b. 1825 Derby, Connecticut, d. 1890.
Black banjoist. Son of Jube Weston, music and dancing teacher; toured states in minstrel groups during the 1850s and in Europe in the late 1860s; wrote "Minor Jig."

WESTON, PAUL (WETSTEIN)

b. 1912 Springfield, Massachusetts.
Orchestra leader and arranger. Graduated Dartmouth College, Hanover, N.H. (1933); arranged for Phil Harris, Joe Haymes, and Rudy Vallee; for Tommy Dorsey (1936-40); also for Dinah Shore and Ginny Simms; joined Capital Records in Hollywood (1943).

WESTON, RANDY

b. 1926 Brooklyn, New York.
Black jazz pianist. Served in army in World War II; played with Art Blakey and others; then led his own trio.

WETHERFORD QUARTET *see* HENRY T. SLAUGHTER

WETTLING, GEORGE GODFREY

b. 1907 Topeka, Kansas, d. 1968.
Jazz drummer. Played in Paul Whiteman's band; also with Red Norvo (1938) and later with Artie Shaw.

WETZLER, HERMANN HANS

b. 1870 Frankfort, Germany, d. 1943 New York City. Conductor and composer. Studied with Frau Schumann and others; pianist and teacher in New York City (1893); conducted his own symphony orchestra after 1902; directed the Hamburg Opera (1905); conductor in Russia (1905); composed the opera, *The Basque Venus.*

WHALE, THOMAS BERNARD

b. 1778, d. 1838 New York City.
Dancing master and composer. Conducted dancing classes in Philadelphia (ca. 1809-12), in New York (1813-20), in Boston (ca. 1821-29), and in New York (1830-38); wrote *A New Set of Cotillions* (1809) and *Whale's Minuets* (1824).

WHEATLEY, JULIA

b. 1817, d. 1875.
Singer. Gave concerts in the Musical Fund Society Hall, Philadelphia (1841).

WHEELER, BILLY ED

b. 1932 Whitesville, West Virginia.
Singer, guitarist, and songwriter. Graduated Berea College, Berea, Kentucky; served in U.S. Navy (1957-58); taught at Berea College (1959-61); wrote "The Reverend Mister Black" (recorded by Kingston Trio), "Rock Boll Weevil," "Coal Tattoo," "Ode to the Little Brown Shack Out Back" (1965), "Lonesome Lovesick Puppy Dog," "Jackson" (1967, recorded by June Carter and Johnny Cash).

WHEELER, LYMAN WARREN

b. 1837 Swampscott, Massachusetts, d. 1900.
Singer and teacher. Studied under C.A. Adams of Lynn, Mass., at the Philharmonic Institute, Boston (1853-55), at the Royal Academy, London, in Milan with Prati and San Giovanni, and others; tenor at Emanuel Church, Boston, after 1863; with Handel and Haydn Society in Boston; taught at the New England Conservatory.

WHEELER, ONIE D.

b. 1921 Senath, Missouri.
Singer and songwriter. Attended high school in Vanduser, Mo.; wrote "Onie's Bop," "When We All Get There," "Run-em-off," "I Saw Mom," "Closing Time."

WHELPTON, GEORGE

b. 1847 Redbourne, England, d. 1930 Oxford, Ohio. Composer. Came to America with his family (1851); served in the Union Army during the Civil War; choir director in Buffalo, N.Y. (1903-25); wrote the hymn "Hear Our Prayer, O Lord."

WHITAKER, EPHRAIM MALLORY

b. 1816, d. 1880.
Composer. After his marriage he lived in Ann Arbor, Michigan; in 1865 moved to Albany, N.Y., where he became a clerk in the State Department of Agriculture; one of his tunes is in the *Presbyterian Hymn Book* (1872), compiled by Edwin F. Hatfield.

WHITE, BENJAMIN FRANKLIN

b. 1800, d. 1879.
Compiler. Compiled *The Sacred Harp* (1844), with E.J. King.

WHITE BROTHERS (band) *see* WILLIAM WARD PINKETT

WHITE, CAROLINA

b. 1886 Dorchester, Massachusetts, d. 1935. Opera singer. Studied with Weldon Hunt; concert debut (1905); at the San Carlo Theatre, Naples (1908); with the Chicago Opera (1910); with the Boston Opera after 1911.

WHITE, CHARLES ALBERT

b. 1830 Boston, Massachusetts, d. there 1892. Popular composer. With W. Frank Smith and John F. Perry formed the music publishing house of White-Smith and Company in Boston about 1867; he wrote the words and music "The Widow in the Cottage by the Seashore" (1868), "Come Birdie" (1870), "I'se Gwine Back to Dixie," "The President Cleveland March," and "Marguerite" (1883, which Denman Thompson included in *The Old Homestead*).

WHITE, CLARENCE CAMERON

b. 1880 Clarksville, Tennessee, d. 1960 New York City. Noted black composer and violinist. His father was a doctor in Oberlin, Ohio; graduated Howard University, Washington, D.C.; graduated the Oberlin Conservatory of Music (1901); taught at the Washington (D.C.) Conservatory of Music after 1901; studied with Samuel Coleridge-Taylor, noted black composer, in London (1908-11); taught music in Boston (1912-23); taught at West Virginia State College, Institute, West Va. (1924-31); director of music at the Hampton Institute, Hampton, Va. (1931-35); composed the ballet number "Meringue" in the play *Tambour* (1928, w. John F. Mathews), the opera *Ouanga* (w. Mathews—on the life of Haiti's ruler, Dessalines, first presented by the American Opera Society in Chicago, 1932, and numerous times thereafter), a string quartet performed by l'Ecole Normale de Musique in Paris (1932), Symphony in D Minor, the ballet *A Night in Sans Souci.*

WHITE, COOL

b. 1821 Philadelphia, Pennsylvania, d. 1891 Chicago, Illinois. Composer and minstrel showman. Born John Hodges; wrote "Lubly Fan" (1844), introduced by the Virginia Serenaders; this tune was used for "Buffalo Gals" (1858, w. Henry Russell, "Girls, won't you come out tonight?"); later used for "Dance with Dolly" (1944).

WHITE, ELLERTON O. ("SONNY")

b. 1917 Panama City, Canal Zone, d. 1971 New York City. Jazz pianist. Led his own band, Sonny White and His Melody Knights, during the 1930s, a twenty-man combination including a violin section, unusual in those days; also appeared with Jonah Jones, Benny Carter, Wilbur De Paris, Willie Bryant, and Teddy Hill; accompanied Billie Holiday in her recording of "Strange Fruit."

WHITE, GEORGE LEONARD

b. 1838 Cadiz, New York, d. 1895 Ithaca, New York. Director and compiler. Organized the Jubilee Singers of Fisk University, Nashville, which toured America and Europe in the 1870s and sang Negro spirituals in order to raise funds for Fisk University; with Theodore F. Seward compiled *Jubilee Songs* (1884), in which many Negro spirituals were published for the first time.

WHITE, JOHN

b. 1855 W. Springfield, Massachusetts, d. 1902 Bad Neuheim, Germany. Organist and composer. Studied with Dudley Buck and others; organist in various German cities; organist in New York (1887-96); resided in Munich after 1897; composed *Alpha and Omega,* an oratorio.

WHITE, JOSEPH (JOSE)

b. 1833 Cuba, d. 1920.
Black violinist. Studied at the Paris Conservatory; appeared with the New York Philharmonic (1876); also with Theodore Thomas' Orchestra.

WHITE, JOSEPH

b. ca. 1838 New Orleans, Louisiana, d. 1890. Black violinist and composer. Studied at the Paris Conservatory; returned to the United States (1875); made successful concert tour of the U.S.; wrote *Violin Concerto* (1867).

WHITE, JOSHUA DANIEL (JOSH)

b. 1908 Greenville, South Carolina, d. 1969 Manhasset, L.I., New York. Black singer, guitarist, and songwriter. Accompanied singer Leroy Carr in the 1930s; with the Southernaires on NBC radio; sang with Libby Holman (1941); sang in New York City night clubs; albums—*Empty Bed Blues, House I Live In, In Memorium—Josh White, Josh, Josh at Midnight, Spirituals and Blues, Josh White, Josh White Chain Gang Songs, Josh White Sings, Josh White 25th Anniversary Album.*

WHITE, PAUL TAYLOR

b. 1895 Bangor, Maine, d. 1973.
Composer. Graduated Eastman School of Music, Rochester, N.Y.; taught there; composed Symphony in E Minor (Rochester Philharmonic under Hanson, 1934), *Five Miniatures* (Rochester Civic Orchestra under composer, 1934), *Boston Sketches* ("Four Spokes from the Hub," Boston Pops Orchestra under Fiedler, 1938), *Lake Spray* for orchestra (Rochester Philharmonic under Iturbi, 1939), *Sea Chanty Quintet, Voyage of the Mayflower* for choir and orchestra.

WHITEFIELD, GEORGE

b. 1714 Gloucester, England, d. 1770 Newburyport, Massachusetts. Hymnist. Graduated Pembroke College, Oxford (1736); ordained in 1737 as a Methodist preacher; came to Savannah, Georgia, in 1738; traveled through the American colonies, England, and Scotland, and returned to America in 1769; wrote "Hark! the Herald Angels Sing" (1753, m. Mendelssohn) based on "Hark, How All the Welkin Rings" by Charles Wesley (1743).

WHITEHEAD, ALFRED ERNEST

b. 1887 Peterborough, England.
Composer. Emigrated to Truro, Nova Scotia, then taught organ at Mt. Allison University, Sackville, New Brunswick; organist at St. Peter's, Sherbrooke (1916-21), at Christ Church Cathedral, Montreal, Quebec (1922-47), when he became Dean of Music at Mt. Allison; composed the tune "Chichester" (1941, "Day by Day," w. unknown).

WHITEHILL, CLARENCE EUGENE

b. 1871 Marengo, Iowa, d. 1932 New York City. Bass. Debut in *Romeo et Juliette* in Brussels (1899); sang in the Paris Opera Comique and at Bayreuth; with the Metropolitan Opera, New York City (1900-10), the Chicago Opera (1911-15), and the Metropolitan again (1915-31).

WHITEMAN, PAUL

b. 1890 Denver, Colorado, d. 1967.
Noted bandleader. Played first viola in the Denver Symphony Orchestra when in his teens; formed his own band after World War I; introduced George Gershwin's *Rhapsody in Blue* (1924) and Ferde Grofe's *Grand Canyon Suite* (1931); became known as the "King of Jazz."

WHITHORNE (WHITTERN), EMERSON

b. 1884 Cleveland, Ohio, d. 1958 New York City. Composer. Studied with Leschetizky and others; critic of *Pall Mall Gazette,* London (1913-14); editor of *Art Publication Society,* St. Louis (1915-20); composed symphonies—

Fata Morgana, New York Days and Nights (Salzburg Festival, 1923), *Ranga, The City of Ys, The Aeroplane, Saturday's Child* for mezzo-soprano, tenor, and orchestra, *Three Greek Impressions* (string quartet), *Sooner or Later* (dance satire produced in New York), *Sierra Morena* and *The Dream Pedlar* for orchestra, songs.

WHITING, ARTHUR BATTELLE

b. 1861 Cambridge, Massachusetts, d. 1936 Beverly, Massachusetts. Pianist and composer. Nephew of G.E. Whiting; pupil of W.H. Sherwood; debut in Boston at age nineteen; pupil of Rheinberger in Munich; organist at the New England Conservatory, Boston, until 1897; taught in Boston; composed a concert overture, a concert etude, fantasy with orchestra, concerto, song cycles.

WHITING, GEORGE

b. 1884 Chicago, Illinois, d. 1943 Bronx, New York City. Singer and lyricist. Vaudeville entertainer and cafe singer; wrote "My Blue Heaven" (1927, m. Walter Donaldson).

WHITING, GEORGE ELBRIDGE

b. 1840 Holliston, Massachusetts, d. 1924 Cambridge, Massachusetts. Teacher. Studied in New York City, Liverpool, England, and Berlin, Germany; taught at the New England Conservatory (1875-79), at the Cincinnati College of Music (1879-82), and again at the New England Conservatory (1882-97); organist-choirmaster at the Church of the Immaculate Conception, but resigned in 1910 over Pope Puis X's encyclical on church music.

WHITING, RICHARD A.

b. 1891 Peoria, Illinois, d. 1938 Beverly Hills, California. Popular composer. Worked for Remick in Detroit for a time; wrote "It's Tulip Time in Holland" (1915, w. Dave Radford); with lyricist Ray Egan—"And They Called It Dixieland" (1916), "Mammy's Little Coal Black Rose" (1916), "Some Sunday Morning" (also with Gus Kahn), "Till We Meet Again" (1918), "Sleepy Time Gal (also with Ange Lorenzo and Joseph R. Alden); also "Horses" (w. Byron Gay), "Honey" (w. Haven Gillespie and Seymour Simons), "She's Funny That Way" (w. Neil Moret); for *George White Scandals* (1932) wrote "Eadie Was a Lady" and "You're an Old Smoothie" (w. Buddy De Sylva, sung by Ethel Merman); wrote "Louise" (1929, w. Leo Robin sung by Maurice Chevalier), "Beyond the Blue Horizon" (with W. Franke Harling, w. Robin), "One Hour with You" (Robin), "On the Good Ship Lollipop" (w. Sidney Clarke, for Shirley Temple), "I've Got a Heart Full of Music" (w. Johnny Mercer, sung by Dick Powell).

WHITING, WILLIAM

b. 1826, d. 1878.
Composer. Wrote "Eternal Father, Strong to Save" (w. Robert Nelson Spencer) which appeared in the *Missionary Service Book;* "O Lord, Our Little Ones to Thee."

WHITMAN, OTIS DEWEY, JR. ("SLIM")

b. 1924 Tampa, Florida.
Singer and guitarist. Served in the navy in World War II; radio debut on WDAE, Tampa (1948); then on KWKH, Shreveport, La.; albums—*Anytime, Birmingham Jail, Cool Water, Country Favorites, Country Memories, Country Hits, Country Songs—City Hits, Favorites, 15th Anniversary, God's Hand in Mine, Happy Street, I'll Never Stop Loving You, I'll Walk with God, I'm a Lonely Wanderer, In Love the Whitman Way, Lonesome Heart.*

WHITMAN, WALT

b. 1819 West Hills, Long Island, New York, d. 1892 Camden, New Jersey. Poet. From 1836 on edited papers in Huntington and Brooklyn, N.Y., and New Orleans; volunteer nurse in Washington, D.C. during the Civil War; moved to Camden in 1873; wrote the poem "Pioneers, O Pioneers," the lines "All the past we leave behind" from his eighth edition of *Leaves of Grass* (1882) which was set to music by Martin Shaw in 1925, tune "Pioneers." (*See also* F.S. Converse, Howard Hanson)

WHITNEY, MYRON WILLIAM

b. 1836 Ashby, Massachusetts, d. 1910 Sandwich, Massachusetts. Bass singer. Debut in *The Messiah* at Tremont Temple, Boston (1858); studied in Florence (1868) under Luigi Vannuccini and under Randegger in London; as Elijah in the Birmingham Festivals; toured United States; sang with Thomas' orchestra; sang as the king in *Lohengrin* under Theodore Thomas.

WHITNEY, SAMUEL BRENTON

b. 1842 Woodstock, Vermont, d. 1914 Brattleboro, Vermont. Teacher. Taught at the New England Conservatory; organist at the Church of the Advent, Boston (1871-1909).

WHITSON, BETH SLATER

b. 1879 Goodrich, Tennessee, d. 1930 Nashville, Tennessee. Lyricist. Educated at George Peabody College; wrote verses for magazines

(1900-07); wrote "Let Me Call You Sweetheart" (1910, m. Leo Friedman).

WHITTIER, JOHN GREENLEAF

b. 1807 Haverhill, Massachusetts, d. 1892 Hampton Falls, New Hampshire. Poet and lyricist. Served in the Massachusetts legislature; edited the *Pennsylvania Freeman*, Philadelphia; then lived in Amesbury, Mass.; wrote the lyrics "Songs of the Negro Boatman" (1862, m. J.W. Dadmun), "Whittier's Service Song" (m. H.S. Oakeley, tune "Abends"), "It May Not Be Our Lot to Wield," "The Centennial Hymn" (1876, m. J.K. Paine), "We May Not Climb the Heavenly Steps" (1856, tune "Serenity"—W.V. Wallace), "All as God Wills, Who Wisely Heed" (tune "Stracathro"—Charles Hutcheson), "Dear Lord and Father of Mankind" (tune "Rest" or "Elton"—F.C. Maker), "Our Thought of Thee Is Glad with Hope" (tune "Beloit"—C.G. Reissiger), "I Know Not What the Future Hath" (tune "Cooling"—A.J. Abbey), "When on My Day of Life the Night Is Falling" (tune "Journey's End"—W.K. Anderson).

WHITTINGHAM, WILLIAM ROLLINSON

b. 1805 New York City, d. 1879 Baltimore, Maryland. Hymnist and compiler. Graduated General Theological Seminary, New York (1825); Episcopal rector in New York City; then professor at the General Theological Seminary (1835), Bishop of Maryland (1840); published *Specimens of a Church Hymnal* (Baltimore, 1865).

WHITTLE, MAJOR DANIEL W.

b. 1840, d. 1891.
Hymnist and evangelist. Philip P. Bliss, the singer, toured with Major Whittle; six of his hymns under the pseudonym "El Nathan" appeared in Sankey's *Sacred Songs and Solos* (1881).

WIESENTHAL, THOMAS VAN DYKE

b. 1790 Chestertown, Maryland, d. 1833 Portsmouth, Virginia. Popular composer. Surgeon-major, Sixth Infantry, U.S. Army (1813), Surgeon's mate, U.S. Navy (1814-29); composed "Cheer Up! Pull Away" (ca. 1818), "In a Far Distant Clime" (ca. 1819), "The Harper's Song" (1821, w. Rokeby), "Hymn to the Evening Star" (1821, w. Lord Byron), "La Festa de la Rosa" (1823, arranged for the pianoforte), "I Oft Have Seen the Timid Tear" (1824, w. R.T. Spence, U.S. Navy), "My Soul Is Dark" (Byron).

WIGHT, FREDERICK COIT

b. 1859 New London, Connecticut, d. 1933. Composer. Composed marches.

WIGNELL, THOMAS

b. ca. 1753 England, d. 1803 Philadelphia, Pennsylvania. Manager. Came to America before 1791; planned the New Theatre in Philadelphia with Alexander Reinagle (1791), construction delayed because of the plague, completed (1793); operas and other productions there (1793-1803), with George Gillingham and Jean Gehot, violinists.

WILBURN, THURMAN THEODORE (TEDDY)

b. 1931 Thayer, Missouri.
Singer and guitarist. With his brother, Doyle, formed the Wilburn Brothers; their albums—*Carefree Moments, Cool Country, Country Gold, I Walk the Line, I'm Gonna Tie One on Tonight, It Looks Like the Sun's Gonna Shine, It's Another World, Let's Go Country, Little Johnny from Down the Street, Livin' in God's Country, Side by Side, Take Up Thy Cross, That Country Feeling, Trouble's Back in Town, We Need a Lot More Happiness.*

WILBURN, VIRGIL DOYLE

b. 1930 Thayer, Missouri.
Singer and guitarist. The Wilburn Family joined Grand Ole Opry, Nashville, Tenn. (1941); became the Wilburn Brothers, Teddy and Doyle (1953).

WILD, HARRISON MAJOR

b. 1861 Hoboken, New Jersey, d. 1929. Organist and conductor. Studied in Chicago and Leipzig, Germany; organist-choirmaster in churches in Chicago after 1879; directed the Chicago Mendelssohn Club after 1894; Apollo Club (1898); became deaf when about sixty-five; later became very depressed and killed himself.

WILDER, JOSEPH BENJAMIN

b. 1922 Colwyn, Pennsylvania.
Black jazz trumpeter. With L. Wolfe Gilbert wrote the words for "All the Cats Join In" (m. Ed Sauter) from *Make Mine Music;* played in Les Hite's band.

WILDER, THORNTON NIVEN

b. 1897 Madison, Wisconsin.
Librettist and playwright. Wrote the libretto for *The Alcestiad* (an opera, m. Louise J. Talma, premiered in West Germany, 1962), *Hello Dolly!* (1964, m. Jerry Herman, book—Michael Stewart, based on Wilder's *Matchmaker*).

WILGUS, D.K.

b. 1918 Mansfield, Ohio.
Compiler and teacher. Graduated Ohio State University, Columbus (1941); served in World War II; taught at Western Kentucky State College, Bowling Green, after 1950 (Ph.D. 1954); edited *Folklore International* (Hatboro, Pa., 1967), *Folksongs of the Southern United States* (Austin, Texas, 1967).

WILKINS, HERVE D.

b. 1848 Italy, New York, d. 1913.
Organist, pianist, and teacher. Choir singer at age seven; organist in Auburn, N.Y. (1866); graduated the University of Rochester, N.Y.; studied under Haupt, Kullak, and Kotzolt in Berlin; concert pianist, tenor, and teacher in Rochester, N.Y.; invented various mechanical devices to improve the organ; composed *Scene Militaire.*

WILLARD, EMMA C. HART

b. 1787 Berlin, Connecticut, d. 1870 Troy, New York. Lyricist. Headed the Middlebury (Vermont) Academy (1807-09), then her own school in Middlebury, then Waterford, N.Y. (1819); then the Troy Female Seminary (1821); wrote "Rocked in the Cradle of the Deep" (m. Joseph P. Knight) while on an ocean voyage, and introduced by basso Knight at a concert in New York City (1839); song later appeared in Henry W. Beecher's *Plymouth Collection* (1855).

WILLARD, SAMUEL

b. 1776 Petersham, Massachusetts, d. 1859 Deerfield, Massachuseets. Hymnist. Graduated Harvard (1803); became a Congregational minister in Deerfield (1807); his own hymns were published in *Regular Hymns* (1823), and *An Index to the Bible with Juvenile Hymns* (1826) and a compilation *Sacred Music and Poetry Reconciled* (1830) which included almost 180 of his own; best known for *The Deerfield Collection of Sacred Music* (1814); went blind in 1829 and lived in Hingham, Mass., for a few years, but then moved back to Deerfield.

WILLCOX, JOHN HENRY

b. 1827 Savannah, Georgia, d. 1875 Boston, Massachusetts. Organist and organ maker. Graduated Trinity College, Hartford, Conn. (1849); organist at St. Paul's P.E. church after 1850; later at the Church of Immaculate Conception until 1874.

WILLEKE, WILLEM

b. 1878 The Hague, Netherlands, d. 1950 Pittsfield, Massachusetts. Cellist and conductor. Studied at The Hague and the Amsterdam Conservatory; solo cellist at the Leipzig Philharmonic (1901-03); later at Covent Garden, London, and the Vienna Opera; member of Kneisel Quartet (1907-17); cellist of Elshuco Trio (1917); conducted orchestra and taught at the Institute of Musical Art, New York City.

WILLET, SLIM

b. 1919 Dublin, Texas.
Singer and songwriter. Born Winston Lee Moore; graduated Hardin-Simmons University, Abilene, Texas (1949); leader of the Hired Hands (1950-55); wrote "Don't Let the Stars Get in Your Eyes," "The Red Rose," "Let Me Know," " My Long Song to You."

WILLIAMS, ANDY

b. 1932 Wall Lake, Iowa.
Singer. With his brothers, Bob, Dick, and Don, sang on radio in Des Moines, Iowa, also Chicago and Cincinnati; then with Kay Thompson in night club shows in California; then went alone on Steve Allen's "Tonight" show; replaced Pat Boone on his weekly "Chevy Showroom"; later had his own show on NBC-TV; master of ceremonies at the Grammy Awards (1972) held in the Felt Forum, New York City.

WILLIAMS, CHARLES

b. 1929 Jackson, Mississippi.
Songwriter. Graduated Texas Christian University, Fort Worth; served in the U.S. Navy; disk jockey on KXLA, Pasadena, Calif.; later on KFOX, Long Beach, Calif.; wrote "I Got Stripes" (1959, with Johnny Cash), "A Million Years or So" (1963), "500 Miles Away from Home" (1963, with Bobby Bare and Hedy West).

WILLIAMS, CHARLES MELVIN ("COOTIE")

b. 1908 Mobile, Alabama.
Black trumpeter. Played with Duke Ellington's band; considered one of the truly great trumpeters.

WILLIAMS, CHICKIE

b. 1919 Bethany, West Virginia.
Singer and songwriter. Born Jessie Wanda Crupe; married Andrew J. Smik, Jr., known as "Doc Williams"; wrote "Whippoorwill Valley," "North Winds," "I Watch the Trains Passing By."

WILLIAMS, CLARENCE

b. 1893 Plaquemine, Louisiana, d. 1965 New York City. Black pianist, bandleader, and composer. Accompanist to Bessie Smith and

Ethel Waters; made some historical recordings with Louis Armstrong (1924-25); wrote "Royal Garden Blues" (1919, with Spencer Williams), "Sugar Blues" (1920), "Baby, Won't You Please Come Home (1920, w. Charles Warfield), "Gulf Coast Blues" (1924), "Cushion Foot Stomp" (1927), "I Wish I Could Shimmy Like My Sister Kate" (1919, with Louis Armstrong and Armand Piron).

WILLIAMS, DAVID MC K

b. 1887 Carnarvonshire, Wales.
Noted composer. His family came to Denver, Colorado (1887); at age thirteen organist-choirmaster of St. Peter's Church, Denver; studied in Paris and served with the 10th Siege Battery of the Royal Canadian Artillery in World War I; organist at St. Bartholomew's Church, New York City (1921-47), and also taught at Juilliard and Union Theological Seminary; composed "In the Year that King Uzziah Died" and "Thirty-four Hymn Decants" (1948); festival service honoring his eighty-fifth birthday was held at St. Bartholomew's Church (1972).

WILLIAMS, DOC

b. 1914 Cleveland, Ohio.
Singer, bandleader, and songwriter. Born Andrew J. Smik, Jr.; leader of "Doc Williams Show," WWVA, Wheeling, West Virginia, after 1937; previously with Doc McCaully's Kansas Klodhoppers (1934-35), and Billie Walker's Texas Longhorns (1935-36); wrote "Whisper Through the Stars," "Willie Roy the Crippled Boy" (1948), "I Love You Little Darling," "My Sinner Friend."

WILLIAMS, EGBERT AUSTIN (BERT)

b. 1877 New Providence, Bahamas, d. 1922 New York City. Black composer. With George Walker formed a vaudeville team; they wrote "Mammy's Little Pickaninny Boy" (1896), "De Darkies' Jubilee" (1897), "The Medicine Man" (1899), "Snap Shot Sal" (1899), "The Ghost of a Coon" (1900), "The Voodoo Man" (1900).

WILLIAMS, FRANK WALTER

b. 1901 Newark, New Jersey.
Teacher and organist. Educated at Harvard (1923) and studied in Paris; organist-choirmaster in Providence, R.I. (1928-35), and taught at Brown University there; organist in Cambridge, Mass. (1937-39); assistant rector at St. Paul's, Oakland, Calif. (1939-43), and rector of St. Mark's, Denver, Colorado (1943-50).

WILLIAMS, HANK, SR.

b. 1923 Georgiana, Alabama, d. 1953 Montgomery, Alabama. Singer and composer. Radio debut on WSFA, Montgomery Alabama at age fourteen; later on KWKH, Shreveport, La.; wrote "Mind Your Own Business" and "You're Gonna Change" (1949); "Moaning the Blues," "Why Don't You Love Me," "I Just Don't Like This Kind of Livin' " and "Long Gone Lonesome Blues" (1950); "Cold, Cold Heart" (recorded by Tony Bennett), "Baby, We're Really in Love," "Crazy Heart," "Dear John," "Hey, Good Lookin'," "I Can't Help It," "Howlin' at the Moon" (all 1951); "Jambalaya," "Kaw-Liga" (with Fred Rose), "Your Cheatin' Heart" (all 1952); performed as "Luke the Drifter."

WILLIAMS, HENRY R.

b. 1813 Boston, Massachusetts, d. 1889.
Black violinist and composer. Played in Frank Johnson's band in Philadelphia; later taught in Boston; arranged music for Patrick S. Gilmore, bandleader; played at Gilmore's World Peace Jubilee in Boston (1872); wrote "Lauriette" (1840), "Come, Love and List Awhile" (1842), "It Was by Chance We Met" (1866), "I Would I'd Never Met Thee" (1876); also *Parisien Waltzes* (1854).

WILLIAMS, JOE

b. 1918 Cordele, Georgia.
Black singer. Born Joseph Goreed; sang with Coleman Hawkins' band; also with Lionel Hampton, Andy Kirk, and Count Basie; hit records were "Every Day I Have the Blues" and "All Right, Okay, You Win"; appeared regularly at the Newport Jazz Festivals.

WILLIAMS, JOE ("MISSISSIPPI BIG JOE")

b. 1903 Crawford, Mississippi.
Black singer and guitarist. Known for his nine-string guitar; later lived in Chicago; albums—*Hand Me Down My Walking Stick, Big Joe Williams, Mississippi's Big Joe Williams.*

WILLIAMS, JOHN

b. 1817 Old Deerfield, Massachusetts, d. 1899 Middletown, Connecticut. Compiler. Graduated Trinity College, Hartford, Conn. (1835); rector in Schenectady, N.Y. (1842-48); president of Trinity College (1848-53); Bishop of Connecticut (1865); compiled *Ancient Hymns of the Holy Church* (Hartford, Conn., 1845).

WILLIAMS, MARY LOU

b. 1910 Atlanta, Georgia.
Black pianist and composer. Born Mary

Elfrieda Winn; played in Andy Kirk's band; also in Sidney Bechet's group at the Pied Piper in the Village, New York City, later known as the Cafe Bohemia, with Bill Coleman on trumpet and Wilbur De Paris on trombone; wrote "Black Christ of the Andes" (jazz hymn), "Anima Christi: Praise the Lord"; Mary Lou Williams Trio at the Newport Jazz Festival, New York City (1972); married saxist John Williams.

WILLIAMS, MASON

b. 1938 Abilene, Texas.
Composer. Composed *Classical Gas;* albums—*Ear Show, Hand Made, Music by Mason Williams, Sharepickers, Listening Matter, Phonograph Record.*

WILLIAMS, RANDALL HANK, JR.

b. 1949 Shreveport, Louisiana.
Singer. Son of Hank Williams, singer and composer; raised in Nashville, Tenn.; at fourteen toured with his mother, Audrey Williams, and her "Caravan of Stars"; albums—*Ballads of the Hills and Plains, Best of Hank Williams, Jr., Blues My Name, Country Shadows, Great Country Favorites, Luke the Drifter, Jr., My Own Way, My Songs, Songs My Father Left Me, Sunday Morning, Time to Sing, Your Cheatin' Heart.*

WILLIAMS, ROGER

b. 1926 Omaha, Nebraska.
Pianist and arranger. Born Louis Weertz; his mother was a teacher and director of the symphony orchestra at Emporia State College, Kansas; played the piano from age three; conducted high school orchestra in Des Moines, Iowa; served in the navy; his hand crushed by the breech of a gun, but saved (1945); graduated Idaho State, Pocatello (1950); master's degree at Drake University, Des Moines, later doctorate; studied at Juilliard, New York City; signed with David Kapp of Kapp Records; made a hit with "Autumn Leaves."

WILLIAMS, B. ALEXANDER ("SANDY")

b. 1906 Somerville, South Carolina.
Black jazz trombonist. Played in Fletcher Henderson's band; recorded with Sidney Bechet in the 1940s; recorded on Victor, "Nobody Knows the Way I Feel This Morning," "Shake It and Break It," and "Old Man Blues," with Sidney De Paris on trumpet and Sidney Catlett on drums.

WILLIAMS, SOL ("TEX")

b. 1917 Ramsey, Illinois.
Singer and bandleader. Attended high school in Bingham, Ill.; radio debut on WJBL, Decatur, Ill., at age thirteen; on WDZ, Tuscola, Ill., at fourteen; later appeared in numerous films; formed The Western Caravan (1946); albums—*Two Sides of Tex Williams, Voice of Authority, Tex Williams.*

WILLIAMS, SPENCER

b. 1889 New Orleans, Louisiana, d. 1965 Flushing, New York. Black pianist and composer. Raised by his aunt, Lulu White, who operated Mahogany Hall saloon on Basin Street in New Orleans; moved to Chicago (1907) and to New York (1913); went to Paris (1925) to write material for Josephine Baker for the *Folies Bergère*; settled in London (1932); married Agnes Bage, English dancer; lived in Stockholm (1951-57), then returned to New York; wrote "I Ain't Got Nobody" (1908, with Roger Graham and Bert Williams), "Tishomingo Blues" (1918), "I Ain't Gonna Give Nobody None of My Jelly Roll" (1919, with Clarence Williams, no relation), "I Found a New Baby" (1919), "Arkansas Blues" (1919), "Basin Street Blues" (1923, words added in 1931 by Jack Teagarden and Glenn Miller), "Mahogany Hall Stomp" (1924), "Everybody Loves My Baby" (1924, w. Jack Palmer).

WILLIAMS, WILLIAM CARLOS

b. 1883 Rutherford, New Jersey, d. 1963.
Poet and doctor. Studied medicine, and practiced in New Jersey; wrote "The Widow's Lament in Springtime" which was set to music by Milton B. Babbitt (1950).

WILLIAMSON, JOHN LEE ("SONNY BOY")

b. 1914 Jackson, Tennessee, d. 1948 Chicago, Illinois. Black harmonica player. Known as a great blues harmonica player; recorded for Bluebird; stabbed to death with icepick and his assailant was never apprehended.

WILLIAMSON, "SONNY BOY"

Black harpist. Born Willie Rice Miller; from Glendora, Miss.; on radio station KFFA, Helena, Arkansas, and WROX, Clarksdale, Mississippi, during 1930s on the "King Biscuit Time" show; married Howlin' Wolf's sister; albums—*Bummer Road, Sonny Boy Williamson/Yardbirds.*

WILLIAMSON, STUART LEE

b. 1933 Brattleboro, Vermont.
Jazz trumpeter. Brother of pianist Claude B. Williamson; with Woody Herman, Charlie Barnet, Skinnay Ennis and others.

WILLIG, GEORGE

b. 1764 Germany, d. 1851 Philadelphia, Pennsylvania. Music publisher and teacher. Took over the business of J.C. Moller, Philadelphia (1794-1851); published Willig's *Collection of Popular Country Dances* (1812), Willig's *Instruction for the Violin* (ca. 1817), Willig's *Pocket Companion* (1822), Willig's *Waltz* (1816); purchased the business of Thomas Carr in Baltimore (1822), which was later taken over by his son, George Willig, Jr.

WILLIS, CHUCK

b. (?), d. 1958.
Black singer and songwriter. Raised in Atlanta, Georgia; sang in Red McAllister's band; wrote and recorded "Don't Deceive Me" ("Please Don't Go") (1953); wrote "Oh What a Dream" (recorded by Ruth Brown, 1954, also recorded by Patti Page), "Close Your Eyes" (recorded, 1955, by Steve and Eydie); wrote and recorded "It's Too Late" (1956, won BMI Award), and ("I Don't Want to") "Hang Up My Rock and Roll Shoes" (1958).

WILLIS, JAMES ("GUY")

b. 1915 Alex, Arkansas.
Singer and songwriter. Raised in Schulter, Oklahoma; formed the Willis Brothers with Skeeter and Vic; radio debut on KGEF, Shawnee, Oklahoma (1932); wrote "I Miss Old Oklahoma" (1932), later numerous other songs; served in World War II; the brothers were with Grand Ole Opry, Nashville, Tenn. (1946-49, also after 1960); toured with USO shows overseas.

WILLIS, LOVE MARIA (WHITCOMB)

b. 1824 Hancock, New Hampshire, d. 1908. Hymnist. Married to Frederick L.H. Willis, M.D., and resided in Rochester, N.Y., and Glenora, on Seneca Lake; wrote the lyrics "Father, Hear the Prayer We Offer" (1864, m. J.L. Steiner, 1723, tune "Gott Will's Machen").

WILLIS, RICHARD

b. ca. 1795 Ireland, d. 1830 West Point, New York. Popular composer. Music teacher in New York City (1816), then became the first teacher of music and leader of the band at the U.S. Military Academy (1817-30); composed "Boston Cadets March" (1822), "DeWitt Clinton's Grand March" (1823), "General LaFayette's March" (1825), "The Harp of Love" (ca. 1822), "They Know Not My Heart" (ca. 1825, w. T. Moore), "West Point March and Quick Step" (ca. 1825).

WILLIS, RICHARD STORRS

b. 1819 Boston, Massachusetts, d. 1900 Detroit, Michigan. Composer. Graduated Yale University (1841); became editor of the *New York Music World;* his brother, Nathaniel P. Willis, was a poet; composed the music for the Christmas carol "It Came Upon a Midnight Clear" (1850, w. E.H. Sears), also "There Is a Green Hill Far Away" (w. C. Frances Humphreys); arranged the music "Fairest Lord Jesus, Ruler of All Nations" (from the German tune).

WILLIS, "SKEETER"

b. 1917 Coalton, Oklahoma.
Singer and fiddler. Joined with Guy and Vic as the Willis Brothers; their albums—*Bummin' Around with the Willis Brothers, Give Me 40 Acres, Hey, Mister Truck Driver, Road Stop—Juke Box Hits, Wild Side of Life, Willis Brothers—Go To Town.*

WILLIS, VICTOR

b. 1922 Schulter, Oklahoma.
Singer, pianist, and accordian player. Member of the Willis Brothers, with Guy and Skeeter.

WILLMAN, ALLAN ARTHUR

b. 1909 Hinckley, Illinois.
Composer. Awarded a scholarship at the Knox College Conservatory of Music, Galesburg, Ill., when he was sixteen; earned M.M. at the Chicago Musical College (1930); pupil of Boulanger in Paris; his *Solitude,* symphonic poem, won Paderewski award (1935).

WILLS, ROBERT (BOB)

b. 1905 Hall County, Texas, d. 1975.
Bandleader and songwriter. Radio debut as fiddler in Fort Worth, Texas (1933); organized the Texas Playboys on KVOO, Tulsa, Oklahoma; also in films; wrote "Texas Playboy Rag," "Lone Star Rag," "Texas Two Step," "Wills Breakdown," "Betty's Waltz"; albums—*Country Walk, Here's That Man Again, King of Western Swing, Living Legend, Mr. Words and Mr. Music, Together, Western Swing Along.*

WILLSON, JOSEPH

b. ca. 1770, d. 1822.
Popular composer, teacher, and music publisher. Music publisher in New Brunswick, N.J. (1801-03) and New York City (1804-22); wrote "I Knew by the Smoke That So Gracefully Curl'd" (1807, w. Thomas Moore), "The Fall of the Dew" (1808), "The Light House" (1814, w. Moore), "Clinton's Grand

March" (1817), "Should Ee'r I Brave the Foaming Seas," "The Stolen Kiss" (the last two songs published by John Butler); his son, Joseph Willson, Jr., published music in New York City (1820).

WILLSON, MEREDITH

b. 1902 Mason City, Iowa.
Popular composer. Studied the flute at the Institute of Musical Art in New York City with Georges Barrere, then was flutist with the bands of J.P. Sousa, Hugo Riesenfeld, and with the New York Philharmonic; wrote the symphonies *San Francisco* (performed by the San Francisco Symphony, 1936), and *The Missions of California* (performed by the Los Angeles Philharmonic, 1940, with Albert Coates conducting); served in the armed forces radio services during World War II; wrote the words and music for "You and I" (1941), "Iowa, I See the Moon," and "May the Good Lord Bless and Keep You" (1950); wrote the text and score *The Music Man* (1957, which included "Seventy-Six Trombones") and *The Unsinkable Molly Brown* (1960, book—Richard Morris, which starred Tammy Grimes).

WILSON, ALFRED

b. ca. 1880 New Orleans, Louisiana, d. 1905.
Black pianist and singer. Played at the Frenchman's and at Lulu White's Mahogany Hall, New Orleans; took to "hop" (opium).

WILSON, BRIAN

b. 1942.
Singer and songwriter. Member of the Beach Boys; wrote "Surf's Up" (1966, with Van Dyke Parks), "Fun, Fun, Fun," "Girls on the Beach," "Car Crazy Cutie," "Little Deuce Coupe."

WILSON, GARLAND

b. 1909 Martinsburg, West Virginia, d. 1954 Paris, France. Jazz pianist. Went to Paris (1932) as accompanist for Nina Mae McKinney.

WILSON, GEORGE H.

b. 1854, d. 1908.
Singer and manager. Annotator for the Boston Symphony Orchestra (1888-92).

WILSON, GLENVILLE DEAN

b. 1833, d. 1897.
Conductor, composer, and teacher. Wrote "Song of the Brook."

WILSON, GRACE

b. 1890 Owosso, Michigan, d. 1962.
Singer. In vaudeville and musical comedy shows (1906-24); with WLS "National Barn Dance," Chicago (1924-60); died of cancer.

WILSON, HAMILTON K. ("SMILEY")

b. 1922 Etowah County, Alabama.
Singer and guitarist. Raised in Attala, Alabama; joined Tex Bynum's Rogers County Cowboys (1939); Rio Grande Cowboys (1940-42); married Kitty Wilson, singer; in films (1949-50); joined Grand Ole Opry, Nashville, Tenn. (1950); retired in the 1960s to live in Hendersonville, Tennessee.

WILSON, HENRY

b. 1828 Greenfield, Massachusetts, d. 1878.
Organist and composer. Wrote "Christ Is Risen, Alleluia," "Ring On, Ye Joyous Christmas Bells."

WILSON, JACKIE

b. 1935.
Black singer. Attended schools in Detroit, Mich.; joined Billy Ward's Dominoes (1953) as lead singer; went solo (1957); sang at the Copacabana, New York City and other well-known clubs; shot and critically wounded by a fan (1961), but survived; first recorded in 1958; albums—*Lonely Teardrops, Baby Workout, Body and Soul, Do Your Thing, I Get the Sweetest Feeling, It's All a Part of Love, Jackie Sings the Blues, Manufacturers of Soul, Soul Galore, Soul Time, Spotlight on Jackie Wilson, Whispers.*

WILSON, JAMES H.

b. 1843 Newport, Rhode Island, d. 1915.
Pianist, composer, and teacher. Graduated the Leipzig Conservatory (1868); pianist and teacher of singing in Newport; composed piano pieces.

WILSON, MARY K. ("KITTY")

b. 1927 Rome, Georgia.
Singer, bassist, and songwriter. Raised in Gadsden, Alabama; played at local functions at age nine; married Smiley Wilson, singer; they joined Circle 3 Ranch Gang (1945); "Louisiana Hayride" (1949); she wrote "Sing and Shout," "We Lived It Up" (1960, recorded by Jimmy Dickens), "I Know" (recorded by Hank Snow).

WILSON, MORTIMER

b. 1876 Chariton, Iowa, d. 1932 New York City. Teacher and composer. Studied in Chicago; taught at the University School of Music, Lincoln, Nebr. (1901-07); conducted the Atlanta Symphony Orchestra and taught there (1911); at Brenau College, Gainesville, Georgia (1916-18); later with the National Academy of Music, New York City.

WILSON, NANCY

b. 1937 Chillicothe, Ohio.
Black singer. Attended high school in Columbus, Ohio; had her own show on WTVN-TV (1952); attended Central State College, Wilberforce, Ohio; sang for Rusty Bryant's band, also for Cannonball Adderley; signed with Capital Records; sang for George Shearing; married drummer Kenny Dennis; at the Apollo Theatre, Harlem, New York City (1972).

WILSON, OLLY W.

b. 1937 St. Louis, Missouri.
Black double bass player and composer. Graduated Washington University, St. Louis (1959); University of Illinois (M.Mus., 1960), the State University of Iowa (Ph.D., 1964); studied electronic music at the University of Illinois; played in symphony orchestras in St. Louis and Cedar Rapids, Iowa; taught at Florida A&M, Tallahassee, West Virginia University Graduate School, Morgantown, Indiana University, and then Oberlin; composed *Wry Fragments* for tenor and percussion (1961), *Sextet* (performed by the Atlanta Symphony, 1963), *And Death Shall Have No Dominion* for tenor and percussion (1963), *Three Movements for Orchestra* (1964), *Chanson Innocent* for contralto and two bassoons (1965), *Cetus* (1967, electronic work, won 1968 Dartmouth College Arts Council Prize), *In Memoriam: Martin Luther King, Jr.* for chorus and electronic sounds (1968).

WILSON, ROBERT EDWARD ("JUICE")

b. 1904 St. Louis, Missouri, d. 1964. Black jazz violinist. Raised in Chicago; played with Freddie Keppard, Lucky Roberts and others; with Noble Sissle in Europe (1929), later in Africa, in Tangier.

WILSON, TEDDY

b. 1912 Austin, Texas.
Black jazz pianist. Played in Benny Goodman's band, especially in small groups; organized his own band (1939); disbanded (1940); formed a sextet; composed *Little Things That Mean So Much;* at the Newport Jazz Festival, New York City (1972).

WILSON, WESLEY ("KID")

b. 1900.
Pianist, singer, and composer. Vaudeville actor, with his wife, Leola "Coot" Grant; with her composed "Come on Coot and Do That Thing"; "You Can't Do That to Me"; he wrote a number of songs and blues recorded by Bessie Smith—"Take Me for a Buggy Ride," "I'm Down in the Dumps," "Do Your Duty," "Levee Blues," "Gimme a Pigfoot."

WINCHELL, JAMES M.

b. 1791, d. 1820.
Composer. Compiled *Sacred Harmony* (Boston, 1819).

WINCHESTER, CALEB THOMAS

b. 1847 Montville, Connecticut, d. 1920 Middletown, Connecticut. Hymnist. Educated at Wesleyan University, Middletown (1869), and became professor of English literature there; wrote the hymn "The Lord Our God Alone Is Strong" (1871, tune "Truro"), which appeared in the *Methodist Episcopal Hymnal* (1878).

WINDING, KAI CHRESTEN

b. 1922 Aarhus, Denmark.
Jazz trombonist. Played in Stan Kenton's band and with others; later formed a septet; toured Europe; at the Newport Jazz Festival, New York City (1972).

WINKLER, EDWIN THEODORE

b. 1823 Savannah, Georgia, d. 1883 Marion, Alabama. Hymnist and compiler. Educated at Brown University, Providence, R.I.; became Baptist minister (1846); compiled *The Sacred Lute* (1855, which included eight of his hymns).

WINNER, JOSEPH

b. 1802 Philadelphia, Pennsylvania, d. there 1878. Instrument maker. Violin maker in Philadelphia; also made furniture and was a cooper (barrel maker); father of Septimus Winner, composer of "Listen to the Mocking Bird" and of Joseph Eastburn Winner, composer of "Little Brown Jug."

WINNER, JOSEPH EASTBURN

b. 1837 Philadelphia, Pennsylvania, d. there 1918. Popular composer. Brother of Septimus Winner, the composer; wrote his music under the pseudonym "Eastburn"; wrote the words and music "Little Brown Jug" (1869), "Oil on the Brain," "The Yankees Boast That They Can Make Clocks," "The Kettle and the Clock," "That's Where the Laugh Comes In" (1893); his Civil War songs were "The Contraband's Song of Freedom," "The Last of the Alabama," "The Prisoner's Release," and "Triumph to Our Dear Old Flag"; also wrote "Meet Me With a Kiss," "Sallie of the Dell," "Friends of Our Early Days," "Only This I Ask of Thee," "We Have Met, Loved and Parted."

WINNER, SEPTIMUS

b. 1827 Philadelphia, Pennsylvania, d. there 1902. Popular composer. Wrote the words and music to some of the top songs of the 19th century, including "Listen to the Mocking Bird" (1855), "Oh Where Has My Little Dog Gone?" (1864, adapted from the German tune "Lauterbach"), "Ten Little Indians" (1868), and "Whispering Hope" (1868); wrote many songs under the pseudonym Alice Hawthorne, which became known as the Hawthorne Ballads; wrote "Village Polkas" (1850), "How Sweet Are the Roses" (1853), "My Cottage Home" (1853), "What Is Home Without a Mother?" (1854), "I Set My Heart Upon a Flower" (1854), "Years Ago" (1856), "This Land of Ours" (1857), "Motherless Kate" (1858), "Abraham's Daughter" (or "Raw Recruits," 1861), "Give Us Back Our Old Commander" (1862), "He's Gone to the Arms of Abraham," "Yes, I Would the Cruel War Were Over," "Parting Whispers" (1863), "Look with Fond Eyes Upon Me" (1864), "Our Sweethearts at Home" (1864), "Ellie Rhee" (or "Carry Me Back to Tennessee," 1865), "A Nation Mourns Her Martyr'd Son" (1865, on the death of President Lincoln), "What Care I?" (1866), "Gone Where the Woodbine Twineth" (1870), "Gipsy Song" (1882), "On the Boardwalk at Cape May," "Out of Work," and "God Save Our President" (1881, as James A. Garfield lay dying of an assassin's bullet). As a youth he spent his summers in Williamsport, Pa., and as an adult the family spent a few weeks every summer with relatives in Aberdeen, Maryland, and Cape May, N.J. After President Lincoln removed General George B. McClellan from command, Winner wrote "Give Us Back Our Old Commander" in support of General McClellan. Then Edwin M. Stanton, the Secretary of War, ordered the arrest of Winner for writing the "seditious" song, but he was pardoned by Lincoln. (For other arrests, *see* A.E. Blackmar, Will Hays, John Howard Payne)

WINTERHALTER, HUGO

b. 1909 Wilkes-Barre, Pennsylvania, d. 1973. Conductor and arranger. Educated at St. Mary's College of Maryland, and the New England Conservatory; arranger for Tommy Dorsey, Vaughn Monroe, Count Basie and others; his record "Canadian Sunset" sold 1,500,000 discs in the 1950s; conducted at the Hollywood Bowl, Calif., and the National Symphony in Washington, D.C.; musical director of RCA Victor (1950-63), Kapp after 1963; resided in Greenwich, Conn.; one of his sons was killed in Vietnam (1966).

WIRGES, WILLIAM

b. 1894 Buffalo, New York, d. 1971 Syosset, New York. Conductor and composer. Led theater and hotel bands in Buffalo while teaching piano, theory, and harmony; served in army in World War I; pianist at the American Music Festival at Chautauqua, N.Y. (1920-21); conducted radio programs after 1923; soloist with Cliquot Club Eskimos, a band; guest artist on "The Goodrich Hour"; wrote "Chiquita Banana," "I Had That Dream Again," "A Toast to Love," "Dear Friends and Gentle Hearts," *Mississippi Lament* (choral composition).

WISEMAN, MAC

b. 1925 Crimora, Virginia.
Singer. Attended the Conservatory of Music, Dayton, Virginia; albums—*Golden Hits of Mac Wiseman; Mac Wiseman Sings "Johnny's Cash and Charley's Pride."*

WISEMAN, SCOTT ("SKYLAND SCOTTY")

b. 1909 Spruce Pine, North Carolina.
Singer, banjoist, and songwriter. Attended school in Crossmore, N.C.; attended Duke University, Durham, N.C.; graduated Fairmont State College, Fairmont, W. Va. (1932); radio debut on WRVA, Richmond, Va. (1927); married Myrtle Eleanor Cooper, singer; they sang as Lulu Belle and Scotty (1933); wrote "Home Coming Time" (1933), "Mountain Dew" (1935, with Bascom Lunsford), "Empty Christmas Stocking" (1938), "Remember Me" (1940), "Time Will Tell" (1945), "That New Vitamine" (1946), "Dontcha" (1947), "Old Time Bible" (1953) "Tenderly He Watches O'er Me" (1954), "Between You and Me" (1955), "Come as You Are" (1957).

WISKE, C. MORTIMER

b. 1853 Troy, New York, d. 1934 Lewiston, Maine. Organist and conductor. Organist in Brooklyn, N.Y., after 1872; conductor and director of festivals in New Jersey, New York and other cities; composed organ and church music.

WITEK, ANTON

b. 1872 Saaz, Czechoslovakia, d. 1933 Winchester, Massachusetts. Violinist. Studied at the Prague Conservatory; concertmaster of the Berlin Philharmonic (1894); formed a trio with his wife, Vita Gerhardt, and Joseph Malkin (1903); concertmaster of the Boston Symphony (1910-18); teacher and soloist after 1918; after his wife died he married Alma Rosengron, a former pupil.

WITHERSPOON, HERBERT

b. 1873 Buffalo, New York, d. 1935 New York City. Basso cantante. Graduated Yale University; studied in New York and Paris; sang with the Boston Symphony and in opera with the Castle Square Company, New York; debut in recital in New York (1902); with the Metropolitan Opera, New York City (1908-16); later choral conductor in New York and Chicago; president of Chicago Musical College (1925-29); general manager of the Metropolitan Opera (1935), where he died of a heart attack in his office; married singer Greta Hughes, divorced; then Florence Hinkle, soprano (d. 1933), and Mrs. B. Skeath.

WITHINGTON, LEONARD

b. 1789 Dorchester, Massachusetts, d. 1885 Newburyport, Massachusetts. Hymnist. Graduated Yale (1814); minister of First Congregational Church, Newburyport, Mass. (1816); wrote "O Saviour of a World Undone," which appeared in E. Mason's *Congregational Hymn Book* (1857).

WITNESSES, THE *see* LOUIS PRIMA

WITT, CHRISTOPHER

b. 1675 England, d. 1765 Philadelphia, Pennsylvania. Organ maker and portrait painter. Came to Philadelphia (1704) and joined the Hermits of the Wissahickon for whom he built the first organ in America, moved the organ shortly after 1708 to his home in Germantown; painted the first known portrait in America of John Kelpius, organist and composer.

WODEHOUSE, P.G.

b. 1881 Guildford, England, d. 1975.
Lyricist and writer. Educated at Dulwich College; wrote musical comedy lyrics and humorous novels of British aristocracy; captured by the Germans in France (1940) and held in a prison camp; became an American citizen (1955); wrote the lyrics "Oh Boy" (1917, m. Jerome Kern), also with Kern—"Mr. Chamberlain" (1903, about Joseph Chamberlain, British Foreign Secretary, 1895-1903); the musicals—*Oh, Lady! Lady!* (1918, with Guy Bolton), *Sally* (1920, with Guy Bolton).

WOLCOTT, SAMUEL

b. 1813 South Windsor, Connecticut, d. 1886 Longmeadow, Massachusetts. Hymnist. Graduated Yale (1833) and Andover Theological Seminary; served as a minister in Congregational churches in Providence, R.I., Chicago, and Cleveland; wrote the lyrics "Christ for the World We Sing" (1869, tune "Moscow"—Felice de Giardini, 1769); his hymns appeared in D.E. Jones' *Songs for the New Life* (1869), Dale's *English Hymn Book* (1874), *Oberlin Manual of Praise* (1880), *Evangelical Association Hymn Book* (1881).

WOLFE, JACQUES

b. 1896 Botoshan, Rumania.
Popular composer. His family came to New York City when he was a child; studied piano with James Friskin at the Institute of Musical Art; clarinetist in the 50th Infantry Band in World War I; wrote "De Glory Road" and "Short'nin' Bread" (1928, based on a 1905 tune by Reese d'Pree, black composer, w. Clement Bread), "Gwine to Hebbin'," "Hallelujah Rhythm," "Sailormen"; with lyricist Carl Sandburg—*Lost* and *Prairie Waters by Night;* an opera, *The Trysting Tree* (libretto—Irving Rowan) presented in Miami, Florida (1957).

WOLFES, HELMUTH

b. 1901 Germany, d. 1971 Cleveland Heights, Ohio. Conductor. Studied piano at age five; studied at the Universities of Berlin, Heidelberg, Halle, and Munich; music director of the Monte Carlo Opera; conductor of the Berlin State Opera; came to U.S. (1938) as assistant conductor of the City Center Opera in New York; conducted on USO tours in Europe, the Philippines, Okinawa, and Japan; chorus director of the New Orleans Opera House; music director of Karamu House, Cleveland, after 1953.

WOLFF, CHRISTIAN

b. 1934 Nice, France.
Composer. Came to U.S. (1941); studied composition with John Cage; Ph.D. at Harvard University (1963), taught there after 1962; wrote *Nine* for nine instruments (1951), *For Six or Seven Players* (1959), *Summer* for string quartet (1961), *Duo for Violinist and Pianist* (1961), *For Five or Ten Players* (1962), *In Between Pieces* for three players (1963), *Septet for Any Instrument* (1964).

WOLFF, ERICH

b. 1874 Vienna, Austria, d. 1913 New York City. Composer. Studied at Vienna Musikfreunde; toured as accompanist for Lieder singers in Europe and the United States; composed *Zlatorog* ballet produced in Prague, (1913), a violin concerto, numerous Lieder songs.

WOLFSOHN, CARL

b. 1834 Alzey, Reinhessen, Germany, d. 1907 Deal Beach, New Jersey. Pianist. Pupil of Aloys Schmitt in Frankfort (1846-48); debut in Frankfort (1848); studied under Vincent Lachner and Mme. Heinfeiter; came to America (1854) and settled in Philadelphia; gave recitals of all the sonatas of Beethoven in 1863-66 in Philadelphia and in Steinway Hall, New York; later works of Chopin; lived in Chicago after 1873; conductor of Beethoven society there.

WOLLE, JOHN FREDERICK

b. 1863 Bethlehem, Pennsylvania, d. there 1933. Composer. Organist of Trinity Episcopal Church, Bethlehem (1881-84); in 1885 became organist of the Moravian Church, and in 1887 organist at Lehigh University, holding both positions until 1905; organized the Bethlehem Choral Union, (1882) and the Bethlehem Bach Choir (1888); composed the tune "Palmarum" (1888, "Fling Out the Banner," w. G.W. Doane, 1848).

WOLLENHAUPT, HEINRICH ADOLPH

b. 1827 Schkeuditz, Germany, d. 1865 New York City. Pianist and composer. Taught piano in New York City after 1845.

WOLPE, STEFAN

b. 1902 Berlin, Germany, d. 1972 New York City. Composer. Studied with Paul Juon, Ferruccio Busoni, and Anton Webern; fled Germany (1933) via Rumania and Israel, then came to America; composed *The Man from Midian* (depicting the life of Moses), the oratorio *Israel and His Land,* the cantata *Yigdal, Palestinian Songs* (ISCM Festival, New York), *Fourteen Palestinian Songs* for alto and piano, many cantatas, and sonatas; stricken with Parkinson's disease (1963); his music destroyed in a fire in his apartment in New York City (1969).

WOLTMANN, FREDERICK

b. 1908 Flushing, New York.
Composer. Graduated the Eastman School of Music, Rochester, N.Y., studied there with Hanson and Rogers; won Juilliard Fellowship at American Academy, Rome; composed *Song of the Forest Dweller, Dance of the Torch Bearers, Songs from a Chinese Lute* and *Pool of Pegasus,* all for orchestra; *Songs for Autumn* for baritone, soprano and orchestra, *Poem* for flute and orchestra, *Scherzo* for eight wind instruments.

WOLVERINES (jazz band)

Featured Bix Beiderbecke and Jimmy McPartland.

WONDER, STEVIE

b. 1951 Saginaw, Michigan.
Black singer. Born Steveland Morris; blind from birth; raised in Detroit; plays the piano, organ, clarinet, harmonica, and drums; first recorded in 1963 at age twelve and became a sensation; albums—*Twelve-Year-Old Genius, Tribute to Uncle Ray, Jazz Soul, With a Song in My Heart, For Once in My Life, I Was Made to Love Her, My Cherie Amour, Up Tight, Stevie Wonder, Steve Wonder's Greatest Hits;* at the Bitter End, New York City (1972).

WOOD, ABRAHAM

b. 1752 Northboro, Massachusetts, d. there 1804. Composer. Fuller (dresser of cloth) and a composer; served as a drummer during the Revolutionary War in the summer months of 1777-78; with Joseph Stone published *The Columbian Harmony,* which included twenty-six of his tunes; also wrote "Anthem on Peace" (1784), *Divine Songs* (1789), and a *Funeral Elegy* (1800, on the death of George Washington).

WOOD, DAVID DUFFIELD ("DUFFLE")

b. 1838 Pittsburgh, Pennsylvania, d. 1910 Philadelphia, Pennsylvania. Organist and teacher. Blinded at the age of two; student at the Pennsylvania Institution for the Blind, Philadelphia; studied only six months under Wilhelm Schnabel but learned to play the violin, flute, piano, and organ; became organist at St. Stephen's Church, Philadelphia (1864), choirmaster there (1870); played the organ there forty-six years to the day (Easter, 1910); also taught at the School for the Blind (1853-1910).

WOOD, DEL

b. (?) Nashville, Tennessee.
Singer and pianist. Born Adelaide Hazelwood; with WSM Grand Ole Opry, Nashville, Tenn., after 1952; albums—*Honky Tonk Piano, It's Honky Tonk Time, There's a Tavern in the Town, Upright, Low Down and Honky Tonk.*

WOOD, SIMEON

b. 1774 South Bridgewater, Massachusetts, d. 1822 Boston, Massachusetts. Musician and music publisher. Music publisher in Boston (1818-22); compiled *S. Wood's Songs* (1818), which included "Here Shall Soft Charity Repair" (Boyce), "Oh! Sweet Was the Scene" (Bishop), "Eagle Wings" (King), "This Blooming Rose" (Philipps), *Waltz* (Eckhard), "To Sigh Yet Feel No Pain" (Haydn), "The Star of Bethlehem" (Granger), *Duett* (Kozeluch), *Masquerade Sonata* (Hook), "The Minute Gun at Sea" (King).

WOODBURY, ISAAC BAKER

b. 1819 Beverly, Massachusetts, d. 1858 Columbia, South Carolina. Popular composer. Blacksmith's apprentice with a strong voice, so he devoted his career to singing and composing; taught music in Boston (1839-45); joined the Bay State Glee Club and toured New England; when he reached Bellow Falls, Vermont, the local storekeeper prevailed upon Woodbury to remain there, where he organized the New Hampshire and Vermont Musical Association and was its conductor for several years; on a visit to the South when he died; composed the music "Rainy Day" (1847, w. H.W. Longfellow), "Stars of the Summer Night" (1856, Longfellow), "If I Were a Voice, a Persuasive Voice" (w. Charles Mackay), "By Cool Siloam's Shady Rill" (w. R. Heber), "Speed Away! Speed Away!" (1848, w. F.J. Crosby, 1890), "Dorrnance" (1845, "Sweet the Moments Rich in Blessing," w. James Allen, 1757), "Selena" (1850, "O Love Divine, What Hast Thou Done," w. Charles Wesley, 1742), "Lake Enon" (1854, "Jesus, I Live to Thee," w. Henry Harbaugh), "Eucharist" (1856, "When I Survey the Wondrous Cross," w. Isaac Watts, 1707), "Woodbury" or "Near Home" (w. Phebe Cary), also "The Sailor Boy's Last Dream" (1846), "Be Kind to the Loved Ones at Home" (1847), "Strike the Harp Gently" (1849), "Oh, Give Me a Home 'Neath the Old Oak Tree" (1855); with B.F. Baker compiled *The Boston Musical Education Society's Collection* (1842) and *The Choral* (1845); also wrote *The Dulcimer* (1850), *The Cythera* (1854), *The Lute of Zion* (1856), *The Harp of the South* (1853), and *The Casket* (1855).

WOODCHOPPERS, THE (band) *see* CLYDE MOODY

WOODHULL, ALFRED ALEXANDER

b. 1810 Cranbury, New Jersey, d. 1836 Princeton, New Jersey. Hymnist. Educated at Princeton and the University of Pennsylvania medical college; practiced medicine in Marietta, Pa., and Princeton, N.J., where he died when only twenty-six years old; wrote the hymn "Great God of Nations, Now to Thee" (1828, tune "Mendon"—German, arr. by Samuel Dyer); his hymn was published in *Psalms and Hymns* (Princeton, N.J. 1829).

WOODMAN, BRITT

b. 1920 Los Angeles, California.
Black trombonist. Played in Duke Ellington's band.

WOODMAN, JONATHAN CALL

b. 1813 Newburyport, Massachusetts, d. 1894 Brooklyn, New York. Composer, organist, teacher, and compiler. Organist of St. George's Chapel, Flushing, N.Y.; published *The Musical Casket* (1858); composed the tune "State Street" (1844) tune for "And Will the Judge Descend?," (w. Philip Doddridge), and "Your Harps, Ye Trembling Saints" (w. A.M. Toplady, second tune "Olmutz" by Lowell Mason); "State Street" was published in William B. Bradbury's *Psalmodist* (1844).

WOODMAN, RAYMOND HUNTINGTON

b. 1861 Brooklyn, New York, d. there 1943. Teacher. Studied in Paris under Cesar Frank; became an organist in churches in Flushing, N.Y. (1875-79), Norwich, Conn., then at the First Presbyterian Church, Brooklyn, N.Y. (1880-1941); also taught at the Metropolitan College of Music (1889-98), the Packer College Institute after 1894, and the American Institute of Applied Music after 1909.

WOODRUFF, ARTHUR D.

b. 1853, d. 1934.
Singer, conductor, and teacher. Conductor of the Orpheus Club, Philadelphia (1914-30).

WOODS, HARRY MAC GREGOR

b. 1896 North Chelmsford, Massachusetts, d. 1970 Phoenix, Arizona. Popular composer. Educated at Harvard; served in the army in World War I; wrote the words and music for "When the Red, Red Robin Comes Bob, Bob, Bobbin' Along" (1926), "I'm Looking Over a Four Leaf Clover," "River Stay Away from My Door" (1931, w. Mort Dixon, introduced by Jimmy Savo), "Here Comes the Sun" (w. Arthur Freed), "The Man from the South" (with Rube Bloom), "When the Moon Comes Over the Mountain" (1931, w. H.E. Johnson, introduced by Kate Smith), "Try a Little Tenderness" (with Reginald Connelly and Jimmy Campbell); retired in Glendale, Arizona; even though he had no fingers on his left hand, he became proficient on the piano.

WOODS, PATRICIA RUDY

b. 1946 Nashville, Tennessee.
Singer. Graduated Belmot College, Nashville (1968); with her sister, Caroline Rudy Moore, member of the Rudy Sisters, gospel singers.

WOODWARD, CHARLES

b. (?), d. ca. 1808.
Compiler. Published *Ecclesia Harmonia* (Philadelphia, 1807); a second edition was published by W.W. Woodward (1809).

WOODWARD, SIDNEY

b. 1860 Georgia, d. 1924.
Black singer. Born a slave; studied in Boston; toured United States (1890); joined Isham's Oriental America Company (1896); toured England (1897), left the group there and remained in England (1897-1900); taught at the Music Settlement School, New York City, after 1900.

WOODWORTH, SAMUEL

b. 1784 Scituate, Massachusetts, d. 1842 New York City. Lyricist. With George P. Morris founded the *New York Mirror* (1823); wrote the lyrics "Hibernias Tears" (1816, m. Charles Gilfert), "The Minstrel" (1816, m. Gilfert); "The Old Oaken Bucket" (1826, m. George Kiallmark), "The Hunters of Kentucky" (sung by Noah Ludlow in a theater in New Orleans, 1822).

WOOLER, ALFRED

b. 1867 Shipley, Yorkshire, England, d. 1937. Composer. Came to western New York as a young man; largely self-educated, and took his exam for his degree Mus.Doc. from the University of New York (1908); composed the tune "Incarnation" ("O Son of God Incarnate," w. W.F. Tillett, 1921).

WOOLETT, WILFRED

b. 1872 Janesville, Wisconsin, d. (?).
Violinist and teacher. Taught violin at Woolett School of Music in Chicago.

WOOLEY, SHELBY F. ("SHEB")

b. 1921 Erick, Oklahoma.
Singer, guitarist, and songwriter. Sang on radio on WBAP, Fort Worth, Texas; formed his own band (1946); moved to Los Angeles; in films after 1949; sang also under the name Ben Colder; wrote "Purple People Eater," "That's My Pa" (1962), "Blue Guitar," "Too Young to Tango," "Sweet Chile," "Meet Mr. Lonely," "Are You Satisfied," "The Middle of the Night Is My Cryin' Time."

WOOLF, BENJAMIN EDWARD

b. 1836 London, England, d. 1901 Boston, Massachusetts. Composer and critic. Brought to America as a boy; music critic of the *Boston Herald;* publisher and editor of the *Saturday Evening Gazette* (1871); wrote light operas; wrote *Pounce and Company, or Capital vs. Labor* (1882).

WOOLS (WOOLLS), STEPHEN

b. 1729 Bath, England, d. 1799 New York City. Singer and actor. Studied with Dr. Thomas Arne in London; debut in New York City as Gibbet in *The Beaux Stratagem* at the opening of the John Street Theater (1767); sang with the Old American Company; as Macheath in *The Beggar's Opera,* Hawthorn in *Love in a Village;* also in *Henry IV* and *The Archers* (w. William Dunlap, m. Benjamin Carr, produced in New York City, 1796).

WORK, HENRY CLAY

b. 1832 Middletown, Connecticut, d. 1884 Hartford, Connecticut. Popular composer. Settled in Chicago (1855) where he became a printer and started writing music; "We're Coming, Sister Mary" was performed by Christy's Minstrels; wrote "Grafted into the Army" (1861), "Kingdom Coming" (1862), "Babylon Is Fallen" (1863), "Girls at Home" (1863), "Wake Nicodemus" (1864), "Come Home Father" (1864, "Ten Nights in a Barroom"), "Marching Through Georgia" (a song which was hated in the South), " 'Tis Finished" (or "Sing Hallelujah!," 1865), "The Lost Letter," "The Ship That Never Returned," and "Grandfather's Clock" (1876).

WORK, JOHN WESLEY, JR.

b. 1901 Tullahoma, Tennessee, d. 1968.
Black composer and teacher. Graduated Fisk University, Nashville, Tenn., Columbia University (M.A.), Yale University (B.Mus.); studied at Juilliard on Julius Rosenwald Fellowship; conducted Men's Glee Club, Fisk University (1927-31), taught there after 1933; director of the Fisk Jubilee Singers (1948-57); wrote *The Singers* (cantata for chorus and orchestra, first prize, Fellowship of American composers, 1946), *Yenvalou* for strings, *Isaac Watts Contemplates the Cross* (choral cycle).

WORK, JOHN WESLEY, SR.

b. 1873 Tennessee, d. 1925.
Black composer and compiler. Graduated Fisk University, Nashville, Tenn.; took the annual groups of Jubilee Singers on tour

(1900-1916); wrote "Song of the Warrior," "If You Were Only Here," "Negro Lullaby" and "Negro Love Song"; with his brother, Frederick, compiled *New Jubilee Songs,* also *Folk Songs of the American Negro* (1907).

WORTMAN, DENIS

b. 1835 East Fishkill, New York, d. 1922 East Orange, New Jersey. Hymnist. Graduated Amherst (1857), Reformed Church Theological Seminary, New Brunswick, N.J. (1860), D.D. from Union College, Schenectady, N.Y. (1870); pastor in Brooklyn, Philadelphia, Schenectady, Fort Plain, and Saugerties, N.Y.; wrote the hymn "God of the Prophets, Bless the Prophet's Sons" (1884, tune "Toulon," abbr. of "Old Hundred Twenty-fourth," 1551).

WRAY, LINK

b. 1929 Florida.
Rock singer and guitarist. Half Shawnee Indian; founding father of electric rock and roll; hit records were "Rumble" and "Rawhide" (1959); album—*Link Wray* (1972); gave concert at Danbury Prison, Danbury, Conn. (1972).

WRIGHT, JOHNNY

b. 1914 Mt. Juliet, Tennessee.
Singer and guitarist. Radio debut on WSIX, Nashville, Tenn. (1936); married Kitty Wells, singer (1938); joined with Jack Anglin in the team of Johnny and Jack (1938); joined KWKH, Shreveport, La. (1947); Jack was killed in a car crash (1963); albums—*We'll Stick Together, Johnny Wright Sings Country Favorites.*

WRIGHT, NATHAN EDWARD ("SONNY")

b. 1943 Flager, Colorado.
Singer and bandleader. Attended schools in Arriba, Colo.; leader of the Country Rebels (1961-67); album—*I Love You, Loretta Lynn.*

WRIGHT, RUBY

b. 1939 Nashville, Tennessee.
Singer. Attended schools in Madison, Tenn.; with Wright Sisters, Carol and Ruby; album—*Dern Ya.*

WRIGHTSON, EARL

b. 1916 Baltimore, Maryland.
Singer. Albums—*Enchanted Evening on Broadway, Soldier of Fortune Ballads, Night with Jerome Kern, Night with Sigmund Romberg.*

WRUBEL, ALLIE

b. 1905 Middletown, Connecticut, d. 1973. Pianist, piccolo player, and composer. He was one of seven children; wrote "You'll Do It Some Day" (1926), "Now You're in My Arms" (1931 w. Morton Downey), "Flirtation Walk" (1934, w. Mort Dixon), "Fare Thee Well" (1935, Dixon), "The Lady in Red" (1935, Dixon), "Mine Alone" (1935, Dixon), "The First Time I Saw You" (1937, w. Nat Shilkret), "Music, Maestro Please" (1938, Herb Magidson), "I Met Her on Monday" (1942, Charles Newman).

WUORINEN, CHARLES

b. 1938 New York City.
Composer. Graduated Columbia University, New York City (1961), M.A. (1963); taught at Columbia after 1964; wrote three symphonies, chamber and electronic music, *Invention for Percussion Quintet* (1962), *Octet* (1962), *Duuiensela* for cello and piano (1962), *Orchestral and Electronic Exchanges* (1965), *Chamber Concerto* for oboe and ten players (1965), *Harpsichord Divisions* (1966), *Piano Concerto* (1966), *John Bull, Slave Regina Versus Septem* (1966); his *Concerto for Amplified Violin* presented at Tanglewood (1972).

WYETH, JOHN

b. 1770 Cambridge, Massachusetts, d. 1858 Philadelphia, Pennsylvania. Composer and publisher. Postmaster of Harrisburg, Pa. (1793-98); published Joseph Doll's *Der leichter Unterricht* (1810), *Repository of Sacred Music* (1810), *Part Second* (1813), Johannes Rothbaust's *Die Franklin Harmonie* (1821); wrote the tune "Nettleton" (1813, "Come, Thou Fount of Every Blessing," w. Robert Robertson, 1758); publisher in Harrisburg (1810-21).

WYNETTE, TAMMY

b. 1942 Tupelo, Mississippi.
Singer, guitarist, and pianist. Radio debut on WBRC, Birmingham, Alabama; also on TV shows; later joined Grand Ole Opry, Nashville, Tenn.; albums—*D-I-V-O-R-C-E, Inspiration, My Elusive Dreams, Run, Angel, Run, Stand by Your Man, Take Me to Your World, Tammy's Greatest Hits, Tammy's Touch, Ways to Love a Man, Your Good Girl's Gonna Go Bad.*

WYNN, ALBERT

b. 1907 New Orleans, Louisiana.
Black jazz trombonist. Played with Earl Hines, Fletcher Henderson and others.

YANCEY, JIMMY

b. 1894 Chicago, Illinois, d. there 1951. Black pianist, singer, and dancer. Known for his "boogie-woogie" tunes.

YARBROUGH, GLENN

b. 1930 Milwaukee, Wisconsin.
Tenor. Attended St. John's College, Annapolis, Maryland; served in Korea during the Korean War; attended Mexico City College, Mexico (1955); with singer Alex Hassilev owned the Limelight, Colorado Springs, Colorado; with Lou Gottlieb formed The Limeliters (1959); albums—*Baby the Rain Must Fall, Best of Glenn Yarbrough, Bitter and the Sweet, Come Share My Life, Each of Us Alone, Honey and Wine.*

YARNOLD, BENJAMIN

b. (?) England, d. 1787.
Composer. Came to Charleston, S.C., in 1753 as organist at St. Philip's Church, until about 1764, then at St. Michael's; his *Anthem and Ode* was performed about 1762.

YARROW, PETER

b. 1938 New York City.
Singer. Graduated Cornell University in psychology; sang and played the guitar on "Folk Sound" on CBS, New York (1960); joined with Noel Paul Stookey and Mary Ellin Travers to form the team of "Peter, Paul and Mary"; their albums—*Album, Late Again, Peter, Paul and Mary, Peter, Paul and Mary—Album, In Concert, In the Wind, Moving, Peter, Paul and Mommy, See What Tomorrow Brings, A Song Will Rise;* at the Philadelphia Folk Festival, Upper Salford Twp., Pa. (1972).

YELLEN, JACK

b. 1892 Poland.
Lyricist and publisher. Brought to U.S. at age five; graduated the University of Michigan; reporter for the Buffalo (N.Y.) *Courier*; co-founder of Ager, Yellen and Bernstein Music Company; wrote "Happy Days Are Here Again" (1929, m. Milton Ager) which was Franklin D. Roosevelt's 1932 campaign song.

YELLOW PAYGES (rock group)

Dan Hortter, lead vocals and harmonica; Dan Gorman, drums; Bill Ham, lead guitar; Bob Barnes, bass guitar; started in California (1968); album—*The Yellow Payges.*

YERBA BUENA BAND *see* LU WATTERS

YON, PIETRO

b. 1886 Settino-Vittone, Italy, d. 1943 Huntington, New York. Composer. Studied at the Milan Conservatory and the Academy of St. Caecilia, Rome (1905); organist-choirmaster at St. Francis Xavier's Church, New York City (1907-26), then St. Patrick's Cathedral, New York City (1926-43); composed masses, motets, and plainsongs.

YORK, SARAH EMILY WALDO

b. 1819, d. 1851.
Hymnist. Wrote "I'm Weary of Straying, O Fain Would I Rest," which appeared in *Reformed Dutch Psalms and Hymns* (1847).

YOUMANS, VINCENT MILLER

b. 1898 New York City, d. 1946 Denver, Colorado. Popular composer. Attended Yale; served in the navy in World War I; became a song plugger for Max Dreyfus, head of Harms, the music publisher; wrote the score for *Two Little Girls in Blue* (1922, with Paul Lannin, w. Ira Gershwin), *Wildflower* (1923, with Herbert Stothart, w. Otto Harbach and Oscar Hammerstein II), *No No Nanette* (1924 and revived 1971, book—Harbach and Frank Mandel, w. Harbach and Irving Caesar, which included "Tea for Two"), *Hit the Deck* (1927 and revived 1960, play—Herbert Fields, w. Leo Robin and Clifford Grey, which included "Hallelujah"); wrote "I Know That You Know" (1926, w. Anne Caldwell), "Without a Song" (1929, w. William Rose and Edward Eliscu), "Drums in My Heart" (1932, w. Edward Heyman), "Time on My Hands" (1930, w. Harold Adamson and Mack Gordon), "Rise 'n Shine" (w. Buddy De Sylva), "I Want a Man" (1928, Hammerstein), "Flying Down to Rio" (1932, w. Gus Kahn and Edward Eliscu); died of tuberculosis.

YOUNG, FARON

b. 1932 Shreveport, Louisiana.
Singer, guitarist, and songwriter. Attended Centenary College, Shreveport, La.; radio debut on KWKH, Shreveport; served in the Korean War; appeared in films; wrote "Goin' Steady" (1953); albums—*All-Time Great Hits of Faron Young, Best of Faron Young, Here's Faron Young, I've Got Precious Memories, This Is Faron, Unmitigated Gall, Wine Me Up, Faron Young's Greatest Hits.*

YOUNG, JAMES OLIVER ("TRUMMY")

b. 1912 Savannah, Georgia.
Black jazz trombonist. Played with Louis Armstrong; also sang in Jimmie Lunceford's band.

YOUNG, JOSEPH

1889 New York City, d. there 1939.
Lyricist. Singer for music publishing firms; with Sam Lewis wrote "How Ya Gonna Keep 'em Down on the Farm?" (m. Walter Donaldson), "My Mammy" (m. Donaldson, made famous by Al Jolson), "There's a Cradle in Caroline" (m. Fred Ahlert), "Dinah" (1925, m. Harry Akst), "In a Little Spanish Town" (1926, m. Mabel Wayne), "Daddy Long Legs" (m. Harry Ruby), "Five Foot Two, Eyes of Blue" (m. Ray Henderson), "Laugh, Clown, Laugh" (m. Ted Fiorito), "King for a Day" (m. Fiorito), "A Night in Spain" (1927, m. Jean Schwartz), "Absence Makes the Heart Grow Fonder for Someone Else" (m. Harry Warren).

YOUNG, LA MONTE

b. 1935 Bern, Idaho.
Composer. Studied at the University of California at Los Angeles and Berkeley (1957-60), and composition with Stockhausen in Darmstadt (1959); wrote *Poem for Chairs, Tables and Benches* (1960); also two stage spectacles for voice, song and strings—*The Tortoise Droning Selected Pitches from the Holy Numbers for the Two Black Tigers, the Green Tiger and the Hermit* (1964) and *The Tortoise Recalling the Drone of the Holy Numbers as They Were Revealed in the Dreams of the Whirlwind.*

YOUNG, LESTER ("PREZ")

b. 1909 Woodville, Mississippi, d. 1959 New York City. Black tenor-saxophonist. Son of William Young, who played in Allen's Brass Band (1912); older brother of Lee Young, drummer; played the tenor-saxophone in Count Basie's band.

YOUNG, MAUDE J. FULLER

b. 1826 Beaufort, North Carolina, d. 1882 Houston, Texas. Poetess and lyricist. The family moved to Houston (1837); married Dr. S.O. Young in Houston (1846), but he died during their first year of marriage; their only son, S.O. Young, served in General John B. Hood's Texas Brigade during the Civil War; she was principal of a public school in Houston (1868-73); State Botanist (1872-73); best known for her poem "The Legend of Sour Lake" and "The Song of the Texas Rangers" (1861, tune "The Yellow Rose of Texas," 1858); known as the "Confederate Lady."

YOUNG RASCALS, THE *see* THE RASCALS

YOUNG, RITA JOHNSON

b. 1869 Baltimore, Maryland, d. 1926 Stamford, Connecticut. Lyricist. Educated at Wilson College; actress with E.H. Southern and others; wrote "Mother Machree" (1910, m. Ernest R. Ball and Chauncey Olcott), "Will You Remember" (1917, m. Sigmund Romberg), "Ah, Sweet Mystery of Life" (1910, m. Victor Herbert), "My Dream Girl" (1924, m. Victor Herbert).

YOUNG TUXEDO BAND *see* PAUL D. BARNES

YOUNG, VICTOR

b. 1900 Chicago, Illinois, d. 1956 Palm Springs, California. Popular composer. Studied violin with Isidor Lotto at the Warsaw (Poland) Conservatory; for a while violinist and arranger with the Ted Fiorito orchestra; later he moved to Los Angeles; wrote "Sweet Sue" (1928, w. Will Harris), "Can't You Understand" (1929, w. Jack Osterman), "Sweet Madness" (1933, w. Ned Washington), "The Searching Wind" (w. Edward Heyman), "Golden Earrings" (w. Jay Livingston and Ray Evans), "Around the World in 80 Days" (1956, Washington, for Michael Todd).

YOUNGBLOODS, THE (country-blues-rock group)

Jesse Colin Young, vocals and bass; Joe Bauer, drums; Banana, vocals, guitar, and electric piano; Jerry Corbitt, former member; group started in Boston; first recorded in 1967; later moved to New York City and San Francisco; albums—*The Youngbloods, Earth Music, Elephant Mountain.*

Z

ZACH, MAX WILHELM

b. 1864 Lemberg, Austria, d. 1921 St. Louis, Missouri. Violist, conductor, and composer. Studied at the Vienna Conservatory; with the Boston Symphony (1886-1907) and conductor of summer concerts; member of Adamowski String Quartet (1890-1906); conductor of the St. Louis Symphony (1907-21); wrote marches and waltzes.

ZACK, JIMMIE

b. 1924 Fair Oaks, Arkansas.
Singer and songwriter. Born Henry Z. Yingst; attended high school in Ames, Iowa; wrote "Wake Me Up" (1958), "Somebody's Been Rockin' My Boat," "Why Don't You Heed His Call" (1959), "Jesus Has Saved My Soul" (1959).

ZADOR, EUGEN

b. 1894 Batazek, Hungary.
Composer. Studied in Vienna; taught at the New Conservatory in Vienna; film composer in Hollywood after 1939; composed operas—*Diana* (Budapest, 1923), *Die Insel der Toten* (Budapest, 1927), *Christopher Columbus* (NBC, 1939); *Bank-Ban* (symphonic poem), *Hannele* (symphonic prelude), suite from the ballet *Machine Men* (Minneapolis Symphony under Ormandy), *Variations on a Hungarian Song* for orchestra.

ZALKIND, RONALD

b. 1949 Yeadon, Pennsylvania.
Pianist, conductor, and manager. Studied with David Sokoloff and Eleanor Sokoloff (no relation); debut at the Philadelphia Orchestra children's concert at age thirteen; studied at the Juilliard School, New York City, with Beveridge Webster; organized and conducted the Empire Sinfonietta, debut at Riverside Church, New York City (June, 1968); Oscar Shumsky, guest conductor of the Sinfonietta at the opening of the remodeled Walnut Street Theater, Philadelphia (1971), also Aaron Copland, guest conductor.

ZAPPA, FRANK

b. 1940.
Guitarist. Resides in Los Angeles; between the ages of eighteen and twenty-one was alternately kicked out of the house or kept in "protective custody," as he called it; lead guitarist of the Mothers of Invention; at the Felt Forum, New York City (1972).

ZAROVICH, JOSEPH H.

b. ca. 1890 St. Petersburg, Russia, d. 1971 Moscow, Russia. Concert manager. Came to the U.S. (ca. 1935); became U.S. citizen (1937), made his headquarters in New York City (1940); booked Soviet talent for tours of the United States; among the Soviet artists brought here were composer-conductor Aram Khachaturian, and Mstislav Rostropovich and Karine Georgyan, cellists; was in Moscow arranging for the first coast-to-coast tour of the Don Coccaks of Aostav when he died.

ZECKWER, CAMILLE

b. 1875 Philadelphia, Pennsylvania, d. 1924. Pianist and composer. Son of Richard Zeckwer; studied at the Philadelphia Musical Academy; succeeded his father as director there (1917-24), name changed to Zeckwer-Hahn Philadelphia Musical Academy; composed chamber music.

ZECKWER, RICHARD

b. 1850 Stendal, East Germany, d. 1922 Philadelphia, Pennsylvania. Pianist. Studied at the Leipzig Conservatory; organist in Philadelphia after 1870; director of the Philadelphia Musical Academy (1876-1917, later known as the Zeckwer-Hahn Philadelphia Musical Academy).

ZEISL, ERIC

b. 1905 Vienna, Austria, d. 1959 Los Angeles, California. Teacher and composer. Came to California and taught at the Los Angeles City College; wrote the overture *Job* and the *Requiem Ebraico.*

ZEISLER, FANNY B. *see* FANNY BLOOMFIELD-ZEISLER

ZEMACHSON, ARNOLD

b. 1892 Vilna, Lithuania, d. 1956.
Composer. Came to America to live; com-

posed Chorale and Fugue in D Minor (Philadelphia Orchestra under Stokowski, 1930), Concerto Grosso in E Minor (Chicago Symphony under Stock, 1934), Suite in F (WOR Sinfonietta under Wallenstein, 1941).

ZEMLINSKY, ALEXANDER VON *see* VON ZEMLINSKY

ZENATELLO, GIOVANNI

b. 1879 Verona, Italy, d. 1949 New York City. Tenor. Sang at Covent Garden, London (1905); with the Manhattan Opera Company, New York City (1907-09), and the Boston Opera (1909-14); later a voice teacher in New York City; married Maria Gay, contralto.

ZENO, HENRY

b. ca. 1884, d. 1917.
Black drummer. Played with King Oliver in the Storyville section (red light district) of New Orleans.

ZERR, ANNA

b. 1822, d. 1881.
Singer. Sang "Old Folks at Home" ("Swanee River" by Stephen Foster) at Castle Garden, New York City (1853).

ZERRAHN, KARL

b. 1826 Malchow, East Germany, d. 1909 Milton, Massachusetts. Conductor. Studied in Hanover and Berlin; member of the Germania Orchestra in New York City (1848); conductor of the Germania Orchestra in Boston (1849-54); conductor of the Handel and Haydn Society in Boston (1854-95); taught at the New England Conservatory, Boston; conducted the Harvard Symphony concerts.

ZEUNER, HEINRICH CHRISTOPHER (CHARLES)

b. 1795 Eisleben, Saxony, Germany, d. 1857 Philadelphia, Pennsylvania. Composer. Came to New York (1827) and was organist at the Park Street Church; in 1854 moved to Philadelphia, where he was organist of St. Andrew's Church and later the Arch Street Presbyterian Church; wrote the music for "Ye Christian Heralds, Go Proclaim" (w. B.H. Draper) which appeared in the fourth edition of *Hymns for the Use of Christians* (1810), compiled by Abner Jones of Newark, N.J., and Elias Smith, (first edition, Portland, Maine, 1805).

ZIEGFELD, FLORENZ

b. 1841 Jener, Oldenburg, Germany, d. 1923. Teacher and educator. Studied at the Leipzig Conservatory under Moscheles, Richter, Papperitz, et al.; came to Chicago (1863); established the Chicago Musical College (1867), also taught piano there.

ZIEGFELD, FLORENZ

b. 1869 Chicago, Illinois, d. 1932 Hollywood, California. Famous producer. Son of the founder of the Chicago Musical College; in 1907 produced the first of his annual *Ziegfeld Follies;* produced numerous musical comedies, including *Show Boat* (1927); Ruth Etting introduced "Shaking the Blues Away" (m. Irving Berlin) in the *Follies* of 1927; Fannie Brice introduced "The Vamp from East Broadway" (m. Irving Berlin and Harry Ruby) in the *Follies* of 1920.

ZIEGLER, EDWARD

b. 1870 Baltimore, Maryland, d. 1947 New York City. Critic and manager. Pupil of F.X. Arens; critic of the *New York World* (1903-08), *Herald* (1908-17), and *American* (1920); with the Metropolitan Opera, New York City after 1917, and general manager after 1920.

ZIEHN, BERNARD

b. 1845 Erfurt, Germany, d. 1912 Chicago, Illinois. Teacher and writer. Came to Chicago (1868); active as an organist and teacher there; wrote *Harmonie und Modulationslehre* (Berlin, 1888), *Five and Six Part Harmonies* (Milwaukee, Wisc., 1911).

ZIMBALIST, EFREM

b. 1889 Rostov-on-Don, Russia.
Famous violinist. Married Alma Gluck, the singer; became director of the Curtis Institute of Music, Philadelphia (1938); in 1943 married Mary Curtis Bok, daughter of Cyrus H.K. Curtis, founder of the *Saturday Evening Post*; his son, Efrem Zimbalist, Jr., a movie and TV actor.

ZIMMER, NORMA

b. (?) Larsen, Idaho.
Singer. With the "Lawrence Welk Show"; appeared with Billy Graham Crusade; albums—*Beautiful Savior, Beyond the Sunset, Whispering Hope, Norma Zimmer Sings Her Most, Norma Zimmer Sings Songs of Faith and Inspiration;* on Lawrence Welk TV show; also guest star touring with evangelist Billy Graham (1972).

ZIMMERMAN, CHARLES A.

b. 1861 Rhode Island, d. 1916 Annapolis, Maryland. Composer and conductor. Musical director of the United States Naval Academy; with Alfred H. Miles wrote "Anchors Aweigh" (1906).

ZINZENDORF, NIKOLAUS LUDWIG VON
see VON ZINZENDORF

ZUNDEL, JOHN

b. 1815 Hochdorf, Germany, d. 1882 Cannstadt, Germany. Composer and compiler. Came to America (1847) and was an organist in New York City; organist and choirmaster of Henry Ward Beecher's Plymouth Church, Brooklyn, N.Y. (1850-80); composed the tune "Beecher" (1870, "Love Divine, All Loves Excelling," w. Charles Wesley) and "There's a Wideness in God's Mercy" (1862, F.W. Faber), published *The Choral Friend* (1852), *Christian Heart Songs* (1870), and assisted Beecher with *The Plymouth Collection* (1855).

ZURKE, ROBERT

b. 1912 Detroit, Michigan, d. 1944 Los Angeles, California. Jazz pianist. Known as a barrelhouse player; played with Bob Crosby's band; later led his own band (1939).

ZWEIG, FRITZ

b. 1893 Olmuetz, Czechoslovakia.
Teacher and conductor. Conductor of the Berlin State Opera (1927-33) and in Prague (1933-37), but the rise of Nazism forced him to leave; went to Paris, then came to America (1940); became a teacher in Hollywood.